# THE BOOK OF
# AMERICAN
# CITY RANKINGS

# THE BOOK OF
# AMERICAN
# CITY RANKINGS

## BY
### John Tepper Marlin and James S. Avery
### with Stephen T. Collins

**Facts On File Publications**
460 Park Avenue South
New York, N.Y. 10016

# THE BOOK OF AMERICAN CITY RANKINGS

Library of Congress Cataloging in Publication Data

Main entry under title:

Marlin, John Tepper.
    The Book of American City Rankings.

    Includes index.
    1. Cities and towns—United States—Handbooks,
manuals, etc.    I. James S. Avery
HT123.B64    306'.0973            82-2437
ISBN 0-87196-685-9              AACR2
ISBN 0-8160-0095-6 (pbk)
Printed in the United States of America
10  9  8  7  6  5  4  3  2

7-16-84

# TABLE OF CONTENTS

# HOW TO USE THIS BOOK

While this book was formally begun in late 1980, its roots go back to 1973, with the creation of the Council on Municipal Performance (COMP). COMP published comparative municipal surveys in pursuit of its mission to make local government more accessible to its citizens.

However, this book's usefulness goes beyond COMP's own interests. The information in this book and the resources it identifies can be used to learn about other cities to which one might move—or to learn more about one's own city. It can be used to decide where to locate businesses, concentrate marketing efforts or focus government programs.

It contains 267 tables with information on life in America's 100 largest cities, where 22 per cent of Americans live (see Table 30). Their metro areas are home to over half of the nation's populace (see Table 31). The data have been organized to be as useful a reference as possible for a wide range of people and organizations. Accompanied by interpretive abstracts, the tables allow the reader to compare and rank the diverse characteristics of U.S. cities. In the second part of the book, the rankings for each city have been summarized to assist the business executive or individual further in evaluating the appeal or problems of a particular city.

*Using This Book to Decide Where to Live*. Those considering a move to another city can utilize the tables in *The Book of American City Rankings* as a guide to which area would be most suitable. Career-minded individuals, for example, would be more attracted to the fast-growing satellite cities, while many retirees prefer to live in the warm climate cities of the southeast and southwest, and in those cities where fixed budgets are less vulnerable (see Tables 100 and 101). Opportunity seekers will desire to establish themselves in a city that has a diverse economic base, high per capita income and the potential for further growth. Indicators of these important economic opportunities are emphasized in several tables.

Individuals, such as ministers, tied to religious groups can use the religion section to determine the number of adherents to different religious groups; aspiring political leaders may also be interested in this information. Parents concerned with the education of their children can analyze the average class size, pupil-teacher ratio and spending on education in each city. For those concerned about safety and law enforcement, tables on crime, arrests and police personnel are supplied.

We have provided readers with the raw data with which to construct their own index. The index can be constructed informally, as readers put together their impression from the various tables, or it can be constructed methodically. The advantage of the methodical approach is that it allows one family member to argue the case before others—a parent vis-à-vis a child, for example, or one spouse vis-à-vis the other spouse.

Rather than pre-select the tables that should be used for this purpose, we suggest that readers make a list of things that they care about, and then go through the book looking for tables which bear on their decision. Let's say a husband is required to move to a warmer and drier climate for health reasons, and his wife is a Presbyterian minister. The couple might construct a table that looks like this:

| Concern | Selected Relevant Tables from This Book |
|---|---|
| 1. Climate Factors | 6, 9, 10, 11 |
| 2. Pollution | 14, 16, 23, 24 |
| 3. Health Care | 171, 172, 175, 176 |
| 4. Jobs | 93, 123, 124, 125 |
| 5. Cost of Living | 99, 138, 139 |
| 6. Religious Adherents | 79, 80 |
| 7. Education | 216, 226, 228 |
| 8. Safety | 191, 192, 193 |

Having decided which tables to include, the next step is to decide which cities are of genuine interest. For example, if one of the two incomes is in health care, the availability of specialized hospital facilities may limit the number of cities under consideration. Based on these factors, the size of the list can probably be reduced to 15 tables and perhaps 10 cities among which you wish to make a selection. The next step is to write in the ranks of the cities that are of interest. Cities should be ranked in every table from what is best in the reader's mind to what is worst; if not, recalculate the rank by subtracting the original rank from the total number of cities in the table. In the case of a table with missing data for a city, take the average of the other cities for which data are included.

The final step is to add up the ranks for each of the cities, as in the following example:

## Selected Tables

| Cities | 11 Temperature | 14 Ozone | 79 Presby-terians | 93 Income | 124 Unemployment | 172 Death Rate | 175 Cardio-vascular | Final Score | Rank |
|---|---|---|---|---|---|---|---|---|---|
| New York | 50 | 40 | 70 | 22 | 47 | 45 | 76 | 350 | 2 |
| Chicago | 73 | 24 | 67 | 43 | 24 | 48 | 74 | 353 | 3 |
| Los Angeles | 18 | 46 | 69 | 33 | 29 | 27 | 57 | 279 | 1 |

Note that the rank is from lowest to highest, since 1 is considered best. This approach assumes giving equal weight to each table or indicator. It is easy to change this assumption—just assign double or triple weight to certain tables. Tables 172 and 175 are really being used as one indicator and could be given half weight, by dividing their total by two. Note that the rank in this example is derived mainly from Table 11, showing that the final results depend on what tables are included and on how readers set up their system of aggregation or weights.

# ON INDICATORS, INDICES AND METRO AREAS

Much of the data included in this book represent Quality of Life (QOL) indicators, defined by the Federal Government as "statistics of direct normative interest which facilitate concise, comprehensive and balanced judgment about the condition of major aspects of a society." A social index is a combination of several such indicators.

*State Surveys.* The use of QOL indicators was pioneered by C. Angoff and the noted journalist H. L. Mencken when they surveyed the 48 states and the District of Columbia to identify "The Worst American State" (*The American Mercury,* September 1931). To define the QOL in each state, they combined 106 indicators into five indices. Their conclusion that Mississippi was the "worst" state was admirably couched in caveats and apologies.

The *Mercury* survey was completed over 50 years ago. Some indicators valid then—like compliance with Prohibition—could no longer be used to measure QOL today because laws and social values have changed. In the same way, many current indicators such as air and water quality were not included then because they were not yet recognized as social problems. Nevertheless, the homicide rate that they used as an indicator of crime is still a good one (although probably less useful than the robbery rate) and one's overall impression is that Angoff and Mencken did their work well.

More recently, the Midwest Research Institute published a series of QOL studies. The first was "Quality of Life in the United States" (1968) by economist John O. Wilson. Like Angoff and Mencken, Wilson chose the state as his unit of analysis because the states have a more dominant role in providing services than the national government, and because state data were more readily available than data for smaller units.

*Substate Surveys.* A later survey, *The Geography of Social Well Being in the United States* (1973) by David M. Smith, was described as "an introduction to territorial social indicators." Smith chose to examine a variety of indicators at various geographical levels—inter-state, inter-city and intra-city. Smith concluded that states are actually poor territorial units by which to observe social well-being, since one or two large cities may influence the average for a state. He therefore preferred substate analysis.

We agree with Smith that national and statewide surveys have some value as "ballpark" social measures, but that differences within nations and states are hidden by QOL indicators averaged at this high level. Comparisons among cities are more useful because cities are homogeneous in more ways than states. City residents fight the same traffic, ride the same buses, face the same crime, drink the same water and breathe the same air. People can and do act on information about urban life, whereas state averages mask local realities.

In *The Good Life Index* (1981) authors H. McKinley Conway and Linda L. Liston review state data, metropolitan area indicators and city indicators. They include an admirable review of some QOL surveys not mentioned here, and also take care to point out that appropriate QOL measures depend on the user. They identify a number of distinct groups: Career Starters, Family and Community Builders, Retiring or Retired, Sophisticates, Frontier People, Blue Collar Workers, even "All-Americans." The book suffers from a scarcity of comparable data at the substate level, although it is an excellent sourcebook for industrial site selection purposes.

*Aggregation Problems.* The problems of aggregation— i.e., creating indices out of several indicators—are illustrated by the Midwest Research Institute's study by Ben-Chieh Liu entitled "Variations in the Quality of Life in the United States, 1970: Index, Rating and Statistics" (1974). Liu combined a number of 1970 measures to create an overall QOL index for the nation's 243 metropolitan areas. However, the raw material for the reader was not provided, so that it was extremely difficult for the reader to break apart the index and reconstruct it according to his or her own preferences. Many probers disagreed with him on the construction of the indices.

Another index-oriented book is *The Places Rated Almanac* by Richard Boyer and David Savageau (1981). It ranks 277 metro areas on the basis of nine QOL indices. Some of the indices combine three variables, others as many as ten. Some metro areas end up at the top of the rankings because they score moderately well in all categories. Others (usually the ones with the largest cities at their core) have low ratings in one category not fully offset by high ratings in others. Where cities are at one extreme or another, the weighting system used by the authors is crucial in determining their final rankings. A slight change in the weighting might produce a large shift in the ranking. Under these conditions, the value of the ranking depends on the degree to which one agrees with the weighting system.

A few years ago, one of us met with a Nobel Prize-winning economist, Professor Wassily Leontief, to discuss indicator concepts that are used in this book. Dr. Leontief said succinctly: "Yes, but don't aggregate." The intelligence of his comment became more apparent as we continued our research. QOL rankings reflect the values of the person who assembles them. Someone who thinks that crime is unimportant but that the availability of dance performances is important will rank New York City highly. Someone who thinks that crime is a crucial factor and climate is unimportant will put Miami at the bottom of the list.

A recent QOL survey which avoids aggregation problems is *Finding Your Best Place to Live in America* (1981), by Drs. Thomas Bowman, George A. Giuliani and M. Ronald Mingé. The authors were very careful to respect the range of individual reader preferences. They chose not to aggregate any of their data. However, they include only 59 tables of data for the 80 metro areas, and nearly one-fourth of them compare states rather than metro areas or cities.

*Performance Measures.* We have taken a special interest in those social indicators that measure not only QOL but also local government performance. Many QOL indicators are totally beyond the control of a city government —climate, for example, or the availability of certain types of recreation (skiing in Atlanta, yachting in Phoenix). Other indicators, however, reflect the performance of a city and its officials. Such performance measures are often more difficult to ascertain than QOL measures. They must relate not only to something that makes people better off, but also to being made better off through conscious human action. Heavy snowfall is a QOL indicator. A measure of the impassibility of major city streets following a snowstorm (say miles per hour of traffic) is both a QOL and a performance indicator.

Performance measures can sometimes become very complex. Many surveys of performance in relation to size conclude that the optimum city size is about 100,000 people. Cities over that size suffer from an efficiency handicap in providing certain services. Should it be considered poor performance then to let a city grow above a certain size? Do neighborhood government or participation systems offer any hope of offsetting some of the diseconomies of large cities? Asking questions like these opens up the areas over which a city may be said to have control.

Performance measures are a special kind of social indicator, of special interest to people who believe that this world can be made better and that government has a legitimate role in this task. Performance measures show us what areas of life can be improved through better management, better organization and better preparedness.

Objective measures of government performance are still very scarce. The best ones, which allow us accurately to compare what and how other cities are doing, are in this book. By providing such data we seek to encourage further refining of the standards by which they are calculated.

*Metro Areas.* Wherever possible we have sought to obtain central city data. Tables with such data are labeled "cities." In other cases, we have obtained "metro area" data, which generally means the Standard Metropolitan Statistical Area (SMSA). The large SMSAs are composed of one or more counties, except for Boston and Providence, which include only a portion of some counties. In the case of the tables on politics and religion only county data are available. For these tables, we have included entire counties instead of portions of counties. The

Boston "metro area" is therefore larger than the SMSA by a small fraction. Providence is defined in these tables as the entire state of Rhode Island plus Bristol County, Massachusetts. The portions of Worcester County and Norfolk County that would have been attributed to Providence are instead allocated to the Worcester and Boston metro areas, respectively. A full description of areas in each SMSA is provided at the end of this book, immediately before the index.

# ACKNOWLEDGMENTS

Stephen T. Collins, an attorney who joined the Council on Municipal Performance (COMP) at the end of 1982, did substantial writing on the chapters on health and police, wrote most of the city summaries and played a crucial role in the final editing process—checking tables, reviewing the publisher's galleys and generally bringing the book to completion. His special role in the production of this book is only partly reflected on the title page.

We also thank the following student interns at COMP in 1982 and 1983 who assisted greatly in the development and production of this book: Immanuel Ness (Columbia University), who was a major resource in assembling data and operating the computer that did the rankings; Harriet Papastergiou (Princeton University), who worked both on the preparation of the water data for the Environment section and then (the following summer) on final editing of the book; Cheryl Norman (Wheaton College), who worked on the computer program that ranked the cities; and Oliver Avens (Yale University) and Doug Lowell (Duke University), who worked on final editing.

We greatly appreciate permission to use information copyrighted by other sources as acknowledged immediately preceding each table.

Since this book represents an outgrowth of the activities of COMP, the authors thank COMP's Board of Directors for their support of comparative municipal research, of which this project is an expression; to early supporters of COMP such as the POINT Foundation, the Robert Sterling Clark Foundation and the Rockefeller Family Fund; and to the many continuing regular corporate supporters of COMP such as AT&T, Exxon Corporation, J.C. Penney Company and RCA.

The authors thank Dr. Eleanora W. Schoenebaum, Editorial Director at Facts On File, Inc., who has shepherded the manuscript patiently from an idea that we gave her at the end of 1980 to this finished book.

We both appreciate the accommodations and understanding shown by our spouses, Alice Tepper Marlin and Joan Avery, when the demands of this book created disruptions in our family schedules.

Finally, we gratefully dedicate this book to our parents —to the continued good health of the Marlin parents and to the memory of the Avery parents—who gave us the start in life that encouraged and allowed us to delve into the deeper mysteries of the world.

John Tepper Marlin
James S. Avery

July 1983

# CORRECTIONS AND UPDATES

Any reference book of this sort soon needs to be updated. For example, as we went to press in July 1983, New York Mayor Edward I. Koch's salary was raised from the $80,000 that he had been collecting to $110,000, which affects the abstract of Table 145; his deputies' salaries were also increased.

This book's value over time is in providing benchmark numbers against which to compare more recent information, and in providing the sources of such information.

For those who wish to keep current on new information— whether data for subsequent years or any corrections to data for prior years—the Council on Municipal Performance (COMP) publishes a Newsletter. The authors would welcome any comments on the usefulness of tables in this book for this Newsletter and for future revised editions of this book. For more information about the Newsletter write to John Tepper Marlin at COMP, 84 Fifth Avenue, New York, NY 10011.

# PREFACE

## Metro Areas

Wherever possible we have sought to obtain central city data. Tables showing such data are labeled "cities." In other cases we have obtained "metro area" data, which generally means the Standard Metropolitan Statistical Area (SMSA). The large SMSAs are composed of one or more counties, except for Boston and Providence, which include only a portion of some counties. In the case of certain tables—notably those on politics and religion—only county data are available. For these tables we have included entire counties instead of portions of counties. The Boston "metro area" in these tables is therefore larger than the SMSA by a small fraction. Providence is defined in these tables as the entire state of Rhode Island plus Bristol County, Massachusetts. The portions of Worcester County and Norfolk County that would have been attributed to Providence are instead allocated to the Worcester and Boston metro areas, respectively.

# CHAPTER ONE

# LAND AND CLIMATIC FACTORS

One of the first things to be considered about any city is its physical features. How large is it in area? How high is it above sea level? What is its rainfall, sunshine pattern, average windiness? How hot and cold does it get? How good is its water? Is the air polluted?

These features greatly affect a city's economy and its desirability as a place to live. A city with a small land area may have affluent suburban areas to which people commute, draining tax revenues.

Land and climatic factors affect a city's potential as a recreational, tourist and even a convention center. Tourists are going to check out how cold a city is in the winter and how hot it is in the summer. Even with the best of

facilities, a city with a record of subfreezing temperatures in certain winter months is going to have trouble attracting large conventions during those months.

Climatic measurements are commonly taken at airports, where air traffic controllers have a continuing need for up-to-date weather information. Most of the 100 largest cities have their own airports (see Tables 234 and 235 below), so that the climatic tables (Tables 5–11) below are labeled "City". In four notable cases, however, two or more large cities are served by a common airport so that the climatic data must serve both cities. These cities are Dallas-Fort Worth, Minneapolis-St. Paul, Tampa-St. Petersburg and Kansas City, Kan.-Mo.

# 1. Largest Cities (Area)

One of the major determinants of a city's financial solvency in the United States is its land area. A sprawling city can take advantage of growth. New developments in the fringe areas add value to the tax rolls. The added services that new developments may require are not necessarily provided immediately, so that in the meantime the developments are a boon.

A city with a small area, on the other hand, does not necessarily benefit from area growth. While the suburbs may burgeon with new housing, shopping malls and industrial parks, this suburbanization hurts the downtown area, contributing to urban decay, loss of jobs and social burdens (transportation, caring for the newly unemployed).

The land area of cities is related to their history and that of each state. Many New England and New Jersey cities like Boston, Providence, Jersey City and Newark are hemmed in because of the historic town meeting

form of government, which encouraged small-sized localities.

One reason why Texas and Oklahoma cities are big is state laws that permit them to grow. Houston, by design, is the largest of them in area. It was incorporated in 1837 under laws that permitted it to annex any unincorporated territories beyond its formal borders. Taking advantage of a Texas law that prohibited a locality from incorporating unless it had the permission of any other incorporated area within three miles, Houston purchased and annexed strips of suburban land to ensure that no suburban area could incorporate around it. Oklahoma City was incorporated in 1890 under state laws permitting easy annexation.

Alaska and Hawaii also have large cities. Of the nation's 100 most populous cities, Anchorage is the largest in area, with 1,955 square miles, and Honolulu is the fourth largest, with 604 square miles. Alaska has the room. Hawaii is much more cramped and permitted the city of Honolulu to merge functions with its much larger county (they were incorporated in 1907) for reasons of efficiency.

Many states show a mixed picture, with cities at both ends of the area spectrum. For example, Jacksonville, with 827 square miles, is the second largest city in Florida; yet Miami, at the other end of the state, is among the ten smallest, with 34 square miles. Clearly, the age of the city plays a part. Miami was already a thriving port when Jacksonville was incorporated in 1822 under state laws that permitted broad annexation. Cali-

fornia has similar extremes, ranging from large Los Angeles to much smaller cities like San Francisco. New York City is large in area because it annexed most of the Bronx in 1874 and three other boroughs in 1898, but generally the cities in New York State are smaller than the national average.

Some small-sized cities like Boston, Miami and San Francisco are hemmed in by surrounding water. They are trapped in another sense within suburban areas that have fought vigorously to retain their independence of the problems of the central city.

SOURCE: Survey of city chambers of commerce and economic development agencies based on 1981 data, by the authors, 1982.

| Rank | City | Area (sq. mi.) | Rank | City | Area (sq. mi.) | Rank | City | Area (sq. mi.) |
|---|---|---|---|---|---|---|---|---|
| 1 | Anchorage | 1,955.0 | 35 | Colorado Springs | 109.9 | 69 | Akron | 56.0 |
| 2 | Jacksonville | 827.0 | 36 | Charlotte | 108.4 | 70 | Pittsburgh | 55.5 |
| 3 | Oklahoma City | 650.0 | 37 | Jackson | 105.4 | 71 | St. Paul | 55.4 |
| 4 | Honolulu | 604.0 | 38 | Wichita | 105.2 | 72 | Las Vegas | 55.0 |
| 5 | Houston | 556.0 | 39 | Tucson | 101.6 | 73 | Madison | 53.9 |
| 6 | Nashville | 533.0 | 40 | Portland, Ore. | 100.0 | 74 | Oakland | 53.4 |
| 7 | Los Angeles | 463.9 | 41 | Birmingham | 98.4 | 75 | Norfolk | 52.6 |
| 8 | Dallas | 378.0 | 42 | Shreveport | 97.0 | 76 | Spokane | 52.1 |
| 9 | Indianapolis | 375.2 | 43 | Milwaukee | 95.8 | 77 | Fort Wayne | 51.9 |
| 10 | Phoenix | 325.2 | 44 | Sacramento | 93.9 | 78 | Aurora | 51.7 |
| 11 | San Diego | 322.9 | 45 | Seattle | 91.6 | 79 | Lincoln | 51.5 |
| 12 | Kansas City, Mo. | 316.3 | 46 | Baltimore | 91.0 | 80 | Long Beach | 50.1 |
| 13 | New York | 303.7 | 47 | Little Rock | 90.7 | 81 | Buffalo | 49.6 |
| 14 | Memphis | 290.0 | 48 | Albuquerque | 87.1 | 82 | Salt Lake City | 49.4 |
| 15 | Lexington | 283.0 | 49 | Toledo | 85.3 | 83 | Dayton | 48.7 |
| 16 | San Antonio | 263.6 | 50 | Tampa | 84.4 | 84 | Tacoma | 47.7 |
| 17 | Virginia Beach | 258.7 | 51 | Chattanooga | 82.9 | 85 | Boston | 46.0 |
| 18 | Ft. Worth | 250.0 | 52 | Lubbock | 82.2 | 86 | San Francisco | 45.4 |
| 19 | El Paso | 240.0 | 53 | Omaha | 81.7 | 87 | Grand Rapids | 44.9 |
| 20 | Chicago | 228.1 | 54 | Arlington, Texas | 79.0 | 88 | Anaheim | 38.2 |
| 21 | Columbus, Ga. | 220.2 | 55 | Cincinnati | 78.1 | 89 | Worcester | 37.4 |
| 22 | New Orleans | 202.5 | 56 | Knoxville | 77.6 | 90 | Rochester | 36.7 |
| 23 | Columbus, Ohio | 183.0 | 57 | Cleveland | 75.9 | 91 | Miami | 34.3 |
| 24 | Tulsa | 177.3 | 58 | Riverside | 72.1 | 92 | Warren, Mich. | 34.2 |
| 25 | Corpus Christi | 155.8 | 59 | Fresno | 72.0 | 93 | Flint | 32.8 |
| 26 | San Jose | 151.0 | 60 | Baton Rouge | 66.3 | 94 | Huntington Beach | 27.3 |
| 27 | Mobile | 142.0 | 61 | Des Moines | 66.0 | 95 | Santa Ana | 27.2 |
| 28 | Detroit | 139.6 | 62 | Louisville | 65.2 | 96 | Syracuse | 25.8 |
| 29 | Atlanta | 136.0 | 62 | St. Louis | 65.2 | 97 | Newark | 24.1 |
| 30 | Philadelphia | 130.0 | 64 | Richmond | 62.5 | 98 | Yonkers | 21.5 |
| 31 | Montgomery | 128.9 | 65 | Washington, D.C. | 61.4 | 99 | Providence | 18.9 |
| 32 | Austin | 123.8 | 66 | Greensboro | 60.6 | 100 | Jersey City | 15.1 |
| 33 | Denver | 116.4 | 67 | Minneapolis | 58.7 | | | |
| 34 | Kansas City, Kan. | 110.0 | 68 | St. Petersburg | 56.8 | | | |

# 2.  City-County Consolidations

One way for a city to grow is to consolidate its functions with those of its surrounding county. This usually results in a more efficient government but often means the city

loses control over some human services. The National Association of Counties defines a city-county consolidation as the unification of the governments of one or more cities with that of the surrounding county. Under that definition the only New York City consolidation was the first one between the city and county, in 1874. The addition to the city in 1874 of areas that were part of Westchester County (areas that subsequently became part of Bronx County during World War I), and the addition of Brooklyn, Staten Island and Queens to New York City in 1898, are better described as annexations.

The impetus for consolidation comes from two sources: (1) civic-minded concern about having efficient government, and (2) political concern regarding control of services by downtown elected officials. Consolidations mean diffusing control of services over a larger area. The big question for city officials is: What services will be left for them to control? Since minorities have tended to be clustered in the central city, they have generally been the political losers in recent consolidations, as most services have been transferred to the county government.

As William J. Belanger Jr., a Louisville official, has said of the continuing loss to the surrounding county of central city control over services: "By the time the racial balance gets to 50–50, you'll see the first black mayor of Louisville, and he'll be the Mayor of Nothing."

States have tended either to prohibit consolidations or to mandate them. Historically, they have mainly prohibited them. Of 85 attempts to consolidate between 1921 and 1979, only 7 were passed up to 1969, while 10 were passed in the next 10 years. Consolidations have historically been opposed because they would involve a change in the status quo. Vested interests took their case to the state legislature or the voters, and without strong state leadership on behalf of consolidations, the proposals were rejected as much out of apathy as out of reasoned opposition.

Eight of the 14 city-county consolidations shown on the following table were state-mandated (Las Vegas was also required, in 1975, to consolidate with surrounding

Clark County, but the consolidation was voided by the Nevada Supreme Court; New York City's 1898 expansion, which we have called an annexation, was also state-mandated).

In recent years state legislatures have taken a middle road, being responsive to local consolidation initiatives because they have become more professional and view consolidated areas as more rational approaches to the delivery of urban services. The increased professionalism and urban sympathy of state legislatures in turn reflects the reapportionments (required by rulings during the 1960s resulting from civil rights litigation) following the 1970 Census and the increased representation of urban residents in state capitals. In the 1970–79 period 16 states adopted general constitutional statutory authorization for city-county consolidation. The move toward consolidation has been left to flow out of local interests rather than statewide imposition.

SOURCE: Derived from International City Management Association, *The Municipal Year Book*, p. 8 (1982) and pp. 69–71 (1980).

| Rank | City | County | Year Consolidated |
|---|---|---|---|
| 1 | New Orleans | Orleans Parish | 1805 |
| 2 | Boston | Suffolk County | 1821 |
| 3 | Philadelphia | Philadelphia County | 1854 |
| 4 | San Francisco | San Francisco County | 1856 |
| 5 | New York | New York County | 1874 |
| 6 | Denver | Denver County | 1904 |
| 7 | Honolulu | Honolulu County | 1907 |
| 8 | Baton Rouge | East Baton Rouge Parish | 1947 |
| 9 | Nashville-Davidson | Davidson County | 1962 |
| 10 | Jacksonville | Duval County | 1967 |
| 11 | Indianapolis | Mason County | 1969 |
| 12 | Columbus, Ga. | Muscogee County | 1970 |
| 13 | Lexington | Fayette County | 1974 |
| 14 | Anchorage | Anchorage Area Borough | 1975 |

# 3. City Annexations

Annexations are preferable to consolidations from a city's point of view, because control remains with the city officials. In the case of consolidations, control of many services shifts to the county officials.

Probably the largest annexation in American history was the 1898 addition of Brooklyn, Staten Island and Queens to New York City. Most of what is now called the Bronx was annexed to New York City in 1874, the same year that New York City and New York County were

consolidated; the remaining part of Bronx County was annexed in 1895 by N.Y.C.; the Bronx was given the status of a separate county within the City in 1914.

For each of the three decades of the 1950s, 1960s and 1970s, there were corporate boundary changes in over three-fifths of all municipalities in the United States. If New England and the Middle Atlantic states are excluded (since they have laws making annexation difficult), approximately three out of four municipalities with more than 2,500 population have been annexed in each of the three decades.

The degree of annexation in the major cities is shown in the following table. City-county consolidations and city mergers are excluded. Only annexations of 5,000 or more persons are shown. Figures are net of any "detachments" (transfers of population and area away from the city, to another jurisdiction). Houston continues to be the fastest-annexing city, adding 77,500 people during the 1970–78 period.

SOURCES: Derived from International City Management Association, *Municipal Yearbook* (1980), pp. 64–67, which summarizes data from the annual Boundary and Annexation survey of the Geography Division of the U.S. Census Bureau. The figures on population added are based on the population data for the annexed areas as of the 1970 Census.

| Rank | City | Population Added 1970–78 (Based on 1970 Census) | Rank | City | Population Added 1970–78 (Based on 1970 Census) | Rank | City | Population Added 1970–78 (Based on 1970 Census) |
|---|---|---|---|---|---|---|---|---|
| 1 | Houston | 77,494 | 5 | Baton Rouge | 36,741 | 9 | Shreveport | 11,175 |
| 2 | San Antonio | 54,429 | 6 | Memphis | 33,412 | 10 | Kansas City, Kan. | 10,672 |
| 3 | Chattanooga | 47,915 | 7 | Jackson | 26,846 | 11 | Fresno | 8,521 |
| 4 | Charlotte, N.C. | 46,049 | 8 | Colorado Springs | 24,800 | 12 | Montgomery | 6,716 |

# 4. Highest Cities

Our data on city altitude identify the highest point within city limits. Altitude is therefore related to area. A city with more land area is more likely to have a high point within its boundaries. This explains why Los Angeles is in fourth place, even though much of it is at sea level, and people who live on a hillside in Riverside look down on Los Angeles as a valley. Los Angeles is seventh largest in land area of the 100 cities, and some of the hills in the area are within city limits.

No one will be surprised to see Colorado Springs and Denver at the top of the 100 cities ranked by altitude, even though they are dwarfed by the Rockies to their west.

At the other end of the scale are coastal cities that do not have "mountains which run down to the sea" and instead have gradual slopes to the water's edge. They include Miami, New Orleans, Jacksonville, Houston, Long Beach and Boston—all of which are subject to the dangers of groundwater pollution, fog and humidity but have the joys of easy access to the water. San Jose and Newark, on the other hand, just happen to be located on flatlands.

SOURCE: Survey of city chambers of commerce and economic development agencies based on 1981 data, by the authors, 1982.

| Rank | City | Altitude At Highest Point (feet) | Rank | City | Altitude At Highest Point (feet) | Rank | City | Altitude At Highest Point (feet) |
|---|---|---|---|---|---|---|---|---|
| 1 | Colorado Springs | 6,145 | 10 | Tucson | 2,390 | 19 | Little Rock | 1,200 |
| 2 | Denver | 5,470 | 11 | Spokane | 2,365 | 20 | Lincoln | 1,189 |
| 3 | Albuquerque | 5,354 | 12 | Las Vegas | 2,180 | 21 | Nashville | 1,100 |
| 4 | Los Angeles | 5,081 | 13 | Oakland | 1,700 | 22 | Portland, Ore. | 1,073 |
| 5 | Salt Lake City | 4,327 | 14 | San Diego | 1,591 | 23 | Atlanta | 1,050 |
| 6 | Honolulu | 4,025 | 15 | Oklahoma City | 1,320 | 24 | Kansas City, Mo. | 1,014 |
| 7 | El Paso | 3,762 | 16 | Wichita | 1,280 | 25 | Lexington | 989 |
| 8 | Lubbock | 3,241 | 17 | Omaha | 1,270 | 26 | Des Moines | 963 |
| 9 | Phoenix | 2,740 | 18 | Pittsburgh | 1,240 | 27 | Cincinnati | 960 |

| Rank | City | Altitude At Highest Point (feet) | Rank | City | Altitude At Highest Point (feet) | Rank | City | Altitude At Highest Point (feet) |
|---|---|---|---|---|---|---|---|---|
| 28 | Minneapolis | 945 | 48 | Tulsa | 674 | 68 | Newark | 273 |
| 29 | Knoxville | 936 | 49 | Toledo | 630 | 69 | Shreveport | 259 |
| 30 | San Francisco | 925 | 50 | Birmingham | 620 | 70 | Mobile | 211 |
| 31 | Columbus, Ohio | 902 | 51 | St. Louis | 616 | 71 | Montgomery | 202 |
| 32 | Greensboro | 897 | 52 | Milwaukee | 581 | 72 | Richmond | 177 |
| 33 | Cleveland | 865 | 53 | Chicago | 578 | 73 | Long Beach | 170 |
| 34 | Riverside | 851 | 54 | Louisville | 565 | 74 | Santa Ana | 135 |
| 35 | Madison | 846 | 55 | Seattle | 540 | 75 | Jacksonville | 71 |
| 36 | Indianapolis | 840 | 56 | Baltimore | 490 | 76 | San Jose | 67 |
| 37 | Fort Wayne | 828 | 57 | Worcester | 484 | 77 | Corpus Christi | 60 |
| 38 | Grand Rapids | 785 | 58 | Philadelphia | 440 | 77 | St. Petersburg | 60 |
| 39 | Ft. Worth | 780 | 58 | Tacoma | 440 | 77 | Tampa | 60 |
| 40 | Charlotte | 765 | 60 | Austin | 425 | 80 | Houston | 49 |
| 41 | Dallas | 750 | 61 | Washington, D.C. | 420 | 81 | Sacramento | 25 |
| 42 | Kansas City, Kan. | 726 | 62 | New York | 410 | 82 | New Orleans | 15 |
| 43 | San Antonio | 700 | 63 | Syracuse | 408 | 83 | Miami | 12 |
| 44 | Buffalo | 698 | 64 | Memphis | 331 | 83 | Norfolk | 12 |
| 45 | St. Paul | 687 | 65 | Boston | 330 | 83 | Virginia Beach | 12 |
| 46 | Detroit | 685 | 66 | Fresno | 328 | | | |
| 47 | Chattanooga | 682 | 67 | Jackson | 296 | | | |

# 5.  Windiest Cities

In the following table, windiness is measured by the average wind velocity during the year 1980. Windiness can be a blessing in the summer, just as it can be painful in the winter. Consider it as an adjustment to the temperature data, which follow. Where temperatures are hot, windiness reduces the impact; where they are cold, windiness increases the impact.

Surprise! Chicago is *not* the windiest city. It's not even among the top 20. Corpus Christi is the windiest, with Boston and Wichita close behind.

The least windy cities are Chattanooga and Columbus, Georgia.

SOURCE: Derived from U.S. National Oceanic and Atmospheric Administration (NOAA), National Weather Service, *Local Climatological Data* (1981).

| Rank | City | Average Wind Speed (mph) | Rank | City | Average Wind Speed (mph) | Rank | City | Average Wind Speed (mph) |
|---|---|---|---|---|---|---|---|---|
| 1 | Corpus Christi | 12.7 | 17 | Las Vegas | 10.1 | 35 | Akron | 9.0 |
| 2 | Boston | 12.5 | 17 | Lincoln | 10.1 | 35 | Albuquerque | 9.0 |
| 3 | Wichita | 12.4 | 17 | Norfolk | 10.1 | 35 | Grand Rapids | 9.0 |
| 4 | Honolulu | 11.9 | 17 | San Francisco | 10.1 | 35 | Salt Lake City | 9.0 |
| 5 | Newark | 11.6 | 22 | Chicago | 9.9 | 35 | Toledo | 9.0 |
| 6 | New York | 11.4 | 22 | Dallas-Fort Worth | 9.9 | 40 | Columbus, Ohio | 8.9 |
| 6 | Oklahoma City | 11.4 | 22 | Flint | 9.9 | 40 | Lexington-Fayette | 8.9 |
| 8 | Milwaukee | 11.2 | 25 | Tulsa | 9.8 | 42 | Cincinnati | 8.7 |
| 9 | Buffalo | 11.1 | 25 | Washington, D.C. | 9.8 | 43 | Austin | 8.6 |
| 10 | St. Louis | 10.9 | 27 | Atlanta | 9.6 | 43 | Baltimore | 8.6 |
| 11 | Cleveland | 10.7 | 27 | Minneapolis-St. Paul | 9.6 | 43 | Tucson | 8.6 |
| 12 | Lubbock | 10.6 | 29 | Fort Wayne | 9.5 | 46 | Indianapolis | 8.5 |
| 13 | Des Moines | 10.4 | 30 | Miami | 9.2 | 46 | Nashville | 8.5 |
| 14 | Rochester | 10.3 | 30 | Philadelphia | 9.2 | 46 | Omaha | 8.5 |
| 15 | Kansas City, Mo.-Kan. | 10.2 | 30 | San Antonio | 9.2 | 49 | Louisville | 8.4 |
| 15 | Providence | 10.2 | 30 | Syracuse | 9.2 | 50 | Madison | 8.3 |
| 17 | Dayton | 10.1 | 34 | Memphis | 9.1 | 50 | Seattle | 8.3 |

| Rank | City | Average Wind Speed (mph) | Rank | City | Average Wind Speed (mph) | Rank | City | Average Wind Speed (mph) |
|---|---|---|---|---|---|---|---|---|
| 50 | Spokane | 8.3 | 61 | Shreveport | 7.8 | 73 | Long Beach | 6.7 |
| 50 | Tacoma | 8.3 | 64 | Little Rock | 7.6 | 73 | Los Angeles | 6.7 |
| 54 | Detroit | 8.2 | 65 | Charlotte | 7.5 | 76 | Birmingham | 6.6 |
| 54 | Houston | 8.2 | 65 | San Diego | 7.5 | 76 | Oakland | 6.6 |
| 54 | Mobile | 8.2 | 67 | Anchorage | 7.4 | 78 | Knoxville | 6.5 |
| 57 | Colorado Springs | 8.1 | 67 | Tampa-St. Petersburg | 7.4 | 79 | Montgomery | 6.4 |
| 57 | Pittsburgh | 8.1 | 69 | El Paso | 7.1 | 80 | Baton Rouge | 6.3 |
| 59 | Denver | 8.0 | 70 | Fresno | 7.0 | 80 | Phoenix | 6.3 |
| 59 | Portland, Ore. | 8.0 | 70 | Jacksonville | 7.0 | 82 | Jackson | 6.2 |
| 61 | Richmond | 7.8 | 70 | New Orleans | 7.0 | 83 | Chattanooga | 5.8 |
| 61 | Sacramento | 7.8 | 73 | Greensboro | 6.7 | 84 | Columbus, Ga. | 5.7 |

# 6. Wettest Cities

Water is essential for human life and industry, which is why deserts are deserted. Coastal areas usually have ample rainfall. One of the important features of the industrial heartland of the United States around the Great Lakes is the availability of water to use in making steel and in manufacturing cars and other durable products. Rainfall is also crucial for agriculture, as farmers well know, and for a reliable drinking water supply.

Cities are ranked according to the average number of inches of rain that fall in a year, based on historical records as far back as they go for a particular day—i.e., to the 1930s and before.

The wettest cities are located around the Gulf of Mexico and the Mississippi Delta. Mobile is by far the wettest city, with a rainfall of 67 inches a year, nearly an inch of rain every five days. The next five wettest cities are Miami, New Orleans, Jacksonville, Baton Rouge and Birmingham, with 51–60 inches a year. Las Vegas, by contrast, has just 4 inches of rain during the entire year—a good place to play.

SOURCE: U.S. National Oceanic and Atmospheric Administration (NOAA), National Weather Service, *Local Climatological Data* (1981).

| Rank | City | Annual Rainfall (inches) | Rank | City | Annual Rainfall (inches) | Rank | City | Annual Rainfall (inches) |
|---|---|---|---|---|---|---|---|---|
| 1 | Mobile | 66.98 | 22 | Louisville | 43.11 | 43 | Fort Wayne | 35.80 |
| 2 | Miami | 59.80 | 23 | Providence | 42.75 | 44 | Seattle | 35.65 |
| 3 | New Orleans | 56.77 | 24 | Richmond | 42.59 | 45 | Akron | 35.13 |
| 4 | Jacksonville | 54.47 | 25 | Boston | 42.52 | 46 | Cleveland | 34.99 |
| 5 | Baton Rouge | 54.05 | 26 | Newark | 41.45 | 47 | Dayton | 34.36 |
| 6 | Birmingham | 53.23 | 27 | Greensboro | 41.36 | 48 | Grand Rapids | 32.39 |
| 7 | Chattanooga | 51.92 | 28 | Baltimore | 40.46 | 49 | Dallas-Fort Worth | 32.30 |
| 8 | Columbus, Ga. | 50.94 | 29 | New York | 40.19 | 50 | Chicago | 31.72 |
| 9 | Montgomery | 49.86 | 30 | Philadelphia | 39.93 | 51 | Toledo | 31.51 |
| 10 | Tampa-St. Petersburg | 49.38 | 31 | Cincinnati | 39.04 | 52 | Oklahoma City | 31.37 |
| 11 | Jackson | 49.19 | 32 | Washington, D.C. | 38.89 | 53 | Rochester | 31.33 |
| 12 | Memphis | 49.10 | 33 | Tacoma | 38.79 | 54 | Detroit | 30.96 |
| 13 | Little Rock | 48.52 | 34 | Indianapolis | 38.74 | 55 | Des Moines | 30.85 |
| 14 | Atlanta | 48.34 | 35 | Portland, Ore. | 37.61 | 56 | Wichita | 30.58 |
| 15 | Houston | 48.19 | 36 | Columbus, Ohio | 37.01 | 57 | Madison | 30.25 |
| 16 | Knoxville | 46.18 | 37 | Kansas City, Mo., Kan | 37.00 | 58 | Omaha | 30.18 |
| 17 | Nashville-Davidson | 46.00 | 38 | Tulsa | 36.90 | 59 | Flint | 29.77 |
| 18 | Worcester | 45.24 | 39 | Syracuse | 36.41 | 60 | Milwaukee | 29.07 |
| 19 | Shreveport | 44.72 | 40 | Pittsburgh | 36.23 | 61 | Lincoln | 28.61 |
| 20 | Norfolk | 44.68 | 41 | Buffalo | 36.11 | 62 | Corpus Christi | 28.53 |
| 21 | Lexington-Fayette | 44.49 | 42 | St. Louis | 35.89 | 63 | San Antonio | 27.54 |

| Rank | City | Annual Rainfall (inches) |
|---|---|---|
| 64 | Minneapolis-St. Paul | 25.94 |
| 65 | Honolulu | 22.90 |
| 66 | San Francisco | 20.66 |
| 67 | Oakland | 18.69 |
| 68 | Lubbock | 18.41 |
| 69 | Spokane | 17.42 |
| 70 | Sacramento | 17.22 |
| 71 | Colorado Springs | 15.73 |

| Rank | City | Annual Rainfall (inches) |
|---|---|---|
| 72 | Denver | 15.51 |
| 73 | Salt Lake City | 15.17 |
| 74 | Anchorage | 14.74 |
| 75 | Los Angeles | 14.05 |
| 76 | Charlotte | 12.48 |
| 77 | Austin | 12.31 |
| 78 | Tucson | 11.05 |
| 79 | Long Beach | 10.25 |

| Rank | City | Annual Rainfall (inches) |
|---|---|---|
| 80 | Fresno | 10.24 |
| 81 | San Diego | 9.45 |
| 82 | Albuquerque | 7.77 |
| 82 | El Paso | 7.77 |
| 84 | Phoenix | 7.05 |
| 85 | Las Vegas | 3.76 |

# 7. Heaviest Snowfall

Because snow requires both precipitation and cold weather, it shows less uniformity from year to year than either temperature or rainfall separately. We therefore use the heaviest snowfall in a single month, based on records that go back to the 1930s or before (in the case of New York City, to the 19th century), as an indicator of what might happen in the future.

Three cities in New York State and two in Washington State rank ahead of Alaska in maximum snowfall. Syracuse was subjected to nearly 73 inches of snow—over 6 feet—in February 1958. Rochester received 65 inches the same month. Buffalo had its worst month during 1977, with 68 inches.

At the other end of the spectrum are Phoenix, Los Angeles and Tampa, with less than an inch of snow in a one-month period.

SOURCE: U.S. National Oceanic and Atmospheric Administration (NOAA), National Weather Service, *Local Climatological Data* (1981).

| Rank | City | Month | Maximum Monthly Snowfall (inches) |
|---|---|---|---|
| 1 | Syracuse | 2/58 | 72.6 |
| 2 | Buffalo | 1/77 | 68.3 |
| 3 | Rochester | 2/58 | 64.8 |
| 4 | Tacoma-Seattle | 1/50 | 57.2 |
| 5 | Spokane | 1/50 | 56.9 |
| 6 | Anchorage | 2/55 | 48.5 |
| 7 | Grand Rapids | 1/79 | 45.5 |
| 8 | Worcester | 2/62 | 45.2 |
| 9 | Cleveland | 1/78 | 42.8 |
| 10 | Colorado Springs | 4/57 | 42.7 |
| 11 | Milwaukee | 2/74 | 42.0 |
| 12 | Salt Lake City | 3/77 | 41.9 |
| 13 | Boston | 2/69 | 41.3 |
| 14 | Portland, Ore. | 1/50 | 41.1 |
| 15 | Dayton | 1/78 | 40.2 |
| 15 | Pittsburgh | 10/54 | 40.2 |
| 17 | Minneapolis-St. Paul | 3/51 | 40.0 |
| 18 | Denver | 11/46 | 39.1 |
| 19 | Akron | 1/78 | 37.5 |
| 20 | Chicago | 12/78 | 35.3 |
| 21 | Columbus, Ohio | 1/78 | 34.4 |
| 22 | Baltimore | 2/79 | 33.1 |
| 23 | Providence | 3/56 | 31.6 |
| 24 | Cincinnati | 1/78 | 31.5 |
| 25 | Seattle | 1/50 | 31.0 |
| 26 | Toledo | 1/78 | 30.8 |
| 27 | Indianapolis | 1/78 | 30.6 |

| Rank | City | Month | Maximum Monthly Snowfall (inches) |
|---|---|---|---|
| 27 | Washington, D.C. | 1/79 | 30.6 |
| 29 | New York | 3/1896 | 30.5 |
| 30 | Newark | 12/47 | 29.1 |
| 31 | Flint | 1/76 | 28.5 |
| 31 | Richmond | 1/40 | 28.5 |
| 33 | Louisville | 1/78 | 28.4 |
| 34 | Philadelphia | 2/79 | 27.6 |
| 35 | Omaha | 3/48 | 27.2 |
| 36 | Madison | 1/79 | 26.9 |
| 37 | St. Louis | 12/73 | 26.3 |
| 38 | Fort Wayne | 1/78 | 25.3 |
| 39 | Detroit | 12/51 | 24.0 |
| 40 | Des Moines | 12/61 | 23.9 |
| 41 | Knoxville | 2/60 | 23.3 |
| 42 | Greensboro | 1/66 | 22.9 |
| 43 | Lexington-Fayette | 1/78 | 21.9 |
| 44 | Lubbock | 11/80 | 21.4 |
| 45 | Lincoln | 12/73 | 19.8 |
| 46 | Charlotte | 3/60 | 19.3 |
| 47 | Nashville-Davidson | 2/79 | 18.9 |
| 47 | Norfolk | 1/80 | 18.9 |
| 49 | Wichita | 1/62 | 18.5 |
| 50 | Memphis | 3/68 | 17.3 |
| 50 | Oklahoma City | 1/49 | 17.3 |
| 52 | Las Vegas | 1/49 | 16.7 |
| 53 | Albuquerque | 12/59 | 14.7 |
| 54 | Kansas City, Mo., Kan. | 1/77 | 14.2 |

| Rank | City | Month | Maximum Monthly Snowfall (inches) |
|---|---|---|---|
| 55 | Columbus, Ga. | 2/73 | 14.0 |
| 56 | Dallas-Fort Worth | 2/78 | 13.5 |
| 57 | El Paso | 11/76 | 12.7 |
| 57 | Tulsa | 1/79 | 12.7 |
| 59 | Little Rock | 1/66 | 12.0 |
| 60 | Chattanooga | 2/60 | 10.4 |
| 61 | Atlanta | 1/40 | 8.3 |
| 62 | Birmingham | 2/63 | 8.0 |
| 63 | Austin | 1/44 | 7.0 |
| 64 | Tucson | 12/71 | 6.8 |
| 65 | Montgomery | 1/77 | 6.0 |
| 66 | Shreveport | 1/78 | 5.9 |
| 67 | Jackson | 1/77 | 5.8 |
| 68 | San Antonio | 1/49 | 4.7 |
| 69 | Mobile | 2/73 | 3.6 |
| 70 | Houston | 2/73 | 2.8 |
| 71 | New Orleans | 12/63 | 2.7 |
| 72 | Fresno | 1/62 | 2.2 |
| 73 | Sacramento | 2/76 | 2.0 |
| 74 | Baton Rouge | 2/73 | 1.8 |
| 75 | Jacksonville | 2/58 | 1.5 |
| 76 | Corpus Christi | 1/40 | 1.2 |
| 77 | Oakland | 2/76 | 1.0 |
| 78 | Phoenix | 2/39 | .6 |
| 79 | Los Angeles | 1/49 | .3 |
| 80 | Tampa-St. Petersburg | 1/77 | .2 |

# 8. Coldest Cities

It is impressive that it got as cold as 80 degrees Fahrenheit below zero in Prospect Creek, Alaska (January 1971), the record low U.S. temperature, or that it dropped to 37 below in Madison (January 1981) and 34 below in Anchorage (January 1975). But so long as we are inside and tucked in our beds, we usually don't care how cold it may get outside in the middle of the night. The more serious question is: How many days during the year, on average (based on historical data), did the temperature remain below zero *throughout the day*?

Based on this measure, the coldest American cities in our survey of the 100 largest are in the northern portion of the temperate zone. Three cities—Anchorage (the coldest city), Minneapolis and Madison—have seen the temperature remain below zero for enough days during the year to equal a whole month.

Based on the average of historical records, more than half of the 100 largest cities had no days in which the temperature remained below zero all day.

SOURCE: U.S. National Oceanic and Atmospheric Administration (NOAA), National Weather Service, *Local Climatological Data* (1981).

| Rank | City | Days Temperature Did Not Rise Above zero° F | Rank | City | Days Temperature Did Not Rise Above zero° F | Rank | City | Days Temperature Did Not Rise Above zero° F |
|---|---|---|---|---|---|---|---|---|
| 1 | Anchorage | 36 | 15 | Cincinnati | 7 | 27 | Wichita | 3 |
| 2 | Minneapolis-St. Paul | 35 | 15 | Cleveland | 7 | 32 | Detroit | 2 |
| 3 | Madison | 28 | 15 | Colorado Springs | 7 | 32 | Louisville | 2 |
| 4 | Des Moines | 17 | 15 | Rochester | 7 | 32 | San Francisco | 2 |
| 5 | Milwaukee | 16 | 15 | Worcester | 7 | 35 | Albuquerque | 1 |
| 6 | Omaha | 15 | 21 | Columbus, Ohio | 6 | 35 | Boston | 1 |
| 7 | Chicago | 13 | 21 | Denver | 6 | 35 | Knoxville | 1 |
| 8 | Fort Wayne | 12 | 23 | Buffalo | 5 | 35 | Lubbock | 1 |
| 9 | Flint | 10 | 23 | Pittsburgh | 5 | 35 | Nashville-Davidson | 1 |
| 9 | Grand Rapids | 10 | 23 | Spokane | 5 | 35 | Newark | 1 |
| 9 | Kansas City, Mo., Kan. | 10 | 26 | St. Louis | 4 | 35 | Oakland | 1 |
| 9 | Syracuse | 10 | 27 | Lexington-Fayette | 3 | 35 | Oklahoma City | 1 |
| 9 | Toledo | 10 | 27 | Lincoln | 3 | 35 | Richmond | 1 |
| 14 | Indianapolis | 9 | 27 | Providence | 3 | 35 | Tulsa | 1 |
| 15 | Akron | 7 | 27 | Salt Lake City | 3 | | | |

# 9. Hottest Cities

Heat is related to health and quality of life. An extremely high level of heat is especially unpleasant and unhealthful when it is associated with a high level of humidity.

To determine upper extremes of heat, the 100 largest cities are ranked on the average number of days during the year that are "hot," i.e., days on which the temperature exceeded 90 degrees F, based on each city's historical records.

In Phoenix nearly half of all the days are hot. Phoenix is also the city that has the record high temperature

of 118 F in July 1958. The runners-up are Las Vegas, 116 (August 1977) and Sacramento, 115 (June 1961). The highest temperature ever recorded in the United States was 134 F in Death Valley, California (July 1913). Eight cities show more than 100 days of hot weather. Each of these cities, however, ranks low in average relative humidity (see next table), which makes the heat less severe.

By contrast, in 12 cities fewer than 10 days in the year were hot. The three lowest are San Francisco, Buffalo and Seattle.

SOURCE: U.S. National Oceanic and Atmospheric Administration (NOAA), National Weather Service, *Local Climatological Data* (1981), and NOAA, Environmental Data Service.

| Rank | City | Number of Days 90° F or Above | Rank | City | Number of Days 90° F or Above | Rank | City | Number of Days 90° F or Above |
|---|---|---|---|---|---|---|---|---|
| 1 | Phoenix | 165 | 29 | Birmingham | 48 | 57 | Chicago | 16 |
| 2 | Tucson | 139 | 30 | Lincoln | 44 | 57 | Indianapolis | 16 |
| 3 | Las Vegas | 133 | 31 | Nashville-Davidson | 42 | 57 | Lexington-Fayette | 16 |
| 4 | San Antonio | 111 | 31 | Richmond | 42 | 57 | Madison | 16 |
| 5 | Fresno | 108 | 33 | Kansas City, Mo., Kan. | 40 | 57 | Oakland | 16 |
| 6 | El Paso | 105 | 33 | St. Louis | 40 | 62 | Honolulu | 15 |
| 7 | Austin | 103 | 35 | Omaha | 38 | 62 | Minneapolis-St. Paul | 15 |
| 8 | Corpus Christi | 101 | 35 | Washington, D.C. | 38 | 64 | Anchorage | 14 |
| 9 | Dallas-Fort Worth | 95 | 37 | Charlotte | 34 | 64 | Columbus, Ohio | 14 |
| 10 | Houston | 89 | 37 | Denver | 34 | 64 | Detroit | 14 |
| 10 | Shreveport | 89 | 39 | Baltimore | 31 | 64 | Fort Wayne | 14 |
| 12 | Baton Rouge | 83 | 39 | Miami | 31 | 68 | Boston | 13 |
| 13 | Jacksonville | 82 | 39 | Norfolk | 31 | 68 | Toledo | 13 |
| 14 | Mobile | 81 | 42 | Greensboro | 29 | 70 | Grand Rapids | 11 |
| 14 | Tampa-St. Petersburg | 81 | 43 | Louisville | 27 | 70 | Rochester | 11 |
| 16 | Jackson | 80 | 43 | San Diego | 27 | 72 | Portland, Ore. | 10 |
| 17 | Lubbock | 79 | 45 | Atlanta | 26 | 73 | Providence | 9 |
| 18 | Sacramento | 75 | 46 | Des Moines | 23 | 74 | Cleveland | 8 |
| 19 | Columbus, Ga. | 74 | 47 | Knoxville | 22 | 74 | Milwaukee | 8 |
| 19 | Tulsa | 74 | 47 | Long Beach | 22 | 76 | Akron | 7 |
| 21 | Montgomery | 70 | 47 | Los Angeles | 22 | 76 | Pittsburgh | 7 |
| 21 | New Orleans | 70 | 50 | Newark | 21 | 76 | Syracuse | 7 |
| 21 | Oklahoma City | 70 | 51 | Philadelphia | 20 | 78 | Flint | 5 |
| 24 | Wichita | 68 | 51 | Spokane | 20 | 79 | Tacoma | 3 |
| 25 | Memphis | 66 | 53 | Cincinnati | 19 | 79 | Worcester | 3 |
| 26 | Albuquerque | 64 | 54 | Colorado Springs | 17 | 81 | Buffalo | 2 |
| 27 | Salt Lake City | 58 | 54 | Dayton | 17 | 81 | San Francisco | 2 |
| 28 | Chattanooga | 49 | 54 | New York | 17 | 81 | Seattle | 2 |

# 10. Most Humid Cities

Humidity affects the health of residents because it reduces the ability of the body to lower its own temperature through perspiration. Instead of evaporating and carrying away the body heat, perspiration remains on the skin. This makes heat much harder for the body to bear and increases the likelihood of heat stroke, fatigue and heat exhaustion, and respiratory ailments.

Cities are ranked on their historic (back to the 1930s and before) average relative humidity during the evening hours, 4 p.m.–8 p.m., since that is the period during which people travel home from work, and the buildup of humidity will be especially uncomfortable. During other hours of the day humidity can be eased through air conditioning. The data, as one would expect, show similarities to the rainfall figures.

Jacksonville is the most humid, with an average relative humidity of 73 percent. Miami trails several points behind. One would not expect that Anchorage would rank as high as it does here. The high degree of humidity probably reflects the presence of the Alaskan Range to the north and the Gulf of Alaska to the south. Cities with less moisture—such as Las Vegas, Tucson and El Paso—are at the other end of the list, with low relative humidities of 20 percent, 25 percent and 27 percent, respectively.

SOURCE: U.S. National Oceanic and Atmospheric Administration (NOAA), National Weather Service, *Local Climatological Data* (1981)

| Rank | City | Percentage Relative Humidity | Rank | City | Percentage Relative Humidity | Rank | City | Percentage Relative Humidity |
|---|---|---|---|---|---|---|---|---|
| 1 | Jacksonville | 73 | 28 | Boston | 65 | 55 | Memphis | 60 |
| 2 | Miami | 71 | 28 | Dayton | 65 | 55 | Minneapolis-St. Paul | 60 |
| 3 | Anchorage | 70 | 28 | Fort Wayne | 65 | 55 | Portland, Ore. | 60 |
| 3 | Buffalo | 70 | 28 | Greensboro | 65 | 55 | Shreveport | 60 |
| 3 | New Orleans | 70 | 28 | Madison | 65 | 61 | Kansas City, Mo., Kan. | 59 |
| 3 | Tampa-St. Petersburg | 70 | 34 | Cincinnati | 64 | 61 | Washington, D.C. | 59 |
| 7 | Honolulu | 69 | 34 | Detroit | 64 | 63 | Lincoln | 58 |
| 7 | Norfolk | 69 | 34 | Lexington-Fayette | 64 | 63 | Omaha | 58 |
| 7 | Richmond | 69 | 37 | Birmingham | 63 | 65 | Tulsa | 55 |
| 7 | Rochester | 69 | 37 | Chicago | 63 | 66 | Wichita | 54 |
| 7 | Syracuse | 69 | 37 | Columbus, Ohio | 63 | 67 | Austin | 53 |
| 12 | Corpus Christi | 68 | 37 | Montgomery | 63 | 67 | Dallas-Fort Worth | 53 |
| 12 | Milwaukee | 68 | 37 | Philadelphia | 63 | 67 | Long Beach | 53 |
| 14 | Cleveland | 67 | 42 | Atlanta | 62 | 67 | Los Angeles | 53 |
| 14 | Grand Rapids | 67 | 42 | Baltimore | 62 | 67 | Oklahoma City | 53 |
| 14 | Houston | 67 | 42 | Chattanooga | 62 | 72 | San Antonio | 52 |
| 14 | Jackson | 67 | 42 | Knoxville | 62 | 73 | Spokane | 51 |
| 14 | Mobile | 67 | 42 | Nashville-Davidson | 62 | 74 | Sacramento | 46 |
| 14 | Oakland | 67 | 42 | Pittsburgh | 62 | 75 | Salt Lake City | 42 |
| 14 | Toledo | 67 | 42 | Seattle-Tacoma | 62 | 76 | Fresno | 41 |
| 21 | Akron | 66 | 49 | Charlotte | 61 | 77 | Denver | 40 |
| 21 | Columbus, Ga. | 66 | 49 | Louisville | 61 | 77 | Lubbock | 40 |
| 21 | Flint | 66 | 49 | Newark | 61 | 77 | Phoenix | 40 |
| 21 | Indianapolis | 66 | 49 | New York | 61 | 80 | Colorado Springs | 39 |
| 21 | Providence | 66 | 49 | St. Louis | 61 | 81 | Albuquerque | 28 |
| 21 | San Francisco | 66 | 49 | San Diego | 61 | 82 | El Paso | 27 |
| 21 | Worcester | 66 | 55 | Des Moines | 60 | 83 | Tucson | 25 |
| 28 | Baton Rouge | 65 | 55 | Little Rock | 60 | 84 | Las Vegas | 20 |

# 11. Average Temperature

The average temperature gives a quick summary of what to expect in a city. The previous tables on hottest and coldest temperatures are important to bear in mind as we review the averages. The overall U.S. historical average (high of 134 degrees and low of minus 80 degrees) is 27 degrees, but this does not mean that the normal U.S. temperature is below the 32-degree freezing point.

To obtain a measure of the average temperature, the 100 largest cities are ranked by the historical average of monthly average temperatures in degrees Fahrenheit.

Five cities exceed 70 degrees F: Honolulu (range: 53 degrees to 93 degrees), Miami, Tampa, Corpus Christi and Phoenix.

Three cities are below 45 degrees F: Madison, Minneapolis and Anchorage (range: minus 34 degrees to 85 degrees).

SOURCE: U.S. National Oceanic and Atmospheric Administration (NOAA), National Weather Service, *Local Climatological Data* (1981).

| Rank | City | Average Temperature | Rank | City | Average Temperature | Rank | City | Average Temperature |
|---|---|---|---|---|---|---|---|---|
| 1 | Honolulu | 76.6 | 8 | Jacksonville | 68.4 | 15 | Las Vegas | 65.8 |
| 2 | Miami | 75.5 | 9 | New Orleans | 68.3 | 16 | Dallas-Fort Worth | 65.5 |
| 3 | Tampa-St. Petersburg | 72.2 | 10 | Austin | 68.1 | 17 | Jackson | 65.0 |
| 4 | Corpus Christi | 71.9 | 11 | Tucson | 67.8 | 18 | Los Angeles | 64.8 |
| 5 | Phoenix | 70.3 | 12 | Baton Rouge | 67.4 | 18 | Montgomery | 64.8 |
| 6 | Houston | 68.9 | 12 | Mobile | 67.4 | 20 | Columbus, Ga. | 64.3 |
| 7 | San Antonio | 68.8 | 14 | Shreveport | 65.9 | 21 | El Paso | 63.4 |

| Rank | City | Average Temperature | Rank | City | Average Temperature | Rank | City | Average Temperature |
|------|------|---------------------|------|------|---------------------|------|------|---------------------|
| 22 | Long Beach | 63.3 | 44 | Wichita | 56.6 | 66 | Providence | 50.0 |
| 23 | San Diego | 62.9 | 45 | St. Louis | 55.9 | 67 | Detroit | 49.9 |
| 24 | Birmingham | 62.4 | 46 | Louisville | 55.6 | 67 | Fort Wayne | 49.9 |
| 25 | Fresno | 62.3 | 47 | Lexington-Fayette | 55.2 | 69 | Cleveland | 49.7 |
| 26 | Memphis | 61.6 | 48 | Baltimore | 55.0 | 70 | Akron | 49.6 |
| 27 | Little Rock | 61.0 | 49 | Philadelphia | 54.6 | 71 | Toledo | 49.3 |
| 28 | Atlanta | 60.8 | 50 | New York | 54.5 | 72 | Des Moines | 49.0 |
| 29 | Charlotte | 60.5 | 51 | Cincinnati | 54.0 | 73 | Chicago | 48.9 |
| 30 | Sacramento | 60.3 | 52 | Newark | 53.9 | 74 | Colorado Springs | 48.4 |
| 31 | Tulsa | 60.2 | 53 | Kansas City, Mo., Kan. | 53.7 | 75 | Syracuse | 48.1 |
| 32 | Oklahoma City | 59.9 | 54 | Portland, Ore. | 52.6 | 76 | Rochester | 47.9 |
| 33 | Chattanooga | 59.8 | 55 | Seattle | 52.5 | 77 | Grand Rapids | 47.8 |
| 34 | Knoxville | 59.7 | 56 | Indianapolis | 52.3 | 78 | Spokane | 47.3 |
| 34 | Lubbock | 59.7 | 57 | Dayton | 52.0 | 79 | Buffalo | 47.1 |
| 36 | Nashville | 59.4 | 58 | Tacoma | 51.9 | 79 | Worcester | 47.1 |
| 37 | Norfolk | 59.3 | 59 | Columbus, Ohio | 51.5 | 81 | Flint | 46.8 |
| 38 | Greensboro | 58.1 | 59 | Omaha | 51.5 | 82 | Milwaukee | 45.7 |
| 39 | Richmond | 57.8 | 61 | Boston | 51.3 | 83 | Madison | 44.9 |
| 40 | Oakland | 57.4 | 62 | Lincoln | 51.0 | 84 | Minneapolis-St. Paul | 44.1 |
| 41 | Washington, D.C. | 57.3 | 62 | Salt Lake City | 51.0 | 85 | Anchorage | 35.0 |
| 42 | Albuquerque | 56.8 | 64 | Pittsburgh | 50.4 | | | |
| 43 | San Francisco | 56.7 | 65 | Denver | 50.1 | | | |

# CHAPTER TWO

# ENVIRONMENT

The 1970s have been called the Decade of the Environment. The Clean Air Act was signed in 1970. Since then air quality has continued to improve. The number of days metro areas were in violation of the National Ambient Air Quality Standards (NAAQS) decreased 18 percent between 1974 and 1978. The data for 37 metropolitan areas show that the *average* for many areas in 1978–80 was lower than their *minimum* reading in 1976–78. The latest available information for 1981 shown in the air quality tables below indicate continuing improvement.

However, air quality has deteriorated in a few cities. Also, while national average concentrations of carbon monoxide (CO), nitrogen dioxide (NO$_2$), and particulates have dropped, ozone concentrations—which produce smog—have continued to be a problem, especially in the Los Angeles and Riverside metro areas.

Finally, the building of tall stacks to disperse the emission of sulfur dioxide and nitrogen dioxide into the ambient air has produced a new problem—the interaction and crystallization of these chemicals in the outer atmosphere and their return to earth as "acid rain." The Council on Environmental Quality has described this phenomenon as the "airmailing of pollution."

On the water quality side, the urban data are harder to obtain and less reliable than for air quality, but water quality in the big cities is now considered to be very good, because the water is treated under the supervision of qualified engineers and scientists. Smaller communities have relied on ground water, which is contaminated in many areas by chemicals that are known or suspected carcinogens or mutagens, such as light molecular weight chlorinated hydrocarbons, for which medical and scientific evidence indicates no "safe" levels of exposure. "The biggest problems are in smaller communities that don't spend money on water treatment" (USEPA official, letter to the authors, July 1982).

Urban runoff is a big problem, on which no progress was made during the 1970s. In 1979 the water supply systems of 11,300 communities were microbiologically contaminated. Three-fifths of the systems were small, serving fewer than 500 people. The most frequently reported source of fecal, toxic and other ground water contamination is the septic tank or cesspool. Another source is the municipal "dump" or landfill. Only 35 percent of 14,000 active landfills identified in 1978 by *Waste Age* were in compliance with state regulations. Many surface waters (rivers, lakes) are still polluted, but their quality is no longer deteriorating. A few bodies of water, such as the Hackensack River, have improved markedly.

Better data are needed on upstream and downstream pollution of rivers by cities with sewage treatment plants. Under the Clean Water Act, permits are required for municipal discharges. Sewage discharge permits were issued to 15,400 municipalities as of February 1980. Under the Federal Water Pollution Control Act Amendments of 1972, all municipal sewage treatment plants were to achieve secondary treatment by 1977 and to use "best practicable" waste treatment by 1983. Many municipalities have not been meeting these requirements, partly because monitoring of river water quality in the cities has been inadequate.

SOURCES: Council on Environmental Quality, *Environmental Quality—1979*, pp. 122, 133, 136, 146, 174; *Environmental Quality—1980*, pp. 81–82, 86, 89, 100, 108, 130.

# 12. Air Pollution: Carbon Monoxide

When materials containing carbon are burned, one by-product is carbon monoxide (CO). Motor vehicles are the largest single source of CO. Concentrations are highest along well-traveled expressways and congested urban areas dependent upon the automobile. Respiratory disease is a special threat to urban residents because of the concentration of pollutants.

Most people know that CO from an idling car confined in a garage can kill by asphyxiation in a matter of minutes. Smaller amounts are also dangerous because CO replaces oxygen in the blood forming carboxyhemoglobin, hampering the delivery of oxygen to the body's vital tissues and organs.

CO is by far the most common pollutant in the ambient air. Human senses cannot detect it because it is colorless, odorless and tasteless. Human activities produce all but a small fraction of the millions of tons of CO that envelop our urban areas. In contrast to ozone, which is a summer pollutant in most of the United States (only the Los Angeles-Long Beach area has both serious wintertime smog and CO), CO is usually primarily a winter pollutant. Ozone requires sunlight to create the chemical reaction that causes smog.

CO concentrations in cities and along busy roads nowadays rarely exceed 15 parts per million (ppm). Levels as low as 10–15 ppm are believed to affect reaction time. Clinical research has shown adverse effects on heart patients of exposure to a concentration of 15 ppm or more of CO for an 8-hour period.

The Federal ambient air quality standard for CO to prevent adverse health effects was set at 9 ppm, which was designed to provide for a margin of safety below the clinically proven danger level of 15 ppm. The maximum allowable one-hour CO concentration was set in the 1970's at 35 ppm. In August 1980, the maximum was lowered to 25 ppm.

In the following table, three metropolitan areas show pollution levels of 9 ppm exceeded on more than 80 days in 1981. Residents and workers in Los Angeles-Long Beach, New York, and Phoenix experienced CO levels above federal standards more than one out of every five days. Denver's mile-high location contributed to its high CO air pollution levels—60 days above 9 ppm in 1981. At the low end of the ranking are 10 cities with only one day where pollution levels exceeded 9 ppm.

The trends in CO levels were also reviewed, using three-year running averages, not shown in the following table. The good news from this analysis is that in large cities CO levels have been dropping, thanks primarily to emission controls on automobiles. The number of days for which the national 9 ppm CO standard was exceeded, using a three-year running average, fell in the Albuquerque area from 88 in 1976 to 34 in 1981; in the Anaheim area from 82 to 32; and in the Boston area from 65 to 21. The number of days that the Chicago area's CO level exceeded the standard fell by two-thirds, from 90 in 1976 to 31 in 1981. Denver's rate fell from 118 to 76; and Jersey City's from 120 to 14. Las Vegas dropped less drastically, from 66 to 45. Los Angeles fell from the high level of 156 in 1976 to 95 in 1981, and Newark from 143 to 31. Philadelphia fell from 54 to 14, and Portland from 66 to 29. Providence fell from 58 to 9 and St. Louis from 57 to 8. Salt Lake City dropped from 63 to 16 and San Jose from 44 to 11. The Spokane area fell from 90 to 12 and the Washington, D.C. area from 79 to 18.

SOURCES: Background information from U.S. Environmental Protection Agency (EPA) *Air Quality Data—1979 Annual Statistics*, EPA-450/4-80-014, September 1980; Council on Environmental Quality (CEQ), Executive Office of the President, *Environmental Quality—1977, —1979,* and *—1980;* and Daphne Gemmill, *City Air* (New York: Council on Municipal Performance, 1974). Trend data for 1981 provided to the authors by the CEQ in advance of publication of its 1982 Annual Report. All other ambient air data provided from a national air quality data bank maintained by Roy F. Weston, Inc., West Chester, Pennsylvania. All air quality data are derived from EPA's SAROAD data bank.

| Rank | Metro Area | Number of days CO Exceeded 9 ppm in 1981 | Rank | Metro Area | Number of days CO Exceeded 9 ppm in 1981 | Rank | Metro Area | Number of days CO Exceeded 9 ppm in 1981 |
|---|---|---|---|---|---|---|---|---|
| 1 | Los Angeles-Long Beach | 88 | 3 | Phoenix | 82 | 5 | Albuquerque | 48 |
| 2 | New York | 87 | 4 | Denver | 60 | 6 | Las Vegas | 39 |

| Rank | Metro Area | Number of days CO Exceeded 9 ppm in 1981 | Rank | Metro Area | Number of days CO Exceeded 9 ppm in 1981 | Rank | Metro Area | Number of days CO Exceeded 9 ppm in 1981 |
|------|------------|-------------------------------------------|------|------------|-------------------------------------------|------|------------|-------------------------------------------|
| 6 | Anchorage | 39 | 20 | Salt Lake City | 9 | 36 | Rochester | 3 |
| 8 | Seattle | 32 | 20 | Washington, D.C. | 9 | 38 | Atlanta | 2 |
| 9 | Minneapolis-St. Paul | 31 | 20 | Wichita | 9 | 38 | Columbus, Ohio | 2 |
| 10 | Newark (1980 data) | 29 | 25 | El Paso | 8 | 38 | Richmond | 2 |
| 11 | Anaheim | 22 | 26 | Cleveland | 7 | 41 | Birmingham | 1 |
| 12 | Portland, Ore. | 21 | 26 | Detroit | 7 | 41 | Buffalo | 1 |
| 13 | Louisville | 16 | 26 | Pittsburgh | 7 | 41 | Cincinnati | 1 |
| 14 | Boston | 15 | 29 | Providence | 6 | 41 | Dayton | 1 |
| 15 | Indianapolis | 12 | 29 | Tucson | 6 | 41 | Houston | 1 |
| 15 | Lincoln | 12 | 31 | Jersey City | 5 | 41 | Milwaukee | 1 |
| 17 | Nashville | 11 | 31 | Philadelphia | 5 | 41 | Riverside | 1 |
| 17 | Spokane | 11 | 31 | San Jose | 5 | 41 | St. Louis | 1 |
| 19 | Charlotte | 10 | 31 | Tulsa | 5 | 41 | San Diego | 1 |
| 20 | Chicago | 9 | 35 | Colorado Springs | 4 | 41 | Toledo | 1 |
| 20 | Fresno | 9 | 36 | Akron | 3 | | | |

# 13. Air Pollution: Particulates

Total suspended particulates (TSP) are produced generally by burning fuel at factories and power plants. They include droplets of oil and acid mists, soil particles, chemical dusts, asbestos, lead and rubber particles, soot and grime. Some of these contaminants, depending on size and chemical structure, are more toxic than others, and federal officials are continuing to seek more precise measures of particulates. Particulates impair the filtering action of the nasal and lung passages and lodge in the lungs, often depositing a surface-carried sulfur oxide directly on the lung's delicate linings. In some urban areas, airborne particulates significantly reduce direct sunlight. Particulates also soil and rot clothing, corrode metals, statues and buildings, and make housekeeping difficult and expensive.

Particulates are monitored extensively. The good news for urban areas is that their estimated annual emissions have dropped significantly in recent years. Every major industrial source of particulates is under some sort of pollution control system or timetable.

The bad news for the nation is that serious new sources of particulate pollution are being created in rural areas, especially through strip mining and associated developments such as coal gasification and operation of coal-fired electric plants. In all areas, new fuel-efficient diesel-powered light vehicles emit a pound of deadly particulates per 1,000 miles—20 to 100 times more than gasoline-powered vehicles fitted with catalytic equipment. The diesel emissions have been shown to be car-cinogenic, mutagenic, and aggravating to respiratory ailments.

The national ambient air quality standard for total suspended particulates issued by the U.S. Environmental Protection Agency is that the maximum 24-hour concentration of 260 micrograms per cubic meter not be exceeded more than once per year.

Using this standard, the following table shows that nine cities exceeded the standard by a factor of 10 or more—i.e., they had at least 10 days in 1981 on which they exceeded the 260 $\mu g/m^3$ ceiling. These metro areas were Denver (31 days), El Paso (28 days), Riverside, St. Louis, Houston, Birmingham, Phoenix, Pittsburgh and Spokane.

Nine metro areas in 1981 were barely within the limit—Albuquerque, Baltimore, Baton Rouge, Cincinnati, Dallas, Dayton, Fresno, San Diego and Salt Lake City. They each had one day on which the concentration exceeded the 260 ceiling.

Particulate pollution has improved markedly in recent years in most metro areas. Comparing the 1976–78 average with the 1979–81 average, it dropped in the Birmingham, Buffalo, Chicago, Cleveland, Mobile, Omaha, Phoenix, Pittsburgh, St. Louis, Salt Lake City, Tucson and Washington, D.C. metro areas. However, particulate pollution *increased* in Anchorage, Denver, El Paso, Houston, Riverside and Spokane.

Metro areas not cited in the above paragraph have not had a serious problem with particulate air pollution.

SOURCES: Background information from U.S. Environmental Protection Agency (EPA) *Air Quality Data—1979 Annual Statistics*, EPA-450/4-80-014, September 1980; Council on Environmental Quality (CEQ), Executive Office of the President, *Environmental Quality—1977, —1979,* and *—1980;* and Daphne Gemmill, *City Air* (New York: Council on Municipal Performance, 1974). Trend data for 1981 provided to the authors by the CEQ in advance of publication of its 1982 Annual Report. All other ambient air data provided from a national air quality data bank maintained by Roy F. Weston, Inc., West Chester, Pennsylvania. All air quality data are derived from EPA's SAROAD data bank.

| Rank | Metro Area | Number of days TSP Exceeded 260 µg/m³ in 1981 | Rank | Metro Area | Number of days TSP Exceeded 260 µg/m³ in 1981 | Rank | Metro Area | Number of days TSP Exceeded 260 µg/m³ in 1981 |
|---|---|---|---|---|---|---|---|---|
| 1 | Denver | 31 | 12 | Las Vegas | 6 | 22 | Tulsa | 2 |
| 2 | El Paso | 28 | 13 | Portland, Ore. | 5 | 24 | Albuquerque | 1 |
| 3 | Riverside | 17 | 14 | Anaheim | 4 | 24 | Baltimore | 1 |
| 4 | St. Louis | 16 | 14 | Buffalo | 4 | 24 | Baton Rouge | 1 |
| 5 | Houston | 14 | 14 | Detroit | 4 | 24 | Cincinnati | 1 |
| 6 | Birmingham | 13 | 14 | Philadelphia | 4 | 24 | Dallas-Forth Worth | 1 |
| 7 | Phoenix | 10 | 14 | Seattle | 4 | 24 | Dayton | 1 |
| 7 | Pittsburgh | 10 | 19 | Chicago | 3 | 24 | Fresno | 1 |
| 7 | Spokane | 10 | 19 | Los Angeles-Long Beach | 3 | 24 | Salt Lake City | 1 |
| 10 | Anchorage | 8 | 19 | Minneapolis-St. Paul | 3 | 24 | San Diego | 1 |
| 10 | Cleveland | 8 | 22 | Indianapolis | 2 | | | |

# 14. Air Pollution: Ozone

Ozone is a pollutant which is the source of what we see as smog, that burning haze first recognized in the Los Angeles basin. It begins to form when the sun's ultraviolet rays in a calm environment (also called air "stagnation" or "inversion") trigger a reaction between hydrocarbons, to a lesser extent nitrogen dioxide and other volatile organic compounds resulting in secondary pollutants known as photochemical oxidants. Hydrocarbons are produced, along with carbon monoxide, largely by automobile emissions, as well as by stationary sources. The health hazard created by hydrocarbons is related primarily to the production of ozone.

Ozone formation is therefore worst when the sunshine is brightest, the air is calmest and where there are large sources of hydrocarbons, especially places with high automobile concentration or many oil refineries and chemical plants. The adverse effect of ozone is to cause people on the street to suffer from eye irritation, coughing, headache, and fatigue. The emission control systems now used on automobiles have helped reduce ozone formation.

The primary National Ambient Air Quality standard for ozone is 0.12 parts per million (ppm) averaged over one hour. Two metro areas have clearly had the most ozone pollution in recent years—Los Angeles and Riverside. This reflects their high auto use, the frequency of sunny days and the frequency of air inversions. Whereas most other metro areas have ozone problems only in the July–September summer season, these two areas have them year-round.

The data below show the number of days that the 0.12 ppm standard for ozone was exceeded in 1981. The two Californian metro areas continue to be far ahead of any others in ozone levels with the pollution level above the 100 Pollutant Standards Index (PSI) level every day for half the year. The next four metro areas with high ozone levels are sunbelt cities—Anaheim, San Diego, Houston and Fresno. Data for two metro areas, Newark and Atlanta, are for 1980.

As an example of the downward trend in ozone levels, the Boston area exceeded the national standard on 24 days in 1976 and on only 3 days in 1981. Cincinnati declined from 22 days to 1, and Cleveland from 32 to 3. Dallas dropped slightly from 22 to 17. The Denver area showed a drop of from 25 to 5 days, and Jersey City from 18 to 7 days. Philadelphia dropped from 52 to 23 days. St.

Louis fell from 64 to 9 days and Salt Lake City from 26 to 17 days. The Washington, D.C. area dropped from 50 to 12 days. However, Baltimore showed less improve-ment, 28 days in 1976 vs. 22 in 1981. Chicago decreased from 17 to 6 days, and Louisville from 12 to 4 days, and the New York City area increased from 28 to 29 days.

SOURCES: Background information from U.S. Environmental Protection Agency (EPA) *Air Quality Data—1979 Annual Statistics*, EPA-450/4-80-014, September 1980; Council on Environmental Quality (CEQ), Executive Office of the President, *Environmental Quality—1977, —1979* and *—1980;* and Daphne Gemmill, *City Air* (New York: Council on Municipal Performance, 1974). Trend data for 1981 provided to the authors by the CEQ in advance of publication of its 1981 Annual Report. All other ambient air data provided from a national air quality data bank maintained by Roy F. Weston, Inc., West Chester, Pennsylvania. All air quality data are derived from EPA's SAROAD data bank.

| Rank | Metro Area | Number of days ozone exceeded 0.12 ppm for one hour in 1981 | Rank | Metro Area | Number of days ozone exceeded 0.12 ppm for one hour in 1981 | Rank | Metro Area | Number of days ozone exceeded 0.12 ppm for one hour in 1981 |
|---|---|---|---|---|---|---|---|---|
| 1 | Riverside | 175 | 16 | Detroit | 12 | 32 | Kansas City | 4 |
| 2 | Los Angeles-Long Beach | 170 | 16 | Washington, D.C. | 12 | 32 | Louisville | 4 |
| 3 | Anaheim | 69 | 19 | Providence | 10 | 32 | Toledo | 4 |
| 4 | San Diego | 67 | 19 | Phoenix | 10 | 36 | Boston | 3 |
| 5 | Houston | 61 | 19 | Milwaukee | 10 | 36 | Cleveland | 3 |
| 6 | Fresno | 36 | 22 | St. Louis | 9 | 36 | Dayton | 3 |
| 7 | Newark (1980 data) | 30 | 23 | Atlanta (1980 data) | 8 | 36 | El Paso | 3 |
| 8 | New York | 29 | 24 | Chicago | 6 | 40 | Buffalo | 2 |
| 9 | Philadelphia | 23 | 25 | Akron | 5 | 40 | Indianapolis | 2 |
| 10 | Baltimore | 22 | 25 | Denver | 5 | 40 | Nashville | 2 |
| 11 | Baton Rouge | 17 | 25 | Jersey City | 5 | 40 | Tampa-St. Petersburg | 2 |
| 11 | Dallas-Fort Worth | 17 | 25 | Portland, Ore. | 5 | 44 | Cincinnati | 1 |
| 11 | Salt Lake City | 17 | 25 | San Francisco | 5 | 44 | Minneapolis-St. Paul | 1 |
| 14 | Las Vegas | 16 | 25 | San Jose | 5 | 44 | Seattle | 1 |
| 15 | Birmingham | 15 | 25 | Tulsa | 5 | 44 | Tucson | 1 |
| 16 | Pittsburgh | 12 | 32 | Charlotte | 4 | | | |

# 15. Overall Air Quality: Pollutant Standards Index

Official rankings of U.S. cities on overall air quality are developed by the Council on Environmental Quality (CEQ) in its annual report. CEQ uses its Pollutant Standards Index (PSI), based on the U.S. Environmental Protection Agency's (EPA) SAROAD data base.

The PSI uses measures of five air pollutants—ozone ($O_3$), carbon monoxide (CO), total suspended particulates (TSP), sulfur dioxide ($SO_2$) and nitrogen dioxide ($NO_2$). The measures of daily pollution levels for each area are compared against a national standard that is described in more detail under each of the different types of pollution in the tables that follow. No data are provided below on $NO_2$ because among the areas covered by this book the standard was exceeded only in Los Angeles.

The PSI for a given area will range between 0 and 500. The critical number in terms of interpreting the tables below is 100. A PSI of 0 means no significant pollution for any of the five criteria pollutants. The PSI will rise above 100 and indicate "unhealthful" conditions when any one of the five pollutants is measured at a station located within the metro area reaches a level judged to have adverse short-term effects on health—i.e., a level in excess of National Ambient Air Quality Standards. Above 100, persons with existing heart or respiratory ailments should reduce physical exertion and outdoor activity.

PSI levels can rise above 200, in which case it means air quality conditions are "very unhealthful" at such times those with heart or lung ailments, and elderly people in general should reduce physical exertion and stay indoors. A PSI above 300 means air quality is "hazardous" and the cautionary advice to stay indoors and avoid exertion is expanded to include the entire population. A PSI above 400 implies such effects as premature death of the ill and elderly; in such cases in addition to the other cautions, windows and doors of buildings should be kept closed.

The table below, and the following tables, focus on the number of days on which the PSI exceeds 100, i.e., the number of days on which the air quality exceeds the lowest of the national air quality standards.

The overall PSI data below for 1981 include 51 metro areas with cities among the 100 largest, of the 61 such metro areas for which data have been provided by the source. Eight of the 61 areas are not included in the table because they had no data for one or more pollutants: Colorado Springs, Grand Rapids, Memphis, Newark, Norfolk, Sacramento, Syracuse, and Wichita. Two areas have insufficient data: Cincinnati and Baltimore.

The Los Angeles area continues to have the worst overall air pollution problem with a PSI above 100 for at least one pollutant on 137 days in 1981. New York wasn't far behind with 102 days. Three other areas showed unhealthful air at least one-fifth of the year 1981: Riverside, Phoenix and Anaheim.

Nine areas—Richmond; Columbus, Ohio; Tampa; Rochester; Providence; Dayton; San Francisco; Buffalo and Tucson—showed unhealthful air for less than one week.

Ozone and carbon monoxide account for most of the violations in the areas with severe air pollution problems. CEQ notes that the siting of monitors is still not standardized and that differences in siting practices may account for some of the differences among air quality findings.

---

SOURCES: Data for 1981 provided to the authors by the U.S. Council on Environment Quality (CEQ) in advance of publication of its 1982 Annual Report. The CEQ data are based on EPA's SAROAD data bank. Additional information provided by the National Air Qualtiy Data Bank as maintained by Roy F. Weston, Inc., West Chester, Pennsylvania.

---

| Rank | City | PSI | Rank | City | PSI | Rank | City | PSI |
|------|------|-----|------|------|-----|------|------|-----|
| 1 | Los Angeles-Long Beach | 137 | 17 | St. Louis | 27 | 35 | Charlotte-Gastonia | 14 |
| 2 | New York | 102 | 19 | Portland | 26 | 36 | Nashville-Davidson | 13 |
| 3 | Riverside-San Bernardino-Ontario | 92 | 20 | Birmingham | 25 | 37 | Milwaukee | 12 |
| 4 | Phoenix | 79 | 21 | Detroit | 23 | 38 | Atlanta | 11 |
| 5 | Anaheim-Santa Ana-Garden Grove | 75 | 22 | El Paso | 22 | 38 | Tulsa | 11 |
| 6 | San Diego | 67 | 23 | Washington | 21 | 40 | Akron | 10 |
| 7 | Denver-Boulder | 56 | 24 | Jersey City | 20 | 40 | San Jose | 10 |
| 8 | Houston | 53 | 25 | Louisville | 19 | 42 | Lincoln | 8 |
| 9 | Las Vegas | 48 | 26 | Baton Rouge | 18 | 43 | Buffalo | 6 |
| 10 | Fresno | 45 | 26 | Boston | 18 | 43 | Tucson | 6 |
| 11 | Anchorage | 40 | 26 | Chicago | 18 | 45 | Dayton | 5 |
| 12 | Minneapolis-St. Paul | 36 | 26 | Dallas-Fort Worth | 18 | 45 | Providence-Warwick-Pawtucket | 5 |
| 13 | Seattle-Everett | 34 | 26 | Kansas City | 18 | 45 | San Francisco-Oakland | 5 |
| 14 | Philadelphia | 33 | 31 | Toledo | 17 | 48 | Rochester | 3 |
| 15 | Albuquerque | 31 | 32 | Spokane | 16 | 49 | Columbus, Ohio | 2 |
| 16 | Salt Lake City-Ogden | 30 | 33 | Cleveland | 15 | 49 | Richmond | 2 |
| 17 | Pittsburgh | 27 | 33 | Indianapolis | 15 | 49 | Tampa-St. Petersburg | 2 |

# 16. Overall Air Quality: 1975–81 Trends

The Pollutant Standards Index (PSI) has been falling, overall. That is, air quality has been improving. If we take the 1981 PSI as a percentage of the 1978–80 average PSI, in all but three of the 30 cities for which we are able to make this comparison the PSI has fallen. The number of days that pollution level maximum standards were exceeded dropped by about 7 percent in the case of metro San Diego (i.e., not much improvement), ranging up to 81 percent in metro Chicago (dramatic improvement). Along with Chicago, the metro areas that achieved remarkable pollution control results are Pittsburgh (down 77 percent), Tampa (down 75 percent), Louisville (down 73 percent) and San Francisco (down 72 percent). Three metro areas saw an increase in the PSI and therefore the level of their pollution in 1981 compared with the average of the previous three years: Phoenix and Toledo (both up 13 percent) and Akron (up 150 percent; the area started with very little air pollution).

We do not show the above data in the following table, because we are advised by their source that they may be affected by changes in monitoring stations. A comparison which avoids this possibility of bias is provided in the table below, which compares metro areas which have the same monitoring stations in 1981 that they had in 1975. Such comparisons are possible for ten metro areas. For these areas, Chicago showed the greatest overall improvement in air quality, from 195 unhealthy days in 1975 to 18 unhealthy days in 1981. Denver improved the least, from 145 unhealthy days in 1975 to 79 unhealthy days in 1981.

The figures show a marked improvement, reflecting primarily the reduction in emissions resulting from federal requirements for controls on automobiles.

SOURCES: Background information from U.S. Environmental Protection Agency (EPA) *Air Quality Data—1979 Annual Statistics*, EPA-450/4-80-014, September 1980; Council on Environmental Quality (CEQ), Executive Office of the President, *Environmental Quality—1977, —1979* and *—1980*; and Daphne Gemmill, *City Air* (New York: Council on Municipal Performance, 1974). Trend data for 1981 provided to the authors by the CEQ in advance of publication of its 1981 Annual Report. All other ambient air data provided from a national air quality data bank maintained by Roy F. Weston, Inc., West Chester, Pennsylvania. All air quality data are derived from EPA's SAROAD data bank.

| Rank | Metro Area | Days PSI Exceeded 100 ("Unhealthy") 1975 | 1981 | Difference | Percent decline 1975–81 |
|------|------------|------|------|------|------|
| 1 | Chicago | 195 | 18 | 177 | 90.8 |
| 2 | Louisville | 185 | 20 | 165 | 89.2 |
| 3 | San Francisco | 29 | 5 | 24 | 82.8 |
| 4 | Washington | 110 | 21 | 89 | 80.9 |
| 5 | St. Louis | 130 | 29 | 101 | 77.7 |
| 6 | Philadelphia | 143 | 33 | 110 | 76.9 |
| 7 | Milwaukee | 40 | 13 | 27 | 67.5 |
| 8 | Portland, Ore. | 83 | 30 | 53 | 63.9 |
| 9 | New York | 270 | 106 | 164 | 60.7 |
| 10 | Denver | 145 | 79 | 66 | 45.5 |

# 17. Water Use

Cities with populations under 5,000 have the most problems in providing an adequate and high-quality drinking water supply. Populations over 10,000 have very few reported quality violations. Most of the water officials' problems are in the areas of ensuring future supplies, obtaining money for capital projects, and maintaining and replacing aging system parts, according to a survey by the authors.

Citizens tend not to notice how their community's water is supplied unless something goes wrong. Complaints from their end primarily concern billing—perceived as too high, in all cases—and meter readings and estimates. Complaints about the taste and odor of tap water are also common, as are problems with slow service and repairs after breaks and main replacements.

Most of the cities studied are provided water by municipal organizations. Among the exceptions are San Jose (San Jose Water Works), Oakland (East Bay Municipal Utilities District), Indianapolis (Indianapolis Water Company), Long Beach and Santa Ana. There does not seem to be a significant difference in the quality and price of water supplied by private companies.

Per resident gallons of water used tell us which cities use the most water relative to population. Our data include agricultural and industrial as well as residential and commercial usage of water. Thus, it is not surprising to find that cities that are tourist centers and/or home to industries that traditionally require large amounts of water (e.g., farming, paper, oil and manufacturing) have high per capita rates. Pittsburgh, for instance, which tops the list with 1,022 gallons per resident used each day in 1981, requires high water use for its steel industry. So does Rochester, in third place, with its photographic industry. Las Vegas in second place needs water for its tourist traffic. Tacoma is the site of many pulp mills.

Near the bottom are found cities such as St. Petersburg, Charlotte, Tampa and Madison which do not have heavy industrial activity. In the middle to lower range, cities in areas with relatively less water have lower per capita consumption figures.

SOURCE: Questionnaires to city water resource officials on 1981 water use, designed and collected for this book by the authors, 1982.

| Rank | City | Per Capita Treated Water Consumed Daily (gallons) | Rank | City | Per Capita Treated Water Consumed Daily (gallons) | Rank | City | Per Capita Treated Water Consumed Daily (gallons) |
|---|---|---|---|---|---|---|---|---|
| 1 | Pittsburgh | 1,022.2 | 29 | Dayton | 203.1 | 57 | Knoxville | 160.0 |
| 2 | Las Vegas | 520.3 | 30 | Lincoln | 202.2 | 57 | Nashville | 160.0 |
| 3 | Rochester | 357.1 | 31 | Jersey City | 200.0 | 59 | Columbus, Ga. | 158.4 |
| 4 | Tacoma | 353.3 | 32 | El Paso | 195.2 | 60 | Worcester | 157.4 |
| 5 | Spokane | 341.6 | 33 | New York | 193.7 | 61 | Jackson | 156.6 |
| 6 | Chicago | 325.1 | 34 | Denver | 192.2 | 62 | Montgomery | 153.6 |
| 7 | Sacramento | 309.7 | 35 | Memphis | 191.7 | 63 | Fort Wayne | 152.5 |
| 8 | Dallas | 305.3 | 36 | Philadelphia | 189.7 | 64 | Lexington-Fayette | 152.3 |
| 9 | San Antonio | 302.0 | 37 | Minneapolis | 189.5 | 65 | Greensboro | 151.1 |
| 10 | Corpus Christi | 293.9 | 38 | Los Angeles | 188.5 | 66 | Warren | 148.9 |
| 11 | Syracuse | 289.4 | 39 | Honolulu | 186.9 | 67 | Little Rock | 148.3 |
| 12 | Fresno | 287.5 | 40 | Portland, Ore. | 186.1 | 68 | Des Moines | 147.3 |
| 13 | Chattanooga | 278.7 | 41 | Arlington, Texas | 184.8 | 69 | Akron | 146.8 |
| 14 | Omaha | 256.7 | 42 | Austin | 184.0 | 70 | Seattle | 144.2 |
| 14 | Riverside | 256.7 | 43 | Oakland | 181.8 | 71 | Mobile | 141.9 |
| 16 | Phoenix | 254.2 | 44 | Long Beach | 180.8 | 72 | Norfolk | 137.7 |
| 17 | Lubbock | 251.4 | 45 | Kansas City, Kan. | 176.9 | 72 | Toledo | 137.7 |
| 18 | Houston | 249.9 | 46 | Kansas City, Mo. | 175.0 | 74 | Indianapolis | 137.3 |
| 19 | Washington, D.C. | 246.1 | 47 | Fort Worth | 173.9 | 75 | Shreveport | 136.9 |
| 20 | Miami | 243.1 | 48 | Cleveland | 169.6 | 76 | Birmingham | 135.1 |
| 21 | Albuquerque | 240.0 | 49 | Wichita | 168.4 | 77 | Tucson | 135.0 |
| 22 | Atlanta | 235.5 | 50 | Detroit | 167.7 | 78 | St. Paul | 131.2 |
| 23 | Boston | 227.2 | 51 | Milwaukee | 167.0 | 79 | Santa Ana | 125.4 |
| 24 | Providence | 226.9 | 52 | Newark | 166.7 | 80 | St. Petersburg | 123.8 |
| 25 | San Diego | 224.7 | 53 | San Jose | 165.3 | 81 | Charlotte | 121.2 |
| 26 | New Orleans | 224.5 | 54 | Columbus, Ohio | 162.8 | 82 | Tampa | 108.9 |
| 27 | Colorado Springs | 211.0 | 55 | Louisville | 160.3 | 83 | Madison | 103.0 |
| 28 | Salt Lake City | 210.2 | 56 | Huntington Beach | 160.2 | | | |

# 18. Water Availability

Treated water available (gallons per capita) is based upon the population served. It measures how well prepared a municipality is to provide peak amounts of treated water to its residents and industry.

The increasing volume of waste produced in cities has reduced the number of available high-quality water sources, a trend which technological advances in treatment have not been able to offset. The quality of the cities' original water sources appears more significant than the effects of their treatment processes.

Thirty-one cities have per capita use exceeding 200 gallons daily. Pittsburgh leads the cities, reporting treated water volume of over 1000 gallons per capita. In response to the authors' survey, some cities consider themselves already currently at peak availability with their present resources. This is indicated by the information provided by San Jose, Providence and Lubbock.

Both Denver and New York report finding themselves perilously close to running out of water in the next decade.

Oakland, Indianapolis and Washington, D.C. will face serious supply dilemmas in the near future, resulting from supplies only marginally greater than demand.

Houston, Milwaukee, St. Louis, San Francisco and Seattle all show high percentages of industrial water use, between 30 percent and 60 percent, but none faces serious supply shortages. There seems to be no direct connection between heavy industrial consumption and adequacy of supply.

Santa Ana's 9.3 million gallons available refers to the water obtained from the Metropolitan Water District, serving 66,280 people. Roughly twice that number of people in the area rely on deep water wells which yield about 17 million gallons per day of water which is not treated because the well water meets state standards. Santa Ana is concerned about water supply adequacy after 1985 when it will be harder to import water.

SOURCE: Questionnaires to city water resource officials on 1981 water availability, designed and collected for this book by the authors, 1982. In the case of Greensboro, Environmental Protection Agency is the source.

| Rank | City | Total (million gallons) | Per Capita Treated Water Available (gallons) |
|---|---|---|---|
| 1 | Spokane | 280.9 | 1,594 |
| 2 | Pittsburgh | 460.0 | 1,022 |
| 3 | Sacramento | 210.0 | 747 |
| 4 | Anaheim | 172.3 | 737 |
| 5 | Fort Worth | 277.0 | 719 |
| 6 | Buffalo | 360.0 | 645 |
| 7 | Las Vegas | 252.0 | 639 |
| 8 | Tacoma | 128.0 | 602 |
| 9 | Oklahoma City | 232.0 | 575 |
| 10 | Riverside | 100.0 | 556 |
| 11 | Milwaukee | 465.0 | 547 |
| 12 | Minneapolis | 200.0 | 539 |
| 13 | Phoenix | 480.0 | 518 |
| 14 | Albuquerque | 190.0 | 507 |
| 15 | Dallas | 424.0 | 469 |
| 16 | Cleveland | 910.0 | 455 |
| 17 | Austin | 177.0 | 454 |
| 18 | Oakland | 485.0 | 441 |
| 19 | Corpus Christi | 103.0 | 420 |
| 20 | New Orleans | 232.0 | 417 |
| 21 | Philadelphia | 806.0 | 413 |
| 22 | Wichita | 120.0 | 412 |
| 23 | Detroit | 150.0 | 392 |
| 24 | Salt Lake City | 141.3 | 379 |
| 25 | Kansas City, Kan. | 60.0 | 375 |
| 26 | St. Paul | 142.9 | 373 |
| 27 | Miami | 126.6 | 365 |
| 28 | Madison | 66.0 | 364 |
| 29 | Kansas City, Mo. | 210.0 | 350 |
| 30 | Des Moines | 96.0 | 349 |
| 31 | Fort Wayne | 72.0 | 343 |
| 32 | Portland, Ore. | 225.0 | 341 |
| 33 | Chattanooga | 62.3 | 335 |
| 34 | Nashville-Davidson | 150.0 | 333 |
| 35 | Long Beach | 117.0 | 331 |
| 36 | El Paso | 140.0 | 330 |
| 37 | Colorado Springs | 73.0 | 322 |
| 38 | Little Rock | 98.0 | 311 |
| 39 | Washington, D.C. | 200.0 | 308 |
| 40 | San Antonio | 151.0 | 302 |
| 41 | Fresno | 69.0 | 288 |
| 42 | Memphis | 200.0 | 286 |
| 43 | Boston | 176.1 | 276 |
| 44 | Columbus, Ga. | 44.9 | 270 |
| 44 | Houston | 430.0 | 270 |
| 46 | Atlanta | 175.0 | 269 |
| 47 | Jersey City | 60.0 | 267 |
| 48 | Montgomery | 50.0 | 263 |
| 49 | Syracuse | 61.0 | 260 |
| 50 | Tucson | 114.0 | 253 |
| 51 | Lubbock | 44.0 | 251 |
| 52 | Denver | 230.0 | 242 |
| 53 | Toledo | 120.0 | 240 |
| 54 | Norfolk | 107.0 | 238 |
| 55 | Honolulu | 172.2 | 234 |
| 56 | Dayton | 70.0 | 219 |
| 57 | Worcester | 37.4 | 217 |
| 58 | San Diego | 191.0 | 215 |
| 59 | Birmingham | 149.0 | 213 |
| 60 | Rochester | 50.0 | 204 |
| 61 | Lincoln | 34.4 | 202 |
| 62 | Los Angeles | 561.0 | 189 |
| 63 | Greensboro | 30.5 | 188 |
| 64 | Arlington, Texas | 32.8 | 185 |
| 65 | Akron | 57.0 | 184 |
| 66 | Providence | 82.0 | 182 |
| 67 | Lexington-Fayette | 29.5 | 176 |
| 68 | Indianapolis | 118.5 | 168 |
| 69 | Newark | 100.0 | 167 |
| 70 | Tampa | 65.7 | 164 |
| 71 | Jackson | 45.0 | 162 |
| 72 | Huntington Beach | 28.2 | 160 |
| 72 | Knoxville | 32.0 | 160 |
| 72 | St. Petersburg | 50.0 | 160 |
| 75 | Shreveport | 36.0 | 150 |
| 76 | Warren | 24.0 | 149 |
| 77 | Columbus, Ohio | 107.6 | 148 |
| 78 | Mobile | 33.0 | 145 |
| 79 | Seattle | 157.0 | 144 |
| 80 | Charlotte | 40.0 | 121 |
| 81 | Santa Ana | 9.3 | 47 |
| 82 | San Jose | 20.0 | 33 |

# 19. Water Cost Per Capita

Water cost per capita is an indicator of expenditures made and revenues received by localities in providing residents with water. Arlington, Texas, stands out, reporting costs of $433.13 for every resident in 1981 and charges of $123.38 per capita. Austin, with costs of $224.45, and Kansas City, Kansas, with $160.64 are next on the list.

Fresno, at the other end of the list, spends a mere $3.08 per capita and charges $2.42. This is explained by the fact that the city reports that it does not treat the raw water with any chemicals or treatments. However, the nitrate content is quite high, and a major customer complaint concerns the presence of sand in the water. Costs vary from year to year for each locality. Much of this fluctuation is due to new facilities being constructed to provide expanded service and repairs.

Austin pumps its water from Lake Austin, and it requires extensive treatment to screen the water, reduce the hardness, settle suspended matter and destroy bacteria. Water taken in by such cities as Fresno, San Antonio and Detroit does not require as extensive treatment; thus, the cost is less.

Costs vary from year to year for each locality as new facilities are constructed and services and maintenance needs change. Other cost variables include labor, operating and maintenance expenses, depreciation, bond and note interest, and capital additions.

SOURCE: Questionnaires to city water resource officials on 1981 data, designed and collected for this book by the authors, 1982.

| Rank | City | Water Cost per Capita ($) | Rank | City | Water Cost per Capita ($) | Rank | City | Water Cost per Capita ($) |
|---|---|---|---|---|---|---|---|---|
| 1 | Arlington, Texas | 433.13 | 19 | Fort Worth | 47.84 | 37 | Nashville-Davidson | 30.85 |
| 2 | Austin | 224.45 | 20 | Columbus, Ohio | 47.43 | 38 | Tampa | 30.00 |
| 3 | Kansas City, Kan. | 160.64 | 21 | Tacoma | 47.25 | 39 | Toledo | 29.60 |
| 4 | Colorado Springs | 152.80 | 22 | Phoenix | 46.20 | 40 | Madison | 28.65 |
| 5 | Memphis | 148.00 | 23 | Huntington Beach | 44.23 | 41 | Pittsburgh | 28.00 |
| 6 | Milwaukee | 140.00 | 24 | New Orleans | 40.91 | 42 | Honolulu | 27.00 |
| 7 | Washington, D.C. | 96.76 | 25 | Los Angeles | 39.40 | 43 | Cleveland | 26.52 |
| 8 | Las Vegas | 96.40 | 26 | Indianapolis | 38.28 | 44 | Santa Ana | 26.44 |
| 9 | Riverside | 94.44 | 27 | Albuquerque | 38.00 | 45 | Portland, Ore. | 26.24 |
| 10 | Des Moines | 77.25 | 28 | Salt Lake City | 37.73 | 46 | Little Rock | 26.21 |
| 11 | Tucson | 75.00 | 29 | Oakland | 37.00 | 47 | Birmingham | 25.71 |
| 12 | Greensboro | 73.03 | 30 | St. Petersburg | 36.98 | 48 | Sacramento | 24.43 |
| 13 | Corpus Christi | 65.40 | 31 | Fort Wayne | 35.17 | 49 | Seattle | 21.40 |
| 14 | Houston | 61.00 | 32 | Warren | 35.03 | 50 | Norfolk | 21.00 |
| 15 | San Diego | 59.13 | 33 | St. Paul | 35.00 | 51 | Lincoln | 18.21 |
| 16 | Denver | 58.79 | 34 | Philadelphia | 34.11 | 52 | Detroit | 15.77 |
| 17 | Knoxville | 55.00 | 35 | Dayton | 34.00 | 53 | San Antonio | 6.68 |
| 18 | Rochester | 50.66 | 36 | Shreveport | 32.90 | 54 | Fresno | 3.08 |

# 20. Water Charges Per Capita

Water charges to customers reflect the financial requirements inherent in operating the water supply system. Austin heads the list of those cities reporting per capita water charges. The reason is the high cost of treating and adequate water supplies in Texas, where groundwater reserves have been depleted by rapid urban growth. Water engineers must drill deeper wells or look elsewhere for water—a costly process. Another Texas city is in second place. Colorado Springs purchases its water from the Denver Regional Authority, and therefore pays even higher rates than the $59.79 per capita in high-cost Denver.

Fresno appears at the lower end. Its rate reflects only water sales and does not include other charges. Interestingly, Corpus Christi's water charges are well below those of other Texas cities.

SOURCE: Questionnaires to city water resource officials on 1981 data, designed and collected for this book by the authors, 1982.

| Rank | City | Water Charge Per Capita ($) | Rank | City | Water Charge Per Capita ($) | Rank | City | Water Charge Per Capita ($) |
|---|---|---|---|---|---|---|---|---|
| 1 | Austin | 196.16 | 16 | Oakland | 51.00 | 30 | Toledo | 30.00 |
| 2 | Arlington, Texas | 123.38 | 17 | Kansas City, Kan. | 49.45 | 32 | Portland, Ore. | 29.81 |
| 3 | Colorado Springs | 87.10 | 18 | New Orleans | 49.22 | 33 | Madison | 29.35 |
| 4 | Greenboro | 83.95 | 19 | Little Rock | 46.25 | 34 | Memphis | 28.00 |
| 5 | Houston | 73.05 | 20 | Columbus, Ohio | 45.22 | 34 | Philadelphia | 28.00 |
| 6 | Tucson | 70.00 | 21 | Phoenix | 42.74 | 36 | Milwaukee | 27.00 |
| 7 | Knoxville | 65.00 | 22 | Fort Wayne | 42.20 | 37 | Cleveland | 23.54 |
| 8 | San Diego | 59.13 | 23 | Birmingham | 40.00 | 38 | Seattle | 20.21 |
| 9 | Denver | 58.79 | 24 | Los Angeles | 39.40 | 39 | Detroit | 15.87 |
| 10 | Rochester | 57.58 | 25 | Albuquerque | 38.00 | 40 | Pittsburgh | 14.00 |
| 11 | Tacoma | 56.51 | 26 | Santa Ana | 37.60 | 41 | Norfolk | 13.00 |
| 12 | Nashville-Davidson | 53.57 | 27 | Dayton | 36.00 | 42 | San Antonio | 9.20 |
| 13 | Fort Worth | 53.07 | 28 | St. Paul | 35.00 | 43 | Lincoln | 5.57 |
| 14 | Honolulu | 52.50 | 29 | Salt Lake City | 34.48 | 44 | Corpus Christi | 5.40 |
| 15 | Indianapolis | 51.58 | 30 | Tampa | 30.00 | 45 | Fresno | 2.42 |

# 21. Water Losses

The more water "lost" by a city, the worse off its water supply. "Loss" covers a wide range of contributing factors, including leaky pipes, main breaks and incomplete metering of supplied water. A finite, but small, amount of water loss inevitably occurs in operating a water supply system, especially where open reservoirs are used to store water, where the water piping system is old and where areas are affected by weather factors that cause ground freezing.

New Orleans heads the list in this category, with 35.3 percent of its water reported as being lost. New Orleans officials point out that the loss is due essentially to unmetered free use, leaks and underregistration. Sacramento's pipes are also unmetered, and its loss percentage is not known. Syracuse is next with 35 percent. Spokane follows with 30 percent Most of the cities lose 10 percent to 15 percent. Some of this loss may be explained by insufficient maintenance and inspection, as well as by the aging infrastructure of central city areas.

SOURCE: Questionnaires to city water resource officials on 1981 data, designed and collected for this book by the authors, 1982.

| Rank | City | Percentage Water Lost | Rank | City | Percentage Water Lost | Rank | City | Percentage Water Lost |
|---|---|---|---|---|---|---|---|---|
| 1 | New Orleans | 35.3 | 19 | Lubbock | 15.0 | 43 | Lincoln | 8.7 |
| 2 | Syracuse | 35.0 | 19 | Seattle | 15.0 | 44 | Huntington Beach | 8.0 |
| 3 | Spokane | 30.0 | 19 | Toledo | 15.0 | 44 | Little Rock | 8.0 |
| 4 | Cleveland | 25.0 | 19 | Washington, D.C. | 15.0 | 44 | Oakland | 8.0 |
| 5 | Pittsburgh | 22.0 | 26 | Shreveport | 14.5 | 44 | San Jose | 8.0 |
| 6 | Houston | 21.0 | 27 | Greensboro | 14.0 | 44 | Tucson | 8.0 |
| 7 | Portland | 20.0 | 27 | Memphis | 14.0 | 49 | Los Angeles | 7.8 |
| 7 | Rochester | 20.0 | 29 | Kansas City, Kan. | 13.0 | 50 | Phoenix | 7.0 |
| 9 | Columbus, Ohio | 19.0 | 30 | Dayton | 12.0 | 50 | Providence | 7.0 |
| 10 | Corpus Christi | 17.6 | 30 | Honolulu | 12.0 | 52 | Denver | 6.0 |
| 11 | Akron | 17.4 | 30 | Las Vegas | 12.0 | 53 | Milwaukee | 5.8 |
| 12 | Knoxville | 17.0 | 30 | Norfolk | 12.0 | 54 | Colorado Springs | 5.0 |
| 13 | St. Paul | 16.5 | 34 | St. Petersburg | 11.8 | 54 | Salt Lake City | 5.0 |
| 14 | Fort Worth | 16.3 | 35 | Memphis | 11.0 | 56 | Austin | 4.8 |
| 15 | Birmingham | 16.0 | 36 | Montgomery | 10.5 | 57 | Jersey City | 3.0 |
| 15 | Philadelphia | 16.0 | 37 | Arlington, Texas | 10.0 | 57 | Riverside | 3.0 |
| 15 | San Antonio | 16.0 | 37 | Newark | 10.0 | 57 | Tacoma | 3.0 |
| 18 | Fort Wayne | 15.6 | 37 | Tampa | 10.0 | 57 | Wichita | 3.0 |
| 19 | Detroit | 15.0 | 40 | Madison | 9.4 | 61 | Santa Ana | 2.8 |
| 19 | Indianapolis | 15.0 | 41 | Des Moines | 9.0 | 62 | Albuquerque | 2.0 |
| 19 | Kansas City, Mo. | 15.0 | 41 | San Diego | 9.0 | 63 | Warren | 1.0 |

# 22.  Water Quality: Solids

In water quality analysis, the term "solids" include both dissolved and suspended matter in water. Although they may not necessarily damage health, higher levels of total solids in water decrease consumer acceptance. The suspended solids mainly contribute to turbidity, thereby altering the appearance of water. Dissolved solids in high concentrations are known to cause corrosion of pipes. Because of the wide range of minerals in water, no specific standard has been recommended for total solids, although there are guidelines for certain minerals.

Most water with less than 500 parts per million

(ppm) of dissolved solids—about one-quarter of a level teaspoon of salt in each gallon—is satisfactory for domestic and some industrial uses.

The cities are ranked using measurements on milligrams per liter (mg/L). This measure produces a ranking of water samples that is virtually identical to the other prevalent measure, parts per million (ppm). The two cities with the highest concentration of solids in water are in Texas—Lubbock and Corpus Christi. The only other city with solids in excess of 500 ppm is Kansas City, Kansas.

SOURCES: Questionnaires to city water resource officials on 1981 data, designed and collected for this book by the authors, 1982; unpublished research for the Council on Municipal Performance by biochemist Dr. Archana Telang, 1976.

| Rank | City | Total Solids (mg/L) | Rank | City | Total Solids (mg/L) | Rank | City | Total Solids (mg/L) |
|---|---|---|---|---|---|---|---|---|
| 1 | Lubbock | 1,200 | 6 | Seattle | 418 | 13 | Columbus, Ohio | 359 |
| 2 | Corpus Christi | 600 | 8 | Lincoln | 412 | 14 | Riverside | 349 |
| 3 | Kansas City, Kan. | 534 | 9 | Colorado Springs | 405 | 15 | Kansas City, Mo. | 348 |
| 4 | Las Vegas | 488 | 10 | Santa Ana | 404 | 16 | Long Beach | 338 |
| 5 | Madison | 434 | 11 | San Antonio | 386 | 17 | Phoenix | 333 |
| 6 | San Diego | 418 | 12 | Indianapolis | 380 | 18 | Wichita | 328 |

| Rank | City | Total Solids (mg/L) | Rank | City | Total Solids (mg/L) | Rank | City | Total Solids (mg/L) |
|---|---|---|---|---|---|---|---|---|
| 19 | Tucson | 300 | 32 | Honolulu | 200 | 49 | St. Paul | 130 |
| 20 | Huntington Beach | 269 | 35 | Birmingham | 195 | 50 | Toledo | 128 |
| 21 | Dayton | 262 | 36 | Shreveport | 194 | 51 | Knoxville | 124 |
| 22 | Houston | 261 | 37 | Pittsburgh | 191 | 52 | Norfolk | 110 |
| 23 | San Jose | 250 | 38 | Cleveland | 190 | 53 | Greensboro | 96 |
| 24 | Tampa | 244 | 39 | Fort Wayne | 189 | 54 | Oakland | 92 |
| 25 | New Orleans | 240 | 39 | Fresno | 189 | 55 | Sacramento | 87 |
| 26 | Washington, D.C. | 238 | 41 | St. Petersburg | 175 | 56 | Newark | 84 |
| 27 | Austin | 220 | 42 | Denver | 172 | 57 | Memphis | 82 |
| 28 | Akron | 219 | 43 | Milwaukee | 169 | 58 | Jersey City | 80 |
| 29 | Salt Lake City | 218 | 44 | Nashville | 148 | 59 | Providence | 64 |
| 30 | Los Angeles | 215 | 45 | Spokane | 141 | 60 | Little Rock | 38 |
| 31 | Fort Worth | 206 | 46 | Rochester | 140 | 61 | Tacoma | 33 |
| 32 | Albuquerque | 200 | 46 | Syracuse | 140 | 62 | Portland, Ore. | 28 |
| 32 | Arlington, Texas | 200 | 48 | Detroit | 135 | 63 | Montgomery | 19 |

# 23. Water Quality: Coliform Bacteria

Coliform bacteria have been used to measure the occurrence and intensity of fecal contamination in stream-pollution investigations for nearly 70 years. Treatment technology hasn't yet been able to cope with increasing urban waste.

The total coliform group—a heterogenous collection of bacterial species having a few broad characteristics in common—merits consideration as an indicator of pollution. It is always present in the intestinal tract of humans and other warmblooded animals and is eliminated in large amounts in fecal wastes. The presence of any type of coliform organism in treated water suggests residual fecal wastes and may indicate that chlorination has resulted in inadequate treatment of contamination. The measure of coliform bacteria is the count per 100 mililiters (i.e., per tenths of a liter).

SOURCE: Questionnaires to city water resource officials on 1981 data, designed and collected for this book by the authors, 1982.

| Rank | City | Coliform (Count per 100 ml) | Rank | City | Coliform (Count per 100 ml) | Rank | City | Coliform (Count per 100 ml) |
|---|---|---|---|---|---|---|---|---|
| 1 | San Diego | 3.00 | 7 | Greensboro | 1.00 | 19 | Shreveport | .90 |
| 2 | Phoenix | 2.20 | 7 | Kansas City, Mo. | 1.00 | 20 | Los Angeles | .73 |
| 2 | Riverside | 2.20 | 7 | Las Vegas | 1.00 | 21 | Honolulu | .40 |
| 2 | Sacramento | 2.20 | 7 | Memphis | 1.00 | 22 | Indianapolis | .13 |
| 2 | Syracuse | 2.20 | 7 | Portland, Ore. | 1.00 | 23 | Columbus, Ohio | .03 |
| 6 | St. Paul | 2.00 | 7 | Rochester | 1.00 | 24 | Denver | .01 |
| 7 | Albuquerque | 1.00 | 7 | St. Petersburg | 1.00 | 24 | San Antonio | .01 |
| 7 | Arlington, Texas | 1.00 | 7 | Toledo | 1.00 | | | |
| 7 | Cleveland | 1.00 | 7 | Tucson | 1.00 | | | |

# 24. Water Quality: Hardness

Hardness of water for the consumer most visibly means the readiness with which one can turn soap into lather. Hardness measures dissolved minerals in water—generally concentrations of calcium and magnesium. Arsenic traces are also associated with hard water and are suspected of causing cancer.

According to a rather general classification determined by the U.S. Geological Survey in 1962, water that has less than 60 parts per million (ppm) of hardness is rated soft. Water ranging in hardness from 61 to 120 ppm is considered moderately hard. Water that has hardness in the range of 121 to 180 ppm is considered hard. Water above 180 ppm will in all likelihood require some softening before use.

Hard water makes washing difficult and can reduce the fabric life of clothing. Each year it costs the average American family about $200 (in 1980 dollars).

On the other hand, soft water is suspected of contributing to heart attacks. The Council on Environmental Quality has found a significant (90 percent confidence level) correlation between soft water and cardiovascular diseases, especially acute ischemic heart disease (heart attacks). But hypertension, which can lead to strokes, is more likely in locations with *hard* water.

SOURCES: Data from questionnaires to city water resource officials on 1981 data, designed and collected for this book by the authors, 1982. Carcinogen information from U.S. Environmental Protection Agency (EPA), *Preliminary Assessments of Suspected Carcinogens in Drinking Water, Report to Congress* (December 1975), pp. 31, 45. Cardiovascular data from U.S. Council on Environmental Quality, *Environmental Quality* (December 1977), pp. 260, 262, 266.

| Rank | City | Dissolved Minerals (ppm) | Rank | City | Dissolved Minerals (ppm) | Rank | City | Dissolved Minerals (ppm) |
|---|---|---|---|---|---|---|---|---|
| 1 | Madison | 408 | 24 | Huntington Beach | 128 | 47 | Denver | 89 |
| 2 | Las Vegas | 340 | 25 | Kansas City, Mo. | 126 | 48 | Fort Wayne | 88 |
| 3 | Kansas City, Kan. | 284 | 25 | Philadelphia | 126 | 49 | Knoxville | 87 |
| 4 | San Jose | 280 | 27 | Tacoma | 125 | 50 | Jersey City | 80 |
| 5 | Indianapolis | 260 | 28 | St. Petersburg | 122 | 51 | Toledo | 79 |
| 6 | Corpus Christi | 250 | 28 | Spokane | 122 | 52 | Shreveport | 78 |
| 7 | Lincoln | 248 | 30 | Sacramento | 120 | 53 | Houston | 77 |
| 8 | San Antonio | 237 | 30 | Syracuse | 120 | 54 | St. Paul | 75 |
| 9 | Santa Ana | 218 | 32 | Pittsburgh | 118 | 55 | Chattanooga | 68 |
| 10 | Lubbock | 212 | 33 | Akron | 117 | 56 | Albuquerque | 67 |
| 11 | Riverside | 199 | 33 | Fresno | 117 | 57 | Colorado Springs | 55 |
| 12 | San Diego | 190 | 33 | New Orleans | 117 | 55 | Newark | 54 |
| 13 | Omaha | 170 | 36 | Long Beach | 116 | 59 | Greensboro | 53 |
| 14 | Minneapolis | 158 | 37 | Columbus, Ohio | 115 | 59 | Oakland | 53 |
| 14 | Phoenix | 158 | 38 | Arlington, Texas | 105 | 61 | Birmingham | 51 |
| 16 | Salt Lake City | 156 | 38 | Los Angeles | 105 | 62 | Honolulu | 50 |
| 17 | Des Moines | 155 | 40 | Austin | 103 | 63 | Memphis | 45 |
| 18 | Washington, D.C. | 150 | 41 | Detroit | 100 | 64 | Montgomery | 40 |
| 19 | Dayton | 145 | 41 | Warren | 100 | 64 | Norfolk | 40 |
| 20 | Tampa | 143 | 41 | Wichita | 100 | 66 | Providence | 29 |
| 21 | Fort Worth | 140 | 44 | Nashville-Davidson | 94 | 67 | Little Rock | 20 |
| 21 | Tucson | 140 | 45 | Milwaukee | 90 | 68 | Seattle | 19 |
| 23 | Cleveland | 130 | 45 | Rochester | 90 | 69 | Portland, Ore. | 11 |

# 25. Water Quality: pH

The balance between acids and alkalies in a solution, known as pH, is very important, as anyone tending a fish tank or swimming pool knows. A pH of 7.0 indicates neutral water. Above a pH of 7.0 the water is alkaline; below 7.0 it is acid. The range is 0–14. Since pH is difficult to measure in the field, no great importance should be attached to differences of one or two units of the decimal place in the table below.

The pH of water is extremely important both for consumption and for industrial uses. It must also be controlled in the treatment process, or chemicals such as chlorine will not function as effectively for as long in killing bacteria. Depending on their water source, some cities use a more extensive treatment process than others. Most of them end up with a pH in the 6–8 range for natural fresh water. According to the data shown below, treated water in Austin, New Orleans, Fort Wayne and Toledo is the most alkaline. The cities in the northwestern United States—Portland, Tacoma and Seattle—fall at the acid end of the range.

Clearly, city water officials consider exceeding the alkalinity ceiling of 8 to be acceptable; 15 of the cities have a pH in the 8.1–10.1 range. None of them, however, has allowed the pH to drop below the acid floor of 6.0

SOURCES: Questionnaires to city water resource officials on 1981 data, designed and collected for this book by the authors, 1982. Background data from U.S. Department of the Interior, Geological Survey, *A Primer on Water Quality* (1965), p. 19.

| Rank | City | pH Factor | Rank | City | pH Factor | Rank | City | pH Factor |
|---|---|---|---|---|---|---|---|---|
| 1 | Austin | 10.1 | 18 | Arlington, Texas | 7.9 | 34 | Colorado Springs | 7.5 |
| 2 | New Orleans | 9.9 | 18 | Huntington Beach | 7.9 | 34 | Fresno | 7.5 |
| 3 | Fort Wayne | 9.5 | 18 | Kansas City, Kan. | 7.9 | 34 | Honolulu | 7.5 |
| 4 | Toledo | 9.2 | 18 | Long Beach | 7.9 | 34 | Knoxville | 7.5 |
| 5 | Des Moines | 9.1 | 18 | Salt Lake City | 7.9 | 34 | Rochester | 7.5 |
| 6 | Birmingham | 9.0 | 18 | Washington, D.C. | 7.9 | 40 | Chattanooga | 7.4 |
| 7 | Fort Worth | 8.8 | 24 | Columbus, Ohio | 7.8 | 40 | Indianapolis | 7.4 |
| 8 | Corpus Christi | 8.7 | 24 | Phoenix | 7.8 | 40 | Little Rock | 7.4 |
| 9 | Dayton | 8.6 | 26 | Lincoln | 7.7 | 43 | Albuquerque | 7.3 |
| 9 | St. Paul | 8.6 | 26 | Los Angeles | 7.7 | 43 | Greensboro | 7.3 |
| 11 | Houston | 8.2 | 26 | Tucson | 7.7 | 43 | Madison | 7.3 |
| 11 | Pittsburgh | 8.2 | 29 | Denver | 7.6 | 43 | Memphis | 7.3 |
| 11 | San Diego | 8.2 | 29 | Detroit | 7.6 | 43 | Newark | 7.3 |
| 11 | Santa Ana | 8.2 | 29 | Milwaukee | 7.6 | 48 | Norfolk | 7.2 |
| 15 | San Antonio | 8.1 | 29 | Philadelphia | 7.6 | 49 | Portland, Ore. | 7.0 |
| 16 | Nashville-Davidson | 8.0 | 29 | Tampa | 7.6 | 49 | Tacoma | 7.0 |
| 16 | Oakland | 8.0 | 34 | Cleveland | 7.5 | 51 | Seattle | 6.6 |

# 26. Water Quality: Residual Chlorine

Residual chlorine is the harmful byproduct of chlorination, which is the most common process used to disinfect water supplies. As the Federal Environmental Protection Agency has said, "as yet, no acceptable substitute exists for chlorine as a disinfectant." Originally hailed in the 19th century as the way to eliminate typhoid, today chlorination remains the most important component in the treatment process. Industrial chemical pollutants such as ammonia, cyanide and various organic compounds reduce the effectiveness of chlorine and thus necessitate the addition of even greater amounts of it.

Chlorine's attraction to organic industrial wastes

forms compounds. Some are odorous, such as chloramines and chloraphenols. Some compounds are also worrisome pollutants: chloroform, bromodichloromethane, bromoform.

A high rate of residual chlorine is primarily a nuisance. It generates customer complaints because of chlorine's smell and its "swimming-pool" taste. Maintaining a residual chlorine level of about 0.3 milligrams per liter (mg/l) in a system can control the general bacterial population below 500 organisms per milliliter. Increasing chlorine above 0.3 mg/l to levels of 0.6 mg/l and 1.0 mg/l does not further reduce the bacterial population by any appreciable amount.

In 1981, five cities had a high level of residual chlorine, above 2 mg/l: St. Paul (3.2), Akron (2.7), Philadelphia (2.3), Knoxville (2.2) and Shreveport (2.1).

With a few East Coast exceptions, most of the cities with a low rate of residual chlorine are in the western part of the United States. Interestingly, the industrial city of Detroit ranks with this group.

SOURCES: Data for 1981 from questionnaires to city water resource officials, designed and collected for this book by the authors, 1982. Background information from U.S. Environmental Protection Agency, *Preliminary Assessments of Suspected Carcinogens in Drinking Water, Report to Congress* (December 1975), p. 37.

| Rank | City | Residual Chlorine (mg/l) | Rank | City | Residual Chlorine (mg/l) | Rank | City | Residual Chlorine (mg/l) |
|---|---|---|---|---|---|---|---|---|
| 1 | St. Paul | 3.20 | 22 | Corpus Christi | 1.10 | 42 | Detroit | .60 |
| 2 | Akron | 2.70 | 22 | Newark | 1.10 | 42 | Jersey City | .60 |
| 3 | Philadelphia | 2.30 | 22 | Norfolk | 1.10 | 42 | Las Vegas | .60 |
| 4 | Knoxville | 2.20 | 25 | Little Rock | 1.04 | 42 | Warren | .60 |
| 5 | Shreveport | 2.10 | 26 | Cleveland | 1.00 | 47 | Pittsburgh | .57 |
| 6 | Nashville-Davidson | 2.00 | 26 | Fort Wayne | 1.00 | 48 | Colorado Springs | .52 |
| 7 | Greensboro | 1.98 | 26 | Kansas City, Mo. | 1.00 | 49 | Lincoln | .50 |
| 8 | Washington, D.C. | 1.80 | 26 | Memphis | 1.00 | 50 | Phoenix | .45 |
| 9 | Arlington, Texas | 1.60 | 26 | Montgomery | 1.00 | 51 | Sacramento | .41 |
| 10 | Birmingham | 1.50 | 26 | Spokane | 1.00 | 52 | Oakland | .30 |
| 10 | Fort Worth | 1.50 | 26 | Syracuse | 1.00 | 52 | Rochester | .30 |
| 10 | Houston | 1.50 | 26 | Toledo | 1.00 | 54 | Tampa | .21 |
| 10 | Lubbock | 1.50 | 34 | Seattle | .95 | 55 | Providence | .20 |
| 14 | Wichita | 1.45 | 35 | Portland, Ore. | .90 | 55 | San Antonio | .20 |
| 15 | Kansas City, Kan. | 1.40 | 36 | Milwaukee | .85 | 55 | Tacoma | .20 |
| 16 | Dayton | 1.35 | 37 | St. Petersburg | .80 | 58 | Riverside | .17 |
| 17 | Indianapolis | 1.25 | 37 | Salt Lake City | .80 | 59 | Madison | .10 |
| 18 | Austin | 1.20 | 39 | Albuquerque | .70 | 60 | Des Moines | .09 |
| 18 | Columbus, Ohio | 1.20 | 40 | Santa Ana | .68 | 61 | Honolulu | .02 |
| 18 | San Diego | 1.20 | 41 | San Jose | .65 | 61 | Tucson | .02 |
| 21 | New Orleans | 1.13 | 42 | Denver | .60 | 63 | Fresno | 0.00 |

# 27. Water Quality: Nitrates

The presence of nitrates in water indicates contamination by sewage or other organic matter such as fertilizers. Although there is no potential danger from nitrates as such, they could easily be converted by some bacteria within the body to toxic nitrites (nitrosoamine). Nitrate in water is known to cause methemoglobinema in babies (blue babies). The susceptibility of infants to nitrates may be because of low pH levels in their gastric juices, which enhance the growth of nitrate-converting bacteria. Older children and adults are not so affected by nitrate contamination, but it is a suspected carcinogen. There is as yet no economical method to eliminate nitrates from water, although ion exchange methods (substituting ions for nitrites) have been investigated. So the only alternative is for people to be informed about the potential dangers of consumption of nitrate-contaminated water by infants.

The presence of nitrates in fertilizers may be the principal reason for the high nitrate levels in three California cities—Riverside, San Jose and Fresno—that top this ranking of cities.

SOURCES: Questionnaires to city water resource officials on 1981 data, designed and collected for this book by the authors, 1982. Background information from U.S. Environmental Protection Agency, *Preliminary Assessments of Suspected Carcinogens in Drinking Water, Report to Congress* (December 1975), p. 45.

| Rank | City | Nitrates (mg/l as N) | Rank | City | Nitrates (mg/l as N) | Rank | City | Nitrates (mg/l as N) |
|---|---|---|---|---|---|---|---|---|
| 1 | Riverside | 22.00 | 23 | Kansas City, Mo. | .60 | 43 | Warren | .23 |
| 2 | San Jose | 15.00 | 24 | Long Beach | .57 | 46 | Corpus Christi | .22 |
| 3 | Fresno | 11.50 | 25 | Chattanooga | .50 | 47 | Cleveland | .20 |
| 4 | Tucson | 8.00 | 25 | Knoxville | .50 | 47 | Montgomery | .20 |
| 5 | Spokane | 3.50 | 25 | Milwaukee | .50 | 49 | Toledo | .17 |
| 6 | Columbus, Ohio | 3.40 | 28 | Jersey City | .42 | 50 | Rochester | .15 |
| 7 | Wichita | 3.10 | 29 | Birmingham | .40 | 50 | Sacramento | .15 |
| 8 | Des Moines | 2.80 | 29 | Kansas City, Kan. | .40 | 52 | St. Paul | .12 |
| 9 | Fort Wayne | 2.10 | 29 | Las Vegas | .40 | 53 | Oakland | .11 |
| 10 | Philadelphia | 1.92 | 29 | Memphis | .40 | 54 | Arlington, Texas | .10 |
| 11 | San Diego | 1.90 | 29 | Tacoma | .40 | 54 | Newark | .10 |
| 12 | Indianapolis | 1.85 | 34 | Colorado Springs | .34 | 56 | Providence | .09 |
| 13 | Huntington Beach | 1.71 | 35 | Salt Lake City | .33 | 56 | Seattle | .09 |
| 14 | San Antonio | 1.60 | 36 | Akron | .30 | 58 | Syracuse | .08 |
| 15 | Madison | 1.49 | 36 | Lincoln | .30 | 59 | Lubbock | .05 |
| 16 | New Orleans | 1.32 | 36 | Nashville-Davidson | .30 | 59 | Portland | .05 |
| 17 | Albuquerque | 1.00 | 36 | Shreveport | .30 | 61 | Greensboro | .04 |
| 18 | Washington, D.C. | .87 | 40 | Los Angeles | .28 | 61 | Portland | .04 |
| 19 | Phoenix | .80 | 41 | Austin | .27 | 61 | St. Petersburg | .04 |
| 20 | Honolulu | .78 | 42 | Denver | .25 | 64 | Little Rock | .01 |
| 21 | Houston | .76 | 43 | Detroit | .23 | 64 | Norfolk | .01 |
| 22 | Pittsburgh | .72 | 43 | Tampa | .23 | 66 | Fort Worth | .00 |

# 28. Water Projections and Planning: 1981–2000

Benjamin Franklin once said, "When the well runs dry, we know the worth of water." The prevention of such an eventuality is one of the major challenges facing officials of water resource systems.

The following table shows the per capita volume of water expected to be available in 10–20 years for the cities responding to the survey. (The per capita figures were based upon current population served.) Arlington, Texas and then Spokane appear to be the cities with the greatest prospect of water supply security. Cities like San Jose, Norfolk and Providence have growing challenges ahead to assure adequate water supplies for the next generation.

California cities have a particularly challenging problem. Presently, agricultural users are pumping ground water to irrigate crop and pastureland to supplement the water they receive from state and federal water projects. The state's ground water supplies are suffering from a net loss of 2 million acre feet per year. This is causing a gradual drain on available water for consumers and a gradual deterioration in quality of remaining supplies. Programs for ground water management are needed.

Water is being used at an exceptional pace everywhere in the country, making water resource and water quality management one of the most important factors in future planning. Research continues on such problems as eutrophication, the solubility of minerals, the reduction of evaporation from lakes and reservoirs, and—among other important areas of concern—ground water contamination.

Fortunately, the field of water resource modeling has become increasingly sophisticated and important in analyzing the consequences of water resource development. Mathematical models are extensively relied on to improve the accuracy of information on water supplies, floods and droughts, water quality, and the economic and social consequences of water-related development and controls. Cities that see serious supply problems ahead will be placing greater emphasis on such computerized

technology.

In their water quality survey of the 100 largest cities in the United States, the authors included a question on the major complaint received by utility officials responsible for supplying water and what they perceived to be their major problem area. The primary consumer complaint by far was the high rates. Taste, turbidity and odor were other serious concerns.

Water resource officials mentioned two major problem areas: (1) the steadily increasing demand for water supplies that seem to be getting scarce; (2) the challenge posed by the variations found in the chemical properties of raw water.

SOURCE: Questionnaires to city water resource officials on 1981 data designed and collected for this book by the authors, 1982.

| Rank | City | Per Capita Water Expected to Be Available Daily (gallons) | Rank | City | Per Capita Water Expected to Be Available Daily (gallons) | Rank | City | Per Capita Water Expected to Be Available Daily (gallons) |
|---|---|---|---|---|---|---|---|---|
| 1 | Arlington, Texas | 3,880 | 21 | Detroit | 488 | 41 | Birmingham | 264 |
| 2 | Spokane | 1,702 | 22 | Oakland | 485 | 42 | Fort Wayne | 262 |
| 3 | Tacoma | 1,312 | 23 | Houston | 454 | 43 | Washington, D.C. | 254 |
| 4 | Las Vegas | 1,045 | 24 | Fort Worth | 452 | 44 | Lubbock | 251 |
| 5 | Pittsburgh | 1,022 | 25 | Montgomery | 421 | 45 | Greensboro | 247 |
| 6 | Riverside | 833 | 26 | Colorado Springs | 418 | 46 | Honolulu | 246 |
| 7 | Phoenix | 821 | 27 | Fresno | 416 | 47 | Tucson | 244 |
| 8 | Austin | 782 | 28 | Little Rock | 359 | 48 | Akron | 226 |
| 9 | Albuquerque | 720 | 29 | Memphis | 357 | 49 | Newark | 208 |
| 10 | Corpus Christi | 714 | 30 | Des Moines | 349 | 50 | Indianapolis | 196 |
| 11 | St. Paul | 649 | 31 | Nashville-Davidson | 333 | 51 | St. Petersburg | 193 |
| 12 | Kansas City, Kan. | 625 | 32 | Denver | 331 | 51 | Seattle | 193 |
| 13 | San Antonio | 600 | 33 | Long Beach | 330 | 51 | Tampa | 193 |
| 14 | Milwaukee | 547 | 33 | San Diego | 330 | 54 | Knoxville | 190 |
| 15 | Cleveland | 520 | 35 | Shreveport | 317 | 54 | Los Angeles | 190 |
| 16 | Salt Lake City | 502 | 36 | New Orleans | 314 | 56 | Norfolk | 182 |
| 17 | Kansas City, Mo. | 500 | 37 | Dayton | 312 | 56 | Providence | 182 |
| 18 | Madison | 496 | 38 | Toledo | 300 | 58 | Santa Ana | 96 |
| 19 | Portland, Ore. | 492 | 39 | Syracuse | 289 | 59 | San Jose | 43 |
| 20 | Philadelphia | 489 | 40 | Columbus, Ohio | 265 | | | |

# 29. Future Water Availability

We asked each water supply agency for its projection of water available to the city in 20 years.

Of the 58 cities providing this information, 15 expect their water availability to increase by at least 50 percent. Most of these cities are located in the southwestern part of the United States.

The cities with the largest projected increase are Arlington, Texas and Santa Ana, which expect their water availability to more than double.

At the other end of the spectrum, six cities expect to require less water: Norfolk; Washington, D.C.; Fort Wayne; New Orleans; Tucson; and Fresno.

SOURCE: Questionnaires to city water resource officials on 1981 data, designed and collected for this book by the authors, 1982.

| Rank | City | Percentage Change in Volume of Water | Rank | City | Percentage Change in Volume of Water | Rank | City | Percentage Change in Volume of Water |
|---|---|---|---|---|---|---|---|---|
| 1 | Tacoma | 117.97 | 21 | Madison | 36.32 | 41 | Spokane | 6.80 |
| 2 | Shreveport | 111.11 | 22 | Seattle | 33.76 | 42 | Honolulu | 5.11 |
| 3 | Arlington, Texas | 105.68 | 23 | Salt Lake City | 32.55 | 43 | Philadelphia | 2.48 |
| 4 | Santa Ana | 104.30 | 24 | Greensboro | 31.32 | 44 | Los Angeles | .89 |
| 5 | San Antonio | 98.68 | 25 | Colorado Springs | 29.86 | 45 | Lubbock | 0.00 |
| 6 | Columbus, Ohio | 79.37 | 26 | Newark | 25.00 | 45 | Milwaukee | 0.00 |
| 7 | Corpus Christi | 69.90 | 26 | Toledo | 25.00 | 45 | Nashville-Davidson | 0.00 |
| 8 | Houston | 68.60 | 28 | Detroit | 24.36 | 45 | Oakland | 0.00 |
| 9 | Austin | 66.67 | 29 | Birmingham | 24.16 | 45 | Pittsburgh | 0.00 |
| 9 | Kansas City, Kan. | 66.67 | 30 | Akron | 22.81 | 45 | Portland, Ore. | 0.00 |
| 11 | Las Vegas | 63.49 | 31 | St. Paul | 22.74 | 45 | Providence | 0.00 |
| 12 | Montgomery | 60.00 | 32 | St. Petersburg | 20.00 | 45 | San Jose | 0.00 |
| 13 | Phoenix | 58.33 | 33 | Knoxville | 18.76 | 53 | Washington, D.C. | −17.05 |
| 14 | San Diego | 53.93 | 34 | Indianapolis | 16.88 | 54 | Norfolk | −17.76 |
| 15 | Riverside | 50.00 | 35 | Little Rock | 15.31 | 55 | Fort Wayne | −23.61 |
| 16 | Portland, Ore. | 44.44 | 36 | Fort Worth | 14.44 | 56 | New Orleans | −24.57 |
| 17 | Dayton | 42.86 | 37 | Cleveland | 14.29 | 57 | Fresno | −44.93 |
| 17 | Kansas City, Mo. | 42.86 | 38 | Tampa | 13.64 | 58 | Tucson | −55.56 |
| 19 | Albuquerque | 42.11 | 39 | Syracuse | 11.48 | | | |
| 20 | Denver | 36.96 | 40 | Memphis | 7.93 | | | |

# CHAPTER THREE

# THE PEOPLE

Adam Smith said in *The Wealth of Nations* the true wealth of a community is its people. The true wealth of a city is the energy of its residents.

We look at population characteristics in absolute terms—number of people—and then in relative terms. The density of population says something about the quality of life. Suburbanization tells us how the central city relates to the rest of the metropolitan area. Birth rates suggest the extent to which the city is family-oriented and also the extent to which it will need teachers and the taxes to pay for them.

From the perspective of what kind of people one would want to live with, and what the interests of the bulk of city residents are likely to be, we have included tables showing the marital status, age, and racial composition of the different cities.

Finally, we focus on residents as a labor pool. To what extent are residents working at all? (Some cities are retirement havens.) What proportion of women work? What are some key occupations?

# 30. Biggest Cities (Population)

Official population figures are collected every 10 years in the United States. The 1980 Census figures show a total population of 226.5 million, of which 74.8 percent live in metropolitan areas and 30.0 percent live in central cities.

Some cities, especially those like New York City with many illegal aliens, argue that the Census figures are incomplete and therefore too low.

The 1980 data show just six cities with populations over 1 million: New York, Chicago, Los Angeles, Philadelphia, Houston and Detroit. Many more cities would exceed a population of 1 million if the entire metropolitan area were included in the count. See the metropolitan population figures in Table 31.

The cumulative population of the 100 largest cities is impressive. The top 10 have a combined population of 20.9 million; they constitute 9.2 percent of the total U.S. population, 12.3 percent of all metropolitan areas' population of 169.4 million and 30.8 percent of all central cities' population of 67.9 million.

The top 20 cities have a population of 27.3 million; the top 30, 32.0 million; the top 40, 35.7 million; the top 50, 39.0 million.

The combined population of all 100 central cities is 48.6 million, which is 21.5 percent of the total U.S. population, 28.7 percent of all metropolitan areas' population and 71.6 percent of all central cities' population. In other words, the 100 largest cities include nearly three-fourths of the population of all the cities in the nation.

SOURCE: U.S. Department of Commerce, Bureau of the Census, *1980 Census of Population: Standard Metropolitan Statistical Areas and Standard Consolidated Statistical Areas: 1980* (October 1981).

| Rank | City | Population (× 1,000) | Rank | City | Population ('000) | Rank | City | Population ('000) |
|---|---|---|---|---|---|---|---|---|
| 1 | New York | 7,071 | 35 | Portland, Ore. | 366 | 68 | Lexington-Fayette | 204 |
| 2 | Chicago | 3,005 | 36 | Honolulu | 365 | 68 | Santa Ana | 204 |
| 3 | Los Angeles | 2,967 | 37 | Long Beach | 361 | 71 | Jackson | 203 |
| 4 | Philadelphia | 1,688 | 37 | Tulsa | 361 | 72 | Mobile | 200 |
| 5 | Houston | 1,594 | 39 | Buffalo | 358 | 73 | Yonkers | 195 |
| 6 | Detroit | 1,203 | 40 | Toledo | 355 | 74 | Des Moines | 191 |
| 7 | Dallas | 904 | 41 | Miami | 347 | 75 | Knoxville | 183 |
| 8 | San Diego | 876 | 42 | Austin | 345 | 76 | Grand Rapids | 182 |
| 9 | Phoenix | 790 | 43 | Oakland | 339 | 77 | Montgomery | 178 |
| 10 | Baltimore | 787 | 44 | Albuquerque | 332 | 78 | Lubbock | 174 |
| 11 | San Antonio | 785 | 45 | Tucson | 331 | 79 | Anchorage | 173 |
| 12 | Indianapolis | 701 | 46 | Newark | 329 | 80 | Fort Wayne | 172 |
| 13 | San Francisco | 679 | 47 | Charlotte | 314 | 80 | Lincoln | 172 |
| 14 | Memphis | 646 | 48 | Omaha | 312 | 82 | Huntington Beach | 171 |
| 15 | Washington, D.C. | 638 | 49 | Louisville | 298 | 82 | Madison | 171 |
| 16 | San Jose | 637 | 50 | Birmingham | 284 | 82 | Riverside | 171 |
| 17 | Milwaukee | 636 | 51 | Wichita | 279 | 82 | Spokane | 171 |
| 18 | Cleveland | 574 | 52 | Sacramento | 276 | 86 | Chattanooga | 170 |
| 19 | Columbus, Ohio | 565 | 53 | Tampa | 272 | 86 | Syracuse | 170 |
| 20 | Boston | 563 | 54 | St. Paul | 270 | 88 | Columbus, Ga. | 169 |
| 21 | New Orleans | 557 | 55 | Norfolk | 267 | 89 | Las Vegas | 165 |
| 22 | Jacksonville | 541 | 56 | Virginia Beach | 262 | 90 | Salt Lake City | 163 |
| 23 | Seattle | 494 | 57 | Rochester | 242 | 91 | Worcester | 162 |
| 24 | Denver | 491 | 58 | Akron | 237 | 92 | Kansas City, Kan. | 161 |
| 25 | Nashville-Davidson | 456 | 58 | St. Petersburg | 237 | 92 | Warren | 161 |
| 26 | St. Louis | 453 | 60 | Corpus Christi | 232 | 94 | Arlington, Texas | 160 |
| 27 | Kansas City, Mo | 448 | 61 | Jersey City | 224 | 94 | Flint | 160 |
| 28 | Atlanta | 425 | 62 | Anaheim | 222 | 96 | Aurora | 159 |
| 28 | El Paso | 425 | 63 | Baton Rouge | 219 | 96 | Tacoma | 159 |
| 30 | Pittsburgh | 424 | 63 | Richmond | 219 | 98 | Little Rock | 158 |
| 31 | Oklahoma City | 403 | 65 | Fresno | 218 | 99 | Providence | 157 |
| 32 | Cincinnati | 385 | 66 | Colorado Springs | 215 | 100 | Greensboro | 156 |
| 32 | Fort Worth | 385 | 67 | Shreveport | 206 | | | |
| 34 | Minneapolis | 371 | 68 | Dayton | 204 | | | |

# 31. Metro Population

The metro area may be thought of as the total area dependent on the central city or central cities—some metro areas have more than one downtown. In cases where there are two major downtowns, the second city is usually included in the name of the metro area. Oakland is added to San Francisco; Fort Worth is added to Dallas. However, this is not done for three cities that are dwarfed by the other member of the pair: Yonkers (included in New York City's metro area), Warren (included in Detroit's metro area) and Aurora (included in Denver's metro area).

A complete list of the components of the standard metropolitan statistical areas is shown at the front of the book.

While only six cities have a population over 1 million, 36 metro areas do, and 15 metro areas have a population over 2 million. The smallest metro area population is that of Anchorage, with 173,000 people.

The 10 largest metro areas have 28.2 percent of all metro areas' population and 21.1 percent of the total U.S. population. All 87 metro areas, which encompass the 100 largest cities, include 68.1 percent of all metro areas' population and 51.0 percent of the total U.S. population.

In other words, *over half of all Americans live in the metro areas covered by this book.* Many more work in or derive their income from these areas.

SOURCE: U.S. Department of Commerce, Bureau of the Census, *1980 Census of Population: Standard Metropolitan Statistical Areas and Standard Consolidated Statistical Areas: 1980* (October 1981).

| Rank | Metro Area | Population | Rank | Metro Area | Population | Rank | Metro Area | Population |
|------|-----------|-----------|------|-----------|-----------|------|-----------|-----------|
| 1 | New York | 9,119,737 | 30 | Buffalo | 1,242,573 | 59 | Austin | 536,450 |
| 2 | Los Angeles-Long Beach | 7,477,657 | 31 | Portland, Ore. | 1,242,187 | 60 | Tucson | 531,263 |
| 3 | Chicago | 7,102,328 | 32 | New Orleans | 1,186,725 | 61 | Flint | 521,589 |
| 4 | Philadelphia | 4,716,818 | 33 | Indianapolis | 1,166,929 | 62 | Fresno | 515,013 |
| 5 | Detroit | 4,352,762 | 34 | Columbus, Ohio | 1,093,293 | 63 | Baton Rouge | 493,973 |
| 6 | San Francisco-Oakland | 3,252,721 | 35 | San Antonio | 1,071,954 | 64 | Tacoma | 485,643 |
| 7 | Washington, D.C. | 3,060,240 | 36 | Sacramento | 1,014,002 | 65 | El Paso | 479,899 |
| 8 | Dallas-Ft. Worth | 2,974,878 | 37 | Rochester | 971,879 | 66 | Knoxville | 476,517 |
| 9 | Houston | 2,905,350 | 38 | Toledo | 971,599 | 67 | Las Vegas | 461,816 |
| 10 | Boston | 2,763,357 | 39 | Salt Lake City | 936,255 | 68 | Albuquerque | 454,499 |
| 11 | St. Louis | 2,355,276 | 40 | Providence | 919,216 | 69 | Mobile | 442,819 |
| 12 | Pittsburgh | 2,263,894 | 41 | Memphis | 912,887 | 70 | Chattanooga | 426,540 |
| 13 | Baltimore | 2,174,023 | 42 | Louisville | 906,240 | 71 | Wichita | 411,313 |
| 14 | Minneapolis-St. Paul | 2,114,256 | 43 | Nashville-Davidson | 850,505 | 72 | Little Rock | 393,494 |
| 15 | Atlanta | 2,029,618 | 44 | Birmingham | 847,360 | 73 | Fort Wayne | 382,961 |
| 16 | Newark | 1,965,304 | 45 | Oaklahoma City | 834,088 | 74 | Shreveport | 376,646 |
| 17 | Anaheim-Santa Ana | 1,931,570 | 46 | Dayton | 830,070 | 75 | Worcester | 372,940 |
| 18 | Cleveland | 1,898,720 | 47 | Greensboro | 827,385 | 76 | Spokane | 341,835 |
| 19 | San Diego | 1,861,846 | 48 | Norfolk-Virginia Beach | 806,691 | 77 | Des Moines | 338,048 |
| 20 | Miami | 1,625,979 | 49 | Honolulu | 762,874 | 78 | Corpus Christi | 326,228 |
| 21 | Denver | 1,619,921 | 50 | Jacksonville | 737,519 | 79 | Madison | 323,545 |
| 22 | Seattle | 1,606,765 | 51 | Tulsa | 689,628 | 80 | Jackson | 320,425 |
| 23 | Tampa-St. Petersburg | 1,569,492 | 52 | Akron | 660,328 | 81 | Lexington-Fayette | 318,136 |
| 24 | Riverside | 1,557,080 | 53 | Syracuse | 642,375 | 82 | Colorado Springs | 317,458 |
| 25 | Phoenix | 1,508,030 | 54 | Charlotte | 637,218 | 83 | Montgomery | 272,687 |
| 26 | Cincinnati | 1,401,403 | 55 | Richmond | 632,015 | 84 | Columbus, Ga. | 239,196 |
| 27 | Milwaukee | 1,397,143 | 56 | Grand Rapids | 601,680 | 85 | Lubbock | 211,651 |
| 28 | Kansas City, Mo., Kan. | 1,327,020 | 57 | Omaha | 570,399 | 86 | Lincoln | 192,884 |
| 29 | San Jose | 1,295,071 | 58 | Jersey City | 556,972 | 87 | Anchorage | 173,017 |

# 32. City Population Growth

Unlike the metro area figures, city figures are affected by annexation. Metro areas expand only gradually as the federal government decides what is statistically most descriptive of the reality of population and commuting patterns.

Cities, on the other hand, are legal entities. The boundaries of the older cities were mostly settled by World War I, whereas they have continued to change greatly for the younger cities, which have grown up since then. The large-scale annexations since the 1950s have all been in the rapidly growing younger cities.

Anchorage grew the fastest in the 1970s, mostly by annexation. The metro area, now coextensive with the city, grew 36.9 percent. Three other cities grew by over 50 percent: Lexington (also by annexation), Colorado Springs and Virginia Beach.

The only city in the broadly defined Northeast that grew at all in the 1970s was Columbus, Ohio, All of the other 48 cities showing growth are in the sunbelt.

The cities that lost ground most rapidly were the large industrial centers of the Northeast. St. Louis, Cleveland, Buffalo, Detroit, Pittsburgh, and Rochester all shrank by over 18 percent.

Interestingly, Louisville ranks among the seven cities that lost the most population (−17.5 percent), while her sister Kentucky city, Lexington, ranks only after Anchorage in population growth (+88.8 percent). The explanation is only partly that Lexington was consolidated with Fayette county in 1974 (see Table 2 above). Metro area population changes show Lexington growing substantially faster than Louisville.

SOURCES: U.S. Department of Commerce, Bureau of the Census, *1980 Census of Population: Standard Metropolitan Statistical Areas and Standard Consolidated Statistical Areas: 1980* (October 1981); R. D. Norton, *City Life–Cycles and American Urban Policy* (New York: Academic Press, 1981), pp. 29, 40.

| Rank | City | Percentage Change 1970–80 | Rank | City | Percentage Change 1970–80 | Rank | City | Percentage Change 1970–80 |
|---|---|---|---|---|---|---|---|---|
| 1 | Anchorage | 259.8 | 33 | Oklahoma City | 9.5 | 65 | Toledo | −7.4 |
| 2 | Aurora | 111.5 | 34 | Columbus, Ga. | 9.3 | 66 | Grand Rapids | −8.0 |
| 3 | Lexington-Fayette | 88.8 | 34 | Tulsa | 9.3 | 67 | Omaha | −10.2 |
| 4 | Arlington, Texas | 77.5 | 36 | Greensboro | 8.0 | 68 | New York | −10.4 |
| 5 | Colorado Springs | 58.8 | 37 | Jacksonville | 7.3 | 69 | Chicago | −10.8 |
| 6 | Virginia Beach | 52.3 | 38 | Sacramento | 7.2 | 70 | Milwaukee | −11.3 |
| 7 | Chattanooga | 41.4 | 39 | Dallas | 7.1 | 71 | Kansas City, Mo., Kan. | −11.7 |
| 8 | San Jose | 38.4 | 40 | Nashville-Davidson | 7.0 | 72 | Richmond | −12.1 |
| 9 | Austin | 36.3 | 41 | Los Angeles | 5.5 | 73 | Boston | −12.2 |
| 10 | Albuquerque | 35.7 | 41 | Mobile | 5.5 | 74 | Providence | −12.5 |
| 11 | Montgomery | 33.6 | 43 | Knoxville | 4.9 | 75 | Baltimore | −13.1 |
| 12 | Anaheim | 33.3 | 44 | Columbus, Ohio | 4.6 | 76 | Norfolk | −13.3 |
| 13 | Baton Rouge | 32.3 | 45 | Memphis | 3.6 | 77 | Philadelphia | −13.4 |
| 14 | El Paso | 32.0 | 45 | Miami | 3.6 | 78 | Newark | −13.8 |
| 15 | Jackson | 31.8 | 47 | Tacoma | 2.7 | 78 | Syracuse | −13.8 |
| 16 | Fresno | 31.7 | 48 | Wichita | 1.0 | 79 | Akron | −13.9 |
| 17 | Las Vegas | 30.9 | 49 | Long Beach | 0.7 | 80 | Atlanta | −14.1 |
| 17 | Phoenix | 30.9 | 50 | Spokane | 0.5 | 80 | Jersey City | −14.1 |
| 19 | Santa Ana | 30.8 | 51 | Madison | −0.7 | 82 | Minneapolis | −14.6 |
| 20 | Charlotte | 30.2 | 52 | Fort Worth | −2.1 | 83 | Cincinnati | −15.0 |
| 21 | Houston | 29.2 | 53 | Tampa | −2.2 | 84 | Washington, D.C. | −15.7 |
| 22 | Tucson | 25.7 | 54 | Fort Wayne | −3.4 | 85 | Dayton | −16.2 |
| 23 | San Diego | 25.5 | 55 | Portland, Ore. | −3.6 | 86 | Flint | −17.4 |
| 24 | Riverside | 22.0 | 56 | Denver | −4.5 | 87 | Louisville | −17.5 |
| 25 | San Antonio | 20.1 | 57 | Indianapolis | −4.9 | 88 | Rochester | −18.1 |
| 26 | Little Rock | 19.6 | 58 | San Francisco | −5.1 | 89 | Pittsburgh | −18.5 |
| 27 | Lubbock | 16.7 | 59 | Des Moines | −5.2 | 90 | Detroit | −20.5 |
| 28 | Lincoln | 15.0 | 60 | Birmingham | −5.5 | 91 | Buffalo | −22.7 |
| 29 | Corpus Christi | 13.4 | 61 | New Orleans | −6.1 | 92 | Cleveland | −23.6 |
| 30 | Shreveport | 13.0 | 62 | Oakland | −6.2 | 93 | St. Louis | −27.2 |
| 31 | Honolulu | 12.4 | 63 | Seattle | −7.0 | | | |
| 32 | St. Petersburg | 9.6 | 64 | Salt Lake City | −7.3 | | | |

# 33.  Metro Population Growth

Metro population growth is a valuable measure independent of central city growth, because the central city data reflect two different sets of developments: (1) decentralization *within* metro areas from the city to the suburbs, and (2) decentralization *among* metro areas, from the older industrial centers to the newer cities of the sunbelt.

The metro area data show a steady population drift away from the broadly defined Northeast (i.e., New England; the middle Atlantic states of New York, New Jersey, Pennsylvania, Maryland; and the Central states of Michigan, Illinois, Ohio, Indiana, Minnesota), paralleling an economic drift away from these states. The great strength of this area was its machine tool industry, over which it had complete domination as of World War I, when one-fifth of all such firms were concentrated in

Ohio alone. The machine tool industry supported and was in turn nourished by the diversified range of manufacturing industries in the Northeast. The complex was highly innovative, and the resulting prosperity meant that workers were highly paid and unionized.

The high wage scale and unionization became a contributing factor toward the area's decline, as the component industries moved from their growth phase into a more mature and stable era. The maturity meant a decline in innovativeness and therefore a decline in the ability of the area to generate unique "exports" (goods sold by the region to other regions, based on indigenously developed technology). The wage differential between the Northeast and the rest of the country (with the exception of California, which had begun to develop its own industrial centers in a more fluid environment) created incentives for industrial managers to move their factories to lower-cost areas. Once the technology was established, cost-cutting became the major motivation of managers. The exodus was led by shoe, textile and apparel manufacturers, which set up new plants in the sunny, nonunion Carolinas and elsewhere in the South.

Innovativeness moved away, too. Innovators tend to be freewheeling entrepreneurs who expend themselves in pursuit of an idea. They often have little patience with the bureaucratic ways of mature, stable industries, especially when those ways interfere with hiring personnel with similarly entrepreneurial motivations.

Thus, the centers of new industries like chemicals and electronics have moved to Texas and California. In the 1970s Texas was the leading gainer in manufacturing employment. Back in the Northeast, efforts by state and local governments to promote economic development were notable for their failure. Even with the best of intentions, government entities are unlikely to remedy problems caused for industrial entrepreneurs by the inflexible environment created by regional industrial maturity. Given a choice, the entrepreneur will pick the newer areas to start new industries.

These developments continue to show up in our data on metro population growth. Besides showing regional population trends that suggest regional economic trends, the metro population growth figures have the additional advantage, compared to central city data, of being less subject to large changes from annexation. Changes in metro area definitions tend to be more modest and gradual than is sometimes the case with the central city figures when a large annexation occurs during the period.

Twelve metro areas grew by over one-third during the 1970s—all of them except Anchorage are sunbelt cities. Twelve metro areas declined by over 1 percent—all of them older cities in the Northeast.

SOURCES: U.S. Department of Commerce, Bureau of the Census, *1980 Census of Population: Standard Metropolitan Statistical Areas and Standard Consolidated Statistical Areas: 1980* (October 1981). R. D. Norton, *City Life-Cycles and American Urban Policy* (New York: Academic Press, 1981), pp. 125, 129, 171.

| Rank | Metro Area | Percentage Change 1970–80 | Rank | Metro Area | Percentage Change 1970–80 | Rank | Metro Area | Percentage Change 1970–80 |
|---|---|---|---|---|---|---|---|---|
| 1 | Las Vegas | 69.0 | 29 | San Antonio | 20.7 | 59 | Washington, D.C. | 5.2 |
| 2 | Phoenix | 55.3 | 31 | Lexington-Fayette | 19.3 | 60 | Omaha | 5.1 |
| 3 | Tucson | 51.1 | 31 | Oklahoma City | 19.3 | 61 | Baltimore | 5.0 |
| 4 | Austin | 48.8 | 33 | Spokane | 18.9 | 61 | Indianapolis | 5.0 |
| 5 | Houston | 45.3 | 34 | Jacksonville | 18.6 | 63 | San Francisco-Oakland | 4.6 |
| 6 | Tampa-St. Petersburg | 44.2 | 35 | Lubbock | 18.0 | 64 | Louisville | 4.5 |
| 7 | San Diego | 37.1 | 36 | Tacoma | 17.8 | 65 | Kansas City, Mo., Kan. | 4.2 |
| 8 | Anchorage | 36.9 | 37 | Mobile | 17.6 | 66 | Toledo | 3.8 |
| 9 | Riverside | 36.7 | 38 | Knoxville | 16.4 | 67 | Flint | 2.5 |
| 10 | Albuquerque | 36.4 | 39 | Richmond | 15.4 | 68 | Chicago | 1.8 |
| 11 | Anaheim-Santa Ana | 35.9 | 40 | Chattanooga | 15.0 | 69 | Providence | 1.1 |
| 12 | El Paso | 33.6 | 41 | Lincoln | 14.8 | 69 | Rochester | 1.1 |
| 13 | Colorado Springs | 32.7 | 42 | Corpus Christi | 14.5 | 71 | Cincinnati | 1.0 |
| 13 | Salt Lake City | 32.7 | 43 | Greensboro | 14.3 | 72 | Syracuse | 0.9 |
| 15 | Baton Rouge | 31.5 | 44 | Charlotte | 14.2 | 73 | Columbus, Ga. | 0.3 |
| 16 | Denver | 30.7 | 45 | New Orleans | 13.4 | 74 | Worcester | 0.2 |
| 17 | Miami | 28.3 | 46 | Seattle | 12.8 | 75 | Milwaukee | -0.5 |
| 18 | Atlanta | 27.2 | 47 | Shreveport | 12.1 | 76 | Detroit | -1.9 |
| 19 | Sacramento | 26.2 | 48 | Grand Rapids | 11.6 | 77 | Philadelphia | -2.2 |
| 20 | Tulsa | 25.6 | 49 | Madison | 11.5 | 78 | St. Louis | -2.3 |
| 21 | Dallas-Ft. Worth | 25.1 | 50 | Birmingham | 10.4 | 79 | Dayton | -2.6 |
| 22 | Fresno | 24.6 | 51 | Norfolk-Virginia Beach | 10.1 | 80 | Akron | -2.8 |
| 23 | Jackson | 23.8 | 52 | Memphis | 9.4 | 81 | Newark | -4.5 |
| 24 | Portland, Ore. | 23.3 | 53 | Des Moines | 7.8 | 82 | Boston | -4.7 |
| 25 | Little Rock | 21.7 | 54 | Minneapolis-St. Paul | 7.6 | 83 | Pittsburgh | -5.7 |
| 26 | Nashville-Davidson | 21.6 | 55 | Columbus, Ohio | 7.4 | 84 | Buffalo | -7.9 |
| 26 | San Jose | 21.6 | 56 | Los Angeles | 6.2 | 85 | Cleveland | -8.0 |
| 28 | Honolulu | 21.0 | 57 | Fort Wayne | 5.8 | 86 | Jersey City | -8.4 |
| 29 | Montgomery | 20.7 | 58 | Wichita | 5.6 | 87 | New York | -8.6 |

# 34. Density

The combined effects of large downtown populations in a small area show up in the density figures, i.e., the number of people per square mile. Density affects the character of urban life. A smaller city like Greensboro has a genuine urban environment with a strong community social life because its location makes it very densely packed. More populous cities like Newark and Detroit lack such an urban social texture because they have suburbs to which workers retire in the evening, depriving the cities of the bustle of out of office communication and interaction.

New York City's density of 23,283 people per square mile means that there are 133 square yards per person, or an area under twelve yards square. By contrast, Anchorage's 88 people per square mile means 35,056 more square yards per person.

New York's tight squeeze needs to be put into per-spective. On the one hand, it understates the problem for Manhattan residents, because the large land area of Staten Island is occupied by relatively few people, while Manhattan takes the brunt of the population. It also doesn't take note of the burdens imposed on the city by commuters and visitors. On the other hand, it overstates the problem because skyscrapers greatly increase the real living and working space provided by the sites on which they stand. Similar points can be made about other cities like Houston, Chicago and San Francisco with skyscrapers and a wide range of density.

Nine of the 13 densest cities are located in the "Bos-Wash" (Boston to Washington) corridor or megalopolis. This could become, in due course, a solidly urbanized area, with the only greenery in parks and recreational facilities.

SOURCE: Derived from population and area figures previously shown.

| Rank | City | Density per square mile | Rank | City | Density per square mile | Rank | City | Density per square mile |
|---|---|---|---|---|---|---|---|---|
| 1 | New York | 23,282.94 | 35 | Honolulu | 4,359.99 | 69 | Salt Lake City | 2,744.66 |
| 2 | San Francisco | 14,955.37 | 36 | Akron | 4,235.30 | 70 | San Diego | 2,711.38 |
| 3 | Jersey City | 14,803.44 | 37 | Worcester | 4,231.51 | 71 | Wichita | 2,653.42 |
| 4 | Newark | 13,639.10 | 38 | Denver | 4,221.62 | 72 | Greensboro | 2,568.35 |
| 5 | Chicago | 13,173.44 | 39 | San Jose | 4,215.56 | 73 | Phoenix | 2,428.36 |
| 6 | Philadelphia | 12,986.23 | 40 | Dayton | 4,179.59 | 74 | Dallas | 2,417.32 |
| 7 | Boston | 12,239.00 | 41 | St. Petersburg | 4,165.52 | 75 | Riverside | 2,369.99 |
| 8 | Washington, D.C. | 10,385.19 | 42 | Toledo | 4,157.50 | 76 | Knoxville | 2,360.04 |
| 9 | Miami | 10,114.61 | 43 | Grand Rapids | 4,049.95 | 77 | Memphis | 2,228.81 |
| 10 | Yonkers | 9,086.09 | 44 | Omaha | 3,814.94 | 78 | Shreveport | 2,121.80 |
| 11 | Baltimore | 8,645.88 | 45 | Albuquerque | 3,809.04 | 79 | Lubbock | 2,116.53 |
| 12 | Detroit | 8,619.91 | 46 | Portland, Ore. | 3,663.83 | 80 | Chattanooga | 2,045.42 |
| 13 | Providence | 8,292.12 | 47 | Richmond | 3,507.42 | 81 | Tulsa | 2,027.63 |
| 14 | Pittsburgh | 7,638.52 | 48 | Tacoma | 3,341.79 | 82 | Arlington, Texas | 2,026.87 |
| 15 | Cleveland | 7,560.24 | 49 | Lincoln | 3,338.48 | 83 | Colorado Springs | 1,957.69 |
| 16 | Santa Ana | 7,489.45 | 50 | Fort Wayne | 3,314.01 | 84 | Jackson | 1,925.00 |
| 17 | St. Louis | 7,403.35 | 51 | Baton Rouge | 3,310.50 | 85 | Indianapolis | 1,867.82 |
| 18 | Buffalo | 7,215.12 | 52 | Spokane | 3,294.23 | 86 | El Paso | 1,771.91 |
| 19 | Long Beach | 7,212.25 | 53 | Tucson | 3,253.32 | 87 | Little Rock | 1,747.09 |
| 20 | Milwaukee | 6,641.04 | 54 | Tampa | 3,217.09 | 88 | Fort Worth | 1,540.56 |
| 21 | Syracuse | 6,588.11 | 55 | Madison | 3,165.42 | 89 | Corpus Christi | 1,489.08 |
| 22 | Rochester | 6,586.95 | 56 | Atlanta | 3,125.16 | 90 | Kansas City, Kan. | 1,464.43 |
| 23 | Los Angeles | 6,395.26 | 57 | Columbus, Ohio | 3,086.72 | 91 | Kansas City, Mo. | 1,418.22 |
| 24 | Oakland | 6,353.71 | 58 | Aurora | 3,067.47 | 92 | Mobile | 1,411.63 |
| 25 | Minneapolis | 6,319.44 | 59 | Fresno | 3,030.58 | 93 | Montgomery | 1,381.28 |
| 26 | Huntington Beach | 6,245.60 | 60 | Las Vegas | 2,994.07 | 94 | Virginia Beach | 1,013.52 |
| 27 | Anaheim | 5,807.51 | 61 | San Antonio | 2,979.55 | 95 | Nashville | 854.88 |
| 28 | Seattle | 5,391.33 | 62 | Sacramento | 2,936.54 | 96 | Columbus, Ga. | 769.49 |
| 29 | Norfolk | 5,075.65 | 63 | Charlotte | 2,900.80 | 97 | Lexington | 721.43 |
| 30 | Cincinnati | 4,935.43 | 64 | Des Moines | 2,893.98 | 98 | Jacksonville | 654.05 |
| 31 | St. Paul | 4,873.40 | 65 | Birmingham | 2,890.38 | 99 | Oklahoma City | 620.33 |
| 32 | Flint | 4,866.19 | 66 | Houston | 2,867.06 | 100 | Anchorage | 88.50 |
| 33 | Warren | 4,711.52 | 67 | Austin | 2,790.08 | | | |
| 34 | Louisville | 4,577.47 | 68 | New Orleans | 2,752.99 | | | |

# 35. Suburbanization

This table provides a measure of the degree of suburbanization of major cities. The higher the suburbanization, the higher the likelihood of central city problems that stem from the lack of an adequate tax base.

Newark tops the list. In column 4 we see that its metropolitan area includes five times more people outside Newark itself than live in the central city area. Many of these suburbanites in Short Hills, or Montclair commute to New York City, which is one of the reasons why the Census Bureau sometimes lumps New York and northeastern New Jersey together. The wealth in Essex County, for the most part, does not directly help municipal officials in Newark, who are seeking taxes to provide more services to the poor in their midst. The only way it helps Newark is that Essex County residents contribute taxes to New Jersey, and the state aids Newark.

Other heavily suburbanized cities are Pittsburgh, St. Louis, Boston, Washington, Atlanta and Miami. At the other extreme are Lubbock, El Paso and Lincoln, the areas of which are so large that there are virtually no suburbs, and Anchorage, which has no suburbs.

Another way of looking at the information is shown in column 3. Over 83 percent of the Newark metro area population is suburban, while under 11 percent of the Lincoln population reside outside the city. Anchorage, of course, is its own metro area and therefore has no suburbs.

The eleven starred (*) metro areas have more central cities than the one or two that are indicated in the name used in this table. The additional cities are as follows:

Anaheim: Garden Grove and Santa Ana
Dallas-Fort Worth: Arlington
Denver: Aurora
Detroit: Warren
Little Rock: North Little Rock
Los Angeles: Long Beach
New York: Yonkers
Providence: Warwick
Riverside: San Bernadino and Ontario
Salt Lake City: Ogden
Seattle: Everett

---

SOURCE: U.S. Department of Commerce, Bureau of the Census, *1980 Census of Population: Standard Metropolitan Statistical Areas and Standard Consolidated Statistical Areas: 1980* (October 1981).

---

| Rank | Metro Area | Central City Population | Outside City Population | Percentage Suburban | Suburban Population/100 City |
|------|------------|------------------------:|------------------------:|--------------------:|----------------------------:|
| 1 | Newark | 329,248 | 1,636,056 | 83.25 | 496.91 |
| 2 | Pittsburgh | 423,938 | 1,839,956 | 81.27 | 434.02 |
| 3 | St. Louis | 453,085 | 1,902,191 | 80.76 | 419.83 |
| 4 | Boston | 562,994 | 2,200,363 | 79.63 | 390.83 |
| 5 | Washington, D.C. | 637,651 | 2,422,589 | 79.16 | 379.92 |
| 6 | Atlanta | 425,022 | 1,604,596 | 79.06 | 377.53 |
| 7 | Miami | 346,931 | 1,279,048 | 78.66 | 368.68 |
| 8 | Riverside* | 377.753 | 1,179,327 | 75.74 | 312.20 |
| 9 | Salt Lake City* | 227,440 | 708,815 | 75.71 | 311.65 |
| 10 | Dayton | 203,588 | 626,482 | 75.47 | 307.72 |
| 11 | Rochester | 241,741 | 730,138 | 75.13 | 302.03 |
| 12 | Syracuse | 170,105 | 472,270 | 73.52 | 277.63 |
| 13 | Sacramento | 275,741 | 738,261 | 72.81 | 267.74 |
| 14 | Cincinnati | 385,457 | 1,015,946 | 72.49 | 263.57 |
| 15 | Detroit* | 1,203,339 | 3,149,423 | 72.35 | 261.72 |
| 16 | Anaheim* | 548,911 | 1,382,659 | 71.58 | 251.89 |
| 17 | Buffalo | 357,870 | 884,703 | 71.20 | 247.21 |
| 18 | Portland, Ore. | 366,383 | 875,804 | 70.51 | 239.04 |
| 19 | Cleveland | 573,822 | 1,324,898 | 69.78 | 230.89 |
| 20 | Grand Rapids | 181,843 | 419,837 | 69.78 | 230.88 |
| 21 | Minneapolis-St. Paul | 641,181 | 1,473,075 | 69.67 | 229.74 |
| 22 | Flint | 159,611 | 361,978 | 69.40 | 226.79 |

| Rank | Metro Area | Central City Population | Outside City Population | Percentage Suburban | Suburban Population/100 City |
|---|---|---|---|---|---|
| 23 | San Francisco-Oakland | 1,018,262 | 2,234,459 | 68.70 | 219.44 |
| 24 | Tampa-St. Petersburg | 508,416 | 1,016,076 | 67.61 | 208.70 |
| 25 | Tacoma | 158,501 | 327,142 | 67.36 | 206.40 |
| 26 | Louisville | 298,451 | 607,789 | 67.07 | 203.65 |
| 27 | Birmingham | 284,413 | 562,947 | 66.44 | 197.93 |
| 28 | Seattle* | 548,259 | 1,058,506 | 65.88 | 193.07 |
| 29 | Providence* | 315,131 | 604,085 | 65.72 | 191.69 |
| 30 | Richmond | 219,214 | 412,801 | 65.32 | 188.31 |
| 31 | Denver* | 568,081 | 1,051,840 | 64.93 | 185.16 |
| 32 | Las Vegas | 164,674 | 297,142 | 64.34 | 180.44 |
| 33 | Philadelphia | 1,688,210 | 3,028,608 | 64.21 | 179.40 |
| 34 | Akron | 237,177 | 423,151 | 64.08 | 178.41 |
| 35 | Baltimore | 786,775 | 1,387,248 | 63.81 | 176.32 |
| 36 | Knoxville | 183,139 | 293,378 | 61.57 | 160.19 |
| 37 | Chattanooga | 169,565 | 256,975 | 60.25 | 151.55 |
| 38 | Jersey City | 223,532 | 333,440 | 59.87 | 149.17 |
| 39 | Kansas City, Kan., Mo. | 609,246 | 878,861 | 59.06 | 144.25 |
| 40 | Chicago | 3,005,072 | 4,097,256 | 57.69 | 136.34 |
| 41 | Fresno | 218,202 | 296,811 | 57.63 | 136.03 |
| 42 | Greensboro | 351,634 | 475,751 | 57.50 | 135.30 |
| 43 | Dallas-Ft. Worth* | 1,289,219 | 1,685,659 | 56.66 | 130.75 |
| 44 | Worcester | 161,799 | 211,141 | 56.62 | 130.50 |
| 45 | Baton Rouge | 219,486 | 274,487 | 55.57 | 125.06 |
| 46 | Los Angeles* | 3,328,097 | 4,149,560 | 55.49 | 124.68 |
| 47 | Toledo | 354,635 | 436,964 | 55.20 | 123.22 |
| 48 | Fort Wayne | 172,196 | 210,765 | 55.04 | 122.40 |
| 49 | Mobile | 200,452 | 242,367 | 54.73 | 120.91 |
| 50 | Milwaukee | 636,212 | 760,931 | 54.46 | 119.60 |
| 51 | New Orleans | 557,482 | 629,243 | 53.02 | 112.87 |
| 52 | San Diego | 875,504 | 986,342 | 52.98 | 112.66 |
| 53 | Honolulu | 365,048 | 397,826 | 52.15 | 108.98 |
| 54 | Oklahoma City | 403,213 | 430,875 | 51.66 | 106.86 |
| 55 | San Jose | 636,550 | 658,521 | 50.85 | 103.45 |
| 56 | Spokane | 171,300 | 170,535 | 49.89 | 99.55 |
| 57 | Phoenix | 764,911 | 743,119 | 49.28 | 97.15 |
| 58 | Columbus, Ohio | 564,871 | 528,442 | 48.33 | 93.55 |
| 59 | Tulsa | 360,919 | 328,709 | 47.66 | 91.08 |
| 60 | Madison | 170,616 | 152,929 | 47.27 | 89.63 |
| 61 | Charlotte | 314,447 | 275,438 | 46.69 | 87.59 |
| 62 | Nashville | 455,651 | 394,854 | 46.43 | 86.66 |
| 63 | Omaha | 311,681 | 258,718 | 45.36 | 83.01 |
| 64 | Shreveport | 205,815 | 170,831 | 45.36 | 83.00 |
| 65 | Houston | 1,594,086 | 1,311,264 | 45.13 | 82.26 |
| 66 | Des Moines | 191,003 | 147,045 | 43.50 | 76.99 |
| 67 | Little Rock* | 222,880 | 170,614 | 43.36 | 76.55 |
| 68 | Indianapolis | 700,537 | 466,122 | 39.94 | 66.51 |
| 69 | Tucson | 330,537 | 200,726 | 37.78 | 60.73 |
| 70 | Jackson | 202,895 | 117,530 | 36.68 | 57.93 |
| 71 | Lexington-Fayette | 204,165 | 113,971 | 35.82 | 55.82 |
| 72 | Austin | 345,496 | 190,954 | 35.60 | 55.27 |
| 73 | Montgomery | 178,157 | 94,530 | 34.67 | 53.06 |
| 74 | Colorado Springs | 215,150 | 102,308 | 32.23 | 47.55 |
| 75 | Wichita | 279,272 | 132,041 | 32.10 | 47.28 |
| 76 | Memphis | 646,356 | 266,531 | 29.20 | 41.24 |
| 77 | Columbus, Ga. | 169,441 | 69,775 | 29.17 | 41.18 |
| 78 | Corpus Christi | 231,999 | 94,229 | 28.88 | 40.62 |
| 79 | Albuquerque | 331,767 | 122,732 | 27.00 | 36.99 |
| 80 | San Antonio | 785,410 | 286,544 | 26.73 | 36.48 |
| 81 | Jacksonville | 540,898 | 196,621 | 26.66 | 36.35 |
| 82 | New York* | 7,071,030 | 2,048,707 | 22.46 | 28.97 |
| 83 | Norfolk-Virginia Beach | 633,755 | 172,936 | 21.44 | 27.29 |
| 84 | Lubbock | 173,979 | 37,672 | 17.80 | 21.65 |
| 85 | El Paso | 425,259 | 54,640 | 11.39 | 12.85 |
| 86 | Lincoln | 171,932 | 20,952 | 10.86 | 12.19 |
| 87 | Anchorage | 173,017 | 0 | 0.00 | 0.00 |

# 36. Suburban Share: 1930–80

The dominant demographic shifts since World War II have been to the suburban areas. Suburban areas—defined as metropolitan areas excluding the central cities—grew 35 percent in the 1940s (vs. 14 percent for the nation as a whole), 49 percent in the 1950s (vs. 18 percent), and 27 percent in the 1960s (vs. 13 percent). This growth slowed down considerably in the 1970s, to 18 percent (vs. 11 percent nationwide), but was still substantial compared to the central cities, which showed virtually no increase in population during this decade.

The explanation for the growth lies primarily in governmental policies. The tax exemption for mortgage interest payments made home ownership more attractive than renting. Veterans' benefits made it easier to buy a house. Federal subsidies to highway construction made it easier to commute into and out of the cities. Local government zoning policies were favorable to developers. The preference in the postwar period for large families can be viewed as another causal factor.

In the 1960s a contributing factor to suburbanization was a distressing by-product of civil rights achievements. In order to improve minority schools, white children were ordered to be bussed to them, and minorities to predominantly white schools, to equalize the racial balance within central city school systems. The response of some parents was to move to suburban areas, where the school systems were less affected by the court-ordered busing requirements. This led what has come to be called the "white flight" of the 1960s and 1970s.

The table below shows the suburbanization affecting each of the major cities. Between 1930 and 1976 in 56 out of 73 metro areas the population of residents located outside of the central city areas grew. Between 1976 and 1980 the trend continued more strongly, although five cities have bucked it—notably New York, Kansas City, Missouri and Columbus, Georgia.

An unfortunate result of suburbanization—which amounts to spreading urbanization—is to shift farmland to residential use. During the 1970s there was increasing concern about the average of 6,000 acres a year that have been converted to residential use. The San Joaquin Valley is the home of two major cities—Bakersfield in the south and Fresno in the center—and is also a prime agricultural area. The eight-county area, with 4.8 million cultivated acres, produced more farm products in 1977 than all but three states. Urbanization is expected to claim some 400,000 acres of farmland in this area by the end of the century. One result of development is that the breakup of the land's natural ecology destroys drainage and contributes to soil erosion. Federal policies that discourage crop rotation and planting of permanent cover have also contributed to this degradation of land and its "desertification."

Partly because of concerns about spreading development, many communities have introduced zoning laws that prohibit further development of suburban areas or make it very costly. In many states the heyday of suburbanization is over.

SOURCES: Advisory Commission on Intergovernmental Relations, *Central City-Suburban Fiscal Disparity and City Distress* (1977); Council on Environmental Quality, *Environmental Quality* (1979), pp. 345, 346, 357, 358; U.S. Department of Commerce, Bureau of the Census, *1980 Census of Population: Standard Metropolitan Statistical Areas and Standard Consolidated Statistical Areas: 1980* (October 1981).

| Rank | Metro Area | Suburban Share of Metropolitan Population | | | Percentage Increase 1930–80 | Percentage Increase 1976–80 |
|---|---|---|---|---|---|---|
| | | 1930 | 1976 | 1980 | | |
| 1 | Austin | 0.33 | 0.13 | 0.36 | 9 | 176.9 |
| 2 | Nashville-Davidson | 0.31 | 0.25 | 0.46 | 78 | 84.0 |
| 3 | Memphis | 0.26 | 0.16 | 0.29 | 12 | 81.3 |
| 4 | Birmingham | 0.38 | 0.40 | 0.66 | 74 | 65.0 |
| 5 | Fort Wayne | 0.22 | 0.36 | 0.55 | 150 | 52.8 |
| 6 | San Antonio | 0.28 | 0.19 | 0.27 | – 4 | 42.1 |
| 7 | Tulsa | 0.53 | 0.34 | 0.48 | – 9 | 41.2 |
| 8 | Charlotte | 0.36 | 0.36 | 0.47 | 31 | 30.6 |
| 9 | Omaha | 0.32 | 0.36 | 0.45 | 41 | 25.0 |
| 10 | Des Moines | 0.18 | 0.35 | 0.43 | 139 | 22.9 |
| 11 | El Paso | 0.23 | 0.09 | 0.11 | –52 | 22.2 |
| 13 | Tampa-St. Petersburg | 0.35 | 0.56 | 0.68 | 94 | 21.4 |
| 13 | Albuquerque | 0.42 | 0.23 | 0.27 | –36 | 17.4 |
| 14 | Spokane | 0.24 | 0.43 | 0.50 | 108 | 16.3 |
| 15 | Tucson | 0.42 | 0.33 | 0.38 | –10 | 15.2 |
| 16 | Toledo | 0.36 | 0.48 | 0.55 | 53 | 14.6 |
| 17 | Fresno | 0.64 | 0.60 | 0.68 | 6 | 13.3 |
| 18 | Houston | 0.37 | 0.40 | 0.45 | 22 | 12.5 |
| 19 | Louisville | 0.27 | 0.60 | 0.67 | 148 | 11.7 |
| 20 | Phoenix | 0.69 | 0.44 | 0.49 | –29 | 11.4 |
| 21 | Oklahoma City | 0.33 | 0.47 | 0.52 | 58 | 10.6 |
| 22 | Richmond | 0.29 | 0.59 | 0.65 | 124 | 10.2 |
| 23 | Dallas | 0.49 | 0.51 | 0.56 | 14 | 9.8 |
| 24 | Atlanta | 0.42 | 0.72 | 0.79 | 88 | 9.7 |
| 25 | Worcester | 0.29 | 0.52 | 0.57 | 97 | 9.6 |
| 26 | Portland, Ore. | 0.34 | 0.65 | 0.71 | 109 | 9.2 |
| 27 | Columbus, Ohio | 0.30 | 0.44 | 0.48 | 60 | 9.1 |
| 28 | Knoxville | 0.50 | 0.57 | 0.62 | 24 | 8.8 |
| 29 | New Orleans | 0.13 | 0.49 | 0.53 | 308 | 8.2 |

| Rank | Metro Area | Suburban Share of Metropolitan Population | | | Percentage Increase 1930–80 | Percentage Increase 1976–80 |
|---|---|---|---|---|---|---|
| | | 1930 | 1976 | 1980 | | |
| 30 | Minneapolis-St. Paul | 0.17 | 0.65 | 0.70 | 312 | 7.6 |
| 31 | Seattle | 0.31 | 0.62 | 0.66 | 113 | 6.4 |
| 32 | Detroit | 0.28 | 0.68 | 0.72 | 157 | 5.8 |
| 33 | Jackson | 0.55 | 0.35 | 0.37 | −33 | 5.7 |
| 34 | Rochester | 0.40 | 0.71 | 0.75 | 88 | 5.6 |
| 34 | Syracuse | 0.48 | 0.72 | 0.76 | 58 | 5.6 |
| 36 | Indianapolis | 0.37 | 0.38 | 0.40 | 8 | 5.3 |
| 37 | Baltimore | 0.25 | 0.61 | 0.64 | 156 | 4.9 |
| 38 | Tacoma | 0.35 | 0.64 | 0.67 | 91 | 4.7 |
| 39 | Grand Rapids | 0.43 | 0.67 | 0.70 | 63 | 4.5 |
| 40 | Madison | 0.49 | 0.45 | 0.47 | − 4 | 4.4 |
| 41 | Cincinnati | 0.47 | 0.70 | 0.73 | 53 | 4.3 |
| 42 | Boston | 0.64 | 0.77 | 0.80 | 25 | 3.9 |
| 42 | Miami | 0.23 | 0.76 | 0.79 | 243 | 3.9 |
| 42 | San Diego | 0.30 | 0.51 | 0.53 | 77 | 3.9 |
| 42 | Washington, D.C. | 0.32 | 0.76 | 0.79 | 147 | 3.9 |
| 46 | St. Louis | 0.43 | 0.78 | 0.81 | 88 | 3.8 |
| 47 | Chicago | 0.25 | 0.56 | 0.58 | 132 | 3.6 |
| 47 | Corpus Christi | 0.64 | 0.28 | 0.29 | 55 | 3.6 |
| 49 | Jersey City | 0.55 | 0.58 | 0.60 | 9 | 3.4 |
| 50 | Providence | 0.52 | 0.64 | 0.66 | 27 | 3.1 |
| 51 | Cleveland | 0.31 | 0.68 | 0.70 | 126 | 2.9 |
| 51 | Flint | 0.35 | 0.67 | 0.69 | 97 | 2.9 |
| 53 | Sacramento | 0.51 | 0.71 | 0.73 | 43 | 2.8 |
| 54 | Salt Lake City | 0.33 | 0.74 | 0.76 | 130 | 2.7 |
| 55 | Newark | 0.65 | 0.81 | 0.83 | 28 | 2.5 |
| 56 | Milwaukee | 0.30 | 0.53 | 0.54 | 80 | 1.9 |
| 57 | Fort Worth | 0.30 | 0.55 | 0.56 | 87 | 1.8 |
| 58 | Akron | 0.35 | 0.63 | 0.64 | 83 | 1.6 |
| 58 | Philadelphia | 0.38 | 0.63 | 0.64 | 68 | 1.6 |
| 60 | San Francisco-Oakland | 0.30 | 0.68 | 0.69 | 130 | 1.5 |
| 61 | Buffalo | 0.38 | 0.70 | 0.71 | 87 | 1.4 |
| 62 | Anaheim | 0.66 | 0.72 | 0.72 | 8 | 0.0 |
| 62 | Baton Rouge | 0.55 | 0.56 | 0.56 | 2 | 0.0 |
| 62 | Dayton | 0.48 | 0.76 | 0.76 | 58 | 0.0 |
| 62 | Jacksonville | 0.00 | 0.27 | 0.27 | 27 | 0.0 |
| 62 | Los Angeles-Long Beach | 0.38 | 0.56 | 0.56 | 47 | 0.0 |
| 62 | Pittsburgh | 0.67 | 0.81 | 0.81 | 21 | 0.0 |
| 62 | Wichita | 0.36 | 0.32 | 0.32 | −11 | 0.0 |
| 69 | Denver | 0.26 | 0.66 | 0.65 | 150 | − 1.5 |
| 70 | San Jose | 0.60 | 0.52 | 0.51 | −18 | − 1.9 |
| 71 | Kansas City, Mo. | 0.43 | 0.64 | 0.59 | 37 | − 7.8 |
| 72 | Columbus, Ga. | 0.55 | 0.35 | 0.29 | −47 | −17.1 |
| 73 | New York | 0.14 | 0.34 | 0.23 | 64 | −32.4 |

**Area in 1976 represented land incorporated into city boundaries after that date.

# 37. Suburban Growth: 1970–80

The table below differs from the previous one in that it looks only at the population of the suburban areas and the change between 1970 and 1980, whereas the previous table compares the ratio of the suburban population to that of the entire metro area. The differences are interesting.

Broadly speaking, all but 10 of the 91 suburban areas grew in population between 1970 and 1980. At least 2 of the suburban areas that shrank did so because of jurisdictional changes: The Lexington and Anchorage suburban areas dropped drastically (in Anchorage to zero) because of consolidations (see Table 2).

Tucson, Las Vegas and Phoenix are at the top of the list with 160 percent, 120 percent and 86 percent increases, respectively, in their suburban populations during the 1970s, whereas on the previous table Tucson ranks only 16th and Phoenix ranks 20th. The explanation could be the updating by the Census Bureau of the defi-

nition of their metro areas, which would enlarge their 1980 base and raise the suburban share ratio.

SOURCE: U.S. Department of Commerce, Bureau of the Census, *1980 Census of Population: Standard Metropolitan Statistical Areas and Standard Consolidated Statistical Areas: 1980* (October 1981).

| Rank | Metro Area | Outside City | | Percentage Change |
|---|---|---|---|---|
| | | 1970 | 1980 | |
| 1 | Tucson | 88,734 | 200,726 | 126.21 |
| 2 | Las Vegas | 147,501 | 297,142 | 101.45 |
| 3 | Phoenix | 386,925 | 719,348 | 85.91 |
| 4 | Austin | 106,924 | 190,954 | 78.59 |
| 5 | Tampa-St. Petersburg | 594,676 | 1,058,964 | 78.07 |
| 6 | Houston | 765,781 | 1,310,215 | 71.10 |
| 7 | Jacksonville | 117,562 | 196,621 | 67.25 |

| Rank | Metro Area | Outside City 1970 | Outside City 1980 | Percentage Change | Rank | Metro Area | Outside City 1970 | Outside City 1980 | Percentage Change |
|---|---|---|---|---|---|---|---|---|---|
| 8 | Denver | 657,997 | 1,051,840 | 59.85 | 47 | Toledo | 379,596 | 436,964 | 15.11 |
| 9 | Salt Lake City | 460,095 | 708,815 | 54.06 | 48 | Flint | 315,347 | 361,978 | 14.79 |
| 10 | Tulsa | 218,804 | 328,515 | 50.14 | 49 | Fort Wayne | 183,715 | 210,765 | 14.72 |
| 11 | San Diego | 660,383 | 986,308 | 49.35 | 50 | Kansas City, Kan.-Mo. | 766,596 | 878,947 | 14.66 |
| 12 | Dallas-Fort Worth | 1,139,767 | 1,685,659 | 47.90 | 51 | Chicago | 3,605,398 | 4,097,256 | 13.64 |
| 13 | El Paso | 37,030 | 54,640 | 47.56 | 52 | Lincoln | 18,454 | 20,952 | 13.54 |
| 14 | Atlanta | 1,100,478 | 1,604,596 | 45.81 | 53 | Washington, D.C. | 2,153,443 | 2,422,589 | 12.50 |
| 15 | Spokane | 116,971 | 170,535 | 45.79 | 54 | Jackson | 104,938 | 117,530 | 11.00 |
| 16 | Nashville-Davidson | 273,242 | 394,854 | 44.51 | 55 | Shreveport | 153,936 | 170,890 | 11.01 |
| 17 | Riverside | 828,073 | 1,180,996 | 42.62 | 56 | Milwaukee | 686,512 | 760,931 | 10.84 |
| 18 | Anaheim | 977,960 | 1,382,659 | 41.38 | 57 | Columbus, Ohio | 477,822 | 528,422 | 10.59 |
| 19 | Portland | 627,163 | 876,211 | 38.71 | 58 | San Jose | 605,400 | 665,629 | 9.95 |
| 20 | New Orleans | 452,999 | 629,558 | 38.98 | 59 | San Francisco- | | | |
| 21 | Richmond | 298,210 | 412,801 | 38.43 | | Oakland | 2,032,014 | 2,232,319 | 9.86 |
| 22 | Albuquerque | 88,765 | 122,732 | 38.27 | 60 | Rochester | 666,505 | 729,489 | 9.45 |
| 23 | Miami | 932,933 | 1,278,916 | 37.09 | 61 | Cincinnati | 933,693 | 1,015,946 | 8.81 |
| 24 | Sacramento | 546,688 | 738,261 | 35.04 | 62 | Worcester | 195,572 | 211,141 | 7.96 |
| 25 | Des Moines | 112,158 | 147,045 | 31.11 | 63 | Detroit | 2,920,988 | 3,150,074 | 7.84 |
| 26 | Baton Rouge | 209,707 | 274,487 | 30.89 | 64 | Syracuse | 439,299 | 472,866 | 7.64 |
| 27 | Omaha | 195,717 | 255,359 | 30.47 | 65 | Los Angeles- | | | |
| 28 | Oklahoma City | 330,928 | 430,875 | 30.20 | | Long Beach | 3,871,300 | 4,149,319 | 7.18 |
| 29 | Honolulu | 305,657 | 397,517 | 30.05 | 66 | St. Louis | 1,788,648 | 1,903,375 | 6.41 |
| 30 | Madison | 118,463 | 152,929 | 29.09 | 67 | Providence | 569,093 | 604,085 | 6.15 |
| 31 | Knoxville | 234,822 | 301,487 | 28.39 | 68 | Philadelphia | 2,874,114 | 3,028,608 | 5.38 |
| 32 | Memphis | 210,115 | 267,116 | 27.13 | 69 | Akron | 403,814 | 423,151 | 4.79 |
| 33 | Tacoma | 257,937 | 327,142 | 26.83 | 70 | Dayton | 609,508 | 626,482 | 2.78 |
| 34 | Seattle | 840,152 | 1,059,210 | 26.07 | 71 | Chattanooga | 250,934 | 256,975 | 2.41 |
| 35 | Lubbock | 30,194 | 37,672 | 24.77 | 72 | Charlotte | 269,043 | 275,438 | 2.38 |
| 36 | Indianapolis | 374,496 | 465,768 | 24.37 | 73 | Cleveland | 1,312,850 | 1,324,898 | 0.92 |
| 37 | Greensboro | 383,141 | 476,345 | 24.33 | 74 | Baltimore | 673,823 | 968,702 | 0.44 |
| 38 | Grand Rapids | 341,576 | 419,837 | 22.91 | 75 | Buffalo | 886,443 | 884,703 | − 0.20 |
| 39 | Norfolk- | | | | 76 | Colorado Springs | 103,771 | 102,308 | − 1.41 |
| | Virginia Beach | 141,580 | 173,196 | 22.33 | 77 | New York | 2,078,153 | 2,048,707 | − 1.42 |
| 40 | San Antonio | 234,026 | 286,074 | 22.24 | 78 | Pittsburgh | 1,881,273 | 1,839,956 | − 2.20 |
| 41 | Birmingham | 466,320 | 562,947 | 20.72 | 79 | Newark | 1,675,538 | 1,636,271 | − 2.34 |
| 42 | Minneapolis- | | | | 80 | Boston | 2,258,030 | 2,200,363 | − 2.55 |
| | St. Paul | 1,221,125 | 1,472,352 | 20.57 | 81 | Jersey City | 347,489 | 333,440 | − 4.04 |
| 43 | Louisville | 505,624 | 607,701 | 20.19 | 82 | Columbus, Ga. | 83,556 | 69,755 | − 16.52 |
| 44 | Fresno | 247,674 | 296,419 | 19.68 | 83 | Lexington-Fayette | 158,564 | 113,464 | − 28.44 |
| 45 | Corpus Christi | 80,307 | 94,229 | 17.34 | 84 | Anchorage | 78,304 | 0 | −100.00 |
| 46 | Wichita | 112,798 | 132,041 | 17.06 | | | | | |

# 38.  Singles Centers

The big three singles centers are Boston, Washington and San Francisco. That should come as no surprise because of their large student and preprofessional populations and, in the case of San Francisco, the city's avant garde life-style. That Syracuse should be in fourth place probably reflects the importance of the student population at Syracuse University in relation to the relatively small size of the city. The same goes for the impact of Brown University and Providence College students in Providence.

At the other extreme, the low percentage of singles in Oklahoma City, Tulsa and Aurora reflect their rapid growth (see Table 32), in Aurora's case largely as a residential area; in the case of the two Oklahoma cities as manufacturing and commercial centers.

SOURCE: U.S. Department of Commerce, Bureau of the Census, *1980 Census of Population: Population Characteristics*, Table 31, state volumes (various publication dates for each volume, 1981–82).

| Rank | City | Single Population (Aged 15 and Over) | Percentage Single | Rank | City | Single Population (Aged 15 and Over) | Percentage Single |
|------|------|---------------------------------------|-------------------|------|------|---------------------------------------|-------------------|
| 1 | Boston | 220,631 | 39.19 | 27 | Long Beach | 84,964 | 23.51 |
| 2 | Washington, D.C. | 230,542 | 36.15 | 28 | Huntington Beach | 38,631 | 22.66 |
| 3 | San Francisco | 231,161 | 34.05 | 29 | Santa Ana | 45,849 | 22.51 |
| 4 | Syracuse | 54,073 | 31.79 | 30 | Sacramento | 61,985 | 22.48 |
| 5 | Providence | 48,392 | 30.86 | 31 | Jackson | 45,403 | 22.38 |
| 6 | Atlanta | 121,845 | 28.67 | 32 | Birmingham | 62,243 | 21.88 |
| 7 | Worcester | 46,266 | 28.59 | 33 | Charlotte | 68,417 | 21.76 |
| 8 | Buffalo | 100,175 | 27.99 | 34 | Albuquerque | 72,094 | 21.73 |
| 9 | Rochester | 67,380 | 27.87 | 35 | Fresno | 46,757 | 21.43 |
| 10 | Baltimore | 217,578 | 27.65 | 36 | Mobile | 42,805 | 21.35 |
| 11 | Lincoln | 46,921 | 27.41 | 37 | San Jose | 134,161 | 21.08 |
| 12 | Newark | 89,137 | 27.07 | 38 | Anaheim | 46,105 | 20.78 |
| 13 | Oakland | 91,726 | 27.03 | 39 | Anchorage | 35,428 | 20.48 |
| 14 | San Diego | 236,126 | 26.97 | 40 | Little Rock | 31,697 | 20.00 |
| 15 | New York | 1,902,263 | 26.90 | 41 | Montgomery | 35,582 | 19.97 |
| 16 | Baton Rouge | 58,768 | 26.78 | 42 | Riverside | 33,860 | 19.82 |
| 17 | Honolulu | 97,254 | 26.64 | 43 | Phoenix | 151,604 | 19.20 |
| 18 | Los Angeles | 780,991 | 26.32 | 44 | Columbus, Ga. | 32,466 | 19.16 |
| 19 | Jersey City | 58,792 | 26.30 | 45 | Kansas City, Kan. | 30,730 | 19.08 |
| 20 | New Orleans | 145,178 | 26.04 | 46 | Las Vegas | 31,332 | 19.03 |
| 21 | Denver | 125,115 | 25.46 | 46 | Wichita | 53,162 | 19.03 |
| 22 | Greensboro | 38,688 | 24.86 | 48 | Colorado Springs | 40,794 | 18.96 |
| 23 | Tucson | 79,341 | 24.00 | 49 | Shreveport | 38,509 | 18.71 |
| 24 | Yonkers | 46,808 | 23.96 | 50 | Aurora | 29,017 | 18.30 |
| 25 | Memphis | 153,027 | 23.68 | 51 | Tulsa | 65,489 | 18.15 |
| 26 | Omaha | 73,666 | 23.64 | 52 | Oklahoma City | 67,976 | 16.86 |

# 39.  Singles

The following table shows the proportion of singles (15 years of age and over) who are women. Only six of 52 cities have a percentage of single women higher than 50 percent. Although the metropolitan New York City area has a predominance of women, as we saw in the earlier table, there are a smidgeon more single men than single women in the city.

A single woman going to San Diego will be outnumbered more than three to two by single men, in part because of the location of a naval base in that city. Anchorage, Columbus, Georgia and Las Vegas aren't far behind.

However, the fact that single women are in a minority in all but 6 cities suggests that many of them choose not to live in the cities at all. Instead, they live in suburban areas, judging by Table 40. Men therefore appear to be more attracted either to the rustic challenge or the central city challenge. Single women are relatively more attracted to suburbia, perhaps because they earn less money and are forced into suburbia to obtain cheaper housing. If the economic explanation doesn't entirely explain the data, it could be that single women associate central cities with street harrassment and danger.

Figures for single men can be derived by subtracting the figures for single women from 100.

SOURCE: U.S. Department of Commerce, Bureau of the Census, *1980 Census of Population: Population Characteristics,* Table 31, state volumes (various publication dates depending on each state, 1981–82).

| Rank | City | Single Population (Aged 15 and Over) | Percentage Female |
|------|------|---------------------------------------|-------------------|
| 1 | Greensboro | 38,688 | 52.71 |
| 2 | Washington, D.C. | 230,542 | 51.41 |
| 3 | Newark | 89,137 | 50.73 |
| 4 | Jackson | 45,403 | 50.72 |
| 5 | Buffalo | 100,175 | 50.35 |
| 6 | Providence | 48,392 | 50.33 |
| 7 | Little Rock | 31,697 | 49.89 |
| 8 | New York | 1,902,263 | 49.79 |

| Rank | City | Single Population (Aged 15 and Over) | Percentage Female | Rank | City | Single Population (Aged 15 and Over) | Percentage Female |
|------|------|------|------|------|------|------|------|
| 9 | Syracuse | 54,073 | 49.76 | 31 | Denver | 125,115 | 45.65 |
| 10 | Yonkers | 46,808 | 49.71 | 31 | Tucson | 79,341 | 45.65 |
| 11 | Montgomery | 35,582 | 49.49 | 33 | Riverside | 33,860 | 45.45 |
| 12 | Boston | 220,631 | 49.47 | 34 | Sacramento | 61,985 | 45.39 |
| 13 | Charlotte | 68,417 | 49.35 | 35 | Aurora | 29,017 | 45.38 |
| 14 | Omaha | 73,666 | 49.16 | 36 | Oklahoma City | 67,967 | 45.36 |
| 15 | Birmingham | 62,243 | 49.15 | 37 | Colorado Springs | 40,794 | 45.32 |
| 15 | Worcester | 46,266 | 49.15 | 38 | Tulsa | 65,489 | 45.13 |
| 17 | Baltimore | 217,578 | 49.00 | 39 | Honolulu | 97,254 | 45.08 |
| 18 | Shreveport | 38,509 | 48.92 | 40 | Wichita | 53,162 | 44.61 |
| 19 | Memphis | 153,027 | 48.68 | 41 | Los Angeles | 780,991 | 44.42 |
| 20 | Rochester | 67,380 | 48.65 | 42 | San Jose | 134,161 | 44.20 |
| 21 | Jersey City | 58,792 | 48.47 | 43 | Phoenix | 151,604 | 44.00 |
| 22 | New Orleans | 145,178 | 48.42 | 44 | Anaheim | 46,105 | 43.61 |
| 23 | Mobile | 42,805 | 47.86 | 45 | Huntington Beach | 38,631 | 43.36 |
| 24 | Atlanta | 121,845 | 47.84 | 46 | San Francisco | 231,161 | 42.44 |
| 25 | Kansas City, Kan. | 30,730 | 47.63 | 47 | Long Beach | 84,964 | 42.28 |
| 26 | Oakland | 91,726 | 47.59 | 48 | Santa Ana | 45,849 | 41.49 |
| 27 | Baton Rouge | 58,768 | 47.43 | 49 | Las Vegas | 31,332 | 40.96 |
| 28 | Lincoln | 46,921 | 47.35 | 50 | Columbus, Ga. | 32,466 | 39.86 |
| 29 | Fresno | 46,757 | 46.33 | 51 | Anchorage | 35,482 | 39.19 |
| 30 | Albuquerque | 72,094 | 46.19 | 52 | San Diego | 236,126 | 37.98 |

# 40. Women in the Population

Frenchman Alexis de Tocqueville said after his travels in America: "If I were asked . . . to what the singular prosperity and growing strength of the American people ought mainly to be attributed, I should reply—to the superiority of their women."

If you are a man and want to improve the odds of meeting one of these superior women, move to New York. The ratio of women to all residents is 53.4 percent, higher than anywhere else in the country.

If you are a woman and want to improve the odds of meeting a man, move to Anchorage, where only 48.1 percent of residents are women.

The divorce rate data indicate that the romance in New York is more likely to endure than one in Anchorage. The table below shows female percentages; figures for males can be derived by subtracting the figure for females from 100.

SOURCE: U.S. Department of Commerce, Bureau of the Census, *1980 Census of Population: Population Characteristics*, Table 26, state volumes (Washington, D.C.: Government Printing Office, various publication printing dates for each state volume, 1981–82).

| Rank | Metro Area | Females | Total Percentage Female |
|------|-----------|---------|------|
| 1 | New York | 4,867,952 | 53.37 |
| 1 | Yonkers | 104,250 | 53.37 |
| 3 | Jackson | 168,920 | 52.72 |
| 4 | Birmingham | 446,469 | 52.68 |
| 5 | Boston | 1,453,819 | 52.61 |
| 6 | Providence | 482,975 | 52.54 |
| 7 | Shreveport | 197,529 | 52.44 |
| 8 | Montgomery | 142,896 | 52.40 |
| 9 | Buffalo | 649,950 | 52.30 |
| 10 | Greensboro | 432,377 | 52.27 |
| 11 | Worcester | 194,779 | 52.23 |
| 12 | Memphis | 475,937 | 52.10 |
| 13 | Chattanooga | 221,972 | 52.04 |
| 14 | Kansas City, Kan. | 690,367 | 52.02 |
| 14 | Little Rock | 204,824 | 52.02 |
| 16 | Charlotte | 331,407 | 52.01 |
| 17 | New Orleans | 617,094 | 51.98 |
| 18 | Mobile | 229,911 | 51.84 |
| 19 | Syracuse | 332,884 | 51.77 |
| 20 | Atlanta | 1,050,434 | 51.75 |
| 21 | Washington, D.C. | 1,583,545 | 51.73 |
| 22 | Baltimore | 1,124,106 | 51.71 |
| 23 | Omaha | 294,279 | 51.66 |
| 23 | Rochester | 501,772 | 51.66 |
| 25 | Oklahoma City | 428,986 | 51.43 |
| 26 | Tulsa | 354,502 | 51.42 |
| 27 | Baton Rouge | 253,542 | 51.31 |
| 28 | Los Angeles | 3,829,142 | 51.21 |

| Rank | Metro Area | Females | Total Percentage Female |
|---|---|---|---|
| 29 | Tucson | 272,123 | 51.20 |
| 30 | Albuquerque | 232,330 | 51.12 |
| 31 | Wichita | 210,179 | 51.10 |
| 32 | Lincoln | 98,526 | 51.08 |
| 32 | San Francisco-Oakland | 1,660,313 | 51.08 |
| 34 | Sacramento | 5.7,587 | 51.04 |
| 35 | Phoenix | 769,261 | 50.98 |
| 36 | Fresno | 261,420 | 50.80 |
| 36 | Riverside | 791,536 | 50.80 |
| 38 | Denver | 821,558 | 50.69 |

| Rank | Metro Area | Females | Total Percentage Female |
|---|---|---|---|
| 39 | Anaheim | 979,104 | 50.66 |
| 40 | Aurora | 80,307 | 50.64 |
| 41 | San Jose | 653,628 | 50.47 |
| 42 | Las Vegas | 229,539 | 49.57 |
| 43 | Colorado Springs | 157,282 | 49.54 |
| 44 | Columbus, Ga. | 118,104 | 49.38 |
| 45 | Norfolk | 396,630 | 49.15 |
| 46 | San Diego | 914,300 | 49.11 |
| 47 | Honolulu | 370,662 | 48.61 |
| 48 | Anchorage | 83,964 | 48.14 |

# 41. Women Anticipating Marriage

A city where a large portion of young women are preparing for marriage by reading about what to do is presumably one where traditional American family values are more likely to be treasured and where long engagements are more likely.

The highest readership of two major magazines devoted to marriage—*Bride's* and *Modern Bride*—is in the Des Moines area. From other magazine circulation tables we know that people in the Des Moines area are heavy buyers of magazines of all kinds. But the readership of 8.08 per thousand residents is well ahead of the next ranked metro area, Omaha, with 6.88 per thousand. Boston and Austin, with their high student populations, are next.

At the low end of the spectrum are Las Vegas with 2 readers of these two publications per thousand residents, and Tacoma and Albuquerque with about 1.8 readers per thousand. In these cities, fewer women read up on what to do at their wedding.

SOURCE: Metro data for February–March 1981 (*Modern Bride*) and February–March 1982 (*Bride's*) from Audit Bureau of Circulation report prepared for this book at the authors' request.

| Rank | Metro Area | Females Anticipating Marriage | Females Anticipating Marriage Per 1000 Population |
|---|---|---|---|
| 1 | Des Moines | 2,732 | 8.08 |
| 2 | Omaha | 2,547 | 6.88 |
| 3 | Boston | 19,567 | 5.34 |
| 4 | Austin | 2,851 | 5.31 |
| 5 | Newark | 9,970 | 5.07 |

| Rank | Metro Area | Females Anticipating Marriage | Females Anticipating Marriage Per 1000 Population |
|---|---|---|---|
| 6 | Madison | 1,638 | 5.06 |
| 7 | New Orleans | 5,847 | 4.93 |
| 8 | Chicago | 34,941 | 4.92 |
| 9 | Pittsburgh | 10,589 | 4.68 |
| 10 | Cleveland | 8,753 | 4.61 |
| 11 | Lexington-Fayette | 1,454 | 4.57 |
| 12 | Philadelphia | 21,457 | 4.55 |
| 13 | Dallas-Ft. Worth | 13,462 | 4.53 |
| 14 | Fort Wayne | 1,706 | 4.45 |
| 15 | Rochester | 4,246 | 4.37 |
| 16 | Buffalo | 5,389 | 4.34 |
| 16 | Jersey City | 2,416 | 4.34 |
| 16 | Milwaukee | 6,067 | 4.34 |
| 19 | Jackson | 1,386 | 4.33 |
| 20 | Washington, D.C. | 13,183 | 4.31 |
| 21 | Anaheim-Santa Ana | 8,243 | 4.27 |
| 22 | Minneapolis-St. Paul | 9,008 | 4.26 |
| 23 | Worcester | 2,748 | 4.25 |
| 24 | Atlanta | 8,525 | 4.20 |
| 24 | New York | 38,347 | 4.20 |
| 26 | St. Louis | 9,660 | 4.10 |
| 27 | Wichita | 1,678 | 4.08 |
| 28 | Grand Rapids | 2,438 | 4.05 |
| 29 | Syracuse | 2,512 | 3.91 |
| 30 | Miami | 6,149 | 3.78 |
| 31 | Houston | 10,868 | 3.74 |
| 32 | Denver | 6,049 | 3.73 |
| 33 | Cincinnati | 5,150 | 3.67 |
| 34 | Columbus, Ohio | 3,956 | 3.62 |
| 35 | Detroit | 15,699 | 3.61 |
| 36 | San Antonio | 3,824 | 3.57 |
| 37 | Baltimore | 7,713 | 3.55 |
| 38 | Knoxville | 1,687 | 3.54 |
| 39 | Indianapolis | 4,106 | 3.52 |
| 40 | Birmingham | 2,952 | 3.48 |
| 41 | Salt Lake City | 3,248 | 3.47 |
| 42 | Los Angeles | 25,713 | 3.44 |
| 42 | Toledo | 2,724 | 3.44 |
| 44 | Little Rock | 1,350 | 3.43 |
| 45 | Oklahoma City | 2,823 | 3.38 |
| 46 | Kansas City | 4,434 | 3.34 |

| Rank | Metro Area | Females Anticipating Marriage | Females Anticipating Marriage Per 1000 Population |
|---|---|---|---|
| 46 | Richmond | 2,113 | 3.34 |
| 48 | Akron | 2,197 | 3.33 |
| 49 | El Paso | 1,588 | 3.31 |
| 50 | Greensboro | 2,728 | 3.30 |
| 50 | Nashville-Davidson | 2,805 | 3.30 |
| 50 | San Jose | 4,108 | 3.30 |
| 53 | Fresno | 1,693 | 3.29 |
| 54 | Baton Rouge | 1,611 | 3.26 |
| 55 | Dayton | 2,701 | 3.25 |
| 56 | Phoenix | 4,822 | 3.20 |
| 57 | San Diego | 5,946 | 3.19 |
| 58 | Charlotte | 2,023 | 3.17 |
| 59 | Providence | 2,989 | 3.16 |
| 60 | Montgomery | 859 | 3.15 |
| 61 | Chattanooga | 1,319 | 3.09 |
| 61 | Tulsa | 2,129 | 3.09 |
| 63 | Mobile | 1,356 | 3.06 |
| 64 | Spokane | 1,024 | 3.00 |
| 65 | Shreveport | 1,125 | 2.99 |

| Rank | Metro Area | Females Anticipating Marriage | Females Anticipating Marriage Per 1000 Population |
|---|---|---|---|
| 66 | Seattle | 4,779 | 2.97 |
| 67 | San Francisco | 9,450 | 2.91 |
| 68 | Flint | 1,513 | 2.90 |
| 69 | Tampa-St. Petersburg | 4,464 | 2.84 |
| 70 | Riverside | 4,357 | 2.80 |
| 71 | Colorado Springs | 885 | 2.79 |
| 72 | Honolulu | 2,062 | 2.70 |
| 72 | Norfolk-Virginia Beach | 2,176 | 2.70 |
| 72 | Sacramento | 2,734 | 2.70 |
| 75 | Portland, Ore. | 3,312 | 2.67 |
| 76 | Tucson | 1,373 | 2.58 |
| 77 | Louisville | 2,328 | 2.57 |
| 78 | Jacksonville | 1,872 | 2.54 |
| 79 | Memphis | 2,301 | 2.52 |
| 80 | Corpus Christi | 753 | 2.31 |
| 81 | Las Vegas | 949 | 2.05 |
| 82 | Tacoma | 879 | 1.81 |
| 83 | Albuquerque | 800 | 1.76 |

# 42. Married Men

If the reason that so many divorced women are concentrated in Oklahoma City is that they have heard of Oklahoma's new oil wealth, they may not have heard of another fact: Oklahoma City men are mostly hitched. Of every 100 men 15 and over, more than 69 are married. That means that a large percentage of the unmarried ones are very young.

Colorado cities are next in line—Aurora and Colorado Springs both show a 64 percent married rate for men 15 and over, suggesting that couples move to these two cities in order to set up house.

At the other extreme, Washington and Boston head the list of single men concentrations. In both cities only 39 out of 100 men 15 and over are married. Both cities are educational and preprofessional centers, which accounts in large part for their showing. When couples get married in both of these cities, they often move to suburban locations. In the case of Boston, the central city is so small in area that M.I.T., across the Charles River from downtown, counts as being in a suburb of Boston.

San Francisco and Atlanta have the third and fourth highest concentrations of single men, as they have of single women.

SOURCE: U.S. Department of Commerce, Bureau of the Census, *1980 Census of Population: Population Characteristics*, Table 31, state volumes (various publication dates depending on each state, 1981–82).

| Rank | Metro Area | All Men (Aged 15 and over) | Married Men | Percentage Married |
|---|---|---|---|---|
| 1 | Oklahoma City | 131,462 | 91,188 | 69.36 |
| 2 | Aurora | 56,791 | 36,447 | 64.18 |
| 3 | Colorado Springs | 76,696 | 49,180 | 64.12 |
| 4 | Shreveport | 64,524 | 41,064 | 63.64 |
| 5 | Wichita | 100,869 | 63,181 | 62.64 |
| 6 | Sacramento | 87,949 | 54,688 | 62.18 |
| 7 | Yonkers | 68,632 | 42,609 | 62.08 |
| 8 | Montgomery | 57,508 | 35,613 | 61.93 |
| 9 | Riverside | 59,393 | 36,708 | 61.81 |
| 10 | Kansas City, Kan. | 53,878 | 33,298 | 61.80 |
| 11 | Phoenix | 280,845 | 172,281 | 61.34 |
| 12 | Charlotte | 105,454 | 64,595 | 61.25 |
| 13 | Little Rock | 52,389 | 32,083 | 61.24 |
| 14 | Columbus, Ga. | 59,142 | 35,739 | 60.43 |
| 15 | Tulsa | 129,426 | 78,934 | 60.99 |
| 16 | Mobile | 67,035 | 40,116 | 59.84 |
| 17 | Fresno | 73,686 | 44,007 | 59.72 |
| 18 | Memphis | 232,631 | 138,694 | 59.62 |

| Rank | Metro Area | All Men (Aged 15 and over) | Married Men | Percentage Married |
|---|---|---|---|---|
| 19 | Anaheim | 80,664 | 48,055 | 59.57 |
| 20 | Albuquerque | 119,446 | 70,834 | 59.30 |
| 21 | San Jose | 222,807 | 132,092 | 59.29 |
| 22 | Jackson | 67,779 | 39,435 | 58.18 |
| 23 | Anchorage | 65,384 | 37,993 | 58.11 |
| 24 | Huntington Beach | 63,544 | 36,720 | 57.79 |
| 25 | Omaha | 108,964 | 62,877 | 57.70 |
| 26 | Birmingham | 92,429 | 52,910 | 57.24 |
| 27 | Las Vegas | 60,625 | 34,428 | 56.79 |
| 28 | Tucson | 120,435 | 68,065 | 56.52 |
| 29 | Santa Ana | 72,934 | 41,216 | 56.51 |
| 30 | Lincoln | 64,732 | 36,354 | 56.16 |
| 31 | Honolulu | 140,296 | 77,260 | 55.07 |
| 32 | New York | 2,358,276 | 1,290,451 | 54.72 |
| 33 | Baton Rouge | 76,244 | 41,313 | 54.19 |
| 34 | Worcester | 56,945 | 30,328 | 53.26 |
| 35 | Jersey City | 70,763 | 37,387 | 52.83 |

| Rank | Metro Area | All Men (Aged 15 and over) | Married Men | Percentage Married |
|---|---|---|---|---|
| 36 | Denver | 182,100 | 95,120 | 52.24 |
| 37 | Los Angeles | 1,074,822 | 549,963 | 51.17 |
| 38 | New Orleans | 178,544 | 91,339 | 51.16 |
| 39 | San Diego | 349,381 | 175,868 | 50.34 |
| 40 | Buffalo | 117,590 | 58,381 | 49.65 |
| 41 | Providence | 53,996 | 26,669 | 49.39 |
| 42 | Rochester | 79,692 | 39,195 | 49.18 |
| 43 | Baltimore | 251,596 | 122,493 | 48.69 |
| 44 | Newark | 94,350 | 45,790 | 48.53 |
| 45 | Greensboro | 52,171 | 25,053 | 48.02 |
| 46 | Oakland | 116,413 | 55,440 | 47.62 |
| 47 | Syracuse | 58,460 | 27,804 | 47.56 |
| 48 | Long Beach | 133,202 | 59,992 | 45.04 |
| 49 | Atlanta | 138,214 | 61,329 | 44.37 |
| 50 | San Francisco | 272,814 | 113,918 | 41.76 |
| 51 | Boston | 202,245 | 79,480 | 39.30 |
| 52 | Washington, D.C. | 213,197 | 83,458 | 39.15 |

# 43. Married Women

For married women with children, it helps to have other families in the area because they will work together for better schools, safer neighborhoods, child care and recreational activities.

For such married women, Omaha is the place to be. Seven out of 10 women 15 and over are married. Three cities are close behind, with 65 married women for every 100: Columbus, Georgia, Colorado Springs and Aurora. Doubtless because there are so few women there to begin with, Anchorage boasts the next highest percentage of married women, 64 out of 100, tied with Oklahoma City (which is also high on the list of divorced women).

At the other extreme, the place for single men to be is Washington, where only 36 out of 100 women 15 and over are married; or Boston, where only 39 out of 100 are married. Atlanta and San Francisco are next, with under 45 married women per 100. In these cities, single women will also find a lot of company for social activities and shared housing.

SOURCE: U.S. Department of Commerce, Bureau of the Census, *1980 Census of Population: Population Characteristics*, Table 31, state volumes (various publication dates depending on each state, 1981–82).

| Rank | Metro Area | All Women (Aged 15 and over) | Married Women | Percentage Married |
|---|---|---|---|---|
| 1 | Omaha | 90,717 | 63,821 | 70.35 |
| 2 | Columbus, Ga. | 54,800 | 35,471 | 64.73 |
| 3 | Colorado Springs | 76,339 | 49,297 | 64.58 |
| 4 | Aurora | 56,220 | 36,287 | 64.54 |
| 5 | Anchorage | 58,322 | 37,437 | 64.19 |
| 6 | Oklahoma City | 141,613 | 90,662 | 64.02 |
| 7 | Wichita | 98,751 | 62,940 | 63.74 |
| 8 | Phoenix | 272,580 | 171,656 | 62.97 |
| 9 | Riverside | 58,916 | 36,687 | 62.27 |
| 10 | Las Vegas | 55,869 | 34,213 | 61.24 |
| 11 | Anaheim | 77,504 | 47,437 | 61.21 |
| 12 | San Jose | 214,796 | 131,383 | 61.17 |
| 13 | Yonkers | 70,316 | 42,660 | 60.67 |
| 14 | Kansas City, Kan. | 55,142 | 33,292 | 60.38 |
| 15 | Huntington Beach | 60,894 | 36,625 | 60.15 |
| 16 | Santa Ana | 65,770 | 39,411 | 59.92 |
| 17 | Charlotte | 108,798 | 64,498 | 59.28 |
| 18 | Albuquerque | 119,769 | 70,882 | 59.18 |
| 19 | Tulsa | 138,686 | 81,731 | 58.93 |
| 20 | Montgomery | 60,182 | 35,453 | 58.91 |
| 21 | Mobile | 67,774 | 39,893 | 58.86 |
| 22 | Shreveport | 69,970 | 41,145 | 58.80 |
| 23 | Fresno | 74,542 | 43,645 | 58.55 |
| 24 | Memphis | 238,439 | 138,374 | 58.03 |
| 25 | Little Rock | 55,600 | 32,076 | 57.69 |
| 26 | Tucson | 118,598 | 67,980 | 57.32 |
| 27 | Honolulu | 134,206 | 76,477 | 56.98 |
| 28 | Lincoln | 63,718 | 36,132 | 56.71 |
| 29 | Sacramento | 96,203 | 54,253 | 56.39 |

| Rank | Metro Area | All Women (Aged 15 and over) | Married Women | Percentage Married |
|---|---|---|---|---|
| 30 | Jackson | 69,970 | 39,403 | 56.31 |
| 31 | Long Beach | 122,573 | 68,182 | 55.63 |
| 32 | Greensboro | 56,631 | 31,068 | 54.86 |
| 33 | San Diego | 305,294 | 167,247 | 54.78 |
| 34 | Birmingham | 96,671 | 52,849 | 54.67 |
| 35 | Baton Rouge | 76,212 | 41,132 | 53.97 |
| 36 | Denver | 177,209 | 93,976 | 53.03 |
| 37 | New York | 2,438,457 | 1,288,015 | 52.82 |
| 38 | Los Angeles | 1,019,374 | 537,531 | 52.73 |
| 39 | Jersey City | 70,817 | 37,299 | 52.67 |
| 40 | Worcester | 58,393 | 30,400 | 52.06 |

| Rank | Metro Area | All Women (Aged 15 and over) | Married Women | Percentage Married |
|---|---|---|---|---|
| 41 | New Orleans | 180,132 | 90,717 | 50.36 |
| 42 | Buffalo | 121,954 | 60,078 | 49.26 |
| 43 | Syracuse | 80,230 | 39,095 | 48.73 |
| 44 | Baltimore | 254,741 | 121,750 | 47.79 |
| 45 | Providence | 56,247 | 26,585 | 47.26 |
| 46 | Oakland | 116,966 | 54,911 | 46.95 |
| 47 | Newark | 98,437 | 45,535 | 46.26 |
| 48 | San Francisco | 253,855 | 112,022 | 44.13 |
| 49 | Atlanta | 138,407 | 60,372 | 43.62 |
| 50 | Boston | 204,218 | 78,756 | 38.56 |
| 51 | Washington, D.C. | 225,721 | 81,755 | 36.22 |

# 44. Divorces

The divorce rate in American cities appears to be related to demographic trends as well as to differences among state laws. The legal differences are illustrated by the high divorce rate in Las Vegas. Nevada has a short residency requirement for divorce, so that cities like Las Vegas or the smaller city of Reno, are centers for couples that wish to divorce with a minimum of judicial inquiry. What started as a new phenomenon in the Northeast in the 1950s and 1960s rapidly shifted to the West Coast in the late 1960s and 1970s. Cities in the Midwest and sunbelt (except those in California) were not as affected by divorce. The staggering rates in the Northeast and on the West Coast have since declined and stabilized at lower levels. At the same time, the trend toward divorce has become glaringly prevalent in major cities in the Midwest and Southwest (Texas cities are notable for their above average divorce rates).

Causes for the decline of divorce in the Northeast and on the West Coast might be related to the changing conceptions of life-style and ethics. Young people are now choosing to live alone or live in group quarters. Couples are deciding to live together instead of making the long-term commitment entailed by marriage.

The figures shown below are for 1978 and indicate the number of divorces per thousand residents. Las Vegas is at the top, for reasons described above. Anchorage's high divorce rate probably reflects the stress of family life in a city that has a high degree of transience. Little Rock's high rate is surprising and may reflect a northward spread of a free-wheeling sunbelt life-style.

In the more conservative and traditional Southwest, changing conventions of life-style have not caught on as quickly, meaning there are more marriages and, consequently, more divorces.

The lowest divorce rates are in family-oriented Riverside and the northeastern population centers of New Jersey, New York and Pennsylvania.

SOURCE: National Center for Health Statistics, *Vital Statistics of the U.S.*, 1981.

| Rank | Metro Area | Population | Total Divorces | Divorces Per 1,000 Population |
|---|---|---|---|---|
| 1 | Las Vegas | 461,816 | 5,874 | 12.72 |
| 2 | Anchorage | 173,017 | 2,106 | 12.17 |
| 3 | Little Rock | 393,494 | 4,073 | 10.35 |
| 4 | Jacksonville | 737,519 | 6,520 | 8.84 |
| 5 | Tulsa | 689,628 | 5,854 | 8.49 |
| 6 | Wichita | 411,313 | 3,213 | 7.81 |
| 7 | Albuquerque | 454,499 | 3,452 | 7.60 |
| 8 | Oklahoma City | 834,088 | 6,183 | 7.41 |
| 9 | Spokane | 341,835 | 2,525 | 7.39 |
| 10 | Phoenix | 1,508,030 | 11,051 | 7.33 |
| 11 | Tucson | 531,263 | 3,880 | 7.30 |
| 12 | Birmingham | 847,360 | 5,975 | 7.05 |
| 13 | Colorado Springs | 317,458 | 2,206 | 6.95 |
| 14 | Tacoma | 485,643 | 3,335 | 6.87 |
| 15 | Dallas-Fort Worth | 2,974,878 | 20,098 | 6.76 |
| 16 | Columbus, Ga. | 239,196 | 1,591 | 6.65 |
| 17 | Seattle | 1,606,765 | 10,564 | 6.57 |
| 18 | Miami | 1,625,979 | 10,549 | 6.49 |
| 19 | Mobile | 442,819 | 2,868 | 6.48 |
| 20 | San Jose | 1,295,071 | 8,260 | 6.38 |
| 21 | Austin | 536,450 | 3,408 | 6.35 |
| 21 | Dayton | 830,070 | 5,270 | 6.35 |
| 23 | Columbus, Ohio | 1,093,293 | 6,920 | 6.33 |
| 23 | Kansas City, Mo., Kan. | 1,327,020 | 8,398 | 6.33 |

| Rank | Metro Area | Population | Total Divorces | Divorces Per 1,000 Population |
|---|---|---|---|---|
| 25 | Knoxville | 476,517 | 3,006 | 6.31 |
| 26 | Louisville | 904,240 | 5,654 | 6.25 |
| 27 | Tampa- St. Petersburg | 1,569,492 | 9791 | 6.24 |
| 27 | Worcester | 372,940 | 2328 | 6.24 |
| 29 | Portland, Ore. | 1,242,187 | 7,704 | 6.20 |
| 30 | Anaheim | 1,931,570 | 11,962 | 6.19 |
| 30 | Houston | 2,905,350 | 17,971 | 6.19 |
| 32 | Atlanta | 2,029,618 | 12,408 | 6.11 |
| 33 | Nashville-Davidson | 850,505 | 5,186 | 6.10 |
| 34 | San Francisco- Oakland | 3,252,721 | 19,791 | 6.08 |
| 35 | San Antonio | 1,071,954 | 6,425 | 5.99 |
| 36 | Corpus Christi | 326,228 | 1,946 | 5.97 |
| 37 | Akron | 660,328 | 3,926 | 5.95 |
| 38 | San Diego | 1,861,846 | 11,017 | 5.92 |
| 39 | Des Moines | 338,048 | 1,950 | 5.77 |
| 40 | Flint | 521,589 | 2,954 | 5.66 |
| 41 | Memphis | 912,887 | 5,085 | 5.57 |
| 42 | Los Angeles | 7,477,657 | 40,497 | 5.42 |
| 43 | El Paso | 479,899 | 2,585 | 5.39 |
| 44 | Lexington-Fayette | 318,136 | 1,708 | 5.37 |
| 45 | Fort Wayne | 382,961 | 2,049 | 5.35 |
| 46 | Lubbock | 211,651 | 1,114 | 5.26 |
| 46 | Montgomery | 272,687 | 1,433 | 5.26 |
| 48 | Sacramento | 1,014,002 | 5,282 | 5.21 |
| 49 | Cleveland | 1,898,720 | 9,881 | 5.20 |

| Rank | Metro Area | Population | Total Divorces | Divorces Per 1,000 Population |
|---|---|---|---|---|
| 50 | Honolulu | 762,874 | 3,941 | 5.17 |
| 51 | Lincoln | 192,884 | 986 | 5.11 |
| 52 | Toledo | 791,599 | 4,033 | 5.09 |
| 53 | Cincinnati | 1,401,403 | 7,019 | 5.01 |
| 54 | Salt Lake City | 936,255 | 4,642 | 4.96 |
| 55 | Fresno | 515,013 | 2,551 | 4.95 |
| 56 | Omaha | 570,399 | 2,819 | 4.94 |
| 57 | Greensboro | 827,385 | 3,963 | 4.79 |
| 58 | Grand Rapids | 601,680 | 2,873 | 4.77 |
| 59 | Detroit | 4,352,762 | 20,280 | 4.66 |
| 60 | Jackson | 320,425 | 1,490 | 4.65 |
| 61 | Charlotte | 637,218 | 2,724 | 4.27 |
| 62 | Chicago | 7,102,328 | 29,330 | 4.13 |
| 63 | Syracuse | 642,375 | 2,637 | 4.11 |
| 64 | Boston | 2,763,357 | 10,804 | 3.91 |
| 65 | Rochester | 971,879 | 3,666 | 3.77 |
| 66 | Milwaukee | 1,397,143 | 4,952 | 3.54 |
| 67 | Baton Rouge | 493,973 | 1,740 | 3.52 |
| 68 | Buffalo | 1,242,573 | 4,340 | 3.49 |
| 69 | Madison | 323,545 | 1,102 | 3.41 |
| 70 | Pittsburgh | 2,263,894 | 7,353 | 3.25 |
| 71 | Philadelphia | 4,716,818 | 14,006 | 2.97 |
| 72 | New York | 9,119,737 | 26,534 | 2.91 |
| 73 | Newark | 1,965,304 | 5,543 | 2.82 |
| 74 | Jersey City | 556,972 | 1,367 | 2.45 |
| 75 | Riverside | 1,557,080 | 2,987 | 1.91 |

# 45. Divorced Men

An unmarried woman should know that the odds of an unmarried man she meets being divorced will be very different in Las Vegas or a big city in Oklahoma compared to, say, Boston or most other large northeastern cities.

The fact is, the odds are over three times as high. In Las Vegas, Oklahoma City and Tulsa, the odds are nearly one in four that a currently unmarried man 15 years old or over will have been divorced. Divorced men should be aware that residents of these cities are likely to be sympathetic to their plight.

In the Northeast—whether because financial constraints are more pressing, because life-styles are more conventional or because main-line religious institutions are more strongly entrenched—an unmarried man is much less likely to be divorced. The six cities with the smallest proportion of divorced men to all unmarried men are in Massachusetts (Boston), New York (Yonkers and New York City), and New Jersey (Jersey City and Newark). Not even 1 out of 10 unmarried men 15 or over is divorced in four of these cities.

The northeastern city with the highest proportion of divorced to unmarried men is Rochester, which still shows half the ratio that prevails in Las Vegas.

SOURCE: U.S. Department of Commerce, Bureau of the Census, *1980 Census of Population: Population Characteristics*, State Volumes, 1981–82.

| Rank | City | All Divorced Men | All Unmarried Men | Percentage Divorced |
|---|---|---|---|---|
| 1 | Las Vegas | 7,703 | 26,202 | 29.4 |
| 2 | Oklahoma City | 13,135 | 50,274 | 26.1 |
| 3 | Tulsa | 11,468 | 47,405 | 24.2 |
| 4 | Long Beach | 14,166 | 63,210 | 22.4 |
| 5 | Aurora | 4,494 | 20,344 | 22.1 |
| 5 | Wichita | 8,339 | 37,688 | 22.1 |
| 7 | Sacramento | 9,553 | 43,401 | 22.0 |
| 8 | Denver | 18,983 | 86,980 | 21.8 |
| 8 | Kansas City, Kan. | 4,486 | 20,580 | 21.8 |
| 8 | Little Rock | 4,422 | 20,306 | 21.8 |
| 8 | Phoenix | 23,663 | 108,564 | 21.8 |

| Rank | City | All Divorced Men | All Unmarried Men | Percentage Divorced |
|---|---|---|---|---|
| 12 | Anchorage | 5,849 | 27,391 | 21.4 |
| 13 | Oakland | 12,899 | 60.973 | 21.2 |
| 14 | Anaheim | 6,612 | 32.609 | 20.3 |
| 15 | Albuquerque | 9,821 | 48,612 | 20.2 |
| 16 | Birmingham | 7,970 | 39,619 | 20.1 |
| 17 | Colorado Springs | 5,210 | 27,516 | 18.9 |
| 18 | Riverside | 4,214 | 22,685 | 18.6 |
| 19 | Huntington Beach | 4,913 | 26,794 | 18.3 |
| 20 | Fresno | 5,586 | 30,679 | 18.2 |
| 21 | Montgomery | 3,927 | 21,898 | 17.9 |
| 22 | Tucson | 9,251 | 52,370 | 17.7 |
| 23 | San Jose | 15,857 | 90,715 | 17.5 |
| 24 | Atlanta | 13,335 | 76,885 | 17.3 |
| 24 | Los Angeles | 90,747 | 524,859 | 17.3 |
| 26 | Mobile | 4,599 | 26,919 | 17.1 |
| 27 | Omaha | 7,632 | 45,087 | 16.9 |
| 28 | Columbus, Ga. | 3,877 | 23,403 | 16.6 |
| 29 | Memphis | 15,399 | 93,937 | 16.4 |
| 30 | San Francisco | 25,830 | 158,896 | 16.3 |
| 31 | Shreveport | 3,790 | 23,460 | 16.2 |
| 32 | San Diego | 27,077 | 173,513 | 15.6 |

| Rank | City | All Divorced Men | All Unmarried Men | Percentage Divorced |
|---|---|---|---|---|
| 33 | Santa Ana | 4,890 | 31,718 | 15.4 |
| 34 | Honolulu | 9,622 | 63,036 | 15.3 |
| 35 | Charlotte | 6,203 | 40,859 | 15.2 |
| 36 | Jackson | 3,972 | 26,348 | 15.1 |
| 37 | Rochester | 5,895 | 40,497 | 14.6 |
| 38 | New Orleans | 12,317 | 87,205 | 14.1 |
| 39 | Baltimore | 18,128 | 129,103 | 14.0 |
| 40 | Washington, D.C. | 17,726 | 129,739 | 13.7 |
| 41 | Buffalo | 7,691 | 57,429 | 13.4 |
| 41 | Greensboro | 2,823 | 21,118 | 13.4 |
| 43 | Lincoln | 3,675 | 28,378 | 13.0 |
| 44 | Providence | 3,290 | 27,327 | 12.0 |
| 45 | Baton Rouge | 4,037 | 34,931 | 11.6 |
| 45 | Worcester | 3,092 | 26,617 | 11.6 |
| 47 | Syracuse | 3,492 | 30,656 | 11.4 |
| 48 | New York | 112,727 | 1,067,825 | 10.6 |
| 49 | Newark | 4,638 | 48,560 | 9.6 |
| 50 | Yonkers | 2,483 | 26,023 | 9.5 |
| 51 | Boston | 11,297 | 122,775 | 9.2 |
| 51 | Jersey City | 3,083 | 33,376 | 9.2 |

# 46. Divorced Women

The leading cities for divorced women are Las Vegas, Oklahoma City, Tulsa, Long Beach, Aurora and Phoenix. Other than Las Vegas they are much more highly ranked than older communities. Women divorced in Anchorage or Little Rock, for example, seem to move to one of these cities. There are fewer than two years' worth of divorced women in Little Rock (7,711 divorced women in 1980 versus 4,073 divorces in 1978), whereas there are three years' worth of divorced women in Tulsa.

Women after divorce are often drained of emotional energy. They are burdened with children and inadequate financial resources. The court settlement, if any, may well be meager and in any case may take time to enforce if the husband chooses not to comply. Under these circumstances the explanation for the large number of divorced women in Las Vegas has nothing to do with the city's glamor but rather the fact that Nevada is an easy state in which to obtain a divorce, and that the divorced woman may remain for lack of energy or resources.

In the table below we have ranked cities on the proportion of all unmarried women (age 15 and over) residing in the city in 1980 who are divorced. The range is from 41 percent for Las Vegas to 14 percent for Baton Rouge.

SOURCE: U.S. Department of Commerce, Bureau of the Census, *1980 Census of Population: Population Characteristics*, State Volumes, 1981–82.

| Rank | City | Divorced Women | All Unmarried Women | Percentage Divorced |
|---|---|---|---|---|
| 1 | Las Vegas | 8,823 | 21,656 | 40.74 |
| 2 | Oklahoma City | 20,084 | 50,921 | 39.44 |
| 3 | Tulsa | 18,403 | 47,955 | 38.38 |
| 4 | Long Beach | 18,471 | 54,391 | 33.96 |
| 5 | Aurora | 6,766 | 19,933 | 33.94 |
| 6 | Phoenix | 34,221 | 100,924 | 33.91 |
| 7 | Wichita | 12,098 | 35,811 | 33.78 |
| 8 | Anaheim | 9,959 | 30,067 | 33.12 |
| 9 | Anchorage | 6,863 | 20,749 | 33.08 |
| 10 | Columbus, Ga. | 6,389 | 19,329 | 33.05 |
| 11 | Kansas City, Kan. | 7,214 | 21,850 | 33.02 |
| 12 | Sacramento | 13,813 | 41,950 | 32.93 |
| 13 | Little Rock | 7,711 | 23,524 | 32.78 |
| 14 | Riverside | 7,464 | 22,853 | 32.66 |
| 15 | Albuquerque | 15,584 | 48,887 | 31.88 |
| 16 | Colorado Springs | 8,554 | 27,042 | 31.63 |
| 17 | Denver | 26,115 | 83,283 | 31.38 |
| 18 | Huntington Beach | 7,519 | 24,269 | 30.98 |
| 19 | Birmingham | 13,228 | 43,882 | 30.19 |
| 20 | San Diego | 38,357 | 128,047 | 29.96 |
| 21 | Fresno | 9,233 | 30,897 | 29.88 |
| 22 | Oakland | 18,403 | 62,055 | 29.66 |

| Rank | City | Divorced Women | All Unmarried Women | Percentage Divorced |
|------|------|---------------|--------------------|--------------------|
| 23 | San Jose | 24,115 | 83,418 | 28.91 |
| 24 | Montgomery | 7,118 | 24,729 | 28.78 |
| 25 | Tucson | 14,396 | 50,618 | 28.44 |
| 26 | Los Angeles | 134,964 | 481,843 | 28.01 |
| 27 | Santa Ana | 7,338 | 26,359 | 27.84 |
| 27 | Shreveport | 7,209 | 26,048 | 27.68 |
| 29 | Mobile | 7,396 | 27,881 | 26.53 |
| 30 | Memphis | 25,576 | 100,065 | 25.56 |
| 31 | Atlanta | 19,740 | 78,035 | 25.30 |
| 32 | San Francisco | 32,748 | 130,843 | 25.03 |
| 33 | Omaha | 11,874 | 48,085 | 24.69 |
| 34 | Jackson | 7,540 | 30,567 | 24.67 |
| 35 | Honolulu | 13,889 | 57,729 | 24.06 |
| 36 | Charlotte | 10,539 | 44,300 | 23.79 |
| 37 | New Orleans | 19,125 | 89,415 | 21.39 |

| Rank | City | Divorced Women | All Unmarried Women | Percentage Divorced |
|------|------|---------------|--------------------|--------------------|
| 38 | Rochester | 8,357 | 41.135 | 20.32 |
| 39 | Greensboro | 5,170 | 25,563 | 20.22 |
| 40 | Baltimore | 26,388 | 132,991 | 19.84 |
| 41 | Lincoln | 5,368 | 27,586 | 19.46 |
| 42 | Worcester | 5,252 | 27,993 | 18.76 |
| 43 | Buffalo | 11,439 | 61,876 | 18.49 |
| 44 | Providence | 5,307 | 29,662 | 17.89 |
| 45 | New York | 203,277 | 1,150,442 | 17.67 |
| 45 | Washington, D.C. | 25,437 | 143,966 | 17.67 |
| 47 | Syracuse | 5,608 | 32,517 | 17.25 |
| 48 | Yonkers | 4,388 | 27,656 | 15.87 |
| 49 | Boston | 16,309 | 106,626 | 15.30 |
| 50 | Jersey City | 5,019 | 33,518 | 14.97 |
| 51 | Newark | 7,687 | 52,902 | 14.53 |
| 52 | Baton Rouge | 4,564 | 32,438 | 14.07 |

# 47.  Births

The birth rate is a good way of looking at what is going on in a city. If the rate is high, it means maternity wards of hospitals are busy, social conversations will turn to children, parents are remodeling their homes or are looking for a bigger place. In the longer term it means that teachers will have jobs and children's wear retailers will have customers.

The health of the central city is more affected by children born and educated within its boundaries than by those born to suburban families and educated outside of the city. The data therefore show central city rates.

Santa Ana, Salt Lake City and Anaheim lead the country in births per 1,000 population. The explanation in Salt Lake City is partly the importance of child-rearing in the Mormon religion, which is based there. In Santa Ana and Anaheim an explanation is the youthful character of the population and, in part, the rearing preference of Hispanic residents (44 percent and 17 percent) in these cities for many children.

At the other end of the table, Anchorage has a low birth rate because of the predominance of people who have come to Alaska in search of work rather than to build a family.

SOURCES: Births (1978) from computer printout provided to the authors by the National Center for Vital Statistics; population from U.S. Census Bureau, *1980 Census of Population: Population Characteristics*, State Volumes, 1981–82.

| Rank | City | Total Births | Births Per 1,000 Population |
|------|------|-------------|----------------------------|
| 1 | Santa Ana | 9,762 | 47.92 |
| 2 | Salt Lake City | 7,233 | 44.37 |
| 3 | Anaheim | 9,762 | 44.00 |
| 4 | Kansas City, Kan. | 6,977 | 43.31 |
| 5 | Oakland | 13,109 | 38.64 |
| 6 | Greensboro | 4,520 | 29.04 |
| 7 | Little Rock | 4,418 | 27.88 |
| 8 | St. Petersburg | 6,422 | 27.11 |
| 9 | Miami | 8,809 | 25.39 |
| 10 | Minneapolis | 8,857 | 23.88 |
| 11 | Tampa | 6,422 | 23.65 |
| 12 | Fort Worth | 8,447 | 21.93 |
| 13 | Rochester | 5,032 | 20.82 |
| 14 | Cincinnati | 7,971 | 20.68 |
| 15 | Flint | 3,271 | 20.49 |
| 16 | Worcester | 3,216 | 19.88 |
| 17 | El Paso | 8,447 | 19.86 |
| 18 | Sacramento | 5,459 | 19.80 |
| 19 | Newark | 6,480 | 19.68 |
| 20 | San Francisco | 13,109 | 19.31 |
| 21 | Colorado Springs | 4,146 | 19.27 |
| 22 | Norfolk | 5,075 | 19.01 |
| 23 | Corpus Christi | 4,409 | 19.00 |
| 24 | Los Angeles | 55,289 | 18.64 |
| 25 | Columbus, Ga. | 3,131 | 18.48 |
| 26 | Providence | 2,885 | 18.40 |
| 26 | Wichita | 5,138 | 18.40 |
| 28 | Shreveport | 3,760 | 18.27 |
| 29 | Mobile | 3,648 | 18.20 |
| 30 | San Antonio | 14,228 | 18.12 |
| 31 | Chicago | 53,693 | 17.87 |
| 31 | New Orleans | 9,961 | 17.87 |
| 33 | Cleveland | 10,248 | 17.86 |
| 34 | Las Vegas | 2,934 | 17.82 |
| 35 | Baton Rouge | 3,860 | 17.59 |
| 36 | Columbus, Ohio | 9,886 | 17.50 |

| Rank | City | Total Births | Births Per 1,000 Population |
|---|---|---|---|
| 37 | Omaha | 5,442 | 17.46 |
| 38 | Fort Wayne | 2,984 | 17.33 |
| 39 | Lubbock | 3,012 | 17.31 |
| 40 | St. Louis | 7,806 | 17.23 |
| 41 | Detroit | 20,325 | 16.89 |
| 42 | Houston | 26,600 | 16.69 |
| 43 | Jersey City | 3,723 | 16.66 |
| 44 | Oklahoma City | 6,707 | 16.63 |
| 45 | Milwaukee | 10,564 | 16.60 |
| 46 | San Jose | 10,524 | 16.53 |
| 47 | Jacksonville | 8,931 | 16.51 |
| 48 | Grand Rapids | 3,000 | 16.50 |
| 49 | Dayton | 3,345 | 16.43 |
| 49 | Indianapolis | 11,516 | 16.43 |
| 51 | Akron | 3,854 | 16.25 |
| 52 | Memphis | 10,457 | 16.18 |
| 53 | Louisville | 4,801 | 16.09 |
| 54 | Albuquerque | 5,330 | 16.07 |
| 55 | Toledo | 5,697 | 16.06 |
| 56 | Fresno | 3,486 | 15.98 |
| 57 | Birmingham | 4,521 | 15.90 |
| 58 | Des Moines | 3,018 | 15.80 |
| 59 | Tulsa | 5,624 | 15.58 |
| 60 | Kansas City, Mo. | 6,977 | 15.57 |
| 61 | Dallas | 14,042 | 15.53 |
| 62 | Tucson | 5,126 | 15.51 |
| 63 | Tacoma | 2,418 | 15.26 |
| 64 | Buffalo | 5,459 | 15.25 |

| Rank | City | Total Births | Births Per 1,000 Population |
|---|---|---|---|
| 65 | Washington, D.C. | 9,700 | 15.21 |
| 66 | Denver | 7,381 | 15.02 |
| 67 | New York | 105,751 | 14.96 |
| 67 | Spokane | 2,562 | 14.96 |
| 69 | Syracuse | 2,537 | 14.91 |
| 70 | Lexington-Fayette | 3,035 | 14.87 |
| 71 | Jackson | 2,989 | 14.73 |
| 72 | Philadelphia | 24,777 | 14.68 |
| 73 | Nashville | 6,616 | 14.52 |
| 74 | Austin | 4,967 | 14.38 |
| 75 | Charlotte | 4,520 | 14.37 |
| 76 | Riverside | 2,448 | 14.33 |
| 77 | Baltimore | 11,182 | 14.21 |
| 78 | Montgomery | 2,523 | 14.16 |
| 79 | Phoenix | 11,141 | 14.11 |
| 80 | Honolulu | 5,130 | 14.05 |
| 81 | Portland, Ore. | 5,093 | 13.90 |
| 82 | Virginia Beach | 3,617 | 13.79 |
| 83 | Lincoln | 2,367 | 13.77 |
| 84 | Pittsburgh | 5,744 | 13.55 |
| 85 | Richmond | 2,925 | 13.34 |
| 86 | Seattle | 6,310 | 12.78 |
| 87 | Boston | 7,140 | 12.68 |
| 88 | San Diego | 11,064 | 12.64 |
| 89 | Knoxville | 2,144 | 11.71 |
| 90 | Atlanta | 4,967 | 11.69 |
| 91 | Madison | 1,932 | 11.32 |
| 92 | Anchorage | 1,598 | 9.24 |

# 48. Average Age of Residents

The age of city residents affects many aspects of city life. Cities with older residents must have more recreational facilities and nursing homes. They require fewer educational facilities, an expensive burden on cities with younger populations.

The cities with the oldest residents are St. Petersburg (median age 42.6) and Miami (median age 38.4)—no surprise in view of the steady migration of retired people to Florida to benefit from the warmer climate. Yonkers is in third place—a surprise for those who aren't familiar with this northern outpost of New York City to which many elderly people go when they retire from their New York City jobs. Yonkers has 12 senior citizens' centers, an Office for Aging and a dense concentration of nursing homes.

The youngest cities are Aurora, Lubbock and Toledo. Aurora's youthful population can be explained by its own youthfulness: It is one of the fastest-growing of all the cities and quickly joined the ranks of the 100 largest in 1980.

Anchorage has a higher median age than Toledo but a much smaller proportion of people 50 and over. This may be explained by the relative absence of children in Anchorage and the relatively high number of children in Toledo families.

SOURCE: *Sales & Marketing Management*, "1982 Survey of Buying Power," 25 Oct. 1982.

| Rank | City | Percentage 50 and Over | Median Age |
|---|---|---|---|
| 1 | St. Petersburg | 43.5 | 42.6 |
| 2 | Miami | 35.8 | 38.4 |
| 3 | Yonkers | 33.3 | 34.9 |
| 4 | San Francisco | 31.4 | 34.4 |
| 5 | Pittsburgh | 34.0 | 33.6 |
| 6 | New York | 29.6 | 33.3 |
| 7 | Seattle | 30.8 | 33.0 |
| 8 | Tampa | 31.2 | 32.9 |
| 9 | Louisville | 31.8 | 32.8 |
| 9 | St. Louis | 33.7 | 32.8 |

| Rank | City | Percentage 50 and Over | Median Age | Rank | City | Percentage 50 and Over | Median Age |
|---|---|---|---|---|---|---|---|
| 11 | Philadelphia | 31.0 | 32.6 | 53 | Milwaukee | 26.9 | 29.9 |
| 12 | Portland, Ore. | 29.8 | 32.2 | 55 | Atlanta | 24.2 | 29.8 |
| 12 | Sacramento | 29.3 | 32.2 | 55 | Jacksonville | 24.1 | 29.8 |
| 12 | Worcester | 32.8 | 32.2 | 55 | Mobile | 25.6 | 29.8 |
| 15 | Denver | 26.9 | 32.1 | 55 | Shreveport | 26.1 | 29.8 |
| 15 | Honolulu | 26.9 | 32.1 | 59 | Dallas | 23.0 | 29.7 |
| 17 | Buffalo | 31.5 | 32.0 | 59 | Detroit | 27.0 | 29.7 |
| 18 | Long Beach | 29.2 | 31.9 | 59 | Fort Wayne | 25.9 | 29.7 |
| 18 | Oakland | 27.5 | 31.9 | 59 | Greensboro | 24.0 | 29.7 |
| 20 | Washington, D.C. | 26.8 | 31.8 | 59 | New Orleans | 25.7 | 29.7 |
| 21 | Richmond | 29.7 | 31.7 | 64 | Dayton | 26.7 | 29.5 |
| 22 | Spokane | 30.4 | 31.6 | 65 | Albuquerque | 21.8 | 29.4 |
| 22 | Warren | 25.6 | 31.6 | 65 | Huntington Beach | 18.0 | 29.4 |
| 24 | Chattanooga | 28.2 | 31.5 | 65 | Memphis | 24.5 | 29.4 |
| 25 | Kansas City, Mo. | 27.4 | 31.3 | 68 | San Diego | 22.9 | 29.3 |
| 26 | Baltimore | 28.8 | 31.2 | 69 | Grand Rapids | 27.3 | 29.2 |
| 27 | Akron | 29.4 | 31.1 | 69 | Montgomery | 23.7 | 29.2 |
| 27 | Cleveland | 29.4 | 31.1 | 71 | Colorado Springs | 20.9 | 29.0 |
| 27 | Los Angeles | 25.1 | 31.1 | 72 | Fresno | 23.6 | 28.9 |
| 27 | Minneapolis | 28.3 | 31.1 | 73 | Lexington-Fayette | 21.1 | 28.7 |
| 27 | Providence | 31.0 | 31.1 | 73 | Riverside | 22.0 | 28.7 |
| 32 | Birmingham | 28.8 | 30.9 | 75 | Columbus, Ga. | 22.9 | 28.6 |
| 33 | Oklahoma City | 25.4 | 30.8 | 76 | Houston | 18.8 | 28.4 |
| 33 | St. Paul | 29.0 | 30.8 | 76 | Jackson | 22.6 | 28.4 |
| 33 | Tacoma | 28.0 | 30.8 | 78 | Lincoln | 22.5 | 28.2 |
| 36 | Des Moines | 27.1 | 30.7 | 79 | Columbus, Ohio | 21.5 | 28.1 |
| 36 | Jersey City | 27.4 | 30.7 | 79 | San Antonio | 22.9 | 28.1 |
| 36 | Knoxville | 28.9 | 30.7 | 79 | San Jose | 17.3 | 28.1 |
| 36 | Las Vegas | 23.1 | 30.7 | 82 | Corpus Christi | 21.3 | 28.0 |
| 36 | Nashville-Davidson | 25.3 | 30.7 | 83 | Madison | 20.0 | 27.8 |
| 41 | Syracuse | 26.4 | 30.6 | 83 | Newark | 22.4 | 27.8 |
| 42 | Cincinnati | 28.8 | 30.5 | 85 | Arlington, Texas | 14.8 | 27.7 |
| 42 | Omaha | 27.1 | 30.5 | 86 | Flint | 23.1 | 27.6 |
| 44 | Chicago | 26.4 | 30.4 | 87 | Virginia Beach | 15.0 | 27.5 |
| 44 | Ft. Worth | 26.6 | 30.4 | 88 | Baton Rouge | 21.7 | 27.3 |
| 44 | Tulsa | 23.7 | 30.4 | 89 | Santa Ana | 18.4 | 27.1 |
| 47 | Boston | 26.4 | 30.0 | 90 | Anchorage | 10.6 | 26.9 |
| 47 | Charlotte | 22.4 | 30.0 | 90 | Austin | 17.6 | 26.9 |
| 47 | Indianapolis | 25.0 | 30.0 | 92 | El Paso | 19.2 | 26.4 |
| 47 | Rochester | 27.4 | 30.0 | 93 | Norfolk | 22.0 | 26.3 |
| 47 | Salt Lake City | 27.9 | 30.0 | 94 | Aurora | 14.7 | 26.1 |
| 47 | Wichita | 25.4 | 30.0 | 95 | Lubbock | 19.1 | 25.9 |
| 53 | Kansas City, Kan. | 26.9 | 29.9 | 96 | Toledo | 27.8 | 20.4 |

# 49. White Population

In Census Bureau parlance a person is white if he or she says so. The category "white" includes all persons who said they were white as well as persons who did not classify themselves but entered a response suggesting a European origin. Nonwhites include blacks, Asians and Pacific Islanders, Amerindians, Eskimos and Aleutian islanders.

Hispanics identify themselves as "white" (about 56 percent) "black" (4 percent) or "other" (40 percent). Being Hispanic is not a racial category, although some Census tables indentify Hispanics separately.

The proportion of a city's population that is white is important for a number of reasons. Whites earn more and spend more. Cities with more nonwhites have greater challenges in the educational area and show higher rates of the types of crimes reflected in the FBI's Uniform Crime Report. They are also, because of their heterogeneity, more varied cities, which provides a flavor that other cities lack.

The most homogeneously white cities are Lincoln (95.5 percent white), Madison and Spokane (both 94.3 percent white). The cities with the most nonwhites are Washington, D.C. (26.9 percent white), Honolulu (28.7 percent white) and Newark (30.8 percent white).

SOURCE: U.S. Census Bureau, *1980 Census of Population: Population Characteristics*, state volumes, 1981–82.

| Rank | City | Percentage of Population White | Rank | City | Percentage of Population White | Rank | City | Percentage of Population White |
|---|---|---|---|---|---|---|---|---|
| 1 | Lincoln | 95.47 | 32 | Oklahoma City | 79.95 | 63 | Columbus, Ga. | 63.57 |
| 2 | Madison | 94.33 | 33 | Seattle | 79.53 | 64 | Mobile | 62.75 |
| 2 | Spokane | 94.33 | 34 | San Antonio | 78.63 | 65 | Dayton | 62.08 |
| 4 | Worcester | 93.94 | 35 | Indianapolis | 77.09 | 66 | Baton Rouge | 61.85 |
| 5 | Des Moines | 90.37 | 36 | Akron | 76.78 | 67 | Dallas | 61.41 |
| 6 | Salt Lake City | 89.76 | 37 | Columbus, Ohio | 76.24 | 68 | Houston | 61.32 |
| 7 | Colorado Springs | 87.89 | 38 | San Diego | 76.16 | 69 | Los Angeles | 61.23 |
| 8 | Minneapolis | 87.29 | 39 | Nashville-Davidson | 75.69 | 70 | Norfolk | 60.79 |
| 9 | Portland, Ore. | 86.51 | 40 | Austin | 75.59 | 71 | New York | 60.72 |
| 10 | Virginia Beach | 86.49 | 41 | Denver | 74.75 | 72 | Montgomery | 60.05 |
| 11 | Anaheim | 85.95 | 42 | Long Beach | 74.71 | 73 | El Paso | 58.60 |
| 12 | Lexington-Fayette | 85.52 | 43 | Pittsburgh | 74.70 | 74 | Philadelphia | 58.23 |
| 13 | Omaha | 85.36 | 44 | Tampa | 73.93 | 75 | San Francisco | 58.18 |
| 14 | Anchorage | 85.15 | 45 | San Jose | 73.83 | 76 | Shreveport | 58.07 |
| 15 | Knoxville | 84.66 | 46 | Milwaukee | 73.34 | 77 | Jersey City | 57.12 |
| 16 | Wichita | 84.44 | 47 | Jacksonville | 72.97 | 78 | Flint | 56.16 |
| 17 | Tacoma | 84.20 | 48 | Fresno | 71.72 | 79 | Cleveland | 53.54 |
| 18 | Phoenix | 83.93 | 49 | Louisville | 71.06 | 80 | St. Louis | 53.53 |
| 19 | Fort Wayne | 83.24 | 50 | Buffalo | 70.51 | 81 | Jackson | 52.38 |
| 20 | Tulsa | 82.59 | 51 | Boston | 69.97 | 82 | Memphis | 51.65 |
| 21 | Providence | 81.91 | 52 | Kansas City, Mo. | 69.80 | 83 | Chicago | 49.59 |
| 22 | Tucson | 81.74 | 53 | Rochester | 69.53 | 84 | Richmond | 47.78 |
| 23 | St. Petersburg | 81.58 | 54 | Fort Worth | 68.91 | 85 | Baltimore | 43.86 |
| 24 | Las Vegas | 81.57 | 55 | Chattanooga | 67.66 | 86 | Birmingham | 43.85 |
| 25 | Syracuse | 81.25 | 56 | Sacramento | 67.62 | 87 | New Orleans | 42.50 |
| 26 | Corpus Christi | 81.15 | 57 | Charlotte | 67.41 | 88 | Oakland | 38.22 |
| 27 | Albuquerque | 80.99 | 58 | Miami | 66.60 | 89 | Detroit | 34.38 |
| 28 | Grand Rapids | 80.93 | 59 | Little Rock | 66.46 | 90 | Atlanta | 32.44 |
| 29 | Lubbock | 80.85 | 60 | Greensboro | 65.74 | 91 | Newark | 30.80 |
| 30 | Riverside | 80.46 | 61 | Cincinnati | 65.15 | 92 | Honolulu | 28.67 |
| 31 | Toledo | 80.05 | 62 | Santa Ana | 64.83 | 93 | Washington, D.C. | 26.94 |

# 50. White Married Men

The percentage of white married men out of all white men is highest in Shreveport (70.55 percent). Closely following are Montgomery, Memphis and Charlotte. The other end of the ranking shows Washington, San Francisco and Boston as cities having less than 40 percent married in this category.

Of the 47 cities ranked, the arithmetic average of white married men as a percentage of all white men is nearly 59 percent. The southern cities show high percentages (except for Atlanta, which is highly cosmopolitan as compared to other southern cities), which reflect the more firmly established traditional family concept.

SOURCE: U.S. Census Bureau, *1980 Census of Population: Population Characteristics*, state volumes, 1981–82.

| Rank | Metro Area | All White Men | Married White Men | Percentage Married |
|---|---|---|---|---|
| 1 | Shreveport | 41,446 | 29,239 | 70.55 |
| 2 | Montgomery | 37,894 | 25,915 | 68.39 |
| 3 | Memphis | 145,630 | 97,227 | 66.76 |
| 4 | Charlotte | 75,755 | 50,117 | 66.16 |
| 5 | Kansas City, Kan. | 39,343 | 25,923 | 65.89 |
| 6 | Little Rock | 37,864 | 24,819 | 65.55 |
| 7 | Greensboro | 35,906 | 23,504 | 65.46 |

| Rank | Metro Area | All White Men | Married White Men | Percentage Married |
|------|------------|--------------:|------------------:|-------------------:|
| 8 | Tulsa | 109,072 | 71,340 | 65.41 |
| 9 | Aurora | 49,178 | 32,121 | 65.32 |
| 10 | Colorado Springs | 65,421 | 42,632 | 65.17 |
| 10 | Mobile | 45,331 | 29,420 | 64.90 |
| 12 | Wichita | 86,233 | 55,852 | 64.77 |
| 13 | Columbus, Ga. | 39,927 | 25,655 | 64.25 |
| 14 | Jackson | 40,536 | 25,992 | 64.12 |
| 15 | Yonkers | 57,141 | 36,310 | 63.54 |
| 16 | Riverside | 45,222 | 28,719 | 63.51 |
| 17 | Birmingham | 45,930 | 29,050 | 63.25 |
| 18 | Phoenix | 227,211 | 143,554 | 63.18 |
| 19 | Albuquerque | 76,065 | 47,478 | 62.42 |
| 20 | Fresno | 49,138 | 30,617 | 62.31 |
| 21 | San Jose | 147,859 | 90,633 | 61.30 |
| 22 | Omaha | 94,885 | 57,603 | 60.71 |
| 23 | Anaheim | 62,507 | 37,794 | 60.46 |
| 24 | Anchorage | 56,374 | 33,398 | 59.24 |
| 25 | Las Vegas | 48,587 | 28,455 | 58.57 |
| 26 | Sacramento | 63,558 | 37,141 | 58.44 |
| 27 | Huntington Beach | 54,765 | 31,946 | 58.33 |

| Rank | Metro Area | All White Men | Married White Men | Percentage Married |
|------|------------|--------------:|------------------:|-------------------:|
| 28 | Santa Ana | 34,358 | 19,994 | 58.19 |
| 29 | New York | 1,361,026 | 791,680 | 58.17 |
| 30 | Tucson | 87,375 | 50,093 | 57.33 |
| 31 | Lincoln | 61,085 | 34,873 | 57.09 |
| 32 | Baltimore | 123,150 | 70,210 | 57.01 |
| 33 | Baton Rouge | 50,843 | 28,652 | 56.35 |
| 34 | Long Beach | 122,573 | 68,182 | 55.63 |
| 35 | New Orleans | 85,962 | 46,861 | 54.51 |
| 36 | Buffalo | 86,856 | 47,155 | 54.29 |
| 37 | Worcester | 53,193 | 28,719 | 53.99 |
| 38 | Honolulu | 40,817 | 21,980 | 53.85 |
| 39 | Denver | 128,413 | 68,465 | 53.32 |
| 40 | Los Angeles | 563,488 | 296,892 | 52.69 |
| 41 | Oakland | 45,416 | 23,190 | 51.06 |
| 42 | San Diego | 254,609 | 129,105 | 50.71 |
| 43 | Providence | 44,224 | 22,397 | 50.64 |
| 44 | Atlanta | 54,649 | 25,577 | 46.80 |
| 45 | Boston | 147,080 | 57,319 | 38.97 |
| 46 | San Francisco | 155,288 | 57,586 | 37.08 |
| 47 | Washington, D.C. | 66,214 | 24,444 | 36.92 |

# 51. White Married Women

For a white married woman, as for married women in general, the presence in a city of a high percentage of others with the same description implies greater attention to family needs. This should be the case in Shreveport and Columbus, Georgia, where 7 out of 10 white women 15 and over are married.

On the other hand, single white woman may find a culture more conducive to their career and social interests in cities where the proportion of white women who are married is low. That is the case in Washington, Boston and San Francisco, where less than 40 out of 100 white women 15 and over are married.

SOURCE: U.S. Census Bureau, *1980 Census of Population: Population Characteristics*, state volumes, 1981–82.

| Rank | Metro Area | All White Women | Married White Women | Percentage Married |
|------|------------|----------------:|--------------------:|-------------------:|
| 1 | Shreveport | 41,807 | 29,117 | 69.65 |
| 2 | Columbus, Ga. | 36,270 | 25,198 | 69.47 |
| 3 | Oklahoma City | 115,059 | 77,116 | 67.02 |
| 4 | Memphis | 146,116 | 96,845 | 66.28 |
| 5 | Kansas City, Kan. | 39,261 | 26,019 | 66.27 |
| 6 | Wichita | 84,406 | 55,773 | 66.08 |

| Rank | Metro Area | All White Women | Married White Women | Percentage Married |
|------|------------|----------------:|--------------------:|-------------------:|
| 7 | Aurora | 48,567 | 31,829 | 65.54 |
| 8 | Anchorage | 49,123 | 32,078 | 65.30 |
| 9 | Colorado Springs | 65,037 | 42,322 | 65.07 |
| 10 | Jackson | 39,804 | 25,887 | 65.04 |
| 11 | Charlotte | 76,996 | 50,062 | 65.02 |
| 12 | Mobile | 45,176 | 29,187 | 64.61 |
| 13 | Phoenix | 221,466 | 142,967 | 64.55 |
| 14 | Las Vegas | 44,042 | 28,119 | 63.85 |
| 14 | Riverside | 44,993 | 28,729 | 63.85 |
| 16 | Yonkers | 57,179 | 36,175 | 63.27 |
| 17 | Little Rock | 39,335 | 24,778 | 62.99 |
| 18 | San Jose | 144,023 | 90,264 | 62.67 |
| 19 | Birmingham | 46,498 | 28,937 | 62.23 |
| 20 | Albuquerque | 75,190 | 46,330 | 61.62 |
| 21 | Fresno | 50,075 | 30,696 | 61.30 |
| 22 | Greensboro | 38,696 | 23,579 | 60.93 |
| 23 | Anaheim | 61,767 | 37,624 | 60.91 |
| 24 | Tulsa | 118,130 | 71,194 | 60.27 |
| 25 | Huntington Beach | 52,624 | 31,596 | 60.04 |
| 26 | Omaha | 96,976 | 57,735 | 59.54 |
| 27 | Baltimore | 118,041 | 69,945 | 59.25 |
| 28 | Santa Ana | 33,649 | 19,747 | 58.69 |
| 29 | Sacramento | 63,192 | 37,061 | 58.65 |
| 30 | Baton Rouge | 49,274 | 28,622 | 58.09 |
| 31 | New York | 1,353,282 | 785,555 | 58.05 |
| 32 | Tucson | 85,647 | 49,497 | 57.79 |
| 33 | New Orleans | 80,570 | 46,319 | 57.49 |
| 34 | Lincoln | 61,093 | 34,865 | 57.07 |
| 35 | Long Beach | 87,576 | 49,555 | 56.59 |
| 36 | Los Angeles | 531,601 | 291,889 | 54.91 |
| 37 | San Diego | 221,997 | 120,315 | 54.20 |
| 38 | Honolulu | 36,676 | 19,873 | 54.19 |

| Rank | Metro Area | All White Women | Married White Women | Percentage Married | | Rank | Metro Area | All White Women | Married White Women | Percentage Married |
|---|---|---|---|---|---|---|---|---|---|---|
| 39 | Denver | 125,972 | 68,129 | 54.08 | | 43 | Providence | 46,268 | 22,457 | 48.54 |
| 40 | Worcester | 54,760 | 28,895 | 52.77 | | 44 | San Francisco | 142,889 | 55,645 | 38.94 |
| 41 | Atlanta | 49,157 | 25,251 | 51.37 | | 45 | Boston | 147,455 | 56,821 | 38.53 |
| 42 | Oakland | 45,267 | 23,155 | 51.15 | | 46 | Washington, D.C. | 68,438 | 23,736 | 34.68 |

# 52. City White Migration

The steady flow of whites from the older central cities has been dubbed "white flight." Although the term connotes fear, and this may be too strong a term for the motivation of many whites, it certainly is an accurate summary of the data for the era since World War II.

There are perhaps six major reasons for white flight:

1. A natural process of urban growth resulting from rapid overall population growth in the postwar era, in part following jobs of companies that established office buildings in the suburban areas, where property was cheaper and more accessible.
2. Subsidy of suburban growth by the federal government through veterans' loans for single-family mortgages and the tax-deductibility of mortgage payments.
3. The inability of the territorially settled older cities to annex growing suburban areas, while the younger cities "captured" these areas through annexation.
4. Immigration to cheaper and more accessible rental housing in the older central cities by minorities, who were excluded by minimum area zoning from the suburban areas and preferred to live in the older cities where there were existing pockets of settled people.
5. A hastening of flight due to a decline in the quality of central city services, such as education, as the tax base was eroded in the older cities and residents left for a better quality of public service or an improved quality of life.
6. Acceleration of this trend by court-ordered busing in the central cities, which some city residents interpreted as meaning that the quality of available public education would have to suffer.

Whatever the predominant reason, the actuality of what has happened in the older cities since World War II is hard to exaggerate. Professor R. D. Norton estimated based on a regression equation that nationwide, between 1950 and 1970, a central city with no metro area growth and no city annexation would see its white population decline by two-thirds—even counting over half of the incoming Hispanics as whites because they were mostly so classified in 1970.

Norton predicted that, with a decline in white birthrates in the 1970s, the white population in the metro areas would grow less and the central city white population would drop even faster. He was right, as the figures below show.

Syndicated columnist George Will chose a strong, apt phrase to describe the postwar changes in New York City—a phrase that could be applied to almost every other old city. He said there is a booming downtown fed by corporations and the entertainment industry. Around this downtown, however, there is industrial decline, with pockets of extreme poverty such as the South Bronx. He called these pockets the "growing necropolis."

One in three of the 1950 whites in the typical old city was gone by 1970; somewhat over 1.5 percent of them left each year. A good portion of the remaining two-thirds were Hispanic newcomers, so that the loss of English-speaking whites was between one-third and one-half. The result was that the median income of people in the central city became lower than that of those in the suburbs.

Between 1970 and 1980 the rate of white flight almost doubled, to nearly 30 percent for the decade, or over 3 percent a year. Of the 21 older cities, from Philadelphia to Detroit, that show the most rapid white flight in the table below, the median white flight is 31 percent.

The younger cities show an entirely different picture. In 1970 the typical young city had two-thirds more whites than it did in 1950. In 1970 the median income of central city dwellers remained greater than that of suburbanites.

Ten central cities showed a growth in their white

population of 20 percent or more in the 1970s: Anchorage; Lexington; Aurora; Arlington, Texas; Colorado Springs; Virginia Beach; Huntington Beach; Charlotte; Las Vegas; and Montgomery. The first two grew in large part through annexation.

In nine central cities, whites declined by more than 31 percent in the 1970s: Detroit (−51 percent), Newark (−40 percent), Oakland (−39 percent), Jersey City, Providence, Flint, St. Louis, Cleveland and Chicago.

SOURCES: U.S. Department of Commerce, Bureau of the Census, *1980 Census of Population Standard Metropolitan Consolidated Areas and Standard Consolidated Statistical Areas: 1980* (October 1981). Background information based in part on Anthony Downs, *Opening Up the Suburbs: An Urban Strategy for America* (New Haven: Yale University Press, 1973); R. D. Norton, *City Life-Cycles and American Urban Policy* (New York: Academic Press, 1981).

| Rank | City | 1970 White Population | 1980 White Population | Absolute Change | Percentage Change |
|---|---|---|---|---|---|
| 1 | Anchorage | 41,899 | 147,334 | 105,435 | 251.64 |
| 2 | Lexington | 89,268 | 174,605 | 85,337 | 95.60 |
| 3 | Aurora | 73,048 | 138,872 | 66,824 | 91.48 |
| 4 | Arlington, Texas | 89,720 | 148,944 | 59,224 | 66.01 |
| 5 | Colorado Springs | 126,474 | 189,113 | 62,639 | 49.53 |
| 6 | Virginia Beach | 154,823 | 226,788 | 71,965 | 46.48 |
| 7 | Huntington Beach | 113,610 | 154,156 | 40,546 | 35.69 |
| 8 | Charlotte | 167,287 | 211.980 | 44,693 | 26.72 |
| 9 | Las Vegas | 109,923 | 134,330 | 24,407 | 22.20 |
| 10 | Montgomery | 88,608 | 106,984 | 18,376 | 20.74 |
| 11 | Austin | 219,609 | 261,166 | 41,557 | 18.92 |
| 12 | Phoenix | 542,510 | 642,059 | 99,549 | 18.35 |
| 13 | Anaheim | 163,517 | 190,679 | 27,162 | 16.61 |
| 14 | Albuquerque | 233,154 | 268,731 | 35,577 | 15.26 |
| 15 | Jackson | 92,651 | 106,285 | 13,634 | 14.72 |
| 16 | Baton Rouge | 119,129 | 135,766 | 16,637 | 13.97 |
| 17 | Fresno | 143,872 | 156,501 | 12,629 | 8.78 |
| 18 | Tucson | 249,299 | 270,188 | 20,889 | 8.38 |
| 19 | Houston | 903,534 | 977,530 | 73,996 | 8.19 |
| 20 | San Diego | 616,796 | 666,829 | 50,033 | 8.11 |
| 21 | Oklahoma City | 298,479 | 322,372 | 23,895 | 8.01 |
| 22 | Little Rock | 99,087 | 105,315 | 6,228 | 6.29 |
| 23 | Riverside | 130,357 | 137,500 | 7,143 | 5.48 |
| 24 | St. Petersburg | 183,765 | 193,277 | 9,512 | 5.18 |
| 25 | Tulsa | 285,869 | 298,114 | 12,245 | 4.28 |
| 26 | Mobile | 122,237 | 125,786 | 3,549 | 2.90 |
| 27 | Lubbock | 137,200 | 140,665 | 3,465 | 2.53 |
| 28 | San Jose | 466,788 | 470,013 | 3,225 | .69 |
| 29 | Lincoln | 164,178 | 164,155 | − 23 | − .01 |
| 30 | Greensboro | 102,694 | 102,320 | − 374 | − .36 |
| 31 | Jacksonville | 397,485 | 394,678 | − 2,807 | − .71 |
| 32 | Columbus, Ohio | 437,255 | 430,678 | − 6,577 | − 1.50 |
| 33 | Spokane | 165,339 | 161,597 | − 3,742 | − 2.26 |
| 34 | Nashville | 358,780 | 344,754 | −14,026 | − 3.91 |
| 35 | Madison | 168,467 | 160,944 | − 7,523 | − 4.47 |
| 36 | Wichita | 246,943 | 235,818 | −11,125 | − 4.51 |
| 37 | Columbus, Ga. | 113,010 | 107,730 | − 5,280 | − 4.67 |
| 38 | Tacoma | 140,301 | 133,471 | − 6,830 | − 4.87 |
| 39 | Honolulu | 110,097 | 104,688 | − 5,409 | − 4.91 |
| 40 | Knoxville | 167,682 | 155,050 | −12,632 | − 7.53 |
| 41 | Des Moines | 188,179 | 172,618 | −15,561 | − 8.27 |
| 42 | Fort Wayne | 157,993 | 143,344 | −14,649 | − 9.27 |
| 43 | Santa Ana | 145,701 | 132,070 | −13,629 | − 9.35 |
| 44 | Tampa | 222,082 | 200,741 | −21,341 | − 9.61 |
| 45 | Miami | 256,377 | 231,069 | −25,308 | − 9.87 |
| 46 | Portland, Ore. | 352,635 | 316,993 | −35,642 | −10.11 |
| 47 | Indianapolis | 606,714 | 540,294 | −66,420 | −10.95 |
| 48 | Shreveport | 119,489 | 106,285 | −13,204 | −11.05 |
| 49 | Warren | 178,415 | 158,283 | −20,132 | −11.28 |
| 50 | Dallas | 626,247 | 555,270 | −70,977 | −11.33 |
| 51 | Worcester | 172,489 | 152,001 | −20,488 | −11.88 |

| Rank | City | 1970 White Population | 1980 White Population | Absolute Change | Percentage Change |
|------|------|----------------------|----------------------|-----------------|-------------------|
| 52 | Yonkers | 189,873 | 164,359 | − 25,514 | −13.44 |
| 53 | Toledo | 329,068 | 283,920 | − 45,148 | −13.72 |
| 54 | Kansas City, Kan. | 132,770 | 114,315 | − 18,455 | −13.90 |
| 55 | Salt Lake City | 170,241 | 146,342 | − 23,899 | −14.04 |
| 56 | Omaha | 310,599 | 266,070 | − 44,529 | −14.34 |
| 57 | Fort Worth | 312,521 | 265,428 | − 47,093 | −15.07 |
| 58 | Seattle | 463,870 | 392,766 | − 71.104 | −15.33 |
| 59 | Grand Rapids | 174,025 | 147,171 | − 26,854 | −15.43 |
| 60 | Los Angeles | 2,173,600 | 1,816,683 | − 356,917 | −16.42 |
| 61 | St. Paul | 295,741 | 243,226 | − 52,515 | −17.76 |
| 62 | Washington, D.C. | 209,272 | 171,796 | − 37,476 | −17.91 |
| 63 | Long Beach | 329,084 | 269,953 | − 59,131 | −17.97 |
| 64 | Memphis | 407,295 | 333,789 | − 73,506 | −18.05 |
| 65 | Kansas City, Mo. | 386,282 | 312,836 | − 73,446 | −19.01 |
| 66 | Akron | 226,362 | 182,114 | − 44,248 | −19.55 |
| 67 | Denver | 458,187 | 367,344 | − 90,843 | −19.83 |
| 68 | El Paso | 311,489 | 249,214 | − 62,275 | −19.99 |
| 69 | Minneapolis | 406,414 | 323,832 | − 82,582 | −20.32 |
| 70 | Syracuse | 173,611 | 138,223 | − 35,388 | −20.38 |
| 71 | San Francisco | 511,186 | 395,082 | − 116,104 | −22.71 |
| 72 | Louisville | 274,511 | 212.102 | − 62,409 | −22.73 |
| 73 | Cincinnati | 325,394 | 251,144 | − 74,250 | −22.82 |
| 74 | Milwaukee | 605,372 | 466,620 | − 138,752 | −22.92 |
| 75 | Philadelphia | 1,278,717 | 983,084 | − 295,633 | −23.12 |
| 76 | Pittsburgh | 412,280 | 316,694 | − 95,586 | −23.18 |
| 77 | Chattanooga | 149,566 | 114,741 | − 34,825 | −23.28 |
| 78 | Norfolk | 215,069 | 162,300 | − 52,769 | −24.54 |
| 79 | Boston | 524,709 | 393,937 | − 130,772 | −24.92 |
| 80 | Dayton | 168,407 | 126,389 | − 42,018 | −24.95 |
| 81 | New Orleans | 321,473 | 236,967 | − 84,506 | −26.29 |
| 82 | Richmond | 143,857 | 104,743 | − 39,114 | −27.19 |
| 83 | Birmingham | 173,911 | 124,730 | − 49,181 | −28.28 |
| 84 | New York | 6,048,841 | 4,293,695 | −1,755,146 | −29.02 |
| 85 | Buffalo | 364,367 | 252,365 | − 112,002 | −30.74 |
| 86 | Rochester | 244,118 | 168,102 | − 76,016 | −31.14 |
| 87 | Chicago | 2,207,767 | 1,490,217 | − 717,550 | −32.50 |
| 88 | Cleveland | 458,084 | 307,264 | − 150,820 | −32.92 |
| 89 | St. Louis | 364,992 | 242,576 | − 122,416 | −33.54 |
| 90 | Flint | 138,065 | 89,647 | − 48.418 | −35.07 |
| 91 | Providence | 161,694 | 102,320 | − 59,374 | −36.72 |
| 92 | Jersey City | 202,813 | 127,699 | − 75,114 | −37.04 |
| 93 | Oakland | 213,512 | 129,690 | − 83,822 | −39.26 |
| 94 | Newark | 168,382 | 101,417 | − 66,965 | −39.77 |
| 95 | Detroit | 837,877 | 413,730 | — 424,147 | −50.62 |

# 53.  White Suburbanites

Whites have significantly higher median incomes than blacks and most other racial groups (Asians excluded). This is an important factor that helps most whites to leave urban residential areas they consider undesirable. Conversely, most blacks are unable to do so. Urbanologist Anthony Downs argues that the concentration of whites in the suburban areas is the result of exclusionary practices in the suburbs. When the minimum lot size is kept high, most blacks are unable to afford to buy property. He deplores the "trickle down" approach to housing, whereby only the deteriorated housing stock in the central city is left to the poor.

Of the 94 relevant suburban areas, 44, or nearly half, are 90 percent or more white; 77, or over four-fifths, are 80 percent or more white.

SOURCES: U.S. Department of Commerce, Bureau of the Census, *1980 Census of Population*. Background information based in part on Anthony Downs, *Opening Up the Suburbs: An Urban Strategy for America* (New Haven: Yale University Press, 1973).

| Rank | Metro Area | Percentage Suburban Population White | Rank | Metro Area | Percentage Suburban Population White | Rank | Metro Area | Percentage Suburban Population White |
|---|---|---|---|---|---|---|---|---|
| 1 | Lincoln | 99.02 | 32 | Detroit | 94.06 | 63 | Tucson | 85.96 |
| 2 | Worcester | 98.88 | 33 | Louisville | 93.69 | 64 | San Diego | 85.89 |
| 3 | Des Moines | 98.44 | 34 | Denver | 93.38 | 65 | Atlanta | 85.42 |
| 4 | Milwaukee | 98.37 | 35 | Lexington-Fayette | 92.65 | 66 | New Orleans | 85.36 |
| 5 | Fort Wayne | 98.35 | 36 | Kansas City, Mo., Kan. | 92.38 | 67 | Anchorage | 85.15 |
| 6 | Indianapolis | 98.32 | 37 | Dallas | 92.14 | 68 | Birmingham | 85.09 |
| 7 | Madison | 98.25 | 37 | Fort Worth | 92.14 | 69 | Riverside | 84.07 |
| 8 | Syracuse | 98.12 | 39 | Cleveland | 91.74 | 70 | Richmond | 83.71 |
| 9 | Providence | 97.87 | 40 | Greensboro | 91.64 | 71 | Corpus Christi | 83.67 |
| 10 | St. Paul | 97.86 | 41 | Nashville-Davidson | 91.53 | 72 | Newark | 83.28 |
| 11 | Salt Lake City | 97.57 | 42 | Oklahoma City | 90.94 | 73 | San Jose | 83.19 |
| 12 | Grand Rapids | 97.44 | 43 | Chicago | 90.76 | 74 | Oakland | 81.09 |
| 13 | Akron | 97.35 | 44 | Philadelphia | 89.82 | 74 | San Francisco | 81.09 |
| 14 | Columbus, Ohio | 97.33 | 45 | Anaheim | 89.62 | 76 | Miami | 80.64 |
| 15 | Chattanooga | 97.17 | 45 | Santa Ana | 89.62 | 77 | Washington, D.C. | 78.47 |
| 16 | Toledo | 97.02 | 47 | Phoenix | 89.40 | 78 | Baton Rouge | 78.33 |
| 17 | Knoxville | 96.87 | 47 | Tacoma | 89.40 | 79 | Memphis | 77.87 |
| 18 | Boston | 96.66 | 49 | Jersey City | 89.24 | 80 | Mobile | 76.77 |
| 19 | Rochester | 96.63 | 50 | Tulsa | 89.19 | 81 | Shreveport | 75.73 |
| 20 | Wichita | 96.55 | 51 | Baltimore | 89.16 | 82 | Fresno | 75.18 |
| 21 | Spokane | 96.53 | 52 | New York | 89.00 | 83 | Jackson | 73.89 |
| 22 | Buffalo | 96.49 | 53 | St. Louis | 88.37 | 84 | Montgomery | 73.31 |
| 23 | Portland, Ore. | 96.01 | 54 | Charlotte | 88.13 | 85 | Huntington Beach | 71.98 |
| 24 | Omaha | 95.84 | 55 | Jacksonville | 88.08 | 85 | Long Beach | 71.98 |
| 25 | Pittsburgh | 95.37 | 56 | Sacramento | 87.98 | 85 | Los Angeles | 71.98 |
| 26 | Cincinnati | 95.11 | 58 | San Antonio | 87.95 | 88 | Albuquerque | 70.29 |
| 27 | St. Petersburg | 94.89 | 58 | Austin | 87.29 | 89 | Norfolk | 66.59 |
| 27 | Tampa | 94.89 | 59 | Colorado Springs | 87.05 | 89 | Virginia Beach | 66.59 |
| 29 | Flint | 94.88 | 60 | Little Rock | 86.87 | 91 | Columbus, Ga. | 60.37 |
| 30 | Seattle | 94.49 | 61 | Houston | 86.32 | 92 | El Paso | 58.23 |
| 31 | Dayton | 94.18 | 62 | Las Vegas | 86.05 | 93 | Honolulu | 37.10 |

# 54. City Blacks

Cities with the highest black populations are in the South or in the industrialized areas of the Northeast. Blacks migrated extensively in the period after the Civil War to the northeastern industrialized centers. They have been the last to take advantage of a general pattern of southwestern and suburban migration. This is due to a number of factors. While migration patterns have in large measure followed movement of industry, the job level of most blacks have been in the blue collar or white collar levels of the more industrialized firms that have remained in the northern regions. Most blacks in urban areas have incomes well below the median income for all Americans. Their disproportionate numbers in the central cities are a factor contributing to the decline of the tax base and therefore to the decreasing ability of cities in the Northeast to maintain and improve their infrastructure and services.

Cities such as Huntington Beach, Lincoln, Salt Lake City and Madison, which are in the upper levels of the income bracket, all have under 3 percent black populations.

SOURCE: U.S. Department of Commerce, Bureau of the Census, *1980 Census of Population: Standard Metropolitan Statistical Areas and Standard Consolidated Statistical Areas: 1980* (October 1981).

| Rank | City | Black Population | Percentage Black |
|---|---|---|---|
| 1 | Washington, D.C. | 448,229 | 70.29 |
| 2 | Atlanta | 282,912 | 66.56 |
| 3 | Detroit | 758,939 | 63.07 |
| 4 | Newark | 191,743 | 58.24 |
| 5 | Birmingham | 158,223 | 55.63 |
| 6 | New Orleans | 308,136 | 55.27 |
| 7 | Baltimore | 431,151 | 54.80 |
| 8 | Richmond | 112,357 | 51.25 |
| 9 | Memphis | 307,702 | 47.61 |
| 10 | Jackson | 95,357 | 47.00 |
| 11 | Oakland | 159,234 | 46.93 |
| 12 | St. Louis | 206,386 | 45.55 |
| 13 | Cleveland | 251,347 | 43.80 |
| 14 | Flint | 66,124 | 41.43 |
| 15 | Shreveport | 84,627 | 41.12 |
| 16 | Chicago | 1,197,000 | 39.83 |
| 17 | Montgomery | 69,765 | 39.16 |
| 18 | Philadelphia | 638,878 | 37.84 |
| 19 | Dayton | 75,031 | 36.85 |
| 20 | Baton Rouge | 80,119 | 36.50 |
| 21 | Mobile | 72,568 | 36.20 |
| 22 | Norfolk | 93,987 | 35.20 |
| 23 | Columbus, Ga. | 57,884 | 34.16 |
| 24 | Cincinnati | 130,467 | 33.89 |
| 25 | Greensboro | 51,373 | 33.01 |
| 26 | Little Rock | 51,091 | 32.24 |
| 27 | Chattanooga | 53,716 | 31.68 |
| 28 | Charlotte | 97,627 | 31.05 |
| 29 | Dallas | 265,594 | 29.38 |
| 30 | Louisville | 84,080 | 28.17 |
| 31 | Jersey City | 61,954 | 27.72 |
| 32 | Houston | 440,257 | 27.62 |
| 33 | Kansas City, Mo. | 122,699 | 27.38 |
| 34 | Buffalo | 95,116 | 26.58 |
| 35 | Rochester | 62,332 | 25.78 |
| 36 | Jacksonville | 137,324 | 25.39 |
| 37 | Tampa | 68,835 | 25.35 |
| 38 | Kansas City, Kan. | 40,826 | 25.34 |
| 39 | New York | 1,784,124 | 25.23 |
| 40 | Miami | 87,110 | 25.11 |
| 41 | Pittsburgh | 101,813 | 24.02 |
| 42 | Nashville-Davidson | 105,942 | 23.25 |
| 43 | Milwaukee | 146,940 | 23.10 |
| 44 | Fort Worth | 87,723 | 22.78 |
| 45 | Akron | 52,719 | 22.23 |
| 46 | Columbus, Ohio | 124,880 | 22.11 |
| 47 | Indianapolis | 152,626 | 21.78 |
| 48 | Boston | 126,229 | 19.69 |
| 49 | Toledo | 61,750 | 17.41 |
| 50 | St. Petersburg | 41,000 | 17.31 |
| 51 | Los Angeles | 505,208 | 17.03 |
| 52 | Syracuse | 26,767 | 15.74 |
| 53 | Grand Rapids | 28,602 | 15.73 |
| 54 | Oklahoma City | 58,702 | 14.56 |
| 55 | Fort Wayne | 25,063 | 14.55 |
| 56 | Knoxville | 25,881 | 14.13 |
| 57 | Sacramento | 36,866 | 13.37 |
| 58 | Lexington-Fayette | 27,121 | 13.28 |
| 59 | Las Vegas | 21,054 | 12.79 |
| 60 | San Francisco | 86,414 | 12.73 |
| 61 | Austin | 42,118 | 12.19 |
| 62 | Omaha | 37,852 | 12.14 |
| 63 | Denver | 59,252 | 12.06 |
| 64 | Providence | 18,546 | 11.83 |
| 65 | Tulsa | 42,594 | 11.80 |
| 66 | Long Beach | 40,732 | 11.27 |
| 67 | Wichita | 30,200 | 10.81 |
| 68 | Yonkers | 20,583 | 10.54 |
| 69 | Virginia Beach | 26,291 | 10.03 |
| 70 | Fresno | 20,665 | 9.47 |
| 70 | Seattle | 46,755 | 9.47 |
| 72 | Tacoma | 14,507 | 9.15 |
| 73 | San Diego | 77,700 | 8.87 |
| 74 | Lubbock | 14,204 | 8.16 |
| 75 | Minneapolis | 28,433 | 7.66 |
| 76 | Portland, Ore. | 27,734 | 7.57 |
| 77 | Riverside | 11,776 | 6.89 |
| 78 | Aurora | 10,889 | 6.87 |
| 79 | Des Moines | 13,054 | 6.83 |
| 80 | Colorado Springs | 11,961 | 5.56 |
| 81 | Anchorage | 9,242 | 5.34 |
| 82 | Corpus Christi | 11,889 | 5.12 |
| 83 | Phoenix | 37,682 | 4.93 |
| 84 | St. Paul | 13,305 | 4.92 |
| 85 | San Jose | 29,157 | 4.58 |
| 86 | Santa Ana | 8,232 | 4.04 |
| 87 | Tucson | 12,301 | 3.72 |
| 88 | El Paso | 13,466 | 3.17 |
| 89 | Arlington, Texas | 4,660 | 2.91 |
| 90 | Worcester | 4,625 | 2.86 |
| 91 | Madison | 4,603 | 2.70 |
| 92 | Albuquerque | 8,361 | 2.52 |
| 93 | Lincoln | 3,444 | 2.00 |
| 94 | Spokane | 2,767 | 1.62 |
| 95 | Salt Lake City | 2,523 | 1.55 |
| 96 | Honolulu | 4,247 | 1.16 |
| 97 | Anaheim | 2,557 | 1.15 |
| 98 | Huntington Beach | 1,218 | .71 |
| 99 | Warren | 297 | .18 |

# 55.  Black Migration

We are interested in differential migration patterns of whites and blacks because whites are wealthier than blacks. Asians alone among nonwhites do as well as whites economically. If whites are moving in, it is usually a sign of prosperity. If they are moving out, it is a sign of decline. On this basis America's largest cities were in a decline in the 1970s. Of the largest 30, 26 saw whites leaving. In 28 cities there was a net influx of whites. They tend to be smaller, sunbelt cities with warm climates, more recreational facilities and more attractive occupational opportunities.

As with any analysis, the deeper one probes, the more complex the interpretation. While the black-white contrast outlined above is generally valid, one must distinguish between poor and middle-class blacks. The blacks that moved to Aurora, Colorado, for example, are probably skilled or professional people attracted by the energy boom in Colorado (a boom that has faded significantly in the early 1980s). On the other hand, the growth of the black populations in most of the older cities is probably attributable primarily to their high birth rates rather than to migration.

Interestingly, the black population grew in all but eight cities. The city where the black population declined most rapidly was St. Louis. The obliteration of the giant Pruitt-Igoe housing project may have contributed to the dispersion of blacks from the city. In the case of Washington, D.C., recent urban renewal projects in southwest Washington and elsewhere have reduced the amount of low-income housing and many of the blacks who used to live in such housing have probably moved to the less expensive residential areas of suburban northern Virginia or southern Maryland.

SOURCE: 1970 and 1980 black population data from the U.S. Census Bureau; calculations by the authors.

| Rank | City | 1970 Black Population | 1980 Black Population | Absolute Change | Percentage Change |
|---|---|---|---|---|---|
| 1 | Aurora | 902 | 10,889 | 9,987 | 1,107.20 |
| 2 | Arlington, Texas | 507 | 4,660 | 4,153 | 819.13 |
| 3 | Anchorage | 2,810 | 9,242 | 6,432 | 228.89 |
| 4 | Long Beach | 18,991 | 48,732 | 29,741 | 156.60 |
| 5 | Warren | 132 | 297 | 165 | 125.00 |
| 6 | El Paso | 7,413 | 13,466 | 6,053 | 81.65 |
| 7 | Madison | 2,607 | 4,603 | 1,996 | 76.56 |
| 8 | Baton Rouge | 46,198 | 80,119 | 33,921 | 73.42 |
| 9 | Honolulu | 2,488 | 4,247 | 1,759 | 70.69 |
| 10 | Colorado Springs | 7,045 | 11,961 | 4,916 | 69.77 |
| 11 | Virginia Beach | 15,693 | 26,291 | 10,598 | 67.53 |
| 12 | San Jose | 17,821 | 29,157 | 11,336 | 63.61 |
| 13 | Riverside | 7,222 | 11,776 | 4,554 | 63.05 |
| 14 | Yonkers | 13,003 | 20,583 | 7,580 | 58.29 |
| 15 | Montgomery | 44,523 | 69,765 | 25,242 | 56.69 |
| 16 | Jackson | 61,063 | 95,357 | 34,294 | 56.16 |
| 17 | Little Rock | 33,074 | 51,091 | 18,017 | 54.47 |
| 18 | Albuquerque | 5,425 | 8,361 | 2,936 | 54.11 |
| 19 | Anaheim | 1,700 | 2,557 | 857 | 50.41 |
| 20 | Minneapolis | 19,005 | 28,433 | 9,428 | 49.60 |
| 21 | Las Vegas | 14,082 | 21,054 | 6,972 | 49.51 |
| 22 | Lexington-Fayette | 18,414 | 27,121 | 8,707 | 47.28 |
| 23 | San Diego | 52,925 | 77,700 | 24,775 | 46.81 |
| 24 | Columbus, Ga. | 40,422 | 57,884 | 17,462 | 43.19 |
| 25 | Lincoln | 2,432 | 3,444 | 1,012 | 41.61 |
| 26 | Austin | 29,816 | 42,118 | 12,302 | 41.25 |
| 27 | Worcester | 3,294 | 4,625 | 1,331 | 40.40 |
| 28 | Milwaukee | 105,088 | 146,940 | 41,852 | 39.82 |
| 29 | Tacoma | 10,407 | 14,507 | 4,100 | 39.39 |
| 30 | Houston | 316,503 | 440,257 | 123,754 | 39.10 |
| 31 | Shreveport | 62,152 | 84,627 | 22,475 | 36.16 |
| 32 | Sacramento | 27,244 | 36,866 | 9,622 | 35.31 |
| 33 | Phoenix | 27,896 | 37,682 | 9,786 | 35.08 |
| 34 | Tucson | 9,179 | 12,301 | 3,122 | 34.01 |
| 35 | Charlotte | 72,972 | 97,627 | 24,655 | 33.78 |
| 36 | Fort Wayne | 18,921 | 25,063 | 6,142 | 32.46 |
| 37 | Fresno | 15,875 | 20,665 | 4,790 | 30.17 |
| 38 | Lubbock | 10,912 | 14,204 | 3,292 | 30.16 |
| 39 | Portland, Ore. | 21,572 | 27,734 | 6,162 | 28.56 |
| 40 | St. Petersburg | 31,911 | 41,000 | 9,089 | 28.48 |

| Rank | City | 1970 Black Population | 1980 Black Population | Absolute Change | Percentage Change |
|---|---|---|---|---|---|
| 41 | Grand Rapids | 22,296 | 28,602 | 6,306 | 28.28 |
| 42 | Spokane | 2,161 | 2,767 | 606 | 28.04 |
| 43 | Oakland | 124,710 | 159,234 | 34,524 | 27.68 |
| 44 | Greensboro | 40,633 | 51,373 | 10,740 | 26.43 |
| 45 | Dallas | 210,238 | 265,594 | 55,356 | 26.33 |
| 46 | Denver | 47,000 | 59,252 | 12,252 | 26.06 |
| 47 | Rochester | 49,647 | 62,332 | 12,685 | 25.55 |
| 48 | Birmingham | 126,388 | 158,223 | 31,835 | 25.19 |
| 49 | Syracuse | 21,383 | 26,767 | 5,384 | 25.17 |
| 50 | Memphis | 245,885 | 307,702 | 61,817 | 25.14 |
| 51 | Columbus, Ohio | 100,000 | 124,980 | 24,980 | 24.98 |
| 52 | Providence | 14,875 | 18,546 | 3,671 | 24.67 |
| 53 | Seattle | 37,868 | 46,755 | 8,887 | 23.46 |
| 54 | Huntington Beach | 990 | 1,218 | 228 | 23.03 |
| 55 | Santa Ana | 6,731 | 8,232 | 1,501 | 22.29 |
| 56 | Flint | 54,237 | 66,124 | 11,887 | 21.91 |
| 57 | St. Paul | 10,930 | 13,305 | 2,375 | 21.72 |
| 58 | Tulsa | 35,262 | 42,594 | 7,332 | 20.79 |
| 59 | Nashville-Davidson | 87,851 | 105,942 | 18,091 | 20.59 |
| 60 | Boston | 104,707 | 126,229 | 21,522 | 20.55 |
| 61 | Chattanooga | 44,693 | 53,716 | 9,023 | 20.18 |
| 62 | Kansas City, Kan. | 34,345 | 40,826 | 6,481 | 18.87 |
| 63 | Oklahoma City | 49,678 | 58,707 | 9,029 | 18.17 |
| 63 | Salt Lake City | 2,135 | 2,523 | 388 | 18.17 |
| 65 | Knoxville | 22,166 | 25,881 | 3,715 | 16.75 |
| 66 | Jacksonville | 117,674 | 137,324 | 19,650 | 16.69 |
| 66 | Toledo | 52,915 | 61,750 | 8,835 | 16.69 |
| 68 | Tampa | 54,720 | 63,835 | 9,115 | 16.65 |
| 69 | New Orleans | 267,294 | 308,136 | 40,842 | 15.27 |
| 70 | Miami | 76,156 | 87,110 | 10,954 | 14.38 |
| 71 | Des Moines | 11,425 | 13,054 | 1,629 | 14.25 |
| 72 | Detroit | 668,428 | 758,939 | 90,511 | 13.54 |
| 73 | Jersey City | 54,595 | 61,954 | 7,359 | 13.47 |
| 74 | Indianapolis | 134,848 | 152,626 | 17,778 | 13.18 |
| 75 | Corpus Christi | 10,526 | 11,889 | 1,363 | 12.94 |
| 76 | Wichita | 26,841 | 30,200 | 3,359 | 12.51 |
| 77 | Fort Worth | 78,324 | 87,723 | 9,399 | 12.00 |
| 78 | Atlanta | 255,051 | 282,912 | 27,861 | 10.92 |
| 79 | Omaha | 34,431 | 37,852 | 3,421 | 9.93 |
| 80 | Kansas City, Mo. | 112,004 | 122,699 | 10,695 | 9.54 |
| 81 | Akron | 48,205 | 52,719 | 4,514 | 9.36 |
| 82 | Chicago | 1,102,620 | 1,197,000 | 94,380 | 8.55 |
| 83 | Mobile | 67,356 | 72,568 | 5,212 | 7.73 |
| 84 | Norfolk | 87,261 | 93,987 | 6,726 | 7.70 |
| 85 | Richmond | 104,766 | 112,357 | 7,591 | 7.24 |
| 86 | New York | 1,668,115 | 1,784,124 | 116,009 | 6.95 |
| 87 | Cincinnati | 125,000 | 130,467 | 5,467 | 4.37 |
| 88 | Baltimore | 420,210 | 431,151 | 10,941 | 2.60 |
| 89 | Dayton | 74,248 | 75,031 | 783 | 1.05 |
| 90 | Buffalo | 94,329 | 95,116 | 787 | .83 |
| 91 | Los Angeles | 503,606 | 505,208 | 1,602 | .31 |
| 92 | Louisville | 86,040 | 84,080 | − 1,960 | − 2.27 |
| 93 | Philadelphia | 653,791 | 638,878 | −14,913 | − 2.28 |
| 94 | Pittsburgh | 104,904 | 101,813 | − 3,091 | − 2.94 |
| 95 | Newark | 207,458 | 191,743 | −15,715 | − 7.57 |
| 96 | San Francisco | 96,078 | 86,414 | − 9,664 | −10.05 |
| 97 | Cleveland | 286,000 | 251,347 | −36,653 | −12.72 |
| 98 | Washington, D.C. | 537,712 | 448,229 | −89,483 | −16.64 |
| 99 | St. Louis | 254,191 | 206,386 | −47,805 | −18.80 |

# 56. Black Married Men

In terms of relative numbers of black men, the places to look are New York, Los Angeles, Washington, D.C. and Baltimore. If we are interested in knowing where married black men are living in terms of relative percentages, then five cities in four states top the list. Four of them are the same cities that top the list of those with the highest proportion of married black women (see next table). The top cities are Colorado Springs, Anchorage, Honolulu, Aurora and Columbus, Georgia. We might interpret these results as indicating that blacks are more likely to have mobility into the middle class in these cities because prejudice against them fades in the face of the multiracial communities in Honolulu and Anchorage; in the face of the strong influence of blacks in Atlanta; and in the face of the progressive attitudes of people moving to the young cities of Colorado Springs and Aurora.

The high rates of unmarried black men in San Francisco, Providence and Boston, on the other hand, are probably simply a reflection of the high student and preprofessional populations in those cities.

SOURCE: Derived from U.S. Census Bureau, *1980 Census of Population: Population Characteristics*, Table 31, State volumes (1981–82).

| Rank | Metro Area | All Black Men | Married Black Men | Percentage Married |
|------|-----------|--------------:|------------------:|-------------------:|
| 1 | Colorado Springs | 2,362 | 4,057 | 58.22 |
| 2 | Honolulu | 1,019 | 1,857 | 54.87 |
| 3 | Anchorage | 1,835 | 3,346 | 54.84 |
| 4 | Aurora | 1,906 | 3,524 | 54.09 |
| 5 | Columbus, Ga. | 8,947 | 16,992 | 52.65 |

| Rank | Metro Area | All Black Men | Married Black Men | Percentage Married |
|------|-----------|--------------:|------------------:|-------------------:|
| 6 | Birmingham | 23,249 | 45,413 | 51.19 |
| 7 | Oklahoma City | 8,604 | 16,866 | 51.01 |
| 8 | Shreveport | 11,136 | 21,874 | 50.91 |
| 9 | Tulsa | 6,108 | 12,053 | 50.68 |
| 10 | Baton Rouge | 11,400 | 22,561 | 50.53 |
| 11 | Riverside | 1,802 | 3,569 | 50.49 |
| 12 | Jackson | 13,013 | 26,309 | 49.46 |
| 13 | Little Rock | 6,669 | 13,531 | 49.29 |
| 14 | Huntington Beach | 219 | 445 | 49.21 |
| 15 | Anaheim | 456 | 927 | 49.19 |
| 16 | Montgomery | 9,212 | 18,781 | 49.05 |
| 17 | Mobile | 9,941 | 20,305 | 48.96 |
| 18 | Kansas City, Kan. | 5,554 | 11,385 | 48.78 |
| 19 | Albuquerque | 1,343 | 2,769 | 48.50 |
| 20 | Charlotte | 12,962 | 27,024 | 47.96 |
| 21 | Yonkers | 2,436 | 5,080 | 47.95 |
| 22 | New Orleans | 39,574 | 83,178 | 47.58 |
| 23 | San Jose | 4,464 | 9,389 | 47.54 |
| 24 | Memphis | 39,593 | 83,546 | 47.39 |
| 25 | Wichita | 4,161 | 8,789 | 47.34 |
| 26 | Tucson | 1,960 | 4,172 | 46.98 |
| 27 | Phoenix | 5,416 | 11,615 | 46.63 |
| 28 | Santa Ana | 1,278 | 2,745 | 46.56 |
| 29 | Sacramento | 5,180 | 11,269 | 45.97 |
| 30 | Greensboro | 6,986 | 15,226 | 45.88 |
| 31 | Fresno | 2,642 | 5,761 | 45.86 |
| 32 | Denver | 8,702 | 19,076 | 45.62 |
| 33 | New York | 215,259 | 475,010 | 45.32 |
| 34 | Las Vegas | 2,679 | 6,082 | 44.05 |
| 35 | Long Beach | 5,143 | 11,950 | 43.04 |
| 36 | Omaha | 4,452 | 10,383 | 42.88 |
| 37 | Atlanta | 34,325 | 80,077 | 42.86 |
| 38 | Oakland | 20,566 | 48,249 | 42.62 |
| 39 | Los Angeles | 62,697 | 152,879 | 41.01 |
| 40 | San Diego | 11,556 | 28,303 | 40.83 |
| 41 | Baltimore | 49,468 | 122,792 | 40.29 |
| 42 | Washington, D.C. | 54,793 | 136,709 | 40.08 |
| 43 | Worcester | 530 | 1,326 | 39.97 |
| 44 | Boston | 13,533 | 35,761 | 37.84 |
| 45 | Providence | 1,893 | 5,062 | 37.40 |
| 46 | San Francisco | 10,952 | 29.318 | 37.36 |
| 47 | Lincoln | 500 | 1,462 | 34.20 |

# 57. Black Married Women

As is the case with black married men, the proportion of women who are married is much lower for black women than for the rest of the population.

The proportion of women 15 and over who are married nationwide is 54.8 percent (23 percent are single; 12.3 percent are widowed; 7.2 percent are divorced; and 2.6 percent are separated). Only in three cities—Honolulu, Anchorage and Colorado Springs—do black women come up to the national average. In all the other cities they are below it. The median rate for black women for the 47 cities for which we have data is 44 percent, over 10 percentage points below the national average.

A substantial number of the unmarried women have children. Of all women with their own children under 18, 35.0 percent of black women were below the poverty level, compared to only 9.2 percent of white women. Approximately the same proportion of such black and white women, 41 percent to 42 percent, worked in 1978. Of the 35 percent of all black women who did not work at all in 1978, 68 percent said it was because they had to be in the home. A slightly lower proportion of black women below the poverty level, 63 percent, gave this reason.

The table below shows that in Honolulu and Anchorage black women will find most other black women are married. The married black woman will find it relatively easy to identify social companions. In New England and Washington, D.C., however, most black women are single. Single black women in these cities will find it relatively easy to find social companions.

SOURCES: U.S. Census Bureau, *1980 Census of Population: Population Characteristics*, Table 31, state volumes 1981–82. Background data from *Sales and Marketing Management* (July 26, 1982), p. A-33; and *Statistical Abstract of the United States* (1980), Table 780, p. 469.

| Rank | Metro Area | All Black Women | Married Black Women | Percentage Married |
|------|-----------|-----------------|---------------------|--------------------|
| 1 | Honolulu | 991 | 635 | 64.08 |
| 2 | Anchorage | 2,547 | 1,488 | 58.42 |
| 3 | Colorado Springs | 3,473 | 1,918 | 55.23 |
| 4 | Columbus, Ga. | 16,528 | 8,782 | 53.13 |
| 5 | Anaheim | 723 | 378 | 52.28 |

| Rank | Metro Area | All Black Women | Married Black Women | Percentage Married |
|------|-----------|-----------------|---------------------|--------------------|
| 6 | Huntington Beach | 334 | 170 | 50.90 |
| 7 | Aurora | 3,326 | 1,629 | 48.98 |
| 8 | Birmingham | 49,041 | 23,294 | 47.50 |
| 9 | Mobile | 21,322 | 9,932 | 46.58 |
| 10 | Tucson | 3,655 | 1,698 | 46.46 |
| 11 | Shreveport | 24,115 | 11,193 | 46.42 |
| 12 | Albuquerque | 2,456 | 1,135 | 46.03 |
| 13 | Riverside | 3,583 | 1,644 | 45.88 |
| 14 | Baton Rouge | 24,801 | 11,347 | 45.75 |
| 15 | Oklahoma City | 18,180 | 8,313 | 45.73 |
| 16 | Tulsa | 12,958 | 5,892 | 45.47 |
| 17 | Phoenix | 10,755 | 4,883 | 45.40 |
| 18 | Jackson | 29,358 | 13,067 | 44.51 |
| 19 | Memphis | 88,889 | 39,439 | 44.37 |
| 20 | Santa Ana | 2,426 | 1,072 | 44.19 |
| 21 | Charlotte | 29,489 | 12,962 | 43.96 |
| 22 | Little Rock | 15,215 | 6,685 | 43.94 |
| 23 | Montgomery | 21,034 | 9,240 | 43.93 |
| 24 | New Orleans | 90,596 | 39,603 | 43.71 |
| 25 | San Jose | 8,772 | 3,813 | 43.47 |
| 26 | San Diego | 21,957 | 9,459 | 43.08 |
| 27 | Wichita | 9,231 | 3,970 | 43.01 |
| 28 | Kansas City, Kan. | 12,851 | 5,510 | 42.88 |
| 29 | Sacramento | 11,065 | 4,682 | 42.31 |
| 30 | Fresno | 5,859 | 2,470 | 42.16 |
| 31 | Denver | 18,692 | 7,791 | 41.68 |
| 32 | Las Vegas | 6,084 | 2,499 | 41.07 |
| 33 | Greensboro | 17,038 | 6,957 | 40.83 |
| 34 | Lincoln | 855 | 345 | 40.35 |
| 35 | New York | 539,984 | 216,493 | 40.09 |
| 36 | Oakland | 50,791 | 19,934 | 39.25 |
| 37 | Atlanta | 86,426 | 33,768 | 39.07 |
| 38 | Long Beach | 11,980 | 4,659 | 38.89 |
| 39 | Yonkers | 6,334 | 2,461 | 38.85 |
| 40 | San Francisco | 26,886 | 10,067 | 37.44 |
| 41 | Baltimore | 131,432 | 49,138 | 37.39 |
| 41 | Los Angeles | 159,124 | 59,489 | 37.39 |
| 43 | Omaha | 11,476 | 4,258 | 37.10 |
| 44 | Washington, D.C. | 145,976 | 53,628 | 36.74 |
| 45 | Worcester | 1,270 | 441 | 34.72 |
| 46 | Boston | 38,667 | 13,318 | 34.44 |
| 47 | Providence | 5,415 | 1,786 | 32.98 |

# 58. Hispanics

The Hispanic population remains predominantly in the southwestern (California, Texas, Arizona, New Mexico, etc.) southeastern (Florida) and northeastern (New York, New Jersey, Connecticut) urban areas of the United States. While most demographic movements within the United States reflect regional and national migration patterns, the Hispanic influx is unique in that it is linked to international labor migration from less developed regions to Western industrialized countries in Western Europe and North America. The migration from Mexico has been primarily to southern California, Texas, Arizona, Colorado and New Mexico; from Puerto Rico primarily to New York, New Jersey and Connecticut; and from Cuba primarily to Florida and the New York metropolitan region.

SOURCE: U.S. Department of Commerce, Bureau of the Census, *1980 Census of Population: Standard Metropolitan Statistical Areas and Standard Consolidated Statistical Areas: 1980*, October 1981.

| Rank | City | Total Hispanic Population | Percentage Hispanic | | Rank | City | Total Hispanic Population | Percentage Hispanic |
|---|---|---|---|---|---|---|---|---|
| 1 | El Paso | 265,819 | 62.51 | | 48 | Oklahoma City | 11,295 | 2.80 |
| 2 | Miami | 194,987 | 56.20 | | 49 | Washington, D.C. | 17,652 | 2.77 |
| 3 | San Antonio | 421,774 | 53.70 | | 50 | Buffalo | 9,499 | 2.65 |
| 4 | Corpus Christi | 108,175 | 46.63 | | 51 | Seattle | 12,646 | 2.56 |
| 5 | Santa Ana | 90,646 | 44.50 | | 52 | Flint | 3,974 | 2.49 |
| 6 | Albuquerque | 112,084 | 33.78 | | 53 | Tacoma | 3,869 | 2.44 |
| 7 | Los Angeles | 815,989 | 27.50 | | 54 | Detroit | 28,970 | 2.41 |
| 8 | Tucson | 82,189 | 24.87 | | 55 | Omaha | 7,304 | 2.34 |
| 9 | Fresno | 51,489 | 23.60 | | 56 | Norfolk | 6,074 | 2.28 |
| 10 | San Jose | 140,574 | 22.08 | | 57 | Fort Wayne | 3,786 | 2.20 |
| 11 | New York | 1,405,957 | 19.88 | | 58 | Portland, Ore. | 7,807 | 2.13 |
| 12 | Lubbock | 32,791 | 18.85 | | 59 | Columbus, Ga. | 3,521 | 2.08 |
| 13 | Austin | 64,766 | 18.75 | | 60 | Virginia Beach | 5,160 | 1.97 |
| 14 | Denver | 91,937 | 18.71 | | 61 | Des Moines | 3,523 | 1.84 |
| 15 | Jersey City | 41,672 | 18.64 | | 62 | Baton Rouge | 3,985 | 1.82 |
| 16 | Newark | 61,254 | 18.60 | | 63 | Jacksonville | 9,775 | 1.81 |
| 17 | Houston | 281,224 | 17.64 | | 64 | St. Petersburg | 4,210 | 1.78 |
| 18 | Anaheim | 38,015 | 17.14 | | 65 | Tulsa | 6,189 | 1.71 |
| 19 | Riverside | 27,604 | 16.15 | | 66 | Syracuse | 2,819 | 1.66 |
| 20 | Phoenix | 115,572 | 15.11 | | 67 | Lincoln | 2,745 | 1.60 |
| 21 | San Diego | 130,610 | 14.92 | | 68 | Spokane | 2,554 | 1.49 |
| 22 | Sacramento | 39,160 | 14.20 | | 69 | Atlanta | 5,842 | 1.37 |
| 23 | Chicago | 422,061 | 14.04 | | 70 | Shreveport | 2,769 | 1.35 |
| 24 | Long Beach | 50,700 | 14.03 | | 71 | Madison | 2,242 | 1.31 |
| 25 | Tampa | 35,982 | 13.25 | | 72 | Minneapolis | 4,684 | 1.26 |
| 26 | Fort Worth | 48,696 | 12.64 | | 73 | St. Louis | 5,531 | 1.22 |
| 27 | Dallas | 111,082 | 12.29 | | 74 | Mobile | 2,265 | 1.13 |
| 28 | San Francisco | 83,373 | 12.28 | | 75 | Charlotte | 3,418 | 1.09 |
| 29 | Oakland | 32,491 | 9.58 | | 76 | Louisville | 2,005 | 1.01 |
| 30 | Colorado Springs | 18,268 | 8.49 | | 76 | Richmond | 2,210 | 1.01 |
| 31 | Las Vegas | 12,787 | 7.77 | | 78 | Baltimore | 7,641 | .97 |
| 32 | Salt Lake City | 12,311 | 7.55 | | 79 | Montgomery | 1,641 | .92 |
| 33 | Boston | 36,068 | 6.41 | | 80 | Indianapolis | 6,145 | .88 |
| 34 | Providence | 9,071 | 5.78 | | 81 | Dayton | 1,748 | .86 |
| 35 | Rochester | 13,153 | 5.44 | | 82 | Little Rock | 1,315 | .83 |
| 36 | Honolulu | 19,127 | 5.24 | | 83 | Columbus, Ohio | 4,651 | .82 |
| 37 | Worcester | 6,877 | 4.25 | | 84 | Memphis | 5,225 | .81 |
| 38 | Milwaukee | 26,111 | 4.10 | | 85 | Nashville-Davidson | 3,627 | .80 |
| 39 | Philadelphia | 65,570 | 3.88 | | 86 | Birmingham | 2,227 | .78 |
| 40 | Wichita | 9,902 | 3.55 | | 86 | Cincinnati | 2,988 | .78 |
| 41 | New Orleans | 19,219 | 3.45 | | 88 | Greensboro | 1,201 | .77 |
| 42 | Kansas City, Mo. | 14,703 | 3.28 | | 88 | Chattanooga | 1,295 | .76 |
| 43 | Grand Rapids | 5,752 | 3.16 | | 90 | Pittsburgh | 3,196 | .75 |
| 44 | Cleveland | 17,772 | 3.10 | | 91 | Jackson | 1,508 | .74 |
| 45 | Anchorage | 5,209 | 3.01 | | 92 | Lexington-Fayette | 1,488 | .73 |
| 45 | Toledo | 10,667 | 3.01 | | 93 | Knoxville | 1,260 | .69 |
| 47 | St. Paul | 7,864 | 2.91 | | 94 | Akron | 1,534 | .65 |

# 59. Asians and Pacific Islanders

Historically, there has been a steady immigration of Asians to the United States. It has become a flood from time to time as a result of wars.

War—especially where the United States was involved—brought Asians to this country as refugees. The Korean and Vietnam Wars are prominent examples. A substantial number of GIs brought war brides home with them. Some of their relatives followed. Public sympathy for the plight of Asian children without parents has resulted in a substantial flow of children to the United States.

Meanwhile the flow of immigrants continues. Traditional small Korean churches are a major source of help to new immigrants from Korea. The most recent flood of immigrants from Southeast Asia because of political tensions and war has become a source of problems for the communities that have been attempting to cope with them.

The largest single concentration of Asians and Pacific Islanders is in Honolulu, where this group numbers 240,000 and represents 65.8 percent of Honolulu's total population. What is more remarkable is that the number in New York, 232,000, is virtually the same. Los Angeles and San Francisco are far behind, although percentage-wise they rank ahead of New York.

Generally Asians and Pacific Islanders have stayed near the oceans. They are mostly located in cities on the two coasts. The fact that these cities have now developed large Asian communities maintains the lure for new immigrants. At the other end of the spectrum, Birmingham has only 793 Asians.

SOURCE: U.S. Department of Commerce, Bureau of the Census, *1980 Census of Population: Standard Metropolitan Statistical Areas and Standard Consolidated Statistical Areas: 1980* (October 1981).

| Rank | City | Total Asian/ Pacific Islander Population | Percentage Asian/ Pacific Islander |
|---|---|---|---|
| 1 | Honolulu | 240,322 | 65.83 |
| 2 | San Francisco | 147,426 | 21.71 |
| 3 | San Jose | 52,448 | 8.24 |
| 4 | Oakland | 26,341 | 7.76 |
| 5 | Seattle | 36,613 | 7.41 |
| 6 | Los Angeles | 196,024 | 6.61 |
| 7 | San Diego | 57,207 | 6.53 |
| 8 | Long Beach | 19,609 | 5.43 |
| 9 | Santa Ana | 10,631 | 5.22 |
| 10 | Jersey City | 9,793 | 4.38 |
| 11 | Anaheim | 8,913 | 4.02 |
| 12 | New York | 231,505 | 3.27 |
| 13 | Tacoma | 4,737 | 2.99 |
| 14 | Portland, Ore. | 10,636 | 2.90 |
| 15 | Fresno | 6,111 | 2.80 |
| 16 | Boston | 15,150 | 2.69 |
| 17 | Norfolk | 7,149 | 2.68 |
| 18 | Virginia Beach | 6,570 | 2.51 |
| 19 | Anchorage | 4,019 | 2.32 |
| 20 | Chicago | 69,191 | 2.30 |
| 21 | Houston | 32,898 | 2.06 |
| 22 | Salt Lake City | 3,329 | 2.04 |
| 23 | Las Vegas | 3,350 | 2.03 |
| 24 | Riverside | 3,391 | 1.98 |
| 25 | Madison | 2,688 | 1.58 |
| 26 | Colorado Springs | 3,144 | 1.46 |
| 27 | Denver | 7,007 | 1.43 |
| 28 | Wichita | 3,895 | 1.39 |
| 29 | Spokane | 2,337 | 1.36 |
| 30 | New Orleans | 7,332 | 1.32 |
| 31 | Minneapolis | 4,104 | 1.11 |
| 32 | Providence | 1,694 | 1.08 |
| 33 | Tucson | 3,523 | 1.07 |
| 34 | Austin | 3,642 | 1.05 |
| 34 | Philadelphia | 17,764 | 1.05 |
| 36 | Washington, D.C. | 6,635 | 1.04 |
| 37 | Columbus, Ga. | 1,740 | 1.03 |
| 37 | Oklahoma City | 4,167 | 1.03 |
| 39 | St. Paul | 2,695 | 1.00 |
| 40 | Lincoln | 1,681 | .98 |
| 41 | Jacksonville | 5,240 | .97 |
| 42 | Albuquerque | 3,162 | .95 |
| 43 | Phoenix | 6,979 | .91 |
| 44 | Lubbock | 1,522 | .87 |
| 45 | Dallas | 7,678 | .85 |
| 46 | Des Moines | 1,596 | .84 |
| 47 | Columbus, Ohio | 4,714 | .83 |
| 47 | El Paso | 3,544 | .83 |
| 49 | Kansas City, Mo. | 3,499 | .78 |
| 49 | Tulsa | 2,813 | .78 |
| 51 | Charlotte | 2,367 | .75 |
| 52 | Baton Rouge | 1,603 | .73 |
| 53 | Newark | 2,366 | .72 |
| 53 | Syracuse | 1,219 | .72 |
| 55 | Tampa | 1,903 | .70 |
| 56 | Lexington-Fayette | 1,360 | .67 |
| 57 | San Antonio | 5,086 | .65 |
| 58 | Rochester | 1,536 | .64 |
| 59 | Baltimore | 4,949 | .63 |
| 60 | Grand Rapids | 1,130 | .62 |
| 61 | Pittsburgh | 2,596 | .61 |
| 61 | Fort Worth | 2,340 | .61 |
| 63 | Knoxville | 1,101 | .60 |
| 63 | Worcester | 974 | .60 |
| 65 | Cleveland | 3,384 | .59 |
| 66 | Cincinnati | 2,216 | .57 |
| 66 | Little Rock | 900 | .57 |
| 66 | Milwaukee | 3,600 | .57 |
| 69 | Omaha | 1,734 | .56 |
| 69 | Sacramento | 1,536 | .56 |
| 71 | Corpus Christi | 1,277 | .55 |
| 71 | Detroit | 6,621 | .55 |
| 73 | Indianapolis | 3,792 | .54 |
| 73 | Miami | 1,861 | .54 |
| 73 | St. Petersburg | 1,272 | .54 |
| 76 | Mobile | 972 | .48 |
| 76 | Nashville | 2,202 | .48 |
| 78 | Atlanta | 2,000 | .47 |
| 78 | Toledo | 1,653 | .47 |
| 80 | Richmond | 976 | .45 |
| 81 | Fort Wayne | 756 | .44 |
| 81 | Greensboro | 680 | .44 |
| 83 | Dayton | 869 | .43 |
| 84 | Memphis | 2,701 | .42 |
| 85 | Flint | 633 | .40 |
| 86 | Montgomery | 688 | .39 |
| 87 | Shreveport | 773 | .38 |
| 88 | Buffalo | 1,322 | .37 |
| 88 | St. Louis | 1,696 | .37 |
| 90 | Akron | 858 | .36 |
| 91 | Chattanooga | 583 | .34 |
| 92 | Jackson | 621 | .31 |
| 92 | Louisville | 931 | .31 |
| 94 | Birmingham | 793 | .28 |

# 60. Amerindians, Eskimos, Aleuts

The races grouped together under the heading "Amerindians, Eskimos and Aleuts" have three things in common: (1) They were indigenous to the United States; (2) they lived off the land or the sea according to their own elaborate customs; and (3) as their traditional livelihood and customs have been destroyed by the advance of civilization, many have moved to cities, where they have sought to adapt themselves to Western ways.

All three of the groups have had difficulty making the double adjustment to city life and to Western culture. They have continued to be an object of concern for urban social agencies. That these groups predated the arrival of the European American adds to the feeling of responsibility such agencies have.

Even though the 48 continental American states were once virtually entirely populated by American Indians, Eskimos and Aleutian Islanders, today their numbers are small. The largest single concentration is in Los Angeles, with 16,595 mostly Amerindians, and this number constitutes barely 0.5 percent of all Los Angeles residents.

Oklahoma cities have the highest proportion of Amerindians. Tulsa and Oklahoma City together have 24,145 Amerindians—3.8 percent of the population of Tulsa and 2.6 percent of the population of Oklahoma City.

The major concentration of Eskimos and Aleutian Islanders is naturally in Anchorage. The 8,900 Arctic Circle inhabitants constitute 5.1 percent of Anchorage's population. The fact that they aren't an even higher percentage is evidence of the growth of Anchorage and perhaps of an aversion to the city on the part of the Eskimos and Aleutian Islanders.

SOURCE: U.S. Department of Commerce, Bureau of the Census, *1980 Census of Population: Standard Metropolitan Statistical Areas and Standard Consolidated Statistical Areas: 1980* (October 1981).

| Rank | City | Total Population Amerindian/ Eskimo/ Aleut | Percentage Amerindian/ Eskimo/ Aleut |
|---|---|---|---|
| 1 | Anchorage | 8,901 | 5.14 |
| 2 | Tulsa | 13,740 | 3.81 |
| 3 | Oklahoma City | 10,405 | 2.58 |
| 4 | Minneapolis | 8,932 | 2.41 |

| Rank | City | Total Population Amerindian/ Eskimo/ Aleut | Percentage Amerindian/ Eskimo/ Aleut |
|---|---|---|---|
| 5 | Albuquerque | 7,341 | 2.21 |
| 6 | Tacoma | 2,895 | 1.83 |
| 7 | Spokane | 2,694 | 1.57 |
| 8 | Phoenix | 10,771 | 1.41 |
| 9 | Tucson | 4,341 | 1.31 |
| 10 | Salt Lake City | 2,116 | 1.30 |
| 11 | Seattle | 6,253 | 1.27 |
| 12 | Sacramento | 3,322 | 1.20 |
| 13 | Riverside | 1,734 | 1.01 |
| 13 | Syracuse | 1,722 | 1.01 |
| 15 | Fresno | 2,097 | .96 |
| 15 | Portland, Ore. | 3,526 | .96 |
| 17 | St. Paul | 2,538 | .94 |
| 18 | Wichita | 2,579 | .92 |
| 19 | Long Beach | 2,982 | .83 |
| 20 | Santa Ana | 1,627 | .80 |
| 21 | Milwaukee | 5,018 | .79 |
| 22 | Denver | 3,847 | .78 |
| 23 | Anaheim | 1,686 | .76 |
| 24 | Grand Rapids | 1,260 | .69 |
| 25 | Providence | 1,048 | .67 |
| 26 | Oakland | 2,199 | .65 |
| 27 | Las Vegas | 1,050 | .64 |
| 28 | Flint | 971 | .61 |
| 29 | San Diego | 5,065 | .58 |
| 29 | San Jose | 3,680 | .58 |
| 31 | Omaha | 1,792 | .57 |
| 32 | Los Angeles | 16,595 | .56 |
| 33 | Lincoln | 922 | .54 |
| 34 | San Francisco | 3,548 | .52 |
| 35 | Colorado Springs | 1,100 | .51 |
| 36 | Greensboro | 768 | .49 |
| 37 | Buffalo | 2,383 | .42 |
| 37 | Rochester | 1,014 | .42 |
| 39 | Dallas | 3,732 | .41 |
| 40 | Kansas City, Mo. | 1,622 | .36 |
| 41 | Charlotte | 1,039 | .33 |
| 41 | Norfolk | 885 | .33 |
| 43 | Fort Worth | 1,227 | .32 |
| 44 | Austin | 1,003 | .29 |
| 44 | Corpus Christi | 924 | .29 |
| 44 | Des Moines | 556 | .29 |
| 44 | El Paso | 1,251 | .29 |
| 48 | Detroit | 3,420 | .28 |
| 49 | Baltimore | 2,108 | .27 |
| 50 | Columbus, Ga. | 421 | .25 |
| 50 | Little Rock | 389 | .25 |
| 50 | Madison | 425 | .25 |
| 50 | Worcester | 399 | .25 |
| 54 | Lubbock | 423 | .24 |
| 54 | Virginia Beach | 633 | .24 |
| 56 | Boston | 1,302 | .23 |
| 56 | San Antonio | 1,782 | .23 |
| 58 | Jacksonville | 1,198 | .22 |
| 59 | Honolulu | 779 | .21 |
| 60 | Chicago | 6,072 | .20 |
| 60 | Fort Wayne | 353 | .20 |
| 60 | Houston | 3,228 | .20 |
| 60 | Tampa | 545 | .20 |
| 64 | Cleveland | 1,094 | .19 |

| Rank | City | Total Population Amerindian/ Eskimo/ Aleut | Percentage Amerindian/ Eskimo/ Aleut |
|------|------|-------------------------------------------|--------------------------------------|
| 64 | Toledo | 661 | .19 |
| 66 | Mobile | 368 | .18 |
| 67 | Newark | 551 | .17 |
| 67 | New York | 11,824 | .17 |
| 69 | Akron | 368 | .16 |
| 69 | Columbus, Ohio | 924 | .16 |
| 69 | Richmond | 357 | .16 |
| 69 | Washington, D.C. | 1,031 | .16 |
| 73 | Dayton | 300 | .15 |
| 73 | Knoxville | 283 | .15 |
| 75 | Indianapolis | 994 | .14 |
| 75 | Philadelphia | 2,235 | .14 |
| 75 | St. Louis | 642 | .14 |
| 75 | St. Petersburg | 331 | .14 |
| 75 | Shreveport | 292 | .14 |

| Rank | City | Total Population Amerindian/ Eskimo/ Aleut | Percentage Amerindian/ Eskimo/ Aleut |
|------|------|-------------------------------------------|--------------------------------------|
| 80 | Baton Rouge | 288 | .13 |
| 81 | Jersey City | 261 | .12 |
| 81 | Nashville | 529 | .12 |
| 83 | Chattanooga | 182 | .11 |
| 83 | Cincinnati | 425 | .11 |
| 83 | Lexington-Fayette | 225 | .11 |
| 83 | Louisville | 336 | .11 |
| 83 | Montgomery | 188 | .11 |
| 83 | Pittsburgh | 482 | .11 |
| 89 | Atlanta | 422 | .10 |
| 90 | Miami | 329 | .09 |
| 90 | New Orleans | 524 | .09 |
| 92 | Memphis | 530 | .08 |
| 93 | Birmingham | 185 | .07 |
| 93 | Jackson | 142 | .07 |

# 61. Foreign Born

Cities with larger proportions of foreign-born populations frequently are those that were entry points for immigrant populations during the turn of the century and after World War II.

Of the top 10 metro areas with foreign-born populations, 9 have boundaries with the Atlantic or Pacific Ocean. Slightly over 35 percent of Miami's population is foreign born, primarily due to the large entrepreneurial Cuban community, which settled in the region after the Cuban revolution and which periodically continues to migrate from Cuba. New York seems to accommodate a larger proportion of European emigres (mainly those migrating to the area after World War II). There is also a large Chinese, Greek and Italian-born population in New York. California cities such as Los Angeles and San Francisco have large Mexican-born populations as well as sizable numbers of Chinese and Philippine aliens.

During the 20 years 1960–80 the largest single source of new immigrants nationwide has been Italy. The next four largest sources of new immigrants are Germany, Canada, Mexico and the United Kingdom.

The country's immigration policies, which favor Europeans, do seem to be maintaining a higher level of immigration from Europe than from Asia or Latin America, although from the perspective of someone living in California, the immigration seems to come primarily from the less developed countries.

The national average of foreign-born Americans was 19 percent in 1960 and 16.5 percent in 1970. The Miami metro area in 1980 therefore had over double (35 percent) the national average of foreign-born individuals. Miami has had to absorb a large flood of immigrants from Cuba and other Caribbean islands.

The next largest proportion of foreign-born residents is in the Los Angeles metro area, where 23 percent were foreign-born—probably mostly Asian and Mexican. New York was in third place, with 21 percent foreign-born.

Indianapolis showed the lowest proportion of foreign-born Americans—less than 2 percent.

SOURCE: U.S. Department of Commerce, Bureau of the Census, *1980 Census of Population: Supplementary Report: Provisional Estimates of Social, Economic and Housing Characteristics* (March 1982).

| Rank | Metro Area | Total Foreign-Born Population | Percentage Foreign-Born |
|------|-----------|------------------------------|-------------------------|
| 1 | Miami | 573,898 | 35.30 |
| 2 | Los Angeles-Long Beach | 1,614,105 | 22.68 |
| 3 | New York | 1,898,765 | 20.82 |
| 4 | San Francisco-Oakland | 514,341 | 15.82 |
| 5 | Anaheim | 248,475 | 15.47 |
| 6 | San Jose | 166,531 | 12.86 |
| 7 | San Diego | 228,802 | 12.29 |
| 8 | Newark | 231,338 | 11.77 |

| Rank | Metro Area | Total Foreign-Born Population | Percentage Foreign-Born |
|---|---|---|---|
| 9 | Chicago | 764,516 | 10.76 |
| 10 | Boston | 286,065 | 10.35 |
| 11 | Riverside | 136,058 | 10.06 |
| 12 | Washington, D.C. | 252,748 | 7.63 |
| 13 | Sacramento | 76,597 | 7.55 |
| 14 | Houston | 217,214 | 7.48 |
| 15 | Seattle | 119,950 | 7.46 |
| 16 | San Antonio | 73,666 | 6.87 |
| 17 | Tampa-St. Petersburg | 109,535 | 6.53 |
| 18 | Detroit | 280,228 | 6.44 |
| 19 | Philadelphia | 270,118 | 5.73 |
| 20 | Cleveland | 106,937 | 5.63 |
| 21 | Phoenix | 84,036 | 5.57 |
| 22 | Buffalo | 67,771 | 5.45 |

| Rank | Metro Area | Total Foreign-Born Population | Percentage Foreign-Born |
|---|---|---|---|
| 23 | Portland, Ore. | 59,605 | 4.80 |
| 24 | Dallas-Fort Worth | 123,757 | 4.78 |
| 25 | Denver | 71,841 | 4.65 |
| 26 | Milwaukee | 56,793 | 4.08 |
| 27 | Minneapolis-St. Paul | 70,533 | 3.83 |
| 28 | Baltimore | 66,913 | 3.81 |
| 29 | New Orleans | 44,253 | 3.73 |
| 30 | Pittsburgh | 76,954 | 3.40 |
| 31 | Columbus, Ohio | 30,112 | 2.75 |
| 32 | Atlanta | 49,145 | 2.42 |
| 33 | Kansas City, Mo., Kan. | 29,897 | 2.25 |
| 34 | St. Louis | 50,216 | 2.13 |
| 35 | Cincinnati | 26,302 | 1.88 |
| 36 | Indianapolis | 19,363 | 1.66 |

# 62. "Other" Married Men

The table below shows the proportion of men 15 and over classified by the U.S. Census as neither black nor white who are married. The percentage of "other" men married reflects both the tendency of people in certain minorities to marry as well as the availability of women in the area.

Factors which contribute to a larger or lower marriage ratio among "other" men in a given city are social conventions, housing availability, and entertainment facilities.

At the top of the range of ratios, between 41 percent and 94 percent, are Fresno and Yonkers with about 94 and 60 percent married. At the low end of the range are Atlanta and Washington, D.C., with about 41 percent married. Fresno has less than 22 percent population single (see Table 38 above), while Washington, D.C. (ranking 2nd) and Atlanta (6th) are among the major single centers in America. Most "other" minorities such as Asians, Pacific Islanders, Amerindians, Eskimos and Aleuts therefore show a propensity to follow the general trend in the city.

The fact that under 11,000 "other" women in Fresno are married (see Table 63) suggests a high degree of interracial marriage on the part of "other" men in the city.

SOURCE: U.S. Department of Commerce, Bureau of the Census, *1980 Census of Population: Supplementary Report: Provisional Estimates of Social, Economic and Housing Characteristics* (March, 1982).

| Rank | Metro Area | All "Other" Married Men (15 Years and over) | "Other" Men (15 Years and over) | Percentage Married |
|---|---|---|---|---|
| 1 | Atlanta | 3,488 | 1,427 | 40.91 |
| 2 | Washington, D.C. | 10,274 | 4,221 | 41.08 |
| 3 | Baton Rouge | 2,840 | 1,261 | 44.40 |
| 4 | Boston | 19,404 | 8,628 | 44.47 |
| 4 | Worcester | 2,426 | 1,079 | 44.48 |
| 6 | Lincoln | 2,185 | 981 | 44.90 |
| 7 | Buffalo | 4,445 | 2,003 | 45.06 |
| 8 | Jackson | 934 | 430 | 46.04 |
| 9 | Anchorage | 5,691 | 2,766 | 48.60 |
| 10 | Omaha | 3,696 | 1,822 | 49.30 |
| 11 | Baltimore | 5,645 | 2,815 | 49.87 |
| 12 | Providence | 4,710 | 2,379 | 50.51 |
| 13 | Columbus, Ga. | 2,223 | 1,137 | 51.15 |
| 14 | Oakland | 22,748 | 11,684 | 51.36 |
| 15 | San Francisco | 88,208 | 45,380 | 51.45 |
| 16 | Denver | 34,611 | 17,953 | 51.87 |
| 17 | New Orleans | 9,404 | 4,904 | 52.15 |
| 18 | San Diego | 66,469 | 35,207 | 52.97 |
| 19 | Los Angeles | 358,455 | 190,374 | 53.11 |
| 20 | Sacramento | 23,262 | 12,367 | 53.16 |
| 21 | Long Beach | 26,052 | 13,883 | 53.29 |
| 22 | Mobile | 1,399 | 755 | 53.97 |
| 23 | Greensboro | 1,039 | 563 | 54.19 |
| 23 | Wichita | 5,847 | 3,168 | 54.18 |
| 25 | Albuquerque | 40,612 | 22,013 | 54.20 |
| 26 | Memphis | 3,455 | 1,874 | 54.24 |
| 27 | New York | 522,240 | 283,512 | 54.29 |
| 28 | Huntington Beach | 8,304 | 4,555 | 54.85 |
| 29 | Tulsa | 8,301 | 4,573 | 55.09 |
| 30 | Las Vegas | 5,956 | 3,294 | 55.31 |
| 31 | Tucson | 28,888 | 16,012 | 55.43 |
| 32 | Phoenix | 42,019 | 23,311 | 55.48 |
| 33 | Honolulu | 97,622 | 54,261 | 55.58 |
| 34 | Santa Ana | 35,831 | 19,944 | 55.66 |
| 35 | Oklahoma City | 9,182 | 5,123 | 55.79 |

| Rank | Metro Area | All "Other" Married Men (15 Years and over) | "Other" Men (15 Years and over) | Percentage Married |
|---|---|---|---|---|
| 36 | Birmingham | 1,086 | 611 | 56.26 |
| 37 | San Jose | 65,559 | 36,995 | 56.43 |
| 38 | Charlotte | 2,675 | 1,516 | 56.67 |
| 39 | Anaheim | 17,230 | 9,805 | 56.91 |
| 40 | Shreveport | 1,204 | 689 | 57.23 |
| 41 | Colorado Springs | 7,218 | 4,186 | 58.00 |
| 42 | Montgomery | 833 | 486 | 58.34 |

| Rank | Metro Area | All "Other" Married Men (15 Years and over) | "Other" Men (15 Years and over) | Percentage Married |
|---|---|---|---|---|
| 43 | Riverside | 10,602 | 6,187 | 58.36 |
| 44 | Aurora | 4,089 | 2,420 | 59.18 |
| 45 | Little Rock | 994 | 595 | 59.86 |
| 46 | Yonkers | 6,411 | 3,863 | 60.26 |
| 47 | Kansas City, Kan. | 3,150 | 1,821 | 84.70 |
| 48 | Fresno | 18,787 | 17,748 | 94.47 |

# 63. "Other" Married Women

More women in the "other" category (neither black nor white) are married than men. That may reflect the fact that they are heavily outnumbered—the result in part of U.S. immigration policies that, in effect, given the opportunities for education overseas, favor men.

The smallest proportion of "other" women who are married is in Washington, D.C. The explanation for this may be the fact that many of the 11,000 or so"other" women are in Washington because they have had diplomatic connections or are students. The Census counts aliens with "green cards" (meaning they are allowed to work in the United States) and alien students who have their residence in the United States.

The low proportion of "other"married women in cities like Worcester or Buffalo may be explained by the fact that there are many single people in these two cities (see Table 38 above; they both rank in the top 10 cities for singles), and that "other" residents follow the same prevailing social patterns and respond to the same pressures.

The city with the highest proportion of married women to all "other" women is Columbus, Georgia, which is also low in the table on singles.

SOURCE: U.S. Department of Commerce, Bureau of the Census, *1980 Census of Population: Population Characteristics*, State Volumes, 1981–82.

| Rank | Metro Area | All "Other" Women (15 years and over) | "Other" Married Women | Percentage Married |
|---|---|---|---|---|
| 1 | Washington, D.C. | 11,307 | 4,391 | 38.83 |
| 2 | Worcester | 2,363 | 1,064 | 45.03 |
| 3 | Buffalo | 4,192 | 1,900 | 45.32 |
| 4 | Boston | 18,096 | 8,617 | 47.62 |
| 5 | Atlanta | 2,824 | 1,353 | 47.91 |
| 6 | Baltimore | 5,268 | 2,667 | 50.63 |
| 7 | Providence | 4,552 | 2,342 | 51.45 |
| 8 | Lincoln | 1,770 | 922 | 52.09 |
| 9 | New York | 545,191 | 285,967 | 52.45 |
| 10 | Omaha | 3,454 | 1,828 | 52.92 |
| 11 | New Orleans | 8,966 | 4,795 | 53.46 |
| 12 | Baton Rouge | 2,137 | 1,163 | 54.42 |
| 13 | Birmingham | 1,132 | 618 | 54.59 |
| 14 | San Francisco | 84,090 | 46,310 | 55.07 |
| 15 | Denver | 32,545 | 18,056 | 55.48 |
| 16 | Jackson | 808 | 449 | 55.57 |
| 17 | Albuquerque | 42,113 | 23,417 | 55.61 |
| 18 | Fresno | 18,608 | 10,479 | 56.31 |
| 19 | Shreveport | 1,371 | 775 | 56.53 |
| 20 | Oakland | 20,908 | 11,822 | 56.54 |
| 21 | Los Angeles | 328,649 | 186,153 | 56.64 |
| 22 | Sacramento | 21,946 | 12,510 | 57.00 |
| 23 | Tucson | 29,296 | 16,785 | 57.29 |
| 24 | Honolulu | 96,538 | 55,969 | 57.98 |
| 25 | Kansas City, Kan. | 3,030 | 1,763 | 58.18 |
| 26 | Little Rock | 1,050 | 613 | 58.38 |
| 27 | Phoenix | 40,359 | 23,806 | 58.99 |
| 28 | Yonkers | 6,803 | 4,024 | 59.15 |
| 29 | Greensboro | 897 | 532 | 59.31 |
| 30 | Anchorage | 6,552 | 3,907 | 59.63 |
| 31 | San Jose | 62,001 | 37,306 | 60.17 |

| Rank | Metro Area | All "Other" Women (15 years and over) | "Other" Married Women | Percentage Married | Rank | Metro Area | All "Other" Women (15 years and over) | "Other" Married Women | Percentage Married |
|------|-----------|--------|--------|--------|------|-----------|--------|--------|--------|
| 32 | Mobile | 1,276 | 774 | 60.66 | 41 | Las Vegas | 5,743 | 3,595 | 62.60 |
| 33 | Long Beach | 23,017 | 13,968 | 60.69 | 41 | Santa Ana | 29,695 | 18,592 | 62.61 |
| 34 | Memphis | 3,434 | 2,090 | 60.86 | 43 | Anaheim | 15,014 | 9,435 | 62.84 |
| 35 | Riverside | 10,340 | 6,314 | 61.06 | 44 | Charlotte | 2,313 | 1,474 | 63.73 |
| 36 | San Diego | 61,340 | 37,473 | 61.09 | 45 | Colorado Springs | 7,829 | 5,057 | 64.59 |
| 37 | Tulsa | 7,598 | 4,645 | 61.13 | 46 | Montgomery | 925 | 602 | 65.08 |
| 38 | Huntington Beach | 7,936 | 4,859 | 61.23 | 47 | Aurora | 4,327 | 2,829 | 65.38 |
| 39 | Oklahoma City | 8,374 | 5,233 | 62.49 | 48 | Columbus, Ga. | 2,002 | 1,491 | 74.40 |
| 40 | Wichita | 5,114 | 3,197 | 62.51 | | | | | |

# CHAPTER FOUR

# Religion

Religion has played a crucial part in American history. The original settlers came to the American Colonies in search of religious freedom, and the Thanksgiving holiday is in large part a reminder of the religious origins of the nation.

The growth of the United States has seen waves of migrations that were religiously motivated. After the Puritans and the Huguenots came the Jews and the Irish to the eastern seaboard, seeking not only a better material life but also the ability to practise their religion without interference. Scandinavian and German Lutherans tended to migrate directly to the Middlewest.

Although the importation of blacks into the South to work on plantations did not have a religious origin, slavery was ended through the intervention of a religiously based movement—abolitionism, which had its second wave in the civil rights movement. The revival of religion in the United States in the 1970s, notably under the banner of the Moral Majority, has taken the form of opposition to abortion. Some view this as an echo of the repudiated religious movement of Prohibition, others as a reassertion of the rights of unborn children.

The data on religion by city in the tables that follow are taken primarily from two surveys in 1971 and 1980 prepared by the Glenmary Center for the National Council of Churches. They are derived from county data and have been combined into metropolitan area figures by the authors. In three cities—Boston, Worcester and Providence—the metro areas do not coincide exactly with county lines, so that whole counties were assigned to the metro areas with which they were most closely associated. For these three cities, the data are for an area larger than the official standard metropolitan statistical area. The Worcester metro area includes all of Worcester County. The Providence metro area includes all of Rhode Island plus Bristol County, Massachusetts. (The same procedure was followed for the chapter on voting

records for the 1976 and 1980 elections, for which county data were again the only information available.)

The data below are usually reported by the county of congregation rather than place of residence. There were no Mormons identified as living in Washington, D.C. proper in 1980 whereas there were many in 1971, because the Mormon Tabernacle was moved to a suburban (Maryland) location during the period.

The data below for 1980 represent over four-fifths of all Christians and a substantial portion of practicing Jews (Orthodox and Hasidic Jews excluded).

The major omissions are some Eastern Orthodox churches and some primarily black churches (mostly Baptist and Methodist churches that didn't provide data). The data should be viewed as providing a rough idea of membership; due account should be taken of the difficulty of keeping track of church adherents. Christian Scientists, for example, are by their By-Laws expressly forbidden from enumerating their members.*

The Glenmary Center data represent the results of surveys in 1980 and 1971 sponsored by the Department of Records and Research of the African Methodist Episcopal Zion Church; the Research Services Department of the Sunday School Board of the Southern Baptist Convention; the Office of Research, Evaluation and Planning of the National Council of Churches of Christ in the U.S.A.; the Lutheran Council in the U.S.A.; the Department of Research and Statistics of the Lutheran Church —Missouri Synod; and the Glenmary Research Center.

The 1980 information was reported by 111 church bodies who participated in the survey cited above, with 112.54 million adherents. The authors have also obtained

---

*Letter to the authors of November 16, 1982, from Mrs. Ruth Elizabeth Jenks, Clerk of the Mother Church, The First Church of Christ, Scientist, Boston.

independent information from the Buddhist Churches of America, which were not in the survey. The trend data use the 1971 survey, which included information submitted by 53 church bodies with a combined membership of 100.81 million.

Information on religious affiliation is based on "adherents" rather than "members." That is, it includes family members and regular participants even if they are not fully members by being baptized or confirmed.

For space reasons, we could not show each of the 112 churches in a table by itself. Therefore, religious groups were selected and grouped in the tables which follow according to the following principles:

1. All three major non-Protestant Judaeo-Christian religious groups: Reform Jews, Conservative Jews and Roman Catholics.
2. Protestant churches which dominate multiple counties: Baptist, Methodist, Lutheran, Latter-Day Saints, Churches of Christ.
3. Other Fundamentalist Protestant churches that have shown rapid growth in certain areas of the country: Brethren, Reformed, Churches of God, Pentecostals.
4. Other Highly Independent Protestant churches with many adherents: Adventist, Mennonite.
5. One non-Judaeo-Christian church, the Buddhists, to exemplify Eastern religions that have grown rapidly in adherents during the 1970s, and are likely to grow further in the 1980s with the influx of Asians.

6. All other religious groups in the Glenmary Survey. A number of influential churches are combined in this table because they have relatively few adherents.

The tables on Protestant churches are shown in order of the relative number of their adherents—i.e., the proportion of residents who adhere to each denomination, in the metro area where the denomination has its highest concentration of adherents.

In addition to caveats already cited, special care should be taken in interpreting the trend information provided where comparative data are available for 1971 and 1980 for two reasons:

1. The trends are calculated in terms of the change in metro church adherents relative to the metro population. If the metro area showed a decline and church membership showed a decline, the sign would be positive. If both showed an increase, the sign would again be positive. If, however, the church membership went the opposite direction from the population change, there will be a negative sign.
2. The 1980 survey included more Protestant denominations than the 1971 survey. For example, the 1971 survey did not include the Baptist General Conference, whereas the 1980 survey did. Detailed information on the surveys may be found in the sources cited below the first table for each church group.

# 64. Reform Jews

Figures on Jews vary considerably depending on the source and the purpose. Jews themselves traditionally count as Jews those who have Jewish mothers. Some Jewish denominations, such as Hasidic Jews, are opposed to providing data on their membership, having seen historically how the information has been used to identify and persecute their people. Jews continue to live primarily in cities, where they pursue—out of all proportion to their numbers—their traditional livelihoods in commerce, finance and the professions.

The broadest definition of Jewishness is ethnic rather than religious. Using this definition, based on estimates of secular Jewish organizations rather than syn-

agogue or temple membership rolls, the cities with the largest Jewish populations are greater New York City, with 2.0 million, of which 1.2 million are in New York City proper; Los Angeles metro, with 503,000; Chicago metro, with 253,000; Miami metro, with 225,000; and Boston metro, with 170,000. No other city has as many as 100,000 Jews.

An oft-cited statistic is that there are more Jews in New York City than in Tel Aviv. The fact is, there are more Jews in Brooklyn alone, or Los Angeles, than in Tel Aviv. There are 50 percent more Jews in New York City proper than Tel Aviv, Jerusalem and Haifa combined.

Looking at religious adherents, we get an entirely

different picture. The percentage of Jews that actually attend a temple or synagogue is a small fraction of the above numbers.

Apart from the data on ethnic Jews, the only published information is on Conservative and Reform Jews. Adding up what we might call "practising" Jews from both of these two major groups, only two metro areas had more than 1 Jew per 100 residents in 1980—New York and Miami.

As one would expect, Reform Jews are most in evidence in the New York metro area, where over 10 of every 1,000 people are adherents, for a total of nearly 96,000 people. Five other cities—Cleveland, Miami, Baltimore, Boston and St. Louis—have more than 5 per thousand. Five metro areas have no reform Jews: Columbus, Georgia and Columbus, Ohio; Little Rock; Norfolk; and Spokane.

No trend information is provided below for Reform Jews because comparable data for years prior to 1980 are not available.

SOURCES: Metro religious adherence data for 1980 derived by the authors from county data in Bernard Quinn, Herman Anderson, Martin Bradley, Paul Goetting and Peggy Shriver, *Churches and Church Membership in the United States, 1980: An Enumeration by Region, State and County Based on Data Reported by 111 Church Bodies* (Atlanta: Glenmary Research Center, 1982). Metro population data for 1980 derived by the authors from county data in Hana Umlauf Lane, Ed., *The World Almanac & Book of Facts 1983* (New York: Newspaper Enterprise Association, Inc., 1981), pp. 246–263.

| Rank | Metro Area | Reform Jews | Reform Jews per 1,000 Population |
|---|---|---|---|
| 1 | New York | 95,788 | 10.50 |
| 2 | Cleveland | 15,381 | 8.10 |
| 3 | Miami | 12,946 | 7.96 |
| 4 | Baltimore | 13,702 | 6.30 |
| 5 | Boston | 20,902 | 5.71 |
| 6 | St. Louis | 13,319 | 5.65 |
| 7 | San Francisco | 16,040 | 4.93 |
| 8 | Cincinnati | 6,673 | 4.83 |
| 9 | Worcester | 3,071 | 4.75 |
| 10 | Buffalo | 5,448 | 4.38 |
| 11 | New Orleans | 5,101 | 4.30 |
| 12 | Milwaukee | 5,724 | 4.10 |
| 13 | Washington, D.C. | 12,466 | 4.07 |
| 14 | Tucson | 2,069 | 3.89 |

| Rank | Metro Area | Reform Jews | Reform Jews per 1,000 Population |
|---|---|---|---|
| 15 | Chicago | 27,271 | 3.84 |
| 15 | Memphis | 3,509 | 3.84 |
| 17 | Pittsburgh | 8,144 | 3.60 |
| 18 | Los Angeles | 26,720 | 3.57 |
| 19 | Kansas City, Mo., Kan. | 4,679 | 3.52 |
| 19 | Rochester | 3,436 | 3.54 |
| 21 | Madison | 1,091 | 3.37 |
| 22 | Providence | 3,172 | 3.35 |
| 23 | Phoenix | 5,004 | 3.32 |
| 24 | Dayton | 2,504 | 3.02 |
| 25 | Denver | 4,594 | 2.84 |
| 26 | Syracuse | 1,816 | 2.81 |
| 27 | Omaha | 1,599 | 2.80 |
| 28 | Philadelphia | 12,928 | 2.74 |
| 29 | Seattle | 4,332 | 2.70 |
| 30 | Akron | 1,776 | 2.69 |
| 30 | Richmond | 1,703 | 2.69 |
| 32 | Minneapolis-St. Paul | 5,591 | 2.64 |
| 33 | Houston | 7,456 | 2.57 |
| 34 | Atlanta | 5,167 | 2.55 |
| 35 | Louisville | 2,280 | 2.52 |
| 36 | Dallas | 7,444 | 2.50 |
| 37 | Tampa | 3,881 | 2.47 |
| 38 | Montgomery | 654 | 2.40 |
| 39 | Detroit | 10,351 | 2.38 |
| 39 | El Paso | 1,143 | 2.38 |
| 41 | San Antonio | 2,419 | 2.26 |
| 42 | Shreveport | 847 | 2.25 |
| 43 | Riverside | 3,436 | 2.21 |
| 44 | Toledo | 1,744 | 2.20 |
| 45 | Albuquerque | 924 | 2.03 |
| 46 | Indianapolis | 2,337 | 2.00 |
| 47 | Des Moines | 669 | 1.98 |
| 48 | Nashville | 1,667 | 1.96 |
| 49 | Jersey City | 1,082 | 1.94 |
| 50 | Birmingham | 1,623 | 1.92 |
| 51 | Anaheim | 3,693 | 1.91 |
| 51 | Lexington-Fayette | 608 | 1.91 |
| 53 | San Diego | 3,493 | 1.88 |
| 54 | Baton Rouge | 900 | 1.86 |
| 54 | Jacksonville | 1,374 | 1.86 |
| 56 | Tulsa | 1,259 | 1.83 |
| 57 | Portland, Ore. | 2,158 | 1.74 |
| 58 | Fort Wayne | 647 | 1.69 |
| 59 | Anchorage | 287 | 1.66 |
| 59 | Jackson | 523 | 1.66 |
| 61 | Corpus Christi | 501 | 1.54 |
| 62 | Austin | 753 | 1.40 |
| 63 | Charlotte | 872 | 1.37 |
| 64 | Las Vegas | 621 | 1.34 |
| 65 | Mobile | 576 | 1.30 |
| 66 | Chattanooga | 533 | 1.25 |
| 67 | Colorado Springs | 386 | 1.22 |
| 68 | Greensboro | 1000 | 1.21 |
| 69 | Flint | 624 | 1.20 |
| 70 | Wichita | 491 | 1.19 |
| 71 | Fresno | 608 | 1.18 |
| 71 | Tacoma | 573 | 1.18 |
| 73 | Honolulu | 874 | 1.15 |
| 74 | Oklahoma City | 935 | 1.12 |
| 75 | Salt Lake City | 1,017 | 1.09 |
| 76 | Grand Rapids | 621 | 1.03 |
| 77 | Sacramento | 1,025 | 1.01 |

# 65. Conservative Jews

Conservative Jews are closer to strictly observant Ortho-dox Judaism than are Reform Jews. It can generally be said that the less rigorous Jewish denominations have obtained more adherents. Hence, the Conservative tem-ples have fewer adherents than the Reform temples. In New York City there are about 6 adherents to Conser-vative Judaism per 1,000 population, versus 10 adherents to Reform Judaism. Miami shows 3 and 8 per 1,000, respectively. Only 22 metro areas have more than 1 Con-servative Jew per 1,000 residents.

Eight metro areas have no Conservative Jews, i.e. no Conservative congregations. Another 20 have fewer than 500 Conservative Jews in total and also fewer than

SOURCES: Metro religious adherence data for 1980 de-rived by the authors from county data in Bernard Quinn, Herman Anderson, Martin Bradley, Paul Goetting and Peggy Shriver, *Churches and Church Membership in the United States, 1980: An Enumeration by Region, State and County Based on Data Reported by 111 Church Bodies* (Atlanta: Glenmary Research Center, 1982). Me-tro population data for 1980 derived by the authors from county data in Hana Umlauf Lane, Ed., *The World Al-manac & Book of Facts 1983* (New York: Newspaper Enterprise Association, Inc., 1981), pp. 246–263.

0.45 Conservative Jews per 1,000 residents and are not shown in the table below.

No trend information is provided below for Conser-vative Jews because comparable information for years prior to 1980 is not available.

| Rank | Metro Area | Conservative Jews | Conservative Jews per 1,000 Population |
|---|---|---|---|
| 1 | New York | 57,013 | 6.25 |
| 2 | Miami | 5,540 | 3.41 |
| 3 | Boston | 12,358 | 3.37 |
| 4 | Philadelphia | 14,381 | 3.05 |
| 5 | Washington, D.C. | 7,909 | 2.58 |
| 6 | Providence | 2,084 | 2.20 |
| 7 | Buffalo | 2,544 | 2.05 |
| 8 | Syracuse | 1,221 | 1.89 |
| 9 | Rochester | 1,738 | 1.79 |
| 10 | Baltimore | 3,719 | 1.71 |
| 11 | Cleveland | 3,206 | 1.69 |
| 12 | Houston | 4,504 | 1.55 |
| 13 | Pittsburgh | 3,346 | 1.48 |
| 14 | Jacksonville | 1,041 | 1.41 |
| 15 | Chicago | 9,444 | 1.33 |
| 16 | Los Angeles | 9,868 | 1.32 |
| 17 | Richmond | 800 | 1.27 |
| 18 | Detroit | 5,481 | 1.26 |
| 19 | Kansas City, Mo., Kan. | 1,655 | 1.25 |
| 20 | Toledo | 866 | 1.09 |
| 21 | Lincoln | 196 | 1.02 |
| 21 | Minneapolis-St. Paul | 2,161 | 1.02 |

# 66. Catholics

Roman Catholics are by far the largest single religious group in the United States. The religious affiliation of many key ethnic groups—Irish, Italians, Hispanics, French, Eastern Europeans—is predominantly Roman Catholic.

In four metro areas Roman Catholic adherents rep-resent more than half the population: Providence (64 per cent), Jersey City (60 per cent), Boston (55 per cent) and Worcester (51 per cent). In the New England states the Catholics are primarily Irish. In New Jersey they are more likely to be Italian. The large Catholic contingents in New York and San Antonio include many Hispanics. In Buffalo and Chicago the Catholics are mostly Eastern

Europeans. In New Orleans Catholicism goes back to the French influence.

Baltimore was named after a British peer whose home was on the southern coast of Ireland and who founded the Maryland city in 1632 as a Catholic refuge. However, in 1980 Baltimore ranked 38th of the 86 cities. Relative to other cities, Baltimore has become more of a haven for Jews than for Catholics.

Cities with the fewest Catholics are those in the southern Bible belt (Columbus, Georgia; Greensboro, North Carolina). Blacks have tended to follow southern Protestants into the Methodist and Baptist churches. A small minority follow the Islamic religion.

SOURCES: Metro religious adherence data for 1980 derived by the authors from county data in Bernard Quinn, Herman Anderson, Martin Bradley, Paul Goetting and Peggy Shriver, *Churches and Church Membership in the United States, 1980: An Enumeration by Region, State and County Based on Data Reported by 111 Church Bodies* (Atlanta: Glenmary Research Center, 1982). Metro population data for 1980 derived by the authors from county data in Hana Umlauf Lane, Ed., *The World Almanac & Book of Facts 1983* (New York: Newspaper Enterprise Association, Inc., 1981), pp. 246–263. Metro data for 1971 derived by the authors from county data in Douglas W. Johnson, Paul R. Picard and Bernard Quinn, *Churches and Church Membership in the United States: An Enumeration by Region, State and County* (Atlanta: Glenmary Research Center, 1974).

| Rank | Metro Area | Catholics | Catholics per 100 Population |
|---|---|---|---|
| 1 | Providence | 602,907 | 63.65 |
| 2 | Jersey City | 335,641 | 60.26 |
| 3 | Boston | 2,030,466 | 55.43 |
| 4 | Worcester | 331,320 | 51.26 |
| 5 | New York | 4,370,154 | 47.92 |
| 6 | Pittsburgh | 1,060,218 | 46.83 |
| 7 | Buffalo | 524,886 | 42.24 |
| 8 | Chicago | 2,897,723 | 40.80 |
| 9 | New Orleans | 482,581 | 40.66 |
| 10 | Cleveland | 750,901 | 39.55 |
| 11 | San Antonio | 392,904 | 36.65 |
| 12 | Philadelphia | 1,660,064 | 35.19 |
| 13 | Albuquerque | 158,552 | 34.89 |
| 14 | Syracuse | 208,150 | 32.15 |
| 15 | Milwaukee | 410,273 | 29.37 |
| 16 | Rochester | 281,687 | 28.98 |
| 17 | San Francisco | 906,709 | 27.88 |
| 18 | El Paso | 131,742 | 27.45 |
| 19 | Detroit | 1,187,263 | 27.28 |
| 20 | Corpus Christi | 87,421 | 26.79 |
| 21 | Cincinnati | 375,206 | 26.77 |
| 22 | St. Louis | 622,206 | 26.42 |
| 23 | Toledo | 207,886 | 26.26 |
| 24 | Miami | 426,437 | 26.23 |
| 25 | Madison | 84,575 | 26.14 |
| 26 | Omaha | 148,801 | 26.09 |
| 27 | Baton Rouge | 124,819 | 25.79 |
| 28 | Los Angeles | 1,904,617 | 25.47 |
| 29 | Minneapolis-St. Paul | 537,934 | 25.44 |
| 30 | Grand Rapids | 149,525 | 24.85 |
| 31 | Akron | 162,705 | 24.64 |
| 32 | Louisville | 193,833 | 21.39 |
| 33 | Tucson | 113,100 | 21.29 |
| 34 | Fresno | 107,396 | 20.85 |
| 35 | Honolulu | 148,000 | 19.40 |
| 36 | Anaheim | 351,081 | 18.18 |
| 37 | Washington, D.C. | 538,548 | 17.60 |
| 38 | Baltimore | 381,157 | 17.53 |
| 39 | Flint | 86,568 | 16.60 |
| 40 | San Diego | 308,464 | 16.57 |
| 41 | Phoenix | 238,210 | 15.80 |
| 42 | Riverside | 235,572 | 15.13 |
| 43 | Fort Wayne | 57,598 | 15.04 |
| 44 | Austin | 77,148 | 14.38 |
| 45 | Denver | 230,997 | 14.26 |
| 46 | Sacramento | 143,918 | 14.19 |
| 47 | Columbus, Ohio | 152,995 | 13.99 |
| 48 | Des Moines | 46,589 | 13.78 |
| 49 | Spokane | 47,001 | 13.75 |
| 50 | Las Vegas | 63,262 | 13.70 |
| 50 | Portland, Ore. | 170,179 | 13.70 |
| 52 | Houston | 386,645 | 13.31 |
| 53 | Wichita | 53,950 | 13.12 |
| 54 | Lincoln | 23,464 | 12.16 |
| 55 | Tampa | 180,555 | 11.50 |
| 56 | Lubbock | 24,225 | 11.45 |
| 57 | Dayton | 94,665 | 11.40 |
| 58 | Kansas City, Mo., Kan. | 134,293 | 10.11 |
| 59 | Colorado Springs | 30,800 | 9.70 |
| 60 | Indianapolis | 111,467 | 9.55 |
| 61 | Seattle | 142,467 | 8.87 |
| 62 | Anchorage | 15,175 | 8.77 |
| 63 | Mobile | 37,605 | 8.49 |
| 64 | Tacoma | 39,460 | 8.13 |
| 65 | Dallas | 216,361 | 7.27 |
| 66 | Jacksonville | 50,766 | 6.88 |
| 67 | Lexington-Fayette | 20,628 | 6.48 |
| 68 | Shreveport | 21,183 | 5.62 |
| 69 | Oklahoma City | 42,753 | 5.13 |
| 70 | Salt Lake City | 47,374 | 5.06 |
| 71 | Memphis | 44,394 | 4.86 |
| 72 | Norfolk | 37,952 | 4.70 |
| 73 | Richmond | 28,873 | 4.57 |
| 74 | Tulsa | 28,233 | 4.10 |
| 75 | Little Rock | 15,361 | 3.90 |
| 76 | Atlanta | 78,692 | 3.88 |
| 77 | Nashville | 28,935 | 3.40 |
| 78 | Birmingham | 27,803 | 3.28 |
| 79 | Montgomery | 8,545 | 3.13 |
| 80 | Jackson | 9,505 | 2.97 |
| 81 | Charlotte | 17,554 | 2.75 |
| 82 | Knoxville | 12,316 | 2.58 |
| 83 | Chattanooga | 9,571 | 2.24 |
| 84 | Newark | 37,952 | 1.93 |
| 85 | Greensboro | 15,039 | 1.82 |
| 86 | Columbus, Ga. | 1,438 | .60 |

# 67. Catholics: Trends

The table below shows the trends in Catholicism in the metro areas between 1971 and 1980 relative to trends in the overall population between 1970 and 1980. Care should be taken in interpreting the signs. The positive numbers mean that the Catholic population changed *in the same direction* as the overall population. In Detroit Catholics left the metro area (or the church) at a rate over three times as fast as city residents as a group. Milwaukee Catholics left the metro area (or the church) at a rate nearly three times as fast as all residents. In Columbus, Georgia, however, while the metro area grew by 612 people, the Catholic population grew by 38 percent more than that. At the other end of the spectrum, the Akron area saw a *loss* of 19,000 people and an *increase* of nearly 27,000 in the Catholic population, meaning that the Catholic population changed in the opposite direction. By contrast, the Syracuse area saw a growth in its population by nearly 11,000 people, but a loss of nearly 70 per cent of that number of Catholics—i.e., over 7,400 people.

The fastest-growing Roman Catholic ethnic group is the Hispanics. This group represents 35 percent of Catholics in New York City.

SOURCES: Kenneth A. Briggs, "Among Hispanic Catholics, Another Pattern of Practice," *New York Times*, January 9, 1983, p. E-24. For sources of data see previous table.

| Rank | Metro Area | Total Population Change (1970–80) | Catholic Population Change as a Percentage of Total Population Change |
|---|---|---|---|
| 1 | Detroit | − 82,289 | 314.44 |
| 2 | Milwaukee | − 6,741 | 268.86 |
| 3 | Columbus, Ga. | 612 | 137.75 |
| 4 | Los Angeles | 435,677 | 128.75 |
| 5 | Dayton | − 22,461 | 123.19 |
| 6 | Washington, D.C. | 150,129 | 108.53 |
| 7 | Grand Rapids | 62,455 | 90.68 |
| 8 | Boston | − 135,744 | 87.26 |
| 9 | Buffalo | − 106,638 | 81.04 |
| 10 | Rochester | 10,363 | 76.97 |
| 11 | Columbus, Ohio | 75,446 | 63.30 |
| 12 | Wichita | 21,961 | 51.18 |
| 13 | Cincinnati | 14,196 | 45.05 |
| 14 | Lubbock | 32,356 | 43.96 |
| 15 | Miami | 358,187 | 35.23 |
| 16 | Toledo | 28,941 | 26.29 |
| 17 | New York | − 853,979 | 23.04 |
| 18 | Omaha | 27,753 | 21.92 |
| 19 | Louisville | 38,910 | 20.48 |
| 20 | Baton Rouge | 108,345 | 20.44 |
| 21 | Portland, Ore. | 235,057 | 19.54 |
| 22 | Albuquerque | 121,233 | 15.45 |
| 23 | Anaheim | 510,337 | 14.44 |
| 24 | Madison | 33,273 | 13.77 |
| 25 | Minneapolis-St. Paul | 148,865 | 13.38 |
| 26 | Lincoln | 24,912 | 12.59 |
| 27 | Tampa | 480,943 | 12.49 |
| 28 | Jacksonville | 115,692 | 12.47 |
| 29 | Houston | 906,034 | 12.43 |
| 30 | Dallas | 597,255 | 11.63 |
| 31 | Phoenix | 536,802 | 10.49 |
| 32 | Mobile | 66,129 | 9.68 |
| 33 | Fresno | 101,684 | 9.24 |
| 34 | San Antonio | 183,775 | 8.58 |
| 35 | Corpus Christi | 41,456 | 8.11 |
| 36 | Memphis | 78,784 | 7.95 |
| 37 | Tucson | 179,596 | 7.70 |
| 38 | Oklahoma City | 134,996 | 6.92 |
| 39 | Colorado Springs | 78,159 | 6.01 |
| 40 | Riverside | 417,931 | 5.93 |
| 41 | Charlotte | 79,433 | 5.48 |
| 42 | Las Vegas | 188,528 | 5.05 |
| 43 | Atlanta | 434,101 | 4.77 |
| 44 | Chattanooga | 55,683 | 4.67 |
| 45 | Montgomery | 46,776 | 4.59 |
| 46 | Birmingham | 80,130 | 4.11 |
| 47 | Greensboro | 103,256 | 4.08 |
| 48 | San Diego | 503,992 | 3.95 |
| 49 | Chicago | 127,573 | 3.88 |
| 50 | Lexington-Fayette | 51,435 | 3.50 |
| 51 | Knoxville | 67,108 | 3.31 |
| 52 | Austin | 175,987 | 2.66 |
| 53 | Denver | 380,376 | 2.52 |
| 54 | Richmond | 84,473 | 2.49 |
| 55 | Pittsburgh | − 137,468 | 2.38 |
| 56 | Des Moines | 24,486 | 2.17 |
| 57 | Salt Lake City | 230,767 | 2.10 |
| 58 | Indianapolis | 55,577 | 1.82 |
| 59 | Providence | 38,267 | 1.50 |
| 60 | Jackson | 61,519 | .61 |
| 61 | Jersey City | − 50,867 | .49 |
| 62 | Norfolk | 74,091 | .45 |
| 63 | Little Rock | 70,198 | .10 |
| 64 | Newark | − 92,164 | − .36 |
| 65 | Nashville | 151,234 | − .37 |
| 65 | Sacramento | 210,209 | − .37 |
| 67 | Shreveport | 40,646 | − .57 |
| 68 | Tulsa | 140,114 | − 1.12 |
| 69 | Honolulu | 132,346 | − 2.04 |
| 70 | Worcester | 646,352 | − 2.06 |
| 71 | Seattle | 182,160 | − 3.24 |
| 72 | Flint | 12,925 | − 3.33 |
| 73 | Spokane | 54,348 | − 4.12 |
| 74 | New Orleans | 140,255 | − 5.35 |
| 75 | Tacoma | 73,309 | − 6.01 |
| 76 | Philadelphia | − 107,292 | − 9.42 |
| 77 | El Paso | 120,608 | − 11.83 |

| Rank | Metro Area | Total Population Change (1970–80) | Catholic Population Change as a Percentage of Total Population Change |
|------|-----------|-----------------------------------|---------------------------------------------------------------------|
| 78 | St. Louis | − 55,608 | − 23.25 |
| 79 | San Francisco | 143,472 | − 23.71 |
| 80 | Cleveland | −165,009 | − 28.03 |
| 81 | Anchorage | 46,632 | − 28.56 |
| 82 | Fort Wayne | 20,977 | − 29.58 |

| Rank | Metro Area | Total Population Change (1970–80) | Catholic Population Change as a Percentage of Total Population Change |
|------|-----------|-----------------------------------|---------------------------------------------------------------------|
| 83 | Baltimore | 157,007 | − 31.35 |
| 84 | Syracuse | 10,779 | − 68.76 |
| 85 | Kansas City, Mo., Kan. | 54,000 | − 81.83 |
| 86 | Akron | − 18,911 | −141.18 |

# 68.  Baptists

Baptists baptize adults (by total immersion) and keep their congregations autonomous. They rely on the Bible and reject any authority between the believer and God.

Baptists are heavily concentrated in the South, where they generally constitute 10 percent to 30 percent of the population. In Knoxville they are nearly four-fifths of the population. Baptists are less in evidence in metro areas in the rest of the country, where they generally constitute only 1 percent to 5 percent of the metro area population. In the Grand Rapids, Madison and Milwaukee metro areas, fewer than 1 person in 100 is a Baptist.

The Baptist adherents included as "Baptists" in the table below cover the following churches: American Baptist Association, American Baptist Churches in the U.S.A., Baptist General Conference, Baptist Missionary Association of America, Bethel Ministerial Association,

Inc., Conservative Baptist Association of America, North American Baptist Conference, Separate Baptists in Christ, Seventh-Day Baptist General Conference and Southern Baptist Convention.

| Rank | Metro Area | Baptists | Baptists per 1,000 Population |
|------|-----------|----------|-------------------------------|
| 1 | Knoxville | 378,392 | 794.08 |
| 2 | Jackson | 97,240 | 303.47 |
| 3 | Birmingham | 250,917 | 296.12 |
| 4 | Shreveport | 105,915 | 281.21 |
| 5 | Little Rock | 105,944 | 269.24 |
| 6 | Lubbock | 53,844 | 254.40 |
| 7 | Oklahoma City | 210,639 | 252.54 |
| 8 | Mobile | 110,474 | 249.48 |
| 9 | Chattanooga | 102,287 | 239.81 |
| 10 | Montgomery | 64,418 | 236.23 |
| 11 | Columbus, Ga. | 54,623 | 228.36 |
| 12 | Charlotte | 140,913 | 221.14 |
| 13 | Tulsa | 148,228 | 214.94 |
| 14 | Dallas | 638,929 | 214.77 |
| 15 | Memphis | 194,988 | 213.59 |
| 16 | Atlanta | 406,574 | 200.32 |
| 17 | Richmond | 121,907 | 192.89 |
| 18 | Nashville | 162,763 | 191.37 |
| 19 | Jacksonville | 134,702 | 182.64 |
| 20 | Lexington-Fayette | 53,242 | 167.36 |
| 21 | Louisville | 149,608 | 165.09 |
| 22 | Greensboro | 127,777 | 154.43 |
| 23 | Kansas City, Mo., Kan. | 192,137 | 144.69 |
| 24 | Houston | 402,115 | 138.41 |
| 25 | Austin | 73,222 | 136.49 |
| 26 | Baton Rouge | 64,348 | 130.27 |
| 27 | Norfolk | 94,958 | 117.71 |
| 28 | San Antonio | 102,936 | 96.03 |
| 29 | Wichita | 37,862 | 92.05 |
| 30 | Tampa | 132,438 | 84.38 |
| 31 | St. Louis | 169,407 | 71.93 |
| 32 | Anchorage | 11,687 | 67.55 |
| 33 | El Paso | 30,133 | 62.79 |
| 34 | Cincinnati | 85,112 | 60.73 |
| 35 | Washington, D.C. | 185,342 | 60.56 |
| 36 | Colorado Springs | 18,952 | 59.70 |
| 37 | Dayton | 46,735 | 56.30 |
| 38 | Albuquerque | 25,337 | 55.75 |

SOURCES: Metro religious adherence data for 1980 derived by the authors from county data in Bernard Quinn, Herman Anderson, Martin Bradley, Paul Goetting and Peggy Shriver, *Churches and Church Membership in the United States, 1980: An Enumeration by Region, State and County Based on Data Reported by 111 Church Bodies* (Atlanta: Glenmary Research Center, 1982). Metro population data for 1980 derived by the authors from county data in Hana Umlauf Lane, Ed., *The World Almanac & Book of Facts 1983* (New York: Newspaper Enterprise Association, Inc., 1981), pp. 246–263. Metro data for 1971 derived by the authors from county data in Douglas W. Johnson, Paul R. Picard and Bernard Quinn, *Churches and Church Membership in the United States: An Enumeration by Region, State and County* (Atlanta: Glenmary Research Center, 1974).

| Rank | Metro Area | Baptists | Baptists per 1,000 Population |
|---|---|---|---|
| 39 | Phoenix | 78,636 | 52.14 |
| 40 | New Orleans | 61,046 | 51.44 |
| 41 | Fresno | 23,932 | 46.47 |
| 42 | Miami | 72,905 | 44.84 |
| 43 | Tucson | 23,255 | 43.77 |
| 44 | Riverside | 60,317 | 38.74 |
| 45 | Sacramento | 34,681 | 34.20 |
| 46 | Denver | 54,950 | 33.92 |
| 47 | Philadelphia | 148,453 | 31.47 |
| 48 | Worcester | 11,436 | 30.66 |
| 49 | Columbus, Ohio | 33,401 | 30.55 |
| 50 | Portland, Ore. | 37,640 | 30.30 |
| 51 | Baltimore | 65,817 | 30.27 |
| 52 | San Francisco | 98,018 | 30.13 |
| 53 | Corpus Christi | 9,567 | 29.32 |
| 54 | Flint | 15,165 | 29.07 |
| 55 | Tacoma | 13,716 | 28.24 |
| 56 | Las Vegas | 12,847 | 27.82 |
| 57 | Providence | 25,924 | 27.37 |
| 58 | Spokane | 9,051 | 26.48 |
| 59 | Los Angeles | 192,585 | 25.75 |
| 60 | San Diego | 45,672 | 24.53 |
| 61 | Rochester | 23,455 | 24.13 |
| 62 | Indianapolis | 27,158 | 23.27 |

| Rank | Metro Area | Baptists | Baptists per 1,000 Population |
|---|---|---|---|
| 63 | Anaheim | 43,694 | 22.62 |
| 64 | Seattle | 35,290 | 21.96 |
| 65 | Cleveland | 38,896 | 20.49 |
| 66 | Toledo | 15,918 | 20.11 |
| 67 | Omaha | 11,101 | 19.46 |
| 68 | Syracuse | 12,197 | 18.99 |
| 69 | Honolulu | 13,218 | 17.33 |
| 70 | Fort Wayne | 6,316 | 16.49 |
| 71 | Lincoln | 3,027 | 15.69 |
| 72 | Minneapolis-St. Paul | 32,888 | 15.56 |
| 73 | Detroit | 66,025 | 15.17 |
| 74 | New York | 136,734 | 14.99 |
| 75 | Des Moines | 4,787 | 14.16 |
| 76 | Buffalo | 17,446 | 14.04 |
| 77 | Boston | 51,141 | 13.96 |
| 78 | Akron | 9,014 | 13.65 |
| 79 | Newark | 26,213 | 13.34 |
| 80 | Chicago | 93,577 | 13.18 |
| 81 | Pittsburgh | 26,610 | 11.75 |
| 82 | Salt Lake City | 9,512 | 10.16 |
| 83 | Jersey City | 5,594 | 10.04 |
| 84 | Milwaukee | 12,356 | 8.84 |
| 85 | Madison | 2,795 | 8.64 |
| 86 | Grand Rapids | 2,338 | 3.89 |

# 69.  Baptists: Trends

The table below shows that relative to the metro area population Baptists increased fastest in Columbus, Georgia. They grew over 7 times as fast as Columbus did. In Knoxville they grew three times as fast. In Kansas City they grew over twice as fast.

Overall, it is interesting that Baptists are increasing in virtually every metro area except Boston, Providence, Baton Rouge, Greensboro, Rochester, Indianapolis, Syracuse and Corpus Christi.

One reason for the increase between 1971 and 1980 is the fact that there were 9 congregations included in the 1980 data and only 5 congregations in the 1971 data. The five included in 1971 are as follows: American Baptist Churches in the U.S.A., Baptist Missionary Association of America, North American Baptist Conference, Seventh-Day Baptist General Conference and Southern Baptist Convention.

SOURCES: See previous table.

| Rank | Metro Area | Total Population Change (1970–80) | Baptists Population Change as a Percentage of Total Population Change |
|---|---|---|---|
| 1 | Columbus, Ga. | 612 | 750.33 |
| 2 | Knoxville | 67,108 | 298.38 |
| 3 | Kansas City, Mo., Kan. | 54,000 | 112.01 |
| 4 | Cincinnati | 14,196 | 67.80 |
| 5 | Little Rock | 70,198 | 45.03 |
| 6 | Washington, D.C. | 150,129 | 31.53 |
| 7 | Oklahoma City | 134,996 | 26.59 |
| 8 | Birmingham | 80,130 | 25.57 |
| 9 | Memphis | 78,784 | 25.33 |
| 10 | Chicago | 127,573 | 24.92 |
| 11 | Charlotte | 79,433 | 24.28 |
| 12 | Mobile | 66,129 | 24.01 |
| 13 | Jackson | 61,519 | 22.77 |
| 14 | San Francisco | 143,472 | 21.89 |
| 15 | Jacksonville | 115,692 | 20.37 |
| 16 | Shreveport | 40,646 | 19.70 |
| 17 | Norfolk | 74,091 | 18.98 |
| 18 | Tulsa | 140,474 | 18.17 |
| 19 | Richmond | 84,473 | 17.22 |
| 20 | Flint | 12,925 | 17.05 |
| 21 | Montgomery | 46,776 | 16.84 |
| 22 | Louisville | 38,910 | 16.79 |
| 23 | Nashville | 151,234 | 16.64 |

| Rank | Metro Area | Total Population Change (1970–80) | Baptists Population Change as a Percentage of Total Population Change | Rank | Metro Area | Total Population Change (1970–80) | Baptists Population Change as a Percentage of Total Population Change |
|---|---|---|---|---|---|---|---|
| 24 | Minneapolis-St. Paul | 148,865 | 16.61 | 56 | Lincoln | 24,912 | 2.69 |
| 25 | Dallas | 597,255 | 14.99 | 57 | Las Vegas | 188,528 | 2.60 |
| 26 | Lexington-Fayette | 51,435 | 14.18 | 58 | San Diego | 503,992 | 2.12 |
| 27 | San Antonio | 183,775 | 13.35 | 59 | El Paso | 120,608 | 1.99 |
| 28 | Columbus, Ohio | 75,446 | 13.33 | 60 | Honolulu | 132,346 | 1.56 |
| 29 | Chattanooga | 55,683 | 12.79 | 61 | Grand Rapids | 62,455 | 1.32 |
| 30 | Los Angeles | 435,677 | 11.31 | 62 | Anaheim | 510,337 | 1.31 |
| 31 | Lubbock | 32,356 | 10.04 | 63 | New Orleans | 140,255 | 1.15 |
| 32 | Akron | − 18,911 | 9.83 | 64 | Salt Lake City | 230,767 | 1.02 |
| 33 | Tacoma | 73,299 | 9.80 | 65 | Miami | 358,187 | .27 |
| 34 | Austin | 175,987 | 8.73 | 66 | Boston | 135,744 | .04 |
| 35 | Portland, Ore. | 235,057 | 8.57 | 67 | Fort Wayne | 20,977 | .04 |
| 36 | Baltimore | 157,007 | 8.53 | 68 | Worcester | 372,940 | − .07 |
| 37 | Atlanta | 434,101 | 7.07 | 69 | Buffalo | −106,638 | − 5.07 |
| 38 | Houston | 906,034 | 6.46 | 69 | Jersey City | − 50,867 | − 5.07 |
| 39 | Wichita | 21,961 | 6.21 | 71 | Providence | 38,267 | − 5.44 |
| 40 | Fresno | 101,684 | 6.14 | 72 | St. Louis | − 55,608 | − 8.69 |
| 41 | Omaha | 27,753 | 6.06 | 73 | Newark | − 92,164 | − 9.12 |
| 42 | Seattle | 182,160 | 5.95 | 74 | Baton Rouge | 118,345 | −10.19 |
| 43 | Spokane | 54,348 | 5.71 | 75 | Greensboro | 103,256 | −10.25 |
| 44 | Denver | 380,376 | 5.51 | 76 | New York | −853,979 | −10.39 |
| 45 | Phoenix | 536,802 | 5.30 | 77 | Cleveland | −165,009 | −12.08 |
| 46 | Colorado Springs | 78,170 | 4.63 | 78 | Rochester | 10,363 | −12.44 |
| 47 | Tampa | 480,943 | 4.62 | 79 | Pittsburgh | −137,468 | −14.08 |
| 48 | Riverside | 417,931 | 4.21 | 80 | Detroit | − 82,289 | −17.07 |
| 49 | Sacramento | 210,209 | 4.09 | 81 | Indianapolis | 55,577 | −21.86 |
| 50 | Tucson | 179,596 | 3.43 | 82 | Syracuse | 5,779 | −30.40 |
| 51 | Anchorage | 46,632 | 3.18 | 83 | Dayton | − 22,461 | −37.10 |
| 52 | Toledo | 28,941 | 3.04 | 84 | Milwaukee | − 6,741 | −56.58 |
| 53 | Des Moines | 24,486 | 2.93 | 85 | Philadelphia | −107,292 | −73.41 |
| 54 | Madison | 33,272 | 2.88 | 86 | Corpus Christi | 41,456 | −87.78 |
| 55 | Albuquerque | 121,233 | 2.84 | | | | |

# 70. Latter-Day Saints (Mormons)

The Church of Jesus Christ of Latter-Day Saints (Mormons) sprang from visions by the founder of the church, Joseph Smith, in 1827. The Bible and *The Book of Mormon* form the basis for the Mormon faith, which includes belief in the afterlife. Brigham Young led the Mormons to the Great Salt Lake, where they founded Salt Lake City, as a spiritual center for followers.

The major Mormon community is metro Salt Lake City, which leads the 1980 ranking below with more than 622 adherents per 1,000 population. Metro Phoenix is next with nearly 77 per 1,000 residents, or one-eighth as many adherents. The top 20 metro areas in the following table are all in the West or the Rocky Mountains. The remainder of the cities all have fewer than 10 adherents per 1,000 population.

Figures below include adherents to both the Church of Jesus Christ of the Latter-Day Saints and the Church of Jesus Christ (Bickertonites). No trend information is available because 1971 data are not published.

SOURCES: Metro data for 1980 derived by the authors from county data in Bernard Quinn, Herman Anderson, Martin Bradley, Paul Goetting and Peggy Shriver, *Churches and Church Membership in the United States, 1980: An Enumeration by Region, State and County Based on Data Reported by 111 Church Bodies* (Atlanta: Glenmary Research Center, 1982). Metro population data for 1980 derived by the authors from county data in Hana Umlauf Lane, Ed. *The World Almanac & Book of Facts 1983* (New York: Newspaper Enterprise Association, Inc., 1981) pp. 246–263.

| Rank | Metro Area | Latter-Day Saints | Latter-Day Saints per 1,000 Population |
|---|---|---|---|
| 1 | Salt Lake City | 582,949 | 622.66 |
| 2 | Las Vegas | 35,293 | 76.42 |
| 3 | Phoenix | 73,657 | 48.84 |
| 4 | Anchorage | 4,900 | 28.32 |
| 5 | Sacramento | 27,150 | 26.78 |
| 6 | Spokane | 8,937 | 26.14 |
| 7 | Honolulu | 19,828 | 25.99 |
| 8 | Portland, Ore. | 31,212 | 25.13 |
| 9 | Riverside | 34,637 | 22.24 |
| 10 | Tacoma | 10,537 | 21.70 |
| 11 | Anaheim | 41,375 | 21.42 |
| 12 | San Francisco | 69,194 | 21.27 |
| 13 | Seattle | 33,186 | 20.65 |
| 14 | Tucson | 9,530 | 17.94 |
| 15 | San Diego | 31,946 | 17.16 |
| 16 | Fresno | 8,638 | 16.77 |
| 17 | Colorado Springs | 4,825 | 15.20 |
| 18 | Denver | 24,347 | 15.03 |
| 19 | Albuquerque | 6,134 | 13.50 |
| 20 | Los Angeles | 97,051 | 12.98 |
| 21 | El Paso | 4,606 | 9.60 |
| 22 | Jacksonville | 4,972 | 6.74 |
| 23 | Omaha | 3,792 | 6.65 |
| 24 | Lincoln | 1,167 | 6.05 |
| 25 | Baton Rouge | 2,605 | 5.27 |
| 26 | Lubbock | 1,107 | 5.23 |
| 27 | Columbus, Ga. | 1,232 | 5.15 |
| 28 | San Antonio | 5,449 | 5.08 |
| 29 | Washington, D.C. | 15,433 | 5.04 |
| 30 | Mobile | 2,177 | 4.92 |
| 31 | Oklahoma City | 4,085 | 4.90 |
| 32 | Lexington-Fayette | 1,551 | 4.88 |
| 33 | Houston | 14,122 | 4.86 |
| 34 | Dallas | 13,578 | 4.56 |
| 35 | Richmond | 2,873 | 4.55 |
| 36 | Corpus Christi | 1,466 | 4.49 |
| 36 | Wichita | 1,845 | 4.49 |
| 38 | Shreveport | 1,662 | 4.41 |
| 39 | Austin | 2,307 | 4.30 |
| 40 | Little Rock | 1,662 | 4.22 |
| 41 | Atlanta | 8,410 | 4.14 |
| 42 | Norfolk | 3,276 | 4.06 |
| 43 | Tulsa | 2,769 | 4.02 |
| 44 | Kansas City, Mo., Kan. | 5,315 | 4.00 |
| 45 | Montgomery | 1,034 | 3.79 |
| 46 | Jackson | 1,106 | 3.45 |
| 47 | Madison | 1,110 | 3.43 |
| 48 | Indianapolis | 3,994 | 3.42 |
| 49 | Dayton | 2,809 | 3.38 |
| 50 | Rochester | 3,148 | 3.24 |
| 51 | Fort Wayne | 1,214 | 3.17 |
| 52 | Knoxville | 1,486 | 3.12 |
| 53 | Columbus, Ohio | 3,336 | 3.05 |
| 54 | Tampa | 4,567 | 2.91 |
| 55 | Des Moines | 981 | 2.90 |
| 56 | Birmingham | 2,337 | 2.76 |
| 57 | Memphis | 2,425 | 2.66 |
| 58 | Charlotte | 1,643 | 2.58 |
| 58 | St. Louis | 6,077 | 2.58 |
| 60 | Louisville | 2,310 | 2.54 |
| 61 | Flint | 1,212 | 2.32 |
| 62 | New Orleans | 2,584 | 2.18 |
| 63 | Nashville | 1,743 | 2.05 |
| 64 | Baltimore | 4,434 | 2.04 |
| 65 | Chattanooga | 852 | 2.00 |
| 65 | Greensboro | 1,651 | 2.00 |
| 67 | Syracuse | 1,275 | 1.98 |
| 68 | Cincinnati | 2,660 | 1.90 |
| 69 | Akron | 1,241 | 1.88 |
| 70 | Miami | 2,906 | 1.79 |
| 71 | Toledo | 1,395 | 1.76 |
| 72 | Grand Rapids | 1,040 | 1.73 |
| 73 | Detroit | 7,172 | 1.65 |
| 73 | Pittsburgh | 3,725 | 1.65 |
| 73 | Worcester | 617 | 1.65 |
| 76 | Minneapolis-St. Paul | 2,925 | 1.38 |
| 77 | Newark | 2,490 | 1.27 |
| 78 | Cleveland | 2,399 | 1.26 |
| 79 | Buffalo | 1,544 | 1.24 |
| 80 | Boston | 4,249 | 1.16 |
| 81 | Providence | 1,051 | 1.11 |
| 82 | Philadelphia | 5,092 | 1.08 |
| 83 | New York | 6,223 | .68 |
| 84 | Jersey City | 350 | .63 |
| 85 | Milwaukee | 350 | .25 |
| 86 | Chicago | 1,150 | .16 |

# 71. Reformed Churches

The largest number of adherents to the Reformed Churches in 1980 relative to metro population was in the Grand Rapids area, where there were 213 adherents per 1,000 population. The next largest concentration of Reformed Church adherents was in the Flint and New York City areas, with 18 and 12 adherents per 1,000 residents, respectively.

Three churches are counted in the 1980 data that follow (the Christian Reformed Church,* the Protestant Reformed Churches in America and the Reformed Church in America*)—the largest of these is the Christian Reformed Church. The two churches that are starred are the ones included in 1971 data used in the trend table.

SOURCES: Metro religious adherence data for 1980 derived by the authors from county data in Bernard Quinn, Herman Anderson, Martin Bradley, Paul Goetting and Peggy Shriver, *Churches and Church Membership in the United States, 1980: An Enumeration by Region, State and County Based on Data Reported by 111 Church Bodies* (Atlanta: Glenmary Research Center, 1982). Metro population data for 1980 derived by the authors from county data in Hana Umlauf Lane, Ed., *The World Almanac & Book of Facts 1983* (New York: Newspaper Enterprise Association, Inc., 1981), pp. 246–263. Metro data for 1971 derived by the authors from county data in Douglas W. Johnson, Paul R. Picard and Bernard Quinn, *Churches and Church Membership in the United States: An Enumeration by Region, State and County* (Atlanta: Glenmary Research Center, 1974).

| Rank | Metro Area | Reformed | Reformed per 1,000 Population |
|---|---|---|---|
| 1 | Grand Rapids | 127,955 | 212.66 |
| 2 | Flint | 9,410 | 18.04 |
| 3 | New York | 111,423 | 12.22 |
| 4 | Anaheim | 15,500 | 8.02 |
| 5 | Newark | 14,045 | 7.15 |
| 6 | Jersey City | 3,111 | 5.59 |
| 7 | Lincoln | 940 | 4.87 |
| 8 | Rochester | 4,555 | 4.69 |
| 9 | Riverside | 7,143 | 4.59 |
| 10 | Chicago | 28,154 | 3.96 |
| 11 | Des Moines | 1,206 | 3.57 |
| 12 | Denver | 5,319 | 3.28 |
| 13 | Sacramento | 1,993 | 1.97 |
| 14 | Phoenix | 2,905 | 1.93 |
| 15 | Worcester | 1,129 | 1.75 |

| Rank | Metro Area | Reformed | Reformed per 1,000 Population |
|---|---|---|---|
| 16 | Seattle | 2,737 | 1.70 |
| 17 | Los Angeles | 11,850 | 1.58 |
| 18 | Minneapolis-St. Paul | 3,108 | 1.47 |
| 19 | Syracuse | 919 | 1.43 |
| 20 | Madison | 449 | 1.39 |
| 21 | Tucson | 710 | 1.34 |
| 22 | Colorado Springs | 422 | 1.33 |
| 23 | Cleveland | 2,418 | 1.27 |
| 24 | Anchorage | 216 | 1.25 |
| 25 | Detroit | 4,890 | 1.12 |
| 26 | Omaha | 614 | 1.08 |
| 27 | Philadelphia | 4,955 | 1.05 |
| 28 | Tampa | 1,485 | .95 |
| 29 | San Diego | 1,623 | .87 |
| 30 | Albuquerque | 369 | .81 |
| 30 | Oklahoma City | 674 | .81 |
| 32 | San Francisco | 2,522 | .78 |
| 33 | Milwaukee | 783 | .56 |
| 33 | Tacoma | 270 | .56 |
| 35 | Salt Lake City | 469 | .50 |
| 36 | Indianapolis | 542 | .46 |
| 37 | Spokane | 140 | .41 |
| 38 | Portland, Ore. | 471 | .38 |
| 39 | Miami | 607 | .37 |
| 40 | Akron | 121 | .18 |
| 41 | Jackson | 48 | .15 |
| 41 | Norfolk | 122 | .15 |
| 41 | Washington, D.C. | 471 | .15 |
| 44 | El Paso | 60 | .13 |
| 45 | Jacksonville | 58 | .08 |
| 46 | Dayton | 55 | .07 |
| 47 | Honolulu | 45 | .06 |
| 47 | Kansas City, Mo., Kan. | 83 | .06 |
| 47 | St. Louis | 142 | .06 |
| 50 | Boston | 137 | .05 |
| 50 | Buffalo | 66 | .05 |
| 50 | Greensboro | 45 | .05 |
| 53 | Pittsburgh | 92 | .04 |
| 54 | Atlanta | 51 | .03 |
| 54 | Cincinnati | 42 | .03 |
| 56 | Houston | 55 | .02 |
| 56 | Louisville | 15 | .02 |

# 72. Reformed Churches: Trends

The largest increase in adherents relative to population for the Reformed Churches was in metro Flint, where between 1971 and 1980 adherents grew by 65 percent of the increase in the area's population. The next largest increase was in Grand Rapids, where Reformed Church adherents grew by nearly 10 percent of the increase in area population.

SOURCE: See previous table.

| Rank | Metro Area | Total Population Change (1970–80) | Reformed Population Change as a Percentage of Total Population Change |
|---|---|---|---|
| 1 | Flint | 12,925 | 65.30 |
| 2 | Grand Rapids | 62,455 | 9.55 |
| 3 | Jersey City | − 50,867 | 3.53 |
| 4 | Newark | − 92,164 | 2.60 |
| 5 | Lincoln | 24,912 | 1.20 |
| 6 | Detroit | − 82,289 | 1.09 |
| 7 | Anaheim | 510,337 | .94 |
| 8 | Milwaukee | − 6,741 | .83 |

| Rank | Metro Area | Total Population Change (1970–80) | Reformed Population Change as a Percentage of Total Population Change |
|------|------------|----------------------------------|----------------------------------------------------------------------|
| 9  | Philadelphia | −107,292 | .73 |
| 10 | Madison | 33,273 | .70 |
| 11 | Oklahoma City | 134,996 | .50 |
| 12 | Omaha | 27,753 | .46 |
| 13 | Sacramento | 210,209 | .45 |
| 14 | San Francisco | 143,472 | .39 |
| 15 | Akron | − 18,911 | .38 |
| 16 | Riverside | 417,931 | .30 |
| 17 | Buffalo | −103,638 | .21 |
| 17 | Colorado Springs | 78,170 | .21 |
| 19 | Albuquerque | 121,233 | .17 |
| 19 | Anchorage | 46,632 | .17 |
| 21 | Norfolk | 74,091 | .16 |
| 22 | Minneapolis-St. Paul | 148,865 | .14 |
| 23 | Tampa | 480,943 | .11 |
| 24 | Cleveland | −165,009 | .08 |
| 24 | Jackson | 61,519 | .08 |
| 24 | Phoenix | 536,802 | .08 |
| 27 | Tucson | 179,596 | .07 |
| 28 | El Paso | 120,608 | .05 |
| 28 | Jacksonville | 115,692 | .05 |
| 28 | Tacoma | 73,299 | .05 |
| 31 | Boston | 135,744 | .04 |
| 31 | Louisville | 38,910 | .04 |
| 31 | Washington, D.C. | 150,129 | .04 |
| 34 | Atlanta | 434,101 | .01 |

| Rank | Metro Area | Total Population Change (1970–80) | Reformed Population Change as a Percentage of Total Population Change |
|------|------------|----------------------------------|----------------------------------------------------------------------|
| 34 | Houston | 906,034 | .01 |
| 34 | Indianapolis | 1,055,797 | .01 |
| 34 | Kansas City, Mo., Kan. | 54,000 | .01 |
| 34 | Portland, Ore. | 235,057 | .01 |
| 34 | Salt Lake City | 230,767 | .01 |
| 34 | Spokane | 84,348 | .01 |
| 41 | Worcester | 301,718 | − .04 |
| 42 | Miami | 358,187 | − .05 |
| 42 | Seattle | 182,160 | − .05 |
| 44 | Dayton | − 22,461 | − .06 |
| 45 | St. Louis | − 55,608 | − .08 |
| 46 | Greensboro | 103,256 | − .09 |
| 47 | Des Moines | 24,486 | − .13 |
| 48 | Fresno | 101,684 | − .14 |
| 49 | Syracuse | 5,779 | − .21 |
| 50 | Denver | 380,376 | − .23 |
| 51 | Los Angeles | 435,677 | − .31 |
| 52 | Toledo | 28,941 | − .40 |
| 53 | Columbus, Ohio | 75,446 | − .54 |
| 54 | Chicago | 127,573 | − .72 |
| 55 | Honolulu | 132,346 | − .78 |
| 56 | Cincinnati | 14,196 | − 1.14 |
| 57 | Rochester | 10,363 | − 4.64 |
| 58 | San Diego | 503,992 | − 5.35 |
| 59 | New York | −853,979 | − 6.11 |

# 73.  Lutherans

In the United States for 1980 13 different varieties of Lutheranism provided data on their adherents shown in the table below.

Lutherans are strongest in the Midwest, where German and Scandinavian immigrants settled in large numbers. Lutheranism is still strongly tied to its northern European antecedents.

The four metro areas where Lutherans constitute more than 10 percent of the population are those of Minneapolis-St. Paul, Madison, Fort Wayne and Milwaukee. In the Toledo area Lutherans constitute just a smidgeon below 10 percent.

The Minneapolis area has the largest single metro congregation, about 433,000 adherents. The next largest is in the Chicago area, about 345,000 adherents.

Lutherans are least prevalent in the South. Apart from Honolulu, the dozen metro areas with the fewest Lutherans (under 6.9 per 1,000 population) are all in the South. The smallest metro congregation is the one in Columbus, Georgia, with under 1,300 adherents.

The metro data cover the following groups (the four starred cities are the major Lutheran churches, which also filed data in 1971): The American Lutheran Church*, Apostolic Lutheran Church of America, Church of the Lutheran Brethren of America, Church of the Lutheran Confession, Estonian Evangelical Lutheran Church, Evangelical Lutheran Churches, Association of Evangelical Lutheran Synod, Free Lutheran Congregations, The Association of Latvian Evangelical Lutheran Church of America, Lutheran Church of America*, the Lutheran Church-Missouri Synod*, The Protestant Conference of the Wisconsin Synod, Wisconsin Evangelical Lutheran Synod*.

SOURCES: John Kent, "Christianity: Protestantism," and T. Corbishley, "Christianity: The Catholic Church Since the Reformation," in R. C. Zaehner, Ed., *The Concise Encyclopedia of Living Faiths* (Boston: Beacon Press, 1959), pp. 117–119, 153. Metro religious adherence data for 1980 derived by the authors from county data in Bernard Quinn, Herman Anderson, Martin Bradley, Paul Goetting and Peggy Shriver, *Churches and Church Membership in the United States, 1980: An Enumeration by Region, State and County Based on Data Reported by 111 Church Bodies* (Atlanta: Glenmary Research Center, 1982). Metro population data for 1980 derived by the authors from county data in Hana Umlauf Lane, Ed., *The World Almanac & Book of Facts 1983* (New York: Newspaper Enterprise Association, Inc., 1981), pp. 246–263. Metro data for 1971 derived by the authors from county data in Douglas W. Johnson, Paul R. Picard and Bernard Quinn, *Churches and Church Membership in the United States: An Enumeration by Region, State and County* (Atlanta: Glenmary Research Center, 1974).

| Rank | Metro Area | Lutherans | Lutherans per 1,000 Population |
|---|---|---|---|
| 1 | Minneapolis-St. Paul | 432,828 | 204.72 |
| 2 | Madison | 57,690 | 178.31 |
| 3 | Fort Wayne | 49,252 | 128.61 |
| 4 | Milwaukee | 164,091 | 117.48 |
| 5 | Toledo | 78,830 | 99.58 |
| 6 | Omaha | 53,855 | 94.42 |
| 7 | Lincoln | 17,132 | 88.82 |
| 8 | Des Moines | 24,779 | 73.30 |
| 9 | Tacoma | 23,807 | 49.02 |
| 10 | Chicago | 344,932 | 48.57 |
| 11 | Spokane | 16,331 | 47.77 |
| 12 | St. Louis | 109,965 | 46.69 |
| 13 | Seattle | 73,950 | 46.02 |
| 14 | Buffalo | 57,304 | 46.01 |
| 15 | Detroit | 192,761 | 44.28 |
| 16 | Pittsburgh | 98,195 | 43.37 |
| 17 | Flint | 22,373 | 42.89 |
| 18 | Baltimore | 91,273 | 41.98 |
| 19 | Austin | 22,306 | 41.58 |
| 20 | Columbus, Ohio | 43,427 | 39.72 |
| 21 | Denver | 62,150 | 38.37 |
| 22 | Portland, Ore. | 47,284 | 38.07 |
| 23 | Cleveland | 72,111 | 37.98 |
| 24 | Grand Rapids | 22,757 | 37.82 |
| 25 | Philadelphia | 162,588 | 34.47 |
| 26 | Colorado Springs | 10,373 | 32.68 |
| 27 | Dayton | 26,874 | 32.38 |
| 28 | Rochester | 27,514 | 28.31 |
| 29 | Phoenix | 41,849 | 27.75 |
| 30 | San Antonio | 29,567 | 27.58 |
| 31 | Akron | 18,072 | 27.37 |
| 32 | Anchorage | 4,578 | 26.46 |
| 33 | Charlotte | 16,027 | 25.15 |
| 34 | Oklahoma City | 19,923 | 23.89 |
| 35 | Wichita | 9,756 | 23.72 |
| 36 | Tucson | 11,939 | 22.47 |
| 37 | San Francisco | 71,411 | 21.95 |
| 38 | Indianapolis | 25,074 | 21.49 |
| 39 | Sacramento | 20,678 | 20.39 |
| 40 | Houston | 57,005 | 19.62 |
| 41 | Albuquerque | 8,870 | 19.52 |
| 42 | New York | 175,389 | 19.23 |
| 43 | Washington, D.C. | 57,943 | 18.93 |
| 44 | Tampa | 29,610 | 18.87 |
| 45 | Corpus Christi | 6,012 | 18.43 |
| 46 | Kansas City, Mo., Kan. | 23,672 | 17.83 |
| 47 | San Diego | 31,614 | 16.98 |
| 48 | Syracuse | 10,130 | 15.77 |
| 49 | Fresno | 7,970 | 15.48 |
| 50 | Anaheim | 29,670 | 15.36 |
| 51 | Riverside | 23,758 | 15.26 |
| 52 | Greensboro | 12,222 | 14.77 |
| 53 | New Orleans | 17,421 | 14.68 |
| 54 | Worcester | 9,270 | 14.34 |
| 55 | Los Angeles | 96,160 | 12.86 |
| 56 | Las Vegas | 5,817 | 12.60 |
| 57 | Newark | 24,008 | 12.22 |
| 58 | Cincinnati | 17,076 | 12.18 |
| 59 | Dallas | 34,245 | 11.51 |
| 60 | Jersey City | 6,255 | 11.23 |
| 61 | Richmond | 6,939 | 10.98 |
| 62 | Mobile | 4,838 | 10.93 |
| 63 | Lubbock | 2,175 | 10.28 |
| 64 | Tulsa | 7,083 | 10.27 |
| 65 | Norfolk | 8,056 | 9.99 |
| 66 | Louisville | 9,003 | 9.93 |
| 67 | Little Rock | 3,804 | 9.67 |
| 68 | Knoxville | 4,419 | 9.27 |
| 69 | Atlanta | 17,313 | 8.53 |
| 70 | Salt Lake City | 7,628 | 8.15 |
| 71 | Miami | 13,035 | 8.02 |
| 72 | Boston | 20,302 | 7.35 |
| 73 | Chattanooga | 3,025 | 7.09 |
| 74 | Providence | 6,576 | 6.94 |
| 75 | Memphis | 6,173 | 6.76 |
| 76 | El Paso | 3,177 | 6.62 |
| 77 | Shreveport | 2,161 | 5.74 |
| 78 | Jacksonville | 4,199 | 5.69 |
| 79 | Montgomery | 1,537 | 5.64 |
| 80 | Lexington-Fayette | 1,751 | 5.50 |
| 81 | Columbus, Ga. | 1,292 | 5.40 |
| 82 | Nashville | 4,587 | 5.39 |
| 83 | Baton Rouge | 2,579 | 5.22 |
| 84 | Honolulu | 3,749 | 4.91 |
| 85 | Birmingham | 3,935 | 4.64 |
| 86 | Jackson | 1,335 | 4.17 |

# 74. Lutherans: Trends

Despite the fact that 1980 data for adherents includes more Lutheran congregations than the 1971 data, the number of Lutherans showed a substantial decline in many metro areas.

In the Milwaukee area for example, Lutherans declined between 1971 and 1980 by 3.6 times the population decline of about 6,700. That is, Lutheran adherents declined by about 24,000 persons.

Similarly, at the other end of the table, in the Toledo metro area, Luterans declined by about 41 percent of the population increase in the area, i.e., by about 12,000 persons.

The bright spots for the Lutheran churches are in the Minneapolis-St. Paul area; Columbus, Ga.; Madison; Washington, D.C. and Oklahoma City. The coverage of churches is described in the previous table.

SOURCE: See previous table.

| Rank | Metro Area | Total Population Change (1970-80) | Lutheran Population Change as a Percentage of Total Population Change |
|------|-----------|-----------------------------------|----------------------------------------------------------------------|
| 1 | Milwaukee | − 6,741 | 357.77 |
| 2 | Minneapolis-St. Paul | 148,865 | 140.77 |
| 3 | Detroit | − 82,289 | 34.00 |
| 4 | Dayton | − 22,461 | 31.64 |
| 5 | St. Louis | − 55,608 | 25.94 |
| 6 | Akron | − 18,911 | 25.23 |
| 7 | Columbus, Ga. | 612 | 15.52 |
| 8 | Philadelphia | −107,292 | 14.38 |
| 9 | Pittsburgh | −137,468 | 10.36 |
| 10 | Madison | 33,273 | 7.56 |
| 11 | Washington, D.C. | 150,129 | 7.54 |
| 12 | Oklahoma City | 134,996 | 7.38 |
| 13 | Jersey City | − 50,867 | 6.90 |
| 14 | New York | −853,979 | 3.51 |
| 15 | Newark | − 92,164 | 3.44 |
| 16 | Cleveland | −165,009 | 3.15 |
| 17 | Buffalo | −103,638 | 2.63 |
| 18 | Grand Rapids | 62,455 | 2.61 |
| 19 | Norfolk | 74,091 | 2.45 |
| 20 | Omaha | 27,753 | 2.32 |
| 21 | Charlotte | 79,433 | 2.19 |
| 22 | Knoxville | 67,108 | 1.60 |
| 23 | Flint | 12,925 | 1.52 |
| 24 | Phoenix | 536,802 | 1.51 |
| 25 | Rochester | 10,363 | 1.49 |
| 26 | Chattanooga | 55,683 | 1.38 |
| 27 | Tampa | 480,943 | 1.37 |
| 28 | Colorado Springs | 78,170 | 1.29 |

| Rank | Metro Area | Total Population Change (1970-80) | Lutheran Population Change as a Percentage of Total Population Change |
|------|-----------|-----------------------------------|----------------------------------------------------------------------|
| 29 | Austin | 175,987 | 1.17 |
| 30 | Atlanta | 434,101 | 1.06 |
| 31 | Anchorage | 46,632 | 1.01 |
| 32 | Little Rock | 70,198 | .99 |
| 33 | Mobile | 66,129 | .94 |
| 34 | Richmond | 84,473 | .77 |
| 35 | Dallas | 597,255 | .75 |
| 36 | Birmingham | 80,130 | .70 |
| 37 | Lubbock | 32,356 | .66 |
| 38 | Nashville | 151,234 | .64 |
| 39 | Boston | 135,744 | .56 |
| 39 | Tulsa | 140,474 | .56 |
| 41 | Baton Rouge | 118,345 | .55 |
| 42 | Las Vegas | 188,528 | .51 |
| 43 | Houston | 906,034 | .49 |
| 44 | Greensboro | 103,256 | .46 |
| 45 | Salt Lake City | 230,767 | .27 |
| 45 | Spokane | 84,348 | .27 |
| 47 | Memphis | 78,784 | .21 |
| 48 | Jackson | 61,519 | .19 |
| 49 | Riverside | 417,931 | .11 |
| 50 | Montgomery | 46,776 | .09 |
| 51 | Albuquerque | 121,233 | .06 |
| 52 | San Antonio | 183,775 | .04 |
| 53 | Indianapolis | 1,055,797 | .01 |
| 54 | Lexington-Fayette | 51,435 | .00 |
| 55 | El Paso | 120,608 | − .04 |
| 56 | Honolulu | 132,346 | − .07 |
| 56 | Shreveport | 40,646 | − .07 |
| 58 | Louisville | 38,910 | − .13 |
| 59 | Sacramento | 210,209 | − .25 |
| 60 | Worcester | 301,718 | − .26 |
| 61 | Tucson | 179,596 | − .55 |
| 62 | Corpus Christi | 41,456 | − .65 |
| 63 | Denver | 380,376 | − .69 |
| 64 | Portland, Ore. | 235,057 | − .70 |
| 65 | Fresno | 101,684 | − .72 |
| 66 | San Diego | 503,992 | − .81 |
| 67 | Baltimore | 157,007 | − .91 |
| 68 | New Orleans | 140,255 | − 1.04 |
| 69 | Miami | 358,187 | − 1.09 |
| 70 | Wichita | 21,954 | − 1.23 |
| 71 | Jacksonville | 115,692 | − 2.45 |
| 72 | Tacoma | 73,299 | − 2.72 |
| 73 | Anaheim | 510,337 | − 3.73 |
| 74 | Seattle | 182,160 | − 3.79 |
| 75 | Providence | 34,413 | − 3.89 |
| 76 | Columbus, Ohio | 75,446 | − 4.99 |
| 77 | San Francisco | 143,472 | − 7.16 |
| 78 | Syracuse | 5,779 | − 7.65 |
| 79 | Los Angeles | 435,677 | − 7.83 |
| 80 | Des Moines | 24,486 | − 8.87 |
| 81 | Fort Wayne | 20,977 | − 9.05 |
| 82 | Lincoln | 24,912 | −14.56 |
| 83 | Cincinnati | 14,196 | −15.88 |
| 84 | Chicago | 127,573 | −18.96 |
| 85 | Kansas City, Mo., Kan. | 54,000 | −21.70 |
| 86 | Toledo | 28,941 | −40.97 |

# 75. Methodists

The Methodists have their strongest congregations in the South. They have many black adherents, the largest group of black members of any church other than the Baptists. Methodists are weakest in numbers in New England.

In Montgomery 19.3 percent of all residents are Methodists. In Charlotte Methodists comprise 18.1 percent of all residents.

At the other extreme, less than 2 residents in 1,000 in Greensboro are Methodists. The metro data below are for 1980 and cover the following Methodist churches (the two starred churches also filed 1971 data):

African Methodist Episcopal Zion Church
Christian Methodist Episcopal Church
Evangelical Methodist Church
Free Methodist Church of North America*
Primitive Methodist Church, U.S.A.
The Southern Methodist Church
The United Methodist Church
Wesleyan Methodist Church*

SOURCES: John Kent, "Christianity: Protestantism," in R. C. Zaehner, Ed., *The Concise Encyclopedia of Living Faiths* (Boston: Beacon Press, 1959), p. 131. Metro religious adherence data for 1980 derived by the authors from county data in Bernard Quinn, Herman Anderson, Martin Bradley, Paul Goetting and Peggy Shriver, *Churches and Church Membership in the United States, 1980: An Enumeration by Region, State and County Based on Data Reported by 111 Church Bodies* (Atlanta: Glenmary Research Center, 1982). Metro population data for 1980 derived by the authors from county data in Hana Umlauf Lane, Ed., *The World Almanac Book of Facts 1983* (New York: Newspaper Enterprise Association, Inc., 1981), pp. 246–263. Metro data for 1971 derived by the authors from county data in Douglas W. Johnson, Paul R. Picard and Bernard Quinn, *Churches and Church Membership in the United States: An Enumeration by Region, State and County* (Atlanta: Glenmary Research Center, 1974).

| Rank | Metro Area | Methodists | Methodists per 1,000 Population |
|---|---|---|---|
| 1 | Montgomery | 52,648 | 193.07 |
| 2 | Charlotte | 115,528 | 181.30 |
| 3 | Birmingham | 120,442 | 142.14 |

| Rank | Metro Area | Methodists | Methodists per 1,000 Population |
|---|---|---|---|
| 4 | Little Rock | 50,864 | 129.26 |
| 5 | Knoxville | 58,408 | 122.57 |
| 6 | Columbus, Ga. | 27,890 | 116.60 |
| 7 | Shreveport | 42,593 | 113.08 |
| 8 | Memphis | 102,209 | 112.00 |
| 9 | Jackson | 33,778 | 105.42 |
| 10 | Oklahoma City | 87,862 | 105.34 |
| 11 | Mobile | 45,097 | 101.84 |
| 12 | Providence | 96,455 | 101.83 |
| 13 | Nashville | 80,977 | 95.21 |
| 14 | Tulsa | 65,545 | 95.04 |
| 15 | Chattanooga | 40,421 | 94.76 |
| 16 | Atlanta | 186,508 | 91.89 |
| 17 | Richmond | 56,768 | 89.82 |
| 18 | Lincoln | 17,322 | 89.81 |
| 19 | Lubbock | 17,886 | 84.51 |
| 20 | Wichita | 34,751 | 84.49 |
| 21 | Indianapolis | 98,128 | 84.09 |
| 22 | Dallas | 248,669 | 83.59 |
| 23 | Syracuse | 53,514 | 83.31 |
| 24 | Fort Wayne | 30,959 | 80.84 |
| 25 | Columbus, Ohio | 87,650 | 80.17 |
| 26 | Norfolk | 64,505 | 79.96 |
| 27 | Des Moines | 26,186 | 77.46 |
| 28 | Washington, D.C. | 220,070 | 71.91 |
| 29 | Dayton | 58,318 | 70.26 |
| 30 | Baltimore | 152,207 | 70.01 |
| 31 | Lexington-Fayette | 22,198 | 69.78 |
| 32 | Pittsburgh | 149,653 | 66.10 |
| 33 | Akron | 40,573 | 61.44 |
| 34 | Toledo | 47,327 | 59.79 |
| 35 | Houston | 173,235 | 59.63 |
| 36 | Louisville | 50.298 | 55.50 |
| 37 | Tampa | 86,695 | 55.24 |
| 38 | Cincinnati | 76,202 | 54.38 |
| 39 | Baton Rouge | 26,502 | 53.65 |
| 40 | Jacksonville | 38,924 | 52.78 |
| 41 | Flint | 26,483 | 50.77 |
| 42 | Rochester | 48,151 | 49.54 |
| 43 | Austin | 25,362 | 47.28 |
| 44 | Kansas City, Mo., Kan. | 62,742 | 47.25 |
| 45 | Corpus Christi | 15,107 | 46.30 |
| 46 | New York | 420,059 | 46.06 |
| 47 | Cleveland | 86,795 | 45.71 |
| 48 | Buffalo | 56,218 | 45.13 |
| 49 | Omaha | 23,784 | 41.70 |
| 50 | San Antonio | 40,859 | 38.12 |
| 51 | St. Louis | 89,141 | 37.85 |
| 52 | Colorado Springs | 11,440 | 36.04 |
| 53 | Philadelphia | 167,284 | 35.47 |
| 54 | Albuquerque | 14,840 | 32.65 |
| 55 | El Paso | 15,216 | 31.71 |
| 56 | Madison | 10,011 | 30.94 |
| 57 | Grand Rapids | 18,177 | 30.21 |
| 58 | Detroit | 128,531 | 29.53 |
| 59 | Minneapolis-St. Paul | 59,600 | 28.19 |
| 60 | Denver | 45,213 | 27.91 |
| 61 | Newark | 52,193 | 26.56 |
| 62 | New Orleans | 30.543 | 25.74 |
| 63 | Chicago | 175,287 | 24.68 |
| 64 | Seattle | 38,997 | 24.27 |
| 65 | Phoenix | 36,419 | 24.15 |

| Rank | Metro Area | Methodists | Methodists per 1,000 Population |
|------|------------|-----------|-------------------------------|
| 66 | Tacoma | 11,543 | 23.77 |
| 67 | Spokane | 7,756 | 22.69 |
| 68 | Portland, Ore. | 27,062 | 21.79 |
| 69 | San Francisco | 65,562 | 20.16 |
| 70 | Tucson | 10,585 | 19.92 |
| 71 | Boston | 54,121 | 19.59 |
| 72 | Miami | 31,333 | 19.27 |
| 73 | Milwaukee | 25,982 | 18.60 |
| 74 | Honolulu | 1,174 | 17.45 |
| 75 | Worcester | 11,114 | 17.19 |
| 76 | Anchorage | 2,896 | 16.74 |

| Rank | Metro Area | Methodists | Methodists per 1,000 Population |
|------|------------|-----------|-------------------------------|
| 77 | Los Angeles | 120,990 | 16.18 |
| 78 | Riverside | 25,166 | 16.16 |
| 79 | San Diego | 27,279 | 14.65 |
| 80 | Fresno | 7,461 | 14.49 |
| 81 | Sacramento | 14,616 | 14.41 |
| 82 | Anaheim | 26,842 | 13.90 |
| 83 | Jersey City | 6,973 | 12.52 |
| 84 | Las Vegas | 3,095 | 6.70 |
| 85 | Salt Lake City | 5,386 | 5.75 |
| 86 | Greensboro | 1,174 | 1.42 |

# 76. Methodists: Trends

Between 1971 and 1980, Methodist adherents grew 19 times faster in metro Columbus, Georgia, than the population as a whole, i.e., by about 11,400 adherents. In Birmingham, Methodists grew twice as fast, by about 160,000 adherents. Similar rapid growth has occurred in many other southern metro areas.

A few metro areas have seen declines, notably Fort Wayne, Lincoln and Kansas City. The losses are concentrated in the Midwest.

The data reflect the inclusion of five new churches between 1971 and 1980, rather than growth within existing churches. The seven churches included in the 1971 and 1980 data are listed in the previous table.

SOURCES: See previous table.

| Rank | Metro Area | Total Population Change (1970-80) | Methodist Population Change as a Percentage of Total Population Change |
|------|------------|------------------------------------|------------------------------------------------------------------------|
| 1 | Columbus, Ga. | 612 | 1918.80 |
| 2 | Birmingham | 80,130 | 101.82 |
| 3 | Charlotte | 79,433 | 73.02 |
| 4 | Montgomery | 46,776 | 72.41 |
| 5 | Omaha | 27,753 | 60.93 |
| 6 | Memphis | 78,784 | 52.60 |
| 7 | Shreveport | 40,646 | 41.77 |
| 8 | Rochester | 10,363 | 40.94 |
| 9 | Washington, D.C. | 150,129 | 38.49 |
| 10 | Milwaukee | − 6,741 | 36.11 |
| 11 | Mobile | 66,129 | 35.31 |
| 12 | Jacksonville | 115,692 | 29.69 |
| 13 | Knoxville | 67,108 | 26.98 |

| Rank | Metro Area | Total Population Change (1970-80) | Methodist Population Change as a Percentage of Total Population Change |
|------|------------|------------------------------------|------------------------------------------------------------------------|
| 14 | Little Rock | 70,198 | 23.28 |
| 15 | Akron | − 18,911 | 22.13 |
| 16 | Cincinnati | 14,196 | 21.15 |
| 17 | Baton Rouge | 118,345 | 19.83 |
| 18 | Norfolk | 74,091 | 18.71 |
| 19 | Chattanooga | 55,683 | 17.15 |
| 20 | Louisville | 38,910 | 13.00 |
| 21 | Atlanta | 434,101 | 12.16 |
| 22 | Jackson | 61,519 | 11.46 |
| 23 | San Francisco | 143,472 | 10.08 |
| 24 | Lexington-Fayette | 51,435 | 9.57 |
| 25 | Dallas | 597,255 | 8.24 |
| 26 | Nashville | 151,234 | 7.29 |
| 27 | Richmond | 84,473 | 7.05 |
| 28 | Oklahoma City | 134,996 | 6.29 |
| 29 | Tulsa | 140,474 | 5.50 |
| 30 | New Orleans | 140,255 | 5.47 |
| 31 | Houston | 906,034 | 3.98 |
| 32 | Chicago | 127,573 | 3.69 |
| 33 | Providence | 34,413 | 2.13 |
| 34 | Tampa | 480,943 | 2.10 |
| 35 | Indianapolis | 1,055,797 | 1.92 |
| 36 | St. Louis | − 55,608 | 1.36 |
| 37 | Austin | 175,987 | 1.29 |
| 38 | Denver | 380,376 | .91 |
| 39 | San Antonio | 183,775 | .50 |
| 40 | Phoenix | 536,802 | .42 |
| 41 | Salt Lake City | 230,767 | − .01 |
| 42 | Worcester | 301,718 | − .03 |
| 43 | Boston | 135,744 | − .07 |
| 44 | Sacramento | 210,209 | − .13 |
| 45 | Riverside | 417,931 | − .28 |
| 46 | Las Vegas | 188,528 | − .35 |
| 47 | Anchorage | 179,596 | − .42 |
| 48 | Tucson | 179,596 | − .43 |
| 49 | San Diego | 503,992 | − .44 |
| 50 | Fresno | 101,684 | − .48 |
| 51 | Spokane | 84,348 | − .61 |

| Rank | Metro Area | Total Population Change (1970-80) | Methodist Population Change as a Percentage of Total Population Change |
|------|------------|----------------------------------|----------------------------------------------------------------------|
| 52 | Miami | 358,187 | – .64 |
| 53 | Grand Rapids | 62,455 | – .65 |
| 54 | Lubbock | 32,356 | – .70 |
| 55 | Portland, Ore. | 235,057 | – .73 |
| 56 | Anaheim | 510,337 | – .87 |
| 57 | El Paso | 120,608 | – 1.09 |
| 58 | Seattle | 182,160 | – 1.18 |
| 59 | Baltimore | 157,007 | – 1.55 |
| 60 | Los Angeles | 435,677 | – 1.95 |
| 61 | Albuquerque | 121,233 | – 1.97 |
| 62 | Tacoma | 73,299 | – 3.10 |
| 63 | Colorado Springs | 78,170 | – 3.15 |
| 64 | Corpus Christi | 41,456 | – 3.43 |
| 65 | Honolulu | 132,346 | – 4.63 |
| 66 | Greensboro | 103,256 | – 5.94 |
| 67 | Syracuse | 5,779 | – 6.00 |
| 68 | Jersey City | – 50,867 | – 6.08 |
| 69 | Cleveland | –165,009 | – 6.83 |

| Rank | Metro Area | Total Population Change (1970-80) | Methodist Population Change as a Percentage of Total Population Change |
|------|------------|----------------------------------|----------------------------------------------------------------------|
| 70 | Flint | 12,925 | – 6.86 |
| 71 | Dayton | – 22,461 | – 9.51 |
| 72 | Minneapolis-St. Paul | 148,865 | – 9.55 |
| 73 | Madison | 33,273 | –10.37 |
| 74 | Columbus, Ohio | 75,446 | –10.87 |
| 75 | Newark | – 92,164 | –10.96 |
| 76 | Buffalo | –103,638 | –13.12 |
| 77 | Toledo | 28,941 | –19.10 |
| 78 | Des Moines | 24,486 | –20.44 |
| 79 | Wichita | – 21,954 | –25.72 |
| 80 | Detroit | – 82,289 | –30.05 |
| 81 | Pittsburgh | –137,468 | –30.36 |
| 82 | Kansas City, Mo., Kan. | 54,000 | –30.93 |
| 83 | Lincoln | 24,912 | –32.41 |
| 84 | New York | –853,979 | –33.84 |
| 85 | Philadelphia | –107,292 | –36.41 |
| 86 | Fort Wayne | 20,977 | –47.85 |

# 77. Churches of Christ

Nashville has the largest number of adherents of the Churches of Christ relative to its size—98 per 1,000 residents, nearly 10 percent. Lexington is close behind with 92 per 1,000, showing the religious continuity with its Kentucky antecedents. Boston and Providence have the smallest representation.

Metro data provided below cover 1980 adherents from three branches of the Churches of Christ (the two starred churches also provided 1971 data):

Christian Church (Disciples of Christ)*
Christian Churches and Churches of Christ*
Churches of Christ

SOURCES: Metro religious adherence data for 1980 derived by the authors from county data in Bernard Quinn, Herman Anderson, Martin Bradley, Paul Goetting and Peggy Shriver, *Churches and Church Membership in the United States, 1980: An Enumeration by Region, State and County Based on Data Reported by 111 Church Bodies* (Atlanta: Glenmary Research Center, 1982). Metro population data for 1980 derived by the authors from county data in Hana Umlauf Lane, Ed., *The World Almanac & Book of Facts 1983* (New York: Newspaper Enterprise Association, Inc., 1981), pp. 246–263. Metro data for 1971 derived by the authors from county data in Douglas W. Johnson, Paul R. Picard and Bernard Quinn, *Churches and Church Membership in the United States: An Enumeration by Region, State and County* (Atlanta: Glenmary Research Center, 1974). Note that the three metro areas in New England do not correspond to Census Bureau definitions of standard metropolitan statistical areas because they are aggregated from country data. See note at the beginning of the chapter.

| Rank | Metro Area | Churches of Christ | Churches of Christ per 1,000 Population |
|------|------------|--------------------|-----------------------------------------|
| 1 | Nashville | 83,596 | 98.29 |
| 2 | Lexington-Fayette | 29,309 | 92.13 |
| 3 | Indianapolis | 95,544 | 81.88 |
| 4 | Lubbock | 17,316 | 81.81 |
| 5 | Wichita | 25,298 | 61.51 |
| 6 | Oklahoma City | 49,099 | 58.87 |
| 7 | Tulsa | 37,574 | 54.48 |
| 8 | Fort Wayne | 18,309 | 47.81 |
| 9 | Dallas | 131,457 | 44.19 |
| 10 | Des Moines | 14,128 | 41.79 |
| 11 | Louisville | 37,715 | 41.62 |
| 12 | Kansas City, Mo., Kan | 54,466 | 41.02 |
| 13 | Memphis | 32,293 | 35.37 |
| 14 | Montgomery | 8,475 | 31.08 |
| 15 | Little Rock | 11,937 | 30.34 |
| 16 | Cincinnati | 41,722 | 29.77 |

| Rank | Metro Area | Churches of Christ | Churches of Christ per 1,000 Population |
|------|-----------|--------------------|----------------------------------------|
| 17 | Chattanooga | 12,106 | 28.38 |
| 18 | Birmingham | 22,343 | 26.37 |
| 19 | Akron | 17,200 | 26.05 |
| 20 | Lincoln | 4,652 | 24.12 |
| 21 | Corpus Christi | 7,241 | 22.19 |
| 22 | Shreveport | 8,120 | 21.56 |
| 23 | Atlanta | 42,963 | 21.17 |
| 24 | St. Louis | 47,007 | 19.96 |
| 25 | Columbus, Ohio | 21,710 | 19.86 |
| 26 | Austin | 9,826 | 18.32 |
| 27 | Omaha | 10,388 | 18.21 |
| 28 | Colorado Springs | 5,775 | 18.19 |
| 29 | Knoxville | 8,464 | 17.76 |
| 30 | Portland, Ore. | 21,811 | 17.56 |
| 31 | Houston | 50,753 | 17.47 |
| 32 | Jacksonville | 12,152 | 16.48 |
| 33 | Greensboro | 13,377 | 16.17 |
| 34 | San Antonio | 17,036 | 15.89 |
| 35 | Flint | 8,108 | 15.54 |
| 36 | Richmond | 9,812 | 15.52 |
| 37 | Dayton | 12,378 | 14.91 |
| 38 | Albuquerque | 6,659 | 14.65 |
| 39 | Tampa | 22,911 | 14.60 |
| 40 | Spokane | 4,875 | 14.26 |
| 41 | Toledo | 11,285 | 14.26 |
| 42 | Mobile | 5,871 | 13.26 |
| 43 | Fresno | 6,676 | 12.96 |
| 44 | Norfolk | 9,693 | 12.02 |
| 45 | Jackson | 3,481 | 10.86 |
| 46 | Denver | 17,321 | 10.69 |
| 47 | Anaheim | 20,407 | 10.56 |
| 48 | Tucson | 5,380 | 10.13 |
| 49 | Cleveland | 19,143 | 10.08 |
| 50 | Riverside | 15,526 | 9.97 |
| 51 | El Paso | 4,781 | 9.96 |

| Rank | Metro Area | Churches of Christ | Churches of Christ per 1,000 Population |
|------|-----------|--------------------|----------------------------------------|
| 52 | Tacoma | 4,499 | 9.26 |
| 53 | Seattle | 14,562 | 9.06 |
| 54 | Pittsburgh | 18,863 | 8.33 |
| 55 | Grand Rapids | 4,868 | 8.09 |
| 56 | Phoenix | 11,766 | 7.80 |
| 57 | San Diego | 13,444 | 7.22 |
| 58 | San Francisco | 21,835 | 6.71 |
| 59 | Las Vegas | 3,064 | 6.63 |
| 60 | Columbus, Ga. | 1,464 | 6.12 |
| 61 | Sacramento | 5,990 | 5.91 |
| 62 | Detroit | 24,194 | 5.56 |
| 63 | Washington, D.C. | 16,333 | 5.34 |
| 64 | Los Angeles | 34,862 | 4.66 |
| 65 | Miami | 6,776 | 4.17 |
| 66 | Charlotte | 2,581 | 4.05 |
| 67 | Baltimore | 7,930 | 3.65 |
| 68 | Anchorage | 625 | 3.61 |
| 69 | Chicago | 23,742 | 3.34 |
| 70 | Honolulu | 2,272 | 2.98 |
| 71 | Buffalo | 3,567 | 2.87 |
| 72 | Baton Rouge | 1,224 | 2.48 |
| 72 | New Orleans | 2,948 | 2.48 |
| 74 | Rochester | 2,272 | 2.34 |
| 75 | Salt Lake City | 1,803 | 1.93 |
| 76 | Minneapolis-St. Paul | 3,391 | 1.86 |
| 77 | Syracuse | 1,146 | 1.78 |
| 78 | Madison | 556 | 1.72 |
| 79 | Newark | 3,105 | 1.58 |
| 80 | Worcester | 576 | 1.54 |
| 81 | New York | 12,528 | 1.37 |
| 82 | Jersey City | 513 | .92 |
| 83 | Milwaukee | 1,210 | .87 |
| 84 | Philadelphia | 3,882 | .82 |
| 85 | Boston | 1,906 | .52 |
| 86 | Providence | 223 | .24 |

# 78.  Churches of Christ: Trends

Between 1971 and 1980 adherents to the Churches of Christ increased most rapidly—nearly fourfold—relative to population growth in metro Columbus, Ga. In second and third place were metro Nashville and Fort Wayne, where the Churches of Christ grew by a number equal to 52 percent of the growth of the two metro areas as a whole.

The Churches of Christ included in the 1971 and 1980 data are listed in the previous table.

SOURCES: See previous table.

| Rank | Metro Area | Total Population Change (1970-80) | Churches of Christ Population Change as a Percentage of Total Population Change |
|------|-----------|-----------------------------------|-------------------------------------------------------------------------------|
| 1 | Columbus, Ga. | 612 | 391.18 |
| 2 | Nashville | 151,234 | 51.75 |
| 3 | Fort Wayne | 20,977 | 51.52 |
| 4 | Lubbock | 32,356 | 43.59 |
| 5 | Cincinnati | 14,196 | 39.98 |
| 6 | Louisville | 38,910 | 34.72 |
| 7 | Flint | 12,925 | 34.58 |
| 8 | Indianapolis | 55,577 | 31.91 |
| 9 | Memphis | 78,784 | 30.29 |
| 10 | Wichita | 21,961 | 27.20 |
| 11 | Birmingham | 80,130 | 24.94 |
| 12 | Oklahoma City | 134,996 | 21.90 |

| Rank | Metro Area | Total Population Change (1970-80) | Churches of Christ Population Change as a Percentage of Total Population Change |
|------|-----------|----------------------------------|-------------------------------------------------------------------------------|
| 13 | Chattanooga | 55,683 | 17.79 |
| 14 | Rochester | 10,363 | 17.46 |
| 15 | Montgomery | 46,776 | 15.48 |
| 16 | Dallas | 597,255 | 14.29 |
| 17 | Shreveport | 40,646 | 12.81 |
| 18 | Little Rock | 70,198 | 12.34 |
| 19 | Omaha | 27,753 | 11.25 |
| 20 | Tulsa | 140,474 | 11.05 |
| 21 | Corpus Christi | 41,456 | 10.58 |
| 22 | Toledo | 28,941 | 10.21 |
| 23 | Kansas City, Mo., Kan. | 54,000 | 10.04 |
| 24 | Syracuse | 5,779 | 8.13 |
| 25 | San Francisco | 143,472 | 7.65 |
| 26 | Knoxville | 67,108 | 6.75 |
| 27 | Chicago | 127,573 | 6.63 |
| 28 | Jacksonville | 115,692 | 6.56 |
| 29 | Mobile | 66,129 | 6.47 |
| 30 | Lincoln | 24,912 | 6.08 |
| 31 | San Antonio | 183,775 | 5.59 |
| 32 | Des Moines | 24,486 | 4.99 |
| 33 | Norfolk | 74,091 | 4.75 |
| 34 | Washington, D.C. | 150,129 | 4.71 |
| 35 | Fresno | 101,684 | 4.45 |
| 36 | Greensboro | 103,256 | 4.27 |
| 37 | Houston | 906,034 | 4.19 |
| 38 | Grand Rapids | 62,455 | 4.12 |
| 39 | Seattle | 182,160 | 3.83 |
| 40 | Portland, Ore. | 235,057 | 3.45 |
| 41 | Atlanta | 434,101 | 3.37 |
| 42 | Jackson | 61,519 | 3.35 |
| 43 | Spokane | 54,348 | 3.31 |
| 44 | Austin | 175,987 | 3.24 |
| 45 | Colorado Springs | 78,170 | 3.16 |
| 46 | Tampa | 480,943 | 2.67 |
| 47 | Albuquerque | 121,233 | 2.59 |
| 48 | Columbus, Ohio | 75,446 | 2.58 |
| 49 | Baltimore | 157,007 | 2.21 |

| Rank | Metro Area | Total Population Change (1970-80) | Churches of Christ Population Change as a Percentage of Total Population Change |
|------|-----------|----------------------------------|-------------------------------------------------------------------------------|
| 50 | El Paso | 120,608 | 2.13 |
| 51 | Charlotte | 79,433 | 2.00 |
| 52 | Richmond | 84,473 | 1.94 |
| 53 | Denver | 380,376 | 1.64 |
| 54 | Tacoma | 73,299 | 1.42 |
| 55 | Anaheim | 510,337 | 1.39 |
| 56 | Tucson | 179,596 | 1.29 |
| 57 | Sacramento | 210,209 | 1.24 |
| 58 | Las Vegas | 188,528 | 1.22 |
| 59 | San Diego | 503,992 | 1.12 |
| 60 | New Orleans | 140,255 | 1.06 |
| 61 | Miami | 358,187 | 1.00 |
| 62 | Riverside | 417,931 | .77 |
| 63 | Anchorage | 46,632 | .70 |
| 64 | Providence | 38,267 | .52 |
| 65 | Honolulu | 132,346 | .45 |
| 66 | Phoenix | 536,802 | .38 |
| 67 | Madison | 33,272 | .33 |
| 68 | Baton Rouge | 118,345 | .17 |
| 69 | Salt Lake City | 230,767 | .14 |
| 70 | Worcester | 372,940 | − .11 |
| 71 | Minneapolis-St. Paul | 148,865 | − .21 |
| 72 | Buffalo | − 106,638 | − .37 |
| 73 | New York | − 853,979 | − .82 |
| 74 | Jersey City | − 50,867 | − 1.01 |
| 75 | Boston | 135,744 | − 1.14 |
| 76 | Cleveland | − 165,009 | − 2.25 |
| 77 | Los Angeles | 435,677 | − 2.49 |
| 78 | Philadelphia | − 107,292 | − 2.60 |
| 78 | Pittsburgh | − 137,468 | − 2.60 |
| 80 | Newark | − 92,164 | − 2.87 |
| 81 | Akron | − 18,911 | − 9.51 |
| 82 | Milwaukee | − 6,741 | −11.96 |
| 83 | Dayton | − 22,461 | −18.06 |
| 84 | Detroit | − 82,289 | −21.42 |
| 85 | St. Louis | − 55,608 | −51.27 |
| 86 | Lexington-Fayette | 51,435 | −95.98 |

# 79. Presbyterians

The largest number of Presbyterians relative to the population is in Charlotte, where nearly 1 person in 100 was a Presbyterian in 1980. Greensboro, Columbus, Georgia, Worchester and Honolulu rank near the bottom.

Eight Presbyterian churches are included in the 1980 data (six starred churches also provided 1971 data):

Associate Reformed Presbyterian Church (General Synod)*

Cumberland Presbyterian Church*
The Orthodox Presbyterian Church*
Presbyterian Church in America
Presbyterian Church in the United States*
Reformed Presbyterian Church, Evangelical Synod*
Reformed Presbyterian Church of North America
The United Presbyterian Church in the U.S.A.*

SOURCES: Metro religious adherence data for 1980 derived by the authors from county data in Bernard Quinn, Herman Anderson, Martin Bradley, Paul Goetting and Peggy Shriver, *Churches and Church Membership in the United States, 1980: An Enumeration by Region, State and County Based on Data Reported by 111 Church Bodies* (Atlanta: Glenmary Research Center, 1982). Metro population data for 1980 derived by the authors from county data in Hana Umlauf Lane, Ed., *The World Almanac & Book of Facts 1983* (New York: Newspaper Enterprise Association, Inc., 1981), pp. 246–263. Metro data for 1971 derived by the authors from county data in Douglas W. Johnson, Paul R. Picard and Bernard Quinn, *Churches and Church Membership in the United States: An Enumeration by Region, State and County* (Atlanta: Glenmary Research Center, 1974).

| Rank | Metro Area | Presbyterians | Presbyterians per 1,000 Population |
|---|---|---|---|
| 1 | Charlotte | 57,483 | 90.21 |
| 2 | Pittsburgh | 168,351 | 74.36 |
| 3 | Newark | 143,113 | 72.82 |
| 4 | Lincoln | 8,834 | 45.80 |
| 5 | Rochester | 35,906 | 36.94 |
| 6 | Chattanooga | 15,315 | 35.91 |
| 7 | Knoxville | 16,794 | 35.24 |
| 8 | Omaha | 20,036 | 35.13 |
| 9 | Des Moines | 11,093 | 32.81 |
| 10 | Greensboro | 26,573 | 32.12 |
| 11 | Montgomery | 8,597 | 31.53 |
| 12 | Richmond | 19,918 | 31.52 |
| 13 | Atlanta | 60,739 | 29.93 |
| 14 | Philadelphia | 137,161 | 29.08 |
| 15 | Nashville | 23,836 | 28.03 |
| 16 | Cincinnati | 38,995 | 27.83 |
| 17 | Jackson | 8,864 | 27.66 |
| 18 | Memphis | 24,427 | 26.76 |
| 19 | Columbus, Ohio | 29,128 | 26.64 |
| 20 | Spokane | 8,455 | 24.73 |
| 21 | Buffalo | 30,172 | 24.22 |
| 22 | Wichita | 9,580 | 23.29 |
| 23 | Lexington-Fayette | 7,400 | 23.26 |
| 24 | Tulsa | 16,023 | 23.23 |
| 25 | Indianapolis | 26,963 | 23.11 |
| 26 | Birmingham | 19,400 | 22.89 |
| 27 | Louisville | 20,449 | 22.56 |
| 28 | Colorado Springs | 7,085 | 22.32 |
| 29 | Dayton | 18,090 | 21.79 |
| 30 | Fort Wayne | 8,272 | 21.60 |
| 31 | St. Louis | 48,047 | 20.40 |
| 32 | Syracuse | 12,895 | 20.07 |
| 33 | Norfolk | 15,897 | 19.71 |
| 34 | Denver | 31,307 | 19.33 |
| 35 | Tacoma | 9,281 | 19.11 |
| 36 | Portland, Ore. | 23,352 | 18.80 |
| 37 | Dallas | 55,387 | 18.62 |
| 38 | Flint | 9,529 | 18.27 |
| 39 | Washington, D.C. | 55,631 | 18.18 |
| 40 | Albuquerque | 8,198 | 18.04 |
| 41 | Jacksonville | 13,298 | 18.03 |
| 42 | Austin | 9,476 | 17.66 |
| 43 | Baltimore | 37,932 | 17.45 |
| 44 | San Francisco | 56,163 | 17.27 |
| 44 | Seattle | 27,755 | 17.27 |
| 46 | Detroit | 75,005 | 17.23 |
| 47 | Kansas City, Mo., Kan. | 21,680 | 16.33 |
| 47 | Minneapolis-St. Paul | 34,516 | 16.33 |
| 49 | Lubbock | 3,348 | 15.82 |
| 50 | Mobile | 6,945 | 15.68 |
| 51 | Shreveport | 5,763 | 15.30 |
| 52 | Oklahoma City | 12,637 | 15.15 |
| 53 | Akron | 9,905 | 15.00 |
| 54 | Tucson | 7,664 | 14.43 |
| 55 | Cleveland | 26,792 | 14.11 |
| 56 | Tampa | 22,092 | 14.08 |
| 57 | Houston | 40,461 | 13.93 |
| 58 | Grand Rapids | 8,255 | 13.72 |
| 59 | Anaheim | 26,453 | 13.70 |
| 60 | Madison | 4,413 | 13.64 |
| 61 | Corpus Christi | 4,351 | 13.33 |
| 62 | Toledo | 10,370 | 13.10 |
| 63 | Sacramento | 13,218 | 13.04 |
| 64 | Baton Rouge | 6,326 | 12.81 |
| 65 | Phoenix | 18,697 | 12.40 |
| 66 | San Diego | 23,036 | 12.37 |
| 67 | Chicago | 85,465 | 12.03 |
| 68 | Fresno | 5,663 | 11.00 |
| 69 | Los Angeles | 77,174 | 10.32 |
| 70 | New York | 91,230 | 10.00 |
| 71 | Miami | 15,922 | 9.79 |
| 72 | San Antonio | 10,197 | 9.51 |
| 73 | New Orleans | 10,899 | 9.18 |
| 74 | Riverside | 12,526 | 8.04 |
| 75 | Little Rock | 3,142 | 7.98 |
| 76 | Milwaukee | 11,084 | 7.93 |
| 77 | El Paso | 3,796 | 7.91 |
| 78 | Anchorage | 1,280 | 7.40 |
| 79 | Salt Lake City | 5,389 | 5.76 |
| 80 | Las Vegas | 1,955 | 4.23 |
| 81 | Jersey City | 1,993 | 3.58 |
| 82 | Providence | 3,122 | 3.30 |
| 83 | Boston | 5,015 | 1.81 |
| 84 | Honolulu | 1,176 | 1.75 |
| 85 | Worcester | 612 | .95 |
| 86 | Columbus, Ga. | 134 | .56 |

# 80. Presbyterians: Trends

Like other main line Protestant religions, Presbyterians are losing adherents in some areas and gaining in others. Among metro areas that were growing, there was an 8 percent increase in Mobile (that is, Presbyterians grew by 8 percent of the 66,000 metro increase, or by about 5,300 persons); Among metro areas that were declining, Presbyterians grew by 65 percent of the Newark metro area decline, i.e., by about 60,000 persons.

The Presbyterian churches for which we have shown 1971 and 1980 data are listed in the previous table.

SOURCES: See previous table.

| Rank | Metro Area | Total Population Change (1970-80) | Presbyterian Population Change as a Percentage of Total Population Change |
|---|---|---|---|
| 1 | Milwaukee | − 6,741 | 54.43 |
| 2 | Detroit | − 82,289 | 27.95 |
| 3 | Pittsburgh | −137,468 | 26.65 |
| 4 | St. Louis | − 55,608 | 21.23 |
| 5 | Philadelphia | −107,292 | 18.58 |
| 6 | Dayton | − 22,461 | 17.59 |
| 7 | Akron | − 18,911 | 16.72 |
| 8 | Mobile | 66,129 | 8.19 |
| 9 | Columbus, Ga. | 612 | 7.03 |
| 10 | Cleveland | −165,009 | 6.03 |
| 11 | Montgomery | 46,776 | 5.15 |
| 12 | Washington, D.C. | 150,129 | 4.90 |
| 13 | Tacoma | 73,299 | 4.75 |
| 14 | New York | −853,979 | 3.60 |
| 15 | Nashville | 151,234 | 2.81 |
| 16 | Charlotte | 79,433 | 1.64 |
| 17 | Boston | 135,744 | 1.28 |
| 18 | Atlanta | 434,101 | 1.24 |
| 18 | Jersey City | − 50,867 | 1.24 |
| 20 | Colorado Springs | 78,170 | 1.04 |
| 21 | Austin | 175,987 | .55 |
| 22 | Phoenix | 536,802 | .42 |
| 23 | Las Vegas | 188,528 | .15 |
| 24 | Salt Lake City | 230,767 | .10 |
| 25 | Anchorage | 46,632 | .09 |
| 26 | Tucson | 179,596 | .08 |
| 27 | Greensboro | 103,256 | .06 |
| 28 | Houston | 906,034 | .05 |
| 29 | Honolulu | 132,346 | .01 |
| 30 | Worcester | 301,718 | − .12 |
| 31 | Jackson | 61,519 | − .16 |
| 32 | Dallas | 597,255 | − .34 |
| 33 | Indianapolis | 1,055,797 | − .47 |
| 34 | Baton Rouge | 118,345 | − .49 |
| 35 | Grand Rapids | 62,455 | − .51 |
| 36 | Sacramento | 210,209 | − .52 |
| 37 | Riverside | 417,931 | − .61 |
| 38 | Albuquerque | 121,233 | − .63 |
| 39 | Lexington-Fayette | 51,435 | − .67 |
| 40 | Miami | 358,187 | − .72 |
| 41 | Tulsa | 140,474 | − .76 |
| 42 | San Diego | 503,992 | − .80 |
| 43 | El Paso | 120,608 | − .82 |
| 44 | Fresno | 101,684 | − .91 |
| 45 | Denver | 380,376 | − .96 |
| 46 | Anaheim | 510,337 | − 1.00 |
| 47 | Birmingham | 80,130 | − 1.22 |
| 48 | Richmond | 84,473 | − 1.33 |
| 49 | Seattle | 182,160 | − 1.54 |
| 50 | Buffalo | −103,638 | − 1.55 |
| 51 | Tampa | 480,943 | − 1.60 |
| 52 | Oklahoma City | 134,996 | − 1.86 |
| 53 | New Orleans | 140,255 | − 1.90 |
| 54 | Chattanooga | 55,683 | − 2.21 |
| 55 | Spokane | 84,348 | − 2.25 |
| 56 | San Antonio | 183,775 | − 2.31 |
| 57 | Portland, Ore. | 235,057 | − 2.33 |
| 58 | Corpus Christi | 41,456 | − 2.38 |
| 59 | Jacksonville | 115,692 | − 3.06 |
| 60 | Madison | 33,273 | − 3.21 |
| 60 | Shreveport | 40,646 | − 3.21 |
| 62 | Knoxville | 67,108 | − 3.31 |
| 63 | Providence | 34,413 | − 3.79 |
| 64 | Minneapolis-St. Paul | 148,865 | − 4.02 |
| 65 | Norfolk | 74,091 | − 4.09 |
| 66 | Lincoln | 24,912 | − 4.16 |
| 67 | Baltimore | 157,007 | − 4.25 |
| 68 | Lubbock | 32,356 | − 4.33 |
| 69 | Little Rock | 70,198 | − 6.20 |
| 70 | San Francisco | 143,472 | − 6.23 |
| 71 | Los Angeles | 435,677 | − 6.34 |
| 72 | Memphis | 78,784 | − 6.57 |
| 73 | Columbus, Ohio | 75,446 | − 6.81 |
| 74 | Toledo | 28,941 | − 7.40 |
| 75 | Wichita | 21,954 | − 7.79 |
| 76 | Des Moines | 24,486 | − 8.14 |
| 77 | Fort Wayne | 20,977 | − 8.74 |
| 78 | Louisville | 38,910 | − 8.88 |
| 79 | Omaha | 27,753 | − 14.37 |
| 80 | Chicago | 127,573 | − 15.20 |
| 81 | Kansas City, Mo., Kan. | 54,000 | − 32.59 |
| 82 | Cincinnati | 14,196 | − 44.91 |
| 83 | Syracuse | 5,779 | − 62.50 |
| 84 | Newark | − 92,164 | − 65.48 |
| 85 | Flint | 12,925 | − 69.97 |
| 86 | Rochester | 10,363 | −107.08 |

# 81. Brethren

The Brethren are an offshoot of the Baptists originating in German-speaking countries. Data for 1980 below show they are strongest in the Baton Rouge metro area, where they represent 45 persons per 1,000 population. Metro Dayton has the second largest concentration of Brethren, 13 per 1,000, followed by Fort Wayne with 7 per 1,000. Only two other metro areas—Akron and Columbus, Ohio—have as many as 2 Brethren per 1,000.

Metro data for 1980 included in the following table cover the following three Congregations of the Brethren (the starred church also provided 1971 data):

Lrethren Church (Ashland, Ohio)
Church of the Brethren*
Fellowship of Grace Brethren Churches, Inc.

SOURCES: Metro religious adherence data for 1980 derived by the authors from county data in Bernard Quinn, Herman Anderson, Martin Bradley, Paul Goetting and Peggy Shriver, *Churches and Church Membership in the United States, 1980: An Enumeration by Region, State and County Based on Data Reported by 111 Church Bodies* (Atlanta: Glenmary Research Center, 1982). Metro population data for 1980 derived by the authors from county data in Hana Umlauf Lane, Ed., *The World Alamanac & Book of Facts 1983* (New York: Newspaper Enterprise Association, Inc., 1981), pp. 246–263. Metro data for 1971 derived by the authors from county data in Douglas W. Johnson, Paul R. Picard and Bernard Quinn, *Churches and Church Membership in the United States: An Enumeration by Region, State and County* (Atlanta: Glenmary Research Center, 1974).

| Rank | Metro Area | Brethren | Brethren per 1,000 Population |
|---|---|---|---|
| 1 | Baton Rouge | 22,362 | 45.27 |
| 2 | Dayton | 10,764 | 12.97 |
| 3 | Fort Wayne | 2,556 | 6.67 |

| Rank | Metro Area | Brethren | Brethren per 1,000 Population |
|---|---|---|---|
| 4 | Akron | 1,680 | 2.54 |
| 5 | Columbus, Ohio | 2,625 | 2.40 |
| 6 | Wichita | 752 | 1.83 |
| 7 | Fresno | 874 | 1.70 |
| 8 | Pittsburgh | 3,387 | 1.50 |
| 9 | Los Angeles | 10,231 | 1.37 |
| 10 | Baltimore | 2,881 | 1.33 |
| 11 | Washington, D.C. | 3,964 | 1.30 |
| 12 | Des Moines | 432 | 1.28 |
| 13 | Toledo | 720 | .91 |
| 14 | Philadelphia | 4,265 | .90 |
| 15 | Tucson | 425 | .80 |
| 16 | Colorado Springs | 243 | .77 |
| 17 | Anaheim | 1,469 | .76 |
| 18 | Lincoln | 141 | .73 |
| 19 | Kansas City, Mo., Kan. | 709 | .53 |
| 19 | Phoenix | 801 | .53 |
| 21 | Greensboro | 421 | .51 |
| 22 | Cleveland | 956 | .50 |
| 22 | Riverside | 785 | .50 |
| 24 | Norfolk | 377 | .47 |
| 25 | Indianapolis | 530 | .45 |
| 26 | Grand Rapids | 267 | .44 |
| 26 | Seattle | 705 | .44 |
| 28 | Denver | 696 | .43 |
| 29 | Omaha | 232 | .41 |
| 29 | Richmond | 256 | .41 |
| 31 | Honolulu | 290 | .38 |
| 32 | Sacramento | 357 | .35 |
| 33 | Tampa | 526 | .34 |
| 34 | Anchorage | 56 | .32 |
| 35 | Mobile | 111 | .25 |
| 36 | Albuquerque | 107 | .24 |
| 36 | Chicago | 1,683 | .24 |
| 36 | Portland, Ore. | 293 | .24 |
| 36 | San Diego | 451 | .24 |
| 40 | Spokane | 52 | .15 |
| 40 | Tacoma | 73 | .15 |
| 42 | Jacksonville | 100 | .14 |
| 43 | Cincinnati | 177 | .13 |
| 44 | Detroit | 529 | .12 |
| 44 | Knoxville | 59 | .12 |
| 46 | Atlanta | 228 | .11 |
| 47 | Flint | 50 | .10 |
| 48 | Miami | 106 | .07 |
| 48 | San Francisco | 221 | .07 |
| 50 | Birmingham | 37 | .04 |
| 51 | Charlotte | 17 | .03 |
| 52 | Louisville | 18 | .02 |
| 53 | New York | 112 | .01 |

# 82. Brethren: Trends

The Brethren are not growing much relative to the population. The most rapid growth by this measure between 1971 and 1980 was in the Baton Rouge area where the Brethren grew one-fifth as fast as the population. It was as if nearly one of every five newcomers to the area were one of the Brethren.

SOURCES: See previous table.

| Rank | Metro Area | Total Population Change (1970-80) | Brethren Population Change as a Percentage of Total Population Change |
|------|-----------|------|------|
| 1 | Baton Rouge | 118,345 | 18.90 |
| 2 | Fort Wayne | 20,977 | 3.44 |
| 3 | Columbus, Ohio | 75,446 | 3.25 |
| 4 | Los Angeles | 435,677 | 1.46 |
| 5 | Wichita | 21,961 | .93 |
| 6 | Washington, D.C. | 150,129 | .72 |
| 7 | Detroit | − 82,289 | .26 |
| 7 | Norfolk | 74,091 | .26 |
| 9 | Anaheim | 510,337 | .24 |
| 10 | Honolulu | 132,346 | .22 |
| 11 | Grand Rapids | 62,455 | .21 |
| 12 | Riverside | 417,931 | .19 |
| 13 | Indianapolis | 55,577 | .17 |
| 14 | Omaha | 27,753 | .16 |
| 15 | Colorado Springs | 78,170 | .15 |
| 16 | Richmond | 84,473 | .14 |
| 16 | Tucson | 179,596 | .14 |
| 18 | Anchorage | 46,632 | .12 |
| 19 | Spokane | 54,348 | .10 |
| 20 | Portland, Ore. | 235,057 | .07 |

| Rank | Metro Area | Total Population Change (1970-80) | Brethren Population Change as a Percentage of Total Population Change |
|------|-----------|------|------|
| 21 | Greensboro | 103,256 | .06 |
| 21 | Sacramento | 210,209 | .06 |
| 23 | Atlanta | 434,101 | .05 |
| 23 | Louisville | 38,910 | .05 |
| 25 | Phoenix | 536,802 | .04 |
| 25 | Tampa | 480,943 | .04 |
| 27 | Denver | 380,376 | .03 |
| 27 | San Diego | 503,992 | .03 |
| 29 | Albuquerque | 121,233 | .02 |
| 29 | Charlotte | 79,433 | .02 |
| 31 | Miami | 358,187 | .01 |
| 32 | Toledo | 28,941 | .01 |
| 33 | Birmingham | 80,130 | − .01 |
| 33 | Mobile | 66,129 | − .01 |
| 35 | Knoxville | 67,108 | − .02 |
| 36 | Jacksonville | 115,692 | − .03 |
| 36 | San Francisco | 143,472 | − .03 |
| 38 | Tacoma | 73,299 | − .04 |
| 39 | Minneapolis-St. Paul | 148,865 | − .05 |
| 40 | Oklahoma City | 134,996 | − .06 |
| 41 | Baltimore | 157,007 | − .07 |
| 41 | Cleveland | −165,009 | − .07 |
| 43 | Des Moines | 24,486 | − .13 |
| 43 | Fresno | 101,684 | − .13 |
| 43 | Lincoln | 24,912 | − .13 |
| 43 | Seattle | 182,160 | − .13 |
| 47 | Chicago | 127,753 | − .23 |
| 48 | Kansas City, Mo., Kan. | 54,000 | − .27 |
| 49 | Philadelphia | −107,292 | − .42 |
| 50 | Pittsburgh | −137,468 | − .60 |
| 51 | Flint | 12,925 | − 1.11 |
| 52 | Akron | − 18,911 | − 2.99 |
| 53 | Dayton | − 22,461 | − 9.43 |
| 54 | Cincinnati | 14,196 | −12.91 |

# 83. Pentecostal Churches

The Pentecostal Church is a fundamentalist and revivalist movement that grew up in the first decade of the 20th century within the Methodist Church and other Protestant denominations to rekindle religious fervor. It eventually became a separate church as well as a force within other churches.

Pentecostal Church adherents predominate in the sunbelt, and the church continues strong in the areas in which it originated. In 1980, adherents constituted over 3 percent of the populations of the Columbus, Georgia and Mobile areas. They constituted over 2 percent in seven other cities.

The 1980 data cover the following eight churches (two starred churches also provided 1971 data):

Assemblies of God
Bible Church of Christ, Inc.
Church of God (Cleveland, Tenn.)*
Congregational Holiness Church
International Church of the Four-Square Gospel
Open Bible Standard Churches, Inc.
Pentecostal Free Will Baptist Church, Inc.
Pentecostal Holiness Church, Inc.*

SOURCES: Metro religious adherence data for 1980 derived by the authors from county data in Bernard Quinn, Herman Anderson, Martin Bradley, Paul Goetting and Peggy Shriver, *Churches and Church Membership in the United States, 1980: An Enumeration by Region, State and County Based on Data Reported by 111 Church Bodies* (Atlanta: Glenmary Research Center, 1982). Metro population data for 1980 derived by the authors from county data in Hana Umlauf Lane, Ed., *The World Almanac Book of Facts 1983* (New York: Newspaper Enterprise Association, Inc., 1981), pp. 246–263. Metro data for 1971 derived by the authors from county data in Douglas W. Johnson, Paul R. Picard and Bernard Quinn, *Churches and Church Membership in the United States: An Enumeration by Region, State and County* (Atlanta: Glenmary Research Center, 1974).

| Rank | Metro Area | Pentecostals | Pentecostals per 1,000 Population |
|---|---|---|---|
| 1 | Columbus, Ga. | 8,197 | 34.27 |
| 2 | Mobile | 13,765 | 31.08 |
| 3 | Tulsa | 20,169 | 29.25 |
| 4 | Chattanooga | 11,189 | 26.23 |
| 5 | Birmingham | 21,887 | 25.83 |
| 6 | Oklahoma City | 20,096 | 24.09 |
| 7 | Fresno | 12,280 | 23.84 |
| 8 | Des Moines | 7,247 | 21.44 |
| 9 | Charlotte | 12,918 | 20.27 |
| 10 | Jacksonville | 14,737 | 19.98 |
| 11 | Little Rock | 7,409 | 18.83 |
| 12 | Dallas | 48,629 | 16.35 |
| 13 | Tacoma | 7,584 | 15.62 |
| 14 | Portland, Ore. | 18,603 | 14.98 |
| 15 | Spokane | 5,112 | 14.95 |
| 16 | Anchorage | 2,566 | 14.83 |
| 17 | Los Angeles | 110,606 | 14.79 |
| 18 | Lubbock | 3,070 | 14.51 |
| 19 | Riverside | 22,447 | 14.42 |
| 20 | Colorado Springs | 4,453 | 14.03 |
| 21 | Sacramento | 13,857 | 13.67 |
| 22 | Wichita | 5,617 | 13.66 |
| 23 | Las Vegas | 6,288 | 13.62 |
| 24 | Tampa | 21,284 | 13.56 |
| 25 | Memphis | 11,742 | 12.86 |
| 26 | Kansas City, Mo., Kan. | 17,010 | 12.81 |
| 27 | Seattle | 20,131 | 12.53 |
| 28 | Dayton | 10,281 | 12.39 |
| 29 | Shreveport | 4,374 | 11.61 |
| 30 | Jackson | 3,704 | 11.56 |

| Rank | City | Pentecostals | Pentecostals per 1,000 Population |
|---|---|---|---|
| 31 | Montgomery | 3,104 | 11.38 |
| 32 | Atlanta | 22,314 | 10.99 |
| 33 | Corpus Christi | 3,582 | 10.98 |
| 34 | Houston | 31,793 | 10.94 |
| 35 | Louisville | 9,485 | 10.47 |
| 36 | St. Louis | 23,694 | 10.06 |
| 37 | San Francisco | 30,213 | 9.29 |
| 38 | Albuquerque | 4,200 | 9.24 |
| 39 | New Orleans | 10,756 | 9.06 |
| 40 | Honolulu | 5,987 | 8.90 |
| 41 | Flint | 4,598 | 8.82 |
| 42 | Akron | 5,817 | 8.81 |
| 43 | Lincoln | 1,696 | 8.79 |
| 44 | Denver | 14,058 | 8.68 |
| 45 | Knoxville | 3,909 | 8.20 |
| 46 | Indianapolis | 9,479 | 8.12 |
| 47 | Lexington-Fayette | 2,493 | 7.84 |
| 48 | Tucson | 4,034 | 7.59 |
| 49 | Omaha | 4,308 | 7.55 |
| 50 | Austin | 4,051 | 7.55 |
| 51 | Norfolk | 6,009 | 7.45 |
| 52 | Greensboro | 5,987 | 7.24 |
| 53 | Anaheim | 13,964 | 7.23 |
| 54 | Richmond | 4,473 | 7.08 |
| 55 | San Diego | 13,043 | 7.01 |
| 56 | San Antonio | 7,468 | 6.97 |
| 57 | Phoenix | 10,109 | 6.70 |
| 58 | Nashville | 5,081 | 5.97 |
| 59 | Toledo | 4,656 | 5.88 |
| 60 | Baton Rouge | 2,824 | 5.72 |
| 61 | Detroit | 24,781 | 5.69 |
| 62 | Syracuse | 3,635 | 5.66 |
| 63 | Grand Rapids | 3,381 | 5.62 |
| 64 | Minneapolis-St. Paul | 11,424 | 5.40 |
| 65 | El Paso | 2,556 | 5.33 |
| 66 | Cleveland | 9,739 | 5.13 |
| 67 | Rochester | 4,753 | 4.89 |
| 68 | Columbus, Ohio | 5,339 | 4.88 |
| 69 | Pittsburgh | 10,809 | 4.77 |
| 70 | Washington, D.C. | 14,521 | 4.75 |
| 71 | Miami | 7,383 | 4.54 |
| 72 | New York | 39,071 | 4.28 |
| 73 | Baltimore | 9,291 | 4.27 |
| 74 | Cincinnati | 5,661 | 4.04 |
| 75 | Jersey City | 2,031 | 3.65 |
| 76 | Worcester | 2,268 | 3.51 |
| 77 | Buffalo | 4,322 | 3.47 |
| 78 | Salt Lake City | 3,190 | 3.41 |
| 79 | Milwaukee | 4,542 | 3.25 |
| 80 | Chicago | 23,006 | 3.24 |
| 81 | Fort Wayne | 1,165 | 3.04 |
| 82 | Philadelphia | 12,082 | 2.56 |
| 83 | Newark | 4,593 | 2.34 |
| 84 | Boston | 5,690 | 2.06 |
| 85 | Madison | 583 | 1.80 |
| 86 | Providence | 1,439 | 1.52 |

# 84. Pentecostal Church Trends

The most rapid increase in adherents to Pentecostal churches in the 1970s was in the Columbus, Georgia area, where adherents increased 12 times as fast as the overall population.

In the Syracuse and Rochester areas, there were over 42 new adherents to Pentecostal churches for every 100 new residents.

SOURCES: The churches covered in 1971 and 1980 and sources for data are listed in the previous table.

| Rank | Metro Area | Total Population Change (1970–80) | Pentecostal Population Change as a Percentage of Total Population Change |
|---|---|---|---|
| 1 | Columbus, Ga. | 612 | 1,199.18 |
| 2 | Syracuse | 5,779 | 62.78 |
| 3 | Rochester | 10,363 | 42.11 |
| 4 | Kansas City, Mo., Kan. | 54,000 | 30.75 |
| 5 | Des Moines | 24,486 | 28.76 |
| 6 | Flint | 12,925 | 27.42 |
| 7 | Los Angeles | 435,677 | 24.71 |
| 8 | Wichita | 21,954 | 22.46 |
| 9 | San Francisco | 143,472 | 19.79 |
| 10 | Louisville | 38,910 | 19.32 |
| 11 | Birmingham | 80,130 | 17.09 |
| 12 | Chicago | 127,573 | 15.13 |
| 13 | Mobile | 66,129 | 14.59 |
| 14 | Cincinnati | 14,196 | 14.33 |
| 15 | Omaha | 27,753 | 14.25 |
| 16 | Tulsa | 140,474 | 12.93 |
| 17 | Oklahoma City | 134,996 | 12.07 |
| 18 | Memphis | 78,784 | 11.99 |
| 19 | Fresno | 101,684 | 10.97 |
| 20 | Seattle | 182,160 | 10.90 |
| 21 | Shreveport | 40,646 | 10.20 |
| 22 | Tacoma | 73,299 | 10.18 |
| 23 | Toledo | 28,941 | 9.98 |
| 24 | Little Rock | 70,198 | 9.80 |
| 25 | Jacksonville | 115,692 | 8.70 |
| 26 | Charlotte | 79,433 | 8.56 |
| 27 | Lubbock | 32,356 | 8.27 |
| 28 | Corpus Christi | 41,456 | 8.09 |
| 29 | Washington, D.C. | 150,129 | 7.72 |
| 30 | Portland, Ore. | 235,057 | 7.67 |
| 31 | Dallas | 597,255 | 7.57 |
| 32 | Minneapolis-St. Paul | 148,865 | 7.55 |
| 33 | New Orleans | 140,255 | 6.60 |
| 34 | Lincoln | 24,912 | 6.51 |

| Rank | Metro Area | Total Population Change (1970–80) | Pentecostal Population Change as a Percentage of Total Population Change |
|---|---|---|---|
| 35 | Sacramento | 210,209 | 6.27 |
| 36 | Spokane | 84,348 | 5.97 |
| 37 | Greensboro | 103,256 | 5.53 |
| 38 | Colorado Springs | 78,170 | 5.48 |
| 39 | Norfolk | 74,091 | 5.20 |
| 40 | Chattanooga | 55,683 | 5.16 |
| 41 | Riverside | 417,931 | 5.06 |
| 42 | Anchorage | 46,632 | 5.01 |
| 43 | Montgomery | 46,776 | 4.83 |
| 44 | Grand Rapids | 62,455 | 4.69 |
| 45 | Fort Wayne | 20,977 | 4.44 |
| 46 | Honolulu | 132,346 | 4.32 |
| 47 | Columbus, Ohio | 75,446 | 4.31 |
| 48 | Jackson | 61,519 | 4.07 |
| 49 | San Antonio | 183,775 | 3.92 |
| 50 | Baltimore | 157,007 | 3.71 |
| 51 | Denver | 380,376 | 3.55 |
| 52 | Providence | 34,413 | 3.43 |
| 53 | Houston | 906,034 | 3.36 |
| 54 | Albuquerque | 121,233 | 3.31 |
| 55 | Richmond | 84,473 | 3.25 |
| 56 | Las Vegas | 188,528 | 3.24 |
| 57 | Tampa | 480,843 | 3.19 |
| 58 | Atlanta | 434,100 | 2.73 |
| 59 | Lexington-Fayette | 51,435 | 2.58 |
| 60 | Anaheim | 510,337 | 2.54 |
| 61 | San Diego | 503,992 | 2.51 |
| 62 | Nashville | 151,234 | 2.38 |
| 63 | Austin | 175,987 | 2.19 |
| 64 | El Paso | 120,608 | 2.05 |
| 65 | Tucson | 179,596 | 1.97 |
| 66 | Baton Rouge | 118,345 | 1.86 |
| 67 | Madison | 33,273 | 1.70 |
| 68 | Miami | 358,187 | 1.64 |
| 69 | Phoenix | 536,802 | 1.47 |
| 70 | Salt Lake City | 230,767 | 1.36 |
| 71 | Knoxville | 67,108 | 1.02 |
| 72 | Indianapolis | 1,055,797 | .77 |
| 73 | Worcester | 301,718 | .70 |
| 74 | Boston | − 135,744 | − 2.67 |
| 75 | Jersey City | − 50,867 | − 3.86 |
| 76 | Buffalo | − 103,638 | − 4.03 |
| 77 | New York | − 853,979 | − 4.36 |
| 78 | Newark | − 92,164 | − 4.50 |
| 79 | Cleveland | − 165,009 | − 4.84 |
| 80 | Pittsburgh | − 137,468 | − 7.07 |
| 81 | Philadelphia | − 107,292 | − 10.53 |
| 82 | Detroit | − 82,289 | − 22.89 |
| 83 | Akron | − 18,911 | − 25.83 |
| 84 | Dayton | − 22,461 | − 30.20 |
| 85 | St. Louis | − 55,608 | − 38.61 |
| 86 | Milwaukee | − 6,741 | − 63.73 |

# 85. Mennonites

Of the major urban areas, the largest concentration of Mennonites relative to population in 1980 was in Fort Wayne, where over 2 percent of the population are Mennonites. Other concentrations are in areas like Fresno and Wichita, which include farming communities, or midwestern and southern communities that serve as hubs for farm produce.

Metro Philadelphia has the largest absolute number of Mennonites—12,404. Many of these Mennonites came there when it was mostly farming country. The city grew up around them. The Pennsylvania Dutch country to the west of Philadelphia, with its well-manicured farms and tourist areas, is well known for its Amish population.

The following eight churches are included in 1980 data on Mennonite adherents (three starred churches also provided 1971 data):

Beachy Amish Mennonite Churches
Church of God in Christ (Mennonite)
Evangelical Mennonite Bretheren Conference*
General Conference of Mennonite Bretheren Churches
Mennonite Church*
The General Conference, Mennonite Church*
Old Order Amish Church

SOURCES: Metro religious adherence data for 1980 derived by the authors from county data in Bernard Quinn, Herman Anderson, Martin Bradley, Paul Goetting and Peggy Shriver, *Churches and Church Membership in the United States, 1980: An Enumeration by Region, State and County Based on Data Reported by 111 Church Bodies* (Atlanta: Glenmary Research Center, 1982). Metro population data for 1980 derived by the authors from county data in Hana Umlauf Lane, Ed., *The World Almanac Book of Facts 1983* (New York: Newspaper Enterprise Association, Inc., 1981), pp. 246–263. Metro data for 1971 derived by the authors from county data in Douglas W. Johnson, Paul R. Picard and Bernard Quinn, *Churches and Church Membership in the United States: An Enumeration by Region, State and County* (Atlanta: Glenmary Research Center, 1974).

| Rank | Metro Area | Mennonites | Mennonites per 1,000 Population |
|---|---|---|---|
| 1 | Fort Wayne | 8,511 | 22.22 |
| 2 | Fresno | 3,368 | 6.54 |
| 3 | Wichita | 2,269 | 5.52 |
| 4 | Toledo | 3,864 | 4.88 |
| 5 | Cleveland | 7,965 | 4.19 |
| 6 | Philadelphia | 12,404 | 2.63 |
| 7 | Tulsa | 1,263 | 1.83 |
| 8 | Columbus, Ohio | 1,526 | 1.40 |
| 9 | Corpus Christi | 330 | 1.01 |
| 10 | Knoxville | 411 | .86 |
| 11 | Omaha | 413 | .72 |
| 12 | Colorado Springs | 225 | .71 |
| 13 | Denver | 1,043 | .64 |
| 13 | Phoenix | 959 | .64 |
| 13 | Portland, Ore. | 799 | .64 |
| 16 | Kansas City, Mo., Kan. | 835 | .63 |
| 17 | Oklahoma City | 461 | .55 |
| 18 | Norfolk | 403 | .50 |
| 19 | Buffalo | 430 | .35 |
| 20 | Akron | 210 | .32 |
| 21 | Flint | 146 | .28 |
| 21 | Lincoln | 54 | .28 |
| 23 | San Francisco | 854 | .26 |
| 24 | Richmond | 132 | .21 |
| 25 | Anchorage | 34 | .20 |
| 25 | Grand Rapids | 119 | .20 |
| 27 | Chicago | 1,327 | .19 |
| 27 | Riverside | 301 | .19 |
| 29 | Indianapolis | 185 | .16 |
| 30 | Washington, D.C. | 445 | .15 |
| 31 | Minneapolis-St. Paul | 301 | .14 |
| 32 | Des Moines | 39 | .12 |
| 32 | Tampa | 183 | .12 |
| 32 | Tucson | 62 | .12 |
| 35 | Baltimore | 231 | .11 |
| 36 | Albuquerque | 39 | .09 |
| 36 | Cincinnati | 127 | .09 |
| 36 | St. Louis | 206 | .09 |
| 36 | Seattle | 142 | .09 |
| 40 | Birmingham | 58 | .07 |
| 40 | Los Angeles | 500 | .07 |
| 42 | Anaheim | 121 | .06 |
| 42 | Miami | 97 | .08 |
| 44 | Houston | 155 | .05 |
| 44 | New York | 412 | .05 |
| 44 | Sacramento | 50 | .05 |
| 47 | Boston | 101 | .04 |
| 47 | Louisville | 34 | .04 |
| 49 | Atlanta | 52 | .03 |
| 49 | Detroit | 130 | .03 |
| 49 | Milwaukee | 36 | .03 |
| 52 | Jackson | 8 | .02 |
| 52 | Rochester | 19 | .02 |
| 52 | Syracuse | 13 | .02 |
| 55 | Dallas | 24 | .01 |
| 55 | Mobile | 6 | .01 |
| 55 | Newark | 16 | .01 |
| 55 | Pittsburgh | 27 | .01 |

# 86.  Mennonites: Trends

Metro areas where Mennonites have been increasing in number are generally the same areas where they are already strong, such as Fort Wayne, where they grew by 27 percent of the area's 21,000-person increase, i.e., by about 5,700 persons. Other metro areas that show a strong increase relative to area population changes are Wichita, Toledo, Cleveland and Fresno—all of which are among the top five in the previous table.

SOURCES: Churches covered by 1971 and 1980 data are identified in the previous table.

| Rank | Metro Area | Total Population Change (1970–80) | Mennonite Population Change as a Percentage of Total Population Change |
|---|---|---|---|
| 1 | Fort Wayne | 20,977 | 27.34 |
| 2 | Wichita | 21,954 | 6.42 |
| 3 | Toledo | 28,941 | 4.89 |
| 4 | Fresno | 101,684 | 2.42 |
| 5 | Columbus, Ohio | 75,446 | .97 |
| 6 | Omaha | 27,753 | .61 |
| 7 | San Francisco | 143,472 | .60 |
| 7 | Tulsa | 140,474 | .60 |
| 9 | Knoxville | 67,108 | .50 |
| 10 | Chicago | 127,573 | .46 |
| 11 | Corpus Christi | 41,456 | .35 |
| 12 | Dayton | − 22,461 | .33 |
| 13 | Oklahoma City | 134,996 | .32 |
| 14 | Kansas City, Mo., Kan. | 54,000 | .30 |
| 15 | Washington, D.C. | 150,129 | .24 |
| 16 | Norfolk | 74,091 | .22 |

| Rank | Metro Area | Total Population Change (1970–80) | Mennonite Population Change as a Percentage of Total Population Change |
|---|---|---|---|
| 16 | Syracuse | 5,779 | .22 |
| 18 | Pittsburgh | − 137,468 | .19 |
| 19 | Rochester | 10,363 | .18 |
| 20 | Minneapolis-St. Paul | 148,865 | .16 |
| 21 | Cincinnati | 14,196 | .13 |
| 22 | Denver | 380,376 | .12 |
| 23 | Louisville | 38,910 | .09 |
| 24 | Anchorage | 46,632 | .07 |
| 25 | Phoenix | 536,802 | .07 |
| 26 | Baltimore | 157,007 | .06 |
| 26 | Flint | 12,925 | .06 |
| 28 | Buffalo | − 103,638 | .05 |
| 28 | Portland, Ore. | 235,057 | .05 |
| 30 | Richmond | 84,473 | .04 |
| 31 | Birmingham | 80,130 | .03 |
| 31 | Tucson | 179,596 | .03 |
| 33 | Anaheim | 510,337 | .02 |
| 33 | Sacramento | 210,209 | .02 |
| 35 | Houston | 906,034 | .01 |
| 35 | Jackson | 61,519 | .01 |
| 35 | Miami | 358,187 | .01 |
| 38 | Boston | − 135,744 | − .01 |
| 39 | Los Angeles | 435,677 | − .01 |
| 40 | Colorado Springs | 78,170 | − .02 |
| 41 | Detroit | − 82,289 | − .03 |
| 42 | Des Moines | 24,486 | − .05 |
| 42 | Riverside | 417,931 | − .05 |
| 42 | Seattle | 182,160 | − .05 |
| 45 | St. Louis | − 55,608 | − .09 |
| 46 | Milwaukee | − 6,741 | − .15 |
| 47 | Akron | − 18,911 | − .19 |
| 48 | Lincoln | 24,912 | − .26 |
| 49 | Philadelphia | − 107,292 | − .80 |
| 50 | Cleveland | − 165,009 | − 4.17 |

# 87.  Adventists

The Adventists are a sect of fundamentalist Christians who have readopted Saturday (the original Jewish Sabbath) as their day of rest and worship. They believe in the imminent return ("advent") of Jesus. Founded in the mid-19th century by people persuaded of beliefs enunciated by William Miller, the Adventists have had a strong missionary zeal and have increased their numbers in many areas. The strongest concentrations in 1980 were Riverside and Lincoln metro areas (18 per 1,000 residents), Chattanooga (17 per 1,000) and Portland, Oregon (12 per 1,000).

The 1980 metro data cover three Adventists churches (starred church also provided 1971 data).

Advent Christian Church
Primitive Advent Christian Church
Seventh-Day Adventists*

SOURCE: Metro religious adherence data for 1980 derived by the authors from county data in Bernard Quinn, Herman Anderson, Martin Bradley, Paul Goetting and Peggy Shriver, *Churches and Church Membership in the United States, 1980: An Enumeration by Region, State and County Based on Data Reported by 111 Church Bodies* (Atlanta: Glenmary Research Center, 1982). Metro population data for 1980 derived by the authors from county data in Hana Umlauf Lane, Ed., *The World Almanac & Book of Facts 1983* (New York: Newspaper Enterprise Association, Inc., 1981), pp. 246–263. Metro data for 1971 derived by the authors from county data in Douglas W. Johnson, Paul R. Picard and Bernard Quinn, *Churches and Church Membership in the United States: An Enumeration by Region, State and County* (Atlanta: Glenmary Research Center, 1974).

| Rank | Metro Area | Adventists | Adventists per 1,000 Population |
|------|-----------|-----------|-------------------------------|
| 1 | Riverside | 28,682 | 18.42 |
| 2 | Lincoln | 3,397 | 17.61 |
| 3 | Chattanooga | 7,192 | 16.86 |
| 4 | Portland, Ore. | 14,494 | 11.67 |
| 5 | Worcester | 3,550 | 9.52 |
| 6 | Spokane | 2,921 | 8.55 |
| 7 | Fresno | 3,802 | 7.38 |
| 8 | Nashville | 5,536 | 6.51 |
| 9 | Sacramento | 5,957 | 5.87 |
| 10 | Montgomery | 1,561 | 5.72 |
| 11 | San Diego | 9,473 | 5.09 |
| 12 | Los Angeles | 37,593 | 5.03 |
| 13 | Baton Rouge | 2,360 | 4.78 |
| 14 | Columbus, Ga. | 1,141 | 4.77 |
| 15 | Honolulu | 3,622 | 4.75 |
| 16 | Denver | 7,609 | 4.70 |
| 17 | Charlotte | 2,831 | 4.44 |
| 18 | Seattle | 6,900 | 4.29 |
| 19 | San Francisco | 13,827 | 4.25 |
| 20 | Shreveport | 1,515 | 4.02 |
| 21 | Jackson | 1,224 | 3.82 |
| 22 | Mobile | 1,639 | 3.70 |
| 23 | Greensboro | 3,021 | 3.65 |
| 24 | Jacksonville | 2,633 | 3.57 |
| 25 | Dayton | 2,936 | 3.54 |
| 25 | Tampa | 5,556 | 3.54 |
| 27 | Chicago | 24,833 | 3.50 |
| 28 | Omaha | 1,976 | 3.46 |
| 29 | Birmingham | 2,894 | 3.42 |
| 30 | Miami | 5,552 | 3.41 |

| Rank | Metro Area | Adventists | Adventists per 1,000 Population |
|------|-----------|-----------|-------------------------------|
| 31 | Tacoma | 1,631 | 3.36 |
| 32 | Phoenix | 4,893 | 3.24 |
| 33 | Flint | 1,658 | 3.18 |
| 34 | Albuquerque | 1,432 | 3.15 |
| 35 | Wichita | 1,290 | 3.14 |
| 36 | Anaheim | 6,025 | 3.12 |
| 37 | New York | 27,797 | 3.05 |
| 38 | Kansas City, Mo., Kan. | 4,013 | 3.02 |
| 39 | Dallas | 8,899 | 2.99 |
| 40 | Grand Rapids | 1,727 | 2.87 |
| 41 | Memphis | 2,589 | 2.84 |
| 42 | Indianapolis | 3,288 | 2.82 |
| 43 | Washington, D.C. | 8,534 | 2.79 |
| 44 | Tulsa | 1,900 | 2.76 |
| 45 | Richmond | 1,708 | 2.70 |
| 46 | Louisville | 2,442 | 2.69 |
| 47 | Des Moines | 900 | 2.66 |
| 47 | Colorado Springs | 846 | 2.66 |
| 47 | Oklahoma City | 2,219 | 2.66 |
| 50 | St. Louis | 6,077 | 2.58 |
| 51 | Madison | 791 | 2.44 |
| 52 | Columbus, Ohio | 2,571 | 2.35 |
| 53 | Knoxville | 1,072 | 2.25 |
| 54 | New Orleans | 2,651 | 2.23 |
| 55 | Tucson | 1,180 | 2.22 |
| 56 | Baltimore | 4,778 | 2.20 |
| 57 | Anchorage | 375 | 2.17 |
| 58 | Detroit | 9,230 | 2.12 |
| 59 | Cleveland | 3,913 | 2.06 |
| 60 | Lexington-Fayette | 566 | 1.78 |
| 61 | Cincinnati | 2,463 | 1.76 |
| 62 | Akron | 1,158 | 1.75 |
| 63 | El Paso | 793 | 1.65 |
| 64 | Rochester | 1,560 | 1.61 |
| 65 | Syracuse | 978 | 1.52 |
| 66 | Las Vegas | 686 | 1.49 |
| 67 | Atlanta | 2,970 | 1.46 |
| 68 | Norfolk | 1,139 | 1.41 |
| 69 | Philadelphia | 6,550 | 1.39 |
| 70 | Minneapolis-St. Paul | 2,823 | 1.34 |
| 71 | Toledo | 1,043 | 1.32 |
| 72 | San Antonio | 1,367 | 1.28 |
| 73 | Milwaukee | 1,747 | 1.25 |
| 74 | Jersey City | 685 | 1.23 |
| 75 | Newark | 2,352 | 1.20 |
| 76 | Providence | 1,123 | 1.19 |
| 77 | Little Rock | 457 | 1.16 |
| 78 | Fort Wayne | 431 | 1.13 |
| 79 | Boston | 4,089 | 1.12 |
| 80 | Houston | 3,236 | 1.11 |
| 81 | Lubbock | 232 | 1.10 |
| 82 | Corpus Christi | 356 | 1.09 |
| 83 | Buffalo | 1,303 | 1.05 |
| 84 | Austin | 478 | .89 |
| 84 | Salt Lake City | 831 | .89 |
| 86 | Pittsburgh | 1,757 | .78 |

# 88. Adventists: Trends

The most rapid increase in Adventists relative to population between 1971 and 1980 was 94 percent in metro Columbus Ga., nearly the rate of population growth, i.e., about 560 new Adventists (which may have come from inclusion of a third Adventist church) vs. a population increase of about 600.

In the Chicago area there were 11 new Adventists for every 100 new residents.

SOURCES: Churches covered by 1971 and 1980 data are identified in the previous table.

| Rank | Metro Area | Total Population Change (1970–80) | Adventist Population Change as a Percentage of Total Population Change |
|---|---|---|---|
| 1 | Columbus, Ga. | 612 | 94.28 |
| 2 | Chicago | 127,573 | 11.38 |
| 3 | Chattanooga | 55,683 | 3.09 |
| 4 | Rochester | 10,363 | 2.60 |
| 5 | Louisville | 38,910 | 2.55 |
| 6 | Kansas City, Mo., Kan. | 54,000 | 2.42 |
| 7 | Omaha | 27,753 | 2.35 |
| 8 | Montgomery | 46,776 | 1.79 |
| 9 | Charlotte | 79,433 | 1.78 |
| 10 | Wichita | 21,961 | 1.77 |
| 11 | Lincoln | 24,912 | 1.66 |
| 12 | Shreveport | 40,646 | 1.65 |
| 13 | Memphis | 78,784 | 1.30 |
| 14 | Providence | 38,267 | 1.29 |
| 15 | Jackson | 61,519 | 1.18 |
| 16 | Los Angeles | 435,677 | 1.17 |
| 17 | Miami | 358,187 | 1.14 |
| 18 | Baton Rouge | 118,345 | 1.04 |
| 18 | Riverside | 417,931 | 1.04 |
| 20 | Flint | 12,925 | 1.02 |
| 21 | Nashville | 151,234 | 1.01 |
| 22 | Birmingham | 80,130 | .95 |
| 23 | Greensboro | 103,256 | .93 |
| 23 | Spokane | 54,348 | .93 |
| 25 | Indianapolis | 55,577 | .91 |
| 26 | Jacksonville | 115,692 | .90 |
| 27 | Mobile | 66,129 | .86 |
| 28 | Portland, Ore. | 235,057 | .84 |
| 29 | Des Moines | 24,486 | .80 |
| 30 | Fresno | 101,684 | .68 |
| 31 | Columbus, Ohio | 75,446 | .65 |
| 32 | Honolulu | 132,346 | .59 |
| 33 | Knoxville | 67,108 | .48 |
| 34 | Richmond | 84,473 | .47 |

| Rank | Metro Area | Total Population Change (1970–80) | Adventist Population Change as a Percentage of Total Population Change |
|---|---|---|---|
| 35 | Fort Wayne | 20,977 | .46 |
| 35 | New Orleans | 140,255 | .46 |
| 37 | Colorado Springs | 78,170 | .43 |
| 37 | Tampa | 480,943 | .43 |
| 39 | Sacramento | 210,209 | .41 |
| 40 | San Diego | 503,992 | .40 |
| 41 | Tulsa | 140,474 | .38 |
| 42 | Dallas | 597,255 | .37 |
| 43 | San Francisco | 143,472 | .36 |
| 44 | Lexington-Fayette | 51,435 | .35 |
| 44 | Oklahoma City | 134,996 | .35 |
| 46 | Norfolk | 74,091 | .34 |
| 47 | Baltimore | 157,007 | .32 |
| 48 | Seattle | 182,160 | .30 |
| 49 | Corpus Christi | 41,456 | .24 |
| 49 | Denver | 380,376 | .24 |
| 51 | El Paso | 120,608 | .23 |
| 52 | Phoenix | 536,802 | .22 |
| 52 | Toledo | 28,941 | .22 |
| 54 | Anaheim | 510,337 | .21 |
| 54 | Madison | 33,272 | .21 |
| 56 | Las Vegas | 188,528 | .17 |
| 57 | Worcester | 372,940 | .16 |
| 58 | San Antonio | 183,775 | .15 |
| 59 | Salt Lake City | 230,767 | .12 |
| 59 | Tucson | 179,596 | .12 |
| 61 | Albuquerque | 121,233 | .11 |
| 61 | Minneapolis-St. Paul | 148,865 | .11 |
| 63 | Houston | 906,034 | .09 |
| 64 | Tacoma | 73,299 | .08 |
| 65 | Little Rock | 70,198 | .01 |
| 66 | Austin | 175,987 | − .01 |
| 67 | Lubbock | 32,356 | − .02 |
| 68 | Akron | − 18,911 | − .07 |
| 69 | Grand Rapids | 62,455 | − .12 |
| 70 | Buffalo | −106,638 | − .15 |
| 71 | Anchorage | 46,632 | − .16 |
| 72 | Pittsburgh | −137,468 | − .28 |
| 73 | Jersey City | − 50,867 | − .33 |
| 74 | Atlanta | 434,101 | − .34 |
| 75 | Newark | − 92,164 | − .37 |
| 76 | Cleveland | −165,009 | − .48 |
| 77 | Boston | 135,744 | − .92 |
| 78 | New York | − 853,979 | − 1.01 |
| 79 | Philadelphia | −107,292 | − 1.09 |
| 80 | Syracuse | 5,779 | − 1.16 |
| 81 | Detroit | − 82,289 | − 1.49 |
| 82 | Washington, D.C. | 150,129 | − 2.33 |
| 83 | Dayton | − 22,461 | − 2.42 |
| 84 | Cincinnati | 14,196 | − 3.71 |
| 85 | St. Louis | − 55,608 | − 6.08 |
| 86 | Milwaukee | − 6,741 | −15.90 |

# 89. Churches of God

The Churches of God are strongest in metro Dayton (13 per 1,000); Akron and Lexington (10 per 1,000); Wichita and Fort Wayne (9 per 1,000).

The 1980 data cover the following two churches (the starred church also provided 1971 data):

Church of God General Conference (Abrahamic Faith) Oregon, Ill.*
Church of God (Seventh Day), Denver, Colorado

SOURCES: Metro religious adherence data for 1980 derived by the authors from county data in Bernard Quinn, Herman Anderson, Martin Bradley, Paul Goetting and Peggy Shriver, *Churches and Church Membership in the United States, 1980: An Enumeration by Region, State and County Based on Data Reported by 111 Church Bodies* (Atlanta: Glenmary Research Center, 1982). Metro population data for 1980 derived by the authors from county data in Hana Umlauf Lane, Ed., *The World Almanac & Book of Facts 1983* (New York: Newspaper Enterprise Association, Inc., 1981), pp. 246–263. Metro data for 1971 derived by the authors from county data in Douglas W. Johnson, Paul R. Picard and Bernard Quinn, *Churches and Church Membership in the United States: An Enumeration by Region, State and County* (Atlanta: Glenmary Research Center, 1974).

| Rank | Metro Area | Churches of God Members | Churches of God Members per 1,000 Population |
|---|---|---|---|
| 1 | Dayton | 10,205 | 12.29 |
| 2 | Akron | 6,936 | 10.50 |
| 3 | Lexington-Fayette | 3,240 | 10.18 |
| 4 | Wichita | 3,868 | 9.40 |
| 5 | Fort Wayne | 3,513 | 9.17 |
| 6 | Flint | 4,529 | 8.68 |
| 7 | Little Rock | 3,271 | 8.31 |
| 8 | Tulsa | 5,200 | 7.54 |
| 9 | Indianapolis | 7,215 | 6.18 |
| 10 | Toledo | 4,782 | 6.04 |
| 11 | Louisville | 5,292 | 5.84 |
| 12 | Portland, Ore. | 6,864 | 5.53 |
| 13 | Cincinnati | 7,287 | 5.20 |
| 14 | Oklahoma City | 3,936 | 4.72 |
| 15 | St. Louis | 9,894 | 4.20 |
| 16 | Birmingham | 3,352 | 3.96 |
| 16 | Columbus, Ohio | 4,333 | 3.96 |
| 18 | Shreveport | 1,284 | 3.41 |
| 19 | Tampa | 4,164 | 2.65 |
| 20 | Detroit | 11,132 | 2.56 |
| 21 | Chattanooga | 1,078 | 2.53 |

| Rank | Metro Area | Churches of God Members | Churches of God Members per 1,000 Population |
|---|---|---|---|
| 22 | Houston | 7,336 | 2.52 |
| 23 | Tacoma | 1,177 | 2.42 |
| 24 | Kansas City, Mo., Kan. | 3,173 | 2.39 |
| 25 | Jackson | 756 | 2.36 |
| 26 | Grand Rapids | 1,390 | 2.31 |
| 27 | Fresno | 1,185 | 2.30 |
| 28 | Spokane | 779 | 2.28 |
| 29 | Riverside | 3,453 | 2.22 |
| 30 | Jacksonville | 1,620 | 2.20 |
| 31 | Sacramento | 2,218 | 2.19 |
| 32 | Phoenix | 3,277 | 2.17 |
| 33 | Corpus Christi | 640 | 1.96 |
| 34 | Lubbock | 408 | 1.93 |
| 35 | Tucson | 1,012 | 1.90 |
| 36 | Mobile | 774 | 1.75 |
| 37 | Colorado Springs | 543 | 1.71 |
| 38 | Los Angeles | 11,682 | 1.56 |
| 39 | Albuquerque | 695 | 1.53 |
| 40 | Seattle | 2,394 | 1.49 |
| 41 | Nashville | 1,226 | 1.44 |
| 42 | San Diego | 2,578 | 1.38 |
| 43 | Charlotte | 870 | 1.37 |
| 44 | Denver | 2,169 | 1.34 |
| 44 | Miami | 2,184 | 1.34 |
| 46 | Baltimore | 2,865 | 1.32 |
| 47 | Greensboro | 1,086 | 1.31 |
| 48 | Lincoln | 246 | 1.28 |
| 49 | San Francisco | 4,026 | 1.24 |
| 50 | Chicago | 8,515 | 1.20 |
| 51 | Baton Rouge | 588 | 1.19 |
| 52 | Pittsburgh | 2,670 | 1.18 |
| 53 | Montgomery | 316 | 1.16 |
| 53 | Omaha | 662 | 1.16 |
| 55 | San Antonio | 1,153 | 1.08 |
| 56 | Washington, D.C. | 3,289 | 1.07 |
| 57 | Memphis | 792 | .87 |
| 58 | Norfolk | 642 | .80 |
| 59 | Milwaukee | 1,086 | .78 |
| 60 | Knoxville | 360 | .76 |
| 61 | Atlanta | 1,467 | .72 |
| 62 | Philadelphia | 3,351 | .71 |
| 63 | Columbus, Ga. | 168 | .70 |
| 64 | New Orleans | 804 | .68 |
| 65 | Des Moines | 228 | .67 |
| 66 | Jersey City | 350 | .63 |
| 66 | Rochester | 609 | .63 |
| 68 | Buffalo | 771 | .62 |
| 69 | El Paso | 285 | .59 |
| 69 | Richmond | 375 | .59 |
| 71 | New York | 5,288 | .58 |
| 72 | Anaheim | 1,107 | .57 |
| 73 | Cleveland | 1,043 | .55 |
| 74 | Las Vegas | 196 | .42 |
| 74 | Providence | 399 | .42 |
| 76 | Madison | 123 | .38 |
| 76 | Newark | 744 | .38 |
| 78 | Dallas | 1,091 | .37 |
| 79 | Austin | 176 | .33 |
| 80 | Minneapolis-St. Paul | 605 | .29 |
| 81 | Boston | 519 | .14 |
| 82 | Honolulu | 33 | .04 |

# 90. Churches of God: Trends

The previous table provides information on 1980 representation of two Churches of God. The table below shows the change between 1971 and 1980. The 1971 data include only one church—the Church of God General Conference (Abraham Faith) Oregon, Ill.

The church included in 1971 data and the two churches included in 1980 data are listed in the previous table.

SOURCES: See previous table.

| Rank | Metro Area | Total Population Change (1970–80) | Churches of God Population Change as a Percentage of Total Population Change |
|---|---|---|---|
| 1 | Flint | 12,925 | 13.61 |
| 2 | Cincinnati | 14,196 | 7.40 |
| 3 | Toledo | 28,941 | 6.79 |
| 4 | Wichita | 21,961 | 5.86 |
| 5 | Louisville | 38,910 | 5.06 |
| 6 | Indianapolis | 55,577 | 4.33 |
| 7 | Little Rock | 70,198 | 3.58 |
| 8 | Chicago | 127,573 | 3.17 |
| 9 | Fort Wayne | 20,977 | 3.14 |
| 10 | Rochester | 10,363 | 2.42 |
| 11 | Lexington-Fayette | 51,435 | 2.22 |
| 12 | Columbus, Ohio | 75,446 | 2.11 |
| 13 | Kansas City, Mo., Kan. | 54,000 | 1.44 |
| 14 | Omaha | 27,753 | 1.30 |
| 15 | Los Angeles | 435,677 | 1.15 |
| 16 | Tacoma | 73,299 | 1.10 |
| 17 | Portland, Ore. | 235,057 | 1.03 |
| 18 | Lubbock | 32,356 | .92 |
| 19 | Washington, D.C. | 150,129 | .86 |
| 20 | San Francisco | 143,472 | .74 |
| 21 | Baltimore | 157,007 | .70 |
| 22 | Cleveland | −165,009 | .61 |
| 22 | Oklahoma City | 134,996 | .61 |
| 22 | Shreveport | 40,646 | .61 |
| 25 | Jackson | 61,519 | .56 |
| 25 | Jacksonville | 115,692 | .56 |
| 27 | Corpus Christi | 41,456 | .55 |
| 28 | Mobile | 66,129 | .52 |
| 28 | Spokane | 54,348 | .52 |
| 30 | Memphis | 78,784 | .50 |
| 31 | Sacramento | 210,209 | .48 |
| 32 | Greensboro | 103,256 | .47 |
| 32 | Houston | 906,034 | .47 |
| 34 | Lincoln | 24,912 | .44 |
| 35 | Tampa | 480,943 | .38 |
| 36 | Des Moines | 24,486 | .37 |
| 37 | Tucson | 179,596 | .31 |
| 38 | Albuquerque | 121,233 | .27 |
| 39 | New Orleans | 140,255 | .26 |
| 40 | San Antonio | 183,775 | .25 |
| 41 | Charlotte | 79,433 | .24 |
| 41 | Norfolk | 74,091 | .24 |
| 43 | Miami | 358,187 | .22 |
| 43 | Riverside | 417,931 | .22 |
| 45 | El Paso | 120,608 | .20 |
| 46 | Phoenix | 536,802 | .18 |
| 46 | San Diego | 503,992 | .18 |
| 48 | Denver | 380,376 | .17 |
| 48 | Madison | 33,272 | .17 |
| 50 | Providence | 38,267 | .15 |
| 51 | Jersey City | − 50,867 | .11 |
| 51 | Nashville | 151,234 | .11 |
| 53 | Colorado Springs | 78,170 | .10 |
| 53 | Knoxville | 67,108 | .10 |
| 53 | Seattle | 182,160 | .10 |
| 53 | Tulsa | 140,474 | .10 |
| 57 | Atlanta | 434,101 | .09 |
| 57 | Fresno | 101,684 | .09 |
| 59 | Richmond | 84,473 | .08 |
| 60 | Dallas | 597,255 | .06 |
| 61 | Baton Rouge | 118,345 | .04 |
| 61 | Las Vegas | 188,528 | .04 |
| 63 | Anaheim | 510,337 | .02 |
| 63 | Minneapolis-St. Paul | 148,865 | .02 |
| 65 | Austin | 175,987 | .01 |
| 65 | Chattanooga | 55,683 | .01 |
| 65 | Montgomery | 46,776 | .01 |
| 68 | Grand Rapids | 62,455 | − .03 |
| 69 | Honolulu | 132,346 | − .14 |
| 70 | Buffalo | − 106,638 | − .17 |
| 71 | Newark | − 92,164 | − .22 |
| 72 | Boston | 135,744 | − .23 |
| 73 | New York | − 853,979 | − .36 |
| 74 | Pittsburgh | − 137,468 | − .82 |
| 75 | Anchorage | 46,632 | − 1.11 |
| 76 | Milwaukee | − 6,741 | − 1.45 |
| 77 | Philadelphia | − 107,292 | − 1.75 |
| 78 | Detroit | − 82,289 | − 6.24 |
| 79 | Columbus, Ga. | 612 | − 7.52 |
| 80 | St. Louis | − 55,608 | − 7.53 |
| 81 | Dayton | − 22,461 | − 8.66 |
| 82 | Akron | − 18,911 | −16.84 |

# 91. Jehovah's Witnesses

There are two reasons for including Jehovah's Witnesses in this book despite having incomplete data on them: (1) They reportedly have between 500,000 and a million members, making them one of the largest churches in the country, and (2) their members are highly active, making door-to-door calls and standing silently on many urban street corners holding aloft their publications, *The Watchtower* and *Awake*.

The data below represent the number of congregations of Jehovah's Witnesses in each city. Information on membership numbers is not available because the church says "we do not keep membership rolls or lists."

New York City has the most congregations of Jehovah's Witnesses, with 297. Los Angeles and Chicago are in second and third place. The church has at least two congregations in every city, suggesting that a systematic attempt has been made by its members to ensure representation through the country. Two cities, Anchorage and Honolulu, are missing, because no information is maintained on these cities by the source.

SOURCE: Response to questionnaire from the authors to the Jehovah's Witnesses, letter from Watchtower Bible and Tract Society of New York, Inc., Brooklyn, New York, November 29, 1982.

| Rank | City | Congregations of Jehovah's Witnesses | Rank | City | Congregations of Jehovah's Witnesses | Rank | City | Congregations of Jehovah's Witnesses |
|---|---|---|---|---|---|---|---|---|
| 1 | New York | 297 | 30 | Oakland | 17 | 66 | St. Paul | 8 |
| 2 | Los Angeles | 143 | 30 | Buffalo | 17 | 66 | Lubbock | 8 |
| 3 | Chicago | 102 | 36 | Pittsburgh | 16 | 66 | Anaheim | 8 |
| 4 | Miami | 67 | 36 | New Orleans | 16 | 70 | Jersey City | 7 |
| 4 | Philadelphia | 67 | 36 | Atlanta | 16 | 70 | Grand Rapids | 7 |
| 6 | Detroit | 62 | 39 | Fort Worth | 15 | 70 | Santa Ana | 7 |
| 7 | Houston | 52 | 39 | Kansas City, Mo. | 15 | 70 | Mobile | 7 |
| 8 | San Antonio | 46 | 39 | Dayton | 15 | 70 | Des Moines | 7 |
| 9 | Baltimore | 43 | 42 | Tulsa | 14 | 70 | Tacoma | 7 |
| 10 | Cleveland | 40 | 42 | Corpus Christi | 14 | 76 | Fort Wayne | 6 |
| 11 | Phoenix | 37 | 44 | Toledo | 13 | 76 | Salt Lake City | 6 |
| 12 | El Paso | 32 | 44 | Albuquerque | 13 | 76 | Chattanooga | 6 |
| 13 | San Diego | 30 | 44 | Long Beach | 13 | 76 | Aurora | 6 |
| 14 | Dallas | 29 | 44 | Oklahoma City | 13 | 76 | Syracuse | 6 |
| 15 | Milwaukee | 27 | 48 | Minneapolis | 12 | 76 | Knoxville | 6 |
| 15 | San Jose | 27 | 48 | Omaha | 12 | 82 | Montgomery | 5 |
| 17 | Indianapolis | 26 | 50 | St. Petersburg | 11 | 82 | Lincoln | 5 |
| 17 | Washington, D.C. | 26 | 50 | Nashville | 11 | 82 | Shreveport | 5 |
| 19 | Denver | 24 | 50 | Birmingham | 11 | 82 | Jackson | 5 |
| 20 | Tucson | 23 | 50 | Richmond | 11 | 82 | Madison | 5 |
| 21 | Seattle | 21 | 50 | Rochester | 11 | 82 | Columbus, Ga. | 5 |
| 21 | San Francisco | 21 | 50 | Las Vegas | 11 | 88 | Little Rock | 4 |
| 21 | St. Louis | 21 | 56 | Austin | 10 | 88 | Huntington Beach | 4 |
| 24 | Sacramento | 20 | 56 | Louisville | 10 | 88 | Kansas City, Kan. | 4 |
| 24 | Tampa | 20 | 56 | Colorado Springs | 10 | 88 | Greensboro | 4 |
| 26 | Boston | 19 | 56 | Riverside | 10 | 88 | Worcester | 4 |
| 26 | Columbus, Ohio | 19 | 60 | Charlotte | 10 | 93 | Warren | 3 |
| 28 | Cincinnati | 18 | 60 | Flint | 10 | 93 | Arlington, Texas | 3 |
| 28 | Jacksonville | 18 | 60 | Wichita | 10 | 93 | Providence | 3 |
| 30 | Fresno | 17 | 63 | Akron | 9 | 93 | Lexington | 3 |
| 30 | Portland, Ore. | 17 | 63 | Norfolk | 9 | 97 | Yonkers | 4 |
| 30 | Memphis | 17 | 63 | Spokane | 9 | 98 | Virginia Beach | 2 |
| 30 | Newark | 17 | 66 | Baton Rouge | 8 | | | |

# 92. Buddhism

Buddhism is one of the world's five major religions, with an estimated 257 million adherents. It ranks with Roman Catholics (581 million), Protestants (344 million, all churches combined), Muslims (592 million) and Hindus (481 million). It is the major religion of China and Japan, which account for one-fourth of the earth's inhabitants. Immigrants from these and other eastern countries along with second-generation families and converts make up the diverse Buddhist following in the United States.

The highest concentration of Buddhists in the United States are found in the West Coast cities of Fresno, San Jose and Sacramento. Fresno, ranked first in the following table, has nearly 12 adherents per 1,000 population. San Jose and Sacramento have more than 6 followers per 1,000 population.

Chicago, New York, Detroit and Washington, D.C. are the last 4 on the table, indicating that Buddhists are not as firmly established on the East Coast.

SOURCES: Data on Buddhist church membership provided in response to a questionnaire from the authors by the Buddhist Churches of America, San Francisco. Trends are not reviewed because data for earlier years were not provided. Background information from R. C. Zaehner, ed., *The Concise Encyclopedia of Living Faiths* (Boston: Beacon Press, 1959), pp. 267–268, 279, 307–308, 317, 344–347, 402. World religion information from *Encyclopedia Britannica Book of the Year: 1982* (Chicago: Encyclopaedia Britannica, 1982).

| Rank | Metro Areas | Population | Members | Members per 1,000 Population |
|------|-------------|-----------:|--------:|----------------------------:|
| 1 | Fresno | 515,013 | 6,080 | 11.80 |
| 2 | San Jose | 1,295,071 | 8,185 | 6.32 |
| 3 | Sacramento | 1,014,002 | 6,130 | 6.04 |
| 4 | Seattle | 1,606,765 | 4,780 | 2.97 |
| 5 | Denver | 1,619,921 | 3,805 | 2.34 |
| 6 | Tacoma | 485,643 | 985 | 1.92 |
| 7 | Riverside | 1,557,080 | 2,915 | 1.87 |
| 8 | San Francisco-Oakland | 3,252,721 | 4,965 | 1.52 |
| 9 | Salt Lake City | 936,225 | 1,335 | 1.42 |
| 10 | Spokane | 341,835 | 390 | 1.14 |
| 11 | San Diego | 1,861,846 | 1,960 | 1.05 |
| 12 | Portland | 1,242,187 | 1,230 | .99 |
| 13 | Los Angeles | 7,477,657 | 7,050 | .94 |
| 14 | Phoenix | 1,508,030 | 560 | .37 |
| 15 | Anaheim-Santa Ana-Garden Grove | 1,931,570 | 500 | .26 |
| 16 | Chicago | 7,012,328 | 1,190 | .17 |
| 17 | New York | 9,119,737 | 640 | .07 |
| 18 | Detroit | 4,352,762 | 250 | .06 |
| 19 | Washington, D.C. | 3,060,240 | 125 | .04 |

# CHAPTER FIVE

# WEALTH AND INCOME

Some would say that the best test of a city's performance is its economy. If a city is well run, it will attract new businesses. Visitors, residents and its economy will benefit as a result.

There are different ways that cities can build up their economic base. They can sell goods, like Akron's rubber tires; or government services, as in Austin or Washington, D.C.; or tourism, as in Honolulu and in an increasing number of cities. One way or another, cities as a whole have to provide services to those outside their borders as well as to their own citizens. The people in a city who sell to the rest of the world are in a real sense the economic foundation of the city.

Cities go through cycles of boom and bust. If they are the centers of growing businesses or government activities then they grow. If their business activities decline, they do also. If the U.S. auto industry declines, Detroit's economy for example, will do so as well unless it finds new business growth elsewhere. The Detroit suburb of Southfield did fine because some businesses there grew despite the prevailing area downtrend.

Basic measures of a city's economic performance are its per capita income and the growth in incomes. Income should be adjusted for cost of living; we provide several such measures. Cost data for housing, health, transportation and communications will also be found elsewhere in this book.

# 93. City Per Capita Income

Younger cities are the leaders in 1980 city per capita income. Many of these cities are recently built complexes that grew out of the suburban sprawl from the major urbanized cities. The population that migrates to these areas is by and large comprised of middle- and upper-class professional workers who want to raise their families away from the fast-paced, urban environment.

Cities like Huntington Beach (a young suburb of Los Angeles) and Yonkers (an aging suburban city north of New York City) rank first and seventh, respectively, in per capita income. Cities clustered at the bottom of the income continuum tend to have higher proportions of racial minorities and are predominately in the South and Northeast. Baltimore, which ranks last in this table, is an example of the result of the urban exodus of the 1950s,

1960s and 1970s. A poor population was left in the remains of what was at one time a thriving urban industrialized port center, while the general infrastructure of the city continued to be used by commuters and tourists. Newark, Buffalo and Cleveland (all ranking in the bottom 15 percent) have undergone the same type of changes. El Paso (ranking 99th) is heavily affected by the migrations from Mexico and therefore requires a somewhat different interpretation.

The development of sections like Baltimore's Inner Harbor into a major commercial, residential and recreational center will bring a significant positive upward change in the city's economy. Development agencies in many other cities are instituting renovations that will improve the localities' income flow.

SOURCE: *Marketing Economics Guide: 1981–82* (New York: Marketing Economics Institute, Ltd., 1981), Section II.

| Rank | City | Per Capita Income ($) | Rank | City | Per Capita Income ($) | Rank | City | Per Capita Income ($) |
|---|---|---|---|---|---|---|---|---|
| 1 | Huntington Beach | 12,225 | 35 | Indianapolis | 8,447 | 69 | Richmond | 7,220 |
| 2 | Anchorage | 11,542 | 36 | San Diego | 8,416 | 70 | Syracuse | 7,151 |
| 3 | Madison | 11,249 | 37 | St. Paul | 8,402 | 71 | Phoenix | 7,123 |
| 4 | Sacramento | 10,971 | 38 | Denver | 8,360 | 72 | Lincoln | 7,106 |
| 5 | Houston | 10,958 | 39 | Des Moines | 8,306 | 73 | Columbus, Ga. | 7,077 |
| 6 | Anaheim | 10,789 | 40 | Tulsa | 8,277 | 74 | St. Petersburg | 7,069 |
| 7 | Yonkers | 10,508 | 41 | Aurora | 8,233 | 75 | Detroit | 7,028 |
| 8 | San Jose | 10,196 | 42 | Pittsburgh | 8,116 | 76 | Louisville | 7,001 |
| 9 | Dallas | 10,120 | 43 | Chicago | 8,097 | 77 | Philadelphia | 6,966 |
| 10 | Washington, D.C. | 10,117 | 44 | Baton Rouge | 8,094 | 78 | Akron | 6,807 |
| 11 | Knoxville | 9,902 | 45 | Charlotte | 8,061 | 79 | Corpus Christi | 6,781 |
| 12 | Honolulu | 9,791 | 46 | Las Vegas | 8,054 | 80 | Tacoma | 6,767 |
| 13 | Oklahoma City | 9,768 | 47 | Virginia Beach | 8,045 | 81 | Flint | 6,714 |
| 14 | Grand Rapids | 9,621 | 48 | Kansas City, Mo. | 8,025 | 82 | San Antonio | 6,710 |
| 15 | Austin | 9,605 | 49 | Greensboro | 7,912 | 83 | Montgomery | 6,695 |
| 16 | San Francisco | 9,542 | 50 | Fort Wayne | 7,878 | 84 | St. Louis | 6,675 |
| 17 | Cincinnati | 9,534 | 51 | Wichita | 7,876 | 85 | Tampa | 6,658 |
| 18 | Nashville-Davidson | 9,429 | 52 | Boston | 7,870 | 86 | Birmingham | 6,650 |
| 19 | Jackson | 9,006 | 53 | Arlington, Texas | 7,824 | 87 | Lexington-Fayette | 6,636 |
| 20 | Oakland | 8,824 | 54 | Kansas City, Kan. | 7,722 | 88 | Cleveland | 6,537 |
| 21 | Fresno | 8,741 | 55 | Shreveport | 7,681 | 89 | Ft. Worth | 6,536 |
| 22 | New York | 8,739 | 56 | Memphis | 7,630 | 90 | Atlanta | 6,499 |
| 23 | Little Rock | 8,687 | 57 | Albuquerque | 7,612 | 91 | Norfolk | 6,417 |
| 24 | Long Beach | 8,659 | 58 | Riverside | 7,595 | 92 | Jacksonville | 6,320 |
| 25 | Columbus, Ohio | 8,656 | 59 | Jersey City | 7,560 | 93 | Buffalo | 6,294 |
| 26 | Santa Ana | 8,601 | 60 | Lubbock | 7,530 | 94 | Dayton | 6,287 |
| 27 | Toledo | 8,591 | 61 | New Orleans | 7,429 | 95 | Mobile | 6,244 |
| 28 | Spokane | 8,562 | 62 | Salt Lake City | 7,384 | 96 | Miami | 5,898 |
| 29 | Seattle | 8,548 | 63 | Milwaukee | 7,337 | 97 | Newark | 5,672 |
| 30 | Portland, Ore. | 8,527 | 64 | Omaha | 7,331 | 98 | Chattanooga | 5,660 |
| 31 | Minneapolis | 8,491 | 65 | Worcester | 7,312 | 99 | El Paso | 4,808 |
| 31 | Warren | 8,491 | 66 | Providence | 7,274 | 100 | Baltimore | 4,797 |
| 33 | Los Angeles | 8,469 | 67 | Rochester | 7,245 | | | |
| 34 | Colorado Springs | 8,453 | 68 | Tucson | 7,233 | | | |

# 94. City Income Per Household

Everything about a city—its housing, its amenities, its problems—is so tied up with the income of residents that it is crucial to understand a city's income situation.

The table below shows city income per household in 1980. It takes into account the number of people per household. A city where people are mostly single will have a household income well below that of a city where households have several members, if per capita incomes are the same.

The table showing average number of people per household, which is provided below along with the other tables on housing, should explain the differences between the per capita and per household figures.

Income per household has special relevance for people who are concerned about the problem of poverty. Poverty is a household rather than an individual problem. Traditionally, household incomes primarily reflected the earning power of the male head of the household. Increasingly, the household includes two or more people earning separate incomes. In poorer families there is less likelihood of having multiple wage earners and more likelihood of reliance on government relief.

The top two cities of Huntington Beach and Anchorage are the same whether one looks at household or per capita income, but San Jose and Anaheim are higher on per household income, suggesting that these two cities have more dual wage earners than the cities they replace, Madison and Sacramento.

At the low end of the scale, the cities with the lowest 1980 incomes per household are Buffalo, Miami and Baltimore.

SOURCE: *Marketing Economics Guide: 1981–82* (New York: Marketing Economics Institute, Ltd., 1981), Section II.

| Rank | City | Income Per Household ($) | Rank | City | Income Per Household ($) | Rank | City | Income Per Household ($) |
|---|---|---|---|---|---|---|---|---|
| 1 | Huntington Beach | 34,206 | 35 | Greensboro | 21,648 | 69 | Minneapolis | 19,262 |
| 2 | Anchorage | 33,115 | 36 | Charlotte | 21,601 | 70 | Milwaukee | 19,046 |
| 3 | San Jose | 30,464 | 37 | San Francisco | 21,560 | 71 | Detroit | 18,945 |
| 4 | Anaheim | 29,929 | 38 | Lubbock | 21,556 | 72 | Montgomery | 18,944 |
| 5 | Houston | 29,012 | 39 | Las Vegas | 21,544 | 73 | Philadelphia | 18,884 |
| 6 | Madison | 28,965 | 40 | Memphis | 21,344 | 74 | Lincoln | 18,719 |
| 7 | Yonkers | 27,721 | 41 | Shreveport | 21,145 | 75 | Flint | 18,427 |
| 8 | Honolulu | 27,355 | 42 | St. Paul | 21,137 | 76 | Richmond | 18,362 |
| 9 | Warren | 27,099 | 43 | Des Moines | 21,015 | 77 | Providence | 18,065 |
| 10 | Grand Rapids | 26,436 | 44 | Corpus Christi | 20,810 | 78 | Lexington-Fayette | 17,886 |
| 11 | Sacramento | 26,347 | 45 | Kansas City, Kan. | 20,754 | 79 | Rochester | 17,781 |
| 12 | Jackson | 25,619 | 46 | Arlington, Texas | 20,741 | 80 | Syracuse | 17,672 |
| 13 | Santa Ana | 25,567 | 47 | Oakland | 20,673 | 81 | Mobile | 17,620 |
| 14 | Washington, D.C. | 25,398 | 48 | Spokane | 20,553 | 82 | Akron | 17,522 |
| 15 | Dallas | 25,209 | 49 | Tulsa | 20,444 | 83 | Birmingham | 17,480 |
| 16 | Nashville-Davidson | 25,168 | 50 | Long Beach | 20,391 | 84 | Louisville | 17,472 |
| 17 | Knoxville | 25,077 | 51 | Columbus, Ga. | 20,387 | 85 | Ft. Worth | 17,469 |
| 18 | Austin | 24,870 | 52 | Worcester | 20,363 | 86 | Salt Lake City | 17,458 |
| 19 | Virginia Beach | 24,632 | 53 | San Antonio | 20,350 | 87 | Tampa | 17,438 |
| 20 | Riverside | 24,413 | 54 | Jersey City | 20,345 | 88 | Jacksonville | 17,379 |
| 21 | Oklahoma City | 24,264 | 55 | Albuquerque | 20,316 | 89 | St. Louis | 16,923 |
| 22 | Fresno | 23,205 | 56 | Phoenix | 20,311 | 90 | Tacoma | 16,913 |
| 23 | San Diego | 23,050 | 57 | Fort Wayne | 20,257 | 91 | Atlanta | 16,804 |
| 24 | Toledo | 22,718 | 58 | Kansas City, Mo. | 20,212 | 92 | St. Petersburg | 16,523 |
| 25 | Baton Rouge | 22,594 | 59 | Pittsburgh | 20,164 | 93 | Cleveland | 16,490 |
| 26 | Indianapolis | 22,577 | 60 | Boston | 20,096 | 94 | Newark | 16,185 |
| 27 | Cincinnati | 22,549 | 61 | New Orleans | 19,973 | 95 | El Paso | 15,904 |
| 28 | Little Rock | 22,536 | 62 | Wichita | 19,810 | 96 | Dayton | 15,753 |
| 29 | Colorado Springs | 22,384 | 63 | Portland, Ore. | 19,544 | 97 | Chattanooga | 15,305 |
| 30 | Columbus, Ohio | 22,112 | 64 | Omaha | 19,500 | 98 | Buffalo | 15,244 |
| 31 | New York | 22,096 | 65 | Norfolk | 19,426 | 99 | Miami | 15,220 |
| 32 | Aurora | 22,057 | 66 | Tucson | 19,371 | 100 | Baltimore | 13,348 |
| 33 | Los Angeles | 21,984 | 67 | Denver | 19,359 | | | |
| 34 | Chicago | 21,868 | 68 | Seattle | 19,274 | | | |

# 95. Metro Per Capita Income

City per capita income doesn't fully capture the presence of wealth in a metro area. As the table below shows, a city like St. Louis with a wealthy suburban area and a constricted downtown—what we might call the "doughnut" syndrome—ranks 84th in city per capita income ($6,675) and 23rd in metro area per capita income ($8,539). Since we are using averages, the data imply a suburban per capita income much higher than the metro area figure of $8,539.

Newark is the most dramatic case of all. Its city per capita income is the fourth lowest in the nation, $5,672. Its metro area per capita income is the 13th highest in the nation, $19,155.

The data for city and metro area per capita income

are from the same source and are comparable. However, Anchorage has a slightly higher metro per capita income than city per capita income. The two figures should be the same.

Another measure of per capita income is provided below, based on 1980 Census data. It shows the Washington, D.C. area with the highest 1980 per capita income, $15,654.

Anchorage and Anaheim follow with per capita incomes of $11,607 and $11,525, respectively.

SOURCE: *Marketing Economics Guide: 1981-82* (New York: Marketing Economics Institute, Ltd., 1981), Section II.

| Rank | Metro Area | Per Capita Income ($) | Rank | Metro Area | Per Capita Income ($) | Rank | Metro Area | Per Capita Income ($) |
|---|---|---|---|---|---|---|---|---|
| 1 | Washington, D.C. | 13,058 | 30 | Seattle | 8,394 | 59 | Flint | 7,307 |
| 2 | Anchorage | 11,607 | 31 | Spokane | 8,385 | 60 | Tampa-St. Petersburg | 7,223 |
| 3 | Anaheim-Santa Ana | 11,525 | 32 | Philadelphia | 8,380 | 61 | Louisville | 7,174 |
| 4 | Madison | 11,339 | 33 | Fresno | 8,331 | 62 | Syracuse | 7,164 |
| 5 | Sacramento | 11,320 | 34 | Honolulu | 8,266 | 63 | Akron | 7,099 |
| 6 | Houston | 10,617 | 35 | Cleveland | 8,232 | 64 | Dayton | 7,062 |
| 7 | San Francisco-Oakland | 10,335 | 36 | Indianapolis | 8,174 | 65 | San Antonio | 7,040 |
| 8 | Grand Rapids | 10,011 | 37 | Las Vegas | 8,132 | 66 | Shreveport | 6,999 |
| 9 | Cincinnati | 9,777 | 38 | Milwaukee | 8,122 | 67 | Greensboro | 6,993 |
| 10 | Knoxville | 9,522 | 39 | New Orleans | 8,105 | 67 | Lubbock | 6,993 |
| 11 | New York | 9,290 | 40 | Nashville-Davidson | 8,041 | 69 | Lincoln | 6,988 |
| 12 | Oklahoma City | 9,215 | 41 | Colorado Springs | 8,026 | 70 | Birmingham | 6,985 |
| 13 | Newark | 9,155 | 42 | Jersey City | 7,960 | 71 | Norfolk-Virginia Beach | 6,981 |
| 14 | Boston | 9,147 | 43 | Rochester | 7,953 | 72 | Tacoma | 6,977 |
| 15 | Austin | 9,123 | 44 | Little Rock | 7,784 | 73 | Albuquerque | 6,946 |
| 16 | Columbus, Ohio | 8,927 | 45 | Charlotte | 7,716 | 74 | Tulsa | 6,944 |
| 17 | Minneapolis-St. Paul | 8,877 | 46 | Fort Wayne | 7,680 | 75 | Buffalo | 6,871 |
| 18 | Chicago | 8,839 | 47 | Omaha | 7,651 | 76 | Columbus, Ga. | 6,822 |
| 18 | Toledo | 8,839 | 48 | Riverside | 7,649 | 77 | Lexington-Fayette | 6,649 |
| 20 | Kansas City, Mo.-Kan. | 8,716 | 49 | Providence | 7,610 | 78 | Salt Lake City | 6,499 |
| 21 | Detroit | 8,613 | 50 | Richmond | 7,594 | 79 | Corpus Christi | 6,395 |
| 22 | Des Moines | 8,544 | 51 | Wichita | 7,492 | 80 | Montgomery | 6,377 |
| 23 | St. Louis | 8,539 | 52 | Worcester | 7,477 | 81 | Chattanooga | 6,062 |
| 24 | Denver | 8,535 | 53 | Miami | 7,454 | 82 | Jacksonville | 5,922 |
| 25 | Jackson | 8,525 | 54 | Phoenix | 7,382 | 83 | Baltimore | 5,913 |
| 26 | Dallas-Ft. Worth | 8,504 | 55 | Los Angeles-Long Beach | 7,371 | 84 | Mobile | 5,721 |
| 27 | Pittsburgh | 8,484 | 56 | Baton Rouge | 7,368 | 85 | El Paso | 4,667 |
| 28 | San Diego | 8,478 | 57 | Memphis | 7,340 | | | |
| 29 | Portland, Ore. | 8,451 | 58 | Atlanta | 7,339 | | | |

# 96. Where Rich People Live

What is the source of cities' wealth? Is the way to a strong economy perhaps to attract people with inherited or accumulated bank accounts and investment portfolios?

To provide a crude indicator of where rich people live, we have counted the number of residences in the top 100 cities of wealthy people as defined by *Forbes* magazine in its "Forbes 400." *Forbes* estimates the net worth of individuals and assigns them to different classes. Those who make the list have a net worth of about $100 million or more.

The top category is reserved for those with a net worth of $1 billion or more. A baker's dozen of the elite make this group. At the top of the list is Daniel Keith Ludwig, a New York City resident, worth over $2 billion. Next is Gordon Peter Getty of San Francisco. The remaining 11 people live in Dallas (5), neighboring Fort Worth (2), Denver (2), Las Vegas and Los Altos Hills.

Well over half the "Forbes 400," 227 people, have homes in the top 100 cities. A few have homes in smaller cities like Midland, Texas, but most of the rest simply live in comfortable rural areas such as the horse country around Upperville and Middleburg, Virginia. The largest contingent by far of the city-based people lives in New York City, 58 out of 227, about one-fourth. The 4 other major cities are Houston, Los Angeles, Dallas and Chicago, which add another one-fourth. Half of this group achieved their wealth through personal efforts and inheritance from real estate holdings. Almost all those listed in Houston and Dallas derive their wealth from oil and oil-related activities. In Chicago the wealth is principally from financial activities and retail manufacturing. In Los Angeles the wealth stemmed from a mixture of oil, computer, movie and hotel businesses. Many of the wealthy found in New York and Texas cities have inherited their money.

These richest individuals choose not to live in the other 54 of the top 100 cities. In fact, many of them simply reside where their money is—i.e., where it is managed. The money is there because it has generally stayed where it was earned.

To answer the question posed above, most wealthy people live where wealth is, as much as the other way around. Wealthy people need Wall Street and its regional equivalents as much as these financial centers need the wealthy.

SOURCE: Harold Seneker with Jonathan Greenberg and John Dorfman, "The Forbes Four Hundred," *Forbes*, September 13, 1982, pp. 100–160.

| Rank | City | Resident Members of "Forbes 400" | Rank | City | Resident Members of "Forbes 400" | Rank | City | Resident Members of "Forbes 400" |
|---|---|---|---|---|---|---|---|---|
| 1 | New York | 58 | 14 | San Jose | 4 | 30 | Colorado Springs | 1 |
| 2 | Houston | 20 | 18 | Baltimore | 3 | 30 | Louisville | 1 |
| 3 | Dallas | 16 | 18 | Detroit | 3 | 30 | Memphis | 1 |
| 3 | Los Angeles | 16 | 18 | Newark | 3 | 30 | Milwaukee | 1 |
| 5 | Chicago | 10 | 18 | San Diego | 3 | 30 | Nashville | 1 |
| 6 | Pittsburgh | 7 | 22 | Cleveland | 2 | 30 | Norfolk | 1 |
| 6 | Washington, D.C. | 7 | 22 | Columbus, Ohio | 2 | 30 | Oakland | 1 |
| 8 | Atlanta | 6 | 22 | Honolulu | 2 | 30 | Omaha | 1 |
| 8 | San Francisco | 6 | 22 | Minneapolis | 2 | 30 | St. Louis | 1 |
| 10 | Boston | 5 | 22 | Portland, Ore. | 2 | 30 | St. Paul | 1 |
| 10 | Denver | 5 | 22 | Richmond | 2 | 30 | Seattle | 1 |
| 10 | Miami | 5 | 22 | San Antonio | 2 | 30 | Tampa | 1 |
| 10 | Philadelphia | 5 | 22 | Tulsa | 2 | 30 | Toledo | 1 |
| 14 | Fort Worth | 4 | 30 | Anaheim | 1 | 30 | Wichita | 1 |
| 14 | Las Vegas | 4 | 30 | Chattanooga | 1 | | | |
| 14 | Oklahoma City | 4 | 30 | Cincinnati | 1 | | | |

# 97. Poor Families

The figures below show what proportion of all families in each city are poor. This measures the burden of poverty on the city's taxpayers and government.

Nationwide, in 1980 (based on 1979 income) there were 27.5 million poor people in America, about the same as in 1970. The proportion of people who were poor dropped from 13.7 percent to 12.5 percent, a positive sign.

The table shows, for the 36 largest U.S. metro areas, the number and proportion of families in 1979 who are below certain poverty levels based on size of family, number of children and age of family householder.

The federal government-defined poverty levels for 1979 are: $3,774 for a person under 65 years; $3,479 for a person 65 or over; $4,876 for two persons with the householder under 65; $4,389 with the householder 65 years or over; $5,787 for a three-person household; $7,412 for a four-person household; $8,776 for a five-person household; $9,915 for a six-person household; $11,237 for a seven-person household; $12,484 for an eight-person household; and $14,812 for a household of nine or more persons.

The data on families do not include persons living alone or individuals living together who are unrelated. Such people represent in almost every metro area (New Orleans, San Antonio and Newark excepted) a larger number of poor people than those included in poor families. The difference is that children are involved in the family data and they are of special concern—quite apart from humanitarian considerations—because early public assistance could help steer them into more productive and self-reliant lives.

SOURCES: U.S. Census Bureau, *1980 Census of Population: Supplementary Report: Provisional Estimates of Social, Economic and Housing Characteristics*, (March, 1982), Table P-4 and p. B-6; data for the year 1979, as reported in 1980. John Tepper Marlin, *The Wealth of Cities* (New York: Council on Municipal Performance, 1974), pp. 5–8.

| Rank | Metro Area | Number of Families Below Poverty Level | Percentage of Families Below Poverty Level |
|------|-----------|------------------|------------------|
| 1 | New York | 339,432 | 14.74 |
| 2 | New Orleans | 441,195 | 14.56 |
| 3 | San Antonio | 38,772 | 14.55 |
| 4 | Miami | 47,258 | 11.29 |

| Rank | Metro Area | Number of Families Below Poverty Level | Percentage of Families Below Poverty Level |
|------|-----------|------------------|------------------|
| 5 | Newark | 53,452 | 10.49 |
| 6 | Los Angeles-Long Beach | 183,006 | 10.08 |
| 7 | Atlanta | 51,784 | 9.68 |
| 8 | Chicago | 171,290 | 9.52 |
| 9 | Philadelphia | 111,896 | 9.28 |
| 10 | Baltimore | 50,624 | 8.97 |
| 11 | Sacramento | 23,690 | 8.89 |
| 12 | Tampa-St. Petersburg | 39,519 | 8.95 |
| 13 | Detroit | 98,703 | 8.82 |
| 14 | Riverside | 36,498 | 8.78 |
| 15 | Houston | 62,252 | 8.29 |
| 16 | San Diego | 37,605 | 8.21 |
| 17 | Cleveland | 40,873 | 8.19 |
| 18 | Columbus, Ohio | 22,622 | 8.16 |
| 19 | Cincinnati | 29,379 | 8.08 |
| 20 | Boston | 53,669 | 8.02 |
| 21 | Indianapolis | 23,646 | 7.60 |
| 22 | Buffalo | 24,461 | 7.55 |
| 23 | St. Louis | 46,388 | 7.47 |
| 24 | Milwaukee | 26,682 | 7.39 |
| 25 | Dallas-Fort Worth | 57,716 | 7.37 |
| 26 | San Francisco-Oakland | 53,310 | 6.66 |
| 27 | Phoenix | 24,299 | 6.19 |
| 28 | Denver | 25,191 | 6.18 |
| 29 | Washington, D.C. | 46,315 | 6.11 |
| 30 | Portland, Ore. | 19,816 | 6.06 |
| 31 | Kansas City, Mo., Kan. | 21,284 | 6.01 |
| 32 | San Jose | 19,289 | 5.94 |
| 33 | Pittsburgh | 35,090 | 5.70 |
| 34 | Anaheim | 24,078 | 4.89 |
| 35 | Seattle | 19,883 | 4.83 |
| 36 | Minneapolis-St. Paul | 23,446 | 4.41 |

# 98.  Households Receiving Public Assistance

This table differs significantly from the earlier one showing the percentage of families below the official poverty level. This table includes unrelated individuals, who make up the majority of persons below the poverty level in almost all the cities. It also indicates whether these people or families are receiving public assistance.

The 10 metro areas with the lowest proportion of households (families and unrelated individuals) receiving public assistance in 1980 are in the sunbelt, from Washington, D.C. southward, the Northwest (Seattle and Portland, Oregon) and the midwestern areas of Denver, Minneapolis, Indianapolis and Kansas City, Kansas and Missouri. The reason is partly the more favorable econo-

mies of these cities and partly the greater difficulty in qualifying for public assistance.

The dozen metro areas with the highest proportion of residents receiving public assistance are in the Boston-New York City-Newark-Philadelphia-Baltimore corridor; in California (Sacramento, Riverside, Los Angeles); plus Chicago, Detroit, Miami and New Orleans.

SOURCE: U.S. Department of Commerce, Bureau of the Census, *1980 Census of Population and Housing: Supplementary Report: Provisional Estimates of Social, Economic and Housing Characteristics*, March 1982.

| Rank | Metro Area | Total Households | Households Receiving Assistance | Percentage Receiving Assistance | Rank | Metro Area | Total Households | Households Receiving Assistance | Percentage Receiving Assistance |
|---|---|---|---|---|---|---|---|---|---|
| 1 | New York | 3,504,748 | 459,674 | 13.12 | 18 | Cincinnati | 499,358 | 38,994 | 7.81 |
| 2 | Sacramento | 385,354 | 44,342 | 11.51 | 19 | St. Louis | 839,659 | 64,497 | 7.68 |
| 3 | Detroit | 1,503,806 | 171,741 | 11.42 | 20 | Milwaukee | 501,106 | 37,774 | 7.54 |
| 4 | Riverside | 550,304 | 58,392 | 10.61 | 21 | Cleveland | 690,126 | 49,947 | 7.24 |
| 5 | New Orleans | 422,543 | 43,730 | 10.35 | 22 | Atlanta | 722,228 | 49,375 | 6.84 |
| 6 | Chicago | 2,497,831 | 252,443 | 10.11 | 23 | San Jose | 458,405 | 29,864 | 6.51 |
| 7 | Newark | 673,806 | 66,971 | 9.94 | 24 | Columbus | 395,024 | 24,231 | 6.13 |
| 8 | Los Angeles-Long Beach | 2,725,968 | 267,221 | 9.80 | 25 | Anaheim | 685,698 | 40,672 | 5.93 |
| 9 | Baltimore | 760,869 | 73,764 | 9.69 | 26 | Tampa-St. Petersburg | 640,738 | 37,333 | 5.83 |
| 9 | Philadelphia | 1,636,379 | 158,506 | 9.69 | 27 | Kansas City, Mo., Kan. | 491,832 | 28,312 | 5.76 |
| 11 | Miami | 606,722 | 58,391 | 9.62 | 28 | Portland, Ore. | 479,321 | 27,112 | 5.66 |
| 12 | Boston | 989,967 | 91,749 | 9.27 | 29 | Indianapolis | 419,383 | 23,443 | 5.59 |
| 13 | Buffalo | 444,442 | 40,734 | 9.17 | 30 | Minneapolis-St. Paul | 761,179 | 42,133 | 5.54 |
| 14 | San Francisco-Oakland | 1,282,416 | 110,151 | 8.59 | 31 | Washington, D.C. | 1,115,707 | 58,258 | 5.22 |
| | | | | | 32 | Denver | 606,596 | 29,911 | 4.93 |
| 15 | San Diego | 669,289 | 56,636 | 8.46 | 33 | Houston | 1,032,784 | 50,537 | 4.89 |
| 16 | Pittsburgh | 831,095 | 67,184 | 8.08 | 34 | Seattle | 617,114 | 29,665 | 4.81 |
| 17 | San Antonio | 347,963 | 27,937 | 8.03 | 35 | Dallas-Fort Worth | 1,074,860 | 49,593 | 4.61 |
| | | | | | 36 | Phoenix | 548,688 | 23,665 | 4.31 |

# CHAPTER SIX

# COST OF LIVING

The following tables show how cities compare in relation to various components of the cost of living such as fuel and light; meat, milk and eggs; clothing and housing rental. Basic income requirements for retired people are also compared.

Many cost differences can be explained by supply and demand in and around the areas we review. In addition, relative prices in geographic regions often depend on competition. These general aspects of cost of living do not apply to the largest cities, where overall prices are generally higher.

# 99. Cost of Living

The overall cost of living is a measure of what a dollar will buy at different times and different places. An official price index for urban consumers has been developed by the Department of Labor's Bureau of Labor Statistics. It shows that, with 1967 as the base of 100, the price index rose as follows: 1920: 60.0; 1930: 50.0; 1940: 42.0; 1950: 72.1; 1960: 88.7; 1970: 116.3; 1980: 246.8. Prices showed a steady creep upward between 1913 and 1920. They hovered around 51 in the 1920s, then dropped precipitously between 1930 and 1933, when they hit 37.6 in April 1933. They touched 43.8 in 1937, then slipped back to 42 in 1940. Since 1940 there has been a steady rise. More recently, the cost of living rose to 272.4 in 1981 and hit 293.3 in September 1982.

The difficulty with the official cost of living figures is that they aren't isolated for very many cities. To obtain a larger number of cities, we have used data collected by the American Chamber of Commerce Researchers Association (ACCRA). The raw data are collected by participating chambers of commerce or similar organizations. The data ACCRA collects are similar to those of the Bureau of Labor Statistics: cost of food, housing, utilities, transportation, health care and miscellaneous services such as entertainment, dry cleaning and appliance re-

pair. Many of the ACCRA components are shown in more detail in other tables in this chapter. ACCRA cautions that the cost of living index should be considered accurate only with a margin of three index whole numbers. Intercity differences smaller than this margin should not be considered definitive. For example, in the table below cities ranked from 25 to 37 should be considered a single group, within which it would be preferable to minimize the significance of the rank order.

Overall, New York City emerges as the most expensive city. The next 5 cities are in California and Texas. Interestingly, two New Jersey cities rank among the 10 most expensive. Denver ranks seventh.

At the other end of the spectrum, we have ample representation of cities in states that are also represented by cities at the top of the list—Buffalo and Syracuse in New York State, Lubbock and San Antonio in Texas, Colorado Springs in Colorado.

The difference in overall cost of living seems therefore to have more to do with size than with region of the country. The two Nebraska cities at the end of the list are also smaller cities. Within states, the larger cities are the more expensive.

SOURCE: American Chamber of Commerce Researchers Association, Inter-City Cost of Living Indicators, second quarter 1982.

| Rank | City | Index | Rank | City | Index | Rank | City | Index |
|------|------|-------|------|------|-------|------|------|-------|
| 1 | New York | 133.2 | 22 | Flint | 103.3 | 43 | Columbus, Ohio | 99.4 |
| 2 | San Jose | 117.2 | 22 | Sacramento | 103.3 | 44 | Fort Worth | 99.3 |
| 3 | San Diego | 114.7 | 24 | Madison | 103.1 | 45 | Fort Wayne | 99.1 |
| 4 | Houston | 111.6 | 25 | Miami | 102.7 | 46 | Dayton | 98.9 |
| 5 | Anaheim | 110.6 | 25 | Oklahoma City | 102.7 | 47 | Knoxville | 98.7 |
| 6 | Fresno | 110.5 | 27 | Atlanta | 102.5 | 47 | Mobile | 98.7 |
| 7 | Denver | 109.8 | 28 | Wichita | 102.4 | 49 | Indianapolis | 98.5 |
| 8 | Jersey City | 109.3 | 29 | Cincinnati | 102.2 | 50 | Kansas City, Kan. | 98.4 |
| 8 | Newark | 109.3 | 29 | Little Rock | 102.2 | 51 | Greensboro | 98.3 |
| 10 | Minneapolis | 107.8 | 29 | Tulsa | 102.2 | 51 | Nashville-Davidson | 98.3 |
| 10 | St. Paul | 107.8 | 32 | Memphis | 101.2 | 53 | St. Louis | 98.1 |
| 12 | Las Vegas | 106.8 | 33 | El Paso | 100.9 | 54 | Lincoln | 98.0 |
| 13 | Baltimore | 106.2 | 33 | Salt Lake City | 100.9 | 55 | San Antonio | 97.8 |
| 14 | Shreveport | 105.5 | 35 | Norfolk | 100.6 | 56 | Omaha | 97.5 |
| 15 | Phoenix | 105.1 | 35 | Virginia Beach | 100.6 | 57 | Buffalo | 96.5 |
| 16 | Riverside | 105.0 | 37 | Baton Rouge | 100.0 | 58 | Louisville | 95.7 |
| 16 | Tacoma | 105.0 | 37 | Charlotte | 100.0 | 58 | Syracuse | 95.7 |
| 18 | Kansas City, Mo. | 104.8 | 39 | Columbus, Ga. | 99.7 | 60 | Colorado Springs | 94.9 |
| 19 | Portland, Ore. | 104.5 | 40 | Birmingham | 99.6 | 61 | Chattanooga | 93.0 |
| 20 | Arlington, Texas | 104.0 | 41 | Albuquerque | 99.5 | 62 | Lubbock | 90.7 |
| 20 | Corpus Christi | 104.0 | 41 | Lexington-Fayette | 99.5 | | | |

# 100. Budget for Retired People

With the decline in the extended family, older people in the larger cities are in some ways more vulnerable than in smaller communities. They are likely to feel more alienated and abandoned. For that reason the elderly tend to cluster in groups and look after each other. An advantage of the cities is good health care, but it is costly. Fixed incomes can be devastated by increased housing and food costs, and health care may suffer.

Figures for the 1980 cost of living for retired people in 25 metropolitan areas encompassing 29 of the 100 largest cities are provided below. The table shows where retired people on fixed incomes are likely to be having trouble making ends meet. Retired people are defined as a husband who is 65 years of age or older and a wife, both of whom are able to care for themselves and are self-supporting. Budget components are food, housing, transportation, clothing, personal care, medical care and other family budget items (recreation, tobacco, reading matter, liquor). The Bureau of Labor Statistics identifies the cost in each city of an identical "basket" of such budget components.

The data show one drawback to Anchorage's lure as a retirement center. The intermediate budget is a high $12,900. Honolulu, Boston and New York are next in line as the most costly places to live.

At the other end of the spectrum, Atlanta, Dallas and San Diego were the cheapest areas to retire in. It costs only $9,516 for the intermediate budget in Atlanta. Although the data are for a couple, the budget for a single person can be approximated at somewhere around two-thirds of this amount. The major savings from living together are rent and food, which are the two largest budget items.

The budget levels are calculated independently for three levels. The "lower" budget levels tend to be approximately one-half the "upper" budget levels. "Intermediate" budget levels (which are the levels shown in the table) are on the lower side of the midpoint between upper and lower budgets.

SOURCE: U.S. Department of Labor, Bureau of Labor Statistics, "News," August 10, 1981.

| Rank | Metro Area | Budget ($) | Rank | Metro Area | Budget ($) | Rank | Metro Area | Budget ($) |
|---|---|---|---|---|---|---|---|---|
| 1 | Atlanta | 9,516 | 10 | St. Louis | 10,108 | 19 | San Francisco-Oakland | 10,921 |
| 2 | Dallas | 9,768 | 11 | Minneapolis-St. Paul | 10,121 | 20 | Washington, D.C. | 11,000 |
| 3 | San Diego | 9,827 | 12 | Los Angeles-Long Beach | 10,238 | 21 | Seattle | 11,343 |
| 4 | Kansas City, Mo., Kan. | 9,978 | 13 | Detroit | 10,395 | 22 | New York | 11,623 |
| 5 | Houston | 9,996 | 14 | Cleveland | 10,500 | 23 | Boston | 11,925 |
| 6 | Denver | 10,028 | 15 | Pittsburgh | 10,503 | 24 | Honolulu | 12,157 |
| 7 | Cincinnati | 10,038 | 16 | Philadelphia | 10,646 | 25 | Anchorage | 12,900 |
| 8 | Baltimore | 10,051 | 17 | Milwaukee | 10,673 | | | |
| 9 | Chicago | 10,070 | 18 | Buffalo | 10,744 | | | |

# 101. Change in Budget for Retired People

While the previous table shows the absolute differences among budget costs, the table below shows where intermediate budget costs for a retired couple have been increasing most rapidly. It shows where recent strains are most likely to be showing up in the ability of those on fixed incomes to keep pace with expenses.

The fastest increase in costs for retired persons has been in Honolulu, where they have risen by 11 percent. The least rapid increase has been in Anchorage, where the rise has been kept to 5 percent.

The rise in costs for elderly people has been in line with the rate of overall inflation.

SOURCE: U.S. Department of Labor, Bureau of Labor Statistics, "News," August 1980 and 1981.

| Rank | Metro Area | Budget 1979 | Budget 1980 | Percentage Change |
|---|---|---|---|---|
| 1 | Honolulu | 10,979 | 12,157 | 10.73 |
| 2 | Milwaukee | 9,698 | 10,673 | 10.05 |

| Rank | Metro Area | Budget 1979 | Budget 1980 | Percentage Change |
|---|---|---|---|---|
| 3 | Seattle | 10,311 | 11,343 | 10.01 |
| 4 | Los Angeles-Long Beach | 9,383 | 10,238 | 9.11 |
| 5 | Pittsburgh | 9,650 | 10,503 | 8.84 |
| 6 | Detroit | 9,553 | 10,395 | 8.81 |
| 7 | New York | 10,700 | 11,623 | 8.63 |
| 8 | Denver | 9,238 | 10,028 | 8.55 |
| 9 | Dallas | 9,001 | 9,768 | 8.52 |
| 10 | Chicago | 9,290 | 10,070 | 8.40 |
| 11 | Philadelphia | 9,835 | 10,646 | 8.25 |
| 12 | Houston | 9,240 | 9,996 | 8.18 |
| 13 | Cincinnati | 9,290 | 10,038 | 8.05 |
| 14 | San Francisco-Oakland | 10,108 | 10,921 | 8.04 |
| 15 | Boston | 11,051 | 11,925 | 7.91 |
| 15 | San Diego | 9,107 | 9,827 | 7.91 |
| 17 | Atlanta | 8,759 | 9,516 | 7.76 |
| 18 | St. Louis | 9,417 | 10,108 | 7.74 |
| 19 | Buffalo | 9,991 | 10,744 | 7.54 |
| 20 | Baltimore | 9,348 | 10,051 | 7.52 |
| 21 | Washington, D.C. | 10,269 | 11,000 | 7.12 |
| 22 | Kansas City, Kan., Mo. | 9,320 | 9,978 | 7.06 |
| 23 | Cleveland | 9,832 | 10,500 | 6.79 |
| 24 | Minneapolis-St. Paul | 9,553 | 10,121 | 5.95 |
| 25 | Anchorage | 12,268 | 12,900 | 5.15 |

# 102. Housing Rental Cost

The largest single component in the cost of living data is housing cost. To show the range of such costs, we indicate below the cost of renting a comparably sized unfurnished, two-bedroom, one-bathroom apartment in each city. Utilities are excluded, except water. The cost of utilities is shown in the next table.

It used to be a rule of thumb that rent (or, in the case of homeowners, the carrying costs of the mortgage plus maintenance costs) should not exceed one-fourth of one's income. This rule has been shattered by the realities of urban life. The figures below explain why the old rule of thumb is no longer valid. If the average rental for a two-bedroom apartment in New York City in mid-1982 is $625 (up 16 percent from a year earlier), rental in a desirable neighborhood may require twice or three times that amount. Few young people earn enough to fit such a monthly rental into one-fourth of their salary. Many young career people are prepared to pay one-third or even one-half of their income to live in a desirable neighborhood in a big city. Their considerations include safety and meeting the right people.

No one will be surprised to see New York at the top of the list. It is also to be expected that California cities will be near the top. Minneapolis and St. Paul rank higher than some people might expect. Despite all the migration out of Newark, its rental was the 8th highest of the 59 cities for which we had data in 1981 but dropped to 24th place in 1982.

At the other end of the spectrum, apartments in Memphis rent for 40 percent of what they cost in New York City. Lubbock's rental is a real bargain, especially in view of the strong local economy centered on high technology companies. Further housing data are provided in later tables on housing.

SOURCE: American Chamber of Commerce Researchers Association, "Inter-City Cost of Living Indicators," second quarter 1982.

| Rank | Monthly Housing Rental Cost City | ($) | Rank | Monthly Housing Rental Cost City | ($) | Rank | Monthly Housing Rental Cost City | ($) |
|---|---|---|---|---|---|---|---|---|
| 1 | New York | 625 | 24 | Jersey City | 334 | 47 | Fort Wayne | 297 |
| 2 | San Jose | 532 | 24 | Newark | 334 | 47 | Fresno | 297 |
| 3 | San Diego | 460 | 26 | Riverside | 329 | 47 | Nashville-Davidson | 297 |
| 4 | Minneapolis | 428 | 27 | El Paso | 325 | 50 | Omaha | 296 |
| 4 | St. Paul | 428 | 28 | Baton Rouge | 323 | 51 | Portland, Ore. | 295 |
| 6 | Houston | 425 | 29 | Norfolk | 322 | 52 | Cincinnati | 293 |
| 7 | Denver | 407 | 29 | Virginia Beach | 322 | 53 | Dayton | 288 |
| 8 | Corpus Christi | 402 | 31 | Kansas City | 321 | 54 | Baltimore | 281 |
| 9 | Las Vegas | 400 | 32 | Indianapolis | 320 | 54 | Jacksonville | 281 |
| 10 | Anaheim | 396 | 33 | Wichita | 318 | 56 | Kansas City, Kan. | 279 |
| 11 | Oklahoma City | 390 | 34 | Lincoln | 315 | 56 | Mobile | 279 |
| 11 | Tulsa | 390 | 35 | Salt Lake City | 314 | 56 | Syracuse | 279 |
| 13 | Chicago | 385 | 35 | San Antonio | 314 | 59 | Sacramento | 278 |
| 14 | Miami | 384 | 37 | Akron | 310 | 60 | Columbus, Ga. | 277 |
| 15 | Tucson | 375 | 37 | Chattanooga | 310 | 60 | Jackson | 277 |
| 16 | Fort Worth | 369 | 37 | Little Rock | 310 | 62 | Tacoma | 275 |
| 17 | Shreveport | 365 | 37 | St. Louis | 310 | 63 | Columbus, Ohio | 270 |
| 18 | Flint | 364 | 41 | Charlotte | 307 | 64 | Louisville | 269 |
| 19 | Arlington, Texas | 354 | 42 | New Orleans | 304 | 65 | Buffalo | 263 |
| 20 | Colorado Springs | 351 | 43 | Albuquerque | 300 | 65 | Birmingham | 263 |
| 21 | Phoenix | 350 | 43 | Knoxville | 300 | 67 | Lubbock | 262 |
| 22 | Atlanta | 348 | 43 | Madison | 300 | 68 | Memphis | 258 |
| 23 | Lexington-Fayette | 345 | 46 | Greensboro | 298 | | | |

# 103. Cost of Fuel and Light

Because the previous table on the cost of housing excludes utilities, we need to examine the cost of fuel and light in each of the cities. This cost has been growing rapidly in the 1970s and varies widely among cities.

Tacoma residents' energy costs were less than one-fourth what New Yorkers have had to pay. However, Washington State's nuclear power fiasco will probably be raising energy costs for residents in that state. The cheapest power in the Northeast or Midwest is in Madison and Akron—$74 and $83 per month, respectively, for consumption of energy (electricity and other usual services) for a house with 1,800 square feet of living space. The most costly power in the second quarter of 1982 was in New York City—$238.41 a month.

Boston is a good sample city to review for components of fuel and light costs. It is not included in the table below but is included in data from the Bureau of Labor Statistics. The average price in Boston in December 1981 for 500 KWH (=1.7 million BTUs) of electricity was $38.54. The national average was $34.96. Utility gas costs in Boston for 40 therms were $33.01; for 100 therms (=10 million BTUs), $73.67. The U.S. city average price for 40 therms was $20.71; for 100 therms, $46.37.

The average Boston price of fuel oil No. 2 (=140,000 BTU) for home heating was $1.272, 2.5 cents more than the national average of $1.247 a gallon. Average prices for fuel oil ranged from $1.164 in the Milwaukee area to $1.298 a gallon in the Seattle-Everett metropolitan area.

SOURCE: American Chamber of Commerce Researchers Association, "Inter-City Cost of Living Indicators," second quarter 1982.

| Rank | Average Monthly Fuel and Light — City | Cost ($) | Rank | Average Monthly Fuel and Light — City | Cost ($) | Rank | Average Monthly Fuel and Light — City | Cost ($) |
|---|---|---|---|---|---|---|---|---|
| 1 | New York | 238.41 | 24 | Nashville-Davidson | 107.30 | 47 | Lubbock | 94.30 |
| 2 | Jersey City | 140.50 | 25 | Knoxville | 106.82 | 48 | Corpus Christi | 93.44 |
| 2 | Newark | 140.50 | 26 | Baton Rouge | 106.51 | 49 | Flint | 92.32 |
| 4 | Houston | 139.51 | 27 | Kansas City, Kan. | 106.14 | 50 | Chattanooga | 92.00 |
| 5 | Fresno | 136.38 | 28 | Memphis | 105.87 | 51 | Denver | 91.37 |
| 6 | Columbus, Ga. | 131.93 | 29 | Jackson | 105.65 | 52 | Salt Lake City | 88.10 |
| 7 | Dayton | 125.24 | 30 | Norfolk | 103.87 | 53 | Oklahoma City | 87.87 |
| 8 | Arlington, Texas | 123.36 | 30 | Virginia Beach | 103.87 | 54 | Lincoln | 87.60 |
| 9 | Syracuse | 122.27 | 32 | Buffalo | 103.20 | 55 | Portland, Ore. | 87.50 |
| 10 | Kansas City, Mo. | 120.70 | 33 | Fort Worth | 103.15 | 56 | Tulsa | 86.73 |
| 11 | Jacksonville | 119.70 | 34 | St. Louis | 102.83 | 57 | Indianapolis | 86.47 |
| 12 | Cincinnati | 118.07 | 35 | Lexington-Fayette | 102.13 | 58 | Shreveport | 85.10 |
| 12 | Columbus, Ohio | 118.07 | 36 | Little Rock | 101.40 | 59 | Las Vegas | 84.54 |
| 14 | Miami | 117.23 | 37 | Louisville | 100.89 | 60 | Tucson | 84.41 |
| 15 | Birmingham | 116.39 | 38 | San Jose | 100.60 | 61 | Akron | 82.76 |
| 16 | Minneapolis | 114.36 | 39 | Riverside | 100.57 | 62 | Anaheim | 77.26 |
| 16 | St. Paul | 114.36 | 40 | San Antonio | 98.76 | 63 | Madison | 73.92 |
| 18 | Charlotte | 113.82 | 41 | Baltimore | 98.73 | 64 | Sacramento | 71.44 |
| 18 | Greensboro | 113.82 | 42 | Omaha | 98.09 | 65 | San Diego | 70.71 |
| 20 | Phoenix | 111.13 | 43 | New Orleans | 98.07 | 66 | Albuquerque | 63.04 |
| 21 | Chicago | 111.03 | 44 | Atlanta | 96.33 | 67 | Colorado Springs | 59.83 |
| 22 | Mobile | 110.09 | 45 | Fort Wayne | 95.53 | 68 | Tacoma | 54.85 |
| 23 | Wichita | 108.95 | 46 | El Paso | 95.21 | | | |

# 104. Cost of Meat

One important measure of the cost of the food we eat is the cost of common varieties of meat. We have used two basic meats (chicken and beef) as measures for this cost, adding the cost of two pounds of chicken and one pound of beef. In the second quarter 1982, Tacoma proved to be the most costly city, Miami the least expensive.

The results do not suggest that proximity to the place where the animals are raised or slaughtered has much to do with cost. Cities like Arlington, Texas that are near cattle-growing territory have meat that is just about as costly as in Newark, which is not. Chicago, a big meat-processing center, is in the middle of the scale. However, both of the Kansas Cities have inexpensive meat.

SOURCE: American Chamber of Commerce Researchers Association, "Inter-City Cost of Living Indicators," second quarter 1982.

| Rank | Cost of Meat City | ($) | Rank | Cost of Meat City | ($) | Rank | Cost of Meat City | ($) |
|---|---|---|---|---|---|---|---|---|
| 1 | Tacoma | 3.76 | 24 | Cincinnati | 2.81 | 47 | Columbus, Ohio | 2.60 |
| 2 | Jersey City | 3.59 | 24 | Houston | 2.81 | 47 | Kansas City, Kan. | 2.60 |
| 2 | Newark | 3.59 | 24 | Lexington-Fayette | 2.81 | 49 | Phoenix | 2.54 |
| 4 | New York | 3.17 | 27 | Corpus Christi | 2.77 | 50 | Nashville-Davidson | 2.53 |
| 5 | Tucson | 3.16 | 28 | Chattanooga | 2.73 | 51 | Ft. Wayne | 2.52 |
| 6 | Baltimore | 3.13 | 29 | Arlington, Texas | 2.70 | 51 | Omaha | 2.52 |
| 7 | Akron | 3.11 | 29 | Mobile | 2.70 | 53 | Shreveport | 2.51 |
| 8 | Baton Rouge | 3.07 | 29 | San Diego | 2.70 | 54 | Kansas City, Mo. | 2.50 |
| 9 | Atlanta | 3.01 | 32 | Charlotte | 2.69 | 54 | Norfolk | 2.50 |
| 9 | Portland, Ore. | 3.01 | 32 | Jackson | 2.69 | 54 | Virginia Beach | 2.50 |
| 11 | Oklahoma City | 2.98 | 34 | Indianapolis | 2.68 | 57 | Syracuse | 2.49 |
| 12 | Greensboro | 2.97 | 34 | New Orleans | 2.68 | 58 | Denver | 2.44 |
| 12 | Tulsa | 2.97 | 36 | Chicago | 2.67 | 58 | Las Vegas | 2.44 |
| 14 | Flint | 2.94 | 36 | Memphis | 2.67 | 58 | Wichita | 2.44 |
| 15 | Albuquerque | 2.92 | 36 | San Antonio | 2.67 | 61 | Minneapolis | 2.41 |
| 15 | Salt Lake City | 2.92 | 39 | Lincoln | 2.65 | 61 | St. Paul | 2.41 |
| 17 | Fresno | 2.91 | 40 | Birmingham | 2.64 | 63 | Columbus, Ga. | 2.40 |
| 18 | Little Rock | 2.90 | 40 | Lubbock | 2.64 | 64 | Anaheim | 2.36 |
| 19 | Jacksonville | 2.89 | 42 | Louisville | 2.63 | 65 | Dayton | 2.31 |
| 20 | Fort Worth | 2.88 | 42 | Madison | 2.63 | 66 | Colorado Springs | 2.30 |
| 21 | Sacramento | 2.87 | 42 | Riverside | 2.63 | 67 | St. Louis | 2.28 |
| 22 | Knoxville | 2.83 | 45 | El Paso | 2.62 | 68 | Miami | 1.73 |
| 23 | Buffalo | 2.82 | 46 | San Jose | 2.61 | | | |

# 105. Cost of Milk and Eggs

Cities are ranked on the cost of a half-gallon carton of milk and one dozen grade A eggs, second quarter 1982. As one would expect, buyers in cities close to dairy country were paying over 25 cents less for a carton of milk than New York City residents, who, according to the state attorney general's office, were being systematically over-

charged by price-fixing dairy marketeers during the period.

Some Tennessee and North Carolina residents are having to pay surprisingly more for their milk. Either there are special problems in transporting and retailing milk in these cities or competition is weak. Chattanooga residents can get their milk and eggs for nearly one-fifth less than their neighbors all around them—to the west in Memphis, the northeast in Knoxville or the south in Columbus, Georgia. This suggests that competition is keen in Chattanooga and that the city serves as a major regional wholesale center for dairy goods.

SOURCE: American Chamber of Commerce Researchers Association, Inter-City Cost of Living Indicators, second quarter 1982.

| Rank | Cost of Milk and Eggs City | ($) | Rank | Cost of Milk and Eggs City | ($) | Rank | Cost of Milk and Eggs City | ($) |
|---|---|---|---|---|---|---|---|---|
| 1 | Charlotte | 2.33 | 23 | Newark | 2.05 | 47 | Akron | 1.94 |
| 1 | Columbus, Ga. | 2.33 | 23 | San Diego | 2.05 | 47 | Tacoma | 1.94 |
| 3 | New York | 2.31 | 26 | Anaheim | 2.04 | 49 | Nashville-Davidson | 1.91 |
| 4 | Shreveport | 2.28 | 26 | Corpus Christi | 2.04 | 50 | Kansas City, Kan. | 1.90 |
| 5 | Memphis | 2.23 | 26 | Jacksonville | 2.04 | 50 | Lincoln | 1.90 |
| 6 | Houston | 2.21 | 26 | Lubbock | 2.04 | 50 | Salt Lake City | 1.90 |
| 7 | Atlanta | 2.18 | 30 | Lexington-Fayette | 2.03 | 53 | Dayton | 1.89 |
| 7 | Colorado Springs | 2.18 | 30 | Oklahoma City | 2.03 | 53 | Sacramento | 1.89 |
| 7 | Greensboro | 2.18 | 32 | Jackson | 2.02 | 55 | Phoenix | 1.88 |
| 10 | Albuquerque | 2.16 | 32 | San Antonio | 2.02 | 56 | Fresno | 1.87 |
| 11 | Arlington, Texas | 2.15 | 34 | El Paso | 2.01 | 56 | Syracuse | 1.87 |
| 12 | Fort Worth | 2.11 | 34 | Wichita | 2.01 | 58 | Birmingham | 1.86 |
| 12 | Riverside | 2.11 | 36 | Baton Rouge | 2.00 | 59 | New Orleans | 1.84 |
| 14 | Flint | 2.10 | 36 | Tucson | 2.00 | 60 | San Jose | 1.82 |
| 14 | Las Vegas | 2.10 | 38 | Baltimore | 1.99 | 61 | Chicago | 1.80 |
| 14 | Miami | 2.10 | 39 | Columbus, Ohio | 1.98 | 62 | St. Louis | 1.79 |
| 17 | Denver | 2.09 | 39 | Fort Wayne | 1.98 | 63 | Madison | 1.78 |
| 17 | Indianapolis | 2.09 | 39 | Kansas City, Mo. | 1.98 | 64 | Minneapolis | 1.77 |
| 19 | Norfolk | 2.07 | 42 | Knoxville | 1.97 | 64 | St. Paul | 1.77 |
| 19 | Virginia Beach | 2.07 | 43 | Little Rock | 1.96 | 66 | Cincinnati | 1.74 |
| 21 | Buffalo | 2.06 | 44 | Mobile | 1.95 | 67 | Chattanooga | 1.71 |
| 21 | Louisville | 2.06 | 44 | Portland, Ore. | 1.95 | 68 | Omaha | 1.63 |
| 23 | Jersey City | 2.05 | 44 | Tulsa | 1.95 | | | |

# 106. Clothing Costs

Clothing costs are necessary expenses. As with the price of other dry goods, they are constantly increasing. Clothing costs for boy's underwear, adult's jeans, a man's dress shirt and dry cleaning for a two-piece suit were totaled in the following table.

The highest costs were in New York, despite the proximity of its textile and apparel industry, with a total cost of $50.37. San Diego was slightly behind, with $50.31. Chattanooga and Baton Rouge were at the end of the ranking showing the lowest cost for these goods— $36.77 and $35.72, respectively.

California cities are on the expensive side, but the differences in costs do not seem to follow entirely consistent patterns.

How do we explain the fact that costs in Kansas City, Kansas were low in the second quarter of 1982, while across the state line Kansas City, Missouri is one of the most expensive places to buy clothing? Add to this anomaly the fact that their positions were reversed from the previous quarter. The state laws in Missouri seem to be favorable to competition, since St. Louis is inexpensive.

Why is clothing so expensive in New Jersey? Why is Nashville so much more costly than Chattanooga?

The answer to these questions is that prices depend on supply and demand in each market area, and the factors in the highly competitive clothing industry change quickly from one quarter to the next. The fact that cities that are under the same state laws can differ in costs as widely as they do in Tennessee suggests again that retail cost differences reflect competition as well as transportation costs. Chattanooga is a major wholesale trade center with over $2 billion a year of such business. This business clearly promotes competition among local retailers, as well as permitting them to undercut prices of retailers in other cities because the latter may do their buying from Chattanooga wholesalers and must cover the costs of transportation and handling.

SOURCE: American Chamber of Commerce Researchers Association (ACCRA), "Inter-City Cost of Living Indicators," second quarter 1982.

| Rank | Clothing Costs City | ($) | Rank | Clothing Costs City | ($) | Rank | Clothing Costs City | ($) |
|------|------|------|------|------|------|------|------|------|
| 1 | New York | 50.37 | 21 | San Jose | 45.41 | 41 | Fort Worth | 42.54 |
| 2 | San Diego | 50.31 | 22 | Shreveport | 45.31 | 42 | Lincoln | 42.52 |
| 3 | Riverside | 49.66 | 23 | Denver | 44.96 | 43 | Buffalo | 42.49 |
| 4 | Columbus, Ga. | 48.38 | 24 | Mobile | 44.73 | 44 | Nashville-Davidson | 42.36 |
| 5 | Knoxville | 48.34 | 25 | El Paso | 44.61 | 45 | Memphis | 42.25 |
| 6 | Fort Wayne | 48.25 | 25 | Miami | 44.61 | 46 | Dayton | 42.24 |
| 7 | Houston | 47.33 | 27 | Baltimore | 44.43 | 47 | Wichita | 42.13 |
| 8 | Sacramento | 46.92 | 28 | Little Rock | 44.20 | 48 | Arlington, Texas | 41.63 |
| 9 | Charlotte | 46.64 | 29 | Lubbock | 44.02 | 49 | Columbus, Ohio | 41.38 |
| 10 | Fresno | 46.46 | 30 | Phoenix | 43.95 | 50 | Lexington-Fayette | 40.72 |
| 10 | Jersey City | 46.46 | 31 | Oklahoma City | 43.77 | 51 | St. Louis | 40.68 |
| 10 | Newark | 46.46 | 32 | Madison | 43.58 | 52 | Greensboro | 40.26 |
| 13 | Tulsa | 46.29 | 33 | Colorado Springs | 43.28 | 53 | Indianapolis | 40.23 |
| 14 | Tacoma | 46.28 | 34 | Minneapolis | 43.23 | 54 | Syracuse | 40.18 |
| 15 | San Antonio | 45.79 | 34 | St. Paul | 43.23 | 55 | Salt Lake City | 40.01 |
| 16 | Portland, Ore. | 45.74 | 36 | Anaheim | 42.97 | 56 | Louisville | 39.82 |
| 17 | Cincinnati | 45.67 | 37 | Las Vegas | 42.83 | 57 | Kansas City, Kan. | 37.87 |
| 18 | Flint | 45.56 | 38 | Albuquerque | 42.73 | 58 | Omaha | 37.83 |
| 19 | Corpus Christi | 45.44 | 39 | Atlanta | 42.65 | 59 | Chattanooga | 36.77 |
| 19 | Kansas City, Mo. | 45.44 | 40 | Birmingham | 42.56 | 60 | Baton Rouge | 35.72 |

# 107. Cost of Cigarettes and Whiskey

The cost of cigarettes and whiskey is important to many people, because these two items—which are included in the sparse group of items covered by the Bureau of Labor Statistics—constitute a substantial portion of their budgets.

Based on the cost of the carton of king-sized cigarettes and 750 ml of Seagram's 7-Crown Whiskey in the fourth quarter 1981, milk and eggs may be expensive in Charlotte and Greensboro, North Carolina, but cigarettes and whiskey are relatively cheap. As we have seen in the previous table, North Carolinians pay a half-dollar more for a half gallon of milk and a dozen eggs than do residents of Tacoma, Washington or Birmingham, Alabama, but the latter pay over $2.50 more for a carton of cigarettes and a bottle of whiskey.

Compared to the second quarter of 1981, Kansas City, Kansas showed only a $.01 increase, while residents' costs jumped appreciably in New York ($1.12) and Tacoma ($1.18) for the fourth quarter of 1981.

New Jersey seems to have the highest cigarette and liquor cost, and North Carolina seems to have the lowest. One difference is in tax rates. The 1981 New Jersey tax on liquor was $2.80 per gallon. The North Carolina tax on liquor was 22.5 percent of the retail price. The ad valorem tax on liquor in North Carolina came to a $1.08 tax on 750 ml of Seagram's (the retail price in 1981, including the tax, being $5.90). This is substantially higher than the equivalent New Jersey tax, which came to 55 cents for a 750 ml bottle (there are 3.78 liters to the gallon). So the big question is why liquor costs over $1.00

a bottle more in New Jersey than in North Carolina even though the tax in New Jersey is half what it is in North Carolina.

The 1981 New Jersey tax on cigarettes was 19 cents per package of 20 cigarettes (Connecticut, Florida and Massachusetts were even higher—21 cents a package), whereas the North Carolina tax was only 2 cents per package. The 17-cent difference in state taxes adds up to a $1.70 difference on a carton of 10 packages which is approximately the difference in prices.

An explanation for North Carolina's low cigarette prices is that it is one of the nation's largest tobacco producers.

SOURCES: Cost data from American Chamber of Commerce Researchers Association (ACCRA), fourth quarter 1981 and (for comparisons) second quarter 1981. Tax information from Tax Foundation, *Facts and Figures on Government Finance*, 1981, pp. 240, 241, 244.

| Rank | Cigarette and Whiskey Costs City | ($) | Rank | Cigarette and Whiskey Costs City | ($) | Rank | Cigarette and Whiskey Costs City | ($) |
|---|---|---|---|---|---|---|---|---|
| 1 | Tacoma | 14.43 | 20 | Albuquerque | 12.93 | 39 | Anaheim | 12.02 |
| 2 | Jersey City | 13.95 | 21 | Baltimore | 12.91 | 40 | Flint | 11.95 |
| 2 | Newark | 13.95 | 22 | Lincoln | 12.89 | 41 | Shreveport | 11.90 |
| 4 | Chattanooga | 13.77 | 23 | Fresno | 12.87 | 42 | St. Louis | 11.83 |
| 5 | Minneapolis | 13.66 | 24 | Lubbock | 12.85 | 43 | Colorado Springs | 11.57 |
| 6 | Birmingham | 13.53 | 25 | Buffalo | 12.81 | 44 | Oklahoma City | 11.48 |
| 7 | Mobile | 13.51 | 26 | Houston | 12.79 | 45 | San Jose | 11.45 |
| 8 | New York | 13.35 | 26 | San Antonio | 12.79 | 46 | Denver | 11.38 |
| 9 | Madison | 13.29 | 28 | Riverside | 12.71 | 46 | Indianapolis | 11.38 |
| 10 | Arlington, Texas | 13.24 | 29 | Corpus Christi | 12.69 | 48 | Baton Rouge | 11.36 |
| 10 | Portland | 13.24 | 30 | San Diego | 12.61 | 49 | Tulsa | 11.34 |
| 12 | Dayton | 13.20 | 30 | Syracuse | 12.61 | 50 | Lexington-Fayette | 11.32 |
| 13 | Nashville-Davidson | 13.18 | 32 | Omaha | 12.60 | 50 | Louisville | 11.32 |
| 14 | Columbus, Ga. | 13.01 | 33 | Salt Lake City | 12.59 | 52 | New Orleans | 11.25 |
| 15 | Fort Worth | 13.00 | 34 | El Paso | 12.57 | 53 | Fort Wayne | 11.24 |
| 15 | Memphis | 13.00 | 35 | Norfolk | 12.48 | 54 | Las Vegas | 10.97 |
| 17 | Columbus, Ohio | 12.97 | 36 | Kansas City, Mo. | 12.38 | 55 | Greensboro | 10.96 |
| 18 | Phoenix | 12.96 | 37 | Kansas City, Kan. | 12.21 | 56 | Charlotte | 10.84 |
| 19 | Akron | 12.94 | 38 | Sacramento | 12.15 | | | |

# 108. Telephone Costs

The table below shows estimated monthly phone costs for a family of four in the second quarter of 1981.

As of 1981 three of the top four cities listed were in New York State, with Buffalo at the top. Its estimated cost was $17.32. Least expensive were five California cities—Fresno, San Jose, San Diego, Riverside and Sacramento—with Sacramento being the lowest, at $5.70. The differences can be explained by the differing philosophies of the two state utility regulatory bodies concerning charges on business or residential users.

Phone costs are significant because they vary widely among cities. Cities that have higher costs will margi-nally inhibit communications among their residents and between their residents and the outside world.

With the breakup of the Bell Telephone System, which subsidized local charges at the expense of long-distance rates, one may expect to see long-distance charges decline steadily, while local charges will increase.

The independence of the component parts of the new telephone system can be expected to increase rather than reduce the differences among phone charges in different cities. Above all, one can expect the charges listed below to increase faster than the overall cost of living.

SOURCE: American Chamber of Commerce Researchers Association, Inter-City Cost of Living Indicators, second quarter 1982.

| Rank | City | Monthly Costs ($) | Rank | City | Monthly Costs ($) | Rank | City | Monthly Costs ($) |
|---|---|---|---|---|---|---|---|---|
| 1 | Buffalo | 17.32 | 21 | Knoxville | 11.75 | 41 | Albuquerque | 9.52 |
| 2 | Lexington | 14.53 | 21 | Nashville | 11.75 | 42 | Fort Worth | 9.50 |
| 2 | New York | 14.53 | 23 | Salt Lake City | 11.59 | 43 | El Paso | 9.48 |
| 4 | Syracuse | 14.35 | 24 | Columbus, Ga. | 11.10 | 44 | Wichita | 9.41 |
| 5 | Norfolk | 14.31 | 25 | Phoenix | 10.88 | 45 | Charlotte | 9.38 |
| 6 | Jackson | 14.25 | 26 | Cincinnati | 10.81 | 46 | St. Louis | 9.26 |
| 7 | Fort Wayne | 14.14 | 27 | Shreveport | 10.72 | 47 | San Antonio | 8.95 |
| 8 | Louisville | 14.11 | 28 | Baton Rouge | 10.71 | 48 | Tacoma | 8.85 |
| 9 | New Orleans | 14.08 | 29 | Dayton | 10.70 | 49 | Denver | 8.81 |
| 10 | Minneapolis | 13.72 | 30 | Chicago | 10.55 | 50 | Greensboro | 8.75 |
| 10 | St. Paul | 13.72 | 31 | Akron | 10.50 | 51 | Corpus Christi | 8.27 |
| 12 | Memphis | 13.66 | 32 | Houston | 10.45 | 52 | Portland, Ore. | 8.21 |
| 13 | Birmingham | 13.60 | 33 | Omaha | 10.06 | 53 | Colorado Springs | 7.95 |
| 14 | Columbus, Ohio | 12.83 | 34 | Lubbock | 9.95 | 54 | Newark | 7.65 |
| 15 | Mobile | 12.51 | 35 | Lincoln | 9.77 | 55 | Oklahoma City | 7.47 |
| 16 | Chattanooga | 12.48 | 36 | Kansas City, Kan. | 9.76 | 56 | Fresno | 6.70 |
| 17 | Tucson | 12.42 | 37 | Madison | 9.70 | 57 | San Jose | 6.60 |
| 18 | Jacksonville | 12.37 | 38 | Kansas City, Mo. | 9.67 | 58 | San Diego | 5.90 |
| 19 | Indianapolis | 11.88 | 39 | Arlington, Texas | 9.60 | 59 | Riverside | 5.70 |
| 20 | Baltimore | 11.81 | 39 | Flint | 9.60 | 59 | Sacramento | 5.70 |

# CHAPTER SEVEN

# ECONOMY AND THE WORK FORCE

The following tables examine the economic base of cities and their metro areas. Three major economic attributes are represented. First, what industries employ the most people. Second, what types of purchases are made by residents and workers. Third, what is the complexion of the labor force.

Based upon employment patterns, metro areas are described as having a base in retailing, finance or other industry.

Broadly speaking, urban centers have been losing manufacturing jobs and have been attracting service jobs. For example in 1977 manufacturing employed 30 percent more people in New York City than financial services (finance, insurance and real estate). By 1982 manufacturing employed nearly 5 percent *fewer* people

than financial services.* The shift away from traditional heavy manufacturing to higher technology industries has also changed the relative importance of different manufacturing centers.

Food sales, retail sales and drugstore sales are also chosen as indicative of local spending patterns. Per capita sales of food and drugs continue to rise in some cities that have been relatively recession-resistant because they are not dependent on only one industry.

---

*Samuel M. Ehrenhalt, Regional Commissioner of Labor Statistics, U.S. Department of Labor, "Some Perspectives on Changing Profiles of Work and Workers in the New York City Economy," address to the City Club of New York, March 11, 1983.

# 109. Manufacturing Centers

Cities became manufacturing centers because of their location, especially in relation to transportation facilities. Cities located near ports, crossroads and rivers ("mill towns") became the initial industrial centers. Since World War II manufacturing centers have shifted out of the older central cities to suburban areas and to younger cities. Growth has been slower inside the older cities than outside them. In fact, a 1974 study "The Density Gradient for Manufacturing Industry" of five metropolitan areas—New York, Cleveland, Cincinnati, Kansas City and Minneapolis–St. Paul—showed that:

1. Decentralization of manufacturing was a dominant pattern in many cities. Central densities fell

and density gradients flattened out over the 1967–71 period.
2. Employment is less centralized than manufacturing firms themselves. That is, larger firms tend to locate at greater distances from the city center than smaller firms.
3. In all five cities, regardless of the overall degree of centralization, apparel, printing and publishing are heavily centralized.

Centers with higher numbers of industrial workers have historically been located in the older cities of the Northeast and the upper Midwest. The table below showing manufacturing workers in the major metro areas in 1980 still reflects the prominence of such work in these areas. These industries tend to be capital-intensive, based on production of heavy machinery or durable goods.

During the 1970s there has been a major shift to computer technology and aero-dynamics industries located in the West (e.g., San Jose, Anaheim) and South (Dallas). The employment figures can be expected to shift in their favor.

SOURCES: U.S. Census Bureau, *1980 Census of Population Supplementary Report: Provisional Estimates of Social, Economic and Housing Characteristics*, states and Standard Metropolitan Statistical Areas (March 1982). Peter Kemper and Roger Schmenner, "The Density Gradient for Manufacturing Industry," *Journal of Urban Economics* 1 (October 1974): 410–27.

| Rank | Metro Area | Total Labor Force | Labor Force in Manufacturing | Percentage of Labor Force in Manufacturing |
|---|---|---|---|---|
| 1 | San Jose | 658,043 | 226,578 | 34.43 |
| 2 | Detroit | 1,722,372 | 548,297 | 31.83 |
| 3 | Milwaukee | 649.181 | 204,676 | 31.53 |
| 4 | Cleveland | 849,689 | 255,907 | 30.12 |
| 5 | Buffalo | 516,027 | 148,490 | 28.78 |
| 6 | Cincinnati | 604,834 | 169,497 | 28.02 |
| 7 | Chicago | 3,179,676 | 869,018 | 27.33 |
| 8 | Anaheim | 965,074 | 255,539 | 26.48 |

| Rank | Metro Area | Total Labor Force | Labor Force in Manufacturing | Percentage of Labor Force in Manufacturing |
|---|---|---|---|---|
| 9 | Newark | 888,497 | 235,156 | 26.47 |
| 10 | Pittsburgh | 950,751 | 243,704 | 25.63 |
| 11 | Los Angeles | 3,488,192 | 863,841 | 24.76 |
| 12 | Indianapolis | 539,776 | 131,804 | 24.42 |
| 13 | Philadelphia | 1,964,490 | 478,907 | 24.38 |
| 14 | Minneapolis-St. Paul | 1,074,666 | 253,974 | 23.63 |
| 15 | St. Louis | 1,024,411 | 236,865 | 23.12 |
| 16 | Seattle | 792,278 | 181,575 | 22.92 |
| 17 | Dallas-Fort Worth | 1,482,436 | 315,004 | 21.25 |
| 18 | Portland, Ore. | 589,090 | 124,075 | 21.06 |
| 19 | Boston | 1,315,200 | 273,802 | 20.82 |
| 20 | Kansas City, Mo., Kan. | 635,700 | 123,768 | 19.47 |
| 21 | Houston | 1,440,981 | 275,129 | 19.09 |
| 22 | Columbus, Ohio | 501,328 | 94,233 | 18.80 |
| 23 | Riverside | 613,956 | 111,767 | 18.20 |
| 24 | Phoenix | 670,608 | 121,408 | 18.10 |
| 25 | New York | 3,878,401 | 683,965 | 17.64 |
| 26 | Baltimore | 970,022 | 170,031 | 17.53 |
| 27 | San Diego | 758,579 | 126,389 | 16.66 |
| 28 | Atlanta | 974,914 | 158,754 | 16.28 |
| 29 | Denver | 820,574 | 126,452 | 15.41 |
| 30 | Miami | 731,889 | 109,100 | 14.91 |
| 31 | San Francisco-Oakland | 1,585,385 | 228,374 | 14.40 |
| 32 | Tampa-St. Petersburg | 604,612 | 86,675 | 14.34 |
| 33 | New Orleans | 448,542 | 58,413 | 13.02 |
| 34 | San Antonio | 418,790 | 50,075 | 11.96 |
| 35 | Sacramento | 434,301 | 34,475 | 7.94 |
| 36 | Washington, D.C. | 1,536,620 | 93,141 | 6.06 |

# 110. Retail Centers

One would imagine that Newark's and New York's metro areas would fare better than they do in this 1980 ranking of retail centers of the major American metro areas.

Possible explanations for New York's poor showing are: The retail trade is so efficient that it uses fewer employees; the inclusion of the entire metro area dilutes the heavy retail activity in Manhattan; much of New York's commercial activity is at the wholesale level; and there are so many other business activities that, proportionately, the retail business is not as important as in other cities.

Tampa-St. Petersburg, the leader here, and the remaining top five cities—San Antonio, Phoenix, San Diego and New Orleans—are all sunbelt, resort and retirement cities.

SOURCE: U.S. Department of Commerce, Bureau of the Census, *1980 Census of Population and Housing: Supplementary Report: Provisional Estimates of Social, Economic and Housing Characteristics* (Washington, D.C.: Government Printing Office, March 1982).

| Rank | Metro Area | Total Labor Force | Labor Force in Retail Trade | Percentage of Labor Force in Retail Trade |
|---|---|---|---|---|
| 1 | Tampa-St. Petersburg | 604,612 | 125,324 | 20.73 |
| 2 | San Antonio | 418,790 | 77,007 | 18.39 |
| 3 | Phoenix | 670,608 | 122,352 | 18.24 |

| Rank | Metro Area | Total Labor Force | Labor Force in Retail Trade | Percentage of Labor Force in Retail Trade |
|---|---|---|---|---|
| 4 | New Orleans | 448,542 | 81,593 | 18.19 |
| 4 | San Diego | 758,579 | 138,000 | 18.19 |
| 6 | Indianapolis | 539,776 | 98,145 | 18.18 |
| 7 | Miami | 731,889 | 131,341 | 17.95 |
| 8 | Sacramento | 434,301 | 77,901 | 17.94 |
| 9 | Columbus, Ohio | 501,328 | 69,701 | 17.89 |
| 10 | Buffalo | 516,027 | 91,434 | 17.72 |
| 11 | Riverside | 613,956 | 108,140 | 17.61 |
| 12 | Detroit | 1,722,372 | 301,060 | 17.48 |
| 13 | Portland, Ore. | 589,090 | 102,396 | 17.38 |
| 14 | Anaheim | 965,074 | 164,788 | 17.08 |
| 15 | Pittsburgh | 950,751 | 161,554 | 16.99 |
| 16 | Dallas-Fort Worth | 1,482,436 | 247,402 | 16.69 |
| 17 | Seattle | 792,278 | 131,586 | 16.61 |
| 18 | Kansas City, Mo., Kan. | 635,700 | 104,517 | 16.44 |
| 19 | Cleveland | 649,689 | 139,380 | 16.40 |
| 20 | Cincinnati | 604,834 | 98,868 | 16.35 |

| Rank | Metro Area | Total Labor Force | Labor Force in Retail Trade | Percentage of Labor Force in Retail Trade |
|---|---|---|---|---|
| 21 | Minneapolis-St. Paul | 1,074,686 | 175,420 | 16.32 |
| 22 | Milwaukee | 649,181 | 104,972 | 16.17 |
| 23 | Atlanta | 974,914 | 157,438 | 16.15 |
| 24 | Denver | 820,574 | 131,890 | 16.07 |
| 25 | Chicago | 3,179,676 | 510,449 | 16.05 |
| 26 | San Francisco-Oakland | 1,585,385 | 254,371 | 16.04 |
| 27 | Boston | 1,315,200 | 206,994 | 15.74 |
| 28 | Baltimore | 970,022 | 150,825 | 15.55 |
| 29 | Los Angeles | 3,488,192 | 537,287 | 15.40 |
| 30 | Philadelphia | 1,964,490 | 299,531 | 15.25 |
| 31 | Houston | 1,440,981 | 214,993 | 14.92 |
| 32 | San Jose | 658,043 | 93,871 | 14.27 |
| 33 | New York | 3,878,401 | 539,072 | 13.90 |
| 34 | Newark | 888,497 | 121,388 | 13.66 |
| 35 | Washington, D.C. | 1,536,620 | 209,110 | 13.61 |
| 36 | St. Louis | 1,024,411 | 72,631 | 7.09 |

# 111. Retail Sales

One important measure of the extent to which a city has maintained its economy is retail sales per capita. This largely reflects the variety and size of the downtown business area and its use by consumers. Even if people who work in the city commute in the evenings, the downtown area can be healthy. But when downtown retail sales deteriorate, that suggests a more serious problem related to buyer preferences.

Northeastern and midwestern cities that have suffered residential population declines also have the lowest per capita retail sales. As workers took up residence in suburban areas, they attracted retail stores, which opened in suburban malls and plazas. The large urban centers attempted to counteract this trend with programs to revitalize blighted urban shopping areas, but the results have not been strong enough to reverse the long-term trend. Southern and southwestern cities, conversely, have a high level of retail sales per capita because many of them encompass urban, suburban and rural areas and districts, and have been able to retain a sizable portion of higher-income populations. Many, like Houston, have annexed adjacent areas to solidify their taxing capacity.

SOURCE: *Sales & Marketing Management*, "1982 Survey of Buying Power, Part II," October 25, 1982, pp. 61–94.

| Rank | City | Retail Sales ($ Billion) 1981 | Retail Sales Per Capita 1981 |
|---|---|---|---|
| 1 | Arlington, Texas | 1.4 | 8,067 |
| 2 | Greensboro | 1.3 | 8,026 |
| 3 | Tulsa | 2.8 | 7,814 |
| 4 | Houston | 12.9 | 7,781 |
| 5 | Knoxville | 1.3 | 7,550 |
| 6 | Lubbock | 1.3 | 7,343 |
| 7 | Honolulu | 2.7 | 7,216 |
| 8 | Austin | 2.6 | 7,206 |
| 9 | Tampa | 1.9 | 7,147 |
| 10 | Anchorage | 1.3 | 7,094 |
| 11 | Des Moines | 1.3 | 6,966 |
| 12 | Salt Lake City | 1.1 | 6,857 |
| 13 | Oklahoma City | 2.8 | 6,831 |
| 14 | Lexington-Fayette | 1.4 | 6,797 |
| 15 | Dallas | 6.2 | 6,766 |
| 16 | Baton Rouge | 1.6 | 6,658 |
| 17 | Wichita | 1.8 | 6,530 |
| 18 | Tacoma | 1.0 | 6,484 |
| 19 | Aurora | 1.0 | 6,269 |
| 20 | Little Rock | 1.1 | 6,248 |
| 21 | Albuquerque | 2.2 | 6,207 |
| 22 | Seattle | 3.0 | 6,195 |
| 23 | Indianapolis | 4.3 | 6,180 |
| 24 | Madison | 1.0 | 6,106 |
| 25 | Fort Worth | 2.3 | 6,026 |
| 26 | Spokane | 1.0 | 5,985 |
| 27 | Nashville-Davidson | 2.7 | 5,933 |
| 28 | Santa Ana | 1.2 | 5,920 |
| 29 | Richmond | 1.3 | 5,918 |
| 30 | Fresno | 1.4 | 5,889 |
| 31 | Portland, Ore. | 2.1 | 5,811 |
| 32 | Riverside | 1.0 | 5,799 |

| Rank | City | Retail Sales ($ Billion) 1981 | Retail Sales Per Capita 1981 | Rank | City | Retail Sales ($ Billion) 1981 | Retail Sales Per Capita 1981 |
|---|---|---|---|---|---|---|---|
| 33 | Mobile | 1.2 | 5,794 | 67 | St. Petersburg | 1.1 | 4,693 |
| 34 | Las Vegas | 1.0 | 5,708 | 68 | Charlotte | 1.6 | 4,689 |
| 35 | San Francisco | 3.8 | 5,698 | 69 | Boston | 2.6 | 4,670 |
| 36 | Omaha | 1.8 | 5,686 | 69 | Los Angeles | 14.0 | 4,670 |
| 37 | Fort Wayne | 1.0 | 5,658 | 69 | Virginia Beach | 1.3 | 4,670 |
| 38 | Colorado Springs | 1.3 | 5,609 | 72 | San Jose | 3.0 | 4,526 |
| 39 | San Antonio | 4.5 | 5,573 | 73 | San Diego | 4.1 | 4,514 |
| 40 | Chattanooga | 1.0 | 5,532 | 74 | Long Beach | 1.6 | 4,476 |
| 41 | Shreveport | 1.2 | 5,493 | 75 | Toledo | 1.5 | 4,386 |
| 42 | Corpus Christi | 1.3 | 5,481 | 76 | Pittsburgh | 1.8 | 4,306 |
| 43 | Jackson | 1.2 | 5,471 | 77 | Louisville | 1.2 | 4,241 |
| 44 | Birmingham | 1.5 | 5,417 | 78 | New Orleans | 2.3 | 4,183 |
| 45 | Akron | 1.2 | 5,361 | 79 | Washington, D.C. | 2.6 | 4,181 |
| 46 | Tucson | 1.8 | 5,352 | 80 | Flint | .6 | 4,160 |
| 47 | Atlanta | 2.2 | 5,318 | 81 | St. Louis | 1.8 | 4,144 |
| 48 | Lincoln | .9 | 5,250 | 82 | Phoenix | 3.4 | 4,130 |
| 49 | Worcester | .8 | 5,229 | 83 | Cincinnati | 1.5 | 4,091 |
| 50 | Denver | 2.5 | 5,178 | 84 | Minneapolis | 1.5 | 4,036 |
| 51 | Montgomery | 1.0 | 5,146 | 85 | Oakland | 1.4 | 4,032 |
| 52 | Jacksonville | 2.8 | 5,126 | 86 | Milwaukee | 2.5 | 3,938 |
| 53 | Miami | 2.0 | 5,095 | 87 | Syracuse | .6 | 3,861 |
| 54 | Huntington Beach | .9 | 5,088 | 88 | Providence | .6 | 3,776 |
| 55 | Warren | .8 | 5,048 | 89 | New York | 23.6 | 3,405 |
| 56 | Memphis | 3.3 | 5,028 | 90 | Baltimore | 2.6 | 3,359 |
| 57 | Anaheim | 1.1 | 5,025 | 91 | Rochester | .8 | 3,345 |
| 58 | Columbus, Ga. | .8 | 5,024 | 92 | Yonkers | .6 | 3,300 |
| 59 | Grand Rapids | .9 | 5,000 | 93 | Chicago | 9.4 | 3,197 |
| 60 | Columbus, Ohio | 2.8 | 4,997 | 94 | Philadelphia | 5.2 | 3,192 |
| 61 | Kansas City, Mo. | 2.2 | 4,982 | 95 | Dayton | .6 | 3,115 |
| 62 | Sacramento | 1.4 | 4,970 | 96 | Cleveland | 1.6 | 3,009 |
| 63 | Norfolk | 1.3 | 4,952 | 97 | Jersey City | .6 | 2,966 |
| 64 | El Paso | 2.1 | 4,770 | 98 | Buffalo | 1.0 | 2,903 |
| 65 | Kansas City, Kan. | .8 | 4,764 | 99 | Detroit | 3.2 | 2,768 |
| 66 | St. Paul | 1.2 | 4,714 | 100 | Newark | .6 | 1,891 |

# 112. Retail Sales Per Household

Retail sales per household are a measure of the disposable income available to families after they have met the necessary expenses required for food and shelter. Retail sales encompass taxable items and include automobiles, clothing, furniture, and miscellaneous gifts and nonessential luxuries.

Anchorage leads this survey of 87 metropolitan areas in per capita retail sales per household during 1981. The high cost of living in Anchorage relates to the concomitant high cost of bringing goods to the relatively small and remote Alaska market. People have been lured to Alaska by the promise of higher incomes from the oil and petroleum product industries. The large city area and weakly developed city transportation services have increased the demand for large-ticket items such as pickup trucks, cars and motorcycles. New York City ranks second to last (86th). Possible explanations for this are the large market, which reduces costs; the high cost of shelter, which limits the amount of money left for retail items; and the efficient transportation system, which limits the interest of residents in large-ticket consumer items such as cars.

SOURCE: *Sales and Marketing Management,* "Survey of Buying Power, Part II," October 25, 1982, pp. 61–94.

| Rank | Retail Sales Per Household Metro Area | ($) |
|---|---|---|
| 1 | Anchorage | 19,753 |
| 2 | Lubbock | 18,407 |
| 3 | Houston | 17,983 |
| 4 | Des Moines | 16,068 |
| 5 | Dallas-Fort Worth | 15,960 |
| 6 | Anaheim | 15,681 |
| 6 | Honolulu | 15,681 |
| 8 | San Jose | 15,470 |
| 9 | Washington, D.C. | 15,132 |
| 10 | Corpus Christi | 15,068 |
| 11 | Lexington-Fayette | 15,010 |
| 12 | Las Vegas | 14,994 |
| 13 | Flint | 14,973 |
| 14 | Richmond | 14,918 |
| 15 | Oklahoma City | 14,754 |
| 16 | Minneapolis-St. Paul | 14,614 |
| 17 | Detroit | 14,609 |
| 18 | Tulsa | 14,600 |
| 19 | El Paso | 14,469 |
| 20 | Kansas City, Mo., Kan. | 14,439 |
| 21 | Miami | 14,407 |
| 22 | San Antonio | 14,316 |
| 23 | Austin | 14,308 |
| 23 | Wichita | 14,308 |
| 25 | Seattle | 14,244 |
| 26 | Denver | 13,773 |
| 27 | Atlanta | 13,767 |
| 28 | Little Rock | 13,624 |
| 29 | Indianapolis | 13,538 |

| Rank | Retail Sales Per Household Metro Area | ($) |
|---|---|---|
| 30 | Jacksonville | 13,505 |
| 31 | Baton Rouge | 13,497 |
| 32 | Norfolk | 13,427 |
| 33 | Albuquerque | 13,381 |
| 34 | Rochester | 13,363 |
| 35 | Grand Rapids | 13,358 |
| 36 | Portland, Ore. | 13,318 |
| 37 | Milwaukee | 13,267 |
| 38 | Worcester | 13,218 |
| 39 | Baltimore | 13,174 |
| 40 | Salt Lake City | 13,143 |
| 41 | Boston | 13,138 |
| 42 | Sacramento | 13,127 |
| 43 | Charlotte | 13,119 |
| 44 | Jackson | 13,117 |
| 45 | San Francisco-Oakland | 13,087 |
| 46 | Chicago | 13,081 |
| 47 | Syracuse | 13,069 |
| 48 | Lincoln | 13,055 |
| 49 | Fresno | 13,043 |
| 50 | Los Angeles | 13,022 |
| 51 | Madison | 13,018 |
| 52 | Nashville | 12,975 |
| 53 | Louisville | 12,959 |
| 54 | Buffalo | 12,938 |
| 55 | St. Louis | 12,923 |
| 56 | Cleveland | 12,903 |
| 57 | Columbus, Ohio | 12,893 |
| 58 | Fort Wayne | 12,849 |

| Rank | Retail Sales Per Household Metro Area | ($) |
|---|---|---|
| 59 | Birmingham | 12,845 |
| 60 | San Diego | 12,743 |
| 61 | Newark | 12,633 |
| 62 | New Orleans | 12,623 |
| 63 | Toledo | 12,611 |
| 64 | Omaha | 12,594 |
| 65 | Cincinnati | 12,520 |
| 66 | Greensboro | 12,502 |
| 67 | Akron | 12,472 |
| 68 | Knoxville | 12,359 |
| 69 | Mobile | 12,245 |
| 70 | Columbus, Ga. | 12,240 |
| 71 | Memphis | 12,205 |
| 72 | Tampa-St. Petersburg | 12,195 |
| 73 | Colorado Springs | 12,192 |
| 74 | Shreveport | 12,146 |
| 75 | Dayton | 12,088 |
| 75 | Montgomery | 12,088 |
| 77 | Riverside | 12,084 |
| 77 | Spokane | 12,084 |
| 79 | Phoenix | 12,041 |
| 80 | Philadelphia | 11,967 |
| 81 | Pittsburgh | 11,762 |
| 82 | Chattanooga | 11,557 |
| 83 | Tucson | 11,231 |
| 84 | Tacoma | 11,220 |
| 85 | Providence | 10,604 |
| 86 | New York | 9,731 |
| 87 | Jersey City | 8,494 |

# 113. Change in Retail Sales

Broadly speaking, manufacturing began to move to suburban areas after World War I, as a means of obtaining space for expansion. Encouraged by GI Bill mortgages, workers began to move to suburban residences immediately after World War II. Large retail outlets began to move to the suburbs a few years later with the development of the shopping center. Some have called the shopping center movement, which reached its peak in the 1960s, the "malling of America."

To city officials, suburban shopping centers often look like giant leeches, drawing away the lifeblood of downtown stores.

Aurora shows the biggest "leech effect." Its retailing grew by over eightfold between 1971 and 1981, drawing business from downtown Denver. Arlington, Texas grew by nearly sixfold, drawing retailing away from Fort Worth and possibly Dallas. Virginia Beach retailing grew by over fourfold, pulling retail sales away from Norfolk. Austin and Houston retailing grew rapidly in suburban areas, but they did not suffer as cities because the growth was within city limits.

By contrast, Newark saw a net decline of over 2 percent in city retail sales, on a basis that is not adjusted for inflation. In real money terms, Newark's city retail sales dropped by one-half during the period. Rochester, Dayton and Buffalo showed some nominal increases in retail sales, but in real terms their retailing business was disastrously drained away to suburban areas.

SOURCES: *Sales & Marketing Management*, "1972 Survey of Buying Power," July 10, 1972, pp. D-3–D-137 and "1982 Survey of Buying Power, Part II," October 25, 1982, pp. 61–94.

| Rank | City | Retail Sales 1971 ($000) | Retail Sales 1981 ($000) | Percentage Change |
|---|---|---|---|---|
| 1 | Aurora | 110.2 | 1,039.4 | 842.81 |
| 2 | Arlington | 208.4 | 1,427.8 | 584.95 |
| 3 | Virginia Beach | 244.2 | 1,303.4 | 433.74 |
| 4 | Austin | 538.9 | 2,598.5 | 382.15 |

| Rank | City | Retail Sales 1971 ($000) | Retail Sales 1981 ($000) | Percentage Change | Rank | City | Retail Sales 1971 ($000) | Retail Sales 1981 ($000) | Percentage Change |
|---|---|---|---|---|---|---|---|---|---|
| 5 | Houston | 2,895.4 | 12,908.4 | 345.82 | 53 | San Francisco | 1,761.8 | 3,831.1 | 117.45 |
| 6 | Colorado Springs | 315.0 | 1,291.8 | 309.99 | 54 | Omaha | 821.0 | 1,753.0 | 113.46 |
| 7 | Lubbock | 327.8 | 1,311.4 | 300.01 | 55 | Long Beach | 767.0 | 1,618.8 | 111.04 |
| 8 | Lexington-Fayette | 357.0 | 1,420.5 | 297.66 | 56 | Sacramento | 673.0 | 1,389.4 | 106.33 |
| 9 | Albuquerque | 573.9 | 2,166.3 | 277.44 | 57 | Denver | 1,242.0 | 2,522.9 | 103.08 |
| 10 | Huntington Beach | 241.2 | 906.6 | 275.80 | 58 | Miami | 996.6 | 2,019.7 | 102.66 |
| 11 | San Antonio | 1,215.5 | 4,502.0 | 270.38 | 59 | Seattle | 1,492.2 | 3,019.8 | 102.37 |
| 12 | Tulsa | 792.1 | 2,841.8 | 258.74 | 60 | Spokane | 507.9 | 1,027.0 | 102.21 |
| 13 | El Paso | 626.9 | 2,117.2 | 237.71 | 61 | Charlotte | 785.2 | 1,571.3 | 100.10 |
| 14 | San Jose | 928.1 | 3,021.0 | 225.58 | 62 | Anchorage | 659.8 | 1,309.6 | 98.48 |
| 15 | Corpus Christi | 421.8 | 1,296.2 | 207.28 | 63 | New Orleans | 1,190.3 | 2,318.4 | 94.77 |
| 16 | Greensboro | 421.6 | 1,255.2 | 197.69 | 64 | Tampa | 990.5 | 1,903.1 | 92.13 |
| 17 | Santa Ana | 421.1 | 1,247.2 | 196.13 | 65 | Chattanooga | 494.5 | 947.4 | 91.58 |
| 18 | Jackson | 389.7 | 1,153.8 | 196.02 | 66 | Salt Lake City | 576.0 | 1,098.4 | 90.41 |
| 19 | Oklahoma City | 954.4 | 2,789.1 | 195.00 | 67 | Fort Wayne | 511.0 | 967.4 | 89.33 |
| 20 | Baton Rouge | 534.5 | 1,572.6 | 194.20 | 68 | St. Paul | 675.3 | 1,242.2 | 83.92 |
| 21 | San Diego | 1,404.5 | 4,080.6 | 190.53 | 69 | St. Petersburg | 624.5 | 1,125.9 | 80.29 |
| 22 | Dallas | 2,133.6 | 6,163.9 | 188.90 | 70 | Jersey City | 361.0 | 646.3 | 78.68 |
| 23 | Indianapolis | 1,484.4 | 4,271.2 | 187.74 | 71 | Toledo | 868.0 | 1,533.8 | 76.70 |
| 24 | Wichita | 648.6 | 1,833.0 | 182.70 | 72 | Kansas City, Mo. | 1,252.4 | 2,188.1 | 74.70 |
| 25 | Riverside | 363.3 | 1,021.7 | 181.21 | 73 | New York | 13,559.4 | 23,649.2 | 74.41 |
| 26 | Lincoln | 332.2 | 926.0 | 178.69 | 74 | Milwaukee | 1,413.7 | 2,454.4 | 73.60 |
| 27 | Columbus, Ohio | 1,026.1 | 2,843.9 | 177.14 | 75 | Grand Rapids | 521.9 | 895.9 | 71.66 |
| 28 | Nashville-Davidson | 983.5 | 2,725.6 | 177.12 | 76 | Portland, Ore. | 1,237.9 | 2,117.0 | 71.02 |
| 29 | Mobile | 427.0 | 1,166.2 | 173.08 | 77 | Birmingham | 909.0 | 1,523.7 | 67.61 |
| 30 | Anaheim | 422.2 | 1,141.6 | 170.36 | 78 | Oakland | 812.6 | 1,354.7 | 66.70 |
| 31 | Knoxville | 497.2 | 1,321.9 | 165.85 | 79 | Richmond | 759.0 | 1,262.9 | 66.26 |
| 32 | Montgomery | 368.9 | 950.9 | 157.71 | 80 | Boston | 1,618.4 | 2,561.8 | 58.30 |
| 33 | Columbus, Ga. | 331.0 | 847.5 | 156.00 | 81 | Philadelphia | 3,321.4 | 5,230.8 | 57.49 |
| 34 | Worcester | 328.2 | 836.0 | 154.67 | 82 | Providence | 378.9 | 579.2 | 52.87 |
| 35 | Tucson | 711.0 | 1,809.1 | 154.10 | 83 | Baltimore | 1,722.5 | 2,566.0 | 48.96 |
| 36 | Akron | 492.0 | 1,233.9 | 150.63 | 84 | Cleveland | 1,117.3 | 1,641.4 | 46.91 |
| 37 | Shreveport | 461.8 | 1,154.6 | 150.01 | 85 | Yonkers | 448.2 | 639.5 | 42.70 |
| 38 | Madison | 419.4 | 1,036.0 | 147.03 | 86 | Syracuse | 460.6 | 639.0 | 38.74 |
| 39 | Memphis | 1,335.6 | 3,270.6 | 144.88 | 87 | Louisville | 880.6 | 1,218.3 | 38.34 |
| 40 | Las Vegas | 393.7 | 961.2 | 144.12 | 89 | Chicago | 6,907.0 | 9,421.6 | 36.40 |
| 41 | Jacksonville | 1,165.0 | 2,809.8 | 141.18 | 89 | Minneapolis | 1,066.0 | 1,454.0 | 36.39 |
| 41 | Little Rock | 443.5 | 1,069.6 | 141.18 | 90 | St. Louis | 1,317.3 | 1,767.1 | 34.14 |
| 43 | Fresno | 579.0 | 1,385.1 | 139.18 | 91 | Cincinnati | 1,146.4 | 1,530.9 | 33.54 |
| 44 | Phoenix | 1,426.6 | 3,395.6 | 138.02 | 92 | Pittsburgh | 1,317.5 | 1,759.3 | 33.53 |
| 45 | Honolulu | 1,135.0 | 2,672.8 | 135.48 | 93 | Atlanta | 1,648.8 | 2,563.5 | 32.96 |
| 46 | Fort Worth | 975.0 | 2,293.0 | 135.16 | 94 | Washington, DC. | 1,962.2 | 2,563.5 | 30.64 |
| 47 | Tacoma | 444.3 | 1,039.3 | 133.92 | 95 | Detroit | 2,503.9 | 3,178.0 | 26.92 |
| 48 | Los Angeles | 6,021.6 | 13,978.7 | 132.14 | 96 | Flint | 579.0 | 640.2 | 10.57 |
| 49 | Des Moines | 573.3 | 1,317.2 | 129.73 | 97 | Buffalo | 917.0 | 990.0 | 7.96 |
| 50 | Kansas City, Kan. | 331.1 | 758.0 | 129.17 | 98 | Dayton | 569.8 | 612.7 | 7.53 |
| 51 | Warren | 353.4 | 795.6 | 125.09 | 99 | Rochester | 776.5 | 778.9 | .34 |
| 52 | Norfolk | 575.0 | 1,280.0 | 122.69 | 100 | Newark | 618.4 | 605.1 | −2.16 |

# 114. Food Sales Per Capita

The following table shows per capita food (i.e., mostly supermarket) sales for 1981 in each of the 100 largest cities. Cities that have the highest per capita food sales are most likely to have prosperous downtown business and commercial districts with little competition from suburban malls.

It is no surprise to see cities like Anaheim, Lincoln and Anchorage in the top rank of this survey. Anaheim's stores are near its residents, because the city grew up as a suburb. The Lincoln and Anchorage city limits are so expansive that suburban areas are included in them. Not one northeastern city is in the top 15 percent of the survey, indicating that in this region many city dwellers with larger food budgets have deserted the in-city corner grocery store or fruit market for the shopping plaza. Conversely, cities in the bottom 20 percent include Newark, Minneapolis, Detroit, Cleveland and Jersey City, all of which experienced a significant decline in middle- and upper-middle class populations and a corresponding growth in suburban malls.

SOURCE: *Sales & Marketing Management,* "1982 Survey of Buying Power, Part I," July 26, 1982.

| Rank | City | Food Sales ($ Million) | Food Sales Per Capita ($) |
|---|---|---|---|
| 1 | Little Rock | 1,069,696 | 6,248 |
| 2 | Anaheim | 1,141,665 | 5,025 |
| 3 | Lincoln | 402,866 | 2,284 |
| 4 | Anchorage | 320,015 | 1,734 |
| 5 | Warren | 270,830 | 1,718 |
| 5 | Aurora | 261,587 | 1,578 |
| 7 | Syracuse | 258,846 | 1,564 |
| 8 | St. Petersburg | 359,771 | 1,500 |
| 9 | Austin | 520,567 | 1,444 |
| 10 | Des Moines | 272,061 | 1,439 |
| 11 | Tulsa | 522,267 | 1,436 |
| 12 | Greensboro | 224,410 | 1,435 |
| 13 | Lubbock | 255,505 | 1,431 |
| 14 | Sacramento | 366,465 | 1,311 |
| 15 | Honolulu | 483,833 | 1,306 |
| 15 | Lexington-Fayette | 272,943 | 1,306 |
| 17 | Buffalo | 437,848 | 1,284 |
| 18 | Huntington Beach | 228,179 | 1,280 |
| 19 | Knoxville | 221,298 | 1,264 |
| 20 | Louisville | 362,528 | 1,261 |
| 21 | San Francisco | 830,691 | 1,235 |
| 22 | Oklahoma City | 502,372 | 1,230 |
| 23 | Tucson | 411,667 | 1,218 |
| 24 | Memphis | 788,739 | 1,213 |
| 25 | Corpus Christi | 283,248 | 1,198 |
| 26 | Denver | 580,977 | 1,192 |
| 27 | Nashville-Davidson | 541,558 | 1,179 |
| 28 | Yonkers | 223,081 | 1,151 |
| 29 | Colorado Springs | 264,899 | 1,150 |
| 30 | Kansas City, Kan. | 180,080 | 1,130 |
| 31 | Fresno | 265,640 | 1,129 |
| 32 | Indianapolis | 770,725 | 1,115 |
| 33 | Jackson | 233,982 | 1,109 |
| 34 | Jacksonville | 598,853 | 1,092 |
| 35 | St. Paul | 286,497 | 1,087 |
| 36 | Albuquerque | 376,302 | 1,078 |
| 37 | Los Angeles | 3,223,421 | 1,077 |
| 39 | San Antonio | 855,736 | 1,059 |
| 39 | Wichita | 297,365 | 1,059 |
| 41 | Spokane | 180,883 | 1,054 |

| Rank | City | Food Sales ($ Million) | Food Sales Per Capita ($) |
|---|---|---|---|
| 42 | Tampa | 279,022 | 1,048 |
| 43 | Omaha | 320,365 | 1,039 |
| 44 | Seattle | 502,785 | 1,031 |
| 45 | Akron | 236,374 | 1,027 |
| 46 | Worcester | 163,711 | 1,024 |
| 47 | Arlington, Texas | 180,563 | 1,020 |
| 48 | Santa Ana | 214,771 | 1,019 |
| 49 | San Jose | 678,108 | 1,016 |
| 50 | Toledo | 352,474 | 1,008 |
| 51 | Shreveport | 210,402 | 1,001 |
| 52 | Kansas City, Mo. | 438,993 | 999 |
| 53 | Riverside | 174,986 | 993 |
| 54 | San Diego | 894,817 | 990 |
| 55 | Las Vegas | 166,371 | 988 |
| 56 | Long Beach | 356,571 | 986 |
| 57 | El Paso | 436,714 | 984 |
| 58 | Milwaukee | 612,511 | 983 |
| 59 | Norfolk | 253,675 | 981 |
| 60 | Virginia Beach | 272,293 | 976 |
| 61 | Richmond | 207,348 | 972 |
| 62 | New Orleans | 529,999 | 956 |
| 63 | Salt Lake City | 152,037 | 949 |
| 64 | St. Louis | 402,866 | 945 |
| 65 | Columbus, Ga. | 159,092 | 943 |
| 66 | Oakland | 314,888 | 937 |
| 67 | Boston | 504,848 | 920 |
| 68 | Phoenix | 753,501 | 917 |
| 69 | Chattanooga | 163,128 | 914 |
| 70 | New York | 6,275,419 | 904 |
| 71 | Columbus, Ohio | 513,299 | 902 |
| 72 | Charlotte | 299,538 | 894 |
| 73 | Birmingham | 243,575 | 866 |
| 74 | Montgomery | 158,640 | 858 |
| 75 | Baton Rouge | 201,922 | 855 |
| 76 | Fort Wayne | 145,173 | 849 |
| 77 | Tacoma | 133,722 | 834 |
| 78 | Cincinnati | 308,359 | 824 |
| 78 | Portland, Ore. | 300,277 | 824 |
| 80 | Fort Worth | 311,037 | 817 |
| 81 | Miami | 321,702 | 812 |
| 82 | Jersey City | 175,049 | 803 |
| 82 | Philadelphia | 1,315,538 | 803 |
| 84 | Mobile | 160,921 | 799 |
| 85 | Pittsburgh | 319,924 | 783 |
| 86 | Flint | 120,195 | 781 |
| 87 | Atlanta | 321,450 | 780 |
| 88 | Baltimore | 567,633 | 743 |
| 89 | Washington, D.C. | 454,434 | 741 |
| 90 | Grand Rapids | 126,313 | 705 |
| 91 | Cleveland | 381,434 | 699 |
| 92 | Madison | 113,972 | 672 |
| 93 | Detroit | 748,045 | 652 |
| 94 | Chicago | 1,915,978 | 650 |
| 95 | Providence | 97,271 | 634 |
| 96 | Minneapolis | 227,096 | 630 |
| 97 | Rochester | 134,093 | 576 |
| 98 | Dayton | 97,391 | 495 |
| 99 | Newark | 136,441 | 426 |
| 100 | Houston | 436,714 | 263 |

# 115. Drugstore Sales Per Capita

Drugstore sales are important because they include a substantial volume of dry goods and home appliance sales in many cities with large national chains (e.g., Drug Fair, Dart Drug).

The high 1981 drugstore expenditures in Honolulu and Anchorage probably reflect the impact of high retail prices generally in these two cities, resulting from the considerable cost of transporting goods to them.

There are differences in drugstore sales that reflect the differing roles of drugstores. Miami (in 7th place on the following table) and Washington, D.C. (in 21st place) have many more large drugstores than New York (in 91st place) and Newark (in 99th place). Some cities appear to reflect statewide patterns. Drug store chains do well in Florida, Indiana, Massachusetts and Alaska. They do less well in New York and New Jersey. California and Texas have chains which are prospering and others which are floundering.

SOURCE: *Sales & Marketing Management*, "1982 Survey of Buying Power, Part I," July 26, 1982.

| Rank | City | Drugstore Sales ($000) | Drugstore Sales Per Capita ($) |
|---|---|---|---|
| 1 | Honolulu | 162,910 | 440 |
| 2 | Anchorage | 72,673 | 394 |
| 3 | Lincoln | 60,613 | 344 |
| 4 | Little Rock | 55,762 | 326 |
| 5 | Greensboro | 49,407 | 316 |
| 6 | Fort Worth | 113,097 | 297 |
| 7 | Miami | 102,716 | 259 |
| 8 | Fresno | 58,760 | 250 |
| 9 | Tampa | 66,057 | 248 |
| 10 | Knoxville | 38,106 | 218 |
| 11 | Fort Wayne | 36,936 | 216 |
| 11 | Seattle | 105,091 | 216 |
| 13 | Charlotte | 71,779 | 214 |
| 14 | Omaha | 63,416 | 206 |
| 15 | Boston | 110,934 | 202 |
| 16 | Indianapolis | 139,180 | 201 |
| 16 | Toledo | 70,145 | 201 |
| 18 | Spokane | 34,118 | 199 |
| 19 | Richmond | 42,061 | 197 |
| 20 | Worcester | 31,243 | 195 |
| 21 | Santa Ana | 40,582 | 193 |
| 21 | Washington, D.C. | 118,511 | 193 |
| 23 | Jacksonville | 105,486 | 192 |
| 24 | Flint | 29,417 | 191 |
| 25 | Dallas | 172,197 | 189 |
| 26 | Akron | 42,992 | 187 |
| 27 | Madison | 30,944 | 182 |
| 28 | Memphis | 116,407 | 179 |
| 29 | Chattanooga | 31,758 | 178 |

| Rank | City | Drugstore Sales ($000) | Drugstore Sales Per Capita ($) |
|---|---|---|---|
| 30 | Tacoma | 28,346 | 177 |
| 31 | Oakland | 58,980 | 176 |
| 32 | Louisville | 50,381 | 175 |
| 33 | Los Angeles | 514,097 | 172 |
| 33 | Mobile | 34,639 | 172 |
| 35 | Albuquerque | 59,112 | 169 |
| 35 | Lexington-Fayette | 35,374 | 169 |
| 37 | Austin | 60,521 | 168 |
| 37 | Cincinnati | 62,911 | 168 |
| 37 | El Paso | 74,698 | 168 |
| 40 | San Francisco | 111,639 | 166 |
| 41 | Tucson | 55,269 | 164 |
| 41 | Warren | 25,928 | 164 |
| 43 | Birmingham | 45,415 | 161 |
| 43 | Houston | 267,786 | 161 |
| 45 | Wichita | 44,237 | 158 |
| 46 | Baton Rouge | 37,176 | 157 |
| 46 | Chicago | 463,891 | 157 |
| 48 | Nashville-Davidson | 71,746 | 156 |
| 49 | Minneapolis | 55,590 | 154 |
| 50 | Columbus, Ga. | 25,612 | 152 |
| 51 | Phoenix | 121,131 | 147 |
| 52 | New Orleans | 80,463 | 145 |
| 53 | Tulsa | 51,955 | 143 |
| 54 | Cleveland | 77,674 | 142 |
| 54 | St. Louis | 60,752 | 142 |
| 56 | Des Moines | 26,654 | 141 |
| 57 | St. Paul | 36,765 | 140 |
| 58 | Detroit | 159,084 | 139 |
| 59 | Kansas City, Mo. | 60,752 | 138 |
| 60 | Baltimore | 105,031 | 137 |
| 61 | Las Vegas | 22,891 | 136 |
| 61 | Long Beach | 49,293 | 136 |
| 61 | Milwaukee | 83,853 | 136 |
| 64 | Pittsburgh | 54,918 | 134 |
| 64 | Salt Lake City | 21,499 | 134 |
| 66 | Anaheim | 30,219 | 133 |
| 67 | Corpus Christi | 31,210 | 132 |
| 68 | Atlanta | 53,807 | 131 |
| 69 | St. Petersburg | 30,761 | 128 |
| 69 | San Jose | 85,291 | 128 |
| 71 | Columbus, Ohio | 72,279 | 127 |
| 71 | Huntington Beach | 22,657 | 127 |
| 73 | Riverside | 22,014 | 125 |
| 74 | Providence | 18,757 | 122 |
| 74 | Rochester | 28,529 | 122 |
| 76 | Lubbock | 20,222 | 113 |
| 77 | Shreveport | 23,544 | 112 |
| 78 | Denver | 53,986 | 111 |
| 78 | Philadelphia | 182,241 | 111 |
| 80 | Montgomery | 20,408 | 110 |
| 81 | Jackson | 22,954 | 109 |
| 82 | Virginia Beach | 30,229 | 108 |
| 83 | Sacramento | 29,911 | 107 |
| 84 | Norfolk | 27,410 | 106 |
| 84 | Oklahoma City | 43,430 | 106 |
| 86 | Grand Rapids | 18,815 | 105 |
| 86 | San Antonio | 84,801 | 105 |
| 88 | Buffalo | 34,322 | 101 |
| 88 | Colorado Springs | 23,184 | 101 |
| 90 | San Diego | 88,837 | 98 |

| Rank | City | Drugstore Sales ($000) | Drugstore Sales Per Capita ($) |
|------|------|------------------------|--------------------------------|
| 91 | New York | 633,182 | 91 |
| 92 | Aurora | 14,713 | 89 |
| 92 | Yonkers | 17,218 | 89 |
| 94 | Dayton | 17,346 | 88 |
| 95 | Jersey City | 18,933 | 87 |

| Rank | City | Drugstore Sales ($000) | Drugstore Sales Per Capita ($) |
|------|------|------------------------|--------------------------------|
| 96 | Syracuse | 14,248 | 86 |
| 97 | Arlington, Texas | 14,955 | 84 |
| 98 | Kansas City, Kan. | 12,498 | 78 |
| 99 | Newark | 19,275 | 60 |
| 100 | Portland, Ore. | 20,897 | 57 |

# 116. Wholesale Trade Centers

Wholesale trade is the business of buying and selling products in bulk. A wholesaler buys goods from a large variety of sources and sells them to retail stores or to large institutional buyers. Sometimes wholesalers operate showrooms or markets in central locations and are called on by retail store buyers. In other cases wholesalers call on retail stores and when they make a sale deliver directly to retailers. Some businesses simultaneously sell on a wholesale and a retail basis, with price depending on the volume purchased by the buyer.

Wholesale trade centers require good transportation facilities. It is therefore to be expected that with its wealth of sea, air, road and rail facilities New York leads the list of the 36 metro areas below with over 11 percent of its labor force engaged in wholesale trade. Transportation is in fact New York's 4th largest "export" industry after finance, insurance and real estate. Wholesale trade is substantially less important. In Dallas-Fort Worth, however, wholesale trade is the area's second largest "export" industry.

The other large wholesale centers have transportation facilities such as warehouses for truckers to shop to and from; large airports; seaports or riverports; or railheads. Wholesale trade is Atlanta's third largest export industry, with trucking and warehousing close behind. Its new airport is a major transit station for both passengers and freight. Portland, New Orleans and Houston are seaports. Kansas City is a riverport. All of these metro areas show 5.9 percent or more of their labor force in wholesale trade.

At the other end of the spectrum are Washington, with 2.3 percent of its employees in wholesale trade, San Diego (3.1 percent) and Riverside (3.3 percent).

An advantage of living in a city with a large wholesale activity is that a careful shopper can find bargains. In the chapter on the cost of living above we saw the advantages to Chattanooga buyers of being a wholesale city with a large wholesaling activity.

SOURCES: Derived from Bureau of the Census, *Supplementary Report: Provisional Estimates of Social, Economic and Housing Characteristics*, March, 1982. "Export industry" concept described in John Tepper Marlin, *The Wealth of Cities* (New York: Council on Municipal Performance, Report 3, 1974), pp. 16–21.

| Rank | Metro Area | Total Labor Force | Labor Force in Wholesale Trade | Percentage of Labor Force in Wholesale Trade |
|------|-----------|-------------------|-------------------------------|----------------------------------------------|
| 1 | New York | 3,878,401 | 431,941 | 11.14 |
| 2 | Atlanta | 974,914 | 65,525 | 6.72 |
| 3 | Portland, Ore. | 589,090 | 38,315 | 6.50 |
| 4 | Dallas-Fort Worth | 482,436 | 93,401 | 6.30 |
| 5 | New Orleans | 448,542 | 28,084 | 6.26 |
| 6 | Houston | 1,440,981 | 89,157 | 6.19 |
| 7 | Kansas City, Mo., Kan. | 635,700 | 37,225 | 5.86 |
| 8 | Minneapolis-St. Paul | 1,074,686 | 62,103 | 5.78 |
| 9 | Miami | 731,889 | 42,039 | 5.74 |
| 10 | Chicago | 3,179,676 | 180,422 | 5.67 |
| 11 | Denver | 820,574 | 45,809 | 5.58 |
| 12 | Los Angeles | 3,488,192 | 180,897 | 5.19 |
| 13 | Indianapolis | 539,776 | 27,723 | 5.14 |
| 14 | Seattle | 792,278 | 40,609 | 5.13 |
| 15 | Newark | 888,497 | 45,480 | 5.12 |
| 16 | San Francisco-Oakland | 1,585,385 | 80,851 | 5.10 |
| 17 | Cleveland | 849,689 | 43,105 | 5.07 |
| 18 | Anaheim | 865,074 | 48,141 | 4.99 |
| 19 | Cincinnati | 604,834 | 30,124 | 4.98 |
| 20 | San Antonio | 418,790 | 20,767 | 4.96 |
| 21 | Phoenix | 670,608 | 32,723 | 4.88 |
| 22 | St. Louis | 1,024,411 | 49,305 | 4.81 |
| 23 | Tampa-St. Petersburg | 604,612 | 28,927 | 4.78 |

| Rank | Metro Area | Total Labor Force | Labor Force in Wholesale Trade | Percentage of Labor Force in Wholesale Trade |
|---|---|---|---|---|
| 24 | Philadelphia | 1,964,490 | 92,938 | 4.73 |
| 25 | Pittsburgh | 950,751 | 43,693 | 4.60 |
| 26 | Columbus, Ohio | 501,328 | 22,881 | 4.56 |
| 27 | Boston | 1,315,200 | 58,003 | 4.41 |
| 28 | Buffalo | 516,027 | 22,234 | 4.31 |
| 29 | Sacramento | 434,301 | 18,443 | 4.25 |
| 30 | Detroit | 1,722,372 | 69,188 | 4.22 |

| Rank | Metro Area | Total Labor Force | Labor Force in Wholesale Trade | Percentage of Labor Force in Wholesale Trade |
|---|---|---|---|---|
| 31 | Milwaukee | 649,181 | 26,041 | 4.01 |
| 32 | Baltimore | 970,022 | 36,629 | 3.78 |
| 33 | San Jose | 658,043 | 23,157 | 3.52 |
| 34 | Riverside | 613,956 | 20,454 | 3.33 |
| 35 | San Diego | 758,579 | 23,229 | 3.06 |
| 36 | Washington, D.C. | 1,536,620 | 35,457 | 2.31 |

# 117. Financial Centers

Cities that have strong financial centers are healthy for two reasons. First, financial services, like services generally, are resistant to recessions. There will be a much higher percentage of layoffs in manufacturing than in banking or securities firms. Financial services tend to be managed conservatively so that there is adequate provision for "off years."

Second, financial services have tended to be concentrated in the central cities. They have been the bedrock of the downtown areas—the banks, brokerage firms, insurance agents and so forth. They have tended not to follow manufacturing and retailing out to the suburban and rural areas.

A measure of the importance of the financial service sector of the economy is the number of financial workers as a percentage of all workers. Of 36 cities for which 1980 data are available, New York and San Francisco have the largest financial sectors, and Detroit and Buffalo have the smallest.

SOURCE: U.S. Department of Commerce, Bureau of the Census, *1980 Census of Population and Housing: Supplementary Report: Provisional Estimates of Social, Economic and Housing Characteristics*, March 1982.

| Rank | Metro Area | Labor Force | Labor Force in Finance | Percentage of Labor Force in Finance |
|---|---|---|---|---|
| 1 | New York | 3,878,401 | 396,856 | 10.23 |
| 2 | San Francisco-Oakland | 1,585,385 | 156,926 | 9.90 |

| Rank | Metro Area | Labor Force | Labor Force in Finance | Percentage of Labor Force in Finance |
|---|---|---|---|---|
| 3 | Tampa-St. Petersburg | 604,612 | 52,781 | 8.73 |
| 4 | Miami | 731,889 | 60,525 | 8.27 |
| 5 | Phoenix | 670,608 | 54,686 | 8.15 |
| 6 | Kansas City, Mo., Kan. | 635,700 | 51,161 | 8.05 |
| 7 | Newark | 888,497 | 71,211 | 8.01 |
| 8 | Dallas-Fort Worth | 1,482,436 | 115,792 | 7.81 |
| 9 | Anaheim | 965,074 | 74,520 | 7.72 |
| 10 | Columbus, Ohio | 501,328 | 38,236 | 7.63 |
| 11 | Atlanta | 974,914 | 74,166 | 7.61 |
| 12 | Minneapolis-St. Paul | 1,074,686 | 81,369 | 7.57 |
| 13 | Boston | 1,315,200 | 98,451 | 7.49 |
| 14 | Denver | 820,574 | 60,174 | 7.33 |
| 15 | Indianapolis | 539,776 | 39,400 | 7.30 |
| 16 | San Diego | 758,579 | 55,254 | 7.28 |
| 17 | Seattle | 792,278 | 57,031 | 7.20 |
| 18 | Los Angeles-Long Beach | 3,488,192 | 248,869 | 7.13 |
| 19 | San Antonio | 418,790 | 29,648 | 7.08 |
| 20 | Chicago | 3,179,676 | 222,339 | 6.99 |
| 20 | Portland, Ore. | 589,090 | 41,206 | 6.99 |
| 22 | Sacramento | 434,301 | 29,808 | 6.86 |
| 23 | Philadelphia | 1,964,490 | 134,138 | 6.83 |
| 24 | Washington, D.C. | 1,536,620 | 104,298 | 6.79 |
| 25 | New Orleans | 448,542 | 30,004 | 6.69 |
| 26 | Milwaukee | 649,181 | 41,987 | 6.47 |
| 27 | St. Louis | 1,024,411 | 65,395 | 6.38 |
| 28 | Houston | 1,440,981 | 89,920 | 6.24 |
| 29 | Cleveland | 849,689 | 50,625 | 5.96 |
| 30 | Riverside | 613,956 | 36,022 | 5.87 |
| 31 | Cincinnati | 604,834 | 34,124 | 5.64 |
| 32 | Baltimore | 970,022 | 54,322 | 5.60 |
| 33 | Pittsburgh | 950,751 | 52,509 | 5.52 |
| 34 | San Jose | 658,043 | 36,221 | 5.50 |
| 35 | Buffalo | 516,027 | 26,937 | 5.22 |
| 36 | Detroit | 1,722,372 | 86,843 | 5.04 |

# 118. Centers of Tourism and Other Services

The following table shows employment in what the Department of Labor calls "Services and Miscellaneous." The Anaheim area ranks at the top of the list with 17.8 percent of its labor force in this category because of Disneyland. The admissions tax for amusement centers puts Anaheim at the top of another table in our chapter on city finances.

The New Orleans area also has a high tourism component and ranks second with 15.2 percent of its labor force in this type of activity. In the case of Tampa-St. Petersburg, the high service component reflects the lack of heavy industry and the dependence of the elderly people who populate the area so heavily on services. In San Diego the high service component reflects the needs of the naval base and the lack of heavy industry.

The relatively low service industry components in the Houston and Dallas-Fort Worth areas reflects the relatively young age of residents of these metro areas and the relative lack of a tourist industry.

SOURCE: Derived from Bureau of the Census, *Supplementary Report: Provisional Estimates of Social, Economic and Housing Characteristics*, March, 1982.

| Rank | Metro Area | Labor Force | Total Workers in "Services & Misc." | Service Workers as Percentage of Total Labor Force |
|---|---|---|---|---|
| 1 | Anaheim | 965,074 | 171,755 | 17.80 |
| 2 | New Orleans | 448,542 | 68,137 | 15.19 |
| 3 | Tampa-St. Petersburg | 604,612 | 86,753 | 14.35 |
| 4 | San Diego | 758,579 | 107,614 | 14.19 |
| 5 | St. Louis | 1,024,411 | 144,523 | 14.11 |
| 6 | Pittsburgh | 950,751 | 132,055 | 13.89 |
| 7 | Detroit | 1,722,372 | 237,255 | 13.77 |
| 8 | New York | 3,878,401 | 533,509 | 13.76 |
| 9 | Sacramento | 434,301 | 59,621 | 13.73 |
| 10 | San Antonio | 418,790 | 57,436 | 13.71 |
| 11 | Boston | 1,315,200 | 180,066 | 13.69 |
| 12 | Buffalo | 516,027 | 70,279 | 13.62 |
| 13 | Baltimore | 970,022 | 131,785 | 13.59 |
| 14 | Riverside | 613,956 | 83,247 | 13.56 |
| 15 | Miami | 731,889 | 99,202 | 13.55 |
| 16 | Indianapolis | 539,776 | 71,280 | 13.21 |
| 17 | Cincinnati | 604,834 | 79,205 | 13.10 |
| 18 | Philadelphia | 1,964,490 | 250,319 | 12.74 |
| 19 | Chicago | 3,179,676 | 402,082 | 12.65 |
| 20 | Minneapolis-St. Paul | 1,074,686 | 135,318 | 12.59 |
| 21 | Seattle | 792,278 | 98,968 | 12.49 |
| 22 | Columbus, Ohio | 501,318 | 62,440 | 12.46 |
| 23 | Milwaukee | 649,181 | 80,261 | 12.36 |
| 24 | Phoenix | 670,608 | 82,665 | 12.33 |
| 25 | Portland, Ore. | 589,090 | 72,453 | 12.30 |
| 26 | Cleveland | 849,689 | 104,369 | 12.28 |
| 27 | Los Angeles | 3,488,192 | 426,096 | 12.18 |
| 28 | San Francisco | 1,585,385 | 192,795 | 12.16 |
| 29 | Kansas City, Mo.-Kan. | 635,700 | 76,481 | 12.03 |
| 30 | Newark | 888,497 | 105,366 | 11.86 |
| 31 | Atlanta | 974,914 | 112,269 | 11.52 |
| 32 | Washington, D.C. | 1,536,620 | 176,472 | 11.48 |
| 33 | Denver | 820,574 | 89,583 | 10.92 |
| 34 | San Jose | 658,043 | 67,176 | 10.21 |
| 35 | Dallas-Fort Worth | 1,482,436 | 150,956 | 10.18 |
| 36 | Houston | 1,440,981 | 144,077 | 10.00 |

# 119. Savings and Loans: Savings Withdrawn

The table below is an indicator of financial difficulties for the savings institutions in the different cities. In all but four cities, savings withdrawn were higher in 1981 than in 1976. The four cities with the healthiest savings industry were Corpus Christi, Tampa, Akron and Riverside.

In Toledo, on the other hand, there was a 17-fold increase in savings withdrawn between 1976 and 1981. Toledo, which traditionally has had a strong manufacturing base, is the home for 7 of the country's largest companies. The economic conditions that affected industrial activity in the country may have led to layoffs and work slowdowns that would affect savings withdrawals.

Houston is ranked second here. This city has been growing faster than most major localities. Residential and commercial development in the Houston area has directly affected the degree of savings withdrawals.

SOURCE: Federal Home Loan Bank Board, *Savings and Home Financing Source Book* (Washington, D.C.: 1976, 1981).

| Rank | Metro Area | Savings Withdrawn 1976 ($) | Savings Withdrawn 1981 ($) | Absolute Change ($) | Percentage Change |
|---|---|---|---|---|---|
| 1 | Toledo | 491,625 | 8,979,739 | 8,488,114 | 1,726.54 |
| 2 | Houston | 1,483,038 | 13,944,711 | 12,461,673 | 840.28 |
| 3 | Knoxville | 119,835 | 1,112,953 | 993,118 | 828.74 |
| 4 | Mobile | 164,442 | 1,190,043 | 1,025,601 | 623.69 |
| 5 | Wichita | 148,359 | 982,598 | 834,239 | 562.31 |
| 6 | Salt Lake City | 1,041,002 | 5,991,131 | 4,950,129 | 475.52 |
| 7 | San Diego | 2,115,150 | 11,927,668 | 9,812,518 | 463.92 |
| 8 | Newark | 1,789,460 | 9,465,628 | 7,676,168 | 428.97 |
| 9 | Albuquerque | 219,684 | 1,147,111 | 927,427 | 422.16 |
| 10 | San Antonio | 381,601 | 1,957,643 | 1,576,042 | 413.01 |
| 11 | Rochester | 504,805 | 2,571,181 | 2,066,376 | 409.34 |
| 12 | New Orleans | 596,410 | 2,943,008 | 2,346,598 | 393.45 |
| 13 | Dallas-Fort Worth | 1,263,201 | 6,132,722 | 4,869,521 | 385.49 |
| 14 | Anaheim-Santa Ana | 1,349,073 | 6,301,623 | 4,952,550 | 367.11 |
| 15 | Shreveport | 43,672 | 201,622 | 157,950 | 361.67 |
| 16 | Miami | 3,500,767 | 16,136,187 | 12,635,420 | 360.93 |
| 17 | Tulsa | 390,649 | 1,766,153 | 1,375,504 | 352.11 |
| 18 | Charlotte | 208,768 | 935,338 | 726,570 | 348.03 |
| 19 | Denver | 1,854,155 | 8,204,760 | 6,350,605 | 342.51 |
| 20 | Seattle | 841,192 | 3,676,414 | 2,835,222 | 337.05 |
| 21 | Los Angeles | 15,192,004 | 65,860,388 | 50,668,384 | 333.52 |
| 22 | Providence | 227,041 | 962,948 | 735,907 | 324.13 |
| 23 | Austin | 265,149 | 1,111,982 | 846,833 | 319.38 |
| 24 | Detroit | 2,384,838 | 9,955,573 | 7,570,735 | 317.45 |
| 25 | Oklahoma City | 246,966 | 1,012,579 | 765,613 | 310.01 |
| 26 | Chicago | 6,277,081 | 25,447,868 | 19,170,787 | 305.41 |
| 27 | El Paso | 99,940 | 404,572 | 304,632 | 304.81 |
| 28 | Little Rock | 233,562 | 924,932 | 691,370 | 296.01 |
| 29 | Nashville | 249,530 | 955,788 | 706,258 | 283.04 |
| 30 | Norfolk | 259,686 | 992,100 | 732,414 | 282.04 |
| 31 | Lubbock | 86,486 | 323,486 | 237,000 | 274.03 |
| 32 | Fort Wayne | 126,659 | 468,666 | 342,007 | 270.02 |
| 33 | Sacramento | 373,598 | 1,375,393 | 1,001,795 | 268.15 |
| 34 | Richmond | 464,296 | 1,696,872 | 1,232,576 | 265.47 |
| 35 | Cleveland | 2,691,823 | 9,774,453 | 7,082,630 | 263.12 |
| 36 | Pittsburgh | 1,630,002 | 5,916,105 | 4,286,103 | 262.95 |
| 37 | Cincinnati | 1,039,403 | 3,686,529 | 2,647,126 | 254.68 |
| 38 | Tucson | 426,426 | 1,509,200 | 1,082,774 | 253.92 |
| 39 | Jersey City | 379,503 | 1,309,187 | 929,684 | 244.97 |
| 40 | Baton Rouge | 124,832 | 427,251 | 302,419 | 242.26 |
| 41 | Grand Rapids | 137,366 | 457,058 | 319,692 | 232.73 |
| 42 | Honolulu | 986,192 | 3,272,057 | 2,285,865 | 231.79 |
| 43 | San Francisco | 5,031,853 | 16,526,438 | 11,494,585 | 228.44 |
| 45 | Washington, D.C. | 2,644,848 | 8,536,119 | 5,891,271 | 222.75 |
| 46 | St. Louis | 1,702,984 | 5,490,738 | 3,787,754 | 222.42 |
| 47 | Milwaukee | 1,492,120 | 4,797,426 | 3,305,306 | 221.52 |
| 48 | Indianapolis | 321,487 | 1,030,986 | 709,499 | 220.69 |
| 49 | Jacksonville | 372,743 | 1,180,773 | 808,030 | 216.78 |
| 50 | Kansas City, Mo., Kan. | 554,576 | 1,752,593 | 1,198,017 | 216.02 |
| 51 | Philadelphia | 2,246,805 | 7,094,512 | 4,847,707 | 215.76 |
| 52 | Madison | 233,144 | 723,010 | 489,866 | 210.11 |
| 53 | Portland, Ore. | 1,564,356 | 4,818,100 | 3,253,744 | 207.99 |
| 54 | Lexington-Fayette | 53,620 | 156,937 | 103,317 | 192.68 |
| 55 | Boston | 628,110 | 1,818,811 | 1,190,701 | 189.57 |
| 56 | Dayton | 696,477 | 1,916,991 | 1,220,514 | 175.24 |
| 57 | Atlanta | 1,345,012 | 3,696,883 | 2,351,871 | 174.86 |
| 58 | Birmingham | 373,606 | 1,007,770 | 634,164 | 169.74 |
| 59 | Omaha | 504,066 | 1,315,449 | 811,383 | 160.97 |
| 60 | New York | 5,416,113 | 14,062,779 | 8,646,666 | 159.65 |
| 61 | Minneapolis-St. Paul | 1,673,850 | 4,304,277 | 2,630,427 | 157.15 |
| 62 | Louisville | 428,932 | 1,098,575 | 669,643 | 156.12 |
| 63 | Des Moines | 438,299 | 1,088,693 | 650,394 | 148.39 |
| 64 | Baltimore | 1,386,210 | 3,427,662 | 2,041,452 | 147.27 |
| 65 | Columbus, Ohio | 1,491,598 | 3,573,817 | 2,082,219 | 139.60 |
| 66 | Memphis | 311,173 | 732,560 | 421,387 | 135.42 |
| 67 | Columbus, Ga. | 161,427 | 362,921 | 201,494 | 124.82 |
| 68 | Greensboro | 457,003 | 925,087 | 468,084 | 102.42 |
| 69 | Riverside | 612,868 | 1,108,764 | 495,896 | 80.91 |
| 70 | Akron | 411,066 | 734,065 | 322,999 | 78.58 |
| 71 | Tampa | 2,172,504 | 1,477,938 | − 694,566 | − 31.97 |
| 72 | Corpus Christi | 189,936 | 68,457 | − 121,479 | − 63.96 |

# 120. Savings and Loans: New Net Savings

Is the previous table too hard on the savings industry? Did the institutions in fact have offsetting deposits? The table below indicates not. Every single city saw its savings institutions decline in deposits between 1976 and 1981.

The metro area of New Orleans showed the least deterioration in deposits, with a 46 percent decline. The largest decrease was in metro Columbus, Ohio, where new net savings dropped from an increase of $241 million in 1976 to an outflow of $814 million in 1981, over three times the level of the 1976 increase.

SOURCE: Federal Home Loan Bank Board, *Savings and Home Financing Source Book* (Washington, D.C.: 1976, 1981).

| Rank | Metro Area | New Net Savings Received 1976 ($000) | New Net Savings Received 1981 ($000) | Absolute Change ($000) | Percentage Change in New Net Savings |
|---|---|---|---|---|---|
| 1 | New Orleans | 255,975 | 137,331 | − 118,644 | − 46.35 |
| 2 | Newark | 366,654 | 125,192 | − 241,462 | − 65.86 |
| 3 | Austin | 108,238 | 32,301 | − 75,937 | − 70.16 |
| 4 | San Diego | 443,056 | 81,827 | − 361,229 | − 81.53 |
| 5 | Corpus Christi | 37,784 | − 1,238 | − 39,022 | − 103.28 |
| 6 | Oklahoma City | 104,466 | − 13,051 | − 117,517 | − 112.49 |
| 7 | Miami | 908,368 | − 124,704 | − 1,033,072 | − 113.73 |
| 8 | Tulsa | 77,485 | − 12,670 | − 90,155 | − 116.35 |
| 9 | Columbus, Ga. | 48,471 | − 8,849 | − 57,320 | − 118.26 |
| 10 | Mobile | 48,965 | − 8,989 | − 57,954 | − 118.36 |
| 11 | Norfolk-Virginia Beach | 107,517 | − 27,215 | − 134,732 | − 125.31 |
| 12 | St. Louis | 521,368 | − 136,782 | − 658,150 | − 126.24 |
| 13 | Richmond | 124,296 | − 36,370 | − 160,666 | − 129.26 |
| 14 | San Antonio | 141,981 | − 42,519 | − 184,500 | − 129.95 |
| 15 | Omaha | 119,723 | − 37,180 | − 156,903 | − 131.06 |
| 16 | Houston | 541,542 | − 174,559 | − 716,101 | − 132.23 |
| 17 | Wichita | 63,810 | − 22,192 | − 86,002 | − 134.78 |
| 18 | Jacksonville | 98,834 | − 39,711 | − 138,545 | − 140.18 |
| 19 | El Paso | 61,242 | − 25,315 | − 86,557 | − 141.34 |
| 20 | Albuquerque | 77,187 | − 35,135 | − 112,322 | − 145.52 |
| 21 | Honolulu | 190,113 | − 92,454 | − 282,567 | − 148.63 |
| 22 | Akron | 91,911 | − 47,263 | − 139,174 | − 151.42 |
| 23 | Denver | 413,096 | − 232,364 | − 645,460 | − 156.25 |
| 24 | Greensboro | 124,926 | − 76,073 | − 200,999 | − 160.89 |
| 25 | Louisville | 153,807 | − 97,269 | − 251,076 | − 163.24 |
| 26 | Sacramento | 117,297 | − 77,351 | − 194,648 | − 165.94 |
| 27 | Jersey City | 72,840 | − 48,805 | − 121,645 | − 167.00 |
| 28 | Tampa-St. Petersburg | 421,827 | − 295,728 | − 717,555 | − 170.11 |
| 29 | Riverside | 114,076 | − 83,699 | − 197,775 | − 173.37 |
| 30 | Lubbock | 30,572 | − 22,897 | − 53,469 | − 174.90 |
| 31 | Knoxville | 49,180 | − 38,588 | − 87,768 | − 178.46 |
| 32 | Milwaukee | 420,483 | − 330,987 | − 751,470 | − 178.72 |
| 33 | Atlanta | 300,896 | − 240,317 | − 541,213 | − 179.87 |
| 34 | Kansas City, Mo., Kan. | 169,041 | − 135,567 | − 304,628 | − 180.21 |
| 35 | Dallas-Fort Worth | 467,683 | − 376,175 | − 843,858 | − 180.43 |
| 36 | Pittsburgh | 501,514 | − 417,349 | − 918,863 | − 183.22 |
| 37 | Philadelphia | 498,043 | − 423,469 | − 921,512 | − 185.03 |
| 38 | Dayton | 187,537 | − 162,110 | − 349,647 | − 186.44 |
| 39 | Little Rock | 79,246 | − 69,187 | − 148,433 | − 187.31 |
| 40 | Tucson | 95,393 | − 83,664 | − 179,057 | − 187.70 |
| 41 | Anaheim-Santa Ana | 296,617 | − 270,067 | − 566,684 | − 191.05 |
| 42 | Chicago | 1,807,879 | − 1,708,079 | − 3,515,958 | − 194.48 |
| 43 | Nashville | 88,098 | − 84,028 | − 172,126 | − 195.38 |
| 44 | Baton Rouge | 51,761 | − 50,267 | − 102,028 | − 197.11 |
| 45 | Los Angeles | 4,455,415 | − 4,394,550 | − 8,849,965 | − 198.63 |
| 46 | Madison | 74,308 | − 77,457 | − 151,765 | − 204.24 |
| 47 | Cleveland | 545,867 | − 572,981 | − 1,118,848 | − 204.97 |
| 48 | Charlotte | 90,367 | − 96,017 | − 186,384 | − 206.25 |
| 49 | Cincinnati | 235,123 | − 260,356 | − 495,479 | − 210.73 |
| 50 | Shreveport | 34,208 | − 39,965 | − 74,173 | − 216.83 |
| 51 | Boston | 57,876 | − 72,356 | − 130,232 | − 225.02 |
| 52 | Toledo | 107,522 | − 135,329 | − 242,851 | − 225.86 |
| 53 | Seattle | 224,771 | − 284,473 | − 509,244 | − 226.56 |
| 54 | Washington, D.C. | 547,372 | − 703,939 | − 1,251,311 | − 228.60 |
| 55 | Memphis | 65,685 | − 65,254 | − 150,939 | − 229.79 |
| 56 | Birmingham | 138,007 | − 179,557 | − 317,564 | − 230.11 |
| 57 | Baltimore | 286,148 | − 387,528 | − 673,676 | − 235.43 |
| 58 | Des Moines | 134,527 | − 189,080 | − 323,607 | − 240.55 |
| 59 | Providence | 19,922 | − 28,890 | − 48,812 | − 243.02 |
| 60 | Detroit | 612,709 | − 889,408 | − 1,502,117 | − 245.16 |
| 61 | San Francisco-Oakland | 1,086,379 | − 1,584,540 | − 2,670,919 | − 245.86 |
| 62 | Grand Rapids | 40,628 | − 59,786 | − 100,414 | − 247.15 |
| 63 | New York | 715,876 | − 1,094,815 | − 1,810,691 | − 252.93 |
| 64 | Phoenix | 110,830 | − 175,739 | − 286,569 | − 258.57 |
| 65 | Lexington-Fayette | 26,438 | − 42,756 | − 69,194 | − 261.72 |
| 66 | Indianapolis | 110,743 | − 185,211 | − 295,954 | − 267.24 |
| 67 | Salt Lake City | 226,582 | − 380,257 | − 606,839 | − 267.82 |
| 68 | Fort Wayne | 29,974 | − 52,327 | − 82,301 | − 274.57 |
| 69 | Minneapolis-St. Paul | 333,008 | − 597,095 | − 930,913 | − 279.55 |
| 70 | Rochester | 70,395 | − 136,782 | − 207,177 | − 294.31 |
| 71 | Portland, Ore. | 286,906 | − 619,556 | − 906,462 | − 315.94 |
| 72 | Columbus, Ohio | 241,114 | − 572,981 | − 814,095 | − 337.64 |

# 121. Savings and Loan Assets

A final way of looking at institutional resources for home mortgages is to compare the total assets per capita of savings and loan associations in each city. The larger their assets, the more money they have to make available for lending and the greater the likelihood of a turnover in mortgages in each year.

The two urban areas in which the savings and loans had more than $10,000 assets per resident in 1981 were metro Miami and Lincoln.

The four urban areas with less than $1,000 per capita invested in savings and loans were metro Providence, Chattanooga, Boston and Corpus Christi.

SOURCE: Federal Home Loan Bank Board, *Savings and Home Financing Source Book* (Washington, D.C.: FHLBB, 1981).

| Rank | Metro Area | Total Assets 1981 | Assets Per Capita ($) |
|---|---|---|---|
| 1 | Miami | 18,464 | 11,356 |
| 2 | Lincoln | 2,175 | 11,276 |
| 3 | Los Angeles-Long Beach | 74,348 | 9,943 |
| 4 | San Francisco-Oakland | 22,105 | 6,796 |
| 5 | Cleveland | 12,779 | 6,730 |
| 6 | Tampa-St. Petersburg | 9,980 | 6,359 |
| 7 | Des Moines | 2,078 | 6,147 |
| 8 | Newark | 11,373 | 5,787 |
| 9 | Denver | 8,905 | 5,497 |
| 10 | Salt Lake City | 5,117 | 5,465 |
| 11 | Houston | 10,792 | 5,150 |
| 12 | Chicago | 34,947 | 4,920 |
| 13 | Milwaukee | 6,751 | 4,832 |
| 14 | Tacoma | 2,186 | 4,501 |
| 15 | St. Louis | 9,950 | 4,225 |
| 16 | Portland, Ore. | 5,243 | 4,221 |
| 17 | Honolulu | 3,203 | 4,199 |
| 18 | Columbus, Ohio | 4,354 | 3,982 |
| 19 | Phoenix | 5,754 | 3,816 |
| 20 | New Orleans | 4,480 | 3,775 |
| 21 | Cincinnati | 5,215 | 3,721 |
| 22 | Anaheim-Santa Ana | 7,019 | 3,634 |
| 23 | Omaha | 2,068 | 3,627 |
| 24 | Pittsburgh | 8,142 | 3,596 |
| 25 | Minneapolis-St. Paul | 7,540 | 3,566 |
| 26 | Dayton | 2,913 | 3,509 |
| 27 | Madison | 1,128 | 3,486 |
| 28 | Las Vegas | 1,584 | 3,430 |
| 29 | Rochester | 3,327 | 3,423 |
| 30 | Washington, D.C. | 10,340 | 3,379 |
| 31 | Dallas-Fort Worth | 9,872 | 3,318 |
| 32 | Richmond | 2,093 | 3,312 |
| 33 | Wichita | 1,317 | 3,202 |
| 34 | Atlanta | 6,315 | 3,111 |
| 35 | Jersey City | 1,730 | 3,106 |
| 36 | Jackson | 958 | 2,990 |
| 37 | Albuquerque | 1,344 | 2,957 |
| 38 | Toledo | 2,316 | 2,926 |
| 39 | Baltimore | 6,156 | 2,832 |
| 40 | Louisville | 2,447 | 2,700 |
| 41 | Tulsa | 1,857 | 2,693 |
| 42 | Greensboro | 2,193 | 2,651 |
| 43 | Little Rock | 1,032 | 2,623 |
| 44 | Charlotte | 1,655 | 2,597 |
| 45 | Detroit | 11,284 | 2,592 |
| 46 | Tucson | 1,361 | 2,562 |
| 47 | Seattle | 4,081 | 2,540 |
| 48 | Kansas City, Kan.-Mo. | 3,308 | 2,493 |
| 49 | Birmingham | 2,023 | 2,387 |
| 50 | Philadelphia | 11,202 | 2,375 |
| 51 | Knoxville | 1,119 | 2,348 |
| 52 | Mobile | 1.039 | 2,346 |
| 53 | Austin | 1,217 | 2,269 |
| 54 | Columbus, Ga. | 541 | 2,262 |
| 54 | Norfolk-Virginia Beach | 1,825 | 2,262 |
| 56 | Oklahoma City | 1,864 | 2,235 |
| 57 | Lubbock | 458 | 2,164 |
| 58 | San Antonio | 2,237 | 2,087 |
| 59 | Jacksonville | 1,483 | 2,011 |
| 60 | Nashville-Davidson | 1,705 | 2,005 |
| 61 | Fort Wayne | 725 | 1,893 |
| 62 | New York | 17,074 | 1,872 |
| 63 | Baton Rouge | 889 | 1,800 |
| 64 | Sacramento | 1,787 | 1,762 |
| 65 | Indianapolis | 2,024 | 1,734 |
| 66 | Memphis | 1,484 | 1,626 |
| 67 | Colorado Springs | 485 | 1,528 |
| 68 | Akron | 947 | 1,434 |
| 69 | El Paso | 642 | 1,338 |
| 70 | Grand Rapids | 772 | 1,283 |
| 71 | Shreveport | 443 | 1,176 |
| 72 | Riverside | 1,741 | 1,118 |
| 73 | Lexington-Fayette | 341 | 1,072 |
| 74 | Providence | 800 | 870 |
| 75 | Chattanooga | 325 | 762 |
| 76 | Boston | 1,738 | 629 |
| 77 | Corpus Christi | 102 | 313 |

# 122. Average Weekly Hours of Production Workers in Manufacturing

Workers stay on the job longer hours in some metro areas compared to others. The reason has to do with the complex interaction of technological changes, type of industry and in some places union strength. Locations where the oil industry is strong seem to lead the list.

On average, Houston manufacturing production workers in 1981 put in 6½ hours per week more than New York City workers; the other cities are spread out in between. The reason for long hours in metro areas where the oil industry is a prominent employer—like Houston, Baton Rouge and Corpus Christi— is probably the fact that this industry has a relatively small ratio of labor to capital. That is, there are relatively few employees compared to capital invested.

Union strength in many older cities is a factor keeping hours from creeping up during recessionary hard times, although it does not seem to be a determining factor. Union areas like Akron and Dayton are high up on the long-hour list, while many metro areas in the relatively union-weak sunbelt are at the other end with shorter hours. Asterisks indicate metro areas, e.g. Norfolk includes Virginia Beach, Los Angeles includes Long Beach and Anaheim includes Santa Ana.

SOURCE: Metro data from U.S. Department of Labor, Bureau of Labor Statistics, *Average Weekly Hours 1981, Gross Hours of Production Workers on Manufacturing Payrolls.*

| Rank | Metro Area | Average Weekly Hours 1981 | Rank | Metro Area | Average Weekly Hours 1981 | Rank | Metro Area | Average Weekly Hours 1981 |
|---|---|---|---|---|---|---|---|---|
| 1 | Houston | 43.6 | 26 | Nashville-Davidson | 40.6 | 48 | Phoenix | 39.8 |
| 2 | Baton Rouge | 42.3 | 29 | Tampa-St. Petersburg | 40.5 | 56 | Knoxville | 39.7 |
| 3 | Jacksonville | 41.9 | 30 | Baltimore | 40.4 | 56 | Worcester | 39.7 |
| 4 | Akron | 41.8 | 30 | Jersey City | 40.4 | 58 | Denver | 39.6 |
| 5 | Corpus Christi | 41.5 | 30 | Pittsburgh | 40.4 | 58 | Seattle | 39.6 |
| 5 | Wichita | 41.5 | 33 | Anaheim* | 40.3 | 60 | Chicago | 39.5 |
| 7 | Dayton | 41.4 | 33 | Boston | 40.3 | 60 | Little Rock | 39.5 |
| 7 | Newark | 41.4 | 33 | Memphis | 40.3 | 60 | Omaha | 39.5 |
| 7 | Shreveport | 41.4 | 33 | Richmond | 40.3 | 63 | Minneapolis-St. Paul | 39.4 |
| 10 | Rochester | 41.2 | 37 | Buffalo | 40.2 | 63 | Riverside | 39.4 |
| 11 | Austin | 41.1 | 37 | Charlotte | 40.2 | 63 | St. Louis | 39.4 |
| 11 | Cincinnati | 41.1 | 37 | Jackson | 40.2 | 66 | San Francisco | 39.3 |
| 11 | Cleveland | 41.1 | 40 | Albuquerque | 40.1 | 67 | Madison | 39.2 |
| 11 | New Orleans | 41.1 | 40 | Salt Lake City | 40.1 | 67 | Washington, D.C. | 39.2 |
| 11 | Norfolk* | 41.1 | 42 | Atlanta | 40.0 | 69 | Greensboro | 38.9 |
| 11 | Miami | 41.1 | 42 | Columbus, Ohio | 40.0 | 69 | Lexington-Fayette | 38.9 |
| 17 | Detroit | 41.0 | 42 | Milwaukee | 40.0 | 69 | San Diego | 38.9 |
| 18 | Mobile | 40.9 | 42 | Philadelphia | 40.0 | 72 | Sacramento | 38.7 |
| 18 | Toledo | 40.9 | 46 | El Paso | 39.9 | 73 | Des Moines | 38.6 |
| 20 | Dallas-Fort Worth | 40.8 | 46 | San Jose | 39.9 | 73 | Tacoma | 38.6 |
| 20 | Syracuse | 40.8 | 48 | Birmingham | 39.8 | 75 | Lincoln | 38.3 |
| 20 | Tulsa | 40.8 | 48 | Grand Rapids | 39.8 | 75 | Tucson | 38.3 |
| 23 | Lubbock | 40.7 | 48 | Kansas City, Mo. | 39.8 | 77 | Fresno | 38.1 |
| 23 | Chattanooga | 40.7 | 48 | Las Vegas | 39.8 | 78 | Honolulu | 37.5 |
| 23 | San Antonio | 40.7 | 48 | Los Angeles* | 39.8 | 78 | Spokane | 37.5 |
| 26 | Flint | 40.6 | 48 | Louisville | 39.8 | 80 | New York | 37.1 |
| 26 | Indianapolis | 40.6 | 48 | Oklahoma City | 39.8 | | | |

# 123. Change in the Labor Force

The wealth of metro areas is far more dependent on the breadth of its labor force and the health of its commerce and industry than on the presence of inherited wealth.

Change in the labor force is a good measure of economic change. If jobs are being created, that is the healthiest of signs, a "bottom line" for an area. Growth in labor force is a complementary measure to the unemployment rate, because a metro area can have heavy immigration which could worsen its unemployment while the labor force is nonetheless increasing.

On that basis, Oklahoma was the shining economic star during the 1980–81 period. Two of the top four metro areas in labor force growth were Oklahoma City and Tulsa. Two Florida metro areas also made the top six cities—Jacksonville and Tampa. Despite the recession,

between 1980 and 1981 many sunbelt metro areas and some northern areas showed such an increase. Minneapolis and Boston—perhaps because of the relative health of the food processing, electronics and financial services industries on which their economies rest in part—chalked up 4–6 percent labor force increases.

The table below shows the labor force change between December 1981 and December 1982. Of the 76 metro areas in the table, more than half, 43, showed an increase in the labor force.

The big winners in 1980–81 became the big losers of 1981–82. Tulsa and Oklahoma City were in the bottom dozen cities in the table and posted labor force declines of 3.6 percent and 1.0 percent, respectively. Their declines, and those of other areas dependent on oil, were clearly related to the vicissicitudes of the oil industry, as the "oil glut" which replaced the oil shortage of the previous few years.

Florida metro areas, however, held on to the gains they showed in the previous year. Jacksonville, Tampa-St. Petersburg and Miami remained in the top ten cities in labor force growth. Washington cities—Seattle and Tacoma—joined Florida in the top ten.

SOURCE: United States Department of Labor, Bureau of Labor Statistics, *News: State and Metropolitan Area Employment and Unemployment: December 1982* (February 15, 1983).

| Rank | Metro Area | Labor Force Dec. 1981 | Labor Force Dec. 1982 | Percent Change in Labor Force |
|------|------------|-----------------------|-----------------------|-------------------------------|
| 1 | Jacksonville | 341.7 | 366.9 | 7.37 |
| 2 | Albuquerque | 210.2 | 224.7 | 6.90 |
| 3 | Tampa-St. Petersburg | 710.3 | 756.6 | 6.52 |
| 4 | Seattle | 871.1 | 924.8 | 6.16 |
| 5 | Fresno | 276.6 | 293.3 | 6.04 |
| 6 | Tucson | 237.1 | 251.4 | 6.03 |
| 7 | Tacoma | 181.1 | 191.9 | 5.96 |
| 8 | Dallas-Fort Worth | 1,670.4 | 1,768.3 | 5.86 |
| 9 | San Jose | 793.1 | 837.1 | 5.55 |
| 10 | Miami | 819.6 | 861.8 | 5.15 |
| 11 | Riverside | 622.8 | 651.3 | 4.58 |
| 12 | San Francisco-Oakland | 1,713.8 | 1,791.8 | 4.55 |
| 13 | San Antonio | 457.2 | 477.5 | 4.44 |
| 14 | Birmingham | 375.6 | 392.1 | 4.39 |
| 15 | Mobile | 187.5 | 195.7 | 4.37 |
| 16 | Anaheim-Santa Ana | 1,176.8 | 1,227.7 | 4.33 |
| 17 | Madison | 185.1 | 193.1 | 4.32 |
| 18 | Phoenix | 790.7 | 823.6 | 4.16 |
| 19 | Newark | 949.7 | 984.9 | 3.71 |
| 20 | Chattanooga | 198.3 | 205.3 | 3.53 |
| 21 | Milwaukee | 717.7 | 741.5 | 3.32 |
| 22 | Salt Lake City | 430.3 | 444.5 | 3.30 |
| 23 | Sacramento | 502.5 | 518.9 | 3.26 |
| 24 | Las Vegas | 264.1 | 272.2 | 3.07 |
| 25 | Houston | 1,707.3 | 1,758.3 | 2.99 |
| 26 | Atlanta | 1,082.4 | 1,113.6 | 2.88 |
| 27 | Norfolk-Virginia Beach | 337.6 | 346.5 | 2.64 |
| 28 | Knoxville | 228.5 | 234.4 | 2.58 |
| 29 | Little Rock | 195.3 | 200.3 | 2.56 |
| 30 | Charlotte | 372.5 | 381.3 | 2.36 |
| 31 | Honolulu | 348.1 | 356.0 | 2.27 |
| 32 | Richmond | 335.1 | 342.6 | 2.24 |
| 33 | Spokane | 149.8 | 152.7 | 1.94 |
| 34 | Detroit | 1,971.1 | 2,006.1 | 1.78 |
| 35 | Grand Rapids | 326.7 | 332.0 | 1.62 |
| 36 | Denver-Boulder | 921.8 | 936.1 | 1.55 |
| 37 | Flint | 222.3 | 225.5 | 1.44 |
| 38 | Pittsburgh | 1,026.5 | 1,041.0 | 1.41 |
| 39 | Philadelphia | 2,168.3 | 2,197.4 | 1.34 |
| 40 | Montgomery | 121.1 | 122.7 | 1.32 |
| 41 | Omaha | 284.9 | 288.6 | 1.30 |
| 42 | Chicago | 3,463.6 | 3,503.6 | 1.15 |
| 43 | Portland, Ore. | 651.5 | 658.5 | 1.07 |
| 44 | Rochester | 475.8 | 479.2 | .71 |
| 45 | Providence | 477.7 | 480.5 | .59 |
| 46 | Toledo | 365.3 | 367.2 | .52 |
| 47 | Washington, D.C. | 1,712.2 | 1,720.4 | .48 |
| 48 | Syracuse | 300.0 | 301.2 | .40 |
| 49 | Baltimore | 1,076.6 | 1,077.8 | .11 |
| 49 | Des Moines | 179.9 | 180.1 | .11 |
| 51 | Nashville-Davidson | 433.1 | 433.2 | .02 |
| 52 | Lincoln | 112.2 | 112.2 | 0.00 |
| 52 | Akron | 302.7 | 302.7 | 0.00 |
| 52 | Jersey City | 242.7 | 242.7 | 0.00 |
| 55 | Cleveland | 921.1 | 920.7 | − .04 |
| 56 | Worcester | 206.2 | 205.9 | − .15 |
| 56 | Memphis | 411.7 | 411.1 | − .15 |
| 58 | Columbus, Ohio | 563.4 | 561.8 | − .28 |
| 59 | Los Angeles-Long Beach | 3,745.0 | 3,733.0 | − .32 |
| 59 | Minneapolis-St. Paul | 1,171.9 | 1,168.1 | − .32 |
| 61 | Boston | 1,472.1 | 1,466.4 | − .39 |
| 62 | Wichita | 229.8 | 228.8 | − .44 |
| 63 | Dayton | 391.4 | 388.4 | − .77 |
| 64 | Jackson | 160.7 | 159.2 | − .93 |
| 65 | Oklahoma City | 458.1 | 453.7 | − .96 |
| 66 | Indianapolis | 618.3 | 612.2 | − .99 |
| 67 | St. Louis | 1,112.4 | 1,098.9 | − 1.21 |
| 68 | Baton Rouge | 229.3 | 226.4 | − 1.26 |
| 69 | Buffalo | 561.0 | 553.9 | − 1.27 |
| 70 | Columbus, Ga. | 92.0 | 90.3 | − 1.85 |
| 71 | New York | 3,608.3 | 3,514.6 | − 2.60 |
| 72 | New Orleans | 512.4 | 498.2 | − 2.77 |
| 73 | Kansas City, Mo., Kan. | 679.0 | 657.7 | − 3.14 |
| 74 | Fort Wayne | 194.7 | 188.4 | − 3.24 |
| 75 | Tulsa | 364.4 | 351.4 | − 3.57 |
| 76 | Shreveport | 162.8 | 156.6 | − 3.81 |

# 124. Unemployment Rates

High unemployment rates imply an added burden on local government in an area of providing social welfare programs with reduced city taxes.

The national unemployment rate in December 1982 was 10.5 percent. In nearly one-half of the 77 metro areas in the following table the unemployment rate was greater than 10 percent. The median unemployment rate was 9.3 percent and the average was 9.9 percent, 0.6 percent below the national average. This indicates that the urban areas in the United States have been coping better than the rest of the nation. However, unemployment has severely hurt some areas that rely on one industry.

Flint, which is tied to Detroit's automotive industry, leads the list with 22 percent unemployment. Other cities, starting with Detroit (17.7 percent unemployment) are dependent on industry or manufacturing: Mobile (16.1 percent), Birmingham (15.9 percent) and Fresno (15.3 percent).

Six cities have unemployment rates below 6 percent. Oklahoma City has the lowest rate (5.1 percent), followed by Dallas-Forth Worth (5.2 percent), Washington (5.4 percent), Honolulu (5.5 percent), Boston (5.6 percent) and Lincoln (5.9).

SOURCE: United States Department of Labor, Bureau of Statistics, *News: State and Metropolitan Area Employment and Unemployment: December 1982* (February 15, 1983).

| Rank | Metro Area | Unemployment Rate (Dec. 1982) | Rank | Metro Area | Unemployment Rate (Dec. 1982) | Rank | Metro Area | Unemployment Rate (Dec. 1982) |
|---|---|---|---|---|---|---|---|---|
| 1 | Flint | 22.0 | 27 | Seattle | 10.6 | 52 | Rochester | 8.3 |
| 2 | Detroit | 17.7 | 28 | San Diego | 10.5 | 52 | Worcester | 8.3 |
| 3 | Mobile | 16.1 | 29 | Los Angeles-Long Beach | 10.4 | 55 | Little Rock | 8.2 |
| 4 | Birmingham | 15.9 | 29 | Memphis | 10.4 | 56 | Houston | 8.1 |
| 5 | Fresno | 15.3 | 31 | Knoxville | 10.2 | 57 | Albuquerque | 8.0 |
| 6 | Pittsburgh | 15.2 | 32 | Columbus, Ga. | 10.1 | 58 | Anaheim-Santa Ana | 7.9 |
| 7 | Toledo | 14.3 | 32 | Tucson | 10.1 | 59 | Denver-Boulder | 7.8 |
| 8 | Akron | 13.5 | 34 | Wichita | 9.9 | 60 | Greensboro-Winston Salem | 7.7 |
| 9 | Las Vegas | 13.3 | 35 | Indianapolis | 9.8 | 61 | Norfolk-Virginia Beach | 7.6 |
| 10 | Riverside | 13.1 | 36 | Nashville-Davidson | 9.7 | 61 | Omaha | 7.6 |
| 11 | Buffalo | 13.0 | 37 | Miami | 9.6 | 63 | Minneapolis-St. Paul | 7.5 |
| 12 | Tacoma | 12.9 | 38 | New Orleans | 9.3 | 64 | Des Moines | 7.4 |
| 13 | Montgomery | 12.7 | 39 | Columbus, Ohio | 9.2 | 64 | Jackson | 7.4 |
| 14 | Grand Rapids | 12.6 | 40 | Baltimore | 9.1 | 64 | Madison | 7.4 |
| 15 | Cleveland | 12.5 | 41 | Baton Rouge | 9.0 | 64 | Tulsa | 7.4 |
| 16 | Milwaukee | 12.2 | 42 | Tampa-St. Petersburg | 8.8 | 68 | Charlotte | 6.8 |
| 17 | Dayton | 12.1 | 43 | Kansas City, Mo.-Kan. | 8.7 | 69 | Atlanta | 6.5 |
| 17 | Fort Wayne | 12.1 | 44 | Philadelphia | 8.6 | 70 | San Antonio | 6.3 |
| 17 | Spokane | 12.1 | 44 | San Jose | 8.6 | 71 | Richmond | 6.2 |
| 20 | Sacramento | 11.9 | 44 | Syracuse | 8.6 | 72 | Lincoln | 5.9 |
| 21 | Shreveport | 11.7 | 47 | New York | 8.5 | 73 | Boston | 5.6 |
| 22 | Chattanooga | 11.4 | 47 | San Francisco-Oakland | 8.5 | 74 | Honolulu | 5.5 |
| 22 | St. Louis | 11.4 | 49 | Newark | 8.4 | 75 | Washington, D.C. | 5.4 |
| 24 | Chicago | 11.1 | 49 | Phoenix | 8.4 | 76 | Dallas-Fort Worth | 5.2 |
| 25 | Providence | 10.9 | 49 | Salt Lake City | 8.4 | 77 | Oklahoma City | 5.1 |
| 26 | Portland, Ore. | 10.7 | 52 | Jacksonville | 8.3 | | | |

# 125.  Unemployment Trends

Unemployment rates continued to rise across the United States in 1982. Nationwide, the increase was 2.2 percentage points, i.e. from 8.3 to 10.5 percent. This represented a 26.5 percent increase in the unemployment rate. Every state experienced decreases in manufacturing employment between December 1981 and December 1982.

As shown in the following table, the increases in unemployment in the first 39 cities exceed the national increase in the unemployment rate. Only 4 cities of the 77 listed in the following table showed decreases in unemployment: Columbus, Georgia; Fort Wayne, Boston and Baltimore. Metro areas like Tulsa and Houston heavily dependent on the oil industry suffered significantly, more than a doubling of their unemployment. Metro areas like Wichita and Pittsburgh dependent on aerospace and steel fabrication also suffered substantially. Flint's high unemployment at the end of 1981, 16.8 percent, worsened to 22.0 percent, an increase of 31 percent. Along with manufacturing and petroleum, other hard-hit areas of employment were mining, construction, transportation, public utilities and trade. One-half of the states recorded reductions in government employment. On a positive note, some of the slack in employment was taken up by employment increases in finance and insurance services and real estate. Financial institutions and insurance companies as well as the high technology and light manufacturing services located in the Boston area accounted for its decrease in unemployment from its low 1981 base of 5.8 percent.

SOURCE: United States Department of Labor, Bureau of Labor Statistics, *News: State and Metropolitan Area Employment and Unemployment: December 1982* (February 15, 1983).

| Rank | Metro Area | Unemployment Rate Dec. 1981 | Dec. 1982 | Percentage Change |
|------|-----------|------|------|------|
| 1 | Wichita | 4.5 | 9.9 | 120.00 |
| 2 | Tulsa | 3.5 | 7.4 | 111.43 |
| 3 | Houston | 3.9 | 8.1 | 107.92 |
| 4 | Pittsburgh | 8.3 | 15.2 | 83.13 |
| 5 | Tucson | 5.7 | 10.1 | 77.19 |
| 6 | Mobile | 10.1 | 16.1 | 59.41 |
| 7 | Birmingham | 10.0 | 15.9 | 59.00 |
| 8 | Phoenix | 5.3 | 8.4 | 58.49 |
| 9 | Milwaukee | 7.8 | 12.2 | 56.41 |
| 10 | Minneapolis-St. Paul | 4.8 | 7.5 | 56.26 |
| 11 | Denver | 5.0 | 7.8 | 56.00 |
| 12 | Oklahoma City | 3.3 | 5.1 | 54.55 |
| 13 | Las Vegas | 8.7 | 13.3 | 52.87 |
| 14 | Anaheim-Santa Ana | 5.3 | 7.9 | 49.06 |
| 15 | Shreveport | 8.0 | 11.7 | 46.26 |
| 16 | Greensboro | 5.3 | 7.7 | 45.28 |
| 17 | Providence | 7.6 | 10.9 | 43.42 |
| 18 | St. Louis | 8.0 | 11.4 | 42.50 |
| 19 | Charlotte | 4.8 | 6.8 | 41.67 |
| 20 | Richmond | 4.4 | 6.2 | 40.91 |
| 21 | Lincoln | 4.2 | 5.9 | 40.48 |
| 22 | Los Angeles-Long Beach | 7.5 | 10.4 | 38.67 |
| 23 | Montgomery | 9.2 | 12.7 | 38.04 |
| 24 | Riverside | 9.7 | 13.1 | 35.05 |
| 25 | Jacksonville | 6.2 | 8.3 | 33.87 |

| Rank | Metro Area | Unemployment Rate Dec. 1981 | Dec. 1982 | Percentage Change |
|------|-----------|------|------|------|
| 26 | Chicago | 8.3 | 11.1 | 33.73 |
| 27 | Dallas-Fort Worth | 3.9 | 5.2 | 33.33 |
| 27 | Miami | 7.2 | 9.6 | 33.33 |
| 27 | Omaha | 5.7 | 7.6 | 33.33 |
| 30 | Chattanooga | 8.6 | 11.4 | 32.56 |
| 31 | Knoxville | 7.7 | 10.2 | 32.47 |
| 32 | Worcester | 6.3 | 8.3 | 31.75 |
| 33 | San Diego | 8.0 | 10.5 | 31.26 |
| 34 | Flint | 16.8 | 22.0 | 30.95 |
| 35 | Rochester | 6.4 | 8.3 | 29.69 |
| 36 | Salt Lake City | 6.5 | 8.4 | 29.23 |
| 37 | Nashville-Davidson | 7.6 | 9.7 | 27.63 |
| 38 | Tampa-St. Petersburg | 6.9 | 8.8 | 27.54 |
| 39 | San Francisco-Oakland | 6.7 | 8.5 | 26.87 |
| 40 | Madison | 5.9 | 7.4 | 25.42 |
| 41 | Newark | 6.7 | 8.4 | 25.37 |
| 42 | Cleveland | 10.0 | 12.5 | 25.00 |
| 43 | San Jose | 6.9 | 8.6 | 24.64 |
| 44 | Buffalo | 10.5 | 13.0 | 23.81 |
| 45 | Akron | 11.1 | 13.5 | 21.62 |
| 46 | Syracuse | 7.1 | 8.6 | 21.13 |
| 47 | Dayton | 10.0 | 12.1 | 21.00 |
| 48 | Kansas City, Mo.-Kan. | 7.2 | 8.7 | 20.83 |
| 49 | San Antonio | 5.3 | 6.3 | 18.87 |
| 50 | New Orleans | 7.9 | 9.3 | 17.72 |
| 51 | Detroit | 15.1 | 17.7 | 17.22 |
| 52 | Norfolk-Virginia Beach | 6.5 | 7.6 | 16.92 |
| 53 | Seattle | 9.1 | 10.6 | 16.48 |
| 54 | Tacoma | 11.1 | 12.9 | 16.22 |
| 55 | Toledo | 12.4 | 14.3 | 15.32 |
| 56 | Memphis | 9.1 | 10.4 | 14.29 |
| 57 | Atlanta | 5.7 | 6.5 | 14.04 |
| 58 | Jackson | 6.5 | 7.4 | 13.85 |
| 59 | Fresno | 13.5 | 15.3 | 13.33 |
| 60 | Albuquerque | 7.1 | 8.0 | 12.68 |
| 61 | Portland, Ore. | 9.5 | 10.7 | 12.63 |
| 62 | Honolulu | 4.9 | 5.5 | 12.24 |
| 63 | Sacramento | 10.7 | 11.9 | 11.21 |
| 64 | Baton Rouge | 8.1 | 9.0 | 11.11 |
| 65 | Little Rock | 7.5 | 8.2 | 9.33 |
| 66 | Grand Rapids | 11.6 | 12.6 | 8.62 |
| 67 | Philadelphia | 8.0 | 8.6 | 7.50 |
| 68 | Spokane | 11.4 | 12.1 | 6.14 |
| 69 | Columbus, Ohio | 8.7 | 9.2 | 5.75 |
| 70 | Des Moines | 7.2 | 7.4 | 2.78 |
| 71 | New York | 8.3 | 8.5 | 2.41 |
| 72 | Washington, D.C. | 5.3 | 5.4 | 1.89 |
| 73 | Indianapolis | 9.8 | 9.8 | 0.00 |
| 74 | Baltimore | 9.2 | 9.1 | − 1.09 |
| 75 | Boston | 5.8 | 5.6 | − 3.45 |
| 76 | Fort Wayne | 12.9 | 12.1 | − 6.20 |
| 77 | Columbus, Ga. | 11.1 | 10.1 | − 9.01 |

# 126. Women in the Workforce

Women constitute between 40.0 and 47.5 percent of the labor force in the 36 metro areas for which information is available.

The highest proportion of women is in Washington, D.C. with 47 percent, followed by Miami, Boston and Tampa, all of which are above 45 percent. This is largely due to the degree of office occupations being held by women particularly in the Federal government and in the insurance field. The lowest proportion of women in the workforce is in Pittsburgh, where 40 percent of the workers are women. Two other cities are below the 41 percent mark: Houston, Riverside and Detroit.

SOURCE: Bureau of the Census, *Supplementary Report: Provisional Estimates of Social, Economic and Housing Characteristics*, March, 1982.

| Rank | Metro Area | Total Labor Force | Total Women in Labor Force | Percentage of Women in Total Labor Force |
|------|-----------|------------------|---------------------------|------------------------------------------|
| 1 | Washington, D.C. | 1,602,826 | 761,481 | 47.51 |
| 2 | Miami | 774,415 | 352,207 | 45.48 |
| 3 | Boston | 1,376,461 | 622,369 | 45.22 |
| 4 | Tampa | 636,592 | 286,743 | 45.04 |
| 5 | Minneapolis-St. Paul | 1,120,213 | 499,525 | 44.59 |
| 6 | New York | 4,169,579 | 1,850,142 | 44.37 |
| 7 | Atlanta | 1,022,054 | 453,348 | 44.36 |
| 8 | Columbus, Ohio | 531,490 | 234,581 | 44.14 |
| 9 | San Francisco-Oakland | 1,682,948 | 741,634 | 44.07 |

| Rank | Metro Area | Total Labor Force | Total Women in Labor Force | Percentage of Women in Total Labor Force |
|------|-----------|------------------|---------------------------|------------------------------------------|
| 10 | San Diego | 811,185 | 357,276 | 44.04 |
| 11 | Kansas City, Mo., Kan. | 671,156 | 295,454 | 44.02 |
| 12 | Newark | 950,206 | 417,994 | 43.99 |
| 13 | Baltimore | 1,039,358 | 455,531 | 43.83 |
| 14 | Sacramento | 476,779 | 208,699 | 43.77 |
| 15 | Milwaukee | 689,318 | 301,342 | 43.72 |
| 16 | Denver | 856,558 | 372,536 | 43.49 |
| 17 | St. Louis | 1,110,974 | 482,894 | 43.47 |
| 18 | Indianapolis | 575,288 | 250,009 | 43.46 |
| 19 | Portland, Ore. | 626,648 | 270,876 | 43.23 |
| 20 | San Jose | 688,524 | 297,228 | 43.17 |
| 21 | Dallas-Fort Worth | 1,528,058 | 659,429 | 43.15 |
| 22 | Chicago | 3,428,148 | 1,475,257 | 43.03 |
| 23 | San Antonio | 440,283 | 188,123 | 42.73 |
| 24 | Los Angeles-Long Beach | 3,712,316 | 1,576,990 | 42.48 |
| 25 | Seattle | 838,696 | 356,090 | 42.46 |
| 26 | Philadelphia | 2,148,304 | 909,805 | 42.35 |
| 27 | Cleveland | 912,264 | 385,577 | 42.27 |
| 28 | Anaheim | 1,008,291 | 425,002 | 42.15 |
| 29 | New Orleans | 519,314 | 217,997 | 41.98 |
| 30 | Phoenix | 707,244 | 296,378 | 41.91 |
| 31 | Cincinnati | 649,924 | 271,510 | 41.78 |
| 32 | Buffalo | 568,092 | 235,609 | 41.47 |
| 33 | Detroit | 1,980,028 | 811,800 | 41.00 |
| 34 | Riverside | 661,434 | 269,860 | 40.80 |
| 35 | Houston | 1,492,307 | 600,767 | 40.26 |
| 36 | Pittsburgh | 1,024,599 | 409,796 | 40.00 |

# 127. Females as Percent of Total Employed

During the 1970s the median age of working Americans dropped from 39 to 34. The great majority of younger women—two-thirds of those between 18 and 34—are in the workforce. Over half of all women are working or seeking work. A declining proportion of men—77 percent in 1981 versus 87 percent in 1951—were working or seeking work.

Of the 35 metro areas listed in the following table, Washington's leads, with women accounting for 47.5 percent of all those employed. Washington's high proportion of women in the workforce reflects the large number of positions in the federal government that are attractive to women.

At the bottom end of the scale—metro areas with lower percentages of women in the workforce—another factor may be present. For example, heavy industrial plants and their corporate headquarters dominate the Cincinnati, Cleveland, Detroit, Houston and Pittsburgh areas' economies. Heavy industry has a higher need for skills that have traditionally been male preserves than do retail or service industry or light manufacturing.

SOURCES: U.S. Department of Commerce, Bureau of the Census, *Supplementary Report Provisional Estimates of Social, Economic and Housing Characteristics*, March 1982. Background information from "The Work Revolution," *Newsweek*, January 17, 1983, p. 30.

| Rank | Metro Area | Total Labor Force | Females Employed in Labor Force | Females Employed in Labor Force as a Percentage of All Employed |
|------|-----------|------------------|--------------------------------|----------------------------------------------------------------|
| 1 | Washington, D.C. | 1,536,620 | 729,821 | 47.50 |
| 2 | Boston | 1,315,200 | 595,254 | 45.26 |
| 3 | Miami | 731,889 | 330,633 | 45.18 |

| Rank | Metro Area | Total Labor Force | Females Employed in Labor Force | Females Employed in Labor Force as a Percentage of All Employed | Rank | Metro Area | Total Labor Force | Females Employed in Labor Force | Females Employed in Labor Force as a Percentage of All Employed |
|---|---|---|---|---|---|---|---|---|---|
| 4 | Tampa-St. Petersburg | 604,612 | 271,894 | 44.97 | 20 | Chicago | 3,179,676 | 1,374,784 | 43.24 |
| 5 | Minneapolis-St. Paul | 1,074,686 | 483,023 | 44.95 | 21 | Dallas-Fort Worth | 1,482,436 | 638,086 | 43.04 |
| 6 | New York | 3,878,401 | 1,716,402 | 44.26 | 22 | San Jose | 658,043 | 281,708 | 42.81 |
| 7 | Kansas City, Mo.-Kan. | 635,700 | 281,235 | 44.24 | 23 | Cleveland | 849,689 | 363,059 | 42.73 |
| 8 | Sacramento | 434,301 | 191,800 | 44.16 | 24 | Seattle | 792,278 | 337,807 | 42.64 |
| 9 | Milwaukee | 649,181 | 286,392 | 44.12 | 25 | Los Angeles-Long Beach | 3,488,192 | 1,484,402 | 42.56 |
| 10 | Atlanta | 974,913 | 429,998 | 44.11 | 26 | San Antonio | 418,790 | 178,007 | 42.51 |
| 11 | Columbus, Ohio | 501,328 | 220,829 | 44.05 | 27 | Philadelphia | 1,964,490 | 828,252 | 42.16 |
| 12 | San Diego | 758,579 | 333,638 | 43.98 | 28 | Buffalo | 516,027 | 216,494 | 41.95 |
| 13 | St. Louis, Mo., Ill. | 1,024,411 | 449,668 | 43.90 | 29 | Detroit | 1,722,372 | 720,092 | 41.81 |
| 14 | Baltimore | 970,022 | 425,628 | 43.88 | 30 | Phoenix | 670,608 | 280,052 | 41.76 |
| 15 | Newark | 888,497 | 389,656 | 43.86 | 31 | New Orleans | 488,542 | 203,247 | 41.60 |
| 16 | San Francisco-Oakland | 1,585,385 | 694,303 | 43.79 | 32 | Cincinnati | 604,834 | 251,101 | 41.52 |
| 17 | Indianapolis | 539,776 | 235,262 | 43.59 | 33 | Riverside | 613,956 | 249,534 | 40.64 |
| 18 | Denver | 820,574 | 356,690 | 43.47 | 34 | Pittsburgh | 950,751 | 383,349 | 40.32 |
| 19 | Portland, Ore. | 589,090 | 255,183 | 43.32 | 35 | Houston | 1,440,981 | 578,130 | 40.12 |

# CHAPTER EIGHT

# CITY FINANCES

How is government organized at the local level? How much of a burden on the economy does government represent? Where does it get its money? How much does it spend? Government is big business. One out of six workers in America is employed by government. Four out of five civilian government workers are employed by state and local governments. Local governments shape the character as well as the economy of a city. The number of employees and the cost of government need to be carefully monitored by government and the taxpayer alike. Good indicators of government efficiency must relate the delivery of services to their cost.

The trend of the past two decades in the United States is that federal civilian employment has been fairly constant at around 3 million people. State and local government, however, increased by one-third, from 8 to 12 million people. That trend was checked by California's Proposition 13, Massachusetts' Proposition 2½ and similar initiatives that restricted state and local government taxation. The result has been a growth in user charges.

In the tables that follow, we examine employment, revenue sources and spending of federal, state and local governments in each city. Some cities besides Washington—notably San Antonio, Baltimore and Portland—have a very high concentration of federal employees. This is very good for their economies. The same goes for cities with many state employees. The burden of paying for the employees is spread out beyond the city in which the employees live. How revenues are raised affects the impact of government taxation on local residents. The basic tax is on property. Cities with a high tourist traffic can seek to impose costs on visitors through sales taxes. Income taxes on people who work as well as live in cities capture revenue from commuters.

# 128. Federal Government Centers

A school of regional economic analysis has developed the concept of "export industries"—i.e., types of activities that generate money for the city and metro area. Dry cleaners are not exporters in this sense. Manufacturing employees are. So are hotel employees, because they service out-of-towners who bring money into the economy. Every city must have an export sector, because cities are net importers of food and other raw materials. They must provide goods and services to pay for what they eat.

One industry that is misunderstood is government. An extra-large *local* government employment is not usually an asset, because it represents a burden on businesses and residents in the area. A high level of *federal* and *state* employment, on the other hand, is an asset to the community, because the money for the personnel comes from outside the community, and higher levels of government provide a generally more stable flow of income than local governments or business.

In this light, it is clear that metro Washington, D.C., with 23.3 percent of its workers in federal government employ, is fortunate, indeed. San Antonio (with two large military bases) and Baltimore (with a large tax-processing center) are the next largest beneficiaries. Milwaukee and Houston have about 2 percent of their workers on the federal payroll.

SOURCE: U.S. Department of Commerce, Bureau of the Census, *1980 Census of Population Supplementary Report: Provisional Estimates of Social, Economic and Housing Characteristics* (March 1982).

| Rank | Metro Area | Total Labor Force | Federal Government Employees | Percentage |
|------|-----------|------------------:|----------------------------:|-----------:|
| 1 | Washington, D.C. | 1,602,826 | 372,990 | 23.27 |
| 2 | San Antonio | 440,283 | 39,876 | 9.52 |
| 3 | Baltimore | 1,039,358 | 89,707 | 9.25 |
| 4 | Portland, Ore. | 626,648 | 47,186 | 8.01 |
| 5 | Sacramento | 476,779 | 29,645 | 6.83 |
| 6 | San Diego | 811,185 | 48,432 | 6.38 |
| 7 | New York | 4,619,579 | 205,751 | 5.31 |
| 8 | Denver | 856,558 | 42,640 | 5.20 |
| 9 | New Orleans | 519,314 | 23,232 | 5.18 |
| 10 | Kansas City, Mo.-Kan. | 635,700 | 32,424 | 5.10 |
| 11 | San Francisco-Oakland | 1,585,385 | 76,729 | 4.84 |
| 12 | Atlanta | 974,914 | 43,927 | 4.51 |
| 13 | Philadelphia | 1,964,490 | 85,263 | 4.34 |
| 14 | St. Louis | 1,024,411 | 41,560 | 4.06 |
| 15 | Indianapolis | 539,776 | 21,626 | 4.01 |
| 16 | Riverside | 613,956 | 22,579 | 3.68 |
| 17 | Boston | 1,315,200 | 46,016 | 3.50 |
| 18 | Phoenix | 670,608 | 22,686 | 3.38 |
| 19 | Columbus, Ohio | 501,328 | 15,801 | 3.17 |
| 19 | Newark | 888,497 | 28,133 | 3.17 |
| 21 | Cincinnati | 604,834 | 18,864 | 3.12 |
| 22 | Chicago | 3,179,676 | 97,930 | 3.08 |
| 23 | Dallas-Fort Worth | 1,482,436 | 44,847 | 3.03 |
| 23 | Seattle | 792,278 | 24,029 | 3.03 |
| 23 | Tampa-St. Petersburg | 604,612 | 18,291 | 3.03 |
| 26 | Miami | 731,889 | 21,161 | 2.89 |
| 27 | Los Angeles-Long Beach | 3,488,192 | 98,612 | 2.83 |
| 28 | Cleveland | 849,689 | 23,655 | 2.78 |
| 29 | Pittsburgh | 950,751 | 24,354 | 2.56 |
| 30 | Buffalo | 516,027 | 12,839 | 2.49 |
| 31 | Minneapolis-St. Paul | 1,074,686 | 26,610 | 2.48 |
| 32 | San Jose | 658,043 | 15,997 | 2.43 |
| 33 | Detroit | 1,722,372 | 39,949 | 2.32 |
| 34 | Anaheim | 965,074 | 22,212 | 2.30 |
| 35 | Houston | 1,440,981 | 28,006 | 2.01 |
| 36 | Milwaukee | 689,813 | 12,473 | 1.80 |

# 129. Direct Federal Aid Per Capita

Federal aid per capita is an important indicator overall, in that the aid given to each state and locality is rarely unrestricted. It is usually earmarked for specific program areas such as housing, health care, education, highways and welfare and is usually channeled through state or county governments.

The latest Census of Government was in 1977; the data were released in 1980. They show that Washington, D.C. had no state aid. Federal aid that might have gone through a state went directly to the city. But its aid of nearly $1,200 a person is very high, even so. At the other end of the spectrum, Yonkers had hardly any federal aid.

While 1980 data are available only for the broad category of federal aid, we obtained unpublished 1976 data showing in detail how the federal aid was distributed in that year in the 100 largest U.S. cities:

1. *Housing and Urban Renewal Aid.* Pittsburgh received no direct federal money in 1976 other than its $5.0 million for housing and urban renewal. Other federal aid went through either the state of Pennsylvania or Allegheny County. Some will show up as state aid to Pittsburgh in later tables. Money going to Allegheny County will not show at all in Pittsburgh's finances, except insofar as the Allegheny debt burden adversely affects Pittsburgh's ability to borrow cheaply in the municipal bond market.

2. *Health and Hospital Aid.* Cities that have consolidated with their counties are receiving money directly from the federal government: Anchorage, Nashville, Jacksonville, Indianapolis, New York. The inclusion of other cities is largely dependent upon state laws. Flint apparently handles all the federal money for health and hospitals directly. New York City does not.

3. *Education.* In some states, such as Texas, school boards operate independently of the cities, so that no educational aid would be expected to come through the city. In New Jersey and New York states, on the other hand, six cities were major recipients in 1976 of federal educational aid. In Yonkers it amounted to all the city's federal aid. Rochester, Buffalo and New York City also have received substantial amounts of federal educational aid.

4. *Highways*. Two cities received more than 6 percent of their 1976 federal aid in the form of highway money: Spokane ($2.6 million, 40.4 percent) and Tacoma ($2.3 million, 16.8 percent). Only 18 other cities received federal highway money, and only three besides the two already mentioned received more than 2.5 percent of their federal aid in this form in 1976.

5. *Welfare*. Washington, D.C. was the only city to receive substantial welfare aid. It received $177.9 million in 1976, 24.2 percent of all federal aid. Only four other cities received welfare aid directly from the federal government. None received as much as 1 percent of its federal aid in this form in 1976.

## CHANGE IN FEDERAL AID

Federal aid to localities is based on a number of factors: (1) needs, as measured through general revenue-sharing formulas and the like; (2) local grantsmanship, i.e., competence in communicating local needs through proposals, political know-how and follow-up with federal officials. States raise money from the federal government for localities within their borders and in some cases may deserve much of the credit for growth in city aid.

Although the end of the 1977–80 period saw the Carter administration seeking to reduce domestic spending as part of its war on inflation, 71 out of 100 cities obtained an increase in federal aid between 1977 and 1980. In real terms, given that the cost of living rose 33 percent between the beginning of 1977 and the beginning of 1980, only 43 cities out of 100 saw an increase in federal aid. The cities that show the greatest increase in federal aid per capita are Fresno, Anaheim and Riverside. They all tripled their per capita federal aid during the period.

The increases in federal aid per capita appear to reflect the impact of broad entitlement programs such as federal revenue sharing on suburban communities that did not previously have significant amounts of direct federal assistance. Such aid had previously been channeled through the states. Under the entitlement programs it was dispersed directly to each locality based on a formula. Larger localities have been required to undergo independent audits, but otherwise there have been few strings attached. The increases may also reflect special demonstration programs for which cities were able to obtain federal funds.

Interestingly, two cities in California as well—San Jose and Oakland—saw their federal aid drop 76 percent and 42 percent, respectively. Madison sustained an incredible 97 percent drop in real federal aid dollars.

Since the Reagan administration began reducing direct federal aid to cities in 1981–82, the data for 1982 and subsequent years can be expected to show a higher number of cities with declines in per capita federal aid. Federal assistance will tend to revert to funding through the states in the form of block grants to be allocated under state-determined formulas and procedures.

SOURCES: U.S. Department of Commerce, Bureau of the Census, *City Government Finances in 1979–80* (Washington, DC: Government Printing Office, 1981). Unpublished data from the 1977 Census of Governments, specially commissioned for this book in 1982 from the Maxwell School, Syracuse University.

| Rank | City | Federal Aid Per Capita | | Absolute Change ($) | Percentage Change |
|------|------|------------------------|------------------|---------------------|-------------------|
| | | 1977 ($) | 1980 ($) | | |
| 1 | Fresno | 21.20 | 91.49 | 70.29 | 331.56 |
| 2 | Anaheim | 9.55 | 38.72 | 29.17 | 305.45 |
| 3 | Riverside | 12.62 | 50.17 | 37.55 | 297.54 |
| 4 | Long Beach | 54.32 | 179.01 | 124.69 | 229.55 |
| 5 | Salt Lake City | 26.36 | 78.96 | 52.60 | 199.54 |
| 6 | Miami | 27.99 | 72.61 | 44.62 | 159.41 |
| 7 | El Paso | 43.78 | 112.69 | 68.91 | 157.40 |
| 8 | Atlanta | 52.76 | 127.83 | 75.07 | 142.29 |
| 9 | Huntington Beach | 9.32 | 21.21 | 11.89 | 127.58 |
| 10 | St. Louis | 111.01 | 235.82 | 124.81 | 112.43 |
| 11 | Nashville-Davidson | 66.04 | 138.24 | 72.20 | 109.33 |
| 12 | Flint | 161.36 | 336.11 | 174.75 | 108.30 |
| 13 | Chicago | 79.26 | 163.58 | 84.32 | 106.38 |
| 14 | Anchorage | 74.84 | 145.45 | 70.61 | 94.35 |
| 15 | Columbus, Ga. | 39.89 | 74.56 | 34.67 | 86.91 |

| | | Federal Aid Per Capita | | Absolute | Percentage |
|---|---|---|---|---|---|
| Rank | City | 1977 ($) | 1980 ($) | Change ($) | Change |
| 16 | Sacramento | 34.58 | 63.79 | 29.21 | 84.47 |
| 17 | New Orleans | 116.32 | 213.59 | 97.27 | 83.62 |
| 18 | Baton Rouge | 70.86 | 128.40 | 57.54 | 81.20 |
| 19 | Lexington-Fayette | 47.23 | 84.35 | 37.12 | 78.59 |
| 20 | Akron | 89.75 | 157.47 | 67.72 | 75.45 |
| 21 | San Francisco | 195.54 | 342.86 | 147.32 | 75.34 |
| 22 | Pittsburgh | 84.06 | 146.36 | 62.30 | 74.11 |
| 23 | Indianapolis | 90.13 | 153.92 | 63.79 | 70.78 |
| 24 | Lincoln | 41.83 | 69.41 | 27.58 | 65.93 |
| 25 | Tucson | 54.42 | 88.12 | 33.70 | 61.93 |
| 26 | Colorado Springs | 48.30 | 77.85 | 29.55 | 61.18 |
| 27 | Cleveland | 152.61 | 242.88 | 90.27 | 59.15 |
| 28 | San Antonio | 66.68 | 105.77 | 39.09 | 58.62 |
| 29 | Phoenix | 70.44 | 111.65 | 41.21 | 58.50 |
| 30 | Corpus Christi | 65.84 | 102.27 | 36.43 | 55.33 |
| 31 | Rochester | 135.40 | 206.80 | 71.40 | 52.73 |
| 32 | Dallas | 43.03 | 65.19 | 22.16 | 51.50 |
| 33 | Columbus, Ohio | 59.45 | 90.03 | 30.58 | 51.44 |
| 34 | Knoxville | 54.38 | 80.83 | 26.45 | 48.64 |
| 35 | Houston | 32.33 | 47.61 | 15.28 | 47.26 |
| 36 | Wichita | 81.31 | 117.39 | 36.08 | 44.37 |
| 37 | Aurora | 11.95 | 17.16 | 5.21 | 43.60 |
| 38 | Syracuse | 114.65 | 164.08 | 49.43 | 43.11 |
| 39 | Minneapolis | 96.91 | 137.02 | 40.11 | 41.39 |
| 40 | Kansas City, Kan. | 108.07 | 152.45 | 44.38 | 41.07 |
| 41 | Toledo | 99.39 | 139.02 | 39.63 | 39.87 |
| 42 | Charlotte | 91.65 | 127.84 | 36.19 | 39.49 |
| 43 | New York | 128.52 | 179.11 | 50.59 | 39.36 |
| 44 | Richmond | 102.59 | 136.54 | 33.95 | 33.09 |
| 45 | Portland, Ore. | 92.67 | 122.09 | 29.42 | 31.75 |
| 46 | Detroit | 165.12 | 215.64 | 50.52 | 30.60 |
| 47 | St. Paul | 105.64 | 136.71 | 31.07 | 29.41 |
| 48 | Arlington, Texas | 13.52 | 17.32 | 3.80 | 28.11 |
| 49 | San Diego | 59.49 | 73.61 | 14.12 | 23.74 |
| 50 | Baltimore | 214.29 | 265.05 | 50.76 | 23.69 |
| 51 | Los Angeles | 74.41 | 89.67 | 15.26 | 20.51 |
| 52 | Greensboro | 64.30 | 77.16 | 12.86 | 20.20 |
| 53 | Memphis | 101.29 | 120.56 | 19.27 | 19.02 |
| 54 | Virginia Beach | 52.07 | 61.51 | 9.44 | 18.13 |
| 55 | Washington, D.C. | 1,020.84 | 1,196.00 | 175.16 | 17.16 |
| 56 | Denver | 106.61 | 123.88 | 17.27 | 16.20 |
| 57 | Providence | 133.01 | 154.53 | 21.52 | 16.18 |
| 58 | Des Moines | 36.26 | 41.86 | 5.60 | 15.44 |
| 59 | St. Petersburg | 69.04 | 76.67 | 7.63 | 11.05 |
| 60 | Kansas City, Mo. | 133.03 | 147.41 | 14.38 | 10.81 |
| 61 | Jackson | 82.31 | 91.07 | 8.76 | 10.64 |
| 62 | Las Vegas | 24.09 | 26.52 | 2.43 | 10.09 |
| 63 | Boston | 180.60 | 198.25 | 17.65 | 9.77 |
| 64 | Little Rock | 51.42 | 55.97 | 4.55 | 8.85 |
| 65 | Shreveport | 78.76 | 85.24 | 6.48 | 8.23 |
| 66 | Dayton | 94.51 | 101.14 | 6.63 | 7.02 |
| 67 | Oklahoma City | 159.10 | 168.31 | 9.21 | 5.79 |
| 68 | Milwaukee | 51.07 | 53.35 | 2.28 | 4.46 |
| 69 | Louisville | 206.83 | 215.50 | 8.67 | 4.19 |
| 70 | Lubbock | 70.20 | 72.57 | 2.37 | 3.38 |
| 71 | Worcester | 107.47 | 109.69 | 2.22 | 2.07 |
| 72 | Austin | 69.53 | 69.32 | − .21 | − .30 |
| 73 | Jacksonville | 78.22 | 77.84 | − .38 | − .49 |
| 74 | Seattle | 111.30 | 109.45 | − 1.85 | − 1.66 |
| 75 | Albuquerque | 104.00 | 100.31 | − 3.69 | − 3.55 |
| 76 | Santa Ana | 47.90 | 45.01 | − 2.89 | − 6.03 |
| 77 | Honolulu | 131.00 | 122.26 | − 8.74 | − 6.67 |
| 78 | Tacoma | 91.66 | 85.16 | − 6.50 | − 7.09 |
| 79 | Omaha | 97.84 | 90.25 | − 7.59 | − 7.76 |
| 80 | Birmingham | 85.39 | 77.33 | − 8.06 | − 9.44 |
| 81 | Fort Worth | 89.74 | 76.85 | − 12.89 | − 14.36 |
| 82 | Cincinnati | 212.99 | 180.22 | − 32.77 | − 15.39 |
| 83 | Tulsa | 109.49 | 91.41 | − 18.08 | − 16.51 |
| 84 | Yonkers | 10.92 | 8.99 | − 1.93 | − 17.67 |
| 85 | Chattanooga | 158.52 | 130.08 | − 28.44 | − 17.94 |

| Rank | City | Federal Aid Per Capita | | Absolute Change ($) | Percentage Change |
|------|------|---------|---------|---------|---------|
| | | 1977 ($) | 1977 ($) | | |
| 86 | Buffalo | 295.04 | 240.42 | − 54.62 | − 18.51 |
| 87 | Grand Rapids | 179.90 | 140.22 | − 39.68 | − 22.06 |
| 88 | Oakland | 188.69 | 144.31 | − 44.38 | − 23.52 |
| 89 | Tampa | 170.73 | 130.05 | − 40.68 | − 23.83 |
| 90 | Fort Wayne | 130.07 | 96.38 | − 33.69 | − 25.90 |
| 91 | Philadelphia | 138.21 | 102.24 | − 35.97 | − 26.03 |
| 92 | Norfolk | 187.22 | 120.58 | − 66.64 | − 35.59 |
| 93 | Warren | 72.53 | 46.69 | − 25.84 | − 35.63 |
| 94 | Newark | 143.91 | 77.56 | − 66.35 | − 46.11 |
| 95 | Montgomery | 82.46 | 43.97 | − 38.49 | − 46.68 |
| 96 | Jersey City | 59.53 | 30.48 | − 29.05 | − 48.80 |
| 97 | Mobile | 52.91 | 25.81 | − 27.10 | − 51.22 |
| 98 | Spokane | 127.07 | 58.03 | − 69.04 | − 54.33 |
| 99 | San Jose | 83.66 | 29.76 | − 53.90 | − 64.43 |
| 100 | Madison | 262.15 | 26.00 | − 236.15 | − 90.08 |

# 130. Dependence on Federal Aid

This table shows how important federal aid is to the overall funding of each city. It also shows the vulnerability of each city to federal aid cuts.

The surprising result is that Anchorage in 1980 was much more dependent on federal funds than Washington, D.C. Washington raises nearly 60 percent of its income from property taxes, sales taxes and other nonfederal revenues. Anchorage raises less than half that proportion.

Anchorage's dependence on federal aid reflects its relative youth, which means it has comparatively few services and low taxes. Because the city consolidated with the county, Anchorage receives federal aid for health and other services that in other cities would go to the county. Health aid for Chicago, for example, would mostly go to Cook County.

At the other extreme are cities like Yonkers, Jersey City, Madison and Aurora, which received less than 4 percent of their revenues from the federal government in 1980. They will be the least affected by federal domestic cuts. The impact on them will be felt primarily through a likely reduction in state aid.

Compared to 1977, most cities saw a decline in federal aid in 1980. The cuts in domestic assistance began even before the Reagan administration took office in 1981. Federal aid to the largest cities as a proportion of total revenues fell on an average from 16.0 percent in 1980 to 14.7 percent in 1981.

The trend for the next few years is likely to be continued sharp cuts in most cities. They will probably lead to increases in local taxes and user charges to maintain minimum service levels.

SOURCES: U.S. Department of Commerce, Bureau of the Census, *City Government Finances in 1979–80* (Washington, D.C.: Government Printing Office, 1981). Unpublished data from the 1977 Census of Governments, especially commissioned for this book in 1982 from the Maxwell School, Syracuse University. Joint Economic Committee, *Trends in the Fiscal Condition of Cities: 1980–82.*

### FEDERAL GOVERNMENT REVENUE AS A PERCENTAGE OF LOCAL REVENUES

| Rank | City | 1977 (%) | 1980 (%) |
|------|------|----------|----------|
| 1 | Anchorage | 12.50 | 71.29 |
| 2 | Washington, D.C. | 43.84 | 40.82 |
| 3 | El Paso | 46.72 | 37.35 |
| 4 | Louisville | 41.41 | 37.06 |
| 5 | San Antonio | 46.49 | 34.46 |
| 6 | Corpus Christi | 38.82 | 32.72 |
| 7 | Kansas City, Kan. | 43.03 | 32.07 |

| Rank | City | 1977 (%) | 1980 (%) |
|------|------|----------|----------|
| 8 | Oklahoma City | 39.10 | 31.07 |
| 9 | Toledo | 31.38 | 30.63 |
| 10 | Akron | 37.33 | 30.59 |
| 11 | New Orleans | 36.21 | 30.38 |
| 12 | Chicago | 30.26 | 29.63 |
| 13 | Honolulu | 28.42 | 28.11 |
| 14 | Fort Worth | 25.94 | 27.36 |

## FEDERAL GOVERNMENT REVENUE AS A PERCENTAGE OF LOCAL REVENUES

| Rank | City | 1977 (%) | 1980 (%) | Rank | City | 1977 (%) | 1980 (%) |
|------|------|----------|----------|------|------|----------|----------|
| 15 | Flint | 46.31 | 27.14 | 58 | Rochester | 22.33 | 17.54 |
| 15 | Fort Wayne | 33.46 | 27.14 | 59 | Seattle | 22.72 | 16.41 |
| 17 | Grand Rapids | 33.41 | 26.80 | 60 | Atlanta | 24.04 | 16.29 |
| 18 | Baton Rouge | 28.18 | 26.61 | 61 | Tacoma | 21.53 | 16.12 |
| 19 | Indianapolis | 30.40 | 26.31 | 62 | Memphis | 21.90 | 16.01 |
| 20 | Pittsburgh | 25.56 | 26.20 | 63 | Spokane | 15.76 | 15.92 |
| 21 | St. Louis | 27.96 | 25.89 | 64 | Santa Ana | 13.75 | 15.91 |
| 22 | Charlotte | 32.12 | 25.71 | 65 | Birmingham | 15.67 | 15.84 |
| 23 | Tampa | 31.00 | 24.98 | 66 | Austin | 25.17 | 15.80 |
| 24 | Long Beach | 21.80 | 24.51 | 67 | Montgomery | 12.19 | 15.70 |
| 25 | Shreveport | 27.11 | 24.08 | 68 | Dallas | 16.54 | 15.65 |
| 26 | Lubbock | 27.68 | 23.94 | 69 | Nashville-Davidson | 21.04 | 15.19 |
| 27 | Phoenix | 32.78 | 23.66 | 70 | Miami | 13.16 | 15.12 |
| 28 | Portland, Ore. | 28.88 | 23.32 | 71 | Little Rock | 13.48 | 14.69 |
| 29 | Oakland | 32.63 | 23.16 | 72 | Jacksonville | 19.06 | 14.50 |
| 30 | Cleveland | 27.40 | 22.57 | 73 | Salt Lake City | 16.54 | 13.63 |
| 31 | St. Paul | 28.41 | 22.53 | 74 | Warren | 11.25 | 13.49 |
| 32 | Columbus, Ga. | 20.16 | 22.47 | 75 | Sacramento | 20.31 | 13.48 |
| 33 | Cincinnati | 29.13 | 22.34 | 76 | Lincoln | 21.10 | 13.40 |
| 34 | Detroit | 26.32 | 22.16 | 77 | Denver | 16.20 | 12.87 |
| 35 | Wichita | 36.77 | 21.82 | 78 | Riverside | 12.99 | 12.64 |
| 36 | Albuquerque | 24.59 | 21.18 | 79 | Boston | 11.98 | 12.55 |
| 37 | Kansas City, Mo. | 23.27 | 21.08 | 80 | Knoxville | 15.21 | 12.19 |
| 38 | Minneapolis | 23.70 | 21.06 | 81 | Richmond | 11.36 | 12.01 |
| 39 | Lexington-Fayette | 17.52 | 20.95 | 82 | Houston | 12.96 | 11.92 |
| 40 | San Francisco | 25.53 | 20.81 | 83 | Philadelphia | 10.50 | 11.73 |
| 41 | Tucson | 20.16 | 20.69 | 84 | Anaheim | 19.13 | 10.99 |
| 42 | St. Petersburg | 28.20 | 20.66 | 85 | Milwaukee | 8.76 | 9.99 |
| 43 | Buffalo | 23.44 | 20.26 | 86 | Worcester | 8.52 | 9.39 |
| 44 | Fresno | 22.86 | 20.20 | 87 | Des Moines | 9.03 | 8.73 |
| 45 | Omaha | 21.04 | 20.16 | 88 | Virginia Beach | 6.97 | 8.65 |
| 46 | Columbus, Ohio | 26.52 | 20.01 | 89 | New York | 7.35 | 8.09 |
| 47 | Baltimore | 19.38 | 19.16 | 90 | San Jose | 8.12 | 7.89 |
| 48 | Jackson | 21.13 | 19.01 | 91 | Huntington Beach | 5.14 | 7.69 |
| 49 | Syracuse | 24.86 | 18.81 | 92 | Las Vegas | 8.74 | 7.46 |
| 50 | San Diego | 25.28 | 18.80 | 93 | Newark | 4.36 | 6.53 |
| 51 | Colorado Springs | 28.39 | 18.79 | 93 | Norfolk | 12.00 | 6.53 |
| 52 | Greensboro | 22.63 | 18.64 | 95 | Arlington, Texas | 4.57 | 6.40 |
| 53 | Providence | 15.85 | 18.21 | 96 | Mobile | 1.18 | 6.30 |
| 54 | Tulsa | 28.16 | 18.19 | 97 | Aurora | 2.82 | 3.94 |
| 55 | Dayton | 19.13 | 17.98 | 98 | Madison | 1.10 | 3.04 |
| 56 | Chattanooga | 22.04 | 17.85 | 99 | Jersey City | .55 | 3.01 |
| 57 | Los Angeles | 25.14 | 17.84 | 100 | Yonkers | .02 | 1.11 |

# 131. Impact of Federal Aid Cuts

The table that follows is derived from a 1981 survey conducted by the U.S. Conference of Mayors to determine the likely impact of federal cutbacks on cities. The questionnaire asked the city officials what fiscal adjustments would have to be made by each city in fiscal 1982. Las Vegas and Tacoma are the mostly seriously affected, since they would not only have to reduce their municipal work force and cut needed services but also increase school student costs and raise local taxes. The challenge of cutting municipal services while raising taxes to pay for them is difficult to confront.

We have summarized the results by assigning one point for each of the following expected impacts:

A. Cutting services.
B. Laying off workers.
C. Raising taxes.
D. Increasing school lunch costs.
E. Additional burdens on the city budget as a result of cuts in income transfer programs.

SOURCE: U.S. Conference of Mayors, Survey, 1981.

**INDEX OF FINANCIAL STRESS FROM FEDERAL CUTBACKS, 1981**

| Rank | City | A | B | C | D | E | Total Points |
|---|---|---|---|---|---|---|---|
| 1 | Las Vegas | x | x | x | x | x | 5 |
| 1 | Tacoma | x | x | x | x | x | 5 |
| 3 | Akron | x | x | x | x | | 4 |
| 3 | Buffalo | x | x | x | x | | 4 |
| 3 | Fresno | x | x | | x | x | 4 |
| 3 | New Orleans | x | x | x | | x | 4 |
| 3 | New York | x | x | | x | x | 4 |
| 3 | Philadelphia | x | x | | x | x | 4 |
| 3 | St. Louis | x | x | x | | x | 4 |
| 3 | Salt Lake City | x | x | x | | x | 4 |
| 3 | San Francisco | x | x | | x | x | 4 |
| 3 | Toledo | x | x | x | | x | 4 |
| 13 | Boston | x | x | | | x | 3 |
| 13 | Cleveland | x | | | x | x | 3 |
| 13 | Fort Wayne | x | | | x | | 3 |
| 13 | Madison | x | x | x | | | 3 |
| 13 | Miami | x | x | | | x | 3 |
| 13 | Minneapolis | x | | x | | x | 3 |
| 13 | Nashville-Davidson | x | x | | | x | 3 |
| 13 | Newark | x | | x | | x | 3 |
| 13 | Oakland | x | x | | | x | 3 |
| 13 | Providence | x | x | x | | | 3 |
| 13 | Portland, Ore. | | x | x | | x | 3 |
| 13 | Rochester | x | x | | | x | 3 |
| 13 | San Diego | x | x | | | x | 3 |
| 13 | Seattle | x | x | | x | | 3 |
| 13 | Syracuse | | x | x | | x | 3 |

| Rank | City | A | B | C | D | E | Total Points |
|---|---|---|---|---|---|---|---|
| 13 | Yonkers | x | x | x | | | 3 |
| 29 | Anchorage | x | | x | | | 2 |
| 29 | Atlanta | | | | x | x | 2 |
| 29 | Baltimore | | x | | | x | 2 |
| 29 | Birmingham | x | x | | | | 2 |
| 29 | Corpus Christi | | | x | | x | 2 |
| 29 | Dayton | | | | x | x | 2 |
| 29 | Denver | x | | | | x | 2 |
| 29 | Flint | x | x | | | | 2 |
| 29 | Lincoln | x | x | | | | 2 |
| 29 | Louisville | x | x | | | | 2 |
| 29 | Omaha | x | x | | | | 2 |
| 29 | Riverside | x | x | | | | 2 |
| 29 | San Jose | x | | | | x | 2 |
| 42 | Cincinnati | | | | | x | 1 |
| 42 | Dallas | | | x | | | 1 |
| 42 | Des Moines | | x | | | | 1 |
| 42 | Indianapolis | x | | | | | 1 |
| 42 | Long Beach | | | | x | | 1 |
| 42 | Los Angeles | | | | | x | 1 |
| 42 | Memphis | | | | x | | 1 |
| 42 | Norfolk | | | | | x | 1 |
| 42 | Oklahoma City | | | | | x | 1 |
| 42 | St. Paul | | | | | x | 1 |
| 42 | Tucson | | | | | x | 1 |
| 42 | Tulsa | | | | | x | 1 |

# 132. State Government Centers

A high percentage of state government workers in a city is desirable for the city. The money these employees spend in the city contributes to the economy and enhances buying power, while the tax burden is spread out across the state.

Six of the top 10-ranked cities are state capitals. The metro area most dependent upon the state government is Sacramento (Austin, another major state capital, is not included in the Census Bureau's metro area data on this subject). Columbus, Ohio; Baltimore, New Orleans and Seattle follow. After these cities no state payroll accounts for as much as 5 percent of metro area employment.

SOURCE: U.S. Department of Commerce, Bureau of the Census, *1980 Census of Population and Housing: Supplementary Report: Provisional Estimates of Social, Economic and Housing Characteristics*, March 1982.

| Rank | Metro Area | Total Labor Force | State Government Employees | Percentage of State Goverment Employees |
|---|---|---|---|---|
| 1 | Sacramento | 476,779 | 59,826 | 12.55 |
| 2 | Columbus, Ohio | 531,490 | 45,246 | 8.51 |
| 3 | Baltimore | 1,039,358 | 58,809 | 5.66 |
| 4 | Seattle | 838,696 | 40,913 | 4.88 |
| 5 | New Orleans | 519,314 | 23,549 | 4.53 |
| 6 | Minneapolis-St. Paul | 1,120,213 | 47,045 | 4.20 |
| 7 | Buffalo | 568,092 | 23,744 | 4.18 |
| 8 | Denver | 856,558 | 35,197 | 4.11 |
| 9 | Phoenix | 707,244 | 28,420 | 4.02 |
| 10 | Atlanta | 1,022,054 | 40,508 | 3.96 |
| 11 | Indianapolis | 575,288 | 20,995 | 3.64 |
| 12 | Boston | 1,376,461 | 50,003 | 3.63 |
| 13 | San Francisco-Oakland | 1,682,948 | 59,515 | 3.54 |
| 14 | Riverside | 661,434 | 22,693 | 3.43 |
| 15 | San Diego | 811,185 | 27,514 | 3.40 |
| 16 | Portland, Ore. | 626,648 | 18,815 | 3.00 |
| 17 | Kansas City, Mo., Kan. | 671,156 | 19,018 | 2.83 |

| Rank | Metro Area | Total Labor Force | State Government Employees | Percentage of State Goverment Employees | Rank | Metro Area | Total Labor Force | State Government Employees | Percentage of State Goverment Employees |
|---|---|---|---|---|---|---|---|---|---|
| 18 | San Antonio | 440,283 | 12,385 | 2.81 | 28 | Los Angeles-Long Beach | 3,488,192 | 79,696 | 2.28 |
| 19 | Washington, D.C. | 1,602,826 | 44,946 | 2.80 | 29 | Pittsburgh | 1,024,599 | 23,126 | 2.26 |
| 20 | Cincinnati | 649,924 | 17,644 | 2.71 | 30 | San Jose | 688,524 | 15,239 | 2.21 |
| 21 | Tampa-St. Petersburg | 636,952 | 16,771 | 2.63 | 31 | Miami | 774,415 | 17,022 | 2.20 |
| 22 | Anaheim | 1,008,291 | 26,402 | 2.62 | 32 | Detroit | 1,980,028 | 42,090 | 2.13 |
| 23 | Philadelphia | 2,148,304 | 56,060 | 2.61 | 33 | Houston | 1,492,307 | 29,547 | 1.98 |
| 24 | St. Louis | 1,110,974 | 28,611 | 2.58 | 34 | Chicago | 3,428,148 | 65,638 | 1.91 |
| 25 | Newark | 950,206 | 24,312 | 2.56 | 35 | Milwaukee | 689,813 | 11,958 | 1.73 |
| 25 | New York | 4,619,579 | 118,050 | 2.56 | 36 | Cleveland | 912,264 | 11,326 | 1.24 |
| 27 | Dallas-Fort Worth | 1,528,058 | 37,427 | 2.45 | | | | | |

# 133. State Aid Per Capita

State aid for cities is desirable because the burden of paying for it is spread over all state taxpayers. State programs are heavily concentrated in health, education and social services.

The 1980 data show that New York, Baltimore and Newark have the highest amounts of state aid per capita and have the most to lose from state funding cutbacks. Each resident of these three cities would get a lump annual sum of over $500 if the state aid were paid out in cash instead of in public services.

Four out of the top nine cities are in New York state. This is very generous of the state, except that city dwellers help pay the state taxes, and on balance the city dwellers may be worse off than if they did not send money to, or receive it from, the state. Senator Daniel Patrick Moynihan has claimed that New York state is a net loser from federal taxation. The cities within the state could be net losers from state taxation, although state voters don't appear to think so. In the 1982 gubernatorial election, the candidate who advocated a 40 percent cut in state taxes won handily in rural areas but lost in New York City.

The data for 1980 do not provide details of the sources of state aid, but we were able to obtain unpublished computer printouts based on Census tapes that show detailed categories for 1976.

1. *Housing and urban renewal.* Of the 100 largest cities, 15 received a significant amount of state aid for this purpose. The highest was Milwaukee, which received 3.5 percent ($4.5 million) of its aid from Wisconsin in this area, followed by 3.2 percent for New Orleans, 1.4 percent for New York City and 1.1 percent for Baton Rouge. In all other cities, this form of aid amounted to less than 1 percent of state aid.

2. *Health and hospitals.* Of the 100 cities, 52 received state aid in this area. The highest percentages were 69.6 percent ($3.0 million) of state aid in Columbus, Georgia, 41.8 percent in Flint, 32.9 percent in Houston, 24.4 percent in San Antonio, 23.9 percent in Cincinnati, 22.8 percent in Anchorage and 21.2 percent in Philadelphia. In all other cities the percentage was less than 20 percent.

3. *Education.* Of the 100 cities, 22 received state aid for this purpose. It's 81.6 percent ($55.1 million) of Rochester's state aid, 78.8 percent of Virginia Beach's, 78.5 percent in Knoxville, 74.9 percent in Memphis, 70.9 percent in Chattanooga, 65.6 percent in Providence, 63.8 percent in Buffalo and Nashville, 60.6 percent in Boston, 60.2 percent in Newark, 60.1 percent in Syracuse, 59.5 percent in Norfolk, 58.8 percent in Worcester, 56.1 percent in Jersey City, 52.2 percent in Richmond, 46.9 percent in Yonkers, 45.3 percent in Baltimore, 43.1 percent in Madison, 31.0 percent in New York City and 28.9 percent in Anchorage. In the other 80 cities the percentage of state aid was zero or less than 6 percent.

4. *Highways.* All but seven cities received some share of their state aid in the form of highway allocations. In three cities this money accounted

for more than 60 percent of state aid: Birmingham ($3.3 million, 66.2 percent), Wichita and Omaha. In four cities it accounted for between 50 and 57 percent: Lincoln, Kansas City, Kansas; Akron, and Fort Wayne. Eleven cities were between 42 percent and 49 percent; four were between 30 percent and 39 percent. The rest were below 30 percent of state revenues.

5. *Public welfare.* Of the 100 cities, 19 received state aid for public welfare. Two received more than half their state aid for this purpose: Denver ($51.4 million, 74.1 percent) and San Francisco ($140.8 million, 51.9 percent). Four received between one-fourth and one-half of their aid in this form: St. Louis, Indianapolis, New York and Richmond. The rest received under 18 percent of state aid for this purpose.

## CHANGE IN STATE AID

State aid to cities grew rapidly in some states during the two decades 1960–80. It is now shrinking, although the difference between states like New York, Massachusetts, Virginia, Pennsylvania, Alaska, California and Maryland, with high levels of state aid, and states like Texas and Oklahoma, with low levels of state aid, will probably diminish.

This equalization of state aid differentials may be seen in the next table, which shows the 1977–80 change in per capita state aid. Texas cities that rank low on state aid rank high on change in state aid, showing a move toward the higher aid in other states.

The big winners from state aid between 1977 and 1980 were Memphis; Columbus, Georgia; Warren; Salt Lake City; Riverside; and Lexington. Corpus Christi saw a tripling of its per capita state aid, but from the small base of $1.00 (to $3.00). Worcester and Philadelphia also more than doubled their aid. Austin and El Paso doubled their aid, but like Corpus Christi from a very small base, so that the increase was not substantial.

On the other end of the scale, three cities stayed the same, which meant they lost ground because of inflation, while an unlucky 13 cities lost what aid they were getting in 1977. The biggest losers were Cincinnati and three cities in the oil and gas states—Oklahoma City, Shreveport and Tulsa. These declines appear to reflect state budget vagaries. The two Oklahoma cities and Shreveport have small levels of aid. Cincinnati's large amount of aid in 1977 appears to have been a one-time grant, since Ohio's level of city aid tends to be closer to the 1980 figure.

The Reagan administration's policy of reducing direct aid to cities and increasing its reliance on block grants to states for dispersal in turn to governments within each state implies an increase in the state aid in those states that have not up to now provided much help to cities. On the other hand, the overall reduction in domestic spending and the fiscal constraints on the states suggest that those states that have provided a high level of assistance to cities may have difficulty maintaining this level, even with increased discretionary federal aid to the states.

Hence, increased state aid alone will not offset the loss in revenues from federal aid cuts. State aid to cities is expected to increase by only 1.2 percent, roughly equivalent to projected state revenue growth. This increase is well below the 1982 rate of inflation.

Of the 100 largest cities, data for 99 are shown. Washington, D.C., is excluded because it is ineligible for state aid.

SOURCES: U.S. Department of Commerce, Bureau of the Census, *City Government Finances in 1977–78* and *City Government Finances in 1979–80* (Washington, D.C.: Government Printing Office, 1979, 1981); Joint Economic Committee, *Trends in the Fiscal Condition of Cities: 1980–1982* (Washington, D.C.: Government Printing Office, 1982); unpublished data from the 1977 Census of Governments, specially commissioned for this book in 1982 from the Maxwell School, Syracuse University.

| Rank | City | Per Capita State Aid 1980 | Absolute Change from 1977 ($) | Percentage Change |
|------|------|---------------------------|-------------------------------|-------------------|
| 1 | Memphis | 384 | 270 | 236.84 |
| 2 | Corpus Christi | 3 | 2 | 200.00 |
| 3 | Columbus, Ga. | 26 | 17 | 188.88 |
| 4 | Warren | 94 | 60 | 176.47 |
| 5 | Salt Lake City | 23 | 13 | 130.00 |
| 6 | Riverside | 108 | 61 | 129.78 |
| 7 | Lexington-Fayette | 27 | 15 | 125.00 |
| 8 | Worcester | 389 | 207 | 113.73 |
| 9 | Philadelphia | 163 | 85 | 108.97 |
| 10 | Jersey City | 420 | 211 | 100.95 |
| 11 | Austin | 8 | 4 | 100.00 |
| 11 | El Paso | 4 | 2 | 100.00 |
| 13 | Honolulu | 37 | 18 | 94.73 |
| 14 | St. Louis | 100 | 47 | 88.67 |
| 15 | Jackson | 144 | 65 | 82.27 |
| 16 | Tacoma | 98 | 41 | 71.92 |
| 17 | Chicago | 75 | 30 | 66.66 |
| 17 | Wichita | 35 | 14 | 66.66 |
| 19 | Boston | 456 | 178 | 64.02 |
| 20 | San Diego | 53 | 20 | 60.60 |
| 21 | Omaha | 53 | 19 | 55.88 |
| 22 | Flint | 177 | 61 | 52.58 |
| 23 | Fort Wayne | 61 | 20 | 48.78 |

| Rank | City | Per Capita State Aid 1980 | Absolute Change from 1977 ($) | Percentage Change |
|------|------|---------|---------|---------|
| 24 | Milwaukee | 203 | 66 | 48.17 |
| 25 | Grand Rapids | 106 | 34 | 47.22 |
| 26 | Des Moines | 100 | 32 | 47.05 |
| 27 | Minneapolis | 171 | 54 | 46.15 |
| 28 | Pittsburgh | 73 | 23 | 46.00 |
| 29 | Jacksonville | 116 | 36 | 45.00 |
| 30 | Providence | 188 | 57 | 43.51 |
| 31 | Buffalo | 452 | 137 | 43.49 |
| 32 | San Francisco | 399 | 120 | 43.01 |
| 33 | Mobile | 30 | 9 | 42.85 |
| 34 | Miami | 78 | 23 | 41.81 |
| 35 | Lincoln | 52 | 15 | 40.54 |
| 36 | Albuquerque | 118 | 34 | 40.47 |
| 37 | Madison | 310 | 89 | 40.27 |
| 38 | Houston | 7 | 2 | 40.00 |
| 38 | Louisville | 21 | 6 | 40.00 |
| 40 | Atlanta | 96 | 27 | 39.13 |
| 41 | Charlotte | 57 | 16 | 39.02 |
| 42 | Tucson | 93 | 26 | 38.80 |
| 43 | Montgomery | 18 | 5 | 38.46 |
| 44 | Newark | 725 | 199 | 37.83 |
| 45 | Baton Rouge | 71 | 19 | 36.53 |
| 46 | Anchorage | 675 | 174 | 34.73 |
| 47 | Cleveland | 57 | 14 | 32.55 |
| 48 | Detroit | 211 | 50 | 31.05 |
| 49 | Kansas City, Kan. | 30 | 7 | 30.43 |
| 50 | Long Beach | 73 | 17 | 30.35 |
| 51 | Columbus, Ohio | 39 | 9 | 30.00 |
| 52 | Kansas City, Mo. | 31 | 7 | 29.16 |
| 53 | Anaheim | 45 | 10 | 28.57 |
| 54 | Little Rock | 115 | 25 | 27.77 |
| 55 | Phoenix | 94 | 20 | 27.02 |
| 56 | Portland, Ore. | 33 | 7 | 26.92 |
| 57 | Sacramento | 53 | 11 | 26.19 |
| 58 | Knoxville | 168 | 34 | 25.37 |
| 59 | Arlington, Texas | 5 | 1 | 25.00 |
| 60 | St. Paul | 131 | 26 | 24.76 |
| 61 | Fresno | 59 | 11 | 22.91 |
| 62 | Greensboro | 54 | 10 | 22.72 |
| 63 | Seattle | 58 | 10 | 20.83 |
| 64 | Indianapolis | 129 | 21 | 19.44 |
| 65 | Los Angeles | 44 | 7 | 18.91 |
| 66 | Aurora | 14 | 2 | 16.66 |
| 66 | San Antonio | 7 | 1 | 16.66 |
| 68 | Chattanooga | 192 | 27 | 16.36 |
| 69 | Dayton | 43 | 6 | 16.21 |
| 69 | Denver | 43 | 6 | 16.21 |
| 71 | Toledo | 36 | 5 | 16.12 |
| 72 | Akron | 38 | 5 | 15.15 |
| 73 | Nashville-Davidson | 177 | 23 | 14.93 |
| 74 | New Orleans | 67 | 8 | 13.55 |
| 75 | St. Petersburg | 44 | 5 | 12.82 |
| 76 | Rochester | 280 | 27 | 10.67 |
| 77 | Norfolk | 256 | 20 | 8.47 |
| 78 | Richmond | 297 | 23 | 8.39 |
| 79 | Colorado Springs | 16 | 1 | 6.66 |
| 80 | Oakland | 46 | 2 | 4.54 |
| 81 | Virginia Beach | 228 | 9 | 4.10 |
| 82 | San Jose | 43 | 1 | 2.38 |
| 83 | New York | 789 | 3 | .38 |
| 84 | Dallas | 6 | 0 | .00 |
| 84 | Fort Worth | 5 | 0 | .00 |
| 84 | Lubbock | 3 | 0 | .00 |
| 87 | Spokane | 69 | − 1 | − 1.42 |
| 88 | Santa Ana | 37 | − 1 | − 2.63 |
| 89 | Syracuse | 244 | − 7 | − 2.78 |
| 90 | Las Vegas | 44 | − 2 | − 4.34 |
| 91 | Yonkers | 186 | − 23 | −11.00 |
| 92 | Tampa | 50 | − 7 | −12.28 |
| 93 | Baltimore | 545 | − 87 | −13.76 |
| 94 | Birmingham | 18 | − 3 | −14.28 |
| 95 | Huntington Beach | 38 | − 18 | −32.14 |
| 96 | Tulsa | 12 | − 7 | −36.84 |
| 97 | Shreveport | 15 | − 11 | −42.30 |
| 98 | Oklahoma City | 10 | − 8 | −44.44 |
| 99 | Cincinnati | 60 | −145 | −70.73 |

# 134. Dependence on State Aid

One way of evaluating the impact on cities of actual or potential cuts in state aid is to look at the cities' dependence on such aid, i.e., the proportion of their revenues that comes from their state.

By this measure, two New Jersey cities—Newark and Jersey City—are the most vulnerable to cuts, with 61 percent and 42 percent dependence in 1980 on state aid. However, the cities are less vulnerable than they were in 1976, when over 66 percent of Newark's revenues and over 54 percent of Jersey City's revenues came from the state of New Jersey.

At the other extreme, Washington, D.C., not being part of a state, has no state aid. Money that would have been channeled through the state shows up as federal aid in the earlier table. The 11 cities after Washington that show the lowest dependence on state aid are all in Texas and Oklahoma.

Overall, the differences in dependence on state aid in 1980 seem to reflect primarily state funding policies. As the federal government reduces direct aid to cities, state aid policies can be expected to grow in significance for cities.

SOURCES: U.S. Department of Commerce, Bureau of the Census, *City Government Finances in 1979–80* (Washington, D.C.: Government Printing Office, 1981); unpublished data from the 1977 Census of Governments, especially commissioned for this book in 1983 from the Maxwell School, Syracuse University.

| Rank | City | Revenue from State Sources as a Percentage of Local Revenue | Rank | City | Revenue from State Sources as a Percentage of Local Revenue | Rank | City | Revenue from State Sources as a Percentage of Local Revenue |
|---|---|---|---|---|---|---|---|---|
| 1 | Newark | 60.98 | 35 | Phoenix | 20.50 | 69 | Columbus, Ohio | 8.71 |
| 2 | Jersey City | 41.50 | 36 | Grand Rapids | 20.32 | 70 | Los Angeles | 8.67 |
| 3 | Baltimore | 39.38 | 37 | Nashville-Davidson | 19.43 | 71 | Toledo | 7.83 |
| 4 | Buffalo | 38.08 | 38 | Spokane | 19.06 | 72 | Columbus, Ga. | 7.79 |
| 5 | Milwaukee | 38.07 | 39 | Philadelphia | 18.71 | 73 | Dayton | 7.57 |
| 6 | Anchorage | 37.27 | 39 | Pittsburgh | 18.71 | 74 | Akron | 7.37 |
| 7 | Madison | 36.26 | 41 | Tacoma | 18.45 | 75 | Oakland | 7.36 |
| 8 | New York | 35.68 | 42 | Fort Wayne | 17.44 | 76 | Mobile | 7.32 |
| 9 | Worcester | 33.33 | 43 | Miami | 16.25 | 77 | Lexington-Fayette | 6.81 |
| 10 | Virginia Beach | 32.10 | 44 | Denver | 14.66 | 78 | Wichita | 6.34 |
| 11 | Norfolk | 31.30 | 45 | Flint | 14.31 | 79 | Kansas City, Kan. | 6.32 |
| 12 | Little Rock | 30.28 | 46 | Huntington Beach | 13.92 | 79 | Montgomery | 6.32 |
| 13 | Jackson | 29.98 | 47 | Chicago | 13.58 | 81 | Kansas City, Mo. | 4.39 |
| 14 | Syracuse | 28.03 | 47 | Cincinnati | 13.58 | 82 | Shreveport | 4.31 |
| 15 | Boston | 27.65 | 49 | San Diego | 13.48 | 83 | Honolulu | 4.11 |
| 16 | Memphis | 27.35 | 50 | Santa Ana | 13.25 | 84 | Salt Lake City | 4.03 |
| 17 | Riverside | 27.17 | 51 | Portland, Ore. | 13.12 | 85 | Colorado Springs | 3.82 |
| 18 | Warren | 27.09 | 52 | Greensboro | 13.08 | 86 | Louisville | 3.66 |
| 19 | Chattanooga | 26.36 | 53 | Fresno | 13.01 | 87 | Birmingham | 3.63 |
| 20 | Minneapolis | 26.23 | 54 | Anaheim | 12.71 | 88 | Aurora | 3.19 |
| 21 | Richmond | 26.10 | 55 | Atlanta | 12.28 | 89 | San Antonio | 2.41 |
| 22 | Knoxville | 25.34 | 56 | St. Petersburg | 11.92 | 90 | Tulsa | 2.38 |
| 22 | Las Vegas | 25.34 | 57 | Omaha | 11.75 | 91 | Arlington, Texas | 1.98 |
| 24 | Albuquerque | 24.97 | 58 | San Jose | 11.50 | 92 | Austin | 1.83 |
| 25 | San Francisco | 24.25 | 59 | Charlotte | 11.47 | 93 | Oklahoma City | 1.77 |
| 26 | Rochester | 23.71 | 60 | Sacramento | 11.11 | 94 | Houston | 1.68 |
| 27 | Yonkers | 22.97 | 61 | St. Louis | 11.02 | 95 | El Paso | 1.41 |
| 28 | Indianapolis | 22.13 | 62 | Lincoln | 9.98 | 96 | Dallas | 1.38 |
| 28 | Providence | 22.13 | 63 | Long Beach | 9.95 | 97 | Fort Worth | 1.34 |
| 30 | Tucson | 21.74 | 64 | Tampa | 9.66 | 98 | Lubbock | 1.05 |
| 31 | Detroit | 21.66 | 65 | New Orleans | 9.58 | 99 | Corpus Christi | .67 |
| 32 | St. Paul | 21.59 | 66 | Baton Rouge | 9.38 | 100 | Washington, D.C. | .00 |
| 33 | Jacksonville | 21.58 | 67 | Cleveland | 9.24 | | | |
| 34 | Des Moines | 20.96 | 68 | Seattle | 8.75 | | | |

# 135.  State Revenue Sharing Aid

Revenue sharing—aid that is essentially unrestricted as to local use—is the most common form of intergovernmental aid. Revenue sharing is a system of financial aid to states and localities in which a predetermined amount of money is given, based on a formula relating to population and need elements. This type of aid is desirable, for it allows flexibility in applying revenues, unlike categorical grants, which are for specific uses.

Unrestricted aid permits the recipient government

to use the funds in the best way possible. Restricted aid may come with matching requirements that make the locality worse off financially than it would have been without the money. Examples of crippling restricted aid are the financing of construction of a community center without providing any money for its operation, or construction of costly roads and bridges without providing for their maintenance.

The Reagan administration's block grant program is

an attempt to reduce the number of restrictions on federal assistance to the states. From the point of view of the advocates of restricted or categorical grants, the disadvantage of block grants is that they reduce the ability of the federal government to ensure that certain goals are met. For example, under Title XX (which has now become the Social Service Block Grant under the Reagan Administration), funds were earmarked to provide day care facilities to free more mothers for work and thereby reduce the welfare burden. Under the new block grant system, the logic of this program may be lost in many states. Day care funds may be buried by advocates of more money for the criminal justice system or transportation or (at best, from a social service standpoint) for more highly visible social programs.

Shreveport is fortunate in receiving all of its aid from the state of Louisiana in unrestricted form. At the other extreme is Louisville, which is provided with no unrestricted state aid.

SOURCE: Unpublished data from the 1977 Census of Governments, specially commissioned for this book in 1982 from the Maxwell School, Syracuse University.

| Rank | City | Total State Aid ($000) | Unrestricted State Aid ($000) | Percentage Unrestricted Aid |
|---|---|---|---|---|
| 1 | Shreveport | 3,139 | 3,139 | 100.00 |
| 2 | St. Petersburg | 10,479 | 9,384 | 89.55 |
| 3 | Las Vegas | 7,171 | 6,269 | 87.42 |
| 4 | Tampa | 13,651 | 11,556 | 84.65 |
| 5 | Albuquerque | 39,233 | 33,053 | 84.25 |
| 6 | Tucson | 30,606 | 23,423 | 76.53 |
| 7 | Greensboro | 8,428 | 5,905 | 70.06 |
| 8 | Phoenix | 73,995 | 51,135 | 69.11 |
| 9 | Cleveland | 32,783 | 22,642 | 69.07 |
| 10 | St. Paul | 35,416 | 23,413 | 66.11 |
| 11 | Dayton | 8,665 | 5,398 | 62.30 |
| 12 | Milwaukee | 129,336 | 80,474 | 62.22 |
| 13 | New Orleans | 37,564 | 22,409 | 59.66 |
| 14 | Honolulu | 13,645 | 8,078 | 59.20 |
| 15 | Santa Ana | 7,638 | 4,208 | 55.09 |
| 16 | Huntington Beach | 6,548 | 3,591 | 54.84 |
| 17 | Jackson | 29,140 | 15,856 | 54.41 |
| 18 | Yonkers | 36,325 | 19,190 | 52.83 |
| 19 | Portland, Ore. | 12,219 | 6,413 | 52.48 |
| 20 | San Jose | 27,647 | 14,411 | 52.13 |
| 21 | Los Angeles | 129,349 | 65,750 | 50.83 |
| 22 | Oakland | 15,567 | 7,900 | 50.75 |
| 23 | Toledo | 12,598 | 6,305 | 50.05 |
| 24 | Charlotte | 17,935 | 8,947 | 49.89 |
| 25 | Corpus Christi | 487 | 242 | 49.69 |
| 26 | Warren | 15,111 | 7,484 | 49.53 |
| 27 | Anaheim | 9,923 | 4,656 | 46.92 |
| 28 | Miami | 27,070 | 12,649 | 46.73 |
| 29 | Columbus, Ohio | 22,142 | 9,975 | 45.05 |
| 30 | Lubbock | 555 | 238 | 42.88 |
| 31 | Grand Rapids | 19,330 | 8,094 | 41.87 |
| 32 | Sacramento | 14,494 | 6,038 | 41.66 |
| 33 | San Diego | 46,212 | 18,183 | 39.35 |
| 34 | Detroit | 253,640 | 98,272 | 38.74 |
| 35 | Cincinnati | 23,215 | 8,754 | 37.71 |
| 36 | Fresno | 12,860 | 4,651 | 36.17 |
| 37 | Colorado Springs | 3,403 | 1,226 | 36.03 |
| 38 | Dallas | 5,206 | 1,833 | 35.21 |
| 39 | Jacksonville | 62,669 | 21,332 | 34.04 |
| 40 | Aurora | 2,201 | 741 | 33.67 |
| 41 | Madison | 52,845 | 17,470 | 33.06 |
| 42 | Syracuse | 41,583 | 12,844 | 30.89 |
| 43 | Flint | 28,280 | 7,998 | 28.28 |
| 44 | Houston | 10,719 | 2,913 | 27.18 |
| 45 | Seattle | 28,807 | 7,352 | 25.52 |
| 46 | Chicago | 225,268 | 56,673 | 25.16 |
| 47 | Akron | 8,997 | 1,905 | 21.17 |
| 48 | El Paso | 1,806 | 380 | 21.04 |
| 49 | Fort Worth | 2,051 | 431 | 21.01 |
| 50 | Baton Rouge | 15,663 | 3,152 | 20.12 |
| 51 | Arlington, Texas | 856 | 169 | 19.74 |
| 52 | Riverside | 18,431 | 3,630 | 19.70 |
| 53 | Birmingham | 5,034 | 955 | 18.97 |
| 54 | Spokane | 11,901 | 2,252 | 18.92 |
| 55 | Montgomery | 3,157 | 578 | 18.31 |
| 56 | Columbus, Ga. | 4,378 | 801 | 18.30 |
| 57 | Buffalo | 161,693 | 27,763 | 17.17 |
| 58 | Austin | 2,774 | 452 | 16.29 |
| 59 | Knoxville | 30,781 | 4,954 | 16.09 |
| 60 | Chattanooga | 32,562 | 4,907 | 15.07 |
| 61 | Des Moines | 19,191 | 2,812 | 14.65 |
| 62 | Worcester | 63,013 | 9,165 | 14.54 |
| 63 | New York | 5,581,796 | 776,403 | 13.91 |
| 64 | Providence | 29,448 | 3,947 | 13.40 |
| 65 | Memphis | 133,132 | 17,737 | 13.32 |
| 66 | Tacoma | 15,455 | 2,048 | 13.25 |
| 67 | Mobile | 6,011 | 791 | 13.16 |
| 68 | Oklahoma City | 3,878 | 488 | 12.58 |
| 69 | Lincoln | 8,884 | 1,110 | 12.49 |
| 70 | Little Rock | 18,287 | 2,268 | 12.40 |
| 71 | Nashville | 80,539 | 9,893 | 12.28 |
| 72 | San Antonio | 5,809 | 705 | 12.14 |
| 73 | Kansas City, Kan. | 4,842 | 551 | 11.38 |
| 74 | Tulsa | 4,311 | 466 | 10.81 |
| 75 | Fort Wayne | 10,576 | 1,088 | 10.29 |
| 76 | Wichita | 9,520 | 939 | 9.86 |
| 77 | San Francisco | 271,198 | 26,309 | 9.70 |
| 78 | Salt Lake City | 3,804 | 319 | 8.39 |
| 79 | Boston | 256,889 | 18,089 | 7.04 |
| 80 | Atlanta | 40,882 | 2,583 | 6.32 |
| 81 | Denver | 69,321 | 4,217 | 6.08 |
| 82 | Anchorage | 32,405 | 1,792 | 5.53 |
| 83 | Indianapolis | 90,743 | 4,964 | 5.47 |
| 84 | Long Beach | 154,690 | 7,993 | 5.17 |
| 85 | Pittsburgh | 31,060 | 1,604 | 5.16 |
| 86 | Omaha | 16,396 | 701 | 4.28 |
| 87 | Norfolk | 68,256 | 2,763 | 4.05 |
| 88 | Richmond | 65,041 | 2,112 | 3.25 |
| 89 | Virginia Beach | 56,845 | 1,839 | 3.24 |
| 90 | Philadelphia | 275,220 | 8,200 | 2.98 |
| 91 | Baltimore | 428,582 | 12,322 | 2.88 |
| 92 | St. Louis | 45,458 | 1,291 | 2.84 |
| 93 | Jersey City | 93,974 | 2,546 | 2.71 |
| 94 | Rochester | 67,567 | 1,643 | 2.43 |
| 95 | Kansas City, Mo. | 13,754 | 330 | 2.40 |
| 96 | Newark | 238,590 | 2,632 | 1.10 |
| 97 | Minneapolis | 63,310 | 105 | .17 |
| 98 | Lexington-Fayette | 5,599 | 1 | .02 |
| 99 | Louisville | 6,360 | 0 | .00 |

# 136. City Revenue Independence

City finances are ultimately dependent on a city's own resources, because city officials cannot mandate a higher level of government to provide aid. While it is desirable for a city to bring in money from higher levels of government, economically speaking, it is dangerous. When the money is cut back, the city is placed in a critical position. Self-reliance implies revenue independence.

Providence is by this measure the most self-reliant of cities. Of every dollar of revenue, 92 cents comes out of the pockets of its residents. In Mobile the relationship is almost reversed. Only 6 cents come from residents, and 94 cents comes from federal and state aid.

Revenue from local sources is primarily a function of property taxes. When property value in central city areas declines, the tax base shrinks, and the city's revenues shrink, too. Many older industrial cities suffer from lower assessed property valuations when central city areas do not have new construction or urban development.

When a city must depend largely on its own tax revenues, not supplemented to any great extent by the state or federal government, it must encourage construction and urban renewal projects to maintain a tax base that can adequately support city government and city services.

SOURCE: U.S. Department of Commerce, Bureau of the Census, *City Government Finances in 1979–80* (Washington, D.C.: Government Printing Office, 1981).

| Rank | City | Revenue from Local Sources as a Percentage of All Revenues | Rank | City | Revenue from Local Sources as a Percentage of All Revenues | Rank | City | Revenue from Local Sources as a Percentage of All Revenues |
|---|---|---|---|---|---|---|---|---|
| 1 | Providence | 92.08 | 35 | Corpus Christi | 38.93 | 69 | Philadelphia | 19.27 |
| 2 | Boston | 77.89 | 36 | Houston | 37.09 | 70 | Denver | 18.67 |
| 3 | Madison | 73.84 | 37 | Las Vegas | 36.88 | 71 | Cleveland | 18.29 |
| 4 | Worcester | 73.07 | 37 | New York | 36.88 | 72 | New Orleans | 17.95 |
| 5 | Rochester | 70.23 | 39 | Lubbock | 36.60 | 73 | Baton Rouge | 17.85 |
| 6 | Honolulu | 67.54 | 40 | Omaha | 34.60 | 74 | Sacramento | 17.79 |
| 7 | Syracuse | 64.66 | 41 | St. Paul | 33.96 | 75 | Salt Lake City | 17.65 |
| 8 | Warren | 64.27 | 42 | Chicago | 33.51 | 76 | Spokane | 17.48 |
| 9 | Buffalo | 61.83 | 43 | El Paso | 32.09 | 77 | Oakland | 17.47 |
| 10 | Yonkers | 60.69 | 44 | Fort Worth | 31.76 | 78 | San Diego | 17.09 |
| 11 | Charlotte | 60.03 | 45 | Wichita | 31.61 | 79 | Oklahoma City | 16.59 |
| 12 | Greensboro | 57.68 | 46 | Jacksonville | 30.23 | 80 | Tacoma | 16.21 |
| 13 | Indianapolis | 57.19 | 47 | Detroit | 30.06 | 81 | San Jose | 15.04 |
| 14 | Newark | 55.36 | 48 | San Francisco | 28.73 | 82 | Cincinnati | 14.46 |
| 15 | Chattanooga | 55.19 | 49 | San Antonio | 28.67 | 83 | Akron | 14.06 |
| 16 | Fort Wayne | 54.78 | 50 | Columbus, Ga. | 27.93 | 84 | Riverside | 14.02 |
| 17 | Kansas City, Kan. | 53.18 | 51 | Albuquerque | 27.85 | 85 | Anaheim | 14.01 |
| 18 | Minneapolis | 50.48 | 52 | Atlanta | 27.52 | 86 | Birmingham | 13.71 |
| 19 | Miami | 50.11 | 53 | Arlington, Texas | 27.14 | 87 | St. Louis | 13.15 |
| 20 | Milwaukee | 50.02 | 54 | Tampa | 26.86 | 88 | Dayton | 13.09 |
| 21 | Baltimore | 47.66 | 55 | Shreveport | 26.19 | 89 | Tucson | 11.42 |
| 22 | Des Moines | 47.21 | 56 | St. Petersburg | 25.24 | 90 | Long Beach | 11.34 |
| 23 | Jersey City | 46.82 | 57 | Huntington Beach | 25.23 | 91 | Colorado Springs | 11.21 |
| 24 | Richmond | 46.08 | 58 | Lexington-Fayette | 23.02 | 91 | Kansas City, Mo. | 11.21 |
| 25 | Pittsburgh | 45.99 | 59 | Lincoln | 22.48 | 93 | Aurora | 10.86 |
| 26 | Knoxville | 44.67 | 60 | Santa Ana | 22.31 | 93 | Austin | 10.86 |
| 27 | Jackson | 44.24 | 61 | Los Angeles | 22.04 | 95 | Montgomery | 10.19 |
| 28 | Portland, Ore. | 43.25 | 62 | Louisville | 21.96 | 96 | Flint | 9.90 |
| 29 | Anchorage | 42.69 | 63 | Grand Rapids | 20.62 | 97 | Toledo | 8.92 |
| 30 | Virginia Beach | 41.21 | 64 | Washington, D.C. | 20.40 | 98 | Tulsa | 6.77 |
| 31 | Memphis | 39.96 | 65 | Phoenix | 19.98 | 99 | Columbus, Ohio | 5.81 |
| 32 | Dallas | 39.62 | 66 | Seattle | 19.89 | 100 | Mobile | 4.28 |
| 33 | Norfolk | 39.31 | 67 | Fresno | 19.71 | | | |
| 34 | Nashville-Davidson | 39.02 | 68 | Little Rock | 19.46 | | | |

# 137. Local Government Employment

While it is economically advantageous for a city to have a lot of federal aid or state employees located there, it is not necessarily a good thing to have a lot of local government employees, because they represent a burden on local taxpayers.

Total local government employment declined in all cities between 1980 and 1981. The average decline was 0.7 percent. However, full-time employment increased slightly (1.2 percent) in the largest cities during the same period. Part-time work forces have borne the brunt of reductions in all cities, with an average decline of 14.8 percent. This trend is expected to continue.

Local employees constitute the highest proportion of the labor force in New York, Riverside, Baltimore, San Antonio, San Diego and Buffalo, and the lowest in Seattle, Cleveland and San Jose.

SOURCES: U.S. Department of Commerce, Bureau of the Census, *1980 Census of Population and Housing: Supplementary Report: Provisional Estimates of Social, Economic and Housing Characteristics*, March 1982. Joint Economic Committee, *Trends in the Fiscal Condition of Cities: 1980–1982* (Washington, D.C.: Government Printing Office, 1982).

| Rank | Metro Area | Labor Force | Total Employees | Local Government Employees as a Percentage of Total Government Labor Force |
|---|---|---|---|---|
| 1 | New York | 4,619,579 | 431,941 | 10.36 |
| 2 | Riverside | 661,434 | 67,778 | 10.25 |
| 3 | Baltimore | 1,039,358 | 98,872 | 9.51 |

| Rank | Metro Area | Labor Force | Total Employees | Local Government Employees as a Percentage of Total Government Labor Force |
|---|---|---|---|---|
| 4 | San Antonio | 440,283 | 40,932 | 9.30 |
| 5 | San Diego | 811,185 | 72,934 | 8.99 |
| 6 | Buffalo | 568,092 | 50,424 | 8.88 |
| 7 | Boston | 1,376,461 | 122,100 | 8.87 |
| 8 | Newark | 950,206 | 82,859 | 8.72 |
| 9 | Sacramento | 476,779 | 40,194 | 8.43 |
| 10 | Milwaukee | 689,813 | 57,682 | 8.36 |
| 11 | San Francisco-Oakland | 1,682,948 | 137,777 | 8.19 |
| 12 | Washington, D.C. | 1,602,286 | 130,867 | 8.16 |
| 13 | Los Angeles-Long Beach | 3,488,192 | 283,323 | 8.12 |
| 14 | Philadelphia | 2,148,304 | 171,307 | 7.97 |
| 15 | Chicago | 3,428,148 | 269,798 | 7.87 |
| 16 | Tampa-St. Petersburg | 636,592 | 49,559 | 7.79 |
| 17 | Denver | 856,558 | 64,845 | 7.57 |
| 18 | Pittsburgh | 1,024,599 | 76,800 | 7.50 |
| 19 | Columbus, Ohio | 531,490 | 39,681 | 7.47 |
| 19 | Detroit | 1,980,028 | 147,986 | 7.47 |
| 21 | Cincinnati | 649,924 | 47,914 | 7.37 |
| 22 | Dallas-Fort Worth | 1,528,058 | 110,920 | 7.26 |
| 23 | Miami | 774,415 | 55,408 | 7.15 |
| 24 | Atlanta | 1,022,054 | 72,350 | 7.08 |
| 25 | New Orleans | 519,314 | 36,670 | 7.06 |
| 26 | Portland, Ore. | 626,648 | 44,065 | 7.03 |
| 27 | Minneapolis-St. Paul | 1,120,213 | 77,662 | 6.93 |
| 28 | St. Louis | 1,110,974 | 76,745 | 6.91 |
| 29 | Anaheim | 1,008,291 | 68,563 | 6.80 |
| 30 | Indianapolis | 575,288 | 39,034 | 6.79 |
| 31 | Houston | 1,492,307 | 100,652 | 6.74 |
| 32 | Phoenix | 707,244 | 47,336 | 6.69 |
| 33 | Kansas City, Kan., Mo. | 671,156 | 44,806 | 6.68 |
| 34 | Seattle | 838,696 | 48,361 | 5.77 |
| 35 | Cleveland | 912,264 | 27,911 | 3.06 |
| 36 | San Jose | 688,524 | 19,796 | 2.88 |

# 138. Property Tax Dependence

Property taxes represent an important part, about one-fourth, of homeowners' costs. In the early 1970s, property taxes rose by about 10 percent a year. The steady rise in taxes—in part reflecting increased assessments—was the result of the upward march in local government services (set in motion by the educational needs of the post-

war baby boom). The tax increases led in turn to California's Proposition 13 and subsequent tax revolts.

Property taxes have been attacked because they tend to be higher in poorer areas than in rich ones. However, the reason for this pattern is slowness to change assessments. Property assessments, should be raised more rapidly in growing areas and reduced more rapidly in declining areas. The trouble with this prescription is that increasing assessments are precisely the scenario that has fueled the tax revolts.

Overall, property taxes are the most important single source of city revenues. Limitations on that tax, such as Proposition 13 and Massachusetts's Proposition 2½, have had an immediate, visible impact on service delivery and education. However, local governments continue to rely on property taxes as their main source of revenue. All 165 of the largest cities responding to a survey by the Joint Economic Committee projected that the proportion of local revenues generated by property taxes would *increase* in 1982 over 1981.

Other tax forms, such as user fees and charges, sales tax and income tax usually account for a total less than property tax alone. The average for the 82 cities in the following table is that 56 percent of all revenues are derived from the property tax.

The cities most dependent on property taxes are Fort Wayne, Worcester, Providence, Boston, Warren and Madison. All are 97 percent or more dependent on property taxes for local revenue.

The cities with the least dependence on property taxes are Sacramento, Mobile, Columbus, Ohio, Montgomery and Toledo. In all cities under 15 percent of local revenues comes from this source.

Data on city revenues in Tables 138–144 rely on several sources. The unpublished data used in Tables 138, 140, 141, 143, and 144 are the most complete. They are from the 1977 Census of Governments which covered the cities' fiscal years ending between July 1, 1976 and June 30, 1977. Published data used in Tables 139 and 142 are less complete and more recent. Population figures used for per capita calculations are from the 1980 Census (see Table 30 above).

SOURCES: Unpublished data from the 1977 Census of Governments, specially commissioned for this book in 1982 from the Maxwell School, Syracuse University. Joint Economic Committee, *Trends in the Fiscal Condition of Cities: 1980–1982* (Washington, D.C.: Government Printing Office, 1982).

| Rank | City | Total Locally Generated Revenue per capita ($) | Property Tax per capita ($) | Property Tax as a Percentage of Locally Generated Revenue (%) |
|---|---|---|---|---|
| 1 | Fort Wayne | 106 | 106 | 99.89 |
| 2 | Worcester | 488 | 486 | 99.53 |
| 3 | Providence | 467 | 463 | 99.11 |
| 4 | Boston | 781 | 772 | 98.83 |
| 5 | Warren | 135 | 132 | 97.98 |
| 6 | Madison | 385 | 374 | 97.21 |
| 7 | Milwaukee | 142 | 136 | 95.65 |
| 8 | Indianapolis | 180 | 172 | 95.64 |
| 9 | Greensboro | 151 | 145 | 95.62 |
| 10 | Charlotte | 177 | 166 | 93.76 |
| 11 | Rochester | 388 | 363 | 93.66 |
| 12 | Anchorage | 459 | 430 | 93.54 |
| 13 | Kansas City, Kan. | 145 | 132 | 90.86 |
| 14 | Buffalo | 276 | 246 | 89.04 |
| 15 | Des Moines | 173 | 154 | 88.89 |
| 16 | Jackson | 119 | 106 | 88.88 |
| 17 | Minneapolis | 203 | 168 | 82.88 |
| 18 | Knoxville | 159 | 129 | 81.43 |
| 19 | Honolulu | 495 | 397 | 80.27 |
| 20 | Wichita | 149 | 118 | 79.53 |
| 21 | Jersey City | 350 | 259 | 73.94 |
| 22 | Memphis | 158 | 112 | 71.28 |
| 23 | Yonkers | 540 | 373 | 69.04 |
| 24 | Jacksonville | 153 | 104 | 67.67 |
| 25 | St. Paul | 166 | 111 | 66.46 |
| 26 | Newark | 320 | 211 | 65.87 |
| 27 | Miami | 244 | 161 | 65.72 |
| 28 | Syracuse | 318 | 205 | 64.59 |
| 29 | Baltimore | 424 | 270 | 63.64 |
| 30 | Lubbock | 134 | 81 | 60.74 |
| 31 | Philadelphia | 189 | 114 | 60.67 |
| 32 | Austin | 158 | 96 | 60.57 |
| 33 | Nashville | 382 | 231 | 60.38 |
| 34 | Corpus Christi | 134 | 80 | 59.81 |
| 35 | Atlanta | 251 | 149 | 59.27 |
| 36 | Fort Worth | 170 | 99 | 58.08 |
| 37 | Richmond | 556 | 321 | 57.73 |
| 38 | Houston | 221 | 127 | 57.57 |
| 39 | Albuquerque | 122 | 70 | 57.32 |
| 40 | Dallas | 239 | 136 | 56.84 |
| 40 | Pittsburgh | 273 | 155 | 56.84 |
| 42 | Virginia Beach | 304 | 172 | 56.70 |
| 43 | El Paso | 103 | 58 | 56.34 |
| 44 | Lincoln | 153 | 86 | 56.22 |
| 45 | San Antonio | 99 | 55 | 55.51 |
| 46 | Las Vegas | 139 | 73 | 52.54 |
| 47 | San Francisco | 508 | 260 | 51.08 |
| 48 | Arlington | 133 | 66 | 49.78 |
| 49 | St. Petersburg | 123 | 61 | 49.49 |
| 50 | Norfolk | 358 | 176 | 49.30 |
| 51 | Detroit | 300 | 147 | 48.89 |
| 52 | New York | 948 | 456 | 48.13 |
| 53 | Tampa | 187 | 88 | 46.87 |
| 54 | Omaha | 218 | 102 | 46.71 |
| 55 | Shreveport | 155 | 66 | 42.86 |
| 56 | Chicago | 245 | 105 | 42.83 |
| 57 | Little Rock | 97 | 40 | 41.48 |
| 58 | Grand Rapids | 136 | 56 | 41.17 |
| 59 | Flint | 180 | 72 | 39.85 |
| 60 | Los Angeles | 227 | 80 | 35.45 |
| 61 | Columbus, Ga. | 174 | 65 | 35.22 |
| 62 | Oakland | 216 | 75 | 34.63 |
| 63 | Denver | 378 | 130 | 34.44 |
| 64 | Seattle | 247 | 84 | 34.10 |
| 65 | Huntington Beach | 164 | 54 | 33.04 |
| 66 | Salt Lake City | 254 | 84 | 33.01 |
| 67 | San Diego | 134 | 44 | 32.72 |

| Rank | City | Total Locally Generated Revenue per capita ($) | Property Tax per capita ($) | Property Tax as a Percentage of Locally Generated Revenue (%) | Rank | City | Total Locally Generated Revenue per capita ($) | Property Tax per capita ($) | Property Tax as a Percentage of Locally Generated Revenue (%) |
|---|---|---|---|---|---|---|---|---|---|
| 68 | Phoenix | 153 | 49 | 32.34 | 85 | Washington, D.C. | 1,476 | 344 | 23.32 |
| 69 | Fresno | 186 | 60 | 31.94 | 86 | Akron | 198 | 45 | 22.60 |
| 70 | Cleveland | 243 | 76 | 31.48 | 87 | Cincinnati | 315 | 69 | 22.00 |
| 71 | Long Beach | 170 | 53 | 31.34 | 88 | Birmingham | 247 | 52 | 20.97 |
| 72 | Chattanooga | 45 | 14 | 31.03 | 89 | Aurora | 209 | 43 | 20.79 |
| 73 | Spokane | 134 | 41 | 30.70 | 90 | Portland, Ore. | 77 | 16 | 20.28 |
| 74 | New Orleans | 250 | 76 | 30.36 | 91 | Dayton | 280 | 52 | 18.45 |
| 75 | Louisville | 236 | 70 | 29.88 | 92 | St. Louis | 433 | 76 | 17.45 |
| 76 | Santa Ana | 149 | 44 | 29.47 | 93 | Kansas City, Mo. | 371 | 58 | 15.75 |
| 77 | Lexington | 235 | 67 | 28.45 | 94 | Tucson | 182 | 28 | 15.24 |
| 78 | Oklahoma City | 218 | 60 | 27.63 | 95 | Tulsa | 180 | 27 | 15.04 |
| 79 | Anaheim | 65 | 37 | 27.45 | 96 | Toeldo | 173 | 24 | 14.18 |
| 80 | San Jose | 167 | 44 | 26.19 | 97 | Montgomery | 156 | 22 | 14.09 |
| 81 | Tacoma | 213 | 56 | 26.10 | 98 | Columbus, Ohio | 164 | 18 | 11.10 |
| 82 | Baton Rouge | 339 | 87 | 25.66 | 99 | Mobile | 175 | 15 | 8.52 |
| 83 | Riverside | 135 | 33 | 24.30 | 100 | Sacramento | 138 | 6 | 4.56 |
| 84 | Colorado Springs | 146 | 35 | 24.22 | | | | | |

# 139.  Change in Property Taxes

In early June 1978 Californians voted on a proposal to put a ceiling on property taxes of 1 percent of assessed value, with a maximum 2 percent increase in assessed value annually thereafter. Since property taxes were running at about 3 percent of assessed value, this represented a 67 percent cut in taxes.

This proposition was opposed by every major interest group in the state, from the municipal unions to then-Governor Jerry Brown and the business community. However, it passed. Economist Paul Samuelson described the passage as the major politicoeconomic event of the decade.

Observers hailed the awakening of citizens' conscience. *Time* magazine put Howard Jarvis, the realtor who was given the most credit for the initiative, on its cover. Readers flooded the magazine with letters of support for tax reduction. Popular papers like the *National Enquirer* urged their readers to clip, sign and send a printed letter demanding that their elected officials support tax cut propositions. Movements began in other states. A national tax cut bill, the Kemp-Roth bill, was introduced in Washington.

Even Governor Brown, faced with the massive problem of supporting local services in California with state funds, decided that he, too, was in favor of Proposition 13. "The voter has spoken," was his response. Some

$5 billion of surplus state funds were put at the disposal of localities to cushion the impact of Proposition 13.

So popular was Proposition 13 immediately after its passage (except among municipal employee unions), that a national magazine parodied the situation with a cartoon strip showing Congressmen cheering, "I will support Proposition 13"; business cheering, "I support Proposition 13"; and Jimmy Carter shouting: "Ah support Proposition 13." A meek citizen asks the obvious question: "Whose revolution is this, anyway?"

Proposition 2½ won passage in Massachusetts, and similar initiatives took root in other states. By reducing property tax rates in these states, pressure for providing revenues fell heavily on the states. If the revenue shortfall was made up by the state, it tended to create more centralized government and erode the state's fiscal position. By the end of 1982 a majority of states were facing fiscal difficulties of one form or another.

Arlington, Texas shows the most rapid increase in property taxes. They grew over eightfold between 1977 and 1980. Eleven other cities show an increase of one-third or more.

These cities are an exception. More indicative of the overall trend during the period, which included the Proposition 13 rebellion, is the fact that 24 cities *reduced* their property taxes. Another 22 cities held their increase to 10 percent or less between 1977 or 1980, during a period when inflation soared well above that.

SOURCES: Unpublished data from the 1977 Census of Government especially commissioned for this book in 1982 from the Maxwell School, Syracuse University and *City Government Finances in 1979–80* (Washington, D.C.: Government Printing Office, September 1981).

| Rank | City | Property Tax 1977-78 ($ 000) | Property Tax 1979-80 ($ 000) | Absolute Change ($ 000) | Percentage Change |
|---|---|---|---|---|---|
| 1 | Arlington, Texas | 6,771 | 63,232 | 56,461 | 833.87 |
| 2 | Pittsburgh | 41,626 | 65,789 | 24,163 | 58.05 |
| 3 | Miami | 38,033 | 55,672 | 17,639 | 46.38 |
| 4 | Aurora | 4,738 | 6,897 | 2,159 | 45.57 |
| 5 | Las Vegas | 8,644 | 12,053 | 3,409 | 39.44 |
| 6 | Tampa | 17,160 | 23,820 | 6,660 | 38.81 |
| 7 | Toledo | 6,373 | 8,664 | 2,291 | 35.95 |
| 8 | Salt Lake City | 10,066 | 13,668 | 3,602 | 35.78 |
| 9 | Jacksonville | 41,330 | 56,027 | 14,697 | 35.56 |
| 10 | New Orleans | 31,209 | 42,236 | 11,027 | 35.33 |
| 11 | Houston | 151,028 | 202,982 | 51,954 | 34.40 |
| 12 | Birmingham | 11,039 | 14,752 | 3,713 | 33.64 |
| 13 | Washington, D.C. | 165,824 | 219,395 | 53,571 | 32.31 |
| 14 | Austin | 25,410 | 33,026 | 7,616 | 29.97 |
| 15 | Wichita | 25,451 | 33,071 | 7,620 | 29.94 |
| 16 | Charlotte | 40,252 | 52,117 | 11,865 | 29.48 |
| 17 | Albuquerque | 17,860 | 23,123 | 5,263 | 29.47 |
| 18 | Honolulu | 114,326 | 145,003 | 30.677 | 26.83 |
| 19 | Fort Wayne | 14,541 | 18,314 | 3,773 | 25.95 |
| 20 | Jackson | 17,085 | 21,515 | 4,430 | 25.93 |
| 21 | Knoxville | 18,816 | 23,681 | 4,865 | 25.86 |
| 22 | Providence | 57,697 | 72,604 | 14,907 | 25.84 |
| 23 | Portland, Ore. | 45,786 | 57,120 | 11,334 | 24.75 |
| 24 | Des Moines | 23,650 | 29,447 | 5,797 | 24.51 |
| 25 | Mobile | 2,407 | 2,994 | 587 | 24.39 |
| 26 | Colorado Springs | 6,178 | 7,607 | 1,429 | 23.13 |
| 27 | Grand Rapids | 8,354 | 10,177 | 1,823 | 21.82 |
| 28 | Columbus, Ohio | 8,501 | 10,291 | 1,790 | 21.06 |
| 29 | Fort Worth | 31,527 | 38,086 | 6,559 | 20.80 |
| 30 | Tacoma | 7,292 | 8,807 | 1,515 | 20.78 |
| 31 | Norfolk | 38,190 | 46,122 | 7,932 | 20.77 |
| 32 | Riverside | 4,672 | 5,611 | 939 | 20.10 |
| 33 | Lubbock | 11,892 | 14,167 | 2,275 | 19.13 |
| 34 | Phoenix | 32,827 | 39,059 | 6,232 | 18.98 |
| 35 | Montgomery | 3,319 | 3,911 | 592 | 17.84 |
| 36 | Flint | 9,733 | 11,421 | 1,688 | 17.34 |
| 37 | Anchorage | 63,526 | 74,337 | 10,811 | 17.02 |
| 38 | Greensboro | 19,266 | 22.535 | 3,269 | 16.97 |
| 39 | Lexington-Fayette | 11,722 | 13,644 | 1,922 | 16.40 |
| 40 | Madison | 54,882 | 63,879 | 8,997 | 16.39 |
| 41 | Shreveport | 11,850 | 13,666 | 1,816 | 15.32 |
| 42 | El Paso | 21,494 | 24,782 | 3,288 | 15.30 |
| 42 | Nashville-Davidson | 91,168 | 105,119 | 13,951 | 15.30 |
| 44 | Corpus Christi | 16,202 | 18,623 | 2,421 | 14.94 |
| 44 | Denver | 55,618 | 63,926 | 8,308 | 14.94 |
| 46 | St. Petersburg | 12,623 | 14,439 | 1,816 | 14.39 |
| 47 | Akron | 9,143 | 10,397 | 1,254 | 13.72 |
| 48 | Baton Rouge | 16,823 | 19,075 | 2,252 | 13.39 |
| 49 | Yonkers | 64,246 | 72,833 | 8,587 | 13.37 |
| 50 | San Antonio | 38,068 | 43,082 | 5,014 | 13.17 |
| 51 | St. Paul | 26,833 | 29,897 | 3,064 | 11.42 |
| 52 | Chattanooga | 21,160 | 23,550 | 2,390 | 11.29 |
| 53 | Cleveland | 39,520 | 43,867 | 4,347 | 10.00 |
| 54 | Philadelphia | 174,420 | 193,466 | 19,046 | 10.92 |
| 55 | Richmond | 63,472 | 70,350 | 6,878 | 10.84 |
| 56 | Warren | 19,383 | 21,292 | 1,909 | 9.85 |
| 57 | Little Rock | 5,847 | 6,405 | 558 | 9.54 |
| 58 | Atlanta | 57,747 | 63,232 | 5,485 | 9.50 |
| 59 | Memphis | 66,627 | 72,751 | 6,124 | 9.19 |
| 60 | Lincoln | 13,593 | 14,831 | 1,238 | 9.11 |
| 61 | Oklahoma City | 22,318 | 24,306 | 1,988 | 8.91 |
| 62 | Milwaukee | 79,773 | 86,304 | 6,531 | 8.19 |
| 63 | Omaha | 29,347 | 31,727 | 2,380 | 8.11 |
| 64 | Dayton | 9,779 | 10.514 | 735 | 7.52 |
| 65 | Worcester | 73,169 | 78,587 | 5,418 | 7.40 |
| 66 | Syracuse | 32,614 | 34,896 | 2,282 | 6.00 |
| 67 | Minneapolis | 58,335 | 62,336 | 4,001 | 6.86 |
| 68 | Dallas | 115,266 | 122,733 | 7,467 | 6.48 |
| 69 | Kansas City, Mo. | 24,600 | 26,169 | 1,569 | 6.38 |
| 70 | Baltimore | 199,531 | 212,230 | 12,699 | 6.36 |
| 71 | Seattle | 39,529 | 41,676 | 2,147 | 5.43 |
| 72 | Detroit | 167,545 | 176,469 | 8,924 | 5.33 |
| 73 | Rochester | 83,423 | 87,782 | 4,359 | 5.23 |
| 74 | Boston | 433,348 | 434,762 | 1,414 | .33 |
| 75 | St. Louis | 34,666 | 34,238 | − 428 | − 1.23 |
| 76 | New York | 3,270,500 | 3,228,047 | − 42,453 | − 1.30 |
| 77 | Chicago | 319,623 | 315,344 | − 4,279 | − 1.34 |
| 78 | Tucson | 9,372 | 9,188 | − 184 | − 1.96 |
| 79 | Kansas City, Kan. | 22,089 | 21,251 | − 838 | − 3.79 |
| 80 | Cincinnati | 27,771 | 26,703 | − 1,068 | − 3.85 |
| 81 | Columbus, Ga. | 11,788 | 10,942 | − 846 | − 7.18 |
| 82 | Buffalo | 95,427 | 88,061 | − 7,366 | − 7.72 |
| 83 | Fresno | 14,422 | 12,989 | − 1,433 | − 9.94 |
| 84 | Huntington Beach | 10,550 | 9,231 | − 1,319 | −12.50 |
| 85 | Jersey City | 66,685 | 57,870 | − 8,815 | −13.22 |
| 86 | Santa Ana | 10,472 | 8,903 | − 1,542 | −14.72 |
| 87 | Tulsa | 11,577 | 9,751 | − 1,826 | −15.77 |
| 88 | San Jose | 33,021 | 27,770 | − 5,251 | −15.90 |
| 89 | San Diego | 47,488 | 38,254 | − 9,234 | −19.44 |
| 90 | Spokane | 8,823 | 7,064 | − 1,759 | −19.94 |
| 91 | Los Angeles | 299,289 | 239,057 | − 60,232 | −20.13 |
| 92 | Sacramento | 22,376 | 17,359 | − 5,017 | −22.42 |
| 93 | San Francisco | 242,043 | 176,308 | − 65,735 | −27.16 |
| 94 | Newark | 99,766 | 69,419 | − 30,347 | −30.42 |
| 95 | Oakland | 38,561 | 25,439 | − 13,122 | −34.03 |
| 96 | Long Beach | 30,074 | 19,222 | − 10,852 | −36.08 |
| 97 | Anaheim | 13,257 | 8,244 | − 5,013 | −37.81 |
| 98 | Indianapolis | 989,039 | 120,347 | −868,692 | −87.83 |

# 140.  Sales Taxes

General sales and user taxes are advantageous for cities that have a high tourist trade and large retail businesses. They are regressive in that they are borne equally by rich and poor. The usual response to this concern is to exempt food and clothing and to impose the sales taxes on items that are considered of a luxury nature, such as restaurant meals. The trend is toward using sales taxes, because the tax is collected for the city by businesses and is therefore viewed as administratively efficient and politically neutral by city officials.

The figures provided below for 1976 do not include state sales taxes, which are in effect in 46 of the 50 states. In New York City, for example, the 4 percent tax is in addition to a 4 percent state tax, making it, along with Yonkers, the highest of all the cities. Some states have higher sales taxes than New York, however: Connecticut tops the list with 7.5 percent, followed by Pennsylvania and Rhode Island with 6 percent, Kentucky, Maine, Maryland and Massachusetts with 5 percent, and California with 4.75 percent. In states with high state sales taxes, the ability of localities to impose sales taxes is preempted.

In the figures below, the three Louisiana cities' rates include the parish school board tax. The California, Illinois, New York and Washington state cities' rates include county taxes. In California city taxes are credited against county taxes. The San Francisco and Oakland rates include a 0.5 percent Bay Area Rapid Transit (BART) tax. The local tax for cities in Georgia, Nevada, North Carolina, Ohio and Utah is entirely county-originated.

SOURCES: Unpublished data from the 1977 Census of Governments, especially commissioned for this book in 1982 from the Maxwell School, Syracuse University. Tax Foundation, *Facts and Figures on Government Finance*, (1981 report based on Commerce Clearing House data).

| Rank | City | Sales Taxes ($ 000) | Sales Taxes Per Capita ($) |
|---|---|---|---|
| 1 | Baton Rouge | 47,491 | 216.36 |
| 2 | Denver | 86,199 | 175.42 |
| 3 | New York | 1,143,383 | 161.70 |
| 4 | Aurora | 22,481 | 141.75 |
| 5 | Yonkers | 26,682 | 136.62 |
| 6 | Oklahoma City | 53,918 | 133.73 |
| 7 | Tulsa | 47,150 | 130.61 |
| 8 | Tucson | 42,930 | 129.89 |
| 9 | Colorado Springs | 21,261 | 98.80 |
| 10 | Nashville | 44,082 | 96.76 |
| 11 | Mobile | 19,246 | 96.04 |
| 12 | Omaha | 28,661 | 91.98 |
| 13 | Salt Lake City | 14,643 | 89.83 |
| 14 | St. Louis | 37,345 | 82.44 |
| 15 | Montgomery | 14,641 | 82.21 |
| 16 | Fresno | 17,305 | 79.31 |
| 17 | Anaheim | 15,001 | 77.11 |
| 18 | Santa Ana | 15,137 | 74.31 |
| 19 | San Francisco | 49,922 | 73.52 |
| 20 | Sacramento | 19,217 | 69.70 |
| 21 | Phoenix | 54,528 | 69.22 |
| 22 | Kansas City, Mo. | 30,138 | 67.24 |
| 23 | Shreveport | 13,221 | 64.24 |
| 24 | Riverside | 10,781 | 61.19 |
| 25 | Houston | 97,297 | 61.04 |
| 26 | Dallas | 54,438 | 60.22 |
| 27 | Richmond | 12,912 | 58.91 |
| 28 | Los Angeles | 171,062 | 57.66 |
| 29 | San Diego | 48,384 | 55.26 |
| 30 | Oakland | 19,075 | 56.36 |
| 31 | Birmingham | 15,168 | 53.33 |
| 32 | Lincoln | 8,605 | 50.03 |
| 33 | San Jose | 31,523 | 49.53 |
| 34 | Huntington Beach | 8,221 | 48.22 |
| 35 | Fort Worth | 18,466 | 47.94 |
| 36 | Long Beach | 17,313 | 47.92 |
| 37 | Lubbock | 8,161 | 46.90 |
| 38 | Seattle | 22,573 | 45.71 |
| 39 | Norfolk | 12,123 | 45.40 |
| 40 | Austin | 15,228 | 44.08 |
| 41 | Arlington, Texas | 6,770 | 42.29 |
| 42 | Corpus Christi | 9,219 | 39.74 |
| 43 | Chicago | 111,104 | 36.97 |
| 44 | Spokane | 5,884 | 34.35 |
| 45 | Tacoma | 5,426 | 34.23 |
| 46 | Virginia Beach | 8,777 | 33.47 |
| 47 | San Antonio | 26,244 | 33.41 |
| 48 | El Paso | 11,892 | 27.96 |
| 49 | Albuquerque | 7,450 | 22.45 |

# 141.  Sales Tax Dependence

Sales taxes are attractive to cities looking for revenue in that they are collected in small amounts that add up because they apply to a large number of transactions.

Their drawback is that they are a nuisance for consumers and merchants and put the city at a competitive disadvantage for retail sales vis-a-vis neighboring areas that do not impose a sales tax. They also have a more significant impact on the poor because they are not progressive.

Does a sales tax really hurt retail sales? To consider this question we need to know how high sales taxes are. The table below, using information from the 1977 Census of Governments, the latest available, is one approach to an answer. It shows how dependent the local government is on the sales tax. For each city it shows the ratio of sales tax revenues to all locally generated revenues.

Tulsa leads, with nearly 73 percent. That is, nearly three-fourths of its local revenues are derived from sales taxes. Tucson, Aurora and Colorado Springs also have figures of over two-thirds of all local tax revenues. In none of these cities is there strong regional competition for retail trade. Shoppers have little choice but to shop in the city.

New York City, widely believed to have the broadest range of taxes in the nation, doesn't raise nearly as much from its sales tax, relative to other sources, as the just-cited top four. Its comparatively low 17 percent figure reflects competition from neighboring Connecticut and New Jersey which have lower sales taxes (7.5 percent and 5.0 percent, respectively).

Of cities with sales taxes, Richmond has the lowest sales tax relative to other local taxes. It generates 10.6 percent of its income from this source, perhaps reflecting competition from a broad variety of suburban areas. Nearly half the 100 cities (48) as of the survey had no sales taxes at all.

SOURCE: Unpublished data from the 1977 Census of Governments, especially commissioned for this book in 1982 from the Maxwell School, Syracuse University.

| Rank | City | Total Locally Generated Revenues ($ 000) | General Sales Tax Revenue ($ 000) | Percentage of General Sales Tax to Total Local Generated Revenues |
|------|------|------|------|------|
| 1 | Tulsa | 64,854 | 47,150 | 72.70 |
| 2 | Tucson | 60,300 | 42,930 | 71.19 |

| Rank | City | Total Locally Generated Revenues ($ 000) | General Sales Tax Revenue ($ 000) | Percentage of General Sales Tax to Total Local Generated Revenues |
|------|------|------|------|------|
| 3 | Aurora | 33,150 | 22,481 | 67.82 |
| 4 | Colorado Springs | 31,402 | 21,261 | 67.71 |
| 5 | Baton Rouge | 74,329 | 47,491 | 63.89 |
| 6 | Oklahoma City | 87,977 | 53,918 | 61.29 |
| 7 | Mobile | 35,148 | 19,246 | 54.76 |
| 8 | Montgomery | 27,748 | 14,641 | 52.76 |
| 9 | Sacramento | 38,118 | 19,217 | 50.41 |
| 10 | Anaheim | 30,033 | 15,001 | 49.95 |
| 11 | Santa Ana | 30,307 | 15,137 | 49.95 |
| 12 | Riverside | 23,187 | 10,781 | 46.50 |
| 13 | Denver | 185,614 | 86,199 | 46.44 |
| 14 | Phoenix | 120,789 | 54,528 | 45.14 |
| 15 | Fresno | 40,665 | 17,305 | 42.56 |
| 16 | Omaha | 67,918 | 28,661 | 42.20 |
| 17 | New Orleans | 139,117 | 57,741 | 41.51 |
| 18 | Shreveport | 31,888 | 13,221 | 41.46 |
| 19 | San Diego | 116,925 | 48,384 | 41.38 |
| 20 | Salt Lake City | 41,404 | 14,643 | 35.37 |
| 21 | San Antonio | 77,606 | 26,244 | 33.82 |
| 22 | Lincoln | 26,379 | 8,605 | 32.62 |
| 23 | Lubbock | 25,377 | 8,161 | 32.16 |
| 24 | Arlington, Texas | 21,342 | 6,770 | 31.72 |
| 25 | Columbus, Ga. | 31,064 | 9,509 | 30.61 |
| 26 | San Jose | 106,026 | 31,523 | 29.73 |
| 27 | Corpus Christi | 31,139 | 9,219 | 29.61 |
| 28 | Huntington Beach | 27,943 | 8,221 | 29.42 |
| 29 | Long Beach | 61,334 | 17,313 | 28.23 |
| 30 | Fort Worth | 65,572 | 18,466 | 28.16 |
| 31 | Austin | 54,522 | 15,228 | 27.93 |
| 32 | Houston | 352,532 | 97,297 | 27.60 |
| 33 | El Paso | 43,989 | 11,892 | 27.03 |
| 34 | Oakland | 73,463 | 19,075 | 25.97 |
| 35 | Spokane | 23,012 | 5,884 | 25.57 |
| 36 | Los Angeles | 674,300 | 171,062 | 25.37 |
| 37 | Nashville | 174,085 | 44,082 | 25.32 |
| 38 | Yonkers | 105,490 | 26,682 | 25.29 |
| 39 | Dallas | 215,942 | 54,438 | 25.21 |
| 40 | Birmingham | 70,370 | 15,168 | 21.55 |
| 41 | Washington, D.C. | 940,868 | 194,018 | 20.62 |
| 42 | St. Louis | 196,171 | 37,345 | 19.04 |
| 43 | Seattle | 122,208 | 22,573 | 18.47 |
| 44 | Albuquerque | 40,357 | 7,450 | 18.46 |
| 45 | Kansas City, Mo. | 166,110 | 30,138 | 18.14 |
| 46 | New York | 6,706,898 | 1,143,383 | 17.05 |
| 47 | Tacoma | 33,743 | 5,426 | 16.08 |
| 48 | Chicago | 736,241 | 111,104 | 15.09 |
| 49 | San Francisco | 345,150 | 49,922 | 14.46 |
| 50 | Norfolk | 94,574 | 12,123 | 12.82 |
| 51 | Virginia Beach | 79,650 | 8,777 | 11.02 |
| 52 | Richmond | 121,853 | 12,912 | 10.60 |

# 142.  City Income Taxes

The concept of income taxes was pioneered as a wartime measure by the United States during World War I. It originally was a flat tax. Pleased with the revenue from the tax, the federal government made the income tax a permanent fixture of American life.

Once made acceptable by the federal government,

taxes were instituted by many states. Only 7 states now have no income tax: Alaska, Florida, Nevada, South Dakota, Texas, Washington and Wyoming. Cities were not long in following the lead of higher levels of government. Philadelphia was the first, instituting an income tax in 1939. Toledo was next in 1946. Columbus, Ohio and Washington, D.C. imposed the tax a year later. Half a dozen more cities followed suit in 1948.

The city income taxes are flat rates on income in every city except two—New York and Washington, which have progressive taxes, i.e., tax rates that increase with income. Washington had the highest per capita tax in fiscal 1979, $449. This is easily explained by the absence of state competition for taxes on its residents. Philadelphia, the city income tax pioneer, had the second highest per capita taxes, $270. Of the cities with income taxes, Pittsburgh had the lowest rate, $42.

SOURCES: Tax rates and 1979 per capita taxes for major cities from Commerce Clearing House, as published in Tax Foundation, *Facts and Figures on Government Finance* (1981). Other data from U.S. Department of Commerce, Bureau of the Census, *City Government Fin-*

*ances in 1978–79* (Washington, D.C.: Government Printing Office, September 1980). Fiscal 1979 city income taxes are divided by 1980 population.

| Rank | City | Percentage of Income | Per Capita ($) |
|---|---|---|---|
| 1 | Washington, D.C. | 2.00–11.00* | 449.20 |
| 2 | Philadelphia | 4.31 | 270.15 |
| 3 | Dayton | 1.75 | 200.87 |
| 4 | Cincinnati | 2.00 | 194.94 |
| 5 | New York | 4.30–9.00* | 192.63 |
| 6 | Columbus, Ohio | 1.50 | 133.30 |
| 7 | Lexington-Fayette | 2.00 | 129.88 |
| 8 | Louisville | 2.20** | 127.55 |
| 9 | Akron | 1.80 | 126.83 |
| 10 | Flint | 1.00 | 122.18 |
| 11 | Toledo | 1.50 | 116.11 |
| 12 | Detroit | 2.00 | 109.87 |
| 13 | Cleveland | 2.00 | 109.60 |
| 14 | Kansas City, Mo. | 1.00 | 107.14 |
| 15 | St. Louis | 1.00 | 101.94 |
| 16 | Baltimore | 50.00*** | 71.61 |
| 17 | Grand Rapids | 1.00 | 71.60 |
| 18 | Birmingham | 1.00 | 66.26 |
| 19 | Pittsburgh | 2.25 | 42.40 |

*Progressive (graduated) tax on residents.
**Includes county and school rates.
***Percentage of state tax.

# 143. Other Selective Sales/Gross Taxes

As city officials exhaust their capacity to tax individuals directly based on property, income or sales, they have looked to other forms of taxes that are collected from businesses based on their sales and revenues. An example would be a tax on the net revenues of a resort area located within city limits. The tax might be agreed upon at the time the city gives permission to the developer to build the resort.

The importance of the table below is as a baseline against which to evaluate future tax collection trends.

In fiscal 1977, the latest year for which such detailed information is available, these other taxes didn't amount to a great deal, i.e., under 9 percent of all locally sourced revenues, except in Anaheim, where nearly 14 percent of its local income came from selected sales and gross taxes. Anaheim probably raised the bulk of this money from taxes on Disneyland revenues.

SOURCE: Unpublished data from the 1977 Census of Governments, specially commissioned for this book in 1982 from the Maxwell School, Syracuse University.

| Rank | City | Other Sales/Gross Taxes ($ 000) | Percentage of Locally Generated Revenues |
|---|---|---|---|
| 1 | Anaheim | 4,193 | 13.96 |
| 2 | San Diego | 10,502 | 8.98 |
| 3 | Newark | 9,329 | 8.85 |
| 4 | Atlanta | 8,371 | 7.85 |
| 5 | Pittsburgh | 8,911 | 7.70 |
| 6 | Virginia Beach | 6,054 | 7.60 |
| 7 | San Francisco | 24,037 | 6.96 |
| 8 | Phoenix | 7,585 | 6.28 |
| 9 | Sacramento | 2,268 | 5.95 |
| 10 | Little Rock | 912 | 5.91 |
| 11 | Norfolk | 5,177 | 5.47 |
| 11 | New Orleans | 7,606 | 5.47 |
| 13 | Washington, D.C. | 50,540 | 5.37 |
| 14 | Columbus, Ga. | 1,660 | 5.34 |
| 15 | Lexington | 2,555 | 5.33 |
| 16 | Louisville | 3,479 | 4.94 |
| 17 | Yonkers | 4,585 | 4.35 |
| 18 | Spokane | 952 | 4.14 |
| 19 | New York | 273,954 | 4.08 |
| 20 | Chicago | 27,315 | 3.71 |
| 21 | Seattle | 4,434 | 3.63 |
| 22 | Tacoma | 1,162 | 3.44 |
| 23 | Mobile | 1,202 | 3.42 |
| 24 | Los Angeles | 17,396 | 3.34 |
| 25 | Fresno | 1,336 | 3.29 |

| Rank | City | Other Sales/Gross Taxes ($ 000) | Percentage of Locally Generated Revenues |
|---|---|---|---|
| 26 | Denver | 6,025 | 3.25 |
| 27 | Chattanooga | 930 | 3.23 |
| 28 | Las Vegas | 738 | 3.22 |
| 29 | Minneapolis | 2,194 | 2.92 |
| 30 | San Antonio | 2,256 | 2.91 |
| 31 | Albuquerque | 1,067 | 2.64 |
| 32 | Portland, Ore. | 2,087 | 2.62 |
| 33 | Baltimore | 8,595 | 2.58 |
| 34 | Miami | 2,170 | 2.56 |
| 35 | Arlington, Texas | 530 | 2.48 |
| 36 | Dallas | 5,120 | 2.37 |
| 37 | Des Moines | 782 | 2.36 |
| 38 | Tucson | 1,371 | 2.27 |
| 39 | Austin | 1,222 | 2.24 |
| 40 | Corpus Christi | 685 | 2.20 |
| 41 | Oakland | 1,549 | 2.11 |
| 42 | El Paso | 922 | 2.10 |
| 42 | Tampa | 1,066 | 2.10 |
| 44 | Houston | 7,228 | 2.05 |
| 44 | Indianapolis | 2,581 | 2.05 |
| 46 | St. Louis | 3,962 | 2.02 |
| 46 | St. Petersburg | 589 | 2.02 |
| 48 | Long Beach | 1,191 | 1.94 |
| 49 | Colorado Springs | 540 | 1.72 |
| 50 | Knoxville | 498 | 1.71 |

| Rank | City | Other Sales/Gross Taxes ($ 000) | Percentage of Locally Generated Revenues |
|---|---|---|---|
| 51 | Lubbock | 416 | 1.64 |
| 52 | Richmond | 1,796 | 1.47 |
| 52 | Santa Ana | 445 | 1.47 |
| 54 | Tulsa | 934 | 1.44 |
| 55 | Milwaukee | 1,233 | 1.37 |
| 56 | Madison | 887 | 1.35 |
| 57 | Columbus, Ohio | 1,234 | 1.33 |
| 58 | Jacksonville | 1,077 | 1.30 |
| 59 | San Jose | 1,334 | 1.26 |
| 60 | Nashville | 2,145 | 1.23 |
| 61 | Cincinnati | 1,411 | 1.16 |
| 62 | Riverside | 246 | 1.06 |
| 63 | Memphis | 1,070 | 1.05 |
| 64 | Cleveland | 1,413 | 1.01 |
| 65 | Wichita | 409 | .98 |
| 66 | Oklahoma City | 774 | .88 |
| 67 | Fort Worth | 553 | .84 |
| 68 | St. Paul | 344 | .76 |
| 69 | Toledo | 378 | .62 |
| 70 | Birmingham | 346 | .49 |
| 71 | Philadelphia | 3,515 | .45 |
| 72 | Dayton | 240 | .42 |
| 73 | Buffalo | 314 | .32 |
| 74 | Akron | 109 | .24 |

# 144. Other City Taxes

While 1980 published data do not provide details beyond the broad categories of property taxes, sales taxes, income taxes and other taxes, it is possible to obtain some perspective on the importance of other city taxes by looking at fiscal 1977 data.

The unpublished data show that a major portion of "other taxes" were public utilities taxes. They were highest in Tampa, where they represented 43.8 percent of local taxes or nearly one-half of the 7.2 percent of all other city taxes. They were 42 percent of such taxes in St. Petersburg, 28 percent in Tacoma, 27.7 percent in St. Paul and 27.4 percent in Salt Lake City. Cities in the following states obtain no revenue from public utilities taxes: Alabama (except Birmingham 8.6 percent), Rhode Island, Massachusetts, Tennessee (except Memphis, nearly 6 percent), Michigan, Ohio, Indiana, Pennsylvania, North Carolina and Wisconsin. In New York state only Yonkers fails to generate income from taxation of public utilities.

SOURCE: Unpublished data from the 1977 Census of Governments, especially commissioned for this book in 1982 from the Maxwell School, Syracuse University.

| Rank | City | Other Taxes ($ 000) | Percentage of Locally Generated Revenues |
|---|---|---|---|
| 1 | Los Angeles | 139,781 | 26.86 |
| 2 | Tacoma | 8,904 | 26.39 |
| 3 | San Jose | 27,417 | 25.86 |
| 4 | Las Vegas | 5,770 | 25.15 |
| 5 | Mobile | 8,605 | 24.48 |
| 6 | Sacramento | 8,984 | 23.57 |
| 7 | Montgomery | 6,434 | 23.19 |
| 8 | Seattle | 27,212 | 22.27 |
| 9 | Little Rock | 3,350 | 21.69 |
| 10 | Oakland | 15,844 | 21.57 |
| 11 | San Francisco | 72,344 | 20.96 |
| 12 | Huntington Beach | 5,595 | 20.02 |
| 13 | Birmingham | 13,268 | 18.85 |
| 14 | Pittsburgh | 17,394 | 15.03 |
| 15 | Long Beach | 9,112 | 14.86 |
| 16 | Portland, Ore. | 11,814 | 14.85 |
| 17 | Anaheim | 2,307 | 13.95 |
| 18 | Spokane | 3,009 | 13.08 |
| 19 | Richmond | 15,869 | 13.02 |
| 20 | Columbus, Ga. | 3,634 | 11.70 |
| 21 | Albuquerque | 4,705 | 11.66 |
| 22 | Atlanta | 12,199 | 11.44 |
| 23 | New Orleans | 15,617 | 11.23 |
| 23 | Riverside | 2,605 | 11.23 |
| 25 | Denver | 18,186 | 9.80 |
| 26 | Norfolk | 9,222 | 9.75 |
| 27 | Shreveport | 3,060 | 9.60 |

| Rank | City | Other Taxes ($ 000) | Percentage of Locally Generated Revenues | | Rank | City | Other Taxes ($ 000) | Percentage of Locally Generated Revenues |
|---|---|---|---|---|---|---|---|---|
| 28 | St. Louis | 18,433 | 9.40 | | 65 | Austin | 1,919 | 3.52 |
| 29 | Virginia Beach | 7,336 | 9.21 | | 66 | Columbus, Ohio | 3,171 | 3.42 |
| 30 | Fresno | 3,707 | 9.12 | | 67 | San Antonio | 2,547 | 3.28 |
| 31 | Philadelphia | 70,228 | 8.96 | | 68 | Omaha | 2,220 | 3.27 |
| 32 | Kansas City, Mo. | 13,873 | 8.35 | | 69 | Kansas City, Kan. | 759 | 3.25 |
| 33 | Newark | 8,390 | 7.96 | | 70 | Tulsa | 2,046 | 3.15 |
| 34 | Santa Ana | 2,374 | 7.83 | | 71 | Milwaukee | 2,690 | 2.98 |
| 35 | San Diego | 8,819 | 7.37 | | 72 | Lexington | 1,395 | 2.91 |
| 36 | Chicago | 54,114 | 7.35 | | 73 | Lincoln | 760 | 2.88 |
| 37 | Tampa | 3,664 | 7.21 | | 74 | Anchorage | 2,096 | 2.64 |
| 38 | Minneapolis | 5,234 | 6.96 | | 75 | Dallas | 5,405 | 2.50 |
| 39 | Akron | 3,199 | 6.95 | | 76 | Chattanooga | 691 | 2.40 |
| 40 | Baton Rouge | 5,141 | 6.92 | | 77 | Indianapolis | 2,976 | 2.36 |
| 41 | St. Petersburg | 1,904 | 6.53 | | 78 | Honolulu | 4,252 | 2.35 |
| 42 | Knoxville | 1,851 | 6.36 | | 79 | Oklahoma City | 1,998 | 2.27 |
| 43 | Nashville | 10,232 | 5.88 | | 80 | Cleveland | 3,153 | 2.26 |
| 44 | Miami | 4,851 | 5.73 | | 81 | Detroit | 8,116 | 2.25 |
| 45 | Syracuse | 1,912 | 5.19 | | 82 | Corpus Christi | 686 | 2.20 |
| 46 | St. Paul | 2,299 | 5.11 | | 83 | Buffalo | 2,169 | 2.19 |
| 47 | Baltimore | 16,444 | 4.93 | | 84 | Flint | 622 | 2.17 |
| 48 | Phoenix | 5,903 | 4.89 | | 85 | Houston | 7,380 | 2.09 |
| 49 | Charlotte | 2,590 | 4.66 | | 86 | New York | 138,735 | 2.07 |
| 50 | Cincinnati | 5,630 | 4.64 | | 87 | Warren | 440 | 2.02 |
| 51 | Jacksonville | 3,778 | 4.56 | | 88 | Dayton | 1,110 | 1.95 |
| 52 | Aurora | 1,506 | 4.54 | | 89 | Grand Rapids | 440 | 1.78 |
| 53 | Memphis | 4,591 | 4.50 | | 90 | Colorado Springs | 515 | 1.64 |
| 54 | Jackson | 1,065 | 4.40 | | 91 | Louisville | 1,127 | 1.60 |
| 55 | Greensboro | 1,032 | 4.38 | | 92 | Madison | 944 | 1.44 |
| 56 | Wichita | 1,813 | 4.36 | | 93 | Lubbock | 353 | 1.39 |
| 57 | Salt Lake City | 1,755 | 4.24 | | 94 | Yonkers | 1,390 | 1.32 |
| 57 | Toledo | 2,590 | 4.24 | | 95 | Rochester | 1,174 | 1.25 |
| 59 | Tucson | 2,521 | 4.18 | | 96 | Boston | 5,129 | 1.17 |
| 50 | Arlington, Texas | 834 | 3.91 | | 97 | Jersey City | 719 | .92 |
| 61 | Fort Worth | 2,532 | 3.86 | | 98 | Providence | 652 | .89 |
| 61 | Washington, D.C. | 36,311 | 3.86 | | 99 | Worcester | 372 | .47 |
| 63 | El Paso | 1,668 | 3.79 | | 100 | Fort Wayne | 20 | .11 |
| 64 | Des Moines | 1,191 | 3.60 | | | | | |

# 145.　City Executives' Salaries

The highest paid chief city administrator in the nation, in Dallas, made $82,000 in 1981. The highest paid baseball team is the New York Yankees, with an average salary of $242,937 in 1980. Meanwhile New York City's mayor, Edward I. Koch, is paid just $60,000, and the city's chief administrator, Deputy Mayor Leventhal, makes (along with two other deputies) $64,548. Koch in 1979 rejected a pay increase for himself that would have raised his salary to $80,000. Koch and Leventhal collect less than a penny from each of the city's 7 million residents. They are the lowest paid executives of the country's major league cities on the basis of the population they serve. The next lowest paid executive is the chief administrator of the city of Houston, who collects 2 cents for each

citizen he serves. At the other end of the scale, the chief administrator of Tacoma gets 42 cents from each of Tacoma's 159,000 residents.

Another way of looking at city executives' salaries is in terms of area. On this basis the $50,000 paid to the chief administrator of Yonkers (18 square miles) in 1981 was the most costly, at $2,780 per square mile. The next most costly cities were Jersey City, Anaheim, Santa Ana and Huntington Beach. The least costly were Nashville (508 square miles), $27,000, or $60 per square mile; Jacksonville; Houston; and Indianapolis.

The following table compares the salaries of the chief administrative officers of major cities relative to population.

SOURCE: City salary data from International City Management Association, 1981.

| Rank | City | City Executives' Annual Salary ($) | Salary per 1,000 Population ($) |
|------|------|-----------|-----------|
| 1 | New York | 64,548 | 9.13 |
| 2 | Houston | 36,051* | 22.62 |
| 3 | Chicago | 74,830 | 24.90 |
| 4 | Los Angeles | 78,951 | 26.62 |
| 5 | Philadelphia | 50,000 | 29.62 |
| 6 | Indianapolis | 25,000** | 35.66 |
| 7 | Memphis | 37,500* | 58.05 |
| 8 | Nashville-Davidson | 27,096 | 59.42 |
| 9 | San Diego | 60,462 | 69.02 |
| 10 | Jacksonville | 42,564 | 78.68 |
| 11 | Buffalo | 29,489 | 82.37 |
| 12 | Washington, D.C. | 52,800 | 82.76 |
| 13 | Louisville | 25,979** | 87.18 |
| 14 | San Antonio | 71,500 | 91.08 |
| 15 | Dallas | 82,000 | 91.71 |
| 16 | Phoenix | 73,715 | 93.31 |
| 17 | New Orleans | 53,772 | 96.54 |
| 18 | San Francisco | 68,040 | 100.21 |
| 19 | Boston | 60,000 | 106.57 |
| 20 | San Jose | 68,619 | 107.72 |
| 21 | Seattle | 54,015 | 109.34 |
| 22 | Birmingham | 32,000 | 112.68 |
| 23 | Newark | 42,543 | 129.31 |
| 24 | Albuquerque | 43,014 | 129.56 |
| 25 | Atlanta | 55,125 | 129.71 |
| 26 | Tampa | 35,734 | 131.38 |
| 27 | Honolulu | 50,820 | 139.23 |
| 28 | Kansas City, Mo. | 62,460 | 139.42 |
| 29 | Oklahoma City | 58,840 | 146.00 |
| 30 | Minneapolis | 54,184 | 146.05 |
| 31 | Toledo | 52,805 | 148.75 |
| 32 | Tucson | 51,700 | 156.19 |
| 33 | Fort Worth | 63,690 | 165.43 |
| 34 | Jersey City | 38,000 | 169.64 |
| 35 | Charlotte | 54,810 | 174.55 |
| 36 | Oakland | 59,400 | 175.22 |

| Rank | City | City Executives' Annual Salary ($) | Salary Per 1,000 Population ($) |
|------|------|-----------|-----------|
| 37 | Cincinnati | 67,500 | 175.32 |
| 38 | Shreveport | 37,500* | 182.04 |
| 39 | Long Beach | 65,949 | 182.68 |
| 40 | Austin | 64,457 | 186.83 |
| 41 | Knoxville | 34,320 | 187.54 |
| 42 | Norfolk | 51,076 | 191.30 |
| 43 | Miami | 66,708 | 192.24 |
| 44 | St. Paul | 53,565 | 198.39 |
| 45 | Columbus, Ga. | 35,761 | 211.60 |
| 46 | Baton Rouge | 46,548 | 212.55 |
| 47 | Rochester | 52,000 | 214.88 |
| 48 | Corpus Christi | 50,834 | 219.11 |
| 49 | St. Petersburg | 52,000 | 219.41 |
| 50 | Dayton | 46,000 | 225.49 |
| 51 | Virginia Beach | 59,928 | 228.72 |
| 52 | Wichita | 64,490 | 231.15 |
| 53 | Sacramento | 64,152 | 232.43 |
| 54 | Flint | 38,864 | 242.90 |
| 55 | Richmond | 54,990 | 251.10 |
| 56 | Yonkers | 50,000 | 256.41 |
| 57 | Des Moines | 49,971 | 261.00 |
| 58 | Little Rock | 43,000 | 272.15 |
| 59 | Grand Rapids | 49,789 | 273.57 |
| 60 | Fresno | 59,892 | 274.73 |
| 61 | Aurora | 45,000 | 283.02 |
| 62 | Santa Ana | 58,000 | 284.31 |
| 63 | Las Vegas | 47,000 | 284.85 |
| 64 | Lubbock | 50,003 | 287.37 |
| 65 | Worcester | 46,889 | 289.41 |
| 66 | Colorado Springs | 64,200 | 298.60 |
| 67 | Madison | 51,870 | 303.33 |
| 68 | Greensboro | 48,300 | 309.62 |
| 69 | Huntington Beach | 53,316 | 311.79 |
| 70 | Spokane | 55,018 | 321.74 |
| 71 | Anchorage | 58,000 | 335.26 |
| 72 | Riverside | 58,104 | 339.79 |
| 73 | Arlington, Texas | 55,800 | 348.75 |
| 74 | Anaheim | 74,830 | 355.14 |
| 75 | Tacoma | 66,144 | 416.00 |

*1/1/80 salary data.
**1/1/76 salary data.

# 146. Energy Management

One of the heaviest users of electricity is municipal government. Saving energy by using more efficient lighting systems would mean a lot for the city and the nation. Some cities are making a conscious effort to reduce their consumption of energy, both to save money and to reduce national energy consumption.

The index below has been created by the authors, based on 30 energy management activities selected by the International City Management Association (ICMA) in a 1981 report on the subject. The column headed "Energy Savings in Public Buildings" indicates government installation of energy-saving devices. The two community columns show government efforts to encourage citizens to conserve energy and to involve citizens in conservation programs. The remaining column, "Other," represents energy-saving initiatives not covered in the previous columns. The letter *e* next to the name of the city indicates that energy expenditures represent the second largest item in the city's operating cost.

The highest score is for Los Angeles. Of the 30 possible energy-saving moves, the city is using 27. The city showing the least effort to reduce energy use is Cleveland, with a score of 1.

SOURCE: Urban Data Service, International City Management Association (ICMA), 1981.

| Rank | City | Energy Savings in Public Buildings | Conservation and Community | | Other | Total |
|---|---|---|---|---|---|---|
| | | | Local Government Efforts | Citizen Participation | | |
| | Total Possible Activities | 7 | 5 | 6 | 12 | 30 |
| 1 | Los Angeles (e) | 4 | 5 | 6 | 12 | 27 |
| 2 | Jacksonville | 6 | 5 | 5 | 10 | 26 |
| 3 | Portland, Ore. | 6 | 5 | 5 | 8 | 24 |
| 4 | Kansas City, Mo. | 7 | 3 | 6 | 7 | 23 |
| 5 | Baltimore | 7 | 2 | 6 | 7 | 22 |
| 6 | New York | 5 | 4 | 3 | 9 | 21 |
| 7 | Lincoln (e) | 4 | 4 | 6 | 6 | 20 |
| 7 | Toledo (e) | 5 | 4 | 4 | 7 | 20 |
| 9 | Madison | 6 | 4 | 3 | 5 | 18 |
| 10 | Dayton (e) | 7 | 4 | 4 | 2 | 17 |
| 11 | Austin (e) | 3 | 3 | 4 | 7 | 17 |
| 11 | El Paso (e) | 6 | 3 | 3 | 5 | 17 |
| 11 | Greensboro | 6 | 3 | 4 | 4 | 17 |
| 11 | Nashville-Davidson (e) | 5 | 2 | 4 | 6 | 17 |
| 11 | Riverside (e) | 3 | 4 | 6 | 4 | 17 |
| 16 | Atlanta | 4 | 4 | 4 | 4 | 16 |
| 16 | St. Paul (e) | 1 | 4 | 5 | 6 | 16 |
| 18 | San Diego | 6 | 1 | 3 | 5 | 15 |
| 18 | Worcester (e) | 3 | 0 | 5 | 7 | 15 |
| 20 | Albuquerque | 3 | 2 | 3 | 6 | 14 |
| 20 | Houston | 4 | 3 | 5 | 2 | 14 |
| 20 | Milwaukee (e) | 6 | 0 | 1 | 7 | 14 |
| 20 | Mobile (e) | 3 | 3 | 4 | 4 | 14 |
| 20 | Oakland (e) | 1 | 2 | 5 | 6 | 14 |
| 20 | San Antonio (e) | 1 | 3 | 2 | 8 | 14 |
| 20 | San Jose (e) | 6 | 1 | 1 | 6 | 14 |
| 27 | Anaheim (e) | 3 | 2 | 3 | 5 | 13 |
| 27 | Norfolk (County) | 4 | 1 | 4 | 4 | 13 |
| 27 | Richmond (e) | 2 | 2 | 5 | 5 | 14 |
| 30 | Dallas | 7 | 1 | 0 | 4 | 12 |
| 30 | Kansas City, Kan. | 2 | 3 | 4 | 3 | 12 |
| 30 | Long Beach | 1 | 1 | 3 | 7 | 12 |
| 30 | Omaha | 4 | 0 | 5 | 3 | 12 |
| 30 | Wichita | 4 | 2 | 2 | 4 | 12 |
| 35 | Anchorage (e) | 2 | 2 | 4 | 3 | 11 |
| 35 | Honolulu | 3 | 3 | 1 | 4 | 11 |
| 35 | Phoenix (e) | 7 | 0 | 0 | 4 | 11 |
| 38 | Fresno (e) | 1 | 2 | 1 | 6 | 10 |
| 38 | Jersey City | 0 | 2 | 4 | 4 | 10 |
| 38 | Little Rock (e) | 4 | 1 | 2 | 3 | 10 |
| 38 | Lubbock (e) | 2 | 2 | 2 | 4 | 10 |
| 42 | Fort Worth | 2 | 1 | 2 | 4 | 9 |
| 42 | Tucson | 4 | 0 | 5 | 0 | 9 |
| 44 | Charlotte | 2 | 0 | 4 | 2 | 8 |
| 44 | Cincinnati (e) | 3 | 0 | 1 | 4 | 8 |
| 46 | Arlington, Texas (e) | 4 | 0 | 0 | 3 | 7 |
| 47 | Birmingham (e) | 2 | 0 | 1 | 3 | 6 |
| 47 | Chattanooga | 0 | 1 | 2 | 3 | 6 |

| Rank | City | Energy Savings in Public Buildings | Conservation and Community | | Other | Total |
|---|---|---|---|---|---|---|
| | | | Local Government Efforts | Citizen Participation | | |
| 47 | New Orleans (e) | 1 | 1 | 1 | 3 | 6 |
| 47 | Sacramento | 1 | 1 | 1 | 3 | 6 |
| 47 | San Francisco | 1 | 0 | 3 | 2 | 6 |
| 47 | Tacoma | 3 | 0 | 1 | 2 | 6 |
| 53 | Columbus, Ga. | 2 | 0 | 0 | 3 | 5 |
| 53 | Denver | 2 | 0 | 0 | 3 | 5 |
| 53 | Newark (e) | 1 | 1 | 2 | 1 | 5 |
| 56 | Huntington Beach | 1 | 1 | 0 | 2 | 4 |
| 56 | Las Vegas | 1 | 1 | 0 | 2 | 4 |
| 56 | St. Louis (e) | 3 | 0 | 0 | 1 | 4 |
| 56 | Tulsa (e) | 3 | 0 | 1 | 0 | 4 |
| 56 | Warren | 1 | 0 | 1 | 2 | 4 |
| 61 | Grand Rapids | 1 | 0 | 0 | 2 | 3 |
| 61 | Montgomery | 1 | 0 | 0 | 2 | 3 |
| 63 | Aurora | 2 | 0 | 0 | 0 | 2 |
| 63 | Spokane | 0 | 1 | 1 | 0 | 2 |
| 65 | Cleveland | 0 | 0 | 0 | 1 | 1 |

# 147. Tax Burden of 30 Largest Cities

The following table compares tax burdens for four major taxes (income, sales, auto and property) in the 30 largest cities in the United States based on a family of four—i.e., one wage-earning spouse and one non-wage-earning spouse who have two school-aged children, own their home and live within the city limits.

For residents earning $17,000, Bostonians have a tax burden of $2,679, which is over eight times greater than the tax burden for New Orleans residents ($319). New York, Philadelphia and Milwaukee are also among those cities with the highest tax burden in 1980. The cities with the lowest burdens include El Paso, Nashville-Davidson and Jacksonville.

Cities with above-average income and real estate taxes have higher average tax burdens. Older cities have the highest tax burdens.

State and local tax burdens for individuals vary by city according to:

a. Service demand (northern cities have cold-weather service demands that can increase municipal costs considerably).
b. Wage levels and overhead operating costs.
c. The percentage of tax-exempt property in a city.
d. The amount of municipal services performed by the private sector.
e. Taxes and fees on nonresidents and the exportation of some portion of the local tax burden to an industry (e.g., oil severance taxes).

Because of federal and state aid cuts, local tax burdens can be expected to increase in the largest cities.

SOURCE: Office of Economic and Tax Policy of the Washington, D.C. Department of Finance and Revenue, Joint Economic Committee, *Trends in the Fiscal Condition of Cities: 1980–1982* (May 1982).

| Rank | City | Income Tax ($) | Sales Tax ($) | Automobile Tax ($) | Property Tax ($) | Total Local Taxes ($) | Local Taxes as a Percentage of Income |
|---|---|---|---|---|---|---|---|
| 1 | Boston | 615 | 124 | 133 | 1,807 | 2,679 | 15.8 |
| 2 | New York | 656 | 379 | 99 | 974 | 2,108 | 12.4 |
| 3 | Philadelphia | 1,107 | 156 | 112 | 426 | 1,801 | 10.6 |
| 4 | Milwaukee | 638 | 171 | 85 | 856 | 1,750 | 10.3 |
| 5 | Detroit | 642 | 184 | 108 | 802 | 1,736 | 10.2 |
| 6 | Baltimore | 660 | 179 | 92 | 789 | 1,720 | 10.1 |
| 6 | Chicago | 325 | 304 | 86 | 999 | 1,714 | 10.1 |
| 8 | St. Louis | 557 | 265 | 135 | 562 | 1,519 | 8.9 |
| 9 | Indianapolis | 276 | 196 | 174 | 688 | 1,334 | 7.7 |
| 10 | Honolulu | 524 | 297 | 133 | 345 | 1,299 | 7.6 |
| 10 | Kansas City, Mo. | 557 | 265 | 150 | 319 | 1,291 | 7.6 |
| 12 | Washington, D.C. | 598 | 209 | 116 | 359 | 1,282 | 7.5 |
| 13 | Atlanta | 300 | 261 | 140 | 508 | 1,209 | 7.1 |
| 14 | Cleveland | 410 | 198 | 82 | 508 | 1,198 | 7.0 |
| 15 | Columbus, Ohio | 410 | 162 | 82 | 431 | 1,085 | 6.4 |
| 16 | Houston | 0 | 219 | 124 | 655 | 998 | 5.9 |
| 17 | Dallas | 0 | 182 | 124 | 639 | 945 | 5.6 |
| 18 | Memphis | 0 | 353 | 97 | 462 | 912 | 5.4 |
| 18 | Phoenix | 237 | 265 | 137 | 279 | 918 | 5.4 |
| 20 | Denver | 241 | 258 | 116 | 293 | 908 | 5.3 |
| 21 | San Diego | 183 | 263 | 132 | 315 | 893 | 5.2 |
| 21 | San Francisco | 183 | 284 | 132 | 281 | 280 | 5.2 |
| 21 | San Jose | 183 | 284 | 132 | 289 | 888 | 5.2 |
| 24 | San Antonio | 0 | 200 | 119 | 509 | 828 | 4.9 |
| 25 | Los Angeles | 183 | 263 | 132 | 213 | 791 | 4.6 |
| 25 | Seattle | 0 | 223 | 181 | 387 | 791 | 4.6 |
| 25 | Nashville-Davidson | 0 | 365 | 97 | 323 | 785 | 4.6 |
| 28 | El Paso | 0 | 182 | 100 | 473 | 755 | 4.4 |
| 29 | Jacksonville | 0 | 158 | 84 | 133 | 375 | 2.2 |
| 30 | New Orleans | 0 | 252 | 67 | 0 | 319 | 1.9 |

# 148.　Municipal Contracting

Budget cutbacks are forcing municipalities in the United States to look increasingly at the possibility of contracting with private suppliers to provide public services.

Although a few northeastern cities are heavy contractors, private contracting tends to be more popular in the rest of the country. Of the 10 cities that are most heavily involved in municipal contracting, only Rochester is in the northeast. The cities that contract for the most private services are Anchorage (39); Portland, Ore. and Tucson (33); Rochester (31); and Atlanta (29). The cities that contract out the least are Birmingham, Miami and Louisville (3), and Baltimore (0). The "Both" column may count the same service more than once, if it is contracted for in more than one way.

Half of Rochester's contracted services are contracted to nonprofit organizations, whereas the propor-

tion is much smaller in other cities relying heavily on private contracts (or purchases of service, as they are also called).

Rochester was the only one of the five cities in New York state that responded. Worcester was the only one of the three New England cities.

In the case of Miami, the reason relatively few services are contracted for privately is that many of the services other cities provide are provided for in the Miami area by Dade County. Dade does a considerable amount of private contracting.

SOURCE: Derived by the authors from unpublished questionnaires prepared by the cities for the International City Management Association, 1982.

| Rank | City | No. Services Contracted to: Businesses | No. Services Contracted to: Nonprofit Organizations | No. Services Contracted to: Both | Rank | City | No. Services Contracted to: Businesses | No. Services Contracted to: Nonprofit Organization | No. Services Contracted to: Both |
|---|---|---|---|---|---|---|---|---|---|
| 1 | Anchorage | 29 | 10 | 39 | 30 | El Paso | 7 | 6 | 13 |
| 2 | Portland, Ore. | 24 | 9 | 33 | 30 | Greensboro | 10 | 3 | 13 |
| 2 | Tucson | 23 | 10 | 33 | 30 | Omaha | 13 | 0 | 13 |
| 4 | Rochester | 16 | 15 | 31 | 34 | Charlotte | 6 | 6 | 12 |
| 5 | Atlanta | 19 | 10 | 29 | 34 | Des Moines | 6 | 6 | 12 |
| 6 | Colorado Springs | 20 | 8 | 28 | 34 | Toledo | 10 | 2 | 12 |
| 6 | San Diego | 19 | 9 | 28 | 34 | Virginia Beach | 9 | 3 | 12 |
| 8 | Phoenix | 23 | 4 | 27 | 38 | Aurora | 7 | 4 | 11 |
| 9 | Cincinnati | 12 | 14 | 26 | 38 | Cleveland | 10 | 1 | 11 |
| 10 | Indianapolis | 15 | 10 | 25 | 38 | Corpus Christi | 5 | 6 | 11 |
| 11 | Philadelphia | 17 | 6 | 23 | 38 | Fort Worth | 10 | 1 | 11 |
| 12 | Wichita | 17 | 5 | 22 | 38 | San Antonio | 3 | 8 | 11 |
| 13 | New Orleans | 14 | 7 | 21 | 43 | Lubbock | 10 | 0 | 10 |
| 14 | Flint | 16 | 4 | 20 | 43 | Memphis | 10 | 0 | 10 |
| 14 | Grand Rapids | 14 | 6 | 20 | 43 | Minneapolis | 7 | 3 | 10 |
| 14 | Honolulu | 17 | 3 | 20 | 43 | Pittsburgh | 10 | 0 | 10 |
| 14 | Los Angeles | 14 | 6 | 20 | 47 | Columbus, Ohio | 4 | 5 | 9 |
| 14 | Riverside | 16 | 4 | 20 | 47 | Detroit | 5 | 4 | 9 |
| 14 | Washington, D.C. | 10 | 10 | 20 | 47 | Little Rock | 7 | 2 | 9 |
| 14 | Worcester | 13 | 7 | 20 | 50 | Long Beach | 6 | 2 | 8 |
| 21 | Warren | 17 | 2 | 19 | 51 | Spokane | 7 | 0 | 7 |
| 22 | Norfolk | 10 | 8 | 18 | 52 | Arlington, Texas | 6 | 0 | 6 |
| 23 | Oklahoma City | 12 | 5 | 17 | 53 | Denver | 4 | 1 | 5 |
| 24 | Knoxville | 2 | 13 | 15 | 54 | Jackson | 4 | 0 | 4 |
| 25 | Austin | 12 | 2 | 14 | 54 | San Jose | 4 | 0 | 4 |
| 25 | Kansas City, Mo. | 10 | 4 | 14 | 56 | Birmingham | 2 | 1 | 3 |
| 25 | St. Petersburg | 12 | 2 | 14 | 56 | Louisville | 3 | 0 | 3 |
| 25 | San Francisco | 5 | 9 | 14 | 56 | Miami | 3 | 0 | 3 |
| 25 | Tacoma | 7 | 7 | 14 | 59 | Baltimore | 0 | 0 | 0 |
| 30 | Dallas | 7 | 6 | 13 | | | | | |

# CHAPTER NINE

# VOTING 1980

Aristotle said that people are political animals. A salient feature of a city therefore is the politics of its residents.

The data below are for metro areas because the figures are aggregated from county data, as was the case with the religious data. The politics of central cities is usually to the left of suburban areas, so that metro figures will usually understate the strength of Democratic candidates downtown.

Generally speaking, the three tables which follow— describing how people in different metro areas voted during the 1980 elections—show the strong degree of support that Ronald Reagan obtained in traditionally Democratic areas such as the South. Only New York and Columbus, Georgia remained Jimmy Carter strongholds, above 60 percent of the major candidate vote. His votes were above 50 percent of major candidate votes in only nine other metro areas. Third-party candidate John Anderson did best in New England metro areas.

## 149. Votes for John Anderson

The third-party vote in American politics is a measure of dissatisfaction with the two major parties—Democratic and Republican. In American history the third party has been in the vanguard of social change. Usually the third parties die after they show their strength, because one of the major parties incorporates in its programs the cause for which the third party fought.

The 1980 election differed from the 1976 election in that there was a third-party candidate who obtained a significant percentage of the vote—John B. Anderson. An evangelical Christian, Anderson served as an Illinois Republican in the House of Representatives for 20 years before leaving his party to run as an independent. His campaign was based largely on the unresponsiveness of the major parties to certain social, environmental and global needs, echoing years of previous maverick positions within his party.

Urban voters in Anderson's Illinois home base did not provide the hard core of his support: Chicago ranked only 32nd out of 86 metro areas in the percentage of its major-party vote that it gave to Anderson.

Instead, the Providence and Boston areas showed the largest vote for Anderson. In both cities he obtained over 14 percent of all votes cast for the three major candidates.

Although Ronald Reagan is of Irish ancestry, his

Republican politics may have been unacceptable to the traditional democratic voters in New England's largest cities. The same explanation goes for Worchester's high Anderson vote.

While Anderson apparently appealed to many northwestern Democrats, he had less success pulling votes away from southern Democrats.

SOURCES: Data derived from county data in *1983 World Almanac*. Information on Anderson from Michael Barone, Grant Ujifusa and Douglas Matthews, *The Almanac of American Politics 1980* (New York: E. P. Dutton, 1979), pp. 264–266.

| Rank | Metro Area | Votes for All Major Candidates | Anderson Votes | Anderson Votes as a Percentage of All Votes |
|------|------------|-------------------------------|----------------|---------------------------------------------|
| 1 | Boston | 1,609,109 | 250,424 | 15.56 |
| 2 | Providence | 599,382 | 85,242 | 14.22 |
| 3 | San Jose | 461,524 | 65,481 | 14.19 |
| 4 | Worcester | 275,805 | 38,379 | 13.92 |
| 5 | Tucson | 182,767 | 25,294 | 13.84 |
| 6 | Denver | 664,092 | 86,756 | 13.06 |
| 7 | Seattle | 716,353 | 90,584 | 12.65 |
| 8 | Lincoln | 74,891 | 9,221 | 12.31 |
| 9 | Madison | 162,926 | 19,772 | 12.14 |

| Rank | Metro Area | Carter Reagan Anderson | Anderson Votes | Anderson Votes as a Percentage of All Votes | Rank | Metro Area | Carter Reagan Anderson | Anderson Votes | Anderson Votes as a Percentage of All Votes |
|---|---|---|---|---|---|---|---|---|---|
| 10 | Honolulu | 221,399 | 25,331 | 11.44 | 50 | Austin | 197,484 | 11,332 | 5.74 |
| 11 | San Francisco | 1,267,823 | 140,178 | 11.06 | 51 | Lexington-Fayette | 108,110 | 6,016 | 5.56 |
| 12 | Portland, Ore. | 534,033 | 58,479 | 10.95 | 52 | Columbus, Ohio | 453,538 | 25,189 | 5.55 |
| 13 | Des Moines | 157,298 | 17,188 | 10.93 | 53 | El Paso | 98,454 | 5,096 | 5.18 |
| 14 | Tacoma | 173,036 | 18,345 | 10.60 | 54 | Indianapolis | 473,047 | 22,416 | 4.74 |
| 15 | Minneapolis-St. Paul | 1,045,476 | 106,072 | 10.15 | 54 | Oklahoma City | 306,996 | 14,552 | 4.74 |
| 16 | Washington, D.C. | 1,064,206 | 107,543 | 10.11 | 56 | Cincinnati | 531,931 | 24,316 | 4.57 |
| 17 | Sacramento | 411,052 | 40,680 | 9.89 | 56 | Jersey City | 195,770 | 8,941 | 4.57 |
| 18 | Rochester | 385,688 | 37,559 | 9.74 | 58 | Tampa-St. Petersburg | 682,508 | 30,293 | 4.44 |
| 19 | San Diego | 698,811 | 67,491 | 9.66 | 59 | St. Louis | 1,013,691 | 44,816 | 4.42 |
| 20 | Albuquerque | 166,206 | 15,907 | 9.57 | 60 | Norfolk-Virginia Beach | 255,661 | 10,993 | 4.27 |
| 21 | Syracuse | 254,871 | 24,260 | 9.52 | 61 | Little Rock | 130,962 | 5,300 | 4.05 |
| 22 | Toledo | 285,121 | 26,210 | 9.19 | 62 | Charlotte | 204,489 | 7,870 | 3.85 |
| 23 | Miami | 520,956 | 44,723 | 8.58 | 63 | Richmond | 248,425 | 9,547 | 3.84 |
| 24 | Fort Wayne | 152,486 | 12,735 | 8.35 | 64 | Knoxville | 174,102 | 6,627 | 3.81 |
| 25 | Grand Rapids | 277,862 | 22,816 | 8.21 | 65 | Louisville | 340,951 | 12,888 | 3.78 |
| 25 | Newark | 759,535 | 62,384 | 8.21 | 66 | Tulsa | 264,773 | 9,711 | 3.67 |
| 25 | Phoenix | 475,014 | 38,975 | 8.21 | 67 | Atlanta | 630,236 | 21,373 | 3.39 |
| 28 | Spokane | 138,617 | 11,258 | 8.12 | 68 | Houston | 858,175 | 26,185 | 3.05 |
| 29 | Philadelphia | 1,915,828 | 153,997 | 8.04 | 69 | San Antonio | 335,767 | 10,198 | 3.04 |
| 30 | Colorado Springs | 105,129 | 8,208 | 7.81 | 70 | Greensboro | 280,291 | 8,445 | 3.01 |
| 31 | Omaha | 217,130 | 16,753 | 7.72 | 71 | New York | 2,666,170 | 79,410 | 2.98 |
| 32 | Chicago | 2,856,238 | 220,153 | 7.71 | 72 | Lubbock | 67,395 | 1,952 | 2.90 |
| 33 | Los Angeles | 2,380,245 | 175,882 | 7.39 | 73 | Dallas | 1,008,547 | 26,777 | 2.66 |
| 34 | Anaheim | 762,800 | 56,299 | 7.38 | 74 | Jacksonville | 251,817 | 6,612 | 2.63 |
| 35 | Milwaukee | 668,758 | 49,156 | 7.35 | 75 | Nashville-Davidson | 296,803 | 7,382 | 2.49 |
| 36 | Akron | 256,957 | 18,800 | 7.32 | 76 | New Orleans | 412,897 | 9,312 | 2.26 |
| 37 | Baltimore | 804,047 | 58,260 | 7.25 | 77 | Corpus Christi | 103,288 | 2,325 | 2.25 |
| 38 | Buffalo | 499,251 | 35,594 | 7.13 | 78 | Memphis | 345,650 | 7,711 | 2.23 |
| 39 | Wichita | 158,744 | 11,237 | 7.08 | 79 | Baton Rouge | 181,678 | 4,002 | 2.20 |
| 40 | Las Vegas | 123,209 | 8,702 | 7.06 | 80 | Columbus, Ga. | 52,879 | 1,064 | 2.01 |
| 41 | Cleveland | 758,661 | 51,999 | 6.85 | 81 | Chattanooga | 142,140 | 2,557 | 1.80 |
| 42 | Flint | 211,101 | 14,395 | 6.82 | 82 | Jackson | 113,911 | 1,710 | 1.50 |
| 43 | Riverside | 522,507 | 35,468 | 6.79 | 83 | Montgomery | 90,266 | 1,281 | 1.42 |
| 44 | Fresno | 158,496 | 10,727 | 6.77 | 84 | Birmingham | 307,568 | 4,119 | 1.34 |
| 45 | Salt Lake City | 375,702 | 24,692 | 6.57 | 85 | Mobile | 142,542 | 1,747 | 1.23 |
| 46 | Dayton | 318,249 | 20,093 | 6.31 | 86 | Shreveport | 132,522 | 1,573 | 1.19 |
| 47 | Detroit | 1,754,315 | 109,663 | 6.25 | | | | | |
| 48 | Pittsburgh | 904,016 | 52,657 | 5.82 | | | | | |
| 49 | Kansas City, Kan.-Mo. | 537,080 | 30,996 | 5.77 | | | | | |

# 150.  Votes for Jimmy Carter

Prior to the 1980 election, the high rate of inflation, and several other developments including the long period during which American hostages were kept in the U.S. Embassy in Teheran and the abortive effort to rescue them, contributed to the feeling that things were not going well in Washington.

President Carter's actions during the months leading up to the election did not dispel this feeling. Disturbed by price increases and tax revolts, he imposed heavy cuts in domestic spending.

Ronald Reagan presented the alternative image of a person who would do the cutting back with vigor rather than apology—someone who would also recover America's rightful place in the world of diplomacy.

His appeal was clearly compelling. Looking at the data—i.e., the votes in areas that have traditionally been Democratic Party strongholds—Carter obtained a majority in only 11 out of 86 metro areas. New York City and Columbus, Georgia (Carter's hometown area) were the only areas to give Carter more than 60 percent of their votes.

Seven metro areas gave Carter less than 30 percent

of their votes: Salt Lake City, Anaheim (Reagan's home-town area), Phoenix, Colorado Springs, Lubbock, San Diego and Oklahoma City.

SOURCE: Derived from county population data and county presidential vote data in the *World Almanac and Book of Facts: 1983* (New York: Newspaper Enterprise Association, 1981), pp. 246–63 and 267–96. Providence figures cover all of Rhode Island plus Bristol County, Massachusetts.

| Rank | Metro Area | Votes for All Major Candidates | Votes for Carter | Carter Votes as a Percentage of All Votes |
|------|------------|-------------------------------:|-----------------:|------------------------------------------:|
| 1 | New York | 2,666,170 | 1,853,439 | 69.52 |
| 2 | Columbus, Ga. | 52,879 | 31,871 | 60.27 |
| 3 | Nashville-Davidson | 296,803 | 170,941 | 57.59 |
| 4 | Madison | 162,926 | 85,609 | 52.54 |
| 5 | Atlanta | 630,236 | 328,520 | 52.13 |
| 6 | Baltimore | 804,047 | 415,108 | 51.63 |
| 7 | Memphis | 345,650 | 177,540 | 51.36 |
| 8 | Buffalo | 499,251 | 255,688 | 51.21 |
| 9 | Corpus Christi | 103,288 | 52,051 | 50.39 |
| 10 | Pittsburgh | 904,016 | 453,341 | 50.15 |
| 11 | Minneapolis-St. Paul | 1,045,476 | 523,527 | 50.08 |
| 12 | Little Rock | 130,962 | 65,207 | 49.79 |
| 13 | Jersey City | 195,770 | 95,662 | 48.84 |
| 14 | Flint | 211,101 | 102,378 | 48.50 |
| 15 | Detroit | 1,754,315 | 849,725 | 48.44 |
| 16 | Cleveland | 758,661 | 365,809 | 48.22 |
| 17 | Akron | 256,957 | 123,029 | 47.88 |
| 18 | Rochester | 385,688 | 184,287 | 47.78 |
| 19 | Baton Rouge | 181,678 | 85,881 | 47.27 |
| 20 | Louisville | 340,951 | 160,895 | 47.19 |
| 21 | Providence | 599,382 | 281,802 | 47.02 |
| 22 | Charlotte | 204,489 | 96,084 | 46.99 |
| 23 | Chicago | 2,856,238 | 1,327,392 | 46.47 |
| 24 | Milwaukee | 668,758 | 310,509 | 46.43 |
| 25 | Austin | 197,484 | 91,449 | 46.31 |
| 26 | Toledo | 285,121 | 130,783 | 45.87 |
| 27 | Kansas City, Kan.-Mo. | 537,080 | 246,086 | 45.82 |
| 28 | St. Louis | 1,013,691 | 463,180 | 45.69 |
| 29 | San Francisco | 1,267,823 | 577,866 | 45.58 |
| 30 | Washington, D.C. | 1,064,206 | 484,877 | 45.56 |
| 31 | Lexington-Fayette | 108,110 | 49,186 | 45.50 |
| 31 | Tampa-St. Petersburg | 682,508 | 310,573 | 45.50 |
| 33 | Birmingham | 307,568 | 139,317 | 45.30 |
| 34 | Dayton | 318,249 | 143,487 | 45.09 |

| Rank | Metro Area | Votes for All Major Candidates | Votes for Carter | Carter Votes as a Percentage of All Votes |
|------|------------|-------------------------------:|-----------------:|------------------------------------------:|
| 35 | Jacksonville | 251,817 | 112,455 | 44.66 |
| 36 | New Orleans | 412,897 | 183,256 | 44.38 |
| 37 | Philadelphia | 1,915,828 | 847,203 | 44.22 |
| 38 | Des Moines | 157,298 | 68,594 | 43.61 |
| 39 | San Antonio | 335,767 | 146,332 | 43.58 |
| 40 | Honolulu | 221,399 | 96,472 | 43.57 |
| 41 | Chattanooga | 142,140 | 61,510 | 43.27 |
| 42 | Portland, Ore. | 534,033 | 229,448 | 42.97 |
| 43 | Norfolk-Virginia Beach | 225,881 | 109,111 | 42.64 |
| 44 | Worcester | 275,805 | 117,326 | 42.54 |
| 45 | Montgomery | 90,266 | 38,260 | 42.39 |
| 46 | Boston | 1,609,109 | 676,386 | 42.03 |
| 47 | Greensboro | 280,291 | 117,686 | 41.99 |
| 48 | Jackson | 113,911 | 47,416 | 41.63 |
| 49 | Fresno | 158,496 | 65,254 | 41.17 |
| 49 | Los Angeles | 2,380,245 | 979,830 | 41.17 |
| 51 | Sacramento | 411,052 | 168,869 | 41.08 |
| 52 | Shreveport | 132,522 | 54,367 | 41.02 |
| 53 | Newark | 759,535 | 309,790 | 40.75 |
| 54 | El Paso | 98,454 | 40,082 | 40.71 |
| 55 | Miami | 520,956 | 210,683 | 40.44 |
| 56 | Seattle | 716,353 | 287,049 | 40.07 |
| 57 | Wichita | 158,744 | 61,980 | 39.04 |
| 58 | Dallas | 1,008,547 | 387,190 | 38.39 |
| 59 | Mobile | 142,542 | 54,628 | 38.32 |
| 60 | Knoxville | 174,102 | 66,675 | 38.30 |
| 61 | Houston | 858,175 | 326,629 | 38.06 |
| 62 | Columbus, Ohio | 453,538 | 172,110 | 37.95 |
| 63 | Syracuse | 254,871 | 96,539 | 37.88 |
| 64 | Richmond | 248,425 | 93,983 | 37.83 |
| 65 | Tacoma | 173,036 | 64,444 | 37.24 |
| 66 | Cincinnati | 531,931 | 193,094 | 36.30 |
| 67 | San Jose | 461,524 | 166,995 | 36.18 |
| 68 | Lincoln | 74,891 | 27,040 | 36.11 |
| 69 | Indianapolis | 473,047 | 169,955 | 35.93 |
| 70 | Albuquerque | 166,206 | 595,581 | 35.85 |
| 71 | Spokane | 138,617 | 49,263 | 35.54 |
| 72 | Tucson | 182,767 | 64,418 | 35.25 |
| 73 | Fort Wayne | 152,486 | 51,109 | 33.52 |
| 74 | Denver | 664,092 | 219,904 | 33.11 |
| 75 | Grand Rapids | 277,862 | 91,225 | 32.83 |
| 76 | Riverside | 522,507 | 168,440 | 32.24 |
| 77 | Tulsa | 264,773 | 83,443 | 31.51 |
| 78 | Omaha | 217,130 | 67,891 | 31.27 |
| 79 | Las Vegas | 123,209 | 38,313 | 31.10 |
| 80 | Oklahoma City | 306,996 | 89,706 | 29.22 |
| 81 | San Diego | 698,811 | 195,410 | 27.96 |
| 82 | Lubbock | 67,395 | 18,732 | 27.79 |
| 83 | Colorado Springs | 105,129 | 28,625 | 26.89 |
| 84 | Phoenix | 475,014 | 119,752 | 25.21 |
| 85 | Anaheim | 762,800 | 176,704 | 23.17 |
| 86 | Salt Lake City | 375,702 | 86,073 | 22.91 |

# 151. Votes for Ronald Reagan

Ronald Reagan performed well in 1980 in the major metro areas, despite the traditional Democratic leanings of the older central cities. Metro areas include suburban communities that have voted Republican in larger numbers. In Detroit and Chicago, for example, Reagan received more than 45 percent of the vote, a strong showing. In 46 of the 86 metro areas shown below, he received more than 50 percent of the votes for the three major candidates.

The most significant exception to Reagan's strong showing was New York City, where he captured less than 28 percent of votes cast for the three major candidates, while Jimmy Carter received 70 percent.

In his home state of California, Reagan performed best in the Anaheim metro area, Orange County, receiving 70 percent of the major-candidate votes. He garnered 63 percent of the votes in the San Diego area and 60 percent in Riverside. His weakest support in California was in the San Francisco area, where he obtained 44 percent of the votes.

Of the 86 metro areas, 12 gave more than 60 percent of their vote for major candidates to Reagan. Of these 12 areas, only Mobile is east of the Mississippi. The eastern metro area that gave Reagan the most votes was Syracuse, with barely a majority (52 percent), midway down the list below.

Overall, Reagan did not fare well in the metro areas of the industrialized northeast. However, he did better than many expected—well enough to win the election comfortably.

---

SOURCE: Derived from county population data and county presidential vote data in the *World Almanac and Book of Facts: 1983* (New York: Newspaper Enterprise Association, 1981), pp. 246–63 and 267–96. Providence figures cover all of Rhode Island plus Bristol County, Massachusetts.

| Rank | Metro Area | Votes for All Major Candidates | Votes for Reagan | Reagan Votes as a Percentage of All Votes |
|------|-----------|------|------|------|
| 1 | Salt Lake City | 264,937 | 375,702 | 70.52 |
| 2 | Anaheim | 529,797 | 762,800 | 69.45 |
| 3 | Lubbock | 46,711 | 67,395 | 69.31 |
| 4 | Phoenix | 316,287 | 475,014 | 66.58 |
| 5 | Oklahoma City | 202,738 | 306,966 | 66.04 |
| 6 | Colorado Springs | 68,656 | 105,129 | 65.31 |
| 7 | Tulsa | 171,619 | 264,773 | 64.82 |
| 8 | San Diego | 435,910 | 698,811 | 62.38 |
| 9 | Las Vegas | 76,194 | 123,209 | 61.84 |
| 10 | Omaha | 132,486 | 217,130 | 61.02 |
| 11 | Riverside | 318,599 | 522,507 | 60.98 |
| 12 | Mobile | 86,167 | 142,542 | 60.45 |
| 13 | Indianapolis | 280,676 | 473,047 | 59.33 |
| 14 | Cincinnati | 314,521 | 531,931 | 59.13 |
| 15 | Grand Rapids | 163,821 | 277,862 | 58.96 |
| 16 | Dallas | 594,580 | 1,008,547 | 58.95 |
| 17 | Houston | 505,361 | 858,175 | 58.89 |
| 18 | Richmond | 144,895 | 248,425 | 58.33 |
| 19 | Fort Wayne | 88,642 | 152,486 | 58.13 |
| 20 | Knoxville | 100,800 | 174,102 | 57.90 |
| 21 | Shreveport | 76,582 | 132,522 | 57.79 |
| 22 | Jackson | 64,785 | 113,911 | 56.87 |
| 23 | Columbus, Ohio | 256,239 | 453,538 | 56.50 |

| Rank | City | Votes for All Major Candidates | Votes for Reagan | Reagan Votes as a Percentage of All Votes |
|------|------|------|------|------|
| 24 | Spokane | 78,096 | 138,617 | 56.34 |
| 25 | Montgomery | 50,725 | 90,226 | 56.20 |
| 26 | Greensboro | 154,160 | 280,291 | 55.00 |
| 27 | Chattanooga | 78,073 | 142,140 | 54.93 |
| 28 | Albuquerque | 90,718 | 166,206 | 54.58 |
| 29 | El Paso | 53,276 | 98,454 | 54.11 |
| 30 | Wichita | 85,527 | 158,744 | 53.88 |
| 31 | Denver | 357,432 | 664,092 | 53.82 |
| 32 | San Antonio | 179,237 | 335,767 | 53.38 |
| 33 | Birmingham | 164,132 | 307,568 | 53.36 |
| 33 | New Orleans | 220,329 | 412,897 | 53.36 |
| 35 | Norfolk-Virginia Beach | 135,837 | 255,881 | 53.09 |
| 36 | Jacksonville | 132,750 | 251,817 | 52.72 |
| 37 | Syracuse | 134,072 | 254,871 | 52.60 |
| 38 | Tacoma | 90,247 | 173,036 | 52.16 |
| 39 | Fresno | 82,515 | 158,496 | 52.06 |
| 40 | Lincoln | 38,630 | 74,891 | 51.58 |
| 41 | Los Angeles | 1,224,533 | 2,380,245 | 51.45 |
| 42 | Newark | 387,361 | 759,535 | 51.00 |
| 43 | Miami | 265,550 | 520,956 | 50.97 |
| 44 | Tucson | 93,055 | 182,767 | 50.91 |
| 45 | Baton Rouge | 91,795 | 181,678 | 50.53 |
| 46 | Tampa-St. Petersburg | 341,642 | 682,508 | 50.06 |
| 47 | St. Louis | 505,695 | 1,013,601 | 49.89 |
| 48 | San Jose | 229,048 | 461,524 | 49.63 |
| 49 | Charlotte | 100,533 | 204,489 | 49.16 |
| 50 | Louisville | 167,168 | 340,951 | 49.03 |
| 51 | Sacramento | 201,503 | 411,052 | 49.02 |
| 52 | Lexington-Fayette | 52,908 | 108,110 | 48.94 |
| 53 | Dayton | 154,669 | 318,249 | 48.60 |
| 54 | Kansas City, Kan., Mo. | 259,998 | 537,080 | 48.41 |
| 55 | Austin | 94,703 | 197,484 | 47.95 |
| 56 | Philadelphia | 914,628 | 1,915,828 | 47.74 |
| 57 | Corpus Christi | 489.912 | 103,288 | 47.35 |
| 58 | Seattle | 338,720 | 716,353 | 47.28 |
| 59 | Jersey City | 91,207 | 195,770 | 46.59 |
| 60 | Memphis | 180,399 | 345,650 | 46.41 |
| 61 | Milwaukee | 309,093 | 668,758 | 46.22 |
| 62 | Little Rock | 60,455 | 130,962 | 46.16 |
| 63 | Portland, Ore. | 246,106 | 534,033 | 46.08 |
| 64 | Chicago | 1,308,693 | 2,856,238 | 45.82 |
| 65 | Des Moines | 71,516 | 157,298 | 45.47 |
| 66 | Detroit | 794,927 | 1,754,315 | 45.31 |
| 67 | Honolulu | 99,596 | 221,399 | 44.98 |
| 68 | Toledo | 128,128 | 285,121 | 44.94 |
| 69 | Cleveland | 340,853 | 758,661 | 44.93 |
| 70 | Akron | 115,128 | 256,957 | 44.80 |
| 71 | Flint | 94,328 | 211,101 | 44.68 |
| 72 | Atlanta | 280,343 | 630,236 | 44.48 |
| 73 | Washington, D.C. | 471,786 | 1,064,206 | 44.33 |
| 74 | Pittsburgh | 398,018 | 904,016 | 44.03 |
| 75 | Worcester | 120,100 | 275,805 | 43.55 |
| 76 | San Francisco | 549,779 | 1,267,823 | 43.36 |
| 77 | Rochester | 163,842 | 385,688 | 42.48 |
| 78 | Boston | 682,299 | 1,609,109 | 42.40 |
| 79 | Buffalo | 207,969 | 499,251 | 41.66 |
| 80 | Baltimore | 330,679 | 804,047 | 41.13 |
| 81 | Nashville-Davidson | 118,480 | 296,803 | 39.92 |
| 82 | Minneapolis-St. Paul | 415,877 | 1,045,476 | 39.78 |
| 83 | Providence | 232,338 | 599,382 | 38.76 |
| 84 | Columbus, Ga. | 19,944 | 52,879 | 37.72 |
| 85 | Madison | 57,545 | 162,926 | 35.32 |
| 86 | New York | 733,321 | 2,666,170 | 27.50 |

# CHAPTER TEN

# HOUSING

Congress committed the nation in 1949 to the goal of adequate housing for all Americans. Adequate housing is still in 1983 an elusive local and individual goal. Big city residents in particular are hard-pressed to find adequate housing at a price they can afford. High interest rates have made purchasing a home very costly, while the cost of available uncontrolled rental housing has soared, especially in cities where some part of rental housing is subject to controls. The quality of housing available for the money will affect the willingness of many people to move to—or remain in—a city.

In cities facing budget deficits, housing has tended to be subordinated to other immediate needs, such as transportation. In New York, expected cutbacks in federal aid for housing for Community Block Grant funds have jeopardized adherence to existing housing program commitments. New York City shows a decrease of about $67 million in fiscal 1982 from a projected $221 million for housing.

In many older cities decaying downtown areas are scarred by abandoned and gutted buildings that create a deteriorating base for commercial and industrial businesses and an undesirable neighborhood for families.

Congressional concern over the housing industry's poor state resulted in the passage by Congress in late 1982 of a $5 billion bill designed to stimulate the industry. However, President Reagan vetoed the measure and again signaled his unwillingness to provide more such federal aid to cities until an economic revival increases the revenue side of the federal budget.

When mortgage interest rates remain in the high teens, low- and even middle-income families in the cities despair of attaining the American dream of owning their own home. In the large cities, the single-family dwelling has been replaced in part by condominiums and cooperative conversions—the former (which permit sale of apartments with building approval of the buyer) becoming the more popular approach in recent years. But

such conversions do not address the problem of city housing for the poor.

In fact, upgrading of housing has displaced the poor in older cities. As homeowners and investors rehabilitate blocks of row houses (in a process called "gentrification"), many poor people who had lived in low-rent housing are forced to move. Where they move to is a major concern to municipalities looking for housing for low-income families who are displaced. Many of those dispossessed of their homes by conversion to luxury housing are left to find living accommodations on their own. New York is attempting to obtain revenue from the developers, who deduct large portions of the costs of rehabilitation under the city's tax-abatement program, by decreasing the tax-free amount in order to increase city revenues for housing funding. This reduces the subsidy to landlord-developers converting low-income apartments and single-room hotels to luxury housing.

"Gentrification" is taking place in such cities as New Orleans and Washington, D.C. Baltimore has had success in making home ownership possible for many who were previously unable to own by its "homesteading program." Still, other cities like Little Rock are experiencing an "in-migration" of lower-income individuals and families who are creating housing assistance needs.

Phoenix devoted 17.5 percent of its 1981–82 total budget to housing, more than $74 million of a $424.7 million budget. Greensboro, while its total budget has increased steadily, has cut back its housing component to $3 million in 1982 from 1981 expenditures of nearly $3.8 million.

How to find a means of providing housing for the poor is a major problem facing large city governments. In New York City, in response to a large increase in the number of homeless, an additional $5 million was provided in the fiscal 1983 housing budget for accommodating 500 homeless in privately run shelters. New York had already committed $32 million to this problem in fiscal 1982. In addition, New York's Mayor Koch has been encouraging churches and synagogues to provide shelter and meals to some of the homeless.

In sum, the picture is mixed. Some cities provide considerable housing subsidies; others provide very little. Some cities are cutting back; others are increasing their housing aid. Each city's situation should be considered in light of housing needs and private housing supply.

# 152.  Housing Growth/Population Growth 1970–80

This interesting table shows that while population has grown in most cities, especially in the smaller ones away from the Northeast, housing has grown even faster. The index of housing growth/population growth was in every city greater than 1. Explanation? People want to be on their own. Children are moving away from their parents. It's not just that there are more people but the baby boom is at a housing forming age.

Financial necessity and a desire for larger housing space may bring the extended family concept back to life. The roommate concept may be another approach lasting long beyond the college years. The fastest growing city is Anchorage which saw a population growth of 3½ times and a housing growth of nearly 4½ times. But Aurora with a slightly less spectacular growth in housing and population had the highest ratio of housing growth to population growth. At the other extreme was Lexington-Fayette where the two figures grew at a more equal rate. An imbalance between the two growth figures, as we see in the case of Aurora, indicates more social change —and more housing availability than a more even ratio as in Lexington-Fayette.

SOURCE: U.S. Census Bureau, 1980 Census of Population, *Standard Metropolitan Statistical Areas and Standard Consolidated Statistical Areas: 1980*, October 1981

| Rank | City | Housing Growth/ Population Growth | Growth, (1970=100) Population | Housing Units |
|---|---|---|---|---|
| 1 | Aurora | 129.4 | 211.5 | 273.8 |
| 2 | Virginia Beach | 126.0 | 152.3 | 191.9 |
| 3 | Austin | 125.6 | 136.3 | 171.2 |
| 4 | Albuquerque | 123.4 | 135.7 | 167.5 |
| 5 | Columbus, Ohio | 123.3 | 104.6 | 129.0 |
| 6 | Denver | 122.9 | 95.5 | 117.4 |
| 6 | Honolulu | 122.9 | 112.4 | 138.1 |
| 8 | Madison | 122.6 | 99.3 | 121.7 |

| Rank | City | Housing Growth/ Population Growth | Growth, (1970=100) Population | Housing Units |
|---|---|---|---|---|
| 9 | Tucson | 122.3 | 125.7 | 153.7 |
| 10 | Warren | 122.2 | 89.9 | 109.9 |
| 11 | Arlington, Texas | 121.8 | 177.5 | 216.2 |
| 11 | Atlanta | 121.8 | 85.9 | 104.6 |
| 13 | Buffalo | 121.7 | 77.3 | 94.1 |
| 14 | Dallas | 121.5 | 107.0 | 130.0 |
| 14 | Greensboro | 121.5 | 108.0 | 131.2 |
| 16 | Houston | 120.9 | 129.2 | 156.2 |
| 17 | Knoxville | 120.8 | 104.0 | 125.6 |
| 18 | Huntington Beach | 120.7 | 147.0 | 177.5 |
| 19 | Norfolk | 120.2 | 86.7 | 104.2 |
| 20 | Anchorage | 120.1 | 359.8 | 432.1 |
| 21 | Richmond | 119.7 | 87.9 | 105.2 |
| 22 | Salt Lake City | 119.6 | 92.7 | 110.9 |
| 23 | Memphis | 119.2 | 103.6 | 123.5 |
| 24 | Las Vegas | 119.1 | 130.9 | 155.9 |
| 25 | Colorado Springs | 118.9 | 158.8 | 188.8 |
| 26 | Toledo | 118.9 | 92.6 | 110.1 |
| 27 | Sacramento | 118.8 | 107.2 | 127.4 |
| 28 | Boston | 118.1 | 87.8 | 103.7 |
| 29 | Fort Wayne | 117.9 | 96.6 | 113.9 |
| 30 | Charlotte | 117.7 | 130.2 | 153.3 |
| 30 | St. Paul | 117.7 | 87.2 | 102.6 |
| 30 | Dayton | 117.7 | 83.8 | 98.6 |
| 33 | Spokane | 117.6 | 100.5 | 118.2 |
| 34 | Tulsa | 117.4 | 109.3 | 128.3 |
| 35 | Lubbock | 116.8 | 116.7 | 136.3 |
| 35 | Lincoln | 116.8 | 115.0 | 134.3 |
| 37 | Fresno | 116.6 | 131.7 | 153.6 |
| 37 | Philadelphia | 116.6 | 86.6 | 101.0 |
| 39 | Mobile | 116.5 | 105.5 | 122.9 |
| 40 | Oklahoma City | 116.3 | 109.5 | 127.4 |
| 41 | Wichita | 115.8 | 101.0 | 117.0 |
| 42 | Fort Lauderdale | 115.7 | 109.8 | 127.0 |
| 43 | Tampa | 115.5 | 97.8 | 113.0 |
| 44 | Jacksonville | 114.6 | 107.3 | 123.0 |
| 45 | Riverside | 114.5 | 122.0 | 139.7 |
| 46 | San Antonio | 114.1 | 120.1 | 137.0 |
| 47 | Jackson | 114.0 | 131.8 | 150.3 |
| 48 | Nashville-Davidson | 113.5 | 107.0 | 121.4 |
| 49 | Miami | 113.0 | 103.6 | 117.1 |
| 50 | Phoenix | 112.9 | 135.2 | 152.6 |
| 51 | San Diego | 112.8 | 125.5 | 141.6 |
| 52 | Baton Rouge | 112.0 | 132.2 | 148.0 |
| 53 | San Jose | 111.8 | 138.4 | 154.7 |
| 54 | Montgomery | 111.6 | 133.6 | 149.1 |
| 55 | Lexington-Fayette | 111.1 | 188.8 | 209.7 |

# 153. Housing Growth

The trend toward suburban living has been highlighted by a high rate of growth of housing units in those localities that are best characterized as satellite cities, because they are populated by many workers who commute to their larger associated cities. In addition, many other factors such as water and sewer capacity and cost of heating fuels and electricity become determining factors for homeowners who plan to make their present home their only home.

This table shows how rapidly some cities were growing in the 1970s: between 1970 and 1980, Anchorage had the most rapid increase in housing—a growth by 1980 of over three times as many housing units as there were in 1970.

At the lower end of the ranking are, as expected, many of the older, distressed cities of the Northeast, including Detroit, Cleveland and Buffalo. St. Louis suffered the loss of housing units from the disastrous Pruitt-Igoe public housing project, which provided such inhospitable living conditions that it was prematurely torn down with hardly a protest from its unhappy residents. St. Louis also experienced a loss of 27 percent of its population between 1970 and 1980.

SOURCE: U.S. Census Bureau, 1980 Census of Population, *Standard Metropolitan Statistical Areas and Standard Consolidated Statistical Areas: 1980*, October 1981.

| Rank | City | 1970 Housing Units (000) | 1980 Housing Units (000) | Absolute Change (000) | Percentage Change |
|---|---|---|---|---|---|
| 1 | Anchorage | 16.2 | 69.9 | 53.7 | 331.48 |
| 2 | Virginia Beach | 48.0 | 92.0 | 49.0 | 113.95 |
| 3 | Lexington-Fayette | 39.0 | 81.7 | 42.7 | 109.48 |
| 4 | Colorado Springs | 46.7 | 88.3 | 41.6 | 89.07 |
| 5 | Salt Lake City | 119.8 | 216.7 | 96.9 | 80.88 |
| 6 | Austin | 85.7 | 146.7 | 61.0 | 71.17 |
| 7 | Albuquerque | 79.0 | 132.3 | 53.3 | 67.46 |
| 8 | San Jose | 139.8 | 219.0 | 79.2 | 56.65 |
| 9 | Houston | 428 | 668.4 | 240.4 | 56.16 |
| 10 | Las Vegas | 43.1 | 67.1 | 24.0 | 55.68 |
| 11 | Fresno | 57.3 | 88.7 | 31.4 | 54.79 |
| 12 | Tucson | 89.3 | 137.2 | 47.9 | 53.63 |
| 13 | Charlotte | 80.8 | 123.8 | 43.0 | 53.21 |
| 14 | Phoenix | 196.0 | 299.2 | 103.2 | 52.65 |
| 15 | Chattanooga | 43.9 | 66.6 | 22.7 | 51.70 |
| 16 | Jackson | 50.5 | 75.6 | 25.1 | 49.70 |
| 17 | Baton Rouge | 56.4 | 84.1 | 27.7 | 49.11 |
| 17 | Montgomery | 45.2 | 67.4 | 22.2 | 49.11 |
| 19 | Anaheim | 56.1 | 83.6 | 27.5 | 49.01 |
| 20 | El Paso | 92.7 | 134.4 | 41.7 | 44.98 |
| 21 | Denver | 193.8 | 277.5 | 83.7 | 43.18 |
| 22 | San Diego | 241.4 | 341.9 | 100.5 | 41.63 |
| 23 | Riverside | 45.9 | 64.3 | 18.4 | 40.08 |
| 24 | Honolulu | 103.0 | 142.3 | 39.3 | 38.15 |
| 25 | San Antonio | 203.2 | 277.5 | 74.3 | 36.56 |
| 26 | Lubbock | 49.1 | 67.0 | 17.9 | 36.45 |
| 27 | Santa Ana | 49.7 | 67.2 | 17.5 | 35.21 |
| 28 | Lincoln | 51.5 | 69.1 | 17.6 | 34.17 |
| 29 | Greensboro | 45.6 | 59.9 | 14.3 | 31.35 |
| 30 | Columbus, Ohio | 182.5 | 236.7 | 54.2 | 29.69 |
| 31 | Tulsa | 121.4 | 156.3 | 34.9 | 28.74 |
| 32 | Dallas | 303.3 | 390.4 | 87.1 | 28.71 |
| 33 | Corpus Christi | 63.8 | 81.6 | 17.8 | 27.89 |
| 34 | Sacramento | 96.6 | 123.3 | 26.7 | 27.63 |
| 35 | Oklahoma City | 139.0 | 177.1 | 38.1 | 27.41 |
| 36 | Shreveport | 63.1 | 80.0 | 16.9 | 26.78 |
| 37 | Knoxville | 61.0 | 76.8 | 15.8 | 25.90 |

| Rank | City | 1970 Housing Units (000) | 1980 Housing Units (000) | Absolute Change (000) | Percentage Change |
|------|------|-----------|-----------|-----------|-----------|
| 38 | Memphis | 198.1 | 244.5 | 46.4 | 23.42 |
| 39 | Madison | 56.1 | 69.0 | 12.9 | 22.99 |
| 40 | Mobile | 61.5 | 75.6 | 14.1 | 22.92 |
| 41 | Jacksonville | 174.3 | 213.5 | 39.2 | 22.48 |
| 42 | St. Petersburg | 97.0 | 118.7 | 21.7 | 22.37 |
| 43 | Nashville-Davidson | 147.3 | 179.1 | 31.8 | 21.58 |
| 44 | Columbus, Ga. | 53.3 | 63.6 | 10.3 | 19.32 |
| 45 | Spokane | 64.3 | 76.0 | 11.7 | 18.19 |
| 46 | Wichita | 99.9 | 116.6 | 16.7 | 16.71 |
| 47 | Miami | 125.3 | 145.8 | 20.5 | 16.36 |
| 48 | Tacoma | 58.7 | 67.8 | 9.1 | 15.50 |
| 49 | Fort Wayne | 61.7 | 70.6 | 8.9 | 14.42 |
| 50 | Tampa | 100.8 | 114.2 | 13.4 | 13.29 |
| 51 | Fort Worth | 139.1 | 156.0 | 16.9 | 12.14 |
| 52 | Portland, Ore. | 151.1 | 167.9 | 16.8 | 11.11 |
| 53 | Los Angeles | 1,074.2 | 1,189.4 | 115.2 | 10.72 |
| 54 | Toledo | 130.0 | 143.3 | 13.3 | 10.23 |
| 55 | Des Moines | 72.6 | 79.9 | 7.3 | 10.05 |
| 56 | Birmingham | 105.4 | 114.5 | 9.1 | 8.63 |
| 56 | New Orleans | 208.5 | 226.5 | 18.0 | 8.63 |
| 58 | Long Beach | 150.1 | 159.7 | 9.6 | 6.39 |
| 59 | Omaha | 117.7 | 124.1 | 6.4 | 5.43 |
| 60 | Richmond | 87.0 | 91.5 | 4.5 | 5.17 |
| 61 | Worcester | 58.6 | 61.6 | 3.0 | 5.11 |
| 62 | Atlanta | 171.0 | 178.8 | 7.8 | 4.56 |
| 63 | Norfolk | 91.1 | 94.9 | 3.8 | 4.17 |
| 64 | Boston | 232.4 | 241.4 | 9.0 | 3.87 |
| 65 | Milwaukee | 246.1 | 253.5 | 7.4 | 3.00 |
| 66 | St. Paul | 107.7 | 110.9 | 3.2 | 2.97 |
| 67 | Oakland | 146.6 | 150.3 | 3.7 | 2.52 |
| 68 | Grand Rapids | 68.2 | 69.9 | 1.7 | 2.49 |
| 69 | San Francisco | 310.4 | 316.6 | 6.2 | 1.99 |
| 70 | Syracuse | 71.8 | 73.2 | 1.4 | 1.94 |
| 71 | Dayton | 85.3 | 86.9 | 1.6 | 1.87 |
| 72 | Philadelphia | 674.2 | 685.6 | 11.4 | 1.69 |
| 73 | Minneapolis | 167.2 | 168.9 | 1.7 | 1.01 |
| 74 | Akron | 95.8 | 96.7 | .9 | .93 |
| 75 | New York | 2,924.3 | 2,946.1 | 21.8 | .74 |
| 76 | Cincinnati | 172.8 | 172.7 | − .1 | − .05 |
| 77 | Kansas City, Mo. | 192.4 | 191.9 | − .5 | − .25 |
| 78 | Washington, D.C. | 278.3 | 276.7 | − 1.6 | − .57 |
| 79 | Providence | 68.1 | 67.5 | − .6 | − .88 |
| 80 | Baltimore | 305.5 | 302.7 | − 2.8 | − .91 |
| 81 | Rochester | 105.1 | 102.6 | − 2.5 | − 2.37 |
| 82 | Louisville | 129.7 | 126.1 | − 3.6 | − 2.77 |
| 83 | Chicago | 1,209.4 | 1,174.7 | −34.7 | − 2.86 |
| 84 | Jersey City | 92.0 | 88.0 | − 4.0 | − 4.34 |
| 85 | Newark | 127.2 | 121.4 | − 5.8 | − 4.55 |
| 86 | Flint | 64.2 | 61.0 | − 3.2 | − 4.98 |
| 87 | Pittsburgh | 189.8 | 179.2 | −10.6 | − 5.58 |
| 88 | Buffalo | 166.1 | 156.4 | − 9.7 | − 5.83 |
| 89 | Cleveland | 264.1 | 239.6 | −24.5 | − 9.27 |
| 90 | Detroit | 530.1 | 471.4 | −58.7 | −11.07 |
| 91 | St. Louis | 238.5 | 202.1 | −36.4 | −15.26 |

# 154. Residents Per Housing Unit

Residents per housing unit is a crude indicator of "crowdedness"—the number of people living in the same space.

The U. S. Census Bureau defines a housing unit as: a house, an apartment, or a group of rooms, or a single room, occupied as a separate living quarters or, if vacant, intended for occupancy. Separate living quarters are those in which the occupants live and eat separately from any other persons in the building and which have direct access from the outside of the building or through a common hall.

Cities that have a high number of residents per housing unit are experiencing a relative housing shortage, to the extent that people are looking for larger quarters. Or they may be cities with larger families, either because of high birthrates or because of the presence of many families that are culturally oriented toward having relatives at home (the so-called extended family form of living).

The following table, which shows 1980 population divided by 1980 housing units, indicates that a number of factors are at work. Cities that are growing at a fast rate, like El Paso, Santa Ana and San Jose, have the greatest number of occupants per household. El Paso and Santa Ana have very high birth rates, indicating a larger number of children per family.

At the other extreme, in St. Petersburg, the population includes many retirees, who mostly live alone (or with their spouses), without children. San Francisco has a small number of occupants per household because it has a large number of adults without children, living as couples or alone.

SOURCE: U.S. Census Bureau, *Standard Metropolitan Statistical Areas and Standard Consolidated Statistical Areas: 1980* (Washington, D.C.: Government Printing Office, October 1981).

| Rank | City | People per Number of Housing Unit | Rank | City | People per Number of Housing Unit | Rank | City | People per Number of Housing Unit |
|---|---|---|---|---|---|---|---|---|
| 1 | El Paso | 3.16 | 32 | Charlotte | 2.53 | 63 | Miami | 2.38 |
| 2 | Santa Ana | 3.03 | 32 | Jacksonville | 2.53 | 63 | Tampa | 2.38 |
| 3 | San Jose | 2.91 | 34 | Milwaukee | 2.51 | 66 | Louisville | 2.37 |
| 4 | Virginia Beach | 2.85 | 34 | Omaha | 2.51 | 66 | Pittsburgh | 2.37 |
| 5 | Corpus Christi | 2.84 | 36 | Albuquerque | 2.50 | 68 | Austin | 2.36 |
| 6 | San Antonio | 2.83 | 36 | Lexington-Fayette | 2.50 | 68 | Rochester | 2.36 |
| 7 | Norfolk | 2.81 | 38 | Lincoln | 2.49 | 70 | Houston | 2.35 |
| 8 | Newark | 2.71 | 38 | Los Angeles | 2.49 | 71 | Dayton | 2.34 |
| 9 | Jackson | 2.68 | 40 | Anchorage | 2.48 | 71 | Kansas City, Mo. | 2.34 |
| 10 | Columbus, Ga. | 2.67 | 40 | Birmingham | 2.48 | 71 | Tacoma | 2.34 |
| 11 | Riverside | 2.66 | 42 | Fort Worth | 2.47 | 74 | Boston | 2.33 |
| 12 | Anaheim | 2.65 | 42 | Indianapolis | 2.47 | 75 | Dallas | 2.32 |
| 12 | Mobile | 2.65 | 42 | Madison | 2.47 | 75 | Providence | 2.32 |
| 14 | Memphis | 2.64 | 42 | Toledo | 2.47 | 75 | Syracuse | 2.32 |
| 14 | Montgomery | 2.64 | 46 | Fresno | 2.46 | 78 | Tulsa | 2.31 |
| 16 | Flint | 2.62 | 46 | New Orleans | 2.46 | 79 | Washington, D.C. | 2.30 |
| 16 | Worcester | 2.62 | 46 | Philadelphia | 2.46 | 80 | Buffalo | 2.29 |
| 18 | Baton Rouge | 2.61 | 49 | Akron | 2.45 | 81 | Oklahoma City | 2.28 |
| 19 | Baltimore | 2.60 | 49 | Las Vegas | 2.45 | 82 | Long Beach | 2.26 |
| 19 | Grand Rapids | 2.60 | 49 | Little Rock | 2.45 | 82 | Oakland | 2.26 |
| 19 | Greensboro | 2.60 | 52 | Colorado Springs | 2.44 | 84 | Spokane | 2.25 |
| 19 | Lubbock | 2.60 | 52 | Fort Wayne | 2.44 | 85 | Sacramento | 2.24 |
| 23 | Honolulu | 2.57 | 55 | Tucson | 2.41 | 85 | St. Louis | 2.24 |
| 23 | Shreveport | 2.57 | 56 | Cleveland | 2.40 | 85 | Salt Lake City | 2.24 |
| 25 | Chicago | 2.56 | 56 | New York | 2.40 | 88 | Cincinnati | 2.23 |
| 25 | Phoenix | 2.56 | 56 | Richmond | 2.40 | 89 | Minneapolis | 2.20 |
| 25 | San Diego | 2.56 | 59 | Columbus, Ohio | 2.39 | 90 | Portland, Ore. | 2.18 |
| 28 | Detroit | 2.55 | 59 | Des Moines | 2.39 | 91 | Denver | 2.16 |
| 29 | Chattanooga | 2.54 | 59 | Knoxville | 2.39 | 92 | Seattle | 2.15 |
| 29 | Jersey City | 2.54 | 59 | Wichita | 2.39 | 93 | San Francisco | 2.14 |
| 29 | Nashville-Davidson | 2.54 | 63 | Atlanta | 2.38 | 94 | St. Petersburg | 1.99 |

# 155. Housing Permits

Construction of new housing requires a permit from the local government to ensure that all relevant zoning and building codes will be adhered to. The number of permits has become an indicator of housing growth. To put local housing permits in perspective, the national picture should be considered. Housing permits declined dramatically between 1977 and 1981, largely because of the high cost of borrowing money. Between 1977 and 1978 permits for multiple-unit projects of five and more units increased slightly, but otherwise in every year the two major categories of single-family units and five-or-more-unit projects showed a steady decline. From a total of over 1.8 million units in 1977, permits dropped to under a million in 1981. The proportion of single-unit structures to all private structures decreased significantly during that period, from 68 to 57 percent. Going further back, the proportion of single-unit structures declined between 1967 and 1971 from 57 to 46 percent. Construction of single-unit structures relative to all housing was near its peak in 1977.

Permits for private construction in 1981 showed continued growth for satellite cities like Aurora and Arlington, Texas in the West and Southwest. Other cities near military bases like Colorado Springs, San Antonio and El Paso have avoided the housing construction slump.

Arlington, located in the Dallas-Fort Worth metro region, had a population increase of over 76 percent in the decade 1970–80. The jobs offered by national and regional firms such as General Motors, Southwestern Bell and Xerox have created a sound foundation for housing growth in the area.

Colorado Springs, heavily tied to the military in the early 1940's and late 1950's, has shown healthy growth in the past decade. One of four housing units in Colorado Springs has been constructed since 1970. In 1979 the combined direct and multiplier effects of defense spending were estimated at $1.2 billion, or over half the personal income of city residents.

The number of housing permits for private construction in each of the cities provides a leading indicator of construction activity. A permit issued in 1981 is likely to result in new housing available in 1982 or 1983. The table shows 1981 permits per 1,000 residents, based on 1980 (latest available) population data.

SOURCES: U.S. Census Bureau, *Housing Units Authorized by Building Permits and Public Contracts: Annual 1981* (Washington, D.C.: Government Printing Office, 1982), pp. 1, 44–352. City of Colorado Springs Planning Department, *Community Profile for the City of Colorado Springs, 1981*. Arlington Planning Department, *Arlington, Texas 1980 Growth Prospectus.*

| Rank | City | Total Permits | Permits per 1,000 Residents |
|------|------|---------------|------------------------------|
| 1 | Aurora | 4,690 | 29.57 |
| 2 | Austin | 8,611 | 24.92 |
| 3 | Arlington, Texas | 3,790 | 23.67 |
| 4 | Anchorage | 3,115 | 18.00 |
| 5 | Colorado Springs | 2,737 | 12.72 |
| 6 | Phoenix | 9,878 | 12.51 |
| 7 | Corpus Christi | 2,758 | 11.89 |
| 8 | Las Vegas | 1,661 | 10.09 |
| 9 | Miami | 3,143 | 9.06 |
| 10 | Dallas | 7,612 | 8.42 |
| 11 | Oklahoma City | 3,224 | 8.00 |
| 12 | Lubbock | 1,336 | 7.68 |
| 13 | Charlotte | 2,392 | 7.61 |
| 13 | San Antonio | 5,975 | 7.61 |
| 15 | Honolulu | 2,617 | 7.17 |
| 16 | Wichita | 2,116 | 7.12 |
| 17 | Houston | 12,143 | 6.73 |
| 18 | Tucson | 2,164 | 6.55 |
| 19 | Tulsa | 2,334 | 6.48 |
| 20 | Indianapolis | 4,231 | 6.04 |
| 21 | Fort Worth | 2,255 | 5.85 |
| 22 | San Diego | 4,972 | 5.68 |
| 23 | Sacramento | 1,516 | 5.50 |
| 24 | El Paso | 2,293 | 5.39 |
| 25 | Salt Lake City | 815 | 5.00 |
| 26 | Birmingham | 1,386 | 4.87 |
| 27 | Madison | 778 | 4.56 |
| 27 | Tacoma | 722 | 4.56 |
| 29 | Mobile | 898 | 4.48 |
| 30 | Huntington Beach | 750 | 4.40 |
| 31 | Spokane | 754 | 4.25 |
| 32 | St. Petersburg | 1,002 | 4.23 |
| 33 | Albuquerque | 1,389 | 4.19 |
| 34 | Lexington-Fayette | 840 | 4.11 |
| 35 | Columbus, Ohio | 2,306 | 4.08 |
| 36 | Greensboro | 632 | 4.06 |
| 37 | Worcester | 638 | 3.94 |
| 38 | Little Rock | 610 | 3.85 |
| 39 | Denver | 1,816 | 3.70 |
| 40 | Lincoln | 629 | 3.66 |
| 41 | Knoxville | 646 | 3.53 |
| 42 | Riverside | 599 | 3.51 |
| 43 | St. Paul | 846 | 3.13 |
| 44 | New Orleans | 1,685 | 3.02 |

| Rank | City | Total Permits | Permits per 1,000 Residents |
|------|------|--------------:|----------------------------:|
| 45 | Nashville-Davidson | 1,333 | 2.93 |
| 46 | San Jose | 1,854 | 2.91 |
| 47 | Shreveport | 596 | 2.90 |
| 48 | Seattle | 1,424 | 2.88 |
| 49 | Akron | 656 | 2.77 |
| 50 | Omaha | 805 | 2.58 |
| 51 | Los Angeles | 7,390 | 2.49 |
| 52 | Des Moines | 469 | 2.46 |
| 53 | Fresno | 507 | 2.32 |
| 54 | Montgomery | 407 | 2.28 |
| 55 | Columbus, Ga. | 365 | 2.15 |
| 56 | Toledo | 747 | 2.11 |
| 57 | Jersey City | 467 | 2.09 |
| 58 | Portland, Ore. | 686 | 1.87 |
| 59 | Richmond | 389 | 1.77 |
| 60 | Anaheim | 391 | 1.76 |
| 61 | Chattanooga | 297 | 1.75 |
| 62 | San Francisco | 1,126 | 1.66 |
| 63 | Atlanta | 668 | 1.57 |
| 64 | Washington, D.C. | 981 | 1.54 |
| 65 | Milwaukee | 894 | 1.41 |
| 66 | Long Beach | 507 | 1.40 |
| 67 | Minneapolis | 492 | 1.33 |
| 68 | Newark | 384 | 1.17 |

| Rank | City | Total Permits | Permits per 1,000 Residents |
|------|------|--------------:|----------------------------:|
| 69 | Baton Rouge | 252 | 1.15 |
| 70 | Jackson | 231 | 1.14 |
| 71 | Philadelphia | 1,906 | 1.13 |
| 72 | Kansas City, Mo. | 465 | 1.04 |
| 73 | Oakland | 335 | 0.98 |
| 74 | Detroit | 1,171 | 0.97 |
| 75 | Baltimore | 746 | 0.94 |
| 76 | Memphis | 564 | 0.88 |
| 76 | Rochester | 215 | 0.88 |
| 78 | Boston | 473 | 0.84 |
| 79 | Tampa | 2,318 | 0.83 |
| 80 | Cincinnati | 308 | 0.79 |
| 81 | Chicago | 2,328 | 0.78 |
| 82 | Providence | 113 | 0.73 |
| 83 | St. Louis | 302 | 0.67 |
| 84 | Pittsburgh | 247 | 0.59 |
| 85 | Syracuse | 89 | 0.52 |
| 86 | Kansas City, Kan. | 216 | 0.49 |
| 87 | Fort Wayne | 72 | 0.41 |
| 88 | Buffalo | 133 | 0.38 |
| 89 | Cleveland | 216 | 0.37 |
| 90 | Yonkers | 71 | 0.36 |
| 91 | Flint | 5 | 0.03 |

# 156.  Change in Authorized Housing Permits

While most areas of the country experienced a drop in the amount of authorized housing permits issued between the years 1980 and 1981, some northern cities—notably Rochester, Syracuse, Worcester and New York—showed increased permit activity. Less than one-quarter of the cities ranked in the following table showed positive changes.

Many cities have undergone uncertain periods of construction activity in the past few years. A general decline in housing production in Boston—ranked 81st here, and showing a decline of nearly 64 percent—has raised the percentage of housing units 20 years old and older. This creates an opportunity for new housing construction or rehabilitation as neighborhoods decline. Some neighborhoods, such as Boston's Beacon Hill area, never lack housing upgraders. Other neighborhoods, like Boston's South End or Charlestown, discover them when the demand for housing has outstripped the supply.

Memphis has been experiencing a severe slowdown in the housing market in 1981. Single-family permits were down 80 percent; multifamily permits were down more than 27 percent. Many homes constructed in the preceding years have remained vacant and unsold for long periods of time. Sales of single-family homes fell by 48.3 percent between the third quarter 1980 and the third quarter 1981.

In Worcester, where city officials report that 13 percent of city housing is in need of rehabilitation, the positive increase in housing permits and expected construction activity in the downtown area bodes well for the area's general economy and housing outlook.

SOURCE: Census Bureau, *Housing Units Authorized by Building Permits and Public Contracts: Annual 1981* (Washington, D.C.: Government Printing Office, July 1982), pp. 44–352.

| Rank | City | Number of Permits 1980 | Number of Permits 1981 | Percentage Change |
|------|------|------------:|------------:|------------------:|
| 1 | Rochester | 10 | 153 | 1,430.00 |
| 2 | Syracuse | 22 | 89 | 304.55 |
| 3 | Anchorage | 1,068 | 3,115 | 191.67 |
| 4 | Riverside | 206 | 599 | 304.55 |
| 5 | Worcester | 223 | 638 | 186.10 |
| 6 | Salt Lake City | 553 | 815 | 47.38 |
| 7 | New York | 6,001 | 8,436 | 40.58 |
| 8 | Miami | 1,679 | 2,318 | 38.06 |

| Rank | City | Number of Permits 1980 | Number of Permits 1981 | Percentage Change |
|---|---|---|---|---|
| 8 | Tampa | 1,679 | 2,318 | 38.06 |
| 10 | Austin | 6,243 | 8,611 | 37.93 |
| 11 | St. Paul | 622 | 846 | 36.01 |
| 12 | Spokane | 579 | 754 | 30.22 |
| 13 | Detroit | 928 | 1,171 | 26.19 |
| 14 | Charlotte | 1,931 | 2,392 | 23.87 |
| 15 | Milwaukee | 767 | 894 | 16.56 |
| 16 | Lubbock | 1,183 | 1,336 | 12.93 |
| 17 | Arlington, Texas | 3,462 | 3,790 | 9.47 |
| 18 | Oklahoma City | 3,050 | 3,224 | 5.70 |
| 19 | Phoenix | 9,391 | 9,878 | 5.19 |
| 20 | Colorado Springs | 2,664 | 2,737 | 2.74 |
| 21 | Indianapolis | 4,148 | 4,231 | 2.00 |
| 22 | San Francisco | 1,132 | 1,126 | − .53 |
| 23 | Madison | 788 | 778 | − 1.27 |
| 24 | Aurora | 4,903 | 4,690 | − 4.34 |
| 25 | Corpus Christi | 2,899 | 2,758 | − 4.86 |
| 26 | Dallas | 8,201 | 7.612 | − 7.18 |
| 27 | Baltimore | 823 | 746 | − 9.36 |
| 28 | San Diego | 5,490 | 4,972 | − 9.44 |
| 29 | Huntington Beach | 835 | 750 | − 10.18 |
| 30 | Akron | 732 | 656 | − 10.38 |
| 31 | Wichita | 2,368 | 2,116 | − 10.64 |
| 32 | San Antonio | 6,762 | 5,975 | − 11.64 |
| 33 | Long Beach | 609 | 507 | − 16.75 |
| 34 | Houston | 14,707 | 12,143 | − 17.43 |
| 35 | New Orleans | 2,047 | 1,685 | − 17.68 |
| 36 | Toledo | 923 | 747 | − 19.07 |
| 37 | Greensboro | 781 | 632 | − 19.08 |
| 38 | St. Petersburg | 1,240 | 1,002 | − 19.19 |
| 39 | Des Moines | 601 | 469 | − 21.96 |
| 40 | Philadelphia | 2,467 | 1,906 | − 22.74 |
| 41 | Tucson | 2,871 | 2,164 | − 24.63 |
| 42 | Chicago | 3,167 | 2,328 | − 26.49 |
| 43 | Denver | 2,482 | 1,816 | − 26.83 |
| 44 | El Paso | 3,148 | 2,293 | − 27.16 |
| 45 | Little Rock | 841 | 610 | − 27.47 |
| 46 | Columbus, Ga. | 513 | 365 | − 28.85 |
| 47 | Nashville-Davidson | 1,892 | 1,333 | − 29.55 |
| 48 | Shreveport | 877 | 596 | − 32.04 |

| Rank | City | Number of Permits 1980 | Number of Permits 1981 | Percentage Change |
|---|---|---|---|---|
| 49 | Los Angeles | 10,883 | 7,390 | − 32.10 |
| 50 | Columbus, Ohio | 3,400 | 2,306 | − 32.18 |
| 51 | Minneapolis | 729 | 492 | − 32.51 |
| 52 | Tulsa | 3,478 | 2,334 | − 32.89 |
| 53 | Tacoma | 1,108 | 722 | − 34.84 |
| 54 | Fort Worth | 3,644 | 2,255 | − 38.12 |
| 55 | Kansas City, Kan. | 350 | 216 | − 38.29 |
| 56 | Las Vegas | 2,726 | 1,661 | − 39.07 |
| 57 | Lexington-Fayette | 1,392 | 840 | − 39.66 |
| 58 | Lincoln | 1,043 | 629 | − 39.69 |
| 59 | Seattle | 2,370 | 1,424 | − 39.92 |
| 60 | Sacramento | 2,577 | 1,516 | − 41.17 |
| 61 | Providence | 193 | 113 | − 41.45 |
| 62 | Knoxville | 1,149 | 646 | − 43.78 |
| 63 | Omaha | 1,471 | 805 | − 45.28 |
| 64 | Albuquerque | 2,621 | 1,389 | − 47.00 |
| 65 | Honolulu | 4,952 | 2,617 | − 47.15 |
| 66 | Atlanta | 1,285 | 668 | − 48.02 |
| 67 | Newark | 749 | 384 | − 48.73 |
| 68 | Portland, Ore. | 1,383 | 686 | − 50.40 |
| 69 | Jersey City | 951 | 467 | − 50.89 |
| 70 | Cleveland | 452 | 215 | − 52.43 |
| 71 | Washington, D.C. | 2,129 | 981 | − 53.92 |
| 72 | Cincinnati | 684 | 308 | − 54.97 |
| 73 | Kansas City, Mo. | 1,044 | 465 | − 55.46 |
| 74 | Memphis | 1,324 | 564 | − 57.40 |
| 75 | Fresno | 2,427 | 1,024 | − 57.81 |
| 76 | Oakland | 797 | 335 | − 57.97 |
| 77 | Anaheim | 983 | 391 | − 60.22 |
| 78 | Richmond | 1,002 | 389 | − 61.18 |
| 79 | San Jose | 4,884 | 1,854 | − 62.04 |
| 80 | St. Louis | 821 | 302 | − 63.22 |
| 81 | Boston | 1,307 | 473 | − 63.81 |
| 82 | Pittsburgh | 743 | 247 | − 66.76 |
| 83 | Chattanooga | 1,064 | 297 | − 72.09 |
| 84 | Jackson | 1,044 | 231 | − 77.87 |
| 85 | Flint | 23 | 5 | − 78.26 |
| 86 | Yonkers | 377 | 71 | − 81.17 |
| 87 | Baton Rouge | 1,492 | 252 | − 83.11 |
| 88 | Fort Wayne | 773 | 72 | − 90.69 |

# 157. Permits for Five or More Housing Units

The following table, showing the percentage of permits issued in 1981 for construction projects of five or more units, indicates that the demand for apartments and condominiums is continuing at a significant pace for most cities. The reason for this is the cost of new homes, the high level of interest rates, and the high cost of land in urban locations. Many cities have seen much available vacant land converted to parking lots. When land does become available, its cost is so high that developers tend to plan for multi-unit projects to spread their land purchase costs over a larger number of units.

Newark showed nearly 94 percent of its construction permits for 1981 to be for structures of five or more units. Salt Lake City and Washington, D.C. follow, with better than 91 percent and 89 percent, respectively.

Most cities have experienced a steady growth in the number of apartment units constructed. Los Angeles, ranked 11th, has attributed the bulk of its increase in housing units to construction of new apartment units. Since 1970, apartments increased by a net total of 104,710, while single-family dwellings only showed a net gain of 1,934 units. For the decade 1970–80, apartment

units represented 84 percent of the certificates of occupancy for Los Angeles.

SOURCES: U.S. Census Bureau, *Housing Units Authorized by Building Permits and Public Contracts: Annual
1981* (Washington, D.C.: Government Printing Office,
July 1982), pp. 44–352. City of Los Angeles, Department
of City Planning, *Estimated Housing Inventory by Geographic Areas, January 1, 1981.*

| Rank | City | Total Housing Permits | Permits for 5 or More Housing Units | Percentage of Permits for 5 or More Units |
|---|---|---|---|---|
| 1 | Newark | 384 | 360 | 93.76 |
| 2 | Salt Lake City | 815 | 746 | 91.53 |
| 3 | Washington, D.C. | 981 | 879 | 89.60 |
| 4 | Cleveland | 215 | 188 | 87.44 |
| 5 | Worcester | 638 | 552 | 86.52 |
| 6 | Cincinnati | 308 | 266 | 86.36 |
| 7 | St. Louis | 302 | 259 | 85.76 |
| 8 | Rochester | 153 | 130 | 84.97 |
| 9 | Miami | 3,143 | 2,660 | 84.63 |
| 10 | Detroit | 1,171 | 961 | 82.07 |
| 11 | Los Angeles | 7,390 | 5,955 | 80.58 |
| 12 | Knoxville | 646 | 519 | 80.34 |
| 13 | Buffalo | 133 | 106 | 79.70 |
| 14 | Houston | 12,143 | 9,579 | 78.88 |
| 15 | Providence | 113 | 84 | 74.34 |
| 16 | Jersey City | 467 | 345 | 73.88 |
| 17 | Indianapolis | 4,231 | 3,081 | 72.82 |
| 18 | Chicago | 2,328 | 1,680 | 72.16 |
| 19 | Baltimore | 746 | 532 | 71.31 |
| 20 | San Francisco | 1,126 | 776 | 68.92 |
| 21 | Milwaukee | 894 | 616 | 68.90 |
| 22 | San Diego | 4,972 | 3,407 | 68.52 |
| 23 | Dallas | 7,612 | 5,163 | 67.83 |
| 24 | Honolulu | 2,617 | 1,772 | 67.71 |
| 25 | Philadelphia | 1,906 | 1,284 | 67.37 |
| 26 | Long Beach | 507 | 332 | 65.48 |
| 27 | Pittsburgh | 247 | 161 | 65.18 |
| 28 | Toledo | 747 | 486 | 65.06 |
| 29 | New York | 8,436 | 5,419 | 64.24 |
| 30 | St. Petersburg | 2,318 | 1,477 | 63.72 |
| 30 | Tampa | 2,318 | 1,477 | 63.72 |
| 32 | Boston | 473 | 300 | 63.42 |
| 33 | Akron | 656 | 416 | 63.41 |
| 34 | Huntington Beach | 750 | 467 | 62.27 |
| 35 | Mobile | 898 | 557 | 62.03 |
| 36 | Seattle | 1,424 | 880 | 61.80 |
| 37 | San Antonio | 5,975 | 3,558 | 59.55 |

| Rank | City | Total Housing Permits | Permits for 5 or More Housing Units | Percentage of Permits for 5 or More Units |
|---|---|---|---|---|
| 38 | Richmond | 389 | 228 | 58.61 |
| 39 | Tulsa | 2,334 | 1,313 | 56.26 |
| 40 | Charlotte | 2,392 | 1,345 | 56.23 |
| 41 | Syracuse | 89 | 49 | 55.06 |
| 42 | Denver | 1,816 | 989 | 54.46 |
| 43 | Tucson | 2,164 | 1,159 | 53.56 |
| 44 | Austin | 8,611 | 4,590 | 53.30 |
| 45 | Minneapolis | 492 | 260 | 52.85 |
| 46 | Phoenix | 9,878 | 5,162 | 52.26 |
| 47 | Corpus Christi | 2,758 | 1,413 | 51.23 |
| 48 | Columbus, Ohio | 2,306 | 1,181 | 51.21 |
| 49 | Madison | 778 | 398 | 51.16 |
| 50 | Little Rock | 610 | 289 | 47.38 |
| 51 | Birmingham | 1,386 | 648 | 46.75 |
| 52 | Aurora | 4,690 | 2,190 | 46.70 |
| 53 | New Orleans | 1,685 | 747 | 44.33 |
| 54 | Lubbock | 1,336 | 585 | 43.79 |
| 55 | Des Moines | 469 | 190 | 40.51 |
| 56 | Las Vegas | 1,661 | 663 | 39.92 |
| 57 | Arlington, Texas | 3,790 | 1,511 | 39.87 |
| 58 | Fresno | 1,024 | 385 | 37.60 |
| 59 | El Paso | 2,293 | 851 | 37.11 |
| 60 | Fort Worth | 2,255 | 804 | 35.65 |
| 61 | Chattanooga | 297 | 105 | 35.35 |
| 62 | San Jose | 1,854 | 644 | 34.74 |
| 63 | Lincoln | 629 | 214 | 34.02 |
| 64 | Nashville-Davidson | 1,333 | 443 | 33.23 |
| 65 | Lexington-Fayette | 840 | 277 | 32.98 |
| 66 | Portland, Ore. | 686 | 216 | 31.49 |
| 67 | Oakland | 335 | 105 | 31.34 |
| 68 | Shreveport | 596 | 184 | 30.87 |
| 69 | Sacramento | 1,516 | 462 | 30.47 |
| 70 | Baton Rouge | 252 | 73 | 28.97 |
| 71 | Tacoma | 722 | 207 | 28.67 |
| 72 | Wichita | 2,116 | 568 | 26.84 |
| 73 | Spokane | 754 | 185 | 24.54 |
| 74 | Columbus, Ga. | 365 | 78 | 21.37 |
| 75 | Anaheim | 391 | 78 | 19.95 |
| 76 | Omaha | 805 | 159 | 19.75 |
| 77 | Oklahoma City | 3,224 | 544 | 16.87 |
| 78 | Riverside | 599 | 93 | 15.53 |
| 79 | Kansas City, Kan. | 216 | 33 | 15.28 |
| 80 | Anchorage | 3,115 | 436 | 13.00 |
| 81 | Albuquerque | 1,389 | 168 | 12.10 |
| 82 | Montgomery | 407 | 43 | 10.57 |
| 83 | Greensboro | 632 | 46 | 7.28 |
| 84 | Kansas City, Mo. | 465 | 33 | 7.10 |
| 85 | St. Paul | 846 | 49 | 5.79 |
| 86 | Colorado Springs | 2,737 | 154 | 5.63 |
| 87 | Memphis | 564 | 29 | 5.14 |
| 88 | Atlanta | 668 | 10 | 1.50 |

# 158. City Spending for Housing and Urban Development

Per capita spending by cities in 1979–80 for housing and
urban development is reflected in the table below. This
category covers spending for city housing and redevelopment projects and regulation, promotion and support of
private housing and redevelopment. Data shown for New
York, Buffalo, Rochester, Syracuse, Yonkers, Flint, De-

troit, Grand Rapids, Warren, Phoenix, Tucson, Lexington-Fayette, Richmond, Norfolk and Virginia Beach includes allocations to municipal housing authorities. Many cities in the table below have housing authorities that are not included in the city finance statistics used below because they are usually classified as independent government entities.

In 1979–80 Pittsburgh spent over $206 per person. Washington, D.C. and New York follow with $171 and

$120. The allocation for Pittsburgh was up dramatically over 1977–78 ($10.58) and 1978–79 ($34.45) indicating a shift in the city's responsibility for housing, most likely reflective of the economic problems caused by the recession. New York showed a steady increase, although less dramatic, spending $66.64 in 1977–78 and $88.43 in 1978–79. Seventeen cities spent less than $10 per person. Warren spent less than $1.00 in 1979–80, as it did in 1977–78 ($.74), and in 1978–79 ($.81).

SOURCE: U.S. Department of Commerce, Bureau of the Census, *City Government Finances in 1979–80* (Washington, D.C.: Government Printing Office, 1981).

| Rank | City | Expenditures Per Capita 1979–80 | Rank | City | Expenditures Per Capita 1979–80 | Rank | City | Expenditures Per Capita 1979–80 |
|---|---|---|---|---|---|---|---|---|
| 1 | Pittsburgh | $206.37 | 31 | San Diego | 35.90 | 61 | Kansas City, Kan. | 14.73 |
| 2 | Washington, D.C. | 171.08 | 32 | Kansas City, Mo. | 34.37 | 62 | Lubbock | 14.61 |
| 3 | New York | 120.68 | 33 | Charlotte | 33.96 | 63 | Tacoma | 14.09 |
| 4 | Syracuse | 103.55 | 34 | San Francisco | 33.52 | 64 | Denver | 13.75 |
| 5 | Louisville | 103.25 | 34 | Philadelphia | 33.52 | 65 | Fort Worth | 13.61 |
| 6 | Minneapolis | 101.54 | 36 | Jacksonville | 33.41 | 66 | Dallas | 13.15 |
| 7 | St. Paul | 98.34 | 37 | Flint | 31.99 | 67 | Jersey City | 12.57 |
| 8 | Akron | 95.57 | 38 | Toledo | 31.30 | 68 | Fresno | 11.44 |
| 9 | Buffalo | 91.32 | 39 | Chicago | 30.30 | 69 | Grand Rapids | 11.30 |
| 10 | Rochester | 88.89 | 40 | Phoenix | 27.22 | 69 | Lincoln | 11.30 |
| 11 | Boston | 82.46 | 41 | Miami | 26.62 | 71 | Jackson | 10.17 |
| 12 | Norfolk | 77.68 | 42 | Memphis | 26.05 | 72 | Indianapolis | 9.65 |
| 13 | New Orleans | 74.81 | 42 | Portland, Ore. | 26.05 | 73 | Seattle | 8.78 |
| 14 | Cincinnati | 71.74 | 44 | Yonkers | 25.95 | 74 | Anaheim | 7.19 |
| 15 | Detroit | 70.63 | 45 | Birmingham | 23.84 | 75 | Tampa | 6.43 |
| 16 | Long Beach | 65.75 | 46 | Fort Wayne | 23.48 | 76 | Aurora | 6.38 |
| 17 | Milwaukee | 65.09 | 47 | Columbus, Ga. | 20.13 | 77 | Colorado Springs | 5.21 |
| 18 | Oakland | 65.07 | 48 | Honolulu | 19.54 | 78 | Huntington Beach | 5.11 |
| 19 | St. Louis | 62.88 | 49 | Albuquerque | 18.80 | 79 | Spokane | 4.59 |
| 20 | Dayton | 55.10 | 50 | Shreveport | 18.61 | 80 | Baton Rouge | 4.37 |
| 21 | Providence | 55.09 | 51 | Oklahoma City | 18.34 | 81 | Riverside | 3.93 |
| 22 | Des Moines | 54.75 | 52 | Los Angeles | 17.90 | 82 | Nashville-Davidson | 3.54 |
| 23 | Baltimore | 52.77 | 53 | Tulsa | 17.82 | 83 | Newark | 2.54 |
| 24 | Cleveland | 52.64 | 54 | Omaha | 17.67 | 84 | Virginia Beach | 2.48 |
| 25 | Richmond | 51.11 | 55 | Columbus, Ohio | 17.34 | 85 | Arlington | 1.75 |
| 26 | Lexington-Fayette | 48.48 | 56 | Austin | 17.16 | 86 | Montgomery | 1.64 |
| 27 | Atlanta | 39.64 | 57 | Tucson | 17.13 | 87 | Chattanooga | 1.28 |
| 28 | Greensboro | 37.75 | 58 | St. Petersburg | 17.11 | 88 | Warren | .96 |
| 29 | San Antonio | 36.74 | 59 | Knoxville | 15.11 | | | |
| 30 | Little Rock | 36.17 | 60 | Santa Ana | 14.82 | | | |

# 159. Renter-Occupied Housing Units

The majority of rental housing units are multiunit structures, and larger cities such as New York and Newark have better than 85 percent of rental housing in this category. Overall, renter-occupied units (whether apartments, duplexes or houses) tend to predominate in the major metropolitan areas with higher densities. New

York, for example, suffers from a lack of space, necessitating larger apartment units instead of conventional prefabricated homes. Although there has been a recent trend toward cooperative and condominium ownership, large cities with higher density and urbanization will continue to have a need for rental housing units, especially in light of the soaring price of homes. This, coupled with the rise in construction costs, energy costs and fuel oil prices in the last decade has curtailed new starts of unsubsidized low- to moderate-income rental housing and has caused a rental housing crunch.

Home ownership also seems to correlate with cities that through urban sprawl have incorporated their hinterlands, encompassing urban, suburban and rural zones. Suburbs and rural areas usually have higher proportions of home ownership (Phoenix, Kansas City, Indianapolis, etc.), increasing the percentage of homes occupied by an owner rather than by a renter.

Total housing units for the following metro areas were divided by renter-occupied units to arrive at the percentage of renter-occupied units from 1980 Census of Housing data.

SOURCE: U.S. Bureau of the Census, 1980 Census of Population and Housing: *Provisional Estimates of Social, Economic and Housing Characteristics*, March 1982.

| Rank | Metro Area | Total Housing Units | Renter Occupied | Renter Occupied Housing Units, Percent |
|---|---|---|---|---|
| 1 | New York | 3,498,663 | 2,414,322 | 69.01 |
| 2 | Los Angeles-Long Beach | 2,730,469 | 1,407,072 | 51.53 |
| 3 | San Francisco-Oakland | 1,280,506 | 601,186 | 46.95 |

| Rank | Metro Area | Total Housing Units | Renter Occupied | Renter Occupied Housing Units, Percent |
|---|---|---|---|---|
| 4 | Boston | 990,660 | 463,504 | 46.79 |
| 5 | New Orleans | 418,406 | 193,402 | 46.22 |
| 6 | Washington, D.C. | 1,112,770 | 508,162 | 45.67 |
| 7 | Miami | 609,830 | 277,303 | 45.47 |
| 8 | San Diego | 670,094 | 300,847 | 44.90 |
| 9 | Newark | 677,464 | 296,380 | 43.75 |
| 10 | Chicago | 2,486,724 | 1,061,302 | 42.68 |
| 11 | Houston | 1,027,069 | 423,605 | 41.24 |
| 12 | San Jose | 458,519 | 184,958 | 40.34 |
| 13 | Baltimore | 756,880 | 302,717 | 39.99 |
| 14 | Milwaukee | 500,684 | 199,911 | 39.93 |
| 15 | Columbus, Ohio | 397,034 | 157,927 | 39.78 |
| 16 | Anaheim | 686,267 | 271,169 | 39.51 |
| 17 | Sacramento | 383,841 | 149,759 | 39.02 |
| 18 | Atlanta | 719,799 | 277,758 | 38.59 |
| 19 | Dallas-Ft. Worth | 1,076,297 | 406,156 | 37.74 |
| 20 | Cincinnati | 498,688 | 183,982 | 37.29 |
| 21 | Portland | 477,513 | 177,631 | 37.20 |
| 22 | Denver | 609,360 | 225,673 | 37.03 |
| 23 | Buffalo | 445,475 | 161,798 | 36.32 |
| 24 | Seattle | 617,962 | 223,142 | 36.11 |
| 25 | San Antonio | 349,330 | 125,817 | 36.02 |
| 26 | Cleveland | 694,401 | 246,319 | 35.47 |
| 27 | Indianapolis | 418,485 | 145,425 | 34.75 |
| 28 | Kansas City, Kan.-Mo. | 493,485 | 165,604 | 33.56 |
| 29 | Minneapolis-St. Paul | 762,376 | 250,228 | 32.82 |
| 30 | Philadelphia | 1,639,330 | 527,393 | 32.17 |
| 31 | St. Louis | 837,997 | 266,159 | 31.76 |
| 32 | Riverside | 551,580 | 174,365 | 31.61 |
| 33 | Phoenix | 544,759 | 170,684 | 31.33 |
| 34 | Pittsburgh | 828,504 | 257,185 | 31.04 |
| 35 | Detroit | 1,508,030 | 433,865 | 28.75 |
| 36 | Tampa-St. Petersburg | 638,816 | 180,626 | 28.28 |

# 160. Group Quarters

Group quarters are defined as nonhousehold living quarters—i.e., residential space occupied by unrelated people. This includes persons under care in institutions and others living in such quarters as dormitories and military barracks. People living in group quarters affect a city's ambience. If they are students, they make the city a livelier place; if they are in military barracks, they usually have a subduing effect. Other types of group quarters include hospitals, nursing homes, religious institutions and counterculture communes. The figures for group quarters therefore say something about a very visible type of housing one may expect as well as the type of people who are likely to be living in it.

The table below shows Norfolk far out ahead of other cities in group quarters in 1980. Norfolk has the largest naval concentration in the world. It is headquarters for the Fifth Naval District, Atlantic Fleet and 23 other major naval commands. At the same time, Norfolk is an important exporting center. These factors stimulate temporary or nonhousehold living.

Montgomery, Las Vegas and Houston, on the other hand, have seen their number of households grow, consistent with their commercial and residential development, to the point where the proportion of residents in group quarters has become very small.

SOURCE: U.S. Bureau of the Census, *1980 Census of Population and Housing: Provisional Estimates of Social, Economic and Housing Characteristics*, March 1982.

| Rank | City | Population in Group Quarters | Percentage in Group Quarters |
|------|------|-----------------------------|------------------------------|
| 1 | Norfolk | 33,870 | 12.69 |
| 2 | Madison | 12,452 | 7.30 |
| 3 | San Diego | 63,319 | 7.23 |
| 4 | Worcester | 11,486 | 7.10 |
| 5 | Boston | 39,518 | 7.02 |
| 6 | Lincoln | 11,925 | 6.94 |
| 7 | Syracuse | 10,833 | 6.37 |
| 8 | Providence | 9,906 | 6.32 |
| 9 | Greensboro | 9,381 | 6.03 |
| 10 | Knoxville | 10,784 | 5.89 |
| 11 | Lubbock | 9,917 | 5.70 |
| 12 | Lexington-Fayette | 11,056 | 5.42 |
| 13 | Grand Rapids | 9,470 | 5.21 |
| 14 | Richmond | 11,041 | 5.04 |
| 15 | Washington, D.C. | 31,899 | 5.00 |
| 16 | Austin | 16,991 | 4.92 |
| 17 | Seattle | 23,027 | 4.66 |
| 18 | Minneapolis | 16,861 | 4.55 |
| 19 | Baton Rouge | 9,776 | 4.45 |
| 20 | Nashville-Davidson | 20,006 | 4.39 |
| 21 | Pittsburgh | 18,317 | 4.32 |
| 22 | St. Paul | 11,508 | 4.26 |
| 23 | Columbus, Ohio | 23,508 | 4.16 |
| 24 | Dayton | 8,377 | 4.11 |
| 25 | Columbus, Ga. | 6,917 | 4.08 |
| 26 | Rochester | 9,777 | 4.04 |
| 27 | Atlanta | 16,926 | 3.98 |
| 28 | Cincinnati | 14,281 | 3.70 |
| 29 | Chattanooga | 6,175 | 3.64 |
| 30 | Virginia Beach | 9,460 | 3.61 |
| 31 | San Francisco | 24,453 | 3.60 |
| 32 | Long Beach | 11,788 | 3.26 |
| 33 | Honolulu | 10,884 | 2.98 |
| 34 | Des Moines | 5,642 | 2.95 |
| 35 | Buffalo | 10,536 | 2.94 |
| 36 | Milwaukee | 17,923 | 2.82 |
| 37 | Anchorage | 4,848 | 2.80 |
| 38 | Spokane | 4,694 | 2.74 |
| 39 | Louisville | 8,136 | 2.73 |
| 40 | Fort Worth | 10,371 | 2.69 |
| 41 | Omaha | 8,173 | 2.62 |
| 42 | Tucson | 8,617 | 2.61 |
| 43 | Jackson | 5,229 | 2.58 |
| 44 | Denver | 12,554 | 2.55 |
| 45 | Salt Lake City | 4,114 | 2.52 |
| 46 | New Orleans | 13,700 | 2.46 |

| Rank | City | Population in Group Quarters | Percentage in Group Quarters |
|------|------|-----------------------------|------------------------------|
| 47 | Oakland | 7,968 | 2.35 |
| 48 | Tampa | 6,286 | 2.32 |
| 49 | Tacoma | 3,663 | 2.31 |
| 50 | Los Angeles | 68,059 | 2.29 |
| 51 | Portland, Ore. | 8,359 | 2.28 |
| 52 | Little Rock | 3,544 | 2.24 |
| 52 | Sacramento | 6,190 | 2.24 |
| 52 | St. Petersburg | 5,301 | 2.24 |
| 55 | Philadelphia | 36,845 | 2.18 |
| 56 | St. Louis | 9,780 | 2.16 |
| 57 | Baltimore | 16,821 | 2.14 |
| 58 | Colorado Springs | 4,507 | 2.09 |
| 58 | San Antonio | 16,396 | 2.09 |
| 60 | Tulsa | 7,515 | 2.08 |
| 61 | Akron | 4,892 | 2.06 |
| 61 | Jacksonville | 11,123 | 2.06 |
| 63 | Riverside | 3,436 | 2.01 |
| 64 | Mobile | 3,977 | 1.98 |
| 65 | Cleveland | 10,791 | 1.88 |
| 66 | Kansas City, Mo. | 8,395 | 1.87 |
| 67 | Toledo | 6,449 | 1.82 |
| 68 | Santa Ana | 3,664 | 1.80 |
| 69 | New York | 123,307 | 1.74 |
| 70 | Memphis | 11,097 | 1.72 |
| 71 | Indianapolis | 11,811 | 1.69 |
| 72 | Miami | 5,793 | 1.67 |
| 73 | Wichita | 4,566 | 1.63 |
| 74 | Chicago | 46,534 | 1.55 |
| 75 | Birmingham | 4,394 | 1.54 |
| 76 | Detroit | 18,334 | 1.52 |
| 77 | Corpus Christi | 3,365 | 1.45 |
| 77 | Oklahoma City | 5,836 | 1.45 |
| 79 | San Jose | 9,120 | 1.43 |
| 80 | Dallas | 11,962 | 1.32 |
| 81 | Shreveport | 2,679 | 1.30 |
| 82 | Anaheim | 2,810 | 1.27 |
| 82 | Flint | 2,021 | 1.27 |
| 84 | El Paso | 5,366 | 1.26 |
| 85 | Charlotte | 3,932 | 1.25 |
| 86 | Newark | 4,039 | 1.23 |
| 87 | Jersey City | 2,728 | 1.22 |
| 88 | Phoenix | 9,015 | 1.18 |
| 89 | Albuquerque | 3,505 | 1.06 |
| 90 | Houston | 15,420 | .97 |
| 91 | Las Vegas | 1,281 | .78 |
| 92 | Montgomery | 4,790 | .27 |

# 161. Owner-Occupied Housing Units

The percentage of owner-occupied housing units presents several possibilities—some of which may be characterized by general housing trends. As compared to renter households, owner households tend to be larger, are more likely to have male heads of households and have a higher average income than renter households. In addition, minority households, female heads of households and young households are more likely to rent.

Condominium conversions and cooperative apartments have greatly affected the housing characteristics of many of the larger, older cities. Cooperatives are owned by a corporation in which residents have shares. Prospective buyers are screened by officers of the cooperative. Condominiums are owned by individuals, who may generally sell to anyone who can afford to buy. In New York City condominiums have finally outstripped cooperatives as the dominant form of unit ownership of large buildings. In most other cities condominiums have long since been the predominant form of ownership. The move toward unit rather than building ownership has changed the housing market in larger cities, decreasing available rental units and displacing those who cannot afford to convert.

The 1980 figures below are for metro areas. The percentage of units that are owner-occupied is even lower for New York City proper (probably below 30 percent), and is dramatically lower for Manhattan. The city's policy of controlling rents on apartments has had the effect of discouraging people who might be able to afford to own their own homes from leaving controlled housing that over time has become more and more of a bargain. The countertrend of recent years has been for landlords of controlled buildings to sell them to corporations, which turn them into cooperatives or condominiums, and in some cases evict nonbuyers. New York state has recently made it more difficult to evict tenants who don't buy.

Metro areas with overall higher average housing costs have lower rates of home ownership. The Los Angeles-Long Beach metro area ranks 35th of 36 in home ownership and has the second highest real estate cost per home unit. The average cost per home in Los Angeles is $82,700, while only 48 percent of the homes are occupied by owners. At the other end of the scale, in Pittsburgh 69 percent of housing units are owner-occupied. The average home cost is only $27,100.

SOURCE: U.S. Bureau of the Census, 1980 Census of Population and Housing: *Provisional Estimates of Social, Economic and Housing Characteristics*, March 1982.

| Rank | Metro Area | Percentage of Owner-Occupied Housing Units | Rank | Metro Area | Percentage of Owner-Occupied Housing Units | Rank | Metro Area | Percentage of Owner-Occupied Housing Units |
|---|---|---|---|---|---|---|---|---|
| 1 | Tampa-St. Petersburg | 71.72 | 13 | San Antonio | 63.98 | 25 | San Jose | 59.66 |
| 2 | Detroit | 71.25 | 14 | Seattle | 63.89 | 26 | Houston | 58.76 |
| 3 | Pittsburgh | 68.96 | 15 | Buffalo | 63.68 | 27 | Chicago | 57.32 |
| 4 | Phoenix | 68.67 | 16 | Denver-Boulder | 62.97 | 28 | Newark | 56.25 |
| 5 | Riverside | 68.39 | 17 | Portland, Ore. | 62.80 | 29 | San Diego | 55.10 |
| 6 | St. Louis | 68.24 | 18 | Dallas-Fort Worth | 62.26 | 30 | Miami | 54.53 |
| 7 | Philadelphia | 67.83 | 19 | Atlanta | 61.41 | 31 | Washington, D.C. | 54.33 |
| 8 | Minneapolis-St. Paul | 67.18 | 20 | Sacramento | 60.98 | 32 | New Orleans | 53.78 |
| 9 | Kansas City, Kan., Mo. | 66.44 | 21 | Anaheim | 60.49 | 33 | Boston | 53.21 |
| 10 | Indianapolis | 65.25 | 22 | Columbus, Ohio | 60.22 | 34 | San Francisco-Oakland | 53.05 |
| 11 | Cleveland | 64.53 | 23 | Milwaukee | 60.07 | 35 | Los Angeles-Long Beach | 48.47 |
| 12 | Cincinnati | 64.11 | 24 | Baltimore | 60.01 | 36 | New York | 30.99 |

# 162. Monthly Home Purchase Cost

The table below shows what it costs each month on the average to buy 1,800 square feet of living space. It assumes a 25-year first mortgage with a 25 percent down payment. The monthly amounts shown below are for payments for the interest on the 75 percent principal and repayment of the principal itself. The cost of the house, including interest, comes to $12 \times 25$ the amount below, plus the down payment and closing costs.

Since interest rates do not vary across the country nearly as much as housing prices, the differences in the figures primarily reflect the differences in housing prices. The reason for presenting the data as monthly costs is that this format shows people thinking of moving into an area how much they would need to earn to cover the costs. Since the interest portion of the amount below is tax-deductible, pretax earnings do not have to be quite as high as they would have to be if these amounts were rental costs. On the other hand, there are more expenses related to owning a home than there are to renting an apartment.

San Diego has the highest housing ownership cost, followed by San Jose. They are the only two cities with monthly carrying costs of over $1,100 for principal and interest. Denver is in fourth place. Surprisingly, Shreveport and Newark are in third and fifth place. Lincoln's high monthly cost of $892 is in sharp contrast to its Nebraska neighbor Omaha's cost of $628. The least expensive housing is in Buffalo, Syracuse and Chattanooga—reflecting the lower cost of living, and the relatively weak job availability and therefore the lack of demand for housing.

SOURCE: American Chamber of Commerce Researchers Association (ACCRA), "Cost of Living," second quarter 1981.

| Rank | City | Average Monthly Home Purchase Cost ($) | Rank | City | Average Monthly Home Purchase Cost ($) | Rank | City | Average Monthly Home Purchase Cost ($) |
|---|---|---|---|---|---|---|---|---|
| 1 | San Diego | 1,172 | 21 | Houston | 770 | 40 | St. Louis | 706 |
| 2 | San Jose | 1,122 | 22 | Flint | 769 | 42 | Dayton | 705 |
| 3 | Shreveport | 942 | 23 | Minneapolis | 768 | 43 | Nashville-Davidson | 703 |
| 4 | Denver | 930 | 23 | St. Paul | 768 | 44 | Mobile | 702 |
| 5 | Newark | 924 | 25 | New Orleans | 761 | 45 | Colorado Springs | 696 |
| 6 | Lincoln | 892 | 26 | Corpus Christi | 760 | 45 | Tacoma | 696 |
| 7 | Madison | 871 | 27 | Tucson | 757 | 47 | Lexington-Fayette | 693 |
| 8 | Kansas City, Kan. | 868 | 27 | Wichita | 757 | 48 | Charlotte | 692 |
| 9 | Riverside | 865 | 29 | Arlington, Texas | 754 | 49 | Lubbock | 682 |
| 10 | Fresno | 853 | 30 | Oklahoma City | 742 | 50 | Akron | 672 |
| 11 | New York | 845 | 31 | Jackson | 741 | 50 | Birmingham | 672 |
| 12 | Phoenix | 842 | 32 | Indianapolis | 732 | 52 | Fort Worth | 666 |
| 13 | Baltimore | 838 | 33 | Sacramento | 728 | 53 | Memphis | 641 |
| 14 | Chicago | 815 | 34 | Baton Rouge | 720 | 54 | Omaha | 628 |
| 15 | Portland, Ore. | 801 | 35 | Columbus, Ohio | 719 | 55 | Columbus, Ga. | 624 |
| 16 | Cincinnati | 795 | 36 | San Antonio | 714 | 56 | Louisville | 615 |
| 17 | El Paso | 788 | 37 | Norfolk | 713 | 57 | Fort Wayne | 606 |
| 18 | Greensboro | 784 | 38 | Jacksonville | 709 | 58 | Buffalo | 588 |
| 19 | Salt Lake City | 778 | 39 | Knoxville | 708 | 59 | Syracuse | 553 |
| 20 | Albuquerque | 774 | 40 | Kansas City, Mo. | 706 | 60 | Chattanooga | 533 |

# 163. Average Cost of Single-Family Residences

Despite the growth of rental housing in the midst of the cities, single-family homes are still the dominant mode of living, even in cities. Housing costs have risen in recent years for four main reasons. First, inflation in general has pushed up prices. Second, population growth has increased demand and has added pressure on real estate prices in growth areas. Third, in some parts of the United States, like California, reduced property taxes have made local housing more attractive and have pushed up housing prices. Finally, higher interest rates and reduced credit availability have meant that many sellers are taking back notes from buyers; this concession is commonly reflected in higher selling prices.

The result of the above factors is that the cost of housing has outstripped salary increases. Fewer people can afford to own a home—at least until interest rates come down further and credit is more plentiful.

The average cost of a single-family residence is an important economic measure. When housing costs rise, fewer young couples purchase new homes; they rent longer, postponing childbearing, and new housing starts to decline. In a cyclical fashion, this pattern continues until mortgage rates settle at levels that new home buyers can afford.

The West Coast has by far the highest cost in the United States for single-family residences (because there are few single-family homes in Manhattan, the average price for New York City relates primarily to housing in the other boroughs). Ten of the top 11 cities below (Honolulu is the exception) are located in California and Nevada. Home purchase prices in Albuquerque averaged $46,400, but 77 percent of the homes for sale there had prices over $50,000. Three Alabama cities—Birmingham, Mobile and Montgomery—are at the lower end of the ranking, with average costs below $37,000.

SOURCE: Bureau of National Affairs, August 1981.

| Rank | City | Average Purchase Price for Single-Family Residences ($) | Rank | City | Average Purchase Price for Single-Family Residences ($) | Rank | City | Average Purchase Price for Single-Family Residences ($) |
|---|---|---|---|---|---|---|---|---|
| 1 | San Jose | 144,000 | 35 | Oklahoma City | 66,600 | 68 | Providence | 51,400 |
| 2 | Anaheim | 122,700 | 36 | Tucson | 66,300 | 70 | Lincoln | 51,300 |
| 2 | Santa Ana | 122,700 | 37 | Tulsa | 64,500 | 71 | Wichita | 50,600 |
| 4 | Honolulu | 109,900 | 38 | Nashville | 62,900 | 72 | Corpus Christi | 50,500 |
| 5 | Oakland | 107,400 | 39 | Memphis | 62,000 | 72 | El Paso | 50,500 |
| 5 | San Francisco | 107,400 | 40 | Portland, Ore. | 61,800 | 72 | Lubbock | 50,500 |
| 7 | Long Beach | 100,600 | 41 | Little Rock | 61,400 | 75 | Jacksonville | 50,200 |
| 7 | Los Angeles | 100,600 | 42 | Norfolk | 60,700 | 75 | Louisville | 50,200 |
| 9 | San Diego | 98,000 | 42 | Virginia Beach | 60,700 | 77 | Indianapolis | 49,900 |
| 10 | Las Vegas | 94,500 | 44 | Richmond | 60,400 | 78 | Buffalo | 49,600 |
| 11 | Sacramento | 93,400 | 45 | Chattanooga | 60,300 | 79 | St. Louis | 49,300 |
| 12 | Washington, D.C. | 93,200 | 46 | Cleveland | 59,600 | 80 | Jackson | 47,100 |
| 13 | Anchorage | 87,900 | 47 | Charlotte | 59,300 | 80 | Rochester | 47,100 |
| 14 | Jersey City | 87,600 | 48 | Baltimore | 58,700 | 82 | Columbus, Ga. | 46,900 |
| 14 | Newark | 87,600 | 49 | Cincinnati | 58,600 | 83 | Albuquerque | 46,400 |
| 16 | Houston | 86,200 | 50 | Columbus, Ohio | 57,800 | 84 | Fort Worth | 46,100 |
| 17 | Huntington Beach | 82,300 | 50 | Fresno | 57,800 | 85 | Toledo | 45,900 |
| 17 | Riverside | 82,300 | 50 | Pittsburgh | 57,800 | 85 | Akron | 45,900 |
| 19 | Phoenix | 79,800 | 53 | Spokane | 57,400 | 87 | Greensboro | 45,800 |
| 20 | New York | 79,400 | 53 | Tacoma | 57,400 | 88 | Knoxville | 45,100 |
| 21 | Seattle | 76,500 | 55 | Baton Rouge | 56,200 | 89 | Flint | 45,000 |
| 22 | New Orleans | 74,800 | 55 | Shreveport | 56,200 | 89 | Grand Rapids | 45,000 |
| 23 | Miami | 72,500 | 57 | Madison | 55,200 | 89 | Warren | 45,000 |
| 24 | San Antonio | 71,600 | 57 | Milwaukee | 55,200 | 92 | Dayton | 44,400 |
| 25 | Arlington, Texas | 71,400 | 59 | Aurora | 54,900 | 93 | Lexington-Fayette | 44,300 |
| 25 | Dallas | 71,400 | 59 | Colorado Springs | 54,900 | 94 | Syracuse | 41,800 |
| 25 | Fort Worth | 71,400 | 61 | Salt Lake City | 54,300 | 94 | Yonkers | 41,800 |
| 28 | Chicago | 71,300 | 62 | Detroit | 54,200 | 96 | Kansas City, Kan. | 41,500 |
| 29 | Austin | 70,800 | 62 | Worcester | 54,200 | 97 | Omaha | 40,000 |
| 30 | Denver | 70,200 | 64 | St. Petersburg | 52,700 | 98 | Birmingham | 36,100 |
| 31 | Minneapolis | 68,800 | 64 | Tampa | 52,700 | 98 | Mobile | 36,100 |
| 31 | St. Paul | 68,800 | 66 | Philadelphia | 52,100 | 98 | Montgomery | 36,100 |
| 33 | Boston | 67,900 | 67 | Des Moines | 51,600 | | | |
| 34 | Atlanta | 67,000 | 68 | Kansas City, Mo. | 51,400 | | | |

# 164. Housing Purchase Cost—Middle and Upper Income

The table that follows, derived from 1981 data developed by a private real estate company, provides another look at the cost of housing. The figures are geared toward what white collar company personnel would pay for housing upon relocation to one of the cities identified below. The "middle-income" housing would be the cost of housing for junior executives, and the "upper-income" represents housing for senior executives. The two levels of cost are based on suburban location and the inherent quality of a home.

The relocation firm assumes that no executive coming to New York City from another area would want to live in the city itself. Continuity of life style with other cities indicates to the firm a commute to a New York City suburban community. New York City is represented in the company's survey by upstate (Westchester) suburban communities such as Scarsdale; by Long Island communities such as Great Neck; by Connecticut suburban communities such as Greenwich; and by New Jersey suburban communities such as West Orange.

Cities are ranked according to middle-income housing cost, shown in the second column, which reflects an independent broker survey of what a house might cost, with estimates based on the following characteristics: three bedrooms, two baths, a two-car attached garage, a family room and a total of 2,000 square feet of living space. The first column shows the cost of more expensive housing.

Note that cities like San Francisco and Honolulu have markedly more expensive housing than is indicated by the previous table. Differences in definition, e.g., the inclusion of a two-car garage, explain the discrepancy.

From the table below it is clearly easiest to purchase a home more cheaply in Buffalo. Even an upper-income home could be purchased in 1981 for under $80,000. No other city offered such a bargain.

SOURCE: Derived from "Home Price Comparisons," Nationwide Relocation Service Inc., Hinsdale, Illinois, 1981.

| Rank | City | Housing Purchase Cost | |
| | | Upper Income ($) | Middle Income ($) |
|---|---|---|---|
| 1 | Buffalo | 75,867 | 57,000 |
| 2 | Akron | 86,515 | 65,000 |
| 3 | Norfolk | 87,846 | 66,000 |
| 4 | Colorado Springs | 88,511 | 66,500 |
| 5 | Fort Wayne | 90,508 | 68,000 |
| 6 | Columbus, Ga. | 93,170 | 70,000 |
| 6 | Madison | 93,170 | 70,000 |
| 6 | San Antonio | 93,170 | 70,000 |
| 9 | Salt Lake City | 96,497 | 72,500 |
| 10 | Cincinnati | 99,825 | 75,000 |
| 10 | Kansas City, Mo. | 99,825 | 75,000 |
| 10 | Mobile | 99,825 | 75,000 |
| 10 | Rochester | 99,825 | 75,000 |
| 14 | Little Rock | 101,156 | 76,000 |
| 15 | Grand Rapids | 101,821 | 76,500 |
| 16 | Louisville | 102,487 | 77,000 |
| 17 | Dayton | 103,818 | 78,000 |
| 17 | Philadelphia | 103,818 | 78,000 |
| 19 | Memphis | 105,149 | 79,000 |
| 20 | Fort Worth | 105,814 | 79,500 |
| 21 | Albuquerque | 106,480 | 80,000 |
| 21 | Baltimore | 106,480 | 80,000 |
| 21 | Birmingham | 106,480 | 80,000 |
| 21 | Chicago | 106,480 | 80,000 |
| 21 | Oklahoma City | 106,480 | 80,000 |
| 21 | Omaha | 106,480 | 80,000 |
| 21 | Phoenix | 106,480 | 80,000 |

| Rank | City | Housing Purchase Cost | |
| | | Upper Income ($) | Middle Income ($) |
|---|---|---|---|
| 21 | Pittsburgh | 106,480 | 80,000 |
| 21 | Sacramento | 106,480 | 80,000 |
| 30 | Columbus, Ohio | 107,811 | 81,000 |
| 30 | Spokane | 107,811 | 81,000 |
| 32 | Austin | 109,142 | 82,000 |
| 33 | Milwaukee | 114,466 | 86,000 |
| 34 | Cleveland | 117,128 | 88,000 |
| 34 | Detroit | 117,128 | 88,000 |
| 36 | Nashville-Davidson | 118,459 | 89,000 |
| 37 | Boston | 119,790 | 90,000 |
| 37 | Des Moines | 119,790 | 90,000 |
| 37 | El Paso | 119,790 | 90,000 |
| 37 | Las Vegas | 119,790 | 90,000 |
| 37 | Tampa | 119,790 | 90,000 |
| 37 | Tulsa | 119,790 | 90,000 |
| 43 | Charlotte | 121,121 | 91,000 |
| 44 | New Orleans | 122,452 | 92,000 |
| 45 | Denver | 126,445 | 95,000 |
| 45 | New York (L.I. suburban) | 126,445 | 95,000 |
| 45 | Richmond | 126,445 | 95,000 |
| 45 | Shreveport | 126,445 | 95,000 |
| 49 | Atlanta | 129,772 | 97,500 |
| 50 | Dallas | 130,438 | 98,000 |
| 50 | Fresno | 130,438 | 98,000 |
| 50 | Tucson | 130,438 | 98,000 |
| 53 | Houston | 133,100 | 100,000 |
| 53 | Wichita | 133,100 | 100,000 |
| 55 | Riverside | 136,427 | 102,000 |
| 56 | Newark (suburban) | 141,086 | 106,000 |
| 57 | St. Louis | 146,410 | 110,000 |
| 57 | Seattle | 146,410 | 110,000 |
| 59 | Anchorage | 153,065 | 115,000 |
| 60 | Portland, Ore. | 159,720 | 120,000 |
| 60 | Providence | 159,720 | 120,000 |
| 62 | St. Paul | 162,382 | 122,000 |
| 63 | Washington, D.C. | 179,685 | 135,000 |
| 64 | Minneapolis | 182,347 | 137,000 |
| 65 | San Jose | 186,340 | 140,000 |
| 66 | New York (upstate suburban) | 191,664 | 144,000 |
| 67 | San Diego | 195,657 | 147,000 |
| 68 | Miami | 199,650 | 150,000 |
| 69 | New York (Connecticut suburban) | 212,960 | 160,000 |
| 70 | Los Angeles | 232,925 | 175,000 |
| 71 | Oakland | 252,890 | 190,000 |
| 72 | Honolulu | 306,130 | 230,000 |
| 73 | San Francisco | 312,785 | 235,000 |

# CHAPTER ELEVEN

# HEALTH

Perhaps the single most important measure of personal well-being is health. This is reflected in personal spending. *In 1980 Americans spent an average of $1,067 each for health care alone.* Total health spending was $247 billion, or 9.4 percent of the gross national product.*

The following tables show some factors affecting health care conditions in cities, such as hospital beds, physicians and nurses per 1,000 population, hospital admissions and health care costs. Since community hospi-

---

*OS Report*, Volume 6 (Washington, D.C.: Association of American Medical Colleges, for the Organization of Student Representatives, spring 1982), p. 2.

tals are found in all of the cities, while other special institutions are not, only community hospitals are used to measure hospital admissions, beds, occupancy rates and nursing personnel.

Tables on death rates, deaths from certain diseases and infant mortality rates are included to give an indication of the impact on health of the environment and the quality of health care. The fast pace of city life takes its toll on urban inhabitants, especially the very young and the very old, who succumb to influenza and pneumonia, for example, in greater numbers than any other age groups. Newborns face relatively high infant mortality rates because of health complications, such as from premature birth and congenital diseases.

# 165. Health Care Fees

Health care fees continue to increase nationwide, rising 12.5 percent in 1981. This was the largest yearly increase since 1935. In addition, the fee for a hospital room rose 17 percent between December 1980 and December 1981, compared with increases of 19 percent for housing and 12 percent for energy.

The following table represents a measure of health care costs based on the total of one hospital day, two doctor visits and two dentist visits in the second quarter of 1981. One hospital day's cost is based upon the daily charge for one semiprivate room. Doctor visit costs are based upon the prevailing charge for one office visit. Dental costs represent typical charges for two dentist visits for cleaning teeth.

The table also shows that dental costs vary widely throughout the United States. The typical price for cleaning teeth goes from a low of $14.33 in Norfolk to a

high of $39.60 in Tacoma. Prices vary widely within cities, too. One 1980 survey in New York City found that dental treatment charges could double from one dentist to another. The American Dental Association's explanation for the variability in charges is that dentistry is more of a "cottage" industry than medicine. Costs and charges are much more likely to be discussed by dentists than by doctors in hospitals.

---

SOURCES: *Money* magazine, January 1981. OS Report, Volume 6 (Washington, D.C.: Association of American Medical Colleges, for the Organization of Student Representatives, spring 1982), p. 2. American Chamber of Commerce Researchers Association, "Inter-City Cost of Living Indicators," second quarter 1981.

| Rank | City | One Hospital Day ($) | Two Doctor Visits ($) | Two Dentist Visits ($) | Total Cost ($) |
|---|---|---|---|---|---|
| 1 | Newark | 202.66 | 43.32 | 56.66 | 302.64 |
| 2 | Baltimore | 173.50 | 65.00 | 64.00 | 302.50 |
| 3 | Chicago | 199.00 | 40.00 | 50.00 | 289.00 |
| 4 | San Jose | 188.00 | 48.00 | 51.60 | 287.60 |
| 5 | New York | 176.00 | 40.00 | 70.00 | 286.00 |
| 5 | Sacramento | 172.00 | 70.00 | 44.00 | 286.00 |
| 7 | Riverside | 171.67 | 58.66 | 53.00 | 283.33 |
| 8 | Portland, Ore. | 190.00 | 37.00 | 50.00 | 277.00 |
| 9 | San Diego | 182.20 | 54.40 | 39.20 | 275.80 |
| 10 | Tacoma | 154.40 | 40.00 | 79.20 | 273.60 |
| 11 | Fresno | 167.20 | 41.00 | 52.50 | 260.70 |
| 12 | Denver | 167.40 | 36.00 | 51.20 | 254.60 |
| 13 | Flint | 167.50 | 36.50 | 48.00 | 252.00 |
| 14 | Phoenix | 139.00 | 42.00 | 58.40 | 239.40 |
| 15 | Syracuse | 156.40 | 36.00 | 36.00 | 228.40 |
| 16 | Akron | 150.00 | 35.00 | 38.66 | 223.66 |
| 17 | Colorado Springs | 145.33 | 36.34 | 40.00 | 221.67 |
| 18 | Albuquerque | 135.10 | 44.02 | 42.00 | 221.12 |
| 19 | Dayton | 141.00 | 37.34 | 38.66 | 217.00 |
| 20 | Indianapolis | 134.62 | 38.40 | 41.20 | 214.22 |
| 21 | Kansas City, Kan. | 139.63 | 36.00 | 38.00 | 213.60 |
| 22 | Salt Lake City | 136.63 | 30.50 | 46.40 | 213.53 |
| 23 | Memphis | 143.00 | 30.00 | 37.60 | 210.60 |
| 24 | Wichita | 122.67 | 35.60 | 50.80 | 209.07 |
| 25 | Tucson | 125.00 | 44.00 | 40.00 | 209.00 |
| 26 | Greensboro | 140.50 | 39.00 | 29.00 | 208.50 |
| 27 | Kansas City, Mo. | 123.50 | 32.00 | 51.60 | 207.10 |
| 28 | Houston | 114.13 | 37.84 | 54.00 | 205.97 |
| 29 | Fort Wayne | 123.50 | 30.00 | 50.00 | 203.50 |
| 30 | Norfolk | 143.00 | 31.34 | 28.66 | 203.00 |

| Rank | City | One Hospital Day ($) | Two Doctor Visits ($) | Two Dentist Visits ($) | Total Cost ($) |
|---|---|---|---|---|---|
| 31 | Cincinnati | 136.60 | 33.50 | 32.66 | 202.76 |
| 32 | Minneapolis | 130.00 | 32.00 | 40.00 | 202.00 |
| 32 | St. Paul | 130.00 | 32.00 | 40.00 | 202.00 |
| 34 | Madison | 126.86 | 35.34 | 36.68 | 198.88 |
| 35 | St. Louis | 115.25 | 43.00 | 39.50 | 197.75 |
| 36 | Omaha | 124.80 | 30.80 | 40.20 | 195.80 |
| 37 | Oklahoma City | 116.80 | 33.20 | 45.60 | 195.60 |
| 38 | New Orleans | 123.00 | 30.50 | 42.00 | 195.50 |
| 39 | Birmingham | 117.25 | 34.00 | 44.00 | 195.25 |
| 40 | Arlington, Texas | 106.00 | 37.20 | 51.20 | 194.40 |
| 41 | San Antonio | 104.00 | 44.00 | 46.00 | 194.00 |
| 42 | Louisville | 124.88 | 30.00 | 36.00 | 190.88 |
| 43 | Columbus, Ohio | 108.60 | 38.20 | 44.00 | 190.80 |
| 44 | El Paso | 110.60 | 32.00 | 48.00 | 190.60 |
| 45 | Corpus Christi | 109.00 | 32.00 | 47.20 | 188.20 |
| 46 | Mobile | 108.67 | 32.66 | 45.50 | 186.83 |
| 47 | Charlotte | 111.80 | 35.00 | 38.50 | 185.30 |
| 48 | Lincoln | 116.33 | 28.66 | 40.00 | 184.99 |
| 49 | Jacksonville | 108.20 | 37.50 | 37.20 | 182.90 |
| 50 | Fort Worth | 107.00 | 36.00 | 37.00 | 180.00 |
| 51 | Buffalo | 101.00 | 34.00 | 38.40 | 173.40 |
| 52 | Nashville | 95.60 | 36.80 | 36.80 | 169.20 |
| 53 | Knoxville | 100.87 | 31.00 | 37.20 | 169.07 |
| 54 | Chattanooga | 98.40 | 32.00 | 36.40 | 166.80 |
| 55 | Lubbock | 93.50 | 36.00 | 36.40 | 165.90 |
| 56 | Shreveport | 96.50 | 33.00 | 36.00 | 165.50 |
| 57 | Baton Rouge | 86.67 | 36.40 | 41.20 | 164.27 |
| 58 | Lexington | 85.42 | 30.00 | 42.00 | 157.42 |
| 59 | Jackson | 78.33 | 33.32 | 42.00 | 153.65 |
| 60 | Columbus, Ga. | 89.66 | 32.66 | 30.00 | 152.32 |

# 166. Daily Community Hospital Cost

Hospital expenses are rising along with most other health care costs. Several reasons for the rising cost of hospital stays have been posited: Most of them relate to physicians' fees, procedures and drugs ordered by doctors. Those who feel that doctors contribute to the costs cite the fact that third-party payers remove, for the most part, the financial inhibitions that might otherwise curtail additional tests, procedures and drugs that would not have been used in past years. Some of these charges are valid. Laboratory procedures and radiologic services now account for up to 25 percent of total bills at some hospitals.

However, the greatest portion of hospital expenses are support services provided by nurses, technicians and aides. Another large component of hospital expenses is administration and housekeeping services. Many of these support groups are union-organized and receive built-in cost of living increases, which have an inflationary effect on medical care costs.

This table and the next four tables refer to "community hospitals," which offer a full range of services, and exclude special hospitals—federal and military hospitals, long-term hospitals (e.g., rehabilitation centers) and units of institutions such as state mental hospitals.

The table below differs from the previous one on patient fees in that it shows hospital costs per inpatient day as measured by the hospitals. These costs are generally much higher than the fees indicated in the previous table. It would thus appear that hospitals must operate at a loss. However, in practice, the charges for tests make up the difference. The incremental costs for tests are very small, since the staff overhead is already counted in the average costs indicated below.

The following table shows that in 1980 the highest hospital costs per inpatient day were in Los Angeles, where they approached $500; the lowest costs were in Greensboro, where they were $206.

SOURCE: American Hospital Association, *Hospital Statistics: 1981* (Chicago: AHA, 1981).

| Rank | City | Daily Community Hospital Cost ($) | Rank | City | Daily Community Hospital Cost ($) | Rank | City | Daily Community Hospital Cost ($) |
|---|---|---|---|---|---|---|---|---|
| 1 | Los Angeles | 458.03 | 26 | Albuquerque | 293.00 | 51 | Richmond | 256.31 |
| 2 | Boston | 440.95 | 27 | Oklahoma City | 292.36 | 52 | Norfolk | 255.10 |
| 3 | Oakland | 410.78 | 28 | Riverside | 288.40 | 53 | St. Louis | 253.43 |
| 4 | San Francisco | 388.04 | 29 | Spokane | 286.24 | 54 | El Paso | 251.90 |
| 5 | Sacramento | 384.89 | 30 | Houston | 283.95 | 55 | Memphis | 251.25 |
| 6 | Anaheim | 373.32 | 31 | Baltimore | 282.58 | 56 | Des Moines | 249.82 |
| 7 | Chicago | 347.19 | 32 | Atlanta | 281.43 | 57 | Dallas | 246.97 |
| 8 | San Jose | 342.27 | 33 | Honolulu | 281.25 | 58 | Lubbock | 246.15 |
| 9 | San Diego | 341.50 | 34 | Newark | 279.70 | 59 | Akron | 243.68 |
| 10 | Long Beach | 337.10 | 35 | Pittsburgh | 279.46 | 60 | Austin | 242.37 |
| 11 | Portland, Ore. | 336.78 | 36 | New Orleans | 277.66 | 61 | Columbus, Ohio | 240.62 |
| 12 | Toledo | 325.78 | 37 | Rochester | 277.09 | 62 | Omaha | 239.43 |
| 13 | Detroit | 324.80 | 38 | Flint | 276.19 | 63 | Buffalo | 237.96 |
| 14 | Philadelphia | 320.93 | 39 | Indianapolis | 276.06 | 64 | Nashville | 237.62 |
| 15 | Phoenix | 315.64 | 40 | Jacksonville | 274.10 | 65 | Lincoln | 235.75 |
| 16 | New York | 311.64 | 41 | Tulsa | 273.99 | 66 | Tampa | 232.45 |
| 17 | Salt Lake City | 304.61 | 42 | Syracuse | 271.19 | 67 | Louisville | 229.90 |
| 18 | Milwaukee | 304.55 | 43 | Dayton | 269.54 | 68 | Mobile | 229.24 |
| 19 | Miami | 304.51 | 44 | Birmingham | 269.13 | 69 | Shreveport | 228.84 |
| 20 | Tucson | 303.86 | 45 | Warren | 268.59 | 70 | Fort Worth | 228.09 |
| 21 | Denver | 301.37 | 46 | Kansas City, Mo. | 267.77 | 71 | San Antonio | 227.04 |
| 22 | Providence | 301.06 | 47 | Tacoma | 265.16 | 72 | Charlotte | 217.85 |
| 23 | Cleveland | 300.52 | 48 | Cincinnati | 265.03 | 73 | Corpus Christi | 217.16 |
| 24 | Seattle | 297.67 | 49 | Wichita | 260.56 | 74 | Jersey City | 207.75 |
| 25 | Minneapolis | 296.39 | 50 | St. Paul | 258.49 | 75 | Greensboro | 205.89 |

# 167. Hospital Admissions

The table below shows 1980 patient admissions to hospitals, a measure of the demand for hospital care, with the following table showing 1980 bed availability, a measure of supply. Since supply limits demand, the two tables are interrelated.

The existence in most of the larger cities of Veterans' Administration hospitals, for example, reduces some of the demand for care in community hospitals. In New York City there are 2,418 beds in four Veterans' Administration hospitals alone. St. Louis, Pittsburgh and Minneapolis lead the cities for which we have data in hospital admissions per 100 residents. These cities also lead in community hospital beds.

Two trends that are reducing hospital admissions per capita are the growth of health maintenance organizations (HMOs) and specialty clinics. Many HMOs are offered through employer plans at low cost to participants. HMOs are effective as preventive clinics. By low-ering costs and offering health care earlier to those who need it, a number of more serious illnesses are detected and treated, not requiring hospitalization. To be financially viable and medically successful, HMOs require a large, educated and basically healthy pool of patients. Most major cities also now have abortion clinics as well as clinics for simple plastic surgery. These types of facilities decrease the number of admissions for what would in the past have been hospital procedures.

In addition, more minor surgery is currently being done on an outpatient basis at many hospitals as a direct result of the health insurance industry's changing policies that now cover many of these procedures.

SOURCE: American Hospital Association, *Hospital Statistics: 1981* (Chicago: AHA, 1981).

| Rank | City | Total Hospital Admissions | Admissions per 100 Residents | Rank | City | Total Hospital Admissions | Admissions per 100 Residents |
|------|------|--------------------------|------------------------------|------|------|--------------------------|------------------------------|
| 1 | St. Louis | 311,948 | 68.85 | 46 | Columbus, Ohio | 161,277 | 28.55 |
| 2 | Pittsburgh | 249,069 | 58.75 | 47 | Lubbock | 49,249 | 28.31 |
| 3 | Minneapolis | 209,105 | 56.37 | 48 | Seattle | 139,189 | 28.18 |
| 4 | Birmingham | 159,666 | 56.14 | 49 | Fresno | 61,357 | 28.12 |
| 5 | Richmond | 122,669 | 55.96 | 50 | Kansas City, Kan. | 44,699 | 27.75 |
| 6 | Knoxville | 101,539 | 55.44 | 51 | Houston | 424,697 | 26.64 |
| 7 | Flint | 85,557 | 53.60 | 52 | Newark | 85,220 | 25.88 |
| 8 | Louisville | 154,347 | 51.72 | 53 | Sacramento | 70,240 | 25.47 |
| 9 | Cincinnati | 187,337 | 48.60 | 54 | Corpus Christi | 58,972 | 25.42 |
| 10 | Miami | 165,297 | 47.65 | 55 | Milwaukee | 161,309 | 25.35 |
| 11 | Salt Lake City | 76,212 | 46.75 | 56 | Dallas | 225,514 | 24.94 |
| 12 | Atlanta | 184,488 | 43.41 | 57 | Washington, D.C. | 158,504 | 24.86 |
| 13 | Providence | 68,029 | 43.38 | 58 | Toledo | 87,116 | 24.56 |
| 14 | Jackson | 86,263 | 42.52 | 59 | Detroit | 294,545 | 24.48 |
| 15 | Dayton | 86,263 | 42.37 | 60 | Tucson | 80,772 | 24.44 |
| 16 | Des Moines | 80,473 | 42.13 | 61 | Greensboro | 37,785 | 24.28 |
| 17 | Grand Rapids | 75,917 | 41.75 | 62 | Charlotte | 76,203 | 24.23 |
| 18 | Syracuse | 68,000 | 39.98 | 63 | Tulsa | 83,598 | 23.16 |
| 19 | Buffalo | 141,387 | 39.51 | 64 | San Antonio | 169,117 | 21.53 |
| 20 | Worcester | 63,766 | 39.41 | 65 | Long Beach | 76,834 | 21.26 |
| 21 | Shreveport | 78,944 | 38.36 | 66 | Lincoln | 36,438 | 21.19 |
| 22 | Rochester | 91,672 | 37.92 | 67 | Norfolk | 56,235 | 21.06 |
| 23 | Portland, Ore. | 138,495 | 37.80 | 68 | Philadelphia | 351,031 | 20.79 |
| 24 | Mobile | 74,728 | 37.28 | 69 | Albuquerque | 68,658 | 20.69 |
| 25 | Boston | 208,263 | 36.99 | 70 | Chicago | 614,620 | 20.45 |
| 26 | Omaha | 114,791 | 36.83 | 71 | San Francisco | 138,076 | 20.34 |
| 27 | Denver | 179,223 | 36.47 | 72 | Indianapolis | 142,354 | 20.31 |
| 28 | Madison | 62,032 | 36.36 | 73 | Columbus, Ga. | 34,007 | 20.07 |
| 29 | Cleveland | 206,628 | 36.01 | 74 | Jacksonville | 107,555 | 19.88 |
| 30 | Spokane | 61,227 | 35.74 | 75 | Riverside | 31,629 | 18.51 |
| 31 | Fort Wayne | 59,028 | 34.28 | 76 | Anaheim | 41,031 | 18.50 |
| 32 | Baton Rouge | 75,026 | 34.18 | 77 | El Paso | 78,375 | 18.43 |
| 33 | Tampa | 92,652 | 34.12 | 78 | Honolulu | 65,957 | 18.07 |
| 34 | St. Paul | 92,000 | 34.05 | 79 | Oakland | 61,277 | 18.06 |
| 35 | Wichita | 91,291 | 32.69 | 80 | Phoenix | 141,625 | 17.93 |
| 36 | Tacoma | 51,532 | 32.51 | 81 | Jersey City | 39,664 | 17.74 |
| 37 | Baltimore | 252,489 | 32.09 | 82 | New York | 1,149,931 | 16.26 |
| 38 | Oklahoma City | 127,247 | 31.56 | 83 | Austin | 56,051 | 16.22 |
| 39 | Kansas City, Mo. | 141,402 | 31.55 | 84 | Santa Ana | 26,879 | 13.19 |
| 40 | Nashville-Davidson | 138,573 | 30.41 | 85 | San Jose | 78,995 | 12.41 |
| 41 | New Orleans | 167,141 | 29.98 | 86 | San Diego | 107,376 | 12.26 |
| 42 | Fort Worth | 115,220 | 29.92 | 87 | Yonkers | 23,538 | 12.05 |
| 43 | Akron | 70,777 | 29.84 | 88 | Los Angeles | 336,684 | 11.35 |
| 44 | Memphis | 188,091 | 29.10 | 89 | Virginia Beach | 19,325 | 7.37 |
| 45 | St. Petersburg | 68,201 | 28.79 | | | | |

# 168. Hospital Beds

The 1978 national guidelines for hospital beds indicate that 4 beds per 1,000 residents is a desirable rate. On this basis all the cities listed in the table were well supplied in 1980 except Virginia Beach, Warren and San Jose, which have under 3 community hospital beds per 1,000, and Los Angeles, San Diego, Yonkers and Austin, which have between 3 and 4 per 1,000.

The figures are a good indicator of the underlying local availability of hospital care. However, they do not take fully into account the competititon for such care from suburban and even rural areas. To adjust for metro and regional use of city hospitals, we would have to increase the population base in the bulk of the cities that serve as regional (St. Louis) and in some cases national (Boston, Houston, New York, Buffalo) health centers. That is, if we were to divide hospital beds in a city by the population of the full area served, we would have a much larger population base and therefore a lower figure for beds per 1,000 residents.

Conversely, where city residents use hospitals outside their city—for example, where the city is a newer satellite of another, older city in the metro area or region

—the most appropriate figure for available hospital beds should be larger than that indicated in the newer city. That is the situation in, for example, Virginia Beach (where residents rely on Norfolk hospitals) and Warren (where residents rely on Detroit hospitals).

SOURCE: American Hospital Association, *Hospital Statistics: 1981* (Chicago: AHA, 1981).

| Rank | City | Community Hospital Beds Per 1,000 Residents | Rank | City | Community Hospital Beds Per 1,000 Residents | Rank | City | Community Hospital Beds Per 1,000 Residents |
|---|---|---|---|---|---|---|---|---|
| 1 | St. Louis | 20.61 | 31 | Fort Wayne | 9.36 | 60 | San Francisco | 6.33 |
| 2 | Pittsburgh | 18.05 | 31 | Madison | 9.36 | 62 | Philadelphia | 6.32 |
| 3 | Minneapolis | 17.03 | 33 | Mobile | 9.10 | 63 | Tulsa | 6.15 |
| 4 | Richmond | 16.45 | 34 | New Orleans | 8.99 | 64 | Corpus Christi | 6.12 |
| 5 | Birmingham | 14.81 | 35 | Akron | 8.50 | 65 | Tucson | 6.10 |
| 6 | Miami | 14.52 | 36 | Wichita | 8.23 | 66 | Jersey City | 6.08 |
| 7 | Flint | 13.66 | 37 | Tampa | 8.22 | 67 | Norfolk | 5.92 |
| 8 | Louisville | 13.16 | 38 | Memphis | 8.20 | 68 | Indianapolis | 5.90 |
| 9 | Cincinnati | 13.02 | 39 | Kansas City, Kan. | 8.13 | 69 | Fresno | 5.77 |
| 10 | Knoxville | 12.46 | 40 | Columbus, Ohio | 8.10 | 70 | San Antonio | 5.63 |
| 11 | Worcester | 12.31 | 41 | Nashville-Davidson | 7.96 | 71 | Sacramento | 5.53 |
| 12 | Providence | 12.13 | 42 | Fort Worth | 7.83 | 72 | Columbus, Ga. | 5.48 |
| 13 | Buffalo | 12.06 | 43 | Spokane | 7.81 | 73 | New York | 5.27 |
| 14 | Dayton | 11.93 | 44 | Milwaukee | 7.71 | 74 | Albuquerque | 5.04 |
| 15 | Grand Rapids | 11.81 | 45 | Oklahoma City | 7.60 | 75 | Lincoln | 4.96 |
| 16 | Cleveland | 11.76 | 46 | Baton Rouge | 7.55 | 75 | Riverside | 4.96 |
| 17 | Des Moines | 11.43 | 47 | Detroit | 7.40 | 77 | Anaheim | 4.81 |
| 18 | Omaha | 11.17 | 48 | Newark | 7.33 | 78 | El Paso | 4.75 |
| 19 | Boston | 11.15 | 49 | Lubbock | 7.28 | 79 | Jacksonville | 4.67 |
| 20 | Atlanta | 10.78 | 50 | Washington, D.C. | 7.22 | 80 | Phoenix | 4.55 |
| 21 | Shreveport | 10.63 | 51 | Tacoma | 7.02 | 81 | Oakland | 4.52 |
| 22 | St. Paul | 10.23 | 52 | Houston | 6.88 | 82 | Honolulu | 4.23 |
| 23 | Denver | 10.14 | 53 | Salt Lake City | 6.83 | 83 | Santa Ana | 4.20 |
| 24 | Jackson | 10.01 | 54 | Seattle | 6.62 | 84 | Austin | 3.91 |
| 24 | Rochester | 10.01 | 55 | Greensboro | 6.52 | 85 | Yonkers | 3.42 |
| 26 | Syracuse | 9.78 | 56 | Dallas | 6.51 | 86 | San Diego | 3.34 |
| 27 | Portland, Ore. | 9.66 | 56 | Toledo | 6.51 | 87 | Los Angeles | 3.14 |
| 28 | Baltimore | 9.61 | 58 | Long Beach | 6.38 | 88 | San Jose | 2.96 |
| 29 | Kansas City, Mo. | 9.43 | 59 | Charlotte | 6.37 | 89 | Warren | 2.17 |
| 30 | St. Petersburg | 9.37 | 60 | Chicago | 6.33 | 90 | Virginia Beach | 1.87 |

# 169. Hospital Occupancy Rate

Hospital occupancy rate, the percentage of available beds filled, is a general indicator of the efficiency of the hospital system. A high occupancy rate means that the hospitals are well utilized. A low occupancy rate means that there are probably more hospitals and hospital beds than the city needs. This figure must be evaluated as relating only to community hospitals. However, the pop-

ularity of all hospitals will be higher in a city if it is one that has specialized hospitals that attract patients from all over a region, the nation or the world.

The table that follows shows Rochester, Buffalo, Boston, New York and Baltimore in the top 10 in 1980. Rochester has one of the most advanced health care centers in the United States. It is the home of Strong Memorial Hospital. Buffalo has several hospitals, including the world-famous Roswell Park Cancer Research Institute. Boston is a center for medicine because of its large and highly respected medical institutions—Harvard, Tufts and Boston University—and for its hospitals. In terms of dollars invested, health care is Boston's largest industry. Baltimore has two large teaching hospitals, the University of Maryland and Johns Hopkins, as well as over 25 general and 9 specialty hospitals.

A prima facie explanation advanced for low occupancy rates is that there are too many hospitals. This may be the case in the greater Los Angeles area, where occupancy rates for community hospitals are 70 percent or less. Long Beach, Anaheim and Santa Ana are all within 30 miles of Los Angeles, and there are over 50 community hospitals in these four cities.

SOURCE: American Hospital Association, *Hospital Statistics: 1981* (Chicago: AHA, 1981).

| Rank | City | Percentage Community Hospital Beds Filled | Rank | City | Percentage Community Hospital Beds Filled | Rank | City | Percentage Community Hospital Beds Filled |
|---|---|---|---|---|---|---|---|---|
| 1 | Rochester | 88.7 | 31 | Charlotte | 80.5 | 61 | Minneapolis | 75.9 |
| 2 | Buffalo | 87.3 | 31 | Louisville | 80.5 | 61 | Sacramento | 75.9 |
| 3 | Syracuse | 87.1 | 33 | Corpus Christi | 80.4 | 63 | Denver | 75.3 |
| 4 | Boston | 86.3 | 34 | Kansas City, Kan. | 80.3 | 63 | Madison | 75.3 |
| 5 | Providence | 86.0 | 35 | Baton Rouge | 80.2 | 65 | Fresno | 74.3 |
| 6 | New York | 85.9 | 35 | Tampa | 80.2 | 66 | New Orleans | 74.2 |
| 7 | Baltimore | 85.6 | 37 | Nashville-Davidson | 79.9 | 66 | Worcester | 74.2 |
| 8 | Indianapolis | 85.2 | 38 | Warren | 79.7 | 68 | San Antonio | 74.1 |
| 9 | Cincinnati | 85.0 | 39 | Seattle | 79.6 | 69 | San Jose | 73.6 |
| 10 | Akron | 84.7 | 40 | Cleveland | 79.3 | 70 | Atlanta | 72.9 |
| 11 | Fort Wayne | 84.4 | 40 | Richmond | 79.3 | 71 | Virginia Beach | 72.7 |
| 12 | Dayton | 84.2 | 42 | Jackson | 79.0 | 72 | Miami | 72.4 |
| 13 | Washington, D.C. | 84.1 | 43 | Tucson | 78.9 | 73 | Portland, Ore. | 71.2 |
| 14 | Toledo | 83.7 | 44 | Jacksonville | 78.6 | 74 | Oakland | 71.1 |
| 15 | Newark | 83.6 | 45 | Kansas City, Mo. | 78.5 | 75 | Columbus, Ga. | 70.9 |
| 16 | Detroit | 83.0 | 46 | Memphis | 78.4 | 75 | Lubbock | 70.9 |
| 16 | Grand Rapids | 83.0 | 46 | Oklahoma City | 78.4 | 77 | St. Petersburg | 70.6 |
| 18 | Yonkers | 82.9 | 48 | Chicago | 78.1 | 77 | Tacoma | 70.6 |
| 19 | Norfolk | 82.5 | 49 | Austin | 77.8 | 79 | Fort Worth | 70.5 |
| 20 | Columbus, Ohio | 82.2 | 50 | Milwaukee | 77.7 | 80 | San Francisco | 70.4 |
| 20 | Honolulu | 82.2 | 51 | Greensboro | 77.5 | 81 | Long Beach | 70.3 |
| 22 | Birmingham | 81.7 | 51 | Omaha | 77.5 | 81 | Spokane | 70.3 |
| 22 | Philadelphia | 81.7 | 53 | Dallas | 77.4 | 83 | Los Angeles | 70.1 |
| 24 | Mobile | 81.5 | 54 | Albuquerque | 77.3 | 84 | San Diego | 69.1 |
| 25 | Jersey City | 81.1 | 55 | Pittsburgh | 77.1 | 85 | Shreveport | 68.8 |
| 26 | St. Louis | 81.0 | 56 | Salt Lake City | 76.9 | 86 | El Paso | 65.2 |
| 27 | Flint | 80.8 | 57 | Tulsa | 76.8 | 87 | Riverside | 64.9 |
| 28 | Des Moines | 80.7 | 58 | Houston | 76.7 | 88 | Anaheim | 64.3 |
| 28 | Wichita | 80.7 | 59 | Phoenix | 76.4 | 89 | Santa Ana | 64.1 |
| 30 | Knoxville | 80.6 | 60 | St. Paul | 76.1 | | | |

# 170. Hospital Nurses

The number of nurses in the table below includes registered nurses and licensed practical nurses in community hospitals in 1980.

The cities ranked show a range from a high of nearly 19 per 1,000 population in Minneapolis to a low of 1.5 per 1,000 in Warren. There are additional nursing professionals in these cities employed in long-term facilities, such as rehabilitation hospitals or psychiatric hospitals, state mental health institutions and Veterans' Administration hospitals. Such specialty institutions are excluded from these tables because they do not represent the full-service hospital—where most people go for health care.

The difficulties many inner city hospitals have in recruiting nursing personnel is reflected in the following table. Detroit, Newark, Philadelphia, Houston and Chicago all have less than 7 nurses per 1,000 population. New York, San Diego and Los Angeles all have less than 5 nurses per 1,000 population.

Many nursing professionals are also employed in nursing homes for the elderly. Although Yonkers is ranked 87th in the following table, it has a great number of nurses employed in such nursing homes.

SOURCE: American Hospital Association, *Hospital Statistics: 1981* (Chicago: AHA, 1981).

| Rank | City | Nurses | Nurses per 1,000 Population |
|------|------|--------|------------------------------|
| 1 | Minneapolis | 6,922 | 18.66 |
| 2 | Pittsburgh | 7,405 | 17.47 |
| 3 | St. Louis | 7,562 | 16.69 |
| 4 | Flint | 2,657 | 16.65 |
| 5 | Richmond | 3,406 | 15.54 |
| 6 | Providence | 2,389 | 15.24 |
| 7 | Birmingham | 4,159 | 14.62 |
| 8 | Boston | 8,220 | 14.60 |
| 9 | Worcester | 2,235 | 13.81 |
| 10 | Syracuse | 2,341 | 13.76 |
| 11 | Cincinnati | 5,039 | 13.07 |
| 12 | Rochester | 2,945 | 12.18 |
| 13 | Miami | 4,178 | 12.04 |
| 14 | Salt Lake City | 1,948 | 11.95 |
| 15 | Dayton | 2,348 | 11.53 |
| 16 | Des Moines | 2,184 | 11.43 |
| 17 | Grand Rapids | 2,052 | 11.28 |
| 18 | Buffalo | 3,978 | 11.12 |
| 18 | Louisville | 3,318 | 11.12 |
| 20 | Cleveland | 6,088 | 10.61 |
| 21 | St. Paul | 2,833 | 10.48 |
| 22 | Omaha | 3,100 | 9.95 |
| 23 | Knoxville | 1,806 | 9.86 |
| 24 | Portland, Ore. | 3,592 | 9.80 |
| 25 | Atlanta | 4,154 | 9.77 |
| 26 | Denver | 4,762 | 9.69 |
| 27 | Baltimore | 7,618 | 9.68 |
| 28 | Madison | 1,574 | 9.23 |
| 29 | Fort Wayne | 1,525 | 8.86 |
| 30 | Mobile | 1,750 | 8.73 |
| 31 | Kansas City, Mo. | 3,851 | 8.59 |
| 32 | Spokane | 1,439 | 8.40 |
| 33 | Shreveport | 1,676 | 8.14 |
| 34 | Toledo | 2,857 | 8.06 |
| 35 | Tampa | 2,171 | 8.00 |
| 36 | Seattle | 3,866 | 7.83 |
| 37 | Jackson | 1,540 | 7.59 |
| 38 | Oklahoma City | 3,009 | 7.46 |
| 39 | St. Petersburg | 1,760 | 7.43 |
| 40 | Washington, D.C. | 4,713 | 7.39 |
| 41 | Wichita | 2,043 | 7.32 |
| 42 | Akron | 1,722 | 7.26 |
| 43 | Norfolk | 1,936 | 7.25 |
| 44 | Fort Worth | 2,779 | 7.22 |
| 45 | Tacoma | 1,133 | 7.15 |
| 46 | Milwaukee | 4,504 | 7.08 |
| 47 | Fresno | 1,511 | 6.92 |
| 48 | Detroit | 8,195 | 6.81 |
| 48 | Tucson | 2,250 | 6.81 |
| 50 | Nashville-Davidson | 3,100 | 6.80 |
| 51 | Columbus, Ohio | 3,810 | 6.74 |
| 52 | Newark | 2,206 | 6.70 |
| 53 | New Orleans | 3,568 | 6.40 |
| 54 | San Francisco | 4,323 | 6.37 |
| 55 | Sacramento | 1,727 | 6.26 |
| 56 | Greensboro | 953 | 6.12 |
| 57 | Memphis | 3,931 | 6.08 |
| 58 | Philadelphia | 10,212 | 6.05 |
| 59 | Indianapolis | 4,232 | 6.04 |
| 60 | Lubbock | 1,036 | 5.95 |
| 61 | Oakland | 2,006 | 5.91 |
| 62 | Houston | 9,292 | 5.83 |
| 63 | Baton Rouge | 1,256 | 5.72 |
| 64 | Charlotte | 1,772 | 5.64 |
| 65 | San Antonio | 4,381 | 5.58 |
| 66 | Albuquerque | 1,846 | 5.56 |
| 67 | Long Beach | 1,985 | 5.49 |
| 68 | Chicago | 16,477 | 5.48 |
| 69 | Corpus Christi | 1,230 | 5.30 |
| 70 | Dallas | 4,773 | 5.28 |
| 71 | Lincoln | 889 | 5.17 |
| 72 | Phoenix | 3,996 | 5.06 |
| 73 | Jersey City | 1,125 | 5.03 |
| 74 | New York | 33,678 | 4.76 |
| 75 | Tulsa | 1,695 | 4.70 |
| 76 | Honolulu | 1,646 | 4.51 |
| 77 | Anaheim | 990 | 4.46 |
| 78 | Austin | 1,506 | 4.36 |
| 79 | Jacksonville | 2,256 | 4.17 |
| 80 | Columbus, Ga. | 701 | 4.14 |
| 81 | Riverside | 619 | 3.62 |
| 82 | San Diego | 2,974 | 3.40 |
| 83 | Los Angeles | 9,944 | 3.35 |
| 84 | El Paso | 1,411 | 3.32 |
| 85 | San Jose | 2,007 | 3.15 |
| 86 | Santa Ana | 632 | 3.10 |
| 87 | Yonkers | 580 | 2.97 |
| 88 | Warren | 245 | 1.52 |

# 171. Doctors

The trend toward specialization by many doctors has contributed to the growth of urban and suburban clinics and medical groups. Because of this, and because of constantly emerging technological advances in the medical field, these specialists must locate near centers providing current support assistance for their specialties.

Boston leads the cities studied, with over 16 doctors per 1,000 population. This reflects the abundance of medical schools and teaching hospitals in that city. The rate of doctors in Boston is more than twice the rate for the next-ranked city, Atlanta.

SOURCE: U.S. Census Bureau, *State and Metropolitan Data Book: 1979* (1977 data).

| Rank | City | Doctors per 1,000 Population | Rank | City | Doctors per 1,000 Population | Rank | City | Doctors per 1,000 Population |
|---|---|---|---|---|---|---|---|---|
| 1 | Boston | 16.02 | 32 | Washington, D.C. | 2.43 | 62 | San Antonio | 1.79 |
| 2 | Atlanta | 7.35 | 33 | San Jose | 2.38 | 64 | Louisville | 1.78 |
| 3 | Cleveland | 6.72 | 34 | Seattle | 2.34 | 64 | Providence | 1.78 |
| 4 | Cincinnati | 6.27 | 35 | Des Moines | 2.31 | 66 | Kansas City, Mo. | 1.77 |
| 5 | Buffalo | 5.88 | 36 | New Orleans | 2.30 | 66 | Wichita | 1.77 |
| 6 | Birmingham | 5.84 | 37 | Long Beach | 2.20 | 68 | Milwaukee | 1.76 |
| 7 | Dayton | 5.37 | 38 | Portland, Ore. | 2.18 | 69 | Pittsburgh | 1.72 |
| 8 | Detroit | 4.96 | 39 | Albuquerque | 2.15 | 69 | St. Louis | 1.72 |
| 9 | Denver | 4.90 | 39 | Omaha | 2.15 | 71 | Baton Rouge | 1.68 |
| 10 | Baltimore | 4.57 | 41 | San Diego | 2.14 | 71 | Greensboro | 1.68 |
| 11 | Grand Rapids | 4.50 | 42 | Nashville-Davidson | 2.13 | 71 | Lubbock | 1.68 |
| 12 | Chicago | 4.35 | 43 | Rochester | 2.11 | 74 | Knoxville | 1.66 |
| 13 | Fresno | 3.92 | 44 | Austin | 2.10 | 75 | Riverside | 1.65 |
| 14 | Akron | 3.88 | 45 | Sacramento | 2.09 | 76 | Shreveport | 1.62 |
| 14 | Madison | 3.88 | 46 | Salt Lake City | 2.05 | 77 | St. Petersburg | 1.45 |
| 16 | Columbus, Ohio | 3.52 | 47 | Philadelphia | 2.02 | 77 | Tampa | 1.45 |
| 17 | New York | 3.42 | 48 | Newark | 2.00 | 79 | Lincoln | 1.43 |
| 18 | Dallas | 3.34 | 48 | Oklahoma City | 2.00 | 80 | Jacksonville | 1.42 |
| 19 | Flint | 3.17 | 50 | Houston | 1.99 | 81 | Anchorage | 1.41 |
| 20 | Chattanooga | 3.15 | 51 | Colorado Springs | 1.95 | 81 | Toledo | 1.41 |
| 21 | Lexington-Fayette | 3.00 | 51 | Minneapolis | 1.95 | 83 | Norfolk | 1.37 |
| 22 | Worcester | 2.87 | 53 | Syracuse | 1.93 | 84 | Mobile | 1.34 |
| 23 | Miami | 2.83 | 54 | Corpus Christi | 1.92 | 85 | Jersey City | 1.29 |
| 24 | Jackson | 2.71 | 54 | Indianapolis | 1.92 | 86 | Virginia Beach | 1.24 |
| 24 | Oakland | 2.71 | 56 | Memphis | 1.90 | 87 | El Paso | 1.21 |
| 26 | San Francisco | 2.70 | 57 | Phoenix | 1.87 | 87 | Tacoma | 1.21 |
| 27 | Little Rock | 2.61 | 58 | Santa Ana | 1.84 | 89 | Las Vegas | 1.20 |
| 28 | Charlotte | 2.54 | 58 | Spokane | 1.84 | 90 | Fort Worth | 1.16 |
| 29 | Tucson | 2.53 | 60 | Anaheim | 1.83 | 91 | Montgomery | 1.09 |
| 30 | Richmond | 2.47 | 61 | Tulsa | 1.82 | | | |
| 31 | Fort Wayne | 2.45 | 62 | Honolulu | 1.79 | | | |

# 172. Death Rates

Death rates must be understood within the broader context of urban growth and decline through births, deaths and migration.

One of the most significant factors that contributes

to higher death rates in the Northeast and Midwest appears to be a general trend toward younger populations in search of employment migrating from the industrialized Northeast and Midwest into the southwestern sunbelt cities. Industrial cities such as Pittsburgh and St. Louis have populations with higher median ages (35.3 and 31.9 years, respectively) compared to Dallas-Fort Worth and San Antonio (29.5 and 27.4, respectively).

Southwestern cities are subject to migration (mostly young) from the Northeast as well as a rapidly increasing population base. In addition, Hispanic communities in many of these cities have more offspring, contributing to population growth, and thus decreasing relative death rates in such cities as El Paso, Lubbock and Albuquerque.

The National Center for Health Statistics reported a provisional crude mortality rate for the United States for 1980 of 8.9 per 1,000 population. The figures in the following table are based on data from 1978, the most recent published government data available by region. The higher-than-average figures shown for nearly three-fourths of the cities ranked (computed only two years before) support the general proposition that city living is more stressful.

Florida cities have uniquely high death rates because of the prevalence of large retirement communities, stemming from a different sort of migration. Many elderly couples in the Northeast and Midwest relocate to Florida after retirement to spend their twilight years. The high death rate in St. Petersburg (19.19 per 1,000 population) is a function of its high median age of 40.6 years.

SOURCE: United States Department of Health and Human Services, Division of Vital Statistics, Statistical Research Branch, *Vital Statistics: 1978* (Washington, D.C.: Government Printing Office, 1982).

| Rank | City | Deaths | Deaths per 1,000 Population |
|---|---|---|---|
| 1 | St. Petersburg | 4,545 | 19.19 |
| 2 | St. Louis | 7,224 | 15.94 |
| 3 | Pittsburgh | 6,321 | 14.91 |
| 4 | Sacramento | 4,083 | 14.81 |
| 5 | Buffalo | 5,109 | 14.28 |
| 6 | Louisville | 4,012 | 13.44 |
| 7 | Cincinnati | 5,118 | 13.28 |
| 8 | Cleveland | 7,469 | 13.02 |
| 9 | Portland, Ore. | 4,659 | 12.72 |
| 10 | Miami | 4,325 | 12.47 |
| 11 | Baltimore | 9,741 | 12.38 |
| 12 | Philadelphia | 20,711 | 12.27 |
| 12 | Rochester | 2,966 | 12.27 |
| 14 | Syracuse | 2,082 | 12.24 |
| 15 | Worcester | 1,973 | 12.19 |
| 16 | Tampa | 3,268 | 12.04 |
| 17 | Atlanta | 5,084 | 11.96 |
| 17 | Detroit | 14,386 | 11.96 |
| 19 | Minneapolis | 4,397 | 11.85 |

| Rank | City | Deaths | Deaths per 1,000 Population |
|---|---|---|---|
| 20 | Birmingham | 3,363 | 11.82 |
| 21 | Providence | 1,836 | 11.71 |
| 22 | Long Beach | 4,181 | 11.57 |
| 23 | Fresno | 2,512 | 11.51 |
| 24 | Jersey City | 2,550 | 11.41 |
| 25 | Akron | 2,704 | 11.40 |
| 26 | New Orleans | 6,288 | 11.28 |
| 27 | Fort Wayne | 1,935 | 11.24 |
| 28 | Kansas City, Mo. | 5,029 | 11.22 |
| 29 | Spokane | 1,912 | 11.16 |
| 30 | Washington, D.C. | 7,065 | 11.08 |
| 31 | Seattle | 5,451 | 11.04 |
| 32 | Dayton | 2,230 | 10.95 |
| 33 | Grand Rapids | 1,976 | 10.87 |
| 33 | St. Paul | 2,937 | 10.87 |
| 35 | Toledo | 3,825 | 10.79 |
| 36 | Boston | 6,030 | 10.71 |
| 37 | Oakland | 3,596 | 10.60 |
| 38 | Chicago | 31,828 | 10.59 |
| 39 | Tacoma | 1,668 | 10.52 |
| 40 | Shreveport | 2,157 | 10.48 |
| 41 | New York | 73,767 | 10.43 |
| 42 | Salt Lake City | 1,699 | 10.42 |
| 43 | Chattanooga | 1,762 | 10.39 |
| 44 | Yonkers | 2,015 | 10.31 |
| 45 | Knoxville | 1,875 | 10.24 |
| 46 | Kansas City, Kan. | 1,640 | 10.18 |
| 47 | Norfolk | 2,295 | 10.11 |
| 48 | Omaha | 3,143 | 10.08 |
| 49 | Mobile | 1,992 | 9.94 |
| 50 | Milwaukee | 6,301 | 9.90 |
| 51 | Des Moines | 1,889 | 9.89 |
| 51 | Fort Worth | 3,810 | 9.89 |
| 53 | Flint | 1,651 | 9.73 |
| 54 | Little Rock | 1,540 | 9.72 |
| 55 | Newark | 3,158 | 9.59 |
| 56 | Denver | 4,668 | 9.50 |
| 57 | Oklahoma City | 3,750 | 9.30 |
| 58 | Indianapolis | 6,444 | 9.20 |
| 59 | Los Angeles | 27,031 | 9.11 |
| 60 | Montgomery | 1,617 | 9.08 |
| 61 | Memphis | 5,788 | 8.95 |
| 62 | Tucson | 2,927 | 8.86 |
| 63 | Jacksonville | 4,731 | 8.75 |
| 64 | Tulsa | 3,125 | 8.66 |
| 65 | Wichita | 2,376 | 8.51 |
| 66 | Riverside | 1,448 | 8.47 |
| 67 | Baton Rouge | 1,833 | 8.35 |
| 67 | Nashville-Davidson | 3,806 | 8.35 |
| 69 | Columbus, Ohio | 4,646 | 8.22 |
| 69 | Greensboro | 1,279 | 8.22 |
| 71 | Dallas | 7,348 | 8.13 |
| 72 | Las Vegas | 1,322 | 8.03 |
| 73 | Columbus, Ga. | 1,303 | 7.69 |
| 74 | Jackson | 1,533 | 7.56 |
| 75 | San Antonio | 5,860 | 7.46 |
| 76 | Charlotte | 2,311 | 7.35 |
| 77 | Phoenix | 5,603 | 7.10 |
| 78 | Houston | 11,036 | 6.92 |
| 79 | Lexington-Fayette | 1,403 | 6.87 |
| 80 | San Diego | 5,999 | 6.85 |
| 81 | Lincoln | 1,175 | 6.83 |
| 82 | Warren | 1,090 | 6.76 |
| 83 | Corpus Christi | 1,552 | 6.69 |
| 84 | Albuquerque | 2,206 | 6.65 |
| 85 | Santa Ana | 1,340 | 6.58 |
| 86 | Madison | 1,103 | 6.46 |

| Rank | City | Deaths | Deaths per 1,000 Population | Rank | City | Deaths | Deaths Per 1,000 Population |
|------|------|--------|---------------------------|------|------|--------|---------------------------|
| 87 | Lubbock | 1,083 | 6.22 | 93 | El Paso | 2,279 | 5.36 |
| 88 | Colorado Springs | 1,287 | 5.98 | 94 | Huntington Beach | 762 | 4.47 |
| 89 | Anaheim | 1,273 | 5.74 | 95 | Virginia Beach | 1,071 | 4.08 |
| 90 | Austin | 1,934 | 5.60 | 96 | Arlington, Texas | 644 | 4.02 |
| 91 | Honolulu | 2,017 | 5.53 | 97 | Aurora | 561 | 3.54 |
| 91 | Richmond | 1,214 | 5.53 | 98 | Anchorage | 550 | 3.18 |

# 173. Infant Deaths

Infant mortality refers to the number of deaths of infants under 1 year old per 1,000 live births for the year.

Infant mortality rates are very important measures in the field of public health. Statistics on infant deaths are affected by city environmental and medical factors. Infant mortality rates serve as one of the best indices of the general health of a city. The nationwide infant mortality rate has decreased from 47.0 per 1,000 live births in 1940 to 16.1 per 1,000 live births in 1975.

There are several possible causes of high infant mortality rates. Teen-age mothers who have inadequate or no prenatal education and care often have premature births, which are therefore high-risk births. Poor nutrition and environment are additional associated factors that can contribute to high-risk births. Rates are higher when the mother is poorly educated, when the birth is illegitimate or when the mother is under age 20 or over age 35.

Cities with large poor populations or high immigrant populations have high infant mortality rates, as seen in the following table, which provides data for 1978. For this population, poor nutritional habits as well as educational and language barriers stand in the way of proper prenatal care and training for the expectant mother. Washington, Baltimore and Chicago show relatively high rates, even though these cities have some of the best health care programs and high-risk facilities in the United States.

SOURCES: National Center for Health Statistics, *Vital Statistics of the United States: 1978*, Volume II, Mortality, Table 7-1 (Washington, D.C.: Government Printing Office, 1982).

| Rank | Metro Area | Infant Deaths per 1,000 Live Births | Rank | Metro Area | Infant Deaths per 1,000 Live Births | Rank | Metro Area | Infant Deaths per 1,000 Live Births |
|------|-----------|-------------------------------------|------|-----------|-------------------------------------|------|-----------|-------------------------------------|
| 1 | Washington, D.C. | 27.3 | 10 | Boston | 16.6 | 19 | Indianapolis | 14.4 |
| 2 | Kansas City, Mo. | 25.3 | 11 | Dallas | 16.3 | 19 | Los Angeles | 14.4 |
| 3 | Baltimore | 23.2 | 12 | Memphis | 16.0 | 21 | San Francisco | 13.5 |
| 4 | St. Louis | 22.5 | 12 | New York | 16.0 | 22 | San Antonio | 13.4 |
| 5 | Detroit | 22.3 | 14 | Houston | 15.6 | 22 | Seattle | 13.4 |
| 6 | New Orleans | 22.2 | 15 | Columbus, Ohio | 15.2 | 24 | Denver | 11.6 |
| 7 | Chicago | 21.3 | 16 | Pittsburgh | 15.0 | 25 | San Diego | 11.5 |
| 8 | Cleveland | 20.1 | 17 | Jacksonville | 14.5 | 26 | Milwaukee | 10.2 |
| 9 | Philadelphia | 18.2 | 17 | Phoenix | 14.5 | | | |

# 174. Neonatal Deaths

The following table shows the percentage of deaths of infants up to 1 year old that occur within the first 28 days of birth. This statistic highlights the period within which most newborns succumb to a early death, and it shows that none of the 100 cities has had significant success in keeping this percentage down. Even in those cities with an abundance of health care professionals and facilities—such as Boston, Washington or Baltimore—7 out of 10 deaths recorded within the first year in these cities occurred within the first 28 days.

In addition to those factors discussed in connection with the infant mortality rate (see the previous table), many early infant deaths are also the result of congenital diseases and premature births.

The following table is based on 1978 data, the most recent published government figures available.

SOURCE: U.S. Department of Health and Human Services, Division of Vital Statistics, Statistical Research Branch, *Vital Statistics: 1978* (Washington, D.C.: Government Printing Office, 1982).

| Rank | City | Deaths Under 28 Days | Deaths Under 1 Year | Deaths Under 28 Days as a Percentage of Deaths Under 1 Year |
|---|---|---|---|---|
| 1 | Lincoln | 24 | 29 | 82.76 |
| 2 | Corpus Christi | 59 | 73 | 80.82 |
| 3 | Buffalo | 69 | 87 | 79.31 |
| 3 | Las Vegas | 23 | 29 | 79.31 |
| 3 | Yonkers | 23 | 29 | 79.31 |
| 6 | Warren | 19 | 24 | 79.21 |
| 7 | Chattanooga | 41 | 52 | 78.85 |
| 8 | Boston | 92 | 118 | 77.97 |
| 9 | Charlotte | 72 | 93 | 77.42 |
| 10 | Philadelphia | 352 | 457 | 77.02 |
| 11 | Fort Worth | 91 | 119 | 76.47 |
| 11 | Knoxville | 26 | 34 | 76.47 |
| 11 | Richmond | 39 | 51 | 76.47 |
| 14 | Pittsburgh | 71 | 93 | 76.34 |
| 15 | Jackson | 35 | 46 | 76.09 |
| 16 | Kansas City, Kan. | 41 | 55 | 74.55 |
| 17 | Louisville | 55 | 74 | 74.32 |
| 18 | Phoenix | 130 | 175 | 74.29 |
| 19 | Washington, D.C. | 190 | 256 | 74.22 |
| 20 | Kansas City, Mo. | 138 | 187 | 73.80 |
| 21 | Memphis | 130 | 177 | 73.45 |
| 22 | New Orleans | 166 | 227 | 73.13 |
| 23 | Cincinnati | 81 | 111 | 72.97 |
| 24 | Jersey City | 62 | 85 | 72.94 |
| 25 | St. Petersburg | 8 | 11 | 72.73 |
| 26 | Minneapolis | 53 | 73 | 72.60 |
| 27 | Mobile | 50 | 69 | 72.46 |
| 28 | Toledo | 63 | 87 | 72.41 |
| 29 | Baltimore | 195 | 270 | 72.22 |
| 30 | Rochester | 53 | 74 | 71.62 |
| 31 | Aurora | 20 | 28 | 71.43 |
| 31 | Columbus, Ga. | 30 | 42 | 71.43 |
| 31 | Lexington-Fayette | 20 | 28 | 71.43 |
| 34 | Atlanta | 111 | 156 | 71.15 |
| 35 | Dayton | 46 | 65 | 70.77 |
| 35 | Tampa | 46 | 65 | 70.77 |
| 37 | Baton Rouge | 58 | 82 | 70.73 |
| 38 | El Paso | 72 | 102 | 70.59 |
| 39 | Dallas | 170 | 242 | 70.25 |
| 40 | Los Angeles | 533 | 760 | 70.13 |
| 41 | Des Moines | 30 | 43 | 69.77 |
| 42 | New York | 1,146 | 1,643 | 69.75 |
| 43 | Nashville-Davidson | 69 | 99 | 69.70 |
| 44 | Anchorage | 32 | 46 | 69.57 |
| 45 | St. Louis | 123 | 177 | 69.49 |
| 46 | Virginia Beach | 36 | 52 | 69.23 |
| 47 | Honolulu | 47 | 68 | 69.12 |
| 48 | Albuquerque | 49 | 71 | 69.01 |
| 48 | Shreveport | 49 | 71 | 69.01 |
| 50 | Wichita | 46 | 67 | 68.66 |
| 51 | Huntington Beach | 26 | 38 | 68.42 |
| 52 | Cleveland | 144 | 211 | 68.25 |
| 53 | Spokane | 30 | 44 | 68.18 |
| 54 | Houston | 321 | 471 | 68.15 |
| 55 | Greensboro | 21 | 31 | 67.74 |
| 56 | Jacksonville | 91 | 135 | 67.41 |
| 57 | Fort Wayne | 37 | 55 | 67.27 |
| 57 | Montgomery | 37 | 55 | 67.27 |
| 59 | Anaheim | 20 | 30 | 66.67 |
| 59 | Salt Lake City | 34 | 51 | 66.67 |
| 61 | Columbus, Ohio | 93 | 141 | 65.96 |
| 62 | Sacramento | 56 | 85 | 65.88 |
| 63 | Chicago | 745 | 1,131 | 65.87 |
| 64 | Providence | 23 | 35 | 65.71 |
| 65 | Birmingham | 53 | 81 | 65.43 |
| 66 | Flint | 44 | 68 | 64.71 |
| 67 | St. Paul | 36 | 56 | 64.29 |
| 67 | Worcester | 18 | 28 | 64.29 |
| 69 | Syracuse | 25 | 39 | 64.10 |
| 70 | Indianapolis | 105 | 166 | 63.25 |
| 70 | San Jose | 74 | 117 | 63.25 |
| 72 | Little Rock | 43 | 68 | 63.24 |
| 73 | Detroit | 285 | 451 | 63.19 |
| 74 | Seattle | 48 | 76 | 63.16 |
| 75 | Akron | 29 | 46 | 63.04 |
| 76 | Riverside | 17 | 27 | 62.96 |
| 77 | Denver | 56 | 89 | 62.92 |
| 78 | Fresno | 30 | 48 | 62.50 |
| 79 | Long Beach | 53 | 85 | 62.35 |
| 80 | Tucson | 34 | 55 | 61.82 |
| 81 | San Antonio | 123 | 199 | 61.81 |
| 82 | Milwaukee | 67 | 109 | 61.47 |
| 83 | Austin | 39 | 64 | 60.94 |
| 84 | Newark | 92 | 151 | 60.93 |
| 85 | San Francisco | 67 | 110 | 60.91 |
| 86 | Lubbock | 28 | 46 | 60.87 |

| Rank | City | Deaths Under 28 Days | Deaths Under 1 Year | Deaths Under 28 Days as a Percentage of Deaths Under 1 Year | Rank | City | Deaths Under 28 Days | Deaths Under 1 Year | Deaths Under 28 Days as a Percentage of Deaths Under 1 Year |
|---|---|---|---|---|---|---|---|---|---|
| 87 | Santa Ana | 35 | 58 | 60.34 | 94 | Oklahoma City | 71 | 125 | 56.80 |
| 88 | Portland, Ore. | 60 | 100 | 60.00 | 95 | Arlington, Texas | 13 | 23 | 56.52 |
| 89 | Colorado Springs | 32 | 54 | 59.26 | 96 | Norfolk | 46 | 82 | 56.10 |
| 90 | San Diego | 78 | 134 | 58.21 | 97 | Tacoma | 24 | 43 | 55.81 |
| 91 | Miami | 40 | 70 | 57.14 | 98 | Oakland | 41 | 74 | 55.41 |
| 92 | Omaha | 57 | 100 | 57.00 | 99 | Madison | 10 | 19 | 52.63 |
| 93 | Tulsa | 49 | 86 | 56.98 | 100 | Grand Rapids | 22 | 45 | 48.89 |

# 175. Deaths from Cardiovascular Diseases

The number one cause of death in the United States is cardiovascular diseases. In 1980, 1,012,150 people in the United States died from them. In 1982, approximately 1.5 million people had heart attacks, and of them, half a million died. Four and one-half million people in the United States have a history of angina or prior heart attacks.

The generally faster pace and greater stress of city life can be seen in the following table. With the exception of the last six cities ranked, the percentages are all high— 42 percent or above. In 33 of the 100 cities over half of all the deaths are from cardiovascular diseases.

The percentage of deaths attributed to major cardiovascular diseases ranged from a high of 55.6 in Grand Rapids to a low of 25.1 in Anchorage. Because heart disease is more likely to cause death to those in midlife years and later, Anchorage's ranking showing the lowest percentage of deaths due to heart disease can be attributed to its youthful population.

The following table is based on 1978 data, the most recent published government figures available. The following two tables break down the overall category of cardiovascular disease by showing the percentage of cardiovascular deaths from heart attacks and from strokes.

SOURCE: U.S. Department of Health and Human Services, Statistical Research Branch, Division of Vital Statistics, *Vital Statistics: 1978* (Washington, D.C.: Government Printing Office, 1982).

| Rank | City | Deaths from Cardiovascular Diseases as a Percentage of of All Deaths | Rank | City | Deaths from Cardiovascular Diseases as a Percentage of of All Deaths | Rank | City | Deaths from Cardiovascular Diseases as a Percentage of of All Deaths |
|---|---|---|---|---|---|---|---|---|
| 1 | Grand Rapids | 55.62 | 15 | St. Louis | 52.34 | 29 | Omaha | 50.65 |
| 2 | Lincoln | 54.81 | 15 | Tacoma | 52.34 | 30 | Richmond | 50.28 |
| 3 | St. Petersburg | 54.65 | 17 | Chattanooga | 52.21 | 31 | Greensboro | 50.12 |
| 4 | St. Paul | 54.51 | 18 | Milwaukee | 52.12 | 32 | Madison | 50.05 |
| 5 | Worcester | 53.57 | 19 | Baton Rouge | 52.05 | 33 | Norfolk | 50.02 |
| 6 | Yonkers | 53.25 | 20 | Lexington-Fayette | 52.03 | 34 | Dayton | 49.82 |
| 7 | Pittsburgh | 52.68 | 21 | Des Moines | 51.99 | 35 | Portland, Ore. | 49.80 |
| 8 | Toledo | 52.58 | 22 | Akron | 51.78 | 36 | Indianapolis | 49.75 |
| 9 | Fort Wayne | 52.56 | 23 | Spokane | 51.73 | 37 | Arlington, Texas | 49.69 |
| 10 | Providence | 52.51 | 24 | New York | 51.44 | 38 | Flint | 49.42 |
| 11 | Cincinnati | 52.50 | 25 | Jersey City | 51.41 | 39 | Detroit | 49.28 |
| 11 | Long Beach | 52.50 | 26 | Chicago | 50.80 | 40 | Seattle | 49.20 |
| 13 | Buffalo | 52.40 | 27 | Syracuse | 50.77 | 41 | Rochester | 49.16 |
| 14 | Warren | 52.39 | 28 | Louisville | 50.67 | 42 | Memphis | 49.12 |

| Rank | City | Deaths from Cardiovascular Diseases as a Percentage of of All Deaths | Rank | City | Deaths from Cardiovascular Diseases as a Percentage of of All Deaths | Rank | City | Deaths from Cardiovascular Diseases as a Percentage of of All Deaths |
|---|---|---|---|---|---|---|---|---|
| 43 | Los Angeles | 48.78 | 63 | Baltimore | 47.20 | 83 | Colorado Springs | 44.83 |
| 44 | Cleveland | 48.67 | 64 | Oklahoma City | 47.12 | 84 | Honolulu | 44.77 |
| 45 | Wichita | 48.57 | 65 | Oakland | 47.02 | 85 | Birmingham | 44.60 |
| 46 | Columbus, Ga. | 48.50 | 66 | Lubbock | 46.91 | 86 | Houston | 44.39 |
| 47 | Tulsa | 48.19 | 67 | San Diego | 46.72 | 87 | San Jose | 44.37 |
| 48 | Huntington Beach | 48.16 | 68 | Denver | 46.62 | 88 | Anaheim | 43.44 |
| 49 | Nashville-Davidson | 48.13 | 69 | San Francisco | 46.60 | 89 | Las Vegas | 43.27 |
| 50 | Salt Lake City | 48.03 | 70 | Kansas City, Kan. | 46.52 | 90 | Phoenix | 42.62 |
| 51 | Tampa | 47.98 | 71 | Santa Ana | 46.42 | 91 | Corpus Christi | 42.59 |
| 52 | Minneapolis | 47.94 | 72 | New Orleans | 46.33 | 92 | Virginia Beach | 42.30 |
| 53 | Riverside | 47.93 | 73 | Newark | 46.30 | 93 | Washington, D.C. | 42.09 |
| 54 | Little Rock | 47.92 | 74 | Charlotte | 46.26 | 94 | Philadelphia | 42.08 |
| 55 | Fort Worth | 47.85 | 75 | Austin | 46.17 | 95 | Montgomery | 41.13 |
| 56 | Boston | 47.83 | 76 | Dallas | 46.16 | 96 | El Paso | 40.19 |
| 56 | Columbus, Ohio | 47.83 | 77 | Atlanta | 46.13 | 97 | Knoxville | 39.20 |
| 58 | Fresno | 47.77 | 78 | Jacksonville | 45.78 | 98 | Aurora | 38.15 |
| 59 | Tucson | 47.45 | 79 | Mobile | 45.53 | 99 | Albuquerque | 33.09 |
| 60 | Jackson | 47.42 | 80 | San Antonio | 45.49 | 100 | Anchorage | 25.09 |
| 61 | Sacramento | 47.37 | 81 | Shreveport | 45.34 | | | |
| 62 | Miami | 47.26 | 82 | Kansas City, Mo. | 44.94 | | | |

# 176. Deaths from Heart Attacks

Since cardiovascular diseases are such an important cause of death in U.S. cities, we have separately identified the major component of such diseases—heart attack ("ischemic heart disease"). The table below shows the proportion of all cardiovascular disease deaths attributed to heart attacks in 1978, the latest year for which data are available. Cities high on this heart attack death rate have a correspondingly lower percentage than other cities of cardiovascular disease deaths attributed to strokes. With the exception of Baton Rouge, all of the 10 highest cities in the ratio of heart attacks to all cardiovascular diseases are in the "frostbelt" areas, suggesting that a fatty and high-calorie northeastern diet and the rigor of northeastern winters contribute to heart disease.

Cardiovascular diseases have been linked to diet. Strokes appear to be related more to salt intake and heart attacks to intake of fat and sugar. Heart attacks are also closely related to exercise. An extraordinary in-depth study over time of Harvard graduates showed that vigorous exercise at least twice a week appeared to make a significant difference within the group in the death rate from heart attacks.

New York, Yonkers, Chicago, Baton Rouge and Jersey City ranked at the top for deaths from heart attacks in 1978, relative to other types of cardiovascular diseases. Lubbock ranked lowest of the cities studied, with heart attacks accounting for 48.2 percent of all cardiovascular disease deaths.

SOURCE: U.S. Department of Health and Human Services, Division of Vital Statistics, Statistical Research Branch, *Vital Statistics: 1978* (Washington, D.C.: Government Printing Office, 1982).

| Rank | City | Heart Attack Deaths as a Percentage of Cardiovascular Disease Deaths | Rank | City | Heart Attack Deaths as a Percentage of Cardiovascular Disease Deaths | Rank | City | Heart Attack Deaths as a Percentage of Cardiovascular Disease Deaths |
|---|---|---|---|---|---|---|---|---|
| 1 | New York | 78.92 | 3 | Chicago | 76.01 | 5 | Jersey City | 75.29 |
| 2 | Yonkers | 78.01 | 4 | Baton Rouge | 75.79 | 6 | Cincinnati | 73.99 |

| Rank | City | Heart Attack Deaths as a Percentage of Cardiovascular Disease Deaths | Rank | City | Heart Attack Deaths as a Percentage of Cardiovascular Disease Deaths | Rank | City | Heart Attack Deaths as a Percentage of Cardiovascular Disease Deaths |
|---|---|---|---|---|---|---|---|---|
| 7 | Worcester | 72.09 | 39 | Dallas | 66.36 | 71 | Shreveport | 62.47 |
| 8 | Baltimore | 70.97 | 40 | San Francisco | 66.08 | 72 | Knoxville | 62.45 |
| 9 | Detroit | 70.85 | 41 | Aurora | 65.89 | 73 | New Orleans | 62.44 |
| 10 | Warren | 70.75 | 42 | San Diego | 65.82 | 74 | Washington, D.C. | 62.37 |
| 11 | Santa Ana | 70.74 | 43 | Portland, Ore. | 65.65 | 75 | Fort Wayne | 62.24 |
| 12 | Des Moines | 70.67 | 43 | St. Paul | 65.65 | 76 | Minneapolis | 61.57 |
| 13 | Dayton | 70.66 | 45 | Memphis | 65.60 | 77 | Salt Lake City | 61.27 |
| 14 | Providence | 70.54 | 46 | Riverside | 65.56 | 78 | Kansas City, Mo. | 60.80 |
| 15 | St. Louis | 70.48 | 47 | Nashville | 65.34 | 79 | Denver | 60.57 |
| 16 | Anaheim | 70.16 | 48 | Oakland | 65.11 | 80 | Oklahoma City | 60.55 |
| 17 | Long Beach | 69.89 | 49 | Sacramento | 64.99 | 81 | Jackson | 60.25 |
| 18 | San Jose | 69.81 | 50 | Philadelphia | 64.95 | 82 | Miami | 60.13 |
| 19 | Pittsburgh | 69.79 | 51 | Tampa | 64.86 | 83 | Spokane | 60.06 |
| 20 | Tucson | 69.76 | 52 | Akron | 64.71 | 84 | Madison | 59.96 |
| 21 | Huntington Beach | 69.75 | 53 | Grand Rapids | 64.70 | 85 | Columbus, Ga. | 59.65 |
| 22 | Los Angeles | 69.66 | 54 | Rochester | 64.66 | 86 | Syracuse | 59.60 |
| 23 | Corpus Christi | 69.59 | 55 | Richmond | 64.63 | 87 | Kansas City, Kan. | 59.24 |
| 24 | Milwaukee | 69.43 | 56 | Mobile | 64.61 | 88 | Fort Worth | 59.13 |
| 25 | Boston | 69.07 | 57 | Honolulu | 64.56 | 89 | Norfolk | 58.80 |
| 26 | Newark | 69.02 | 58 | Charlotte | 64.36 | 90 | Columbus, Ohio | 58.55 |
| 27 | Cleveland | 68.89 | 59 | St. Petersburg | 64.05 | 91 | Lincoln | 58.54 |
| 28 | Toledo | 68.87 | 60 | Fresno | 64.00 | 92 | El Paso | 57.97 |
| 29 | Phoenix | 68.43 | 61 | Houston | 63.79 | 93 | Atlanta | 57.65 |
| 30 | Wichita | 68.11 | 62 | Anchorage | 63.77 | 94 | Arlington, Texas | 57.50 |
| 31 | Buffalo | 67.73 | 63 | Tacoma | 63.69 | 95 | Albuquerque | 57.12 |
| 31 | Jacksonville | 67.73 | 64 | San Antonio | 63.58 | 96 | Austin | 57.11 |
| 33 | Greensboro | 67.39 | 65 | Louisville | 63.40 | 97 | Little Rock | 54.74 |
| 34 | Lexington | 67.26 | 66 | Virginia Beach | 63.36 | 98 | Birmingham | 53.87 |
| 35 | Las Vegas | 67.13 | 67 | Omaha | 62.94 | 99 | Montgomery | 52.78 |
| 36 | Tulsa | 67.07 | 68 | Colorado Springs | 62.91 | 100 | Lubbock | 48.23 |
| 37 | Flint | 66.67 | 69 | Seattle | 62.83 | | | |
| 38 | Chattanooga | 66.63 | 70 | Indianapolis | 62.51 | | | |

# 177. Deaths from Strokes

Sometimes death is listed as being caused by a stroke when the reasons for death are related to several cardiovascular diseases or other diseases.

This medical reporting problem is not unique to the United States (nor even to medicine!). Unquestionably other countries' data suffer from systematic biases resulting from medical practice and governmental actions.

Deaths from strokes, as a percentage of major cardiovascular diseases in 1978, were highest in Montgomery (27.7 percent) and six other southern cities. This may reflect a high salt content in the local diet and a higher and earlier incidence of hypertension. It may also reflect inadequate diagnosis and treatment of hypertension. The lowest percentages were found in New York and Miami (9.2 percent), perhaps because expert care is readily available in these two cities and with such care fatalities due to strokes can be cut in half.

SOURCES: U.S. Department of Health and Human Services, Division of Vital Statistics, Statistical Research Branch, *Vital Statistics: 1978* (Washington, D.C.: Government Printing Office, 1982). *Better Homes and Gardens Medical Yearbook: 1979* (Chicago: Encyclopedia Britannica, 1978), p. 314.

| Rank | City | Stroke Deaths as a Percentage of Cardiovascular Disease Deaths | Rank | City | Stroke Deaths as a Percentage of Cardiovascular Disease Deaths | Rank | City | Stroke Deaths as a Percentage of Cardiovascular Disease Deaths |
|---|---|---|---|---|---|---|---|---|
| 1 | Montgomery | 27.67 | 35 | Nashville | 19.81 | 69 | Lubbock | 17.32 |
| 2 | Knoxville | 24.63 | 36 | Flint | 19.73 | 70 | Santa Ana | 17.20 |
| 3 | Birmingham | 24.60 | 37 | Omaha | 19.66 | 71 | Columbus, Ohio | 17.19 |
| 3 | St. Petersburg | 24.60 | 38 | El Paso | 19.65 | 72 | Philadelphia | 17.12 |
| 5 | Columbus, Ga. | 24.21 | 39 | San Francisco | 19.59 | 73 | Milwaukee | 17.08 |
| 6 | Fort Worth | 23.86 | 40 | Fresno | 19.58 | 74 | Greensboro | 16.85 |
| 7 | Arlington, Texas | 23.44 | 41 | Lincoln | 19.57 | 75 | Las Vegas | 16.78 |
| 8 | Honolulu | 23.03 | 41 | Oakland | 19.57 | 76 | Detroit | 16.56 |
| 9 | Shreveport | 22.60 | 43 | Long Beach | 19.41 | 77 | Rochester | 16.53 |
| 10 | Tacoma | 22.45 | 44 | Grand Rapids | 19.29 | 78 | Denver | 15.90 |
| 11 | Oklahoma City | 22.24 | 45 | Portland, Ore. | 19.22 | 79 | Corpus Christi | 15.89 |
| 12 | Jackson | 22.15 | 46 | San Antonio | 19.17 | 80 | Dayton | 15.84 |
| 12 | Minneapolis | 22.15 | 47 | Dallas | 19.10 | 81 | Virginia Beach | 15.67 |
| 14 | Albuquerque | 21.92 | 48 | San Jose | 19.03 | 82 | Des Moines | 15.58 |
| 15 | Fort Wayne | 21.83 | 49 | Akron | 19.00 | 83 | St. Louis | 15.50 |
| 16 | Memphis | 21.42 | 50 | Indianapolis | 18.87 | 84 | Warren | 15.41 |
| 17 | Chattanooga | 21.30 | 51 | Charlotte | 18.80 | 85 | Cleveland | 15.05 |
| 18 | Little Rock | 21.27 | 52 | Buffalo | 18.75 | 86 | Pittsburgh | 15.02 |
| 19 | Salt Lake City | 21.08 | 53 | Syracuse | 18.64 | 87 | Aurora | 14.95 |
| 20 | Colorado Springs | 20.97 | 54 | Lexington | 18.63 | 88 | Newark | 14.84 |
| 21 | Louisville | 20.95 | 55 | Richmond | 18.62 | 89 | Cincinnati | 14.66 |
| 22 | Houston | 20.86 | 55 | Phoenix | 18.59 | 90 | Tucson | 14.54 |
| 23 | Norfolk | 20.73 | 57 | Los Angeles | 18.58 | 91 | Anchorage | 14.49 |
| 23 | Tampa | 20.73 | 58 | Anaheim | 18.44 | 92 | Worcester | 14.29 |
| 25 | Kansas City, Mo. | 20.71 | 59 | Tulsa | 18.13 | 93 | Boston | 13.73 |
| 26 | Mobile | 20.62 | 60 | Toledo | 17.95 | 94 | Baton Rouge | 13.52 |
| 27 | San Diego | 20.59 | 61 | Sacramento | 17.89 | 95 | Chicago | 12.98 |
| 28 | Spokane | 20.53 | 62 | Kansas City, Kan. | 17.69 | 96 | Yonkers | 12.67 |
| 29 | Huntington Beach | 20.44 | 63 | Wichita | 17.68 | 97 | Baltimore | 12.57 |
| 30 | Madison | 20.11 | 64 | Providence | 17.53 | 98 | Jersey City | 12.20 |
| 31 | Seattle | 20.10 | 65 | Washington, D.C. | 17.52 | 99 | New York | 11.29 |
| 32 | Riverside | 20.03 | 66 | Austin | 17.47 | 100 | Miami | 9.25 |
| 33 | Atlanta | 19.91 | 67 | Jacksonville | 17.36 | | | |
| 34 | New Orleans | 19.84 | 67 | St. Paul | 17.36 | | | |

# 178. Deaths from Cancer

There are approximately 100 diseases classified as cancer. In 1978, 397,000 deaths and in 1981 over 420,000 deaths resulted from some form of cancer. Cancer strikes two out of three American families. Although several forms of cancer can now be cured or arrested, it is still the number two cause of death in the United States.

Preventive efforts to control cancer have centered on research into environmental factors. Many scientists and doctors link cancers to substances in our air, water and food. Workplace environments are also being closely studied for carcinogens.

The table that follows shows the number of deaths attributed to some form of cancer as a percentage of total deaths. Yonkers led the 100 cities, with nearly 37 percent of all deaths attributed to cancer in 1978. The figure is high but not surprising, because Yonkers has experienced a steady growth in its elderly population for the past few decades. Cancer is a more likely cause of death (along with heart disease) as one gets older. Therefore, we see retirement cities such as Huntington Beach, Honolulu, Virginia Beach and Tampa in our top 10. St. Petersburg is low on the cancer table but was high (3rd) on the table for deaths from cardiovascular diseases.

SOURCES: Statistical Research Branch, Division of Vital Statistics, United States Department of Health and Human Services, *Vital Statistics: 1978* (Washington, D.C.: Government Printing Office, 1982). Research Department, American Cancer Society.

| Rank | City | Cancer Deaths as a Percentage of All Deaths | Rank | City | Cancer Deaths as a Percentage of All Deaths | Rank | City | Cancer Deaths as a Percentage of All Deaths |
|---|---|---|---|---|---|---|---|---|
| 1 | Yonkers | 36.87 | 35 | Los Angeles | 20.98 | 69 | El Paso | 20.14 |
| 2 | Anaheim | 24.59 | 36 | Cincinnati | 20.97 | 70 | Fort Worth | 20.05 |
| 3 | Huntington Beach | 24.54 | 37 | Worcester | 20.93 | 71 | Santa Ana | 19.85 |
| 4 | Honolulu | 24.34 | 38 | New York | 20.92 | 72 | Boston | 19.77 |
| 5 | Virginia Beach | 23.44 | 39 | Louisville | 20.89 | 73 | Chattanooga | 19.75 |
| 6 | Oakland | 22.61 | 40 | San Jose | 20.87 | 74 | Dayton | 19.73 |
| 7 | Las Vegas | 22.47 | 41 | Pittsburgh | 20.79 | 75 | St. Petersburg | 19.67 |
| 9 | Syracuse | 22.33 | 42 | St. Paul | 20.74 | 76 | Grand Rapids | 19.64 |
| 9 | Tampa | 22.22 | 42 | Tacoma | 20.74 | 77 | Lincoln | 19.57 |
| 10 | Madison | 22.21 | 44 | Aurora | 20.68 | 78 | New Orleans | 19.56 |
| 11 | Milwaukee | 22.16 | 44 | Charlotte | 20.68 | 79 | Little Rock | 19.55 |
| 12 | Providence | 22.11 | 44 | Jackson | 20.68 | 80 | Kansas City, Mo. | 19.49 |
| 13 | Washington, D.C. | 22.07 | 47 | Minneapolis | 20.67 | 81 | Newark | 19.38 |
| 14 | Indianapolis | 22.02 | 48 | Cleveland | 20.62 | 82 | Lexington | 19.32 |
| 15 | Warren | 21.93 | 49 | Tulsa | 20.61 | 83 | Anchorage | 19.27 |
| 16 | Shreveport | 21.88 | 50 | Albuquerque | 20.58 | 83 | Houston | 19.27 |
| 17 | San Diego | 21.80 | 51 | Jersey City | 20.55 | 85 | Greensboro | 19.08 |
| 18 | Memphis | 21.77 | 51 | Toledo | 20.55 | 86 | St. Louis | 19.02 |
| 19 | Mobile | 21.69 | 53 | Phoenix | 20.54 | 87 | Detroit | 18.91 |
| 20 | Omaha | 21.64 | 54 | Austin | 20.53 | 88 | Norfolk | 18.87 |
| 21 | Baltimore | 21.57 | 55 | Fort Wayne | 20.47 | 89 | Colorado Springs | 18.80 |
| 22 | Miami | 21.48 | 56 | Fresno | 20.46 | 90 | Atlanta | 18.65 |
| 23 | Des Moines | 21.44 | 57 | Akron | 20.45 | 91 | Richmond | 18.45 |
| 23 | Spokane | 21.44 | 58 | Knoxville | 20.43 | 92 | Kansas City, Kan. | 18.41 |
| 25 | San Francisco | 21.37 | 59 | Riverside | 20.37 | 93 | Flint | 18.11 |
| 26 | Philadelphia | 21.33 | 60 | Rochester | 20.30 | 94 | Denver | 18.08 |
| 27 | Buffalo | 21.28 | 61 | Oklahoma City | 20.27 | 95 | Arlington, Texas | 17.86 |
| 28 | Jacksonville | 21.24 | 62 | Tucson | 20.26 | 96 | Baton Rouge | 17.68 |
| 29 | Sacramento | 21.23 | 63 | Columbus, Ohio | 20.23 | 97 | Salt Lake City | 17.54 |
| 30 | Nashville | 21.10 | 63 | Corpus Christi | 20.23 | 98 | Lubbock | 17.27 |
| 30 | Portland, Ore. | 21.10 | 65 | Long Beach | 20.19 | 99 | Columbus, Ga. | 16.58 |
| 32 | Wichita | 21.04 | 66 | Dallas | 20.18 | 100 | Montgomery | 16.39 |
| 33 | Seattle | 21.01 | 67 | Chicago | 20.15 | | | |
| 34 | Birmingham | 20.99 | 67 | San Antonio | 20.15 | | | |

# 179. Deaths from Pneumonia and Influenza

Although both pneumonia and influenza ("flu") still pose a threat to life for certain groups (especially the elderly), they are no longer among the major killers. Pneumonia was the number one killer in 1900, with a rate of 304 deaths per 100,000 population. It is now under control because of medicines like penicillin and other antibiotics. In 1918–19 a worldwide epidemic of influenza and pneumonia took over 20 million lives.

Influenza is a virus. It is seldom the direct cause of death, but it takes many forms (called strains) and often strikes a person with pneumonia to cause death. Since the 1950s, when the Asian strain was first identified, the United States has been struck by three significant influenza viruses—the Hong Kong (1968), the Victoria (1975) and the U.S.S.R. or "Russian" (1977). Influenza has its greatest impact on the very young and the very old. The age groups primarily affected are 0–5 years and those over 65.

Richmond, at 7.66 percent, and Boston, at 6.65 percent, are ranked first and second for the highest death rates from pneumonia and influenza as a percentage of all deaths reported in 1978. Lubbock is third, but the remaining top 10 cities are all northern cities. As these diseases are most prevalent in colder climates, this ranking is not surprising.

SOURCE: U.S. Department of Health and Human Services, Division of Vital Statistics, Statistical Research Branch, *Vital Statistics: 1978* (Washington, D.C.: Government Printing Office, 1982).

| Rank | City | Flu and Pneumonia Deaths as a Percentage of All Deaths | | Rank | City | Flu and Pneumonia Deaths as a Percentage of All Deaths | | Rank | City | Flu and Pneumonia Deaths as a Percentage of All Deaths |
|------|------|------|---|------|------|------|---|------|------|------|
| 1 | Richmond | 7.66 | | 35 | St. Petersburg | 3.15 | | 69 | Kansas City, Mo. | 2.68 |
| 2 | Boston | 6.65 | | 36 | San Antonio | 3.14 | | 69 | Nashville | 2.68 |
| 3 | Lubbock | 4.80 | | 37 | Corpus Christi | 3.09 | | 71 | Buffalo | 2.66 |
| 4 | Minneapolis | 4.57 | | 37 | Long Beach | 3.09 | | 72 | Philadelphia | 2.65 |
| 4 | Seattle | 4.57 | | 37 | Phoenix | 3.09 | | 73 | Tacoma | 2.64 |
| 6 | Worcester | 4.46 | | 37 | San Jose | 3.09 | | 74 | Detroit | 2.61 |
| 7 | Rochester | 4.45 | | 41 | Madison | 3.08 | | 75 | Austin | 2.59 |
| 8 | New York | 4.26 | | 41 | Virginia Beach | 3.08 | | 76 | Dayton | 2.56 |
| 9 | St. Paul | 3.92 | | 43 | Providence | 3.05 | | 77 | Baltimore | 2.55 |
| 10 | Denver | 3.83 | | 44 | Albuquerque | 3.04 | | 78 | Little Rock | 2.53 |
| 11 | Colorado Springs | 3.81 | | 44 | Chicago | 3.04 | | 79 | Memphis | 2.51 |
| 12 | Riverside | 3.80 | | 46 | Akron | 3.03 | | 80 | Los Angeles | 2.49 |
| 13 | Cincinnati | 3.77 | | 47 | Fort Worth | 2.97 | | 81 | Toledo | 2.48 |
| 14 | Arlington, Texas | 3.73 | | 48 | St. Louis | 2.96 | | 82 | Fresno | 2.47 |
| 15 | Des Moines | 3.71 | | 49 | Baton Rouge | 2.95 | | 83 | Wichita | 2.40 |
| 16 | San Francisco | 3.67 | | 49 | Columbus, Ohio | 2.95 | | 84 | Sacramento | 2.38 |
| 17 | Omaha | 3.66 | | 49 | Charlotte | 2.95 | | 85 | Indianapolis | 2.37 |
| 18 | Washington, D.C. | 3.48 | | 52 | Jacksonville | 2.94 | | 85 | Newark | 2.37 |
| 19 | Jackson | 3.46 | | 53 | Yonkers | 2.93 | | 87 | Milwaukee | 2.36 |
| 20 | Aurora | 3.39 | | 54 | Anaheim | 2.91 | | 88 | Jersey City | 2.35 |
| 21 | Atlanta | 3.38 | | 54 | Tampa | 2.91 | | 88 | Oklahoma City | 2.35 |
| 22 | Knoxville | 3.37 | | 56 | Pittsburgh | 2.90 | | 90 | Fort Wayne | 2.33 |
| 23 | Santa Ana | 3.36 | | 57 | San Diego | 2.85 | | 91 | New Orleans | 2.32 |
| 24 | Tucson | 3.31 | | 57 | Tulsa | 2.85 | | 92 | Lexington | 2.28 |
| 25 | Columbus, Ga. | 3.30 | | 59 | Louisville | 2.84 | | 93 | Flint | 2.24 |
| 26 | Spokane | 3.29 | | 60 | Oakland | 2.81 | | 94 | Anchorage | 2.00 |
| 27 | Syracuse | 3.27 | | 60 | Houston | 2.81 | | 95 | Montgomery | 1.98 |
| 28 | Dallas | 3.24 | | 61 | Lincoln | 2.80 | | 96 | Greensboro | 1.95 |
| 28 | Salt Lake City | 3.24 | | 63 | Norfolk | 2.79 | | 97 | Warren | 1.93 |
| 30 | Chattanooga | 3.23 | | 64 | Cleveland | 2.78 | | 98 | Mobile | 1.56 |
| 31 | Honolulu | 3.22 | | 65 | Birmingham | 2.77 | | 99 | Las Vegas | 1.51 |
| 32 | Portland, Ore. | 3.20 | | 66 | Huntington Beach | 2.76 | | 100 | Miami | 1.46 |
| 32 | Shreveport | 3.20 | | 67 | Kansas City, Kan. | 2.74 | | | | |
| 34 | El Paso | 3.16 | | 68 | Grand Rapids | 2.73 | | | | |

# 180. Suicides

Why do people commit suicide, and how are these causes reflected by the unusually high incidence of suicides in California and Florida? The 1978 suicide rate per 100,000 population indicates that cities in these states had the most suicidal populations, far exceeding suicides in northeastern and midwestern states. Of the leading 10 cities, 5 are located in California and 3 in Florida. Rounding off the list are Las Vegas (Number 5) and Denver (Number 6). Sacramento led all the cities in suicides per 100,000, with over 34 such cases in 1978.

The continued migration from the Northeast and Midwest to the Southwest and Florida means that many people no longer have families structured around traditional American nuclear and extended family lines. Individuals who migrate lose close friendship ties and organizational memberships, and thereby important mechanisms for support. Psychological and personal problems may be internalized without any social support for their release. (San Francisco, Number 3, is noted for its avant garde life-style, which deemphasizes the importance of raising a family.)

Migration to Florida cities is also linked with retirement. A significant portion of suicides are related to the onset of terminal diseases, which are more likely in the elderly and whose outcome the victims may decide to anticipate through suicide.

At the bottom of the list were northeastern cities such as New York (Number 94, with a rate of 8.9 suicides per 100,000), Boston (Number 95) and Newark (Number 100, with a rate of 6.7 suicides per 100,000 population). In these cities social support systems are strong.

SOURCE: U.S. Department of Health and Human Services, Statistical Research Branch, Division of Vital Statistics, *Vital Statistics: 1978* (Washington, D.C.: Government Printing Office, 1982).

| Rank | City | Suicides Per 100,000 Residents | Rank | City | Suicides Per 100,000 Residents | Rank | City | Suicides Per 100,000 Residents |
|---|---|---|---|---|---|---|---|---|
| 1 | Sacramento | 34.09 | 35 | Detroit | 16.12 | 69 | Dallas | 12.06 |
| 2 | Fresno | 27.04 | 36 | Columbus, Ga. | 15.93 | 70 | Arlington, Texas | 11.87 |
| 3 | San Francisco | 25.48 | 37 | Jacksonville | 15.71 | 71 | Santa Ana | 11.78 |
| 4 | Tampa | 23.94 | 38 | Pittsburgh | 15.57 | 72 | Syracuse | 11.76 |
| 5 | Las Vegas | 23.68 | 39 | Shreveport | 15.55 | 73 | Worcester | 11.74 |
| 6 | Denver | 23.40 | 40 | Rochester | 15.31 | 74 | San Antonio | 11.71 |
| 7 | Long Beach | 22.97 | 41 | Corpus Christi | 15.09 | 75 | Baltimore | 11.69 |
| 8 | Miami | 21.33 | 42 | Honolulu | 15.07 | 76 | New Orleans | 11.66 |
| 9 | Oakland | 20.92 | 43 | Fort Worth | 15.06 | 77 | Grand Rapids | 11.55 |
| 10 | St. Petersburg | 20.26 | 44 | Cleveland | 14.81 | 78 | Nashville | 11.19 |
| 11 | Tacoma | 20.19 | 45 | Cincinnati | 14.79 | 79 | Charlotte | 11.13 |
| 12 | Phoenix | 20.01 | 46 | Minneapolis | 14.56 | 80 | Wichita | 11.10 |
| 13 | Portland, Ore. | 19.92 | 47 | Austin | 14.47 | 81 | Fort Wayne | 11.03 |
| 14 | Colorado Springs | 19.52 | 48 | Tulsa | 14.41 | 82 | Washington, D.C. | 10.98 |
| 15 | Albuquerque | 19.29 | 49 | Houston | 14.30 | 83 | El Paso | 10.82 |
| 16 | Seattle | 19.24 | 50 | Warren | 14.27 | 84 | Little Rock | 10.73 |
| 17 | Louisville | 19.10 | 51 | Dayton | 14.24 | 85 | Chicago | 10.62 |
| 18 | Kansas City, Mo. | 18.97 | 52 | Columbus, Ohio | 14.16 | 86 | Greensboro | 10.28 |
| 19 | Los Angeles | 18.74 | 53 | Huntington Beach | 14.08 | 87 | Yonkers | 10.24 |
| 20 | Oklahoma City | 18.35 | 54 | Birmingham | 14.06 | 88 | Kansas City, Kan. | 9.93 |
| 21 | Akron | 17.71 | 55 | Providence | 14.03 | 89 | Virginia Beach | 9.92 |
| 22 | Norfolk | 17.62 | 56 | St. Louis | 13.90 | 90 | Lexington-Fayette | 9.80 |
| 23 | Spokane | 17.51 | 57 | Richmond | 13.69 | 91 | St. Paul | 9.62 |
| 24 | Toledo | 17.20 | 58 | Baton Rouge | 13.67 | 92 | Memphis | 9.44 |
| 25 | Salt Lake City | 17.17 | 58 | San Jose | 13.67 | 93 | Lincoln | 9.31 |
| 26 | Atlanta | 16.94 | 60 | Knoxville | 13.65 | 94 | New York | 8.90 |
| 27 | Flint | 16.92 | 61 | Madison | 13.48 | 95 | Boston | 8.88 |
| 28 | San Diego | 16.68 | 62 | Mobile | 13.47 | 96 | Buffalo | 8.66 |
| 29 | Tucson | 16.64 | 63 | Jackson | 13.31 | 97 | Montgomery | 7.86 |
| 30 | Aurora | 16.39 | 64 | Philadelphia | 13.21 | 98 | Omaha | 7.70 |
| 30 | Riverside | 16.39 | 65 | Anaheim | 13.07 | 99 | Jersey City | 6.71 |
| 32 | Milwaukee | 16.35 | 66 | Indianapolis | 12.56 | 100 | Newark | 6.68 |
| 33 | Des Moines | 16.23 | 67 | Chattanooga | 12.38 | | | |
| 34 | Anchorage | 16.18 | 68 | Lubbock | 12.07 | | | |

# 181. Nuclear Suicide

Residents of smaller cities often believe they are safer from attack by nuclear weapons than those in large cities, because larger cities are thought of as the likeliest targets. This is not necessarily the case. A medium-sized one megaton (1 Mt) nuclear bomb is equivalent to one million tons of TNT or nearly 80 times the explosive power of the bomb dropped on the city of Hiroshima. In 1985, the Soviet Union will have about 5,000 Mt of strategic (long-range) nuclear weapons to deploy. A single such bomb would leave many residents of a large city like Los Angeles alive. It would, however, completely wipe out all residents of the typical smaller city. The table below, showing what percentage of residents would be killed by a 1 Mt bomb, may provide food for thought.

It may be seen from the table that virtually all of the residents of Lincoln would be killed by a 1 Mt bomb, whereas less than 20 percent of the residents of Los Angeles and New York would be killed by such a bomb.

A Royal Swedish Academy reference scenario includes speculation that the largest U.S. cities would be hit with 3 to 10 Mt of nuclear bombs. However, most military planners do not expect such a heavy assault on large cities, at least in the first phase of a nuclear war. Only cities near military bases, major industrial facilities or energy sources such as oil refineries and nuclear power plants would be annihilated immediately.

The difficult question in terms of city rankings is: What cities would have the highest likelihood of nuclear attack? Two come to mind—Washington, D.C. and the Strategic Air Command headquarters in Omaha. Then the cities near ICBM silos, like Kansas City, or the ones near B-52 bomber bases, like Syracuse. Port cities like Norfolk and Virginia Beach, or Seattle (close enough to Puget Sound) would be targeted because they are the bases for nuclear submarines. Add in oil refineries and other industrial sites, and many more cities are included.

Since prevailing wind patterns take radiation east-ward, west coast cities are likely to have a higher post-nuclear exchange survival rate than other cities.

Many military planners believe that nuclear weapons can be used for "tactical" purposes, i.e., on a limited basis. Other people believe that once into a nuclear war it will be difficult to stop the military machine from proceeding. Stanley Kubrick's "Dr. Strangelove" is still the best lay guide to nuclear reality. In an all-out nuclear war, there is little point to ranking the probability of a city's being a nuclear target. Odds are *it will be*. The only hopeful side to the terrible burden of being a nuclear superpower is that the Soviets must bear the same burden—and since they don't share their weapons with the Warsaw Pact nations, they bear it alone.

SOURCES: Federal data cited in Edward M. Kennedy, Mark O. Hatfield, *Freeze! How You Can Help Prevent Nuclear War* (New York: Bantam Books, 1982). *The New Physician*, Number 5 (1982), p. 14. "Reference Scenario: How a Nuclear War Might be Fought," *Ambio*, Volume II, No. 2–3 (Oxford: Royal Swedish Academy/Pergamon Press, 1982), pp. 94–99 and 175.

| Rank | Metro Area | Percentage Killed in Hit by 1-Megaton Nuclear Warhead | Rank | Metro Area | Percentage Killed in Hit by 1-Megaton Nuclear Warhead | Rank | Metro Area | Percentage Killed in Hit by 1-Megaton Nuclear Warhead |
|---|---|---|---|---|---|---|---|---|
| 1 | Lincoln | 98.21 | 29 | Honolulu | 79.50 | 57 | Birmingham | 57.92 |
| 2 | Montgomery | 98.10 | 30 | Grand Rapids | 79.39 | 58 | Norfolk | 57.85 |
| 3 | Lexington-Fayette | 96.63 | 31 | Tacoma | 78.93 | 59 | Riverside | 55.82 |
| 4 | Lubbock | 96.32 | 32 | Tulsa | 78.32 | 60 | Phoenix | 55.42 |
| 5 | Anchorage | 95.45 | 33 | Tucson | 78.10 | 61 | Dayton | 54.27 |
| 6 | Corpus Christi | 95.24 | 34 | Tampa | 75.76 | 62 | Denver | 53.18 |
| 7 | Greensboro | 94.84 | 35 | Toledo | 75.74 | 63 | Providence | 51.23 |
| 8 | Fresno | 92.39 | 36 | El Paso | 74.81 | 64 | Cincinnati | 49.87 |
| 9 | Fort Wayne | 89.91 | 37 | Rochester | 74.12 | 65 | Cleveland | 49.58 |
| 10 | Shreveport | 89.38 | 38 | Richmond | 71.91 | 66 | Minneapolis | 48.26 |
| 11 | Worcester | 89.18 | 39 | Salt Lake City | 71.43 | 67 | Kansas City, Mo. | 48.20 |
| 12 | Jackson | 88.48 | 40 | Buffalo | 70.71 | 68 | San Diego | 48.18 |
| 13 | Colorado Springs | 87.80 | 41 | Omaha | 70.42 | 69 | St. Louis | 44.00 |
| 14 | Austin | 87.43 | 42 | Akron | 70.19 | 70 | Seattle | 43.69 |
| 15 | Flint | 87.12 | 43 | Memphis | 68.34 | 71 | Houston | 43.28 |
| 16 | Wichita | 86.90 | 44 | Nashville-Davidson | 68.09 | 72 | Atlanta | 42.22 |
| 17 | Albuquerque | 85.56 | 45 | St. Petersburg | 67.90 | 73 | Pittsburgh | 41.78 |
| 18 | Des Moines | 84.76 | 46 | New Orleans | 67.39 | 74 | Washington, D.C. | 37.47 |
| 19 | Spokane | 84.25 | 47 | San Antonio | 67.17 | 75 | Boston | 35.82 |
| 20 | Knoxville | 83.73 | 48 | Jacksonville | 66.36 | 76 | Miami | 34.53 |
| 20 | Madison | 83.73 | 49 | Portland, Ore. | 65.86 | 77 | Detroit | 32.22 |
| 22 | Chattanooga | 83.33 | 50 | Columbus, Ohio | 64.29 | 78 | Philadelphia | 31.95 |
| 23 | Las Vegas | 83.22 | 51 | Baltimore | 62.53 | 79 | Chicago | 31.48 |
| 24 | Baton Rouge | 82.73 | 52 | Indianapolis | 62.05 | 80 | San Francisco | 30.33 |
| 25 | Charlotte | 81.47 | 53 | Oklahoma City | 61.92 | 81 | Dallas | 27.41 |
| 26 | Syracuse | 81.41 | 54 | Louisville | 61.65 | 82 | New York | 18.81 |
| 27 | Mobile | 81.16 | 55 | Milwaukee | 60.95 | 83 | Los Angeles | 17.19 |
| 28 | Little Rock | 79.67 | 56 | Sacramento | 60.67 | | | |

# CHAPTER TWELVE

# POLICE, FIRE, SANITATION

The following tables cover the major "uniformed services"—police, fire and sanitation. These services constitute the principal part of what are sometimes called the "hard" services (in constrast to "soft," or "human," services such as health and education, which we cover in other sections).

Of the uniformed services, police protection is in almost all communities the highest public priority. It and crime will be the subjects of the most attention in the tables that follow. The odds are very high that a city resident or worker will be affected by crime, whereas the same city resident or worker is much less likely nowadays to be the victim of a fire. And while people are aesthetically affronted by streets that are not clean and garbage that has not been picked up, their first concern is for the safety of their bodies and property.

Crime is more prevalent in cities than in rural or suburban areas. The density and anonymity of the cities create an environment in which criminal behavior can flourish. Cities provide ample victims and opportunity for escape. City crime rates are highest in the least affluent neighborhoods, where residents are less well protected and criminal elements can sometimes dictate their own laws.

The outlook for crime in the big cities is not hopeless, however. Crime rates declined in 1981 and 1982 and are likely to continue downward. Potential criminals are on the average becoming older as the baby boom age group matures. Rates of violent crime are therefore likely to decline. As the FBI says, "Individuals between the ages of 16 and 24 are arrested with greater frequency than any other segment of the population."[*]

Crime is also being reduced as potential victims protect themselves through better home security measures and less frequent display of wealth in public.

Private security forces—mostly those hired by businesses, but including doormen and neighborhood block patrols—now exceed public police protection personnel in some cities. This development has played a role in reducing crime. Such private expenditure is in fact probably a better value than public police, because hourly costs are substantially lower and because the service is targeted and supported by the organization paying for the security.

Inequality of income—the existence of a considerable discrepancy between the very poor and the very rich—is closely related to reported crime rates, as is the percentage of families with high incomes. Poverty rates per se are not so related—perhaps because underreporting of crime is more widespread among the poor.

Police approaches to fighting crime seem to be related to how high the local crime rates are. In a 1973 survey described in *City Crime*,[**] four of the five cities with the lowest crime rates cited increasing police-community cooperation as one of their three chief crime control approaches; only one of the five cities with the highest crime rates cited this approach. None of the cities with the lowest crime rates listed lack of community cooperation as an obstacle to crime control, but three of the highest-crime-rate cities did.

In the survey, officials of cities with the lowest crime rates emphasized foot or car patrols as a crime-fighting weapon. The five cities with the highest crime rates placed greater emphasis on team patrols (police working in pairs or groups), perhaps because team patrolling improves police safety. None of the five lowest-crime-rate cities cited an inadequate number of police officers or

---

[*]U.S. Department of Justice, Federal Bureau of Investigation (FBI), *Crime in the U.S.—1981: Uniform Crime Reports* (Washington, D.C.: Government Printing Office, 1982).

[**]Arthur Carol, *City Crime* (New York: Council on Municipal Performance, Municipal Performance Report 1, 1973), pp. 26–27.

lack of funding as one of their three biggest problems, whereas three of the five cities with the highest crime rates (which had more police per capita than those with the lowest crime rates) did.

All of the cities cited the courts as a major obstacle to effective crime control, both for handing out lenient penalties and for inadequate follow-up on arrests. Only the cities with higher crime rates cited inadequate funding for courts (and police) as one of their three most important obstacles to controlling crime.

How much should cities spend on police? The figures suggest many cities could spend less than they have been spending. Police officers are essential for responding to calls and obtaining information on crimes, but crime prevention doesn't follow merely from hiring more police or paying them better salaries. Beyond the tiny enclaves for the rich, cities with more police relative to population have more reported crime, not less; cities with more police are better able to catalog the crimes. In the largest cities, for many crime categories the police do no more than take down the information—e.g., auto thefts in New York City.

Standards for reporting crime data vary from city to city and from year to year. Homicide data are doubtless the most accurate. But murders are infrequent and tend to be domestic crimes, which are not widely feared because most people do not expect someone they know to kill them. Robberies (muggings) are of more interest because they are more common, tend to victimize strangers and are therefore frightening for people who walk the city streets or travel on public transportation. Robbery is also the crime most likely to result in a killing. Robbery data appear to be more consistent and reliable than data on property crimes, which do not involve threats to life (larceny, burglary, auto theft). Robberies can be more clearly categorized than, for example, larcenies, and are less dependent on differences in reporting practices in different cities than, for example, assaults. Property crime rates may reflect different degrees of underreporting, depending on the type of crime. More populous cities, which tend to have higher robbery rates, have lower property crime rates than smaller cities. There is a close and significant relationship among city density, migration rates and robbery. Of the three property crime rates, the rate for auto theft, which is closely watched by insurance companies, is found to be most consistent with other city data. We know of only two cities of the largest 100—St. Louis and Washington, D.C.—that have had independent audits of crime-reporting practices.

Interpreting measures produced by inadequately standardized data is difficult. Since Chicago is known to have decentralized, nonstandardized crime-reporting practices, the overall change in its crime rate from year to year may not be significant. We therefore put greater weight on robbery and homicide figures, which are less subject to arbitrary judgments than are property crime figures. We conclude that Virginia Beach and Huntington Beach—along with Lincoln; Yonkers; and Columbus, Georgia—had the lowest crime rates in 1981. Cities with the largest decrease in crime rates were Chattanooga and Honolulu.

# 182.  Total "Index" Crimes

Information on total index crimes is taken from the Federal Bureau of Investigation (FBI) Uniform Crime Reports (UCR). The information has been collected since 1930, based on standards set between 1927 and 1929 by the Committee on Uniform Crime Records of the International Association of Chiefs of Police.

Index (or "Part I") crimes cover seven varieties of criminal activity. Four are violent personal crimes: homicide, rape, robbery and assault. Three are nonviolent property crimes: burglary, larceny and motor vehicle theft. Recently the FBI has started to add arson to the list of index property crimes, but the FBI says that data so far are inadequate to justify using them for totals.

The highest overall crime rate in 1981 was in Miami, with over 15 crimes per 100 residents. The crime problem continued into 1982. This compares with a national average of 5.8 crimes per 100 and an average for all urban areas (standard metropolitan statistical areas, of SMSAs) of 6.6 crimes per 100. Cities outside of urban areas have an average of 5.2 crimes per 100. Rural areas have an average of only 2.2 crimes per 100. It is still true in 1981 that cities have more crimes than rural areas. That's a price city dwellers pay.

None of the cities can compete with the rural crime rate average. Even the lowest-ranked—Columbus, Georgia—had a crime rate in 1981 of 5.2 per 100, more than double the rural average. Of the 96 cities for which we have 1981 data, only 9 have a crime rate below the average for all metro areas.

SOURCES: U.S. Department of Justice, Federal Bureau of Investigation (FBI), *Crime in the U.S. 1981: Uniform Crime Report* (Washington, D.C.: Government Printing Office, 1982). Arthur Carol, *City Crime* (New York: Council on Municipal Performance, Municipal Performance Report 1, 1973), pp. 7–8.

| Rank | City | Crimes | Crimes Per 100 Population |
|---|---|---|---|
| 1 | Miami | 52,911 | 15.25 |
| 2 | Tampa | 40,856 | 15.05 |
| 3 | Flint | 23,649 | 14.82 |
| 4 | Atlanta | 60,569 | 14.25 |
| 4 | Boston | 79,643 | 14.15 |
| 6 | St. Louis | 62,654 | 13.83 |
| 7 | Portland, Ore. | 50,432 | 13.76 |
| 8 | Sacramento | 36,681 | 13.30 |
| 9 | Dayton | 27,053 | 13.29 |
| 10 | Oakland | 44,679 | 13.17 |
| 11 | Salt Lake City | 20,850 | 12.79 |
| 12 | Dallas | 111,585 | 12.34 |
| 13 | Denver | 60,417 | 12.29 |
| 14 | Birmingham | 34,249 | 12.04 |
| 15 | Detroit | 143,107 | 11.89 |
| 16 | Little Rock | 18,781 | 11.85 |
| 17 | Baton Rouge | 25,917 | 11.81 |
| 18 | Kansas City, Mo. | 51,005 | 11.38 |
| 19 | Rochester | 27,291 | 11.29 |
| 19 | Seattle | 55,764 | 11.29 |
| 21 | Richmond | 24,766 | 11.28 |
| 22 | Fresno | 24,581 | 11.27 |
| 22 | Tucson | 37,241 | 11.27 |
| 24 | Kansas City, Kan. | 18,123 | 11.25 |
| 25 | Omaha | 34,351 | 11.02 |
| 26 | Mobile | 21,998 | 10.97 |
| 27 | Minneapolis | 40,111 | 10.81 |
| 28 | Las Vegas | 43,374 | 10.66 |
| 29 | Washington, D.C. | 67,910 | 10.65 |
| 30 | Cleveland | 60,721 | 10.58 |
| 30 | San Francisco | 71,812 | 10.58 |
| 32 | Des Moines | 19,974 | 10.46 |
| 33 | Phoenix | 81,384 | 10.31 |
| 34 | New York | 725,846 | 10.27 |
| 35 | Los Angeles | 304,101 | 10.25 |
| 36 | Tacoma | 16,193 | 10.22 |
| 37 | Santa Ana | 20,712 | 10.17 |
| 38 | Providence | 15,548 | 9.92 |
| 39 | Baltimore | 77,563 | 9.86 |
| 40 | Toledo | 34,091 | 9.61 |
| 41 | Cincinnati | 36,814 | 9.55 |
| 41 | Columbus, Ohio | 36,814 | 9.55 |
| 43 | Charlotte | 29,646 | 9.43 |
| 44 | Grand Rapids | 17,049 | 9.38 |
| 45 | New Orleans | 52,158 | 9.36 |
| 46 | Albuquerque | 30,614 | 9.23 |
| 47 | Jackson | 18,585 | 9.16 |
| 47 | Spokane | 15,698 | 9.16 |
| 49 | Corpus Christi | 21,216 | 9.14 |
| 50 | Wichita | 25,383 | 9.09 |
| 51 | Riverside | 15,361 | 8.99 |
| 52 | Austin | 30,867 | 8.93 |
| 52 | Long Beach | 32,280 | 8.93 |
| 54 | Jersey City | 19,926 | 8.91 |
| 55 | Lubbock | 15,418 | 8.86 |
| 56 | St. Petersburg | 20,894 | 8.82 |
| 57 | Colorado Springs | 18,836 | 8.75 |
| 58 | Madison | 14,898 | 8.73 |
| 59 | Oklahoma City | 35,128 | 8.71 |
| 60 | San Jose | 54,154 | 8.51 |
| 61 | Syracuse | 14,445 | 8.49 |
| 62 | St. Paul | 22,799 | 8.44 |
| 63 | Tulsa | 30,260 | 8.38 |
| 64 | Jacksonville | 45,070 | 8.33 |
| 65 | Lexington-Fayette | 16,836 | 8.25 |
| 65 | Memphis | 53,325 | 8.25 |
| 67 | Chattanooga | 13,555 | 7.99 |
| 68 | Anchorage | 13,731 | 7.94 |
| 69 | San Antonio | 62,035 | 7.90 |
| 70 | Shreveport | 16,030 | 7.79 |
| 71 | Norfolk | 20,769 | 7.78 |
| 72 | Akron | 18,424 | 7.77 |
| 73 | Anaheim | 17,202 | 7.75 |
| 74 | Greensboro | 12,018 | 7.72 |
| 75 | Fort Wayne | 13,112 | 7.61 |
| 76 | Fort Worth | 29,275 | 7.60 |
| 77 | San Diego | 66,122 | 7.55 |
| 78 | Aurora | 11,903 | 7.51 |
| 78 | Warren | 12,094 | 7.51 |
| 80 | Pittsburgh | 31,384 | 7.40 |
| 81 | Nashville-Davidson | 33,604 | 7.37 |
| 82 | Indianapolis | 33,898 | 7.34 |
| 83 | Arlington, Texas | 11,541 | 7.21 |
| 84 | Louisville | 21,124 | 7.08 |
| 85 | Milwaukee | 44,775 | 7.04 |
| 86 | El Paso | 29,275 | 6.88 |
| 87 | Knoxville | 12,527 | 6.84 |
| 88 | Montgomery | 11,512 | 6.46 |
| 89 | Honolulu | 49,548 | 6.41 |
| 90 | Lincoln | 10,601 | 6.17 |
| 91 | Philadelphia | 100,592 | 5.96 |
| 92 | Virginia Beach | 15,337 | 5.85 |
| 93 | Chicago | 173,316 | 5.77 |
| 94 | Yonkers | 11,219 | 5.74 |
| 95 | Huntington Beach | 9,369 | 5.49 |
| 96 | Columbus, Ga. | 8,776 | 5.18 |

# 183.  Trends in "Total" Crimes

Nationwide, total crimes increased from 8.2 million in 1972 to 13.3 million in 1981, a frightening rise. Per thousand inhabitants the figure rose from 40 in 1972 to 60—a 50 percent increase.

The figures aren't so scary, however, when we look at them by type of crime. The most reliably reported crimes—homicides and auto thefts—are holding steady or are down. The least reliable reported crimes—assaults and larcenies—are the ones that have been increasing.

If the trends hold up, the 1981 and 1982 crime data suggest that the steady yearly rise in city crime is ending. Favorable explanations for this encouraging development are (1) preventive measures by residents and businesses in the big cities; and (2) maturation of the postwar baby boom age group, so that there are fewer young people, who commit a preponderance of violent crimes. An unfavorable explanation is that with city budget cutbacks there are fewer police officers to record crimes, so that fewer crimes make it into the statistics. When New York City police officers went on strike, reported crimes went down.

The good news is that total crimes declined between 1980 and 1981 in 33 of the 96 cities for which we have data. In large cities where crime increased, the increase was lower than in recent years. In 1982 New York City began for the first time to show a decline in total crime.

The bad news is that total crime rates have been increasing in some cities, especially the intermediate size ones. The 10 cities with the fastest rates increase include one large city, Detroit, ranked number seven. Detroit's 1981 increase of 12.3 per cent contrasts sharply with Chicago's reported *decline* of nearly 12 per cent. We interpret Chicago's decline, however, as a reflection of variability in reporting, since the city's crime-reporting system has traditionally been decentralized, so that uniform standards of reporting have not been carefully monitored and crime statistics have changed drastically in both directions.

Portland, Oregon showed the highest rise in the rate of total reported crime, 23.5 percent—nearly 6.5 percent higher than second-ranked Anchorage. Chattanooga had the greatest decrease, with total crime reported down 15.4 percent.

SOURCES: U.S. Department of Justice, Federal Bureau of Investigation (FBI), *Crime in the U.S.—1980: Uniform Crime Reports and Crime in the U.S.—1981:* (Washington, D.C.: Government Printing Office, 1981 and 1982). Also see Arthur Carol, *City Crime* (New York: Council on Municipal Performance, Municipal Performance Report 1, 1973), p. 26.

| Rank | City | 1980 Crime | 1981 Crime | Absolute Change | Percentage Change |
|---|---|---|---|---|---|
| 1 | Portland, Ore. | 40,833 | 50,432 | 9,599 | 23.50 |
| 2 | Anchorage | 11,724 | 13,731 | 2,007 | 17.11 |
| 3 | Richmond | 21,493 | 24,766 | 3,273 | 15.22 |
| 4 | Jackson | 16,209 | 18,585 | 2,376 | 14.65 |
| 5 | Lubbock | 13,492 | 15,418 | 1,926 | 14.27 |
| 6 | Charlotte | 26,208 | 29,646 | 3,438 | 13.11 |
| 7 | Detroit | 127,420 | 143,107 | 15,687 | 12.31 |
| 8 | Minneapolis | 35,820 | 40,111 | 4,291 | 11.97 |
| 9 | Cincinnati | 32,985 | 36,814 | 3,829 | 11.60 |
| 10 | Flint | 21,201 | 23,649 | 2,448 | 11.54 |
| 11 | Colorado Springs | 16,910 | 18,836 | 1,926 | 11.38 |
| 12 | Warren | 10,940 | 12,094 | 1,154 | 10.54 |
| 13 | Corpus Christi | 19,385 | 21,216 | 1,831 | 9.44 |
| 14 | Salt Lake City | 19,086 | 20,850 | 1,764 | 9.24 |
| 15 | Santa Ana | 19,033 | 20,712 | 1,679 | 8.82 |
| 16 | Providence | 14,317 | 15,548 | 1,231 | 8.59 |
| 17 | El Paso | 27,065 | 29,275 | 2,210 | 8.16 |
| 18 | Lexington | 15,566 | 16,836 | 1,270 | 8.15 |
| 19 | Milwaukee | 41,446 | 44,775 | 3,329 | 8.03 |
| 20 | San Antonio | 57,873 | 62,035 | 4,162 | 7.19 |

| Rank | City | 1980 Crime | 1981 Crime | Absolute Change | Percentage Change |
|------|------|-----------:|-----------:|----------------:|------------------:|
| 21 | Washington, D.C. | 63,668 | 67,910 | 4,242 | 6.66 |
| 22 | Sacramento | 34,699 | 36,681 | 1,982 | 5.71 |
| 23 | Cleveland | 57,602 | 60,721 | 3,119 | 5.71 |
| 24 | Grand Rapids | 16,185 | 17,049 | 864 | 5.33 |
| 25 | Louisville | 20,072 | 21,124 | 1,052 | 5.24 |
| 26 | Little Rock | 17,851 | 18,781 | 930 | 5.20 |
| 27 | San Jose | 51,831 | 54,514 | 2,683 | 5.17 |
| 28 | Dallas | 106,101 | 111,585 | 5,484 | 5.16 |
| 29 | Boston | 75,755 | 79,643 | 3,888 | 5.13 |
| 30 | Jacksonville | 42,890 | 45,070 | 2,180 | 5.08 |
| 31 | Tampa | 38,903 | 40,856 | 1,953 | 5.02 |
| 32 | Las Vegas | 41,405 | 43,376 | 1,971 | 4.76 |
| 33 | Memphis | 50,921 | 53,325 | 2,404 | 4.72 |
| 34 | Seattle | 53,294 | 55,764 | 2,470 | 4.53 |
| 35 | Syracuse | 13,828 | 14,445 | 617 | 4.46 |
| 36 | Albuquerque | 29,326 | 30,614 | 1,288 | 4.39 |
| 37 | Mobile | 21,088 | 21,998 | 910 | 4.31 |
| 38 | Tucson | 35,947 | 37,241 | 1,294 | 3.59 |
| 39 | Kansas City, Kan. | 17,495 | 18,123 | 628 | 3.58 |
| 40 | Jersey City | 19,245 | 19,926 | 681 | 3.53 |
| 41 | Kansas City, Mo. | 49,274 | 51,005 | 1,731 | 3.51 |
| 42 | Los Angeles | 293,837 | 304,101 | 10,264 | 3.49 |
| 43 | Wichita | 24,562 | 25,383 | 821 | 3.34 |
| 44 | Pittsburgh | 30,399 | 31,384 | 985 | 3.24 |
| 45 | Des Moines | 19,369 | 19,974 | 605 | 3.12 |
| 46 | St. Paul | 22,134 | 22,799 | 665 | 3.00 |
| 47 | Norfolk | 20,183 | 20,769 | 586 | 2.90 |
| 48 | Denver | 58,782 | 60,417 | 1,635 | 2.78 |
| 49 | Austin | 30,066 | 30,867 | 801 | 2.66 |
| 50 | New York | 710,151 | 725,846 | 15,695 | 2.21 |
| 51 | Atlanta | 59,394 | 60,569 | 1,175 | 1.97 |
| 51 | San Francisco | 70,424 | 71,812 | 1,388 | 1.97 |
| 53 | Virginia Beach | 15,069 | 15,337 | 268 | 1.77 |
| 54 | Arlington, Texas | 11,341 | 11,541 | 200 | 1.76 |
| 55 | Dayton | 26,593 | 27,053 | 460 | 1.72 |
| 56 | Oakland | 44,152 | 44,679 | 527 | 1.19 |
| 57 | Baltimore | 76,704 | 77,563 | 859 | 1.11 |
| 58 | Knoxville | 12,423 | 12,527 | 104 | .83 |
| 59 | Miami | 52,540 | 52,911 | 371 | .70 |
| 60 | Madison | 14,796 | 14,898 | 102 | .68 |
| 61 | Akron | 18,448 | 18,524 | 76 | .41 |
| 61 | Anaheim | 17,131 | 17,202 | 71 | .41 |
| 63 | Toledo | 34,047 | 34,091 | 44 | .12 |
| 64 | Long Beach | 32,314 | 32,280 | − 34 | − .10 |
| 65 | Columbus, Ohio | 55,362 | 55,293 | − 69 | − .12 |
| 66 | Omaha | 24,430 | 24,351 | − 79 | − .32 |
| 67 | Philadelphia | 101,144 | 100,592 | − 552 | − .54 |
| 68 | St. Petersburg | 21,067 | 20,894 | − 173 | − .82 |
| 69 | Fresno | 24,806 | 24,581 | − 225 | − .90 |
| 70 | Baton Rouge | 26,224 | 25,917 | − 307 | − 1.17 |
| 71 | Aurora | 12,089 | 11,903 | − 186 | − 1.53 |
| 72 | Riverside | 15,626 | 15,361 | − 265 | − 1.69 |
| 73 | Tacoma | 16,516 | 16,193 | − 323 | − 1.95 |
| 74 | Yonkers | 11,522 | 11,219 | − 303 | − 2.62 |
| 75 | New Orleans | 53,575 | 52,158 | − 1,417 | − 2.64 |
| 76 | Fort Worth | 48,492 | 47,153 | − 1,339 | − 2.76 |
| 77 | Oklahoma City | 36,191 | 35,128 | − 1,063 | − 2.93 |
| 78 | St. Louis | 64,631 | 62,654 | − 1,977 | − 3.05 |
| 79 | Birmingham | 35,406 | 34,249 | − 1,157 | − 3.26 |
| 80 | Greensboro | 12,462 | 12,018 | − 444 | − 3.56 |
| 81 | Nashville | 34,886 | 33,604 | − 1,282 | − 3.67 |
| 82 | Columbus, Ga. | 9,186 | 8,776 | − 410 | − 4.46 |
| 83 | Spokane | 16,437 | 15,698 | − 739 | − 4.49 |
| 84 | Tulsa | 32,017 | 30,260 | − 1,757 | − 5.48 |
| 85 | Rochester | 28,989 | 27,291 | − 1,698 | − 5.85 |
| 86 | Lincoln | 11,261 | 10,601 | − 660 | − 5.86 |
| 87 | San Diego | 70,505 | 66,122 | − 4,383 | − 6.21 |
| 88 | Phoenix | 88,523 | 81,371 | − 7,152 | − 8.07 |

| Rank | City | 1980 Crime | 1981 Crime | Absolute Change | Percentage Change |
|---|---|---|---|---|---|
| 89 | Indianapolis | 37,220 | 33,898 | − 3,322 | − 8.92 |
| 90 | Huntington Beach | 10,367 | 9,369 | − 998 | − 9.62 |
| 91 | Montgomery | 12,852 | 11,512 | − 1,340 | −10.42 |
| 92 | Chicago | 196,605 | 173,316 | −23,289 | −11.84 |
| 93 | Fort Wayne | 15,101 | 13,112 | − 1,989 | −13.17 |
| 94 | Honolulu | 57,718 | 49,548 | − 8,170 | −14.15 |
| 95 | Shreveport | 18,784 | 16,030 | − 2,754 | −14.66 |
| 96 | Chattanooga | 16,019 | 13,555 | − 2,464 | −15.38 |

# 184. Metro Area Versus Central City Crime

Crime rates are lower in both suburban and rural areas than in cities. The table below shows by how much. It provides an index of total crimes per 100,000 in cities relative to metropolitan areas. The 1981 city crime rate was divided by the metropolitan area crime rate and then multiplied by 100. If the city rate is the same as the metro rate—as is, for example, the case in Honolulu—the index will register 100.

Only three cities showed a higher metro area (and therefore suburban) crime rate than their central city crime rate: Baton Rouge, Virginia Beach and St. Petersburg.

The cities that showed the highest central city crime rate relative to the metro (and therefore suburban) area crime rate were the older industrial cities mostly the northeast: Dayton, Newark, Pittsburgh, St. Louis, Rochester and Boston.

SOURCE: U.S. Department of Justice, Federal Bureau of Investigation (FBI), *Crime in the U.S.—1981: Uniform Crime Reports* (Washington, D.C.: Government Printing Office, 1982).

| Rank | City | Index | Rank | City | Index | Rank | City | Index |
|---|---|---|---|---|---|---|---|---|
| 1 | Baton Rouge | 96 | 23 | New Orleans | 116 | 49 | San Francisco | 131 |
| 2 | St. Petersburg | 98 | 23 | Phoenix | 116 | 49 | Washington, D.C. | 131 |
| 2 | Virginia Beach | 98 | 23 | Tucson | 116 | 53 | Nashville | 132 |
| 4 | Honolulu | 100 | 29 | Jersey City | 117 | 53 | Sacramento | 132 |
| 4 | Lincoln | 100 | 30 | Madison | 118 | 55 | Baltimore | 133 |
| 6 | Lubbock | 101 | 31 | Wichita | 119 | 55 | Denver | 133 |
| 6 | Philadelphia | 101 | 32 | Anaheim | 121 | 55 | Knoxville | 133 |
| 8 | Columbus, Ga. | 104 | 32 | Des Moines | 121 | 55 | Santa Ana | 133 |
| 9 | Chicago | 106 | 32 | Houston | 121 | 55 | Tacoma | 133 |
| 9 | El Paso | 106 | 32 | Milwaukee | 121 | 60 | Lexington | 134 |
| 9 | Las Vegas | 106 | 32 | San Diego | 121 | 61 | Columbus, Ohio | 137 |
| 9 | Long Beach | 106 | 32 | Spokane | 121 | 61 | Dallas | 137 |
| 13 | Jacksonville | 107 | 38 | Seattle | 123 | 63 | Little Rock | 138 |
| 13 | Riverside | 107 | 39 | Greensboro | 124 | 63 | Mobile | 138 |
| 13 | San Jose | 107 | 39 | Indianapolis | 124 | 63 | St. Paul | 138 |
| 16 | Miami | 110 | 39 | Norfolk | 124 | 66 | Toledo | 139 |
| 16 | Omaha | 110 | 42 | Akron | 125 | 67 | Providence | 140 |
| 18 | San Antonio | 111 | 43 | Colorado Springs | 126 | 68 | Tulsa | 141 |
| 19 | Louisville | 112 | 44 | Charlotte | 127 | 69 | Fort Worth | 143 |
| 19 | Memphis | 112 | 44 | Portland, Ore. | 127 | 69 | Fresno | 143 |
| 19 | New York | 112 | 46 | Jackson | 128 | 71 | Richmond | 144 |
| 22 | Albuquerque | 115 | 47 | Detroit | 130 | 72 | Kansas City, Kan. | 145 |
| 23 | Austin | 116 | 47 | Shreveport | 130 | 72 | Kansas City, Mo. | 145 |
| 23 | Corpus Christi | 116 | 49 | Montgomery | 131 | 72 | Salt Lake City | 145 |
| 23 | Los Angeles | 116 | 49 | Oklahoma City | 131 | 75 | Oakland | 146 |

| Rank | City | Index | Rank | City | Index | Rank | City | Index |
|---|---|---|---|---|---|---|---|---|
| 76 | Buffalo | 150 | 83 | Cleveland | 167 | 90 | Rochester | 187 |
| 76 | Cincinnati | 150 | 84 | Flint | 169 | 91 | St. Louis | 192 |
| 78 | Tampa | 154 | 85 | Minneapolis | 172 | 92 | Pittsburgh | 194 |
| 79 | Fort Wayne | 155 | 86 | Worcester | 174 | 93 | Newark | 196 |
| 80 | Chattanooga | 158 | 87 | Birmingham | 176 | 94 | Dayton | 221 |
| 80 | Grand Rapids | 158 | 88 | Atlanta | 178 | | | |
| 82 | Syracuse | 165 | 89 | Boston | 186 | | | |

# 185. Violent Crimes

Violent crimes include homicides, rapes, robberies and assaults. Homocides and rapes are a small fraction of violent crimes. In 1981 less than 7 per cent of all violent crimes were homicides or rapes. Most are robberies and assaults. Robberies are a more reliable indicator than assaults—how do you decide whether an assault is felonious or not? How many domestic assaults are actually reported? The only problem for the cities is that robberies are a peculiarly urban crime. A robbery isn't as likely to succeed in a small town. Strangers are likely to be noticed. In a big city, it's another matter entirely. Moreover, robberies are especially feared because they involve the possibility of loss of life and because they are crimes among strangers.

SOURCE: U.S. Department of Justice, Federal Bureau of Investigation (FBI), *Crime in the U.S.—1981: Uniform Crime Reports* (Washington, D.C.: Government Printing Office, 1982).

| Rank | City | Violent Crimes | Violent Crimes Per 1,000 Population |
|---|---|---|---|
| 1 | Miami | 11,211 | 32.31 |
| 2 | Boston | 14,071 | 24.99 |
| 3 | Atlanta | 10,579 | 24.89 |
| 4 | St. Louis | 10,364 | 22.87 |
| 5 | Washington, D.C. | 14,468 | 22.69 |
| 6 | Baltimore | 17,737 | 22.54 |
| 7 | New York | 145,946 | 22.20 |
| 8 | Cleveland | 12,429 | 21.66 |
| 9 | Flint | 3,377 | 21.16 |
| 10 | Tampa | 5,674 | 20.90 |
| 11 | Oakland | 7,037 | 20.74 |
| 12 | Detroit | 23,176 | 19.26 |
| 13 | Los Angeles | 52,819 | 17.80 |
| 14 | San Francisco | 12,011 | 17.69 |
| 15 | Portland, Ore. | 6,452 | 17.61 |
| 16 | Dayton | 3,509 | 17.24 |
| 17 | Kansas City, Mo. | 7,714 | 17.21 |
| 18 | New Orleans | 8,121 | 14.57 |
| 19 | Little Rock | 2,307 | 14.56 |
| 20 | Jersey City | 3,203 | 14.33 |
| 21 | Pittsburgh | 5,983 | 14.11 |
| 22 | Dallas | 12,661 | 14.00 |
| 23 | Kansas City, Kan. | 2,117 | 13.14 |
| 24 | Mobile | 2,629 | 13.12 |
| 25 | Baton Rouge | 2,861 | 13.04 |
| 26 | Sacramento | 3,555 | 12.89 |
| 27 | Fort Worth | 4,946 | 12.84 |
| 28 | Long Beach | 4,579 | 12.67 |
| 29 | Rochester | 2,971 | 12.29 |
| 30 | Richmond | 2,668 | 12.17 |
| 31 | Birmingham | 3,292 | 11.57 |
| 32 | Las Vegas | 4,648 | 11.42 |
| 33 | Seattle | 5,414 | 10.96 |
| 34 | Memphis | 7,056 | 10.92 |
| 35 | Providence | 1,681 | 10.72 |
| 36 | St. Petersburg | 2,509 | 10.59 |
| 37 | Minneapolis | 3,883 | 10.47 |
| 38 | Denver | 5,085 | 10.35 |
| 39 | Grand Rapids | 1,876 | 10.32 |
| 40 | Philadelphia | 17,299 | 10.25 |
| 41 | Oklahoma City | 4,128 | 10.24 |
| 42 | Cincinnati | 3,891 | 10.09 |
| 43 | Charlotte | 3,166 | 10.07 |
| 44 | Fresno | 2,158 | 9.89 |
| 45 | Indianapolis | 4,539 | 9.83 |
| 46 | Columbus, Ohio | 5,263 | 9.32 |
| 47 | Lubbock | 1,598 | 9.19 |
| 48 | Riverside | 1,567 | 9.17 |
| 49 | Louisville | 2,731 | 9.15 |
| 50 | Norfolk | 2,441 | 9.14 |
| 51 | Aurora | 1,437 | 9.06 |
| 52 | Albuquerque | 2,985 | 9.00 |
| 53 | Santa Ana | 1,758 | 8.63 |
| 54 | Tacoma | 1,356 | 8.56 |
| 55 | St. Paul | 2,309 | 8.54 |
| 56 | Chicago | 25,609 | 8.52 |
| 57 | Tucson | 2,810 | 8.50 |
| 58 | Chattanooga | 1,431 | 8.44 |
| 59 | El Paso | 3,510 | 8.25 |
| 60 | Phoenix | 6,320 | 8.00 |
| 61 | Syracuse | 1,356 | 7.97 |
| 62 | Salt Lake City | 1,269 | 7.78 |
| 63 | Toledo | 2,712 | 7.65 |
| 64 | San Diego | 6,593 | 7.53 |
| 65 | Tulsa | 2,681 | 7.43 |

| Rank | City | Violent Crimes | Violent Crimes Per 1,000 Population |
|------|------|----------------|-------------------------------------|
| 66 | Jackson | 1,393 | 6.87 |
| 67 | Corpus Christi | 1,587 | 6.84 |
| 68 | Colorado Springs | 1,463 | 6.77 |
| 69 | Nashville-Davidson | 3,087 | 6.77 |
| 70 | Shreveport | 1,389 | 6.75 |
| 71 | Jacksonville | 3,634 | 6.72 |
| 72 | Greensboro | 1,034 | 6.64 |
| 73 | San Jose | 4,122 | 6.48 |
| 74 | Spokane | 1,085 | 6.33 |
| 75 | Wichita | 1,729 | 6.19 |
| 76 | Knoxville | 1,094 | 5.97 |
| 77 | San Antonio | 4,651 | 5.92 |
| 78 | Anaheim | 1,255 | 5.66 |
| 79 | Lexington-Fayette | 1,148 | 5.62 |
| 80 | Yonkers | 1,069 | 5.47 |
| 81 | Des Moines | 1,039 | 5.44 |

| Rank | City | Violent Crimes | Violent Crimes Per 1,000 Population |
|------|------|----------------|-------------------------------------|
| 82 | Honolulu | 1,965 | 5.38 |
| 82 | Milwaukee | 3,424 | 5.38 |
| 84 | Anchorage | 924 | 5.34 |
| 85 | Warren | 858 | 5.32 |
| 86 | Akron | 1,236 | 5.21 |
| 87 | Omaha | 1,583 | 5.08 |
| 88 | Montgomery | 853 | 4.79 |
| 89 | Fort Wayne | 821 | 4.77 |
| 90 | Columbus, Ga. | 757 | 4.47 |
| 91 | Austin | 1,542 | 4.46 |
| 92 | Arlington, Texas | 699 | 4.37 |
| 93 | Huntington Beach | 543 | 3.18 |
| 94 | Madison | 463 | 2.71 |
| 95 | Lincoln | 426 | 2.48 |
| 96 | Virginia Beach | 606 | 2.31 |

# 186.  Arrests for Violent Crimes

In the table below and in the tables on arrests for property crimes, murders, rapes, robberies and arsons, we provide information on the ratio of arrests to reported crimes.

The arrest rate we show below is the percentage of reported crimes in each category represented by arrests. Each arrest is considered to pertain to only one reported crime. The arrest rate is an approximation of the "clearance rate," which is the proportion of crimes solved by arrest. One arrest is often considered by the police, however, to solve more than one crime.

For all violent crimes—i.e., murders (homicides), rapes, robberies and assaults—the ratio of arrests to reports in 1981 ranged from a high of 64 percent in Greensboro to a low of 5 percent in Jackson.

On one level, these arrest rates for violent crimes may be viewed as a measure of a city's tolerance for violence. If one man assaults another savagely in a bar, do the police officers responding to the bartender's urgent call take one man (or both men) to the police station, or do they just tell the participants to break it up and go home?

Assuming that Greensboro and Jackson report crimes in the same way—the goal of the Federal Bureau of Investigation's Uniform Crime Reports program— then Greensboro's police have a lower tolerance for violence than do Jackson's. The odds are roughly 6 in 10 in Greensboro that a report of violence will result in an arrest, while in Jackson the odds are only 1 in 20.

Philadelphia and Fresno show an arrest rate of 59 percent. Five other cities show arrest rates greater than 50 percent—Louisville; Columbus, Georgia; Milwaukee; Honolulu; and Virginia Beach.

At the other end of the scale, six cities show arrest rates of 20 percent or less for violent crimes—Fort Wayne; Baltimore; Kansas City; Flint; Miami; and Indianapolis.

SOURCES: Reported violent crimes for 1981 from U.S. Department of Justice, Federal Bureau of Investigation, *Crime in the U.S.—1981: Uniform Crime Reports* (Washington, D.C.: Government Printing Office, 1982). Arrests for violent crimes in 1981 from a special unpublished report provided at the authors' request by the Federal Bureau of Investigation, January 1983.

| Rank | City | Reports of Violent Crimes | Arrests Violent Crimes | Percentage of Arrests Per Violent Crimes Reported |
|------|------|---------------------------|------------------------|---------------------------------------------------|
| 1 | Greensboro | 1,034 | 661 | 63.93 |
| 2 | Philadelphia | 17,616 | 10,472 | 59.45 |
| 3 | Fresno | 2,158 | 1,265 | 58.62 |
| 4 | Louisville | 2,731 | 1,517 | 55.55 |
| 5 | Columbus, Ga. | 757 | 409 | 54.03 |
| 6 | Milwaukee | 3,424 | 1,801 | 52.60 |
| 7 | Honolulu | 1,965 | 987 | 50.23 |
| 8 | Virginia Beach | 606 | 303 | 50.00 |
| 9 | Huntington Beach | 543 | 260 | 47.88 |
| 10 | Oklahoma City | 4,128 | 1,952 | 47.29 |
| 11 | San Diego | 6,593 | 3,009 | 45.64 |

| Rank | City | Reports of Violent Crimes | Arrests Violent Crimes | Percentage of Arrests Per Violent Crimes Reported |
|---|---|---|---|---|
| 12 | Colorado Springs | 1,463 | 654 | 44.70 |
| 13 | Sacramento | 3,555 | 1,582 | 44.50 |
| 14 | Salt Lake City | 1,269 | 562 | 44.29 |
| 15 | Baton Rouge | 2,861 | 1,244 | 43.48 |
| 16 | Santa Ana | 1,758 | 754 | 42.89 |
| 17 | Norfolk | 2,441 | 1,032 | 42.28 |
| 18 | El Paso | 3,510 | 1.438 | 40.97 |
| 19 | Atlanta | 10,579 | 4,283 | 40.49 |
| 20 | Anaheim | 1,255 | 506 | 40.32 |
| 21 | Riverside | 1,567 | 611 | 38.99 |
| 22 | Wichita | 1,729 | 664 | 38.40 |
| 23 | Chicago | 25,609 | 9,721 | 37.96 |
| 24 | Long Beach | 4,431 | 1,652 | 37.28 |
| 25 | Tucson | 2,810 | 1,047 | 37.26 |
| 26 | Charlotte | 3,166 | 1,173 | 37.05 |
| 27 | Knoxville | 1,094 | 403 | 36.84 |
| 28 | Jersey City | 3,203 | 1,178 | 36.78 |
| 29 | Jacksonville | 5,634 | 2,051 | 36.40 |
| 30 | San Jose | 4,122 | 1,478 | 35.86 |
| 31 | Providence | 1,681 | 576 | 34.27 |
| 31 | Shreveport | 1,389 | 476 | 34.27 |
| 33 | Syracuse | 1,356 | 461 | 33.00 |
| 34 | Tulsa | 2,681 | 879 | 32.79 |
| 35 | Phoenix | 6,320 | 2,051 | 32.45 |
| 36 | Detroit | 23,176 | 7,444 | 32.12 |
| 37 | Fort Worth | 4,946 | 1,582 | 31.99 |
| 38 | New Orleans | 8,121 | 2,551 | 31.41 |
| 39 | Los Angeles | 52,819 | 16,463 | 31.17 |
| 40 | Montgomery | 853 | 265 | 31.07 |
| 41 | Richmond | 2,668 | 820 | 30.73 |
| 42 | San Francisco | 12,011 | 3,610 | 30.06 |
| 43 | Rochester | 2,971 | 858 | 28.88 |
| 44 | Las Vegas | 4,648 | 1,337 | 28.77 |
| 45 | Kansas City, Mo. | 7,714 | 2,213 | 28.69 |
| 46 | Mobile | 2,629 | 752 | 28.60 |
| 47 | Tampa | 5,674 | 1,596 | 28.13 |
| 48 | Grand Rapids | 1,876 | 526 | 28.04 |
| 49 | Toledo | 2,712 | 750 | 27.65 |
| 50 | Omaha | 1,983 | 545 | 27.48 |
| 51 | St. Petersburg | 2,509 | 684 | 27.26 |
| 52 | Lexington-Fayette | 1,148 | 310 | 27.00 |
| 53 | Pittsburgh | 5,983 | 1,602 | 26.78 |
| 54 | Washington, D.C. | 14,468 | 3,846 | 26.58 |
| 55 | New York | 156,946 | 39,632 | 25.25 |
| 56 | Lubbock | 1,598 | 399 | 24.97 |
| 57 | Anchorage | 924 | 227 | 24.57 |
| 58 | Dallas | 12,752 | 3,122 | 24.48 |
| 59 | Corpus Christi | 1,587 | 373 | 23.50 |
| 60 | San Antonio | 4,651 | 1.067 | 22.94 |
| 61 | Portland, Ore. | 6,452 | 1,468 | 22.75 |
| 62 | Dayton | 3,509 | 777 | 22.14 |
| 63 | Minneapolis | 3,883 | 836 | 21.53 |
| 64 | Birmingham | 3,292 | 703 | 21.35 |
| 65 | Chattanooga | 3,166 | 670 | 21.16 |
| 66 | Indianapolis | 4,539 | 923 | 20.33 |
| 67 | Miami | 11,211 | 2,268 | 20.23 |
| 68 | Flint | 3,377 | 660 | 19.54 |
| 69 | Kansas City, Kan. | 2,117 | 336 | 15.87 |
| 70 | Baltimore | 17,737 | 1,436 | 8.10 |
| 71 | Fort Wayne | 821 | 52 | 6.33 |
| 72 | Jackson | 5,634 | 308 | 5.47 |

# 187. Trends in Violent Crimes

Historical data (not shown below) reviewed by the Federal Bureau of Investigation may help put recent trends in perspective. Violent crimes were up from 400 per 100,000 in 1972 to 580 per 100,000 in 1981. However, homicides—the most reliable indicators of crime—were hardly up at all, from 9.0 to 9.8 per 100,000 population. In fact, they dropped to 8.8 per 100,000 in 1976–77. Nothing to be proud of, but no big increase. So there may have just been an increase in reporting as opposed to a major increase in actual crimes.

Robberies (defined as taking or trying to take something from someone by force or threat of force) are the next most reliable data after homicides. They were up 39 percent between 1972 and 1981—from 180 per 100,000 to 250 per 100,000. Not good, but not quite as bad as the overall crime rate increases.

The increases in violent crimes were in the other areas, where crime reporting is less reliable. Rapes were up from 22.5 per 100,000 to 35.6 per 100,000, but this could merely indicate a greater willingness of women to come forward and report the crime.

Assaults account for the largest increase in violent crimes. They were up 49 per cent—from 190 per 100,000 in 1972 to 280 per 100,000 in 1981. To some extent this increase, along with the increase in robberies, can be attributed to the coming of age of the postwar baby boom generation. It could also reflect people's greater willingness to tell the police about such incidents.

The table below indicates that between 1979 and 1981 Honolulu sustained a 10.5 percent drop in its already low rate of violent crimes—a drop perhaps related to the recession, which brought fewer tourists to

Honolulu and therefore gave criminals fewer easy targets on whom to prey, or to the deterrent effect of good police work.

At the other end of the scale, violent crimes doubled in Montgomery and were up in 77 out of the 90 cities for which we have data.

---

SOURCES: U.S. Department of Justice, Federal Bureau of Investigation (FBI), *Crime in the U.S.—1979* and *Crime in the U.S.—1981* (Washington, D.C.: Government Printing Office, 1980 and 1982).

---

| Rank | City | 1979 Violent Crimes | 1981 Violent Crimes | Absolute Change in Violent Crimes | Percentage Change in Violent Crimes |
|------|------|---------------------|---------------------|-----------------------------------|-------------------------------------|
| 1 | Montgomery | 415 | 853 | 438 | 105.54 |
| 2 | Miami | 6,825 | 11,211 | 4,386 | 64.26 |
| 3 | El Paso | 2,245 | 3,510 | 1,265 | 56.35 |
| 4 | Mobile | 1,763 | 2,629 | 866 | 49.12 |
| 5 | Lubbock | 1,101 | 1,598 | 497 | 45.14 |
| 6 | Las Vegas | 3,210 | 4,648 | 1,438 | 44.80 |
| 7 | Jersey City | 2,224 | 3,203 | 979 | 44.02 |
| 8 | Portland, Ore. | 4,558 | 6,452 | 1,894 | 41.55 |
| 9 | Tucson | 2,029 | 2,810 | 781 | 38.49 |
| 10 | Washington, D.C. | 10,533 | 14,468 | 3,935 | 37.36 |
| 11 | Providence | 1,234 | 1,681 | 447 | 36.22 |
| 12 | Santa Ana | 1,297 | 1,758 | 461 | 35.54 |
| 13 | Madison | 342 | 463 | 121 | 35.38 |
| 14 | Tampa | 4,206 | 5,674 | 1,468 | 34.90 |
| 15 | Colorado Springs | 1,092 | 1,463 | 371 | 33.97 |
| 16 | Lexington-Fayette | 873 | 1,148 | 275 | 31.50 |
| 17 | Anchorage | 708 | 924 | 216 | 30.51 |
| 18 | Fort Worth | 3,799 | 4,946 | 1,147 | 30.19 |
| 19 | Kansas City, Mo. | 5,942 | 7,714 | 1,772 | 29.82 |
| 20 | Pittsburgh | 4,649 | 5,983 | 1,334 | 28.69 |
| 21 | Cleveland | 9,736 | 12,429 | 2,693 | 27.66 |
| 22 | Charlotte | 2,485 | 3,166 | 681 | 27.40 |
| 23 | San Jose | 3,236 | 4,122 | 886 | 27.38 |
| 24 | Fort Wayne | 649 | 821 | 172 | 26.50 |
| 25 | Columbus, Ohio | 4,242 | 5,263 | 1,021 | 24.07 |
| 26 | St. Paul | 1,882 | 2,309 | 427 | 22.69 |
| 27 | Baton Rouge | 2,332 | 2,861 | 529 | 22.68 |
| 28 | Memphis | 5,785 | 7,056 | 1,271 | 21.97 |
| 29 | Los Angeles | 43,372 | 52,819 | 9,447 | 21.78 |
| 30 | Tacoma | 1,117 | 1,356 | 239 | 21.40 |
| 31 | San Diego | 5,436 | 6,593 | 1,157 | 21.28 |
| 32 | Philadelphia | 14,537 | 17,616 | 3,079 | 21.18 |
| 33 | Richmond | 2,234 | 2,668 | 434 | 19.43 |
| 34 | Wichita | 1,456 | 1,729 | 273 | 18.76 |
| 35 | New York | 132,383 | 156,946 | 24,563 | 18.55 |
| 36 | Grand Rapids | 1,603 | 1,876 | 273 | 17.03 |
| 37 | Tulsa | 2,326 | 2,681 | 355 | 15.26 |
| 38 | Jacksonville | 4,903 | 5,634 | 731 | 14.91 |
| 39 | Yonkers | 931 | 1,069 | 138 | 14.82 |
| 40 | Norfolk | 2,127 | 2,441 | 314 | 14.76 |
| 41 | Virginia Beach | 530 | 606 | 76 | 14.34 |
| 42 | Baltimore | 15,523 | 17,737 | 2,214 | 14.26 |
| 43 | San Antonio | 4,088 | 4,651 | 563 | 13.77 |
| 44 | Salt Lake City | 1,119 | 1,269 | 150 | 13.40 |
| 45 | Shreveport | 1,225 | 1,389 | 164 | 13.39 |
| 46 | St. Petersburg | 2,215 | 2,509 | 294 | 13.27 |
| 47 | Milwaukee | 3,039 | 3,424 | 385 | 12.67 |
| 48 | Arlington, Texas | 626 | 699 | 73 | 11.66 |
| 49 | Seattle | 4,857 | 5,414 | 557 | 11.47 |
| 50 | Albuquerque | 2,679 | 2,985 | 306 | 11.42 |
| 51 | Dallas | 11,453 | 12,752 | 1,299 | 11.34 |
| 52 | Long Beach | 3,990 | 4,431 | 441 | 11.05 |
| 53 | Syracuse | 1,225 | 1,356 | 131 | 10.69 |

| Rank | City | 1979 Violent Crimes | 1981 Violent Crimes | Absolute Change in Violent Crimes | Percentage Change in Violent Crimes |
|------|------|---------------------|---------------------|-----------------------------------|-------------------------------------|
| 54 | Sacramento | 3,212 | 3,555 | 343 | 10.68 |
| 55 | Akron | 1,118 | 1,236 | 118 | 10.55 |
| 56 | Detroit | 21,021 | 23,176 | 2,155 | 10.25 |
| 57 | Dayton | 3,195 | 3,509 | 314 | 9.83 |
| 58 | Fresno | 1,976 | 2,158 | 182 | 9.21 |
| 59 | Phoenix | 5,803 | 6,320 | 517 | 8.91 |
| 60 | San Francisco | 11,041 | 12,011 | 970 | 8.79 |
| 61 | Indianapolis | 4,178 | 4,539 | 361 | 8.64 |
| 62 | Oklahoma City | 3,812 | 4,128 | 316 | 8.29 |
| 63 | Riverside | 1,451 | 1,567 | 116 | 7.99 |
| 64 | Anaheim | 1,176 | 1,255 | 79 | 6.72 |
| 65 | Chattanooga | 1,526 | 1,431 | 95 | 6.23 |
| 66 | Louisville | 2,576 | 2,731 | 155 | 6.02 |
| 67 | Sopkane | 1,029 | 1,085 | 56 | 5.44 |
| 68 | Rochester | 2,846 | 2,971 | 125 | 4.39 |
| 69 | Greensboro | 997 | 1,034 | 37 | 3.71 |
| 70 | Austin | 1,495 | 1,545 | 50 | 3.34 |
| 71 | Columbus, Ga. | 737 | 757 | 20 | 2.71 |
| 72 | Flint | 3,294 | 3,377 | 83 | 2.52 |
| 73 | Cincinnati | 3,808 | 3,891 | 83 | 2.18 |
| 74 | Kansas City, Kan. | 2,084 | 2,117 | 33 | 1.58 |
| 75 | Corpus Christi | 1,589 | 1,587 | — 2 | — .13 |
| 76 | Minneapolis | 3,899 | 3,883 | — 16 | — .41 |
| 77 | Denver | 5,118 | 5,085 | — 33 | — .64 |
| 78 | Birmingham | 3,328 | 3,292 | — 36 | — 1.08 |
| 79 | Atlanta | 10,715 | 10,579 | — 136 | — 1.27 |
| 80 | Omaha | 2,017 | 1,983 | — 34 | — 1.69 |
| 81 | Des Moines | 1,074 | 1,039 | — 35 | — 3.26 |
| 82 | Knoxville | 1,135 | 1,094 | — 41 | — 3.61 |
| 83 | St. Louis | 10,774 | 10,364 | — 410 | — 3.81 |
| 84 | Lincoln | 448 | 426 | — 22 | — 4.91 |
| 85 | Nashville | 3,251 | 3,087 | — 164 | — 5.04 |
| 86 | Huntington Beach | 580 | 543 | — 37 | — 6.38 |
| 87 | Chicago | 27,807 | 25,609 | — 2,198 | — 7.90 |
| 88 | Toledo | 2,966 | 2,712 | — 254 | — 8.56 |
| 89 | New Orleans | 8,894 | 8,121 | — 773 | — 8.69 |
| 90 | Honolulu | 2,196 | 1,965 | — 231 | —10.52 |

# 188. Homicides

Between 1972 and 1981 the fewest murders occurred in the second quarter of 1976 and the first quarter of 1978. The most occurred in the third quarter of 1980. Usually murders are lower in the first half of the year and peak in the second half. However, murders are much less seasonal than other violent crimes.

Blacks are much more likely to be killed than whites. Between 1978 and 1980, *for every 100,000 black males in the age range of 24–30, over 100 were murdered.* That's over 1 in a thousand. The corresponding odds for white males and black females is one-third of the rate for black males, or less. The odds for white females are relatively tiny—less than 1 in 20,000 for any age group. The people least likely to be murdered in America are white children aged 6 to 12. Their odds of being killed drop to less than 1 in 100,000.

Homicides, like robberies, are a good crime indicator because they tend to be reported consistently. If someone dies, the word commonly gets out and reports have to be filed. Assaults and rapes, the other two violent crimes (besides robberies), are less reliably reported to the police and by the police.

Cities with a large transient population, a volatile economic base, and racial and economic tensions—such as Miami, Atlanta and Los Angeles—tend to have higher homicide rates. Cities with the highest homicide rates (Atlanta; Detroit; Cleveland; Washington, D.C.; Dallas; Los Angeles; Chicago and New York) all have metro area populations in excess of 2 million.

As the table below shows, in 1981 Miami had the highest murder rate of the 95 cities surveyed, with 61 homicides per 100,000 population. Miami's racial problems were exacerbated by the 1980 entry of the Cuban refugee "freedom flotilla," many of whose members were convicted criminals exiled by Castro.

At the other end of the table, cities that had the fewest homicides in 1981 tend to have smaller populations and to be in the middle-level income brackets. The bottom five cities (Warren, Des Moines, Madison, Yonkers, Lincoln and Huntington Beach) have populations below 100,000 with small metro areas. Most of these cities have only recently experienced large population gains but are relatively stable because of their racial and ethnic homogeneity.

SOURCE: U.S. Department of Justice, Federal Bureau of Investigation (FBI), *Crime in the U.S.—1981: Uniform Crime Reports* (Washington, D.C.: Government Printing Office, 1982), pp. 325, 341.

| Rank | City | Homicides | Homicides Per 100,000 Population |
|---|---|---|---|
| 1 | Miami | 210 | 60.53 |
| 2 | St. Louis | 265 | 58.49 |
| 3 | El Paso | 205 | 48.21 |
| 4 | Atlanta | 182 | 42.82 |
| 5 | Detroit | 502 | 41.72 |
| 6 | Cleveland | 233 | 40.60 |
| 7 | New Orleans | 217 | 38.93 |
| 8 | Oakland | 119 | 35.07 |
| 9 | Washington, D.C. | 223 | 34.97 |
| 10 | Birmingham | 97 | 34.11 |
| 11 | Dallas | 301 | 33.29 |
| 12 | Dayton | 67 | 32.91 |
| 13 | Los Angeles | 880 | 29.66 |
| 14 | Fort Worth | 113 | 29.34 |
| 15 | Chicago | 877 | 29.18 |
| 16 | Baltimore | 228 | 28.98 |
| 17 | Shreveport | 54 | 26.24 |
| 18 | Las Vegas | 106 | 26.05 |
| 19 | New York | 1,826 | 25.82 |
| 20 | Kansas City, Mo. | 115 | 25.68 |
| 21 | Tampa | 69 | 25.41 |
| 22 | Corpus Christi | 58 | 25.00 |
| 23 | Jackson | 48 | 23.66 |
| 24 | San Antonio | 185 | 23.55 |
| 25 | Baton Rouge | 50 | 22.78 |
| 26 | Little Rock | 36 | 22.72 |
| 27 | Richmond | 48 | 21.90 |
| 28 | Philadelphia | 362 | 21.44 |
| 29 | Flint | 34 | 21.30 |
| 30 | Memphis | 133 | 20.58 |
| 31 | Long Beach | 74 | 20.48 |
| 32 | Denver | 100 | 20.35 |
| 33 | Jersey City | 45 | 20.13 |
| 34 | Lubbock | 34 | 19.54 |
| 35 | Mobile | 39 | 19.46 |

| Rank | City | Homicides | Homicides Per 100,000 Population |
|---|---|---|---|
| 36 | Sacramento | 53 | 19.22 |
| 37 | Kansas City, Kan. | 30 | 18.62 |
| 38 | San Francisco | 126 | 18.56 |
| 39 | Louisville | 55 | 18.43 |
| 40 | Boston | 100 | 17.76 |
| 41 | Nashville | 79 | 17.34 |
| 42 | Chattanooga | 29 | 17.10 |
| 43 | Montgomery | 30 | 16.84 |
| 44 | Jacksonville | 89 | 16.45 |
| 45 | Charlotte | 51 | 16.22 |
| 46 | Oklahoma City | 65 | 16.12 |
| 47 | Columbus, Ohio | 91 | 16.11 |
| 47 | Norfolk | 43 | 16.11 |
| 49 | Rochester | 38 | 15.72 |
| 50 | Wichita | 43 | 15.40 |
| 51 | Fresno | 33 | 15.12 |
| 52 | Providence | 23 | 14.67 |
| 53 | Toledo | 52 | 14.66 |
| 54 | Indianapolis | 65 | 14.07 |
| 55 | Tulsa | 50 | 13.85 |
| 56 | Knoxville | 25 | 13.65 |
| 57 | Albuquerque | 45 | 13.56 |
| 58 | Grand Rapids | 24 | 13.20 |
| 59 | Columbus, Ga. | 22 | 12.98 |
| 60 | Phoenix | 97 | 12.28 |
| 61 | Seattle | 59 | 11.95 |
| 62 | Pittsburgh | 49 | 11.56 |
| 63 | Austin | 39 | 11.29 |
| 64 | Milwaukee | 71 | 11.16 |
| 65 | St. Petersburg | 26 | 10.98 |
| 66 | Cincinnati | 42 | 10.90 |
| 67 | Santa Ana | 22 | 10.80 |
| 68 | San Jose | 68 | 10.68 |
| 69 | San Diego | 93 | 10.62 |
| 70 | Syracuse | 18 | 10.58 |
| 71 | Fort Wayne | 18 | 10.45 |
| 72 | Anchorage | 18 | 10.40 |
| 73 | Portland, Ore. | 38 | 10.37 |
| 74 | Akron | 24 | 10.12 |
| 75 | Omaha | 28 | 8.98 |
| 76 | Lexington-Fayette | 18 | 8.82 |
| 77 | Salt Lake City | 14 | 8.59 |
| 78 | Anaheim | 19 | 8.56 |
| 79 | Tucson | 28 | 8.47 |
| 80 | Colorado Springs | 18 | 8.37 |
| 81 | Riverside | 13 | 7.61 |
| 82 | Minneapolis | 28 | 7.55 |
| 83 | Arlington, Texas | 12 | 7.49 |
| 84 | Spokane | 11 | 6.42 |
| 85 | Aurora | 10 | 6.31 |
| 85 | Tacoma | 10 | 6.31 |
| 87 | Honolulu | 40 | 5.17 |
| 88 | St. Paul | 13 | 4.81 |
| 89 | Virginia Beach | 12 | 4.58 |
| 90 | Warren | 6 | 3.72 |
| 91 | Des Moines | 7 | 3.66 |
| 92 | Madison | 6 | 3.52 |
| 93 | Yonkers | 6 | 3.07 |
| 94 | Lincoln | 5 | 2.91 |
| 95 | Huntington Beach | 4 | 2.35 |

# 189.  Arrests for Homicide

One major function of a police department is to serve as a deterrent to major crimes by ensuring that perpetrators of such crimes are arrested and brought to court, where justice will presumably be meted out.

The higher the ratio of arrests for murder to reports of murder, other things being equal, the safer one ought to feel.

The table below, showing arrests for murder in 1981 relative to reports of murder, suggests that Californians ought to feel safer than anyone else on this basis. Despite heavy cuts in local government spending in the state since Proposition 13 in 1978, half of the 10 cities with the highest ratio of arrests to reported murders are in that state. Huntington Beach in 1981 had a ratio of nearly 6 arrests for murder per report of murder. Los Angeles, Anaheim, Riverside and San Francisco had between 1.9 and 1.6 arrests for murder per report of murder. Five other California cities had a ratio of 1.0 or over. Only San Diego and San Jose were well below 1.0. Apparently police department budgets in California had not been cut enough to hinder their follow-up on murders.

Arrests for murder are likely to be of higher quality than other arrests because of the seriousness of the crime, the attendant publicity and the concern of police departments not to decrease the likelihood of conviction by botching up the arrest process.

At the other end of the spectrum from California cities are cities in New England and New York. They have a low ratio of arrests for murder to reports of murder. New York, Providence and Syracuse are all among the bottom 11 cities in the table below. Boston and Buffalo are not included in the table at all because they had not filed arrest data with the Federal Bureau of Investigation at the time of the preparation of the arrest data for this table. Although Worcester provided arrest data (eight arrests for murder in 1981), no information on the city's reported murders was included in the 1981 Uniform Crime Reports.

The lowest ratio of arrests to murders in 1981 was in Fort Wayne, which had 3 arrests for 18 murders—17 percent.

SOURCES: Reported murders for 1981 from U.S. Department of Justice, Federal Bureau of Investigation, *Crime in the U.S.—1981: Uniform Crime Reports* (Washington, D.C.: Government Printing Office, 1982). Arrests for murders in 1981 from a special unpublished report provided at the authors' request by the Federal Bureau of Investigation, January 1983.

| Rank | City | Reports of Homicide | Arrests for Homicide | Arrests as Percent of Reports |
|---|---|---|---|---|
| 1 | Huntington Beach | 1 | 23 | 575 |
| 2 | El Paso | 35 | 73 | 208 |
| 3 | Warren | 6 | 12 | 200 |
| 4 | Los Angeles | 879 | 1,692 | 192 |
| 5 | Anaheim | 19 | 35 | 184 |
| 6 | Riverside | 13 | 23 | 176 |
| 7 | Greensboro | 11 | 18 | 163 |
| 8 | San Francisco | 126 | 198 | 157 |
| 9 | Columbus, Ga. | 22 | 34 | 154 |
| 10 | Honolulu | 40 | 60 | 150 |
| 10 | Salt Lake City | 14 | 21 | 150 |
| 12 | Virginia Beach | 12 | 17 | 141 |
| 13 | Fresno | 33 | 46 | 139 |
| 13 | Omaha | 28 | 39 | 139 |
| 15 | Colorado Springs | 18 | 25 | 138 |
| 16 | Milwaukee | 71 | 93 | 130 |
| 17 | Chicago | 877 | 1,086 | 123 |
| 17 | Detroit | 502 | 621 | 123 |
| 19 | Philadelphia | 362 | 431 | 119 |
| 20 | Santa Ana | 22 | 26 | 118 |
| 21 | Flint | 34 | 40 | 117 |
| 21 | Toledo | 51 | 60 | 117 |
| 23 | Little Rock | 36 | 41 | 113 |
| 24 | Tucson | 28 | 31 | 110 |
| 25 | Baton Rouge | 50 | 55 | 109 |
| 26 | Mobile | 39 | 42 | 107 |
| 27 | Oakland | 118 | 124 | 105 |
| 28 | Long Beach | 74 | 76 | 102 |
| 28 | Pittsburgh | 49 | 50 | 102 |
| 30 | Chattanooga | 29 | 29 | 100 |
| 30 | Lexington-Fayette | 18 | 18 | 100 |
| 32 | Kansas City, Mo. | 115 | 114 | 99 |
| 33 | Sacramento | 53 | 52 | 98 |
| 34 | Corpus Christi | 57 | 55 | 96 |
| 34 | Louisville | 55 | 53 | 96 |
| 36 | Jacksonville | 89 | 83 | 93 |
| 36 | Norfolk | 43 | 40 | 93 |
| 38 | Charlotte | 51 | 47 | 92 |
| 38 | Knoxville | 25 | 23 | 92 |
| 40 | Newark | 161 | 148 | 91 |
| 41 | Las Vegas | 106 | 96 | 90 |
| 42 | Richmond | 48 | 43 | 89 |
| 43 | Lubbock | 34 | 30 | 88 |
| 43 | St. Petersburg | 26 | 23 | 88 |
| 45 | Oklahoma City | 65 | 57 | 87 |
| 46 | Jersey City | 44 | 38 | 86 |
| 46 | Tampa | 69 | 60 | 86 |
| 46 | Washington, DC. | 223 | 193 | 86 |
| 49 | Atlanta | 182 | 155 | 85 |
| 50 | New Orleans | 217 | 184 | 84 |
| 51 | Shreveport | 54 | 45 | 83 |
| 52 | Minneapolis | 28 | 23 | 82 |
| 53 | Rochester | 38 | 31 | 81 |
| 53 | San Diego | 94 | 77 | 81 |
| 53 | Wichita | 43 | 35 | 81 |
| 56 | Montgomery | 30 | 24 | 80 |
| 57 | Tulsa | 47 | 37 | 78 |
| 58 | Dallas | 298 | 231 | 77 |
| 58 | Dayton | 67 | 52 | 77 |
| 58 | San Jose | 68 | 53 | 77 |
| 61 | Grand Rapids | 24 | 18 | 75 |
| 62 | Kansas City, Ks. | 30 | 22 | 73 |
| 63 | Portland | 38 | 27 | 71 |
| 64 | Phoenix | 96 | 68 | 70 |

| Rank | City | Reports of Homicide | Arrests for Homicide | Arrests as Percent of Reports |
|------|------|---------------------|----------------------|-------------------------------|
| 65 | Fort Worth | 113 | 76 | 67 |
| 66 | San Antonio | 185 | 119 | 64 |
| 67 | New York | 1,826 | 1,142 | 62 |
| 68 | Indianapolis | 65 | 40 | 61 |
| 69 | Providence | 23 | 14 | 60 |
| 70 | Birmingham | 97 | 56 | 57 |
| 71 | Anchorage | 18 | 10 | 55 |

| Rank | City | Reports of Homicide | Arrests for Homicide | Arrests as Percent of Reports |
|------|------|---------------------|----------------------|-------------------------------|
| 72 | Aurora | 10 | 5 | 50 |
| 73 | Miami | 210 | 86 | 40 |
| 74 | Jackson | 48 | 14 | 29 |
| 75 | Syracuse | 18 | 5 | 27 |
| 76 | Baltimore | 288 | 58 | 20 |
| 77 | Fort Wayne | 18 | 3 | 17 |
| 78 | Worcester | n.a. | 8 | n.a. |

# 190. Homicides as a Percentage of All Deaths

In 1978, as the table below shows, the odds of dying from homicide in Anchorage were nearly 1 in 20. That is, of 100 deaths, nearly 5 represented homicides. An explanation of the higher 1978 figure in Anchorage is the relatively youthful age of residents and the lack of social stability produced by a heavily male, unmarried population as compared to other cities.

In New York in 1982 homicide was the leading cause of death among 15–24 year olds, followed in order by accidents, suicides and drug overdoses. In Huntington Beach, on the other hand, homicides relative to all deaths were less than one-seventh of 1 percent.

SOURCES: U.S. Department of Health and Human Services, Division of Vital Statistics, Statistical Research Branch, *Vital Statistics*, 1978, (Washington, D.C.: Government Printing Office, 1982). Statement by Dr. Sol Blumenthal, New York City Health Department, 1982.

| Rank | City | Total Deaths | Homicides | Homicides as a Percentage All Deaths |
|------|------|--------------|-----------|--------------------------------------|
| 1 | Anchorage | 550 | 25 | 4.55 |
| 2 | Houston | 11,036 | 499 | 4.52 |
| 3 | Richmond | 1,214 | 53 | 4.37 |
| 4 | Detroit | 14,386 | 522 | 3.63 |
| 4 | Las Vegas | 1,322 | 41 | 3.63 |
| 6 | New Orleans | 6,288 | 214 | 3.40 |
| 7 | Dallas | 7,348 | 240 | 3.27 |
| 8 | Newark | 3,158 | 101 | 3.20 |
| 9 | Lubbock | 1,083 | 34 | 3.14 |
| 10 | Corpus Christi | 1,552 | 48 | 3.09 |
| 10 | St. Louis | 7,224 | 223 | 3.09 |
| 13 | Los Angeles | 27,031 | 781 | 2.89 |
| 14 | Chicago | 31,828 | 865 | 2.72 |
| 14 | Cleveland | 7,469 | 203 | 2.72 |
| 16 | Dayton | 2,230 | 56 | 2.51 |
| 17 | Washington, D.C. | 7,065 | 172 | 2.43 |

| Rank | City | Total Deaths | Homicides | Homicides as a Percentage All Deaths |
|------|------|--------------|-----------|--------------------------------------|
| 18 | San Antonio | 5,860 | 142 | 2.42 |
| 19 | Charlotte | 2,311 | 55 | 2.38 |
| 19 | Columbus, Ga. | 1,303 | 31 | 2.38 |
| 21 | Montgomery | 1,617 | 37 | 2.29 |
| 22 | Fresno | 2,512 | 56 | 2.23 |
| 22 | Shreveport | 2,157 | 48 | 2.23 |
| 24 | Kansas City, Mo. | 5,029 | 111 | 2.21 |
| 25 | Fort Worth | 3,810 | 83 | 2.18 |
| 25 | Nashville | 3,806 | 83 | 2.18 |
| 27 | Miami | 4,325 | 94 | 2.17 |
| 28 | Mobile | 1,992 | 43 | 2.16 |
| 29 | Birmingham | 3,363 | 72 | 2.14 |
| 30 | Albuquerque | 2,206 | 47 | 2.13 |
| 31 | Memphis | 5,788 | 122 | 2.11 |
| 32 | Austin | 1,934 | 40 | 2.07 |
| 32 | New York | 73,767 | 1,528 | 2.07 |
| 34 | Baltimore | 9,741 | 197 | 2.02 |
| 35 | Flint | 1,651 | 33 | 1.00 |
| 36 | Aurora | 5,61 | 11 | 1.96 |
| 36 | Baton Rouge | 1,833 | 36 | 1.96 |
| 36 | Jackson | 1,533 | 30 | 1.96 |
| 39 | Sacramento | 4,083 | 79 | 1.93 |
| 40 | Norfolk | 2,295 | 44 | 1.92 |
| 41 | Philadelphia | 20,711 | 369 | 1.78 |
| 42 | Oklahoma City | 3,750 | 66 | 1.77 |
| 43 | Little Rock | 1,540 | 27 | 1.75 |
| 44 | Denver | 4,668 | 80 | 1.71 |
| 44 | Kansas City, Kan. | 1,640 | 28 | 1.71 |
| 46 | Oakland | 3,596 | 61 | 1.70 |
| 48 | Jacksonville | 4,731 | 78 | 1.65 |
| 48 | Phoenix | 5,603 | 92 | 1.64 |
| 49 | San Francisco | 7,680 | 118 | 1.54 |
| 50 | Tampa | 3,268 | 50 | 1.53 |
| 51 | Riverside | 1,448 | 22 | 1.52 |
| 52 | Tulsa | 3,125 | 47 | 1.50 |
| 53 | Santa Ana | 1,340 | 20 | 1.49 |
| 54 | Salt Lake City | 1,699 | 25 | 1.47 |
| 55 | Indianapolis | 6,444 | 94 | 1.46 |
| 55 | San Jose | 3,493 | 51 | 1.46 |
| 57 | Louisville | 4,012 | 56 | 1.40 |
| 58 | Long Beach | 4,181 | 58 | 1.39 |
| 59 | Greensboro | 1,279 | 17 | 1.33 |
| 60 | Cincinnati | 5,118 | 64 | 1.25 |
| 61 | Chattanooga | 1,762 | 21 | 1.19 |

| Rank | City | Total Deaths | Homicides | Homicides as a Percentage All Deaths |
|---|---|---|---|---|
| 61 | Honolulu | 2,017 | 24 | 1.19 |
| 63 | Tucson | 2,927 | 34 | 1.16 |
| 64 | Arlington, Texas | 644 | 7 | 1.09 |
| 64 | Pittsburgh | 6,321 | 69 | 1.09 |
| 64 | Wichita | 2,376 | 26 | 1.09 |
| 67 | Seattle | 5,451 | 59 | 1.08 |
| 68 | Boston | 6,030 | 63 | 1.04 |
| 69 | San Diego | 5,999 | 62 | 1.03 |
| 70 | Colorado Springs | 1,287 | 13 | 1.01 |
| 70 | Des Moines | 1,990 | 19 | 1.01 |
| 70 | El Paso | 2,279 | 23 | 1.01 |
| 70 | Rochester | 2,966 | 30 | 1.01 |
| 74 | Fort Wayne | 1,935 | 19 | .98 |
| 75 | Tacoma | 1,668 | 16 | .96 |
| 76 | Warren | 1,090 | 10 | .92 |
| 77 | Knoxville | 1,875 | 17 | .91 |
| 78 | Buffalo | 5,109 | 46 | .90 |
| 79 | Toledo | 3,825 | 34 | .89 |
| 80 | Jersey City | 2,550 | 22 | .88 |
| 81 | Milwaukee | 6,301 | 51 | .81 |

| Rank | City | Total Deaths | Homicides | Homicides as a Percentage All Deaths |
|---|---|---|---|---|
| 82 | Anaheim | 1,273 | 10 | .79 |
| 83 | Yonkers | 2,015 | 15 | .74 |
| 84 | Lexington | 1,403 | 10 | .71 |
| 84 | Providence | 1,836 | 13 | .71 |
| 86 | Omaha | 3,143 | 22 | .70 |
| 86 | St. Petersburg | 4,545 | 32 | .70 |
| 88 | Portland, Ore. | 3,659 | 31 | .66 |
| 89 | Minneapolis | 4,397 | 29 | .66 |
| 90 | Virginia Beach | 1,071 | 7 | .65 |
| 91 | Columbus, Ohio | 4,646 | 26 | .56 |
| 92 | St. Paul | 2,937 | 16 | .54 |
| 93 | Syracuse | 2,082 | 11 | .53 |
| 94 | Grand Rapids | 1,976 | 10 | .51 |
| 95 | Spokane | 1,912 | 9 | .47 |
| 96 | Worcester | 1,973 | 7 | .35 |
| 97 | Akron | 2,704 | 9 | .33 |
| 98 | Madison | 1,103 | 2 | .17 |
| 99 | Lincoln | 1,175 | 2 | .17 |
| 100 | Huntington Beach | 762 | 4 | .13 |

# 191. Robberies

The robbery rate is widely believed to the the best single measure of crime, the "bellwether" crime rate, because it is readily identifiable to and by the police as the taking of property with the threat of violence. If no violence is present, the theft becomes burglary (if it is from a home or business) or larceny (e.g., stealing hubcaps from a car or a purse from a restaurant). Also, because of the seriousness of the crime, it is likely to be reported to, and recorded by, the police. This makes it a better indicator than property crimes, which may be inconsistently reported to, or recorded by, the police. Robbery is especially feared by the public, because it is the chief form of stranger-to-stranger violence. Homicides and assaults are most commonly committed among people who know each other.

We related robberies to resident population because this measure is a common indicator of the incidence of crime, because it sheds light on the relative burden of crime on local residents, and because it is a crude indicator of the probability of the crime's happening to an individual during the year. However, the probability of a resident's being robbed is overstated by crime statistics for cities with a large influx of daytime commuters and visitors. Visitors are much more likely to be robbed than residents.

Cities in economic decline are more likely to have residents affected by inner-city blight. Such residents are more likely to commit economically motivated crimes. This pattern is reflected in the high crime rates in northeastern and midwestern cities and three large California cities. Many of them experienced fiscal crises in the 1970s because of the flight of middle-class and skilled working-class residents to the suburbs and the Southwest. Cities with more inequality of incomes between rich and poor (e.g., New York, Miami, Washington and Los Angeles) are also likely to incur higher rates of economically motivated crime. In Miami there were 1.79 robberies per 100 residents in 1981. This made Miami the leading city in robberies for two consecutive years. Nevertheless, the robbery rate fell from 1980's level of 2.05 per 100, twice Miami's 1979 rate.

Miami's 1981 robbery rate was nearly 36 times as high as Lincoln, Nebraska's. The places where a resident is least likely to get robbed were Lincoln, with .05 robberies per 100 residents, and Virginia Beach, with .09 per 100.

SOURCE: U.S. Department of Justice, Federal Bureau of Investigation (FBI), *Crime in the U.S.—1981: Uniform Crime Reports* (Washington, D.C.: Government Printing Office, 1982).

| Rank | City | Total Robberies | Robberies Per 100 Population | | Rank | City | Total Robberies | Robberies Per 100 Population |
|---|---|---|---|---|---|---|---|---|
| 1 | Miami | 6,196 | 1.79 | | 49 | Norfolk | 1,085 | .41 |
| 2 | Boston | 9,248 | 1.64 | | 50 | Jackson | 793 | .39 |
| 3 | Washington, D.C. | 10,399 | 1.63 | | 50 | St. Paul | 1,061 | .39 |
| 4 | New York | 107,475 | 1.52 | | 52 | San Diego | 3,323 | .38 |
| 5 | Baltimore | 10,715 | 1.36 | | 53 | Oklahoma City | 1,491 | .37 |
| 5 | Cleveland | 7,821 | 1.36 | | 54 | St. Petersburg | 857 | .36 |
| 7 | Detroit | 14,797 | 1.23 | | 54 | Salt Lake City | 587 | .36 |
| 8 | St. Louis | 5,365 | 1.18 | | 56 | Nashville | 1,594 | .35 |
| 9 | Dayton | 2,353 | 1.16 | | 57 | Phoenix | 2,696 | .34 |
| 10 | Oakland | 3,836 | 1.13 | | 57 | Riverside | 578 | .34 |
| 11 | San Francisco | 7,386 | 1.09 | | 59 | Albuquerque | 1,107 | .33 |
| 12 | Atlanta | 4,500 | 1.06 | | 59 | San Jose | 2,070 | .33 |
| 13 | Pittsburgh | 4,288 | 1.01 | | 61 | Grand Rapids | 562 | .31 |
| 14 | Jersey City | 2,180 | .98 | | 61 | Tacoma | 494 | .31 |
| 15 | Los Angeles | 28,152 | .95 | | 63 | Omaha | 899 | .29 |
| 16 | New Orleans | 4,950 | .89 | | 63 | Wichita | 816 | .29 |
| 17 | Tampa | 2,314 | .85 | | 65 | Baton Rouge | 609 | .28 |
| 18 | Portland, Ore. | 3,072 | .84 | | 65 | Milwaukee | 1,806 | .28 |
| 19 | Long Beach | 2,928 | .81 | | 67 | Anaheim | 576 | .26 |
| 20 | Kansas City, Mo. | 3,235 | .72 | | 67 | Colorado Springs | 557 | .26 |
| 21 | Las Vegas | 2,778 | .68 | | 67 | Knoxville | 474 | .26 |
| 22 | Sacramento | 1,833 | .66 | | 67 | Tucson | 872 | .26 |
| 23 | Philadelphia | 10,816 | .64 | | 67 | Tulsa | 949 | .26 |
| 24 | Memphis | 4,092 | .63 | | 72 | Akron | 602 | .25 |
| 25 | Minneapolis | 2,296 | .62 | | 72 | Charlotte | 774 | .25 |
| 25 | Richmond | 1,364 | .62 | | 75 | Spokane | 410 | .24 |
| 27 | Dallas | 5,402 | .60 | | 76 | Aurora | 359 | .23 |
| 27 | Fort Worth | 2,312 | .60 | | 76 | San Antonio | 1,835 | .23 |
| 29 | Columbus, Ohio | 3,356 | .59 | | 78 | Anchorage | 380 | .22 |
| 30 | Louisville | 1,730 | .58 | | 78 | Chattanooga | 370 | .22 |
| 31 | Flint | 891 | .56 | | 78 | Columbus, Ga. | 367 | .22 |
| 32 | Syracuse | 929 | .55 | | 78 | Fort Wayne | 384 | .22 |
| 33 | Chicago | 16,118 | .54 | | 78 | Lexington-Fayette | 455 | .22 |
| 33 | Providence | 852 | .54 | | 83 | Corpus Christi | 490 | .21 |
| 35 | Birmingham | 1,502 | .53 | | 84 | El Paso | 871 | .20 |
| 36 | Rochester | 1,246 | .52 | | 85 | Austin | 669 | .19 |
| 37 | Fresno | 1,102 | .51 | | 85 | Greensboro | 302 | .19 |
| 38 | Toledo | 1,776 | .50 | | 85 | Shreveport | 394 | .19 |
| 39 | Denver | 2,403 | .49 | | 88 | Lubbock | 314 | .18 |
| 40 | Indianapolis | 2,194 | .48 | | 89 | Honolulu | 1,320 | .17 |
| 40 | Kansas City, Kan. | 774 | .48 | | 90 | Warren | 253 | .16 |
| 40 | Little Rock | 759 | .48 | | 91 | Montgomery | 263 | .15 |
| 43 | Mobile | 938 | .47 | | 92 | Arlington, Texas | 212 | .13 |
| 43 | Seattle | 2,344 | .47 | | 92 | Madison | 221 | .13 |
| 45 | Cincinnati | 1,756 | .46 | | 94 | Huntington Beach | 211 | .12 |
| 46 | Yonkers | 853 | .44 | | 95 | Virginia Beach | 235 | .09 |
| 47 | Jacksonville | 2,340 | .43 | | 96 | Lincoln | 90 | .05 |
| 47 | Santa Ana | 867 | .43 | | | | | |

# 192.  Arrests for Robbery

Robberies represent one of the two major categories within the overall total of violent crimes, the other being ("aggravated") assaults. The other two crime categories of homicide and rape are far less numerous. In general, most violent crimes that are not robberies are assaults. Since we provide data on rapes and homicides, this can be confirmed by examining these tables and the one for all violent crimes.

The table below shows that the median arrest rate for robberies was about 25 percent—i.e., roughly one arrest for robbery for every four reports of robberies.

The range was 70 percent in Greensboro to 5 percent in Baltimore. This table shows, in conjunction with the violent crimes table, that robberies accounted for 29 percent of Greensboro's violent crimes in 1981 and 32 percent of its arrests.

Montgomery shows 57 arrests per 100 robberies, a far higher showing than in the total violent crimes table. This suggests that Montgomery places a higher priority on tracking robberies than it does on tracking down, or making arrests for, assaults.

SOURCES: Reported robberies for 1981 from U.S. Department of Justice, Federal Bureau of Investigation, *Crime in the U.S.—1981: Uniform Crime Reports* (Washington, D.C.: Government Printing Office, 1982). Arrests for robberies in 1981 from a special unpublished report provided at the author's request by the Federal Bureau of Investigation, January 1983.

| Rank | City | Reports of Robberies | Arrests for Robberies | Percentage of Arrests per Robberies Reported |
|---|---|---|---|---|
| 1 | Greensboro | 302 | 210 | 69.54 |
| 2 | Montgomery | 263 | 149 | 56.65 |
| 3 | Philadelphia | 10.816 | 5,509 | 50.93 |
| 4 | Milwaukee | 1,806 | 896 | 49.61 |
| 5 | Honolulu | 1,320 | 617 | 46.74 |
| 6 | Virginia Beach | 235 | 100 | 42.55 |
| 7 | Chicago | 16,118 | 6,691 | 41.51 |
| 8 | Chattanooga | 370 | 151 | 40.81 |
| 9 | Salt Lake City | 587 | 228 | 38.84 |
| 10 | El Paso | 871 | 324 | 37.20 |
| 11 | Fresno | 102 | 403 | 36.57 |
| 12 | Wichita | 816 | 293 | 35.91 |
| 13 | Columbus, Ga. | 367 | 129 | 35.15 |
| 14 | Huntington Beach | 211 | 74 | 35.07 |
| 15 | Tucson | 872 | 282 | 32.34 |
| 16 | San Diego | 3,323 | 1,064 | 32.02 |
| 17 | Rochester | 1,246 | 395 | 31.70 |
| 18 | Omaha | 899 | 274 | 30.48 |
| 19 | Baton Rouge | 609 | 185 | 30.38 |
| 20 | Warren | 253 | 76 | 30.04 |
| 21 | Colorado Springs | 557 | 164 | 29.44 |
| 22 | Louisville | 1,730 | 485 | 28.03 |
| 23 | San Jose | 2,070 | 576 | 27.83 |
| 24 | Little Rock | 759 | 210 | 27.67 |
| 25 | Long Beach | 2,928 | 810 | 27.66 |
| 26 | Knoxville | 474 | 130 | 27.43 |
| 27 | Sacramento | 1,833 | 501 | 27.33 |
| 28 | Charlotte | 774 | 208 | 26.87 |

| Rank | City | Reports of Robberies | Arrests for Robberies | Percentage of Arrests per Robberies Reported |
|---|---|---|---|---|
| 29 | Norfolk | 1,085 | 290 | 26.73 |
| 30 | Anaheim | 576 | 151 | 26.22 |
| 31 | Santa Ana | 867 | 225 | 25.95 |
| 32 | Jersey City | 2,180 | 562 | 25.78 |
| 32 | Phoenix | 2,696 | 695 | 25.78 |
| 34 | Birmingham | 381 | 1,502 | 25.37 |
| 34 | Mobile | 938 | 238 | 25.37 |
| 36 | Lexington-Fayette | 455 | 115 | 25.27 |
| 37 | Las Vegas | 2,778 | 689 | 24.80 |
| 38 | Kansas City, Mo. | 3,235 | 793 | 24.51 |
| 39 | Lubbock | 314 | 75 | 23.89 |
| 40 | New Orleans | 4,950 | 1,181 | 23.86 |
| 41 | Jacksonville | 2,340 | 557 | 23.80 |
| 42 | Fort Worth | 2,312 | 548 | 23.70 |
| 43 | Flint | 891 | 210 | 23.57 |
| 44 | Tulsa | 949 | 222 | 23.39 |
| 45 | Oakland | 3,386 | 889 | 23.18 |
| 46 | Los Angeles | 28,152 | 6,470 | 22.98 |
| 47 | Providence | 852 | 194 | 22.77 |
| 48 | San Antonio | 1,835 | 415 | 22.62 |
| 49 | Oklahoma City | 1,491 | 332 | 22.27 |
| 50 | Syracuse | 929 | 203 | 21.85 |
| 51 | Atlanta | 4,567 | 985 | 21.57 |
| 52 | Shreveport | 394 | 83 | 21.07 |
| 53 | Toledo | 1,776 | 371 | 20.89 |
| 54 | Corpus Christi | 490 | 102 | 20.82 |
| 55 | New York | 107,478 | 22,150 | 20.61 |
| 56 | Pittsburgh | 4,288 | 866 | 20.20 |
| 57 | Minneapolis | 2,296 | 463 | 20.17 |
| 58 | Aurora | 359 | 72 | 20.06 |
| 59 | Grand Rapids | 562 | 108 | 19.22 |
| 60 | Detroit | 14,797 | 2,817 | 19.04 |
| 61 | Washington, D.C. | 10,399 | 1,905 | 18.32 |
| 62 | Anchorage | 380 | 69 | 18.16 |
| 63 | Richmond | 1,364 | 246 | 18.04 |
| 64 | San Francisco | 7,386 | 1,328 | 17.98 |
| 65 | Portland, Ore. | 3,072 | 544 | 17.71 |
| 66 | Dallas | 5,402 | 953 | 17.64 |
| 67 | Jackson | 793 | 133 | 16.77 |
| 68 | Dayton | 2,353 | 386 | 16.40 |
| 69 | Tampa | 2,314 | 379 | 16.38 |
| 70 | St. Petersburg | 857 | 133 | 15.52 |
| 71 | Riverside | 578 | 89 | 15.40 |
| 72 | Miami | 6,196 | 913 | 14.74 |
| 73 | Indianapolis | 2,194 | 306 | 13.95 |
| 74 | Kansas City, Kan. | 774 | 93 | 12.02 |
| 75 | Fort Wayne | 384 | 29 | 7.55 |
| 76 | Baltimore | 10,715 | 517 | 4.83 |

# 193. Trends in Robberies

During the 10-year period 1972 to 1981, the moving average robbery trend was relatively stable during 1972 and 1973. This was followed by a trend upward that persisted until 1975 (the peak being reached for this period in the fourth quarter of 1974). Robberies then increased, but not to the 1974 level, and now appear to be stabilizing in the early 1980s.

Miami showed the highest increase, nearly 83 percent. We attribute this increase to the arrival of a large influx of Cuban refugees, some of whom had been released by Premier Fidel Castro from that country's jails, and to the high percentage of poor people in Miami.

The increases in Tampa and Portland, Ore., between 1979 and 1981 are harder to account for. In both cases robbery rates in 1979 were relatively low. The increases may have occurred simply because both cities have had a good press and are attracting new arrivals. Such migrations have a dual effect. They bring into town people who don't know the "bad areas" and set people up to be victimized. Also they bring into town some lawless individuals along with the law-abiding newcomers.

Honolulu's robbery rate declined by approximately 16 percent. We attribute this decline to the recession, which reduced travel and therefore the degree of transience in this major but expensive-to-visit tourist city. Chattanooga and Atlanta also showed strong drops, of 15 percent and 13 percent respectively. Improved police department performance may account for some of the drop in robberies.

SOURCE: U.S. Department of Justice, Federal Bureau of Investigation (FBI), *Crime in the U.S.—1981: Uniform Crime Reports* (Washington, D.C.: Government Printing Office, 1982).

| Rank | City | 1979 Robberies | 1981 Robberies | Absolute Change in Robberies | Percentage Change in Robberies |
|------|------|---------------|---------------|------------------------------|-------------------------------|
| 1 | Miami | 3,390 | 6,196 | 2,806 | 82.77 |
| 2 | Tampa | 1,312 | 2,314 | 1,002 | 76.37 |
| 3 | Portland, Ore. | 1,787 | 3,072 | 1,285 | 71.91 |
| 4 | Mobile | 564 | 938 | 374 | 66.31 |
| 5 | Lexington-Fayette | 275 | 455 | 180 | 65.45 |
| 6 | Jersey City | 1,382 | 2,180 | 798 | 57.74 |
| 7 | Pittsburgh | 2,752 | 4,288 | 1,536 | 55.81 |
| 8 | Greensboro | 196 | 302 | 106 | 54.08 |
| 9 | San Jose | 1,358 | 2,070 | 712 | 52.43 |
| 10 | Colorado Springs | 368 | 557 | 189 | 51.36 |
| 11 | Jacksonville | 1,555 | 2,340 | 785 | 50.48 |
| 12 | Washington, D.C. | 6,920 | 10,399 | 3,479 | 50.27 |
| 13 | Las Vegas | 1,891 | 2,778 | 887 | 46.91 |
| 14 | Tulsa | 651 | 949 | 298 | 45.78 |
| 15 | Riverside | 370 | 528 | 158 | 42.70 |
| 16 | Providence | 614 | 852 | 238 | 38.76 |
| 17 | Richmond | 985 | 1,364 | 379 | 38.48 |
| 18 | Los Angeles | 20,454 | 28,152 | 7,698 | 37.64 |
| 19 | Columbus, Ohio | 2,445 | 3,356 | 911 | 37.26 |
| 20 | Albuquerque | 815 | 1,107 | 292 | 35.83 |
| 21 | Cleveland | 5,760 | 7,821 | 2,061 | 35.78 |
| 22 | Lubbock | 232 | 314 | 82 | 35.34 |
| 23 | St. Petersburg | 649 | 857 | 208 | 32.05 |
| 24 | Yonkers | 655 | 853 | 198 | 30.23 |
| 25 | New York | 82,572 | 107,475 | 24,903 | 30.16 |
| 26 | Fort Worth | 1,783 | 2,312 | 529 | 29.67 |
| 27 | Detroit | 11,413 | 14,797 | 3,384 | 29.65 |
| 28 | Long Beach | 2,278 | 2,928 | 650 | 28.53 |
| 29 | Baltimore | 8,482 | 10,715 | 2,233 | 26.33 |
| 30 | Oklahoma City | 1,188 | 1,491 | 303 | 25.51 |
| 31 | Tucson | 697 | 872 | 175 | 25.11 |
| 32 | Virginia Beach | 188 | 235 | 47 | 25.00 |
| 33 | Baton Rouge | 488 | 609 | 121 | 24.80 |
| 34 | Santa Ana | 699 | 867 | 168 | 24.03 |
| 35 | Memphis | 3,300 | 4,092 | 792 | 24.00 |
| 36 | Akron | 491 | 602 | 111 | 22.61 |
| 37 | Flint | 727 | 891 | 164 | 22.56 |
| 38 | Philadelphia | 8,838 | 10,816 | 1,978 | 22.38 |
| 39 | Wichita | 668 | 816 | 148 | 22.16 |
| 40 | Kansas City, Mo. | 2,651 | 3,235 | 584 | 22.03 |
| 41 | Dallas | 4,456 | 5,402 | 946 | 21.23 |
| 42 | Madison | 184 | 221 | 37 | 20.11 |
| 43 | St. Paul | 894 | 1,061 | 167 | 18.68 |
| 44 | Salt Lake City | 495 | 587 | 92 | 18.59 |

| Rank | City | 1979 Robberies | 1981 Robberies | Absolute Change in Robberies | Percentage Change in Robberies |
|---|---|---|---|---|---|
| 45 | Spokane | 349 | 410 | 61 | 17.48 |
| 46 | Austin | 577 | 669 | 92 | 15.94 |
| 47 | Syracuse | 802 | 929 | 127 | 15.84 |
| 48 | Minneapolis | 1,988 | 2,296 | 308 | 15.49 |
| 49 | Phoenix | 2,337 | 2,696 | 359 | 15.36 |
| 50 | San Diego | 2,884 | 3,323 | 439 | 15.22 |
| 51 | Dayton | 2,067 | 2,353 | 286 | 13.84 |
| 52 | Rochester | 1,096 | 1,246 | 150 | 13.69 |
| 53 | Milwaukee | 1,592 | 1,806 | 214 | 13.44 |
| 54 | Seattle | 2,071 | 2,344 | 273 | 13.18 |
| 55 | Sacramento | 1,640 | 1,833 | 193 | 11.77 |
| 56 | Louisville | 1,548 | 1,730 | 182 | 11.76 |
| 57 | Arlington, Texas | 190 | 212 | 22 | 11.58 |
| 58 | Chicago | 14,464 | 16,118 | 1,654 | 11.44 |
| 59 | Anchorage | 343 | 380 | 37 | 10.79 |
| 60 | San Francisco | 6,694 | 7,386 | 692 | 10.34 |
| 61 | Charlotte | 703 | 774 | 71 | 10.10 |
| 62 | Fresno | 1,009 | 1,102 | 93 | 9.22 |
| 63 | Fort Wayne | 353 | 384 | 31 | 8.78 |
| 64 | Montgomery | 242 | 263 | 21 | 8.68 |
| 65 | San Antonio | 1,689 | 1,835 | 146 | 8.64 |
| 66 | Lincoln | 83 | 90 | 7 | 8.43 |
| 67 | Kansas City, Kan. | 714 | 774 | 60 | 8.40 |
| 68 | El Paso | 813 | 871 | 58 | 7.13 |
| 69 | Indianapolis | 2,053 | 2,194 | 141 | 6.87 |
| 70 | Denver | 2,257 | 2,403 | 146 | 6.47 |
| 71 | Norfolk | 1,021 | 1,085 | 64 | 6.27 |
| 72 | Huntington Beach | 199 | 211 | 12 | 6.03 |
| 73 | Cincinnati | 1,662 | 1,756 | 94 | 5.66 |
| 74 | Tacoma | 468 | 494 | 26 | 5.56 |
| 75 | Corpus Christi | 476 | 490 | 14 | 2.94 |
| 76 | Knoxville | 461 | 474 | 13 | 2.82 |
| 77 | Des Moines | 464 | 476 | 12 | 2.59 |
| 78 | Birmingham | 1,474 | 1,502 | 28 | 1.90 |
| 79 | Columbus, Ga. | 362 | 367 | 5 | 1.38 |
| 80 | St. Louis | 5,386 | 5,365 | − 21 | − .39 |
| 81 | Toledo | 1,784 | 1,776 | − 8 | − .45 |
| 82 | Grand Rapids | 565 | 562 | − 3 | − .53 |
| 83 | Shreveport | 416 | 394 | − 22 | − 5.29 |
| 84 | Omaha | 954 | 899 | − 55 | − 5.77 |
| 85 | Anaheim | 613 | 576 | − 37 | − 6.04 |
| 86 | New Orleans | 5,276 | 4,950 | − 326 | − 6.18 |
| 87 | Nashville | 1,716 | 1,594 | − 122 | − 7.11 |
| 88 | Atlanta | 5,189 | 4,507 | − 682 | − 13.14 |
| 89 | Chattanooga | 434 | 370 | − 64 | − 14.75 |
| 90 | Honolulu | 1,568 | 1,320 | − 248 | − 15.82 |

# 194. Rapes

The rates of rape are higher than the published figures indicate. Only a fraction of rapes are reported, because women are often naturally enough too traumatized or frightened to report them. Rape victims are almost always women (there are only a few cases of males being raped, usually by homosexuals), so that the effective rate for women should be twice the rate for all residents. Some authorities speculate that the rate should be doubled again for adult females, to take account of the fact that rape victims tend to fall within certain age ranges.

The highest rate of rapes in 1981 was in Newark, which showed 18 rapes per 10,000 residents.

Yonkers had the lowest rate of rapes—under 2 per 10,000. This reflects the high average age of residents, reducing the number of both likely victims and likely rapists.

SOURCE: U.S. Department of Justice, Federal Bureau of Investigation (FBI), *Crime in U.S.—Uniform Crime Reports—1981* (Washington, D.C.: Government Printing Office, 1982).

| Rank | City | Total Rapes | Rapes Per 10,000 Population |
|------|------|-------------|----------------------------|
| 1 | Newark | 598 | 17.97 |
| 2 | Atlanta | 644 | 14.78 |
| 3 | Tampa | 409 | 14.32 |
| 4 | Oakland | 430 | 12.37 |
| 5 | Dallas | 1,121 | 11.96 |
| 6 | Memphis | 760 | 11.62 |
| 7 | Flint | 178 | 11.19 |
| 8 | Fort Worth | 435 | 10.92 |
| 9 | Portland, Ore. | 403 | 10.91 |
| 10 | Cleveland | 621 | 10.83 |
| 11 | Tacoma | 174 | 10.75 |
| 12 | Miami | 382 | 10.71 |
| 13 | Grand Rapids | 190 | 10.49 |
| 14 | Detroit | 1,229 | 10.29 |
| 15 | Minneapolis | 367 | 9.84 |
| 16 | Little Rock | 151 | 9.77 |
| 17 | San Francisco | 672 | 9.71 |
| 18 | Anchorage | 173 | 9.66 |
| 19 | Seattle | 485 | 9.63 |
| 20 | Kansas City, Mo. | 429 | 9.53 |
| 21 | Birmingham | 267 | 9.37 |
| 21 | Boston | 531 | 9.37 |
| 23 | Denver | 471 | 9.35 |
| 24 | St. Louis | 413 | 9.09 |
| 25 | Los Angeles | 2,666 | 8.80 |
| 26 | Richmond | 195 | 8.72 |
| 27 | Indianapolis | 400 | 8.66 |
| 27 | Kansas City, Kan. | 140 | 8.66 |
| 29 | Long Beach | 307 | 8.38 |
| 30 | Oklahoma City | 336 | 8.11 |
| 31 | Sacramento | 228 | 8.09 |
| 31 | Salt Lake City | 137 | 8.09 |
| 33 | Akron | 189 | 7.97 |
| 34 | Nashville-Davidson | 363 | 7.92 |
| 34 | New Orleans | 453 | 7.92 |
| 36 | Lubbock | 143 | 7.88 |
| 37 | Las Vegas | 310 | 7.62 |
| 38 | Cincinnati | 289 | 7.54 |
| 39 | Colorado Springs | 158 | 7.42 |
| 40 | Austin | 263 | 7.35 |
| 41 | Dayton | 142 | 7.34 |
| 42 | St. Paul | 197 | 7.29 |
| 43 | San Jose | 465 | 7.21 |
| 44 | Wichita | 202 | 7.15 |

| Rank | City | Total Rapes | Rapes Per 10,000 Population |
|------|------|-------------|----------------------------|
| 45 | Jacksonville | 410 | 7.13 |
| 46 | Baltimore | 565 | 7.09 |
| 47 | Norfolk | 189 | 7.06 |
| 48 | Columbus, Ohio | 396 | 7.04 |
| 49 | Fresno | 155 | 7.01 |
| 50 | Riverside | 121 | 6.94 |
| 51 | Shreveport | 138 | 6.91 |
| 52 | Tulsa | 247 | 6.73 |
| 53 | Washington, D.C. | 414 | 6.51 |
| 54 | Toledo | 229 | 6.45 |
| 55 | Albuquerque | 213 | 6.32 |
| 56 | Charlotte | 198 | 6.26 |
| 57 | San Diego | 559 | 6.22 |
| 58 | Arlington, Texas | 102 | 6.08 |
| 58 | Mobile | 123 | 6.08 |
| 60 | Corpus Christi | 145 | 6.04 |
| 60 | St. Petersburg | 150 | 6.04 |
| 62 | Anaheim | 135 | 6.02 |
| 63 | Jersey City | 132 | 5.88 |
| 64 | Rochester | 141 | 5.81 |
| 65 | Omaha | 186 | 5.76 |
| 66 | Baton Rouge | 129 | 5.74 |
| 67 | Philadelphia | 936 | 5.55 |
| 68 | Des Moines | 104 | 5.47 |
| 69 | New York | 3,862 | 5.46 |
| 70 | Louisville | 158 | 5.27 |
| 71 | Jackson | 105 | 5.19 |
| 72 | Phoenix | 408 | 5.13 |
| 73 | Spokane | 88 | 5.03 |
| 74 | Pittsburgh | 213 | 5.00 |
| 75 | Tucson | 163 | 4.78 |
| 76 | Knoxville | 88 | 4.76 |
| 77 | Aurora | 76 | 4.67 |
| 78 | El Paso | 205 | 4.63 |
| 79 | San Antonio | 376 | 4.58 |
| 80 | Milwaukee | 290 | 4.52 |
| 81 | Lexington-Fayette | 92 | 4.51 |
| 82 | Columbus, Ga. | 78 | 4.49 |
| 83 | Santa Ana | 92 | 4.36 |
| 84 | Chicago | 1,255 | 4.17 |
| 85 | Syracuse | 68 | 3.97 |
| 86 | Huntington Beach | 68 | 3.88 |
| 87 | Madison | 66 | 3.84 |
| 88 | Virginia Beach | 93 | 3.50 |
| 89 | Providence | 55 | 3.49 |
| 90 | Honolulu | 265 | 3.43 |
| 91 | Greensboro | 53 | 3.36 |
| 92 | Chattanooga | 54 | 3.22 |
| 93 | Fort Wayne | 51 | 2.98 |
| 94 | Lincoln | 41 | 2.37 |
| 95 | Warren | 38 | 2.36 |
| 96 | Montgomery | 37 | 2.06 |
| 97 | Yonkers | 32 | 1.64 |

# 195. Arrests for Rape

In the median city, Tampa, the 409 reported rapes resulted in 136 arrests, an arrest rate of 33 percent.

The best arrest record was in Providence. In that city in 1981, 55 rape reports resulted in 66 arrests. Multiple arrests are possible because more than one person may have been involved in a single rape. Also, police may have more than one suspect and therefore arrest more than one person pending judicial process. Six cities besides Providence had arrest rates higher than 70 percent in 1981: Montgomery, Detroit, Jersey City, Philadelphia, Chattanooga and Chicago.

On the low end of the arrest rate schedule, six cities had arrest rates below 15 percent: Fort Wayne, Anchorage, Indianapolis, Norfolk, Minneapolis and Baltimore.

SOURCES: Reported rapes for 1981 from U.S. Department of Justice, Federal Bureau of Investigation, *Crime in the U.S.—1981: Uniform Crime Reports* (Washington, D.C.: Government Printing Office, 1982). Arrests for rapes in 1981 from a special unpublished report provided at the authors' request by the Federal Bureau of Investigation, January 1983.

| Rank | City | Reports of Rapes | Arrests for Rapes | Percentage of Arrests Per Rapes Reported |
|---|---|---|---|---|
| 1 | Providence | 55 | 66 | 120.00 |
| 2 | Montgomery | 37 | 30 | 81.08 |
| 3 | Detroit | 1,229 | 981 | 79.82 |
| 4 | Jersey City | 132 | 96 | 72.73 |
| 5 | Philadelphia | 936 | 678 | 72.44 |
| 6 | Chattanooga | 54 | 39 | 72.22 |
| 7 | Chicago | 1,255 | 897 | 71.47 |
| 8 | Syracuse | 68 | 47 | 69.12 |
| 9 | Grand Rapids | 190 | 112 | 58.95 |
| 10 | Dayton | 142 | 83 | 58.45 |
| 11 | Kansas City, Mo. | 429 | 250 | 58.28 |
| 12 | Sacramento | 228 | 123 | 53.95 |
| 13 | Milwaukee | 290 | 153 | 52.76 |
| 14 | Pittsburgh | 213 | 109 | 51.17 |
| 15 | Virginia Beach | 93 | 47 | 50.54 |
| 16 | Newark | 598 | 300 | 50.17 |
| 17 | Warren | 38 | 18 | 47.37 |
| 18 | Louisville | 158 | 74 | 46.84 |
| 19 | Columbus, Ga. | 78 | 36 | 46.15 |
| 20 | Honolulu | 265 | 120 | 45.28 |
| 21 | Tucson | 163 | 73 | 44.79 |
| 22 | Fresno | 155 | 67 | 43.23 |
| 23 | Richmond | 195 | 82 | 42.05 |
| 24 | Las Vegas | 310 | 129 | 41.61 |
| 24 | Salt Lake City | 137 | 57 | 41.61 |
| 26 | Toledo | 229 | 95 | 41.48 |
| 27 | Santa Ana | 92 | 38 | 41.30 |

| Rank | City | Reports of Rapes | Arrests for Rapes | Percentage of Arrests Per Rapes Reported |
|---|---|---|---|---|
| 28 | Flint | 178 | 73 | 41.01 |
| 29 | Atlanta | 644 | 263 | 40.84 |
| 30 | New York | 3,862 | 1,505 | 38.97 |
| 31 | Jacksonville | 410 | 156 | 38.05 |
| 32 | Rochester | 141 | 53 | 37.59 |
| 33 | Baton Rouge | 129 | 48 | 37.21 |
| 34 | New Orleans | 453 | 168 | 37.09 |
| 35 | Lexington-Fayette | 92 | 34 | 36.96 |
| 36 | Long Beach | 307 | 108 | 35.18 |
| 37 | Colorado Springs | 158 | 55 | 34.81 |
| 38 | San Diego | 559 | 188 | 33.63 |
| 39 | Tampa | 409 | 136 | ,3.25 |
| 40 | Oakland | 430 | 142 | 33.02 |
| 41 | Washington, D.C. | 414 | 136 | 32.85 |
| 42 | Oklahoma City | 336 | 109 | 32.44 |
| 43 | Omaha | 186 | 60 | 32.26 |
| 44 | Aurora | 76 | 24 | 31.58 |
| 45 | Riverside | 121 | 38 | 31.40 |
| 46 | Fort Worth | 435 | 134 | 30.80 |
| 47 | Greensboro | 53 | 16 | 30.19 |
| 48 | Lubbock | 143 | 43 | 30.07 |
| 49 | Charlotte | 198 | 55 | 27.78 |
| 50 | El Paso | 205 | 54 | 26.34 |
| 51 | Wichita | 202 | 53 | 26.24 |
| 52 | Dallas | 1,121 | 293 | 26.14 |
| 53 | Los Angeles | 2,666 | 670 | 25.13 |
| 54 | Knoxville | 88 | 22 | 25.00 |
| 55 | Tulsa | 247 | 61 | 24.70 |
| 56 | Shreveport | 138 | 34 | 24.64 |
| 57 | Little Rock | 151 | 37 | 24.50 |
| 58 | Mobile | 123 | 30 | 24.39 |
| 59 | San Jose | 465 | 113 | 24.30 |
| 60 | Corpus Christi | 145 | 35 | 24.14 |
| 61 | Jackson | 105 | 25 | 23.81 |
| 62 | San Antonio | 376 | 86 | 22.87 |
| 63 | St. Petersburg | 150 | 34 | 22.67 |
| 64 | Portland, Ore. | 403 | 91 | 22.58 |
| 65 | Phoenix | 408 | 92 | 22.55 |
| 66 | Miami | 382 | 86 | 22.51 |
| 67 | San Francisco | 672 | 144 | 21.43 |
| 68 | Birmingham | 267 | 56 | 20.97 |
| 69 | Anaheim | 135 | 28 | 20.74 |
| 70 | Huntington Beach | 68 | 14 | 20.59 |
| 71 | Kansas City, Kan. | 140 | 25 | 17.86 |
| 72 | Baltimore | 565 | 82 | 14.51 |
| 73 | Minneapolis | 367 | 53 | 14.44 |
| 74 | Norfolk | 189 | 27 | 14.29 |
| 75 | Indianapolis | 400 | 57 | 14.26 |
| 76 | Anchorage | 173 | 18 | 10.40 |
| 77 | Fort Wayne | 85 | 5 | 5.88 |

# 196. Property Crimes

"Property crimes," in FBI parlance, include burglary, larceny, theft and auto theft. Burglary means breaking into a home or business. Larceny means stealing from someone's person (including from persons in offices or homes—e.g., snatching a purse off a desk by someone posing as a delivery man) or vehicle by stealth rather than by threat and without breaking in.

Sixty percent of the property crimes are larcenies. In the days when the FBI was run by J. Edgar Hoover, there was built-in inflation in this crime, because thefts of items valued under $50 were excluded from Index Crime figures. The value limit did two things. It permitted police officers to dismiss a larceny, if they wished, as relating to items that were worth too little to bother about; and it meant that as the value of a $50 bill went down every year, more and more items would be included as being worth $50. So the FBI could report every year a steady increase in larcenies for reasons which in part had nothing to do with crime but with the declining value of money. The Council on Municipal Performance pointed this out in 1973. (The FBI changed its data-collection practices a few years later.)

Reporting larcenies is still plagued with questions. Larcenies as the FBI reports them have a middle class bias because they exclude white collar crimes. If a bank teller absconds with $1 million, it's embezzlement, and it's not included. Meanwhile, the teenager who takes a hubcap off a car outside the bank door will be dutifully reported to the police and will show up in the UCR.

Roughly one-fifth of larcenies involve property taken from buildings; two-fifths from motor vehicles (of which half involve hubcaps and other motor vehicle accessories); and the remaining two-fifths involve shoplifting and other thefts. Purse-snatching and pocket-picking—peculiarly urban crimes—represent only 3 percent of all reported larcenies nationwide but double that percentage in the northeastern states, which include the older cities. The worst months for larcenies are July and August, suggesting that school vacations have a lot to do with them.

Larcenies went up every year between 1972 and 1980 (except for 1977, when there was a drop), increasing by over 58 percent. Then between 1980 and 1981 they declined, just 1 percent, but enough to give us hope: *Maybe the trend has turned around.* The early data for 1982 strengthen this impression.

Burglaries and auto thefts are less subject to reporting variability than larcenies and show a smaller increase. Between 1972 and 1981 they were up 43 percent and only 10 percent, respectively. The drop in auto theft may have to do with the improved locking mechanisms on cars.

Tampa is the highest in 1981 property crimes per 100 residents (nearly 13). The elderly are commonly preyed upon and Tampa has many elderly people. Flint is next (13), followed by Miami and Sacramento (12).

At the other end of the spectrum, Chicago, Philadelphia and Columbus, Georgia have low reported property crime rates, under 5 per 100 residents. In large cities like Chicago and Philadelphia, where police officials seem to report crimes with varying degrees of comprehensiveness from year to year, the violent crime figures are more consistent and reliable than the property crime data.

Several cities have had outside accounting firms audit their crime data: Washington, D.C. and St. Louis, for example. Their crime figures are probably more accurate than those of other cities, at least during the years of the audits.

SOURCES: U.S. Department of Justice, Federal Bureau of Investigation (FBI), *Crime in the U.S.—1981: Uniform Crime Report* (Washington, D.C.: Government Printing Office, 1982). Arthur Carol, *City Crime* (New York: Council on Municipal Performance, Municipal Performance Report 1, 1973), pp. 6–8.

| Rank | City | Total Property Crimes | Property Crimes Per 100 Population |
|---|---|---|---|
| 1 | Sacramento | 53,648 | 19.45 |
| 2 | Tampa | 35,182 | 12.96 |
| 3 | Flint | 20,272 | 12.70 |
| 4 | Miami | 41,700 | 12.02 |
| 5 | Salt Lake City | 19,581 | 12.01 |
| 6 | Portland, Ore. | 43,980 | 12.00 |
| 7 | Atlanta | 49,990 | 11.76 |
| 8 | Boston | 65,592 | 11.65 |
| 9 | Dayton | 23,544 | 11.56 |
| 10 | St. Louis | 52,290 | 11.54 |
| 11 | Denver | 55,332 | 11.26 |
| 12 | Oakland | 37,642 | 11.09 |
| 13 | Fort Worth | 42,207 | 10.96 |
| 14 | Dallas | 98,833 | 10.93 |
| 15 | Birmingham | 30,957 | 10.88 |
| 16 | Baton Rouge | 23,056 | 10.50 |
| 17 | Tucson | 34,431 | 10.42 |
| 18 | Little Rock | 16,474 | 10.40 |
| 19 | Fresno | 22,423 | 10.28 |
| 20 | Seattle | 50,350 | 10.20 |
| 21 | Richmond | 22,098 | 10.08 |
| 22 | Rochester | 24,320 | 10.06 |
| 23 | Detroit | 119,931 | 9.97 |
| 24 | Des Moines | 18,935 | 9.91 |
| 25 | Minneapolis | 36,228 | 9.77 |
| 26 | Kansas City, Mo. | 43,291 | 9.66 |
| 26 | Mobile | 19,369 | 9.66 |
| 28 | Las Vegas | 38,728 | 9.52 |
| 29 | Phoenix | 75,051 | 9.50 |
| 30 | Kansas City, Kan. | 15,108 | 9.38 |
| 31 | Tacoma | 14,837 | 9.36 |
| 32 | Santa Ana | 18,954 | 9.30 |
| 33 | Columbus, Ohio | 50,030 | 8.86 |
| 34 | Toledo | 31,379 | 8.85 |
| 35 | Providence | 13,867 | 8.84 |
| 36 | Cincinnati | 32,923 | 8.54 |
| 37 | Spokane | 14,613 | 8.53 |
| 38 | San Francisco | 57,714 | 8.50 |
| 39 | Austin | 29,322 | 8.49 |
| 40 | Shreveport | 17,450 | 8.48 |
| 41 | Jackson | 17,192 | 8.47 |
| 41 | Los Angeles | 251,282 | 8.47 |
| 41 | Wichita | 23,654 | 8.47 |
| 44 | Corpus Christi | 19,629 | 8.46 |
| 44 | Madison | 14,435 | 8.46 |
| 46 | Charlotte | 26,480 | 8.42 |
| 47 | Cleveland | 48,282 | 8.41 |

| Rank | City | Total Property Crimes | Property Crimes Per 100 Population | Rank | City | Total Property Crimes | Property Crimes Per 100 Population |
|---|---|---|---|---|---|---|---|
| 48 | Grand Rapids | 15,173 | 8.34 | 73 | Chattanooga | 12,124 | 7.15 |
| 49 | Albuquerque | 27,629 | 8.33 | 74 | Fort Wayne | 12,291 | 7.14 |
| 50 | Colorado Springs | 17,373 | 8.07 | 75 | Greensboro | 10,984 | 7.06 |
| 50 | Riverside | 13,794 | 8.07 | 76 | Norfolk | 18,346 | 6.87 |
| 52 | New York | 568,900 | 8.05 | 77 | San Diego | 59,529 | 6.80 |
| 53 | Washington, D.C. | 50,896 | 7.98 | 78 | Arlington, Texas | 10,842 | 6.77 |
| 54 | Lubbock | 13,820 | 7.94 | 79 | Nashville | 30,517 | 6.70 |
| 55 | San Jose | 50,392 | 7.92 | 80 | Aurora | 10,466 | 6.60 |
| 56 | New Orleans | 44,037 | 7.90 | 81 | Milwaukee | 41,351 | 6.50 |
| 57 | St. Petersburg | 18,385 | 7.76 | 82 | Warren | 10,320 | 6.40 |
| 58 | Oklahoma City | 31,000 | 7.69 | 83 | Indianapolis | 29,359 | 6.36 |
| 58 | Syracuse | 13,089 | 7.69 | 84 | Louisville | 18,393 | 6.16 |
| 60 | Lexington-Fayette | 15,688 | 7.68 | 85 | Honolulu | 47,583 | 6.15 |
| 61 | Long Beach | 27,701 | 7.67 | 86 | El Paso | 25,765 | 6.06 |
| 62 | Tulsa | 27,579 | 7.64 | 87 | Knoxville | 11,076 | 6.05 |
| 63 | Baltimore | 59,826 | 7.60 | 88 | Pittsburgh | 25,401 | 5.99 |
| 64 | St. Paul | 20,490 | 7.58 | 89 | Montgomery | 10,659 | 5.98 |
| 65 | Jersey City | 16,723 | 7.48 | 90 | Lincoln | 10,175 | 5.92 |
| 66 | Anchorage | 12,807 | 7.40 | 91 | Virginia Beach | 14,539 | 5.55 |
| 67 | San Antonio | 57,384 | 7.31 | 92 | Yonkers | 10,150 | 5.20 |
| 68 | Omaha | 22,768 | 7.30 | 93 | Huntington Beach | 8,826 | 5.18 |
| 69 | Akron | 17,288 | 7.29 | 94 | Chicago | 147,707 | 4.92 |
| 69 | Jacksonville | 39,436 | 7.29 | 94 | Philadelphia | 82,976 | 4.92 |
| 71 | Anaheim | 15,947 | 7.19 | 96 | Columbus, Ga. | 8,091 | 4.78 |
| 72 | Memphis | 46,269 | 7.16 | | | | |

# 197. Arrests for Property Crimes

Property crimes—i.e., the three crime categories of burglary, larceny theft and auto theft—account for the bulk of all index crimes and of all arrests for such crimes. For example, Chicago in 1981 showed reports of about 26,000 violent crimes and 148,000 property crimes. It showed arrests for about 10,000 violent crimes and for about 49,000 property crimes.

A police department may decide as a matter of making full use of its personnel that an arrest has value for deterrence purposes even though the likelihood of conviction may be remote because the police department has gathered inadequate evidence or has not followed proper procedures. Such harassment types of arrests are common for dealing with prostitution, gambling or street peddlers. At the very least, they cut down on the time spent in such activities and reduce their profitability.

The difficulty with such an approach is that it doesn't really represent "solution" of a crime in the sense implied by a clearance rate. The criminal can be expected back on the street within a few hours. Harassment arrests may also violate civil liberties protections.

In this light, note in the table below for 1981 property crimes arrests that Chicago has the highest ratio of all major cities, 33 percent. In the previous table, on violent crimes arrests, Chicago ranked 23rd of 72 cities with an arrest rate of 38 percent.

Given the fact that it is difficult to identify and apprehend criminals in a very large city like Chicago, the question arises whether the property crimes arrests in Chicago are of low quality relative to those in other cities.

To obtain an answer to this question, one would ideally like information on the disposition of each arrest. However, such information is virtually impossible to come by in most cities because police and court data systems are hardly ever interconnected. Once an arrest is made, the information is transferred to the district attorney's office. The office of the district attorney reviews all arrests and dismisses some of them immediately as having inadequate evidence or for having been impaired by improper procedures such as illegal searches. Those arrests that survive what is called this "first judicial screening" are then processed for prosecution. While the later stages of criminal prosecution have much to do with the priorities and practices of the district attorney's office, the first judicial screening might provide a good comparative measure of the quality of arrests.

In the absence of such information, we must rely on internal comparisons of the arrest data to arrive at an understanding of the relative arrest quality prevalent in different cities.

In 1981 New York City and Chicago police departments made about the same number of property crime arrests—57,000 in New York versus 49,000 in Chicago. Yet New York had 567,000 reported property crimes compared to Chicago's 148,000.

This comparison suggests that New York isn't making much of an effort to follow up on property crimes. This is in fact the case. New York's police department as a matter of policy doesn't assign detectives to pursue auto thefts (e.g., by taking fingerprints) beyond obtaining what information is needed to fill out a basic report.

Chicago's arrest rate record suggests that its police department is far more diligent in following up property crimes. That it should show more arrests than any other city, however, suggests that its arrests are not of as high a quality as they would be in many other cities.

Overall, all but three cities show a lower arrest rate for property crimes than for violent crimes. However, three cities buck that eminently understandable difference between arrest rates for violent and property crimes. They appear to devote more resources to property crimes than to violent crimes relative to other cities. They are Fort Wayne, Jackson and Baltimore.

In the first two cities, arrests for property crimes were twice the rate of arrests for violent crimes. For example, Fort Wayne showed an arrest rate of 13.2 percent for property crimes and 6.3 percent for violent crimes. Jackson showed an arrest rate of 11.8 percent for property crimes and 5.5 percent for violent crimes. One suspects that the poorer areas of these two cities have many violent crimes that receive less attention than property crimes in wealthier areas, whether because of relative indifference of the police departments to violent crimes in these areas or—even more likely—a breakdown in relations between police departments and residents of poorer communities.

The median arrest rate is 14.3 percent. That is, in 100 property crimes, there were slightly over 14 arrests. The range is from over 33 in Chicago to slightly over 7 in Knoxville.

SOURCES: Reported property crimes for 1981 from U.S. Department of Justice, Federal Bureau of Investigation, *Crime in the U.S.—1981: Uniform Crime Reports* (Washington, D.C.: Government Printing Office, 1982). Arrests for property crimes in 1981 from a special unpublished report provided at the authors' request by the Federal Bureau of Investigation, January 1983.

| Rank | City | Reports of Property Crimes | Arrests for Property Crimes | Percentage of Arrests Per Property Crimes Reported |
|---|---|---|---|---|
| 1 | Chicago | 147,707 | 48,967 | 33.15 |
| 2 | Montgomery | 10,659 | 2,984 | 28.00 |
| 3 | Greensboro | 10,984 | 3,039 | 27.67 |
| 4 | Newark | 16,723 | 4,414 | 26.39 |
| 5 | Aurora | 10,466 | 2,591 | 24.76 |
| 6 | Colorado Springs | 17,373 | 4,165 | 23.97 |
| 7 | Philadelphia | 82,976 | 18,532 | 22.33 |
| 8 | Milwaukee | 41,351 | 9,086 | 21.97 |
| 9 | El Paso | 25,765 | 5,458 | 21.18 |
| 10 | Salt Lake City | 19,581 | 4,109 | 20.98 |
| 11 | Jacksonville | 39,436 | 8,064 | 20.45 |
| 12 | Fresno | 22,423 | 4,558 | 20.33 |
| 13 | Norfolk | 18,346 | 3,575 | 19.49 |
| 14 | Virginia Beach | 14,539 | 2,775 | 19.09 |
| 15 | Kansas City, Mo. | 43,291 | 8,201 | 18.94 |
| 16 | Chattanooga | 12,124 | 2,292 | 18.90 |
| 17 | St. Petersburg | 18,385 | 3,458 | 18.81 |
| 18 | Columbus, Ga. | 8,091 | 1,489 | 18.40 |
| 19 | New Orleans | 44,037 | 8,094 | 18.38 |
| 20 | Huntington Beach | 8,826 | 1,522 | 17.24 |
| 21 | Las Vegas | 38,728 | 6,589 | 17.01 |
| 22 | Rochester | 24,320 | 4,126 | 16.97 |
| 23 | Omaha | 22,768 | 3,822 | 16.79 |
| 24 | Baton Rouge | 23,056 | 3,854 | 16.72 |
| 25 | Riverside | 13,794 | 2,273 | 16.48 |
| 26 | Honolulu | 47,583 | 7,835 | 16.47 |
| 27 | Oklahoma City | 31,000 | 4,935 | 15.92 |
| 28 | Fort Worth | 42,207 | 6,684 | 15.84 |
| 29 | Oakland | 37,642 | 5,786 | 15.37 |
| 30 | Charlotte | 26,480 | 4,065 | 15.35 |
| 31 | Louisville | 18,383 | 2,813 | 15.30 |
| 31 | Washington, D.C. | 50,896 | 7,785 | 15.30 |
| 33 | Minneapolis | 36,228 | 5,491 | 15.16 |
| 34 | Phoenix | 75,051 | 11,231 | 14.96 |
| 35 | San Diego | 59,529 | 8,788 | 14.76 |
| 36 | Lubbock | 13,820 | 1,981 | 14.33 |
| 37 | Long Beach | 27,701 | 3,967 | 14.32 |
| 38 | Corpus Christi | 19,629 | 2,799 | 14.26 |
| 38 | San Jose | 50,392 | 7,187 | 14.26 |
| 40 | Anaheim | 15,947 | 2,259 | 14.17 |
| 41 | Indianapolis | 29,359 | 4,154 | 14.15 |
| 42 | Anchorage | 12,801 | 1,804 | 14.09 |
| 42 | Little Rock | 16,474 | 2,321 | 14.09 |
| 44 | Atlanta | 49,990 | 7,021 | 14.04 |
| 45 | Richmond | 22,098 | 3,093 | 14.00 |
| 46 | Warren | 10,320 | 1,420 | 13.76 |
| 47 | Los Angeles | 251,282 | 34,428 | 13.70 |
| 48 | Santa Ana | 18,954 | 2,591 | 13.67 |
| 49 | San Antonio | 57,384 | 7,703 | 13.42 |
| 50 | Tampa | 35,182 | 4,699 | 13.36 |
| 51 | Fort Wayne | 12,291 | 1,620 | 13.18 |
| 52 | Dallas | 98,833 | 12,946 | 13.10 |
| 53 | Wichita | 23,654 | 3,049 | 12.89 |
| 54 | Detroit | 119,931 | 15,233 | 12.70 |
| 54 | Miami | 41,700 | 5,295 | 12.70 |
| 56 | Portland, Ore. | 43,980 | 5,528 | 12.57 |
| 57 | San Francisco | 57,714 | 6,825 | 11.83 |
| 58 | Jackson | 17,192 | 2,032 | 11.82 |
| 59 | Pittsburgh | 25,401 | 2,987 | 11.76 |
| 60 | Dayton | 23,544 | 2,669 | 11.34 |
| 61 | Tucson | 34,431 | 3,894 | 11.31 |
| 62 | Lexington-Fayette | 15,688 | 1,732 | 11.04 |
| 63 | Baltimore | 59,826 | 6,498 | 10.86 |
| 64 | Shreveport | 17,450 | 1,880 | 10.77 |
| 65 | Kansas City, Kan. | 15,108 | 1,623 | 10.74 |

| Rank | City | Reports of Property Crimes | Arrests for Property Crimes | Percentage of Arrests Per Property Crimes Reported |
|---|---|---|---|---|
| 66 | Providence | 13,867 | 1,481 | 10.68 |
| 67 | Mobile | 19,369 | 2,056 | 10.61 |
| 68 | Syracuse | 13,089 | 1,345 | 10.28 |
| 69 | Toledo | 31,379 | 3,209 | 10.23 |
| 70 | Grand Rapids | 15,173 | 1,511 | 9.96 |
| 71 | New York | 568,900 | 56,547 | 9.94 |

| Rank | City | Reports of Property Crimes | Arrests for Property Crimes | Percentage of Arrests Per Property Crimes Reported |
|---|---|---|---|---|
| 72 | Birmingham | 30,957 | 3,039 | 9.82 |
| 73 | Tulsa | 27,579 | 2,460 | 8.92 |
| 74 | Sacramento | 53,648 | 4,228 | 7.88 |
| 75 | Flint | 20,272 | 1,571 | 7.75 |
| 76 | Knoxville | 11,076 | 798 | 7.20 |

# 198.  Trends in Property Crimes

Nationwide, property crimes rose in every year from 1972 through 1976, dropped in 1977, rose again every year through 1980, then dropped again in 1981. They continued their decline into 1982.

Whereas in 1972 a person selected at random in the United States would have faced a probability of .036 of having property taken from his office or business, in 1981, the probability had risen to .052 (down from .053 in 1980)—a rise of over 5 percent.

Looking at property crime trends on a quarterly basis, the rate was at its low point in the first quarter of 1973 and at its high point in the third quarter of 1980. During 1972–81 property crime was always lowest during the winter first quarter (January–March) and highest during the summer third quarter (July–September).

Questions about the reliability of property crime data apply with less force to comparative time data. If a city keeps its figures in the same way over time, the fact that its methods are different from those of another city should not be so important when we examine changes in figures for the same city from year to year. On the other hand, some cities have been known to change their data collection methods purposefully—for example, raising crime rates when budgets are up for consideration and lowering them to assist an incumbent mayor before elections. These practices have been observed in the past to have occurred in cities like Chicago and Philadelphia.

Portland, Ore., showed an increase of nearly 40 percent in crimes against property between 1979 and 1981, as its popularity brought in newcomers. Chicago data showed a decrease of a little over 7 percent. San Diego showed the greatest decrease of the cities studied, 10.7 percent, perhaps reflecting the city's new anti-crime measures.

SOURCES: U.S. Department of Justice, Federal Bureau of Investigation (FBI), *Crime in the U.S.—1979 Uniform Crime Report* (Washington, D.C.: Government Printing Office, 1980); *Crime in the U.S.—1981: Uniform Crime Report* (Washington, D.C.: Government Printing Office, 1982), pp. 58–107, 322, 324, 325.

| Rank | City | 1979 Property Crimes | 1981 Property Crimes | Absolute Change | Percentage Change |
|---|---|---|---|---|---|
| 1 | Portland, Ore. | 31,520 | 43,980 | 12,460 | 39.53 |
| 2 | Miami | 30,355 | 41,700 | 11,345 | 37.37 |
| 3 | Detroit | 89,704 | 119,931 | 30,227 | 33.70 |
| 4 | Richmond | 16,594 | 22,098 | 5,504 | 33.17 |
| 5 | Mobile | 14,817 | 19,369 | 4,552 | 30.72 |
| 6 | Charlotte | 20,499 | 26,480 | 5,981 | 29.18 |
| 7 | Tampa | 27,481 | 35,182 | 7,701 | 28.02 |
| 8 | Minneapolis | 28,507 | 36,228 | 7,721 | 27.08 |
| 9 | Colorado Springs | 13,779 | 17,373 | 3,594 | 26.08 |
| 10 | San Jose | 40,073 | 50,392 | 10,319 | 25.75 |

| Rank | City | 1979 Property Crimes | 1981 Property Crimes | Absolute Change | Percentage Change |
|---|---|---|---|---|---|
| 11 | Las Vegas | 30,923 | 38,728 | 7,805 | 25.24 |
| 12 | Wichita | 18,935 | 23,654 | 4,719 | 24.92 |
| 13 | Lexington-Fayette | 12,664 | 15,688 | 3,024 | 23.88 |
| 14 | Corpus Christi | 15,955 | 19,629 | 3,674 | 23.03 |
| 15 | Philadelphia | 68,049 | 82,976 | 14,927 | 21.94 |
| 16 | Providence | 11,418 | 13,867 | 2,449 | 21.45 |
| 17 | Seattle | 41,482 | 50,350 | 8,868 | 21.38 |
| 18 | Santa Ana | 15,695 | 18,954 | 3,259 | 20.76 |
| 19 | Nashville-Davidson | 25,361 | 30,517 | 5,156 | 20.33 |
| 20 | Flint | 16,853 | 20,273 | 3,420 | 20.29 |
| 21 | Dallas | 82,308 | 98,833 | 16,525 | 20.08 |
| 22 | Salt Lake City | 16,334 | 19,581 | 3,247 | 19.88 |
| 23 | Kansas City, Mo. | 36,123 | 43,291 | 7,168 | 19.84 |
| 24 | Tucson | 28,770 | 34,431 | 5,661 | 19.68 |
| 25 | Memphis | 38,714 | 46,269 | 7,555 | 19.51 |
| 26 | Greensboro | 9,304 | 10,984 | 1,680 | 18.06 |
| 27 | Denver | 46,872 | 55,332 | 8,460 | 18.05 |
| 28 | Milwaukee | 35,331 | 41,351 | 6,020 | 17.04 |
| 29 | Los Angeles | 215,263 | 251,282 | 36,019 | 16.73 |
| 30 | Grand Rapids | 13,021 | 15,173 | 2,152 | 16.53 |
| 31 | Washington, D.C. | 45,877 | 53,442 | 7,565 | 16.49 |
| 32 | Sacramento | 28,440 | 33,126 | 4,686 | 16.48 |
| 33 | New York | 488,727 | 568,900 | 80,173 | 16.40 |
| 34 | St. Petersburg | 15,806 | 18,385 | 2,579 | 16.32 |
| 35 | Arlington, Texas | 9,353 | 10,842 | 1,489 | 15.92 |
| 36 | Des Moines | 16,350 | 18,935 | 2,585 | 15.81 |
| 37 | Jersey City | 14,446 | 16,723 | 2,277 | 15.76 |
| 38 | Anchorage | 11,140 | 12,807 | 1,667 | 14.96 |
| 39 | Jacksonville | 34,446 | 39,436 | 4,990 | 14.49 |
| 40 | Cleveland | 42,258 | 48,292 | 6,034 | 14.28 |
| 41 | Akron | 15,140 | 17,288 | 2,148 | 14.19 |
| 42 | Austin | 25,742 | 29,322 | 3,580 | 13.91 |
| 43 | Kansas City, Kan. | 14,115 | 16,006 | 1,891 | 13.40 |
| 44 | Virginia Beach | 13,010 | 14,731 | 1,721 | 13.23 |
| 45 | Knoxville | 10,102 | 11,433 | 1,331 | 13.18 |
| 46 | Lubbock | 12,231 | 13,820 | 1,589 | 12.99 |
| 47 | Riverside | 12,224 | 13,794 | 1,570 | 12.84 |
| 48 | San Antonio | 50,893 | 57,384 | 6,491 | 12.75 |
| 49 | Louisville | 16,316 | 18,393 | 2,077 | 12.73 |
| 50 | St. Louis | 46,439 | 52,290 | 5,851 | 12.60 |
| 51 | Tacoma | 13,207 | 14,837 | 1,630 | 12.34 |
| 52 | Cincinnati | 29,312 | 32,923 | 3,611 | 12.32 |
| 53 | Albuquerque | 24,662 | 27,629 | 2,967 | 12.03 |
| 54 | Lincoln | 9,153 | 10,175 | 1,022 | 11.17 |
| 55 | Long Beach | 24,967 | 27,701 | 2,734 | 10.95 |
| 56 | Tulsa | 25,105 | 27,579 | 2,474 | 9.85 |
| 57 | Pittsburgh | 23,309 | 25,401 | 2,092 | 8.98 |
| 58 | Fort Worth | 38,891 | 42,207 | 3,316 | 8.53 |
| 59 | Birmingham | 28,534 | 30,957 | 2,423 | 8.49 |
| 60 | Madison | 13,321 | 14,435 | 1,114 | 8.36 |
| 61 | Columbus, Ga. | 7,494 | 8,119 | 625 | 8.34 |
| 62 | Phoenix | 69,344 | 75,051 | 5,707 | 8.23 |
| 63 | Columbus, Ohio | 46,363 | 50,030 | 3,667 | 7.91 |
| 64 | Dayton | 21,841 | 23,544 | 1,703 | 7.80 |
| 65 | St. Paul | 19,119 | 20,490 | 1,371 | 7.17 |
| 66 | Yonkers | 9,489 | 10,150 | 661 | 6.97 |
| 67 | Baton Rouge | 21,592 | 23,056 | 1,464 | 6.78 |
| 68 | El Paso | 24,194 | 25,765 | 1,571 | 6.49 |
| 69 | Toledo | 29,637 | 31,379 | 1,742 | 5.88 |
| 70 | Fresno | 21,289 | 22,423 | 1,134 | 5.33 |
| 71 | Oklahoma City | 29,765 | 31,000 | 1,235 | 4.15 |
| 72 | Atlanta | 48,009 | 49,990 | 1,981 | 4.13 |
| 73 | Shreveport | 14,151 | 14,641 | 490 | 3.46 |
| 74 | Norfolk | 17,780 | 18,328 | 548 | 3.08 |
| 75 | Baltimore | 58,221 | 59,826 | 1,605 | 2.76 |
| 76 | Chattanooga | 11,836 | 12,124 | 288 | 2.43 |
| 77 | Omaha | 22,335 | 22,768 | 433 | 1.94 |

| Rank | City | 1979 Property Crimes | 1981 Property Crimes | Absolute Change | Percentage Change |
|---|---|---|---|---|---|
| 78 | New Orleans | 43,585 | 44,037 | 452 | 1.04 |
| 79 | Anaheim | 15,833 | 15,947 | 114 | .72 |
| 80 | San Francisco | 59,704 | 59,801 | 97 | .16 |
| 81 | Spokane | 14,656 | 14,613 | − 43 | − .29 |
| 82 | Montgomery | 10,781 | 10,659 | − 122 | − 1.13 |
| 83 | Rochester | 25,441 | 24,320 | − 1,121 | − 4.41 |
| 84 | Syracuse | 13,738 | 13,089 | − 649 | − 4.72 |
| 85 | Indianapolis | 30,927 | 29,359 | − 1,548 | − 5.07 |
| 86 | Fort Wayne | 12,962 | 12,291 | − 671 | − 5.18 |
| 87 | Honolulu | 50,730 | 47,583 | − 3,147 | − 6.20 |
| 88 | Chicago | 158,921 | 147,7074 | − 11,214 | − 7.06 |
| 89 | Huntington Beach | 9,572 | 8,826 | − 746 | − 7.79 |
| 90 | San Diego | 66,657 | 59,529 | − 7,128 | −10.69 |

# 199.  Police Personnel

The largest cities have the highest average number of police employees as well as the most crime. In 1981, as the table below shows, the average number of police in cities with a population of over 250,000 was 3.3 per 1,000 inhabitants; the range was 1.6 to 6.4. The average declined for the smaller sized groups to 2.3, 2.1 and 2.0 police employees per 1,000 inhabitants. However, for the smallest size group—cities with less than 10,000 population—the average increases to 2.4 police employees per 1,000 residents. Some of these cities have as many as 9.3 police employees per 1,000 residents (i.e., nearly 1 police employee per 100 men, women and children.)

The explanation for the relatively large number of police employees in small communities that have relatively little crime is that some of these communities are wealthy suburban areas. They can *afford* relatively large police forces.

Philadelphia, where a former police chief (Frank Rizzo) was for a while the mayor, has the highest number of police employees relative to the population—nearly 5 per 1,000 residents. Louisville, Baltimore, Jersey City and Des Moines are close behind with 4 or more per 1,000 residents.

At the low end, Riverside and Spokane have fewer than 1.5 police employees per 1,000 residents.

| Rank | City | Total Police Personnel | Police Personnel Per 1,000 Population |
|---|---|---|---|
| 1 | Philadelphia | 8,309 | 4.93 |
| 2 | Louisville | 940 | 4.60 |
| 3 | Baltimore | 3,538 | 4.44 |
| 4 | Jersey City | 958 | 4.27 |
| 5 | Des Moines | 770 | 4.05 |
| 6 | Detroit | 4,778 | 4.00 |
| 7 | Kansas City, Mo. | 1,703 | 3.78 |
| 8 | Milwaukee | 2,359 | 3.68 |
| 9 | Cleveland | 2,029 | 3.54 |
| 10 | Denver | 1,697 | 3.37 |
| 11 | Las Vegas | 1,351 | 3.32 |
| 11 | San Francisco | 2,297 | 3.32 |
| 13 | Dayton | 603 | 3.12 |
| 14 | Chattanooga | 516 | 3.07 |
| 14 | Miami | 1,095 | 3.07 |
| 16 | Los Angeles | 9,288 | 3.06 |
| 17 | Salt Lake City | 503 | 2.97 |
| 18 | Baton Rouge | 655 | 1.91 |
| 19 | Indianapolis | 1,315 | 2.85 |
| 20 | Montgomery | 492 | 2.74 |
| 21 | Seattle | 1,377 | 2.73 |
| 22 | Columbus, Ohio | 1,530 | 2.72 |
| 22 | Phoenix | 2,166 | 2.72 |
| 24 | Jacksonville | 1,560 | 2.71 |
| 25 | Greensboro | 418 | 2.65 |
| 26 | Dallas | 2,475 | 2.64 |
| 27 | Norfolk | 692 | 2.58 |
| 27 | Tampa | 736 | 2.58 |
| 29 | Jackson | 515 | 2.55 |
| 30 | Kansas City, Kan. | 411 | 2.54 |
| 31 | Nashville-Davidson | 1,156 | 2.52 |

SOURCES: International City Management Association (ICMA), *The Municipal Year Book: 1982* (Washington, D.C.: ICMA, 1982). U.S. Department of Justice, Federal Bureau of Investigation (FBI), *Crime in the U.S.—1981* (Washington, D.C.: Government Printing Office, 1982), pp. 236–37, 241–249.

| Rank | City | Total Police Personnel | Police Personnel Per 1,000 Population | Rank | City | Total Police Personnel | Police Personnel Per 1,000 Population |
|------|------|------------------------|--------------------------------------|------|------|------------------------|--------------------------------------|
| 32 | St. Paul | 674 | 2.49 | 52 | Toledo | 723 | 2.04 |
| 33 | Cincinnati | 940 | 2.45 | 52 | Virginia Beach | 541 | 2.04 |
| 34 | New Orleans | 1,376 | 2.40 | 54 | Oklahoma City | 832 | 2.01 |
| 34 | New York | 17,032 | 2.40 | 55 | Akron | 467 | 1.97 |
| 36 | Knoxville | 444 | 2.40 | 56 | San Diego | 1,741 | 1.94 |
| 38 | Little Rock | 370 | 2.39 | 57 | Fort Wayne | 327 | 1.91 |
| 39 | Honolulu | 1,817 | 2.35 | 58 | Anaheim | 424 | 1.89 |
| 40 | Charlotte | 742 | 2.34 | 58 | Portland, Ore. | 697 | 1.89 |
| 41 | Fort Worth | 915 | 2.30 | 58 | Wichita | 533 | 1.89 |
| 42 | Tucson | 770 | 2.26 | 61 | Oakland | 608 | 1.75 |
| 43 | St. Petersburg | 555 | 2.24 | 62 | Huntington Beach | 305 | 1.74 |
| 44 | Lexington-Fayette | 442 | 2.16 | 63 | Tacoma | 276 | 1.70 |
| 45 | Minneapolis | 801 | 2.15 | 64 | Lincoln | 287 | 1.66 |
| 45 | Omaha | 694 | 2.15 | 64 | San Antonio | 1,364 | 1.66 |
| 47 | Aurora | 348 | 2.14 | 66 | Lubbock | 293 | 1.62 |
| 48 | Madison | 366 | 2.13 | 67 | San Jose | 996 | 1.54 |
| 49 | Colorado Springs | 443 | 2.08 | 68 | Riverside | 252 | 1.44 |
| 49 | Mobile | 420 | 2.08 | 69 | Spokane | 247 | 1.41 |
| 51 | Santa Ana | 435 | 2.06 | | | | |

# 200.  Crimes Per Police Employee

The following table provides an indicator of the relative workload for police employees. Since police departments have varying degrees of "civilianization," we consider the total number of employees a better basis for measuring workload than the number of uniformed officers.

The data are for 1981. They include only the seven "Index" crimes described in earlier crime tables and exclude a wide range of white collar and petty crimes. The police employee base is the one relevant to the city police department's jurisdiction and excludes (for example, in a city like Indianapolis) the areas still serviced by county or small independent police departments within the combined city-county area.

As the table below shows, Oakland police employees had the heaviest index crime workload in 1981. Its police employees coped with an average of over 73 crimes each. Police employees may do nothing at all about a crime except write a report on it (the usual situation in a large city), or they may spend weeks going out to gather evidence and waiting in courtrooms for their case to come before a judge. While the average time a police employee would spend on a crime in Oakland is 3.4 days (assuming a 250-day working year), the reality is that most crimes will require just a few minutes to enter on a report. Only a few crimes will take up many days of time.

Philadelphia, which for some years had a former police chief as mayor, has the largest number of police employees relative to crimes, i.e. the lowest index crime workload. With 12 crimes per police employee in 1981, each employee had nearly 21 days to devote to each reported Index crime. New York City ranks at the end of the top third of the table, suggesting that its police employees are busier than the average city's, but not so busy as the ones at the top of the table. The top 5 cities are all on the West Coast.

Police employees in large cities, especially those with a heavy daytime influx of commuters and a high tourist or transit traffic, have more difficulty in tracking down evidence with which to convict a criminal. If two cities have the same number of crimes, we would expect the city with the higher density or larger population to require a larger police force to handle the crimes for purposes of reporting, gathering evidence and testifying. On this basis, we would expect a city like New York to be at the bottom of the list, i.e. with a lower ratio of crimes to police than smaller cities.

The table shows that New York is instead among the top third cities with the busiest workload. This suggests that police employees in New York City are too overloaded with work to offer as high a quality of police service as in other cities.

The reality in New York City is that police employees as a matter of department policy have been instructed to spend no time gathering evidence such as fingerprints in crimes like auto theft that would be considered serious in other cities.

SOURCES: Police employees from International City Management Association (ICMA), *The Municipal Year Book 1982* (Washington, DC: ICMA, 1982), pp. 95–99. Crimes from U.S. Department of Justice, Federal Bureau of Investigation (FBI), *Crimes in the U.S.—1981: Uniform Crime Reports* (Washington, DC: Government Printing Office, 1982).

| Rank | City | Total Crimes | Police Employees | Crimes Per Police Employee |
|---|---|---|---|---|
| 1 | Oakland | 44,678 | 608 | 73.48 |
| 2 | Portland, Ore. | 50,432 | 697 | 72.36 |
| 3 | Riverside | 15,361 | 252 | 60.96 |
| 4 | Spokane | 14,698 | 247 | 59.51 |
| 5 | Tacoma | 16,193 | 276 | 58.67 |
| 6 | Tampa | 40,856 | 736 | 55.51 |
| 7 | Fort Wayne | 13,112 | 237 | 55.32 |
| 8 | San Jose | 54,514 | 996 | 54.73 |
| 9 | Lubbock | 15,418 | 293 | 52.62 |
| 10 | Mobile | 21,998 | 420 | 52.38 |
| 11 | Fort Worth | 47,153 | 915 | 51.53 |
| 12 | Little Rock | 18,781 | 370 | 50.76 |
| 13 | Tucson | 37,241 | 770 | 48.36 |
| 14 | Miami | 52,911 | 1,095 | 48.32 |
| 15 | Minneapolis | 38,215 | 801 | 47.71 |
| 16 | Wichita | 25,383 | 533 | 47.62 |
| 17 | Santa Ana | 20,712 | 435 | 47.61 |
| 18 | Toledo | 34,090 | 723 | 47.15 |
| 19 | San Antonio | 62,035 | 1,364 | 45.48 |
| 20 | Dallas | 111,582 | 2,475 | 45.08 |
| 21 | Dayton | 27,053 | 603 | 44.86 |
| 22 | Kansas City, Kan. | 18,123 | 411 | 44.09 |
| 23 | New York | 725,846 | 17,032 | 42.62 |
| 24 | Colorado Springs | 18,836 | 443 | 42.52 |
| 25 | Oklahoma City | 35,128 | 832 | 42.22 |
| 26 | Salt Lake City | 20,849 | 503 | 41.45 |
| 27 | Madison | 14,898 | 366 | 40.70 |
| 28 | Anaheim | 17,202 | 424 | 40.57 |
| 29 | Seattle | 55,764 | 1,377 | 40.50 |
| 30 | Charlotte | 29,646 | 742 | 39.95 |
| 31 | Akron | 18,525 | 467 | 39.67 |
| 32 | Baton Rouge | 25,917 | 655 | 39.57 |
| 33 | Cincinnati | 36,815 | 940 | 39.16 |
| 34 | Lexington-Fayette | 16,836 | 442 | 38.09 |
| 35 | San Diego | 66,123 | 1,741 | 37.98 |
| 36 | New Orleans | 52,158 | 1,376 | 37.91 |
| 37 | St. Petersburg | 20,894 | 555 | 37.65 |
| 38 | Phoenix | 81,370 | 2,166 | 37.57 |
| 39 | Lincoln | 10,601 | 287 | 36.94 |
| 40 | Columbus, Ohio | 55,293 | 1,530 | 36.14 |
| 41 | Jackson | 18,583 | 515 | 36.08 |
| 42 | Denver | 60,417 | 1,697 | 35.60 |
| 43 | Omaha | 24,351 | 694 | 35.09 |
| 44 | Aurora | 11,903 | 348 | 34.20 |
| 45 | St. Paul | 22,799 | 674 | 33.83 |
| 46 | Shreveport | 16,030 | 480 | 33.40 |
| 47 | Los Angeles | 304,100 | 9,288 | 32.74 |
| 48 | Las Vegas | 43,376 | 1,351 | 32.11 |
| 49 | San Francisco | 7,812 | 2,297 | 31.26 |
| 50 | Huntington Beach | 9,369 | 305 | 30.72 |
| 51 | Norfolk | 20,769 | 692 | 30.01 |
| 52 | Detroit | 143,107 | 4,778 | 29.95 |
| 52 | Kansas City, Mo. | 51,005 | 1,703 | 29.95 |
| 54 | Cleveland | 60,721 | 2,029 | 29.93 |
| 55 | Nashville-Davidson | 33,604 | 1,156 | 29.07 |
| 56 | Jacksonville | 45,070 | 1,560 | 28.89 |
| 57 | Greensboro | 12,014 | 418 | 28.74 |
| 58 | Virginia Beach | 15,337 | 541 | 28.35 |
| 59 | Knoxville | 12,527 | 444 | 28.21 |
| 60 | Honolulu | 49,548 | 1,817 | 27.27 |
| 61 | Chattanooga | 13,555 | 516 | 26.27 |
| 62 | Des Moines | 19,974 | 770 | 25.94 |
| 63 | Indianapolis | 33,898 | 1,315 | 25.78 |
| 64 | Montgomery | 11,512 | 492 | 23.40 |
| 65 | Louisville | 21,124 | 940 | 22.47 |
| 66 | Baltimore | 77,563 | 3,538 | 21.92 |
| 67 | Jersey City | 19,925 | 958 | 20.80 |
| 68 | Milwaukee | 44,775 | 2,359 | 18.98 |
| 69 | Philadelphia | 100,592 | 8,309 | 12.11 |

# 201. Cost Per Police Employee

Total police department expenditures per employee is a crude measure of how well police officers are paid. Civilianization of police departments has become a valuable approach in many cities, because police department costs may be brought down—without lowering uniformed officers' salaries—by increasing the proportion of civilians in the department.

Virginia Beach's relatively low 1981 cost of under $26,000 per employee, shown in the table below, prob-ably reflects the high degree of civilianization in its police department—more than 31 percent in the previous year, 1980. Cincinnati spent a low $9,734 per employee in 1981, and Montgomery spent $15,998.

Cost per employee may be high, on the other hand, because of the purchase of expensive crime-fighting vehicles and communications and other equipment, as well as paying high salaries. Oakland and Detroit are at the top, with $82,618 and $53,806 per employee.

SOURCE: International City Management Association (ICMA), *The Municipal Year Book: 1982* (Washington, D.C.: ICMA, 1982), pp. 95–99.

| Rank | City | Police Personnel | Total Police Expenditure ($ 000) | Cost Per Police Employee ($ 000) |
|---|---|---|---|---|
| 1 | Oakland | 608 | 50,232 | 82.62 |
| 2 | Detroit | 4,778 | 257,083 | 53.81 |
| 3 | Portland | 697 | 34,671 | 49.74 |
| 4 | Anaheim | 424 | 19,946 | 47.04 |
| 5 | San Francisco | 2,297 | 104,136 | 45.34 |
| 6 | Riverside | 252 | 11,289 | 44.80 |
| 7 | Spokane | 247 | 10,568 | 42.79 |
| 8 | New York | 17,032 | 719,088 | 42.22 |
| 9 | Los Angeles | 9,288 | 360,122 | 38.77 |
| 10 | New Orleans | 1,376 | 52,258 | 37.98 |
| 11 | Tacoma | 276 | 10,223 | 37.05 |
| 12 | Madison | 366 | 13,508 | 36.91 |
| 13 | Huntington Beach | 305 | 10,808 | 35.44 |
| 14 | San Jose | 996 | 33,640 | 33.78 |
| 15 | Santa Ana | 435 | 14,687 | 33.76 |
| 16 | Cleveland | 2,029 | 67,775 | 33.40 |
| 17 | Minneapolis | 801 | 26,606 | 33.22 |
| 18 | St. Paul | 674 | 21,968 | 32.59 |
| 19 | Seattle | 1,377 | 43,936 | 31.91 |
| 20 | Philadelphia | 8,309 | 260,391 | 31.34 |
| 21 | Milwaukee | 2,359 | 72,980 | 30.94 |
| 22 | Houston | 3,697 | 113,606 | 30.73 |
| 23 | Omaha | 694 | 20,920 | 30.14 |
| 24 | Phoenix | 2,166 | 64,728 | 29.88 |
| 25 | Salt Lake City | 503 | 14,979 | 29.78 |
| 26 | Buffalo | 1,194 | 35,425 | 29.67 |
| 27 | Akron | 467 | 13,695 | 29.33 |
| 27 | Columbus, Ohio | 1,530 | 44,875 | 29.33 |
| 29 | Jersey City | 958 | 27,858 | 29.08 |
| 30 | Tampa | 736 | 20,811 | 28.28 |
| 31 | St. Petersburg | 555 | 15,689 | 28.27 |
| 32 | Dallas | 2,475 | 68,684 | 27.75 |
| 33 | Colorado Springs | 443 | 12,246 | 27.64 |
| 34 | Aurora | 348 | 9,596 | 27.57 |
| 35 | Las Vegas | 1,351 | 37,184 | 27.52 |
| 36 | Jackson | 515 | 14,088 | 27.36 |
| 37 | Jacksonville | 1,560 | 42,183 | 27.04 |
| 38 | Dayton | 603 | 16,024 | 26.57 |
| 39 | Baltimore | 3,538 | 93,749 | 26.50 |
| 40 | Kansas City, Mo. | 1,703 | 45,110 | 26.49 |
| 41 | Denver | 1,697 | 44,935 | 26.48 |
| 42 | Wichita | 533 | 14,059 | 26.38 |
| 43 | Honolulu | 1,817 | 47,763 | 26.29 |
| 44 | San Antonio | 1,364 | 35,840 | 26.28 |
| 45 | Toledo | 723 | 18,889 | 26.13 |
| 46 | San Diego | 1,741 | 45,452 | 26.11 |
| 47 | Tucson | 770 | 19,986 | 25.96 |
| 48 | Des Moines | 430 | 11,019 | 25.63 |
| 49 | Mobile | 420 | 10,673 | 25.41 |
| 50 | Lexington-Fayette | 442 | 11,228 | 25.40 |
| 51 | Worcester | 572 | 14,494 | 25.34 |
| 52 | Louisville | 940 | 22,654 | 24.10 |
| 53 | Indianapolis | 1,315 | 31,673 | 24.09 |
| 54 | Charlotte | 742 | 17,671 | 23.82 |
| 55 | Kansas City, Kan. | 411 | 9,769 | 23.77 |
| 56 | Oklahoma City | 832 | 19,474 | 23.41 |
| 57 | Fort Worth | 915 | 21,364 | 23.35 |
| 58 | Lubbock | 293 | 6,828 | 23.30 |
| 59 | Greensboro | 418 | 9,618 | 23.01 |
| 60 | Lincoln | 287 | 6,500 | 22.65 |
| 61 | Norfolk | 692 | 15,620 | 22.57 |
| 62 | Nashville-Davidson | 1,156 | 26,068 | 22.55 |
| 63 | Baton Rouge | 655 | 14,578 | 22.26 |
| 64 | Knoxville | 444 | 9,187 | 20.69 |
| 65 | Fort Wayne | 327 | 6,750 | 20.64 |
| 66 | Virginia Beach | 541 | 11,116 | 20.55 |
| 67 | Shreveport | 480 | 9,518 | 19.83 |
| 68 | Little Rock | 370 | 6,810 | 18.41 |
| 69 | Chattanooga | 516 | 9,075 | 17.59 |
| 70 | Montgomery | 492 | 7,871 | 16.00 |
| 71 | Cincinnati | 940 | 9,150 | 9.73 |

# 202. Arson

Inclusion of arson, an increasingly important type of crime, as an Index Crime is a relatively recent development for the FBI Uniform Crime Reports. Hence, arson data are not available for several cities. The causes of arson are attributed variously to vandalism and to laws and practices relating to the insurance industry that permit property owners in distressed neighborhoods to benefit from burning their own property.

A U.S. Department of Justice study concludes that cities that have a higher arrest and conviction rate for arson have a lower arson rate. Cities with less than a 20 percent arson conviction rate had an average of 50 arsons per 100,000 population. Cities with an 80 percent or better arson conviction rate had an average of 10 arsons per 100,000 population. The survey concludes that the chief need is for increased training of arson investigators, who must be familiar both with the technical aspects of fires and fire investigation and with police methods of criminal investigation. Some cities still divide these tasks between fire and police personnel.

The highest reported arson rates in 1981 were in Rochester and Riverside.

SOURCES: John F. Boudreau et al., U.S. Department of Justice, Law Enforcement Assistance Administration, *Arson and Arson Investigation: Survey and Assessment* (Washington, D.C.: Government Printing Office, 1977), pp. 51, 71. U.S. Department of Justice, Federal Bureau of Investigation (FBI), *Crime in the U.S.—1981 Uniform Crime Reports:* (Washington, D.C.: Government Printing Office, 1982).

| Rank | City | Arsons | Arsons Per 10,000 Population |
|---|---|---|---|
| 1 | Riverside | 484 | 27.75 |
| 2 | Dayton | 441 | 22.79 |
| 3 | Los Angeles | 6,895 | 22.75 |
| 4 | San Jose | 1,422 | 22.05 |
| 5 | Flint | 345 | 21.68 |
| 6 | Atlanta | 917 | 21.05 |
| 7 | Toledo | 724 | 20.40 |
| 8 | Cleveland | 1,131 | 19.73 |
| 9 | Providence | 301 | 19.11 |
| 10 | Tucson | 483 | 14.16 |
| 11 | Cincinnati | 535 | 13.95 |
| 12 | Rochester | 324 | 13.39 |
| 13 | Denver | 646 | 12.83 |
| 14 | Tacoma | 206 | 12.72 |
| 15 | New York | 8,962 | 12.68 |
| 16 | El Paso | 558 | 12.61 |
| 17 | Akron | 289 | 12.18 |
| 18 | Memphis | 769 | 11.76 |
| 19 | Las Vegas | 467 | 11.48 |
| 20 | Kansas City, Mo. | 513 | 11.39 |
| 21 | Norfolk | 303 | 11.31 |
| 22 | Sacramento | 317 | 11.25 |
| 23 | Columbus, Ohio | 613 | 10.89 |
| 24 | Des Moines | 200 | 10.52 |
| 25 | Arlington, Texas | 175 | 10.43 |
| 26 | Lubbock | 187 | 10.31 |
| 27 | Baltimore | 817 | 10.25 |
| 28 | Kansas City, Kan. | 162 | 10.02 |
| 29 | Dallas | 917 | 9.78 |
| 30 | Little Rock | 149 | 9.64 |
| 31 | Tulsa | 351 | 9.56 |

| Rank | City | Arsons | Arsons Per 10,000 Population |
|---|---|---|---|
| 32 | Grand Rapids | 153 | 8.45 |
| 33 | Fort Worth | 330 | 8.28 |
| 34 | Fort Wayne | 136 | 7.94 |
| 35 | Miami | 274 | 7.68 |
| 36 | St. Paul | 207 | 7.66 |
| 37 | Wichita | 215 | 7.61 |
| 38 | Mobile | 153 | 7.57 |
| 39 | Tampa | 213 | 7.46 |
| 40 | Shreveport | 145 | 7.26 |
| 41 | Chicago | 2,179 | 7.23 |
| 42 | Washington, D.C. | 429 | 6.75 |
| 43 | Chattanooga | 113 | 6.73 |
| 44 | Colorado Springs | 140 | 6.57 |
| 44 | San Antonio | 539 | 6.57 |
| 46 | Montgomery | 116 | 6.46 |
| 47 | St. Petersburg | 160 | 6.45 |
| 48 | San Francisco | 430 | 6.21 |
| 49 | Fresno | 137 | 6.20 |
| 50 | Birmingham | 177 | 6.19 |
| 51 | Long Beach | 220 | 6.00 |
| 51 | Seattle | 302 | 6.00 |
| 53 | Jackson | 120 | 5.94 |
| 54 | Louisville | 177 | 5.90 |
| 55 | Santa Ana | 123 | 5.82 |
| 56 | Aurora | 91 | 5.59 |
| 57 | Lexington-Fayette | 114 | 5.58 |
| 58 | San Diego | 485 | 5.40 |
| 59 | Baton Rouge | 121 | 5.39 |
| 60 | Jacksonville | 306 | 5.32 |
| 61 | Spokane | 93 | 5.31 |
| 62 | Virginia Beach | 139 | 5.23 |
| 63 | Madison | 86 | 5.01 |
| 64 | Greensboro | 75 | 4.75 |
| 65 | Minneapolis | 176 | 4.72 |
| 66 | New Orleans | 261 | 4.56 |
| 67 | Salt Lake City | 75 | 4.43 |
| 68 | Indianapolis | 192 | 4.16 |
| 69 | Anchorage | 74 | 4.13 |
| 70 | Yonkers | 80 | 4.09 |
| 71 | Milwaukee | 262 | 4.08 |
| 72 | Richmond | 86 | 3.85 |
| 73 | Anaheim | 83 | 3.70 |
| 74 | Austin | 123 | 3.44 |
| 75 | Jersey City | 70 | 3.12 |
| 76 | Corpus Christi | 70 | 2.91 |
| 77 | Lincoln | 50 | 2.89 |
| 78 | Huntington Beach | 41 | 2.34 |

# 203. Arson Trends

Because arson is a new number recently introduced into the index crimes of the FBI's Uniform Crime Reports, the FBI is unwilling to report on trends or even to provide data on totals for each year.

However, since the data on the 100 largest cities are more complete than for most other cities, the comparisons in the table below have validity.

Between 1980 and 1981 arsons were up in 29 cities and down in 49 cities—an encouraging development. Arsons doubled in Richmond, from 43 to 86, and were up by over 50 percent in Aurora; Columbus, Ohio; and Lexington. In the other 25 cities showing increases, arsons rose by less than 50 percent.

SOURCE: U.S. Department of Justice, Federal Bureau of Investigation (FBI), *Crime in the U.S.—1981:* Federal Bureau of Investigation (Washington, D.C.: Government Printing Office, 1982).

| Rank | City | 1980 Arsons | 1981 Arsons | Absolute Change | Percentage Change |
|---|---|---|---|---|---|
| 1 | Richmond | 43 | 86 | 43 | 100.00 |
| 2 | Aurora | 50 | 91 | 41 | 82.00 |
| 3 | Rochester | 189* | 324 | 135 | 71.43 |
| 4 | Columbus, Ohio | 385 | 613 | 228 | 59.22 |
| 5 | Lexington-Fayette | 75 | 114 | 39 | 52.00 |
| 6 | Tacoma | 138 | 206 | 68 | 49.27 |
| 7 | Flint | 250 | 345 | 95 | 38.00 |
| 8 | Montgomery | 86 | 116 | 30 | 34.88 |
| 9 | Baton Rouge | 90 | 121 | 31 | 34.44 |
| 10 | Little Rock | 112 | 149 | 37 | 33.03 |
| 11 | New Orleans | 198 | 261 | 63 | 31.81 |
| 12 | Birmingham | 138 | 177 | 39 | 28.26 |
| 13 | Louisville | 156 | 198 | 42 | 26.92 |
| 14 | Cincinnati | 426 | 535 | 109 | 25.58 |
| 15 | Norfolk | 242 | 303 | 61 | 25.20 |
| 16 | Tampa | 177 | 213 | 36 | 20.33 |
| 17 | St. Petersburg | 134 | 160 | 26 | 19.40 |
| 18 | Washington, D.C. | 373 | 429 | 56 | 15.01 |
| 19 | Chicago | 1,916 | 2,179 | 263 | 13.72 |
| 20 | San Diego | 430 | 485 | 55 | 12.79 |
| 21 | Colorado Springs | 125 | 140 | 15 | 12.00 |
| 22 | Fresno | 125 | 137 | 12 | 9.60 |
| 23 | Tucson | 451 | 483 | 32 | 7.09 |
| 24 | Salt Lake City | 71 | 75 | 4 | 5.63 |
| 25 | Baltimore | 776 | 817 | 41 | 5.28 |
| 26 | Denver | 617 | 646 | 29 | 4.70 |
| 27 | Wichita | 207 | 215 | 8 | 3.86 |
| 28 | New York | 8,658 | 8,962 | 304 | 3.51 |
| 29 | St. Paul | 202 | 207 | 5 | 2.47 |
| 30 | Fort Wayne | 134 | 136 | 2 | 1.49 |
| 31 | Akron | 295 | 289 | − 6 | − 2.03 |
| 32 | Madison | 88 | 86 | − 2 | − 2.27 |
| 33 | Sacramento | 330 | 317 | − 13 | − 3.93 |
| 34 | Dallas | 957 | 917 | − 40 | − 4.17 |
| 35 | Dayton | 463 | 441 | − 22 | − 4.75 |
| 36 | Jackson | 127 | 120 | − 7 | − 5.51 |
| 37 | Toledo | 767 | 724 | − 43 | − 5.60 |
| 38 | Memphis | 822 | 769 | − 53 | − 6.44 |
| 39 | San Antonio | 578 | 539 | − 39 | − 6.74 |
| 40 | Seattle | 326 | 302 | − 24 | − 7.36 |
| 41 | Cleveland | 1,226 | 1,131 | − 95 | − 7.74 |
| 42 | Mobile | 167 | 153 | − 14 | − 8.38 |
| 43 | Los Angeles | 7,594 | 6,895 | −699 | − 9.20 |
| 44 | Santa Ana | 136 | 123 | − 13 | − 9.55 |
| 45 | Spokane | 103 | 93 | − 10 | − 9.70 |
| 46 | San Francisco | 478 | 430 | − 48 | − 10.04 |
| 47 | Las Vegas | 521 | 467 | − 54 | − 10.36 |
| 48 | Greensboro | 84 | 75 | − 9 | − 10.71 |
| 49 | San Jose | 1,612 | 1,422 | −190 | − 11.78 |
| 50 | Tulsa | 399 | 351 | − 48 | − 12.03 |
| 51 | Lubbock | 214 | 187 | − 27 | − 12.61 |
| 52 | Atlanta | 321 | 280 | − 41 | − 12.77 |
| 53 | Minneapolis | 203 | 176 | − 27 | − 13.30 |
| 54 | Anaheim | 96 | 83 | − 13 | − 13.54 |
| 55 | Jacksonville | 355 | 306 | − 49 | − 13.80 |
| 56 | Fort Worth | 383 | 330 | − 53 | − 13.83 |
| 57 | Grand Rapids | 178 | 153 | − 25 | − 14.04 |
| 58 | Virginia Beach | 162 | 139 | − 23 | − 14.19 |
| 59 | Long Beach | 264 | 220 | − 44 | − 16.66 |
| 60 | Austin | 149 | 123 | − 26 | − 17.44 |
| 61 | Des Moines | 246 | 200 | − 46 | − 18.69 |

| Rank | City | 1980 Arsons | 1981 Arsons | Absolute Change | Percentage Change |
|------|------|-------------|-------------|-----------------|-------------------|
| 62 | Huntington Beach | 51 | 41 | − 10 | − 19.60 |
| 63 | Riverside | 618 | 484 | −134 | − 21.68 |
| 64 | Shreveport | 187 | 145 | − 42 | − 22.45 |
| 65 | Jersey City | 92 | 70 | − 22 | − 23.91 |
| 66 | Providence | 400 | 301 | − 99 | − 24.75 |
| 67 | El Paso | 768 | 558 | −210 | − 27.34 |
| 68 | Milwaukee | 362 | 262 | −100 | − 27.62 |
| 69 | Kansas City, Mo. | 724 | 513 | −211 | − 29.14 |
| 70 | Corpus Christi | 112 | 70 | − 42 | − 37.50 |
| 71 | Arlington, Texas | 283 | 175 | −108 | − 38.16 |
| 72 | Miami | 446 | 274 | −172 | − 38.56 |
| 73 | Chattanooga | 184 | 113 | − 71 | − 38.58 |
| 74 | Indianapolis | 348 | 192 | −156 | − 44.82 |
| 74 | Yonkers | 145 | 80 | − 65 | − 44.82 |
| 76 | Kansas City, Kan. | 313 | 162 | −151 | − 48.24 |
| 77 | Anchorage | 170 | 74 | − 96 | − 56.47 |
| 78 | Lincoln | 129 | 50 | − 79 | − 61.24 |

*1979 data

# 204.  Arrests for Arson

While arrest data for arson are complete, many cities are excluded from the table below because they did not report (at least to the satisfaction of the Federal Bureau of Investigation) the number of arsons in 1981. We know, therefore, that Detroit had 289 arrests for arsons and Philadelphia had 253 arrests for arsons in 1981, but we cannot relate these to arson reports.

The median arrest rate for the 61 cities for which we have adequate data is 12 percent—Santa Ana's 15 arrests for 123 reported arsons in 1981.

Colorado Springs leads the list, with a 46 percent arrest rate. Two other cities have arrest rates above 30 percent—Jersey City and New Orleans. Seven cities have arrest rates for arson in 1981 of under 5 percent: Riverside, El Paso, Los Angeles, Dallas, San Jose, Toledo and New York.

SOURCES: Reported arsons for 1981 from U.S. Department of Justice, Federal Bureau of Investigation, *Crime in the U.S.—1981: Uniform Crime Reports* (Washington, D.C.: Government Printing Office, 1982). Arrests for arsons in 1981 from a special unpublished report provided at the authors' request by the Federal Bureau of Investigation, January 1983.

| Rank | City | Reports of Arsons | Arrests for Arsons | Percentage of Arrests per Arsons Reported |
|------|------|-------------------|--------------------|-------------------------------------------|
| 1 | Colorado Springs | 140 | 65 | 46.43 |
| 2 | Jersey City | 70 | 29 | 41.43 |
| 3 | New Orleans | 261 | 84 | 32.18 |
| 4 | Aurora | 91 | 26 | 28.57 |
| 5 | Huntington Beach | 41 | 11 | 26.83 |
| 6 | Richmond | 86 | 23 | 26.74 |
| 7 | Milwaukee | 262 | 69 | 26.34 |
| 8 | Rochester | 324 | 85 | 26.23 |
| 9 | Louisville | 198 | 50 | 25.25 |
| 10 | Baton Rouge | 121 | 28 | 23.14 |
| 11 | Chattanooga | 113 | 25 | 22.12 |
| 12 | Montgomery | 116 | 25 | 21.55 |
| 13 | Greensboro | 75 | 16 | 21.33 |
| 14 | Fresno | 137 | 29 | 21.17 |
| 15 | Minneapolis | 176 | 36 | 20.45 |
| 16 | Salt Lake City | 75 | 15 | 20.00 |
| 17 | Little Rock | 149 | 29 | 19.46 |
| 18 | Corpus Christi | 70 | 13 | 18.57 |
| 19 | Anaheim | 83 | 15 | 18.07 |
| 20 | Fort Worth | 330 | 55 | 16.67 |
| 21 | Jacksonville | 306 | 51 | 16.67 |
| 22 | Norfolk | 303 | 50 | 16.50 |
| 23 | Virginia Beach | 139 | 22 | 15.83 |
| 24 | San Diego | 485 | 73 | 15.05 |
| 25 | Sacramento | 317 | 46 | 14.51 |
| 26 | San Francisco | 430 | 62 | 14.42 |
| 27 | Chicago | 2,179 | 296 | 13.58 |
| 28 | Tampa | 213 | 28 | 13.15 |
| 29 | Flint | 345 | 44 | 12.75 |
| 30 | Wichita | 215 | 27 | 12.56 |

| Rank | City | Reports of Arsons | Arrests for Arsons | Percentage of Arrests per Arsons Reported |
|------|------|------|------|------|
| 31 | St. Petersburg | 160 | 20 | 12.50 |
| 32 | Santa Ana | 123 | 15 | 12.20 |
| 33 | Las Vegas | 467 | 55 | 11.78 |
| 34 | Grand Rapids | 153 | 18 | 11.76 |
| 35 | Kansas City, Mo. | 513 | 58 | 11.31 |
| 36 | Lubbock | 187 | 21 | 11.23 |
| 37 | Mobile | 153 | 17 | 11.11 |
| 38 | Shreveport | 145 | 16 | 11.03 |
| 39 | Birmingham | 177 | 19 | 10.73 |
| 40 | Washington, D.C. | 429 | 43 | 10.02 |
| 41 | San Antonio | 539 | 52 | 9.65 |
| 42 | Long Beach | 220 | 21 | 9.55 |
| 43 | Baltimore | 817 | 77 | 9.42 |
| 44 | Atlanta | 280 | 26 | 9.29 |
| 45 | Tulsa | 351 | 30 | 8.55 |
| 46 | Providence | 301 | 23 | 7.64 |

| Rank | City | Reports of Arsons | Arrests for Arsons | Percentage of Arrests per Arsons Reported |
|------|------|------|------|------|
| 47 | Miami | 274 | 20 | 7.30 |
| 48 | Kansas City, Kan. | 162 | 11 | 6.79 |
| 49 | Anchorage | 74 | 5 | 6.76 |
| 50 | Dayton | 441 | 28 | 6.35 |
| 51 | Fort Wayne | 136 | 8 | 5.88 |
| 52 | Jackson | 120 | 7 | 5.83 |
| 53 | Indianapolis | 192 | 11 | 5.73 |
| 54 | Lexington-Fayette | 114 | 6 | 5.26 |
| 55 | New York | 8,962 | 439 | 4.90 |
| 56 | Toledo | 724 | 35 | 4.83 |
| 57 | San Jose | 1,422 | 64 | 4.50 |
| 58 | Dallas | 917 | 39 | 4.25 |
| 59 | Los Angeles | 6,895 | 235 | 3.41 |
| 60 | El Paso | 558 | 10 | 1.79 |
| 61 | Riverside | 484 | 7 | 1.45 |

# 205.  Fire Losses

The table below shows the losses from all fires in 1981 (or 1980 in the cases where cities are starred, and 1979 if double-starred) ranked by loss per capita. Little Rock had the highest loss rate of the 82 cities for which we have data, $53 per person. New York City and Chicago are conspicuously absent from the table—they do not provide fire loss information.

At the low end of the scale is Omaha, with under $2 fire loss per person. Whether or not this reflects the influence of the insurance industry based in the city, Omaha is well below the next contenders, El Paso and Indianapolis, for both of which we unfortunately have no more recent data than 1979.

SOURCE: Federal Emergency Management Agency, *Statistical Abstract of Fire Experience for Large Cities* (Washington, D.C.: FEMA, November 1982).

| Rank | City | Total Losses (000) | Loss Per Capita ( $ ) |
|------|------|------|------|
| 1 | Little Rock* | 8,453 | 53.34 |
| 2 | Yonkers | 9,806 | 50.20 |
| 3 | Las Vegas** | 7,822 | 47.50 |
| 4 | Atlanta | 19,487 | 45.85 |
| 5 | Birmingham | 12,930 | 45.46 |
| 6 | Buffalo | 15,967 | 44.62 |
| 7 | Oakland | 15,120 | 44.56 |

| Rank | City | Total Losses (000) | Loss Per Capita ( $ ) |
|------|------|------|------|
| 8 | Akron | 10,552 | 44.49 |
| 9 | Oklahoma City | 16,804 | 40.96 |
| 10 | Boston | 20,569 | 36.54 |
| 11 | Fort Worth* | 13,759 | 35.72 |
| 12 | Baton Rouge | 7,737 | 35.25 |
| 13 | Shreveport | 7,164 | 34.81 |
| 14 | Tulsa | 12,393 | 34.34 |
| 15 | Santa Ana | 6,920 | 33.97 |
| 15 | Syracuse | 5,778 | 33.97 |
| 17 | Houston | 53,942 | 33.82 |
| 18 | Anchorage | 5,584 | 32.01 |
| 19 | Spokane | 5,283 | 30.84 |
| 20 | Sacramento | 8,475 | 30.74 |
| 21 | Miami | 10,599 | 30.64 |
| 22 | Minneapolis | 11,331 | 30.55 |
| 23 | Fresno | 6,421 | 20.43 |
| 24 | Kansas City, Mo. | 13,135 | 29.31 |
| 25 | Los Angeles | 86,524 | 29.16 |
| 26 | San Francisco | 19,252 | 28.35 |
| 27 | Detroit | 33,937 | 28.20 |
| 28 | Toledo | 9,901 | 27.92 |
| 29 | Tampa | 7,352 | 27.08 |
| 30 | Portland | 9,754 | 26.62 |
| 31 | Cleveland | 15,236 | 26.55 |
| 32 | Memphis | 16,877 | 26.11 |
| 33 | New Orleans | 14,046 | 25.20 |
| 34 | Jackson | 5,068 | 24.98 |
| 35 | Lexington-Fayette | 4,900 | 24.00 |
| 36 | Charlotte | 7,516 | 23.90 |
| 37 | San Jose | 14,633 | 23.25 |
| 38 | Columbus, Ga. | 3,917 | 23.12 |
| 39 | Tucson | 7,360 | 22.27 |
| 41 | Des Moines | 3,857 | 20.19 |
| 41 | Dayton* | 4,064 | 19.98 |

| Rank | City | Total Losses (000) | Loss Per Capita ($) |
|------|------|-------------------:|--------------------:|
| 42 | Flint | 3,178 | 19.91 |
| 43 | Kansas City, Kan. | 3,121 | 19.37 |
| 44 | San Diego | 16,929 | 19.34 |
| 45 | Knoxville | 3,460 | 18.89 |
| 46 | Worcester | 2,997 | 18.52 |
| 47 | Wichita | 5,117 | 18.32 |
| 48 | Grand Rapids | 3,329 | 18.31 |
| 49 | Warren | 2,916 | 18.10 |
| 50 | Madison | 3,055 | 17.91 |
| 51 | Greensboro | 2,779 | 17.86 |
| 52 | St. Paul | 4,720 | 17.47 |
| 53 | Milwaukee | 10,522 | 16.54 |
| 54 | Columbus, Ohio | 9,256 | 16.39 |
| 55 | Albuquerque | 5,416 | 16.32 |
| 56 | Washington, D.C. | 10,096 | 15.83 |
| 57 | Virginia Beach | 4,118 | 15.71 |
| 58 | Seattle | 7,719 | 15.63 |
| 59 | Montgomery | 2,713 | 15.25 |
| 60 | Austin | 5,277 | 15.10 |
| 61 | Cincinnati | 5,802 | 15.05 |
| 62 | Jacksonville* | 8,067 | 14.91 |

| Rank | City | Total Losses (000) | Loss Per Capita ($) |
|------|------|-------------------:|--------------------:|
| 63 | Baltimore* | 11,620 | 14.77 |
| 64 | Norfolk | 3,569 | 13.37 |
| 65 | Richmond | 2,880 | 13.14 |
| 66 | Anaheim | 2,874 | 13.10 |
| 67 | St. Petersburg | 3,068 | 12.86 |
| 68 | Fort Wayne | 2,210 | 12.83 |
| 69 | Colorado Springs | 2,684 | 12.48 |
| 70 | San Antonio | 9,436 | 12.01 |
| 71 | Mobile* | 2,373 | 11.84 |
| 72 | Riverside | 1,820 | 10.65 |
| 73 | Aurora | 1,519 | 9.58 |
| 74 | Lubbock | 1,655 | 9.51 |
| 75 | Corpus Christi** | 2,144 | 9.24 |
| 76 | Lincoln | 1,558 | 9.06 |
| 77 | Huntington Beach | 1,521 | 8.92 |
| 78 | Denver | 4,171 | 8.47 |
| 79 | Salt Lake City | 1,242 | 7.62 |
| 80 | Indianapolis** | 3,835 | 5.47 |
| 81 | El Paso** | 1,469 | 3.45 |
| 82 | Omaha | 536 | 1.71 |

# 206.  Fire Deaths

As with so many measures of the services of municipal employees, fire deaths show only one aspect of the results of fire fighting efforts. The true worth of firefighters is best measured in lives saved, but this information is difficult to obtain. A common denominator is another measure, response time, which is computed in a few cities but is not yet centrally collected. For example, the median time it took to dispatch fire fighters in New York City's five boroughs was 49 seconds in 1982. The median time it took fire fighters to arrive on the scene was 4 minutes 59 seconds, ranging from averages of 4 minutes 14 seconds in Brooklyn to 5 minutes 18 seconds in Staten Island.

The highest fire death rates in 1981, more than 10 for every 100,000 residents, were in Albuquerque, Jersey City, Montgomery and Birmingham. The larger cities such as New York, Chicago and Los Angeles have a better record than these 4. Chicago's fire death rate of 5.7 per 100,000 is less than half the death rate of these 4. New York's rate of under 3.5 deaths per 100,000 population and Los Angeles's rate of under 2.5 are even better.

Many fire deaths occur in the northern cities in the cold weather. Many of their victims are the poor, who rely on unsafe heating methods. Cities with high death

rates may have suffered major single fire disasters, usually hotels or motels, such as the MGM fire in Las Vegas.

Seven cities had no fire deaths at all in 1981: Aurora, Colorado Springs, Fresno, Honolulu, Las Vegas, Lincoln and Mobile.

SOURCES: National Emergency Management Agency, *Statistical Abstract of Fire Experience for Large Cities* (November 1982). New York City data from *The Mayor's Management Report: Preliminary, January 31, 1983* (New York: Citibooks, 1983), p. 90.

| Rank | City | Number of Deaths from Fires | Deaths per 100,000 Population |
|------|------|----------------------------:|------------------------------:|
| 1 | Albuquerque | 46 | 13.87 |
| 2 | Jersey City | 30 | 13.42 |
| 3 | Montgomery | 22 | 12.37 |
| 4 | Birmingham | 34 | 11.95 |
| 5 | Richmond | 20 | 9.12 |
| 6 | Kansas City, Mo. | 37 | 8.26 |
| 7 | Newark | 26 | 7.90 |
| 8 | Syracuse | 13 | 7.64 |
| 9 | Atlanta | 31 | 7.29 |
| 10 | Cleveland | 40 | 6.97 |
| 11 | Greensboro | 10 | 6.43 |

| Rank | City | Number of Deaths from Fires | Deaths per 100,000 Population | Rank | City | Number of Deaths from Fires | Deaths per 100,000 Population |
|------|------|------|------|------|------|------|------|
| 12 | Worcester | 10 | 6.18 | 55 | Buffalo | 10 | 2.79 |
| 13 | Dayton | 12 | 5.90 | 56 | Grand Rapids | 5 | 2.75 |
| 14 | Rochester | 14 | 5.79 | 57 | Baton Rouge | 6 | 2.73 |
| 15 | Fort Worth | 22 | 5.71 | 58 | Houston | 43 | 2.70 |
| 16 | Chicago | 170 | 5.66 | 59 | Omaha | 8 | 2.55 |
| 17 | Tampa | 15 | 5.52 | 59 | Providence | 4 | 2.55 |
| 18 | St. Louis | 24 | 5.30 | 61 | Little Rock | 4 | 2.52 |
| 19 | Boston | 28 | 4.97 | 62 | Los Angeles | 73 | 2.46 |
| 20 | Jackson | 10 | 4.93 | 63 | Tucson | 8 | 2.42 |
| 21 | Detroit | 59 | 4.90 | 64 | Indianapolis | 16 | 2.28 |
| 22 | Louisville | 14 | 4.69 | 65 | Sacramento | 6 | 2.18 |
| 23 | Oklahoma City | 19 | 4.63 | 66 | San Antonio | 17 | 2.16 |
| 24 | Philadelphia | 78 | 4.62 | 67 | Akron | 5 | 2.11 |
| 25 | Washington, D.C. | 29 | 4.55 | 68 | Lexington-Fayette | 4 | 1.96 |
| 26 | Toledo | 16 | 4.51 | 69 | Kansas City, Ks. | 3 | 1.86 |
| 27 | New Orleans | 25 | 4.48 | 69 | Warren | 3 | 1.86 |
| 28 | St. Petersburg | 10 | 4.19 | 71 | Anaheim | 4 | 1.82 |
| 29 | Tulsa | 15 | 4.16 | 72 | San Jose | 11 | 1.75 |
| 30 | Cincinnati | 16 | 4.15 | 72 | Spokane | 3 | 1.75 |
| 31 | Chattanooga | 7 | 4.13 | 74 | Fort Wayne | 3 | 1.74 |
| 31 | Oakland | 14 | 4.13 | 75 | Jacksonville | 9 | 1.66 |
| 33 | San Francisco | 28 | 4.12 | 76 | Des Moines | 3 | 1.57 |
| 34 | Norfolk | 11 | 4.12 | 77 | Nashville-Davidson | 7 | 1.54 |
| 35 | Portland, Ore. | 15 | 4.09 | 78 | Santa Ana | 3 | 1.47 |
| 36 | Miami | 14 | 4.05 | 79 | Minneapolis | 5 | 1.35 |
| 37 | Flint | 6 | 3.76 | 80 | Corpus Christi | 3 | 1.29 |
| 38 | Baltimore | 29 | 3.69 | 81 | Salt Lake City | 2 | 1.23 |
| 39 | Wichita | 10 | 3.58 | 82 | Madison | 2 | 1.17 |
| 39 | Yonkers | 7 | 3.58 | 83 | St. Paul | 3 | 1.11 |
| 41 | Charlotte | 11 | 3.50 | 84 | El Paso | 4 | 0.94 |
| 42 | New York | 246 | 3.48 | 85 | Austin | 3 | 0.86 |
| 43 | Lubbock | 6 | 3.45 | 86 | San Diego | 7 | 0.80 |
| 44 | Anchorage | 6 | 3.44 | 87 | Huntington Beach | 1 | 0.59 |
| 44 | Seattle | 17 | 3.44 | 88 | Knoxville | 1 | 0.55 |
| 46 | Dallas | 31 | 3.43 | 89 | Virginia Beach | 1 | 0.38 |
| 47 | Denver | 16 | 3.25 | 90 | Aurora | 0 | 0.00 |
| 48 | Memphis | 20 | 3.09 | 90 | Colorado Springs | 0 | 0.00 |
| 49 | Pittsburgh | 13 | 3.07 | 90 | Fresno | 0 | 0.00 |
| 50 | Columbus, Ga. | 5 | 2.95 | 90 | Honolulu | 0 | 0.00 |
| 51 | Riverside | 5 | 2.93 | 90 | Las Vegas | 0 | 0.00 |
| 52 | Shreveport | 6 | 2.92 | 90 | Lincoln | 0 | 0.00 |
| 53 | Columbus, Oh. | 16 | 2.83 | 90 | Mobile | 0 | 0.00 |
| 53 | Milwaukee | 18 | 2.83 | | | | |

# 207. Fire Personnel

Fire personnel per 100,000 population is an important measure of safety for several reasons. First is the prevention and suppression of fires, which in many cases represents about 50 percent or more of fire department expenses. Just as important are emergency medical services provided by fire personnel. Tacoma, for example, allocated more than 70 percent of its budget in 1980 to fire prevention, fire suppression and emergency medical services.

One reason for the low personnel/population ratios

is that civilianization of fire departments in administrative areas reduces costs and allows for reduction in uniformed personnel while maintaining services.

The three cities with the highest number of fire personnel (uniformed and civilian) in 1981 relative to population were all in New York State: Buffalo, Syracuse and Rochester. Of the larger cities, Houston and New York were near the middle of the rankings, with 177 and 176, respectively. Los Angeles showed 106 per 100,000.

SOURCE: International City Management Association, *The Municipal Year Book* (Washington, D.C.: ICMA, 1981), pp. 94–99.

| Rank | City | Total Fire Personnel | Fire Personnel Per 100,000 Population |
|---|---|---|---|
| 1 | Buffalo | 1,057 | 295.36 |
| 2 | Syracuse | 493 | 289.82 |
| 3 | Rochester | 670 | 277.16 |
| 4 | Honolulu | 971 | 265.99 |
| 5 | Kansas City, Kan. | 425 | 263.83 |
| 6 | Richmond | 577 | 263.21 |
| 7 | Baltimore | 2,005 | 254.84 |
| 8 | Pittsburgh | 1,077 | 254.05 |
| 9 | Dayton | 478 | 234.79 |
| 10 | Tampa | 621 | 228.71 |
| 11 | Baton Rouge | 488 | 222.34 |
| 12 | Tacoma | 351 | 221.45 |
| 13 | Cincinnati | 846 | 219.48 |
| 14 | Nashville-Davidson | 983 | 215.74 |
| 15 | Mobile | 428 | 213.52 |
| 16 | Kansas City, Mo. | 945 | 210.86 |
| 17 | Charlotte | 652 | 207.35 |
| 18 | Jackson | 409 | 201.58 |
| 19 | Montgomery | 355 | 199.26 |
| 20 | Seattle | 974 | 197.23 |
| 21 | Little Rock | 309 | 195.00 |
| 22 | Lexington-Fayette | 398 | 194.94 |
| 23 | Las Vegas | 320 | 194.32 |
| 24 | Miami | 671 | 193.41 |
| 25 | Shreveport | 393 | 190.95 |
| 26 | St. Paul | 513 | 189.84 |
| 27 | Greensboro | 292 | 187.61 |
| 28 | Oklahoma City | 741 | 183.77 |
| 29 | Flint | 293 | 183.57 |
| 30 | New Orleans | 1,018 | 182.61 |
| 31 | Omaha | 559 | 179.35 |
| 32 | Spokane | 306 | 178.63 |
| 33 | Houston | 2,830 | 177.53 |
| 34 | Portland, Ore. | 647 | 176.59 |
| 35 | Milwaukee | 1,121 | 176.20 |
| 36 | New York | 12,446 | 176.01 |
| 37 | Akron | 411 | 173.29 |
| 38 | Dallas | 1,566 | 173.22 |
| 39 | Madison | 290 | 169.97 |
| 40 | Sacramento | 459 | 166.46 |
| 41 | Norfolk | 441 | 165.18 |
| 42 | Toledo | 585 | 164.96 |
| 43 | Philadelphia | 2,767 | 163.90 |
| 44 | Des Moines | 313 | 163.87 |
| 45 | Fort Worth | 624 | 162.02 |
| 46 | Atlanta | 664 | 156.23 |
| 47 | Columbus, Ohio | 867 | 153.49 |
| 48 | Lubbock | 266 | 152.89 |
| 49 | Detroit | 1,803 | 149.83 |
| 50 | Grand Rapids | 271 | 149.03 |
| 51 | Wichita | 406 | 145.38 |
| 52 | Fresno | 317 | 145.28 |
| 53 | Minneapolis | 538 | 145.03 |
| 54 | Lincoln | 245 | 142.50 |
| 55 | Aurora | 225 | 141.88 |
| 56 | Jacksonville | 764 | 141.25 |
| 57 | Anchorage | 240 | 138.71 |
| 58 | Tucson | 430 | 130.09 |
| 59 | Long Beach | 466 | 128.97 |
| 60 | St. Petersburg | 302 | 127.48 |
| 61 | Colorado Springs | 268 | 124.56 |
| 62 | Riverside | 194 | 113.53 |
| 63 | Santa Ana | 224 | 109.96 |
| 64 | Phoenix | 850 | 107.64 |
| 65 | Los Angeles | 3,138 | 105.77 |
| 66 | San Antonio | 817 | 104.02 |
| 67 | Anaheim | 221 | 99.62 |
| 68 | San Jose | 629 | 98.81 |
| 69 | Huntington Beach | 160 | 93.84 |
| 70 | Virginia Beach | 227 | 86.58 |

# 208. Fire Department Expenditures

Fire department expenditures per resident reflect directly on health and safety and may also relate to arson crimes. For example, Montgomery's 35 percent increase in arson may be related to its low fire department expenditure of about $30 per resident shown in the table below. The lowest fire expenditure was in Virginia Beach, about $19 per resident. The highest expenditure per resident in 1980 was $94 in Syracuse, followed by $90 in Baltimore and Worcester.

Fire department expenditures are not simply for the maintenance of fire trucks. They also include money for enforcement of fire codes and investigation of fires. In some cities, arson is investigated by the fire department rather than the police department; there is some evidence that fire departments have had better luck with this kind of work.

SOURCES: International City Management Association, *The Municipal Year Book; 1981* (Washington, D.C.: ICMA, 1981), pp. 94–99. 1981 New York City data from "The Mayor's Management Report," January 30, 1982.

| Rank | City | Total Fire Expenditure ($ 000) | Fire Expenditure Per Resident ($) |
|------|------|-------------------------------|-----------------------------------|
| 1 | Syracuse | 16,000 | 94.06 |
| 2 | Worcester | 14,522 | 89.75 |
| 3 | Baltimore | 70,599 | 89.73 |
| 4 | Anchorage | 15,294 | 88.40 |
| 5 | Rochester | 21,045 | 87.06 |
| 6 | Buffalo | 29,634 | 82.81 |
| 7 | Portland, Ore. | 29,170 | 79.62 |
| 8 | Tampa | 19,656 | 72.39 |
| 9 | New Orleans | 38,917 | 69.81 |
| 10 | Miami | 23,520 | 67.79 |
| 11 | Detroit | 78,654 | 65.36 |
| 12 | Flint | 10,424 | 65.31 |
| 13 | Richmond | 13,640 | 62.22 |
| 14 | Seattle | 30,710 | 62.19 |
| 15 | Cincinnati | 23,374 | 60.64 |
| 16 | Tacoma | 9,610 | 60.63 |
| 17 | Dayton | 12,324 | 60.53 |
| 18 | St. Paul | 16,057 | 59.42 |
| 19 | Long Beach | 21,336 | 59.05 |
| 20 | Kansas City, Mo. | 26,317 | 58.72 |
| 21 | Honolulu | 21,421 | 58.68 |
| 22 | Kansas City, Kan. | 9,443 | 57.89 |
| 23 | Madison | 9,877 | 57.89 |
| 24 | Pittsburgh | 23,310 | 54.98 |
| 25 | Las Vegas | 8,619 | 52.34 |
| 26 | New York | 368,005 | 52.04 |
| 27 | Los Angeles | 145,056 | 49.08 |
| 28 | Anaheim | 1,640 | 47.96 |
| 29 | Sacramento | 13,152 | 47.70 |
| 30 | Baton Rouge | 10,335 | 47.08 |
| 31 | Philadelphia | 79,201 | 46.91 |
| 32 | Fresno | 10,169 | 46.60 |
| 33 | Minneapolis | 17,126 | 46.17 |
| 34 | Atlanta | 10,608 | 46.13 |
| 35 | Milwaukee | 29,341 | 46.12 |
| 36 | Mobile | 9,211 | 45.95 |
| 37 | Houston | 72,981 | 45.78 |
| 38 | Grand Rapids | 8,304 | 45.67 |
| 39 | Omaha | 14,044 | 45.06 |
| 40 | Lexington-Fayette | 9,132 | 44.73 |
| 41 | Spokane | 7,640 | 44.60 |
| 42 | Jackson | 8,629 | 42.53 |
| 43 | Dallas | 37,972 | 42.00 |
| 44 | Columbus, Ohio | 23,449 | 41.51 |
| 45 | Aurora | 6,501 | 40.99 |
| 46 | Santa Ana | 8,111 | 39.82 |
| 47 | Shreveport | 8,093 | 39.32 |
| 48 | Toledo | 13,363 | 37.68 |
| 49 | Greensboro | 5,818 | 37.38 |
| 50 | Des Moines | 7,130 | 37.33 |
| 51 | Akron | 8,833 | 37.24 |
| 52 | Charlotte | 11,589 | 36.86 |
| 53 | Tucson | 11,939 | 36.12 |
| 54 | Fort Worth | 13,423 | 34.85 |
| 55 | Jacksonville | 18,734 | 34.63 |
| 56 | Nashville | 15,735 | 34.53 |
| 57 | Lubbock | 5,969 | 34.31 |
| 58 | Riverside | 5,810 | 34.00 |
| 59 | Oklahoma City | 13,536 | 33.57 |
| 60 | Wichita | 9,347 | 33.47 |
| 61 | Norfolk | 8,689 | 32.55 |
| 62 | Huntington Beach | 5,458 | 32.01 |
| 63 | Little Rock | 4,982 | 31.44 |
| 64 | Lincoln | 5,401 | 31.41 |
| 65 | Phoenix | 24,125 | 30.55 |
| 66 | San Jose | 19,182 | 30.13 |
| 67 | Montgomery | 5,295 | 29.72 |
| 68 | St. Petersburg | 7,027 | 29.66 |
| 69 | Colorado Springs | 6,323 | 29.39 |
| 70 | San Antonio | 18,483 | 23.53 |
| 71 | Virginia Beach | 4,857 | 18.52 |

# 209. Fires Per Fire Employee

A good general indicator of the workload of a fire fighter is the number of fires in a year relative to people available to fight them. Since definitions of active fire fighters differ among cities, we include all fire department employees in the fire fighter figure.

In 1981, the heaviest workload was in Sacramento, where 459 fire employees faced 6,189 fires. That works out at 13 fires per fire employee or roughly one fire every month. Since fire fighters work in crews of four or five, and several crews are sent to a fire, a fire employee in Sacramento could be expected to be called to a fire about twice a week.

At the other end of the spectrum, Salt Lake City had 386 fire employees, not many fewer than Sacramento, and one-tenth the number of fires, 693—an average of under 2 fires per employee for the year. In Salt Lake City a fire employee would expect to be called to a fire two or three times a month. The above average figures apply only to structural fires. Fire employees respond to other kinds of requests—for example, vehicular fires, prevention calls, and false alarms.

SOURCE: Fire employees from International City Management Association, *The Municipal Year Book: 1982* (Washington, D.C.: IMCA, 1982), pp. 94–99. Fires from Federal Emergency Management Agency, *Statistical Abstract of Fire Experience for Large Cities* (November 1982).

| Rank | City | Total Fire Personnel | Total Fires | Fires Per Fire Employees | Rank | City | Total Fire Personnel | Total Fires | Fires Per Fire Employees |
|---|---|---|---|---|---|---|---|---|---|
| 1 | Sacramento | 459 | 6,189 | 13.48 | 40 | Fort Wayne | 266 | 1,803 | 6.78 |
| 2 | Virginia Beach | 260 | 3,167 | 12.18 | 41 | Riverside | 194 | 1,294 | 6.67 |
| 3 | Jersey City | 682 | 7,874 | 11.55 | 42 | Dallas | 1,538 | 10,240 | 6.66 |
| 4 | Anaheim | 214 | 2,391 | 11.17 | 43 | Des Moines | 310 | 2,029 | 6.55 |
| 5 | Worcester | 496 | 5,516 | 11.12 | 44 | Huntington Beach | 160 | 1,014 | 6.34 |
| 6 | Lexington-Fayette | 394 | 4,363 | 11.07 | 45 | Buffalo | 1,044 | 6,603 | 6.32 |
| 7 | Detroit | 1,737 | 18,051 | 10.39 | 46 | Santa Ana | 244 | 1,528 | 6.26 |
| 8 | Fort Worth | 670 | 6,738 | 10.06 | 47 | New Orleans | 952 | 5,918 | 6.21 |
| 9 | Cleveland | 856 | 8,546 | 9.98 | 48 | Norfolk | 442 | 2,726 | 6.17 |
| 10 | New York | 12,446 | 122,261 | 9.82 | 49 | Baltimore | 1,929 | 11,818 | 6.13 |
| 11 | San Diego | 728 | 7,125 | 9.79 | 50 | Omaha | 547 | 3,276 | 5.99 |
| 12 | Chattanooga | 455 | 4,448 | 9.78 | 51 | Wichita | 391 | 2,328 | 5.95 |
| 13 | Lubbock | 278 | 2,676 | 9.63 | 52 | Nashville-Davidson | 961 | 5,645 | 5.87 |
| 14 | Indianapolis | 881 | 8,311 | 9.43 | 53 | Grand Rapids | 271 | 1,561 | 5.76 |
| 15 | Jacksonville | 758 | 7,105 | 9.37 | 54 | Dayton | 452 | 2,569 | 5.68 |
| 16 | Kansas City, Mo. | 899 | 8,305 | 9.24 | 55 | Charlotte | 648 | 3,627 | 5.60 |
| 17 | Oklahoma City | 756 | 6,962 | 9.21 | 56 | Akron | 387 | 2,114 | 5.46 |
| 18 | Las Vegas | 332 | 3.019 | 9.09 | 56 | Anchorage | 240 | 1,311 | 5.46 |
| 19 | Atlanta | 664 | 6,020 | 9.07 | 58 | Spokane | 309 | 1,617 | 5.23 |
| 19 | Fresno | 317 | 2,873 | 9.07 | 59 | Knoxville | 416 | 2,094 | 5.03 |
| 21 | San Antonio | 1,059 | 9,538 | 9.01 | 60 | St. Paul | 473 | 2,354 | 4.98 |
| 22 | Tucson | 435 | 3,895 | 8.95 | 61 | Richmond | 577 | 2,846 | 4.93 |
| 23 | Jackson | 448 | 3,965 | 8.85 | 62 | Greensboro | 298 | 1,447 | 4.86 |
| 24 | Philadelphia | 2,909 | 25,324 | 8.71 | 63 | Milwaukee | 1,121 | 5,429 | 4.84 |
| 25 | Mobile | 409 | 3,560 | 8.70 | 63 | Portland, Ore. | 657 | 3,180 | 4.84 |
| 26 | Los Angeles | 3,370 | 29,296 | 8.69 | 65 | Houston | 3,041 | 14,344 | 4.72 |
| 27 | Oakland | 533 | 4,595 | 8.62 | 66 | Flint | 293 | 1,356 | 4.63 |
| 28 | Little Rock | 298 | 2,492 | 8.36 | 67 | Cincinnati | 880 | 4,025 | 4.57 |
| 29 | Toledo | 493 | 4,012 | 8.14 | 68 | Syracuse | 493 | 2,230 | 4.52 |
| 30 | Denver | 933 | 6,941 | 7.44 | 69 | Montgomery | 344 | 1,531 | 4.45 |
| 31 | Kansas City, Kan. | 407 | 3,015 | 7.41 | 70 | Rochester | 670 | 2,967 | 4.43 |
| 32 | Shreveport | 388 | 2,871 | 7.40 | 71 | Aurora | 230 | 996 | 4.33 |
| 33 | Colorado Springs | 281 | 2,041 | 7.26 | 72 | Seattle | 976 | 3,952 | 4.05 |
| 34 | Pittsburgh | 1,077 | 7,738 | 7.18 | 73 | Lincoln | 238 | 937 | 3.94 |
| 35 | Louisville | 617 | 4,372 | 7.09 | 74 | Madison | 271 | 891 | 3.29 |
| 36 | Tampa | 547 | 3,865 | 7.07 | 75 | Baton Rouge | 511 | 1,499 | 2.93 |
| 37 | St. Petersburg | 293 | 2,031 | 6.93 | 76 | Miami | 676 | 1,773 | 2.62 |
| 38 | Columbus, Ohio | 860 | 5,919 | 6.88 | 77 | Salt Lake City | 386 | 693 | 1.80 |
| 39 | Minneapolis | 539 | 3,698 | 6.86 | | | | | |

# 210. Fires

The arson information collected by the FBI is one source of information on fires. The number of fires is another. Where the number of fires relative to population is very high, one might draw the conclusion either that the city properties are fire-prone or that arson rates are very high.

In the table below showing 1981 fires per 1,000 residents (except for six cities for which the data on fires are for 1980—Worcester, Detroit, Louisville, Nashville, Oklahoma City, Albuquerque—and one city, Las Vegas, for which the figures are for 1979) three New England and two New Jersey cities rank among the top six. Only Chattanooga had over 22 fires per 1,000 residents.

Jersey City is in first place with 35 fires per 1,000

residents. This could reflect one of three possibilities: (1) many properties in the city are old and vulnerable to electrical hazards; (2) industries in the city have a high propensity to develop fires; or (3) arsonists have been at work.

At the low end of the spectrum, are several satellite cities like Huntington Beach, Aurora and Warren; cities in relatively sparsely populated regions like Salt Lake City, Madison and Lincoln; and Miami. The low rate of fires in Miami may have to do with the relative lack of need for heating fuels. But given the city's high rate of violent crime, it seems an anomaly that fire rates are so low.

SOURCE: Federal Emergency Management Agency, *Statistical Abstract of Fire Experience in Large Cities*, November 1982.

| Rank | City | Total Fires | Fires per 1,000 Population |
|------|------|-------------|---------------------------|
| 1 | Jersey City | 7,874 | 35.23 |
| 2 | Worcester | 5,516 | 34.09 |
| 3 | Providence | 5,272 | 33.62 |
| 4 | Boston | 15,190 | 26.98 |
| 5 | Chattanooga | 4,448 | 26.23 |
| 6 | Newark | 7,566 | 22.98 |
| 7 | Sacramento | 6,189 | 22.44 |
| 8 | Yonkers | 4,264 | 21.83 |
| 9 | Memphis | 13,962 | 21.60 |
| 10 | St. Louis | 9,778 | 21.58 |
| 11 | Lexington-Fayette | 4,363 | 21.37 |
| 12 | Jackson | 3,965 | 19.54 |
| 13 | Kansas City, Kan. | 3,015 | 18.72 |
| 14 | Kansas City, Mo. | 8,305 | 18.53 |
| 15 | Buffalo | 6,603 | 18.45 |
| 16 | Las Vegas | 3,019 | 18.33 |
| 17 | Pittsburgh | 7,739 | 18.26 |
| 18 | Mobile | 3,560 | 17.76 |
| 19 | Fort Worth | 6,738 | 17.49 |
| 20 | New York | 122,261 | 17.29 |
| 21 | Oklahoma City | 6,962 | 16.97 |
| 22 | Chicago | 50,238 | 16.72 |
| 23 | Little Rock | 2,492 | 15.73 |
| 24 | Lubbock | 2,676 | 15.38 |
| 25 | Albuquerque | 5,043 | 15.20 |
| 26 | Baltimore | 11,818 | 15.02 |
| 27 | Washington, D.C. | 9,571 | 15.01 |
| 28 | Detroit | 18,051 | 15.00 |
| 28 | Philadelphia | 25,324 | 15.00 |
| 30 | Cleveland | 8,546 | 14.89 |
| 31 | Birmingham | 4,190 | 14.73 |
| 32 | Louisville | 4,372 | 14.65 |
| 33 | Tampa | 3,865 | 14.23 |
| 34 | Atlanta | 6,020 | 14.16 |
| 35 | Denver | 6,941 | 14.10 |
| 36 | Shreveport | 2,871 | 13.95 |
| 37 | Oakland | 4,595 | 13.54 |
| 38 | Fresno | 2,873 | 13.17 |
| 39 | Jacksonville | 7,105 | 13.14 |
| 40 | Syracuse | 2,230 | 13.11 |
| 41 | Richmond | 2,846 | 12.98 |
| 42 | Dayton | 2,569 | 12.63 |
| 43 | Nashville-Davidson | 5,645 | 12.39 |

| Rank | City | Total Fires | Fires per 1,000 Population |
|------|------|-------------|---------------------------|
| 44 | Rochester | 2,967 | 12.27 |
| 45 | San Antonio | 9,538 | 12.14 |
| 46 | Virginia Beach | 3,167 | 12.08 |
| 47 | Columbus, Ga. | 2,030 | 11.98 |
| 48 | Indianapolis | 8,311 | 11.86 |
| 49 | Tucson | 3,895 | 11.78 |
| 50 | Charlotte | 3,627 | 11.53 |
| 51 | Knoxville | 2,094 | 11.43 |
| 52 | Dallas | 10,240 | 11.33 |
| 53 | Toledo | 4,012 | 11.31 |
| 54 | San Francisco | 7,544 | 11.11 |
| 55 | Anaheim | 2,391 | 10.90 |
| 56 | Corpus Christi | 2,495 | 10.75 |
| 57 | Des Moines | 2,029 | 10.62 |
| 57 | New Orleans | 5,918 | 10.62 |
| 59 | Columbus, Ohio | 5,919 | 10.48 |
| 60 | Fort Wayne | 1,803 | 10.47 |
| 61 | Cincinnati | 4,025 | 10.44 |
| 62 | Omaha | 3,276 | 10.42 |
| 63 | Norfolk | 2,726 | 10.21 |
| 64 | Tulsa | 3,685 | 10.21 |
| 65 | Minneapolis | 3,698 | 9.97 |
| 65 | El Paso | 4,239 | 9.97 |
| 67 | Los Angeles | 29,296 | 9.87 |
| 68 | Colorado Springs | 2,041 | 9.49 |
| 69 | Spokane | 1,617 | 9.44 |
| 70 | Greensboro | 1,447 | 9.30 |
| 71 | Houston | 14,344 | 8.99 |
| 72 | Akron | 2,114 | 8.91 |
| 73 | St. Paul | 2,354 | 8.71 |
| 74 | Portland | 3,180 | 8.68 |
| 75 | Montgomery | 1,531 | 8.61 |
| 76 | Grand Rapids | 1,561 | 8.58 |
| 77 | Milwaukee | 5,429 | 8.53 |
| 78 | St. Petersburg | 2,031 | 8.51 |
| 79 | Flint | 1,356 | 8.50 |
| 80 | Wichita | 2,328 | 8.34 |
| 81 | San Diego | 7,125 | 8.14 |
| 82 | Seattle | 3,952 | 8.00 |
| 83 | Austin | 2,790 | 7.98 |
| 84 | San Jose | 4,868 | 7.73 |
| 85 | Riverside | 1,294 | 7.57 |
| 86 | Anchorage | 1,311 | 7.52 |
| 87 | Santa Ana | 1,528 | 7.50 |
| 88 | Warren | 1,159 | 7.19 |
| 89 | Baton Rouge | 1,499 | 6.83 |
| 90 | Aurora | 996 | 6.28 |
| 91 | Huntington Beach | 1,014 | 5.95 |
| 92 | Lincoln | 937 | 5.45 |
| 93 | Madison | 891 | 5.22 |
| 94 | Miami | 1,773 | 5.11 |
| 95 | Salt Lake City | 693 | 4.25 |

# 211. Refuse Collection Expenditure

Clean streets are aesthetically valuable, but they are also vital to avoid adverse health effects. The figures below refer to "sanitation other than sewage," and they therefore include the cost of disposal as well as collection.

Refuse expenditure per person reflects differences in quality of service as well as in volume of refuse and productivity. New York City, where disposal of refuse is becoming a major problem, has 3 percent of the nation's population but produces 6 percent of its refuse. The city's sanitation commissioner, looking on the bright side (i.e., prospects for burning refuse for energy), describes it as the "Persian Gulf of garbage." Most cities collect

| Rank | City | Total Refuse Spending ($ 000) | Refuse Spending Per Capita ($) |
|---|---|---|---|
| 4 | Honolulu | 17,648 | 48.34 |
| 5 | Tampa | 12,152 | 44.75 |
| 6 | New York | 310,566 | 43.92 |
| 7 | Milwaukee | 27,094 | 42.59 |
| 8 | Knoxville | 7,778 | 42.47 |
| 9 | St. Petersburg | 10,029 | 42.34 |
| 10 | Tacoma | 6,529 | 41.19 |
| 11 | Philadelphia | 66,539 | 39.41 |
| 12 | Madison | 6,073 | 35.59 |
| 13 | Rochester* | 7,950 | 32.89 |
| 14 | Charlotte | 10,080 | 32.06 |
| 15 | Baton Rouge | 6,669 | 30.38 |
| 16 | Cleveland | 17,332 | 30.20 |
| 17 | Miami* | 10,231 | 29.49 |
| 18 | Lexington-Fayette | 6,001 | 29.39 |
| 19 | Flint* | 4,647 | 29.11 |
| 20 | Pittsburgh* | 12,031 | 28.38 |
| 21 | Montgomery | 4,958 | 27.83 |
| 22 | Dallas | 25,152 | 27.82 |
| 23 | Denver | 13,569 | 27.61 |
| 24 | Phoenix | 21,415 | 27.12 |
| 25 | Spokane | 4,643 | 27.10 |
| 26 | Chattanooga | 4,445 | 26.21 |
| 27 | Fresno* | 5,596 | 25.65 |
| 28 | Columbus, Ohio | 14,429 | 25.54 |
| 29 | Dayton | 5,077 | 24.94 |
| 30 | Tucson | 8,066 | 24.40 |
| 31 | Oklahoma City | 9,483 | 23.52 |
| 32 | Louisville | 6,997 | 23.44 |
| 33 | New Orleans | 12,898 | 23.14 |
| 34 | Virginia Beach | 5,700 | 21.74 |
| 35 | Jackson | 4,398 | 21.68 |
| 36 | Minneapolis | 7,935 | 21.39 |
| 37 | Norfolk | 5,468 | 20.48 |
| 38 | Greensboro* | 3,151 | 20.25 |
| 39 | Arlington, Texas* | 3,141 | 19.62 |
| 40 | Buffalo | 7,017 | 19.61 |
| 41 | Mobile | 3,843 | 19.17 |
| 42 | Sacramento* | 5,005 | 18.15 |
| 43 | Long Beach* | 6,501 | 17.99 |
| 44 | Akron | 4,225 | 17.81 |
| 45 | San Diego | 15,110 | 17.26 |
| 46 | Fort Worth | 6,591 | 17.11 |
| 47 | Houston | 26,901 | 16.88 |
| 48 | Little Rock | 2,641 | 16.67 |
| 49 | Richmond* | 3,632 | 16.57 |
| 50 | Lubbock | 2,849 | 16.38 |
| 51 | Riverside | 2,758 | 16.14 |
| 52 | Des Moines | 3,049 | 15.96 |
| 53 | Worcester | 2,569 | 15.88 |
| 54 | Nashville-Davidson | 7,172 | 15.74 |
| 55 | Kansas City, Mo. | 6,997 | 15.61 |
| 56 | Los Angeles | 42,646 | 14.37 |
| 57 | Seattle | 6,679 | 13.52 |
| 58 | Shreveport | 2,694 | 13.09 |
| 59 | Toledo | 4,635 | 13.07 |
| 60 | Syracuse* | 2,117 | 12.45 |
| 61 | Grand Rapids* | 1,961 | 10.78 |
| 62 | Jacksonville | 5,427 | 10.03 |
| 63 | Cincinnati | 3,530 | 9.16 |
| 64 | Indianapolis | 6,207 | 8.86 |
| 65 | Salt Lake City | 1,430 | 8.77 |
| 66 | Tulsa | 1,448 | 4.01 |
| 67 | Wichita | 1,013 | 3.63 |
| 68 | St. Paul | 805 | 2.98 |

*1980 data

refuse once or twice a week. Toledo, Ohio was down in 1982 to once a fortnight, while Trenton, New Jersey maintains what its mayor describes as a "Cadillac" service, three times a week.

Six cities spent less than $10 a person in 1981 on refuse collection: St. Paul, Wichita, Tulsa, Salt Lake City, Indianapolis and Cincinnati. For a few starred cities the latest available information is for 1980.

At the other extreme, three cities—Detroit, Baltimore and Anchorage—spent over $50 a person per year on refuse collection.

The table below gives more up-to-date and specific information than that provided by the Census Bureau, which collects data on "total sanitation costs (excluding sewerage)." The Census data combine collection and disposal costs. While the bulk of this cost is for collection, disposal can be a significant portion of it in large cities that are using up their landfill areas. The Census data showed that Aurora, Oakland and San Jose all paid less than $3.50 per resident for sanitation in fiscal 1980. These three communities depend upon their residents or businesses or both to pay for much of their collection services. At the other end of the scale, seven communities paid over $35 a person for sanitation: Tacoma; Rochester; New York; Philadelphia; Miami; Albuquerque; and Washington, D.C. Two of the four most expensive sanitation systems are therefore in New York State. In New York City's case the high cost is related to the difficulty of disposal as well as to expensive labor settlements.

Sanitation cost per capita is viewed by many public officials as a less useful measure than cost per ton collected or cost per household. Unfortunately, data on the number of households are less available and less reliable than straight population data.

SOURCES: International City Management Association, *The Municipal Year Book: 1982* (Washington, D.C.: ICMA, 1982), pp. 12–67. U.S. Department of Commerce, Bureau of the Census, *City Government Finances in 1979–80* (Washington, D.C.: Government Printing Office, September 1981). New York City 1981 data from "The Mayor's Management Report," January 30, 1982, and from New York City Department of Sanitation.

| Rank | City | Total Refuse Spending ($ 000) | Refuse Spending Per Capita ($) |
|---|---|---|---|
| 1 | Detroit | 119,280 | 99.12 |
| 2 | Baltimore | 40,958 | 52.06 |
| 3 | Anchorage* | 8,820 | 50.98 |

# CHAPTER THIRTEEN

# EDUCATION

Urban educational systems face pressing fiscal and social challenges. Fiscal pressures result from declining enrollments, inflation and tax-limitation initiatives. Social pressures in urban education result from the new assertiveness of religious, feminist and ethnic groups; from television and technology; and from a decline in the extended family and alienation associated with central city decline.

The drop in student enrollment in the 1970s reflects the passing on of the postwar baby crop. It has affected the mode of educational institutions, giving rise to personnel layoffs, underutilization of school facilities, school closings and decreased funding. The selection of alternative courses of action has become more difficult as resources have become more limited. Since the baby boom generation is bringing children into the classroom again in the 1980s, the problem may not continue to be so serious except in cities that are suffering population declines.

Truancy, delinquency and drop-out rates have reached serious levels. Residents' dissatisfaction with public education may be measured by continuing enrollment in private schools. Taxpayers are looking for ways to ease their local tax burdens, while federal and state aid is cut. School systems are finding citizens reluctant to pay for educational programs considered marginal, extracurricular and not pertinent to basic educational objectives (e.g., high school sports). This has had a direct impact on the teaching profession. Great numbers of teaching positions are being terminated, while thousands are graduating yearly seeking teaching jobs despite the decreasing employment demand.

A little more than one-third of the 100 largest cities will have a large "bubble" of students moving through their middle and high schools for the next 6 to 10 years. This is evident from the high percentage of elementary students presently enrolled in those school systems. The importance of looking at elementary school enrollments is to determine future staffing needs for the whole school system. After a period of steady declines in the 1970s, by 1982 there were signs of another coming wave of new pupils to strengthen elementary school enrollments. But not all cities reflect these broad national trends.

Federal funding has been aimed primarily at elementary education. Relatively few dollars have gone to fund programs in urban secondary education, where the present need appears greatest. Procedures for securing what federal funds are available tend to have been complex and extremely time-consuming, thereby frustrating initiative and budgetary programming. Federal and state funds in the future will be even harder to obtain.

While federal funds have been shrinking, costly federal educational mandates continue in force. A 1979 HEW report states:

> Substantial organizational shifts (in educational policy and programming) required to accommodate desegregation, bilingual and handicapped training, affirmative action and other similar programs require long-term financial planning improbable in the current context of school finance.*

Appropriate and effective student counseling is another present-day problem. Many inner city systems have student-counselor ratios in the range of 600- or 700-to-1! These work loads are far too heavy to permit effective counseling.

More attention must be given to career education. It remains a viable means of achieving success in breaking the cycle of poverty in which many city youths are trapped. As urbanologist Dr. Bernard Watson has said: "The influence of an increasingly technological employment market and abysmally poor secondary schooling

---

*U.S. Department of Health, Education and Welfare, Office of Education, *Urban High School Reform Initiative* (1979).

threatens to create . . . a permanent underclass of under-educated, unemployable citizens."**

Educational planners and researchers will have to place more emphasis on the current educational problems of attendance, finance and programming. Educators today must find ways to integrate the available resources of the urban community into modern-day educational training. This will help develop educational incentives and improve priorities and goal-setting measures necessary for successful and productive lives in this complex living environment.

**Bernard Watson, "Urban Education: Past, Present and Future," paper presented to the Urban Education Conference, Philadelphia, 1978.

# 212. School Enrollment

The following table shows 1980 city school enrollment relative to population (data given are for the county or parish only where indicated). It is interesting in several ways. Those cities with the highest percentage of students per 100 residents—Albuquerque, Charlotte, Virginia Beach—are indicative of communities with more families and therefore lower average ages. They and other such cities, like Shreveport, Anchorage and Fresno, represent communities with a smaller proportion of elderly people. With exceptions such as Houston and San Francisco, cities at the lower end of the percentage scale are largely either cities with retirement communities (St. Petersburg and Phoenix), with resort communities (Honolulu) or just with an older population (Providence and Minneapolis).

SOURCE: Educational systems survey by the authors, 1982.

| Rank | City | Students | Students per 100 Residents |
|---|---|---|---|
| 1 | Albuquerque | 78,668 | 23.71 |
| 2 | Charlotte | 74,149 | 23.58 |
| 3 | Virginia Beach | 58,966 | 22.49 |
| 4 | Shreveport | 45,123 | 21.92 |
| 5 | Anchorage | 36,908 | 21.33 |
| 6 | Fresno | 46,531 | 21.32 |
| 7 | Newark | 63,609 | 19.32 |
| 8 | Las Vegas* | 88,567 | 19.18 |
| 9 | Los Angeles | 534,124 | 18.00 |
| 10 | Atlanta | 76,366 | 17.97 |
| 11 | Jacksonville* | 100,526 | 17.61 |
| 12 | Detroit | 211,825 | 17.60 |
| 12 | Memphis‡ | 113,729 | 17.60 |
| 14 | Baton Rouge‡ | 64,079 | 17.50 |
| 15 | Des Moines | 33,161 | 17.36 |
| 16 | Austin | 59,859 | 17.33 |
| 17 | Tampa* | 111,948 | 17.30 |
| 18 | Tucson | 55,654 | 16.84 |

| Rank | City | Students | Students per 100 Residents |
|---|---|---|---|
| 19 | Mobile*‡ | 60,966 | 16.73 |
| 20 | Tacoma | 26,437 | 16.68 |
| 21 | Washington, D.C. | 106,156 | 16.65 |
| 22 | Fort Worth | 63,862 | 16.58 |
| 23 | Birmingham | 46,698 | 16.42 |
| 24 | Lubbock | 28,320 | 16.28 |
| 25 | Nashville-Davidson* | 73,831 | 16.20 |
| 26 | Anaheim | 35,843 | 16.16 |
| 27 | Norfolk | 43,120 | 16.15 |
| 28 | Wichita | 44,524 | 15.94 |
| 29 | Chicago‡ | 477,339 | 15.88 |
| 30 | Long Beach | 56,145 | 15.57 |
| 31 | Kansas City, Kan. | 25,012 | 15.54 |
| 32 | New Orleans | 85,660 | 15.47 |
| 33 | Lexington-Fayette* | 31,264 | 15.31 |
| 34 | Dayton | 31,119 | 15.29 |
| 35 | Louisville* | 103,309 | 15.09 |
| 35 | Santa Ana | 30,740 | 15.09 |
| 37 | Richmond | 32,815 | 14.97 |
| 38 | Baltimore* | 97,682 | 14.90 |
| 39 | Jackson | 30,103 | 14.84 |
| 40 | Worcester | 23,854 | 14.74 |
| 41 | Oakland | 49,300 | 14.53 |
| 41 | St. Louis | 65,815 | 14.53 |
| 43 | Portland, Ore. | 52,869 | 14.45 |
| 44 | Colorado Springs | 30,989 | 14.40 |
| 45 | Salt Lake City | 23,353 | 14.32 |
| 46 | Omaha | 44,592 | 14.31 |
| 47 | Cleveland | 82,053 | 14.30 |
| 48 | Cincinnati | 54,977 | 14.26 |
| 48 | Dallas | 128,919 | 14.26 |
| 48 | El Paso | 60,648 | 14.26 |
| 51 | Madison | 24,237 | 14.21 |
| 52 | Milwaukee | 88,832 | 13.96 |
| 53 | Miami*‡ | 223,740 | 13.76 |
| 54 | Tulsa | 49,374 | 13.68 |
| 55 | New York | 943,805 | 13.35 |
| 56 | Philadelphia | 224,339 | 13.29 |
| 57 | Toledo | 45,766 | 12.91 |
| 58 | Denver | 63,414 | 12.90 |
| 59 | Columbus, Ohio | 72,821 | 12.89 |
| 60 | Little Rock | 20,201 | 12.75 |
| 61 | Syracuse | 21,655 | 12.73 |
| 62 | San Diego | 110,587 | 12.63 |
| 63 | Houston | 194,043 | 12.16 |

| Rank | City | Students | Students per 100 Residents |
|------|------|----------|---------------------------|
| 64 | St. Petersburg* | 87,561 | 12.02 |
| 65 | St. Paul | 31,665 | 11.72 |
| 66 | Providence | 18,086 | 11.53 |
| 67 | Boston | 62,889 | 11.17 |
| 68 | Minneapolis | 40,032 | 10.79 |
| 69 | Yonkers | 20,874 | 10.70 |
| 70 | Oklahoma City | 41,128 | 10.20 |
| 71 | Indianapolis | 66,037 | 9.42 |
| 72 | Kansas City, Mo. | 38,696 | 8.63 |
| 73 | San Antonio | 66,597 | 8.48 |

| Rank | City | Students | Students per 100 Residents |
|------|------|----------|---------------------------|
| 74 | San Francisco‡ | 55,147 | 8.12 |
| 75 | Riverside | 9,811 | 5.74 |
| 76 | Honolulu† | 164,773 | 4.51 |
| 77 | Huntington Beach | 7,070 | 4.15 |
| 78 | Phoenix | 24,587 | 3.11 |

*County or parish system.
†Statewide system.
‡1979 data.

# 213. Change in Pupil Enrollment

Whether related to teacher staffing, per-pupil cost, state funds or building use, few factors affect the course of the educational process more than changes in enrollment.

It is well-known that pupil enrollments in public schools have been shrinking in most of the school systems in the United States. In the 77 cities for which we have 1977–81 data, enrollment increased in only 12 cities, with no increase exceeding 10 percent. In fact, only one approached it—Jackson (9.7 percent). The cities at the top of the list saw a heavy immigration of younger individuals and families. Overall population increased from 1970 to 1980 in Santa Ana (30.8 percent), Jackson (31.8 percent), Austin (36.3 percent), Riverside (22.0 percent) and Virginia Beach (52.3 percent).

The decrease in student populations identified here implies a serious impact on school budget funding and school buildings used or needed, as well as on personnel requirements—teachers and administrators.

Particularly in the larger cities, some educational researchers forecast that school enrollment will decline by the mid-1980s by as much as 18 percent for the elementary levels and by as much as 25 percent for the secondary levels. Others project that elementary school enrollment will rebound in the early 1980s, so that school buildings leased or sold for other purposes because of enrollment decline may then have to be repurchased or leased back as enrollments rise again.

SOURCE: Educational systems survey by the authors, 1982.

| Rank | City | 1977-1978 School Year | 1980-81 School Year | Absolute Change | Percentage Change |
|------|------|-----------------------|---------------------|-----------------|-------------------|
| 1 | Jackson | 27,441 | 30,103 | 2,662 | 9.70 |
| 2 | Virginia Beach | 55,521 | 58,966 | 3,445 | 6.20 |
| 3 | Santa Ana | 28,983 | 30,740 | 1,757 | 6.06 |
| 4 | Riverside | 9,275 | 9,811 | 536 | 5.78 |
| 5 | San Antonio | 63,381 | 66,597 | 3,216 | 5.07 |
| 6 | Austin | 57,782 | 59,859 | 2,077 | 3.59 |
| 7 | El Paso | 58,854 | 60,648 | 1,794 | 3.05 |
| 8 | Worcester | 23,164 | 23,854 | 690 | 2.98 |
| 9 | Las Vegas* | 86,211 | 88,567 | 2,356 | 2.73 |
| 10 | Tampa* | 110,206 | 111,948 | 1,742 | 1.58 |
| 11 | Louisville* | 101,983 | 103,309 | 1,316 | 1.29 |
| 12 | Atlanta | 76,655 | 76,366 | − 289 | − .38 |
| 13 | Albuquerque | 80,488 | 78,668 | − 1,820 | − 2.26 |
| 14 | Memphis | 117,590 | 113,729‡ | − 3,861 | − 3.28 |
| 15 | Fort Worth | 66,432 | 63,862 | − 2,570 | − 3.87 |
| 16 | Long Beach | 58,499 | 56,145 | − 2,354 | − 4.02 |
| 17 | Charlotte | 77,313 | 74,149 | − 3,164 | − 4.09 |
| 18 | San Diego | 115,435 | 110,587 | − 4,848 | − 4.20 |
| 19 | St. Petersburg* | 91,432 | 87,561 | − 3,871 | − 4.23 |
| 20 | Dallas | 134,621 | 128,919 | − 5,702 | − 4.24 |
| 21 | Nashville-Davidson* | 77,185 | 73,831 | − 3,354 | − 4.35 |
| 22 | Tucson | 58,278 | 55,654 | − 2,624 | − 4.50 |
| 23 | Colorado Springs | 32,452 | 30,989 | − 1,463 | − 4.51 |
| 24 | Mobile*‡ | 63,877 | 60,966 | − 2,911 | − 4.56 |
| 25 | Houston | 203,445 | 194,043 | − 9,402 | − 4.62 |
| 26 | Wichita | 46,742 | 44,524 | − 2,218 | − 4.75 |
| 27 | Honolulu† | 173,871 | 164,773 | − 9,098 | − 5.23 |
| 28 | Norfolk | 45,568 | 43,120 | − 2,448 | − 5.37 |
| 29 | Birmingham | 49,479 | 46,698 | − 2,781 | − 5.62 |
| 30 | Los Angeles | 568,681 | 534,124 | −34,557 | − 6.08 |
| 31 | New Orleans | 91,298 | 85,660 | − 5,638 | − 6.18 |
| 32 | Chicago‡ | 510,591 | 477,339 | −33,252 | − 6.51 |
| 33 | Miami* | 240,566 | 223,740 | −16,826 | − 6.99 |
| 34 | Cincinnati | 59,138 | 54,977 | − 4,161 | − 7.04 |
| 35 | Lexington-Fayette* | 33,671 | 31,264 | − 2,407 | − 7.15 |
| 36 | Baton Rouge*‡ | 69,144 | 64,079 | − 5,065 | − 7.33 |
| 37 | Anchorage | 39,902 | 36,908 | − 2,994 | − 7.50 |
| 38 | Little Rock | 21,852 | 20,201 | − 1,651 | − 7.56 |
| 39 | Portland, Ore. | 57,478 | 52,869 | − 4,609 | − 8.02 |
| 40 | Richmond | 35,839 | 32,815 | − 3,024 | − 8.44 |
| 41 | Shreveport | 49,328 | 45,123 | − 4,205 | − 8.52 |
| 42 | New York | 1,033,813 | 943,805 | −90,008 | − 8.71 |

| Rank | City | 1977-1978 School Year | 1980-81 School Year | Absolute Change | Percentage Change |
|------|------|------|------|------|------|
| 43 | Newark | 69,729 | 63,609 | − 6,120 | − 8.78 |
| 44 | Jacksonville* | 110,298 | 100,526 | − 9,772 | − 8.86 |
| 45 | Kansas City, Kan. | 27,572 | 25,012 | − 2,560 | − 9.28 |
| 45 | Salt Lake City | 25,742 | 23,353 | − 2,389 | − 9.28 |
| 47 | Providence | 19,988 | 18,086 | − 1,902 | − 9.52 |
| 48 | Lubbock | 31,550 | 28,320 | − 3,230 | −10.24 |
| 49 | Philadelphia | 252,021 | 224,339 | −27,682 | −10.98 |
| 50 | Oakland | 55,836 | 49,300 | − 6,536 | −11.71 |
| 51 | Milwaukee | 101,192 | 88,832 | −12,360 | −12.21 |
| 52 | Detroit | 241,998 | 211,825 | −30,173 | −12.47 |
| 53 | Denver | 72,553 | 63,414 | − 9,139 | −12.60 |
| 53 | San Francisco‡ | 63,098 | 55,147 | − 7,951 | −12.60 |
| 55 | Oklahoma City | 47,309 | 41,128 | − 6,181 | −13.07 |
| 56 | Los Angeles | 619,715 | 534,124 | −85,591 | −13.81 |
| 57 | Syracuse | 25,150 | 21,665 | − 3,485 | −13.86 |
| 58 | Kansas City, Mo. | 45,073 | 38,696 | − 6,377 | −14.15 |
| 59 | Madison | 28,472 | 24,237 | − 4,235 | −14.87 |
| 60 | Anaheim | 42,153 | 35,843 | − 6,310 | −14.97 |
| 61 | Washington, D.C. | 124,995 | 106,156 | −18,839 | −15.07 |
| 62 | Indianapolis | 78,191 | 66,037 | −12,154 | −15.54 |

| Rank | City | 1977-1978 School Year | 1980-81 School Year | Absolute Change | Percentage Change |
|------|------|------|------|------|------|
| 63 | Tulsa | 58,687 | 49,374 | − 9,313 | −15.87 |
| 64 | Toledo | 54,644 | 45,766 | − 8,878 | −16.25 |
| 65 | Des Moines | 39,779 | 33,161 | − 6,618 | −16.64 |
| 66 | St. Paul | 38,105 | 31,665 | − 6,440 | −16.90 |
| 67 | Tacoma | 31,841 | 26,437 | − 5,404 | −16.97 |
| 68 | Boston | 76,215 | 62,889 | −13,326 | −17.48 |
| 69 | Fresno | 56,476 | 46,531 | − 9,945 | −17.61 |
| 70 | Omaha | 55,444 | 44,492 | −10,952 | −19.75 |
| 71 | Minneapolis | 50,478 | 40,032 | −10,446 | −20.69 |
| 72 | Yonkers | 26,353 | 20,874 | − 5,479 | −20.79 |
| 73 | Dayton | 39,761 | 31,119 | − 8,642 | −21.73 |
| 74 | Columbus, Ohio | 93,473 | 72,821 | −20,652 | −22.09 |
| 75 | Cleveland | 118,575 | 82,053 | −36,522 | −30.80 |
| 76 | Baltimore‡ | 147,000 | 97,682 | −49,318 | −33.55 |
| 77 | St. Louis | 110,536 | 65,815 | −44,721 | −40.46 |

*County or parish system.
†Statewide system.
‡1979 data.

# 214. Public School Teachers

One of the great differences between public and private schools is in teacher hiring flexibility. In order to ensure minimum standards of competence in teaching, most public schools require teaching certification. Certification has become a series of hurdles to be passed, only a few of which relate to inspired teaching. Private schools, on the other hand, have maintained their flexibility and are able to find people who are qualified in their fields, are inspired, but lack certificates. Both approaches have their logic and their risks.

A result of the usual public school approach is that a high proportion of teachers are full-time. The table below provides some indication of this. It gives the proportion of all public school employees that are full-time teachers. It therefore shows to what extent a school system may have a high degree of administrative overhead.

The figures below indicate that New York City has the highest proportion of full-time teachers to all employees, 78.3 percent (New York's numbers, however, include regular teachers on sabbatical leave). Oakland has the lowest, 36.1 percent. Anchorage, listed among the top 10, includes in its count librarians and guidance counselors.

SOURCE: Educational systems survey by the authors, 1982.

| Rank | City | All Public School Employees | Percentage Full-Time Teachers |
|------|------|------|------|
| 1 | New York | 69,950 | 78.34 |
| 2 | Wichita | 3,088 | 75.56 |
| 3 | Worcester | 2,600 | 74.16 |
| 4 | Honolulu† | 11,914 | 73.68 |
| 5 | Detroit | 12,741 | 69.67 |
| 6 | Madison | 2,240 | 66.97 |
| 7 | Tacoma | 2,982 | 65.48 |
| 8 | Birmingham | 4,126 | 65.20 |
| 9 | Omaha | 4,089 | 63.31 |
| 10 | Anchorage | 3,169 | 62.49 |
| 11 | Denver | 6,495 | 62.44 |
| 12 | Cincinnati | 4,676 | 61.00 |
| 13 | Houston | 17,011 | 61.14 |
| 14 | Tulsa | 4,859 | 60.73 |
| 15 | Newark | 6,963 | 60.63 |
| 16 | Providence | 2,146 | 60.34 |
| 17 | St. Petersburg* | 8,501 | 59.00 |
| 18 | Baton Rouge* | 6,112 | 59.66 |
| 19 | Kansas City, Kan. | 2,575 | 59.34 |
| 20 | Louisville* | 9,471 | 58.90 |
| 21 | Lexington-Fayette* | 3,458 | 58.53 |
| 22 | Norfolk | 4,500 | 57.79 |
| 23 | Chicago | 48,316 | 57.50 |
| 24 | Baltimore* | 10,210 | 56.89 |
| 25 | Austin | 5,592 | 56.88 |
| 26 | Huntington Beach | 699 | 56.80 |
| 27 | Des Moines | 3,222 | 56.70 |
| 28 | Yonkers | 2,411 | 56.62 |
| 29 | Fresno | 2,996 | 56.48 |
| 30 | Colorado Springs | 2,878 | 56.40 |
| 31 | Boston | 8,714 | 56.37 |
| 32 | Virginia Beach | 5,233 | 56.14 |
| 33 | Dayton | 3,226 | 55.80 |

| Rank | City | All Public School Employees | Percentage Full-Time Teachers |
|------|------|----------------------------|-------------------------------|
| 34 | St. Paul | 4,780 | 55.44 |
| 34 | Salt Lake City | 2,091 | 55.44 |
| 36 | Albuquerque | 7,585 | 55.20 |
| 37 | Little Rock | 2,315 | 54.34 |
| 38 | Syracuse | 2,548 | 54.32 |
| 39 | Tucson | 5,069 | 54.30 |
| 40 | Las Vegas* | 8,049 | 54.04 |
| 41 | Santa Ana | 2,720 | 53.31 |
| 42 | Charlotte | 7,367 | 52.94 |
| 43 | El Paso | 5,918 | 52.66 |
| 44 | Jacksonville* | 10,607 | 52.63 |
| 45 | Lubbock | 3,247 | 52.11 |
| 46 | Anaheim | 2,902 | 51.62 |
| 46 | Riverside | 893 | 51.62 |
| 48 | St. Louis | 6,963 | 51.54 |
| 49 | Jackson | 3,300 | 51.51 |
| 50 | Portland, Ore. | 5,264 | 51.47 |
| 51 | Columbus, Ohio | 7,442 | 51.39 |
| 52 | Altanta | 8,500 | 50.97 |
| 53 | San Antonio | 6,056 | 50.18 |
| 54 | Philadelphia | 25,000 | 50.00 |

| Rank | City | All Public School Employees | Percentage Full-Time Teachers |
|------|------|----------------------------|-------------------------------|
| 55 | Milwaukee | 11,269 | 49.94 |
| 56 | Minneapolis | 5,290 | 48.34 |
| 57 | New Orleans | 9,052 | 47.83 |
| 58 | Washington, D.C. | 11,072 | 47.31 |
| 59 | Tampa* | 12,321 | 46.91 |
| 60 | Oklahoma City | 4,565 | 46.70 |
| 61 | Shreveport* | 5,897 | 45.57 |
| 62 | Dallas | 14,137 | 45.32 |
| 63 | Fort Worth | 7,375 | 45.09 |
| 64 | Kansas City, Mo. | 4,887 | 44.42 |
| 65 | Long Beach | 5,427 | 43.77 |
| 66 | Indianapolis | 7,835 | 43.52 |
| 67 | Los Angeles | 57,681 | 42.97 |
| 68 | San Diego | 12,029 | 42.79 |
| 69 | Toledo | 3,902 | 42.76 |
| 70 | Cleveland | 9,833 | 42.16 |
| 71 | Oakland | 6,261 | 36.14 |

*County or parish system.
†Statewide system.

# 215.  Average Class Size

A major consequence of an *average* class size of 30 or more in a school system is that a number of individual classes in the system are going to be extremely large—some upwards of 40 students. As a result, teaching conditions are not the best, and the individual attention that may be present in a class of 25 or less will be diluted.

A number of school systems that find themselves with an average class size greater than 25 will probably have larger classes at the secondary level, where individual attention is not nearly as great. Generally, in such instances, the elementary grades are smaller. This is particularly significant for the early childhood years, when the teaching of fundamentals requires close attention, and a child who falls behind may find it difficult—or impossible—to catch up.

Some school systems have class sizes below 25 because their enrollments have been declining while there has been no corresponding reduction in professional staff.

Those systems with high average class sizes over 25 and pupil-teacher ratios of 24 or more to 1 are likely to have suffered budgetary cutbacks and thus have fewer additional professional resources to complement the basic teaching staff. In such situations a teacher's work load is likely to be increased, meaning additional work time spent outside the classroom performing administrative duties or providing special instruction to individual pupils.

Of those cities that replied to our survey of educational systems, the west coast cities of Santa Ana, Anaheim, Oakland and Long Beach have the highest average class size.

SOURCE: Educational systems survey by the authors, 1982.

| Rank | City | Average Number of Pupils Per Class | Rank | City | Average Number of Pupils Per Class | Rank | City | Average Number of Pupils Per Class |
|------|------|-----------------------------------|------|------|-----------------------------------|------|------|-----------------------------------|
| 1 | Santa Ana | 34.0 | 3 | Long Beach | 31.0 | 7 | New York | 29.5 |
| 2 | Oakland | 31.3 | 5 | Detroit | 30.0 | 8 | St. Louis | 29.1 |
| 3 | Anaheim | 31.0 | 5 | Chicago | 30.0 | 9 | Fresno | 28.5 |

| Rank | City | Average Number of Pupils Per Class | Rank | City | Average Number of Pupils Per Class | Rank | City | Average Number of Pupils Per Class |
|---|---|---|---|---|---|---|---|---|
| 10 | Atlanta | 28.0 | 30 | Charlotte* | 25.0 | 50 | Colorado Springs | 22.4 |
| 10 | Fort Worth | 28.0 | 30 | Dayton | 25.0 | 51 | San Antonio | 22.0 |
| 10 | Milwaukee | 28.0 | 30 | Kansas City, Kan. | 25.0 | 52 | Baltimore* | 21.7 |
| 13 | Cleveland | 27.0 | 33 | Louisville* | 24.7 | 53 | Lexington-Fayette* | 21.4 |
| 13 | Dallas | 27.0 | 34 | Des Moines | 24.6 | 54 | Jacksonville* | 21.1 |
| 13 | Houston | 27.0 | 34 | Norfolk | 24.6 | 55 | Little Rock | 21.0 |
| 13 | Huntington Beach | 27.0 | 36 | Anchorage | 24.0 | 55 | Portland, Ore. | 21.0 |
| 13 | Indianapolis | 27.0 | 36 | Austin | 24.0 | 57 | Worcester | 20.5 |
| 13 | Los Angeles | 27.0 | 36 | Jackson | 24.0 | 58 | Salt Lake City | 20.3 |
| 13 | Minneapolis | 27.0 | 36 | Madison | 24.0 | 59 | Albuquerque | 19.9 |
| 13 | Riverside | 27.0 | 36 | Omaha | 24.0 | 60 | Columbus, Ohio | 19.0 |
| 13 | Tucson | 27.0 | 36 | Providence | 24.0 | 61 | Virginia Beach | 18.5 |
| 22 | Las Vegas* | 26.5 | 36 | St. Paul | 24.0 | 62 | Birmingham | 18.1 |
| 23 | Honolulu† | 26.2 | 36 | St. Petersburg* | 24.0 | 63 | Lubbock | 16.7 |
| 23 | Kansas City, Mo. | 26.2 | 44 | Wichita | 23.3 | 64 | Richmond | 15.0 |
| 25 | Oklahoma City | 26.0 | 45 | Denver | 23.1 | | | |
| 25 | Shreveport* | 26.0 | 45 | Washington, D.C. | 23.1 | *County or parish system. | | |
| 27 | Cincinnati | 25.9 | 47 | Newark | 23.0 | †Statewide system. | | |
| 28 | New Orleans | 25.8 | 47 | Tampa* | 23.0 | | | |
| 29 | Tacoma | 25.6 | 49 | Tulsa | 22.8 | | | |

# 216. Pupil-Teacher Ratio

Generally speaking, the higher the pupil-teacher ratio, the lower the numbers of support staff that are available to assist in broadening the educational process. Support staff includes personnel such as school psychologists; social workers; guidance personnel; and supervisors of art, music, foreign languages and physical education. Some of the wealthier school districts even have professional support staff to teach computer programming.

Cities on the West Coast dominate the top range of the pupil-teacher ratio. However, with the exception of the top five cities listed in the table, the ratios sent to the authors by the school systems appear to reflect reasonable pupil-teacher relationships.

SOURCE: Educational systems survey by the authors, 1982.

| Rank | City | Average Number of Pupils Per Teacher | Rank | City | Average Number of Pupils Per Teacher | Rank | City | Average Number of Pupils Per Teacher |
|---|---|---|---|---|---|---|---|---|
| 1 | Fresno | 27.5 | 14 | Washington, D.C. | 20.3 | 27 | Oklahoma City | 19.3 |
| 2 | Toledo | 27.4 | 15 | Tucson | 20.2 | 28 | Des Moines | 19.2 |
| 3 | Detroit | 23.9 | 16 | Dallas | 20.1 | 28 | Fort Worth | 19.2 |
| 4 | Anaheim | 23.7 | 16 | Virginia Beach | 20.1 | 30 | Colorado Springs | 19.1 |
| 5 | Long Beach | 23.6 | 18 | Cleveland | 19.8 | 31 | Charlotte* | 19.0 |
| 6 | San Antonio | 21.9 | 18 | New Orleans | 19.8 | 32 | Albuquerque | 18.8 |
| 7 | Oakland | 21.8 | 20 | Cincinnati | 19.6 | 32 | Austin | 18.8 |
| 8 | Los Angeles | 21.6 | 20 | Columbus, Ohio | 19.6 | 32 | Honolulu† | 18.8 |
| 9 | San Diego | 21.5 | 22 | El Paso | 19.5 | 35 | Houston | 18.7 |
| 10 | Riverside | 21.3 | 22 | Portland, Ore. | 19.5 | 36 | Anchorage | 18.6 |
| 11 | Santa Ana | 21.2 | 24 | Indianapolis | 19.4 | 37 | Louisville* | 18.5 |
| 12 | Salt Lake City | 21.1 | 24 | Providence | 19.4 | 38 | Jacksonville* | 18.3 |
| 13 | Las Vegas* | 20.4 | 24 | Tampa* | 19.4 | 38 | St. Louis | 18.3 |

| Rank | City | Average Number of Pupils Per Teacher | | Rank | City | Average Number of Pupils Per Teacher | | Rank | City | Average Number of Pupils Per Teacher |
|---|---|---|---|---|---|---|---|---|---|---|
| 40 | Philadelphia | 17.9 | | 52 | Shreveport* | 16.8 | | 66 | Newark | 15.1 |
| 41 | Kansas City, Mo. | 17.8 | | 54 | Lubbock | 16.7 | | 67 | Richmond | 15.0 |
| 42 | Huntington Beach | 17.7 | | 54 | Tulsa | 16.7 | | 68 | Tacoma | 13.5 |
| 42 | Jackson | 17.7 | | 56 | Norfolk | 16.6 | | 69 | Houston | 13.0 |
| 44 | Atlanta | 17.6 | | 57 | Kansas City, Kan. | 16.4 | | 70 | Boston | 12.8 |
| 44 | Baton Rouge* | 17.6 | | 58 | Madison | 16.2 | | 71 | Worcester | 12.4 |
| 46 | Birmingham | 17.4 | | 59 | Little Rock | 16.1 | | 72 | St. Paul | 11.9 |
| 47 | Dayton | 17.3 | | 60 | Milwaukee | 15.8 | | | | |
| 48 | New York | 17.2 | | 61 | Minneapolis | 15.7 | | | | |
| 48 | Omaha | 17.2 | | 61 | Syracuse | 15.7 | | | | |
| 48 | St. Petersburg* | 17.2 | | 63 | Denver | 15.6 | | | | |
| 51 | Chicago | 17.1 | | 64 | Lexington-Fayette* | 15.4 | | *County or parish system. | | |
| 52 | Baltimore* | 16.8 | | 65 | Yonkers | 15.3 | | †Statewide system. | | |

# 217. Special Education

The definition of "special education" may vary among school systems. While such a designation is limited only to the mentally and physically handicapped in some systems, in others it may also include special education programs directed to bilingual education, career counseling, vocational training and special classes for advanced students.

Four of the 66 educational systems responding to the authors' survey reported greater than 10 percent of total enrollment in special education programs. More than 47 percent of the systems have a special education enrollment greater than 5 percent of total enrollment.

Boston ranks first, with 18 percent of total enrollment receiving some form of special education, reflecting the expanding role that counseling and classes for the special student have had in public education.

Colorado Springs, second in this ranking, has a number of specially designed programs to serve the needs of the handicapped and the developmentally disabled pupil.

SOURCE: Educational systems survey by the authors, 1982.

| Rank | City | Percentage of Pupils Enrolled in Special Education | | Rank | City | Percentage of Pupils Enrolled in Special Education | | Rank | City | Percentage of Pupils Enrolled in Special Education |
|---|---|---|---|---|---|---|---|---|---|---|
| 1 | Boston | 18.01 | | 17 | Madison | 6.50 | | 33 | Syracuse | 4.50 |
| 2 | Colorado Springs | 14.57 | | 18 | Yonkers | 6.16 | | 34 | Portland, Ore. | 4.49 |
| 3 | Oakland | 11.82 | | 19 | New York | 6.10 | | 35 | Providence | 4.43 |
| 4 | Tucson | 10.14 | | 19 | Tacoma | 6.10 | | 36 | Chicago | 4.24 |
| 5 | Oklahoma City | 9.84 | | 21 | St. Louis | 5.97 | | 37 | Jackson | 3.57 |
| 6 | Lexington-Fayette* | 9.79 | | 22 | Kansas City, Mo. | 5.86 | | 38 | Louisville* | 3.54 |
| 7 | Little Rock | 9.70 | | 23 | Dayton | 5.67 | | 39 | Fresno | 3.49 |
| 8 | Jacksonville* | 9.62 | | 23 | Honolulu† | 5.67 | | 40 | Baltimore* | 3.12 |
| 9 | Des Moines | 8.99 | | 25 | Cleveland | 5.64 | | 41 | New Orleans | 2.98 |
| 10 | Indianapolis | 8.95 | | 26 | Riverside | 5.34 | | 42 | Kansas City, Kan. | 2.89 |
| 11 | Tulsa | 8.46 | | 27 | Richmond | 5.28 | | 43 | Anchorage | 2.88 |
| 12 | Dallas | 8.19 | | 27 | St. Paul | 5.28 | | 44 | Huntington Beach | 2.57 |
| 13 | Wichita | 7.84 | | 29 | Albuquerque | 5.04 | | 45 | Salt Lake City | 2.45 |
| 14 | Cincinnati | 7.46 | | 30 | Detroit | 4.90 | | 46 | Tampa* | 2.38 |
| 15 | Las Vegas* | 6.95 | | 31 | Shreveport* | 4.74 | | 47 | Denver | 2.29 |
| 16 | Toledo | 6.80 | | 32 | St. Petersburg* | 4.66 | | 48 | Minneapolis | 2.21 |

| Rank | City | Percentage of Pupils Enrolled in Special Education | Rank | City | Percentage of Pupils Enrolled in Special Education | Rank | City | Percentage of Pupils Enrolled in Special Education |
|---|---|---|---|---|---|---|---|---|
| 49 | Fort Worth | 2.19 | 56 | Atlanta | 1.28 | 63 | San Diego | .52 |
| 50 | El Paso | 2.12 | 57 | San Antonio | 1.22 | 64 | Charlotte* | .49 |
| 51 | Washington, D.C. | 2.09 | 58 | Santa Ana | 1.20 | 65 | Austin | .37 |
| 52 | Anaheim | 1.49 | 59 | Virginia Beach | 1.00 | 66 | Columbus, Ohio | .25 |
| 53 | Lubbock | 1.47 | 60 | Omaha | .88 | | | |
| 54 | Philadelphia | 1.38 | 61 | Baton Rouge* | .84 | *County or parish system. | | |
| 55 | Newark | 1.34 | 61 | Los Angeles | .84 | †Statewide system. | | |

# 218.  Black Pupils

The public school systems shown below with large black student populations in 1980 have been forerunners of a trend toward greater minority domination of inner city schools. This trend has continued during the 1970s and into the 1980s. So-called white flight from inner cities has had a damaging effect on inner city schools—giving their systems the image of educationally weak and socially permissive systems. This in turn aggravates the conditions of flight, further deepening the problem of these schools.

Busing, which was designed to remedy educational inequality, probably had the opposite effect in many cities, since white families moved away to be in suburban school systems.

Localities like Washington, D.C., Atlanta, Detroit, New Orleans, Richmond and Birmingham have the largest black student populations. Cities like Cincinnati, Dayton and Norfolk are approaching two-thirds majorities. Communities such as these and others with black pupil populations in excess of 40 percent will probably have black majority city populations in the next decade.

Inner city schools are infected by the most critical influences of the external urban environment—crime and safety problems, negative self-images, and teacher and pupil apathy. Nearly one-third of all students who are enrolled in schools in major cities attend schools in systems of 25,000 or more students. The large number of young people in large city school systems dramatizes the need to place greater emphasis on these institutions to increase the percentage of students who make it through successfully and to decrease the percentage of those brought up with a self-image imbued with failure.

SOURCES: Educational systems survey by the authors, 1982. National Center for Educational Statistics, *The Condition of Education* (Washington, D.C.: Government Printing Office, 1979).

| Rank | City | Percentage of Black Students Enrolled | Rank | City | Percentage of Black Students Enrolled | Rank | City | Percentage of Black Students Enrolled |
|---|---|---|---|---|---|---|---|---|
| 1 | Washington, D.C. | 94.5 | 13 | Little Rock | 63.3 | 25 | Houston | 44.9 |
| 2 | Atlanta | 90.9 | 14 | Philadelphia | 62.6 | 26 | Kansas City, Kan. | 43.1 |
| 3 | Detroit | 85.4 | 15 | Chicago | 60.7 | 27 | Baton Rouge | 41.0 |
| 4 | New Orleans | 84.5 | 16 | Norfolk | 57.6 | 28 | Columbus, Ohio | 39.4 |
| 5 | Richmond | 84.4 | 17 | Cincinnati | 57.2 | 29 | New York | 38.6 |
| 6 | Birmingham | 76.3 | 18 | Dayton | 56.6 | 30 | Charlotte | 38.0 |
| 7 | St. Louis | 75.6 | 19 | Shreveport* | 54.2 | 31 | Fort Worth | 36.5 |
| 8 | Jackson | 73.3 | 20 | Indianapolis | 49.6 | 32 | Jacksonville | 35.4 |
| 9 | Newark | 70.0 | 21 | Dallas | 49.2 | 33 | Oklahoma City | 35.0 |
| 10 | Cleveland | 68.4 | 22 | Milwaukee | 46.9 | 34 | Toledo | 33.4 |
| 11 | Kansas City, Mo. | 67.5 | 23 | Boston | 46.0 | 35 | Syracuse | 32.7 |
| 12 | Oakland | 66.6 | 24 | Los Angeles | 45.2 | 36 | Providence | 25.7 |

| Rank | City | Percentage of Black Students Enrolled |
|------|------|--------------------------------------|
| 37 | Louisville* | 25.3 |
| 37 | Omaha | 25.3 |
| 39 | Los Angeles | 23.3 |
| 40 | Tulsa | 22.9 |
| 41 | Denver | 22.6 |
| 42 | Yonkers | 21.0 |
| 43 | Lexington-Fayette* | 19.9 |
| 43 | Minneapolis | 19.9 |
| 45 | Tampa* | 19.6 |
| 46 | Long Beach | 18.7 |
| 47 | Austin | 18.6 |
| 47 | Wichita | 18.6 |
| 49 | St. Petersburg* | 17.0 |
| 50 | San Diego | 15.4 |

| Rank | City | Percentage of Black Students Enrolled |
|------|------|--------------------------------------|
| 51 | Las Vegas | 15.1 |
| 52 | San Antonio | 14.6 |
| 53 | Tacoma | 14.0 |
| 54 | Portland, Ore. | 13.9 |
| 55 | Lubbock | 13.1 |
| 56 | St. Paul | 12.4 |
| 57 | Baltimore* | 11.6 |
| 58 | Fresno | 11.5 |
| 58 | Virginia Beach | 11.5 |
| 60 | Des Moines | 10.8 |
| 61 | Anchorage | 6.1 |
| 62 | Colorado Springs | 6.0 |
| 62 | Santa Ana | 6.0 |
| 64 | Tucson | 5.2 |

| Rank | City | Percentage of Black Students Enrolled |
|------|------|--------------------------------------|
| 65 | Madison | 5.0 |
| 65 | Worcester | 5.0 |
| 67 | Riverside | 4.4 |
| 68 | El Paso | 4.0 |
| 69 | Albuquerque | 3.4 |
| 70 | Salt Lake City | 2.0 |
| 71 | Honolulu | 1.4 |
| 72 | Anaheim | 1.0 |
| 73 | Huntington Beach | .8 |

*County or parish system.
†Statewide system.

# 219.  Hispanic Pupils

Hispanics represent sizable population minorities in 23 of the 100 largest cities in the United States. And with a median population age of 23 (one-third under 15 years of age), in time they will become majorities in more cities. With the barriers of language and the need for increasing time and attention to skill training, Hispanics will be a particularly important challenge for American education.

The Hispanic population increased over 80 percent between 1970 and 1980. There are several key factors that contributed significantly to this rapid growth. One is the increase in immigration from Mexico and other Latin American countries. Hispanics drawn principally by strong family ties and the lure of steady employment have come into cities in Texas and California in large numbers. New York is another major stronghold and lure for Hispanic families.

Another major influence on the data is Catholicism, to which Hispanics adhere broadly. Catholic opposition to birth control has contributed to the higher birthrate of the Hispanic population. This in turn is increasingly reflected in the school enrollments. Already, Hispanics have majorities in four of the cities' school systems and substantial proportions in 10 others.

In many inner city areas migrating Hispanics have moved into the older and poorer residential areas. As a result, they have become inheritors of the aging school infrastructure that serves the areas. Often, this has had an adverse effect on their educational development. Those systems with increasing Hispanic student populations are those in which greater efforts must be made to make the schools a living part of the total community.

SOURCE: Educational systems survey by the authors, 1982.

| Rank | City | Percentage of Hispanic Students Enrolled |
|------|------|-----------------------------------------|
| 1 | San Antonio | 74.0 |
| 2 | Cleveland | 68.4 |
| 3 | El Paso | 67.0 |
| 4 | Santa Ana | 63.5 |
| 5 | Los Angeles | 45.2 |
| 6 | Albuquerque | 39.5 |
| 7 | Fresno | 32.2 |
| 8 | Denver | 32.1 |
| 9 | New York | 30.5 |

| Rank | City | Percentage of Hispanic Students Enrolled |
|------|------|-----------------------------------------|
| 10 | Lubbock | 30.3 |
| 11 | Tucson | 28.9 |
| 12 | Houston | 27.8 |
| 13 | Austin | 27.2 |
| 14 | Anaheim | 27.0 |
| 15 | Riverside | 21.8 |
| 16 | Newark | 20.0 |
| 17 | Dallas | 19.1 |
| 18 | Long Beach | 18.3 |

| Rank | City | Percentage of Hispanic Students Enrolled |
|------|------|-----------------------------------------|
| 19 | San Diego | 17.8 |
| 20 | Fort Worth | 17.6 |
| 21 | Chicago | 17.2 |
| 22 | Yonkers | 16.0 |
| 23 | Boston | 13.0 |
| 24 | Salt Lake City | 12.0 |
| 25 | Providence | 10.2 |
| 26 | Colorado Springs | 10.0 |
| 26 | Oakland | 10.0 |

| Rank | City | Percentage of Hispanic Students Enrolled |
|------|------|------|
| 28 | Worcester | 8.0 |
| 29 | Philadelphia | 7.1 |
| 30 | Milwaukee | 6.0 |
| 31 | Huntington Beach | 5.5 |
| 32 | Las Vegas* | 5.3 |
| 33 | Kansas City, Kan. | 5.1 |
| 34 | St. Paul | 5.0 |
| 35 | Tampa* | 4.8 |
| 36 | Toledo | 4.2 |
| 37 | Wichita | 4.1 |
| 38 | Oklahoma City | 4.0 |
| 39 | Kansas City, Mo. | 3.5 |
| 40 | Omaha | 2.3 |
| 41 | Des Moines | 2.0 |
| 41 | Honolulu† | 2.0 |
| 41 | Syracuse | 2.0 |
| 41 | Tacoma | 2.0 |

| Rank | City | Percentage of Hispanic Students Enrolled |
|------|------|------|
| 45 | Anchorage | 1.9 |
| 46 | Portland, Ore. | 1.8 |
| 47 | Detroit | 1.7 |
| 48 | Minneapolis | 1.4 |
| 49 | New Orleans | 1.3 |
| 50 | Tulsa | 1.1 |
| 50 | Washington, D.C. | 1.1 |
| 52 | Madison | 1.0 |
| 53 | Virginia Beach | .8 |
| 54 | Atlanta | .6 |
| 54 | Baltimore* | .6 |
| 54 | Jacksonville | .6 |
| 57 | Baton Rouge | .5 |
| 57 | Indianapolis | .5 |
| 57 | Norfolk | .5 |
| 60 | St. Petersburg* | .4 |
| 61 | Charlotte | .3 |

| Rank | City | Percentage of Hispanic Students Enrolled |
|------|------|------|
| 61 | Columbus, Ohio | .3 |
| 61 | Dayton | .3 |
| 64 | Lexington-Fayette* | .2 |
| 64 | St. Louis | .2 |
| 64 | Shreveport | .2 |
| 67 | Cincinnati | .1 |
| 67 | Jackson | .1 |
| 67 | Little Rock | .1 |
| 67 | Richmond | .1 |
| 71 | Birmingham | .0‡ |

*County or parish system.
†Statewide system.
‡Less than .1%.

# 220. Cost Per Pupil

The expenditure of school funds represented by "cost per pupil" reflects teacher salaries, teacher-student ratios and the depth of services in and beyond the classroom. Many systems have increased that portion of their educational budgets for student services because of state and federal regulations, collective bargaining agreements and inflation. Increased special education programs, bilingual education and smaller classes are examples of federal and state mandates.

In this listing Yonkers, New York and Anchorage rank at the top in the expenditure of funds on pupil education. The lowest reported in the survey is Toledo, with $1,205, then Virginia Beach, with $1,404, and Oklahoma City, with $1,590. The median cost per pupil for the 71 systems replying is $2,168. Almost 25 percent of

the systems have costs per pupil that currently exceed $2,500 yearly.

The expenditure per pupil data combine all pupils. To make fair comparisons we need to consider the number of pupils receiving special instruction because of language barriers, physical, mental or emotional handicaps, or intellectual gifts.

Some of the preceding tables (e.g., percentage Hispanics and pupil-teacher ratios) shed light on the problems and practices of individual school districts and should be reviewed as part of the evaluation of the data below. New York, for example, has a large Hispanic population; the overall average class size of 29.5 pupils is large; but the prevalence of special instruction is indicated by the lower pupil-teacher ratio of 17-to-1.

SOURCE: Educational systems survey by the authors, 1982.

| Rank | City | Cost Per Pupil ($) |
|------|------|------|
| 1 | Yonkers | 3,916 |
| 2 | New York | 3,482 |
| 3 | Anchorage | 3,184 |
| 4 | Milwaukee | 3,031 |
| 5 | Richmond | 3,029 |
| 6 | Madison | 2,999 |
| 7 | Denver | 2,965 |

| Rank | City | Cost Per Pupil ($) |
|------|------|------|
| 8 | Philadelphia | 2,818 |
| 9 | Detroit | 2,719 |
| 10 | Honolulu† | 2,658 |
| 11 | Baltimore* | 2,615 |
| 12 | San Diego | 2,602 |
| 13 | Des Moines | 2,598 |
| 14 | Portland, Ore. | 2,541 |

| Rank | City | Cost Per Pupil ($) |
|------|------|------|
| 15 | Dayton | 2,500 |
| 16 | Austin | 2,452 |
| 17 | Minneapolis | 2,430 |
| 18 | Washington, D.C. | 2,419 |
| 19 | Fresno | 2,400 |
| 19 | Tacoma | 2,400 |
| 21 | Jacksonville* | 2,379 |

| Rank | City | Cost Per Pupil ($) |
|---|---|---|
| 22 | St. Paul | 2,365 |
| 23 | St. Louis | 2,364 |
| 24 | Syracuse | 2,327 |
| 25 | Columbus, Ohio | 2,322 |
| 26 | St. Petersburg | 2,286 |
| 27 | Atlanta | 2,255 |
| 28 | Kansas City, Mo. | 2,250 |
| 29 | Fort Worth | 2,249 |
| 30 | Charlotte | 2,227 |
| 31 | Santa Ana | 2,226 |
| 32 | Cleveland | 2,223 |
| 33 | Lubbock | 2,217 |
| 34 | Chicago | 2,201 |
| 35 | Omaha | 2,199 |
| 36 | Wichita | 2,168 |
| 37 | Colorado Springs | 2,166 |
| 38 | Worcester | 2,164 |
| 39 | Dallas | 2,160 |

| Rank | City | Cost Per Pupil ($) |
|---|---|---|
| 40 | Providence | 2,159 |
| 41 | Long Beach | 2,116 |
| 42 | Cincinnati | 2,103 |
| 43 | Indianapolis | 2,071 |
| 44 | Huntington Beach | 2,033 |
| 45 | Little Rock | 2,029 |
| 45 | Tulsa | 2,029 |
| 47 | Albuquerque | 2,019 |
| 48 | Tampa | 2,010 |
| 49 | Houston | 2,000 |
| 50 | Anaheim | 1,980 |
| 51 | Salt Lake City | 1,979 |
| 52 | Shreveport* | 1,953 |
| 53 | Oakland | 1,938 |
| 54 | San Antonio | 1,885 |
| 55 | Baton Rouge* | 1,881 |
| 56 | New Orleans | 1,871 |
| 57 | Louisville* | 1,868 |

| Rank | City | Cost Per Pupil ($) |
|---|---|---|
| 58 | Tucson | 1,866 |
| 59 | Birmingham | 1,850 |
| 60 | Lexington-Fayette* | 1,846 |
| 61 | Las Vegas* | 1,815 |
| 62 | Riverside | 1,800 |
| 63 | Los Angeles | 1,785 |
| 64 | Newark | 1,781 |
| 65 | Jackson | 1,667 |
| 66 | El Paso | 1,651 |
| 67 | Norfolk | 1,637 |
| 68 | Kansas City, Kan. | 1,603 |
| 69 | Oklahoma City | 1,590 |
| 70 | Virginia Beach | 1,404 |
| 71 | Toledo | 1,215 |

*County or parish system.
†Statewide system.

# 221. Spending Per Resident

Historically, public education has been very costly to local taxpayers. The value of the spending per resident figure—as opposed to the cost per pupil and proportion of budget data, which we also review—is that it clearly shows to residents what they are paying for their schools. A childless couple in Charlotte, for example, was paying over $1,000 for public schools in fiscal 1981. Education is a matter of concern even for those without children. Education, after all, is the key to long-term improvement in the quality of life.

The following 1980–81 figures supplied by 72 school districts in the 100 largest U.S. cities may include several variables that would not make them truly comparable. For example, debt service and capital outlay are not treated uniformly by school districts in their reports.

Looking at the figures as submitted, Anchorage ranks highest, with $648.56 in public school expenditures per resident. Good financial health, the higher cost of living and the generally higher cost of goods and services relative to public education needs and requirements add up to the higher per capita expense. A factor to consider also is the high wage scale in Anchorage, which would be reflected in school costs.

Interestingly, each of the top cities listed, such as Charlotte and Fresno, is also highly ranked in the table showing the number of students per 100 residents. It is also true that public school expenditures have remained constant or increased, despite the fact that in most of the school districts enrollment has declined.

SOURCE: Educational systems survey by the authors, 1982.

| Rank | City | Population (000) | Total Public School Spending ($ 000) | Spending Per Capita ($) |
|---|---|---|---|---|
| 1 | Anchorage | 173.0 | 112,201 | 648.56 |
| 2 | Tacoma | 158.5 | 96,752 | 610.42 |
| 3 | Los Angeles | 3,328.0 | 1,801,702 | 541.38 |
| 4 | Newark | 329.3 | 176,901 | 537.20 |
| 5 | Fresno | 218.2 | 116,632 | 534.52 |
| 6 | Charlotte* | 314.4 | 163,600 | 520.36 |
| 7 | Milwaukee | 636.2 | 308,047 | 484.20 |
| 8 | Detroit | 1,203.3 | 576,034 | 478.71 |
| 9 | New York | 7,071.0 | 3,371,000 | 476.74 |
| 10 | St. Paul | 270.2 | 128,312 | 474.88 |
| 11 | Richmond | 219.2 | 103,968 | 474.31 |
| 12 | Albuquerque | 331.7 | 154,681 | 466.33 |
| 13 | Philadelphia | 1,688.2 | 773,455 | 458.15 |
| 14 | Washington, D.C. | 637.7 | 289,487 | 453.95 |
| 15 | Las Vegas* | 461.8 | 205,856 | 445.77 |
| 16 | Des Moines | 191.0 | 85,005 | 445.05 |
| 17 | Chicago | 3,005.1 | 1,319,746 | 439.17 |
| 18 | Shreveport* | 205.8 | 88,115 | 428.16 |
| 19 | Boston | 563.0 | 240,400 | 427.00 |
| 20 | Madison | 170.6 | 72,682 | 426.04 |
| 21 | Austin | 345.5 | 146,754 | 424.76 |
| 22 | Jacksonville* | 571.0 | 239,176 | 418.87 |
| 23 | Yonkers | 195.4 | 81,747 | 418.36 |
| 24 | Denver | 491.4 | 200,988 | 409.01 |
| 25 | Portland, Ore. | 366.4 | 144,017 | 393.06 |
| 26 | Dayton | 203.6 | 80,000 | 392.93 |
| 27 | Anaheim | 221.9 | 86,000 | 387.56 |
| 28 | Virginia Beach | 262.2 | 100,290 | 382.49 |
| 29 | Fort Worth | 385.1 | 143,680 | 373.10 |

| Rank | City | Population (000) | Total Public School Spending ($ 000) | Spending Per Capita ($) |
|---|---|---|---|---|
| 30 | Atlanta | 425.0 | 156,354 | 367.89 |
| 31 | Syracuse | 170.1 | 62,186 | 365.58 |
| 32 | Oakland | 339.3 | 124,000 | 365.46 |
| 33 | Lubbock | 174.0 | 62,796 | 360.90 |
| 34 | San Diego | 875.5 | 307,451 | 351.17 |
| 35 | St. Louis | 453.1 | 154,799 | 341.64 |
| 36 | Santa Ana | 203.7 | 68,555 | 336.55 |
| 37 | Long Beach | 361.3 | 119,660 | 331.19 |
| 38 | Dallas | 904.1 | 297,851 | 329.44 |
| 39 | Baton Rouge* | 366.2 | 120,503 | 329.06 |
| 40 | Lexington-Fayette* | 204.2 | 66,958 | 327.90 |
| 41 | Cleveland | 573.8 | 185,634 | 323.52 |
| 42 | Birmingham | 284.4 | 91,697 | 322.42 |
| 43 | Tampa* | 647.0 | 205,856 | 318.17 |
| 44 | Worcester | 161.8 | 51,017 | 315.31 |
| 45 | Wichita | 279.3 | 85,286 | 305.36 |
| 46 | Baltimore | 786.8 | 240,009 | 305.04 |
| 47 | Omaha | 311.7 | 94,563 | 303.38 |
| 48 | Tucson | 330.5 | 98,695 | 298.62 |
| 49 | Cincinnati | 385.5 | 112,193 | 291.03 |
| 50 | Tulsa | 361.0 | 103,000 | 285.32 |
| 51 | Salt Lake City | 163.0 | 46,352 | 284.37 |
| 52 | Colorado Springs | 215.1 | 59,972 | 278.81 |
| 53 | New Orleans | 557.5 | 153,638 | 275.58 |

| Rank | City | Population (000) | Total Public School Spending ($ 000) | Spending Per Capita ($) |
|---|---|---|---|---|
| 54 | St. Petersburg* | 728.4 | 200,196 | 274.84 |
| 55 | Minneapolis | 371.0 | 101,642 | 273.97 |
| 56 | Columbus, Ohio | 564.9 | 154,747 | 273.94 |
| 57 | Norfolk | 267.0 | 72,706 | 272.31 |
| 58 | Louisville | 684.8 | 183,628 | 268.15 |
| 59 | Toledo | 354.6 | 94,767 | 267.25 |
| 60 | Houston | 1,594.1 | 414,121 | 259.78 |
| 61 | Kansas City, Mo. | 448.2 | 113,344 | 252.89 |
| 62 | Jackson | 202.9 | 50,000 | 246.43 |
| 63 | Little Rock | 158.5 | 38,422 | 242.41 |
| 64 | Kansas City, Kan. | 161.7 | 37,638 | 232.76 |
| 65 | El Paso | 425.3 | 93,463 | 219.76 |
| 66 | Providence | 156.9 | 32,919 | 209.81 |
| 67 | Indianapolis | 700.8 | 136,786 | 195.19 |
| 68 | San Antonio | 785.4 | 131,800 | 167.81 |
| 69 | Oklahoma City | 403.2 | 65,375 | 162.14 |
| 70 | Riverside | 170.9 | 25,000 | 146.28 |
| 71 | Honolulu** | 3,650.5 | 334,400 | 91.60 |
| 72 | Huntington Beach | 170.5 | 14,372 | 84.29 |

*County or parish system.
**State system.

# 222. City Spending on Education

Broadly speaking, about one-fourth of local spending is on education. This proportion has been fairly constant. As educational costs have risen, so have other costs, and vice versa.

In the table below, expenditures for education do not include spending by the separate school districts that administer schools within most municipal areas. Great variations in amount from city to city therefore reflect differences in the relative role of the respective municipal government. Those spending below 20 percent have substantial independent school board funding. Houston, Dallas and Austin represent good examples of cities where the administration of public schools in the state is conducted by independent school districts that are self-governing, taxing jurisdictions.

Another consideration to be borne in mind when reviewing the figures below is that smaller cities have fewer municipal responsibilities. New York City's low percentage spent on education reflects the broad range of noneducational functions for which it is responsible.

Cities like Syracuse, Chattanooga, Rochester and Madison with very high proportions of their city expenditures dedicated to education have surrounding counties that pick up many social services that are handled in places like New York City by the city itself.

SOURCE: U.S. Census Bureau, *City Government Finances in 1979–80* (Washington, D.C.: Government Printing Office, 1981).

| Rank | City | Total Expenditures ($ 000) | Amount Budgeted for Education ($ 000) | Percentage Spent on Education |
|---|---|---|---|---|
| 1 | Chattanooga | 118,156 | 55,074 | 46.61 |
| 2 | Syracuse | 166,922 | 77,464 | 46.41 |
| 3 | Newark | 383,278 | 175,576 | 45.81 |
| 4 | Madison | 147,045 | 67,054 | 45.60 |
| 5 | Rochester | 308,881 | 136,090 | 44.06 |
| 6 | Yonkers | 173,739 | 75,841 | 43.65 |
| 7 | Knoxville | 115,149 | 49,280 | 42.80 |
| 8 | Anchorage | 305,843 | 129,673 | 42.39 |
| 9 | Providence | 122,445 | 51,052 | 41.69 |
| 10 | Virginia Beach | 198,680 | 81,839 | 41.19 |
| 11 | Memphis | 468,011 | 190,584 | 40.72 |
| 12 | Buffalo | 406,909 | 156,491 | 38.46 |
| 13 | Nashville-Davidson | 355,050 | 135,315 | 38.11 |
| 14 | Worcester | 190,757 | 69,366 | 36.36 |
| 15 | Jersey City | 241,934 | 86,507 | 35.76 |
| 16 | Norfolk | 228,812 | 73,878 | 32.29 |
| 17 | Baltimore | 1,035,252 | 315,271 | 30.45 |
| 18 | Boston | 862,762 | 258,562 | 29.97 |
| 19 | Richmond | 273,804 | 81,093 | 29.62 |
| 20 | New York | 13,171,385 | 3,279,277 | 24.90 |
| 21 | Washington | 1,975,878 | 383,387 | 19.40 |
| 22 | Kansas City, Kan. | 294,594 | 16,000 | 5.43 |

| Rank | City | Total Expenditures ($ 000) | Amount Budgeted for Education ($ 000) | Percentage Spent on Education |
|---|---|---|---|---|
| 23 | Birmingham | 146,977 | 3,561 | 2.42 |
| 23 | Philadelphia | 1,615,208 | 39,113 | 2.42 |
| 25 | San Diego | 294,167 | 7,103 | 2.41 |
| 26 | Los Angeles | 1,210,742 | 27,552 | 2.28 |
| 27 | San Francisco | 839,713 | 18,691 | 2.23 |
| 28 | Chicago | 1,569,869 | 33,141 | 2.11 |
| 29 | Phoenix | 384,085 | 5,546 | 1.44 |
| 30 | Detroit | 1,106,224 | 15,780 | 1.43 |
| 30 | San Antonio | 248,217 | 3,543 | 1.43 |
| 32 | Indianapolis | 417,406 | 5,655 | 1.35 |
| 33 | Long Beach | 246,543 | 2,850 | 1.16 |
| 33 | Seattle | 275,526 | 3,195 | 1.16 |
| 35 | Atlanta | 403,769 | 4,338 | 1.07 |
| 36 | St. Louis | 391,944 | 3,835 | .98 |
| 37 | Oakland | 312,930 | 1,246 | .58 |

| Rank | City | Total Expenditures ($ 000) | Amount Budgeted for Education ($ 000) | Percentage Spent on Education |
|---|---|---|---|---|
| 38 | Omaha | 138,367 | 307 | .22 |
| 39 | Little Rock | 57,395 | 111 | .20 |
| 40 | Tulsa | 171,648 | 294 | .17 |
| 41 | Oklahoma City | 208,799 | 285 | .14 |
| 42 | Milwaukee | 313,350 | 334 | .11 |
| 42 | Austin | 157,736 | 168 | .11 |
| 44 | New Orleans | 379,362 | 362 | .09 |
| 45 | Dallas | 369,299 | 238 | .06 |
| 46 | Spokane | 59,877 | 10 | .02 |
| 47 | Cincinnati | 295,806 | 38 | .01 |
| 48 | Houston | 625,838 | 4 | .00* |
| 48 | Minneapolis | 233,648 | 8 | .00* |

*Less than .01%.

# 223. Elementary Pupils

Public school system with a high percentage of students (55 percent and up) in the elementary grades have a sound pupil foundation for maintaining a stable educational system. However, the data also reflect the exodus of pupils to suburban or private schools when they reach high school.

A disproportionately low percentage of students in the elementary grades suggests that parents are sending their children to private or parochial schools, or are moving out of the area or not moving in (for example, because of higher home purchase or rental prices). This could be the case in Anaheim.

SOURCE: Educational systems survey by the authors, 1982.

| Rank | City | Elementary Students | Percentage of Elementary Students |
|---|---|---|---|
| 1 | Newark | 46,380 | 72.91 |
| 2 | Chicago | 337,744 | 70.76 |
| 2 | Dayton | 22,019 | 70.76 |
| 4 | St. Louis | 45,432 | 69.03 |
| 5 | Virginia Beach | 35,308 | 59.88 |
| 6 | Houston | 113,341 | 58.41 |
| 7 | Little Rock | 11,609 | 57.47 |
| 8 | Norfolk | 24,741 | 57.38 |
| 9 | Worcester | 13,666 | 57.22 |
| 10 | El Paso | 34,564 | 56.99 |
| 11 | Fresno | 26,086 | 56.06 |
| 12 | Santa Ana | 17,200 | 55.84 |
| 13 | Long Beach | 31,324 | 55.79 |
| 14 | Oakland | 27,467 | 55.71 |
| 15 | Yonkers | 11,524 | 55.21 |

| Rank | City | Elementary Students | Percentage of Elementary Students |
|---|---|---|---|
| 16 | Atlanta | 42,120 | 55.16 |
| 17 | Dallas | 70,847 | 54.95 |
| 18 | Salt Lake City | 12,819 | 54.89 |
| 19 | Wichita | 24,416 | 54.84 |
| 20 | Lubbock | 15,484 | 54.68 |
| 21 | Cincinnati | 29,987 | 54.54 |
| 22 | Los Angeles | 290,776 | 54.44 |
| 23 | San Diego | 60,165 | 54.26 |
| 24 | Toledo | 24,817 | 54.23 |
| 25 | Austin | 32,383 | 54.10 |
| 26 | Lexington-Fayette* | 16,894 | 54.04 |
| 27 | Miami | 47,952 | 53.98 |
| 28 | Cleveland | 44,280 | 53.97 |
| 29 | Anchorage | 19,822 | 53.71 |
| 30 | Birmingham | 24,528 | 53.21 |
| 31 | Colorado Springs | 16,467 | 53.15 |
| 32 | Charlotte* | 39,393 | 53.13 |
| 33 | Des Moines | 17,556 | 52.94 |
| 34 | Syracuse | 11,442 | 52.81 |
| 35 | Washington, D.C. | 55,772 | 52.54 |
| 36 | Denver | 33,296 | 52.51 |
| 37 | Minneapolis | 20,924 | 52.27 |
| 38 | St. Paul | 16,505 | 52.12 |
| 39 | Jackson | 15,625 | 51.91 |
| 40 | Portland, Ore. | 27,370 | 51.77 |
| 40 | Riverside | 27,370 | 51.77 |
| 42 | Kansas City, Kan. | 13,002 | 51.74 |
| 43 | Omaha | 23,035 | 51.66 |
| 44 | Indianapolis | 33,851 | 51.26 |
| 45 | New Orleans | 43,897 | 51.25 |
| 46 | Shreveport* | 23,107 | 51.21 |
| 47 | Kansas City, Mo. | 19,754 | 51.05 |
| 48 | Oklahoma City | 20,896 | 50.81 |
| 49 | Honolulu† | 83,699 | 50.80 |
| 49 | Tucson | 28,273 | 50.80 |
| 51 | San Antonio | 33,539 | 50.36 |
| 52 | Philadelphia | 112,944 | 50.35 |
| 53 | Tulsa | 24,617 | 49.86 |

| Rank | City | Elementary Students | Percentage of Elementary Students |
|------|------|--------------------|-----------------------------------|
| 54 | Tacoma | 14,176 | 49.85 |
| 55 | Las Vegas* | 43,420 | 49.03 |
| 56 | Fort Worth | 31,251 | 48.94 |
| 57 | Detroit | 103,165 | 48.70 |
| 58 | Columbus, Ohio | 34,817 | 47.81 |
| 59 | Boston | 29,971 | 47.66 |
| 60 | Richmond | 15,429 | 47.02 |
| 61 | Tampa* | 52,632 | 47.01 |
| 62 | Jacksonville* | 46,738 | 46.49 |
| 63 | Baton Rouge | 28,656 | 44.72 |
| 64 | Baltimore* | 43,626 | 44.66 |

| Rank | City | Elementary Students | Percentage of Elementary Students |
|------|------|--------------------|-----------------------------------|
| 65 | New York | 414,398 | 43.91 |
| 66 | Louisville | 43,405 | 42.01 |
| 67 | St. Petersburg* | 36,617 | 41.82 |
| 68 | Providence | 7,400 | 40.92 |
| 69 | Albuquerque | 31,839 | 40.47 |
| 70 | Madison | 9,548 | 39.39 |
| 71 | Anaheim | 11,335 | 31.71 |

*County or parish system.
†Statewide system.

# 224. Private Elementary School Attendance

Private education enrollment has been declining. In part, this reflects the fact that total student enrollments are decreasing. Statistics indicate that between 1970 and 1980 total school enrollment in the United States decreased 7 percent. During the same period, private school enrollment declined 12 percent. Tuition costs alone have increased as much as 15 percent in the one-year period from 1980 to 1981, making the cost of private education more prohibitive and exacerbating the decline in enrollments.

As the table below indicates, in the elementary schools (Kindergarten through 8th Grade) of one-sixth of the 36 largest U.S. SMSAs, one-fifth or more of school-age children are being educated in private schools. With the single exception of New Orleans, at the top with 29.5 per cent, cities in the Northeast and Mid-west sections of the country show the largest percentages of children in private schools. This reflects two main characteristics of the large cities in these areas. First, they were settled by European immigrants who brought with them strong religious traditions—especially Roman Catholic traditions—that include sectarian schooling. Only New Orleans had a comparably deep-rooted Catholic history, distinguished from the northeastern cities by the purity of its French origins. Second, the older cities have a longer tradition of private education quite apart from the sectarian schools. Some of these schools, like the Ethical Culture Society School in New York, were designed for the children of working people and only with great misgivings decided to admit the children of those who could afford to pay. Most of the schools, however, were overtly and from the beginning designed to offer an education that was academically, physically or socially superior to what was available from public institutions of learning.

Private schools were given a boost by court-ordered busing directives in the 1960s and 1970s. Parents who did not wish to move to suburban school districts and who were concerned about the educational quality of the public schools enrolled their children in private schools. While national statistics indicate declining private school enrollment, most of the 36 metro areas shown in the table below still show significant (10 percent or more) private school enrollment. Parents' desire to have their children educated in a more formal or holistic setting by attending religious-oriented schools, academies or other private educational institutions remains a major attraction of private education.

SOURCES: U.S. Census Bureau, *Census of Population and Housing, 1980.* Dena Kleiman and Kenneth A. Briggs, "More Parents Turning Away from Public Schools to Meet Children's Needs," *New York Times*, September 7, 1981; John Herbers, "Private School Rolls Fell By a Third from '64 to '79," *New York Times*, October 8, 1982; *Provisional Estimates of Social, Economic and Housing Characteristics: States and Selected Standard Metropolitan Areas*, Table P-2, "Nativity, Language, Commuting, Educational and Veteran Status, and Disability Characteristics: 1980," (Washington, D.C.: GPO, 1982).

| Rank | Metro Area | All Students, Public and Private, K–8 | Private School Students, K–8 | Percentage of Students in Private Schools, K–8 |
|------|-----------|------|------|------|
| 1 | New Orleans | 181,894 | 53,672 | 29.51 |
| 2 | Milwaukee | 196,919 | 51,459 | 25.87 |
| 3 | Philadelphia | 642,355 | 165,959 | 25.84 |

| Rank | Metro Area | All Students, Public and Private, K–8 | Private School Students, K–8 | Percentage of Students in Private Schools, K–8 |
|---|---|---|---|---|
| 4 | Cleveland | 259,687 | 60,308 | 23.22 |
| 5 | New York | 1,148,188 | 259,924 | 22.64 |
| 6 | St. Louis | 340,323 | 71,229 | 20.93 |
| 7 | Cincinnati | 203,733 | 40,422 | 19.84 |
| 8 | Chicago | 1,016,544 | 198,152 | 19.49 |
| 9 | Pittsburgh | 279,877 | 53,775 | 19.21 |
| 10 | Buffalo | 170,825 | 32,075 | 18.78 |
| 11 | Miami | 198,115 | 33,569 | 16.94 |
| 12 | Atlanta | 308,228 | 32,853 | 16.66 |
| 13 | Minneapolis | 296,483 | 48,197 | 16.25 |
| 14 | San Francisco | 378,793 | 59,970 | 15.83 |
| 15 | Los Angeles | 992,776 | 150,628 | 15.17 |
| 16 | Washington, D.C. | 427,790 | 59,356 | 13.88 |
| 17 | Newark | 273,995 | 37,262 | 13.60 |
| 18 | Kansas City, Kan.-Mo. | 186,996 | 23,305 | 12.46 |
| 19 | San Jose | 175,228 | 18,020 | 12.28 |
| 20 | Baltimore | 302,206 | 37,035 | 12.25 |

| Rank | Metro Area | All Students, Public and Private, K–8 | Private School Students, K–8 | Percentage of Students in Private Schools, K–8 |
|---|---|---|---|---|
| 21 | Boston | 346,159 | 41,988 | 12.13 |
| 22 | Tampa-St. Petersburg | 181,181 | 21,543 | 11.89 |
| 23 | Sacramento | 131,108 | 15,246 | 11.63 |
| 24 | Indianapolis | 173,900 | 20,006 | 11.50 |
| 25 | San Antonio | 173,667 | 19,567 | 11.27 |
| 26 | Columbus, Ohio | 152,560 | 16,613 | 10.89 |
| 27 | Seattle | 204,415 | 22,213 | 10.87 |
| 28 | Detroit | 664,130 | 67,084 | 10.10 |
| 29 | Portland, Ore. | 168,178 | 16,640 | 9.98 |
| 29 | San Diego | 235,797 | 23,528 | 9.98 |
| 31 | Anaheim-Santa Ana | 262,292 | 25,681 | 9.79 |
| 32 | Denver | 222,557 | 19,358 | 8.70 |
| 33 | Riverside | 225,943 | 18,873 | 8.35 |
| 34 | Houston | 445,696 | 35,325 | 7.93 |
| 35 | Dallas-Fort Worth | 438,980 | 34,109 | 7.79 |
| 36 | Phoenix | 21,077 | 14,520 | 6.91 |

# 225. Private High School Attendance

The comments on the previous table apply to this table as well. The table shows the percentage of private school attendance in Grades 9 through 12, i.e., high school.

The New Orleans metro area has the highest percentage of nonpublic enrollment in high school. This is probably due to its large Catholic population (close to 500,000 adherents in 1980). Interestingly, the other leading metro areas in this ranking that have high private school enrollment—New York, Chicago, Philadelphia, Cleveland, Cincinnati, Milwaukee and St. Louis—also have high Catholic populations. According to the National Catholic Education Association, however, Catholic school attendance has been declining (down 44 per cent from 1964 to 1979) and will continue to decline in the 1980s, although at a slower rate.

SOURCES: U.S. Census Bureau, *Census of Population and Housing, 1980:* Dena Kleiman and Kenneth A. Briggs, "More Parents Turning Away From Public Schools to Meet Children's Needs," *New York Times,* September 7, 1981; John Herbers, "Private School Rolls Fell By a Third From '64 to '79," *New York Times,* October 8, 1982; *Provisional Estimates of Social, Economic and Housing Characteristics: States and Selected Standard Metropolitan Areas,* Table P-2, "Nativity, Language, Commuting, Educational and Veteran Status, and Disability Characteristics: 1980," (Washington, D.C.: GPO, 1982).

| Rank | Metro Area | All Students, Public and Private, 9–12 | Private School Students, 9–12 | Percentage of Students in Private Schools, 9–12 |
|---|---|---|---|---|
| 1 | New Orleans | 82,485 | 20,575 | 24.94 |
| 2 | Philadelphia | 340,081 | 77,911 | 22.91 |
| 3 | Cincinnati | 96,761 | 18,841 | 19.47 |
| 4 | New York | 594,380 | 99,205 | 16.69 |
| 5 | St. Louis | 168,527 | 25,102 | 14.89 |
| 6 | Cleveland | 134,570 | 19,650 | 14.60 |
| 7 | Chicago | 478,670 | 67,810 | 14.17 |
| 8 | Miami | 102,611 | 14,021 | 13.66 |
| 9 | Milwaukee | 101,495 | 13,686 | 13.47 |
| 10 | Baltimore | 157,143 | 20,852 | 13.27 |
| 11 | San Francisco | 204,686 | 25,385 | 12.40 |
| 12 | Boston | 185,444 | 22,987 | 12.39 |
| 13 | Los Angeles | 485,570 | 58,182 | 11.98 |
| 14 | Minneapolis | 148,660 | 17,724 | 11.92 |
| 15 | Kansas City, Kan.-Mo. | 86,871 | 10,297 | 11.85 |
| 16 | Buffalo | 90,913 | 10,163 | 11.18 |
| 17 | Newark | 148,589 | 16,465 | 11.08 |
| 17 | Washington, D.C. | 213,476 | 23,650 | 11.08 |
| 19 | Columbus, Ohio | 70,621 | 6,080 | 8.61 |
| 20 | Indianapolis | 77,631 | 6,588 | 8.49 |
| 21 | Detroit | 317,061 | 25,882 | 8.16 |
| 22 | Pittsburgh | 152,112 | 12,274 | 8.07 |
| 23 | Tampa-St. Petersburg | 85,122 | 6,400 | 7.52 |
| 24 | Anaheim-Santa Ana | 134,076 | 9,436 | 7.04 |
| 25 | Seattle | 103,003 | 7,171 | 6.96 |
| 26 | Denver | 109,464 | 7,550 | 6.90 |
| 27 | San Jose | 89,967 | 6,165 | 6.85 |
| 28 | Portland, Ore. | 69,635 | 4,725 | 6.79 |
| 29 | Sacramento | 66,730 | 4,464 | 6.69 |
| 30 | Phoenix | 94,089 | 5,912 | 6.28 |
| 31 | Atlanta | 130,017 | 8,035 | 6.18 |
| 32 | San Antonio | 74,188 | 4,603 | 6.15 |

| Rank | Metro Area | All Students, Public and Private, 9–12 | Private School Students, 9–12 | Percentage of Students in Private Schools, 9–12 | Rank | Metro Area | All Students, Public and Private, 9–12 | Private School Students, 9–12 | Percentage of Students in Private Schools, 9–12 |
|------|-----------|------|------|------|------|-----------|------|------|------|
| 33 | San Diego | 110,366 | 6,376 | 5.69 | 35 | Dallas-Fort Worth | 184,008 | 9,112 | 4.95 |
| 34 | Riverside | 97,345 | 4,950 | 5.09 | 36 | Houston | 171,988 | 7,904 | 4.60 |

# 226. High School Drop-Out Rates

High drop-out rates indicate the presence of a continuing educational problem—one that is affected by a variety of factors, including the home environment, peer influence, educational level, school environment and even teacher competence. One might expect that a lower drop-out rate would go hand-in-hand with a higher college-bound percentage and a higher cost per pupil. However, this relationship does not always hold true. Sixty-three of the 78 school systems responding to the Council on Municipal Performance survey of educational systems submitted figures on their drop-out rate for grades 9–12. Almost one-third (30 percent) have drop-out rates higher than 10 percent. Over 50 percent have rates of 7 percent and up.

All systems reporting a high drop-out rate are making concerted efforts to improve attendance patterns and reduce the number of students choosing to discontinue their formal education. New York City, in recognizing its problem, has organized a high school drop-out task force. This group is working on the early identification of dropouts, career programs, personalizing the school environment and model "holding power" programs. Outreach centers have had some success in reaching dropouts.

SOURCE: Educational systems survey by the authors, 1982.

| Rank | City | Dropouts as a Percentage of Full-Time Enrolled Students | Rank | City | Dropouts as a Percentage of Full-Time Enrolled Students | Rank | City | Dropouts as a Percentage of Full-Time Enrolled Students |
|------|------|------|------|------|------|------|------|------|
| 1 | New York‡ | 44.6 | 23 | Little Rock | 9.0 | 47 | Omaha | 4.8 |
| 2 | Fresno | 29.7 | 25 | Detroit | 8.5 | 48 | Toledo | 4.7 |
| 3 | Indianapolis | 17.1 | 26 | Tampa* | 8.3 | 49 | Des Moines | 4.5 |
| 4 | Minneapolis | 16.0 | 27 | Cincinnati | 8.0 | 49 | El Paso | 4.5 |
| 4 | Riverside | 16.0 | 27 | Los Angeles | 8.0 | 49 | Portland, Ore. | 4.5 |
| 6 | Norfolk | 14.2 | 27 | Tucson | 8.0 | 49 | Virginia Beach | 4.5 |
| 7 | Anaheim | 14.0 | 30 | Cleveland | 7.8 | 53 | Colorado Springs | 3.6 |
| 8 | Philadelphia | 13.7 | 31 | Louisville* | 7.7 | 54 | Houston | 3.0 |
| 8 | Providence | 13.7 | 32 | Newark | 7.6 | 55 | Washington, D.C. | 2.7 |
| 8 | St. Louis | 13.7 | 33 | Shreveport* | 7.2 | 56 | Jacksonville | 2.6 |
| 11 | Richmond | 12.0 | 34 | Syracuse | 6.9 | 57 | Oklahoma City | 2.3 |
| 11 | Wichita | 12.0 | 35 | St. Paul | 6.8 | 58 | Baltimore* | 1.7 |
| 13 | Tacoma | 11.6 | 36 | Austin | 6.7 | 59 | San Antonio | 1.6 |
| 14 | Columbus, Ohio | 11.0 | 37 | Charlotte | 6.4 | 60 | Anchorage | 1.1 |
| 15 | Kansas City, Mo. | 10.8 | 37 | New Orleans | 6.4 | 61 | Yonkers | .8 |
| 16 | Boston | 10.5 | 39 | Albuquerque | 6.2 | 62 | Honolulu† | .6 |
| 17 | Dayton | 10.2 | 39 | Jackson | 6.2 | 63 | Baton Rouge* | .1 |
| 18 | Chicago | 9.9 | 41 | Worcester | 6.0 | | | |
| 19 | Fort Worth | 9.7 | 42 | Las Vegas* | 5.7 | *County or parish system. | | |
| 20 | Denver | 9.6 | 43 | San Diego | 5.6 | †Statewide system. | | |
| 21 | Milwaukee | 9.3 | 44 | Atlanta | 5.2 | ‡Figures are for the class of 1978. | | |
| 22 | St. Petersburg* | 9.1 | 45 | Lubbock | 5.1 | | | |
| 23 | Lexington-Fayette* | 9.0 | 46 | Madison | 5.0 | | | |

# 227. Occupational Programs

Students identified as receiving public and private post-secondary occupational education are those enrolled in programs that consist of planned sequences of courses leading to a specific occupational objective, e.g., X-ray technician, data programmer, auto mechanic.

The information in the table below gives an indication of the degree of formal skills training taking place in the 100 largest cities in 1976–77. To some extent the student enrollment is a function of city size. However, the assessment by local institutions of specific occupational needs remains an extremely important reason why one city may have more such courses than another. This does not necessarily mean that there is a great variation in the nature or degree of skill training. The types of listings include schools identified as cosmetology/barber, art/design, hospital and allied health, technical institutes, and community colleges or even four-year colleges, all with the appropriate accreditation. Chicago leads in total enrolled, with New York City and Washington, D.C. following.

Most of the training in Chicago is for hospital and allied health services and business office skills. In New York City, training for business office skills and marketing predominates. In Los Angeles the state occupational centers, with their variety of programs, conduct the great majority of occupational training.

At the lower enrollment end of the ranking, Virginia Beach has occupational programs for mechanics and general office workers—two basic needs of an affluent, mostly residential area. The emphasis in Yonkers, with its significant older population, is on allied health care.

Generally, each community through its postsecondary occupational programs is serving important needs for health care, mechanical training and general office skills. The larger cities have a need for more sophisticated business office skills such as data processing, accounting, and business and commerce technologies.

SOURCE: National Center for Education Statistics, U.S. Department of Health Education and Welfare *Directory of Postsecondary Schools with Occupational Programs, 1978*. Washington, D.C.: GPO, 1978.

| Rank | City | Student Enrollment in Postsecondary Occupational Programs | Rank | City | Student Enrollment in Postsecondary Occupational Programs | Rank | City | Student Enrollment in Postsecondary Occupational Programs |
|---|---|---|---|---|---|---|---|---|
| 1 | Chicago | 68,611 | 29 | Detroit | 6,252 | 57 | Mobile | 3,304 |
| 2 | New York | 44,743 | 30 | San Diego | 5,583 | 58 | Dayton | 3,249 |
| 3 | Washington, D.C. | 36,241 | 30 | San Antonio | 5,583 | 59 | Oakland | 3,105 |
| 4 | Los Angeles | 28,480 | 32 | Columbus, Ga. | 5,490 | 60 | Honolulu | 3,080 |
| 5 | Pittsburgh | 19,444 | 33 | Albuquerque | 5,474 | 61 | Toledo | 3,077 |
| 6 | Santa Ana | 18,074 | 34 | Seattle | 5,273 | 62 | Syracuse | 3,006 |
| 7 | Minneapolis | 17,823 | 35 | Baltimore | 5,262 | 63 | Colorado Springs | 3,003 |
| 8 | Cleveland | 17,625 | 36 | Providence | 5,185 | 64 | Tucson | 2,950 |
| 9 | Denver | 17,061 | 37 | Cincinnati | 4,819 | 65 | Little Rock | 2,932 |
| 10 | Miami | 16,276 | 38 | Newark | 4,559 | 66 | Charlotte | 2,869 |
| 11 | Boston | 13,491 | 39 | New Orleans | 4,359 | 67 | Akron | 2,852 |
| 12 | Phoenix | 11,783 | 40 | Indianapolis | 4,284 | 68 | Grand Rapids | 2,708 |
| 13 | Omaha | 11,500 | 41 | Buffalo | 4,267 | 69 | Las Vegas | 2,704 |
| 14 | Philadelphia | 11,455 | 42 | Warren | 4,191 | 70 | San Jose | 2,680 |
| 15 | Houston | 11,229 | 43 | Tampa | 4,173 | 71 | Shreveport | 2,595 |
| 16 | St. Louis | 9,994 | 44 | Lexington-Fayette | 4,102 | 72 | Fort Worth | 2,590 |
| 17 | Sacramento | 9,856 | 45 | Columbus, Ohio | 3,948 | 73 | Spokane | 2,358 |
| 18 | Portland, Ore. | 9,634 | 46 | Wichita | 3,936 | 74 | El Paso | 2,353 |
| 19 | Atlanta | 8,611 | 47 | Long Beach | 3,934 | 75 | Anaheim | 2,256 |
| 20 | San Francisco | 8,606 | 48 | Nashville | 3,868 | 76 | Madison | 2,249 |
| 21 | Oklahoma City | 8,246 | 49 | Kansas City, Mo. | 3,864 | 77 | Flint | 2,226 |
| 22 | Memphis | 8,139 | 50 | Baton Rouge | 3,802 | 78 | Worcester | 2,221 |
| 23 | St. Petersburg | 8,084 | 51 | Knoxville | 3,787 | 79 | Fort Wayne | 2,206 |
| 24 | Milwaukee | 7,701 | 52 | Birmingham | 3,658 | 80 | Des Moines | 2,157 |
| 25 | Dallas | 7,331 | 53 | Chattanooga | 3,428 | 81 | Tacoma | 2,067 |
| 26 | St. Paul | 7,261 | 54 | Salt Lake City | 3,407 | 82 | Fresno | 2,041 |
| 27 | Louisville | 6,659 | 55 | Rochester | 3,337 | 83 | Jacksonville | 1,858 |
| 28 | Tulsa | 6,289 | 56 | Montgomery | 3,316 | 84 | Norfolk | 1,830 |

| Rank | City | Student Enrollment in Postsecondary Occupational Programs | | Rank | City | Student Enrollment in Postsecondary Occupational Programs | | Rank | City | Student Enrollment in Postsecondary Occupational Programs |
|---|---|---|---|---|---|---|---|---|---|---|
| 85 | Austin | 1,735 | | 91 | Lubbock | 939 | | 97 | Anchorage | 517 |
| 86 | Lincoln | 1,571 | | 92 | Jersey City | 920 | | 98 | Arlington, Texas | 516 |
| 87 | Aurora | 1,482 | | 93 | Richmond | 867 | | 99 | Yonkers | 330 |
| 88 | Kansas City, Kan. | 1,388 | | 94 | Huntington Beach | 763 | | 100 | Virginia Beach | 284 |
| 89 | Corpus Christi | 1,068 | | 95 | Greensboro | 717 | | | | |
| 90 | Riverside | 1,062 | | 96 | Jackson | 654 | | | | |

# 228. College-Bound Graduates

This table provides a general indication of the percentage of graduates who are college-bound in the public school systems replying to the survey. Some school systems, such as New York City's, included all postsecondary educational development in their figure. Other communities—like Indianapolis; Tacoma; Kansas City, Mo.; Cincinnati; and Chicago—confined the percentage to four-year-college-bound students only.

There is no obvious correlation indicated between attendance rate, size of school system and the percentage of graduates who go to college. The average for the smallest 14 systems listed (52.8 percent) is approximately the same as for the 10 largest (53.0 percent).

The percentage figure for college-bound graduates, however, represents an important indication of the academic level of achievement in the respective school system as it relates to postsecondary professional development. All measures of achievement have their own special problems. College admissions are not exempt, but they have the great advantage of reflecting student motivation and school guidance as well as raw intellectual achievement. A school where a high proportion of pupils go on to college is likely to have more social and intellectual direction than one where a high proportion of pupils do not.

SOURCE: Educational systems survey by the authors, 1982.

| Rank | City | Percentage of Graduates Who Are College-Bound | | Rank | City | Percentage of Graduates Who Are College-Bound | | Rank | City | Percentage of Graduates Who Are College-Bound |
|---|---|---|---|---|---|---|---|---|---|---|
| 1 | Honolulu† | 85.0 | | 20 | Austin | 59.0 | | 39 | Milwaukee | 47.0 |
| 2 | New York | 82.0 | | 20 | Columbus, Ohio | 59.0 | | 39 | Newark | 47.0 |
| 3 | Yonkers | 81.0 | | 20 | Providence | 59.0 | | 39 | Tulsa | 47.0 |
| 4 | Virginia Beach | 76.0 | | 23 | Colorado Springs | 58.0 | | 39 | Wichita | 47.0 |
| 5 | Los Angeles | 74.0 | | 23 | Dallas | 58.0 | | 43 | Omaha | 46.0 |
| 6 | Charlotte | 73.0 | | 23 | Lubbock | 58.0 | | 44 | Anchorage | 44.0 |
| 7 | Long Beach | 72.0 | | 26 | Boston | 57.6 | | 44 | Baton Rouge | 44.0 |
| 8 | Jackson | 71.0 | | 27 | Philadelphia | 57.0 | | 46 | Cincinnati | 43.0 |
| 9 | Birmingham | 69.0 | | 28 | Riverside | 55.0 | | 46 | Tucson | 43.0 |
| 9 | Worcester | 69.0 | | 29 | St. Paul | 54.9 | | 48 | Atlanta | 42.0 |
| 11 | Madison | 64.0 | | 30 | Denver | 54.0 | | 48 | Detroit | 42.0 |
| 12 | Portland, Ore. | 63.0 | | 30 | Salt Lake City | 54.0 | | 48 | Washington, D.C. | 42.0 |
| 12 | Syracuse | 63.0 | | 32 | Las Vegas* | 52.0 | | 51 | Little Rock | 41.0 |
| 14 | Baltimore* | 62.0 | | 32 | Norfolk | 52.0 | | 51 | St. Louis | 41.0 |
| 14 | Houston | 62.0 | | 34 | Des Moines | 51.0 | | 51 | Albuquerque | 40.0 |
| 16 | El Paso | 61.0 | | 34 | San Antonio | 51.0 | | 53 | Anaheim | 40.0 |
| 16 | St. Petersburg* | 61.0 | | 36 | Minneapolis | 50.0 | | 53 | Chicago | 40.0 |
| 18 | Lexington-Fayette | 60.0 | | 37 | Richmond | 48.0 | | 53 | Dayton | 40.0 |
| 18 | San Diego | 60.0 | | 37 | Jacksonville | 48.0 | | 53 | Tampa* | 40.0 |

| Rank | City | Percentage of Graduates Who Are College-Bound | Rank | City | Percentage of Graduates Who Are College-Bound | Rank | City | Percentage of Graduates Who Are College-Bound |
|------|------|-----|------|------|-----|------|------|-----|
| 58 | Kansas City, Mo. | 37.0 | 60 | Indianapolis | 29.0 | *County or parish system. | | |
| 59 | New Orleans | 36.7 | 61 | Tacoma | 22.0 | †Statewide system. | | |

# 229. College-Educated Adults

In cities with fewer college-educated adults (four or more years of college, i.e., presumably with a college degree), a college degree will be rarer and therefore more valuable. However, in such cities there will also be a smaller community of professional people with whom the college-educated person can associate.

The metro area of Washington, D.C., with its government offices and agencies and national and professional association headquarters, has the highest proportion of college-educated adults (persons 25 years old or older), according to 1980 figures. Interestingly, in an earlier table we saw that Washington, D.C. also has one of the lowest proportions of high-school-educated adults, according to 1980 figures. It therefore has extreme inequalities in educational achievement as compared to other cities.

Cosmopolitan San Francisco is next, closely followed by Denver, San Jose and Seattle. Each one is an area with a solid base of professionals and persons with a high level of technological training. San Jose, for example, has approximately 100 business parks in its metro area, most of them in technological manufacture and research and development.

The areas with a high proportion of manufacturing and industrial labor share the lower end of the ranking with areas that have a high level of agricultural activity. Riverside, for example, has industrial activity, with a considerable proportion of storage, warehousing, manufacturing and distribution. Industrial areas rank high on high school education and low on college education. In contrast to Washington, D.C., in metro area Pittsburgh the odds are low (16 percent) that an adult has four years of college education and high (41 percent) that the adult has a high school education. Manufacturing cities have a high degree of *income* equality. They also have a high degree of *educational* equality.

SOURCE: U.S. Census Bureau, *1980 Census of Population and Housing: Provisional Estimates of Social, Economic and Housing Characteristics: States and Selected Standard Metropolitan Statistical Areas*, Table P-5, "General Social and Economic Characteristics by Race and Spanish Origin: 1980," (Washington, D.C.: GPO, 1982).

| Rank | Metro Area | Total Adults 25 and Over | Percentage of Adults 25 and Over with a College Education |
|------|------------|-----|-----|
| 1 | Washington, D.C. | 595,994 | 32.47 |
| 2 | San Francisco | 551,141 | 26.46 |
| 3 | Denver | 250,629 | 26.39 |
| 4 | San Jose | 190,021 | 25.24 |
| 5 | Seattle | 237,706 | 24.21 |
| 6 | Boston | 397,891 | 23.56 |
| 7 | Atlanta | 268,205 | 22.87 |
| 8 | Minneapolis-St. Paul | 265,582 | 21.79 |
| 9 | San Diego | 227,024 | 21.18 |
| 10 | Anaheim | 237,469 | 21.03 |
| 11 | New York | 1,194,331 | 20.66 |
| 12 | Houston | 331,541 | 20.55 |
| 13 | Newark | 243,182 | 20.16 |
| 14 | Columbus, Ohio | 124,250 | 20.06 |
| 15 | Portland, Ore. | 147,051 | 19.55 |
| 16 | Sacramento | 115,388 | 19.29 |
| 17 | Dallas-Fort Worth | 325,168 | 19.15 |
| 18 | Kansas City, Mo.-Kan. | 150,031 | 19.08 |
| 19 | Los Angeles | 835,727 | 18.89 |
| 20 | Phoenix | 159,433 | 18.10 |
| 21 | Milwaukee | 144,084 | 17.62 |
| 22 | Philadelphia | 491,795 | 17.36 |
| 23 | Cincinnati | 134,485 | 16.67 |
| 24 | Baltimore | 213,215 | 16.41 |
| 25 | Miami | 169,473 | 16.16 |
| 26 | New Orleans | 106,609 | 15.93 |
| 27 | Chicago | 662,247 | 15.92 |
| 28 | Pittsburgh | 226,010 | 15.84 |
| 29 | Indianapolis | 105,740 | 15.72 |
| 30 | Cleveland | 180,130 | 15.59 |
| 30 | San Antonio | 90,622 | 15.59 |
| 32 | St. Louis | 206,623 | 14.90 |
| 33 | Detroit | 357,812 | 14.21 |
| 34 | Buffalo | 104,090 | 13.91 |
| 35 | Tampa | 377,659 | 13.39 |
| 36 | Riverside | 119,416 | 13.17 |

# 230.  Singing Teachers

The table below is a measure of the availability of non-academic educational services in a city. Whether as part of a school's program or obtained by parents privately to "enrich" their children's education, singing teachers are a resource that can add a great deal to the learning and growth of a child.

While there are many singing teachers who are not members of the National Association of Teachers of Singing, it is a fair bet that a high percentage of the most dedicated members of the profession will seek membership in their association.

New York City had 143 member singing teachers in 1982. Five cities have over 40 members: Dallas, Minneapolis, Los Angeles, Houston and Chicago. Tucson has 30 member teachers. Other cities have between one and 28 teachers, except three cities which have none: Warren, Huntington Beach and Anchorage. Residents of Warren can go to Detroit for singing lessons, and residents of Huntington Beach can go to Los Angeles. But Anchorage residents have a *long* way to go to obtain a lesson from the nearest member teacher.

SOURCE: Response for this book to the authors' questionnaire by the National Association of Teachers of Singing, 1982.

| Rank | City | Members of Nat'l Assoc of Singing Teachers | Rank | City | Members of Nat'l Assoc of Singing Teachers | Rank | City | Members of Nat'l Assoc of Singing Teachers |
|---|---|---|---|---|---|---|---|---|
| 1 | New York | 143 | 31 | San Antonio | 17 | 66 | Little Rock | 6 |
| 2 | Dallas | 46 | 36 | Boston | 16 | 66 | Mobile | 6 |
| 3 | Los Angeles | 44 | 37 | Atlanta | 14 | 66 | Oakland | 6 |
| 3 | Minneapolis | 44 | 37 | Denver | 14 | 72 | Colorado Springs | 5 |
| 5 | Houston | 43 | 37 | St. Louis | 14 | 72 | Columbus, Ga. | 5 |
| 6 | Chicago | 42 | 40 | Birmingham | 13 | 72 | Dayton | 5 |
| 7 | Tucson | 30 | 40 | Charlotte | 13 | 72 | Des Moines | 5 |
| 8 | Baltimore | 28 | 40 | Indianapolis | 13 | 72 | Las Vegas | 5 |
| 9 | Baton Rouge | 27 | 40 | Madison | 13 | 72 | Long Beach | 5 |
| 9 | Fort Worth | 27 | 40 | Philadelphia | 13 | 72 | St. Petersburg | 5 |
| 11 | San Francisco | 26 | 40 | Rochester | 13 | 72 | Shreveport | 5 |
| 11 | Seattle | 26 | 46 | Grand Rapids | 12 | 72 | Tacoma | 5 |
| 13 | Nashville-Davidson | 25 | 46 | Jacksonville | 12 | 81 | Arlington | 4 |
| 13 | Portland, Ore. | 25 | 48 | Chattanooga | 11 | 81 | Fort Wayne | 4 |
| 15 | Lincoln | 24 | 48 | Jackson | 11 | 81 | Toledo | 4 |
| 15 | St. Paul | 24 | 48 | Norfolk | 11 | 84 | Montgomery | 3 |
| 17 | Cincinnati | 23 | 51 | Lexington-Fayette | 10 | 84 | Riverside | 3 |
| 17 | Wichita | 23 | 51 | Lubbock | 10 | 84 | San Jose | 3 |
| 19 | Austin | 22 | 51 | Richmond | 10 | 84 | Santa Ana | 3 |
| 20 | Milwaukee | 21 | 51 | Syracuse | 10 | 84 | Virginia Beach | 3 |
| 20 | Washington, D.C. | 21 | 51 | Tampa | 10 | 89 | Anaheim | 2 |
| 22 | Oklahoma City | 20 | 51 | Tulsa | 10 | 89 | Kansas City, Kan. | 2 |
| 22 | San Diego | 20 | 57 | Honolulu | 9 | 89 | Newark | 2 |
| 24 | Columbus, Ohio | 19 | 57 | Spokane | 9 | 89 | Providence | 2 |
| 24 | Greensboro | 19 | 59 | Akron | 8 | 93 | Aurora | 1 |
| 24 | Memphis | 19 | 59 | Albuquerque | 8 | 93 | Flint | 1 |
| 24 | New Orleans | 19 | 59 | Detroit | 8 | 93 | Jersey City | 1 |
| 24 | Salt Lake City | 19 | 59 | Sacramento | 8 | 93 | Worcester | 1 |
| 29 | Cleveland | 18 | 63 | El Paso | 7 | 93 | Yonkers | 1 |
| 29 | Pittsburgh | 18 | 63 | Fresno | 7 | 98 | Anchorage | 0 |
| 31 | Kansas City, Mo. | 17 | 63 | Omaha | 7 | 98 | Huntington Beach | 0 |
| 31 | Louisville | 17 | 66 | Buffalo | 6 | 98 | Warren, Mi | 0 |
| 31 | Miami | 17 | 66 | Corpus Christi | 6 | | | |
| 31 | Phoenix | 17 | 66 | Knoxville | 6 | | | |

# CHAPTER FOURTEEN

# TRAVEL AND COMMUNICATIONS

The economic dimensions of the U.S. travel industry are immense. By the end of this century, travel is expected to be one of the largest industries in the world. Travel away from home is an integral part of the American lifestyle. Studies* indicate that close to one out of every two U.S. residents takes at least one trip to a place 100 miles or more away from home in a given year.

According to the proceedings of the 1981 Travel Outlook Forum, total national travel industry receipts for 1980 were up 16 percent over 1979. The Travel Price Index represents the cost of lodging, food, transportation, entertainment, incidentals and other items that a traveler buys when traveling away from home in the United States. Through October 1980 the index was up 21 percent, compared to a 14 percent increase in the

---

*U.S. Travel Center and Travel Research Association.

Consumer Price Index. That is, the Travel Price Index grew 50 percent faster than average consumer prices for this period. Without gasoline price increases, the cost of travel would have been up only 13 percent, or less than the overall Consumer Price Index. Overall, in 1980 travel industry receipts adjusted for inflation fell 3 percent.

Travel industry employment grew by 300,000 jobs in 1980. Employment in travel-related businesses now accounts for almost 8 million U.S. jobs, or 9 percent of total employment in the country. The travel industry stands out among U.S. industries in creating new jobs and providing employment for minorities, women and youth. Also, small businesses dominate the travel (and tourist) industry; 98 percent of the travel-related business firms are classified as small businesses.

For cities it is important to note that travel is disproportionately beneficial economically. Travelers "visiting" in suburban and rural areas usually come into the nearest city and base themselves at city hotels or motels.

# 231. Transportation Centers

Certain metro areas derive a large proportion of their residents' incomes from transportation—i.e., serving as a port, a terminal or a transit station—whether for passenger traffic or for freight. Tonnage and passenger traffic figures provide measures of the importance of specific modes of transportation.

The table below provides an overall measure of the importance of transportation in a metro area's economy. It divides metro transportation employment by total metro employment.

New Orleans shows the highest percentage (nearly 8.4) of the total work force accounted for by transportation workers. Miami is second, with nearly 7.9 percent of the total labor force employed in the transportation areas. Both areas are ports and leaders in tourism and conventions. Atlanta, Kansas City (Mo., Kan.), San Francisco, New York, Chicago, Houston, Dallas-Fort Worth and Seattle complete the top 10 cities ranked in this table. They all have significant air traffic.

SOURCE: Derived from U.S. Census Bureau, *1980 Census: Supplementary Report: Provisional Estimates of Social, Economic and Housing Characteristics* (March 1982).

| Rank | Metro Area | Total Labor Force | Labor Force Employed in Transportation | Percentage of Labor Force Employed in Transportation |
|---|---|---|---|---|
| 1 | New Orleans | 448,542 | 37,526 | 8.37 |
| 2 | Miami | 731,889 | 57,448 | 7.85 |
| 3 | Atlanta | 974,914 | 70,057 | 7.19 |
| 4 | Kansas City, Mo., Kan. | 635,700 | 44,818 | 7.05 |
| 5 | San Francisco | 1,585,385 | 101,140 | 6.38 |
| 6 | New York | 3,878,401 | 239,102 | 6.16 |
| 7 | Chicago | 3,179,676 | 187,365 | 5.89 |
| 8 | Houston | 1,440,981 | 82,357 | 5.72 |
| 9 | Dallas-Fort Worth | 1,482,436 | 83,742 | 5.65 |
| 10 | Seattle | 792,278 | 44,037 | 5.56 |
| 11 | St. Louis | 1,024,411 | 55,034 | 5.37 |
| 12 | Minneapolis-St. Paul | 1,074,686 | 57,164 | 5.32 |
| 13 | Denver | 820,574 | 43,043 | 5.25 |
| 14 | Portland, Ore. | 589,090 | 30,195 | 5.13 |
| 15 | Pittsburgh | 950,751 | 46,110 | 4.85 |
| 16 | Newark | 888,497 | 42,387 | 4.77 |
| 17 | Baltimore | 970,022 | 44,164 | 4.55 |
| 18 | Indianapolis | 539,776 | 24,436 | 4.53 |
| 19 | Cincinnati | 604,834 | 26,839 | 4.44 |
| 20 | Los Angeles | 3,488,192 | 151,405 | 4.34 |
| 21 | Cleveland | 849,689 | 36,564 | 4.30 |
| 22 | Buffalo | 516,027 | 22,076 | 4.28 |
| 23 | Riverside | 613,956 | 26,210 | 4.27 |
| 24 | Philadelphia | 1,964,490 | 83,134 | 4.23 |
| 25 | Columbus, Ohio | 501,318 | 20,207 | 4.03 |
| 25 | Tampa-St. Petersburg | 604,612 | 24,349 | 4.03 |
| 27 | Milwaukee | 649,181 | 25,368 | 3.91 |
| 28 | Washington, D.C. | 1,536,620 | 59,463 | 3.87 |
| 29 | San Antonio | 418,790 | 16,167 | 3.86 |
| 30 | Sacramento | 434,301 | 16,509 | 3.80 |
| 31 | Boston | 1,315,200 | 49,585 | 3.77 |
| 32 | Anaheim | 965,074 | 36,238 | 3.75 |
| 33 | Phoenix | 670,608 | 24,904 | 3.71 |
| 34 | San Jose | 658,043 | 22,577 | 3.43 |
| 35 | Detroit | 1,722,372 | 56,446 | 3.28 |
| 36 | San Diego | 758,579 | 23,265 | 3.07 |

# 232.  Urban Transit, Total Transit Vehicles

New York City leads all American cities in the number of transit vehicles used for urban area transport. This is largely because of its need to accommodate its large urban and suburban workforce. Transit vehicles used to transport New Yorkers include buses, subways, ferrys and tramways, each designed to serve the function of contrasting types of commuters. For instance, the ferry service between Manhattan and Staten Island and the tramway between Manhattan and Roosevelt Island cater to those people that live on islands not accessible to Manhattan by subway. Chicago and Los Angeles are second and third in transit vehicles. Suburban centers and cities in the South and Southwest are less adequately equipped for mass transport. Most people in these areas (as in Los Angeles and other California cities) continue to depend upon the automobile as the primary, and indeed sole source of transportation.

NOTES: Transportation statistics are not based on

metro areas as defined elsewhere in this book, although for smaller cities the areas are the same. When interpreting the following urban area data, note that New York City includes Newark, Jersey City and Yonkers as well as Nassau, Rockland and Suffolk counties. Los Angeles includes Long Beach. San Francisco includes Oakland. Minneapolis includes St. Paul. Kansas City, Mo., includes Kansas City, Kan.

SOURCE: U.S. Department of Transportation, Urban Mass Transportation Administration, *A Directory of Regularly Scheduled, Fixed Route, Local Public Transportation Service in Urbanized Areas over 50,000 Population* (Washington, D.C.: Government Printing Office, 1981).

| Rank | Urbanized Area | Total Number of Transit Vehicles | Rank | Urbanized Area | Total Number of Transit Vehicles | Rank | Urbanized Area | Total Number of Transit Vehicles |
|---|---|---|---|---|---|---|---|---|
| 1 | New York | 15,174 | 30 | Salt Lake City | 244 | 59 | Tulsa | 81 |
| 2 | Chicago | 4,512 | 31 | Louisville | 241 | 60 | Knoxville | 79 |
| 3 | Los Angeles | 2,915 | 32 | Memphis | 239 | 61 | Spokane | 74 |
| 4 | San Francisco-Oakland | 2,466 | 33 | Columbus, Ohio | 227 | 62 | Albuquerque | 72 |
| 5 | Philadelphia | 2,249 | 34 | Providence | 204 | 62 | Fresno | 72 |
| 6 | Washington, D.C. | 2,107 | 35 | Rochester | 203 | 64 | Grand Rapids | 69 |
| 7 | Boston | 1,487 | 36 | Indianapolis | 200 | 64 | Oklahoma City | 69 |
| 8 | Pittsburgh | 966 | 36 | Norfolk | 200 | 64 | Tampa | 69 |
| 9 | Cleveland | 950 | 38 | Phoenix | 198 | 67 | Worcester | 66 |
| 10 | Seattle | 921 | 39 | Dayton | 192 | 68 | Austin | 63 |
| 11 | Minneapolis-St. Paul | 914 | 40 | Sacramento | 191 | 69 | Fort Wayne | 62 |
| 12 | Detroit | 886 | 41 | Syracuse | 190 | 70 | Chattanooga | 59 |
| 13 | Baltimore | 818 | 42 | Richmond | 186 | 71 | Lincoln | 57 |
| 14 | St. Louis | 766 | 43 | Long Beach | 178 | 72 | Wichita | 52 |
| 15 | Atlanta | 727 | 44 | Toledo | 175 | 73 | Shreveport | 50 |
| 16 | Milwaukee | 544 | 45 | Jacksonville | 168 | 74 | Little Rock | 49 |
| 17 | Portland | 488 | 46 | Omaha | 160 | 75 | Columbus, Ga. | 41 |
| 18 | Denver | 466 | 47 | Madison | 146 | 76 | Colorado Springs | 40 |
| 19 | New Orleans | 455 | 48 | Nashville | 143 | 76 | Flint | 40 |
| 20 | Cincinnati | 435 | 49 | Tacoma | 138 | 78 | Baton Rouge | 37 |
| 21 | Miami | 432 | 50 | Akron | 113 | 79 | Lexington-Fayette | 37 |
| 22 | Houston | 430 | 51 | El Paso | 111 | 80 | Mobile | 32 |
| 23 | Dallas | 419 | 52 | Tucson | 104 | 81 | Anchorage | 31 |
| 24 | Buffalo | 394 | 53 | Fort Worth | 102 | 81 | Jackson | 31 |
| 25 | San Antonio | 360 | 54 | Charlotte | 94 | 83 | Corpus Christi | 30 |
| 26 | San Diego | 352 | 55 | Riverside | 92 | 84 | Lubbock | 28 |
| 27 | Honolulu | 336 | 56 | Des Moines | 87 | 85 | Montgomery | 27 |
| 28 | Kansas City, Kan.-Mo. | 289 | 57 | Birmingham | 85 | 86 | Las Vegas | 23 |
| 29 | San Jose | 277 | 58 | St. Petersburg | 82 | 87 | Greensboro | 19 |

# 233. Highway Expenditures Trend

Highway spending has formed a major part of government investment in transportation. With the growth of suburbanization opening in the early period after World War II, national investment on highways was at its peak. With the majority of interstate highways now largely completed, the task is primarily one of maintaining roads that have been built.

The table below—based on Census Bureau data—shows that most localities have spent more nominal dollars on highways in Fiscal 1980 than in Fiscal 1972. Of the table below, 98 cities are included. Anchorage spent $14.776 million on highways in 1980 but no data are available on 1972. The District of Columbia spent $75.169 million on highways in 1980, but its 1972 figure of $62,000 is wrong according to local officials, perhaps related to problems around that time in moving to an automated accounting system. Of the 98 remaining cities, 72 spent more money in 1980 than in 1972. If city spending on highways were adjusted for inflation during the period, using "real" dollars, the majority of cities have spent less in 1980 than in 1972.

As one would expect, the most rapid increases in highway construction have occurred in growing areas, especially satellite cities like Aurora and Virginia Beach.

SOURCE: U.S. Department of Commerce, Bureau of the Census, *City Government Finances in 1979–80* (Washington, D.C.: Government Printing Office, September 1981). District of Columbia Department of Transportation, telephone conversation, February 28, 1983.

## Change in Highway Expenditures, 1972–1980 ('000)

| Rank | City | 1972 | 1980 | Change | Change, Percent |
|---|---|---|---|---|---|
| 1 | Aurora | 1,584 | 7,311 | 5,727 | 361.55 |
| 2 | Virginia Beach | 4,175 | 15,342 | 11,167 | 267.47 |
| 3 | St. Petersburg | 3,780 | 13,601 | 9,821 | 259.81 |
| 4 | Montgomery | 1,534 | 5,439 | 3,905 | 254.56 |
| 5 | Lexington-Fayette | 1,334 | 4,107 | 2,773 | 207.87 |
| 6 | Portland, Ore. | 4,929 | 14,325 | 9,396 | 190.63 |
| 7 | Huntington Beach | 2,334 | 6,520 | 4,186 | 179.35 |
| 8 | Phoenix | 17,745 | 47,665 | 29,920 | 168.61 |
| 9 | Jersey City | 1,714 | 4,456 | 2,742 | 159.98 |
| 10 | Fresno | 6,390 | 15,993 | 9,603 | 150.28 |
| 11 | Oklahoma City | 8,944 | 22,191 | 13,247 | 148.11 |
| 12 | Columbus, Ga. | 1,999 | 4,898 | 2,899 | 145.02 |
| 13 | Las Vegas | 1,706 | 4,161 | 2,455 | 143.90 |
| 14 | Baltimore | 29,616 | 71,867 | 42,251 | 142.66 |
| 15 | Chicago | 60,564 | 146,887 | 86,323 | 142.53 |
| 16 | St. Louis | 8,583 | 20,757 | 12,174 | 141.84 |
| 17 | San Jose | 14,033 | 33,538 | 19,505 | 138.99 |
| 18 | Colorado Springs | 4,636 | 10,751 | 6,115 | 131.90 |
| 19 | Miami | 5,012 | 11,206 | 6,194 | 123.58 |
| 20 | Santa Ana | 4,012 | 8,371 | 4,359 | 108.65 |
| 21 | Kansas City, Mo. | 13,747 | 28,132 | 14,385 | 104.64 |
| 22 | Omaha | 11,566 | 23,617 | 12,051 | 104.19 |
| 23 | Jacksonville | 8,572 | 16,809 | 8,237 | 96.09 |
| 24 | Kansas City, Kan. | 6,466 | 12,505 | 6,039 | 93.40 |
| 25 | Fort Wayne | 4,698 | 9,060 | 4,362 | 92.85 |
| 26 | Spokane | 5,431 | 10,137 | 4,706 | 86.65 |
| 27 | Providence | 3,504 | 6,517 | 3,013 | 85.99 |
| 28 | Albuquerque | 8,209 | 15,000 | 6,791 | 82.73 |
| 29 | Riverside | 4,670 | 8,373 | 3,703 | 79.29 |
| 30 | Denver | 10,718 | 18,728 | 8,010 | 74.73 |
| 31 | Lincoln | 6,229 | 10,846 | 4,617 | 74.12 |
| 32 | Louisville | 4,192 | 7,087 | 2,895 | 69.06 |
| 33 | Worcester | 3,930 | 6,262 | 2,332 | 59.34 |
| 34 | Tulsa | 9,203 | 14,653 | 5,450 | 59.22 |
| 35 | Detroit | 33,796 | 53,397 | 19,601 | 57.00 |
| 36 | Charlotte | 10,118 | 15,754 | 5,636 | 55.70 |
| 37 | Grand Rapids | 5,344 | 8,296 | 2,952 | 55.24 |

## Change in Highway Expenditures, 1972–1980 ('000)

| Rank | City | 1972 | 1980 | Change | Change, Percent |
|---|---|---|---|---|---|
| 38 | Rochester | 15,472 | 23,161 | 7,689 | 49.70 |
| 39 | Long Beach | 9,874 | 14,766 | 4,892 | 49.54 |
| 40 | Cincinnati | 15,609 | 23,305 | 7,696 | 49.30 |
| 41 | Birmingham | 10,953 | 16,249 | 5,296 | 48.35 |
| 42 | Mobile | 4,093 | 6,023 | 1,930 | 47.15 |
| 43 | Anaheim | 4,527 | 6,615 | 2,088 | 46.12 |
| 44 | Little Rock | 2,667 | 3,859 | 1,192 | 44.69 |
| 45 | Richmond | 11,622 | 16,477 | 4,855 | 41.77 |
| 46 | Memphis | 14,437 | 20,190 | 5,753 | 39.85 |
| 47 | Philadelphia | 42,929 | 57,656 | 14,727 | 34.31 |
| 48 | Norfolk | 6,561 | 8,644 | 2,083 | 31.75 |
| 49 | Baton Rouge | 10,356 | 13,549 | 3,193 | 30.83 |
| 50 | Flint | 5,403 | 6,902 | 1,499 | 27.74 |
| 51 | Wichita | 13,934 | 17,761 | 3,827 | 27.47 |
| 52 | Newark | 3,241 | 4,087 | 846 | 26.10 |
| 53 | Atlanta | 10,661 | 13,327 | 2,666 | 25.01 |
| 54 | Fort Worth | 16,682 | 20,653 | 3,971 | 23.80 |
| 55 | San Diego | 17,402 | 20,953 | 3,551 | 20.41 |
| 56 | Chattanooga | 6,089 | 7,318 | 1,229 | 20.18 |
| 57 | Nashville-Davidson | 13,669 | 16,301 | 2,632 | 19.26 |
| 58 | Tampa | 7,887 | 9,382 | 1,495 | 18.96 |
| 59 | Columbus, Ohio | 20,484 | 24,235 | 3,751 | 18.31 |
| 60 | Des Moines | 10,299 | 12,135 | 1,836 | 17.83 |
| 61 | Arlington | 5,931 | 6,838 | 907 | 15.29 |
| 62 | Boston | 23,407 | 26,651 | 3,244 | 13.86 |
| 63 | Knoxville | 4,105 | 4,653 | 548 | 13.35 |
| 64 | Tacoma | 11,983 | 13,308 | 1,325 | 11.06 |
| 65 | Jackson | 8,165 | 9,063 | 898 | 10.00 |
| 66 | Tucson | 10,108 | 11,103 | 995 | 9.84 |
| 67 | Los Angeles | 65,111 | 71,012 | 5,901 | 9.06 |
| 68 | San Antonio | 12,824 | 13,448 | 624 | 4.86 |
| 69 | El Paso | 8,053 | 8,380 | 327 | 4.06 |
| 70 | Houston | 45,720 | 47,238 | 1,518 | 3.32 |
| 71 | Corpus Christi | 6,993 | 7,201 | 208 | 2.97 |
| 72 | Lubbock | 4,162 | 4,252 | 90 | 2.16 |
| 73 | New Orleans | 20,356 | 20,256 | − 100 | − .43 |
| 74 | Indianapolis | 36,239 | 35,739 | − 500 | − 1.38 |
| 75 | Toledo | 16,031 | 15,784 | − 247 | − 1.54 |
| 76 | Dayton | 9,405 | 9,182 | − 223 | − 2.37 |
| 77 | Austin | 11,294 | 10,972 | − 322 | − 2.85 |
| 78 | Shreveport | 8,038 | 7,743 | − 295 | − 3.67 |
| 79 | Milwaukee | 43,755 | 41,739 | − 2,016 | − 4.60 |
| 80 | St. Paul | 15,394 | 14,508 | − 886 | − 5.75 |
| 81 | Oakland | 11,700 | 10,518 | − 1,182 | − 10.10 |
| 82 | Honolulu | 26,718 | 23,436 | − 3,282 | − 12.28 |
| 83 | Pittsburgh | 16,527 | 13,295 | − 3,232 | − 19.56 |
| 84 | Warren | 5,043 | 4,001 | − 1,042 | − 20.66 |
| 85 | Madison | 14,864 | 11,780 | − 3,084 | − 20.75 |
| 86 | Minneapolis | 33,157 | 26,270 | − 6,887 | − 20.77 |
| 87 | Greensboro | 9,455 | 7,396 | − 2,059 | − 21.78 |
| 88 | Dallas | 40,739 | 30,743 | − 9,996 | − 24.54 |
| 89 | New York | 361,266 | 265,414 | − 95,852 | − 26.53 |
| 90 | Cleveland | 22,122 | 15,331 | − 6,791 | − 30.70 |
| 91 | Seattle | 29,057 | 19,233 | − 9,824 | − 33.81 |
| 92 | Sacramento | 8,880 | 5,851 | − 3,029 | − 34.11 |
| 93 | Buffalo | 18,857 | 10,160 | − 8,697 | − 46.12 |
| 94 | Syracuse | 8,301 | 3,890 | − 4,411 | − 53.14 |
| 95 | Akron | 23,156 | 10,408 | − 12,748 | − 55.05 |
| 96 | Yonkers | 5,970 | 2,461 | − 3,509 | − 58.78 |
| 97 | Salt Lake City | 3,282 | 1,246 | − 2,036 | − 62.04 |
| 98 | San Francisco | 34,375 | 12,645 | − 21,730 | − 63.21 |

# 234. Airline Passenger Miles

Nationwide, the number of airline passengers declined nearly 10 percent between 1979 and 1981, from 316,683 to 285,720. Passenger miles declined 5 percent. Meanwhile, available seat miles rose over 2 percent, from 416 million to 425 million. The result is that what we might call the airplane occupancy rate dropped from 63 percent in 1979 to under 59 percent in 1981.

Some airline transit terminals, or "hub-and-spoke" centers, serving as major centers for stopovers. Atlanta, for example, is the major airline center in the Southeast for most major carriers. Its location in the central southeast portion of the United States affords great flexibility for carriers who serve regional as well as national needs. Chicago serves the same function for the Midwest.

Because the airline industry has adequate capacity to meet existing traffic demand, large changes in these centers are not likely. The first 21 cities in the ranking below serve the United States from East Coast to West

and from North to South.

The following table shows the total of both inbound and outbound passenger miles for domestic flights each day for 1981. New York leads this ranking, with more than 906 million passenger miles per day, over 150 million miles more than Los Angeles. New York's preeminence as an air terminal stems from its history as a port city and a center of world trade and from its large population. New York's Kennedy Airport is the major international terminal serving European cities, as well as serving the U.S. interior, Canada, South America and Latin America. New York's LaGuardia Airport is the center of the heavily trafficked Boston-New York-Washington shuttle route. Los Angeles and San Francisco are gateways to Hawaii and the Far East, while Chicago is the hub terminal of the Midwest. San Francisco and Chicago fill out the top four cities listed—all with more than 400 million miles daily.

SOURCES: *Origin and Destination Survey of Airline Passenger Traffic, Domestic: 1982* (Washington, D.C.: Air Transport Association of America, 1982). *World Almanac and Book of Facts: 1983* (New York: Newspaper Enterprise Association, 1981).

| Rank | City (Airport) | Passenger Miles Per Day (× 1,000,000) | Rank | City (Airport) | Passenger Miles Per Day (× 1,000,000) | Rank | City (Airport) | Passenger Miles Per Day (× 1,000,000) |
|------|----------------|---------------------------------------|------|----------------|---------------------------------------|------|----------------|---------------------------------------|
| 1 | New York | 906 | 26 | Baltimore | 76 | 51 | Dayton | 28 |
| 2 | Los Angeles | 748 | 27 | Kansas City, Mo. | 71 | 51 | Louisville | 28 |
| 3 | San Francisco | 489 | 28 | Salt Lake City | 68 | 51 | Rochester | 28 |
| 4 | Chicago | 426 | 29 | San Antonio | 61 | 54 | Syracuse | 25 |
| 5 | Honolulu | 274 | 30 | Oakland | 51 | 55 | Des Moines | 22 |
| 6 | Miami | 263 | 31 | Indianapolis | 48 | 56 | Birmingham | 21 |
| 7 | Boston | 261 | 31 | Milwaukee | 48 | 57 | Greensboro | 20 |
| 8 | Dallas-Fort Worth | 260 | 31 | San Jose | 48 | 58 | Spokane | 19 |
| 9 | Washington, D.C. | 245 | 34 | Sacramento | 45 | 58 | Wichita | 19 |
| 10 | Houston | 235 | 35 | Cincinnati | 43 | 60 | Newark | 18 |
| 11 | Denver | 230 | 36 | Columbus, Ohio | 41 | 61 | Little Rock | 17 |
| 12 | Seattle | 198 | 36 | Memphis | 41 | 61 | Richmond | 17 |
| 13 | Atlanta | 174 | 36 | Tulsa | 41 | 63 | Providence | 15 |
| 14 | Las Vegas | 171 | 39 | Albuquerque | 40 | 64 | Knoxville | 13 |
| 15 | Philadelphia | 160 | 39 | Oklahoma City | 40 | 64 | Lubbock | 13 |
| 16 | Detroit | 157 | 39 | Tucson | 40 | 64 | Shreveport | 13 |
| 17 | Phoenix | 154 | 42 | Anchorage | 38 | 67 | Grand Rapids | 12 |
| 18 | San Diego | 133 | 42 | Buffalo | 38 | 67 | Jackson | 12 |
| 19 | Minneapolis-St. Paul | 131 | 44 | Norfolk | 35 | 69 | Colorado Springs | 11 |
| 20 | Tampa-St. Petersburg | 127 | 45 | Nashville | 34 | 69 | Corpus Christi | 11 |
| 21 | St. Louis | 106 | 46 | Jacksonville | 33 | 71 | Fresno | 10 |
| 22 | New Orleans | 101 | 47 | Austin | 31 | 71 | Lexington | 10 |
| 23 | Cleveland | 96 | 47 | El Paso | 31 | 71 | Toledo | 10 |
| 24 | Portland, Ore. | 91 | 49 | Charlotte | 30 | 74 | Baton Rouge | 9 |
| 25 | Pittsburgh | 84 | 49 | Omaha | 30 | 74 | Madison | 9 |

| Rank | City (Airport) | Passenger Miles Per Day (× 1,000,000) | Rank | City (Airport) | Passenger Miles Per Day (× 1,000,000) | Rank | City (Airport) | Passenger Miles Per Day (× 1,000,000) |
|---|---|---|---|---|---|---|---|---|
| 74 | Mobile | 9 | 79 | Montgomery | 6 | 81 | Columbus, Ga. | 4 |
| 77 | Fort Wayne | 8 | 80 | Lincoln | 5 | 83 | Flint | 1 |
| 78 | Chattanooga | 7 | 81 | Akron | 4 | 84 | Worcester | 0.2 |

# 235.  Airline Traffic

There are three major generators of airline passenger traffic: (1) "hub-and-spoke" centers (transit terminals), (2) business cities and (3) tourist centers. Cities that lead our list of passengers per 1,000 residents per day in 1981 possess at least one of these generators. The large airline terminals all have substantial business and transit activity.

The transit trade is significant for a few smaller cities. Las Vegas, the relatively small tourist and gambling center, heads our list of surveyed cities, and Miami, both a tourist center and a hub-and-spoke center, ranks second. Honolulu ranks ninth.

Other cities combine being tourist and business centers—for example, San Francisco, Boston and Washington. Other metro areas—like Atlanta, Denver, Salt Lake City, Dallas-Fort Worth, St. Louis, Pittsburgh, Minneapolis-St. Paul and Houston—are major air transport hub-and-spoke centers, providing airline transit terminals at which travelers changing planes from other cities can make connections.

New York's position in the middle of the list shows that its preeminent ranking as an airport center stems in large part from its being the nation's largest population center. Other cities have more traffic relative to their populations.

SOURCE: *Origin and Destination Survey of Airline Passenger Traffic, Domestic: 1982* (Washington, D.C.: Air Transport Association of America, 1982).

| Rank | City (Airport) | Airline Passengers | Airline Passengers Per 1,000 |
|---|---|---|---|
| 1 | Las Vegas | 17,083 | 103.78 |
| 2 | Miami | 23,731 | 68.40 |
| 3 | Atlanta | 25,062 | 58.97 |
| 4 | San Francisco | 35,389 | 52.12 |
| 5 | Denver | 24,354 | 49.56 |

| Rank | City (Airport) | Airline Passengers | Airline Passengers Per 1,000 |
|---|---|---|---|
| 6 | Boston | 27,412 | 48.69 |
| 7 | Washington, D.C. | 30,195 | 47.35 |
| 8 | Salt Lake City | 7,396 | 45.37 |
| 9 | Honolulu | 14,662 | 40.16 |
| 10 | Dallas-Fort Worth | 35,780 | 39.58 |
| 11 | St. Louis | 14,343 | 31.66 |
| 12 | Seattle | 15,138 | 30.65 |
| 13 | Pittsburgh | 11,808 | 27.85 |
| 14 | Tampa-St. Petersburg | 13,939 | 27.49 |
| 15 | Minneapolis-St. Paul | 14,526 | 22.66 |
| 16 | New Orleans | 12,205 | 21.89 |
| 17 | Cleveland | 12,225 | 21.30 |
| 18 | Portland, Ore. | 7,724 | 21.08 |
| 19 | Lincoln | 3,599 | 20.93 |
| 20 | Syracuse | 3,494 | 20.54 |
| 21 | Kansas City, Mo. | 8,908 | 19.88 |
| 22 | Sacramento | 5,418 | 19.65 |
| 23 | Greensboro | 3,008 | 19.33 |
| 24 | Norfolk | 5,006 | 18.75 |
| 25 | Houston | 29,802 | 18.70 |
| 26 | Phoenix | 14,661 | 18.57 |
| 27 | Los Angeles | 53,223 | 17.94 |
| 28 | Oakland | 5,953 | 17.55 |
| 29 | Dayton | 3,421 | 16.80 |
| 30 | Buffalo | 6,004 | 16.78 |
| 31 | Chicago | 49,190 | 16.37 |
| 32 | Rochester | 3,893 | 16.10 |
| 33 | Cincinnati | 6,068 | 15.74 |
| 34 | Detroit | 18,911 | 15.72 |
| 35 | Tulsa | 5,565 | 15.42 |
| 36 | Charlotte | 4,645 | 14.77 |
| 37 | Des Moines | 2,788 | 14.60 |
| 38 | Austin | 4,957 | 14.35 |
| 39 | Lubbock | 2,466 | 14.17 |
| 40 | Albuquerque | 4,614 | 13.91 |
| 41 | Little Rock | 2,170 | 13.69 |
| 42 | Spokane | 2,343 | 13.68 |
| 43 | San Diego | 11,783 | 13.46 |
| 44 | Louisville | 3,998 | 13.40 |
| 45 | Oklahoma City | 5,261 | 13.05 |
| 46 | New York | 86,307 | 12.21 |
| 47 | Tucson | 3,799 | 11.49 |
| 48 | Omaha | 3,573 | 11.46 |
| 48 | Providence | 1,797 | 11.46 |
| 50 | Richmond | 2,465 | 11.24 |
| 51 | San Jose | 6,965 | 10.94 |
| 52 | Nashville | 4,901 | 10.76 |

| Rank | City (Airport) | Airline Passengers | Airline Passengers Per 1,000 | Rank | City (Airport) | Airline Passengers | Airline Passengers Per 1,000 |
|---|---|---|---|---|---|---|---|
| 53 | Birmingham | 3,032 | 10.66 | 69 | Jacksonville | 4,228 | 7.82 |
| 54 | San Antonio | 7,802 | 9.93 | 70 | Madison | 1,236 | 7.24 |
| 55 | Philadelphia | 16,501 | 9.77 | 71 | Lexington | 1,412 | 6.92 |
| 56 | Knoxville | 1,781 | 9.72 | 72 | Mobile | 1,253 | 6.25 |
| 57 | Columbus, Ohio | 5,434 | 9.62 | 73 | Fresno | 1,357 | 6.22 |
| 58 | Anchorage | 1,653 | 9.55 | 74 | Chattanooga | 1,043 | 6.15 |
| 59 | Baltimore | 7,391 | 9.39 | 75 | Fort Wayne | 988 | 5.74 |
| 60 | El Paso | 3,925 | 9.23 | 76 | Baton Rouge | 1,220 | 5.56 |
| 61 | Memphis | 5,901 | 9.13 | 77 | Colorado Springs | 1,132 | 5.26 |
| 62 | Milwaukee | 5,687 | 8.94 | 78 | Montgomery | 849 | 4.77 |
| 63 | Indianapolis | 6,254 | 8.92 | 79 | Toledo | 1,111 | 3.13 |
| 64 | Shreveport | 1,831 | 8.90 | 80 | Columbus, Ga. | 506 | 2.99 |
| 65 | Grand Rapids | 1,610 | 8.85 | 81 | Akron | 597 | 2.52 |
| 66 | Corpus Christi | 1,984 | 8.55 | 82 | Flint | 207 | 1.30 |
| 67 | Wichita | 2,332 | 8.35 | 83 | Worcester | 23 | .42 |
| 68 | Jackson | 1,639 | 8.08 | | | | |

# 236.  Committable Hotel Rooms

Intercity travel in practice is limited by the availability of hotel space for stopovers and meetings. The number of committable hotel rooms in a city shows the extent to which it can accommodate convention and last-minute visitors. It is also indicative of the strengths of its business and financial centers as well as its cultural attractions. In the following ranking the top-10 cities are geographically dispersed across the United States.

Since 1980 the governments of large cities have been attempting to attract trade and convention business as well as tourists. One example is New York City's government-subsidized convention center designed by I. M. Pei. Presently under construction, it is large enough to house the Statue of Liberty. Hotels continue to be built in these cities, with increased services and facilities to service convention centers. They are competing for business by offering meeting rooms and restaurants, game rooms, discos and sports facilities.

With the exception of Las Vegas, the top cities listed in the following table (which shows 1982 data) are also the nation's larger business and cultural centers. New York ranks first in this category, with over twice the number of rooms available in Las Vegas. The tourist and convention trade cities in the top-seven cities all had more than 20,000 rooms.

SOURCE: Derived from *Meeting News*, Vol. 7, No. 1 (New York: Gralla Publications, January 1983).

| Rank | City | Hotel Rooms Per 1,000 Population | Rank | City | Hotel Rooms Per 1,000 Population | Rank | City | Hotel Rooms Per 1,000 Population |
|---|---|---|---|---|---|---|---|---|
| 1 | New York | 100.0 | 11 | Kansas City, Mo. | 15.0 | 19 | Louisville | 10.0 |
| 2 | Las Vegas | 49.6 | 12 | Detroit | 14.3 | 19 | Phoenix | 10.0 |
| 3 | Chicago | 44.0 | 13 | Miami | | 22 | Honolulu | 9.6 |
| 4 | Washington, D.C. | 37.0 | | (Including Miami Beach) | 14.0 | 23 | St. Louis | 9.2 |
| 5 | Atlanta | 29.0 | 14 | Indianapolis | 12.0 | 24 | Cleveland | 9.0 |
| 6 | Dallas | 21.0 | 14 | New Orleans | 12.0 | 24 | Nashville | 9.0 |
| 7 | San Francisco | 20.5 | 14 | St. Paul | 12.0 | 24 | San Diego | 9.0 |
| 8 | Anaheim | 16.0 | 17 | Minneapolis | 11.0 | 27 | Tucson | 8.5 |
| 8 | Houston | 16.0 | 18 | Boston | 10.5 | 28 | Cincinnati | 8.0 |
| 8 | Los Angeles | 16.0 | 19 | Jacksonville | 10.0 | 28 | Seattle | 8.0 |

| Rank | City | Hotel Rooms Per 1,000 Population | Rank | City | Hotel Rooms Per 1,000 Population | Rank | City | Hotel Rooms Per 1,000 Population |
|---|---|---|---|---|---|---|---|---|
| 30 | Denver | 7.4 | 50 | Baton Rouge | 4.5 | 65 | Syracuse | 2.5 |
| 31 | Charlotte | 7.0 | 50 | Wichita | 4.5 | 71 | Little Rock | 2.0 |
| 31 | Columbus, Ohio | 7.0 | 52 | Lexington | 4.2 | 71 | Long Beach | 2.0 |
| 31 | Knoxville | 7.0 | 53 | Birmingham | 4.0 | 71 | Richmond | 2.0 |
| 31 | Philadelphia | 7.0 | 54 | Albuquerque | 3.5 | 71 | Rochester | 2.0 |
| 31 | Pittsburgh | 7.0 | 54 | Grand Rapids | 3.5 | 71 | Shreveport | 2.0 |
| 36 | Portland, Ore. | 6.5 | 54 | Sacramento | 3.5 | 71 | Spokane | 2.0 |
| 36 | San Antonio | 6.5 | 57 | Salt Lake City | 3.4 | 71 | Toledo | 2.0 |
| 38 | Des Moines | 6.0 | 58 | Fresno | 3.3 | 78 | Buffalo | 1.8 |
| 38 | Oklahoma City | 6.0 | 59 | Greensboro | 3.0 | 78 | St. Petersburg | 1.8 |
| 38 | Tampa | 6.0 | 59 | Lubbock | 3.0 | 80 | Columbus, Ga. | 1.7 |
| 41 | Dayton | 5.7 | 59 | Madison | 3.0 | 81 | Flint | 1.6 |
| 42 | Austin | 5.0 | 59 | Milwaukee | 3.0 | 82 | Anchorage | 1.5 |
| 42 | Baltimore | 5.0 | 59 | Norfolk | 3.0 | 82 | Lincoln | 1.5 |
| 42 | Chattanooga | 5.0 | 59 | Omaha | 3.0 | 82 | Oakland | 1.5 |
| 42 | Fort Worth | 5.0 | 65 | Colorado Springs | 2.5 | 82 | Providence | 1.5 |
| 42 | Memphis | 5.0 | 65 | Corpus Christi | 2.5 | 86 | Fort Wayne | 1.2 |
| 42 | Tulsa | 5.0 | 65 | El Paso | 2.5 | 86 | Mobile | 1.2 |
| 42 | Virginia Beach | 5.0 | 65 | Montgomery | 2.5 | 88 | Arlington, Texas | 1.1 |
| 49 | Jackson | 4.9 | 65 | San Jose | 2.5 | 89 | Akron | 1.0 |

# 237.  Hotels and Motels

The number of hotels and motels per 1,000 population indicates the degree of tourism and convention activity. Unlike the number of committable hotel rooms, many of which may be in only a few very large hotels, the numbers here also reflect the health of the hotel-motel business. More hotels per capita mean there is more demand, and the area can support greater numbers of hotels and motels as an industry.

Las Vegas is ranked first in the table below which divides hotels and motels as of 1977 (latest available survey) by 1980 population. As a tourist and convention center, this city surpasses all others. "The Strip" in Las Vegas is well-known as a main street of hotels, bars and casinos. St. Petersburg, a retirement and resort city on the Florida gulf coast, and its neighbor Tampa rank second and seventh, respectively. Tampa is a port city (10th largest in 1981) and an industrial city experiencing steady growth because of its diversified industrial base (brewing, steel making and phosphate chemical products) and its center for commercial fishermen.

Salt Lake City and Honolulu are the only state capitals listed in the top 10. Salt Lake City, as the world center of the Mormon religion and as the major industrial and commercial center in the Central Rockies, ranks fifth in hotels-motels per capita.

The remainder of the cities in the top 10 are all resort cities—San Francisco (fourth), Virginia Beach (sixth), Miami (eighth) and Colorado Springs (ninth).

SOURCE: U.S. Department of Commerce, *1977 Census of Service Industries* (Washington, D.C.: Government Printing Office, August 1981).

| Rank | City | Number of Hotels and Motels | Number of Hotels and Motels Per 1,000 Residents |
|---|---|---|---|
| 1 | Las Vegas | 122 | .74 |
| 2 | St. Petersburg | 140 | .59 |
| 3 | Anaheim | 106 | .48 |
| 4 | San Francisco | 305 | .45 |
| 5 | Salt Lake City | 72 | .44 |
| 6 | Virginia Beach | 111 | .42 |
| 7 | Tampa | 111 | .41 |
| 8 | Miami | 118 | .34 |
| 9 | Colorado Springs | 71 | .33 |
| 10 | Honolulu | 115 | .32 |
| 11 | Spokane | 50 | .29 |
| 12 | Knoxville | 51 | .28 |
| 12 | Portland, Ore. | 103 | .28 |
| 12 | Tucson | 93 | .28 |
| 15 | Chattanooga | 46 | .27 |
| 15 | Fresno | 59 | .27 |
| 17 | Albuquerque | 87 | .26 |
| 17 | Corpus Christi | 60 | .26 |
| 19 | Denver | 121 | .25 |

| Rank | City | Number of Hotels and Motels | Number of Hotels and Motels Per 1,000 Residents | Rank | City | Number of Hotels and Motels | Number of Hotels and Motels Per 1,000 Residents |
|---|---|---|---|---|---|---|---|
| 20 | San Diego | 203 | .23 | 59 | Omaha | 39 | .13 |
| 21 | Lubbock | 38 | .22 | 59 | Tulsa | 48 | .13 |
| 21 | Madison | 38 | .22 | 63 | Charlotte | 39 | .12 |
| 21 | Nashville | 102 | .22 | 63 | Fort Wayne | 21 | .12 |
| 21 | Oklahoma City | 90 | .22 | 63 | Houston | 198 | .12 |
| 21 | Seattle | 111 | .22 | 63 | Tacoma | 19 | .12 |
| 26 | Norfolk | 55 | .21 | 67 | Columbus, Ga. | 19 | .11 |
| 26 | Phoenix | 163 | .21 | 67 | St. Louis | 50 | .11 |
| 28 | Anchorage | 34 | .20 | 67 | Syracuse | 18 | .11 |
| 28 | Lexington | 40 | .20 | 67 | Toledo | 38 | .11 |
| 28 | Long Beach | 72 | .20 | 71 | Cleveland | 60 | .10 |
| 28 | Oakland | 67 | .20 | 71 | Columbus, Ohio | 55 | .10 |
| 28 | Sacramento | 55 | .20 | 71 | Detroit | 118 | .10 |
| 28 | Wichita | 55 | .20 | 71 | Santa Ana | 20 | .10 |
| 34 | Greensboro | 30 | .19 | 75 | Chicago | 247 | .08 |
| 34 | Jackson | 39 | .19 | 75 | Cincinnati | 30 | .08 |
| 34 | New Orleans | 104 | .19 | 75 | Grand Rapids | 14 | .08 |
| 37 | Des Moines | 35 | .18 | 75 | Milwaukee | 53 | .08 |
| 37 | Lincoln | 31 | .18 | 79 | Dayton | 15 | .07 |
| 37 | Little Rock | 29 | .18 | 79 | Louisville | 20 | .07 |
| 40 | Atlanta | 72 | .17 | 79 | St. Paul | 19 | .07 |
| 40 | Austin | 58 | .17 | 79 | San Jose | 44 | .07 |
| 40 | Los Angeles | 512 | .17 | 79 | Shreveport | 15 | .07 |
| 43 | Arlington, Texas | 25 | .16 | 84 | Boston | 36 | .06 |
| 43 | Baton Rouge | 36 | .16 | 84 | Kansas City, Kan. | 9 | .06 |
| 43 | El Paso | 68 | .16 | 84 | Huntington Beach | 10 | .06 |
| 43 | Kansas City, Mo. | 72 | .16 | 84 | New York | 398 | .06 |
| 43 | Montgomery | 28 | .16 | 88 | Akron | 13 | .05 |
| 43 | San Antonio | 127 | .16 | 88 | Baltimore | 39 | .05 |
| 49 | Aurora | 23 | .15 | 88 | Buffalo | 17 | .05 |
| 49 | Dallas | 134 | .15 | 88 | Flint | 8 | .05 |
| 49 | Jacksonville | 82 | .15 | 88 | Newark | 17 | .05 |
| 49 | Mobile | 31 | .15 | 88 | Pittsburgh | 22 | .05 |
| 49 | Riverside | 25 | .15 | 88 | Rochester | 12 | .05 |
| 49 | Washington, D.C. | 98 | .15 | 88 | Warren | 8 | .05 |
| 55 | Birmingham | 39 | .14 | 88 | Yonkers | 9 | .05 |
| 55 | Fort Worth | 54 | .14 | 97 | Jersey City | 8 | .04 |
| 55 | Memphis | 91 | .14 | 97 | Philadelphia | 61 | .04 |
| 58 | Richmond | 30 | .14 | 97 | Providence | 6 | .04 |
| 59 | Indianapolis | 92 | .13 | 100 | Worcester | 3 | .02 |
| 59 | Minneapolis | 47 | .13 | | | | |

# 238.  Port Tonnage Per City Resident

Port tonnage per capita is an important economic measure for port cities because busy ports mean jobs and income. The following table (showing 1980 data) indicates tonnage in short tons (2,000 pounds) divided by the city population.

Baton Rouge leads in per capita tonnage with more than 361 tons per resident. It is followed by New Orleans. Those two cities (respectively the fifth largest and largest ports in terms of tonnage in the United States) show how important the Mississippi River is as a destination port and as a transfer point for cargo to the middle of the United States. They handle more tonnage than the combined total of Norfolk, Mobile, Tampa, Corpus Christi, Long Beach and Pittsburgh. New Orleans services more than 100 steamship lines, which send over 4,500 ships from all parts of the world to New Orleans each year.

Mobile, Tampa and Corpus Christi—all located on the Gulf of Mexico—are ranked fourth, fifth and sixth, making five out of the top six cities Gulf ports.

The three Pacific Coast ports of Tacoma, Long Beach and Portland are in the top 10 in tonnage per resident, but the next West Coast city is Oakland, ranking 25th on the list.

While New York rated second to New Orleans in total port tonnage in 1981, its vast city population pulled its port tonnage per resident down to the 24th-ranked city in the table.

SOURCE: World Almanac and Book of Facts: 1983 (New York: Newspaper Enterprise Association, Inc., 1981), p. 155. Port of New Orleans: 1980–81 Annual Directory. (New Orleans: Port of New Orleans 1980.)

| Rank | City | Port Tonnage | Port Tonnage Per Capita |
|---|---|---|---|
| 1 | Baton Rouge | 79,346,780 | 361.51 |
| 2 | New Orleans | 177,315,800 | 318.07 |
| 3 | Norfolk | 54,217,591 | 203.08 |
| 4 | Mobile | 37,568,968 | 187.42 |
| 5 | Tampa | 48,625,160 | 175.21 |
| 6 | Corpus Christi | 39,107,016 | 168.57 |
| 7 | Tacoma | 17,162,210 | 108.27 |
| 8 | Long Beach | 38,779,672 | 107.32 |
| 9 | Pittsburgh | 36,586,155 | 86.30 |

| Rank | City | Port Tonnage | Port Tonnage Per Capita |
|---|---|---|---|
| 10 | Portland, Ore. | 29,314,059 | 80.01 |
| 11 | Houston | 108,937,268 | 68.34 |
| 12 | Baltimore | 50,041,515 | 63.60 |
| 13 | Toledo | 22,263,285 | 62.78 |
| 14 | St. Louis | 24,528,760 | 54.14 |
| 15 | Providence | 7,509,253 | 47.89 |
| 16 | Seattle | 21,288,838 | 43.11 |
| 17 | Boston | 22,033,922 | 39.14 |
| 18 | St. Paul | 10,528,472 | 38.96 |
| 19 | Jacksonville | 15,644,000 | 28.92 |
| 20 | Philadelphia | 47,882,836 | 28.36 |
| 21 | Cincinnati | 10,833,216 | 28.10 |
| 22 | Louisville | 7,694,745 | 25.78 |
| 23 | Cleveland | 14,045,151 | 24.48 |
| 24 | New York | 166,991,220 | 23.62 |
| 25 | Oakland | 7,313,533 | 21.56 |
| 26 | Honolulu | 7,646,270 | 20.95 |
| 27 | Memphis | 11,451,998 | 17.72 |
| 28 | Buffalo | 5,986,470 | 16.73 |
| 29 | Detroit | 19,268,443 | 16.01 |
| 30 | Miami | 3,929,398 | 11.33 |
| 31 | Chicago | 32,993,244 | 10.98 |
| 32 | Los Angeles | 30,151,053 | 10.16 |
| 33 | Milwaukee | 4,079,506 | 6.41 |
| 34 | Minneapolis | 2,246,839 | 3.50 |
| 35 | San Diego | 2,188,859 | 2.50 |

# 239. Houses with Phones

Significant sectors of the population of some cities continue to be without phones. It is not within the means of some families to utilize the more convenient home phone service because of the monthly service charge (or a prior poor credit rating).

In New York City the telephone company charges households an increment of 8 cents for each local call, while it costs 10 cents to use public phones.

Occupied housing units with telephones indicate the degree to which metro area residents have access to the phone. Minneapolis-St. Paul leads here, with more than 98 phones per 100 homes. Minneapolis is also ranked second in phones per capita, with more than 2.5 per resident. All 36 cities listed have telephones in more than 90 percent of occupied housing units.

SOURCE: Metro area data from U.S. Department of Commerce, Bureau of the Census, Provisional Social, Economic and Housing Characteristics: 1980 (Washington, D.C.: Government Printing Office, August 1981).

| Rank | Metro Area | Total Housing Units | Housing Units With Phones | Percentage of Housing Units With Phones |
|---|---|---|---|---|
| 1 | Minneapolis-St. Paul | 762,376 | 748,706 | 98.21 |
| 2 | San Jose | 458,519 | 446,831 | 97.45 |
| 3 | Anaheim | 686,267 | 668,434 | 97.40 |
| 4 | Pittsburgh | 828,504 | 806,594 | 97.36 |
| 5 | Washington, D.C. | 1,112,770 | 1,083,333 | 97.35 |
| 6 | Milwaukee | 500,684 | 486,465 | 97.16 |
| 7 | St. Louis | 837,997 | 810,997 | 96.78 |
| 8 | Kansas City, Mo., Kan. | 493,485 | 474,887 | 96.23 |
| 9 | Seattle | 617,962 | 594,624 | 96.22 |
| 10 | Boston | 990,660 | 952,924 | 96.19 |
| 11 | Philadelphia | 1,639,330 | 1,576,760 | 96.18 |
| 12 | San Francisco-Oakland | 1,280,506 | 1,230,407 | 96.09 |
| 13 | Cleveland | 694,401 | 665,272 | 95.81 |
| 14 | Cincinnati | 498,688 | 477,463 | 95.74 |
| 15 | Baltimore | 756,980 | 724,268 | 95.68 |
| 16 | Denver | 609,360 | 582,821 | 95.64 |
| 17 | Sacramento | 383,841 | 366,880 | 95.58 |
| 18 | Portland, Ore. | 477,513 | 455,729 | 95.44 |
| 19 | Detroit | 1,509,030 | 1,437,995 | 95.29 |
| 20 | San Diego | 670,094 | 637,355 | 95.11 |
| 21 | Indianapolis | 418,485 | 397,042 | 94.88 |

| Rank | Metro Area | Total Housing Units | Housing Units With Phones | Percentage of Housing Units With Phones | Rank | Metro Area | Total Housing Units | Housing Units With Phones | Percentage of Housing Units With Phones |
|---|---|---|---|---|---|---|---|---|---|
| 22 | Columbus, Ohio | 397,034 | 376,134 | 94.74 | 30 | Phoenix | 544,759 | 507,408 | 93.14 |
| 23 | Chicago | 2,486,724 | 2,350,888 | 94.54 | 31 | New Orleans | 418,406 | 387,148 | 92.53 |
| 24 | Buffalo | 445,475 | 420,953 | 94.50 | 32 | San Antonio | 349,330 | 322,976 | 92.46 |
| 25 | Riverside | 551,580 | 521,090 | 94.47 | 33 | Tampa-St. Petersburg | 638,816 | 586,509 | 91.81 |
| 26 | Los Angeles-Long Beach | 2,730,469 | 2,577,258 | 94.39 | 34 | Miami | 609,830 | 553,351 | 90.74 |
| 26 | Newark | 677,464 | 639,445 | 94.39 | 35 | Houston | 1,027,069 | 931,744 | 90.72 |
| 28 | Dallas-Fort Worth | 1,076,297 | 1,015,237 | 94.33 | 36 | New York | 3,498,663 | 3,153,340 | 90.13 |
| 29 | Atlanta | 719,799 | 672,433 | 93.42 | | | | | |

# CHAPTER FIFTEEN

# CULTURE AND RECREATION

This chapter looks at how people in each city spend their leisure time on cultural and recreational activities. Americans are finding themselves with more free time on their hands and are spending their money to get the most out of it. Many people are entering into activities such as tennis or skiing, or are taking up hobbies like photography.

In the following chapter are tables on the 100 cities' cultural and recreational characteristics. Magazine readership is interpreted to reflect cities with dominant hobbyists and enthusiasts from gourmet cooks to golfers. In addition, measures of the various cities commitment to public libraries and parks and recreation facilities are included.

# 240. Library Volumes

Public library holdings are noteworthy as a measure of the sustained interest of local government in obtaining and storing knowledge. In a democratic society the decisions of the government are a reflection of the decisions of the people who live in the area. A lot of books implies, over time, respect for knowledge and a desire to make it readily accessible.

The figures below include only public library holdings. Although private universities and other institutions often make their facilities available to individuals, many of them make it difficult by requiring special introductions and references. In the end it is worth a lot to know that anyone can read a book in a public library. What that privilege is worth depends on how many books are available in the library.

Boston leads the list of the 99 cities reported on, with a little more than 795 volumes per 100 persons in 1981. The Boston Public Library is well-known for its special collections and extensive holdings on such selected subjects as art and architecture, business and management, education, history, music, science and technology.

Chattanooga is ranked second, with nearly 615 volumes per 100 persons. Its ranking second only to Boston might be especially surprising to those who are unaware that Chattanooga is home to a campus of the University of Tennessee (as well as three liberal arts colleges) and two state technical colleges.

SOURCE: *American Library Directory* (New York: R. R. Bowker Company, 1982).

| Rank | City | Library Volumes for 100 Residents | Rank | City | Library Volumes for 100 Residents | Rank | City | Library Volumes for 100 Residents |
|---|---|---|---|---|---|---|---|---|
| 1 | Boston | 795.02 | 34 | Honolulu | 219.83 | 67 | Corpus Christi | 156.15 |
| 2 | Chattanooga | 614.79 | 35 | Milwaukee | 211.72 | 68 | Houston | 155.48 |
| 3 | Fort Wayne | 568.18 | 36 | Sacramento | 210.98 | 69 | Phoenix | 154.52 |
| 4 | Worcester | 515.31 | 37 | Jacksonville | 207.85 | 70 | Yonkers | 153.68 |
| 5 | Minneapolis | 426.53 | 38 | Des Moines | 207.27 | 71 | Montgomery | 151.88 |
| 6 | Cleveland | 422.39 | 39 | Los Angeles | 206.24 | 72 | Huntington Beach | 149.27 |
| 7 | Tacoma | 375.25 | 40 | Columbus, Ga. | 205.99 | 73 | Columbus, Ohio | 148.05 |
| 8 | Cincinnati | 373.96 | 41 | Austin | 204.04 | 74 | Louisville | 147.55 |
| 9 | Birmingham | 354.10 | 42 | Dallas | 202.69 | 75 | Spokane | 137.82 |
| 10 | Kansas City, Mo. | 349.10 | 43 | Oakland | 202.51 | 76 | Colorado Springs | 135.67 |
| 11 | Grand Rapids | 346.70 | 44 | Portland, Ore. | 202.25 | 77 | Pittsburgh | 135.39 |
| 12 | Denver | 335.64 | 45 | Anaheim | 199.59 | 78 | Lubbock | 133.50 |
| 13 | Buffalo | 322.21 | 46 | Long Beach | 196.66 | 79 | Miami | 132.16 |
| 14 | Wichita | 312.84 | 47 | San Diego | 195.43 | 80 | Las Vegas | 127.58 |
| 15 | Newark | 310.66 | 48 | Indianapolis | 195.10 | 81 | Anchorage | 124.72 |
| 16 | Seattle | 307.42 | 49 | Little Rock | 192.11 | 81 | Mobile | 124.72 |
| 17 | Rochester | 297.05 | 50 | Knoxville | 190.82 | 83 | New Orleans | 124.70 |
| 18 | St. Louis | 295.18 | 51 | Fresno | 185.57 | 84 | Chicago | 124.43 |
| 19 | Jersey City | 292.00 | 52 | Kansas City, Kan. | 181.50 | 85 | Lexington | 113.55 |
| 20 | Richmond | 288.06 | 53 | Atlanta | 180.84 | 86 | San Antonio | 111.17 |
| 21 | St. Paul | 283.02 | 54 | San Jose | 180.19 | 87 | Arlington, Texas | 109.19 |
| 22 | Baltimore | 275.38 | 55 | Santa Ana | 179.51 | 88 | Nashville | 108.70 |
| 23 | Madison | 271.98 | 56 | Charlotte | 178.60 | 89 | Shreveport | 106.22 |
| 24 | Salt Lake City | 269.26 | 57 | Omaha | 178.24 | 90 | Fort Worth | 106.17 |
| 25 | San Francisco | 262.97 | 58 | New York | 176.16 | 91 | Syracuse | 105.63 |
| 26 | Norfolk | 249.95 | 59 | Jackson | 176.09 | 92 | Oklahoma City | 104.97 |
| 27 | Toledo | 239.18 | 60 | Philadelphia | 173.59 | 93 | Virginia Beach | 104.06 |
| 28 | Lincoln | 239.13 | 61 | Warren | 169.19 | 94 | Baton Rouge | 103.45 |
| 29 | Greensboro | 234.45 | 62 | Tucson | 169.13 | 94 | El Paso | 103.45 |
| 30 | Dayton | 230.23 | 62 | Tulsa | 169.13 | 96 | Tampa | 99.60 |
| 31 | Flint | 227.62 | 64 | St. Petersburg | 169.06 | 97 | Albuquerque | 85.11 |
| 32 | Washington, D.C. | 223.61 | 65 | Detroit | 165.97 | 98 | Providence | 65.80 |
| 33 | Akron | 223.38 | 66 | Memphis | 165.17 | 99 | Aurora | 41.72 |

# 241. Library Budgets

With budget cuts affecting every level of government, from Washington through the state capitals to the smallest municipality, libraries are one of the first services to suffer. Administrators want to be sure that the public is aware of the cuts. Libraries are one way to make their point. Libraries are, to be sure, not as essential as police, fire or sanitation services, but at some point cuts in libraries seriously impair the quality of life.

Data for Honolulu include the State Library of Hawaii which is located in the city.

Cleveland, Ohio tops all the cities in library budgets per capita with Minneapolis, Boston and Seattle following in that order. This table does not reflect the degree of cutbacks public libraries have suffered in funding. Dependent upon the city, these cuts have caused staff shortages, reduction in the numbers of new books and cutbacks in hours of operation. El Paso's public library staff donated their own money for new library books. Phila-

delphia's Free Library funding cutback eliminated over 100 jobs. New Orleans cut staff 10 percent. New York's public library system had to cut operating hours. Rising costs forced Detroit to close some branches. Chicago still faces the challenge of securing sufficient funds for the completion of a new building.

SOURCE: American Library Association, *American Library Directory* (Chicago: ALA, 1982).

| Rank | City | Total Budget ($) | Library Budget Per Capita ($) |
|---|---|---|---|
| 1 | Cleveland | 17,544,698 | 30.64 |
| 2 | Minneapolis | 9,057,317 | 24.48 |
| 3 | Boston | 12,292,160 | 21.85 |
| 4 | Seattle | 10,535,469 | 21.33 |

| Rank | City | Total Budget ($) | Library Budget Per Capita ($) |
|------|------|-----------------|-------------------------------|
| 5 | Tacoma | 2,943,377 | 18.57 |
| 6 | Long Beach | 6,622,837 | 18.14 |
| 7 | Denver | 9,099,500 | 17.67 |
| 8 | Madison | 3,497,343 | 17.49 |
| 9 | Yonkers | 3,310,107 | 16.20 |
| 10 | Rochester | 4,752,322 | 16.11 |
| 11 | Washington, D.C. | 10,275,50 | 16.09 |
| 12 | Toledo | 7,149,829 | 15.17 |
| 13 | Flint | 2,909,398 | 15.05 |
| 14 | Birmingham | 4,113,000 | 14.43 |
| 15 | Fort Wayne | 4,143,369 | 14.29 |
| 16 | Anchorage | 2,878,600 | 14.06 |
| 17 | San Francisco | 9,027,598 | 14.04 |
| 18 | Austin | 4,715,145 | 13.73 |
| 19 | Worcester | 2,342,609 | 13.59 |
| 20 | Baltimore | 10,624,644 | 13.56 |
| 21 | Anaheim | 2,596,109 | 12.97 |
| 22 | Cincinnati | 11,201,847 | 12.83 |
| 23 | Philadelphia | 21,356,036 | 12.65 |
| 24 | St. Paul | 3,315,690 | 12.36 |
| 25 | Grand Rapids | 2,226,176 | 12.26 |
| 26 | Salt Lake City | 2,232,267 | 12.22 |
| 27 | St. Louis | 5,637,798 | 12.12 |
| 28 | Tulsa | 5,510,300 | 11.95 |
| 29 | Newark | 4,324,200 | 11.38 |
| 30 | Buffalo | 11,470,634 | 11.31 |
| 31 | Miami | 14,250,000 | 10.96 |
| 31 | Santa Ana | 2,015,997 | 10.96 |
| 33 | Oakland | 3,785,053 | 10.88 |
| 34 | Lincoln | 1,980,989 | 10.82 |
| 35 | Kansas City, Mo. | 3,718,516 | 10.62 |
| 36 | Milwaukee | 10,452,195 | 10.42 |
| 37 | New York | 73,594,678 | 10.41 |
| 38 | Richmond | 2,219,205 | 10.11 |
| 39 | Indianapolis | 7,078,595 | 10.10 |
| 39 | Tucson | 5,404,380 | 10.10 |
| 41 | Des Moines | 2,019,602 | 10.03 |
| 42 | Portland, Ore. | 5,582,600 | 9.99 |
| 43 | Akron | 4,304,433 | 9.90 |
| 44 | Detroit | 14,755,850 | 9.75 |
| 45 | Honolulu | 9,168,146 | 9.51 |
| 46 | Chicago | 31,690,811 | 9.41 |
| 47 | Dallas | 8,429,732 | 9.32 |
| 48 | Charlotte | 3,728,589 | 9.31 |
| 49 | Greensboro | 2,052,732 | 9.11 |
| 50 | Dayton | 5,424,000 | 9.04 |
| 51 | Norfolk | 2,367,942 | 9.01 |
| 52 | Wichita | 2,433,608 | 8.90 |
| 53 | Aurora | 1,400,650 | 8.75 |
| 54 | Atlanta | 5,086,645 | 8.72 |
| 55 | Memphis | 6,918,475 | 8.70 |
| 56 | Houston | 13,459,276 | 8.55 |
| 56 | Omaha | 2,664,180 | 8.55 |
| 58 | Sacramento | 6,354,743 | 8.25 |
| 59 | Jersey City | 1,827,009 | 8.17 |
| 60 | Spokane | 1,344,907 | 8.05 |
| 61 | Nashville | 3,821,855 | 8.00 |
| 62 | Virginia Beach | 2,075,626 | 7.96 |
| 63 | Knoxville | 2,479,046 | 7.79 |
| 64 | Syracuse | 3,744,647 | 7.78 |
| 65 | Las Vegas | 2,301,985 | 7.68 |
| 66 | Warren | 1,222,512 | 7.59 |
| 67 | San Jose | 4,654,000 | 7.49 |
| 68 | Arlington | 1,257,874 | 7.40 |
| 69 | Louisville | 5,048,237 | 7.38 |
| 70 | Lexington-Fayette | 1,499,718 | 7.35 |
| 71 | Fresno | 3,524,131 | 7.34 |
| 72 | Phoenix | 5,563,991 | 7.30 |
| 73 | Tampa | 4,594,057 | 7.17 |
| 74 | San Diego | 5,740,311 | 6.82 |
| 75 | Colorado Springs | 1,889,495 | 6.68 |
| 76 | Huntington Beach | 1,094,623 | 6.55 |
| 76 | Los Angeles | 18,470,350 | 6.55 |
| 78 | Chattanooga | 1,735,508 | 6.15 |
| 78 | Jacksonville | 3,716,078 | 6.15 |
| 80 | Kansas City, Kan. | 1,101,066 | 6.08 |
| 81 | Mobile | 1,857,130 | 6.02 |
| 82 | Pittsburgh | 8,683,976 | 5.99 |
| 83 | Shreveport | 1,501,337 | 5.96 |
| 84 | Albuquerque | 2,450,794 | 5.93 |
| 85 | St. Petersburg | 1,403,058 | 5.91 |
| 86 | Jackson | 2,418,879 | 5.82 |
| 87 | El Paso | 2,459,240 | 5.65 |
| 88 | Baton Rouge | 2,046,115 | 5.55 |
| 89 | Columbus, Ga. | 1,073,504 | 5.21 |
| 90 | Oklahoma City | 2,836,877 | 4.99 |
| 91 | Lubbock | 1,044,058 | 4.93 |
| 92 | New Orleans | 2,903,149 | 4.85 |
| 93 | Little Rock | 1,065,961 | 4.58 |
| 94 | Corpus Christi | 903,381 | 4.42 |
| 95 | Fort Worth | 3,028,257 | 4.23 |
| 96 | San Antonio | 3,950,570 | 3.00 |
| 97 | Montgomery | 546,690 | 3.13 |
| 98 | Providence | 2,219,205 | 2.34 |
| 99 | Columbus, Ohio | 1,233,587 | 1.48 |

# 242. Books Loaned by Libraries

The table below measures the use that was made of libraries in different cities in 1981. It shows the extent to which people read, or at least the extent to which they read books they obtain at public libraries. From another perspective, it's a measure of the degree of success local librarians achieve in attracting people to their libraries.

Seattle's public library has the highest ranking in books loaned, nine books per person, evidence of a reasonably well read public. Another Washington state city, Tacoma, is in the top five, along with the Ohio cities of Dayton and Toledo. Birmingham is a strong fifth—all with per capita loans above seven per resident.

For a number of years, libraries have had a variety of programs to stimulate the borrowing of books. In the early 1970s libraries in Miami and Atlanta, among other cities, started offering college-credit studies under the sponsorship of local colleges. New York's public library system was one of the first to set up a computer-operated urban information system. San Antonio had a 24-hour borrowing system using the telephone to order books. Audiovisual materials and media resource personnel are now commonplace in libraries. More and more we see libraries, even with their budgetary restrictions, be-

coming a greater community resource through special cultural programs and other activities to attract public interest.

Note in the following table that the data for Honolulu library circulation represent circulation for the entire state of Hawaii. New York data are not available for 1981 and are taken instead from a 1981 report on libraries by New York City Comptroller Harrison J. Goldin and reflect 1977 data.

SOURCE: *American Library Directory,* (New York: R. R. Bowker Company, 1982).

| Rank | City | Books Loaned Per Capita | Rank | City | Books Loaned Per Capita | Rank | City | Books Loaned Per Capita |
|------|------|-------------------------|------|------|-------------------------|------|------|-------------------------|
| 1 | Seattle | 9.03 | 33 | Newark | 4.66 | 65 | Albuquerque | 3.35 |
| 2 | Dayton | 7.66 | 34 | Greensboro | 4.62 | 66 | Milwaukee | 3.29 |
| 3 | Tacoma | 7.53 | 35 | Charlotte | 4.59 | 67 | Anchorage | 3.25 |
| 4 | Toledo | 7.29 | 36 | Grand Rapids | 4.54 | 68 | El Paso | 3.24 |
| 5 | Birmingham | 7.16 | 37 | Arlington, Texas | 4.53 | 68 | Louisville | 3.24 |
| 6 | Cincinnati | 6.69 | 38 | Oakland | 4.52 | 70 | Baton Rouge | 3.20 |
| 7 | St. Paul | 6.54 | 39 | Phoenix | 4.42 | 70 | Colorado Springs | 3.20 |
| 8 | Minneapolis | 6.48 | 39 | Wichita | 4.42 | 70 | Little Rock | 3.20 |
| 9 | Tucson | 6.36 | 41 | Virginia Beach | 4.41 | 70 | Memphis | 3.20 |
| 10 | Des Moines | 6.18 | 42 | Spokane | 4.39 | 70 | Tampa | 3.20 |
| 11 | Fort Wayne | 6.08 | 43 | San Jose | 4.35 | 75 | Chattanooga | 3.12 |
| 12 | Atlanta | 6.07 | 44 | Fresno | 4.19 | 76 | Oklahoma City | 3.11 |
| 13 | Santa Ana | 5.82 | 45 | Dallas | 4.14 | 77 | New York | 3.07 |
| 14 | Lincoln | 5.78 | 46 | Salt Lake City | 4.03 | 77 | St. Louis | 3.07 |
| 15 | Austin | 5.74 | 47 | Norfolk | 3.97 | 79 | Philadelphia | 2.90 |
| 16 | Buffalo | 5.59 | 48 | Knoxville | 3.96 | 80 | Baltimore | 2.77 |
| 17 | Indianapolis | 5.50 | 49 | Yonkers | 3.87 | 81 | Mobile | 2.75 |
| 18 | Cleveland | 5.45 | 50 | Los Angeles | 3.85 | 82 | Miami | 2.62 |
| 18 | Portland, Ore. | 5.45 | 51 | Nashville | 3.81 | 83 | Montgomery | 2.54 |
| 20 | Denver | 5.44 | 52 | Warren | 3.78 | 84 | Washington, D.C. | 2.32 |
| 21 | Honolulu | 5.41 | 53 | Aurora | 3.76 | 85 | Kansas City, Kan. | 2.30 |
| 22 | Omaha | 5.33 | 54 | Boston | 3.73 | 86 | Kansas City, Mo. | 2.29 |
| 23 | Long Beach | 5.17 | 55 | Lexington-Fayette | 3.69 | 87 | San Antonio | 2.22 |
| 24 | Anaheim | 5.13 | 56 | Tulsa | 3.68 | 88 | Chicago | 2.15 |
| 25 | St. Petersburg | 5.10 | 57 | Houston | 3.66 | 89 | Jersey City | 2.02 |
| 26 | Rochester | 5.07 | 58 | San Francisco | 3.65 | 90 | Pittsburgh | 2.01 |
| 27 | Worcester | 4.96 | 59 | Jacksonville | 3.60 | 91 | Syracuse | 1.85 |
| 28 | Richmond | 4.94 | 60 | Columbus, Ohio | 3.54 | 92 | New Orleans | 1.84 |
| 29 | San Diego | 4.87 | 61 | Corpus Christi | 3.44 | 93 | Detroit | 1.27 |
| 30 | Flint | 4.84 | 62 | Columbus, Ga. | 3.40 | 94 | Madison | 1.01 |
| 31 | Huntington Beach | 4.79 | 63 | Fort Worth | 3.39 | 95 | Las Vegas | .38 |
| 32 | Akron | 4.69 | 63 | Jackson | 3.39 | | | |

# 243. Metropolitan Newspaper Circulation

Newspapers inform people of significant events and serve business and consumer needs by advertising sales and products. Local newspapers are important because they provide an important link between government, busi-

ness and community. People buy papers for a number of reasons. Their special interest might be the sports pages, obituaries, gossip columns, editorials, columns, television listings, even cartoons. People often buy newspapers just to look at the job, housing, supermarket or other advertisements.

While city people continue to be interested in news and information, they have switched increasingly from the printed word to television. One result is that people are much more aware of the relationship between international and national developments such as oil price changes, federal tax cuts and budget deficits, inflation and unemployment. The closing of a local steel mill can be immediately linked on television with lower labor costs in a foreign country.

The following table shows daily metro newspaper circulation (Sunday papers are excluded) per capita in 66 major areas for 1982. Spokane ranks first, with 40 percent saturation. Omaha and Richmond tie for second place, with 39 buyers per 100 residents. Tampa and Salt Lake City rank 65th and 66th, with only 13 percent and 12 percent saturation. Many of the cities at the bottom of the table have seen newspaper readership decline because people have come to rely on alternatives such as weekly newspapers or local television. Certain cities at the bottom of the ranking have seen the closing of afternoon newspapers as people have abandoned these papers in favor of expanded local television news.

SOURCE: *The World Almanac and Book of Facts: 1983* (New York: Newspaper Enterprise Association, Inc., 1981), p. 429.

| Rank | Metro Area | Newspaper Circulation | Newspaper Circulation Per 100 Residents |
|---|---|---|---|
| 1 | Spokane | 135,655 | 39.68 |
| 2 | Omaha | 224,380 | 39.34 |
| 2 | Richmond | 248,644 | 39.34 |
| 4 | Worcester | 142,897 | 38.32 |
| 5 | New York | 3,392,376 | 37.20 |
| 6 | Louisville | 325,964 | 35.97 |
| 7 | Denver | 571,249 | 35.26 |
| 8 | Milwaukee | 485,444 | 34.75 |
| 9 | Oklahoma City | 280,184 | 33.59 |
| 10 | Little Rock | 131,929 | 33.53 |
| 11 | Sacramento | 331,238 | 32.67 |

| Rank | Metro Area | Newspaper Circulation | Newspaper Circulation Per 100 Residents |
|---|---|---|---|
| 12 | Memphis | 292,853 | 32.08 |
| 13 | Charlotte | 214,101 | 31.85 |
| 14 | Buffalo | 391,396 | 31.50 |
| 15 | Tulsa | 214,037 | 31.04 |
| 16 | Indianapolis | 356,981 | 30.59 |
| 17 | Wichita | 124,171 | 30.19 |
| 18 | Minneapolis-St. Paul | 626,600 | 29.64 |
| 19 | Albuquerque | 134,579 | 29.61 |
| 20 | Columbus, Ohio | 319,898 | 29.26 |
| 21 | Syracuse | 186,428 | 29.02 |
| 22 | Norfolk-Virginia Beach | 234,024 | 29.01 |
| 23 | Detroit | 1,257,032 | 28.88 |
| 24 | Dayton | 234,963 | 28.31 |
| 25 | Seattle | 448,046 | 27.88 |
| 26 | Birmingham | 235,365 | 27.78 |
| 27 | Jacksonville | 204,554 | 27.74 |
| 28 | Portland, Ore. | 337,180 | 27.14 |
| 29 | Dallas-Fort Worth | 806,882 | 27.12 |
| 30 | Phoenix | 406,100 | 26.93 |
| 31 | Miami | 435,071 | 26.76 |
| 32 | Fresno | 137,699 | 26.74 |
| 33 | Houston | 770,609 | 26.52 |
| 34 | Honolulu | 198,564 | 26.03 |
| 35 | Boston | 714,798 | 25.87 |
| 36 | Austin | 136,685 | 25.48 |
| 37 | San Antonio | 272,710 | 25.44 |
| 38 | Washington, D.C. | 760,950 | 24.87 |
| 39 | San Francisco-Oakland | 805,971 | 24.78 |
| 40 | Akron | 163,409 | 24.75 |
| 41 | Rochester | 240,387 | 24.73 |
| 42 | Cincinnati | 340,650 | 24.31 |
| 43 | Providence | 219,440 | 23.87 |
| 44 | Nashville | 201,531 | 23.70 |
| 45 | New Orleans | 280,655 | 23.65 |
| 46 | Columbus, Ga. | 55,920 | 23.38 |
| 47 | Madison | 75,423 | 23.31 |
| 48 | Baltimore | 486,281 | 22.37 |
| 49 | Cleveland | 405,842 | 21.37 |
| 50 | Grand Rapids | 128,099 | 21.29 |
| 51 | St. Louis | 499,428 | 21.20 |
| 52 | Knoxville | 100,910 | 21.18 |
| 53 | Newark | 415,406 | 21.14 |
| 54 | Toledo | 165,034 | 20.85 |
| 55 | Flint | 108,533 | 20.81 |
| 56 | Chicago | 1,453,885 | 20.47 |
| 57 | Pittsburgh | 447,704 | 19.78 |
| 58 | Atlanta | 392,526 | 19.34 |
| 59 | San Diego | 342,560 | 18.40 |
| 60 | Los Angeles | 1,348,363 | 18.03 |
| 61 | Philadelphia | 846,927 | 17.96 |
| 62 | San Jose | 226,829 | 17.51 |
| 63 | Tacoma | 107,383 | 15.66 |
| 64 | Tucson | 78,039 | 14.69 |
| 65 | Tampa | 202,363 | 12.89 |
| 66 | Salt Lake City | 114,800 | 12.26 |

# 244. Entertainment Centers

The following table ranks cities based on the number of entertainers, orchestra members and producers per 1,000 population. This is a measure of the availability of talent in music and the performing arts.

Las Vegas, the epitome of a show business city, ranks first in the table below showing 1977 data (latest available). Because of legalized gambling there and the concentration of hotels and casinos, there is great competition among the businesses to lure tourists. The city's well-known high dependence on entertainment means a large number of people there who follow careers in entertainment. Fifth-ranked Honolulu is similarly dependent on entertainment for its tourist trade.

Nashville ranks second. This city of nearly half a million people is the center of the popular field of country music and its related industries. Los Angeles is third.

Minneapolis is ranked fourth. It is the home of the Minnesota Orchestra, one of the 31 major symphony orchestras in the United States and one of the oldest, dating back to 1903. Sixth-ranked Seattle also has a major symphony and the Seattle Opera Association, Seattle Repertory Theater and the ACT Theater. In fact, Seattle has more equity theaters per capita than New York! The University of Washington, located in Seattle, offers one of the country's best programs for drama and theater.

SOURCES: U.S. Department of Commerce, *1977 Annual Survey of Service Industries* (Washington, D.C.: Government Printing Office, August 1981). Seattle data from *Introducing Seattle* (Seattle Chamber of Commerce, 1981).

| Rank | City | Total People in Entertainment | Number of People in Entertainment Per 1,000 Population |
|------|------|------|------|
| 1 | Las Vegas | 280 | 1.70 |
| 2 | Nashville | 689 | 1.51 |
| 3 | Los Angeles | 3,272 | 1.10 |
| 4 | Minneapolis | 353 | .95 |
| 5 | Honolulu | 296 | .81 |
| 6 | Seattle | 361 | .73 |
| 7 | Madison | 123 | .72 |
| 8 | New York | 4,940 | .70 |
| 9 | Portland, Ore. | 223 | .61 |
| 10 | Denver | 294 | .60 |
| 10 | Salt Lake City | 98 | .60 |
| 12 | Lincoln | 95 | .55 |
| 13 | San Francisco | 370 | .54 |
| 14 | Des Moines | 100 | .52 |
| 14 | St. Paul | 140 | .52 |

| Rank | City | Total People in Entertainment | Number of People in Entertainment Per 1,000 Population |
|------|------|------|------|
| 14 | Spokane | 89 | .52 |
| 17 | Miami | 175 | .50 |
| 18 | Austin | 163 | .47 |
| 19 | Omaha | 141 | .45 |
| 20 | Cincinnati | 169 | .44 |
| 20 | Tacoma | 69 | .44 |
| 22 | Fort Wayne | 74 | .43 |
| 22 | Lexington-Fayette | 88 | .43 |
| 22 | Milwaukee | 272 | .43 |
| 22 | Tampa | 118 | .43 |
| 26 | Dallas | 377 | .42 |
| 26 | Kansas City, Mo. | 187 | .42 |
| 26 | San Diego | 366 | .42 |
| 29 | Atlanta | 176 | .41 |
| 29 | Boston | 232 | .41 |
| 29 | Huntington Beach | 70 | .41 |
| 32 | Colorado Springs | 83 | .39 |
| 32 | Rochester | 95 | .39 |
| 34 | Indianapolis | 258 | .37 |
| 34 | Little Rock | 59 | .37 |
| 34 | Louisville | 111 | .37 |
| 34 | Oklahoma City | 149 | .37 |
| 38 | Albuquerque | 119 | .36 |
| 38 | Anchorage | 63 | .36 |
| 38 | Memphis | 230 | .36 |
| 38 | St. Petersburg | 86 | .36 |
| 42 | Anaheim | 77 | .35 |
| 42 | Knoxville | 65 | .35 |
| 42 | Oakland | 120 | .35 |
| 42 | Richmond | 76 | .35 |
| 46 | Charlotte | 108 | .34 |
| 46 | Grand Rapids | 61 | .34 |
| 46 | Santa Ana | 70 | .34 |
| 46 | Tulsa | 121 | .34 |
| 50 | Columbus, Ohio | 184 | .33 |
| 50 | Phoenix | 262 | .33 |
| 52 | Lubbock | 56 | .32 |
| 52 | Syracuse | 54 | .32 |
| 52 | Virginia Beach | 85 | .32 |
| 55 | San Antonio | 246 | .31 |
| 55 | Toledo | 109 | .31 |
| 55 | Tucson | 104 | .31 |
| 58 | Akron | 71 | .30 |
| 58 | Arlington, Texas | 48 | .30 |
| 58 | Fort Worth | 116 | .30 |
| 58 | Houston | 478 | .30 |
| 58 | Sacramento | 82 | .30 |
| 58 | Washington, D.C. | 193 | .30 |
| 64 | Chicago | 869 | .29 |
| 64 | Long Beach | 104 | .29 |
| 64 | Norfolk | 78 | .29 |
| 64 | Providence | 45 | .29 |
| 64 | St. Louis | 130 | .29 |
| 69 | Fresno | 61 | .28 |
| 69 | Greensboro | 44 | .28 |
| 69 | Mobile | 57 | .28 |
| 69 | Pittsburgh | 117 | .28 |
| 69 | San Jose | 178 | .28 |
| 69 | Wichita | 79 | .28 |
| 75 | Chattanooga | 45 | .27 |
| 75 | Jacksonville | 145 | .27 |
| 75 | Warren | 43 | .27 |

| Rank | City | Total People in Entertainment | Number of People in Entertainment Per 1,000 Population |
|---|---|---|---|
| 75 | Worcester | 43 | .27 |
| 75 | Yonkers | 52 | .27 |
| 80 | Baltimore | 193 | .25 |
| 80 | Buffalo | 89 | .25 |
| 80 | Jackson | 50 | .25 |
| 80 | New Orleans | 141 | .25 |
| 84 | El Paso | 95 | .22 |
| 84 | Shreveport | 45 | .22 |
| 86 | Aurora | 33 | .21 |
| 86 | Corpus Christi | 49 | .21 |
| 86 | Kansas City, Kan. | 34 | .21 |
| 89 | Dayton | 40 | .20 |

| Rank | City | Total People in Entertainment | Number of People in Entertainment Per 1,000 Population |
|---|---|---|---|
| 90 | Birmingham | 54 | .19 |
| 90 | Montgomery | 33 | .19 |
| 90 | Philadelphia | 324 | .19 |
| 93 | Baton Rouge | 40 | .18 |
| 93 | Flint | 28 | .18 |
| 95 | Cleveland | 87 | .15 |
| 95 | Detroit | 176 | .15 |
| 95 | Riverside | 25 | .15 |
| 98 | Columbus, Ga. | 17 | .10 |
| 98 | Jersey City | 22 | .10 |
| 100 | Newark | 27 | .08 |

# 245. Opera Performances

This table shows the total number of months that the hometown opera companies are scheduled to perform in their cities in 1982–83. Only New York and Houston audiences have the equivalent of a full year of opera. Only Philadelphia, Seattle, San Francisco, Chicago and Pittsburgh have as much as half a year.

Things aren't quite so bad for opera lovers in the other cities. We don't show the months during which the major opera companies will be visiting them. Also, even the big-city companies may not perform all the months they are scheduled to. They may be closed by strikes, funding difficulties and so forth.

SOURCE: *Opera America* (Washington, D.C.: 1982).

| Rank | City | Months of Scheduled Performances | Rank | City | Months of Scheduled Performances | Rank | City | Months of Scheduled Performances |
|---|---|---|---|---|---|---|---|---|
| 1 | New York | 17 | 13 | Fort Worth | 4 | 29 | Milwaukee | 3 |
| 2 | Houston | 14 | 13 | Indianapolis | 4 | 29 | Mobile | 3 |
| 3 | Philadelphia | 9 | 13 | Kansas City, Mo. | 4 | 29 | Omaha | 3 |
| 4 | Seattle | 8 | 13 | Louisville | 4 | 29 | San Antonio | 3 |
| 5 | Chicago | 7 | 13 | Miami | 4 | 37 | Anchorage | 2 |
| 5 | San Francisco | 7 | 13 | New Orleans | 4 | 37 | Dallas | 2 |
| 7 | Pittsburgh | 6 | 13 | Norfolk | 4 | 37 | Des Moines | 2 |
| 8 | Baltimore | 5 | 13 | Rochester | 4 | 37 | Honolulu | 2 |
| 8 | Portland, Ore. | 5 | 13 | Salt Lake City | 4 | 37 | Little Rock | 2 |
| 8 | St. Paul | 5 | 13 | Syracuse | 4 | 37 | Newark | 2 |
| 8 | San Diego | 5 | 13 | Tucson | 4 | 37 | St. Louis | 2 |
| 8 | Tulsa | 5 | 13 | Washington, D.C. | 4 | 37 | Shreveport | 2 |
| 13 | Boston | 4 | 29 | Charlotte | 3 | 45 | Colorado Springs | 1 |
| 13 | Cincinnati | 4 | 29 | Chattanooga | 3 | 45 | Jackson | 1 |
| 13 | Cleveland | 4 | 29 | Los Angeles | 3 | 45 | San Jose | 1 |
| 13 | Detroit | 4 | 29 | Memphis | 3 | | | |

# 246. Auto Enthusiasts

September 1981 subscribers to *Motor Trend, Hot Rod* and *Petersen Motor Group* are used as the measurement here to identify auto enthusiasts.

Des Moines is the second largest tire manufacturing center in the United States, with Firestone and Armstrong plants, and their employees account for a large portion of the readership of these three magazines. In general, the other metro areas at the top of the list are western and midwestern cities with access to open highways.

Subscribers in New York and Jersey City account for less than 1 percent of sales and exhibit less interest in autos. Residents of these metro areas are less likely to own automobiles, as the majority of them rely on public transportation.

SOURCE: Metro data based on September 1981 circulation from the Audit Bureau of Circulation, report prepared at the authors' request.

| Rank | Metro Area | Total Subscribers | Subscribers as Percentage of Population |
|---|---|---|---|
| 1 | Des Moines | 12,088 | 3.58 |
| 2 | Wichita | 10,955 | 2.66 |
| 3 | Minneapolis-St. Paul | 53,737 | 2.54 |
| 4 | Oklahoma City | 20,861 | 2.50 |
| 5 | Tucson | 12,686 | 2.39 |
| 6 | Dayton | 19,410 | 2.34 |
| 7 | Spokane | 7,930 | 2.32 |
| 8 | Las Vegas | 10,545 | 2.28 |
| 9 | Denver | 36,078 | 2.23 |
| 10 | Tacoma | 10,787 | 2.22 |
| 11 | Jackson | 7,148 | 2.21 |
| 11 | Madison | 7,148 | 2.21 |
| 13 | Fort Wayne | 8,406 | 2.20 |
| 13 | Honolulu | 16,779 | 2.20 |
| 15 | Omaha | 12,426 | 2.18 |
| 15 | San Jose | 28,277 | 2.18 |
| 17 | Colorado Springs | 6,899 | 2.17 |
| 17 | Riverside | 33,751 | 2.17 |
| 17 | Sacramento | 22,024 | 2.17 |
| 20 | Grand Rapids | 12,903 | 2.14 |
| 20 | Indianapolis | 25,019 | 2.14 |
| 20 | Tulsa | 14,786 | 2.14 |
| 23 | Anaheim-Santa Ana | 40,572 | 2.10 |
| 23 | Phoenix | 31,602 | 2.10 |
| 25 | Akron | 13,767 | 2.08 |

| Rank | Metro Area | Total Subscribers | Subscribers as Percentage of Population |
|---|---|---|---|
| 25 | Seattle | 33,434 | 2.08 |
| 27 | Rochester | 19,597 | 2.02 |
| 28 | Kansas City, Kan., Mo. | 26,208 | 1.97 |
| 29 | Houston | 56,871 | 1.96 |
| 30 | Atlanta | 39,376 | 1.94 |
| 31 | Little Rock | 7,513 | 1.91 |
| 32 | Fresno | 9,782 | 1.90 |
| 33 | Milwaukee | 26,063 | 1.87 |
| 33 | Pittsburgh | 42,404 | 1.87 |
| 35 | Columbus, Ohio | 20,332 | 1.86 |
| 36 | St. Louis | 43,369 | 1.84 |
| 37 | Washington, D.C. | 55,532 | 1.81 |
| 38 | Toledo | 14,219 | 1.80 |
| 39 | Buffalo | 22,249 | 1.79 |
| 39 | Syracuse | 11,470 | 1.79 |
| 41 | Dallas-Fort Worth | 52,709 | 1.77 |
| 42 | Cleveland | 33,494 | 1.76 |
| 42 | Knoxville | 8,386 | 1.76 |
| 44 | Cincinnati | 24,213 | 1.73 |
| 45 | Austin | 9,233 | 1.72 |
| 46 | Portland, Ore. | 21,234 | 1.71 |
| 47 | San Diego | 31,411 | 1.69 |
| 48 | Flint | 8,747 | 1.68 |
| 49 | Lexington-Fayette | 5,315 | 1.67 |
| 50 | Norfolk-Virginia Beach | 13,311 | 1.65 |
| 51 | Detroit | 71,472 | 1.64 |
| 52 | Chattanooga | 6,939 | 1.63 |
| 53 | Nashville-Davidson | 13,815 | 1.62 |
| 54 | Albuquerque | 7,248 | 1.59 |
| 55 | Jacksonville | 11,589 | 1.57 |
| 55 | Richmond | 9,894 | 1.57 |
| 57 | Chicago | 110,882 | 1.56 |
| 58 | San Francisco | 61,281 | 1.55 |
| 59 | Worcester | 9,894 | 1.53 |
| 60 | Los Angeles | 111,435 | 1.49 |
| 61 | Greensboro | 12,198 | 1.47 |
| 61 | San Antonio | 15,772 | 1.47 |
| 63 | El Paso | 7,003 | 1.46 |
| 64 | Philadelphia | 67,591 | 1.43 |
| 65 | Charlotte | 9,055 | 1.42 |
| 65 | Shreveport | 5,349 | 1.42 |
| 67 | Louisville | 12,650 | 1.40 |
| 68 | Baltimore | 29,575 | 1.36 |
| 68 | Salt Lake City | 12,732 | 1.36 |
| 70 | Tampa-St. Petersburg | 21,122 | 1.35 |
| 71 | Newark | 26,048 | 1.33 |
| 72 | Baton Rouge | 6,503 | 1.32 |
| 73 | Miami | 20,703 | 1.27 |
| 74 | Boston | 46,023 | 1.26 |
| 75 | Montgomery | 3,358 | 1.23 |
| 76 | Birmingham | 10,337 | 1.22 |
| 77 | Corpus Christi | 4,026 | 1.20 |
| 78 | New Orleans | 13,836 | 1.17 |
| 79 | Memphis | 10,612 | 1.16 |
| 80 | Mobile | 5,045 | 1.14 |
| 81 | Providence | 9,790 | 1.03 |
| 82 | New York | 74,080 | .81 |
| 83 | Jersey City | 3,552 | .64 |

# 247. Black Interests

*Ebony, Jet* and *Essence* are directed primarily at black readers. They report on a variety of subjects, including national news, business, fashion, sports and leisure-time activities. *Ebony* had a paid circulation of more than 1,300,000 in 1981, making it the 47th largest magazine in the United States, with a circulation as large as *Jet* and *Essence* combined.

It is not surprising that metro areas with relatively larger black populations are ranked at the top of the following table. Of the top 10 metro areas, 7 are in the South. Of northern metro areas, Washington ranks 1st, Newark 3rd and Cleveland 10th.

SOURCES: Metro area data based on April 1981 *Ebony, Jet* and *Essence* circulations from Audit Bureau of Circulation report prepared especially for this book at the request of the authors. Additional information from *World Almanac and Book of Facts: 1983* (New York: Newspaper Enterprise Association, Inc., 1981).

| Rank | Metro Area | Total Subscribers | Subscribers Per 100 Population |
|---|---|---|---|
| 1 | Washington, D.C. | 131,671 | 4.30 |
| 2 | Montgomery | 9,083 | 3.33 |
| 3 | Newark | 65,219 | 3.32 |
| 4 | Norfolk-Virginia Beach | 25,438 | 3.15 |
| 5 | Atlanta | 63,632 | 3.14 |
| 6 | Memphis | 26,070 | 2.86 |
| 7 | Baton Rouge | 13,793 | 2.79 |
| 8 | Birmingham | 22,913 | 2.70 |
| 9 | Shreveport | 9,842 | 2.61 |
| 10 | Cleveland | 47,946 | 2.53 |
| 11 | Baltimore | 54,288 | 2.50 |
| 12 | Detroit | 106,670 | 2.45 |
| 13 | Philadelphia | 114,366 | 2.42 |
| 14 | Charlotte | 15,185 | 2.38 |
| 15 | New Orleans | 27,898 | 2.35 |
| 16 | Chicago | 159,624 | 2.25 |
| 17 | Jacksonville | 16,212 | 2.20 |
| 18 | New York | 196,430 | 2.15 |
| 19 | Mobile | 9,477 | 2.14 |
| 20 | Little Rock | 8,310 | 2.11 |
| 21 | Greensboro | 15,956 | 1.93 |
| 22 | Houston | 55,144 | 1.90 |
| 23 | St. Louis | 44,605 | 1.89 |
| 24 | Indianapolis | 21,167 | 1.81 |
| 25 | Dayton | 14,708 | 1.77 |
| 26 | Cincinnati | 24,460 | 1.75 |
| 27 | Nashville-Davidson | 14,607 | 1.72 |
| 28 | Columbus, Ohio | 17,537 | 1.60 |
| 29 | Miami | 25,858 | 1.59 |
| 30 | Kansas City, Kan., Mo. | 20,741 | 1.56 |
| 30 | Los Angeles-Long Beach | 116,780 | 1.56 |
| 32 | Flint | 8,033 | 1.54 |
| 33 | Dallas-Fort Worth | 44,342 | 1.49 |
| 34 | Louisville | 13,427 | 1.48 |
| 35 | San Francisco | 57,807 | 1.46 |
| 36 | Chattanooga | 5,619 | 1.32 |
| 37 | Lexington-Fayette | 4,072 | 1.28 |
| 38 | Akron | 8,01 | 1.21 |
| 39 | Oklahoma City | 9,939 | 1.19 |
| 40 | Las Vegas | 5,434 | 1.18 |
| 41 | Milwaukee | 16,225 | 1.16 |
| 42 | Wichita | 4,734 | 1.15 |
| 43 | Jersey City | 6,127 | 1.10 |
| 44 | Toledo | 8,444 | 1.07 |
| 45 | Tulsa | 7,304 | 1.06 |
| 46 | Austin | 5,581 | 1.04 |
| 47 | Buffalo | 12,385 | 1.00 |
| 48 | Fort Wayne | 3,735 | .98 |
| 49 | Omaha | 5,514 | .97 |
| 49 | Pittsburgh | 21,950 | .97 |
| 51 | Sacramento | 9,754 | .96 |
| 52 | Knoxville | 4,266 | .90 |
| 52 | Rochester | 8,781 | .90 |
| 54 | Tacoma | 4,265 | .88 |
| 55 | Colorado Springs | 2,773 | .87 |
| 55 | Tampa-St. Petersburg | 13,612 | .87 |
| 57 | San Diego | 15,224 | .82 |
| 58 | Denver | 13,181 | .81 |
| 59 | San Antonio | 8,523 | .80 |
| 60 | Grand Rapids | 4,574 | .76 |
| 61 | Des Moines | 2,524 | .75 |
| 62 | Boston | 24,935 | .68 |
| 62 | San Jose | 8,759 | .68 |
| 64 | Seattle | 10,436 | .65 |
| 64 | Syracuse | 4,184 | .65 |
| 66 | Fresno | 3,320 | .64 |
| 67 | Riverside | 9,741 | .63 |
| 68 | El Paso | 2,620 | .55 |
| 69 | Tucson | 2,749 | .52 |
| 70 | Jackson | 1,662 | .51 |
| 70 | Madison | 1,662 | .51 |
| 72 | Minneapolis-St. Paul | 10,041 | .47 |
| 73 | Phoenix | 6,668 | .44 |
| 74 | Albuquerque | 1,870 | .41 |
| 75 | Honolulu | 3,018 | .40 |
| 75 | Portland, Ore. | 5,023 | .40 |
| 77 | Anaheim-Santa Ana | 7,373 | .38 |
| 77 | Corpus Christi | 1,264 | .38 |
| 77 | Providence | 3,623 | .38 |
| 80 | Spokane | 712 | .21 |
| 81 | Richmond | 1,005 | .16 |
| 81 | Worcester | 1,005 | .16 |
| 83 | Salt Lake City | 1,335 | .14 |

# 248. Business Readership

Metro area subscribers to *Forbes*, *Fortune* and *Business Week* are grouped together here. Each subscription is considered to be by a different person. The total is divided by population.

Readers of these magazines are likely to be investors, to operate businesses or to be employed in fields where up-to-date analysis of business and economic trends is a high priority.

The Indianapolis area leads with more than 2 percent of its population subscribing to these magazines. San Jose is next, followed by Washington, Newark and New York.

The lowest proportions of subscribers to business magazines—under half a percent—are found in the Flint and Mobile metro areas.

SOURCE: Metro area data from August 1981 (*Forbes*) and March 1982 (*Business Week* and *Fortune*) circulation from the Audit Bureau of Circulation, report prepared at the authors' request.

| Rank | Metro Area | Subscribers to Business Magazines | Subscribers per 100 Population |
|------|-----------|-----------------------------------|-------------------------------|
| 1 | Indianapolis | 25,069 | 2.15 |
| 2 | San Jose | 25,579 | 1.98 |
| 3 | Washington, D.C. | 54,765 | 1.79 |
| 4 | Newark | 33,262 | 1.69 |
| 5 | New York | 150,615 | 1.65 |
| 6 | Denver | 25,882 | 1.60 |
| 7 | San Francisco | 61,429 | 1.55 |
| 8 | Boston | 56,289 | 1.54 |
| 9 | Anaheim-Santa Ana | 29,552 | 1.53 |
| 9 | Seattle | 24,597 | 1.53 |
| 11 | Houston | 41,864 | 1.44 |
| 12 | Minneapolis-St. Paul | 30,294 | 1.43 |
| 13 | Chicago | 97,205 | 1.37 |
| 14 | Atlanta | 26,509 | 1.31 |
| 15 | Dallas-Forth Worth | 38,431 | 1.29 |
| 15 | Jackson | 4,179 | 1.29 |
| 15 | Madison | 4,179 | 1.29 |
| 18 | Phoenix | 18,690 | 1.24 |
| 19 | Honolulu | 9,202 | 1.21 |
| 20 | Cleveland | 22,550 | 1.19 |
| 20 | Portland, Ore. | 14,788 | 1.19 |
| 22 | Los Angeles | 88,567 | 1.18 |
| 23 | Austin | 6,206 | 1.16 |
| 24 | Philadelphia | 51,386 | 1.09 |
| 25 | Milwaukee | 15,041 | 1.08 |

| Rank | Metro Area | Subscribers to Business Magazines | Subscribers per 100 Population |
|------|-----------|-----------------------------------|-------------------------------|
| 26 | Rochester | 10,445 | 1.07 |
| 26 | San Diego | 19,891 | 1.07 |
| 28 | Charlotte | 6,709 | 1.05 |
| 29 | Des Moines | 3,464 | 1.02 |
| 30 | Tulsa | 6,977 | 1.01 |
| 31 | Kansas City, Mo., Kan. | 12,969 | .98 |
| 31 | Miami | 15,965 | .98 |
| 31 | Omaha | 5,604 | .98 |
| 31 | Pittsburgh | 22,086 | .98 |
| 35 | Wichita | 3,997 | .97 |
| 36 | Columbus, Ohio | 10,524 | .96 |
| 36 | Tucson | 5,102 | .96 |
| 38 | Akron | 6,268 | .95 |
| 39 | Grand Rapids | 5,511 | .92 |
| 39 | Oklahoma City | 7,646 | .92 |
| 41 | Cincinnati | 12,757 | .91 |
| 42 | Richmond | 5,696 | .90 |
| 42 | St. Louis | 21,306 | .90 |
| 44 | Dayton | 7,300 | .88 |
| 44 | Detroit | 38,428 | .88 |
| 44 | Sacramento | 8,875 | .88 |
| 44 | Worcester | 5,696 | .88 |
| 48 | Tampa-St. Petersburg | 13,437 | .86 |
| 49 | Albuquerque | 3,875 | .85 |
| 49 | Colorado Springs | 2,714 | .85 |
| 51 | Syracuse | 5,418 | .84 |
| 52 | Spokane | 2,823 | .83 |
| 53 | Baltimore | 17,548 | .81 |
| 53 | Fort Wayne | 3,118 | .81 |
| 55 | Lexington-Fayette | 2,421 | .76 |
| 55 | Toledo | 6,037 | .76 |
| 57 | Providence | 7,069 | .75 |
| 58 | Louisville | 6,732 | .74 |
| 59 | Greensboro | 6,143 | .74 |
| 60 | Buffalo | 8,949 | .72 |
| 60 | Jacksonville | 5,310 | .72 |
| 60 | New Orleans | 8,521 | .72 |
| 60 | Tacoma | 3,514 | .72 |
| 64 | Fresno | 3,632 | .71 |
| 65 | Birmingham | 5,937 | .70 |
| 65 | Knoxville | 3,342 | .70 |
| 65 | Salt Lake City | 6,554 | .70 |
| 68 | Montgomery | 1,839 | .67 |
| 68 | Nashville-Davidson | 5,671 | .67 |
| 70 | Little Rock | 2,601 | .66 |
| 71 | San Antonio | 7,060 | .66 |
| 72 | Baton Rouge | 3,205 | .65 |
| 72 | Memphis | 5,890 | .65 |
| 74 | Jersey City | 3,492 | .63 |
| 75 | Las Vegas | 2,832 | .61 |
| 76 | Chattanooga | 2,462 | .58 |
| 77 | Corpus Christi | 1,913 | .57 |
| 77 | Riverside | 8,935 | .57 |
| 77 | Shreveport | 2,144 | .57 |
| 80 | El Paso | 2,572 | .54 |
| 80 | Norfolk-Virginia Beach | 4,320 | .54 |
| 82 | Mobile | 2,180 | .49 |
| 83 | Flint | 2,292 | .44 |

# 249. Boating Enthusiasts

The center for boating enthusiasts is Norfolk-Virginia Beach—as measured by the 1981 and 1982 readership of *Boating, Yachting, Motor Boating & Sailing* and *Petersen Marine Group*. No surprise—Norfolk is both a naval center and a shipbuilding area.

The other metro areas in the top 10 in the following table are all located on large bodies of water or have waterway access to them except for Grand Rapids and Des Moines. Grand Rapids can be explained—it is only about 30 miles to Lake Michigan. Des Moines, however, is located nearly equidistant between the Mississippi and Missouri Rivers, which are a full 100 miles away. But the Raccoon and Des Moines Rivers converge in Des Moines, and there are several navigable lakes nearby.

El Paso ranks last. By looking at a map, one will see the dearth of navigable waterways other than the Rio Grande in that portion of the Southwest.

SOURCE: Metro data based on January 1981 (*Boating, Yachting*), September 1981 (*Petersen Marine Group*) and March 1982 (*Motor Boating & Sailing*) circulation from Audit Bureau of Circulation, report prepared at the authors' request.

| Rank | Metro Area | Total Subscribers | Subscribers as Percentage of Population |
|---|---|---|---|
| 1 | Norfolk-Virginia Beach | 10,755 | 1.33 |
| 2 | Seattle | 11,297 | .70 |
| 3 | Miami | 10,399 | .64 |
| 4 | Anaheim-Santa Ana | 11,269 | .58 |
| 5 | Tacoma | 2,554 | .53 |
| 6 | Tampa-St. Petersburg | 8,211 | .52 |
| 7 | Grand Rapids | 2,680 | .45 |
| 8 | Toledo | 3,416 | .43 |
| 9 | Des Moines | 1,406 | .42 |
| 9 | Washington, D.C. | 12,916 | .42 |
| 11 | Jacksonville | 2,930 | .40 |
| 12 | Detroit | 17,116 | .39 |
| 12 | Portland, Ore. | 4,895 | .39 |
| 12 | San Diego | 7,301 | .39 |
| 15 | Baltimore | 8,263 | .38 |
| 15 | Honolulu | 2,864 | .38 |
| 17 | New Orleans | 4,277 | .36 |
| 18 | Houston | 10,301 | .35 |
| 18 | Sacramento | 3,550 | .35 |
| 20 | Boston | 12,628 | .34 |
| 20 | San Francisco | 13,290 | .34 |
| 20 | San Jose | 4,349 | .34 |
| 23 | Cleveland | 6,265 | .33 |
| 23 | Providence | 3,131 | .33 |
| 23 | Spokane | 1,111 | .33 |
| 26 | Las Vegas | 1,483 | .32 |
| 26 | Philadelphia | 14,973 | .32 |
| 28 | Corpus Christi | 1,039 | .31 |
| 28 | Newark | 6,175 | .31 |
| 28 | Rochester | 2,981 | .31 |
| 31 | Atlanta | 6,069 | .30 |
| 31 | Los Angeles | 22,486 | .30 |
| 33 | Mobile | 1,277 | .29 |
| 34 | Flint | 1,313 | .25 |
| 34 | Riverside | 3,937 | .25 |
| 36 | Chicago | 16,712 | .24 |
| 36 | Minneapolis-St. Paul | 5,109 | .24 |
| 38 | Baton Rouge | 1,134 | .23 |
| 38 | Buffalo | 2,815 | .23 |
| 38 | Milwaukee | 3,256 | .23 |
| 38 | New York | 20,728 | .23 |
| 38 | Phoenix | 3,439 | .23 |
| 43 | Akron | 1,476 | .22 |
| 43 | Denver | 3,584 | .22 |
| 43 | Syracuse | 1,428 | .22 |
| 46 | Columbus, Ohio | 2,306 | .21 |
| 46 | Dallas-Fort Worth | 6,103 | .21 |
| 48 | Charlotte | 1,300 | .20 |
| 48 | Jackson | 637 | .20 |
| 48 | Madison | 637 | .20 |
| 51 | Austin | 1,023 | .19 |
| 51 | Cincinnati | 2,717 | .19 |
| 51 | Richmond | 1,171 | .19 |
| 54 | Dayton | 1,499 | .18 |
| 54 | Fort Wayne | 674 | .18 |
| 54 | Indianapolis | 2,086 | .18 |
| 54 | Worcester | 1,171 | .18 |
| 58 | Fresno | 858 | .17 |
| 58 | Jersey City | 932 | .17 |
| 60 | Chattanooga | 667 | .16 |
| 60 | Knoxville | 755 | .16 |
| 60 | Louisville | 1,405 | .16 |
| 60 | Pittsburgh | 3,521 | .16 |
| 60 | St. Louis | 3,864 | .16 |
| 60 | Tucson | 826 | .16 |
| 60 | Tulsa | 1,124 | .16 |
| 67 | Birmingham | 1,265 | .15 |
| 67 | Colorado Springs | 478 | .15 |
| 67 | Greensboro | 1,202 | .15 |
| 67 | Montgomery | 415 | .15 |
| 67 | Oklahoma City | 1,264 | .15 |
| 67 | Salt Lake City | 1,364 | .15 |
| 73 | Kansas City, Kan., Mo. | 1,862 | .14 |
| 73 | Little Rock | 532 | .14 |
| 73 | Nashville-Davidson | 1,214 | .14 |
| 73 | San Antonio | 1,541 | .14 |
| 77 | Albuquerque | 593 | .13 |
| 77 | Lexington-Fayette | 425 | .13 |
| 77 | Memphis | 1,162 | .13 |
| 80 | Omaha | 671 | .12 |
| 80 | Shreveport | 445 | .12 |
| 80 | Wichita | 502 | .12 |
| 83 | El Paso | 332 | .07 |

# 250. Dieters

Dieters who are serious about weight loss use every means available to keep themselves on course. Many of them subscribe to *Weight Watchers* magazine, which had, in 1981, a paid circulation in excess of 733,000. The following table represents 1981 subscribers to *Weight Watchers* magazine as a percentage of population.

The top 15 metro areas account for nearly 8% of the paid circulation, and 3 of them—Grand Rapids, Flint and Detroit—are all in Michigan. Washington residents, too, seem to be weight conscious—Spokane, as well as Seattle and Tacoma are in the top 13.

At the bottom, where the last 10 metro areas account for nearly 3% of the paid circulation, we find Honolulu.

SOURCE: Metro data based on October 1981 circulation from Audit Bureau of Circulation, report prepared for this book at the authors' request.

| Rank | City | Total Subscribers | Subscribers Per 1,000 Population |
|------|------|------------------:|--------------------------------:|
| 1 | Spokane | 1,681 | 4.75 |
| 2 | Des Moines | 1,592 | 4.73 |
| 3 | Grand Rapids | 2,824 | 4.70 |
| 4 | Portland, Ore. | 5,823 | 4.63 |
| 5 | Flint | 2,357 | 4.60 |
| 6 | Sacramento | 4,611 | 4.31 |
| 7 | Seattle | 6,996 | 4.25 |
| 8 | Fort Wayne | 1,601 | 4.22 |
| 9 | Omaha | 2,362 | 4.13 |
| 10 | Fresno | 2,182 | 4.03 |
| 11 | Oklahoma City | 3,516 | 4.02 |
| 12 | Worcester | 2,557 | 3.93 |
| 13 | Tacoma | 1,958 | 3.90 |
| 14 | Wichita | 1,616 | 3.88 |
| 15 | Detroit | 16,158 | 3.82 |
| 16 | San Jose | 5,060 | 3.73 |
| 17 | Washington, D.C. | 11,242 | 3.62 |
| 18 | Milwaukee | 5,025 | 3.60 |
| 19 | Madison | 1,159 | 3.50 |
| 20 | Minneapolis-St. Paul | 7,434 | 3.49 |
| 21 | Columbus, Ohio | 3,816 | 3.46 |
| 22 | Kansas City | 4,608 | 3.44 |
| 23 | Las Vegas | 1,720 | 3.35 |
| 23 | Phoenix | 5,397 | 3.35 |
| 25 | Indianapolis | 3,831 | 3.32 |
| 26 | Albuquerque | 1,564 | 3.26 |
| 26 | Toledo | 2,582 | 3.26 |
| 28 | San Francisco | 10,584 | 3.21 |
| 28 | Tulsa | 2,346 | 3.21 |
| 30 | Riverside | 5,231 | 3.14 |
| 31 | Charlotte | 2,027 | 3.12 |
| 31 | Tucson | 1,763 | 3.12 |
| 33 | Denver | 5,283 | 3.10 |
| 34 | Akron | 2,020 | 3.09 |
| 34 | Chicago | 22,012 | 3.09 |
| 36 | Greensboro | 2,593 | 3.07 |
| 37 | Nashville-Davidson | 2,641 | 3.06 |
| 38 | Dayton | 2,431 | 2.96 |
| 38 | Tampa-St. Petersburg | 5,016 | 2.96 |
| 40 | Dallas-Fort Worth | 9,391 | 2.95 |
| 41 | Anaheim-Santa Ana | 6,026 | 2.91 |
| 42 | Cleveland | 5,373 | 2.89 |
| 43 | Miami | 4,901 | 2.86 |
| 44 | Providence | 2,478 | 2.84 |
| 45 | Atlanta | 5,885 | 2.76 |
| 45 | St. Louis | 6,461 | 2.76 |
| 47 | Austin | 1,634 | 2.75 |
| 47 | Louisville | 2,445 | 2.75 |
| 47 | Memphis | 2,686 | 2.75 |
| 47 | Rochester | 2,686 | 2.75 |
| 51 | Salt Lake City | 2,701 | 2.72 |
| 52 | Norfolk | 2,210 | 2.68 |
| 53 | Colorado Springs | 892 | 2.67 |
| 53 | Jacksonville | 2,034 | 2.67 |
| 55 | Syracuse | 1,703 | 2.63 |
| 56 | Richmond | 1,703 | 2.62 |
| 56 | San Diego | 5,229 | 2.62 |
| 58 | Cincinnati | 3,638 | 2.61 |
| 59 | Boston | 9,509 | 2.59 |
| 59 | New Orleans | 3,204 | 2.59 |
| 61 | Montgomery | 720 | 2.58 |
| 62 | Little Rock | 1,024 | 2.57 |
| 62 | Pittsburgh | 5,745 | 2.57 |
| 64 | Baton Rouge | 1,355 | 2.56 |
| 65 | Houston | 8,130 | 2.54 |
| 66 | Chattanooga | 1,079 | 2.50 |
| 67 | Lexington-Fayette | 797 | 2.49 |
| 68 | Los Angeles-Long Beach | 18,698 | 2.45 |
| 69 | Mobile | 1,098 | 2.43 |
| 70 | Corpus Christi | 822 | 2.40 |
| 71 | New York | 21,306 | 2.37 |
| 72 | Philadelphia | 11,013 | 2.35 |
| 72 | Shreveport | 920 | 2.35 |
| 74 | Knoxville | 1,108 | 2.31 |
| 75 | Buffalo | 2,797 | 2.28 |
| 76 | Birmingham | 1,908 | 2.24 |
| 77 | Baltimore | 4,734 | 2.15 |
| 78 | Jersey City | 1,150 | 2.10 |
| 79 | San Antonio | 2,376 | 2.09 |
| 80 | Jackson | 582 | 1.78 |
| 81 | Newark | 3,367 | 1.73 |
| 82 | El Paso | 894 | 1.72 |
| 83 | Honolulu | 1,250 | 1.60 |

# 251. Flying Enthusiasts

The city of Wichita leads this ranking for flying enthusiasts based upon 1981 subscribers to *Flying* divided by population. The .35 percent of the population that subscribes to *Flying* represents .46 percent of the magazine's entire U.S. circulation.

Wichita is a leading manufacturing center for small aircraft. Beech, Boeing, Cessna and Gates Learjet employ nearly 30,000 workers. They produce 60 percent of the free world's general aircraft and their employees account for the high readership of *Flying*. Wichita is also the headquarters of National Flying Farmers.

*Flying* is mainly directed at those who own or fly smaller aircraft for business or hobby. This is an expensive pastime, and one that requires some space, so it is not surprising to find Phoenix, Tucson, Denver and Colorado Springs in the top 10.

New York, Providence and Jersey City are last in the ranking, with a readership of .06 percent or less.

SOURCE: Metro data based on March 1981 circulation from the Audit Bureau of Circulation, report prepared at the authors' request.

| Rank | Metro Area | Total Subscribers | Subscribers Per 1,000 Population |
|------|-----------|-------------------|----------------------------------|
| 1 | Wichita | 1,447 | 3.47 |
| 2 | San Jose | 3,674 | 2.71 |
| 3 | Denver | 4,580 | 2.69 |
| 4 | Phoenix | 4,238 | 2.63 |
| 5 | Anaheim-Santa Ana | 5,300 | 2.56 |
| 5 | Tucson | 1,443 | 2.56 |
| 7 | Seattle | 4,062 | 2.47 |
| 8 | Sacramento | 2,462 | 2.30 |
| 9 | Colorado Springs | 768 | 2.29 |
| 10 | Las Vegas | 1,148 | 2.24 |
| 11 | Portland, Ore. | 2,728 | 2.17 |
| 11 | Tulsa | 1,584 | 2.17 |
| 13 | San Diego | 4,173 | 2.09 |
| 14 | Spokane | 729 | 2.06 |
| 15 | Dallas-Fort Worth | 6,522 | 2.05 |
| 16 | Fresno | 1,106 | 2.04 |
| 17 | Miami | 3,482 | 2.03 |
| 18 | San Francisco | 6,681 | 2.02 |
| 19 | Des Moines | 664 | 1.97 |
| 19 | Riverside | 3,285 | 1.97 |
| 21 | Oklahoma City | 1,624 | 1.85 |
| 22 | Austin | 1,090 | 1.84 |
| 23 | Kansas City, Kan.-Mo. | 2,401 | 1.79 |

| Rank | Metro Area | Total Subscribers | Subscribers Per 1,000 Population |
|------|-----------|-------------------|----------------------------------|
| 24 | Houston | 5,704 | 1.78 |
| 24 | Minneapolis-St. Paul | 3,800 | 1.78 |
| 26 | Madison | 586 | 1.77 |
| 27 | Atlanta | 3,753 | 1.76 |
| 28 | Albuquerque | 832 | 1.74 |
| 29 | Little Rock | 674 | 1.69 |
| 30 | Los Angeles-Long Beach | 12,753 | 1.67 |
| 30 | Tacoma | 838 | 1.67 |
| 32 | Dayton | 1,368 | 1.66 |
| 33 | Washington, D.C. | 5,137 | 1.65 |
| 34 | Salt Lake City | 1,520 | 1.53 |
| 35 | Omaha | 823 | 1.44 |
| 36 | Columbus, Ohio | 1,571 | 1.42 |
| 37 | Tampa-St. Petersburg | 2,369 | 1.40 |
| 38 | Indianapolis | 1,582 | 1.37 |
| 39 | Shreveport | 530 | 1.35 |
| 40 | Jacksonville | 1,010 | 1.32 |
| 41 | Chicago | 9,315 | 1.31 |
| 41 | Corpus Christi | 450 | 1.31 |
| 43 | Fort Wayne | 494 | 1.30 |
| 44 | Lexington-Fayette | 411 | 1.28 |
| 45 | Honolulu | 996 | 1.27 |
| 46 | Knoxville | 589 | 1.23 |
| 46 | Norfolk | 1,016 | 1.23 |
| 46 | St. Louis | 2,880 | 1.23 |
| 46 | San Antonio | 1,402 | 1.23 |
| 50 | Charlotte | 791 | 1.22 |
| 51 | Grand Rapids | 721 | 1.20 |
| 52 | Flint | 608 | 1.19 |
| 53 | Nashville-Davidson | 1,021 | 1.18 |
| 54 | El Paso | 596 | 1.15 |
| 55 | Birmingham | 959 | 1.13 |
| 55 | Jackson | 371 | 1.13 |
| 57 | Milwaukee | 1,551 | 1.11 |
| 58 | Greensboro | 930 | 1.10 |
| 59 | Detroit | 4,635 | 1.09 |
| 60 | Cleveland | 1,904 | 1.03 |
| 61 | Toledo | 806 | 1.02 |
| 62 | Akron | 660 | 1.01 |
| 62 | Chattanooga | 434 | 1.01 |
| 62 | Memphis | 983 | 1.01 |
| 62 | Rochester | 983 | 1.01 |
| 66 | Newark | 1,949 | 1.00 |
| 67 | Boston | 3,620 | .99 |
| 67 | Montgomery | 277 | .99 |
| 69 | Baton Rouge | 520 | .98 |
| 69 | New Orleans | 1,211 | .98 |
| 71 | Cincinnati | 1,344 | .97 |
| 72 | Pittsburgh | 2,116 | .95 |
| 73 | Richmond | 614 | .94 |
| 74 | Mobile | 409 | .91 |
| 75 | Louisville | 772 | .87 |
| 75 | Syracuse | 565 | .87 |
| 75 | Worcester | 566 | .87 |
| 78 | Philadelphia | 3,982 | .85 |
| 79 | Buffalo | 1,007 | .82 |
| 80 | Baltimore | 1,773 | .80 |
| 81 | New York | 5,570 | .62 |
| 82 | Providence | 515 | .59 |
| 83 | Jersey City | 222 | .41 |

# 252. Golf Enthusiasts

More than 10 million Americans have taken to golf, which is played both by individuals and by teams. A handicapping system allows less skilled players to compete with the more skilled.

Golf is a warm-weather game, though some fanatic golfers play out of season under "winter rules," which take into account bad fairway and green conditions.

The following table measures golf enthusiasts in each metro area by the readership of *Golf* and *Golf Digest*.

The top 14 metro areas, with more than 10 subscribers per 1,000 population, show a wide geographical distribution—from Honolulu (1) and Rochester (5) to San Antonio (12) and Detroit (14). Honolulu is the site of the Hawaiian Open, a prestigious event of the Professional Golf Association (PGA), the ruling body for professionals. Other major PGA tournaments are held in Phoenix and Akron.

SOURCE: Metro data based on August 1981 (*Golf Digest*) and April 1982 (*Golf*) circulation from the Audit Bureau of Circulation, report prepared at the authors' request especially for this book.

| Rank | Metro Area | Total Subscribers | Subscribers Per 1,000 Population |
|------|-----------|------------------|----------------------------------|
| 1 | Honolulu | 12,294 | 16.12 |
| 2 | Omaha | 5,404 | 14.59 |
| 3 | Phoenix | 17,789 | 11.80 |
| 4 | Des Moines | 3,837 | 11.35 |
| 5 | Rochester | 10,923 | 11.24 |
| 6 | Grand Rapids | 6,732 | 11.19 |
| 7 | Charlotte | 7,023 | 11.02 |
| 7 | Tampa-St. Petersburg | 17,291 | 11.02 |
| 9 | Denver | 17,454 | 10.77 |
| 10 | Anaheim-Santa Ana | 20,684 | 10.71 |
| 11 | Akron | 7,001 | 10.60 |
| 12 | San Antonio | 11,005 | 10.27 |
| 13 | Detroit | 44,072 | 10.13 |
| 13 | Sacramento | 10,268 | 10.13 |
| 15 | San Jose | 12,428 | 9.98 |
| 16 | Cleveland | 18,882 | 9.94 |
| 17 | Greensboro | 8,156 | 9.86 |
| 18 | Syracuse | 6,316 | 9.83 |
| 19 | Fort Wayne | 3,708 | 9.68 |
| 20 | Minneapolis-St. Paul | 20,282 | 9.59 |
| 21 | Spokane | 3,247 | 9.50 |
| 22 | Tucson | 4,995 | 9.40 |
| 22 | Wichita | 3,868 | 9.40 |

| Rank | Metro Area | Total Subscribers | Subscribers Per 1,000 Population |
|------|-----------|------------------|----------------------------------|
| 24 | Columbus, Ohio | 10,268 | 9.39 |
| 25 | Las Vegas | 4,241 | 9.18 |
| 26 | Colorado Springs | 2,894 | 9.12 |
| 27 | Pittsburgh | 20,567 | 9.08 |
| 28 | Seattle | 14,492 | 9.02 |
| 29 | Chattanooga | 3,786 | 8.88 |
| 30 | Jacksonville | 6,533 | 8.86 |
| 31 | Oklahoma City | 7,378 | 8.85 |
| 32 | El Paso | 4,241 | 8.84 |
| 33 | Portland, Ore. | 10,819 | 8.71 |
| 34 | Washington, D.C. | 26,497 | 8.66 |
| 35 | Atlanta | 17,470 | 8.61 |
| 35 | Chicago | 61,161 | 8.61 |
| 37 | Dayton | 7,113 | 8.57 |
| 38 | Madison | 2,763 | 8.54 |
| 38 | Milwaukee | 11,937 | 8.54 |
| 40 | Flint | 4,449 | 8.53 |
| 41 | Toledo | 6,707 | 8.47 |
| 42 | San Diego | 15,637 | 8.40 |
| 43 | Dallas-Fort Worth | 24,773 | 8.33 |
| 44 | Kansas City, Kan.-Mo. | 11,022 | 8.30 |
| 45 | Salt Lake City | 7,730 | 8.26 |
| 46 | San Francisco | 26,786 | 8.23 |
| 47 | Cincinnati | 11,428 | 8.15 |
| 48 | Riverside | 12,477 | 8.01 |
| 49 | Tulsa | 5,517 | 8.00 |
| 50 | Richmond | 4,746 | 7.51 |
| 51 | Austin | 4,018 | 7.49 |
| 52 | Newark | 14,652 | 7.46 |
| 53 | Houston | 21,511 | 7.40 |
| 54 | Fresno | 3,802 | 7.38 |
| 55 | Tacoma | 3,503 | 7.21 |
| 56 | Worcester | 4,631 | 7.17 |
| 57 | Lexington-Fayette | 2,251 | 7.08 |
| 58 | Albuquerque | 3,164 | 6.96 |
| 59 | Nashville-Davidson | 5,915 | 6.95 |
| 60 | Louisville | 6,211 | 6.85 |
| 61 | Buffalo | 8,414 | 6.77 |
| 62 | Norfolk-Virginia Beach | 5,422 | 6.72 |
| 63 | Memphis | 6,037 | 6.61 |
| 64 | St. Louis | 15,450 | 6.56 |
| 65 | Knoxville | 3,108 | 6.52 |
| 66 | Little Rock | 2,563 | 6.51 |
| 67 | Los Angeles | 47,853 | 6.40 |
| 68 | Philadelphia | 29,338 | 6.22 |
| 69 | Boston | 22,709 | 6.20 |
| 69 | Providence | 5,876 | 6.20 |
| 71 | Birmingham | 5,199 | 6.14 |
| 72 | Montgomery | 1,595 | 5.85 |
| 73 | Jackson | 1,819 | 5.68 |
| 74 | Indianapolis | 6,411 | 5.49 |
| 75 | Baltimore | 11,799 | 5.43 |
| 76 | New Orleans | 6,111 | 5.15 |
| 77 | Shreveport | 1,933 | 5.13 |
| 78 | Mobile | 2,246 | 5.07 |
| 79 | Corpus Christi | 1,605 | 4.92 |
| 80 | Miami | 7,655 | 4.71 |
| 81 | Baton Rouge | 2,232 | 4.52 |
| 82 | New York | 31,771 | 3.48 |
| 83 | Jersey City | 1,023 | 1.84 |

# 253.  Gourmet Cooks

The following table shows the number of subscribers to *Bon Appetit, Gourmet Magazine* and *Monthly Magazine of Food and Wine* relative to the total metro population for 1980 and 1981. These subscribers are likely to consume a wider diversity of foods and to have a finer appreciation of food delicacies than nonsubscribers, who are more likely to be satisfied with a simple fare of "meat and potatoes."

Four metro areas—San Francisco, Seattle, San Jose and Washington—lead the table with better than 2 percent of their respective populations receiving recipes and other food ideas to help them satisfy their epicurean tastes. The southern metro areas at the bottom of our ranking probably prefer home-style southern meals to the kind of cuisine flaunted in the gourmet magazines.

SOURCE: Metro data based on June 1980 (*Monthly Magazine of Food and Wine*), October 1981 (*Bon Appetit*) and November 1981 (*Gourmet*) circulation from Audit Bureau of Circulation, report prepared at the authors' request.

| Rank | Metro Area | Subscribers | Number of Subscribers Per 1,000 Population |
|---|---|---|---|
| 1 | San Francisco | 93,775 | 23.72 |
| 2 | Seattle | 33,810 | 21.04 |
| 3 | San Jose | 26,821 | 20.71 |
| 4 | Washington, D.C. | 62,259 | 20.34 |
| 5 | Anaheim-Santa Ana | 37,759 | 19.55 |
| 6 | Sacramento | 17,753 | 17.51 |
| 7 | San Diego | 29,839 | 16.03 |
| 8 | Denver | 24,502 | 15.13 |
| 9 | Boston | 55,161 | 15.06 |
| 10 | Newark | 29,536 | 15.03 |
| 11 | Los Angeles | 111,908 | 14.97 |
| 12 | Portland, Ore. | 18,406 | 14.82 |
| 13 | Jackson | 4,370 | 13.51 |
| 13 | Madison | 4,370 | 13.51 |
| 15 | Tucson | 7,152 | 13.46 |
| 16 | Rochester | 12,558 | 12.92 |
| 17 | Albuquerque | 5,492 | 12.08 |
| 18 | Fresno | 6,199 | 12.04 |
| 19 | Las Vegas | 5,510 | 11.93 |
| 20 | Chicago | 84,482 | 11.89 |
| 21 | Phoenix | 17,904 | 11.87 |
| 22 | Tacoma | 5,549 | 11.43 |
| 23 | Austin | 6,035 | 11.25 |
| 24 | New York | 102,256 | 11.21 |
| 25 | Philadelphia | 52,546 | 11.14 |
| 26 | Colorado Springs | 3,533 | 11.13 |
| 27 | Minneapolis-St. Paul | 23,167 | 10.96 |
| 28 | Honolulu | 8,169 | 10.71 |
| 29 | Richmond | 6,515 | 10.31 |
| 30 | Cleveland | 19,445 | 10.24 |
| 31 | Milwaukee | 14,299 | 10.23 |
| 32 | New Orleans | 11,987 | 10.10 |
| 33 | Worcester | 6,515 | 10.08 |
| 34 | Riverside | 15,287 | 9.82 |
| 35 | Omaha | 5,573 | 9.77 |
| 36 | Miami | 15,790 | 9.71 |
| 37 | Houston | 27,584 | 9.49 |
| 38 | Atlanta | 18,771 | 9.25 |
| 39 | Spokane | 3,141 | 9.19 |
| 40 | Dallas-Fort Worth | 27,178 | 9.14 |
| 41 | Providence | 8,528 | 9.00 |
| 42 | Syracuse | 5,773 | 8.99 |
| 43 | Pittsburgh | 20,141 | 8.90 |
| 44 | Baltimore | 19,197 | 8.83 |
| 45 | Kansas City, Kan.-Mo. | 11,656 | 8.78 |
| 46 | Detroit | 36,915 | 8.48 |
| 47 | Tampa-St. Petersburg | 13,104 | 8.35 |
| 48 | Des Moines | 2,779 | 8.22 |
| 49 | Buffalo | 10,111 | 8.14 |
| 50 | Oklahoma City | 6,665 | 7.99 |
| 51 | Cincinnati | 11,062 | 7.89 |
| 52 | Columbus, Ohio | 8,487 | 7.76 |
| 53 | Jacksonville | 5,695 | 7.72 |
| 54 | Tulsa | 5,319 | 7.71 |
| 55 | Baton Rouge | 3,800 | 7.69 |
| 56 | St. Louis | 17,893 | 7.60 |
| 57 | San Antonio | 8,046 | 7.51 |
| 58 | Lexington-Fayette | 2,284 | 7.18 |
| 59 | Grand Rapids | 4,267 | 7.09 |
| 59 | Wichita | 2,918 | 7.09 |
| 61 | Dayton | 5,860 | 7.06 |
| 62 | Toledo | 5,521 | 6.97 |
| 63 | Akron | 4,559 | 6.90 |
| 64 | Norfolk-Virginia Beach | 5,516 | 6.84 |
| 65 | Indianapolis | 7,826 | 6.71 |
| 66 | Little Rock | 2,557 | 6.50 |
| 67 | Fort Wayne | 2,458 | 6.42 |
| 68 | Jersey City | 3,570 | 6.41 |
| 69 | Charlotte | 3,980 | 6.25 |
| 70 | Louisville | 5,593 | 6.17 |
| 71 | Knoxville | 2,931 | 6.15 |
| 72 | Salt Lake City | 5,654 | 6.04 |
| 73 | El Paso | 2,895 | 6.03 |
| 73 | Shreveport | 2,270 | 6.03 |
| 75 | Nashville-Davidson | 5,014 | 5.90 |
| 76 | Corpus Christi | 1,932 | 5.75 |
| 77 | Memphis | 5,195 | 5.69 |
| 78 | Mobile | 2,416 | 5.46 |
| 79 | Greensboro | 4,491 | 5.43 |
| 80 | Montgomery | 1,344 | 4.93 |
| 81 | Birmingham | 4,088 | 4.82 |
| 82 | Flint | 2,440 | 4.68 |
| 83 | Chattanooga | 1,729 | 4.05 |

# 254. Health Enthusiasts

Health and health-related issues have captured public attention throughout the United States in recent years with a proliferation of health clubs and an increased interest among both young and older people in dietary matters and in participation sports such as tennis, racquetball and jogging.

Subscribers to *Health* and *Prevention* are used here to measure area residents' interest in health matters. These two magazines report on current trends in medical practice, health care and nutrition.

Tucson and Philadelphia are first and second in the following table, with more than 20 readers per 1,000 population. The rest of the metro areas in the top 10—all with more than 17 readers per 1,000—are Spokane, Akron, Sacramento, Fort Wayne, Seattle, Atlanta, Riverside and Cleveland.

SOURCE: Metro area data based on March *(Health)* and December *(Prevention)* 1981 circulation from the Audit Bureau of Circulation, report prepared at the authors' request especially for this book.

| Rank | Metro Area | Total Subscribers | Subscribers Per 1,000 Population |
|---|---|---|---|
| 1 | Tucson | 11,632 | 21.89 |
| 2 | Philadelphia | 94,969 | 20.13 |
| 3 | Spokane | 6,744 | 19.73 |
| 4 | Akron | 12,371 | 18.73 |
| 5 | Sacramento | 18,342 | 18.09 |
| 6 | Fort Wayne | 6,873 | 17.95 |
| 7 | Seattle | 28,417 | 17.69 |
| 8 | Atlanta | 35,695 | 17.59 |
| 9 | Riverside | 27,185 | 17.46 |
| 10 | Cleveland | 33,062 | 17.41 |
| 11 | Omaha | 6,372 | 17.20 |
| 12 | Portland, Ore. | 21,302 | 17.15 |
| 13 | Tampa-St. Petersburg | 26,878 | 17.13 |
| 14 | San Diego | 31,483 | 16.91 |
| 15 | Anaheim-Santa Ana | 32,610 | 16.88 |
| 15 | Minneapolis-St. Paul | 35,695 | 16.88 |
| 17 | Tacoma | 8,185 | 16.85 |
| 18 | Columbus, Ohio | 18,342 | 16.78 |
| 19 | Honolulu | 12,332 | 16.17 |
| 20 | Wichita | 6,631 | 16.12 |
| 21 | Dayton | 13,243 | 15.95 |
| 22 | Fresno | 8,091 | 15.71 |
| 23 | Pittsburgh | 35,513 | 15.69 |
| 24 | Phoenix | 23,641 | 15.68 |

| Rank | Metro Area | Total Subscribers | Subscribers Per 1,000 Population |
|---|---|---|---|
| 25 | Denver | 25,316 | 15.63 |
| 26 | San Jose | 19,325 | 15.52 |
| 27 | Newark | 30,418 | 15.48 |
| 28 | San Francisco | 48,801 | 15.00 |
| 29 | New York | 136,502 | 14.97 |
| 30 | Colorado Springs | 4,719 | 14.86 |
| 31 | Washington, D.C. | 45,358 | 14.82 |
| 32 | Madison | 4,685 | 14.48 |
| 32 | Oklahoma City | 12,078 | 14.48 |
| 32 | Rochester | 14,077 | 14.48 |
| 35 | Las Vegas | 6,683 | 14.47 |
| 36 | Buffalo | 17,790 | 14.32 |
| 37 | Milwaukee | 19,885 | 14.23 |
| 38 | Los Angeles | 104,578 | 13.99 |
| 39 | El Paso | 6,683 | 13.93 |
| 40 | Des Moines | 4,679 | 13.84 |
| 40 | Syracuse | 8,889 | 13.84 |
| 42 | Grand Rapids | 8,174 | 13.59 |
| 43 | Indianapolis | 15,791 | 13.53 |
| 44 | Albuquerque | 6,103 | 13.43 |
| 45 | Toledo | 10,540 | 13.31 |
| 46 | Kansas City, Kan.-Mo. | 16,807 | 12.66 |
| 47 | Flint | 6,465 | 12.39 |
| 48 | Jacksonville | 9,080 | 12.31 |
| 49 | Tulsa | 8,432 | 12.23 |
| 50 | Worcester | 7,888 | 12.20 |
| 51 | Detroit | 53,046 | 12.19 |
| 52 | Chicago | 86,319 | 12.15 |
| 53 | Dallas-Fort Worth | 35,710 | 12.00 |
| 54 | Salt Lake City | 11,043 | 11.79 |
| 55 | Jersey City | 6,460 | 11.60 |
| 56 | Greensboro | 9,427 | 11.39 |
| 57 | Cincinnati | 15,560 | 11.10 |
| 58 | Corpus Christi | 3,604 | 11.05 |
| 59 | Austin | 5,915 | 11.03 |
| 60 | St. Louis | 25,952 | 11.02 |
| 61 | Little Rock | 4,256 | 10.82 |
| 62 | Houston | 30,791 | 10.60 |
| 63 | Lexington-Fayette | 3,365 | 10.58 |
| 64 | Chattanooga | 4,481 | 10.51 |
| 65 | Nashville-Davidson | 8,904 | 10.47 |
| 66 | Boston | 37,578 | 10.26 |
| 67 | Mobile | 4,522 | 10.21 |
| 68 | Miami | 16,538 | 10.17 |
| 69 | Richmond | 6,373 | 10.08 |
| 70 | Norfolk-Virginia Beach | 8,045 | 9.97 |
| 71 | Louisville | 8,856 | 9.77 |
| 72 | Baltimore | 21,079 | 9.70 |
| 73 | Providence | 9,004 | 9.51 |
| 74 | Birmingham | 8,029 | 9.48 |
| 75 | Charlotte | 6,033 | 9.47 |
| 76 | Knoxville | 4,501 | 9.45 |
| 77 | Montgomery | 2,507 | 9.19 |
| 78 | Shreveport | 3,318 | 8.81 |
| 79 | Baton Rouge | 4,284 | 8.67 |
| 79 | Jackson | 2,779 | 8.67 |
| 81 | New Orleans | 10,090 | 8.50 |
| 82 | Memphis | 6,420 | 7.03 |
| 83 | San Antonio | 3,632 | 3.39 |

# 255. Motorcycle Enthusiasts

Dedicated motorcyclists can become mystical when they talk of the joys of opening up their throttle on an open stretch of road. Advantages of motorcycles that appeal to less adventurous people are that motorcycles are easier to park in the city, move in traffic when cars are stopped and are cheaper to own and operate than cars.

On the negative side, motorcyclists have higher accident and fatality rates than car drivers and annoy many people with the noise of their engines.

The concentration of motorcyclists is shown below as the combined readership of *Cycle* and *Motorcyclist* magazines. In absolute terms the largest group is in Los Angeles, with over 20,000 readers, followed by Chicago (nearly 15,000), New York, San Francisco and Detroit. Motorcycle transportation is clearly popular in these congested metro areas. The smallest group of motorcyclists is indicated by a readership of just 560 in Jackson.

In relative terms, the largest motorcycle readership is in Indianapolis, with 6.09 per 1,000 residents, followed by Des Moines, with 6.02. The smallest relative readership is in Jersey City, with about 1 reader per 1,000 residents.

SOURCE: Metro area data based on April *(Cycle)* and September *(Motorcyclist)* 1981 circulation from the Audit Bureau of Circulation, report prepared at the authors' request especially for this book.

| Rank | Metro Area | Total Subscribers | Subscribers Per 1,000 Population |
|---|---|---|---|
| 1 | Indianapolis | 7,108 | 6.09 |
| 2 | Des Moines | 2,034 | 6.02 |
| 3 | Buffalo | 5,759 | 4.63 |
| 4 | Tucson | 2,401 | 4.52 |
| 5 | Omaha | 1,580 | 4.27 |
| 6 | Oklahoma City | 3,501 | 4.20 |
| 7 | San Jose | 5,140 | 4.13 |
| 8 | Madison | 1,315 | 4.06 |
| 9 | Sacramento | 4,102 | 4.05 |
| 10 | Tulsa | 2,777 | 4.03 |
| 11 | Spokane | 1,340 | 3.92 |
| 12 | Seattle | 6,277 | 3.91 |
| 13 | Minneapolis-St. Paul | 8,251 | 3.90 |
| 14 | Riverside | 6,054 | 3.89 |
| 14 | Rochester | 3,784 | 3.89 |
| 16 | Tacoma | 1,861 | 3.83 |
| 17 | Anaheim-Santa Ana | 7,247 | 3.75 |
| 18 | Colorado Springs | 1,179 | 3.71 |
| 19 | Denver | 5,958 | 3.68 |
| 20 | Las Vegas | 1,661 | 3.60 |
| 21 | Portland, Ore. | 4,442 | 3.58 |

| Rank | Metro Area | Total Subscribers | Subscribers Per 1,000 Population |
|---|---|---|---|
| 22 | Wichita | 1,459 | 3.55 |
| 23 | Little Rock | 1,392 | 3.54 |
| 24 | Syracuse | 2,260 | 3.52 |
| 25 | Phoenix | 5,121 | 3.40 |
| 26 | Jacksonville | 2,499 | 3.39 |
| 27 | Akron | 2,227 | 3.37 |
| 28 | Houston | 9,741 | 3.35 |
| 29 | Atlanta | 6,763 | 3.33 |
| 30 | Flint | 1,730 | 3.32 |
| 31 | San Francisco | 10,704 | 3.29 |
| 32 | Milwaukee | 4,513 | 3.23 |
| 33 | Austin | 1,718 | 3.20 |
| 34 | Grand Rapids | 1,890 | 3.14 |
| 35 | Dallas-Fort Worth | 9,227 | 3.10 |
| 35 | Kansas City, Kan.-Mo. | 4,114 | 3.10 |
| 37 | Columbus, Ohio | 3,352 | 3.07 |
| 38 | Fort Wayne | 1,171 | 3.06 |
| 39 | Richmond | 1,877 | 2.97 |
| 40 | Washington, D.C. | 9,072 | 2.96 |
| 41 | Albuquerque | 1,339 | 2.95 |
| 42 | San Diego | 5,469 | 2.94 |
| 43 | Dayton | 2,431 | 2.93 |
| 44 | Worcester | 1,856 | 2.87 |
| 45 | Nashville-Davidson | 2,402 | 2.82 |
| 46 | Los Angeles | 20,204 | 2.70 |
| 47 | Fresno | 1,387 | 2.69 |
| 48 | Knoxville | 1,274 | 2.67 |
| 49 | Cleveland | 4,986 | 2.63 |
| 50 | Cincinnati | 3,630 | 2.59 |
| 50 | St. Louis | 6,110 | 2.59 |
| 52 | Tampa-St. Petersburg | 4,053 | 2.58 |
| 53 | Baton Rouge | 1,257 | 2.54 |
| 54 | Chattanooga | 1,051 | 2.46 |
| 55 | Salt Lake City | 2,290 | 2.45 |
| 56 | Miami | 3,970 | 2.44 |
| 56 | Pittsburgh | 5,516 | 2.44 |
| 58 | Detroit | 10,585 | 2.43 |
| 59 | Shreveport | 909 | 2.41 |
| 60 | San Antonio | 2,562 | 2.39 |
| 61 | Montgomery | 644 | 2.36 |
| 62 | Toledo | 1,852 | 2.34 |
| 63 | Greensboro | 1,929 | 2.33 |
| 64 | Newark | 4,536 | 2.31 |
| 65 | Norfolk-Virginia Beach | 1,842 | 2.28 |
| 65 | Philadelphia | 10,756 | 2.28 |
| 67 | Charlotte | 1,449 | 2.27 |
| 68 | Corpus Christi | 720 | 2.21 |
| 69 | Boston | 7,989 | 2.18 |
| 70 | Birmingham | 1,814 | 2.14 |
| 71 | Baltimore | 4,601 | 2.12 |
| 72 | Chicago | 14,972 | 2.11 |
| 72 | Providence | 1,999 | 2.11 |
| 74 | El Paso | 1,001 | 2.09 |
| 75 | New Orleans | 2,432 | 2.05 |
| 76 | Louisville | 1,784 | 1.97 |
| 77 | Honolulu | 1,404 | 1.84 |
| 78 | Mobile | 811 | 1.83 |
| 79 | Lexington-Fayette | 577 | 1.81 |
| 80 | Jackson | 556 | 1.74 |
| 81 | Memphis | 1,533 | 1.68 |
| 82 | New York | 11,257 | 1.23 |
| 83 | Jersey City | 599 | 1.08 |

# 256. Photography Enthusiasts

Photography enthusiasts, as measured by subscribers to *Peterson's Photographic* and *Popular Photography*, represent nearly 0.6 percent of the population in the San Jose area and above 0.5 percent in the next six metro areas. One would expect the Washington and San Francisco areas to rank high, as they do, because of the eminently photographable character of these cities. Photography's wide popularity is evident from a reading of the following table. None of the 83 metro areas listed has less than 0.2 percent readership.

SOURCE: Metro data based on circulation data for *Peterson's Photographic* (October 1981) and *Popular Photography* (April 1981) from Audit Bureau of Circulation, report prepared for this book at the authors' request.

| Rank | Metro Area | Total Subscribers | Subscribers per 1,000 Population |
|------|-----------|-------------------|-----------------------------------|
| 1 | San Jose | 8,135 | 5.99 |
| 2 | Washington, D.C. | 17,415 | 5.61 |
| 3 | San Francisco | 18,267 | 5.54 |
| 4 | Des Moines | 1,855 | 5.51 |
| 5 | Denver | 9,288 | 5.45 |
| 6 | Seattle | 8,841 | 5.37 |
| 7 | Anaheim-Santa Ana | 10,488 | 5.07 |
| 8 | Tucson | 2,783 | 4.93 |
| 9 | Sacramento | 5,258 | 4.91 |
| 10 | Portland, Ore. | 5,803 | 4.61 |
| 11 | Colorado Springs | 1,538 | 4.60 |
| 12 | Honolulu | 3,551 | 4.54 |
| 13 | Wichita | 1,884 | 4.52 |
| 14 | Los Angeles-Long Beach | 34,229 | 4.49 |
| 15 | Madison | 1,481 | 4.48 |
| 16 | Newark | 8,704 | 4.46 |
| 17 | Memphis | 4,189 | 4.29 |
| 17 | Rochester | 4,189 | 4.29 |
| 19 | Phoenix | 6,842 | 4.24 |
| 20 | Kansas City, Kan.-Mo. | 5,655 | 4.23 |
| 20 | Miami | 7,248 | 4.23 |
| 22 | Tacoma | 2,096 | 4.18 |
| 23 | New York | 37,305 | 4.06 |
| 23 | San Diego | 8,102 | 4.06 |
| 25 | Houston | 12,672 | 3.96 |
| 26 | Spokane | 1,386 | 3.92 |
| 27 | Cleveland | 7,219 | 3.89 |
| 27 | Philadelphia | 18,272 | 3.89 |

| Rank | Metro Area | Total Subscribers | Subscribers per 1,000 Population |
|------|-----------|-------------------|-----------------------------------|
| 29 | Boston | 14,217 | 3.87 |
| 30 | Minneapolis-St. Paul | 8,166 | 3.83 |
| 31 | Grand Rapids | 2,278 | 3.79 |
| 32 | Albuquerque | 1,808 | 3.77 |
| 33 | Atlanta | 7,967 | 3.74 |
| 34 | Pittsburgh | 8,282 | 3.71 |
| 35 | Austin | 2,195 | 3.70 |
| 35 | Buffalo | 4,545 | 3.70 |
| 35 | Indianapolis | 4,261 | 3.70 |
| 35 | Riverside | 6,173 | 3.70 |
| 39 | Chicago | 26,148 | 3.67 |
| 40 | Dallas-Fort Worth | 11,658 | 3.66 |
| 41 | Milwaukee | 5,026 | 3.60 |
| 42 | Oklahoma City | 3,131 | 3.58 |
| 43 | Detroit | 15,028 | 3.55 |
| 44 | Little Rock | 1,408 | 3.54 |
| 44 | Syracuse | 2,289 | 3.54 |
| 46 | Columbus, Ohio | 3,862 | 3.50 |
| 46 | Fresno | 1,898 | 3.50 |
| 48 | St. Louis | 8,144 | 3.48 |
| 49 | Akron | 2,248 | 3.44 |
| 49 | Las Vegas | 1,762 | 3.44 |
| 49 | Omaha | 1,968 | 3.44 |
| 49 | Richmond | 2,240 | 3.44 |
| 53 | Knoxville | 1,646 | 3.43 |
| 54 | Dayton | 2,806 | 3.41 |
| 54 | Tampa-St. Petersburg | 5,780 | 3.41 |
| 56 | Baton Rouge | 1,789 | 3.38 |
| 57 | Baltimore | 7,424 | 3.37 |
| 57 | Salt Lake City | 3,351 | 3.37 |
| 59 | Worcester | 2,186 | 3.36 |
| 60 | Lexington-Fayette | 1,073 | 3.35 |
| 61 | Toledo | 2,600 | 3.29 |
| 62 | Flint | 1,669 | 3.26 |
| 63 | Cincinnati | 4,509 | 3.24 |
| 64 | Jersey City | 1,739 | 3.18 |
| 65 | Tulsa | 2,301 | 3.15 |
| 66 | New Orleans | 3,820 | 3.08 |
| 67 | Fort Wayne | 1,151 | 3.04 |
| 68 | Norfolk | 2,460 | 2.99 |
| 69 | Charlotte | 1,937 | 2.98 |
| 70 | Shreveport | 1,147 | 2.93 |
| 71 | Providence | 2,547 | 2.92 |
| 72 | Nashville-Davidson | 2,496 | 2.89 |
| 73 | Birmingham | 2,415 | 2.84 |
| 74 | Chattanooga | 1,218 | 2.83 |
| 74 | Jacksonville | 2,161 | 2.83 |
| 76 | San Antonio | 3,173 | 2.79 |
| 77 | Corpus Christi | 953 | 2.78 |
| 77 | Louisville | 2,471 | 2.78 |
| 79 | Jackson | 839 | 2.56 |
| 80 | Greensboro | 2,126 | 2.52 |
| 81 | El Paso | 1,267 | 2.43 |
| 81 | Mobile | 1,098 | 2.43 |
| 83 | Montgomery | 662 | 2.37 |

# 257. Heterosexual Male Pornography

The giant circulation of pornography in the United States makes it a factor to be considered in intercity comparisons, whether from the perspective of those seeking erotic stimulation or those opposed to the continuing relaxation of social (and criminal) barriers to the dissemination of pornography.

The table below measures the circulation of two major magazines directed to the heterosexual male, *Playboy* and *Penthouse*. Of the two, *Playboy* was founded earlier, and became one of the publishing success stories of all time, combining "soft" pornography with sober articles and stories by well-known writers. *Penthouse* has attempted to catch up to the *Playboy* rabbit by providing even more explicit photography.

The Des Moines area outranks Las Vegas in combined circulation of the two magazines. Over 85 copies of the two magazines (combined) are sold to every 1000 Des Moines area residents, nearly 9 percent.

The table shows some extremely interesting differences. Minneapolis, for example, ranks sixth whereas its regional neighbor Milwaukee ranks 52nd—pointing up perhaps different degrees of tolerance in the two cities. The southwestern and western metro areas rank at the top end of the scale, whereas southern and eastern cities are at the bottom—Atlanta and Austin being major exceptions, followed at a distance by Houston and Dallas.

SOURCE: Metro data based on September 1980 (*Penthouse*) and January 1981 (*Playboy*) circulation from Audit Bureau of Circulation report prepared at the authors' request.

| Rank | Metro Area | Total Subscribers | Subscribers per 1,000 Population |
|---|---|---|---|
| 1 | Des Moines | 28,927 | 85.57 |
| 2 | Las Vegas | 35,619 | 77.13 |
| 3 | Tucson | 40,241 | 75.75 |
| 4 | Omaha | 26,998 | 72.89 |
| 5 | Denver | 107,890 | 66.60 |
| 6 | Minneapolis-St. Paul | 136,512 | 64.57 |
| 7 | Madison | 19,510 | 60.30 |
| 8 | Seattle | 96,383 | 59.99 |
| 9 | San Jose | 72,402 | 58.15 |
| 10 | Atlanta | 115,802 | 57.06 |
| 11 | Sacramento | 56,323 | 55.55 |
| 12 | Colorado Springs | 17,583 | 55.39 |
| 13 | Austin | 29,133 | 54.31 |
| 14 | Washington, D.C. | 165,628 | 54.12 |
| 15 | Anaheim-Santa Ana | 103,967 | 53.83 |
| 16 | San Diego | 97,665 | 52.46 |
| 17 | Houston | 151,726 | 52.22 |
| 18 | San Francisco | 167,043 | 51.35 |
| 19 | Wichita | 20,535 | 49.93 |

| Rank | Metro Area | Total Subscribers | Subscribers per 1,000 Population |
|---|---|---|---|
| 20 | Portland, Ore. | 61,263 | 49.32 |
| 21 | Dallas-Fort Worth | 144,338 | 48.52 |
| 22 | Honolulu | 35.771 | 46.89 |
| 23 | Albuquerque | 21,281 | 46.82 |
| 24 | Spokane | 15,879 | 46.45 |
| 25 | Tacoma | 22,224 | 45.76 |
| 26 | Phoenix | 67,450 | *4.73 |
| 27 | Oklahoma City | 36,468 | 43.72 |
| 28 | Fresno | 22,257 | 43.22 |
| 29 | Chicago | 303,902 | 42.79 |
| 30 | Riverside | 65,811 | 42.27 |
| 31 | Tulsa | 28,931 | 41.95 |
| 32 | Los Angeles | 310,276 | 41.49 |
| 33 | Grand Rapids | 24,789 | 41.20 |
| 34 | Little Rock | 16,144 | 41.03 |
| 35 | Knoxville | 19,438 | 40.79 |
| 36 | New Orleans | 48,029 | 40.47 |
| 37 | Indianapolis | 47,134 | 40.39 |
| 38 | Salt Lake City | 37,360 | 39.90 |
| 39 | Detroit | 172,490 | 39.63 |
| 40 | Pittsburgh | 89,638 | 39.59 |
| 41 | Columbus, Ohio | 42,855 | 39.20 |
| 42 | Baton Rouge | 19,261 | 38.99 |
| 43 | Boston | 142,082 | 38.79 |
| 44 | Dayton | 32,161 | 38.74 |
| 45 | Cleveland | 73,472 | 38.70 |
| 46 | Jacksonville | 28,281 | 38.35 |
| 47 | Miami | 61,141 | 37.60 |
| 48 | Norfolk-Virginia Beach | 30,162 | 37.39 |
| 49 | St. Louis | 86,846 | 36.87 |
| 50 | Flint | 19,181 | 36.77 |
| 51 | Rochester | 35,679 | 36.71 |
| 52 | Toledo | 28,743 | 36.31 |
| 53 | Fort Wayne | 13,748 | 35.90 |
| 54 | Louisville | 32,446 | 35.80 |
| 55 | Kansas City | 47,426 | 35.71 |
| 56 | Charlotte | 22,468 | 35.26 |
| 57 | Cincinnati | 48,802 | 34.82 |
| 58 | Tampa-St. Petersburg | 54,287 | 34.59 |
| 59 | Baltimore | 75,055 | 34.52 |
| 60 | Philadelphia | 162,583 | 34.47 |
| 61 | Richmond | 21,730 | 34.38 |
| 62 | Milwaukee | 48,004 | 34.36 |
| 63 | Lexington-Fayette | 10,909 | 34.29 |
| 64 | Corpus Christi | 11,044 | 33.85 |
| 65 | Montgomery | 9,218 | 33.80 |
| 66 | Akron | 22,201 | 33.62 |
| 67 | San Antonio | 35,397 | 33.02 |
| 68 | Worcester | 21,050 | 32.57 |
| 69 | Syracuse | 20,799 | 32.38 |
| 70 | Newark | 61,208 | 31.14 |
| 71 | Nashville-Davidson | 26,402 | 31.04 |
| 72 | Shreveport | 11,541 | 30.64 |
| 73 | Mobile | 13,443 | 30.36 |
| 74 | Providence | 28,355 | 29.94 |
| 75 | Buffalo | 37,124 | 29.88 |
| 76 | El Paso | 14,218 | 29.63 |
| 77 | Memphis | 26,307 | 28.82 |
| 78 | New York | 259,197 | 28.42 |
| 79 | Chattanooga | 11,796 | 27.66 |
| 80 | Jackson | 8,661 | 27.03 |
| 81 | Greensboro | 21,610 | 26.12 |
| 82 | Birmingham | 21,542 | 25.42 |
| 83 | Jersey City | 13,856 | 24.88 |

# 258. Science Hobbyists

Science and technical magazines are good introductory materials for future engineers and scientists and provide interesting tidbits on the latest inventions and scientific trends. They also report on mechanical and electrical methods and machines that hobbyists or do-it-your-selfers find helpful.

The following table represents the combined subscribers of *Science Digest* and *Popular Science* per 1,000 population. Omaha leads the list, with more than 20 subscribers per 1,000. Seattle, Wichita and Denver are close behind. Atlanta is the only southern metro area in the top 15.

The bottom 20 metro areas are all in the South except Jersey City, Providence and New York.

SOURCE: Metro area data based on April 1982 circulation from the Audit Bureau of Circulation, report prepared at the authors' request especially for this book.

| Rank | Metro Area | Total Subscribers | Subscribers Per 1,000 Population |
|------|-----------|-------------------|----------------------------------|
| 1 | Omaha | 7,480 | 20.19 |
| 2 | Seattle | 27,476 | 17.10 |
| 3 | Wichita | 6,567 | 15.97 |
| 4 | Denver | 25,699 | 15.86 |
| 5 | Atlanta | 30,695 | 15.12 |
| 6 | Minneapolis-St. Paul | 30,695 | 14.52 |
| 7 | San Jose | 17,545 | 14.09 |
| 8 | Des Moines | 4,671 | 13.82 |
| 9 | Tacoma | 6,446 | 13.27 |
| 10 | Madison | 4,199 | 12.98 |
| 11 | Colorado Springs | 4,028 | 12.69 |
| 12 | Las Vegas | 5,799 | 12.56 |
| 13 | Albuquerque | 5,696 | 12.53 |
| 14 | Spokane | 4,238 | 12.40 |
| 15 | Tucson | 6,517 | 12.27 |
| 16 | Rochester | 11,749 | 12.09 |
| 17 | El Paso | 5,799 | 12.08 |
| 18 | Portland, Ore. | 14,978 | 12.06 |
| 19 | Fort Wayne | 4,615 | 12.05 |
| 20 | Sacramento | 12,177 | 12.01 |
| 21 | Milwaukee | 16,334 | 11.69 |
| 22 | Washington, D.C. | 35,468 | 11.59 |
| 23 | Phoenix | 17,346 | 11.50 |
| 24 | San Diego | 21,210 | 11.39 |
| 25 | Honolulu | 8,659 | 11.35 |
| 26 | Austin | 6,034 | 11.25 |

| Rank | City | Total Subscribers | Subscribers Per 1,000 Population |
|------|------|-------------------|----------------------------------|
| 27 | Columbus, Ohio | 12,177 | 11.14 |
| 28 | Kansas City, Kan.-Mo. | 14,543 | 10.95 |
| 29 | Dayton | 9,070 | 10.93 |
| 30 | Anaheim-Santa Ana | 21,058 | 10.90 |
| 30 | Tulsa | 7,516 | 10.90 |
| 32 | Akron | 7,050 | 10.68 |
| 33 | Salt Lake City | 9,958 | 10.64 |
| 34 | Cleveland | 20,176 | 10.63 |
| 34 | Detroit | 46,267 | 10.63 |
| 36 | Buffalo | 13,165 | 10.59 |
| 37 | Oklahoma City | 8,701 | 10.43 |
| 38 | San Francisco | 33,443 | 10.28 |
| 39 | Toledo | 8,114 | 10.25 |
| 40 | Grand Rapids | 6,090 | 10.12 |
| 41 | Chicago | 71,491 | 10.07 |
| 42 | Syracuse | 6,436 | 10.02 |
| 43 | Newark | 19,628 | 9.99 |
| 43 | Riverside | 15,560 | 9.99 |
| 45 | Worcester | 6,340 | 9.81 |
| 46 | Tampa-St. Petersburg | 15,303 | 9.75 |
| 47 | Pittsburgh | 21,954 | 9.70 |
| 48 | Houston | 28,005 | 9.64 |
| 49 | Dallas-Fort Worth | 28,579 | 9.61 |
| 50 | Flint | 4,981 | 9.55 |
| 51 | Boston | 33,885 | 9.25 |
| 51 | Indianapolis | 10,794 | 9.25 |
| 53 | St. Louis | 21,328 | 9.06 |
| 54 | Knoxville | 4,277 | 8.98 |
| 55 | Los Angeles | 66,549 | 8.90 |
| 56 | Norfolk-Virginia Beach | 7,175 | 8.89 |
| 57 | Baltimore | 19,300 | 8.88 |
| 58 | Cincinnati | 12,010 | 8.57 |
| 59 | Philadelphia | 39,084 | 8.29 |
| 60 | Fresno | 4,264 | 8.28 |
| 61 | San Antonio | 8,682 | 8.10 |
| 62 | Charlotte | 5,025 | 7.89 |
| 63 | Baton Rouge | 3,771 | 7.63 |
| 64 | Corpus Christi | 2,460 | 7.54 |
| 65 | Lexington-Fayette | 2,334 | 7.34 |
| 66 | Nashville-Davidson | 6,235 | 7.33 |
| 67 | Miami | 11,880 | 7.31 |
| 68 | Louisville | 6,574 | 7.25 |
| 69 | New Orleans | 8,460 | 7.13 |
| 70 | New York | 64,758 | 7.10 |
| 71 | Little Rock | 2,791 | 7.09 |
| 72 | Shreveport | 2,663 | 7.07 |
| 73 | Jacksonville | 5,186 | 7.03 |
| 74 | Richmond | 4,406 | 6.97 |
| 75 | Providence | 6,549 | 6.91 |
| 76 | Greensboro | 5,354 | 6.47 |
| 77 | Mobile | 2,771 | 6.26 |
| 78 | Chattanooga | 2,580 | 6.05 |
| 79 | Birmingham | 4,831 | 5.70 |
| 80 | Jersey City | 3,169 | 5.69 |
| 81 | Memphis | 5,135 | 5.63 |
| 82 | Jackson | 1,780 | 5.56 |
| 83 | Montgomery | 1,457 | 5.34 |

# 259. Skiing Enthusiasts

Skiing is an expensive sport. The price tag for the equipment—several hundred dollars—is just the beginning. The main cost is getting to the slopes when they have snow on the ground. Because the business of transporting and servicing skiers is a seasonal one, there are few bargains. The suppliers must cover their costs for the year in a few months. The summer trade in ski resorts is where the bargains are to be found.

The implications of the cost of skiing show up in the data below. They represent the 1981 and 1982 subscribers to two magazines—*Ski* and *Skiing*—relative to the total population in the area. Two factors dominate the results: money and geography. No one will be surprised that Denver and Colorado Springs are in first and second place, with 1 subscriber for every 1,000 residents. The Rockies are right there, and so are some of the world's best ski resorts. But *Anaheim?* How much skiing is there in Orange County? Not much, but there are a lot of skiers there who enjoy traveling to Aspen or Vail.

The data show vividly how much more popular skiing is west of the Mississippi. All California metro areas are in the top 19. The best the East Coast can come up with is Rochester in 15th place. Unfair, in light of the fact that upstate New York has more snow than anyplace else. But it's true that the Rockies have the highest mountains. Stratton and Stowe in Vermont do not provide as much of a challenge for the expert skier.

At the bottom of the ski slope shown below nestle metro areas like Montgomery and Mobile, with barely 5 subscribers per 100,000 people, less than 200 people in either metro area (even fewer people if we could delete those who subscribe to both magazines).

SOURCE: Metro data based on January 1981 (*Skiing*) and January 1982 (*Ski*) circulation from the Audit Bureau of Circulation, report prepared at authors' request.

| Rank | Metro Area | Total Subscribers | Number of Subscribers Per 1,000 Population |
|---|---|---|---|
| 1 | Denver | 20,721 | 12.79 |
| 2 | Colorado Springs | 3,497 | 11.02 |
| 3 | Anaheim-Santa Ana | 18,899 | 9.78 |
| 4 | Seattle | 15,463 | 9.62 |
| 5 | Spokane | 2,968 | 8.68 |
| 6 | Sacramento | 8,371 | 8.26 |

| Rank | Metro Area | Total Subscribers | Number of Subscribers Per 1,000 Population |
|---|---|---|---|
| 7 | Salt Lake City | 7,585 | 8.10 |
| 8 | San Jose | 10,200 | 7.88 |
| 9 | Las Vegas | 3,302 | 7.15 |
| 10 | Minneapolis-St. Paul | 14,624 | 6.92 |
| 10 | Portland, Ore. | 8,593 | 6.92 |
| 12 | Albuquerque | 3,046 | 6.70 |
| 13 | Tacoma | 3,109 | 6.40 |
| 14 | Fresno | 3,125 | 6.07 |
| 15 | Rochester | 5,859 | 6.03 |
| 16 | Jackson | 1,938 | 5.99 |
| 16 | Madison | 1,938 | 5.99 |
| 18 | San Diego | 10,794 | 5.80 |
| 19 | Los Angeles | 42,078 | 5.63 |
| 20 | Syracuse | 3,533 | 5.50 |
| 21 | Richmond | 3,319 | 5.25 |
| 22 | Worcester | 3,319 | 5.13 |
| 23 | Boston | 18,702 | 5.11 |
| 24 | San Francisco | 19,865 | 5.03 |
| 25 | Washington, D.C. | 15,260 | 4.99 |
| 26 | Newark | 9,422 | 4.79 |
| 27 | Phoenix | 7,105 | 4.71 |
| 28 | Riverside | 7,133 | 4.58 |
| 29 | Milwaukee | 5,848 | 4.19 |
| 30 | Chicago | 27,853 | 3.92 |
| 31 | Des Moines | 1,319 | 3.90 |
| 32 | Grand Rapids | 2,317 | 3.85 |
| 33 | Wichita | 1,581 | 3.84 |
| 34 | Pittsburgh | 8,119 | 3.59 |
| 35 | Buffalo | 4,335 | 3.49 |
| 36 | Oklahoma City | 2,900 | 3.48 |
| 37 | Tucson | 1,788 | 3.37 |
| 38 | Cleveland | 6,377 | 3.36 |
| 39 | Philadelphia | 15,593 | 3.31 |
| 40 | Detroit | 14,266 | 3.28 |
| 41 | Norfolk-Virginia Beach | 2,641 | 3.27 |
| 42 | Dallas-Fort Worth | 9,575 | 3.22 |
| 43 | Providence | 3,001 | 3.17 |
| 44 | Akron | 2,072 | 3.14 |
| 45 | Flint | 1,604 | 3.08 |
| 46 | Columbus, Ohio | 3,314 | 3.03 |
| 47 | New York | 27,113 | 2.97 |
| 48 | Omaha | 1,654 | 2.90 |
| 49 | Austin | 1,552 | 2.89 |
| 50 | Baltimore | 6,242 | 2.87 |
| 51 | Houston | 7,950 | 2.74 |
| 52 | Kansas City, Kan.-Mo. | 3,178 | 2.39 |
| 53 | Tulsa | 1,500 | 2.18 |
| 54 | Dayton | 1,799 | 2.17 |
| 55 | Indianapolis | 2,496 | 2.14 |
| 56 | Charlotte | 1,353 | 2.12 |
| 57 | Atlanta | 4,285 | 2.11 |
| 58 | Fort Wayne | 789 | 2.06 |
| 59 | Toledo | 1,572 | 1.99 |
| 60 | El Paso | 937 | 1.95 |
| 61 | Knoxville | 767 | 1.61 |
| 62 | Lexington-Fayette | 508 | 1.60 |
| 63 | Cincinnati | 2,128 | 1.52 |
| 64 | Jersey City | 826 | 1.48 |
| 64 | Miami | 2,401 | 1.48 |
| 66 | Greensboro | 1,204 | 1.46 |
| 67 | New Orleans | 1,646 | 1.39 |

| Rank | Metro Area | Total Subscribers | Number of Subscribers Per 1,000 Population |
|---|---|---|---|
| 68 | Honolulu | 1,033 | 1.35 |
| 69 | Louisville | 1,214 | 1.34 |
| 70 | St. Louis | 3,076 | 1.31 |
| 70 | San Antonio | 1,405 | 1.31 |
| 72 | Shreveport | 391 | 1.04 |
| 73 | Little Rock | 404 | 1.03 |
| 74 | Birmingham | 827 | 0.98 |
| 75 | Tampa-St. Petersburg | 1,488 | 0.95 |

| Rank | Metro Area | Total Subscribers | Number of Subscribers Per 1,000 Population |
|---|---|---|---|
| 76 | Nashville-Davidson | 803 | 0.94 |
| 77 | Jacksonville | 684 | 0.93 |
| 78 | Corpus Christi | 292 | 0.87 |
| 79 | Chattanooga | 368 | 0.86 |
| 80 | Memphis | 772 | 0.85 |
| 81 | Baton Rouge | 400 | 0.81 |
| 82 | Montgomery | 129 | 0.47 |
| 83 | Mobile | 183 | 0.41 |

# 260.  Tennis Enthusiasts

Tennis began as an indoor court game in 15th-century France and was first played in America as lawn tennis in the 1870s. It has come full circle with the advent of urban health and racket clubs, which now have indoor facilities to allow tennis players to participate year-round.

Increased interest in this sport has been greatly aided by media attention and by the large purses of professional tournaments (John McEnroe was the top money winner in 1981, with $941,000). The most limiting factor for tennis buffs in a large metro area is the cost and trouble of obtaining court time, which may explain why smaller and medium-size metro areas dominate the top ranks in the following table.

San Jose, located in southern California, leads, with more than 10 tennis enthusiasts per 1,000 residents, based on combined subscriptions to *Tennis* and *World Tennis*. Des Moines, Washington, Atlanta and Richmond follow.

Jersey City, Buffalo and Cleveland are the least enthusiastic tennis followers, with only 2.5 readers or less per 1,000 residents.

SOURCE: Metro data based on August 1981 circulation from the Audit Bureau of Circulation, report prepared at the author's request especially for this book.

| Rank | Metro Area | Total Subscribers | Subscribers Per 1,000 Population |
|---|---|---|---|
| 1 | San Jose | 12,737 | 10.23 |
| 2 | Des Moines | 2,760 | 8.16 |
| 3 | Washington, D.C. | 24,100 | 7.88 |
| 4 | Atlanta | 13,997 | 6.90 |
| 5 | Richmond | 4,194 | 6.64 |

| Rank | Metro Area | Total Subscribers | Subscribers Per 1,000 Population |
|---|---|---|---|
| 6 | Anaheim-Santa Ana | 12,309 | 6.37 |
| 7 | Norfolk-Virginia Beach | 4,633 | 5.74 |
| 8 | Omaha | 2,038 | 5.50 |
| 9 | Oklahoma City | 4,579 | 5.49 |
| 10 | Honolulu | 4,167 | 5.46 |
| 11 | Providence | 5,055 | 5.34 |
| 12 | Miami | 8,447 | 5.20 |
| 13 | San Francisco | 16,891 | 5.19 |
| 14 | Charlotte | 3,273 | 5.14 |
| 15 | Dayton | 4,255 | 5.13 |
| 16 | Houston | 14,231 | 4.90 |
| 16 | Jacksonville | 3,616 | 4.90 |
| 18 | Austin | 2,575 | 4.80 |
| 19 | Colorado Springs | 1,476 | 4.65 |
| 20 | Baton Rouge | 2,279 | 4.61 |
| 21 | Dallas-Fort Worth | 13,511 | 4.54 |
| 22 | Sacramento | 4,485 | 4.42 |
| 23 | New Orleans | 4,997 | 4.21 |
| 24 | Denver | 6,774 | 4.18 |
| 25 | Louisville | 3,775 | 4.17 |
| 26 | San Diego | 7,718 | 4.15 |
| 27 | Wichita | 1,702 | 4.14 |
| 28 | Las Vegas | 1,900 | 4.11 |
| 29 | Columbus, Ohio | 4,485 | 4.10 |
| 30 | Philadelphia | 19,315 | 4.09 |
| 31 | Cincinnati | 5,706 | 4.07 |
| 32 | Phoenix | 6,126 | 4.06 |
| 33 | Lexington-Fayette | 1,285 | 4.04 |
| 34 | Boston | 14,519 | 3.96 |
| 34 | El Paso | 1,900 | 3.96 |
| 36 | Newark | 7,706 | 3.92 |
| 36 | New York | 35,763 | 3.92 |
| 38 | Los Angeles | 29,133 | 3.90 |
| 39 | Greensboro | 3,190 | 3.86 |
| 40 | Tulsa | 2,640 | 3.83 |
| 41 | Indianapolis | 4,436 | 3.80 |
| 42 | Chattanooga | 1,597 | 3.74 |
| 43 | Knoxville | 1,777 | 3.73 |
| 44 | Corpus Christi | 1,198 | 3.67 |
| 45 | Chicago | 25,817 | 3.64 |
| 45 | Kansas City, Kan.-Mo. | 4,831 | 3.64 |
| 47 | Shreveport | 1,357 | 3.60 |

| Rank | Metro Area | Total Subscribers | Subscribers Per 1,000 Population |
|---|---|---|---|
| 48 | Grand Rapids | 2,116 | 3.52 |
| 49 | St. Louis | 8,185 | 3.48 |
| 50 | Seattle | 5,581 | 3.47 |
| 51 | Minneapolis-St. Paul | 7,233 | 3.42 |
| 51 | Nashville-Davidson | 2,907 | 3.42 |
| 53 | Fort Wayne | 1,288 | 3.36 |
| 54 | Baltimore | 7,282 | 3.35 |
| 55 | Little Rock | 1,311 | 3.33 |
| 55 | Tampa-St. Petersburg | 5,233 | 3.33 |
| 57 | Tucson | 1,736 | 3.27 |
| 58 | Albuquerque | 1,454 | 3.20 |
| 58 | Memphis | 2,923 | 3.20 |
| 60 | Rochester | 3,097 | 3.19 |
| 61 | San Antonio | 3,389 | 3.16 |
| 62 | Mobile | 1,384 | 3.13 |
| 63 | Jackson | 1,001 | 3.12 |
| 64 | Milwaukee | 4,346 | 3.11 |
| 65 | Fresno | 1,597 | 3.10 |
| 66 | Birmingham | 2,620 | 3.09 |
| 67 | Portland, Ore. | 3,832 | 3.08 |
| 68 | Madison | 987 | 3.05 |
| 69 | Salt Lake City | 2,800 | 2.99 |
| 70 | Toledo | 2,343 | 2.96 |
| 71 | Syracuse | 1,854 | 2.89 |
| 72 | Montgomery | 769 | 2.82 |
| 72 | Pittsburgh | 6,385 | 2.82 |
| 74 | Riverside | 4,343 | 2.79 |
| 75 | Worcester | 1,790 | 2.77 |
| 76 | Detroit | 11,952 | 2.75 |
| 77 | Akron | 1,772 | 2.68 |
| 78 | Flint | 1,370 | 2.63 |
| 79 | Spokane | 897 | 2.62 |
| 80 | Tacoma | 1,237 | 2.55 |
| 81 | Cleveland | 4,765 | 2.51 |
| 82 | Buffalo | 2,654 | 2.14 |
| 83 | Jersey City | 1,016 | 1.82 |

# 261. Travel Enthusiasts

Most travel and vacation magazine readers are business executives, professionals and government officials who spend a significant proportion of their time flying to and from conferences and meetings. These readers of travel magazines seek the most efficient and comfortable methods of travel and the best hotels and restaurants to patronize during their stay in a particular location.

Other people read travel magazines to plan their next vacation or simply to learn more about a particular place. Because of the reduction of the time-space-cost relationship with the introduction of low-cost air fares and supersonic jets such as the Concorde, many vacation places have become more accessible to individuals for vacation trips.

*Travel and Leisure* and *Signature* are used here to measure the concentration of intercity travelers. They are published for American Express and Diners Club cardholders, respectively.

Travel and vacation magazines are most prevalent in America's major business and resort centers. The largest single cluster of readers, over 120,000, is in New York. On a per capita basis, the leader is the Washington, D.C. area, with over 16 readers per 1,000 residents; followed by Houston and Newark, with 14 each; and New York, with 13 per 1,000. Reminder: The Newark metro area includes most of northern New Jersey, many of whose residents work in New York City. Newark itself is only a small fraction of this area.

SOURCE: Metro area data based on November 1980 (*Travel and Leisure*) and October 1981 (*Signature*) circulation from the Audit Bureau of Circulation, report prepared at the authors' request especially for this book.

| Rank | Metro Area | Total Subscribers | Subscribers Per 1,000 Population |
|---|---|---|---|
| 1 | Washington, D.C. | 49,452 | 16.16 |
| 2 | Houston | 40,377 | 13.90 |
| 3 | Newark | 27,292 | 13.89 |
| 4 | New York | 121,402 | 13.31 |
| 5 | Miami | 20,129 | 12.38 |
| 6 | Chicago | 79,366 | 11.17 |
| 7 | Las Vegas | 5,035 | 10.90 |
| 8 | Jersey City | 5,930 | 10.65 |
| 9 | El Paso | 5,035 | 10.49 |
| 10 | San Francisco | 33,011 | 10.15 |
| 11 | Los Angeles | 70,659 | 9.45 |
| 12 | Denver | 14,531 | 8.97 |
| 13 | Anaheim-Santa Ana | 17,241 | 8.93 |
| 13 | Omaha | 3,308 | 8.93 |
| 15 | San Jose | 10,845 | 8.71 |
| 16 | Philadelphia | 40,592 | 8.61 |
| 17 | New Orleans | 10,037 | 8.46 |
| 18 | Dallas-Fort Worth | 24,837 | 8.35 |
| 19 | Atlanta | 16,654 | 8.21 |
| 20 | Tampa-St. Petersburg | 12,854 | 8.19 |
| 21 | Honolulu | 6,079 | 7.97 |
| 22 | Minneapolis-St. Paul | 16,654 | 7.88 |
| 23 | Detroit | 33,721 | 7.75 |
| 24 | Boston | 28,113 | 7.68 |

| Rank | Metro Area | Total Subscribers | Subscribers Per 1,000 Population |
|---|---|---|---|
| 25 | Oklahoma City | 6,206 | 7.44 |
| 26 | Indianapolis | 8,104 | 6.94 |
| 27 | Baltimore | 14,942 | 6.87 |
| 28 | Kansas City, Kan.-Mo. | 9,074 | 6.83 |
| 29 | Jacksonville | 4,921 | 6.67 |
| 30 | Corpus Christi | 2,156 | 6.61 |
| 31 | Des Moines | 2,213 | 6.55 |
| 32 | San Antonio | 6,902 | 6.44 |
| 33 | Austin | 3,402 | 6.34 |
| 34 | Cleveland | 12,025 | 6.33 |
| 35 | Jackson | 2,026 | 6.32 |
| 36 | Charlotte | 4,005 | 6.29 |
| 37 | Seattle | 9,955 | 6.20 |
| 38 | Memphis | 5,654 | 6.19 |
| 38 | San Diego | 11,521 | 6.19 |
| 40 | Tulsa | 4,255 | 6.17 |
| 41 | Pittsburgh | 13,811 | 6.10 |
| 42 | Nashville-Davidson | 5,151 | 6.06 |
| 43 | Phoenix | 9,012 | 5.98 |
| 44 | Providence | 5,617 | 5.93 |
| 45 | Sacramento | 5,937 | 5.86 |
| 46 | Tucson | 3,075 | 5.79 |
| 47 | Rochester | 5,612 | 5.77 |
| 48 | Albuquerque | 2,612 | 5.75 |
| 49 | Riverside | 8,915 | 5.73 |
| 50 | Wichita | 2,307 | 5.61 |
| 51 | Colorado Springs | 1,745 | 5.50 |
| 52 | Little Rock | 2,149 | 5.46 |
| 53 | Columbus, Ohio | 5,937 | 5.43 |
| 54 | St. Louis | 12,402 | 5.27 |

| Rank | Metro Area | Total Subscribers | Subscribers Per 1,000 Population |
|---|---|---|---|
| 55 | Buffalo | 6,490 | 5.22 |
| 56 | Shreveport | 1,958 | 5.20 |
| 57 | Norfolk-Virginia Beach | 4,179 | 5.18 |
| 58 | Fort Wayne | 1,907 | 4.98 |
| 59 | Knoxville | 2,343 | 4.92 |
| 60 | Portland, Ore. | 6,049 | 4.87 |
| 61 | Worcester | 3,143 | 4.86 |
| 62 | Montgomery | 1,317 | 4.83 |
| 63 | Syracuse | 3,073 | 4.78 |
| 64 | Tacoma | 2,267 | 4.67 |
| 65 | Birmingham | 3,907 | 4.61 |
| 65 | Richmond | 2,911 | 4.61 |
| 67 | Milwaukee | 6,428 | 4.60 |
| 68 | Madison | 1,455 | 4.50 |
| 69 | Fresno | 2,312 | 4.49 |
| 70 | Chattanooga | 1,908 | 4.47 |
| 70 | Lexington-Fayette | 1,423 | 4.47 |
| 72 | Grand Rapids | 2,621 | 4.36 |
| 73 | Baton Rouge | 2,138 | 4.33 |
| 74 | Toledo | 3,398 | 4.29 |
| 75 | Cincinnati | 6,005 | 4.28 |
| 76 | Dayton | 3,518 | 4.24 |
| 77 | Akron | 2,746 | 4.16 |
| 78 | Greensboro | 3,418 | 4.13 |
| 79 | Mobile | 1,802 | 4.07 |
| 80 | Louisville | 3,575 | 3.94 |
| 81 | Salt Lake City | 3,579 | 3.82 |
| 82 | Spokane | 1,299 | 3.80 |
| 83 | Flint | 1,945 | 3.73 |

# 262.  Youth Activities

*Boy's Life* and *Scouting* readership in 1981 is used here as a measure of those interested in youth activities.

A possible reason for the large number of midwestern and western metro areas at the top of the list may be that they have a larger share of families with two parents living at home. Since parents are mainly responsible for magazine subscriptions, many of them are also likely to get involved in youth and community related events. Scouting is not only a youth activity, for parents also get involved in different types of scouting activities—for instance, fishing, hiking and hunting.

Most of the larger American metro areas (for example, New York and Los Angeles) remain conspicuously at the bottom of the ranking. These metro areas have large numbers of senior citizens and young adults who live without children. Naturally, these types of households will have different interests than scouting and other youth activities. These larger metro areas also have substantially higher minority populations, which have not

been exposed as frequently to scouting programs. Children in these metro areas, as well as some southern metro areas, have a greater interest in conventional competitive team sports like baseball, football and basketball, rather than fishing, hiking and hunting, which are more accessible to smaller cities and their rural areas.

SOURCE: Metro data based on October 1981 circulation from Audit Bureau of Circulation, report prepared for this book at the authors' request.

| Rank | Metro Area | People Interested in Youth Activities | Percentage of People Interested in Youth Activities |
|---|---|---|---|
| 1 | Salt Lake City | 35,772 | 3.82 |
| 2 | Des Moines | 7,311 | 2.16 |
| 3 | Kansas City, Kan., Mo. | 22,811 | 1.72 |

| Rank | Metro Area | People Interested in Youth Activities | Percentage of People Interested in Youth Activities |
|---|---|---|---|
| 4 | Las Vegas | 7,068 | 1.53 |
| 4 | Rochester | 14,869 | 1.53 |
| 6 | Spokane | 5,031 | 1.47 |
| 7 | Omaha | 8,352 | 1.46 |
| 8 | Charlotte | 8,567 | 1.34 |
| 9 | Colorado Springs | 4,158 | 1.31 |
| 10 | Jackson | 4,138 | 1.28 |
| 10 | Madison | 4,138 | 1.28 |
| 10 | Milwaukee | 17,858 | 1.28 |
| 13 | Portland, Ore. | 15,736 | 1.27 |
| 14 | Greensboro | 10,408 | 1.26 |
| 14 | St. Louis | 29,775 | 1.26 |
| 16 | Wichita | 5,013 | 1.22 |
| 17 | Richmond | 7,657 | 1.21 |
| 18 | Syracuse | 7,623 | 1.19 |
| 19 | Worcester | 7,657 | 1.18 |
| 20 | Washington, D.C. | 35,919 | 1.17 |
| 21 | Flint | 6,014 | 1.15 |
| 21 | Oklahoma City | 9,604 | 1.15 |
| 23 | Minneapolis-St. Paul | 24,086 | 1.14 |
| 24 | Fort Wayne | 4,284 | 1.12 |
| 25 | Denver | 17,938 | 1.11 |
| 26 | Anaheim-Santa Ana | 21,228 | 1.10 |
| 27 | Toledo | 8,613 | 1.09 |
| 28 | Dallas-Fort Worth | 31,773 | 1.07 |
| 29 | Newark | 20,881 | 1.06 |
| 30 | Seattle | 16,647 | 1.04 |
| 30 | Tacoma | 5,038 | 1.04 |
| 30 | Tulsa | 7,183 | 1.04 |
| 33 | Birmingham | 8,688 | 1.03 |
| 33 | Norfolk-Virginia Beach | 8,295 | 1.03 |
| 35 | Sacramento | 10,321 | 1.02 |
| 36 | Indianapolis | 11,730 | 1.01 |
| 37 | Corpus Christi | 3,329 | .99 |
| 38 | Baltimore | 21,044 | .97 |
| 38 | Baton Rouge | 4,794 | .97 |
| 38 | Columbus, Ohio | 10,643 | .97 |
| 41 | Chicago | 68,111 | .96 |
| 41 | Phoenix | 14,547 | .96 |
| 41 | Pittsburgh | 21,744 | .96 |
| 44 | Philadelphia | 44,930 | .95 |
| 44 | San Jose | 12,340 | .95 |
| 46 | Atlanta | 19,134 | .94 |
| 46 | Tucson | 4,969 | .94 |
| 48 | Austin | 4,976 | .93 |
| 48 | Buffalo | 11,543 | .93 |
| 48 | Little Rock | 3,679 | .93 |
| 48 | Louisville | 8,469 | .93 |
| 52 | Jacksonville | 6,765 | .92 |
| 53 | Cincinnati | 12,756 | .91 |
| 53 | Cleveland | 17,202 | .91 |
| 55 | Dayton | 7,376 | .89 |
| 55 | Houston | 25,878 | .89 |
| 55 | San Antonio | 9,506 | .89 |
| 58 | Albuquerque | 4,002 | .88 |
| 59 | Memphis | 7,931 | .87 |
| 59 | Nashville-Davidson | 7,387 | .87 |
| 61 | Detroit | 37,311 | .86 |
| 61 | San Diego | 16,010 | .86 |
| 63 | Akron | 5,612 | .85 |
| 64 | Chattanooga | 3,580 | .84 |
| 64 | Honolulu | 6,375 | .84 |
| 66 | Providence | 7,738 | .82 |
| 66 | Riverside | 12,795 | .82 |
| 68 | Montgomery | 2,222 | .81 |
| 69 | Boston | 29,388 | .80 |
| 69 | Lexington-Fayette | 2,557 | .80 |
| 71 | Shreveport | 2,896 | .77 |
| 72 | Knoxville | 3,487 | .73 |
| 72 | Mobile | 3,220 | .73 |
| 74 | Grand Rapids | 4,270 | .71 |
| 74 | Tampa-St. Petersburg | 11,111 | .71 |
| 76 | San Francisco | 27,407 | .69 |
| 77 | El Paso | 3,266 | .68 |
| 78 | Los Angeles | 50,382 | .67 |
| 79 | New Orleans | 7,869 | .66 |
| 80 | Fresno | 3,338 | .65 |
| 81 | New York | 47,753 | .52 |
| 82 | Miami | 8,230 | .51 |
| 83 | Jersey City | 2,473 | .44 |

# 263. Bowling Establishments and Pool Halls

Bowling and pool are relatively inexpensive American sports which are popular because of the simplicity of their rules and the consequent catholicity of their appeal and accessibility.

During the 1960s, bowling lounges were built in many malls and plazas and often included game rooms, short order food service and bars. Pool tables were installed as an additional attraction in these indoor recreation centers. Bowling leagues and pool tournaments are integral to the prosperity of these centers.

Cities which lead the list of bowling centers and pool halls have a large number of bowling leagues in which

almost anyone—from women and children to bowling professionals—can play. The three leading cities—Milwaukee, Fort Wayne, and Toledo—are in the Frostbelt, suggesting that the indoor nature of bowling and pool fill a void for those who want to be active and socialize in cold weather. Honolulu's fourth place can be explained by Hawaii's absorption with mainland sports.

Cities at the bottom of the table have fewer bowling centers and pool halls for one of two possible reasons. One is that their residents are too poor to afford the charges required by a downtown location (Providence and Newark). Poorer residents are more likely to spend their leisure time on activities like television-watching that don't require a fee. The other is that residents are too rich to want to play. In Huntington Beach, for example, the residents have a greater interest in outdoor sports such as tennis, golf and water skiing, given the city's sunny year-round climate.

SOURCE: U.S. Department of Commerce, *1977 Census of Service Industries* (Washington, D.C.: Government Printing Office, August, 1981).

| Rank | City | Number of Bowling and Pool Establishments | Number Per 100,000 Residents |
|------|------|-------------------------------------------|------------------------------|
| 1 | Milwaukee | 58 | 9.12 |
| 2 | Fort Wayne | 15 | 8.71 |
| 3 | Toledo | 28 | 7.90 |
| 4 | Honolulu | 28 | 7.67 |
| 5 | Salt Lake City | 12 | 7.36 |
| 6 | Kansas City, Kan. | 11 | 6.83 |
| 7 | Grand Rapids | 12 | 6.60 |
| 8 | Seattle | 32 | 6.48 |
| 9 | Madison | 11 | 6.45 |
| 10 | Greensboro | 10 | 6.43 |
| 11 | Omaha | 20 | 6.42 |
| 12 | Des Moines | 12 | 6.28 |
| 13 | Flint | 10 | 6.27 |
| 14 | Minneapolis | 23 | 6.20 |
| 15 | Cleveland | 34 | 5.93 |
| 16 | Akron | 14 | 5.90 |
| 16 | Columbus, Ga. | 10 | 5.90 |
| 18 | Rochester | 14 | 5.79 |
| 19 | Wichita | 16 | 5.73 |
| 20 | Nashville | 26 | 5.71 |
| 21 | Buffalo | 20 | 5.59 |
| 22 | Tulsa | 20 | 5.54 |
| 23 | Richmond | 12 | 5.47 |
| 24 | Knoxville | 10 | 5.46 |
| 25 | Charlotte | 17 | 5.41 |
| 26 | Spokane | 9 | 5.25 |
| 27 | St. Paul | 14 | 5.18 |
| 28 | Colorado Springs | 11 | 5.11 |
| 29 | Tacoma | 8 | 5.05 |
| 30 | Detroit | 60 | 4.99 |
| 31 | Boston | 28 | 4.97 |
| 32 | Santa Ana | 10 | 4.91 |
| 33 | Columbus, Ohio | 27 | 4.78 |
| 34 | Pittsburgh | 20 | 4.72 |
| 35 | Syracuse | 8 | 4.70 |
| 36 | Tucson | 15 | 4.54 |
| 37 | Mobile | 9 | 4.49 |
| 38 | Kansas City, Mo. | 20 | 4.46 |
| 39 | Jackson | 9 | 4.44 |
| 40 | Dayton | 9 | 4.42 |

| Rank | City | Number of Bowling and Pool Establishments | Number Per 100,000 Residents |
|------|------|-------------------------------------------|------------------------------|
| 41 | Aurora | 7 | 4.41 |
| 42 | Louisville | 13 | 4.36 |
| 43 | Sacramento | 12 | 4.35 |
| 44 | Chicago | 129 | 4.29 |
| 45 | Jacksonville | 23 | 4.25 |
| 45 | Las Vegas | 7 | 4.25 |
| 47 | Cincinnati | 16 | 4.15 |
| 47 | Fort Worth | 16 | 4.15 |
| 49 | Norfolk | 11 | 4.12 |
| 50 | Riverside | 7 | 4.10 |
| 51 | Denver | 20 | 4.07 |
| 52 | Anaheim | 9 | 4.06 |
| 53 | Tampa | 11 | 4.05 |
| 54 | Indianapolis | 28 | 4.00 |
| 55 | Albuquerque | 13 | 3.92 |
| 55 | Lexington-Fayette | 8 | 3.92 |
| 57 | Dallas | 34 | 3.76 |
| 58 | Arlington | 6 | 3.75 |
| 59 | Oklahoma City | 15 | 3.72 |
| 59 | Warren | 6 | 3.72 |
| 61 | Los Angeles | 108 | 3.64 |
| 62 | Yonkers | 7 | 3.58 |
| 63 | San Antonio | 28 | 3.57 |
| 64 | Memphis | 23 | 3.56 |
| 65 | Lincoln | 6 | 3.49 |
| 66 | Austin | 12 | 3.47 |
| 67 | St. Petersburg | 8 | 3.38 |
| 68 | St. Louis | 15 | 3.31 |
| 69 | Portland, Ore. | 12 | 3.28 |
| 70 | Houston | 51 | 3.20 |
| 71 | Baton Rouge | 7 | 3.19 |
| 72 | Baltimore | 25 | 3.18 |
| 73 | Birmingham | 9 | 3.16 |
| 73 | Little Rock | 5 | 3.16 |
| 75 | Jersey City | 7 | 3.13 |
| 76 | San Francisco | 21 | 3.09 |
| 77 | Oakland | 10 | 2.95 |
| 78 | Shreveport | 6 | 2.92 |
| 79 | Phoenix | 23 | 2.91 |
| 80 | Anchorage | 5 | 2.89 |
| 81 | Montgomery | 5 | 2.81 |
| 82 | Long Beach | 10 | 2.77 |
| 83 | New York | 187 | 2.64 |
| 84 | New Orleans | 14 | 2.51 |
| 84 | Washington, D.C. | 16 | 2.51 |
| 86 | San Jose | 15 | 2.36 |
| 87 | Philadelphia | 39 | 2.31 |
| 88 | Lubbock | 4 | 2.30 |
| 89 | Fresno | 5 | 2.29 |
| 89 | Virginia Beach | 6 | 2.29 |
| 91 | Miami | 7 | 2.02 |
| 92 | San Diego | 17 | 1.94 |
| 93 | Atlanta | 8 | 1.88 |
| 94 | Worcester | 3 | 1.85 |
| 95 | Chattanooga | 3 | 1.77 |
| 96 | Corpus Christi | 4 | 1.72 |
| 97 | El Paso | 7 | 1.65 |
| 98 | Huntington Beach | 2 | 1.17 |
| 99 | Newark | 3 | .91 |
| 100 | Providence | 1 | .64 |

# 264. Eating and Drinking Places

Sales at eating and drinking places measure cities' relative prosperity, the degree of socialization and reputation for good places to dine. The eating and drinking places used here are those establishments primarily selling prepared foods and drinks for consumption on or near premises, and include lunch counters, refreshment stands, caterers and in-plant food contractors.

Honolulu (a major resort center, which drives up costs), Anchorage (where costs are burdened by transportation and distance) and cosmopolitan San Francisco all had over $1,000 per capita sales at their eating and drinking places in 1980. This reflects both the presence of a significant percentage of higher income people and higher costs of eating and drinking establishments. In the case of Anchorage, one must add the likelihood of more out of home eating because of the relatively small proportion of residents who are married and have children.

Yonkers, Newark and Jersey City with higher percentages of lower income populations and more "stay at home" eating and drinking habits, are listed at the lower end of the scale, under $300 per person in 1980.

Major cities like Detroit, Chicago, Baltimore and Philadelphia are in the lowest 15 percent of the cities because of their large middle-income and low-income populations. New York City is in the bottom fourth (No. 76 out of 100, $428 per capita) despite its well-known expensive eateries.

SOURCE: *Marketing Economics Guide*, 1981–82 (New York: Marketing Economics Institute, Ltd., 1981).

| Rank | City | Sales at Eating and Drinking Places Per Capita ($) | Rank | City | Sales at Eating and Drinking Places Per Capita ($) | Rank | City | Sales at Eating and Drinking Places Per Capita ($) |
|---|---|---|---|---|---|---|---|---|
| 1 | Honolulu | 1,143.77 | 35 | Kansas City, Mo. | 605.11 | 69 | Virginia Beach | 451.65 |
| 2 | Anchorage | 1,095.46 | 36 | Salt Lake City | 603.82 | 70 | Charlotte | 449.06 |
| 3 | San Francisco | 1,033.38 | 37 | St. Louis | 601.98 | 71 | Mobile | 443.86 |
| 4 | Seattle | 997.81 | 38 | San Diego | 596.81 | 72 | Huntington Beach | 443.01 |
| 5 | Madison | 896.18 | 39 | Santa Ana | 591.75 | 73 | Kansas City, Kan. | 440.33 |
| 6 | Boston | 884.49 | 40 | Tulsa | 585.50 | 74 | Aurora | 432.67 |
| 7 | Portland, Ore. | 850.57 | 41 | Nashville-Davidson | 580.50 | 75 | San Jose | 431.65 |
| 8 | Tampa | 837.48 | 42 | Los Angeles | 578.99 | 76 | New York | 428.11 |
| 9 | Greensboro | 834.15 | 43 | Columbus, Ohio | 578.90 | 77 | Las Vegas | 423.47 |
| 10 | Washington, D.C. | 804.46 | 44 | Louisville | 564.79 | 78 | Shreveport | 411.23 |
| 11 | Wichita | 795.92 | 45 | Milwaukee | 557.03 | 79 | Grand Rapids | 410.50 |
| 12 | Fort Worth | 769.00 | 46 | Lexington-Fayette | 553.50 | 80 | Columbus, Ga. | 410.39 |
| 13 | Austin | 756.82 | 47 | Pittsburgh | 543.90 | 81 | Cleveland | 409.56 |
| 14 | Dallas | 733.63 | 48 | Miami | 541.45 | 82 | Memphis | 400.05 |
| 15 | Houston | 712.52 | 49 | Indianapolis | 539.05 | 83 | El Paso | 398.55 |
| 16 | Fort Wayne | 701.10 | 50 | Riverside | 537.43 | 84 | Jacksonville | 397.22 |
| 17 | Anaheim | 691.48 | 51 | Warren | 532.16 | 85 | Colorado Springs | 396.19 |
| 18 | Atlanta | 682.99 | 52 | Long Beach | 530.59 | 86 | Philadelphia | 391.75 |
| 19 | Omaha | 682.89 | 53 | New Orleans | 518.89 | 87 | Baltimore | 378.55 |
| 20 | Fresno | 665.31 | 54 | Albuquerque | 508.55 | 88 | Chicago | 375.43 |
| 21 | Denver | 663.49 | 55 | Minneapolis | 503.85 | 89 | Worcester | 369.67 |
| 22 | St. Paul | 650.88 | 56 | Norfolk | 502.00 | 90 | St. Petersburg | 351.47 |
| 23 | Richmond | 649.43 | 57 | Oakland | 501.22 | 91 | Tucson | 350.32 |
| 24 | Spokane | 649.37 | 58 | Birmingham | 499.58 | 92 | Providence | 349.80 |
| 25 | Sacramento | 647.81 | 59 | San Antonio | 498.48 | 93 | Dayton | 349.28 |
| 26 | Cincinnati | 635.65 | 60 | Toledo | 496.35 | 94 | Rochester | 347.15 |
| 27 | Lubbock | 634.04 | 61 | Montgomery | 494.58 | 95 | Syracuse | 329.19 |
| 28 | Arlington, Texas | 631.30 | 62 | Baton Rouge | 487.33 | 96 | Detroit | 308.77 |
| 29 | Tacoma | 622.06 | 63 | Flint | 484.93 | 97 | Buffalo | 300.97 |
| 30 | Oklahoma City | 618.29 | 64 | Phoenix | 464.94 | 98 | Jersey City | 287.76 |
| 31 | Des Moines | 617.30 | 65 | Jackson | 461.71 | 99 | Newark | 273.37 |
| 32 | Knoxville | 616.20 | 66 | Little Rock | 461.24 | 100 | Yonkers | 221.17 |
| 33 | Lincoln | 611.48 | 67 | Chattanooga | 456.00 | | | |
| 34 | Akron | 608.56 | 68 | Corpus Christi | 455.75 | | | |

# 265. Spending for Parks and Recreation

Municipal spending for parks and recreation is a residual item which reflects how a city organizes its services. If a sports arena is entirely privately owned, the cost of maintaining the facility does not appear in the municipal budget at all. The fact that Jersey City, Milwaukee and Chicago spend less than one cent per person means that most recreational facilities located in these cities are operated privately or by government agencies rather than by these cities.

Most arenas are owned by municipalities. While the cost of tickets for major sporting events has increased rapidly, revenues to city governments have not gone up with the cost of inflation, which in many cases have forced local government to decrease spending for parks and recreation. One factor that has contribu.ed greatly to the decline of city-owned sporting facilities has been the advent of national pay (cable) television networks such as ESPN and USA which broadcast sporting events.

The relatively low level of spending on parks and recreation (less than 10 cents a person in any city) reflects an American bias that such spending is a luxury compared to other essential services such as education, roads, police, fire, and sanitation.

Detroit's place at the top of the table below probably reflects use of parks maintenance as a means of maintaining employment. Anaheim spends a lot probably because of the importance of the Disneyland tourist trade. Honolulu also needs to maintain its attractive beach areas, which bear heavily on the tourist trade. Per capita spending in all three cities was more than 8 cents.

SOURCE: U.S. Department of Commerce, Bureau of the Census, *City Government Finances in 1979–80* (Washington, D.C.: Government Printing Office, 1981), Table 5.

| Rank | City | Total Spending $ | Spending for Parks and Recreation Per Capita ¢ |
|---|---|---|---|
| 1 | Detroit | 101,554 | 8.44 |
| 2 | Anaheim | 18,600 | 8.38 |
| 3 | Honolulu | 29,970 | 8.21 |
| 4 | San Francisco | 52,559 | 7.74 |
| 5 | Seattle | 35,866 | 7.26 |
| 6 | Sacramento | 16,741 | 6.07 |
| 7 | Denver | 28,806 | 5.86 |
| 8 | Oakland | 19,674 | 5.80 |
| 9 | Portland, Ore. | 20,309 | 5.54 |

| Rank | City | Total Spending $ | Spending for Parks and Recreation Per Capita ¢ |
|---|---|---|---|
| 9 | Long Beach | 20,009 | 5.54 |
| 11 | Greensboro | 8,516 | 5.47 |
| 12 | Madison | 9,291 | 5.45 |
| 13 | Riverside | 8,850 | 5.18 |
| 14 | San Diego | 45,119 | 5.15 |
| 15 | Minneapolis | 19,026 | 5.13 |
| 16 | Albuquerque | 16,989 | 5.12 |
| 17 | New Orleans | 28,399 | 5.09 |
| 18 | Miami | 17,341 | 5.00 |
| 19 | Tampa | 13,187 | 4.86 |
| 20 | Cincinnati | 18,328 | 4.75 |
| 21 | Dallas | 42,872 | 4.74 |
| 22 | Baltimore | 37,248 | 4.73 |
| 23 | Oklahoma City | 18,852 | 4.68 |
| 24 | Norfolk | 12,481 | 4.67 |
| 25 | Fresno | 10,066 | 4.61 |
| 26 | Atlanta | 19,330 | 4.55 |
| 27 | Corpus Christi | 10,437 | 4.50 |
| 28 | Arlington | 7,054 | 4.41 |
| 29 | Memphis | 28,354 | 4.39 |
| 30 | Pittsburgh | 17,395 | 4.10 |
| 31 | Anchorage | 6,877 | 3.97 |
| 32 | Washington, D.C. | 25,149 | 3.94 |
| 33 | Louisville | 11,553 | 3.87 |
| 34 | Aurora | 6,128 | 3.86 |
| 35 | Spokane | 6,590 | 3.85 |
| 36 | Columbus, Ohio | 21,633 | 3.83 |
| 37 | Austin | 13,043 | 3.78 |
| 37 | Grand Rapids | 6,685 | 3.78 |
| 39 | Richmond | 8,256 | 3.77 |
| 40 | St. Louis | 16,882 | 3.73 |
| 40 | Tucson | 12,332 | 3.73 |
| 42 | Boston | 20,935 | 3.72 |
| 43 | Montgomery | 6,578 | 3.69 |
| 44 | Phoenix | 28,462 | 3.60 |
| 45 | Kansas City, Mo. | 15,820 | 3.53 |
| 46 | Des Moines | 6,629 | 3.47 |
| 47 | Charlotte | 12,416 | 3.43 |
| 48 | Baton Rouge | 7,500 | 3.42 |
| 49 | Philadelphia | 57,048 | 3.38 |
| 50 | San Jose | 21,201 | 3.33 |
| 51 | Worcester | 5,201 | 3.21 |
| 52 | Salt Lake City | 5,185 | 3.18 |
| 53 | Flint | 5,008 | 3.14 |
| 54 | Colorado Springs | 6,578 | 3.06 |
| 55 | Birmingham | 8,627 | 3.03 |
| 55 | Omaha | 9,443 | 3.03 |
| 57 | Lincoln | 5,175 | 3.01 |
| 58 | Fort Wayne | 4,953 | 2.88 |
| 59 | Dayton | 5,783 | 2.84 |
| 59 | San Antonio | 22,306 | 2.84 |
| 61 | Las Vegas | 4,664 | 2.83 |
| 62 | Indianapolis | 19,702 | 2.81 |
| 63 | Tulsa | 9,994 | 2.77 |
| 64 | Huntington Beach | 4,647 | 2.73 |
| 65 | Virginia Beach | 6,965 | 2.66 |
| 66 | Houston | 41,825 | 2.62 |
| 67 | Lubbock | 4,537 | 2.61 |
| 68 | Providence | 4,050 | 2.58 |
| 68 | Rochester | 6,242 | 2.58 |
| 70 | Wichita | 7,054 | 2.53 |

| Rank | City | Total Spending $ | Spending for Parks and Recreation Per Capita ¢ | Rank | City | Total Spending | Spending for Parks and Recreation Per Capita ¢ |
|---|---|---|---|---|---|---|---|
| 71 | Shreveport | 5,141 | 2.50 | 85 | Chattanooga | 3,075 | 1.81 |
| 72 | Los Angeles | 73,438 | 2.48 | 86 | Knoxville | 3,215 | 1.76 |
| 73 | Lexington-Fayette | 4,990 | 2.44 | 87 | Toledo | 5,693 | 1.61 |
| 74 | Fort Worth | 9,327 | 2.42 | 88 | Columbus, Ga. | 2,607 | 1.54 |
| 74 | Little Rock | 3,829 | 2.42 | 89 | Cleveland | 8,061 | 1.40 |
| 76 | Buffalo | 8,627 | 2.41 | 90 | Jacksonville | 7,507 | 1.39 |
| 77 | New York | 165,236 | 2.34 | 91 | Yonkers | 2,477 | 1.27 |
| 78 | Syracuse | 3,921 | 2.31 | 92 | Warren | 2,017 | 1.25 |
| 79 | Nashville | 10,276 | 2.26 | 93 | Newark | 3,851 | 1.17 |
| 80 | Santa Ana | 4,592 | 2.25 | 94 | Kansas City, Kan. | 1,871 | 1.16 |
| 81 | El Paso | 9,500 | 2.23 | 95 | Tacoma | 1,681 | 1.06 |
| 82 | Mobile | 4,048 | 2.02 | 96 | Jersey City | 2,157 | 0.97 |
| 83 | Akron | 4,733 | 2.00 | 97 | Milwaukee | 6,057 | 0.95 |
| 84 | Jackson | 3,999 | 1.97 | 98 | Chicago | 16,634 | 0.56 |

# 266. Square Dance Callers

With America's new interest in physical fitness, square dancing may pick up a following from people who decide that prefer it to the lonely life of the daily jogger. Square dance aficionados might make do with a record player instead of a fiddle or two—but they can't do without the caller.

Even though they move into a city, some folks like nothing better than to get out for a rousing square dance every now and again. They will be disappointed in some cities—like Honolulu; Kansas City, Mo.; St. Louis; Washington, D.C.; Anchorage; Jersey City; and Yonkers—if they are looking for a registered member of the International Association of Square Dance Callers (IASDC). These cities have no member callers at all.

Fortunately, there are 27 cities to choose from that had 10 or more registered members of the IASDC in 1982. Los Angeles tops the list, with 35 members, followed by Phoenix, Chicago, Oakland and Dallas. San Francisco and Tampa had 22 registered callers each; Portland, Oregon and San Diego had 21 each.

SOURCE: International Association of Square Dance Callers, data provided for this book in response to authors' questionnaire, 1982.

| Rank | City | Number of Square Dance Callers | Rank | City | Number of Square Dance Callers | Rank | City | Number of Square Dance Callers |
|---|---|---|---|---|---|---|---|---|
| 1 | Los Angeles | 35 | 14 | Detroit | 15 | 28 | Milwaukee | 9 |
| 2 | Phoenix | 27 | 16 | Boston | 14 | 28 | New Orleans | 9 |
| 3 | Chicago | 26 | 17 | Salt Lake City | 13 | 28 | Tacoma | 9 |
| 4 | Oakland | 25 | 18 | Charlotte | 11 | 32 | Greensboro | 8 |
| 5 | Dallas | 24 | 18 | Grand Rapids | 11 | 32 | Lexington-Fayette | 8 |
| 6 | San Francisco | 22 | 18 | Houston | 11 | 32 | New York | 8 |
| 6 | Tampa | 22 | 18 | Indianapolis | 11 | 32 | Spokane | 8 |
| 8 | Portland, Ore. | 21 | 18 | Newark | 11 | 32 | Tulsa | 8 |
| 8 | San Diego | 21 | 18 | Syracuse | 11 | 37 | Fort Worth | 7 |
| 10 | Atlanta | 20 | 24 | Albuquerque | 10 | 37 | Jacksonville | 7 |
| 11 | Seattle | 19 | 24 | Baltimore | 10 | 37 | Knoxville | 7 |
| 12 | Columbus, Ohio | 17 | 24 | Kansas City, Kan. | 10 | 37 | Louisville | 7 |
| 12 | Huntington Beach | 17 | 24 | Rochester | 10 | 37 | Memphis | 7 |
| 14 | Denver | 15 | 28 | Flint | 9 | 37 | Philadelphia | 7 |

| Rank | City | Number of Square Dance Callers | | Rank | City | Number of Square Dance Callers | | Rank | City | Number of Square Dance Callers |
|---|---|---|---|---|---|---|---|---|---|---|
| 37 | Pittsburgh | 7 | | 54 | Norfolk | 4 | | 72 | Miami | 2 |
| 44 | Aurora | 6 | | 54 | Omaha | 4 | | 72 | Mobile | 2 |
| 44 | Austin | 6 | | 54 | San Antonio | 4 | | 72 | Riverside | 2 |
| 44 | Cleveland | 6 | | 54 | Tucson | 4 | | 72 | Sacramento | 2 |
| 44 | Nashville-Davidson | 6 | | 64 | Buffalo | 3 | | 72 | St. Petersburg | 2 |
| 44 | Oklahoma City | 6 | | 64 | Cincinnati | 3 | | 72 | San Jose | 2 |
| 44 | St. Paul | 6 | | 64 | Corpus Christi | 3 | | 72 | Santa Ana | 2 |
| 44 | Warren | 6 | | 64 | Las Vegas | 3 | | 72 | Shreveport | 2 |
| 51 | Des Moines | 5 | | 64 | Montgomery | 3 | | 72 | Virginia Beach | 2 |
| 51 | Long Beach | 5 | | 64 | Providence | 3 | | 72 | Wichita | 2 |
| 51 | Minneapolis | 5 | | 64 | Richmond | 3 | | 87 | Akron | 1 |
| 54 | Chattanooga | 4 | | 64 | Worcester | 3 | | 87 | Baton Rouge | 1 |
| 54 | Colorado Springs | 4 | | 72 | Anaheim | 2 | | 87 | Birmingham | 1 |
| 54 | Dayton | 4 | | 72 | Arlington, Texas | 2 | | 87 | El Paso | 1 |
| 54 | Fort Wayne | 4 | | 72 | Columbus, Ga. | 2 | | 87 | Jackson | 1 |
| 54 | Fresno | 4 | | 72 | Little Rock | 2 | | 87 | Lubbock | 1 |
| 54 | Lincoln | 4 | | 72 | Madison | 2 | | 87 | Toledo | 1 |

# 267.  Historic Places

The following table shows the number of historic places designated in the National Register.

There are no surprises here. The average citizen of the U.S. would probably mention four of the top five if asked (Washington, D.C., New York, Philadelphia and Boston). Once we pass the top six, probably few Americans can name the correct order of cities.

O. Henry, the author, once said that Boston, San Francisco and New Orleans are the three most interesting cities in America—all with dramatic histories. It is somewhat odd that San Francisco and New Orleans are not ranked higher in the listing of historic places.

SOURCE: *National Register of Historic Places*, 1976.

| Rank | City | Historic Places | | Rank | City | Historic Places | | Rank | City | Historic Places |
|---|---|---|---|---|---|---|---|---|---|---|
| 1 | Washington, D.C. | 158 | | 19 | Salt Lake City | 24 | | 39 | Kansas City, Mo. | 14 |
| 2 | New York | 111 | | 21 | Milwaukee | 23 | | 39 | Little Rock | 14 |
| 3 | Philadelphia | 94 | | 22 | Honolulu | 22 | | 39 | Montgomery | 14 |
| 4 | Boston | 62 | | 23 | Detroit | 21 | | 42 | Knoxville | 13 |
| 5 | Richmond | 60 | | 23 | Lexington | 21 | | 42 | Portland, Ore. | 13 |
| 6 | Baltimore | 53 | | 23 | Madison | 21 | | 44 | Syracuse | 12 |
| 7 | Providence | 47 | | 26 | Indianapolis | 20 | | 44 | Toledo | 12 |
| 8 | Cincinnati | 44 | | 26 | Mobile | 20 | | 46 | Dayton | 11 |
| 9 | Cleveland | 42 | | 26 | Pittsburgh | 20 | | 46 | Memphis | 11 |
| 10 | Chicago | 36 | | 29 | St. Louis | 19 | | 46 | Norfolk | 11 |
| 10 | New Orleans | 36 | | 30 | Rochester | 18 | | 49 | Chattanooga | 10 |
| 12 | Austin | 30 | | 30 | San Antonio | 18 | | 49 | Minneapolis | 10 |
| 13 | Nashville | 28 | | 32 | Los Angeles | 17 | | 51 | Buffalo | 9 |
| 13 | San Francisco | 28 | | 32 | Louisville | 17 | | 51 | Jacksonville | 9 |
| 13 | Seattle | 28 | | 32 | St. Paul | 17 | | 51 | Sacramento | 9 |
| 16 | Denver | 27 | | 32 | Tampa | 17 | | 55 | Baton Rouge | 8 |
| 17 | Columbus, Ohio | 26 | | 36 | Atlanta | 16 | | 55 | Jackson | 8 |
| 18 | Columbus, Ga. | 25 | | 36 | Omaha | 16 | | 55 | Tucson | 8 |
| 19 | Newark | 24 | | 36 | San Diego | 16 | | 55 | Virginia Beach | 8 |

| Rank | City | Historic Places | Rank | City | Historic Places | Rank | City | Historic Places |
|------|------|-----------------|------|------|-----------------|------|------|-----------------|
| 55 | Wichita | 8 | 63 | Phoenix | 5 | 80 | Fort Wayne | 2 |
| 59 | Akron | 7 | 63 | Spokane | 5 | 80 | Fresno | 2 |
| 59 | Grand Rapids | 7 | 63 | Tacoma | 5 | 80 | Greensboro | 2 |
| 59 | Lincoln | 7 | 63 | Worcester | 5 | 80 | Jersey City | 2 |
| 59 | Oakland | 7 | 63 | Las Vegas | 4 | 80 | Long Beach | 2 |
| 63 | Birmingham | 5 | 73 | San Jose | 4 | 80 | Riverside | 2 |
| 63 | Des Moines | 5 | 73 | Yonkers | 4 | 80 | Shreveport | 2 |
| 63 | El Paso | 5 | 76 | Charlotte | 3 | 87 | Albuquerque | 1 |
| 63 | Fort Worth | 5 | 76 | Colorado Springs | 3 | 87 | Dallas | 1 |
| 63 | Houston | 5 | 76 | Kansas City, Kan. | 3 | 87 | Lubbock | 1 |
| 63 | Miami | 5 | 76 | Oklahoma City | 3 | 87 | St. Petersburg | 1 |

# SUMMARIES OF THE 100 LARGEST CITIES

## Akron

Akron's 1980 population, slightly over 237,000, makes it the 58th biggest city in the nation. A population loss of nearly 14 percent in the 1970s may be attributed to the shift of manufacturing facilities, especially tire manufacturing, to the South and West and the decline of the auto industry. However, Akron has benefited from the change. Although unemployment was still high (8th in December 1982), the recent rise in auto sales should help those related industries still in Akron. The city is experiencing a change in character as it diversifies its economy and the new industries lean toward services and other non-manufacturing jobs. The downtown area has been slower to recover, but the conversion of many old plants to new industries such as plastics, electrical components, aerospace and other light manufacturing and other uses, such as research and hotels (like the Quaker Hilton, created out of an old Quaker Oats factory at a cost of $10 million), have proved that the conversions work. A similar project was undertaken by Burroughs Corporation in Detroit with great success. Residential developments along the Ohio Canal (such as Landings at Canal Park) and downtown construction of condominiums will provide housing and attract residents to this city.

| Title | City Rank | Total Cities Ranked |
|---|---|---|
| Largest Cities (Area) | 69 | (100) |
| Overall Air Quality, PSI (1981) | 40 | (51) |
| Biggest Cities (Population) | 58 | (100) |
| Births | 51 | (92) |
| City per Capita Income | 78 | (100) |
| Cost of Living | * | (62) |
| City Retail Sales per Capita | 45 | (100) |
| Unemployment Rates | 8 | (77) |

| Title | City Rank | Total Cities Ranked |
|---|---|---|
| Dependence on State Aid | 74 | (100) |
| Housing Growth/Population Growth | * | (55) |
| Daily Community Hospital Cost | 59 | (75) |
| Death Rates | 25 | (98) |
| Total Crimes | 72 | (96) |
| Cost per Police Employee | 28 | (71) |
| Arson | 17 | (78) |
| Spending per Resident on Education | * | (72) |
| Library Budgets | 43 | (99) |

*City not listed in table.

## Albuquerque

Albuquerque's population grew by nearly 36 percent between 1970 and 1980, adding over 87,000 new residents and raising its ranking from 58th to 44th. The growth rate is likely to continue for some time. Albuquerque ranks high in housing growth/population growth (4th). A moderate cost of living (41st) and per capita income (57th) show that labor costs are low and goods and products are not costly, which suggests that Albuquerque has room to grow economically. Major employers in the Albuquerque region are split between government, manufacturing, and medical and health services. This diverse economic base has allowed Albuquerque to withstand the 1981–82 recession's impact on certain industries. Albuquerque is also situated at the foot of the Sandia Mountains and attracts tourists and skiing enthusiasts, further broadening its economic base. In addition, Albuquerque is one of the Southwest's major trade and distribution centers.

| Title | City Rank | Total Cities Ranked |
|---|---|---|
| Largest Cities (Area) | 48 | (100) |
| Overall Air Quality, PSI (1981) | 15 | (51) |
| Biggest Cities (Population) | 44 | (100) |
| Births | 54 | (92) |
| City per Capita Income | 57 | (100) |
| Cost of Living | 41 | (62) |
| City Retail Sales per Capita | 21 | (100) |
| Unemployment Rates | 57 | (77) |
| Dependence on State Aid | 24 | (100) |
| Housing Growth/Population Growth | 4 | (55) |
| Daily Community Hospital Cost | 26 | (75) |
| Death Rates | 84 | (98) |
| Total Crimes | 46 | (96) |
| Cost per Police Employee | * | (71) |
| Arson | * | (78) |
| Spending per Resident on Education | 12 | (72) |
| Library Budgets | 84 | (99) |

*City not listed in table.

# Anaheim

Anaheim, 25 miles southeast of Los Angeles, is the 8th biggest city in California and the 62nd biggest in the country. The city's economy revolves around Disneyland, as over 7 million people visit the amusement park each year. The city collects money directly from Disneyland in the form of an admission tax. Tourism is a broader source of revenue for city shops, restaurants and hotels. Other significant industries include aerospace, electronics and citrus fruit packaging firms. Anaheim is also the home of the California Angels baseball team. The city is growing both by attracting new businesses and by luring young people searching for jobs. Many are choosing to stay in Anaheim and start families. The city has a very high birthrate (3rd highest). Despite the poor air quality (5th worst) and the high cost of living (5th highest), Anaheim is still an attractive city to live in, although congestion is of concern to many residents. The city's per capita income is high (6th), and city officials are dedicated to providing public support for making Anaheim a place to reside, as shown by the city's high budget allocations for such activities as police spending (4th), education (27th) and libraries (21st).

| Title | City Rank | Total Cities Ranked |
|---|---|---|
| Largest Cities (Area) | 88 | (100) |
| Overall Air Quality, PSI (1981) | 5 | (51) |
| Biggest Cities (Population) | 62 | (100) |
| Births | 3 | (92) |
| City per Capita Income | 6 | (100) |

| Title | City Rank | Total Cities Ranked |
|---|---|---|
| Cost of Living | 5 | (62) |
| City Retail Sales per Capita | 57 | (100) |
| Unemployment Rates | * | (77) |
| Dependence on State Aid | 54 | (100) |
| Housing Growth/Population Growth | * | (55) |
| Daily Community Hospital Costs | 6 | (75) |
| Death Rates | 89 | (98) |
| Total Crimes | 73 | (96) |
| Cost per Police Employee | 4 | (71) |
| Arson | 73 | (78) |
| Spending per Resident on Education | 27 | (72) |
| Library Budgets | 21 | (99) |

*City not listed in table.

# Anchorage

The city of Anchorage merged with its surrounding county ("borough") in 1975 and grew to 1955 square miles, the largest city areawise in the nation—and the only city that is coterminous with its own metro area. It is the 79th largest city in the United States, with a population of over 173,000. It has the 11th worst air quality, however. Its birth and death rates are the lowest in the nation, reflecting the pioneer spirit and the youthful average age of many of its residents, who came to Anchorage in pursuit of a good job. It has the 2nd highest per capita income, coupled with a high cost of living and commensurately high retail sales. Incomes are generated primarily by companies in the aviation and oil industries and by national defense (with a major air force base adding to the city economy). Anchorage also serves as the distribution and commercial center for Alaska. It has a low crime rate and the 10th lowest arson rate. It has the highest spending per capita on education and a high library budget.

| Title | City Rank | Total Cities Ranked |
|---|---|---|
| Largest Cities (Area) | 1 | (100) |
| Overall Air Quality, PSI (1981) | 11 | (51) |
| Biggest Cities (Population) | 79 | (100) |
| Births | 92 | (92) |
| City per Capita Income | 2 | (100) |
| Cost of Living | * | (62) |
| City Retail Sales per Capita | 10 | (100) |
| Unemployment Rates | * | (77) |
| Dependence on State Aid | 6 | (100) |
| Housing Growth/Population Growth | 20 | (55) |
| Daily Community Hospital Cost | * | (75) |
| Death Rates | 98 | (98) |
| Total Crimes | 68 | (96) |
| Cost per Police Employee | * | (71) |

| Title | City Rank | Total Cities Ranked |
|---|---|---|
| Arson | 69 | (78) |
| Spending per Resident on Education | 1 | (72) |
| Library Budgets | 16 | (99) |

*City not listed in table.

## Arlington

The least populous of the nine Texas cities that rank among the 100 largest, Arlington has experienced the fastest growth rate, with a population increase of nearly 78 percent between 1970 and 1980, making it the 6th fastest growing city in the country. Arlington's population is now over 160,000, ranked 94th. The city's strategic location between Dallas and Fort Worth has been a prime reason for its growth. Corporate regional headquarters and light industry have settled in Arlington, and with them there has been an influx of workers (a 41 percent increase in the employed population between 1970 and 1979). Arlington is the location of one of the world's largest planned industrial developments, Great Southwest Industrial District (nearly 7,000 acres, most of which lie within city limits) and has recently created the I-20 East Business Park (approximately 26,000 acres) to accommodate industrial development, offices and retail support facilities. In addition, the city benefits from the economic impact of Arlington Stadium (where the Texas Rangers play) and the tourist attractions of Six Flags over Texas, the Southwestern Historical Museum and the International Wildlife Park. Tourism brought $98 million into the city in 1981. Housing growth/population growth is 11th highest in the country, and the outlook is for increases in both housing and population throughout the decade. Arlington's per capita income is not high (53rd), but the attraction of its suburban shopping areas has made it first in retail sales per capita. Total index crimes are low, adding to the city's overall attractiveness.

| Title | City Rank | Total Cities Ranked |
|---|---|---|
| Largest Cities (Area) | 54 | (100) |
| Overall Air Quality, PSI (1981) | * | (51) |
| Biggest Cities (Population) | 94 | (100) |
| Births | * | (92) |
| City per Capita Income | 53 | (100) |
| Cost of Living | 20 | (62) |
| City Retail Sales per Capita | 1 | (100) |
| Unemployment Rates | * | (77) |
| Dependence on State Aid | 91 | (100) |

| Title | City Rank | Total Cities Ranked |
|---|---|---|
| Housing Growth/Population Growth | 11 | (55) |
| Daily Community Hospital Cost | * | (75) |
| Death Rates | 96 | (98) |
| Total Crimes | 83 | (96) |
| Cost per Police Employee | * | (71) |
| Arson | 25 | (78) |
| Spending per Resident on Education | * | (72) |
| Library Budgets | 68 | (99) |

*City not listed in table.

## Atlanta

Atlanta's 1980 census population was slightly over 425,000, making it the 28th largest city in the United States. Although Atlanta lost 14 percent of its population in the 1970s, one explanation for this is that the Atlanta suburban share increased by nearly this amount during the same period. The loss may also be considered the result of a natural decrease in population—more deaths than births—rather than emigration. A shift in the suburban migration trend in Atlanta may be underway in the 1980s—housing growth/population growth is 11th, indicating that developers are preparing for people to move into the city. Like many other cities in the sunbelt, the populations are rearranging themselves in surrounding suburban areas or moving back into the cities, rather than moving to other cities. Atlanta's position as one of the country's largest trade and transportation hubs contributes to suburbanization, as many companies locate outside the city. The Atlanta airport handles more transfer traffic than any other city in the United States (the planes are mostly scheduled to fly in at one time and fly out a short time later in a reasonable inspire-expire pattern). City per capita income is 11th lowest, indicating that labor costs are lower, which contributes to increased business stability in the area. This is supported by the relatively low unemployment rate (9th lowest). One aspect of concern to Atlanta residents is the city's high crime rate (4th highest; arson is 6th highest). Crime has been a preoccupation of Atlanta's two black mayors—Maynard Jackson and Andrew Young. Atlanta is the first large American city to have elected two black mayors in a row.

| Title | City Rank | Total Cities Ranked |
|---|---|---|
| Largest Cities (Area) | 29 | (100) |
| Overall Air Quality, PSI (1981) | 38 | (51) |

| Title | City Rank | Total Cities Ranked |
|---|---|---|
| Biggest Cities (Population) | 28 | (100) |
| Births | 90 | (92) |
| City per Capita Income | 90 | (100) |
| Cost of Living | 27 | (62) |
| City Retail Sales per Capita | 47 | (100) |
| Unemployment Rates | 69 | (77) |
| Dependence on State Aid | 55 | (100) |
| Housing Growth/Population Growth | 11 | (55) |
| Daily Community Hospital Cost | 32 | (75) |
| Death Rates | 17 | (98) |
| Total Crimes | 4 | (96) |
| Cost per Police Employee | * | (71) |
| Arson | 6 | (78) |
| Spending per Resident on Education | 30 | (72) |
| Library Budgets | 54 | (99) |

*City not listed in table.

## Aurora

The 2nd fastest growing city after Anchorage, Aurora in 1980 had nearly 159,000 residents, an increase of 111.5 percent since 1970. Located on the city limits of Denver, Aurora is the number one city in the country in housing growth/population growth. Its proximity to Denver, which became a boom town in the 1970s because of a national focus on energy, has permitted it to benefit from the Denver overflow. Aurora has less crime than Denver and has been able to plan its growth with fewer pressures than Denver. For a small city, Aurora has high retail sales per capita (19th) and above-average per capita income (41st). Insurance, banking, energy and manufacturing (equipment for military aircraft) provide the area with a diverse economic base and jobs for both skilled and un-skilled personnel. The future of both Denver and its satellite Aurora has been clouded by the cancellation of projects in the shale oil, synthetic fuel and solar energy areas because of the return of petroleum prices to earlier, lower levels that do not make energy alternatives as profitable as planned.

| Title | City Rank | Total Cities Ranked |
|---|---|---|
| Largest Cities (Area) | 78 | (100) |
| Overall Air Quality, PSI (1981) | * | (51) |
| Biggest Cities (Population) | 96 | (100) |
| Births | * | (92) |
| City per Capita Income | 41 | (100) |
| Cost of Living | * | (62) |
| City Retail Sales per Capita | 19 | (100) |
| Unemployment Rates | * | (77) |
| Dependence on State Aid | 88 | (100) |

| Title | City Rank | Total Cities Ranked |
|---|---|---|
| Housing Growth/Population Growth | 1 | (55) |
| Daily Community Hospital Cost | * | (75) |
| Death Rates | 97 | (98) |
| Total Crimes | 78 | (96) |
| Cost per Police Employee | 34 | (71) |
| Arson | 56 | (78) |
| Spending per Resident on Education | * | (72) |
| Library Budgets | 53 | (99) |

*City not listed in table.

## Austin

Austin, the capital of Texas, has grown more rapidly than any other city in that state. Its population increased by nearly 100,000 people (over 36 percent) in the 1970s, to 345,000. This growth rate will probably continue, since space for future land use and development is ample. Austin's growth has resulted from its ability to attract skilled engineers and electronics specialists and investment in high-technology plants by such firms as IBM, Texas Instruments and Motorola. Austin offers a pleasant climate, the lowest tax rates in Texas and a low cost of living. Its unemployment rate is much lower than in other U.S. cities—around 3 percent. The University of Texas, now considered among the major universities in the sunbelt, provides a strong pool of skilled labor. Despite Austin's economic progress, its inner city has developed some of the problems associated with the older industrialized cities of the Northeast.

| Title | City Rank | Total Cities Ranked |
|---|---|---|
| Largest Cities (Area) | 32 | (100) |
| Overall Air Quality, PSI (1981) | * | (51) |
| Biggest Cities (Population) | 42 | (100) |
| Births | 74 | (92) |
| City per Capita Income | 15 | (100) |
| Cost of Living | * | (62) |
| City Retail Sales per Capita | 8 | (100) |
| Unemployment Rates | * | (77) |
| Dependence on State Aid | 92 | (100) |
| Housing Growth/Population Growth | 3 | (55) |
| Daily Community Hospital Cost | 60 | (75) |
| Death Rates | 90 | (98) |
| Total Crimes | 52 | (96) |
| Cost per Police Employee | * | (71) |
| Arson | 74 | (78) |
| Spending per Resident on Education | 21 | (72) |
| Library Budgets | 18 | (99) |

*City not listed in table.

## Baltimore

Baltimore lost over 13 percent of its population in the decade between 1970 and 1980, dropping from the 7th largest city to the 10th, with a population of nearly 787,000. Like New York, Chicago, Philadelphia and Detroit, Baltimore has suffered from a deterioration of its physical facilities as businesses have moved their offices or plants to the West, South and Southwest, taking jobs and tax revenues with them. These older, industrialized cities of the Northeast have sought to diversify and expand their economic bases by attracting new businesses. Their central areas have been undergoing a transformation as retailers and city officials seek to create more pedestrian-oriented shopping spaces and cultural centers. Baltimore's famed Inner Harbor and the National Aquarium are two such examples. Efforts to induce residents to remain in the city and to attract new residents have been hampered by the city's sluggish local economy. Baltimore's cost of living is 13th highest in the nation, reflecting its large size, yet retail sales are 11th lowest in the United States. Baltimore's Mayor William Donald Schaefer has kept the city's spirit alive with an effective campaign to increase city efficiency (e.g., in purchasing), raise grants from higher levels of government, attract loans and investments from businesses and promote self-help through neighborhood organizations. The fact that the city's per capita income is the lowest of the nation's largest cities suggests that plant investment opportunities exist for some business that would benefit from an urban location.

| Title | City Rank | Total Cities Ranked |
|---|---|---|
| Largest Cities (Area) | 46 | (100) |
| Overall Air Quality, PSI (1981) | * | (51) |
| Biggest Cities (Population) | 10 | (100) |
| Births | 77 | (92) |
| City per Capita Income | 100 | (100) |
| Cost of Living | 13 | (62) |
| City Retail Sales per Capita | 90 | (100) |
| Unemployment Rates | 40 | (77) |
| Dependence on State Aid | 3 | (100) |
| Housing Growth/Population Growth | * | (55) |
| Daily Community Hospital Cost | 31 | (75) |
| Death Rates | 11 | (98) |
| Total Crimes | 39 | (96) |
| Cost per Police Employee | 39 | (71) |
| Arson | 27 | (78) |
| Spending per Resident on Education | 46 | (72) |
| Library Budgets | 20 | (99) |

*City not listed in table.

## Baton Rouge

Baton Rouge is the capital of Louisiana and its 2nd largest city. Ruled by the Spanish, French and British in the 18th century, it has a unique international flavor. It is situated on the east bank of the Mississippi River and is the closest inland deep-water port on the river. This location makes it a major port, distribution center and commercial center for the region. Natural resources such as salt, gas and fresh water are abundant in the area and are vital to its economy. Air quality is average for large cities. The major industries in Baton Rouge are petroleum and petroleum products, while other significant manufactures include rubber and plastics. Finance and banking are also well represented. Not deterred by the high crime rate (17th highest), residents are inclined to do a great deal of their shopping in historic downtown Baton Rouge (retail sales per capita are 16th highest). The city's relatively high birthrate (35th) and low death rate (67th) reveal its low (9th lowest) median age of 27.3 years. The youthful population bodes well for the city's future. The low rate of housing growth (4th lowest) relative to the city's rapid population growth (11th highest) suggests a pent-up demand for housing, which should show up in new construction in the 1980s.

| Title | City Rank | Total Cities Ranked |
|---|---|---|
| Largest Cities (Area) | 60 | (100) |
| Overall Air Quality, PSI (1981) | 26 | (51) |
| Biggest Cities (Population) | 63 | (100) |
| Births | 35 | (92) |
| City per Capita Income | 44 | (100) |
| Cost of Living | 37 | (62) |
| City Retail Sales per Capita | 16 | (100) |
| Unemployment Rates | 41 | (77) |
| Dependence on State Aid | 66 | (100) |
| Housing Growth/Population Growth | 52 | (55) |
| Daily Community Hospital Cost | * | (75) |
| Death Rates | 67 | (98) |
| Total Crimes | 17 | (96) |
| Cost per Police Employee | 63 | (71) |
| Arson | 59 | (78) |
| Spending per Resident on Education | 39 | (72) |
| Library Budgets | 88 | (99) |

*City not listed in table.

## Birmingham

Birmingham is the largest city in Alabama and, with 284,000 people, is the median city in population (50th) of the 100 biggest. Appropriately named after the English industrial center, Birmingham is the leading iron and steel manufacturer in the South. Due to the decline in the auto industry in the late 1970s and early 1980s, metal fabricators have fallen on hard times. Steel manufacturing in the United States has taken a sharp shift away from capital-extensive production to more capital-intensive operations, which further reduce costs. This process of technological modernization has resulted in the permanent elimination of many traditional steelworker jobs. Birmingham was badly hit with high unemployment (4th highest) in a city that already had a low per capita income (15th lowest). Reflective of the poor economy, the crime rate is very high (14th highest). To solve its economic problems, the city has attempted to diversify its economy by attracting other manufacturers and encouraging the construction of distribution facilities. It is more likely that a turnaround in the overall U.S. economy will lift Birmingham out of its difficulties. U.S. Steel's recent commitment of $650 million to expansion has given Birmingham a significant push and is a favorable signal of the beginning of recovery, but, clearly, the steel industry will never regain the importance that it once held for the American economy.

| Title | City Rank | Total Cities Ranked |
|---|---|---|
| Largest Cities (Area) | 41 | (100) |
| Overall Air Quality, PSI (1981) | 20 | (51) |
| Biggest Cities (Population) | 50 | (100) |
| Births | 57 | (92) |
| City per Capita Income | 86 | (100) |
| Cost of Living | 40 | (62) |
| City Retail Sales per Capita | 44 | (100) |
| Unemployment Rates | 4 | (77) |
| Dependence on State Aid | 87 | (100) |
| Housing Growth/Population Growth | * | (55) |
| Daily Community Hospital Cost | 44 | (75) |
| Death Rates | 20 | (98) |
| Total Crimes | 14 | (96) |
| Cost per Police Employee | * | (71) |
| Arson | 50 | (78) |
| Spending per Resident on Education | 42 | (72) |
| Library Budgets | 14 | (99) |

*City not listed in table.

# Boston

The population of Boston declined by over 12 percent between 1970 and 1980, dropping the city from the 16th to the 20th most populous in the country. A continued loss in population is projected through the year 2000. Most of the loss is from the older, industrialized areas of the city. The city had a low unemployment rate for 1982 but has lost jobs in manufacturing and wholesale/retail

trade to suburban areas. A thriving commercial and industrial area grounded in electronics, which has sprung up along Route 128 since World War II, makes Boston a center for this industry in the Northeast. Health and education continue to be vital and growing parts of the Boston economy. Finance, insurance and related activities also continue to provide a signficant job base. City per capita income is below average, and retail sales are low (69th out of 100). Boston ranks high (5th highest) in total index crimes. Culturally, Boston has something for everyone—symphony, ballet, museums, a planetarium and music of all kinds.

| Title | City Rank | Total Cities Ranked |
|---|---|---|
| Largest Cities (Area) | 85 | (100) |
| Overall Air Quality, PSI (1981) | 26 | (51) |
| Biggest Cities (Population) | 20 | (100) |
| Births | 87 | (92) |
| City per Capita Income | 52 | (100) |
| Cost of Living | * | (62) |
| City Retail Sales per Capita | 69 | (100) |
| Unemployment Rates | 73 | (77) |
| Dependence on State Aid | 15 | (100) |
| Housing Growth/Population Growth | 28 | (55) |
| Daily Community Hospital Cost | 2 | (75) |
| Death Rates | 36 | (98) |
| Total Crimes | 5 | (96) |
| Cost per Police Employee | * | (71) |
| Arson | * | (78) |
| Spending per Resident on Education | 19 | (72) |
| Library Budgets | 3 | (99) |

*City not listed in table.

# Buffalo

Buffalo suffered a loss in population between 1970 and 1980 of nearly 23 percent and a corresponding drop in rank from 28th to 39th. Manufacturing, which plays a large role in many northern industrial cities like Buffalo, declined throughout the early 1980s as the recession cut into heavy manufacturing. Large manufacturers in the Buffalo area had to reduce employment, and companies such as Bethlehem Steel, Chevrolet, Ford, General Motors, Republic Steel and Westinghouse, which employ a large proportion of workers in Buffalo, were unable to maintain their employment levels. Unemployment was 11th highest in the country in 1982. In 1980 alone, the manufacturing sector lost almost 11,000 jobs in the Buffalo area. City per capita income was 93rd. Retail sales per capita were third lowest. To combat this trend in its economy, Buffalo could seek to diversify its economic base or improve its overall business climate. Buffalo's economy is closely tied to the auto industry. Improvement nationally will mean improvement for Buffalo. Buffalo's economy is moving into the service area, and during 1980 services employment increased in Buffalo at the national rate, 3.7 percent. Despite its poor job performance, Buffalo ranks 13th in housing growth/population growth. This positive indicator, if maintained, signals an upswing in the Buffalo economy.

| Title | City Rank | Total Cities Ranked |
|---|---|---|
| Largest Cities (Area) | 81 | (100) |
| Overall Air Quality, PSI (1981) | 43 | (51) |
| Biggest Cities (Population) | 39 | (100) |
| Births | 64 | (92) |
| City per Capita Income | 93 | (100) |
| Cost of Living | 57 | (62) |
| City Retail Sales per Capita | 98 | (100) |
| Unemployment Rates | 11 | (77) |
| Dependence on State Aid | 4 | (100) |
| Housing Growth/Population Growth | 13 | (55) |
| Daily Community Hospital Cost | 63 | (75) |
| Death Rates | 5 | (98) |
| Total Crimes | * | (96) |
| Cost per Police Employee | 26 | (71) |
| Arson | * | (78) |
| Spending per Resident on Education | * | (72) |
| Library Budgets | 30 | (99) |

*City not listed in table.

## Charlotte

Charlotte—ranked 47th in population in 1980, with about 314,000 residents—has increased from its 1970 rank (60th) by growing over 30 percent in that decade. The population increase in Charlotte is largely a result of immigration from the surrounding areas and other cities, with most of the new residents moving to the area in search of jobs. The increased population has resulted in a demand for housing, placing Charlotte 30th in housing growth/population growth. Charlotte is a major transportation center, with over 100 trucking firms. Rail connections to the North, South and West link Charlotte with other major transportation centers in the region. Charlotte is also a center for education—colleges and universities in the area, with a student population of nearly 13,000, contribute greatly to the overall economy. A diverse economic base—with manufacturing, textile production, and agricultural and food products—provides the Charlotte area with employment opportunities for all types of labor. The unemployment rate in December 1982 was well below the national average.

| Title | City Rank | Total Cities Ranked |
|---|---|---|
| Largest Cities (Area) | 36 | (100) |
| Overall Air Quality, PSI (1981) | 35 | (51) |
| Biggest Cities (Population) | 47 | (100) |
| Births | 75 | (92) |
| City per Capita Income | 45 | (100) |
| Cost of Living | * | (62) |
| City Retail Sales per Capita | 68 | (100) |
| Unemployment Rates | 68 | (77) |
| Dependence on State Aid | 59 | (100) |
| Housing Growth/Population Growth | 30 | (55) |
| Daily Community Hospital Cost | 72 | (75) |
| Death Rates | 76 | (98) |
| Total Crimes | 43 | (96) |
| Cost per Police Employee | 54 | (71) |
| Arson | * | (78) |
| Spending per Resident on Education | 6 | (72) |
| Library Budgets | 48 | (99) |

*City not listed in table.

## Chattanooga

Chattanooga, the 86th largest city, is on the Tennessee River in the lower range of the Appalachian Valley. The region has been a focal point of poverty programs since the days of the New Deal. The Tennessee Valley Authority (TVA), established under President Franklin D. Roosevelt, has not, however, remedied the economic woes of Chattanooga, as the city still has a very low (3rd lowest) per capita income. Congress has rejected suggestions to cut funds allocated to the TVA and has instead supported the construction of a multi-million-dollar office building for the TVA in Chattanooga. The city continues to be fairly dependent on the state of Tennessee for aid (19th). With an inflexible budget due to small tax revenues, Chattanooga has reserved limited funds for the police force (3rd lowest spending) and libraries (20th lowest). Residents benefit from the low cost of living (2nd lowest) because of the availability of inexpensive food products and because of a housing surplus. Chattanooga remains an important southern industrial city and a producer of essential goods such as textiles, synthetic fibers and chemicals. With a turnaround in the economy in 1983, Chattanooga can look forward to some relief from its economic blues.

| Title | City Rank | Total Cities Ranked |
|---|---|---|
| Largest Cities (Area) | 51 | (100) |
| Overall Air Quality, PSI (1981) | * | (51) |
| Biggest Cities (Population) | 86 | (100) |

| Title | City Rank | Total Cities Ranked |
|---|---|---|
| Births | * | (92) |
| City per Capita Income | 98 | (100) |
| Cost of Living | 61 | (62) |
| City Retail Sales per Capita | 40 | (100) |
| Unemployment Rates | 22 | (77) |
| Dependence on State Aid | 19 | (100) |
| Housing Growth/Population Growth | * | (55) |
| Daily Community Hospital Cost | * | (75) |
| Death Rates | 43 | (98) |
| Total Crimes | 67 | (96) |
| Cost per Police Employee | 69 | (71) |
| Arson | 43 | (78) |
| Spending per Resident on Education | * | (72) |
| Library Budgets | 79 | (99) |

*City not listed in table.

# Chicago

Chicago is the 2nd most populous city in the nation, with a 1980 population of just over 3 million, despite a loss of nearly 11 percent in population since 1970. As the hub of trade and commerce in the Midwest, the city remains strong because of its diversified economic base. Chicago is the center for health-related industries and finance in the Midwest and is headquarters for many major corporations. Commercial construction and residential renovation have been steady, although new home starts have been down as high interest rates and the 1981–82 recession took their toll. Unemployment, while higher than normal, is not unusually high for a city of this size because of the need for all types of skilled and unskilled employees. The indicators for crime are very low. However, the reporting of crimes in Chicago has long been erratic, and in 1981 Chicago detectives contrived to remove reported crimes from the records if they deemed the reports "unfounded." City per capita income is 43rd, yet retail sales are 8th lowest in the United States, suggesting that many Chicago residents spend most of their shopping money in the malls and plazas in Chicago's northern and western suburbs. In 1983 the city's first female mayor was succeeded by its first black mayor.

| Title | City Rank | Total Cities Ranked |
|---|---|---|
| Largest Cities (Area) | 20 | (100) |
| Overall Air Quality, PSI (1981) | 26 | (51) |
| Biggest Cities (Population) | 2 | (100) |
| Births | 31 | (92) |
| City per Capita Income | 43 | (100) |
| Cost of Living | * | (62) |

| Title | City Rank | Total Cities Ranked |
|---|---|---|
| City Retail Sales per Capita | 93 | (100) |
| Unemployment Rates | 24 | (77) |
| Dependence on State Aid | 47 | (100) |
| Housing Growth/Population Growth | * | (55) |
| Daily Community Hospital Cost | 7 | (75) |
| Death Rates | 38 | (98) |
| Total Crimes | 93 | (96) |
| Cost per Police Employee | * | (71) |
| Arson | 41 | (78) |
| Spending per Resident on Education | 17 | (72) |
| Library Budgets | 46 | (99) |

*City not listed in table.

# Cincinnati

Cincinnati lost 15 percent of its population between 1970 and 1980 as a result of the recent trend of migrations to America's Southwest. Cincinnati's future growth apparently depends on economic diversification beyond manufacturing and commercial industries, while retaining the heavy machine and soap product industries through reindustrializing. This tall order is not beyond Cincinnati's capacity. The city continues to have a large work force. It will require huge long-term capital investments and worker training. Cincinnati is unlikely in any case to lose its importance as a transportation center. Its strategic location as a port on the Ohio River gives it a strong role in servicing the large river traffic. Cincinnati is also the principal financial and commercial city in the Ohio-Kentucky-Indiana tristate region. It is famous for its two sports teams—the Reds (the oldest major league baseball team) and the Bengals (football).

| Title | City Rank | Total Cities Ranked |
|---|---|---|
| Largest Cities (Area) | 55 | (100) |
| Overall Air Quality, PSI (1981) | * | (51) |
| Biggest Cities (Population) | 32 | (100) |
| Births | 14 | (92) |
| City per Capita Income | 17 | (100) |
| Cost of Living | 29 | (62) |
| City Retail Sales per Capita | 83 | (100) |
| Unemployment Rates | * | (77) |
| Dependence on State Aid | 47 | (100) |
| Housing Growth/Population Growth | * | (55) |
| Daily Community Hospital Cost | 48 | (75) |
| Death Rates | 7 | (98) |
| Total Crimes | 41 | (96) |
| Cost per Police Employee | 71 | (71) |
| Arson | 11 | (78) |
| Spending per Resident on Education | 49 | (72) |
| Library Budgets | 22 | (99) |

*City not listed in table.

# Cleveland

Despite a decline in population from 751,000 in 1970 to 574,000 in 1980, Cleveland remains Ohio's largest city and an important port on Lake Erie. The main factor in Cleveland's decline is the national shift toward new high-technology industries based outside of Ohio. At the same time, manufacturers have been seeking cheaper sources of labor in such areas as South America and the Far East and have shifted production away from Cleveland. The city has consequently faced acute economic distress. Cleveland's per capita income ranks 13th lowest and its retail sales per capita 5th lowest. Its 1978 fiscal crisis, related to the election of a socialist mayor, led to a significant decline in public services. The increase in income taxes that followed shortly after the city's fiscal crisis caused additional loss of jobs. The city's economy continues to be closely linked to the health of the traditional heavy industries—steel, metalworking and automobiles. The city must depend on a few aggressive local firms like Eaton and TRW to generate new jobs from the areas of the economy such as military contracting that have prospered in the early 1980s. Cleveland has some enviable strengths. Culturally, it possesses a symphony orchestra with a worldwide reputation. Many of its service firms in accounting, banking and law are recognized nationally as outstanding.

| Title | City Rank | Total Cities Ranked |
|---|---|---|
| Largest Cities (Area) | 57 | (100) |
| Overall Air Quality, PSI (1981) | 33 | (51) |
| Biggest Cities (Population) | 18 | (100) |
| Births | 33 | (92) |
| City per Capita Income | 88 | (100) |
| Cost of Living | * | (62) |
| City Retail Sales per Capita | 96 | (100) |
| Unemployment Rates | 15 | (77) |
| Dependence on State Aid | 67 | (100) |
| Housing Growth/Population Growth | * | (55) |
| Daily Community Hospital Cost | 23 | (75) |
| Death Rates | 8 | (98) |
| Total Crimes | 30 | (96) |
| Cost per Police Employee | 16 | (71) |
| Arson | 8 | (78) |
| Spending per Resident on Education | 41 | (72) |
| Library Budgets | 1 | (99) |

*City not listed in table.

# Colorado Springs

Colorado Springs is one of the fastest-growing cities in the United States. Continued population growth has heightened the need for better highways and more adequate housing. Colorado Springs expects to develop its suburban areas in the coming years, with the bulk of new housing being constructed on the fringes of existing urban development. Water quality is declining due to the population growth, and the Colorado Springs government anticipates changes in the city's present treatment facilities to handle this problem. Like many cities, Colorado Springs is investigating ways to maintain water quality through the end of this century.

| Title | City Rank | Total Cities Ranked |
|---|---|---|
| Largest Cities (Area) | 35 | (100) |
| Overall Air Quality, PSI (1981) | * | (51) |
| Biggest Cities (Population) | 66 | (100) |
| Births | 21 | (92) |
| City per Capita Income | 34 | (100) |
| Cost of Living | 60 | (62) |
| City Retail Sales per Capita | 38 | (100) |
| Unemployment Rates | * | (77) |
| Dependence on State Aid | 85 | (100) |
| Housing Growth/Population Growth | 26 | (55) |
| Community Daily Hospital Cost | * | (75) |
| Death Rates | 88 | (98) |
| Total Crimes | 57 | (96) |
| Cost per Police Employee | 33 | (71) |
| Arson | 44 | (78) |
| Spending per Resident on Education | 52 | (72) |
| Library Budgets | 75 | (99) |

*City not listed in table.

# Columbus, Georgia

Columbus, Georgia is located on the east bank of the Chattahoochee River across from Phenix City, Alabama (a part of the Columbus metro area). The population of Columbus in 1980 was over 169,000, up 9.3 percent over 1970. Columbus city residents outnumber suburban residents by over 2 to 1, making this city one where city per capita spending especially benefits the city economy. Another aspect of the population increase during the 1970s in Columbus is that the natural increase—relatively high births (25th) and low deaths (73rd)—means that young families are staying in the city rather than moving to suburban areas. This does not mean that Columbus is wall-to-wall with high-rise apartments. With a land area over 200 square miles (21st largest) and a relatively small population (88th), there is ample room within city limits for suburban-style living. Nearby Fort Benning, with a military payroll in excess of $450 million, contributes greatly to the economy. Columbus is a textile production center, with Columbus Mills (carpets and rugs) and Swift Spinning Mills (a division of Fieldcrest). It is also a finance and insurance center for the region. Crime in Columbus is the lowest in the nation.

| Title | City Rank | Total Cities Ranked |
|---|---|---|
| Largest Cities (Area) | 21 | (100) |
| Overall Air Quality, PSI (1981) | * | (51) |
| Biggest Cities (Population) | 88 | (100) |
| Births | 25 | (92) |
| City per Capita Income | 73 | (100) |
| Cost of Living | 39 | (62) |
| City Retail Sales per Capita | 58 | (100) |
| Unemployment Rates | 32 | (77) |
| Dependence on State Aid | 72 | (100) |
| Housing Growth/Population Growth | * | (55) |
| Daily Community Hospital Cost | * | (75) |
| Death Rates | 73 | (98) |
| Total Crimes | 96 | (96) |
| Cost per Police Employee | * | (71) |
| Arson | * | (78) |
| Spending per Resident on Education | * | (72) |
| Library Budgets | 89 | (99) |

*City not listed in table.

# Columbus, Ohio

Columbus, the 19th largest city in the United States, with almost 565,000 population, grew nearly 5 percent between 1970 and 1980. One reason is Columbus's annexation policy, which has allowed it to maintain its population and tax base by adding over 80 square miles since 1982. Columbus has not been as affected by recessionary fallout as other large cities of the Northeast because of its diverse economic base. Only 20 percent of the Columbus work force is engaged in manufacturing. The service sector accounts for 19 percent. Another 7 percent are employed in finance, real estate and insurance—more than 50 insurance companies are headquartered in Columbus. Also, 23 percent of the Columbus work force is employed in retail/wholesale trade. City per capita income is 25th in the nation, and cost of living is 43rd—a favorable relationship. Unemployment is moderate—and excellent in comparison with other similar-sized cities in Ohio and elsewhere in the north. Columbus also has a high rate of housing growth to population growth, ranking 5th in the country. This indicator bodes well for future growth and development in the Columbus area.

| Title | City Rank | Total Cities Ranked |
|---|---|---|
| Largest Cities (Area) | 23 | (100) |
| Overall Air Quality, PSI (1981) | 49 | (51) |
| Biggest Cities (Population) | 19 | (100) |
| Births | 36 | (92) |
| City per Capita Income | 25 | (100) |
| Cost of Living | 43 | (62) |
| City Retail Sales per Capita | 60 | (100) |
| Unemployment Rates | 39 | (77) |
| Dependence on State Aid | 69 | (100) |
| Housing Growth/Population Growth | 5 | (55) |
| Daily Community Hospital Cost | 61 | (75) |
| Death Rates | 69 | (98) |
| Total Crimes | 41 | (96) |
| Cost per Police Employee | 27 | (71) |
| Arson | 23 | (78) |
| Spending per Resident on Education | 56 | (72) |
| Library Budgets | 99 | (99) |

# Corpus Christi

Corpus Christi, located on the Gulf of Mexico nearly 160 miles from the Mexican border, is the 60th most populous U.S. city. Its relatively high birthrate (23rd highest) contributed to a population growth in 1970–80 of slightly over 13 percent. Energy companies and port tonnage account for the majority of the revenues to the city on a year-round basis. Tourism also contributes heavily—Padre Island National Seashore is one of the many attractions for visitors to the area. Corpus Christi has a relatively high cost of living (20th) and low (22nd lowest) per capita income. It receives little (2nd least) state aid. Total crimes are higher than for other similar-sized cities. Arson is, however, much lower (3rd lowest), perhaps because in Corpus Christi's petroleum-oriented economy, playing with matches is a fitting taboo.

| Title | City Rank | Total Cities Ranked |
|---|---|---|
| Largest Cities (Area) | 25 | (100) |
| Overall Air Quality, PSI (1981) | * | (51) |
| Biggest Cities (Population) | 60 | (100) |
| Births | 23 | (92) |
| City per Capita Income | 79 | (100) |
| Cost of Living | 20 | (62) |
| City Retail Sales per Capita | 42 | (100) |
| Unemployment Rates | * | (77) |
| Dependence on State Aid | 99 | (100) |
| Housing Growth/Population Growth | * | (55) |
| Daily Community Hospital Cost | 73 | (75) |
| Death Rates | 83 | (98) |
| Total Crimes | 49 | (96) |
| Cost per Police Employee | * | (71) |
| Arson | 76 | (78) |
| Spending per Resident on Education | * | (72) |
| Library Budgets | 94 | (99) |

*City not listed in table.

# Dallas

Dallas is a major center of commerce in the southwestern United States. The Dallas economy is highly diversified, including oil and gas, electronics, consumer household goods and transportation. In the 1970s Dallas matured into one of America's major cities, ranking 7th overall in 1980, with a population of more than 900,000. Unlike many American cities, Dallas has grown steadily. Rather than having population booms or busts, the Dallas economy has absorbed only the population that it can use. Such sustained growth has produced limited social dislocation from the effects of unemployment during down years and few strains on social services. Consequently, the Dallas-Fort Worth (metro) unemployment rate ranks 2nd lowest of the 77 metro areas surveyed. Dallas's dependence on state aid is also quite low compared to other cities, ranking 5th lowest. Workers in Dallas are apparently able to afford a wide range of consumer goods. Dallas ranks 15th of 100 cities surveyed in retail sales per capita, corresponding to Dallas's ranking as 9th in per capita income.

| Title | City Rank | Total Cities Ranked |
|---|---|---|
| Largest Cities (Area) | 8 | (100) |
| Overall Air Quality, PSI (1981) | 26 | (51) |
| Biggest Cities (Population) | 7 | (100) |
| Births | 61 | (92) |
| City per Capita Income | 9 | (100) |
| Cost of Living | * | (62) |
| City Retail Sales per Capita | 15 | (100) |
| Unemployment Rates | 76 | (77) |
| Dependence on State Aid | 96 | (100) |
| Housing Growth/Population Growth | 14 | (55) |
| Daily Community Hospital Cost | 57 | (75) |
| Death Rates | 71 | (98) |
| Total Crimes | 12 | (96) |
| Cost per Police Employee | 32 | (71) |
| Arson | 29 | (78) |
| Spending per Resident on Education | 38 | (72) |
| Library Budgets | 47 | (99) |

*City not listed in table.

# Dayton

Dayton experienced a decline in population of over 16 percent in the 1970s and dropped in rank from 59th to 68th. The loss of nearly 40,000 residents in that period was a result of emigration to other cities and the surrounding suburbs rather than natural causes (births versus deaths). Like Akron, Cleveland and Toledo, Dayton has suffered greatly from unemployment (17th highest), although it was lower than in Toledo (7th), Akron (8th) and Cleveland (15th). The presence of nearly 1 million persons within a 25-mile radius of Dayton with a combined annual income of over $2.5 billion greatly benefits the Dayton area economy but does not seem to benefit retail sales in the downtown area (6th lowest). Manufacturing, services and government are the leading employers in Dayton. The nearby Wright Patterson Air Force Base provides additional revenue to Dayton area merchants. Housing growth/population growth is 30th, indicating that developers anticipate a demand for more single-family homes in the city. Crime is high, both for total index crimes (9th) and for arson (2nd).

| Title | City Rank | Total Cities Ranked |
|---|---|---|
| Largest Cities (Area) | 83 | (100) |
| Overall Air Quality, PSI (1981) | 45 | (51) |
| Biggest Cities (Population) | 68 | (100) |
| Births | 49 | (92) |
| City per Capita Income | 94 | (100) |
| Cost of Living | 46 | (62) |
| City Retail Sales per Capita | 95 | (100) |
| Unemployment Rates | 17 | (77) |
| Dependence on State Aid | 73 | (100) |
| Housing Growth/Population Growth | 30 | (55) |
| Daily Community Hospital Cost | 43 | (75) |
| Death Rates | 32 | (98) |
| Total Crimes | 9 | (96) |
| Cost per Police Employee | 38 | (71) |
| Arson | 2 | (78) |
| Spending per Resident on Education | 26 | (72) |
| Library Budgets | 50 | (99) |

*City not listed in table.

# Denver

Denver is the major city and financial center of the Rocky Mountain region. Its importance lies in its growth as a commercial and financial center for the region, which is rich in energy resources. The city's fortunes expanded with the search for new energy in the 1970s. Denver was in the limelight, as its financial and energy companies expanded into areas such as oil, gas, coal and shale resources. Denver is also important as an administrative center for federal, regional and state governments. Denver is home both to a federal mint and to the headquarters of the Atomic Energy Commission and is the capital of Colorado. The population of Denver proper has declined somewhat in the last decade as a result of the increasing trend toward suburbanization. Its suburb

Aurora has at the same time achieved big-city status on its own. Denver has experienced some of the unwanted effects of becoming an important national city. Its crime index ranks 13th highest of 96 cities, and its air quality has become among the worst in the nation.

| Title | City Rank | Total Cities Ranked |
|---|---|---|
| Largest Cities (Area) | 33 | (100) |
| Overall Air Quality, PSI (1981) | 7 | (51) |
| Biggest Cities (Population) | 24 | (100) |
| Births | 66 | (92) |
| City per Capita Income | 38 | (100) |
| Cost of Living | 7 | (62) |
| City Retail Sales per Capita | 50 | (100) |
| Unemployment Rates | 59 | (77) |
| Dependence on State Aid | 44 | (100) |
| Housing Growth/Population Growth | 6 | (55) |
| Daily Community Hospital Cost | 21 | (75) |
| Death Rates | 56 | (98) |
| Total Crimes | 13 | (96) |
| Cost per Police Employee | 41 | (71) |
| Arson | 13 | (78) |
| Spending per Resident on Education | 24 | (72) |
| Library Budgets | 7 | (99) |

*City not listed in table.

## Des Moines

Des Moines is the capital of, and most populous city in, Iowa. It is located in central Iowa at the confluence of the Raccoon and Des Moines rivers. The city is the commercial center of Iowa and a major producer of manufactured goods such as plastics, tires, dental equipment and concrete blocks. It is also a publishing and communications center—Meredith Corporation (publisher of *Better Homes and Gardens*) and Heritage Communications (cable television) are two large employers. Des Moines is home to more than 50 insurance companies and is the second largest insurance center in the United States after Hartford, Connecticut. City officials have initiated an ambitious urban renewal program to encourage more industries to locate in Des Moines. The project includes construction of high-rise office buildings, condominiums and apartments.

| Title | City Rank | Total Cities Ranked |
|---|---|---|
| Largest Cities (Area) | 61 | (100) |
| Overall Air Quality, PSI (1981) | * | (51) |
| Biggest Cities (Population) | 74 | (100) |
| Births | 58 | (92) |

| Title | City Rank | Total Cities Ranked |
|---|---|---|
| City per Capita Income | 39 | (100) |
| Cost of Living | * | (62) |
| City Retail Sales per Capita | 11 | (100) |
| Unemployment Rates | 64 | (77) |
| Dependence on State Aid | 34 | (100) |
| Housing Growth/Population Growth | * | (55) |
| Daily Community Hospital Cost | 56 | (75) |
| Death Rates | 52 | (98) |
| Total Crimes | 32 | (96) |
| Cost per Police Employee | 48 | (71) |
| Arson | 24 | (78) |
| Spending per Resident on Education | 16 | (72) |
| Library Budgets | 41 | (99) |

*City not listed in table.

## Detroit

Detroit exemplifies the downside potential of cities when their economies go sour, especially when a city is not economically diversified. Detroit in 1980 was the sixth largest city in the United States in population, but like many other industrial cities, it has been losing residents—over 20 percent in 1970–80. The outlook for the remainder of the decade will depend to a large extent on the revival of the auto industry, which is tied closely to the economic condition of another Michigan city, Flint, as well as other industrial cities. An upturn in auto sales will greatly improve the unemployment figures, per capita income and retail sales. Although economic hardships face Detroit residents, the corner may have been turned. Auto production is running 40 percent higher in 1983 than in 1982. The challenge for the auto companies is to sell all the new cars. Despite the city's economic distress, city employee salaries have remained high—cost per police employee ranks second only to Oakland. A problem for Detroit is that Michigan has little money to help out with. The most optimistic prognosis is that the kind of cooperative spirit shown in the 1982 labor contract with the Ford Motor Company will be revived and demonstrated in other parts of the Detroit and Michigan economic scene. Leadership qualities are not lacking in Detroit, since its mayor, Coleman Young, serves as an active president of the U.S. Conference of Mayors.

| Title | City Rank | Total Cities Ranked |
|---|---|---|
| Largest Cities (Area) | 28 | (100) |
| Overall Air Quality, PSI (1981) | 21 | (51) |
| Biggest Cities (Population) | 6 | (100) |

| Title | City Rank | Total Cities Ranked |
|---|---|---|
| Births | 41 | (92) |
| City per Capita Income | 75 | (100) |
| Cost of Living | * | (62) |
| City Retail Sales per Capita | 99 | (100) |
| Unemployment Rates | 2 | (77) |
| Dependence on State Aid | 31 | (100) |
| Housing Growth/Population Growth | * | (55) |
| Daily Community Hospital Cost | 13 | (75) |
| Death Rates | 17 | (98) |
| Total Crimes | 15 | (96) |
| Cost per Police Employee | 2 | (71) |
| Arson | * | (78) |
| Spending per Resident on Education | 8 | (72) |
| Library Budgets | 44 | (99) |

*City not listed in table.

| Title | City Rank | Total Cities Ranked |
|---|---|---|
| Largest Cities (Area) | 19 | (100) |
| Overall Air Quality, PSI (1981) | 22 | (51) |
| Biggest Cities (Population) | 28 | (100) |
| Births | 17 | (92) |
| City per Capita Income | 99 | (100) |
| Cost of Living | 33 | (62) |
| City Retail Sales per Capita | 64 | (100) |
| Unemployment Rates | * | (77) |
| Dependence on State Aid | 95 | (100) |
| Housing Growth/Population Growth | * | (55) |
| Daily Community Hospital Cost | 54 | (75) |
| Death Rates | 93 | (98) |
| Total Crimes | 86 | (96) |
| Cost per Police Employee | * | (71) |
| Arson | 16 | (78) |
| Spending per Resident on Education | 65 | (72) |
| Library Budgets | 87 | (99) |

*City not listed in table.

## El Paso

El Paso benefited from immigration to the Southwest from abroad and from other U.S. regions. The 1980 census showed that El Paso increased its population 32 percent since 1970 to over 425,000—jumping up in the population ranks from 45th to 28th. Projected population figures for El Paso are 500,000–550,000 in 1990 and 600,000 in 2000. The impact of the increase in population will be enhanced by the demographics of the city of Juarez, Mexico, which lies just across the Rio Grande from El Paso and had an estimated population of approximately 650,000 in 1980. The close proximity of these two cities has been beneficial both to El Paso businesses and to Juarez residents. Between 10,000 and 15,000 workers from Juarez are employed in El Paso. The combined crossings of tourists and workers make El Paso first in border crossings in the United States—more than 38.8 million northbound crossings in 1980 alone. A majority of the El Paso economy is based in manufacturing, with nearly 23 percent of all those employed being engaged in the manufacture of apparel and other textile products. Food and food products are the next largest employer group, accounting for nearly 12 percent of employees. Another plus for businesses in the El Paso area is the foreign trade zone created in 1981. El Paso has a moderate cost of living (33rd out of 62) but the second lowest city per capita income in the United States—a boon for business. Total index crimes are very low for a city of its size—86th out of 96. El Paso also benefits from the presence of several military installations. Military expenditures for local purchases and contracts totaled over $125 million in 1980.

## Flint

Flint, the 94th most populous city in the nation, is 60 miles northwest of Detroit and is the 3rd biggest city in Michigan. It is a leading auto manufacturer, 2nd only to Detroit in the production of cars. The severe decline in the American auto industry in the late 1970s and in 1981–82 forced GM, Ford and Chrysler to lay off many workers. Flint was extremely hard hit, leading the nation with a 22 percent rate of unemployment in December 1982. High unemployment has contributed to a very high crime rate (3rd highest), which, in turn, has encouraged many residents to move to the suburbs—the city lost over 17 percent of its population in the 1970s. A strong suburban population is indicated by Flint's low city per capita income (20th lowest) and retail sales per capita (21st lowest). The city's future appears to be brightening as the U.S. auto industry exhibits signs of recovery.

| Title | City Rank | Total Cities Ranked |
|---|---|---|
| Largest Cities (Area) | 93 | (100) |
| Overall Air Quality, PSI (1981) | * | (51) |
| Biggest Cities (Population) | 94 | (100) |
| Births | 15 | (92) |
| City per Capita Income | 81 | (100) |
| Cost of Living | 22 | (62) |
| City Retail Sales per Capita | 80 | (100) |
| Unemployment Rates | 1 | (77) |
| Dependence on State Aid | 45 | (100) |
| Housing Growth/Population Growth | * | (55) |
| Daily Community Hospital Cost | 38 | (75) |

| Title | City Rank | Total Cities Ranked |
|---|---|---|
| Death Rates | 53 | (98) |
| Total Crimes | 3 | (96) |
| Cost per Police Employee | * | (71) |
| Arson | 5 | (78) |
| Spending per Resident on Education | * | (72) |
| Library Budgets | 13 | (99) |

*City not listed in table.

## Fort Wayne

Fort Wayne lies at the confluence of the St. Mary, St. Joseph and Maumee Rivers. It is the 2nd most populous city in Indiana and the 80th most populous in the nation. The retail center for the region, Fort Wayne produces and distributes heavy trucks, copper wire, electrical equipment and foods and grains. The city has been affected by the national recession, with high unemployment (18th highest), but should experience a recovery in 1983 because of its wide economic base. Crime is low (21st lowest) and retail sales per capita are high for a city of its size (37th), indicating that Fort Wayne is attractive to new residents. The city also has a relatively low cost of living (18th lowest).

| Title | City Rank | Total Cities Ranked |
|---|---|---|
| Largest Cities (Area) | 77 | (100) |
| Overall Air Quality, PSI (1981) | * | (51) |
| Biggest Cities (Population) | 80 | (100) |
| Births | 38 | (92) |
| City per Capita Income | 50 | (100) |
| Cost of Living | 45 | (62) |
| City Retail Sales per Capita | 37 | (100) |
| Unemployment Rates | 18 | (77) |
| Dependence on State Aid | 42 | (100) |
| Housing Growth/Population Growth | 29 | (55) |
| Daily Community Hospital Cost | * | (75) |
| Death Rates | 27 | (98) |
| Total Crimes | 75 | (96) |
| Cost per Police Employee | 65 | (71) |
| Arson | 34 | (78) |
| Spending per Resident on Education | * | (72) |
| Library Budgets | 15 | (99) |

*City not listed in table.

## Fort Worth

Fort Worth's population declined slightly (by about 2 percent) in the 1970s, from 393,455 to 385,141. This decline does not indicate the state of Fort Worth's econ-omy, which is strong. Opportunities for industrial and manufacturing development lie in the city's strategic location as a north-south and east-west crossroads, and its diversified economy. With an area of 250 square miles, the city also has a large physical space to accommodate more extensive development. Fort Worth has a network of industrial and business parks to encourage increased capital investment. The Dallas-Fort Worth area is the 9th largest market in the United States and is the home of the world's largest airport. Fort Worth itself is the 5th largest distribution center in the country, noted as a junction of railways and highways, and as a major storage point for the grain and livestock industries. Among other industries are aircraft and oil. Fort Worth is a locus for the market area of the Southwest, a region that has grown economically faster than anywhere else in the United States. Fort Worth can also boast a relatively low unemployment rate—of 77 cities surveyed, Fort Worth ranked 76th in unemployment, with a rate of 5.2 percent in December 1982. As a result, wages have been on the rise, and Fort Worth appears to be an attractive city for new residents and workers from the Northeast. Fort Worth also has a low crime rate (21st lowest), below comparably sized cities.

| Title | City Rank | Total Cities Ranked |
|---|---|---|
| Largest Cities (Area) | 18 | (100) |
| Overall Air Quality, PSI (1981) | 26 | (51) |
| Biggest Cities (Population) | 32 | (100) |
| Births | 12 | (92) |
| City per Capita Income | 89 | (100) |
| Cost of Living | 44 | (62) |
| City Retail Sales per Capita | 25 | (100) |
| Unemployment Rates | 76 | (77) |
| Dependence on State Aid | 97 | (100) |
| Housing Growth/Population Growth | * | (55) |
| Daily Community Hospital Cost | 70 | (75) |
| Death Rates | 51 | (98) |
| Total Crimes | 76 | (96) |
| Cost per Police Employee | 57 | (71) |
| Arson | 33 | (78) |
| Spending per Resident on Education | 29 | (72) |
| Library Budgets | 95 | (99) |

*City not listed in table.

## Fresno

Fresno is roughly equidistant from Los Angeles and San Francisco, in the middle of central California's San Joaquin Valley, one of the most fertile agricultural regions in the world. As the major city in central California,

Fresno is an important outlet for the agricultural products of the valley. Production in Fresno is dominated by the agricultural commodity and food processing industries. These products include canned fruits and vegetables, dried fruits, grapes and raisins. The railroad and trucking industries are essential to enable the Fresno area to handle the large amount of freight that originates there. Fresno has experienced rapid growth in the decade ending in 1980. Its population increased nearly 32 percent in the 1970s, to over 218,000 in 1980 (65th most populous). As a result of this significant population growth, Fresno has expanded development of transportation and retail sales facilities, such as highways and shopping centers. Per capita income in Fresno is high (21st), but its cost of living is even higher (6th). A problem for the area is the competition for land between agriculture and development. As land values increase, the temptation to convert agricultural land to other uses becomes stronger, even though the economic foundation of the area is agricultural.

area—making everything from office supplies, furniture and pollution control equipment to jet avionics—as well as a sound base in insurance, banking and other services are providing Grand Rapids residents with steady employment. The recession did take its toll on Grand Rapids in the form of unemployment (14th highest), but this problem is less deep-rooted in Grand Rapids than in cities more closely tied to heavy manufacturing and the auto industry. Grand Rapids had a high per capita income (14th), reflecting the wealth that has settled into the city. Future development is planned to center around the booming health care industry. The four prominent hospitals in Grand Rapids have seen the advantages of specialization and have become regionally known for their work in special surgery and as burn and poison control centers. Grand Rapids is the home of Steelcase Inc., the world's leading office furniture and systems manufacturer, with a work force of about 7,500. Steelcase has committed $50 million to the construction of its new headquarters. Other major employers are Kelvinator, Amway, Foremost and Gordon Food Sales.

| Title | City Rank | Total Cities Ranked |
|---|---|---|
| Largest Cities (Area) | 59 | (100) |
| Overall Air Quality, PSI (1981) | 10 | (51) |
| Biggest Cities (Population) | 65 | (100) |
| Births | 56 | (92) |
| City per Capita Income | 21 | (100) |
| Cost of Living | 6 | (62) |
| City Retail Sales per Capita | 30 | (100) |
| Unemployment Rates | 5 | (77) |
| Dependence on State Aid | 53 | (100) |
| Housing Growth/Population Growth | 37 | (55) |
| Daily Community Hospital Cost | * | (75) |
| Death Rates | 23 | (98) |
| Total Crimes | 22 | (96) |
| Cost per Police Employee | * | (71) |
| Arson | 49 | (78) |
| Spending per Resident on Education | 5 | (72) |
| Library Budgets | 71 | (99) |

*City not listed in table.

| Title | City Rank | Total Cities Ranked |
|---|---|---|
| Largest Cities (Area) | 87 | (100) |
| Overall Air Quality, PSI (1981) | * | (51) |
| Biggest Cities (Population) | 76 | (100) |
| Births | 48 | (92) |
| City per Capita Income | 14 | (100) |
| Cost of Living | * | (62) |
| City Retail Sales per Capita | 59 | (100) |
| Unemployment Rates | 14 | (77) |
| Dependence on State Aid | 36 | (100) |
| Housing Growth/Population Growth | * | (55) |
| Daily Community Hospital Cost | * | (75) |
| Death Rates | 33 | (98) |
| Total Crimes | 44 | (96) |
| Cost per Police Employee | * | (71) |
| Arson | 32 | (78) |
| Spending per Resident on Education | * | (72) |
| Library Budgets | 25 | (99) |

*City not listed in table.

## Grand Rapids

Grand Rapids, located across from Detroit on the western side of Michigan, is the 76th largest city in the United States, with a 1980 population of nearly 182,000, having dropped from its 1970 ranking (65th) because of a loss of 8 percent of its population. A diverse economy has made the effects of the recession in Grand Rapids less burdensome than in other Michigan cities such as Detroit and Flint. More than 1,500 manufacturers in the

## Greensboro

Greensboro has concentrated its physical growth and development plans on future annexations; housing and neighborhood preservation; urban services; residential development and industrial, commercial and office development. Like many cities, Greensboro has emphasized water quality and protection of existing watersheds. Greensboro's relatively high birthrate (6th) will impact upon the housing growth/population growth ratio as well as educational spending for several years to come. The city economy seems to be very stable. Retail sales per capita are the second highest in the nation, while the cost of living is relatively low (12th lowest). Crime is generally lower than average, which may reflect the above-average (25th highest) number of police employees per 1,000 population (2.65—higher than Dallas, New York and Little Rock).

| Title | City Rank | Total Cities Ranked |
|---|---|---|
| Largest Cities (Area) | 66 | (100) |
| Overall Air Quality, PSI (1981) | * | (51) |
| Biggest Cities (Population) | 100 | (100) |
| Births | 6 | (92) |
| City per Capita Income | 49 | (100) |
| Cost of Living | 51 | (62) |
| City Retail Sales per Capita | 2 | (100) |
| Unemployment Rates | 60 | (77) |
| Dependence on State Aid | 52 | (100) |
| Housing Growth/Population Growth | 14 | (55) |
| Daily Community Hospital Cost | 75 | (75) |
| Death Rates | 69 | (98) |
| Total Crimes | 74 | (96) |
| Cost per Police Employee | 59 | (71) |
| Arson | 64 | (78) |
| Spending per Resident on Education | * | (72) |
| Library Budgets | 49 | (99) |

*City not listed in table.

## Honolulu

Honolulu is the 4th largest city in area and the 36th largest in population. Honolulu City has been made co-extensive with Honolulu County, which has eased its administrative problems. Honolulu generates the greatest revenues from its tourist industry (more than $3 billion annually) and the processing of agricultural crops like pineapples and sugarcane. In addition, its military bases provide Honolulu with a revenue stream that is not influenced by the business cycle. Retail sales are 7th highest in the nation, and city per capita income is 12th highest. Honolulu has a relatively high ratio of housing growth to population growth (6th), which should continue for the near future as retirees and others seek housing. The city's growth rate between 1970 and 1980 was over 12 percent, despite its low birthrate (13th lowest). The growth rate should remain high as migration to Honolulu continues, although some residents oppose continued expansion of high-rise apartment buildings. Crime rates are very low—8th lowest—and enhance the appeal of this island paradise.

| Title | City Rank | Total Cities Ranked |
|---|---|---|
| Largest Cities (Area) | 4 | (100) |
| Overall Air Quality, PSI (1981) | * | (51) |
| Biggest Cities (Population) | 36 | (100) |
| Births | 80 | (92) |
| City per Capita Income | 12 | (100) |
| Cost of Living | * | (62) |
| City Retail Sales per Capita | 7 | (100) |
| Unemployment Rates | 74 | (77) |
| Dependence on State Aid | 83 | (100) |
| Housing Growth/Population Growth | 7 | (55) |
| Daily Community Hospital Cost | 33 | (75) |
| Death Rates | 91 | (98) |
| Total Crimes | 89 | (96) |
| Cost per Police Employee | 43 | (71) |
| Arson | * | (78) |
| Spending per Resident on Education | 71 | (72) |
| Library Budgets | 45 | (99) |

*City not listed in table.

## Houston

Houston has grown rapidly in population, reaching 1.6 million people in 1980—the 5th most populous of the largest cities and challenging Philadelphia for fourth place. Of America's five largest cities, Houston was the only one to register a significant increase in population in the 1970s. Houston is now the South's most important commercial and industrial center. Its strategic location on the Gulf of Mexico has facilitated its growth as the nation's largest oil and gas center, the hub of industrial and petrochemical manufacturing and imported petroleum products, making Houston's port the third largest in the United States. The prognosis for Houston's future growth remains good. It continues to be attractive for business and has now become an important international banking center. Houston has also benefited greatly from being the new home for many skilled and semiskilled workers from the Northeast. Houston's growth is attributable primarily to immigration, since its birthrate ranks only 42nd. Houston is a leader in the space industry and is home of the Johnson Space Center.

| Title | City Rank | Total Cities Ranked |
|---|---|---|
| Largest Cities (Area) | 5 | (100) |
| Overall Air Quality, PSI (1981) | 8 | (51) |
| Biggest Cities (Population) | 5 | (100) |
| Births | 42 | (92) |
| City per Capita Income | 5 | (100) |
| Cost of Living | 4 | (62) |
| City Retail Sales per Capita | 4 | (100) |

| Title | City Rank | Total Cities Ranked |
|---|---|---|
| Unemployment Rates | 56 | (77) |
| Dependence on State Aid | 94 | (100) |
| Housing Growth/Population Growth | 16 | (55) |
| Daily Community Hospital Cost | 30 | (75) |
| Death Rates | 78 | (98) |
| Total Crimes | * | (96) |
| Cost per Police Employee | 22 | (71) |
| Arson | * | (78) |
| Spending per Resident on Education | 49 | (72) |
| Library Budgets | 56 | (99) |

*City not listed in table.

## Huntington Beach

Huntington Beach is a growing city on the California coast, just south of Los Angeles and Long Beach, and southwest of Anaheim and Santa Ana. It registered a 47 percent gain in population in the 1970s, to over 171,000 (82nd). Huntington Beach has a very high city per capita income (1st). Its financial status stems from its history as a wealthy suburb of Los Angeles and increasingly from its growing high-technology economic base, which is concentrated in the aerospace industry and electronics marketing. Because of its historically wealthy population, Huntington Beach has grown to be an important financial center in southern California. Huntington Beach's indicators of crime rank among the lowest (2nd lowest) of the cities for which data are available; hence, Huntington Beach has thus far escaped the most deleterious effects of urban growth. Arson was scarcely present at all (with Huntington Beach ranking lowest). Spending per resident on education ranked 52nd (lowest), undoubtedly because residents are older or prefer to send their children to private schools, keeping down the city's tax rate.

| Title | City Rank | Total Cities Ranked |
|---|---|---|
| Largest Cities (Area) | 94 | (100) |
| Overall Air Quality, PSI (1981) | * | (51) |
| Biggest Cities (Population) | 82 | (100) |
| Births | * | (92) |
| City per Capita Income | 1 | (100) |
| Cost of Living | * | (62) |
| City Retail Sales per Capita | 54 | (100) |
| Unemployment Rates | * | (77) |
| Dependence on State Aid | 46 | (100) |
| Housing Growth/Population Growth | 18 | (55) |
| Daily Community Hospital Cost | * | (75) |
| Death Rates | 94 | (98) |
| Total Crimes | 95 | (96) |
| Cost per Police Employee | 13 | (71) |

| Title | City Rank | Total Cities Ranked |
|---|---|---|
| Arson | 78 | (78) |
| Spending per Resident on Education | 72 | (72) |
| Library Budgets | 76 | (99) |

*City not listed in table.

## Indianapolis

Indianapolis is the capital of Indiana and its largest city. Its population declined 4.9 percent to just over 700,000 in the decade between 1970 and 1980, owing to increasing suburbanization. Indianapolis combines the benefits of an urban financial and retail downtown center with easily accessible suburban and even rural counties outside the center. Because of its relatively large land area compared to most American cities, the city incorporates many affluent suburban areas. This has been beneficial to the city's financial structure, as it has been able to maintain and expand its property tax base. Trends toward suburban shopping and home buying have therefore not yet had a serious detrimental effect on the city's economy but instead have expanded it. Indianapolis is a major highway and railway commodity transport hub and has a large manufacturing base in heavy industries, which have been hurt by the recent recession. The city has been left behind in the early development of more avanced technological industries. Its per capita income ranks 35th of 100 cities surveyed. For a large city, Indianapolis is relatively safe—ranking 82nd in the crime index.

| Title | City Rank | Total Cities Ranked |
|---|---|---|
| Largest Cities (Area) | 9 | (100) |
| Overall Air Quality, PSI (1981) | 33 | (51) |
| Biggest Cities (Population) | 12 | (100) |
| Births | 49 | (92) |
| City per Capita Income | 35 | (100) |
| Cost of Living | * | (62) |
| City Retail Sales per Capita | 23 | (100) |
| Unemployment Rates | 35 | (77) |
| Dependence on State Aid | 29 | (100) |
| Housing Growth/Population Growth | * | (55) |
| Daily Community Hospital Cost | 39 | (75) |
| Death Rates | 58 | (98) |
| Total Crimes | 82 | (96) |
| Cost per Police Employee | 53 | (71) |
| Arson | 68 | (78) |
| Spending per Resident on Education | 67 | (72) |
| Library Budgets | 39 | (99) |

*City not listed in table.

## Jackson

Jackson grew nearly 32 percent in the 1970s, making it the 71st largest city in the country, with a 1980 population of nearly 203,000. Both birthrates and death rates are relatively low. The capital and largest city in Mississippi, it is a major distribution and retailing center for the deep South. More than 350 manufacturers make diverse products, from electrical transformers, switchgear and batteries to snack foods, mattresses, concrete blocks, garden tillers and hydraulic controls (used in aircraft, missiles, ships and space vehicles). Jackson is also home to many oil and gas companies. The relative affluence of Jackson can be seen in its high city per capita income (19th) and its low unemployment rate (14th lowest), reflecting the city's diverse economic base. Jackson is also a major center for education—schools in the area offer degrees ranging from vocational training to graduate programs in business, law and medicine. The city does not spend a great deal on public services like education (10th lowest) or libraries (14th lowest).

| Title | City Rank | Total Cities Ranked |
|---|---|---|
| Largest Cities (Area) | 37 | (100) |
| Overall Air Quality, PSI (1981) | * | (51) |
| Biggest Cities (Population) | 71 | (100) |
| Births | 71 | (92) |
| City per Capita Income | 19 | (100) |
| Cost of Living | * | (62) |
| City Retail Sales per Capita | 43 | (100) |
| Unemployment Rates | 64 | (77) |
| Dependence on State Aid | 13 | (100) |
| Housing Growth/Population Growth | 46 | (55) |
| Daily Community Hospital Cost | * | (75) |
| Death Rates | 74 | (98) |
| Total Crimes | 47 | (96) |
| Cost per Police Employee | 36 | (71) |
| Arson | 53 | (78) |
| Spending per Resident on Education | 62 | (72) |
| Library Budgets | 86 | (99) |

*City not listed in table.

## Jacksonville

Jacksonville is the most populous city in Florida, with a population of over 541,000. Like many Florida cities, it grew with the net influx of retirees and relocating businesses from the Northeast in search of cheaper living costs and lower wages. Jacksonville's population grew by over 7 percent between 1970 and 1980. With the second largest area of the 100 largest cities, it has ample room for growth within the city limits. Some of this growth in population will come from foreign immigration and still more from the continuing migration from other regions of the United States. Florida cities may reach a saturation point as the state's costs and wage levels rise and labor becomes relatively cheaper in other areas of the country. Still, Jacksonville benefits from its port and other transportation revenues. A Navy base contributes to the economy, and further income is generated by tourism, manufacturing, finance and insurance.

| Title | City Rank | Total Cities Ranked |
|---|---|---|
| Largest Cities (Area) | 2 | (100) |
| Overall Air Quality, PSI (1981) | * | (51) |
| Biggest Cities (Population) | 22 | (100) |
| Births | 47 | (92) |
| City per Capita Income | 92 | (100) |
| Cost of Living | * | (62) |
| City Retail Sales per Capita | 52 | (100) |
| Unemployment Rates | 52 | (77) |
| Dependence on State Aid | 33 | (100) |
| Housing Growth/Population Growth | 43 | (55) |
| Daily Community Hospital Cost | 40 | (75) |
| Death Rates | 63 | (98) |
| Total Crimes | 64 | (96) |
| Cost per Police Employee | 37 | (71) |
| Arson | 60 | (78) |
| Spending per Resident on Education | 22 | (72) |
| Library Budgets | 78 | (99) |

*City not listed in table.

## Jersey City

Jersey City is the second most populous city in the state of New Jersey. It lies on the Hudson River across from New York City. Jersey City is in the heart of the world's largest transportation center, with major rail, sea and highway modes. In terms of area, Jersey City is the smallest of the 100 most populous cities. Yet it ranks 61st in total population, so that population density is higher than in most other U.S. cities. Jersey City's cost of living, 8th highest, appears to have had a detrimental effect on retail sales, which are the 4th lowest. Jersey City exemplifies the problems of cities that cannot expand their tax base to cope with social problems in their midst. Fortunately, the state of New Jersey has stepped in and has greatly helped to ameliorate some of Jersey City's problems.

| Title | City Rank | Total Cities Ranked |
|---|---|---|
| Largest Cities (Area) | 100 | (100) |
| Overall Air Quality, PSI (1981) | 24 | (51) |
| Biggest Cities (Population) | 61 | (100) |
| Births | 43 | (92) |
| City per Capita Income | 59 | (100) |
| Cost of Living | 8 | (62) |
| City Retail Sales per Capita | 97 | (100) |
| Unemployment Rates | * | (77) |
| Dependence on State Aid | 2 | (100) |
| Housing Growth/Population Growth | * | (55) |
| Daily Community Hospital Cost | 74 | (75) |
| Death Rates | 24 | (98) |
| Total Crimes | 54 | (96) |
| Cost per Police Employee | 29 | (71) |
| Arson | 75 | (78) |
| Spending per Resident on Education | * | (72) |
| Library Budgets | 59 | (99) |

*City not listed in table.

# Kansas City, Kansas

The Kansas City, Kansas population has been fortunate to maintain an unemployment rate that does not seriously threaten to cut into its present middle-range ranking in per capita income (54th) and its low cost of living (13th lowest). The high birthrate for Kansas City may show its effects in the coming years on total index crimes and housing growth/population growth. There should be an increase in housing costs in the Kansas City area along with the rise in population, but chances are the increases will be less burdensome than in cities of similar population such as Worcester or Salt Lake City.

| Title | City Rank | Total Cities Ranked |
|---|---|---|
| Largest Cities (Area) | 34 | (100) |
| Overall Air Quality, PSI (1981) | 26 | (51) |
| Biggest Cities (Population) | 92 | (100) |
| Births | 4 | (92) |
| City per Capita Income | 54 | (100) |
| Cost of Living | 50 | (62) |
| City Retail Sales per Capita | 65 | (100) |
| Unemployment Rates | 43 | (77) |
| Dependence on State Aid | 79 | (100) |
| Housing Growth/Population Growth | * | (55) |
| Daily Community Hospital Cost | * | (75) |
| Death Rates | 46 | (98) |
| Total Crimes | 24 | (96) |
| Cost per Police Employee | 55 | (71) |
| Arson | 28 | (78) |
| Spending per Resident on Education | 64 | (72) |
| Library Budgets | 80 | (99) |

*City not listed in table.

# Kansas City, Missouri

Kansas City, Missouri is the larger of the two Kansas Cities. It had a 1980 population of slightly over 448,000, the 27th largest city. In the decade between 1970 and 1980, it lost nearly 12 percent of its population, much of it to suburban migration. Kansas City is often called the food capital of the world, since its economy depends heavily on production and distribution of such commodities as grains, animal feeds and livestock. In addition, local, state and federal government employees are heavily concentrated in the area. The federal government alone employed nearly 23,000 people in 1980. The city's foreign trade zone is an inducement to businesses in Europe and the Far East to strengthen their marketing and trade ties to the Kansas Cities. City per capita income is average (48th), but the cost of living is high (18th).

| Title | City Rank | Total Cities Ranked |
|---|---|---|
| Largest Cities (Area) | 12 | (100) |
| Overall Air Quality, PSI (1981) | 26 | (51) |
| Biggest Cities (Population) | 27 | (100) |
| Births | 60 | (92) |
| City per Capita Income | 48 | (100) |
| Cost of Living | 18 | (62) |
| City Retail Sales per Capita | 61 | (100) |
| Unemployment Rates | 43 | (77) |
| Dependence on State Aid | 81 | (100) |
| Housing Growth/Population Growth | * | (55) |
| Daily Community Hospital Cost | 46 | (75) |
| Death Rates | 28 | (98) |
| Total Crimes | 18 | (96) |
| Cost per Police Employee | 40 | (71) |
| Arson | 20 | (78) |
| Spending per Resident on Education | 61 | (72) |
| Library Budgets | 35 | (99) |

*City not listed in table.

# Knoxville

Knoxville is the 3rd largest city in Tennessee and the 75th largest in the nation. The city boasts a very diversified economy, producing goods ranging from clothing to furniture to electronics. Major regional employers include Union Carbide, Levi-Strauss and Standard Knitting Mills. Knoxville is also the home of the University of Tennessee, with a student body of about 30,000 and employment of over 8,000. The city benefited tremendously from the World's Fair held there in 1982. Knoxville has very strong retail sales (5th highest) and a high per capita income (11th highest), even though the cost of living is very low (16th lowest). It has a very low birthrate (4th lowest), suggesting an aging population and suburbanization of young marrieds. Its crime rate is low. Knoxville's future seems very bright as urban renewal projects continue, and both London Fog and Magnavox are committed to expanding their employment in the area.

| Title | City Rank | Total Cities Ranked |
|---|---|---|
| Largest Cities (Area) | 56 | (100) |
| Overall Air Quality, PSI (1981) | * | (51) |
| Biggest Cities (Population) | 75 | (100) |
| Births | 89 | (92) |
| City per Capita Income | 11 | (100) |
| Cost of Living | 47 | (62) |
| City Retail Sales per Capita | 5 | (100) |
| Unemployment Rates | 31 | (77) |
| Dependence on State Aid | 22 | (100) |
| Housing Growth/Population Growth | 17 | (55) |
| Daily Community Hospital Cost | * | (75) |
| Death Rates | 45 | (98) |
| Total Crimes | 87 | (96) |
| Cost per Police Employee | 64 | (71) |
| Arson | * | (78) |
| Spending per Resident on Education | * | (72) |
| Library Budgets | 63 | (99) |

*City not listed in table.

# Las Vegas

Las Vegas grew by nearly 31 percent in the 1970s, making it the 89th largest city in the United States, with a population of nearly 165,000. The majority of its revenues are generated from the gambling casinos located in this entertainment-oriented city and the tourist dollars spent there. Its location in the southernmost part of Nevada, close by the Lake Mead National Recreation Area (and Boulder Dam), enhances its attraction for tourists. Manufacturing and retail sales are other employment leaders. The nearby Nellis Air Force Base also provides revenue to Las Vegas. The revenue has been put to varied use, as the city has financed capital projects such as road construction, upgrading of the city jail and annex, and the construction of three parks. In addition, a sports complex to be completed in 1983 will be the home of an AAA baseball team and will accommodate other sporting events. Las Vegas also realizes the benefits of private management of city facilities—its Municipal Golf Course is expected to generate about $50,000, and significant improvements have been made without use of city funds. Las Vegas is expected to continue to grow into the 1990s, as its tourist traffic and other income earners expand.

| Title | City Rank | Total Cities Ranked |
|---|---|---|
| Largest Cities (Area) | 72 | (100) |
| Overall Air Quality, PSI (1981) | 9 | (51) |
| Biggest Cities (Population) | 89 | (100) |
| Births | 34 | (92) |
| City per Capita Income | 46 | (100) |
| Cost of Living | 12 | (62) |
| City Retail Sales per Capita | 34 | (100) |
| Unemployment Rates | 9 | (77) |
| Dependence on State Aid | 23 | (100) |
| Housing Growth/Population Growth | 24 | (55) |
| Daily Community Hospital Cost | * | (75) |
| Death Rates | 72 | (98) |
| Total Crimes | 28 | (96) |
| Cost per Police Employee | 35 | (71) |
| Arson | 19 | (78) |
| Spending per Resident on Education | 15 | (72) |
| Library Budgets | 65 | (99) |

*City not listed in table.

# Lexington-Fayette

Lexington-Fayette, located in central Kentucky approximately 75 miles east of Louisville and approximately 80 miles south of Cincinnati, is the 3rd fastest-growing city in the United States, having increased its population by nearly 89 percent in the 1970s. An explanation of its strong growth is the merger of Lexington with surrounding Fayette county in 1974. Its 1980 population of over 204,000 makes it the 68th most populous city. The city is a center for trade for the region, with high retail sales (14th). It enjoys a diversified economy, with such products as electrical goods, tobacco products and coal. Major employers in the area are the University of Kentucky, IBM, Square D, Trane, Brown and Williamson, and R.J. Reynolds. Horses and horse breeding are still very much a part of the social and economic life of the Lexington area. Lexington is home to the University Medical Center, one of the finest medical facilities in the central United States.

| Title | City Rank | Total Cities Ranked |
|---|---|---|
| Largest Cities (Area) | 15 | (100) |
| Overall Air Quality, PSI (1981) | * | (51) |
| Biggest Cities (Population) | 68 | (100) |
| Births | 70 | (92) |
| City per Capita Income | 87 | (100) |
| Cost of Living | 41 | (62) |
| City Retail Sales per Capita | 14 | (100) |
| Unemployment Rates | * | (77) |
| Dependence on State Aid | 77 | (100) |
| Housing Growth/Population Growth | 55 | (55) |

| Title | City Rank | Total Cities Ranked |
|---|---|---|
| Daily Community Hospital Cost | * | (75) |
| Death Rates | 79 | (98) |
| Total Crimes | 65 | (96) |
| Cost per Police Employee | 50 | (71) |
| Arson | 57 | (78) |
| Spending per Resident on Education | 40 | (72) |
| Library Budgets | 70 | (99) |

*City not listed in table.

# Lincoln

Lincoln is the 2nd most populous city in Nebraska and the 80th most populous in the nation. As the capital of Nebraska, it is the center for all state agencies and activities. Surrounded by fertile agricultural land, Lincoln is a processing center for grain (flour) and other food products. Other major goods produced in the city include railroad cars and pharmaceuticals. Lincoln's low birthrate (10th lowest) and low death rate (18th lowest) may be explained in part by the fact that the city's residents have a low average age of 28.2 years (19th lowest) and a high population of singles (11th highest). Lincoln is an attractive place to live for people not wedded to the life-style of America's fastest-paced cities. Its cost of living and crime rate are among the 8 lowest; its unemployment rate and arson rate are among the 5 lowest.

| Title | City Rank | Total Cities Ranked |
|---|---|---|
| Largest Cities (Area) | 79 | (100) |
| Overall Air Quality, PSI (1981) | 42 | (51) |
| Biggest Cities (Population) | 80 | (100) |
| Births | 83 | (92) |
| City per Capita Income | 72 | (100) |
| Cost of Living | 54 | (62) |
| City Retail Sales per Capita | 48 | (100) |
| Unemployment Rates | 72 | (77) |
| Dependence on State Aid | 62 | (100) |
| Housing Growth/Population Growth | 35 | (55) |
| Daily Community Hospital Cost | 65 | (75) |
| Death Rates | 81 | (98) |
| Total Crimes | 90 | (96) |
| Cost per Police Employee | 60 | (71) |
| Arson | 77 | (78) |
| Spending per Resident on Education | * | (72) |
| Library Budgets | 34 | (99) |

*City not listed in table.

# Little Rock

Little Rock grew nearly 20 percent in population between 1970 and 1980, to over 158,000, making it the 98th largest U.S. city. Part of this increase may be due to the high birthrate—7th highest in 1980. Some of the population increase also reflects Little Rock's annexation program. Between 1978 and 1980 the city annexed over 23 square miles and added about 12,000 people. Further annexations are planned through the year 2000. A balanced development plan for the suburban areas of Little Rock encourages availability of public facilities and public transportation through ongoing public planning. Environmental concerns are focused on the floodplains (and zoning relating to structures in this area), control of storm floods and water quality. The plan also calls for school and library construction as needed within the suburban areas.

| Title | City Rank | Total Cities Ranked |
|---|---|---|
| Largest Cities (Area) | 47 | (100) |
| Overall Air Quality, PSI (1981) | * | (51) |
| Biggest Cities (Population) | 98 | (100) |
| Births | 7 | (92) |
| City per Capita Income | 23 | (100) |
| Cost of Living | 29 | (62) |
| City Retail Sales per Capita | 20 | (100) |
| Unemployment Rates | 55 | (77) |
| Dependence on State Aid | 12 | (100) |
| Housing Growth/Population Growth | * | (55) |
| Daily Community Hospital Cost | * | (75) |
| Death Rates | 54 | (98) |
| Total Crimes | 16 | (96) |
| Cost per Police Employee | 68 | (71) |
| Arson | 30 | (78) |
| Spending per Resident on Education | 63 | (72) |
| Library Budgets | 93 | (99) |

*City not listed in table.

# Long Beach

Long Beach, with a 1980 population of over 361,000, is the 37th most populous city. A slight population increase in the 1970s (less than 1 percent) should be magnified in the near future as Long Beach's ongoing commitment to revitalize the downtown area and encourage new construction continues there. New construction on the city's waterfront includes a city-owned marina and a tourist development, Shoreline Village. More than $1.2 billion is being pumped into development in downtown Long Beach. The moderate unemployment rate will drop significantly with the reopening of the Navy base in 1985.

While Long Beach should be prosperous in the coming years, it will have to keep an eye on drawbacks to living in this resurgent city such as its number one rank in pollution and its high hospital costs (10th).

| Title | City Rank | Total Cities Ranked |
|---|---|---|
| Largest Cities (Area) | 80 | (100) |
| Overall Air Quality, PSI (1981) | 1 | (51) |
| Biggest Cities (Population) | 37 | (100) |
| Births | * | (92) |
| City per Capita Income | 24 | (100) |
| Cost of Living | * | (62) |
| City Retail Sales per Capita | 74 | (100) |
| Unemployment Rates | 29 | (77) |
| Dependence on State Aid | 63 | (100) |
| Housing Growth/Population Growth | * | (55) |
| Daily Community Hospital Cost | 10 | (75) |
| Death Rates | 22 | (98) |
| Total Crimes | 52 | (96) |
| Cost per Police Employee | * | (71) |
| Arson | 51 | (78) |
| Spending per Resident on Education | 37 | (72) |
| Library Budgets | 6 | (99) |

*City not listed in table.

## Los Angeles

Los Angeles is the nation's third most populous city, with a 1980 population of 2,967,000, only about 40,000 behind Chicago. Los Angeles has stopped growing at its 1960s rate. Its population growth, now expected to be slow, will be contingent on its ability to redevelop its declining areas. The city is concentrating on more intensive development—making more efficient use of land for housing, commerce and industrial development—which is requiring greater coordination between government and private developers. The Los Angeles region is fabled for its complex highway networks. Public transportation is not as significant in Los Angeles as in other similar-sized American cities, in part because of the area's extensive development. Los Angeles's major industries include manufacturing, finance and trade, and it is a center for agricultural products processing. The port of Los Angeles handles a large volume of import/export trade. The city hosts many tourists, who come to visit the major attractions of the film (Hollywood) and television industries.

| Title | City Rank | Total Cities Ranked |
|---|---|---|
| Largest Cities (Area) | 7 | (100) |
| Overall Air Quality, PSI (1981) | 1 | (51) |
| Biggest Cities (Population) | 3 | (100) |
| Births | 24 | (92) |
| City per Capita Income | 33 | (100) |
| Cost of Living | * | (62) |
| City Retail Sales per Capita | 70 | (100) |
| Unemployment Rates | 29 | (77) |
| Dependence on State Aid | 70 | (100) |
| Housing Growth/Population Growth | * | (55) |
| Daily Community Hospital Cost | 1 | (75) |
| Death Rates | 59 | (98) |
| Total Crimes | 35 | (96) |
| Cost per Police Employee | 9 | (71) |
| Arson | 4 | (78) |
| Spending per Resident on Education | 3 | (72) |
| Library Budgets | 76 | (99) |

*City not listed in table.

## Louisville

Louisville is the 49th largest city in the country, with a 1980 population of nearly 300,000. The city suffered a loss of over 17 percent of its population in the 1970s, much of the loss attributable to emigration to the surrounding suburbs. The Louisville metro area grew by over 125 percent in the late 1970s, and this increase in the suburban population has brought with it the development of the surrounding suburbs to the detriment of the central city. The low retail sales in 1980 and the low city per capita income (in both cases in the bottom quartile) suggest that Louisville merchants have lost sales to the suburban areas and that the city has lost tax dollars as those who are better situated financially have left the city for suburban homes. Positive indicators that this trend may be slowing can be seen in new construction in the city. The Galleria and Riverfront projects and the Kentucky Center for the Arts promise to attract tourists and bring more commercial activity back to the central city.

| Title | City Rank | Total Cities Ranked |
|---|---|---|
| Largest Cities (Area) | 62 | (100) |
| Overall Air Quality, PSI (1981) | 25 | (51) |
| Biggest Cities (Population) | 49 | (100) |
| Births | 53 | (92) |
| City per Capita Income | 76 | (100) |
| Cost of Living | 58 | (62) |
| City Retail Sales per Capita | 77 | (100) |
| Unemployment Rates | * | (77) |
| Dependence on State Aid | 86 | (100) |

| Title | City Rank | Total Cities Ranked |
|---|---|---|
| Housing Growth/Population Growth | * | (55) |
| Daily Community Hospital Cost | 67 | (75) |
| Death Rates | 6 | (98) |
| Total Crimes | 84 | (96) |
| Cost per Police Employee | 52 | (71) |
| Arson | 54 | (78) |
| Spending per Resident on Education | 58 | (72) |
| Library Budgets | 69 | (99) |

*City not listed in table.

## Lubbock

Lubbock is located in northwestern Texas 300 miles west of Dallas. It is an important commercial and financial center for western Texas and eastern New Mexico. The city also serves the region's medical, cultural and recreational needs. Lubbock's population increased by nearly 17 percent in the 1970s. Its 1980 population of 173,979 is small (78th), while its land area is larger (52nd), making its density low. Lubbock's economy is centered on vegetable and grain processing, the livestock industry and petroleum and mineral extraction. Lubbock is situated in the hub of an important interstate network, a major trucking and rail freight terminus serving a large part of the southwest region. Lubbock's economy is very stable. Income per capita is modest (60th), but its cost of living is even lower—the lowest of the 62 cities for which data are available. Lubbock is therefore an attractive city for prospective business investors. Prospects for future growth are fairly good. Lubbock's service and educational facilities will have to expand to keep pace with its growing population.

| Title | City Rank | Total Cities Ranked |
|---|---|---|
| Largest Cities (Area) | 52 | (100) |
| Overall Air Quality, PSI (1981) | * | (51) |
| Biggest Cities (Population) | 78 | (100) |
| Births | 39 | (92) |
| City per Capita Income | 60 | (100) |
| Cost of Living | 62 | (62) |
| City Retail Sales per Capita | 6 | (100) |
| Unemployment Rates | * | (77) |
| Dependence on State Aid | 98 | (100) |
| Housing Growth/Population Growth | 35 | (55) |
| Daily Community Hospital Cost | 58 | (75) |
| Death Rates | 87 | (98) |
| Total Crimes | 55 | (96) |
| Cost per Police Employee | 58 | (71) |
| Arson | 26 | (78) |
| Spending per Resident on Education | 33 | (72) |
| Library Budgets | 91 | (99) |

*City not listed in table.

## Madison

Madison has a low birthrate (2nd lowest) and a very low death rate (86th), which suggests a substantial population of young people who moved to Madison with children or who are childless. Two explanations for this phenomenon are that the university's 40,000-student main campus is in the city and that Madison is also Wisconsin's capital city. Both facts would tend to lure well-educated professionals to Madison. Such people tend to have fewer children than average. The city has grown rapidly in recent years and is adding a major commercial sector to its two other primary economic activities (education and government). The city's low unemployment rate (12th lowest) and very high per capita income (3rd highest) suggest that the Wisconsin state government and the state government-run University of Wisconsin pay well and are stable employers—a special boon during a recessionary period such as 1981–82. The city's high spending on its public schools (20th), its libraries (8th) and its police (12th) further illustrates the advantages of living in Madison as well as Wisconsin's historic commitment to providing government with the funds to do a good job. Madison not only benefits from having the state government and state university in the area—it also receives a high level (7th highest) of direct state aid.

| Title | City Rank | Total Cities Ranked |
|---|---|---|
| Largest Cities (Area) | 73 | (100) |
| Overall Air Quality, PSI (1981) | * | (51) |
| Biggest Cities (Population) | 82 | (100) |
| Births | 91 | (92) |
| City per Capita Income | 3 | (100) |
| Cost of Living | 24 | (62) |
| City Retail Sales per Capita | 24 | (100) |
| Unemployment Rates | 66 | (77) |
| Dependence on State Aid | 7 | (100) |
| Housing Growth/Population Growth | 8 | (55) |
| Daily Community Hospital Cost | * | (75) |
| Death Rates | 86 | (98) |
| Total Crimes | 58 | (96) |
| Cost per Police Employee | 12 | (71) |
| Arson | 63 | (78) |
| Spending per Resident on Education | 20 | (72) |
| Library Budgets | 8 | (99) |

*City not listed in table.

## Memphis

With a population of nearly 650,000, Memphis is the 14th largest city in the nation. In the decade between 1970 and 1980, Memphis gained nearly 4 percent in population. Located on the Mississippi River, the city is a transportation and distribution hub for the region and is well connected by rail lines to all parts of the country. The additional features of self-supporting Memphis International Airport and interstate highway routes around it make Memphis the 6th largest distribution center in the United States. River traffic is largely devoted to petroleum and petroleum products, coal and lignite, grains and food products. Motor freight makes up a large portion of the transportation system in Memphis, and there are numerous warehousing facilities in the city. Other revenues are generated by agricultural products sold or processed in Memphis. It has the world's largest spot cotton market and is the world's 2nd largest processor of soybeans, the 3rd largest meat processor and the 3rd largest total food processor. City per capita income is 56th, indicating below-average prevailing wages (especially low for such a large city), and cost of living is 32nd. Memphis is 23rd in housing growth relative to population growth and should continue to grow into the next century. Total index crimes are low for a city of its size.

nearest large city in the United States. The net influx of new residents strained the social service budgets of Miami and surrounding Dade County. It placed great burdens on city agencies, which were already under heavy pressure to maintain services in the wake of mass immigration. The situation was exacerbated by race riots in the summers of 1981 and 1982. Miami's crime rate was number one in the nation. The flood of new residents has pushed down the per capita income level to the 5th lowest in the country, while its cost of living continues to be high (25th). Unemployment remained above average (37th). The city's housing is not keeping up with population—housing growth/population growth is 49th. Miami's economy benefits greatly from its tourist revenues. Its attractions are its beaches, resorts and nightclubs with famous stars performing—much like Las Vegas but without the legalized gambling. Legalized betting does take place (and also aids the economy) at nearby horse tracks, dog tracks and jai alai frontons. Miami's progressive mayor, Maurice Ferre, is one of the nation's three prominent Hispanic mayors, the others being San Antonio's Henry Cisneros and Denver's Federico Pena.

| Title | City Rank | Total Cities Ranked |
|---|---|---|
| Largest Cities (Area) | 14 | (100) |
| Overall Air Quality, PSI (1981) | * | (51) |
| Biggest Cities (Population) | 14 | (100) |
| Births | 52 | (92) |
| City per Capita Income | 56 | (100) |
| Cost of Living | 32 | (62) |
| City Retail Sales per Capita | 56 | (100) |
| Unemployment Rates | 30 | (77) |
| Dependence on State Aid | 16 | (100) |
| Housing Growth/Population Growth | 23 | (55) |
| Daily Community Hospital Cost | 55 | (75) |
| Death Rates | 61 | (98) |
| Total Crimes | 65 | (96) |
| Cost per Police Employee | * | (71) |
| Arson | 18 | (78) |
| Spending per Resident on Education | * | (72) |
| Library Budgets | 55 | (99) |

*City not listed in table.

| Title | City Rank | Total Cities Ranked |
|---|---|---|
| Largest Cities (Area) | 91 | (100) |
| Overall Air Quality, PSI (1981) | * | (51) |
| Biggest Cities (Population) | 41 | (100) |
| Births | 9 | (92) |
| City per Capita Income | 96 | (100) |
| Cost of Living | 25 | (62) |
| City Retail Sales per Capita | 53 | (100) |
| Unemployment Rates | 37 | (77) |
| Dependence on State Aid | 43 | (100) |
| Housing Growth/Population Growth | 49 | (55) |
| Daily Community Hospital Cost | 19 | (75) |
| Death Rates | 10 | (98) |
| Total Crimes | 1 | (96) |
| Cost per Police Employee | * | (71) |
| Arson | 35 | (78) |
| Spending per Resident on Education | * | (72) |
| Library Budgets | 31 | (99) |

*City not listed in table.

## Miami

Miami is the 41st most populous city, with a 1980 population of almost 347,000. In the 1970s it grew by nearly 4 percent. This growth, however, resulted largely from immigration from the Caribbean Islands and brought with it many economic and social problems. The most obvious problems came on the heels of the Haitian refugees and the Cuban immigrants, who gravitated to the

## Milwaukee

Milwaukee, the 12th most populous city in the United States in 1970, dropped to 17th in 1980—a population loss during the 1970s of over 11 percent. Much of this loss may be attributed to the decline in manufacturing that affected all large cities heavily dependent on it. Nearly 30 percent of Milwaukee's workers are employed in manufacturing, making the city one of the most reliant on this industry. Although the city is still a brewery center, several of Milwaukee's breweries have closed. The city's high 1982 unemployment rate—16th highest—shows the impact of the recession on the Milwaukee economy. However, Milwaukee is beginning to establish itself as a specialty manufacturing city. This shift in manufacturing will aid Milwaukee greatly in diversifying its economic base. It now leads the nation in production of industrial controls and X-ray apparatus. Total index crimes are very low for a city Milwaukee's size (12th lowest), making it one of the safest large cities in the country.

| Title | City Rank | Total Cities Ranked |
|---|---|---|
| Largest Cities (Area) | 43 | (100) |
| Overall Air Quality, PSI (1981) | 37 | (51) |
| Biggest Cities (Population) | 17 | (100) |
| Births | 45 | (92) |
| City per Capita Income | 63 | (100) |
| Cost of Living | * | (62) |
| City Retail Sales per Capita | 86 | (100) |
| Unemployment Rates | 16 | (77) |
| Dependence on State Aid | 5 | (100) |
| Housing Growth/Population Growth | * | (55) |
| Daily Community Hospital Cost | 18 | (75) |
| Death Rates | 50 | (98) |
| Total Crimes | 85 | (96) |
| Cost per Police Employee | 21 | (71) |
| Arson | 71 | (78) |
| Spending per Resident on Education | 7 | (72) |
| Library Budgets | 36 | (99) |

*City not listed in table.

## Minneapolis

Minneapolis is the 34th largest city in the United States, with a 1980 population of nearly 371,000, having dropped in rank since 1970 with a population loss of nearly 15 percent. Minneapolis has a diversified economic base with employment opportunities for all types of labor. The trend toward electronic and computer-based technologies has given Minneapolis a high rate of employment for those in technical careers. The professional and technical occupations continue to grow in Minneapolis, with nearly 25 percent of the workers being in this category. Minneapolis is headquarters for Honeywell, Control Data, General Mills and Pillsbury as well as other *Fortune* 500 corporations such as International Multifoods and Peavey and Bemis. Development and new industrial investment helped create jobs in Minneapolis in the late 1970s and continue to be important for maintaining growth in the area. The city pumped over $245 million into its physical plant in 1979 alone and

expects continued reinvestments of this kind into the 1980s, which will create jobs in the city and lend stability to the economy, although it will also build up a debt burden. Total index crimes for Minneapolis are high—27th. Compared to its near neighbor, Milwaukee, Minneapolis has a greater taste for artistic and cultural pursuits. If Milwaukee drinks beer and watches football games, Minneapolis drinks wine and watches "Masterpiece Theater."

| Title | City Rank | Total Cities Ranked |
|---|---|---|
| Largest Cities (Area) | 67 | (100) |
| Overall Air Quality, PSI (1981) | 12 | (51) |
| Biggest Cities (Population) | 34 | (100) |
| Births | 10 | (92) |
| City per Capita Income | 31 | (100) |
| Cost of Living | 10 | (62) |
| City Retail Sales per Capita | 84 | (100) |
| Unemployment Rates | 63 | (77) |
| Dependence on State Aid | 20 | (100) |
| Housing Growth/Population Growth | * | (55) |
| Daily Community Hospital Cost | 25 | (75) |
| Death Rates | 19 | (98) |
| Total Crimes | 27 | (96) |
| Cost per Police Employee | 17 | (71) |
| Arson | 65 | (78) |
| Spending per Resident on Education | 55 | (72) |
| Library Budgets | 2 | (99) |

*City not listed in table.

## Mobile

Although Mobile's population has increased 5.5 percent over the past 10 years, the city's population has not reached the 1960 level of nearly 203,000. This may be due to the high (third highest) unemployment rates that have continued to affect heavy manufacturing and oil and gas industry output over the past several years. The close relationship between the heavy manufacturing industries and unemployment has affected the other Alabama cities, too. Mobile, however, can fall back on its port revenues as one means of diminishing the effects of layoffs. The continued growth of the port tonnage has enhanced the overall character of the city and has kept it from becoming overly dependent upon manufacturing.

| Title | City Rank | Total Cities Ranked |
|---|---|---|
| Largest Cities (Area) | 27 | (100) |
| Overall Air Quality, PSI (1981) | * | (51) |
| Biggest Cities (Population) | 72 | (100) |

| Title | City Rank | Total Cities Ranked |
|---|---|---|
| Births | 29 | (92) |
| City per Capita Income | 95 | (100) |
| Cost of Living | 47 | (62) |
| City Retail Sales per Capita | 33 | (100) |
| Unemployment Rates | 3 | (77) |
| Dependence on State Aid | 76 | (100) |
| Housing Growth/Population Growth | 39 | (55) |
| Daily Community Hospital Cost | 68 | (75) |
| Death Rates | 49 | (98) |
| Total Crimes | 26 | (96) |
| Cost per Police Employee | 49 | (71) |
| Arson | 38 | (78) |
| Spending per Resident on Education | * | (72) |
| Library Budgets | 81 | (99) |

*City not listed in table.

## Montgomery

Montgomery is one of the fastest-growing cities in the South, despite its relatively low birthrate (78th). One explanation is that it has annexed neighboring suburban areas. The 1978 area in square miles was a little over 50; by 1980 that figure had more than doubled to nearly 129 square miles, adding over 20,000 to the population. The city forecasts a population for 1990 of nearly 194,000 and a population for the year 2000 of more than 211,000. Montgomery's figures for total crimes as well as those for arson and robberies are lower than those of Mobile, another Alabama city with only a slightly larger population.

| Title | City Rank | Total Cities Ranked |
|---|---|---|
| Largest Cities (Area) | 31 | (100) |
| Overall Air Quality, PSI (1981) | * | (51) |
| Biggest Cities (Population) | 77 | (100) |
| Births | 78 | (92) |
| City per Capita Income | 83 | (100) |
| Cost of Living | * | (62) |
| City Retail Sales per Capita | 51 | (100) |
| Unemployment Rates | 13 | (77) |
| Dependence on State Aid | 80 | (100) |
| Housing Growth/Population Growth | 53 | (55) |
| Daily Community Hospital Cost | * | (75) |
| Death Rates | 60 | (98) |
| Total Crimes | 88 | (96) |
| Cost per Police Employee | 70 | (71) |
| Arson | 46 | (78) |
| Spending per Resident on Education | * | (72) |
| Library Budgets | 97 | (99) |

*City not listed in table.

## Nashville-Davidson

Nashville has a diverse economic base, which has greatly helped it weather the 1981–82 recessionary maladies. As a broad-based manufacturing city, Nashville was not hurt as much as other cities that rely more on a single industry. In addition, as the state capital and an educational center, Nashville has benefited from the income and job stability of these industries. Its city per capita income is 18th in the nation, and overall retail sales per capita are 27th. Coupled with the relatively low cost of living (51st out of 62), including a low cost of hospital care, Nashville is economically attractive. Culturally, a major phenomenon in the past decade has been the continued growth of its country music industry. Annual tourism revenue attributed to that industry exceeds $200 million.

| Title | City Rank | Total Cities Ranked |
|---|---|---|
| Largest Cities (Area) | 6 | (100) |
| Overall Air Quality, PSI (1981) | 36 | (51) |
| Biggest Cities (Population) | 25 | (100) |
| Births | 73 | (92) |
| City per Capita Income | 18 | (100) |
| Cost of Living | 51 | (62) |
| City Retail Sales per Capita | 27 | (100) |
| Unemployment Rates | 36 | (77) |
| Dependence on State Aid | 37 | (100) |
| Housing Growth/Population Growth | 47 | (55) |
| Daily Community Hospital Cost | 64 | (75) |
| Death Rates | 67 | (98) |
| Total Crimes | 81 | (96) |
| Cost per Police Employee | 62 | (71) |
| Arson | * | (78) |
| Spending per Resident on Education | * | (72) |
| Library Budgets | 61 | (99) |

*City not listed in table.

## Newark

Newark, like Jersey City, is very small in area (4th smallest). With the 46th biggest population, the city is densely populated. Lacking a strategy for itself over the years, the city has seen its wealthier people leave while dependents on government programs have remained. Consequently, even though its metro area is wealthy (9th wealthiest), its central city is very poor (4th poorest). Newark's shopping has deteriorated drastically—its retail sales per capita are the lowest in the nation, despite the city's high cost of living (8th highest). In the 1950s Newark was the shopping center for northern New Jersey; between 1970 and 1981 its retail sales dropped from $614 million to $605 million, a real decline of over 50 percent. By contrast, little Atlantic City, with a population one-eighth as large, had retail sales nearly half Newark's. Some stores in Newark close down in mid-afternoon, and the city's own Chamber of Commerce in early 1983 says that at night "downtown Newark is a ghost town." Its 13 percent unemployment in 1982 was high. With 67 percent of its land exempt from local taxes, its property taxes are extraordinarily high, contributing to the fact that 10 percent of its housing is substandard—the highest figure of any major city. The majority of its population is now black, and a substantial portion of the remainder is Hispanic. Newark has major strengths. The state of New Jersey is helping out by providing substantial aid, more than any other city receives from its state. Newark is a strong educational center, with five colleges, so that its 35,000 students serve as a labor pool for high-technology industry. The city is home to two major insurance companies—Prudential and Mutual Benefit Life—as well as New Jersey's largest bank and its major utilities. Its airport is active (11th busiest) and growing in importance. Its port is the world's largest container cargo center, handling more than half the cargo coming into the Port of New York area and serving as the point of entry for more cars and meat than any other port. Its 50 bus lines with 5,000 daily trips as well as its superb rail and highway network add up to the nation's leading transportation center. The steady upgrading of housing in the Ironbound area and in areas around Newark provide a base for future revival. Signs of life in Newark are its new office buildings, including Gateways One and Two and the Gateway Hilton, with Gateway Three under construction. What Newark needs most is some glamour —a shopping center on the waterfront, with activities going on into the night. At the moment, employees rarely leave their buildings. Renaissance Newark Inc. is seeking to build a new complex on the waterfront near the railroad station and to include in it retail facilities. If this plan is financed and started, it could be the basis for a new image for Newark.

| Title | City Rank | Total Cities Ranked |
|---|---|---|
| Death Rates | 55 | (98) |
| Total Crimes | * | (96) |
| Cost per Police Employee | * | (71) |
| Arson | * | (78) |
| Spending per Resident on Education | 4 | (72) |
| Library Budgets | 29 | (99) |

*City not listed in table.

# New Orleans

New Orleans, with a population of nearly 557,000, is the 21st largest city in the United States. Known as one of the world's busiest ports, its location at the mouth of the nation's longest river has made it the largest port in the United States in tonnage (over 177 million tons in 1980). It relies heavily on the port to generate revenues and to attract industry and commercial ventures to this sunbelt hub. Development has begun in the area called New Orleans East for construction of a 4,800-acre community, which will include residential, industrial and commercial buildings. Commercial and industrial areas will be located on the intercoastal waterway and the Louisville and Nashville railway lines. Housing and schools will be provided for an estimated 50,000 people, and approximately 16,000 new jobs will be created in just the first phase of development. An additional 23,200 acres are slated for eventual development, adding 200,000 to the New Orleans population within 25 years. New Orleans should maintain its importance as a transportation center, and development of areas like New Orleans East should reverse the city's population loss of 6 percent between 1970 and 1980. City per capita income and unemployment rates are both below average. The city pays relatively dearly for police employees (10th highest), although its crime rate is low for a city of its size (45th).

| Title | City Rank | Total Cities Ranked |
|---|---|---|
| Largest Cities (Area) | 97 | (100) |
| Overall Air Quality, PSI (1981) | * | (51) |
| Biggest Cities (Population) | 46 | (100) |
| Births | 19 | (92) |
| City per Capita Income | 97 | (100) |
| Cost of Living | 8 | (62) |
| City Retail Sales per Capita | 100 | (100) |
| Unemployment Rates | 49 | (77) |
| Dependence on State Aid | 1 | (100) |
| Housing Growth/Population Growth | * | (55) |
| Daily Community Hospital Cost | 34 | (75) |

| Title | City Rank | Total Cities Ranked |
|---|---|---|
| Largest Cities (Area) | 22 | (100) |
| Overall Air Quality, PSI (1981) | * | (51) |
| Biggest Cities (Population) | 21 | (100) |
| Births | 31 | (92) |
| City per Capita Income | 61 | (100) |
| Cost of Living | * | (62) |
| City Retail Sales per Capita | 78 | (100) |
| Unemployment Rates | 38 | (77) |
| Dependence on State Aid | 65 | (100) |
| Housing Growth/Population Growth | * | (55) |
| Daily Community Hospital Cost | 36 | (75) |

| Title | City Rank | Total Cities Ranked |
|---|---|---|
| Death Rates | 26 | (98) |
| Total Crimes | 45 | (96) |
| Cost per Police Employee | 10 | (71) |
| Arson | 66 | (78) |
| Spending per Resident on Education | 53 | (72) |
| Library Budgets | 92 | (99) |

*City not listed in table.

# New York

New York exemplifies the absurdity of ranking any city on its "overall quality of life." Even though New York City is the 13th largest in land area, its enormous population puts its density in 1st place, well ahead of San Francisco's. How someone will like New York City depends in part on how that person feels about density. One bad feature, for example, is that New York's overall air quality in 1981 was the second worst after Los Angeles, its high carbon monoxide levels accounting for its severest problem. While its air pollution levels have declined substantially in recent years, New York has not improved as rapidly as other large cities like Chicago. Another negative aspect of density is that New York City has a high cost of living (1st in Table 99, 4th in Table 100) in the country, not fully compensated for by its having above-average (22nd highest) income. The lure of New York is the challenge of its working environment. It is the center of corporate America, of finance, of communications, of fashion, of the arts. A young dancer or artist feels a tremendous pull toward New York, whatever the city's problems (and they have been exaggerated). The city's cost of living and income averages don't show the whole truth, which is that people can and do live on very little as well as on a great deal. The very wealthy people clustered around Central Park in Manhattan are balanced by many poor people elsewhere in the city, and many of the people who earn large incomes in New York City don't show up in the city's average because they live in suburban areas outside the city. New York City is the 8th most dependent on state aid because of its many programs to assist the poor. Its retail sales per capita are among the dozen lowest in the country, because many people don't spend much money. New York City had a below-average birthrate and an above-average death rate, suggesting an elderly population; many people of child-rearing age move to suburban areas and come back when they are older. Like Chicago, New York has a very high heart attack rate and a relatively low rate of strokes. Heart attacks are related to overweight (sugar), lack of exercise and soft water, whereas strokes are related to salt and hard water. Hospital costs are 16th highest—but the care can be the best. New York City's lure and anonymity create opportunities for crime. New York ranks 34th out of 96 cities in total reported index crimes in 1981 and 4th highest in robberies (a better indicator) in 1981. It ranks 15th in arsons. Crime may have peaked nationally, but New York was 26th highest in the change in robberies in 1979–81, showing slightly over a 30 percent increase. It ranks 8th highest in cost per police employee. The city has the 7th highest average class size, even though it ranks 9th in spending on education per resident. It ranks 2nd in the percentage of college-bound seniors, probably reflecting the ample availability of and access to college programs through the State University of New York and the City University of New York.

| Title | City Rank | Total Cities Ranked |
|---|---|---|
| Largest Cities (Area) | 13 | (100) |
| Overall Air Quality, PSI (1981) | 2 | (51) |
| Biggest Cities (Population) | 1 | (100) |
| Births | 67 | (92) |
| City per Capita Income | 22 | (100) |
| Cost of Living | 1 | (62) |
| City Retail Sales per Capita | 89 | (100) |
| Unemployment Rates | 47 | (77) |
| Dependence on State Aid | 8 | (100) |
| Housing Growth/Population Growth | * | (55) |
| Daily Community Hospital Cost | 16 | (75) |
| Death Rates | 41 | (98) |
| Total Crimes | 34 | (96) |
| Cost per Police Employee | 8 | (71) |
| Arson | 15 | (78) |
| Spending per Resident on Education | 9 | (72) |
| Library Budgets | 37 | (99) |

*City not listed in table.

# Norfolk

Norfolk—on the mouth of the James, Elizabeth and Nansemond Rivers opening onto Chesapeake Bay—is located adjacent to Virginia Beach, one of the fastest-growing cities in the United States. Although Norfolk (55th most populous) lost over 13 percent of its population during the 1970s, its present situation may be better off for the loss, for its can now plan the growth of its housing (it is 19th in housing growth/population growth) and development without the pressures that come with population overflow. Industrial development is one of the primary areas that will be important to Norfolk's continued economic success. Locations open to new business include the Norfolk Industrial Park and the Norfolk International Airport, both run by the Norfolk Port and Industrial Authority and the City of Norfolk. Major employers in the area are Norfolk Shipbuilding and Drydock, Ford Motor Company, Landmark Communications and Smith-Douglas. The naval installations at Norfolk are a boon to the local economy because their revenues are not subject to business cycles. Norfolk has the largest naval concentration in the world, with headquarters for the Fifth Naval District, Atlantic Fleet and 23 other major naval commands. It is also the home of NATO and the Armed Forces Staff College. Despite the large infusion of federal salaries, city per capita income is low (10th lowest). The city is heavily dependent upon the state (11th highest) for aid. Crimes are low (71st), adding to the city's attractiveness.

| Title | City Rank | Total Cities Ranked |
|---|---|---|
| Largest Cities (Area) | 75 | (100) |
| Overall Air Quality, PSI (1981) | * | (51) |
| Biggest Cities (Population) | 55 | (100) |
| Births | 22 | (92) |
| City per Capita Income | 91 | (100) |
| Cost of Living | 35 | (62) |
| City Retail Sales per Capita | 63 | (100) |
| Unemployment Rates | * | (77) |
| Dependence on State Aid | 11 | (100) |
| Housing Growth/Population Growth | 19 | (55) |
| Daily Community Hospital Cost | 52 | (75) |
| Death Rates | 47 | (98) |
| Total Crimes | 71 | (96) |
| Cost per Police Employee | 61 | (71) |
| Arson | 21 | (78) |
| Spending per Resident on Education | * | (72) |
| Library Budgets | 51 | (99) |

*City not listed in table.

## Oakland

Oakland, located on the eastern shore of San Francisco Bay, is the 4th largest city in California and the 43rd largest in the nation. It is a major port on the West Coast, handling over 7 million tons in 1980, making shipping and shipbuilding significant industries in the city. Oakland's diverse economy also includes production of electrical equipment, fabricated metals, chemicals and processed food. Young people are attracted to Oakland by relatively high salaries (city per capita income is 20th) and appear to be settling in the area and starting families (the birthrate is 5th highest). The high crime rate (10th highest) is a problem, yet the city government is dedi-

cated to lessening it considerably; it pays more for its police force than any other city in the country. In fact, Oakland's generosity to its police force on the fringe benefits side turned out to be so lavish, with cost of living increases, that it has had to renegotiate its plan drastically for new employees.

| Title | City Rank | Total Cities Ranked |
|---|---|---|
| Largest Cities (Area) | 74 | (100) |
| Overall Air Quality, PSI (1981) | 45 | (51) |
| Biggest Cities (Population) | 43 | (100) |
| Births | 5 | (92) |
| City per Capita Income | 20 | (100) |
| Cost of Living | * | (62) |
| City Retail Sales per Capita | 85 | (100) |
| Unemployment Rates | 47 | (77) |
| Dependence on State Aid | 75 | (100) |
| Housing Growth/Population Growth | * | (55) |
| Daily Community Hospital Cost | 3 | (75) |
| Death Rates | 37 | (98) |
| Total Crimes | 10 | (96) |
| Cost per Police Employee | 1 | (71) |
| Arson | * | (78) |
| Spending per Resident on Education | 32 | (72) |
| Library Budgets | 33 | (99) |

*City not listed in table.

## Oklahoma City

Oklahoma City is a good example for study of city planning and development. The city is even less dependent on state aid than Tulsa (8th least dependent), so its plans are comparatively unrestricted by state requirements. The 31st largest city in the United States in terms of population and 3rd largest in area, it has ample room for growth and development. Downtown business and civic groups have launched a strong drive to revitalize the capital area and the central city industrial district. The population growth rate during the 1970s was nearly 10 percent, and the projected population for Oklahoma City in the year 2000 is nearly 500,000. The plan for Oklahoma City includes protection of the watershed by restricting building in the southeast section of the city. A proposed reservoir for that area would substantially enhance water supply and quality.

| Title | City Rank | Total Cities Ranked |
|---|---|---|
| Largest Cities (Area) | 3 | (100) |
| Overall Air Quality, PSI (1981) | * | (51) |
| Biggest Cities (Population) | 31 | (100) |

| Title | City Rank | Total Cities Ranked |
|---|---|---|
| Births | 44 | (92) |
| City per Capita Income | 13 | (100) |
| Cost of Living | 25 | (62) |
| City Retail Sales per Capita | 13 | (100) |
| Unemployment Rates | 77 | (77) |
| Dependence on State Aid | 93 | (100) |
| Housing Growth/Population Growth | 40 | (55) |
| Daily Community Hospital Cost | 27 | (75) |
| Death Rates | 57 | (98) |
| Total Crimes | 59 | (96) |
| Cost per Police Employee | 56 | (71) |
| Arson | * | (78) |
| Spending per Resident on Education | 69 | (72) |
| Library Budgets | 90 | (99) |

*City not listed in table.

## Omaha

Omaha lost over 10 percent of its population between 1970 and 1980, dropping from 41st to 48th in population rank. Most of the movement of population was to suburban areas surrounding Omaha. While the central city tax base decreased, commuters continued to spend money within city limits, helping to offset other revenue losses. Omaha is a major trade and transportation center for livestock. Its large railroad facilities make it a hub for distribution to all parts of the United States. Omaha is also a manufacturing center—Western Electric and Control Data together account for nearly 6,000 jobs. To regulate suburban growth and oversee the revitalization and stabilization of the inner city areas, Omaha has adopted an Urban Development Policy. Its goals are to ensure that public and private development is conducted at the least cost and with the highest benefit to the public. Omaha has sought to relate intangible factors of human life quality and ethical and moral costs with the tangible factors, delineating and zoning areas for commercial, industrial or residential development. The plan also periodically reviews areas where demand for housing has grown and areas where housing and land values should be protected (for example, the central city area). Omaha has seen a trend toward development in the central city for residential living. Such developments are studied in accordance with the Urban Development Policy's "In City" Program. This is necessary because of the city's concern that the developments not disrupt existing inner city neighborhoods. The program also aids in planning for renovation of or addition to public facilities, services and schools. City income per capita is a little below average, but the cost of living is also relatively low. Unemployment is very low, so that Omaha fared comparatively well in the 1981–82 recession.

| Title | City Rank | Total Cities Ranked |
|---|---|---|
| Largest Cities (Area) | 53 | (100) |
| Overall Air Quality, PSI (1981) | * | (51) |
| Biggest Cities (Population) | 48 | (100) |
| Births | 37 | (92) |
| City per Capita Income | 64 | (100) |
| Cost of Living | 56 | (62) |
| City Retail Sales per Capita | 36 | (100) |
| Unemployment Rates | 61 | (77) |
| Dependence on State Aid | 57 | (100) |
| Housing Growth/Population Growth | * | (55) |
| Daily Community Hospital Cost | 62 | (75) |
| Death Rates | 48 | (98) |
| Total Crimes | 25 | (96) |
| Cost per Police Employee | 23 | (71) |
| Arson | * | (78) |
| Spending per Resident on Education | 47 | (72) |
| Library Budgets | 56 | (99) |

*City not listed in table.

## Philadelphia

Philadelphia, the 4th most populous city in the United States, is facing many of the same problems that most of the older, industrial cities of the North and Northeast have encountered. Philadelphia has lost more than 13 percent of its population between 1970 and 1980. The decreased birthrate shows that families have continued to move to suburban areas. A declining rate of retail sales shows that the downtown area has suffered. Like Washington, D.C., Philadelphia has begun a campaign to revitalize its downtown area (e.g., with a convention center and new shopping areas) and its housing. Philadelphia ranks 37th in housing growth/population growth, indicating that there is a continuing demand for city housing, which has been the least costly among major cities. A renewal and renovation of the port area has contributed greatly to maintaining revenues from that source. Effective lobbying for federal contracts has revived the Navy Yard, nearly doubling its employment within a few years. Unemployment rates have not been as high as in other large cities such as Detroit, Los Angeles or Baltimore. A source of strength is Philadelphia's base in technology (Pennsylvania Bell), education (University of Pennsylvania and Temple University), medicine and chemical companies. During the 1979–83 period, Phildelphia's fiscal ills were ameliorated by its effective, no-nonsense mayor, William Green, who cut back on city spending while improving tax collections.

| Title | City Rank | Total Cities Ranked |
|---|---|---|
| Largest Cities (Area) | 30 | (100) |
| Overall Air Quality, PSI (1981) | 14 | (51) |
| Biggest Cities (Population) | 4 | (100) |
| Births | 72 | (92) |
| City per Capita Income | 77 | (100) |
| Cost of Living | * | (62) |
| City Retail Sales per Capita | 94 | (100) |
| Unemployment Rates | 44 | (77) |
| Dependence on State Aid | 39 | (100) |
| Housing Growth/Population Growth | 37 | (55) |
| Daily Community Hospital Cost | 14 | (75) |
| Death Rates | 12 | (98) |
| Total Crimes | 91 | (96) |
| Cost per Police Employee | 20 | (71) |
| Arson | * | (78) |
| Spending per Resident on Education | 13 | (72) |
| Library Budgets | 23 | (99) |

*City not listed in table.

## Phoenix

Phoenix has experienced the highest percentage population increase of the 10 largest cities in America—up 35.2 percent to over 790,000 between 1970 and 1980. The principal factors behind Phoenix's growth rate are its pleasant year-round climate, its strong and diversifying economy, and the tremendous population influx from the Northeast and California. Phoenix's fast population growth is expected to continue through the year 2000. This growth rate means that the city must meet expanding service and capital improvement requirements in transportation (highways and mass transit), housing and planning, water and land use. Phoenix's growth has been aided by an economic environment friendly to private business, including low taxes and an availability of services. This growth has centered around the technology industries that require skilled labor in engineering, electronics and manufacturing. Phoenix has attracted a significant percentage of the migrants from the Northeast. It has developed a large and ambitious work force amenable to working at lower wages. Its large senior-size population also has a lower than average median income. These facts translate into the city's having a lower than average per capita income (30th lowest). Phoenix has some problems—a high cost of living (15th), for example, and a high rate of violent crime.

| Title | City Rank | Total Cities Ranked |
|---|---|---|
| Largest Cities (Area) | 10 | (100) |
| Overall Air Quality, PSI (1981) | 4 | (51) |
| Biggest Cities (Population) | 9 | (100) |

| Title | City Rank | Total Cities Ranked |
|---|---|---|
| Births | 79 | (92) |
| City per Capita Income | 71 | (100) |
| Cost of Living | 15 | (62) |
| City Retail Sales per Capita | 82 | (100) |
| Unemployment Rates | 51 | (77) |
| Dependence on State Aid | 35 | (100) |
| Housing Growth/Population Growth | 49 | (55) |
| Daily Community Hospital Cost | 15 | (75) |
| Death Rates | 77 | (98) |
| Total Crimes | 33 | (96) |
| Cost per Police Employee | 24 | (71) |
| Arson | * | (78) |
| Spending per Resident on Education | * | (72) |
| Library Budgets | 72 | (99) |

*City not listed in table.

## Pittsburgh

Pittsburgh's 1980 population of nearly 424,000 ranks 30th, having dropped from 23rd place in 1970 with a population loss of nearly 19 percent. Famed as a steel town, Pittsburgh suffered greatly during the recession and will continue to be plagued by the syndrome of economic ills that have affected many other northern industrial cities. In spite of this gloomy background, Pittsburgh has continued to fight the trend by proceeding with the new construction planned under its own Renaissance Plan. Although the name is reminiscent of Detroit's Renaissance Center, Pittsburgh's downtown showcase (the Golden Triangle) predates Detroit's. An upturn in auto sales in 1983 has alleviated some of the pressures brought on by the city's high unemployment— the 6th highest in December 1982. City per capita income is 42nd, not high—but higher than that of the other northeastern industrial cities facing similar economic problems. Total index crimes are very low (17th lowest) for a city of Pittsburgh's size.

| Title | City Rank | Total Cities Ranked |
|---|---|---|
| Largest Cities (Area) | 70 | (100) |
| Overall Air Quality, PSI (1981) | 17 | (51) |
| Biggest Cities (Population) | 30 | (100) |
| Births | 84 | (92) |
| City per Capita Income | 42 | (100) |
| Cost of Living | * | (62) |
| City Retail Sales per Capita | 76 | (100) |
| Unemployment Rates | 6 | (77) |
| Dependence on State Aid | 39 | (100) |
| Housing Growth/Population Growth | * | (55) |
| Daily Community Hospital Cost | 35 | (75) |

| Title | City Rank | Total Cities Ranked |
|---|---|---|
| Death Rates | 3 | (98) |
| Total Crimes | 80 | (96) |
| Cost per Police Employee | * | (71) |
| Arson | * | (78) |
| Spending per Resident on Education | * | (72) |
| Library Budgets | 82 | (99) |

*City not listed in table.

# Portland

Portland—the largest city in Oregon, with a 1980 population of over 366,000—is the 35th most populous city in the country. A small population loss during the 1970s (3.6 percent) is explained by the shift to surrounding suburban areas, which increased their population in the same period by better than 23 percent. An additional 240,000 new residents are expected to move into the metro area during the 1980s. Portland benefits from a diverse economic base. Manufacturing is the leading employer (better than 20 percent), followed by services (20 percent) and retail trade (over 17 percent). Growth in the manufacturing sector is expected to focus on electrical equipment and supplies, which now account for 8.8 percent of employment. Downtown Portland is undergoing considerable development and renewal, including a resurgence of residential construction. Portland's commitment to assist and encourage housing retention, neighborhood conservation and new development has been evident in programs for low-interest loans for homeowners and developers and property tax abatements for some new and rehabilitated housing. Low-income housing accounted for nearly 40 percent of new housing built between 1978 and 1980. City per capita income ranks 30th, and cost of living ranks 19th. Retail sales rank 31st, meaning that the suburban malls have not yet severely cut into downtown merchants' sales. Crime is high—7th highest—even though Portland spends heavily per capita for its police employees (3rd highest).

| Title | City Rank | Total Cities Ranked |
|---|---|---|
| Largest Cities (Area) | 40 | (100) |
| Overall Air Quality, PSI (1981) | 19 | (51) |
| Biggest Cities (Population) | 35 | (100) |
| Births | 81 | (92) |
| City per Capita Income | 30 | (100) |
| Cost of Living | 19 | (62) |
| City Retail Sales per Capita | 31 | (100) |

| Title | City Rank | Total Cities Ranked |
|---|---|---|
| Unemployment Rates | 26 | (77) |
| Dependence on State Aid | 51 | (100) |
| Housing Growth/Population Growth | * | (55) |
| Daily Community Hospital Cost | 11 | (75) |
| Death Rates | 9 | (98) |
| Total Crimes | 7 | (96) |
| Cost per Police Employee | 3 | (71) |
| Arson | * | (78) |
| Spending per Resident on Education | 25 | (72) |
| Library Budgets | 42 | (99) |

*City not listed in table.

# Providence

Founded in 1636 by Roger Williams and located in the Boston-New York corridor, Providence is one of the oldest cities in the United States. It is the second smallest city of the 100 largest in population (157,000, after Greensboro) and area (18.9 square miles, after Jersey City). Providence's economy is dominated by the production of costume jewelry, textiles and silverware. Traditionally dependent on manufacturing, Providence has not diversified swiftly into more promising contemporary service and technology industries. Providence is therefore negatively affected by international competition in its areas of specialization, and its per capita income is below average (66th). Providence is an important rail and highway transportation center and has the third largest port in New England. Its air quality is relatively good (6th lowest). Only five days were recorded as having exceeded the PSI for at least one pollutant. Total index crimes in Providence are 38th; arsons, however, are the 9th highest in the United States, probably resulting from the decaying buildings and factories that have not been renovated or rebuilt during the city's decline. Spending on libraries is next to last, although Providence is the home of two thriving educational institutions—Brown University and the Rhode Island School of Design.

| Title | City Rank | Total Cities Ranked |
|---|---|---|
| Largest Cities (Area) | 99 | (100) |
| Overall Air Quality, PSI (1981) | 45 | (51) |
| Biggest Cities (Population) | 99 | (100) |
| Births | 26 | (92) |
| City per Capita Income | 66 | (100) |
| Cost of Living | * | (62) |
| City Retail Sales per Capita | 88 | (100) |
| Unemployment Rates | 25 | (77) |
| Dependence on State Aid | 28 | (100) |

| Title | City Rank | Total Cities Ranked |
|---|---|---|
| Housing Growth/Population Growth | * | (55) |
| Daily Community Hospital Cost | 22 | (75) |
| Death Rates | 21 | (98) |
| Total Crimes | 38 | (96) |
| Cost per Police Employee | * | (71) |
| Arson | 9 | (78) |
| Spending per Resident on Education | 66 | (72) |
| Library Budgets | 98 | (99) |

*City not listed in table.

# Richmond

Richmond experienced a population loss during the 1970s of over 12 percent and a drop in rank from 57th to 63rd. However, its 1980 census population of slightly over 219,000 is expected to increase in the next decade because of the city's revitalization of its downtown area and the renewal of its economic base in the direction of health care and transportation services. Construction in progress includes the expansion of the Medical College of Virginia, a major teaching and research resource for the mid-Atlantic region. The tobacco processing industry is the key employer in the private sector, giving Richmond residents a stable core of jobs. Other major employers in Virginia's capital city are federal, state and local governments (including Virginia Commonwealth University), which provide nearly 80,000 jobs. Financial and insurance institutions are also concentrated in Richmond, which is headquarters for the Fifth Federal Reserve District. The city is ranked 21st in housing growth/population growth and seems to be stemming the population outflow in the 1980s. Total index crimes are 21st —relatively high for a city of its size.

| Title | City Rank | Total Cities Ranked |
|---|---|---|
| Largest Cities (Area) | 64 | (100) |
| OVerall Air Quality, PSI (1981) | 49 | 51 |
| Biggest Cities (Population) | 63 | (100) |
| Births | 85 | (92) |
| City per Capita Income | 69 | (100) |
| Cost of Living | * | (62) |
| City Retail Sales per Capita | 29 | (100) |
| Unemployment Rates | 71 | (77) |
| Dependence on State Aid | 21 | (100) |
| Housing Growth/Population Growth | 21 | (55) |
| Daily Community Hospital Cost | 51 | (75) |
| Death Rates | 91 | (98) |
| Total Crimes | 21 | (96) |
| Cost per Police Employee | * | (71) |
| Arson | 72 | (78) |

| Title | City Rank | Total Cities Ranked |
|---|---|---|
| Spending per Resident on Education | 11 | (72) |
| Library Budgets | 38 | (99) |

*City not listed in table.

# Riverside

Riverside witnessed a considerable population growth (22 percent) in the 1970s, to become the largest city between Phoenix and Los Angeles and the 82nd most populous city. Its high cost of living, coupled with a high level of unemployment (10th highest), has made the 1981–82 recession very difficult for lower wage earners. Aid from the state of California is not a long-term solution. Riverside has therefore accelerated its plans for downtown revitalization and appears dedicated to developing the city into a commercial and industrial center. Arson (highest) and air pollution (3rd highest) are additional problems facing Riverside. However, other crimes are average, and the city's police (6th most costly) and medical programs are strong.

| Title | City Rank | Total Cities Ranked |
|---|---|---|
| Largest Cities (Area) | 58 | (100) |
| Overall Air Quality, PSI (1981) | 3 | 51 |
| Biggest Cities (Population) | 82 | (100) |
| Births | 76 | (92) |
| City per Capita Income | 58 | (100) |
| Cost of Living | 16 | (62) |
| City Retail Sales per Capita | 32 | (100) |
| Unemployment Rates | 10 | (77) |
| Dependence on State Aid | 17 | (100) |
| Housing Growth/Population Growth | 44 | (55) |
| Daily Community Hospital Cost | 28 | (75) |
| Death Rates | 66 | (98) |
| Total Crimes | 51 | (96) |
| Cost per Police Employee | 6 | (71) |
| Arson | 1 | (78) |
| Spending per Resident on Education | 70 | (72) |
| Library Budgets | * | (99) |

*City not listed in table.

# Rochester

Rochester, the 3rd largest city in New York, is situated on Lake Ontario, with good access to the transportation advantages of the Great Lakes and the St. Lawrence Seaway. This location contributes to the good air quality

(3rd lowest in terms of pollution) and makes Rochester one of the most attractive of American cities. City officials are attempting to improve the area's amenities through downtown revitalization and beautification of the St. Lawrence River area. The rebuilding of downtown plazas is also directed at residents who do much of their shopping outside of Rochester in the city's large metro area. Rochester's retail sales per capita are low (10th lowest). Residents have been inclined to move to suburban locations because of Rochester's high crime rate (19th highest) and the 12th highest arson rate in the country. The Eastman Kodak Company is the biggest employer in the city. An extraordinary 30 percent of all factory workers work for Kodak. A decrease in sales, however, forced Kodak to lay off more than 1,500 workers in early 1983. Xerox is another major employer. Rochester is a noted educational center, home to over five universities, RIT and the University of Rochester being the most notable.

| Title | City Rank | Total Cities Ranked |
|---|---|---|
| Largest Cities (Area) | 90 | (100) |
| Overall Air Quality, PSI (1981) | 48 | (51) |
| Biggest Cities (Population) | 57 | (100) |
| Births | 13 | (92) |
| City per Capita Income | 67 | (100) |
| Cost of Living | * | (62) |
| City Retail Sales per Capita | 91 | (100) |
| Unemployment Rates | 52 | (77) |
| Dependence on State Aid | 26 | (100) |
| Housing Growth/Population Growth | * | (55) |
| Daily Community Hospital Cost | 37 | (75) |
| Death Rates | 12 | (98) |
| Total Crimes | 19 | (96) |
| Cost per Police Employee | * | (71) |
| Arson | 12 | (78) |
| Spending per Resident on Education | * | (72) |
| Library Budgets | 10 | (99) |

*City not listed in table.

## Sacramento

Sacramento is located at the confluence of the Sacramento and American Rivers, in the heart of agriculturally rich eastern California. The capital of California, it is also a transportation center for the West Coast, as two main intercontinental railways (Southern and Western Pacific) converge on it. The high death rate (4th highest) and high birthrate (18th) indicate a high median age (12th highest) as well as young people moving to a city with a large elderly population. Sacramento has a diverse economy, producing goods ranging from food to military hardware.

Mather and McClellan Air Force Bases and the Sacramento Army Depot are all situated in the Sacramento area. The city is one of the most rapidly expanding in the nation and has a high per capita income (4th highest). Living in the capital is not all positive, however, as the crime rate is high (8th). The cost of living is also above average (22nd).

| Title | City Rank | Total Cities Ranked |
|---|---|---|
| Largest Cities (Area) | 44 | (100) |
| Overall Air Quality, PSI (1981) | * | (51) |
| Biggest Cities (Population) | 52 | (100) |
| Births | 18 | (92) |
| City per Capita Income | 4 | (100) |
| Cost of Living | 22 | (62) |
| City Retail Sales per Capita | 62 | (100) |
| Unemployment Rates | 20 | (77) |
| Dependence on State Aid | 60 | (100) |
| Housing Growth/Population Growth | 26 | (55) |
| Daily Community Hospital Cost | 5 | (75) |
| Death Rates | 4 | (98) |
| Total Crimes | 8 | (96) |
| Cost per Police Employee | * | (71) |
| Arson | 22 | (78) |
| Spending per Resident on Education | * | (72) |
| Library Budgets | 58 | (99) |

*City not listed in table.

## St. Louis

St. Louis is one of the nation's leading industrial centers and serves as the 4th most important headquarters city for *Fortune* 500 corporations. Among the major industries based in St. Louis are transportation construction (air/rail), chemicals, steel, agriculture and food processing. In the decade from 1970 to 1980, the city's population declined drastically, by more than 27 percent—from over 622,000 to 453,000. St. Louis' nickname—"Gateway to the West"—has been particularly appropriate in recent years, as many younger St. Louis residents have been moving through the gate to new homes further west. The high emigration rates leaves an older population that has the 2nd highest death rate in the nation. The city's location in the heart of the Midwest and on the Mississippi River makes it an important trucking, rail and river transport center. St. Louis has a large and diversified labor force, which includes skilled, semiskilled and unskilled labor. Overall, its per capita income ranks 17th lowest. This relatively low income, together with high unemployment, accounts for the city's low retail sales per capita (20th lowest). Opportunities for future growth in St. Louis depend on the city's ability—demonstrated in the past—to attract capital investment targeted to specific labor requirements that take advantage of the relatively low cost of such labor in the area.

| Title | City Rank | Total Cities Ranked |
|---|---|---|
| Largest Cities (Area) | 62 | (100) |
| Overall Air Quality, PSI (1981) | 17 | (51) |
| Biggest Cities (Population) | 26 | (100) |
| Births | 40 | (92) |
| City per Capita Income | 84 | (100) |
| Cost of Living | 53 | (62) |
| City Retail Sales per Capita | 81 | (100) |
| Unemployment Rates | 23 | (77) |
| Dependence on State Aid | 61 | (100) |
| Housing Growth/Population Growth | * | (55) |
| Daily Community Hospital Cost | 53 | (75) |
| Death Rates | 2 | (98) |
| Total Crimes | 6 | (96) |
| Cost per Police Employee | * | (71) |
| Arson | * | (78) |
| Spending per Resident on Education | 35 | (72) |
| Library Budgets | 27 | (99) |

*City not listed in table.

## St. Paul

St. Paul, the smaller of the "Twin Cities" of Minneapolis and St. Paul, had a 1980 population of over 270,000 and dropped 8 places in rank to 54th, after experiencing a population loss of nearly 13 percent between 1970 and 1980. Most of the population loss may be attributed to suburbanization, although its impact on central city finances is moderated by the area's innovative tax pooling system. St. Paul is the state capital of Minnesota and is a center for state and local government as well as many federal offices (district offices of the FCC, IRS and Immigration and Naturalization Service as well as other major offices, including the Department of Agriculture and the Department of Defense). Several *Fortune* 500 corporations are headquartered in St. Paul, among them Minnesota Mining and Manufacturing, Economics Laboratory, American Hoist & Derrick, Deluxe Check Printers and Farmers Union Central Exchange. It is also headquarters for Burlington Northern Railroad and West Publishing, the world's largest law book publisher. New construction, centered around Town Square, totaled $298 million just in the three-year period from 1978 to 1980, bolstering the economy in the downtown area. In addition, five major industrial parks are located in St. Paul, and a new development, Metro Center '85, will add 15,600 permanent jobs and generate $400 million in new private investment in St. Paul by 1990.

| Title | City Rank | Total Cities Ranked |
|---|---|---|
| Largest Cities (Area) | 71 | (100) |
| Overall Air Quality, PSI (1981) | 12 | (51) |
| Biggest Cities (Population) | 54 | (100) |
| Births | * | (92) |
| City per Capita Income | 37 | (100) |
| Cost of Living | 10 | (62) |
| City Retail Sales per Capita | 66 | (100) |
| Unemployment Rates | 63 | (77) |
| Dependence on State Aid | 32 | (100) |
| Housing Growth/Population Growth | 30 | (55) |
| Daily Community Hospital Cost | 50 | (75) |
| Death Rates | 33 | (98) |
| Total Crimes | 62 | (96) |
| Cost per Police Employee | 18 | (71) |
| Arson | 36 | (78) |
| Spending per Resident on Education | 10 | (72) |
| Library Budgets | 24 | (99) |

*City not listed in table.

## St. Petersburg

Located on the southern peninsula of Tampa Bay, St. Petersburg is a major tourist, recreation and convention center on Florida's west coast. Its economic base is diversified by the production of military communications equipment, electronics, jewelry manufacturing and utilities. It is a favorite retirement spot for elderly people from the northeast. The large number of retired and semi-retired people in St. Petersburg contribute to the relatively low per capita income, as these people are generally living on fixed retirement incomes and, if they work, occupy low-paid, part-time jobs. St. Petersburg's population growth depends substantially on immigration. It has grown in the 1970s by 9.6 percent, from about 216,000 in 1970 to 237,000 in 1980, making it the 58th largest city in the United States. St. Petersburg is also constrained by its relatively small sized land area (57 square miles, 68th largest). The city's recreational facilities include water sports, jai alai, horse racing, and professional baseball. St. Petersburg has excellent hospital facilities. St. Petersburg's major Waterfront Plan will cover an area of 340 acres on Tampa Bay including the airport and port area. This area includes nearly eight miles of shoreline and represents a public investment of over $70 million.

| Title | City Rank | Total Cities Ranked |
|---|---|---|
| Largest Cities (Area) | 68 | (100) |
| Overall Air Quality, PSI (1981) | 49 | (51) |
| Biggest Cities (Population) | 58 | (100) |

| Title | City Rank | Total Cities Ranked |
|---|---|---|
| Births | 8 | (92) |
| City per Capita Income | 74 | (100) |
| Cost of Living | * | (62) |
| City Retail Sales per Capita | 67 | (100) |
| Unemployment Rates | 42 | (77) |
| Dependence on State Aid | 56 | (100) |
| Housing Growth/Population Growth | * | (55) |
| Daily Community Hospital Cost | * | (75) |
| Death Rates | 1 | (98) |
| Total Index Crimes | 56 | (96) |
| Cost per Police Employee | 31 | (71) |
| Arson | 47 | (78) |
| Spending per Resident on Education | 54 | (72) |
| Library Budgets | 85 | (99) |

*City not listed in table.

## Salt Lake City

Despite being the center of the Mormon religion, whose adherents are noted for having large families, Salt Lake City has lost slightly more than 7 percent of its residents in 1970–80, dropping its 1980 census rank to 90th, compared to its 1970 ranking of 74th. An explanation is that during the same period, the population of suburban areas of Salt Lake County has grown 35 percent. Although the city's population dropped, its housing units grew nearly 11 percent in 1970–80. Total construction—which includes new dwelling units, additions, renovations and nonresidential construction—increased nearly 62 percent in 1980–81. The overall outlook for Salt Lake City is continued growth and prosperity. Its high birthrate (2nd in the United States) will underpin retail sales and additional construction. Unemployment, which was moderate at the end of 1982, should continue to be below the national average.

| Title | City Rank | Total Cities Ranked |
|---|---|---|
| Largest Cities (Area) | 82 | (100) |
| Overall Air Quality, PSI (1981) | 16 | (51) |
| Biggest Cities (Population) | 90 | (100) |
| Births | 2 | (92) |
| City per Capita Income | 62 | (100) |
| Cost of Living | 33 | (62) |
| City Retail Sales per Capita | 12 | (100) |
| Unemployment Rates | 49 | (77) |
| Dependence on State Aid | 84 | (100) |
| Housing Growth/Population Growth | 22 | (55) |
| Daily Community Hospital Cost | 17 | (75) |
| Death Rates | 42 | (98) |
| Total Crimes | 11 | (96) |
| Cost per Police Employee | 25 | (71) |

| Title | City Rank | Total Cities Ranked |
|---|---|---|
| Arson | 67 | (78) |
| Spending per Resident on Education | 51 | (72) |
| Library Budgets | 26 | (99) |

*City not listed in table.

## San Antonio

San Antonio's population increased by over 20 percent between 1970 and 1980, upping its rank from the 15th to the 11th largest city in the United States, with a population of over 785,000 in 1980. San Antonio is fortunate to have a diversified economy with strong bases in manufacturing, agriculture ($39 million in 1980 in cash receipts), government employment (five military installations with over 41,000 military personnel and nearly 30,000 civilian employees), medical facilities (over 11,300 employed by the South Texas Medical Center) and tourism. In addition, San Antonio's city government has embarked on a drive to make San Antonio the region's center for the development of electronics and related industries. Continued migration of workers to the South and Southwest from other countries and other U.S. regions is expected to increase the labor force in cities like San Antonio for years to come. San Antonio is using precise and intelligent planning to prepare for the influx of workers and job seekers and make them—and prospective new employers—welcome and smoothly absorbable into the city's vital economy. Mayor Henry Cisneros has earned a national reputation for his role in facilitating his city's economic development.

| Title | City Rank | Total Cities Ranked |
|---|---|---|
| Largest Cities (Area) | 16 | (100) |
| Overall Air Quality, PSI (1981) | * | (51) |
| Biggest Cities (Population) | 11 | (100) |
| Births | 30 | (92) |
| City per Capita Income | 82 | (100) |
| Cost of Living | 55 | (62) |
| City Retail Sales per Capita | 39 | (100) |
| Unemployment Rates | 70 | (77) |
| Dependence on State Aid | 89 | (100) |
| Housing Growth/Population Growth | 45 | (55) |
| Daily Community Hospital Cost | 71 | (75) |
| Death Rates | 75 | (98) |
| Total Crimes | 69 | (96) |
| Cost per Police Employee | 44 | (71) |
| Arson | 45 | (78) |
| Spending per Resident on Education | 68 | (72) |
| Library Budgets | 96 | (99) |

*City not listed in table.

## San Diego

The city of San Diego has been experiencing a steady rise in population—averaging a 20 percent increase over each of the last two decades. The trend promises to continue throughout the remainder of the century. Current construction in the city is devoted largely to office buildings, while the housing stock continues to grow in the surrounding suburban areas. The drive to create industrial and commercial areas near the city will bolster the city's rosy economic outlook. San Diego has the 3rd highest cost of living. Daily hospital costs are 9th highest in the United States. In spite of these indicators, San Diego lags in retail sales per capita and average city per capita income (36th), probably because a lot of its residents are moderately paid personnel attached to the naval base. San Diego is the 8th largest city in terms of population, but it has a relatively low total index crime rate—77th out of 96.

| Title | City Rank | Total Cities Ranked |
|---|---|---|
| Largest Cities (Area) | 11 | (100) |
| Overall Air Quality, PSI (1981) | 6 | (51) |
| Biggest Cities (Population) | 8 | (100) |
| Births | 88 | (92) |
| City per Capita Income | 36 | (100) |
| Cost of Living | 3 | (62) |
| City Retail Sales per Capita | 73 | (100) |
| Unemployment Rates | 28 | (77) |
| Dependence on State Aid | 49 | (100) |
| Housing Growth/Population Growth | 50 | (55) |
| Daily Community Hospital Costs | 9 | (75) |
| Death Rates | 80 | (98) |
| Total Crimes | 77 | (96) |
| Cost per Police Employee | 46 | (71) |
| Arson | 58 | (78) |
| Spending per Resident on Education | 34 | (72) |
| Library Budgets | 74 | (99) |

*City not listed in table.

## San Francisco

Despite the decline of many other older U.S. cities, San Francisco has not experienced any significant downturn. This can be attributed primarily to the city's diversified and expanding economy. San Francisco is the financial hub of America's West. It is home to America's largest bank, the Bank of America. It is also one of the West Coast's major seaports. Outlying areas have developed major computer industries that have made the Bay Area the principal region for development of American high technology. One of the problems that have accompanied this growth is a relatively high cost of living, pricing some areas out of the reach of many working-class families. San Francisco remains the cultural center of the West Coast, with a major symphony orchestra and an opera company. It is famous for its tourist attractions (Chinatown, Fisherman's Wharf, the Golden Gate Bridge, the cable cars and bay views) and its restaurants. With the 13th largest city population, San Francisco has the 15th smallest city area, making it one of the densest of cities. Its air quality is the 6th best of the 51 largest cities. Its per capita income is 16th.

| Title | City Rank | Total Cities Ranked |
|---|---|---|
| Largest Cities (Area) | 86 | (100) |
| Overall Air Quality, PSI (1981) | 45 | (51) |
| Biggest Cities (Population) | 13 | (100) |
| Births | 20 | (92) |
| City per Capita Income | 16 | (100) |
| Cost of Living | * | (62) |
| City Retail Sales per Capita | 35 | (100) |
| Unemployment Rates | 47 | (77) |
| Dependence on State Aid | 25 | (100) |
| Housing Growth/Population Growth | * | (55) |
| Daily Community Hospital Cost | 4 | (75) |
| Death Rates | * | (98) |
| Total Crimes | 30 | (96) |
| Cost per Police Employee | 5 | (71) |
| Arson | 48 | (78) |
| Spending per Resident on Education | * | (72) |
| Library Budgets | 17 | (99) |

*City not listed in table.

## San Jose

San Jose has increased its population since 1970 by over 38 percent, becoming the 16th largest city in the United States after having been 29th in 1970. In that same 10-year period, 7,000 new jobs were created in San Jose. An additional 10,000–12,000 jobs are projected for the city by 1990. Like many other cities faced with huge population increases, San Jose in 1979 formed a Downtown Development Corporation to advise about and oversee future growth and development in the city. One of the new construction efforts in the downtown area is the San Antonio Plaza, a $200 million project that is expected to be completed in 1985. An additional $100 million is targeted for improvement of Park Center Plaza. Urban renewal is also planned for the downtown area in conjunction with mass transit improvements. Located in the high-technology "Silicon Valley," San Jose has a bright economic outlook, although cost competition in the computer industry is encouraging manufacturers to make electronic components overseas. San Jose has the 2nd highest cost of living in the United States and the 8th highest per capita income. Daily hospital costs are the 8th highest in the nation.

| Title | City Rank | Total Cities Ranked |
|---|---|---|
| Largest Cities (Area) | 26 | (100) |
| Overall Air Quality, PSI (1981) | * | (51) |
| Biggest Cities (Population) | 16 | (100) |
| Births | 46 | (92) |
| City per Capita Income | 8 | (100) |
| Cost of Living | 2 | (62) |
| City Retail Sales per Capita | 72 | (100) |
| Unemployment Rates | 44 | (77) |
| Dependence on State Aid | 58 | (100) |
| Housing Growth/Population Growth | 52 | (55) |
| Daily Community Hospital Cost | 8 | (75) |
| Death Rates | * | (98) |
| Total Crimes | 60 | (96) |
| Cost per Police Employee | 14 | (71) |
| Arson | 4 | (78) |
| Spending per Resident on Education | * | (72) |
| Library Budgets | 67 | (99) |

*City not listed in table.

## Santa Ana

Santa Ana is the 68th largest city in the United States, with a 1980 population of nearly 204,000. It is located just southeast of Anaheim. Its population increased in the 1970s by nearly 31 percent. One reason is that Santa Ana had the nation's highest birthrate (4.8 per 100 residents), reflecting the youthful average age of the population (27.1 years—8th lowest) and the high proportion (44.5 percent) of Hispanics (5th highest), who tend to have larger families than average. Another reason for growth is that people are attracted to the city because its broad-based economy provides jobs for both skilled and unskilled workers. Santa Ana's diverse economy is represented by manufacturing, transportation, finance, retail and service firms as well as government agencies. Major manufacturers include AMF-Voit, ITT Canon Electric, Lear Siegler Instruments, EECO and Kawasaki Motors Corp. (USA). One-fifth of all those employed in manufacturing are in aerospace. Santa Ana's Community Redevelopment Agency is dedicated to keeping the downtown area vital and has been successful in attracting substantial private investment for the construction of new office space, retail space and new housing (700 units in the downtown area in 1981). Rehabilitation and general renovation in the 89-block downtown area will stimulate economic development in conjunction with community development and redevelopment plans.

| Title | City Rank | Total Cities Ranked |
|---|---|---|
| Largest Cities (Area) | 95 | (100) |
| Overall Air Quality, PSI (1981) | 5 | (51) |
| Biggest Cities (Population) | 68 | (100) |
| Births | 1 | (92) |
| City per Capita Income | 26 | (100) |
| Cost of Living | * | (62) |
| City Retail Sales per Capita | 28 | (100) |
| Unemployment Rates | * | (77) |
| Dependence on State Aid | 50 | (100) |
| Housing Growth/Population Growth | * | (55) |
| Daily Community Hospital Cost | * | (75) |
| Death Rates | 85 | (98) |
| Total Crimes | 37 | (96) |
| Cost per Police Employee | 15 | (71) |
| Arson | 55 | (78) |
| Spending per Resident on Education | 36 | (72) |
| Library Budgets | 31 | (99) |

*City not listed in table.

## Seattle

Seattle, the business and financial center of America's Northwest, is the 23rd most populous city in the United States, with nearly 500,000 residents. Its 7 percent loss in population in the 1970s may be attributed to emigration to the surrounding suburbs, the population of which outnumbers Seattle residents 2 to 1. Its economy depends on lumber, manufacturing (including a major aerospace component) and port revenues. The port of Seattle is the 2nd largest handler of container cargo in the country (over 21 million tons in 1980). City per capita income is 29th, and retail sales per capita are 22nd. Seattle's well-off residents continue to shop downtown. The Seattle economy is heavily dependent on the aerospace industry, which is closely linked to the state of the American economy and the ability of Seattle firms to sell their aircraft overseas in a highly competitive market. The Seattle economy, especially heavy manufacturing, was therefore seriously hurt by the 1981–82 recession, with an unemployment rate of about 11 percent. Seattle is focusing on its budget problems and is attempting to create a stronger fiscal environment for the future. Seattle plans to examine the effects of population movement, growth in economies (city and state), households and other factors in an attempt to make city budgets more responsive to these factors. Dependence on state aid was moderate—less than 10 percent of the city's general revenue. Seattle spends heavily for its libraries (4th highest budget).

| Title | City Rank | Total Cities Ranked |
|---|---|---|
| Largest Cities (Area) | 45 | (100) |
| Overall Air Quality, PSI (1981) | 13 | (51) |
| Biggest Cities (Population) | 23 | (100) |
| Births | 86 | (92) |
| City per Capita Income | 29 | (100) |
| Cost of Living | * | (62) |
| City Retail Sales per Capita | 22 | (100) |
| Unemployment Rates | 27 | (77) |
| Dependence on State Aid | 68 | (100) |
| Housing Growth/Population Growth | * | (55) |
| Daily Community Hospital Cost | 24 | (75) |
| Death Rates | 31 | (98) |
| Total Crimes | 19 | (96) |
| Cost per Police Employee | 19 | (71) |
| Arson | 52 | (78) |
| Spending per Resident on Education | * | (72) |
| Library Budgets | 4 | (99) |

*City not listed in table.

## Shreveport

Shreveport is the 3rd biggest city in Louisiana and the 67th most populous in the nation. Louisiana's low corporate income taxes have benefited the city and have successfully stimulated the movement of many industries to it. Western Electric (communications equipment manufacturing) is the largest employer in the area, with over 6,000 workers. Other major firms in Shreveport include ARKLA Inc. (natural gas, motor fuels and industrial chemicals), Crystal Oil Company and Transcontinental Energy Corp. Unemployment in the city at the end of 1982 was above average (21st highest). The cost of living is surprisingly high (14th). Residents of the city are compensated, however, by low hospital costs (7th lowest) and a significant budget allocation to public education (18th highest). Judging by the cost of police employees, municipal workers are not lavishly compensated.

| Title | City Rank | Total Cities Ranked |
|---|---|---|
| Largest Cities (Area) | 42 | (100) |
| Overall Air Quality, PSI (1981) | * | (51) |
| Biggest Cities (Population) | 67 | (100) |
| Births | 28 | (92) |
| City per Capita Income | 55 | (100) |
| Cost of Living | 14 | (62) |
| City Retail Sales per Capita | 41 | (100) |
| Unemployment Rates | 21 | (77) |
| Dependence on State Aid | 82 | (100) |
| Housing Growth/Population Growth | * | (55) |
| Daily Community Hospital Cost | 69 | (75) |
| Death Rates | 40 | (98) |

| Title | City Rank | Total Cities Ranked |
|---|---|---|
| Total Crimes | 70 | (96) |
| Cost per Police Employee | 67 | (71) |
| Arson | 40 | (78) |
| Spending per Resident on Education | 18 | (72) |
| Library Budgets | 83 | (99) |

*City not listed in table.

## Spokane

Spokane's population is second only to Seattle's in Washington state and is 82nd nationwide. Its high death rate (29th) and low birthrate (67th) suggest an elderly downtown population. The city has a strong agricultural and manufacturing base. It is the center for exports of forest products from the prosperous Inland Empire Region of the Northwest. In the late 1970s and early 1980s, when key mining industries curtailed production because of declining auto and (for a while) defense spending, Spokane suffered considerable unemployment (17th highest). Despite hard times, spending on public employees remains high. Relative to population, Spokane's chief executive in 1981 was the 8th highest paid. Police spending is high (7th), although arsons are low and total crimes are average. City officials are looking to new commercial construction to bring employment back up, with overall economic recovery taking up the slack in the longer term.

| Title | City Rank | Total Cities Ranked |
|---|---|---|
| Largest Cities (Area) | 76 | (100) |
| Overall Air Quality, PSI (1981) | 32 | (51) |
| Biggest Cities (Population) | 82 | (100) |
| Births | 67 | (92) |
| City per Capita Income | 28 | (100) |
| Cost of Living | * | (62) |
| City Retail Sales per Capita | 26 | (100) |
| Unemployment Rates | 17 | (77) |
| Dependence on State Aid | 38 | (100) |
| Housing Growth/Population Growth | 33 | (55) |
| Daily Community Hospital Cost | 29 | (75) |
| Death Rates | 29 | (98) |
| Total Crimes | 47 | (96) |
| Cost per Police Employee | 7 | (71) |
| Arson | 61 | (78) |
| Spending per Resident on Education | * | (72) |
| Library Budgets | 60 | (99) |

*City not listed in table.

# Syracuse

Syracuse declined in population by nearly 14 percent in the 1970s, making it the 86th largest city in the United States (down from 66th), with a population of 170,000. Like many other northeastern industrial cities, Syracuse was greatly affected by the 1981–82 recession. The city had to cut back on income-augmenting programs and focus on savings in other areas to maintain such programs as much as possible. In 1981 the Department of Public Works became the nation's first municipal owner of a drum-mix asphalt manufacturing plant. At a repair rate of 20 miles of street a year, the asphalt plant investment of $1.5 million will be recovered within four years. Syracuse has taken an innovative approach to housing by converting three city schools into homes for the elderly. Urban industrial parks are planned to make better use of existing buildings, refurbished to accommodate various small industrial plants and processes. Other downtown construction includes the expansion of the Hotel Syracuse and the companion development of a block of South Salina Street. Syracuse is a center for education, with Syracuse University (over 21,000 students), the State University of New York's Upstate Medical Center (1,000) and three community colleges. Crime programs in Syracuse have been directed at updating police services, introducing neighborhood watch units, zone patrolling and deploying specialized crime units such as the street crime task forces during holiday seasons.

| Title | City Rank | Total Cities Ranked |
|---|---|---|
| Largest Cities (Area) | 96 | (100) |
| Overall Air Quality, PSI (1981) | * | (51) |
| Biggest Cities (Population) | 86 | (100) |
| Births | 69 | (92) |
| City per Capita Income | 70 | (100) |
| Cost of Living | 58 | (62) |
| City Retail Sales per Capita | 87 | (100) |
| Unemployment Rates | 44 | (77) |
| Dependence on State Aid | 14 | (100) |
| Housing Growth/Population Growth | * | (55) |
| Daily Community Hospital Cost | 42 | (75) |
| Death Rates | 14 | (98) |
| Total Crimes | 61 | (96) |
| Cost per Police Employee | * | (71) |
| Arson | * | (78) |
| Spending per Resident on Education | 31 | (72) |
| Library Budgets | 64 | (99) |

*City not listed in table.

# Tacoma

Tacoma prides itself on its stability. Dependent on revenues from the wood and pulp product industries of the Pacific Northwest, it has sought to diversify its economic base to cushion the boom-and-bust cycle of these industries. It receives substantial revenues from the transportation manufacturing industries in the region as well as the military bases located throughout the area. Tacoma's population of 158,500 in 1980 represents growth of nearly 3 percent over 1970, attributable primarily to natural growth (more births than deaths), not immigration. Tacoma has invested heavily in economic development projects to entice industry, commerce, trade and tourism. It is in the process of undergoing a major downtown revitalization and building a large sports facility, the Tacoma Dome.

| Title | City Rank | Total Cities Ranked |
|---|---|---|
| Largest Cities (Area) | 84 | (100) |
| Overall Air Quality, PSI (1981) | * | (51) |
| Biggest Cities (Population) | 96 | (100) |
| Births | 63 | (92) |
| City per Capita Income | 80 | (100) |
| Cost of Living | 16 | (62) |
| City Retail Sales per Capita | 18 | (100) |
| Unemployment Rates | 12 | (77) |
| Dependence on State Aid | 41 | (100) |
| Housing Growth/Population Growth | * | (55) |
| Daily Community Hospital Cost | 47 | (75) |
| Death Rates | 39 | (98) |
| Total Crimes | 36 | (96) |
| Cost per Police Employee | 11 | (71) |
| Arson | 14 | (78) |
| Spending per Resident on Education | 2 | (72) |
| Library Budgets | 5 | (99) |

*City not listed in table.

# Tampa

Tampa's 1980 population was nearly 272,000, making it the 53rd largest city in the United States. A small population loss of slightly more than 2 percent since 1970 may be attributed to a population shift to surrounding suburban areas rather than emigration. The suburban share of the population for the metro area comprising Tampa and St. Petersburg, located across Tampa Bay, is 68 percent. Tampa is located on one of the best-protected natural harbors in the world, and its port facilities add greatly to the economic base of the area. Nearly 49 million tons of cargo passed through Tampa in 1980, making it the 9th largest port in the nation. The city benefits from its attractions as a tourist center as well. Mild winters and a temperature range of about 20 degrees make Tampa attractive to retirees as well as visitors. Tampa is also an industrial city, manufacturing and processing such diverse goods as electronic components, phosphates and fertilizer, seafood, retail goods and nuclear steam generators. Tampa's Downtown Development Authority has ambitious plans for the city's growth. By 1990 it hopes to increase downtown office space by 4.5 million square feet, increase the number of first-class hotel rooms from less than 1,000 to 3,000, add approximately 4,100 downtown residential units and increase retail sales by $180 million. The total investment of over $163 million in construction in 1981 and the $338 million slated for 1982 indicate the tremendous growth in the city's downtown area. The biggest project, Harbour Island—a proposed office, hotel, residential, retail and recreation complex—is due to be completed in 1994 at a cost of $1 billion. It is designed to provide housing for 14,000 residents and jobs for 6,000 by the year 2000.

| Title | City Rank | Total Cities Ranked |
|---|---|---|
| Largest Cities (Area) | 50 | (100) |
| Overall Air Quality, PSI (1981) | 49 | (51) |
| Biggest Cities (Population) | 53 | (100) |
| Births | 11 | (92) |
| City per Capita Income | 85 | (100) |
| Cost of Living | * | (62) |
| City Retail Sales per Capita | 9 | (100) |
| Unemployment Rates | 42 | (77) |
| Dependence on State Aid | 64 | (100) |
| Housing Growth/Population Growth | 43 | (55) |
| Daily Community Hospital Cost | 66 | (75) |
| Death Rates | 16 | (98) |
| Total Crimes | 2 | (96) |
| Cost per Police Employee | 30 | (71) |
| Arson | 39 | (78) |
| Spending per Resident on Education | 43 | (72) |
| Library Budgets | 73 | (99) |

*City not listed in table.

## Toledo

Toledo suffered a population loss of over 7 percent in the 1970s and consequently dropped in rank from 34th to 40th, with a 1980 population of nearly 355,000. Toledo is the major trading center for northwestern Ohio and southeastern Michigan. Toledo is also known as the "glass capital of the world," with such *Fortune* 500 headquarters as Owens-Illinois, Libbey-Owens-Ford and Owens-Corning Fiberglas providing jobs for nearly

12,000. Two major refineries operated by Sohio and Sunoco process more than 8 million barrels of crude oil a month. The city is also a rail transportation center, with more than 1,200 miles of track in the city alone. In addition, more than 100 motor freight companies are located in Toledo. Another important source of income to Toledo and the surrounding area is the Port of Toledo, which handled more than 22 million tons in 1980. The Port Authority oversees development of the Toledo Express Airport as well as the port; it is a self-contained agency with local government powers and maintains staffing in the areas of finance, trade and development, legal, marketing and engineering, and coordinates with the city the development of those areas. City per capita income is high (27th), but retail sales are low (75th), suggesting that the downtown area is losing sales to suburban shopping areas. Toledo took immediate action to cut its municipal spending, going so far as to reduce its refuse collection service frequency to once a fortnight. Residents were advised to add vinegar to the plastic garbage bags to keep dogs and rodents away from the bags during the wait for service. Toledo's relatively high housing growth/population growth ranking (25th) suggests that ample good housing is available for those planning to live and work in Toledo. The city is well poised to take advantage of national economic recovery.

| Title | City Rank | Total Cities Ranked |
|---|---|---|
| Largest Cities (Area) | 49 | (100) |
| Overall Air Quality, PSI (1981) | 31 | (51) |
| Biggest Cities (Population) | 40 | (100) |
| Births | 55 | (92) |
| City per Capita Income | 27 | (100) |
| Cost of Living | * | (62) |
| City Retail Sales per Capita | 75 | (100) |
| Unemployment Rates | 7 | (77) |
| Dependence on State Aid | 71 | (100) |
| Housing Growth/Population Growth | 26 | (55) |
| Daily Community Hospital Cost | 12 | (75) |
| Death Rates | 35 | (98) |
| Total Crimes | 40 | (96) |
| Cost per Police Employee | 45 | (71) |
| Arson | 7 | (78) |
| Spending per Resident on Education | 59 | (72) |
| Library Budgets | 12 | (99) |

*City not listed in table.

## Tucson

Tucson's population grew by nearly 26 percent in the 1970s, making it the 45th largest city in the United States. During that decade, the Tucson metro area grew even faster—over 51 percent. The impact has been an economic boon to the city and to the area. The new Tucson residents are not mostly retirees. The average age is 29.1—lower than the national average of 30.2. The colleges and universities in Tucson as well as several vocational schools provide an ample pool of workers with a broad range of skills. Major employers in the Tucson area are government, wholesale and retail trade, services and manufacturing. Construction workers, miners and those employed by public utilities or communications or transportation companies fill out the work force. Tucson has 25 industrial parks, in which major firms like National Semiconductor, Hughes Aircraft and Gates Learjet maintain manufacturing facilities. Tucson also has a Foreign Trade Zone, allowing many industries to pay lower tax on goods processed or assembled in it. Housing growth/population growth is 9th highest in the country, encompassing single-family, condominium and town house construction. In addition, home owners in Tucson are sinking money into home improvements (60 percent made improvements in 1980), meaning that Tucson residents are staying put rather than moving out. Total index crimes are 22nd—relatively high for a city of its size, and arsons are 10th highest.

| Title | City Rank | Total Cities Ranked |
|---|---|---|
| Largest Cities (Area) | 39 | (100) |
| Overall Air Quality, PSI (1981) | 43 | (51) |
| Biggest Cities (Population) | 45 | (100) |
| Births | 62 | (92) |
| City per Capita Income | 68 | (100) |
| Cost of Living | * | (62) |
| City Retail Sales per Capita | 46 | (100) |
| Unemployment Rates | 33 | (77) |
| Dependence on State Aid | 30 | (100) |
| Housing Growth/Population Growth | 9 | (55) |
| Daily Community Hospital Cost | 20 | (75) |
| Death Rates | 62 | (98) |
| Total Crimes | 22 | (96) |
| Cost per Police Employee | 47 | (71) |
| Arson | 10 | (78) |
| Spending per Resident on Education | 48 | (72) |
| Library Budgets | 39 | (99) |

*City not listed in table.

# Tulsa

Tulsa managed to weather the recession through 1982 because of its diverse economic base. Although unemployment increased during 1982, it was still relatively low. Energy companies and related businesses such as drilling and equipment suppliers as well as fertilizer pro-

ducers are large employers in the Tulsa area. Manufacturing jobs have continued to increase—up over 5 percent from the 4th quarter of 1980 through the 4th quarter of 1981. Certain occupations are in large demand in Tulsa—engineering, computer programming, production and health services. Tulsa is performing slightly better than Oklahoma City in overall economic terms. Retail sales are quite a bit higher in Tulsa (3rd in the United States versus 13th in Oklahoma City). Tulsa has a lower per capita income (40th vs. 13th) and a slightly less expensive cost of living (29th vs. 25th) than Oklahoma City. Although it lost ground in 1982, Tulsa is an attractive city economically.

| Title | City Rank | Total Cities Ranked |
|---|---|---|
| Largest Cities (Area) | 24 | (100) |
| Overall Air Quality, PSI (1981) | 38 | (51) |
| Biggest Cities (Population) | 37 | (100) |
| Births | 59 | (92) |
| City per Capita Income | 40 | (100) |
| Cost of Living | 29 | (62) |
| City Retail Sales per Capita | 3 | (100) |
| Unemployment Rates | 64 | (77) |
| Dependence on State Aid | 90 | (100) |
| Housing Growth/Population Growth | 34 | (55) |
| Daily Community Hospital Cost | 41 | (75) |
| Death Rates | 64 | (98) |
| Total Crimes | 63 | (96) |
| Cost per Police Employee | * | (71) |
| Arson | 31 | (78) |
| Spending per Resident on Education | 50 | (72) |
| Library Budgets | 28 | (99) |

*City not listed in table.

# Virginia Beach

Virginia Beach is one of the fastest-growing cities in America and is taking pains to grow right. In the decade from 1970 to 1980, its population grew by more than half, lured by such attractions as its access to water and its low crime rate (5th lowest). While this growth was not as spectacular as Anchorage or Aurora—both more than doubled their populations in the same period—it still makes Virginia Beach the 11th fastest growing city in the United States. The 1981–82 recession, which cut into production and sales in many other cities, did not affect Virginia Beach as markedly. Its industry and tourism both generate revenue, broadening its economic base. The construction of a major mall, renovation and expansion of an existing mall, and new construction of office buildings in 1981 have all been undertaken in the face of cutbacks in other U.S. cities. Virginia Beach ranks second in housing growth/population growth in the 1970s. To ensure that growth and development will be consistent with the future growth of the city, Virginia Beach in 1979 adopted a comprehensive plan. Significant areas of concern are environmental protection, including water conservation and protection of the natural floodplain; continued development of a diversified and balanced economic base (tourism, military and retail/wholesale trade); zoning and increased emphasis on transportation and other public services.

| Title | City Rank | Total Cities Ranked |
|---|---|---|
| Largest Cities (Area) | 17 | (100) |
| Overall Air Quality, PSI (1981) | * | (51) |
| Biggest Cities (Population) | 56 | (100) |
| Births | 82 | (92) |
| City per Capita Income | 47 | (100) |
| Cost of Living | 35 | (62) |
| City Retail Sales per Capita | 69 | (100) |
| Unemployment Rates | * | (77) |
| Dependence on State Aid | 10 | (100) |
| Housing Growth/Population Growth | 2 | (55) |
| Daily Community Hospital Cost | * | (75) |
| Death Rates | 95 | (98) |
| Total Crimes | 92 | (96) |
| Cost per Police Employee | 66 | (71) |
| Arson | 62 | (78) |
| Spending per Resident on Education | 28 | (72) |
| Library Budgets | 62 | (99) |

*City not listed in table.

## Warren

Warren, located just north of the Detroit city limits, is the 92nd largest city in the United States, with a 1980 population of over 161,000. It has historically been a residential area for well-off Detroit auto employees. In 1970 the city had 132 black residents. During the 1970s, a net of 165 more blacks moved into the city, making 297 blacks. Warren is the only city of the 100 largest with under 1,000 black residents. The city having the next lowest number is Huntington Beach, with 1,218 blacks. As Warren has grown, it has become an industrial city and an automotive center in its own right. It is home to a number of the automotive giants' manufacturing and assembling facilities—among them Chevrolet, Chrysler, Dodge, General Motors and Volkswagen. Like Detroit and other cities heavily tied to the automotive industry, Warren suffered through the 1981–82 recession with high unemployment and a decline in retail sales. The upturn shown in auto sales in early 1983 has already begun to revive the city's economy. A trend toward ex-

pansion of the industrial base into electronics and defense contracting will help the city begin to depend less on the auto industry. City per capita income is above average (31st). Crime is low (78th).

| Title | City Rank | Total Cities Ranked |
|---|---|---|
| Largest Cities (Area) | 92 | (100) |
| Overall Air Quality, PSI (1981) | * | (51) |
| Biggest Cities (Population) | 92 | (100) |
| Births | * | (92) |
| City per Capita Income | 31 | (100) |
| Cost of Living | * | (62) |
| City Retail Sales per Capita | 55 | (100) |
| Unemployment Rates | * | (77) |
| Dependence on State Aid | 18 | (100) |
| Housing Growth/Population Growth | 10 | (55) |
| Daily Community Hospital Cost | 45 | (75) |
| Death Rates | 82 | (98) |
| Total Crimes | 78 | (96) |
| Cost per Police Employee | * | (71) |
| Arson | * | (78) |
| Spending per Resident on Education | * | (72) |
| Library Budgets | 66 | (99) |

*City not listed in table.

## Washington, D.C.

Washington, D.C.'s 1980 population declined significantly—nearly 16 percent between 1970 and 1980 to 637,651. However, Washington's metro area continued to grow, most startlingly on the Virginia side of the Potomac River, as new developments have spung up in Arlington, Alexandria and Crystal City, maintaining a trend toward suburbanization. Washington has historically been a creature of Congress and until the 1970s depended on congressional committees for its funding and authority. In 1975 Washington gained greater autonomy over its local affairs. Its new "home rule" status boosted the morale of the majority of Washington's population, which now plays a greater role in its future. In 1976 Washington's "metro"—a modern underground rail transportation system—began operation. Washington's major industry is administration and support for the federal government, although national associations and lobbies have been catching up as large area employers. Washington residents' per capita income ranks 10th. World-famous cultural attractions include the venerable Smithsonian Institution and Library of Congress as well as the newer Kennedy Center. Washington attracts a large number of tourists to such famed sites as the White House, Capitol Building, Washington Monument, Lincoln Memorial and Arlington Cemetery. While these tourists are a revenue source for Washington residents, they are also a service drain: blocking traffic, littering the streets and creating special needs for police.

| Title | City Rank | Total Cities Ranked |
|---|---|---|
| Largest Cities (Area) | 65 | (100) |
| Overall Air Quality, PSI (1981) | 23 | (51) |
| Biggest Cities (Population) | 15 | (100) |
| Births | 65 | (92) |
| City per Capita Income | 10 | (100) |
| Cost of Living | * | (62) |
| City Retail Sales per Capita | 79 | (100) |
| Unemployment Rates | 75 | (77) |
| Dependence on State Aid | 100 | (100) |
| Housing Growth/Population Growth | * | (55) |
| Daily Community Hospital Cost | * | (75) |
| Death Rates | 30 | (98) |
| Total Crimes | 29 | (96) |
| Cost per Police Employee | * | (71) |
| Arson | 42 | (78) |
| Spending per Resident on Education | 14 | (72) |
| Library Budgets | 11 | (99) |

*City not listed in table.

# Wichita

With over 279,000 residents in 1980, Wichita is the most populous city in Kansas. Its population has remained stable in the 1970s, growing by a mere 1 percent. Wichita's economy is centered almost entirely in general aviation aircraft manufacturing, which is the city's main employer. Among its major aircraft companies are Beech, Boeing, Cessna and Gates Learjet. The city's development as an aircraft center results from its location in the cereal-producing flatlands of central Kansas—a good place to try out airplanes in the early days of aviation. Other major industries that diversify Wichita's economy are agriculture, animal and food processing, minerals and raw materials. The Wichita commercial market is vital for the southern Kansas-northern Oklahoma region, and the city is a major highway, air and railroad junction for the midwestern region. Wichita has excellent educational and cultural facilties and is also a sports center, with professional teams in baseball, hockey and soccer. Wichita ranks in the middle (51st) in per capita income and in cost of living (28th).

| Title | City Rank | Total Cities Ranked |
|---|---|---|
| Largest Cities (Area) | 38 | (100) |
| Overall Air Quality, PSI (1981) | * | (51) |
| Biggest Cities (Population) | 51 | (100) |
| Births | 26 | (92) |
| City per Capita Income | 51 | (100) |
| Cost of Living | 28 | (62) |
| City Retail Sales per Capita | 17 | (100) |
| Unemployment Rates | 34 | (77) |
| Dependence on State Aid | 78 | (100) |
| Housing Growth/Population Growth | 41 | (55) |
| Daily Community Hospital Cost | 49 | (75) |
| Death Rates | 65 | (98) |
| Total Crimes | 50 | (96) |
| Cost per Police Employee | 42 | (71) |
| Arson | 37 | (78) |
| Spending per Resident on Education | 45 | (72) |
| Library Budgets | 52 | (99) |

*City not listed in table.

# Worcester

Worcester, with a population of nearly 162,000, is the 91st largest city in the country. Its population loss of more than 8 percent in the 1970s can be attributed to continuing suburbanization. Worcester has suffered along with other cities because of the 1981–82 recession and receives substantial state aid to help it cope (9th highest). However, an increasing number of people have begun to buy homes in the city, as shown by an upswing in single-family building permits. Also, Worcester's economy is diversified, with 3,500 manufacturing and nonmanufacturing firms in the city. It has a strong educational base, with 7 colleges and universities, including the medical school of the University of Massachusetts. The newly opened Centrum, a civic center designed to handle sporting events and performances, is expected to bring 1 million visitors to Worcester each year. The nearby Worcester Marriott Inn (also completed and opened in 1982) will provide a place for visitors to stay and will create additional new jobs. Already, low unemployment rates (24th lowest) in Worcester make this city a relatively attractive one for individuals concerned about job security. Its broad base will allow it to rebound quickly from the recession.

| Title | City Rank | Total Cities Ranked |
|---|---|---|
| Largest Cities (Area) | 89 | (100) |
| Overall Air Quality, PSI (1981) | * | (51) |
| Biggest Cities (Population) | 91 | (100) |

| Title | City Rank | Total Cities Ranked |
|---|---|---|
| Births | 16 | (92) |
| City per Capita Income | 65 | (100) |
| Cost of Living | * | (62) |
| City Retail Sales per Capita | 49 | (100) |
| Unemployment Rates | 54 | (77) |
| Dependence on State Aid | 9 | (100) |
| Housing Growth/Population Growth | * | (55) |
| Daily Community Hospital Cost | * | (75) |
| Death Rates | 15 | (98) |
| Total Crimes | * | (96) |
| Cost per Police Employee | 51 | (71) |
| Arson | * | (78) |
| Spending per Resident on Education | 44 | (72) |
| Library Budgets | 19 | (99) |

*City not listed in table.

# Yonkers

Located just north of New York City in southern Westchester County, Yonkers is very much intertwined with the economy of New York Ciy. A fairly dense city—ranking 73rd in overall population but only 98th in area of the 100 largest American cities—Yonkers retains some of its suburban qualities. Its population has fallen over 4 percent from 1970 to a little more than 195,000 in 1980. The city retains a population with a high per capita in come (7th). However, its closeness to New York City has had a negative impact on retail sales, as shoppers appear to go downtown for household commodities. Interestingly, Yonkers is one of the safest places to live, ranking 3rd lowest in total index crimes. The city's attraction to some higher-income residents and to elderly people helps maintain its stability. The fiscal crisis that Yonkers experienced in the mid-1970s stemmed from a combination of antiquated accounting and auditing practice and the determination of many local residents to cut taxes for what they believed were unwanted city services.

| Title | City Rank | Total Cities Ranked |
|---|---|---|
| Largest Cities (Area) | 98 | (100) |
| Overall Air Quality, PSI (1981) | * | (51) |
| Biggest Cities (Population) | 73 | (100) |
| Births | * | (92) |
| City per Capita Income | 7 | (100) |
| Cost of Living | * | (62) |
| City Retail Sales per Capita | 92 | (100) |
| Unemployment Rates | * | (77) |
| Dependence on State Aid | 27 | (100) |
| Housing Growth/Population Growth | * | (55) |
| Daily Community Hospital Cost | * | (75) |
| Death Rates | 44 | (98) |
| Total Crimes | 94 | (96) |
| Cost per Police Employee | * | (71) |
| Arson | 70 | (78) |
| Spending per Resident on Education | 23 | (72) |
| Library Budgets | 9 | (99) |

*City not listed in table.

# DEFINITIONS OF STANDARD METROPOLITAN STATISTICAL AREAS

The 87 standard metropolitan statistical area titles and definitions shown in this book are based on the definitions as listed in Standard Metropolitan Areas, 1975, Office of Management and Budget as amended to June 1981. Changes in area definitions due to additions or deletions since 1960 are indicated in parentheses.

**1. Akron, Ohio.** Consists of Portage and Summit Counties, Ohio. (Prior to 1964, definition excludes Portage County, Ohio)

**2. Albuquerque, New Mexico.** Consists of Bernalillo and Sandoval Counties, New Mexico (Prior to 1973, definition excludes Sandoval County, New Mexico)

**3. Anaheim-Santa Ana-Garden Grove, California.** Coextensive with Orange County, California (New area, October 1963)

**4. Anchorage, Alaska.** Coextensive with Anchorage Census Division, Alaska (New area, November 1971)

**5. Atlanta, Georgia.** Consists of Butts, Cherokee, Clayton, Cobb, De Kalb, Douglas, Fayette, Forsyth, Fulton, Gwinnett, Henry, Newton, Paulding, Rockdale, and Walton Counties, Georgia (Prior to 1973, definition excludes Butts, Cherokee, Douglas, Fayette, Forsyth, Henry, Newton, Paulding, Rockdale, and Walton Counties, Georgia)

**6. Austin, Texas.** Consists of Hays, Travis, and Williamson Counties, Texas (Prior to 1977, definition excludes Williamson County, Texas. Prior to 1973, definition excludes Hays County, Texas)

**7. Baltimore, Maryland.** Consists of Baltimore City and Anne Arundel, Baltimore, Carroll, Harford, and Howard Counties, Maryland (Prior to 1967, definition excludes Harford County, Maryland)

**8. Baton Rouge, Louisiana.** Consists of Ascension, East Baton Rouge, Livingston, and West Baton Rouge Parishes, Louisiana (Prior to 1973, definition excludes Ascension, Livingston, and West Baton Rouge Parishes, Louisiana)

**9. Birmingham, Alabama.** Consists of Jefferson, St. Clair, Shelby, and Walker Counties, Alabama (Prior to 1973, definition excludes St. Clair County, and prior to 1967, definition excludes Shelby and Walker Counties, Alabama)

**10. Boston, Massachusetts.** Consists of Beverly, Lynn, Peabody, and Salem cities, and Boxford, Danvers, Hamilton, Lynnfield, Manchester, Marblehead, Middleton, Nahant, Saugus, Swampscott, Topsfield, and Wenham towns in *Essex County;* Cambridge, Everett, Malden, Medford, Melrose, Newton, Somerville, Waltham, and Woburn cities, and Acton, Arlington, Ashland, Bedford, Belmont, Boxborough, Burlington, Carlisle, Concord, Framingham, Holliston, Lexington, Lincoln, Natick, North Reading, Reading, Sherborn, Stoneham, Sudbury, Wakefield, Watertown, Wayland, Weston, Wilmington, and Winchester towns in *Middlesex County;* Quincy city, and Bellingham, Braintree, Brookline, Canton, Cohasset, Dedham, Dover, Foxborough, Franklin, Holbrook, Medfield, Medway, Millis, Milton, Needham, Norfolk, Norwood, Randolph, Sharon, Stoughton, Walpole, Wellesley, Westwood, Weymouth, and Wrentham towns in *Norfolk County;* Abington, Duxbury, Hanover, Hanson, Hingham, Hull, Kingston, Marshfield, Norwell, Pembroke, Rockland and Scituate towns in *Plymouth County;* and all of *Suffolk County*, Massachusetts (Prior to 1973, definition excludes Boxford town in

Essex County; Acton, Boxborough, Carisle, and Holliston towns in Middlesex County; Bellingham, Foxborough, Franklin, Medway, Stoughton and Wrentham towns in Norfolk County; and Abington, Hanson, and Kingston towns in Plymouth County. Prior to 1964, definition excludes Sherborn town in Middlesex County and Millis town in Norfolk County, Massachusetts)

**11. Buffalo, New York.** Consists of Erie and Niagara Counties, New York

**12. Charlotte-Gastonia, North Carolina.** Consists of Gaston, Mecklenburg, and Union Counties, North Carolina (Prior to 1973, area title excludes Gastonia and definition excludes Gaston County. Prior to 1964, definition excludes Union County, North Carolina)

**13. Chattanooga, Tennessee.** Consists of Hamilton, Marion, and Sequatchie Counties, Tennessee and Catoosa, Dade, and Walker Counties, Ga. (Prior to 1973, definition excludes Marion and Sequatchie Counties, Tennessee and Catoosa and Dade Counties, Ga.)

**14. Chicago, Illinois.** Consists of Cook, Du Page, Kane, Lake McHenry, and Will Counties, Illinois

**15. Cincinnati, Ohio-Kentucky-Indiana.** Consists of Clermont, Hamilton, and Warren Counties, Ohio; Boone, Campbell, and Kenton Counties, Kentucky; and Dearborn County, Indiana (Prior to 1964, definition excludes Clermont and Warren Counties, Ohio; Boone County, Kentucky; and Dearborn County, Indiana)

**16. Cleveland, Ohio.** Consists of Cuyahoga, Geauga, Lake, and Medina Counties, Ohio (Prior to 1964, definition excludes Geauga and Medina Counties, Ohio)

**17. Colorado Springs, Colorado.** Consists of El Paso and Teller Counties, Colorado (Prior to 1973, definition excludes Teller County, Colorado. New area, August 1960)

**18. Columbus, Georgia-Alabama.** Consists of Chattahoochee and Muskogee Counties, Georgia; and Russell County, Alabama

**19. Columbus, Ohio.** Consists of Delaware, Fairfield, Franklin, Madison, and Pickaway Counties, Ohio. (Prior to 1973, definition excludes Fairfield and Madison Counties, Ohio. Prior to 1964, definition excludes Delaware and Pickaway Counties, Ohio)

**20. Corpus Christi, Texas.** Consists of Nueces and San Patricio Counties, Texas (Prior to July 1965, definition excludes San Patricio County, Texas)

**21. Dallas-Fort Worth, Texas.** Consists of Collin, Dallas, Denton, Ellis, Hood, Johnson, Kaufman, Parker, Rockwall, Tarrant and Wise Counties, Texas. (Prior to 1973, area title excludes Fort Worth, and definition excludes Hood, Johnson, Parker, Tarrant and Wise Counties, Texas. Prior to 1967, definition excludes Kaufman and Rockwall Counties, Texas) Includes City of Arlington, Texas.

**22. Dayton, Ohio.** Consists of Greene, Miami, Montgomery, and Preble Counties, Ohio. (Prior to 1964, definition excludes Preble County, Ohio)

**23. Denver-Boulder, Colorado.** Consists of Adams, Arapahoe, Boulder, Denver, Douglas, Gilpin, and Jefferson Counties, Colorado. (Prior to 1973, area title excludes Boulder, and definition excludes Gilpin and Douglas Counties, Colorado) Includes City of Aurora, Colorado.

**24. Des Moines, Iowa.** Consists of Polk and Warren Counties, Iowa. (Prior to 1973, definition excludes Warren County, Iowa)

**25. Detroit, Michigan.** Consists of Lapeer, Livingston, Macomb, Oakland, St. Clair and Wayne Counties, Michigan. (Prior to 1973, definition excludes Lapeer, Livingston, and St. Clair Counties, Michigan) Includes City of Warren, Michigan.

**26. El Paso, Texas.** Coextensive with El Paso County, Texas.

**27. Flint, Michigan.** Consists of Genesee and Shiawassee Counties, Michigan (Prior to 1973, definition includes Lapeer and excludes Shiawassee County, Michigan. Prior to 1964, definition excludes Lapeer County, Michigan)

**28. Fort Wayne, Indiana.** Consists of Adams, Allen, De Kalb, and Wells Counties, Indiana (Prior to 1973, definition excludes Adam, De Kalb, and Wells Counties, Indiana)

**29. Fresno, California.** Coextensive with Fresno County, California

**30. Grand Rapids, Michigan.** Consists of Kent and Ottawa Counties, Michigan (Prior to 1964, definition excludes Ottawa County, Michigan)

**31. Greensboro-Winston-Salem-High Point, North Carolina.** Consists of Davidson, Forsyth, Guilford, Randolph, Stokes and Yadkin Counties, North Carolina (Prior to 1973, area definition excludes Davidson and Stokes Counties, North Carolina. Prior to 1967, area title excludes Winston-Salem and definition excludes Forsyth, Randolph, and Yadkin Counties, North Carolina)

**32. Honolulu, Hawaii.** Coextensive with Honolulu County, Hawaii

**33. Houston, Texas.** Consists of Brazoria, Fort Bend, Harris, Liberty, Montgomery, and Waller Counties, Texas (Prior to 1973, definition excludes Waller County. Prior to 1965, definition excludes Brazoria, Fort Bend, Liberty, and Montgomery Counties, Texas)

**34. Indianapolis, Indiana.** Consists of Boone, Hamilton, Hancock, Hendricks, Johnson, Marion, Morgan, and Shelby Counties, Indiana (Prior to 1967, definition excludes Boone County, and prior to 1964, definition excludes Hamilton, Hancock, Hendricks, Johnson, Morgan, and Shelby Counties, Indiana)

**35. Jackson, Mississippi.** Consists of Hinds and Rankin Counties, Mississippi (Prior to 1964, definition excludes Rankin County, Mississippi)

**36. Jacksonville, Florida.** Consists of Baker, Clay, Duval, Nassau, and St. Johns Counties, Florida (Prior to 1973, definition excludes Baker, Clay, Nassau, and St. Johns Counties, Florida)

**37. Jersey City, New Jersey.** Coextensive with Hudson County, New Jersey

**38. Kansas City, Missouri-Kansas.** Consists of Cass, Clay, Jackson, Platte and Ray Counties, Missouri; Johnson and Wyandotte Counties, Kansas (Prior to 1973, definition excludes Ray County, Missouri and prior to 1964, definition excludes Cass and Platte Counties, Missouri)

**39. Knoxville, Tennessee.** Consists of Anderson, Blount, Knox and Union, Tennessee (Prior to 1973, definition excludes Union County, Tennessee)

**40. Las Vegas, Nevada.** Coextensive with Clark County, Nevada. (New area, August 1960)

**41. Lexington-Fayette, Kentucky.** Consists of Bourbon, Clark, Fayette, Jessamine, Scott, and Woodford Counties, Kentucky (Prior to 1973, definition excludes Bourbon, Clark, Jessamine, Scott, and Woodford Counties, Kentucky. Prior to 1974, area title excludes Fayette, Kentucky)

**42. Lincoln, Nebraska.** Coextensive with Lancaster County, Nebraska

**43. Little Rock—North Little Rock, Arkansas.** Consists of Pulaski and Saline Counties, Arkansas. (Prior to 1967 definition excludes Saline County, Ark.)

**44. Los Angeles—Long Beach California.** Coextensive with Los Angeles County, California. (Prior to 1964, definition includes Orange County, California)

**45. Louisville, Kentucky-Indiana.** Consists of Bullitt, Jefferson, and Oldham Counties, Kentucky; Clark and Floyd Counties, Indiana. (Prior to 1973, definition excludes Bullitt and Oldham Counties, Kentucky.)

**46. Lubbock, Texas.** Coextensive with Lubbock County, Texas.

**47. Madison, Wisconsin.** Coextensive with Dane County, Wisconsin

**48. Memphis, Tennessee-Arkansas-Mississippi.** Consists of Shelby and Tipton Counties, Tennessee; Crittenden County, Arkansas; and De Soto County, Mississippi (Prior to 1973, definition excludes Tipton County, Tennessee, and De Soto County, Mississippi. Prior to 1964, definition excludes Crittenden County, Arkansas.

**49. Miami, Florida.** Coextensive with Dade County, Florida

**50. Milwaukee, Wisconsin.** Consists of Milwaukee, Ozaukee, Washington, and Waukesha Counties, Wisconsin. (Prior to 1967, definition excludes Washington County, and prior to 1964, definition excludes Ozaukee County, Wisconsin)

**51. Minneapolis-St. Paul, Minnesota.** Consists of Anoka, Carver, Chisago, Dakota, Hennepin, Ramsey, Scott, Washington and Wright Counties, Minnesota; and St. Croix County, Wisconsin (Prior to 1973, definition excludes Carver, Chisago, Scott, and Wright Counties, Minnesota, and St. Croix County, Wisconsin.)

**52. Mobile, Alabama.** Consists of Baldwin and Mobile Counties, Alabama (Prior to 1964, definition excludes Baldwin County, Alabama.)

**53. Montgomery, Alabama.** Consists of Autauga, Elmore, and Montgomery Counties, Alabama. (Prior to 1973, definition excludes Autauga County, and prior to 1964 definition excludes Elmore County, Alabama.)

**54. Nashville-Davidson, Tennessee.** Consists of Cheatham, Davidson, Dickson, Robertson, Rutherford, Sumner, Williamson, and Wilson Counties, Tennessee. (Prior to 1973, definition excludes Cheatham, Dickson, Robertson, Rutherford, and Williamson Counties, Tennessee, and area title excludes Davidson. Prior to 1964, definition excludes Sumber and Wilson Counties, Tennessee.)

**55. New Orleans, Louisiana.** Consists of Jefferson, Orleans, St. Bernard, and St. Tammany Parishes, Louisiana. (Prior to 1964, definition excludes St. Tammany Parish, Louisiana.)

**56. New York, New York.** Consists of New York City, and Putnam, Rockland, and Westchester Counties, New York; and Bergen County, New Jersey (Prior to 1973, includes Nassau and Suffolk Counties, New York; includes Yonkers, New York and excludes Putnam County, New York, and Bergen County, New Jersey.)

**57. Newark, New Jersey.** Consists of Essex, Morris, Somerset, and Union Counties, New Jersey. (Prior to 1973, definition excludes Somerset County, New Jersey.)

**58. Norfolk-Virginia Beach-Portsmouth, Virginia, North Carolina.** Consists of Chesapeake, Norfolk, Portsmouth, Suffolk, and Virginia Beach cities, Virginia; and Currituck County, North Carolina (Prior to 1973, definition excludes Nanesmond and Suffolk cities, Virginia, which consolidated February 1974 to form Suffolk City, Virginia, and Currituck County, North Carolina (Prior to 1971, area title excludes Virginia Beach city, Virginia.)

**59. Oklahoma City, Oklahoma.** Consists of Canadian, Cleveland, McClain, Oklahoma, and Pottawatomie Counties, Oklahoma. (Prior to 1973, definition excludes McClain and Pottawatomie Counties, and prior to 1961, excludes Canadian County, Oklahoma.)

**60. Omaha, Nebraska-Iowa.** Consists of Douglas and Sarpy Counties, Nebraska; and Pottawattamie County, Iowa.

**61. Philadelphia, Pennsylvania.** Consists of Bucks, Chester, Delaware, Montgomery, and Philadelphia Counties, Pennsylvania; and Burlington, Camden, and Gloucester Counties, New Jersey.

**62. Phoenix, Arizona.** Coextensive with Maricopa County, Arizona.

**63. Pittsburgh, Pennsylvania.** Consists of Allegheny, Beaver, Washington, and Westmoreland Counties, Pennsylvania

**64. Portland, Oregon-Washington.** Consists of Clackamas, Multnomah, and Washington Counties, Oregon; and Clark County, Washington.

**65. Providence-Warwick-Pawtucket, Rhode Island-Massachusetts.** Consists of Barrington, Bristol and Warren towns in Bristol County; Warwick city and Coventry, East Greenwich, and West Warwick towns in Kent County; Jamestown town in Newport County; Central Falls, Cranston, East Providence, Pawtucket, Providence, and Woonsocket cities, and Burrillville, Cumberland, Johnston, Lincoln, North Providence, North Smithfield, Scituate, and Smithfield towns in Providence County; Narragansett, North Kingstown, and South Kingstown towns in Washington County, Rhode Island; Attleboro city and North Attleborough, Norton, Rehoboth and Seekonk towns in Bristol County; Plainville town in Norfolk County; Blackstone and Millville towns in Worcester County, Massachusetts. (Prior to 1973 definition includes Bellingham, Franklin, and Wrentham towns in Norfolk County, Massachusetts; and excludes Scituate town in Providence and South Kingstown town in Washington County, Rhode Island; and also excludes Norton town in Bristol County, Massachusetts. Prior to 1964, definition excludes Rehoboth town in Bristol County, Massachusetts.)

**66. Richmond, Virginia.** Consists of Richmond city, and Charles City, Chesterfield, Goochland, Hanover, Henrico, New Kent and Powhatan Counties, Virginia (Prior to 1975, area definition excludes New Kent County. Prior to 1973, definition excludes Charles City, Goochland, and Powhatan Counties. Prior to 1964, definition excludes Hanover County, Virginia.)

**67. Riverside-San Bernadino, California.** Consists of Riverside and San Bernadino Counties, California. (Area retitled, November 1971)

**68. Rochester, New York.** Consists of Livingston, Monroe, Ontario, Orleans, and Wayne Counties, New York. (Prior to 1973, definition excludes Ontario County; Prior to 1964, definition excludes Livingston, Orleans, and Wayne Counties, New York)

**69. Sacramento, California.** Consists of Placer, Sacramento, and Yolo Counties, California. (Prior to 1964, definition excludes Placer and Yolo Counties, California.)

**70. St. Louis, Missouri-Illinois.** Consists of St. Louis city, and Franklin, Jefferson, St. Charles, and St. Louis Counties, Missouri; Clinton, Madison, Monroe, and St. Clair Counties, Illinois (Prior to 1973, definition excludes Clinton and Monroe Counties, Illinois. Prior to 1964, definition excludes Franklin County, Missouri.)

**71. Salt Lake City-Ogden, Utah.** Consists of Davis, Salt Lake, Tooele, and Weber Counties, Utah. (Prior to 1973, area title excludes Ogden, and definition excludes Tooele and Weber Counties. Prior to 1964, definition excludes Davis County, Utah)

**72. San Antonio, Texas.** Consists of Bexar, Comal, and Guadaloupe Counties, Texas. (Prior to 1973, definition excludes Comal County. Prior to 1964, definition excludes Guadaloupe County, Texas.)

**73. San Diego, California.** Coextensive with San Diego County, California.

**74. San Francisco-Oakland.** Consists of Alameda, Contra Costa, Marin, San Francisco, and San Mateo Counties, California. (Prior to 1964, definition includes Solano County, California.)

**75. San Jose, California.** Coextensive with Santa Clara County, California.

**76. Seattle-Everett, Washington.** Consists of King and Snohomish Counties, Washington. (Prior to 1964, area title excludes Everett, Washington)

**77. Shreveport, Louisiana.** Consists of Bossier, Caddo, and Webster Parishes, Louisiana. (Prior to 1973, definition excludes Webster Parish, Louisiana)

**78. Spokane, Washington.** Coextensive with Spokane County, Washington

**79. Syracuse, New York.** Consists of Madison, Onondaga, and Oswego Counties, New York.

**80. Tacoma, Washington.** Coextensive with Pierce County, Washington.

**81. Tampa-St. Petersburg, Florida.** Consists of Hillborough, Pasco, and Pinellas Counties, Florida. (Prior to 1973, definition excludes Pasco County, Florida)

**82. Toledo, Ohio-Michigan.** Consists of Fulton, Lucas, Ottawa, and Wood Counties, Ohio; and Monroe County, Michigan. (Prior to 1973, definition excludes Fulton and Ottawa Counties, Ohio. Prior to 1964, definition excludes Wood County, Ohio; and Monroe County, Michigan.)

**83. Tucson, Arizona.** Coextensive with Pima County, Arizona.

**84. Tulsa, Oklahoma.** Consists of Creek, Mayes, Osage, Rogers, Tulsa, and Wagoner Counties, Oklahoma. (Prior to 1973, definition excludes Mayes, Rogers, and Wagoner Counties, Oklahoma. Prior to 1961, definition excludes Osage County, Oklahoma.)

**85. Washington, D.C.-Maryland-Virginia.** Consists of Washington, D.C.; Charles, Montgomery, and Prince Georges Counties, Maryland; and Alexandria, Fairfax, Falls Church, Manassas, and Manasses Park cities, and Arlington, Fairfax, Loudoun and Prince William Counties, Virginia. (Prior to 1975, definition includes Manassas and Manassas Park cities in Prince William County, Virginia, from which they were separated and made independent cities. Prior to 1973, definition excludes Charles County, Maryland. Prior to 1967, definition excludes Loudoun and Prince William Counties, Virginia, and prior to 1964, definition includes Fairfax city in Fairfax County, Virginia, from which it was separated and made an independent city.)

**86. Wichita, Kansas.** Consists of Butler and Sedgwick Counties, Kansas. (Prior to 1964, definition excludes Butler County, Kansas)

**87. Worcester, Massachusetts.** Consists of Worcester city, and Auburn, Berlin, Boylston, Brookfield, Charleston, East Brookfield, Grafton, Holden, Leicester, Millbury, Northborough, Northbridge, North Brookfield, Oxford, Paxton, Shrewsbury, Spencer, Sterling, Sutton, Upton, Uxbridge, Webster, Westborough, and West Boylston towns in Worcester County, Massachusetts. (Prior to 1973, definition excludes Charleston, Uxbridge, and Webster towns in Worcester County, Massachusetts. Prior to 1964, definition excludes Paxton and Sterling towns, Massachusetts)

# INDEX